Letters to Shareholders

By Warren E. Buffett

1965 to 2012

Letters to the Shareholders of Berkshire Hathaway Inc.

	Annual Percentage Change		
	Per-Share Book Value of Berkshire	Market Price Per-Share of Berkshire	S&P 500 with Dividends
1965	23.8%	39.6%	10.0%
1966	20.3	(6.8)	(11.7)
1967	11.0	21.7	30.9
1968	19.0	71.4	11.0
1969	16.2	19.4	(8.4)
1970	12.0	(4.7)	3.9
1971	16.4	80.5	14.6
1972	21.7	8.1	18.9
1973	4.7	(2.5)	(14.8)
1974	5.5	(48.7)	(26.4)
1975	21.9	2.5	37.2
1976	59.3	129.3	23.6
1977	31.9	46.8	(7.4)
1978	24.0	14.5	6.4
1979	35.7	102.5	18.2
1980	19.3	32.8	32.3
1981	31.4	31.8	(5.0)
1982	40.0	38.4	21.4
1983	32.3	69.0	22.4
1984	13.6	(2.7)	6.1
1985	48.2	93.7	31.6
1986	26.1	14.2	18.6
1987	19.5	4.6	5.1

	Book Value	Market Price	S&P 500
1988	20.1	59.3	16.6
1989	44.4	84.6	31.7
1990	7.4	(23.1)	(3.1)
1991	39.6	35.6	30.5
1992	20.3	29.8	7.6
1993	14.3	38.9	10.1
1994	13.9	25.0	1.3
1995	43.1	57.4	37.6
1996	31.8	6.2	23.0
1997	34.1	34.9	33.4
1998	48.3	52.2	28.6
1999	0.5	(19.9)	21.0
2000	6.5	26.6	(9.1)
2001	(6.2)	6.5	(11.9)
2002	10.0	(3.8)	(22.1)
2003	21.0	15.8	28.7
2004	10.5	4.3	10.9
2005	6.4	0.8	4.9
2006	18.4	24.1	15.8
2007	11.0	28.7	5.5
2008	(9.6)	(31.8)	(37.0)
2009	19.8	2.7	26.5
2010	13.0	21.4	15.1
2011	4.6	(4.7)	2.1
2012	14.4	16.8	16.0
Compounded annual gain (1965-2012)	19.7%	21.2%	9.4%
Overall gain	586,817%	1,011,674%	7,433%

Notes: Data are for calendar years with these exceptions: 1965 and 1966, year ended 9/30; 1967, 15 months ended 12/31. Starting in 1979, accounting rules required insurance companies to value the equity securities they hold at market rather than at the lower of cost or market, which was previously the requirement. In this table, Berkshire's results through 1978 have been restated to conform to the changed rules. In all other respects, the results are calculated using the numbers originally reported.

The S&P 500 numbers are **pre-tax** whereas the Berkshire numbers are **after-tax**. If a corporation such as Berkshire were simply to have owned the S&P 500 and accrued the appropriate taxes, its results would have lagged the S&P 500 in years when that index showed a positive return, but would have exceeded the S&P 500 in years when the index showed a negative return. Over the years, the tax costs would have caused the aggregate lag to be substantial.

Market Price changes from 1965 to 1968 are based on the asking price for Berkshire shares in the days surrounding fiscal year end.

Introduction

Warren E. Buffett first took control of Berkshire Hathaway Inc., a small textile company, in April of 1965. A share changed hands for around $18 at the time. Forty-eight letters to shareholders later, the same share traded for $134,060, compounding investor capital at just under 21% per year—a multiplier of 7,448 times.

Buffett has said many times that he "was wired at birth to allocate capital." By allocating resources to assets and endeavors that have the greatest potential for gain, Buffett has guided Berkshire to creating enormous value—not only for shareholders, but for the managers, employees, and customers of its holdings.

The numbers and charts you see on the following pages tell the story of a compounding machine. The rest of the book tells of the people, companies, and philosophy that drove it for more than 45 years.

In addition to providing an astounding case study on Berkshire's success, Buffett shows an incredible willingness to share his methods and act as a teacher to his many students.

I put this compilation together as thanks to Warren's positive influence on myself and many, many others.

Max Olson
Salt Lake City, Utah

P.S. I owe a huge thanks to Tracy Britt, for working with me to finish this book, Deb Ray for scouring Warren's archives for the information I needed, and to Guy Spier for suggesting I make the book public.

ON THE COVER: Berkshire Cotton Manufacturing Company, MA (1898), *Mason Machine Works*. Mathat, Asa: Warren Buffett, *Fortune's Most Powerful Women* (2011).

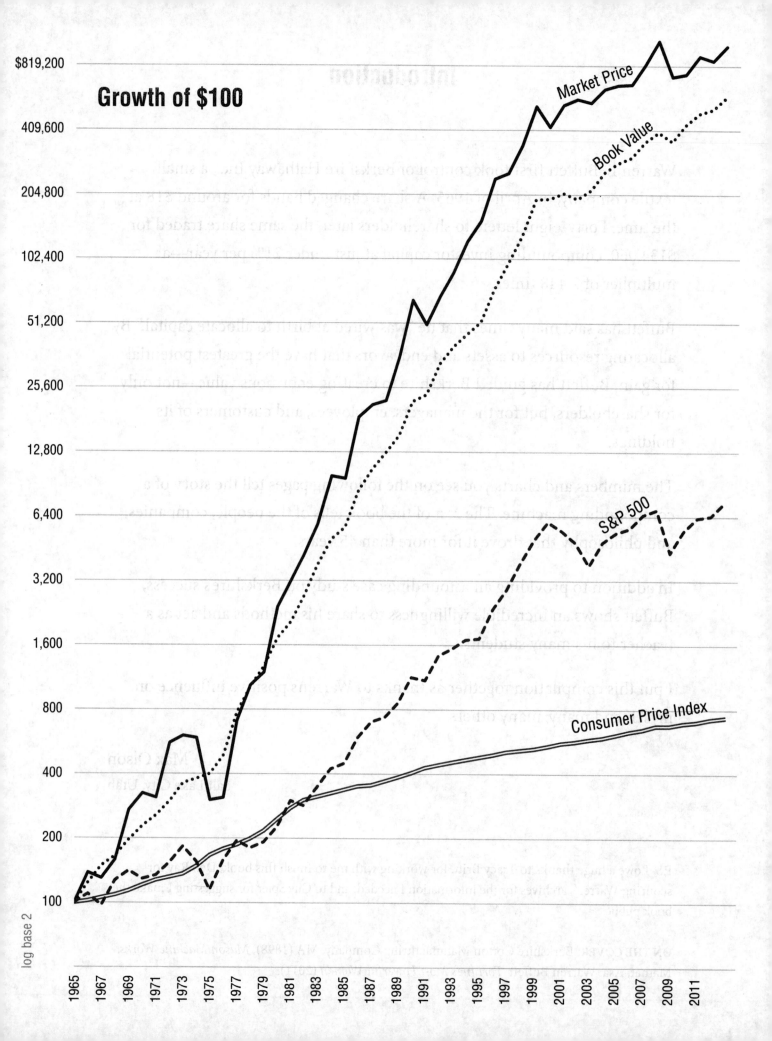

Growth of $100

$819,200

409,600

204,800

102,400

51,200

25,600

12,800

6,400

3,200

1,600

800

400

200

100

log base 2

Market Price

Book Value

S&P 500

Consumer Price Index

1965 1967 1969 1971 1973 1975 1977 1979 1981 1983 1985 1987 1989 1991 1993 1995 1997 1999 2001 2003 2005 2007 2009 2011

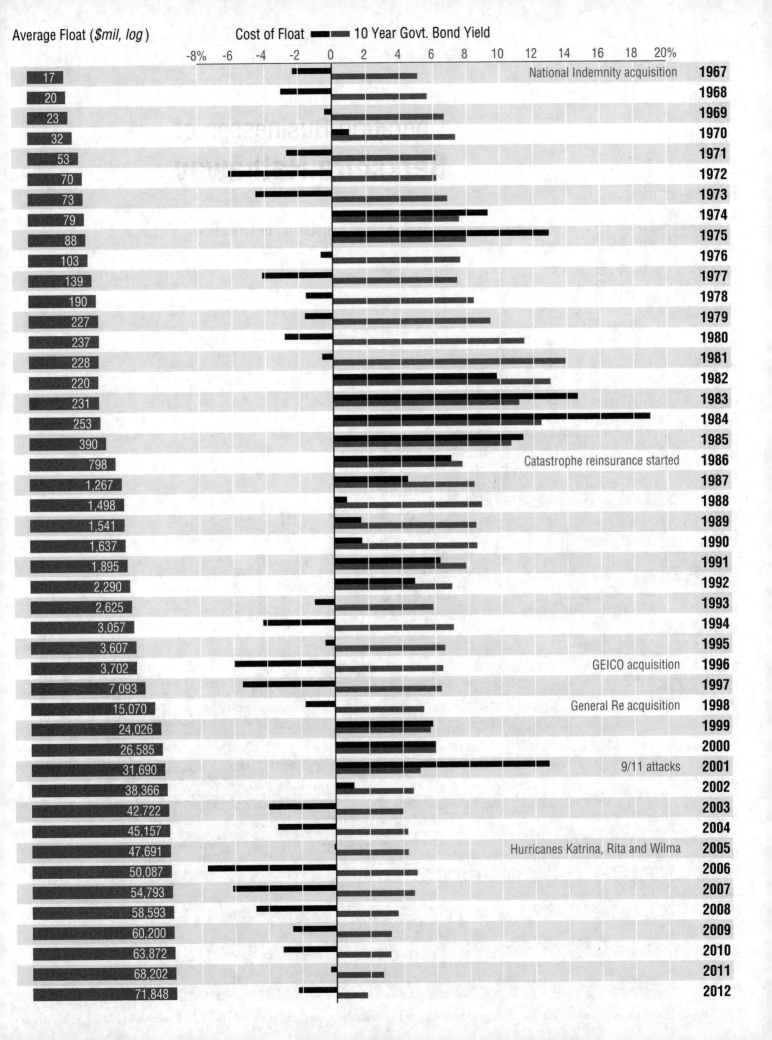

Average Float (*$mil, log*) Cost of Float ▬▬ 10 Year Govt. Bond Yield ▬▬

		-8%	-6	-4	-2	0	2	4	6	8	10	12	14	16	18	20%	

Float	Event	Year
17	National Indemnity acquisition	1967
20		1968
23		1969
32		1970
53		1971
70		1972
73		1973
79		1974
88		1975
103		1976
139		1977
190		1978
227		1979
237		1980
228		1981
220		1982
231		1983
253		1984
390		1985
798	Catastrophe reinsurance started	1986
1,267		1987
1,498		1988
1,541		1989
1,637		1990
1,895		1991
2,290		1992
2,625		1993
3,057		1994
3,607		1995
3,702	GEICO acquisition	1996
7,093		1997
15,070	General Re acquisition	1998
24,026		1999
26,585		2000
31,690	9/11 attacks	2001
38,366		2002
42,722		2003
45,157		2004
47,691	Hurricanes Katrina, Rita and Wilma	2005
50,087		2006
54,793		2007
58,593		2008
60,200		2009
63,872		2010
68,202		2011
71,848		2012

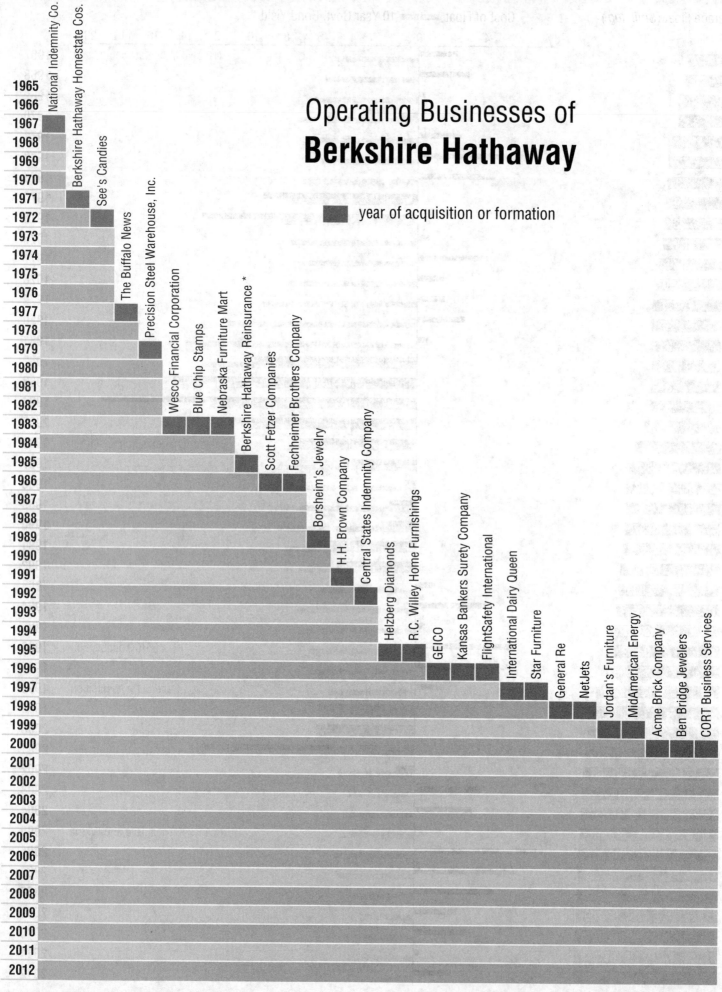

Operating Businesses of
Berkshire Hathaway

■ year of acquisition or formation

Years (left axis): 1965, 1966, 1967, 1968, 1969, 1970, 1971, 1972, 1973, 1974, 1975, 1976, 1977, 1978, 1979, 1980, 1981, 1982, 1983, 1984, 1985, 1986, 1987, 1988, 1989, 1990, 1991, 1992, 1993, 1994, 1995, 1996, 1997, 1998, 1999, 2000, 2001, 2002, 2003, 2004, 2005, 2006, 2007, 2008, 2009, 2010, 2011, 2012

Businesses: National Indemnity Co., Berkshire Hathaway Homestate Cos., See's Candies, The Buffalo News, Precision Steel Warehouse, Inc., Wesco Financial Corporation, Blue Chip Stamps, Nebraska Furniture Mart, Berkshire Hathaway Reinsurance *, Scott Fetzer Companies, Fechheimer Brothers Company, Borsheim's Jewelry, H.H. Brown Company, Central States Indemnity Company, Helzberg Diamonds, R.C. Willey Home Furnishings, GEICO, Kansas Bankers Surety Company, FlightSafety International, International Dairy Queen, Star Furniture, General Re, NetJets, Jordan's Furniture, MidAmerican Energy, Acme Brick Company, Ben Bridge Jewelers, CORT Business Services

Notes: These operating businesses report directly to Berkshire. Many own subsidiaries, and as a result, there are hundreds of additional businesses

Four years ago your management committed itself to the development of more substantial and more consistent earning power than appeared possible if capital continued to be invested exclusively in the textile industry. The funds for this program were temporarily utilized in marketable securities, pending the acquisition of operating businesses meeting our investment and management criteria.

—**Warren Buffett**, April 3, 1970 (*page 12*)

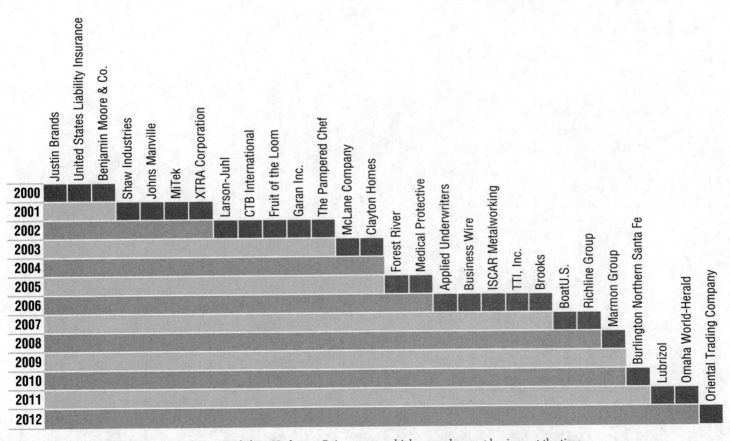

not listed here. * In 1985, Ajit Jain took over Berkshire Hathaway Reinsurance, which was a dormant business at the time.

Topics Index

Berkshire Hathaway Inc.
Corporate Genealogy

In 1929, several textile operations with much common ownership were amalgamated with Berkshire Cotton Manufacturing Co. (incorporated 1889), immediately renamed Berkshire Fine Spinning Associates, Inc. The merging mills were Valley Falls Co., Coventry Co., Greylock Mills, and Fort Dummer Mills, incorporated in 1853, 1865, 1880 and 1910 respectively. Although the documentation is not perfect, it is believed that the earliest progenitor of these corporations began business in 1806.

The resulting operation was a giant, accounting for about 25% of the country's fine cotton textile production. In the 1930s its many mills utilized approximately 1% of the electric output in the New England states. But profitability did not follow volume and preferred dividends were omitted late in 1930 and for six years thereafter.

World War II and the immediate postwar years produced extraordinary profitability and great balance sheet strength. In 1955, Hathaway Manufacturing Co., a New Bedford based manufacturer of both synthetic and cotton textiles was merged into Berkshire Fine Spinning and the name was immediately changed to Berkshire Hathaway Inc. Hathaway was founded in 1888 by Horatio Hathaway and included Hetty Green as an original shareholder with 6¼% ownership.

The combined enterprise had over 10,000 employees and owned close to six million square feet of plant but the subsequent financial record was just as dismal as that which followed the previous grand consolidation of 1929.

After the merger, Berkshire Hathaway's summarized balance sheet was as follows at its fiscal year-end September 30, 1955:

Assets		Liabilities and Stockholders' Equity	
Cash	$ 4,169,000	Accounts Payable and	
Marketable Securities	4,580,000	Accrued Expenses	$ 4,048,000
Accounts Receivable and			
Inventories	28,918,000		
Net Property, Plant and		Stockholders' Equity —	
Equipment	16,656,000	2,294,564 shares outstanding;	
Other Assets	1,125,000	book value $22.40 per share	51,400,000
	$55,448,000		$55,448,000

During the nine following years, sales of Berkshire Hathaway Inc. aggregated approximately $530 million. A reconciliation of shareholders' equity for these nine years follows:

Stockholders' equity at September 30, 1955	$51,400,000
Additions to capital surplus	888,000
Aggregate net loss-from operations 1956-64	(10,138,000)
Cash dividends paid 1956-64	(6,929,000)
Repurchases of common stock	(13,082,000)
Stockholders' equity at October 3, 1964	$22,139,000

Berkshire Hathaway Inc.'s summarized balance sheet at October 3, 1964 was as follows:

Assets		Liabilities and Stockholders' Equity	
Cash	$ 920,000	Notes Payable	$ 2,500,000
Accounts Receivable and		Accounts Payable and	
Inventories	19,140,000	Accrued Expenses	3,248,000
Net Property, Plant and		Total Liabilities	5,746,000
Equipment	7,571,000	Stockholders' Equity —	
Other Assets	256,000	1,137,776 shares outstanding;	
		book value $19.46 per share	22,139,000
	$27,887,000		$27,887,000

BERKSHIRE HATHAWAY INC.

November 9, 1965

TO THE STOCKHOLDERS OF
BERKSHIRE HATHAWAY INC.:

The fiscal year ended October 2, 1965 resulted in net earnings of $2,279,206 as compared to net earnings of $125,586 for the prior year. These net earnings do not reflect any nonrecurring losses incurred on the disposal of assets due to the permanent closing of the King Philip Plants A and E in Fall River, Massachusetts, as such losses have been charged to a reserve previously established for such purpose.

Because of loss carryovers, no federal income taxes were payable by the Corporation with respect to either of these years; however, to prevent any misleading interpretation of future earnings when loss carryovers shall not be available, the Corporation has included in computing net earnings for 1965 and 1964 a charge substantially equal to the federal income taxes that would have been payable with respect to results of operations during each of these years.

The Corporation is continuing to operate King Philip Plant D in Warren, Rhode Island, and the Hathaway Synthetic, Box Loom and Home Fabrics Divisions in New Bedford, Massachusetts.

During 1965 raw material, stock in process and cloth inventories were decreased by $1,411,967 and bank loans of $2,500,000 were paid off. Also, during the year the Corporation purchased 120,231 of its own shares, leaving a total of 1,017,547 shares outstanding at the end of the fiscal year.

The Corporation made a substantial reduction in its overhead costs during the fiscal year just ended. Approximately $811,812 was invested by the Corporation during the year in the purchase of new machinery in a continuing effort to reduce costs and to improve quality. This program will continue during the current fiscal year.

A major portion of the machinery at King Philip Plant E Division has been sold. We expect to dispose of the remaining portion of this plant during the current fiscal year. This will complete the liquidation of our unprofitable plants. The proposed sale of the King Philip E Division will make it necessary to provide storage for raw cotton and grey cloth for the King Philip D Division at the Hathaway Division Plant C (former Langshaw Mill). Plans are under way to accomplish this within the current fiscal year.

After more than fifty years of service, Mr. Seabury Stanton resigned as a director and as President and Mr. Kenneth V. Chace was elected to succeed him. At the same time, Mr. John K. Stanton resigned as a director and as Treasurer and Clerk. Mr. Harold V. Banks was elected to succeed him as Treasurer and Clerk.

All divisions of the Corporation currently have substantial backlogs of unfilled orders and we presently anticipate that operations for the coming year will continue to be profitable.

We wish to express our thanks to all the employees of the Corporation whose loyal cooperation and efforts have helped to make this year successful.

MALCOLM G. CHACE, JR.
Chairman of the Board

KENNETH V. CHACE
President

[*Letter written by Warren E. Buffett*]

BERKSHIRE HATHAWAY INC.

December 2, 1966

TO THE STOCKHOLDERS OF
BERKSHIRE HATHAWAY INC.:

For your information, we have highlighted the financial information for fiscal 1966 in comparison with the five preceding years on the facing page.

In this letter we will discuss in some detail the following areas:

1. Operating Conditions — 1966
2. Survey of Operations 1961-1966
3. Maintenance of Financial Condition
4. Dividends

OPERATING CONDITIONS — 1966

Sales

Although total sales of $49.4 million were very close to last year's, there were significant changes in the product mix. The Synthetic Division sales dropped in dollar volume, but this was offset by a corresponding increase in Home Fabrics sales. The Box Loom Division sales showed some gain, but this was offset by a drop in sales of our King Philip D Division.

The sales picture for the last half of 1966 was one of generally depressed markets. Heavy imports of yarn dyed goods plus a change in styling trends caused loss of sales and depressed prices in our Box Loom Division. Overproduction of acetate fabrics plus importation of nylon fabrics brought more looms into competition with us in our Synthetic Division. The combination of imports and increased domestic production depressed prices of plain polyester/cotton blends. We estimate that this development will cause looms to swing back on to cotton goods and thereby adversely affect our sales position on lawns woven at King Philip D Division.

The negative factors, which prevailed in the last quarter of our 1966 fiscal year, contributed to our decision to avoid inventory buildup by shutting down the Box Loom and Synthetic Divisions in New Bedford for the week of October 9, 1966. Inasmuch as the textile market has not, at this writing, shifted to a more active level, further cutbacks in production may be necessary to avoid inventory buildup.

New Products

The growth of our Home Fabrics Division over the past few years is, in large part, due to our development of both new products and new application of old products. In the past year, we have increased our expenditures for development so as to provide fabrics that will yield more stable prices and volumes.

1

Labor

In early 1966, we signed a contract with the Textile Workers Union of America AFL-CIO for three years ending April 15, 1969. This contract covers wages and benefits with no reopening clause.

Plant and Equipment

We have spent approximately $970,000 for purchase and installation of new equipment in order to lower costs, improve quality, and increase our manufacturing flexibility.

During fiscal 1966, we disposed of the remainder of our unused property.

Income Tax Payments

All but a small portion of our tax carryforward has been used as of the end of fiscal 1966. We therefore will incur income tax liability with respect to future earnings.

SURVEY OF OPERATIONS OCTOBER 1, 1960 — OCTOBER 1, 1966

As one might expect, in a business as highly cyclical as the textile business, the past decade for Berkshire Hathaway has been a recurring story of a period of earnings followed by a period of relatively heavy losses. The past year has been a significant one in this history because, not only was 1966 a year of profitable operations, but, also, it witnessed the restoration of our financial strength to the level that existed at the end of 1960. You will recall that the heavy losses of the years 1957 and 1958 had not yet been fully recouped by the profitable operations of the years 1959 and 1960, when our business was again hit with a three-year period of loss operations.

Not only did our financial condition in these years suffer from the inroads created by these losses, but it also had to absorb the impact of our heavy capital expenditure program of the early 1960s.

The following table summarizes the change in the net worth position of Berkshire Hathaway, Inc. during the past six years:

Net Worth October 1, 1960		$37,981,820
Net Earnings 1961-1966 (after reflecting $6,200,000 losses on disposal of fixed assets)	$ 40,476	
Less Dividends Paid 1961-1966	1,366,273	
Excess of Dividends over Net Earnings 1961-1966		1,325,797
		36,656,023
Repurchases of a total of 607,972 shares of Capital Stock 1961-1966 . .		7,161,103
Net Worth October 1, 1966		$29,494,920

You will note that while dividends exceeded net earnings during this six-year period, the major reason for the 22% decrease in net worth has been the repurchase by the Company of its own stock, pursuant to a program whereby the Company's outstanding shares have been reduced to 1,017,547 shares—a 37% reduction compared with the shares outstanding on October 1, 1960. This decrease in outstanding shares has been appropriate, considering the reduction in scale of the Company's operations due to closing of unprofitable mills.

The benefit to the present stockholders of this program of share repurchases is indicated, in part, by the fact that net worth per share of the Company's outstanding common stock on October 1, 1966 was $28.99, compared with $23.37 six years previously.

In the year ended October 1, 1960, our sales totaled $62.6 million, whereas in 1966, they totaled $49.4 million, a decrease of approximately 21%. This corresponds to the 22% decrease in total net worth. The fact that the Company is now achieving approximately the same net worth turnover as existed at the beginning of this six-year period is again some indication of the restoration of its strength.

MAINTENANCE OF FINANCIAL CONDITION

It has always been among the goals of Berkshire Hathaway to maintain a strong financial condition. Indeed, it has been this practice that has enabled the Company to survive in the light of the highly cyclical nature of its business. The present strength of the Company's financial condition is demonstrated by its $23,158,187 of working capital at October 1, 1966. This figure is about equal to the Company's working capital on October 1, 1960 although on a per share basis, because of the reduction in the number of shares through repurchasing, our working capital is now $22.76 compared with $14.41 six years ago.

In addition to the cyclical nature of our business, there are other reasons why a strong financial condition is advisable. As you have been advised previously, the Company has been searching for suitable acquisitions within, and conceivably without, the textile field. Although to date none has been successfully concluded, we continue to have an active interest in such acquisitions. The present state of the money market, in which funds are virtually unobtainable for acquisition purposes, makes it imperative that we have available the liquid assets with which to consummate such acquisitions, should the hoped-for opportunities present themselves. Present uncertainties such as war, tax rates and decreased level of business activity also all combine to emphasize the continuing need for a strong financial condition.

A second area in which substantial investment may be necessary is our fast-growing Home Fabrics Division. Home Fabrics' sales have nearly doubled in the past three years. Should a corresponding increase be attained in the coming years, we may he called upon to invest up to $7 million in additional inventory and receivables.

Finally, the threat of technological change is ever present in the textile field. We have an investment of $24.4 million ($6.3 million after accrued depreciation) in plant and equipment. This is an investment which the textile machinery industry is constantly striving to render obsolete. An important change at any level of our manufacturing process could require major capital expenditures at tomorrow's replacement prices. We shall continue to weigh most carefully the possible rewards and risks of any capital expenditure program. However, should we decide that it is in our best interests to make capital expenditures, we must be in a financial position to do so. Sufficient working capital would be particularly necessary if the advent of important cost-cutting equipment coincided with a period of depressed textile earnings, making outside capital difficult or impossible to obtain.

It is these considerations which caused the Company at year end to include in its working capital $5.4 million of marketable securities, composed of short-term municipal bonds, commercial paper and common stock. Because of the uncertainties in knowing when the Company may be called upon to produce substantial sums of cash, and the possibility that this might not occur for a considerable period of time, your directors have felt that we should be as zealous to achieve a realistic return on this portion of our capital as we are on the other funds that are at the time invested in plant, inventories, receivables, etc. Accordingly, it is the present intention of the directors to proceed toward the interim investment of a major portion of these funds in marketable common stocks. This should hold promise not only of greater income than can be achieved through alternative investment possibilities in the field of non-equity marketable securities, but also provides us with the opportunity to participate in earnings derived outside of our textile business, even if only temporarily and indirectly.

DIVIDENDS

This restoration of the Company's financial position now permits a dividend policy reflecting the distribution to our stockholders of a reasonable proportion of current after-tax earnings. Such a policy, however, must be consistent with the need for preserving the strength of our present financial position.

To implement this policy, a dividend of 10¢ per share was declared on November 14, 1966, payable January 3, 1967 to stockholders of record on December 2, 1966.

MALCOLM G. CHACE, JR.
Chairman of the Board

KENNETH V. CHACE
President

[*Letter written by Warren E. Buffett*]

BERKSHIRE HATHAWAY INC.

March 8, 1968

To the Stockholders of
Berkshire Hathaway Inc.:

The Company has adopted a calendar year for accounting purposes. This new calendar year end substitutes for the previous September 30 year end. The change was effective December 30, 1967. This report covers the fifteen months ended December 30, 1967.

TEXTILE OPERATIONS

FISCAL YEAR ENDED SEPTEMBER 30, 1967

Sales

Total sales showed a decline from $49.4 million in fiscal 1966 to $39 million in fiscal 1967. The cause of the drop in dollar volume was a combination of a decrease in yardage demand in all divisions and a sharp drop in prices in all areas except the Home Fabrics Division. Although sales and profits of our Home Fabrics Division were down substantially, this area demonstrated the greatest resistance to the depressed conditions of the textile markets in which we operate. Berkshire Hathaway does not produce coarse goods such as heavy ducks, which is the segment of the textile business that was the strongest in 1967.

During the year, we curtailed our production about 15 per cent in an attempt to avoid building inventories. We maintained satisfactory inventory levels but our curtailment resulted in the loss of certain categories of skilled help which will be required if we are to fully utilize our plant capacity. Therefore, abnormally high training costs will be incurred before we again run full.

By the end of the fiscal year, there was some indication that the general textile market was improving with the exception of that for our fine combed lawns, which we manufacture at our King Philip D Division in Warren, Rhode Island. This fabric remained in poor demand, with depressed prices throughout the year. A market survey indicated that the demand for cotton lawn fabrics was gradually being displaced by a demand for polyester blend fabrics.

On the positive side, we expanded our Home Fabrics products line into a wider variety of fabrics and also expanded our sales force in this area. In addition to this, we started an Apparel Fabrics Division, selling finished yarn-dyed box loom goods into the women's apparel market. Both of these moves were part of our general policy of attempting to establish product lines away from areas of direct competition with staple fabric producers. We intend to further implement this policy.

Manufacturing Operation

Because of reduced levels of production, smaller individual orders, and more frequent loom shifts, manufacturing costs were materially higher than in the last several years. A return to full operation should correct this situation to a great extent. Although product development and diversification of fabrics will result in higher manufacturing costs, these higher costs should be more than offset by higher prices for the fabrics and result in greater profits.

Labor Relations

Labor relations remain satisfactory. Our labor contract will carry us through until April of 1969. A general wage rate increase is called for by this contract in April of 1968. The current labor market is a difficult one, as for most industries, with relatively fewer job applications being received from persons possessing the requisite training and skills.

THREE MONTHS ENDED DECEMBER 30, 1967

This quarter showed a very definitive increase in demand in all divisions except King Philip D. We operated at close to normal levels, with some equipment idle only because of our inability to quickly obtain and train sufficient people. Our new Apparel Fabrics Division was off to a good start and our Home Fabrics Division renewed its historical strong growth pattern. Based on current market conditions, we expect a significant improvement in textile operating profits during 1968. Our operating loss carryforward has been fully utilized and any future net profit we realize will be subject to normal federal income taxes.

The portion of our business which proved unsatisfactory was the cotton lawn business. As a result of a second market survey, it was decided to close the King Philip D Division in Warren, Rhode Island where these goods were manufactured. The plant was an efficient one for the manufacture of fine combed lawns, which, unfortunately, are no longer in any sort of demand. The equipment at this plant had little adaptability to other end products, thereby making a conversion attempt uneconomical. The decision to terminate operations was hastened by the very large increase in the cost of new crop cotton, which could not be reflected in increased finished product prices. Any loss from termination of operations at King Philip D will be reflected as incurred in 1968. At this point in time, we can only speculate as to the amount of this loss but we do not envision that it will exceed $1 million pre-tax.

INSURANCE SUBSIDIARIES

We are highly pleased with the results of our insurance subsidiaries since their acquisition in March 1967. These two companies, National Indemnity Company and National Fire and Marine Insurance Company, continue under the very able management of Mr. Jack Ringwalt who has guided them since inception.

Gross premium volume increased only slightly during 1967, but termination of certain reinsurance arrangements resulted in a substantial gain in net premium volume. Underwriting was conducted at a good profit margin and investment income increased substantially, reflecting both a greater base of assets and the higher yields that prevailed throughout the year in the fixed income sector. All earnings of the insurance subsidiaries are being retained to build additional capital strength.

Our investment in the insurance companies reflects a first major step in our efforts to achieve a more diversified base of earning power. The success of this effort is indicated by the attainment of earnings in the subsidiaries during 1967 which substantially exceeded the earnings attributable to a larger capital investment m the textile business. We expect that there will be years in the future when the order of relative profitability is reversed, reflecting different stages in both the insurance and textile cycles. However, we believe it is an added factor of strength to have these two unrelated sources of earnings rather than to be solely exposed to the conditions of one industry, as heretofore.

FUTURE OBJECTIVES

Management continues to be alert to opportunities to expand our operations in either the textile business, the insurance business or unrelated area. We feel it is essential that we not repeat the history of the 1956-1966 period, when over-all earnings on average invested capital of over $30 million were something less than zero. Our present liquid resources held in readily marketable common stocks are available for either acquisition of new businesses or for application toward greater profit opportunities in our present operations. In addition, we will not hesitate to borrow money to take advantage of attractive opportunities. Our goal is to obtain a reasonably stable and substantial level of earning power commensurate with the capital employed in the business.

MALCOLM G. CHACE, JR.
Chairman of the Board

KENNETH V. CHACE
President

[*Letter written by Warren E. Buffett*]

BERKSHIRE HATHAWAY INC.

March 12, 1969

TO THE STOCKHOLDERS OF
BERKSHIRE HATHAWAY INC.:

Earnings in both textile and insurance operations improved somewhat during 1968. Total operating earnings in relation to stockholders' investment still are not satisfactory, but we are expending every effort to bring them to the proper level.

Textile Operations

Sales volume increased about 14% with good gains in both Home Fabrics and Menswear Linings. Over the years, these have been our most consistently profitable areas and their improvement in 1968 reflects strong efforts by Richard Bowen in Home Fabrics and Ralph Rigby in Menswear Linings. The Home Fabrics Division in 1969 will utilize new 150 inch Saurer looms, offering opportunities for expanding our style line. We hold options on additional looms, enabling expansion if profitable projections materialize.

Our Box Loom Division continued to present severe operating problems, as it has over many years. Our history in this area shows occasional periods of strong prices, regularly followed by heavy imports of goods, severe price cutting and curtailed operations. As a result of a careful survey of the future market for Box Loom greige goods and the investment required to service this market, it was decided to phase out our operation of such greige goods during 1969. After the transitional operating period has been completed and some loss has been sustained on the sale of fixed assets, we expect an improved over-all textile operating situation.

Insurance Operations

National Indemnity Company and National Fire & Marine Insurance Company continue their splendid operating performance under Jack Ringwalt. Premium volume increased only slightly in 1968, but more importantly, a good underwriting profit was again produced during a period when the property insurance industry operated at an underwriting loss. Investment income increased substantially in 1968, reflecting both a greater base of assets and higher yields on fixed income securities. Some capital gains again developed from our investments in common stocks.

The insurance companies continue to seek new areas for expansion, both at the direct level and possible in the reinsurance field. The emphasis continues, however, to be on underwriting at a profit rather than volume simply for the sake of size. Due to our policy of retaining all earnings in the insurance subsidiaries, we have substantially augmented their capital funds, increasing our ability to retain greater segments of our originated premium volume.

Marketable Securities and Acquisitions

During 1968, we sold a portion of our marketable securities portfolio at a profit of approximately $1.5 million after tax. At the end of 1968, we had unrealized market appreciation of $6,400,000 in the balance of the portfolio. Such securities were held in marketable common stocks as a temporary investment, pending the utilization of the funds in acquisition or expansion of operating businesses consistent with our program for the development of greater and more diversified earning power.

Immediately after year end, we purchased all of the stock of Sun Newspapers, Inc. and Blacker Printing Company, Inc., which represents an initial entry into the publishing business. This purchase involved only a small portion of our funds available for acquisition. Sun Newspapers, Inc. publishes five weekly newspapers in the Omaha, Nebraska area, with paid circulation of about 50,000. A related printing business is conducted by Blacker Printing Company, Inc. This purchase, while small, has potential for future expansion. The operations will continue under the able management of Stanford Lipsey.

Kenneth V. Chace
President

[*Letter written by Warren E. Buffett*]

BERKSHIRE HATHAWAY INC.

April 3, 1970

To the Stockholders of
Berkshire Hathaway Inc.:

Four years ago your management committed itself to the development of more substantial and more consistent earning power than appeared possible if capital continued to be invested exclusively in the textile industry. The funds for this program were temporarily utilized in marketable securities, pending the acquisition of operating businesses meeting our investment and management criteria.

This policy has proved reasonably successful—particularly when contrasted with results achieved by firms which have continued to commit large sums to textile expansion in the face of totally inadequate returns. We have been able to conclude two major purchases of operating businesses, and their successful operations enabled Berkshire Hathaway to achieve an over-all return of more than 10% on average stockholders' equity last year in the face of less than a 5% return from the portion of our capital employed in the textile business. We have liquidated our entire holdings of marketable securities over the last two years at a profit of more than $5 million after taxes. These gains provided important funds to facilitate our major purchase of 1969, when borrowed money to finance acquisitions was generally most difficult to obtain.

We anticipate no further purchases of marketable securities, but our search for desirable acquisitions continues. Any acquisition will, of course, be dependent upon obtaining appropriate financing.

Textile Operations

Dollar sales volume in 1969 was approximately 12% below 1968. Net earnings were slightly higher despite substantial operating losses incurred in the termination of our Box Loom Division. Earnings on capital employed improved modestly but still remain unsatisfactory despite strenuous efforts toward improvement.

We are presently in the midst of a textile recession of greater intensity than we have seen for some years. There is an over-all lack of demand for textile products in a great many end uses. This lack of demand has required curtailment of production to avoid inventory build-up. Both our Menswear Lining Division and Home Fabrics Division have been forced to schedule two-week shutdowns during the first quarter of 1970, but inventories remain on the high side. The slowdown in demand appears even greater than that normally occurring in the cyclical textile market. Recovery from this cycle will probably be dependent upon Federal Government action on economic factors they can control.

We have concentrated our textile operations in those areas that appear, from historical performance and from our market projections, to be potentially satisfactory businesses. Improvements have been made in our mill operations which, under better industry conditions, should produce substantial cost reductions. However, the present picture is for lower profits in this business during 1970.

Insurance Operations

Jack Ringwalt and his outstanding management group turned in new records in just about every department during 1969. During another year in which the fire and casualty insurance industry experienced substantial underwriting losses, our insurance subsidiaries achieved significant adjusted underwriting profits. Since establishment of the business in 1941, Mr. Ringwalt has held to the principle of underwriting for a profit—a policy which is frequently talked about within the industry but much less frequently achieved.

Our new surety department, although small, made good progress during the year. We are entering the workmen's compensation market in California through the establishment of a branch office in Los Angeles. Our new reinsurance division seems to be off to a strong start, although the nature of this business is such that it takes at least several years to render an intelligent verdict as to operating results. We also have interesting plans for a new "home state" insurance operation.

Phil Liesche—over 20 years a major contributor to outstanding results in the production and underwriting departments—was elected Executive Vice President early this year.

Expectations are for continued growth in our insurance operations.

Banking Operations

The most significant event of 1969 for Berkshire Hathaway was the acquisition of 97.7% of the stock of The Illinois National Bank and Trust Co. of Rockford, Illinois. This bank had been built by Eugene Abegg, without addition of outside capital, from $250,000 of net worth and $400,000 of deposits in 1931 to $17 million of net worth and $100 million of deposits in 1969. Mr. Abegg has continued as Chairman and produced record operating earnings (before security losses) of approximately $2 million in 1969. Such earnings, as a percentage of either deposits or total assets, are close to the top among larger commercial banks in the country which are not primarily trust department operations. It will not be easy to achieve greater earnings in 1970 because (1) our bank is already a highly efficient business, and (2) the unit banking law of Illinois makes more than modest deposit growth difficult for a major downtown bank.

After almost a year of ownership, we are delighted with our investment in Illinois National Bank, and our association with Mr. Abegg.

Kenneth V. Chace
President

[*Letter written by Warren E. Buffett*]

Berkshire Hathaway Inc.

March 15, 1971

To the Stockholders of
Berkshire Hathaway Inc.:

The past year witnessed dramatically diverse earnings results among our various operating units. The Illinois National Bank & Trust reported record earnings and continued to rank right at the top, nationally, among banks in terms of earnings as a percentage of average resources. Our insurance operations had some deterioration in underwriting results, but increased investment income produced a continued excellent return. The textile business became progressively more difficult throughout the year and the final break-even result is understandable, considering the industry environment.

The combination of these factors produced a return of approximately 10% on average shareholder's investment. While this figure is only about average for American industry, it is considerably in excess of what would have been achieved had resources continued to be devoted exclusively to the textile business, as was the pattern until five years ago.

Textile Operations

Sales in both menswear linings and home fabrics declined significantly during the year. Thus we were continuously forced to modify production plans to prevent inventories from mounting. Such production curtailments were costly to the Company and disruptive to the lives of our employees.

Prices continue at poor levels and demand has not strengthened. Inventory levels, while reduced from a year ago through great effort, continue high in relation to current sales levels. We continue to work at making the changes required in manufacturing and marketing areas that will result in profitable operations with more stable employment.

Led by Ken Chace, the effort, attitude and enterprise manifested by management and labor in this operation have been every bit the equal of their counterparts in our much more profitable businesses. But in the past year they have been swimming against a strong tide and, at this writing, that situation still prevails.

Insurance Operations

We enjoyed an outstanding year for growth in our insurance business, accompanied by a somewhat poorer underwriting picture. Our traditional operation experienced a surge in volume as conventional auto insurance markets became more restricted. This is in line with our history as a non-conventional carrier which receives volume gains on a "wave" basis when standard markets are experiencing capacity or underwriting problems. Although our combined loss and expense ratio on the traditional business rose to approximately 100% during the year, our management, led by Jack Ringwalt and Phil Liesche, has the ability and determination to return it to an underwriting profit.

Our new reinsurance division, managed by George Young, made substantial progress during the year. While an evaluation of this division's underwriting will take some years, initial signs are encouraging. We are producing significant volume in diverse areas of reinsurance and developing a more complete staff in order to handle a much larger volume of business in the future.

The surety business, referred to in last year's report, operated at a significant underwriting loss during 1970. The contractor's bond field was a disappointment and we are restricting our writing to the miscellaneous bond area. This will mean much less volume but, hopefully, underwriting profits.

Our "home-state" operations—Cornhusker Casualty Company, formed in early 1970 as a 100% owned subsidiary of National Indemnity, writing standard business through Nebraska agents only—is off to a strong start. The combination of big-company capability and small-company accessibility is providing to be a strong marketing tool with first class agents. John Ringwalt deserves credit for translating the concept into reality. Our present plans envision extension of the home-state approach and we plan to have another company in operation later this year.

Banking Operations

Eugene Abegg had the problem in 1970 of topping a banner year in 1969—and in the face of an unchanged level of deposits, managed to do it. While maintaining a position of above average liquidity, net operating earnings before security gains came to well over 2% of average deposits. This record reflects an exceptionally well-managed banking business.

Bob Kline became President of the Illinois National Bank in January, 1971, with Mr. Abegg continuing as Chairman and Chief Executive Officer. Illinois is a unit banking start, and deposit growth is hard to come by. In the year he has been with the bank, Mr. Kline has demonstrated effort and initiative in generating new deposits. Such deposit growth, in line with national trends, will largely be in the consumer savings area with attendant high costs. With generally lower interest rates prevailing on loans throughout the country, it will be a challenge to management to maintain earnings while utilizing a higher cost deposit mix.

In the closing days of 1970, new bank holding company legislation was passed which affects Berkshire Hathaway because of its controlling ownership of The Illinois National Bank. In effect, we have about ten years to dispose of stock in the bank (which could involve a spin-off of bank stock to our shareholders) and it will probably be some time before we decide on a course of action. In the meantime, certain activities of all entities in the Berkshire Hathaway group—including acquisitions—are subject to the provisions of the Act and Regulations of the Federal Reserve Board.

Warren E. Buffett
Chairman of the Board

Berkshire Hathaway Inc.

To the Stockholders of
Berkshire Hathaway Inc.:

It is a pleasure to report that operating earnings in 1971, excluding capital gains, amounted to more than 14% of beginning shareholders' equity. This result—considerably above the average of American industry—was achieved in the face of inadequate earnings in our textile operation, making clear the benefits of redeployment of capital inaugurated five years ago. It will continue to be the objective of management to improve return on total capitalization (long term debt plus equity), as well as the return on equity capital. However, it should be realized that merely maintaining the present relatively high rate of return may well prove more difficult than was improvement from the very low levels of return which prevailed throughout most of the 1960's.

Textile Operations

We, in common with most of the textile industry, continued to struggle throughout 1971 with inadequate gross margins. Strong efforts to hammer down costs and a continuous search for less price-sensitive fabrics produced only marginal profits. However, without these efforts we would have operated substantially in the red. Employment was more stable throughout the year as our program to improve control of inventories achieved reasonable success.

As mentioned last year, Ken Chace and his management group have been swimming against a strong industry tide. This negative environment has only caused them to intensify their efforts. Currently we are witnessing a mild industry pickup which we intend to maximize with our greatly strengthened sales force. With the improvement now seen in volume and mix of business, we would expect better profitability—although not of a dramatic nature—from our textile operation in 1972.

Insurance Operations

An unusual combination of factors—reduced auto accident frequency, sharply higher effective rates in large volume lines, and the absence of major catastrophes—produced an extraordinarily good year for the property and casualty insurance industry. We shared in these benefits, although they are not without their negative connotations.

Our traditional business—and still our largest segment—is in the specialized policy or non-standard insured. When standard markets become tight because of unprofitable industry underwriting, we experience substantial volume increases as producers look to us. This was the condition several years ago, and largely accounts for the surge of direct volume experienced in 1970 and 1971. Now that underwriting has turned very profitable on an industry-wide basis, more companies are seeking the insureds they were rejecting a short while back and rates are being cut in some areas. We continue to have underwriting profitability as our primary goal and this may well mean a substantial decrease in National Indemnity's direct volume during 1972. Jack Ringwalt and Phil Liesche continue to guide this operation in a manner matched by very few in the business.

Our reinsurance business, which has been developed to a substantial operation in just two years by the outstanding efforts of George Young, faces much the same situation. We entered the reinsurance business late in 1969 at a time when rates had risen substantially and capacity was tight.

17

The reinsurance industry was exceptionally profitable in 1971, and we are now seeing rate-cutting as well as the formation of well-capitalized aggressive new competitors. These lower rates are frequently accompanied by greater exposure. Against this background we expect to see our business curtailed somewhat in 1972. We set no volume goals in our insurance business generally—and certainly not in reinsurance—as virtually any volume can be achieved if profitability standards are ignored. When catastrophes occur and underwriting experience sours, we plan to have the resources available to handle the increasing volume which we will then expect to be available at proper prices.

We inaugurated our "home-state" insurance operation in 1970 by the formation of Cornhusker Casualty Company. To date, this has worked well from both a marketing and an underwriting standpoint. We have therefore further developed this approach by the formation of Lakeland Fire & Casualty Company in Minnesota during 1971, and Texas United Insurance in 1972. Each of these companies will devote its entire efforts to a single state seeking to bring the agents and insureds of its area a combination of large company capability and small company accessibility and sensitivity. John Ringwalt has been in overall charge of this operation since inception. Combining hard work with imagination and intelligence, he has transformed an idea into a well organized business. The "home-state" companies are still very small, accounting for a little over $1.5 million in premium volume during 1971. It looks as though this volume will more than double in 1972 and we will develop a more creditable base upon which to evaluate underwriting performance.

A highlight of 1971 was the acquisition of Home & Automobile Insurance Company, located in Chicago. This company was built by Victor Raab from a small initial investment into a major auto insurer in Cook County, writing about $7.5 million in premium volume during 1971. Vic is cut from the same cloth as Jack Ringwalt and Gene Abegg, with a talent for operating profitably accompanied by enthusiasm for his business. These three men have built their companies from scratch and, after selling their ownership position for cash, retain every bit of the proprietary interest and pride that they have always had.

While Vic has multiplied the original equity of Home & Auto many times since its founding, his ideas and talents have always been circumscribed by his capital base. We have added capital funds to the company, which will enable it to establish branch operations extending its highly-concentrated and on-the-spot marketing and claims approach to other densely populated areas.

All in all, it is questionable whether volume added by Home & Auto, plus the "home-state" business in 1972, will offset possible declines in direct and reinsurance business of National Indemnity Company. However, our large volume gains in 1970 and 1971 brought in additional funds for investment at a time of high interest rates, which will be of continuing benefit in future years. Thus, despite the unimpressive prospects regarding premium volume, the outlook for investment income and overall earnings from insurance in 1972 is reasonably good.

Banking Operations

Our banking subsidiary, The Illinois National Bank & Trust Company, continued to lead its industry as measured by earnings as a percentage of deposits. In 1971, Illinois National earned well over 2% after tax on average deposits while (1) not using borrowed funds except for very occasional reserve balancing transactions; (2) maintaining a liquidity position far above average; (3) recording loan losses far below average; and (4) utilizing a mix of over 50% time deposits with all consumer savings accounts receiving maximum permitted interest rates throughout the year. This reflects a superb management job by Gene Abegg and Bob Kline.

Interest rates received on loans and investments were down substantially throughout the banking industry during 1971. In the last few years, Illinois National's mix of deposits has moved considerably more than the industry average away from demand money to much more expensive time money. For example, interest paid on deposits has gone from under $1.7 million in 1969 to over $2.7 million in 1971. Nevertheless, the unusual profitability of the Bank has been maintained. Marketing efforts were intensified during the year, with excellent results.

With interest rates even lower now than in 1971, the banking industry is going to have trouble achieving gains in earnings during 1972. Our deposit gains at Illinois National continue to come in the time money area, which produces only very marginal incremental income at present. It will take very close cost control to enable Illinois National to maintain its 1971 level of earnings during 1972.

Financial

Because of the volume gains being experienced by our insurance subsidiaries early in 1971, we re-cast Berkshire Hathaway's bank loan so as to provide those companies with additional capital funds. This financing turned out to be particularly propitious when the opportunity to purchase Home & Auto occurred later in the year.

Our insurance and banking subsidiaries possess a fiduciary relationship with the public. We retain a fundamental belief in operating from a very strongly financed position so as to be in a position to unquestionably fulfill our responsibilities. Thus, we will continue to map our financial future for maximum financial strength in our subsidiaries as well as at the parent company level.

Warren E. Buffett
Chairman of the Board

March 13, 1972

Berkshire Hathaway Inc.

To the Stockholders of
Berkshire Hathaway Inc.:

Operating earnings of Berkshire Hathaway during 1972 amounted to a highly satisfactory 19.8% of beginning shareholders' equity. Significant improvement was recorded in all of our major lines of business, but the most dramatic gains were in insurance underwriting profit. Due to an unusual convergence of favorable factors—diminishing auto accident frequency, moderating accident severity, and an absence of major catastrophes—underwriting profit margins achieved a level far above averages of the past or expectations of the future.

While we anticipate a modest decrease in operating earnings during 1973, it seems clear that our diversification moves of recent years have established a significantly higher base of normal earning power. Your present management assumed policy control of the company in May, 1965. Eight years later, our 1972 operating earnings of $11,116,256 represent a return many-fold higher than would have been produced had we continued to devote our resources entirely to the textile business. At the end of the 1964 fiscal year, shareholders' equity totaled $22,138,753. Since that time, no additional equity capital has been introduced into the business, either through cash sale or through merger. On the contrary, some stock has been reacquired, reducing outstanding shares by 14%. The increase in book value per share from $19.46 at fiscal year-end 1964 to $69.72 at 1972 year-end amounts to about 16.5% compounded annually.

Our three major acquisitions of recent years have all worked out exceptionally well—from both the financial and human standpoints. In all three cases, the founders were major sellers and received significant proceeds in cash—and, in all three cases, the same individuals, Jack Ringwalt, Gene Abegg and Vic Raab, have continued to run the businesses with undiminished energy and imagination which have resulted in further improvement of the fine records previously established.

We will continue to search for logical extensions of our present operations, and also for new operations which will allow us to continue to employ our capital effectively.

Textile Operations

As predicted in last year's annual report, the textile industry experienced a pickup in 1972. In recent years, Ken Chace and Ralph Rigby have developed an outstanding sales organization enjoying a growing reputation for service and reliability. Manufacturing capabilities have been restructured to complement our sales strengths.

Helped by the industry recovery, we experienced some payoff from these efforts in 1972. Inventories were controlled, minimizing close-out losses in addition to minimizing capital requirements; product mix was greatly improved. While the general level of profitability of the industry will always be the primary factor in determining the level of our textile earnings, we believe that our relative position within the industry has noticeably improved. The outlook for 1973 is good.

Insurance Underwriting

Our exceptional underwriting profits during 1972 in the large traditional area of our insurance business at National Indemnity present a paradox. They served to swell substantially total corporate profits for 1972, but the factors which produced such profits induced exceptional amounts of new competition at what we believe to be a non-compensatory level of rates. Over-all, we probably would have retained better prospects for the next five years if profits had not risen so dramatically this year.

Substantial new competition was forecast in our annual report for last year and we experienced in 1972 the decline in premium volume that we stated such competition implied. Our belief is that industry underwriting profit margins will narrow substantially in 1973 or 1974 and, in time, this may produce an environment in which our historical growth can be resumed. Unfortunately, there is a lag between deterioration of underwriting results and tempering of competition. During this period we expect to continue to have negative volume comparisons in our traditional operation. Our seasoned management, headed by Jack Ringwalt and Phil Liesche, will continue to underwrite to produce a profit, although not at the level of 1972, and base our rates on long-term expectations rather than short-term hopes. Although this approach has meant dips in volume from time to time in the past, it has produced excellent long-term results.

Also as predicted in last year's report, our reinsurance division experienced many of the same competitive factors in 1972. A multitude of new organizations entered what has historically been a rather small field, and rates were often cut substantially, and we believe unsoundly, particularly in the catastrophe area. The past year turned out to be unusually free of catastrophes and our underwriting experience was good.

George Young has built a substantial and profitable reinsurance operation in just a few years. In the longer term we plan to be a very major factor in the reinsurance field, but an immediate expansion of volume is not sensible against a background of deteriorating rates. In our view, underwriting exposures are greater than ever. When the loss potential inherent in such exposures becomes an actuality, repricing will take place which should give us a chance to expand significantly.

In the "home state" operation, our oldest and largest such company, Cornhusker Casualty Company, operating in Nebraska only, achieved good underwriting results. In the second full year, the home state marketing appeal has been proven with the attainment of volume on the order of one-third of that achieved by "old line" giants who have operated in the state for many decades.

Our two smaller companies, in Minnesota and Texas, had unsatisfactory loss ratios on very small volume. The home state managements understand that underwriting profitably is the yardstick of success and that operations can only be expanded significantly when it is clear that we are doing the right job in the underwriting area. Expense ratios at the new companies are also high, but that is to be expected when they are in the development stage.

John Ringwalt has done an excellent job of launching this operation, and plans to expand into at least one additional state during 1973. While there is much work yet to be done, the home state operation appears to have major long-range potential.

Last year it was reported than we had acquired Home and Automobile Insurance Company of Chicago. We felt good about the acquisition at the time, and we feel even better now. Led by Vic Raab, this company continued its excellent record in 1972. During 1973 we expect to enter the Florida (Dade County) and California (Los Angeles) markets with the same sort of specialized urban auto coverage which Home and Auto has practiced so successfully in Cook County. Vic has the managerial capacity to run a much larger operation. Our expectation is that Home and Auto will expand significantly within a few years.

Insurance Investment Results

We were most fortunate to experience dramatic gains in premium volume from 1969 to 1971 coincidental with virtually record-high interest rates. Large amounts of investable funds were thus received at a time when they could be put to highly advantageous use. Most of these funds were placed in tax-exempt bonds and our investment income, which has increased from $2,025,201 in 1969 to $6,755,242 in 1972, is subject to a low effective tax rate.

Our bond portfolio possesses unusually good call protection, and we will benefit for many years to come from the high average yield of the present portfolio. The lack of current premium growth, however, will moderate substantially the growth in investment income during the next several years.

Banking Operations

Our banking subsidiary, The Illinois Bank and Trust Co. of Rockford, maintained its position of industry leadership in profitability. After-tax earnings of 2.2% on average deposits in 1972 are the more remarkable when evaluated against such moderating factors as: (1) a mix of 50% time deposits heavily weighted toward consumer savings instruments, all paying the maximum rates permitted by law; (2) an unvaryingly strong liquid position and avoidance of money-market borrowings; (3) a loan policy which has produced a net charge-off ratio in the last two years of about 5% of that of the average commercial bank. This record is a direct tribute to the leadership of Gene Abegg and Bob Kline who run a bank where the owners and the depositors can both eat well and sleep well.

During 1972, interest paid to depositors was double the amount paid in 1969. We have aggressively sought consumer time deposits, but have not pushed for large "money market" certificates of deposit although, during the past several years, they have generally been a less costly source of time funds.

During the past year, loans to our customers expanded approximately 38%. This is considerably more than indicated by the enclosed balance sheet which includes $10.9 million in short-term commercial paper in the 1971 loan total, but which has no such paper included at the end of 1972.

Our position as "Rockford's Leading Bank" was enhanced during 1972. Present rate structures, a decrease in investable funds due to new Federal Reserve collection procedures, and a probable increase in already substantial non-federal taxes make it unlikely that Illinois National will be able to increase its earnings during 1973.

Financial

On March 15, 1973, Berkshire Hathaway borrowed $20 million at 8% from twenty institutional lenders. This loan is due March 1, 1993, with principal repayments beginning March 1, 1979. From the proceeds, $9 million was used to repay our bank loan and the balance is being invested in insurance subsidiaries. Periodically, we expect that there will be opportunities to achieve significant expansion in our insurance business and we intend to have the financial resources available to maximize such opportunities.

Our subsidiaries in banking and insurance have major fiduciary responsibilities to their customers. In these operations we maintain capital strength far above industry norms, but still achieve a good level of profitability on such capital. We will continue to adhere to the former objective and make every effort to continue to maintain the latter.

Warren E. Buffett
Chairman of the Board

March 16, 1973

Berkshire Hathaway Inc.

To the Stockholders of
Berkshire Hathaway Inc.:

Our financial results for 1973 were satisfactory, with operating earnings of $11,930,592, producing a return of 17.4% on beginning stockholders' equity. Although operating earnings improved from $11.43 to $12.18 per share, earnings on equity decreased from the 19.8% of 1972. This decline occurred because the gain in earnings was not commensurate with the increase in shareholders' investment. We had forecast in last year's report that such a decline was likely. Unfortunately, our forecast proved to be correct.

Our textile, banking, and most insurance operations had good years, but certain segments of the insurance business turned in poor results. Overall, our insurance business continues to be a most attractive area in which to employ capital.

Management's objective is to achieve a return on capital over the long term which averages somewhat higher than that of American industry generally—while utilizing sound accounting and debt policies. We have achieved this goal in the last few years, and are trying to take those steps which will enable us to maintain this performance in the future. Prospects for 1974 indicate some further decline in rate of return on our enlarged equity base.

Textile Operations

Textile demand remained unusually strong throughout 1973. Our main problems revolved around shortages of fiber, which complicated operations and resulted in something less than full utilization of loom capacity. Prices of some fibers skyrocketed during the year.

Cost of Living Council regulations prevented the pricing of many finished products at levels of some of our competitors. However, profits were reasonably commensurate with our capital investment, although below those that apparently might have been achieved had we been able to price at market levels. The textile business has been highly cyclical and price controls may have served to cut down some of the hills while still leaving us with the inevitable valleys.

Because of the extraordinary price rises in raw materials during 1973, which show signs of continuing in 1974, we have elected to adopt the "lifo" method of inventory pricing. This method more nearly matches current costs against current revenues, and minimizes inventory "profits" included in reported earnings. Further information on this change is included in the footnotes to our financial statements.

Insurance Operations

During 1973, Jack Ringwalt retired as President of National Indemnity Company after an absolutely brilliant record since founding the business in 1940. He was succeeded by Phil Liesche who, fortunately for us, possesses the same underwriting and managerial philosophy that worked so well for Jack.

Our traditional business, specialized auto and general liability lines conducted through National Indemnity Company and National Fire and Marine Insurance Company, had an exceptionally fine underwriting year during 1973. We again experienced a decline in volume. Competition was intense, and we passed up the chance to match rate-cutting by more optimistic underwriters. There currently are faint indications that some of these competitors are learning of the inadequacy of their rates (and also of their loss reserves) which may result in easing of market pressures as the year develops. If so, we may again experience volume increases.

Our reinsurance operation had a somewhat similar year—good underwriting experience, but difficulty in maintaining previous volume levels. This operation, guided by the tireless and well directed efforts of George Young, has been a major profit producer since its inception in 1969.

Our "home state" insurance companies made excellent progress in Nebraska and Minnesota, with both good growth in volume and acceptable loss ratios. We began operations late in the year in Iowa. To date, our big problem has been Texas. In that state we virtually had to start over during 1973 as the initial management we selected proved incapable of underwriting successfully. The Texas experience has been expensive, and we still have our work cut out for us. Overall, however, the home state operation appears to have a promising potential.

Our specialized urban auto operation, Home and Automobile Insurance Company, experienced very poor underwriting in Chicago during 1973. It would appear that rates are inadequate in our primary Cook County marketing area, although the current energy situation confuses the picture. The question is whether possible lowered accident frequency because of reduced driving will more than offset continuing inflation in medical and repair costs, as well as jury awards. We believe that inflation will hurt us more than reduced driving will help us, but some of our competitors appear to believe otherwise.

Home and Auto expanded into Florida and California during the year, but it is too early to know how these moves will prove out financially.

A contributing factor in our unsatisfactory earnings at Home and Auto during 1973 was an accounting system which was not bringing information to management on a sufficiently timely basis. This situation now is being corrected.

On the investment side of our insurance operation, we made substantial additional commitments in common stocks during 1973. We had significant unrealized depreciation—over $12 million—in our common stock holdings at year-end, as indicated in our financial statements. Nevertheless, we believe that our common stock portfolio at cost represents good value in terms of intrinsic business worth. In spite of the large unrealized loss at year-end, we would expect satisfactory results from the portfolio over the longer term.

Banking Operations

The Illinois National Bank & Trust Co. of Rockford again had a record year in 1973. Average deposits were approximately $130 million, of which approximately 60% were time deposits. Interest rates were increased substantially in the important consumer savings area when regulatory maximums were raised at mid-year.

Despite this mix heavily weighted toward interest bearing deposits, our operating earnings after taxes (including a new Illinois state income tax) were again over 2.1% of average deposits.

We continue to be the largest bank in Rockford. We continue to maintain unusual liquidity. We continue to meet the increasing loan demands of our customers. And we continue to maintain our unusual profitability. This is a direct tribute to the abilities of Gene Abegg, Chairman, who has been running the Bank since it opened its doors in 1931, and Bob Kline, our President.

Merger With Diversified Retailing Company, Inc.

Your Directors have approved the merger of Diversified Retailing Company, Inc. into Berkshire Hathaway Inc. on terms involving issuance of 195,000 shares of Berkshire stock for the 1,000,000 shares of Diversified stock outstanding. Because Diversified and its subsidiaries own 109,551 shares of Berkshire, the net increase in the number of shares of Berkshire outstanding after giving effect to this transaction will not exceed 85,449. Various regulatory approvals must be obtained before this merger can be completed, and proxy material will be submitted to you later this year so that you may vote upon it.

Diversified Retailing Company, Inc., through subsidiaries, operates a chain of popular-priced women's apparel stores and also conducts a reinsurance business. In the opinion of your management, its most important asset is 16% of the stock of Blue Chip Stamps.

Blue Chip Stamps

Our holdings of stock in Blue Chip Stamps at year-end amounted to approximately 19% of that company's outstanding shares. Since year-end, we have increased our holdings so that they now represent approximately 22½%; implementation of the proposed merger with Diversified Retailing Company, Inc. would increase this figure to about 38½%.

Our equity in earnings of Blue Chip Stamps became significant for the first time in 1973, and posed an accounting question as to just what period's earnings should be recognized by Berkshire Hathaway Inc. as applicable to the financial statements covered by this annual report.

Blue Chip's fiscal year ends on the Saturday closest to February 28, or two months after the fiscal year-end of Berkshire Hathaway Inc. Or, viewed, alternatively, their year ends ten months prior to Berkshire Hathaway's. An acceptable accounting choice for us, and one which, if made, would not have required an auditor's disclaimer as to scope, was to recognize in our 1973 income an equity of $632,000 in Blue Chip's earnings for their year ended March 3, 1973 with regard to the fewer shares of Blue Chip we owned during this earlier period. But such an approach seemed at odds with reality, and would have meant a ten month lag each year in the future. Therefore, we chose to reflect as 1973 income our equity of $1,008,000 in Blue Chip's earnings based upon unaudited interim earnings through November as publicly reported by Blue Chip Stamps and with regard to our shareholdings during 1973. Because we made this choice of unaudited but current figures, as opposed to the alternative of audited but far from current figures, Peat, Marwick, Mitchell & Co. were unable to express an opinion on our 1973 earnings attributable to Blue Chip Stamps.

The annual report of Blue Chip Stamps, which will contain financial statements for the year ending March 2, 1974 audited by Price, Waterhouse and Company, will be available in early May. Any shareholder of Berkshire Hathaway Inc. who desires an annual report of Blue Chip Stamps may obtain it at that time by writing Mr. Robert H. Bird, Secretary, Blue Chip Stamps, 5801 South Eastern Avenue, Los Angeles, California 90040.

Blue Chip's trading stamp business has declined drastically over the past year or so, but it has important sources of earning power in its See's Candy Shops subsidiary as well as Wesco Financial Corporation, a 54% owned subsidiary engaged in the savings and loan business. We expect Blue Chip Stamps to achieve satisfactory earnings in future years related to capital employed, although certainly at a much lower level than would have been achieved if the trading stamp business had been maintained at anything close to former levels.

Your Chairman is on the Board of Directors of Blue Chip Stamps, as well as Wesco Financial Corporation, and is Chairman of the Board of See's Candy Shops Incorporated. Operating management of all three entities is in the hands of first-class, able, experienced executives.

Sun Newspapers, Inc.

In the 1969 annual report we commented on the purchase of Sun Newspapers Inc., a group of weekly papers published in the metropolitan Omaha area. Since that time we have not commented on their operations in the text of our annual reports, nor have we consolidated their financial results since the operation, because of the small investment involved, has been "financially insignificant."

During 1973 it was made quite apparent that such insignificance did not extend to publishing quality. On May 7th Sun Newspapers was awarded a Pulitzer Prize for local investigative reporting, (the first time in history that a weekly had won in this category) for its special section of March 30: 1972 relating to Boys Town. We reported the extraordinary contrast between decreasing services and mounting wealth that had taken place since Father Flanagan's death in 1948.

In addition to the Pulitzer Prize, the reporting job also won the Public Service Award of Sigma Delta Chi, the national society of professional journalists, as well as seven other national awards.

Our congratulations go to Paul Williams, Editor, and Stan Lipsey, Publisher, as well as the entire editorial staff of Sun Newspapers for their achievement, which vividly illustrated that size need not be equated with significance in publishing.

Warren E. Buffett
Chairman of the Board

March 29, 1974

Berkshire Hathaway Inc.

To the Stockholders of
Berkshire Hathaway Inc.:

Operating results for 1974 overall were unsatisfactory due to the poor performance of our insurance business. In last year's annual report some decline in profitability was predicted but the extent of this decline, which accelerated during the year, was a surprise. Operating earnings for 1974 were $8,383,576, or $8.56 per share, for a return on beginning shareholders' equity of 10.3%. This is the lowest return on equity realized since 1970. Our textile division and our bank both performed very well, turning in improved results against the already good figures of 1973. However, insurance underwriting, which has been mentioned in the last several annual reports as running at levels of unsustainable profitability, turned dramatically worse as the year progressed.

The outlook for 1975 is not encouraging. We undoubtedly will have sharply negative comparisons in our textile operation and probably a moderate decline in banking earnings. Insurance underwriting is a large question mark at this time—it certainly won't be a satisfactory year in this area, and could be an extremely poor one. Prospects are reasonably good for an improvement in both insurance investment income and our equity in earnings of Blue Chip Stamps. During this period we plan to continue to build financial strength and liquidity, preparing for the time when insurance rates become adequate and we can once again aggressively pursue opportunities for growth in this area.

Textile Operations

During the first nine months of 1974 textile demand was exceptionally strong, resulting in very firm prices. However, in the fourth quarter significant weaknesses began to appear, which have continued into 1975.

We currently are operating at about one-third of capacity. Obviously, at such levels operating losses must result. As shipments have fallen, we continuously have adjusted our level of operations downward so as to avoid building inventory.

Our products are largely in the curtain goods area. During a period of consumer uncertainty, curtains may well be high on the list of deferrable purchases. Very low levels of housing starts also serve to dampen demand. In addition, retailers have been pressing to cut inventories generally, and we probably are feeling some effect from these efforts. These negative trends should reverse in due course, and we are attempting to minimize losses until that time comes.

Insurance Underwriting

In the last few years we consistently have commented on the unusual profitability in insurance underwriting. This seemed certain eventually to attract unintelligent competition with consequent inadequate rates. It also has been apparent that many insurance organizations, major as well as minor, have been guilty of significant underreserving of losses, which inevitably produces faulty information as to the true cost of the product being sold. In 1974, these factors, along with a high rate of inflation, combined to produce a rapid erosion in underwriting results.

The costs of the product we deliver (aula repair, medical payments, compensation benefits, etc.) are increasing at a rate we estimate to be in the area of 1%per month. Of course, this increase doesn't proceed in an even flow but, inexorably, inflation grinds very heavily at the repair services—to humans and to property—that we provide. However, rates virtually have been unchanged in the properly and casualty field for the last few years. With costs moving forward rapidly and prices remaining unchanged, it was not hard to predict what would happen to profit margins.

Best's, the authoritative voice of the insurance industry, estimates that in 1974 all auto insurance premiums in the United States increased only about 2%. Such a growth in the pool of dollars available to pay insured losses and expenses was woefully inadequate. Obviously, medical costs applicable to people injured during the year, jury awards for pain and suffering, and body shop charges for repairing damaged cars increased at a dramatically greater rate during the year. Since premiums represent the sales dollar and the latter items represent the cost of goods sold, profit margins turned sharply negative.

As this report is being written, such deterioration continues. Loss reserves for many giant companies still appear to be understated by significant amounts, which means that these competitors continue to underestimate their true costs. Not only must rates be increased sufficiently to match the month-by-month increase in cost levels, but the existing expense-revenue gap must be overcome. At this time it appears that insurers must experience even more devastating underwriting results before they take appropriate pricing action.

All major areas of insurance operations, except for the "home state" companies, experienced significantly poorer results for the year.

The direct business of National Indemnity Company, our largest area of insurance activity, produced an underwriting loss of approximately 4% after several years of high profitability. Volume increased somewhat, but we are not encouraging such increases until rates are more adequate. At some point in the cycle, after major insurance companies have had their fill of red ink, history indicates that we will experience an inflow of business at compensatory rates. This operation, headed by Phil Liesche, a most able underwriter, is staffed by highly profit-oriented people and we believe it will provide excellent earnings in most future years, as it has in the past.

Intense competition in the reinsurance business has produced major losses for practically every company operating in the area. We have been no exception. Our underwriting loss was something over 12%—a horrendous figure, but probably little different from the average of the industry. What is even more frightening is that, while about the usual number of insurance catastrophes occurred during 1974, there really was no "super disaster" which might have accounted for the poor figures of the industry. Rather, a condition of inadequate rates prevails, particularly in the casualty area where we have significant exposure. Our reinsurance department is run by George Young, an exceptionally competent and hardworking manager. He has cancelled a great many contracts where prices are totally inadequate, and is making no attempt to increase volume except in areas where premiums are commensurate with risk. Based upon present rate levels, it seems highly unlikely that the reinsurance industry generally, or we, specifically, will have a profitable year in 1975.

Our "home state" companies, under the leadership of John Ringwalt, made good progress in 1974. We appear to be developing a sound agency group, capable of producing business with acceptable loss ratios. Our expense ratios still are much too high, but will come down as the operation develops into units of economic size. The Texas problem which was commented upon In last year's report seems to be improving. We consider the "home state" operation one of our more promising areas for the future.

Our efforts to expand Home and Automobile Insurance Company into Florida proved disastrous. The underwriting loss from operations in that market will come to over $2 million, a very large portion of which was realized in 1974. We made the decision to drop out of the Florida market in the middle of 1974, but losses in substantial amounts have continued since that time because of the term nature of insurance contracts, as well as adverse development on outstanding claims. We can't blame external insurance industry conditions for this mistake. In retrospect, it is apparent that our management simply did not have the underwriting information and the pricing knowledge necessary to be operating in the area. In Cook County, where Home and Auto's volume traditionally has been concentrated, evidence also became quite clear during 1914 that rates were inadequate. Therefore, rates were increased during the middle of the year but competition did not follow; consequently, our volume has dropped significantly in this area as competitors take business from us at prices that we regard as totally unrealistic.

While the tone of this section is pessimistic as to 1974 and 1975, we consider the insurance business to be inherently attractive. Our overall return on capital employed in this area—even including the poor results of 1974—remains high. We have made every effort to be realistic in the calculation of loss and expense reserves. Many of our competitors are in a substantially weakened financial position, and our strong capital picture leaves us prepared to grow significantly when conditions become right.

Insurance Investment Results

Investment funds generated from the operation of our insurance companies continued to grow during 1974. Investment income grew correspondingly, and produced overall profitability for the insurance group despite the poor underwriting results. As the insurance group balance sheet shows, we have increased liquidity substantially. This trend has continued since yearend. With poor underwriting and with generally weakened capital ratios throughout the insurance industry, such a higher level of liquidity is appropriate and comforting. It eliminates the possible temptation to write business at any price, simply to maintain cash flow, which is a major problem faced by many companies.

Several comments regarding market value of securities may be appropriate. Between the insurance group and the bank, we have approximately $140 million invested in bonds. About $20 million of this investment is in very short-term Treasury securities or commercial paper, neither of which is subject to other than negligible market fluctuation. This leaves about $120 million in bonds of longer maturities, with a very large percentage of this sum in municipal bonds with an average maturity of perhaps twelve to fifteen years. Because of our large liquid position and inherent operating characteristics of our financial businesses, it is quite unlikely that we will be required to sell any quantity of such bonds under disadvantageous conditions. Rather, it is our expectation that these bonds either will be held to maturity or sold at times believed to be advantageous.

However, on any given day the market value of our bond portfolio is determined by yields available on comparable securities. Such market values can swing dramatically. For example, during 1974 a leading index of high-grade municipals increased in yield from a level of 5.18% at the beginning of the year to 7.08% at the end of the year. In the bond market, each 1/100 of 1% change in yield is referred to as a "basis point" and thus, a change of 1% in interest levels is referred to as 100 basis points. As measured by the index, bond yields increased 190 basis points during 1974. On a fifteen-year bond, an increase of 10 basis points translates to about a 1% downward change in market value. On $120 million of such bonds, it is therefore clear that a change of 10 basis points in yields (which easily can happen in one day) changes the market value of our bond portfolio by something over $1 million. Thus, in 1974 our bond portfolio, which probably had a market value roughly approximating its carrying value at the start of the year, had a market value substantially below carrying value at the end of the year. The market value of our bond portfolio will continue to move in both directions in response to changes in the general level of yields but we do not consider such movements, and the unrealized gains and losses that they produce, to be of great importance as long as adequate liquidity is maintained.

Our stock portfolio declined again in 1974—along with most equity portfolios—to the point that at yearend it was worth approximately $17 million less than its carrying value. Again, we are under-no pressure to sell such securities except at times that we deem advantageous and it is our belief that, over a period of years, the overall portfolio will prove to be worth more than its cost. A net capital loss was realized in 1974, and very likely again will occur in 1975. However, we consider several of our major holdings to have great potential for significantly increased values in future years, and therefore feel quite comfortable with our stock portfolio. At this writing, market depreciation of the portfolio has been reduced by more than half from yearend figures, reflecting higher general stock market levels.

Banking Operations

There is little new to say about Illinois National Bank and Trust. With Eugene Abegg running the operation, the exceptional has become the commonplace. Year after year he continues to run one of the most profitable banks in the United States, while paying maximum interest rates to depositors, operating with unusual levels of liquidity, and maintaining a superior level of loan quality.

Two factors specifically should be noted in looking at the separate income statement of the bank. The effect of filing a consolidated tax return is reflected in their figures, with the tax loss of the insurance operations used to offset the tax liability created by banking operations. Also, a property tax formerly paid by the bank now is assessed to the parent company and is reflected in corporate selling and administrative expense. Because of accruals, this had a double effect at both the bank and corporate level in 1974.

Under present money market conditions, we expect bank earnings to be down somewhat in 1975 although we believe they still are likely to compare favorably with those of practically any banking institution in the country.

Blue Chip Stamps

During 1974 we increased our holdings of Blue Chip Stamps to approximately 25½% of the outstanding shares of that company. Overall, we are quite happy about the results of Blue Chip and its prospects for the future. Stamp sales continue at a greatly reduced level, but the Blue Chip management has done an excellent job of adjusting operating costs, The See's Candy Shops, Inc. subsidiary had an outstanding year, and has excellent prospects for the future.

Your Chairman is on the Board of Directors of Blue Chip Stamps, as well as Wesco Financial Corporation, a 64% owned subsidiary, and is Chairman of the Board of See's Candy Shops, Inc. We expect Blue Chip Stamps to be a source of continued substantial earning power for Berkshire Hathaway Inc.

The annual report of Blue Chip Stamps, which will contain financial statements for the year ended March 1, 1975 audited by Price, Waterhouse and Company, will be available in early May. Any shareholder of Berkshire Hathaway Inc. who desires an annual report of Blue Chip Stamps may obtain it at that time by writing Mr. Robert H. Bird, Secretary, Blue Chip Stamps, 5801 South Eastern

Avenue, Los Angeles, California 90040.

Merger with Diversified Retailing Company, Inc.

As you previously have been informed, the proposed merger with Diversified Retailing Company, Inc. was terminated by the respective Boards of Directors on January 28, 1975. We continue to view such a merger as eventually desirable, and hope to reopen the subject at some future time.

Warren E. Buffett
Chairman of the Board

March 31, 1975

Berkshire Hathaway Inc.

To the Stockholders of Berkshire Hathaway Inc.:

Last year, when discussing the prospects for 1975, we stated "the outlook for 1975 is not encouraging." This forecast proved to be distressingly accurate. Our operating earnings for 1975 were $6,713,592, or $6.85 per share, producing a return on beginning shareholder's equity of 7.6%. This is the lowest return on equity experienced since 1967. Furthermore, as explained later in this letter, a large segment of these earnings resulted from Federal income tax refunds which will not be available to assist performance in 1976.

On balance, however, current trends indicate a somewhat brighter 1976. Operations and prospects will be discussed in greater detail below, under specific industry titles. Our expectation is that significantly better results in textiles, earnings added from recent acquisitions, an increase in equity in earnings of Blue Chip Stamps resulting from an enlarged ownership interest, and at least a moderate improvement in insurance underwriting results will more than offset other possible negatives to produce greater earnings in 1976. The major variable—and by far the most difficult to predict with any feeling of confidence—is the insurance underwriting result. Present very tentative indications are that underwriting improvement is in prospect. If such improvement is moderate, our overall gain in earnings in 1976 likewise will prove moderate. More significant underwriting improvement could give us a major gain in earnings.

Textile Operations

During the first half of 1975 sales of textile products were extremely depressed, resulting in major production curtailments. Operations ran at a significant loss, with employment down as much as 53% from a year earlier.

In contrast with previous cyclical slumps, however, most textile producers quickly reduced production to match incoming orders, thus preventing massive industry-wide accumulation of inventories. Such cutbacks caused quite prompt reflection at the mill operating level when demand revived at retail. As a result, beginning about midyear business rebounded at a fairly rapid rate. This "V" shaped textile depression, while one of the sharpest on record, also became one of the shortest ones in our experience. The fourth quarter produced an excellent profit for our textile division, bringing results for the year into the black.

On April 28, 1975 we acquired Waumbec Mills Incorporated and Waumbec Dyeing and Finishing Co., Inc. located in Manchester, New Hampshire. These companies have long sold woven goods into the drapery and apparel trade. Such drapery materials complement and extend the line already marketed through the Home Fabrics Division of Berkshire Hathaway. In the period prior to our acquisition, the company had run at a very substantial loss, with only about 55% of looms in operation and the finishing plant operating at about 50% of capacity. Losses continued on a reduced basis for a few months after acquisition. Outstanding efforts by our manufacturing, administrative and sales people now have produced major improvements, which, coupled with the general revival in textiles, have moved Waumbec into a significant profit position.

We expect a good level of profits from textiles in 1976. Continued progress is being made in the movement of Waumbec goods into areas of traditional marketing strength of Berkshire Hathaway, productivity should improve in both the weaving and finishing areas at Manchester, and textile demand continues to firm at decent prices.

1

We have great confidence in the ability of Ken Chace and his team to maximize our strengths in textiles. Therefore, we continue to look for ways to increase further our scale of operations while avoiding major capital investment in new fixed assets which we consider unwise, considering the relatively low returns historically earned on large scale investment in new textile equipment.

Insurance Underwriting

The property and casualty insurance industry had its worst year in history during 1975. We did our share—unfortunately, even somewhat more. Really disastrous results were concentrated in auto and long-tail (contracts where settlement of loss usually occurs long after the loss event) lines.

Economic inflation, with the increase in cost of repairing humans and property far outstripping the general rate of inflation, produced ultimate loss costs which soared beyond premium levels established in a different cost environment. "Social" inflation caused the liability concept to be expanded continuously, far beyond limits contemplated when rates were established—in effect, adding coverage beyond what was paid for. Such social inflation increased significantly both the propensity to sue and the possibility of collecting mammoth jury awards for events not previously considered statistically significant in the establishment of rates. Furthermore, losses to policyholders which otherwise would result from mushrooming insolvencies of companies inadequately reacting to these problems are divided through Guaranty Funds among remaining solvent insurers. These trends will continue, and should moderate any optimism which otherwise might be justified by the sharply increased rates now taking effect.

Berkshire Hathaway's insurance subsidiaries have a disproportionate concentration of business in precisely the lines which produced the worst underwriting results in 1975. Such lines produce unusually high investment income and, therefore, have been particularly attractive to us under previous underwriting conditions. However, our "mix" has been very disadvantageous during the past two years and it well may be that we will remain positioned in the more difficult part of the insurance spectrum during the inflationary years ahead.

The only segment to show improved results for us during 1975 was the "home state" operation, which has made continuous progress under the leadership of John Ringwalt. Although still operating at a significant underwriting loss, the combined ratio improved from 1974. Adjusted for excess costs attributable to operations still in the start-up phase, underwriting results are satisfactory. Texas United Insurance Company, a major problem a few years ago, has made outstanding progress since George Billing has assumed command. With an almost totally new agency force, Texas United was the winner of the "Chairman's Cup" for achievement of the lowest loss ratio among the home state companies. Cornhusker Casualty Company, oldest and largest of the home state companies, continues its outstanding operation with major gains in premium volume and a combined ratio slightly under 100. Substantial premium growth is expected at the home state operation during 1976; the measurement of success, however, will continue to be the achievement of a low combined ratio.

Our traditional business at National Indemnity Company, representing well over half of our insurance volume, had an extraordinarily bad underwriting year in 1975. Although rates were increased frequently and significantly, they continually lagged loss experience throughout the year. Several special programs instituted in the early 1970s have caused significant losses, as well as a heavy drain on managerial time and energies. Present indications are that premium volume will show a major increase in 1976, and we hope that underwriting results will improve.

Reinsurance suffered the same problems as our direct business during 1975. The same remedial efforts were attempted. Because reinsurance contract settlements lag those of direct business, it well may be that any upturn in results from our direct insurance business will precede those of the reinsurance segment.

At our Home and Automobile Insurance Company subsidiary, now writing auto business only in the Cook County area of Illinois, experience continued very bad in 1975 resulting in a management change in October. John Seward was made President at that time, and has energetically and imaginatively implemented a completely revamped underwriting approach.

Overall, our insurance operation will produce a substantial gain in premium volume during 1976. Much of this will reflect increased rates rather than more policies. Under normal circumstances such a gain in volume would be welcome, but our emotions are mixed at present. Underwriting experience should improve—and we expect it to—but our confidence level is not high. While our efforts will be devoted to obtaining a combined ratio below 100, it is unlikely to be attained during 1976.

Insurance Investments

Gains in investment income were moderate during 1975 because premium volume remained flat and underwriting losses reduced funds available for investment. Invested assets, measured at cost at yearend, were close to identical with the level at the beginning of the year.

At the end of 1974 the net unrealized loss in the stock section of our portfolio amounted to about $17 million, but we expressed the opinion, nevertheless, that this portfolio overall represented good value at its carrying value of cost. During 1975 a net capital loss of $2,888,000 before tax credits was realized, but our present expectation is that 1976 will be a year of realized capital gain. On March 31, 1976 our net unrealized gains applicable to equities amounted to about $15 million. Our equity investments are heavily concentrated in a few companies which are selected based on favorable economic characteristics, competent and honest management, and a purchase price attractive when measured against the yardstick of value to a private owner.

When such criteria are maintained, our intention is to hold for a long time; indeed, our largest equity investment is 467,150 shares of Washington Post "B" stock with a cost of $10.6 million, which we expect to hold permanently.

With this approach, stock market fluctuations are of little importance to us—except as they may provide buying opportunities—but business performance is of major importance. On this score we have been delighted with progress made by practically all of the companies in which we now have significant investments.

We have continued to maintain a strong liquid position in our insurance companies. In last year's annual report we explained how variations of 1/10 of 1% in interest rates result in million dollar swings in market value of our bonds. We consider such market fluctuation of minor importance as our liquidity and general financial strength make it highly improbable that bonds will have to be sold at times other than those of our choice.

Banking

It is difficult to find adjectives to describe the performance of Eugene Abegg, Chief Executive of Illinois National Bank and Trust of Rockford, Illinois, our banking subsidiary.

In a year when many banking operations experienced major troubles, Illinois National continued its outstanding record. Against average loans of about $65 million, net loan losses were $24,000, or .04%. Unusually high liquidity is maintained with obligations of the U. S. Government and its agencies, all due within one year, at yearend amounting to about 75% of demand deposits. Maximum rates of interest are paid on all consumer savings instruments which make up more than half of the deposit base. Yet, despite the maintenance of premier liquidity and the avoidance of "stretching" for high yield loans, the Illinois National continues as about the most profitable bank of its size, or larger, in the country.

In 1975 the thirty largest banks in the United States earned an average of .5% on total assets. The Illinois National earned about four times that much. These same thirty largest banks carried down 7% of operating revenues to net income. Without counting any tax benefits from consolidation, Illinois National carried down 27%.

Gene Abegg opened the doors of the Illinois National Bank in 1931 with paid-in capital of $250,000. In 1932, its first full year of operation, it earned $8,782. No additional capital has been paid in, and we recommend reading its financial statements on pages 28-34 to see what a truly outstanding manager has built in 44 years at the helm.

Under the present interest rate structure, it is expected that earnings of the Bank will be off somewhat during 1976 but still will remain at a highly satisfactory level.

Blue Chip Stamps

During 1975 our holdings of Blue Chip Stamps remained at 25½% of that company's outstanding shares. However, early in 1976 our holdings were increased to 31½%. We expect some increase in our equity in Blue Chip's earnings in 1976 because of this increased ownership.

The stamp business continues its precipitous decline with volume in the year ended February 28, 1976 amounting to only one-sixth that of the peak year ended February 28, 1970. Don Koeppel and Bill Ramsey have done an extraordinary job of cost-cutting, which has served to moderate operating problems resulting from this evaporation of business. In addition, the acquisition of See's Candies in 1972 has proven a real winner. Chuck Huggins's management has been outstanding, and profits have moved up dramatically during the past several years.

Shareholders of Berkshire Hathaway Inc. desiring the current annual report of Blue Chip Stamps should write Mr. Robert H. Bird, Secretary, Blue Chip Stamps, 5801 South Eastern Avenue, Los Angeles, California 90040.

Federal Income Tax Implications

In reading our earnings statement you will notice a significant amount of Federal income taxes paid in earlier years are now recoverable because of the net operating loss, as computed for tax purposes, sustained in 1975. Such loss results from the exclusion from income of 100% of interest from state and local issues, and 85% of dividends from domestic corporations. We have exhausted our reservoir of available tax recoveries and, therefore, a repeat of our overall operating performance in 1976 would produce much smaller net earnings. While we do not expect this result, it is important that you are aware of the absence of this cushion in the event that operating losses, as calculated for Federal tax purposes, should continue.

Acquisition of K & W Products

In addition to the 1975 Waumbec acquisition, we acquired for cash and notes on January 6, 1978, 100% of the assets of K & W Products, including its insurance subsidiaries. The insurance operations are minor in scope, representing business already associated with National Indemnity Company. K & W Products manufactures specialty automotive chemicals for use in automobile maintenance, such as radiator and block sealants, gasket compounds and fuel and oil additives. The company has extensive trademark or trade name protection for its products, which it manufactures at plants in California and Indiana. Although relatively small, with sales of a little over $2 million, it consistently has generated favorable earnings. Positioned as we now are with respect to income taxes, the addition of a solid source of taxable income is particularly welcome.

General Review

Your present management assumed responsibility at Berkshire Hathaway in May, 1965. At the end of the prior fiscal year (September, 1964) the net worth of the Company was $22.1 million, and 1,137,778 common shares were outstanding, with a resulting book value of $19.46 per share. Ten years earlier, Berkshire Hathaway's net worth had been $53.4 million. Dividends and stock repurchases accounted for over $21 million of the decline in company net worth, but aggregate net losses of $9.8 million had been incurred on sales of $595 million during the decade.

In 1965, two New England textile mills were the company's only sources of earning power and, before Ken Chace assumed responsibility for the operation, textile earnings had been erratic and, cumulatively, something less than zero subsequent to the merger of Berkshire Fine Spinning and Hathaway Manufacturing. Since 1964, net worth has been built to $92.9 million, or $94.92 per share. We have acquired total, or virtually total ownership of six businesses through negotiated purchases for cash (or cash and notes) from private owners, started four others, purchased a 31.5% interest in a large affiliate enterprise and reduced the number of outstanding shares of Berkshire Hathaway to 979,569. Overall, equity per share has compounded at an annual rate of slightly over 15%.

While 1975 was a major disappointment, efforts will continue to develop growing and diversified sources of earnings. Our objective is a conservatively financed and highly liquid business—possessing extra margins of balance sheet strength consistent with the fiduciary obligations inherent in the banking and insurance industries—which will produce a long term rate of return on equity capital exceeding that of American industry as a whole.

Warren E. Buffett, Chairman

Berkshire Hathaway Inc.

To the Stockholders of Berkshire Hathaway Inc.:

After two dismal years, operating results in 1976 improved significantly. Last year we said the degree of progress in insurance underwriting would determine whether our gain in earnings would be "moderate" or "major." As it turned out, earnings exceeded even the high end of our expectations. In large part, this was due to the outstanding efforts of Phil Liesche's managerial group at National Indemnity Company.

In dollar terms, operating earnings came to $16,073,000, or $16.47 per share. While this is a record figure, we consider return on shareholders' equity to be a much more significant yardstick of economic performance. Here our result was 17.3%, moderately above our long-term average and even further above the average of American industry, but well below our record level of 19.8% achieved in 1972.

Our present estimate, subject to all the caveats implicit in forecasting, is that dollar operating earnings are likely to improve somewhat in 1977, but that return on equity may decline a bit from the 1976 figure.

Textile Operations

Our textile division was a significant disappointment during 1976. Earnings, measured either by return on sales or by return on capital employed, were inadequate. In part, this was due to industry conditions which did not measure up to expectations of a year ago. But equally important were our own shortcomings. Marketing efforts and mill capabilities were not properly matched in our new Waumbec operation. Unfavorable manufacturing cost variances were produced by improper evaluation of machinery and personnel capabilities. Ken Chace, as always, has been candid in reporting problems and has worked diligently to correct them. He is a pleasure to work with—even under difficult operating conditions.

While the first quarter outlook is for red ink, our quite tentative belief is that textile earnings in 1977 will equal, or exceed modestly, those of 1976. Despite disappointing current results, we continue to look for ways to build our textile operation and presently have one moderate-size acquisition under consideration. It should be recognized that the textile business does not offer the expectation of high returns on investment. Nevertheless, we maintain a commitment to this division—a very important source of employment in New Bedford and Manchester—and believe reasonable returns on average are possible.

Insurance Underwriting

Casualty insurers enjoyed some rebound from the disaster levels of 1975 as rate increases finally outstripped relentless cost increases. Preliminary figures indicate that the stockholder owned portion of the property and casualty industry had a combined ratio of 103.0 in 1976, compared to 108.3 in 1975. (100 represents a break-even position on underwriting—and higher figures represent underwriting losses.) We are unusually concentrated in auto lines where stock companies had an improvement from 113.5 to 107.4. Our own overall improvement was even more dramatic, from 115.4 to 98.7.

Our major insurance sector in insurance, the traditional auto and general liability business of

1

National Indemnity Company, had an outstanding year, achieving profit levels significantly better than the industry generally. Credit for this performance must be given to Phil Liesche, aided particularly by Roland Miller in Underwriting and Bill Lyons in Claims.

Volume at National Indemnity Company grew rapidly during 1976 as competitors finally reacted to the inadequacy of past rates. But, as mentioned in last year's annual report, we are concentrated heavily in lines that are particularly susceptible to both economic and social inflation. Thus present rates, which are adequate for today, will not be adequate tomorrow. Our opinion is that before long, perhaps in 1978, the industry will fall behind on rates as temporary prosperity produces unwise competition. If this happens, we must be prepared to meet the next wave of inadequate pricing by a significant reduction in volume.

Reinsurance underwriting has lagged the improvement in direct business. When mistakes are made in the pricing of reinsurance, the effects continue for even longer than when similar mistakes are made in direct underwriting. George Young, an outstanding manager, has worked tirelessly to achieve his goal of profitable underwriting, and has cancelled a great many contracts where appropriate rate adjustments were not obtainable. Here, as in the direct business, we have had a concentration in casualty lines which have been particularly hard hit by inflationary conditions. The near term outlook still is not good for our reinsurance business.

Our "home state" operation continues to make substantial progress under the management of John Ringwalt. The combined ratio improved from 108.4 in 1975 to 102.7 in 1976. There still are some excess costs reflected in the combined ratio which result from the small size of several operations. Cornhusker Casualty Company, oldest and largest of the home state companies, was the winner of the Chairman's Cup in 1976 for achievement of the lowest loss ratio among the home state companies. Cornhusker also achieved the lowest combined ratio in its history at 94.4, marking the fifth time in its six full years of existence that a ratio below 100 has been recorded. Premium growth was 78% at the home state companies in 1976, as market position improved significantly. We presently plan a new home state operation later this year.

Our Home and Automobile Insurance Company subsidiary, writing primarily automobile business in the Cook County area of Illinois, experienced a strong recovery in 1976. This is directly attributable to John Seward who, in his first full year, has revamped significantly both rating methods and marketing. The auto business has been shifted to a six month direct bill policy, which permits a faster reaction time to underwriting trends. Our general liability business at Home and Automobile has been expanded significantly with good results. While it remains to be proven that we can achieve sustained underwriting profitability at Home and Auto, we are delighted with the progress John Seward has achieved.

Overall, we expect a good year in insurance in 1977. Volume is high and present rate levels should allow profitable underwriting. Longer term, however, there are significant negatives in the insurance picture. Auto lines, in particular, seem highly vulnerable to pricing and regulatory problems produced by political and social factors beyond the control of individual companies.

Insurance Investments

Pre-tax investment income in 1976 improved to $10,820,000 from $8,918,000 as invested assets built up substantially, both from better levels of profitability and from gains in premium volume.

In recent reports we have noted the unrealized depreciation in our bond account, but stated that we considered such market fluctuations of minor importance as our liquidity and general financial strength made it improbable that bonds would have to be sold at times other than those of our choice. The bond market rallied substantially in 1976, giving us moderate net unrealized gains at yearend in the bond portfolios of both our bank and insurance companies. This, too, is of minor importance since our intention is to hold a large portion of our bonds to maturity. The corollary to higher bond prices is that lower earnings are produced by the new funds generated for investment. On balance, we prefer a situation where our bond portfolio has a current market value less than carrying value, but more attractive rates are available on issues purchased with newly-generated funds.

Last year we stated that we expected 1976 to be a year of realized capital gains and, indeed, gains of $9,962,000 before tax, primarily from stocks, were realized during the year. It presently appears that 1977 also will be a year of net realized capital gains. We now have a substantial unrealized gain in our stock portfolio as compared to a substantial unrealized loss several years ago. Here again we consider such market fluctuations from year to year relatively unimportant; unrealized appreciation in our equity holdings, which amounted to $45.7 million at yearend, has declined by about $5 million as this is written on March 21st.

However, we consider the yearly business progress of the companies in which we own stocks to be very important. And here, we have been delighted by the 1976 business performance achieved by most of our portfolio companies. If the business results continue excellent over a period of years, we are certain eventually to achieve good financial results from our stock holdings, regardless of wide year-to-year fluctuations in market values.

Our equity holdings with a market value of over $3 million on December 31, 1976 were as follows:

No. of Shares	Company	Cost
141,987	California Water Service Company	$ 3,608,711
1,986,953	Government Employees Insurance Company Convertible Preferred	19,416,635
1,294,308	Government Employees Insurance Company Common Stock	4,115,670
395,100	Interpublic Group of Companies	4,530,615
562,900	Kaiser Industries, Inc.	8,270,871
188,900	Munsingwear, Inc.	3,398,404
83,400	National Presto Industries, Inc.	1,689,896
170,800	Ogilvy & Mather International	2,762,433
934,300	The Washington Post Company Class B	10,627,604
	Total	$58,420,839
	All other Holdings	16,974,375
	Total Equities	$75,395,214

You will notice that our major equity holdings are relatively few. We select such investments on a long-term basis, weighing the same factors as would be involved in the purchase of 100% of an operating business: (1) favorable long-term economic characteristics; (2) competent and honest management; (3) purchase price attractive when measured against the yardstick of value to a private owner; and (4) an industry with which we are familiar and whose long-term business characteristics we feel competent to judge. It is difficult to find investments meeting such a test, and that is one reason for our concentration of holdings. We simply can't find one hundred different securities that conform to our investment requirements. However, we feel quite comfortable concentrating our holdings in the much smaller number that we do identify as attractive.

Our intention usually is to maintain equity positions for a long time, but sometimes we will make a purchase with a shorter expected time horizon such as Kaiser Industries. Here a distribution of securities and cash from the parent company is expected to be initiated in 1977. Purchases were made in 1976 after the announcement of the distribution plan by Kaiser management.

Banking

Eugene Abegg, Chief Executive of Illinois National Bank and Trust Company of Rockford, Illinois, our banking subsidiary, continues to lead the parade among bankers—just as he has even since he opened the bank in 1931.

Recently, National City Corp. of Cleveland, truly an outstandingly well-managed bank, ran an ad stating "the ratio of earnings to average assets was 1.34% in 1976 which we believe to be the best percentage for any major banking company." Among the really large banks this was the best earnings achievement but, at the Illinois National Bank, earnings were close to 50% better than those of National City, or approximately 2% of average assets.

This outstanding earnings record again was achieved while:

(1) paying maximum rates of interest on all consumer savings instruments (time deposits now make up well over two-thirds of the deposit base at the Illinois National Bank),

(2) maintaining an outstanding liquidity position (Federal Funds sold plus U. S. Government and Agency issues of under six months' duration presently are approximately equal to demand deposits), and

(3) avoiding high-yield but second-class loans (net loan losses in 1976 came to about $12,000, or .02% of outstanding loans, a very tiny fraction of the ratio prevailing in 1976 in the banking industry).

Cost control is an important factor in the bank's success. Employment is still at about the level existing at the time of purchase in 1969 despite growth in consumer time deposits from $30 million to $90 million and considerable expansion in other activities such as trust, travel and data processing.

Blue Chip Stamps

During 1976 we increased our interest in Blue Chip Stamps, and by yearend we held about 33% of that company's outstanding shares. Our interest in Blue Chip Stamps is of growing importance to us. Summary financial reports of Blue Chip Stamps are contained in the footnotes to our attached financial statements. Moreover, shareholders of Berkshire Hathaway Inc. are urged to obtain the current and subsequent annual reports of Blue Chip Stamps by requesting them from Mr. Robert H. Bird, Secretary, Blue Chip Stamps, 5801 South Eastern Avenue, Los Angeles, California 90040.

Miscellaneous

K & W Products has performed well in its first year as a subsidiary of Berkshire Hathaway Inc. Both sales and earnings were up moderately over 1975.

We have less than four years remaining to comply with requirement that our bank be divested by December 31, 1980. We intend to accomplish such a divestiture in a manner that minimizes disruption to the bank and produces good results for our shareholders. Most probably this will involve a spin-off of bank shares in 1980.

We also hope at some point to merge with Diversified Retailing Company, Inc. Both corporate simplification and enhanced ownership position in Blue Chip Stamps would be benefits of such a merger. However, it is unlikely that anything will be proposed in this regard during 1977.

Warren E. Buffett, Chairman

March 21, 1977

Berkshire Hathaway Inc.

To the Stockholders of Berkshire Hathaway Inc.:

Operating earnings in 1977 of $21,904,000, or $22.54 per share, were moderately better than anticipated a year ago. Of these earnings, $1.43 per share resulted from substantial realized capital gains by Blue Chip Stamps which, to the extent of our proportional interest in that company, are included in our operating earnings figure. Capital gains or losses realized directly by Berkshire Hathaway Inc. or its insurance subsidiaries are not included in our calculation of operating earnings. While too much attention should not be paid to the figure for any single year, over the longer term the record regarding aggregate capital gains or losses obviously is of significance.

Textile operations came in well below forecast, while the results of the Illinois National Bank as well as the operating earnings attributable to our equity interest in Blue Chip Stamps were about as anticipated. However, insurance operations, led again by the truly outstanding results of Phil Liesche's managerial group at National Indemnity Company, were even better than our optimistic expectations.

Most companies define "record" earnings as a new high in earnings per share. Since businesses customarily add from year to year to their equity base, we find nothing particularly noteworthy in a management performance combining, say, a 10% increase in equity capital and a 5% increase in earnings per share. After all, even a totally dormant savings account will produce steadily rising interest earnings each year because of compounding.

Except for special cases (for example, companies with unusual debt-equity ratios or those with important assets carried at unrealistic balance sheet values), we believe a more appropriate measure of managerial economic performance to be return on equity capital. In 1977 our operating earnings on beginning equity capital amounted to 19%, slightly better than last year and above both our own long-term average and that of American industry in aggregate. But, while our operating earnings per share were up 37% from the year before, our beginning capital was up 24%, making the gain in earnings per share considerably less impressive than it might appear at first glance.

We expect difficulty in matching our 1977 rate of return during the forthcoming year. Beginning equity capital is up 23% from a year ago, and we expect the trend of insurance underwriting profit margins to turn down well before the end of the year. Nevertheless, we expect a reasonably good year and our present estimate, subject to the usual caveats regarding the frailties of forecasts, is that operating earnings will improve somewhat on a per share basis during 1978.

Textile Operations

The textile business again had a very poor year in 1977. We have mistakenly predicted better results in each of the last two years. This may say something about our forecasting abilities, the nature of the textile industry, or both. Despite strenuous efforts, problems in marketing and manufacturing have persisted. Many difficulties experienced in the marketing area are due primarily to industry conditions, but some of the problems have been of our own making.

A few shareholders have questioned the wisdom of remaining in the textile business which, over the longer term, is unlikely to produce returns on capital comparable to those available in many other businesses. Our reasons are several: (1) Our mills in both New Bedford and Manchester are among the largest employers in each town, utilizing a labor force of high average age possessing relatively non-transferable skills. Our workers and unions have exhibited unusual understanding and effort in cooperating with management to achieve a cost structure and product mix which might allow us to maintain a viable operation. (2) Management also has been energetic and straightforward in its approach to our textile problems. In particular, Ken Chace's efforts after the change in corporate control took place in 1965 generated capital from the textile division needed to finance the acquisition and expansion of our profitable insurance operation. (3) With hard work and some imagination regarding manufacturing and marketing configurations, it seems reasonable that at least modest profits in the textile division can be achieved in the future.

Insurance Underwriting

Our insurance operation continued to grow significantly in 1977. It was early in 1967 that we made our entry into this industry through the purchase of National Indemnity Company and National Fire and Marine Insurance Company (sister companies) for approximately $8.6 million. In that year their premium volume amounted to $22 million. In 1977 our aggregate insurance premium volume was $151 million. No additional shares of Berkshire Hathaway stock have been issued to achieve any of this growth.

Rather, this almost 600% increase has been achieved through large gains in National Indemnity's traditional liability areas plus the starting of new companies (Cornhusker Casualty Company in 1970, Lakeland Fire and Casualty Company in 1971, Texas United Insurance Company in 1972, The Insurance Company of Iowa in 1973, and Kansas Fire and Casualty Company in late 1977), the purchase for cash of other insurance companies (Home and Automobile Insurance Company in 1971, Kerkling Reinsurance Corporation, now named Central Fire and Casualty Company, in 1976, and Cypress Insurance Company at yearend 1977), and finally through the marketing of additional products, most significantly reinsurance, within the National Indemnity Company corporate structure.

In aggregate, the insurance business has worked out very well. But it hasn't been a one-way street. Some major mistakes have been made during the decade, both in products and personnel. We experienced significant problems from (1) a surety operation initiated in 1969, (2) the 1973 expansion of Home and Automobile's urban auto marketing into the Miami, Florida area, (3) a still unresolved aviation "fronting" arrangement, and (4) our Worker's Compensation operation in California, which we believe retains an interesting potential upon completion of a reorganization now in progress. It is comforting to be in a business where some mistakes can be made and yet a quite satisfactory overall performance can be achieved. In a sense, this is the opposite case from our textile business where even very good management probably can average only modest results. One of the lessons your management has learned—and, unfortunately, sometimes re-learned—is the importance of being in businesses where tailwinds prevail rather than headwinds.

In 1977 the winds in insurance underwriting were squarely behind us. Very large rate increases were effected throughout the industry in 1976 to offset the disastrous underwriting results of 1974 and 1975. But, because insurance policies typically are written for one-year periods, with pricing mistakes capable of correction only upon renewal, it was 1977 before the full impact was felt upon earnings of those earlier rate increases.

The pendulum now is beginning to swing the other way. We estimate that costs involved in the insurance areas in which we operate rise at close to 1% per month. This is due to continuous monetary inflation affecting the cost of repairing humans and property, as well as "social inflation", a broadening definition by society and juries of what is covered by insurance policies. Unless rates rise at a comparable 1% per month, underwriting profits must shrink. Recently the pace of rate increases has slowed dramatically, and it is our expectation that underwriting margins generally will be declining by the second half of the year.

We must again give credit to Phil Liesche, greatly assisted by Roland Miller in Underwriting and Bill Lyons in Claims, for an extraordinary underwriting achievement in National Indemnity's traditional auto and general liability business during 1977. Large volume gains have been accompanied by excellent underwriting margins following contraction or withdrawal by many competitors in the wake of the 1974-75 crisis period. These conditions will reverse before long. In the meantime, National Indemnity's underwriting profitability has increased dramatically and, in addition, large sums have been made available for investment. As markets loosen and rates become inadequate, we again will face the challenge of philosophically accepting reduced volume. Unusual managerial discipline will be required, as it runs counter to normal institutional behavior to let the other fellow take away business—even at foolish prices.

Our reinsurance department, managed by George Young, improved its underwriting performance during 1977. Although the combined ratio (see definition on page 12) of 107.1 was unsatisfactory, its trend was downward throughout the year. In addition, reinsurance generates unusually high funds for investment as a percentage of premium volume.

At Home and Auto, John Seward continued to make progress on all fronts. John was a battlefield promotion several years ago when Home and Auto's underwriting was awash in red ink and the company faced possible extinction. Under his management it currently is sound, profitable, and growing.

John Ringwalt's homestate operation now consists of five companies, with Kansas Fire and Casualty Company becoming operational late in 1977 under the direction of Floyd Taylor. The homestate companies had net premium volume of $23 million, up from $5.5 million just three years ago. All four companies that operated throughout the year achieved combined ratios below 100, with Cornhusker Casualty Company, at 93.8, the leader. In addition to actively supervising the other four homestate operations, John Ringwalt manages the operations of Cornhusker which has recorded combined ratios below 100 in six of its seven full years of existence and, from a standing start in 1970, has grown to be one of the leading insurance companies operating in Nebraska utilizing the conventional independent agency system. Lakeland Fire and Casualty Company, managed by Jim Stodolka, was the winner of the Chairman's Cup in 1977 for achieving the lowest loss ratio among the homestate companies. All in all, the homestate operation continues to make excellent progress.

The newest addition to our insurance group is Cypress Insurance Company of South Pasadena, California. This Worker's Compensation insurer was purchased for cash in the final days of 1977 and, therefore, its approximate $12.5 million of volume for that year was not included in our results. Cypress and National Indemnity's present California Worker's Compensation operation will not be combined, but will operate independently utilizing somewhat different marketing strategies. Milt Thornton, President of Cypress since 1968, runs a first-class operation for policyholders, agents, employees and owners alike. We look forward to working with him.

Insurance companies offer standardized policies which can be copied by anyone. Their only products are promises. It is not difficult to be licensed, and rates are an open book. There are no important advantages from trademarks, patents, location, corporate longevity, raw material sources, etc., and very little consumer differentiation to produce insulation from competition. It is commonplace, in corporate annual reports, to stress the difference that people make. Sometimes this is true

3

and sometimes it isn't. But there is no question that the nature of the insurance business magnifies the effect which individual managers have on company performance. We are very fortunate to have the group of managers that are associated with us.

Insurance Investments

During the past two years insurance investments at cost (excluding the investment in our affiliate, Blue Chip Stamps) have grown from $134.6 million to $252.8 million. Growth in insurance reserves, produced by our large gain in premium volume, plus retained earnings, have accounted for this increase in marketable securities. In turn, net investment income of the Insurance Group has improved from $8.4 million pre-tax in 1975 to $12.3 million pre-tax in 1977.

In addition to this income from dividends and interest, we realized capital gains of $6.9 million before tax, about one-quarter from bonds and the balance from stocks. Our unrealized gain in stocks at yearend 1977 was approximately $74 million but this figure, like any other figure of a single date (we had an unrealized loss of $17 million at the end of 1974), should not be taken too seriously. Most of our large stock positions are going to be held for many years and the scorecard on our investment decisions will be provided by business results over that period, and not by prices on any given day. Just as it would be foolish to focus unduly on short-term prospects when acquiring an entire company, we think it equally unsound to become mesmerized by prospective near term earnings or recent trends in earnings when purchasing small pieces of a company; i.e., marketable common stocks.

A little digression illustrating this point may be interesting. Berkshire Fine Spinning Associates and Hathaway Manufacturing were merged in 1955 to form Berkshire Hathaway Inc. In 1948, on a pro forma combined basis, they had earnings after tax of almost $18 million and employed 10,000 people at a dozen large mills throughout New England. In the business world of that period they were an economic powerhouse. For example, in that same year earnings of IBM were $28 million (now $2.7 billion), Safeway Stores, $10 million, Minnesota Mining, $13 million, and Time, Inc., $9 million. But, in the decade following the 1955 merger aggregate sales of $595 million produced an aggregate loss for Berkshire Hathaway of $10 million. By 1964 the operation had been reduced to two mills and net worth had shrunk to $22 million, from $53 million at the time of the merger. So much for single year snapshots as adequate portrayals of a business.

Equity holdings of our insurance companies with a market value of over $5 million on December 31, 1977 were as follows:

No. of Shares	Company	Cost	Market
		(000's omitted)	
246,450	Capital Cities Communications, Inc.	$ 10,909	$ 13,228
1,986,953	Government Employees Insurance Company Convertible Preferred.	19,417	33,033
1,294,308	Government Employees Insurance Company Common Stock.	4,116	10,516
592,650	Interpublic Group of Companies	4,531	17,187
324,580	Kaiser Aluminum & Chemical Corporation	11,218	9,981
1,305,800	Kaiser Industries, Inc.	778	6,039
226,900	Knight-Ridder Newspapers, Inc.	7,534	8,736
170,800	Ogilvy & Mather International	2,762	6,960
934,300	The Washington Post Company Class B	10,628	33,401
	Total.	$ 71,893	$139,081
	All other Holdings	34,996	41,992
	Total Equities	$106,889	$181,073

We select our marketable equity securities in much the same way we would evaluate a business for acquisition in its entirety. We want the business to be (1) one that we can understand, (2) with favorable long-term prospects, (3) operated by honest and competent people, and (4) available at a very attractive price. We ordinarily make no attempt to buy equities for anticipated favorable stock price behavior in the short term. In fact, if their business experience continues to satisfy us, we welcome lower market prices of stocks we own as an opportunity to acquire even more of a good thing at a better price.

Our experience has been that pro-rata portions of truly outstanding businesses sometimes sell in the securities markets at very large discounts from the prices they would command in negotiated transactions involving entire companies. Consequently, bargains in business ownership, which simply are not available directly through corporate acquisition, can be obtained indirectly through stock ownership. When prices are appropriate, we are willing to take very large positions in selected companies, not with any intention of taking control and not foreseeing sell-out or merger, but with the expectation that excellent business results by corporations will translate over the long term into correspondingly excellent market value and dividend results for owners, minority as well as majority.

Such investments initially may have negligible impact on our operating earnings. For example, we invested $10.9 million in Capital Cities Communications during 1977. Earnings attributable to the shares we purchased totaled about $1.3 million last year. But only the cash dividend, which currently provides $40,000 annually, is reflected in our operating earnings figure.

Capital Cities possesses both extraordinary properties and extraordinary management. And these management skills extend equally to operations and employment of corporate capital. To purchase, directly, properties such as Capital Cities owns would cost in the area of twice our cost of purchase via the stock market, and direct ownership would offer no important advantages to us. While control would give us the opportunity—and the responsibility—to manage operations and corporate resources, we would not be able to provide management in either of those respects equal to that now in place. In effect, we can obtain a better management result through non-control than control. This is an unorthodox view, but one we believe to be sound.

Banking

In 1977 the Illinois National Bank continued to achieve a rate of earnings on assets about three times that of most large banks. As usual, this record was achieved while the bank paid maximum rates to savers and maintained an asset position combining low risk and exceptional liquidity. Gene Abegg formed the bank in 1931 with $250,000. In its first full year of operation, earnings amounted to $8,782. Since that time, no new capital has been contributed to the bank; on the contrary, since our purchase in 1969, dividends of $20 million have been paid. Earnings in 1977 amounted to $3.6 million, more than achieved by many banks two or three times its size.

Late last year Gene, now 80 and still running a banking operation without peer, asked that a successor be brought in. Accordingly, Peter Jeffrey, formerly President and Chief Executive Officer of American National Bank of Omaha, has joined the Illinois National Bank effective March 1st as President and Chief Executive Officer.

Gene continues in good health as Chairman. We expect a continued successful operation at Rockford's leading bank.

Blue Chip Stamps

We again increased our equity interest in Blue Chip Stamps, and owned approximately 36½% at the end of 1977. Blue Chip had a fine year, earning approximately $12.9 million from operations and, in addition, had realized securities gains of $4.1 million.

Both Wesco Financial Corp., an 80% owned subsidiary of Blue Chip Stamps, managed by Louis Vincenti, and See's Candies, a 99% owned subsidiary, managed by Chuck Huggins, made good progress in 1977. Since See's was purchased by Blue Chip Stamps at the beginning of 1972, pre-tax operating earnings have grown from $4.2 million to $12.6 million with little additional capital investment. See's achieved this record while operating in an industry experiencing practically no unit growth. Shareholders of Berkshire Hathaway Inc. may obtain the annual report of Blue Chip Stamps by requesting it from Mr. Robert H. Bird, Blue Chip Stamps, 5801 South Eastern Avenue, Los Angeles, California 90040.

Warren E. Buffett, Chairman

March 14, 1978

Berkshire Hathaway Inc.

To the Shareholders of Berkshire Hathaway Inc.:

First, a few words about accounting. The merger with Diversified Retailing Company, Inc. at yearend adds two new complications in the presentation of our financial results. After the merger, our ownership of Blue Chip Stamps increased to approximately 58% and, therefore, the accounts of that company must be fully consolidated in the Balance Sheet and Statement of Earnings presentation of Berkshire. In previous reports, our share of the net earnings only of Blue Chip had been included as a single item on Berkshire's Statement of Earnings, and there had been a similar one-line inclusion on our Balance Sheet of our share of their net assets.

This full consolidation of sales, expenses, receivables, inventories, debt, etc. produces an aggregation of figures from many diverse businesses—textiles, insurance, candy, newspapers, trading stamps—with dramatically different economic characteristics. In some of these your ownership is 100% but, in those businesses which are owned by Blue Chip but fully consolidated, your ownership as a Berkshire shareholder is only 58%. (Ownership by others of the balance of these businesses is accounted for by the large minority interest item on the liability side of the Balance Sheet.) Such a grouping of Balance Sheet and Earnings items—some wholly owned, some partly owned—tends to obscure economic reality more than illuminate it. In fact, it represents a form of presentation that we never prepare for internal use during the year and which is of no value to us in any management activities.

For that reason, throughout the report we provide much separate financial information and commentary on the various segments of the business to help you evaluate Berkshire's performance and prospects. Much of this segmented information is mandated by SEC disclosure rules and covered in "Management's Discussion" on pages 29 to 34. And in this letter we try to present to you a view of our various operating entities from the same perspective that we view them managerially.

A second complication arising from the merger is that the 1977 figures shown in this report are different from the 1977 figures shown in the report we mailed to you last year. Accounting convention requires that when two entities such as Diversified and Berkshire are merged, all financial data subsequently must be presented as if the companies had been merged at the time they were formed rather than just recently. So the enclosed financial statements, in effect, pretend that in 1977 (and earlier years) the Diversified-Berkshire merger already had taken place, even though the actual merger date was December 30, 1978. This shifting base makes comparative commentary confusing and, from time to time in our narrative report, we will talk of figures and performance for Berkshire shareholders as historically reported to you rather than as restated after the Diversified merger.

With that preamble it can be stated that, with or without restated figures, 1978 was a good year. Operating earnings, exclusive of capital gains, at 19.4% of beginning shareholders' investment were within a fraction of our 1972 record. While we believe it is improper to include capital gains or losses in evaluating the performance of a single year, they are an important component of the longer term record. Because of such gains, Berkshire's long-term growth in equity per share has been greater than would be indicated by compounding the returns from operating earnings that we have reported annually.

For example, over the last three years—generally a bonanza period for the insurance industry, our largest profit producer—Berkshire's per share net worth virtually has doubled, thereby compounding at about 25% annually through a combination of good operating earnings and fairly substantial capital gains. Neither this 25% equity gain from all sources nor the 19.4% equity gain from operating earnings in 1978 is sustainable. The insurance cycle has turned downward in 1979, and it is almost certain that operating earnings measured by return on equity will fall this year. However, operating earnings measured in dollars are likely to increase on the much larger shareholders' equity now employed in the business.

In contrast to this cautious view about near term return from operations, we are optimistic about prospects for long term return from major equity investments held by our insurance companies. We make no attempt to predict how security markets will behave; successfully forecasting short term stock price movements is something we think neither we nor anyone else can do. In the longer run, however, we feel that many of our major equity holdings are going to be worth considerably more money than we paid, and that investment gains will add significantly to the operating returns of the insurance group.

Sources of Earnings

To give you a better picture of just where Berkshire's earnings are produced, we show below a table which requires a little explanation. Berkshire owns close to 58% of Blue Chip which, in addition to 100% ownership of several businesses, owns 80% of Wesco Financial Corporation. Thus, Berkshire's equity in Wesco's earnings is about 46%. In aggregate, businesses that we control have about 7,000 full-time employees and generate revenues of over $500 million.

The table shows the overall earnings of each major operating category on a pre-tax basis (several of the businesses have low tax rates because of significant amounts of tax-exempt interest and dividend income), as well as the share of those earnings belonging to Berkshire both on a pre-tax and after-tax basis. Significant capital gains or losses attributable to any of the businesses are not shown in the operating earnings figure, but are aggregated on the "Realized Securities Gain" line at the bottom of the table. Because of various accounting and tax intricacies, the figures in the table should not be treated as holy writ, but rather viewed as close approximations of the 1977 and 1978 earnings contributions of our constituent businesses.

| (in thousands of dollars) | Earnings Before Income Taxes | | | | Net Earnings After Tax | |
| | Total | | Berkshire Share | | Berkshire Share | |
	1978	1977	1978	1977	1978	1977
Total – all entities	$66,180	$57,089	$54,350	$42,234	$39,242	$30,393
Earnings from operations:						
Insurance Group:						
Underwriting	$ 3,001	$ 5,802	$ 3,000	$ 5,802	$ 1,560	$ 3,017
Net investment income . .	19,705	12,804	19,691	12,804	16,400	11,360
Berkshire-Waumbec textiles .	2,916	(620)	2,916	(620)	1,342	(322)
Associated Retail Stores, Inc.	2,757	2,775	2,757	2,775	1,176	1,429
See's Candies	12,482	12,840	7,013	6,598	3,049	2,974
Buffalo Evening News	(2,913)	751	(1,637)	389	(738)	158
Blue Chip Stamps - Parent . .	2,133	1,091	1,198	566	1,382	892
Illinois National Bank and Trust Company	4,822	3,800	4,710	3,706	4,262	3,288
Wesco Financial Corporation – Parent . .	1,771	2,006	777	813	665	419
Mutual Savings and Loan Association	10,556	6,779	4,638	2,747	3,042	1,946
Interest on Debt	(5,566)	(5,302)	(4,546)	(4,255)	(2,349)	(2,129)
Other	720	165	438	102	261	48
Total Earnings from Operations	$52,384	$42,891	$40,955	$31,427	$30,052	$23,080
Realized Securities Gain. . . .	13,796	14,198	13,395	10,807	9,190	7,313
Total Earnings	$66,180	$57,089	$54,350	$42,234	$39,242	$30,393

Blue Chip and Wesco are public companies with reporting requirements of their own. Later in this report we are reproducing the narrative reports of the principal executives of both companies, describing their 1978 operations. Some of the figures they utilize will not match to the penny the ones we use in this report, again because of accounting and tax complexities. But their comments should be helpful to you in understanding the underlying economic characteristics of these important partly-owned businesses. A copy of the full annual report of either company will be mailed to any shareholder of Berkshire upon request to Mr. Robert H. Bird for Blue Chips Stamps, 5801 South Eastern Avenue, Los Angeles, California 90040, or to Mrs. Bette Deckard for Wesco Financial Corporation, 315 East Colorado Boulevard, Pasadena, California 91109.

Textiles

Earnings of $1.3 million in 1978, while much improved from 1977, still represent a low return on the $17 million of capital employed in this business. Textile plant and equipment are on the books for a very small fraction of what it would cost to replace such equipment today. And, despite the age of the equipment, much of it is functionally similar to new equipment being installed by the industry. But despite this "bargain cost" of fixed assets, capital turnover is relatively low reflecting required high investment levels in receivables and inventory compared to sales. Slow capital turnover, coupled with low profit margins on sales, inevitably produces inadequate returns on capital. Obvious approaches to improved profit margins involve differentiation of product, lowered manufacturing costs through more efficient equipment or better utilization of people, redirection toward fabrics enjoying stronger market trends, etc. Our management is diligent in pursuing such objectives. The problem, of course, is that our competitors are just as diligently doing the same thing.

The textile industry illustrates in textbook style how producers of relatively undifferentiated goods in capital intensive businesses must earn inadequate returns except under conditions of tight supply or real shortage. As long as excess productive capacity exists, prices tend to reflect direct operating costs rather than capital employed. Such a supply-excess condition appears likely to prevail most of the time in the textile industry, and our expectations are for profits of relatively modest amounts in relation to capital.

We hope we don't get into too many more businesses with such tough economic characteristics. But, as we have stated before: (1) our textile businesses are very important employers in their communities, (2) management has been straightforward in reporting on problems and energetic in attacking them, (3) labor has been cooperative and understanding in facing our common problems, and (4) the business should average modest cash returns relative to investment. As long as these conditions prevail—and we expect that they will—we intend to continue to support our textile business despite more attractive alternative uses for capital.

Insurance Underwriting

The number one contributor to Berkshire's overall excellent results in 1978 was the segment of National Indemnity Company's insurance operation run by Phil Liesche. On about $90 million of earned premiums, an underwriting profit of approximately $11 million was realized, a truly extraordinary achievement even against the background of excellent industry conditions. Under Phil's leadership, with outstanding assistance by Roland Miller in Underwriting and Bill Lyons in Claims, this segment of National Indemnity (including National Fire and Marine Insurance Company, which operates as a running mate) had one of its best years in a long history of performances which, in aggregate, far outshine those of the industry. Present successes reflect credit not only upon present managers, but equally upon the business talents of Jack Ringwalt, founder of National Indemnity, whose operating philosophy remains etched upon the company.

Home and Automobile Insurance Company had its best year since John Seward stepped in and straightened things out in 1975. Its results are combined in this report with those of Phil Liesche's operation under the insurance category entitled "Specialized Auto and General Liability".

Worker's Compensation was a mixed bag in 1978. In its first year as a subsidiary, Cypress Insurance Company, managed by Milt Thornton, turned in outstanding results. The worker's compensation line can cause large underwriting losses when rapid inflation interacts with changing social concepts, but Milt has a cautious and highly professional staff to cope with these problems. His performance in 1978 has reinforced our very good feelings about this purchase.

Frank DeNardo came with us in the spring of 1978 to straighten out National Indemnity's California Worker's Compensation business which, up to that point, had been a disaster. Frank has the experience and intellect needed to correct the major problems of the Los Angeles office. Our volume in this department now is running only about 25% of what it was eighteen months ago, and early indications are that Frank is making good progress.

George Young's reinsurance department continues to produce very large sums for investment relative to premium volume, and thus gives us reasonably satisfactory overall results. However, underwriting results still are not what they should be and can be. It is very easy to fool yourself regarding underwriting results in reinsurance (particularly in casualty lines involving long delays in settlement), and we believe this situation prevails with many of our competitors. Unfortunately, self-delusion in company reserving almost always leads to inadequate industry rate levels. If major factors in the market don't know their true costs, the competitive "fall-out" hits all—even those with adequate cost knowledge. George is quite willing to reduce volume significantly, if needed, to achieve satisfactory underwriting, and we have a great deal of confidence in the long term soundness of this business under his direction.

The homestate operation was disappointing in 1978. Our unsatisfactory underwriting, even though partially explained by an unusual incidence of Midwestern storms, is particularly worrisome against the backdrop of very favorable industry results in the conventional lines written by our homestate group. We have confidence in John Ringwalt's ability to correct this situation. The bright spot in the group was the performance of Kansas Fire and Casualty in its first full year of business. Under Floyd Taylor, this subsidiary got off to a truly remarkable start. Of course, it takes at least several years to evaluate underwriting results, but the early signs are encouraging and Floyd's operation achieved the best loss ratio among the homestate companies in 1978.

Although some segments were disappointing, overall our insurance operation had an excellent year. But of course we should expect a good year when the industry is flying high, as in 1978. It is a virtual certainty that in 1979 the combined ratio (see definition on page 31) for the industry will move up at least a few points, perhaps enough to throw the industry as a whole into an underwriting loss position. For example, in the auto lines—by far the most important area for the industry and for us—CPI figures indicate rates overall were only 3% higher in January 1979 than a year ago. But the items that make up loss costs—auto repair and medical care costs—were up over 9%. How different than yearend 1976 when rates had advanced over 22% in the preceding twelve months, but costs were up 8%.

Margins will remain steady only if rates rise as fast as costs. This assuredly will not be the case in 1979, and conditions probably will worsen in 1980. Our present thinking is that our underwriting performance relative to the industry will improve somewhat in 1979, but every other insurance management probably views its relative prospects with similar optimism—someone is going to be disappointed. Even if we do improve relative to others, we may well have a higher combined ratio and lower underwriting profits in 1979 than we achieved last year.

We continue to look for ways to expand our insurance operation. But your reaction to this intent should not be unrestrained joy. Some of our expansion efforts—largely initiated by your Chairman have been lackluster, others have been expensive failures. We entered the business in 1967 through purchase of the segment which Phil Liesche now manages, and it still remains, by a large margin, the best portion of our insurance business. It is not easy to buy a good insurance business, but our experience has been that it is easier to buy one than create one. However, we will continue to try both approaches, since the rewards for success in this field can be exceptional.

Insurance Investments

We confess considerable optimism regarding our insurance equity investments. Of course, our enthusiasm for stocks is not unconditional. Under some circumstances, common stock investments by insurers make very little sense.

We get excited enough to commit a big percentage of insurance company net worth to equities only when we find (1) businesses we can understand, (2) with favorable long-term prospects, (3) operated by honest and competent people, and (4) priced very attractively. We usually can identify a small number of potential investments meeting requirements (1), (2) and (3), but (4) often prevents action. For example, in 1971 our total common stock position at Berkshire's insurance subsidiaries amounted to only $10.7 million at cost, and $11.7 million at market. There were equities of identifiably excellent companies available—but very few at interesting prices. (An irresistible footnote: in 1971, pension fund managers invested a record 122% of net funds available in equities—at full prices they couldn't buy enough of them. In 1974, after the bottom had fallen out, they committed a then record low of 21% to stocks.)

The past few years have been a different story for us. At the end of 1975 our insurance subsidiaries held common equities with a market value exactly equal to cost of $39.3 million. At the end of 1978 this position had been increased to equities (including a convertible preferred) with a cost of $129.1 million and a market value of $216.5 million. During the intervening three years we also had realized pre-tax gains from common equities of approximately $24.7 million. Therefore, our overall unrealized and realized pre-tax gains in equities for the three year period came to approximately $112 million. During this same interval the Dow-Jones Industrial Average declined from 852 to 805. It was a marvelous period for the value-oriented equity buyer.

We continue to find for our insurance portfolios small portions of really outstanding businesses that are available, through the auction pricing mechanism of security markets, at prices dramatically cheaper than the valuations inferior businesses command on negotiated sales.

This program of acquisition of small fractions of businesses (common stocks) at bargain prices, for which little enthusiasm exists, contrasts sharply with general corporate acquisition activity, for which much enthusiasm exists. It seems quite clear to us that either corporations are making very significant mistakes in purchasing entire businesses at prices prevailing in negotiated transactions and takeover bids, or that we eventually are going to make considerable sums of money buying small portions of such businesses at the greatly discounted valuations prevailing in the stock market. (A second footnote: in 1978 pension managers, a group that logically should maintain the longest of investment perspectives, put only 9% of net available funds into equities—breaking the record low figure set in 1974 and tied in 1977.)

We are not concerned with whether the market quickly revalues upward securities that we believe are selling at bargain prices. In fact, we prefer just the opposite since, in most years, we expect to have funds available to be a net buyer of securities. And consistent attractive purchasing is likely to prove to be of more eventual benefit to us than any selling opportunities provided by a short-term run up in stock prices to levels at which we are unwilling to continue buying.

Our policy is to concentrate holdings. We try to avoid buying a little of this or that when we are only lukewarm about the business or its price. When we are convinced as to attractiveness, we believe in buying worthwhile amounts.

Equity holdings of our insurance companies with a market value of over $8 million on December 31, 1978 were as follows:

No. of Shares	Company	Cost	Market
		(000's omitted)	
246,450	American Broadcasting Companies, Inc.	$ 6,082	$ 8,626
1,294,308	Government Employees Insurance Company Common Stock	4,116	9,060
1,986,953	Government Employees Insurance Company Convertible Preferred	19,417	28,314
592,650	Interpublic Group of Companies	4,531	19,039
1,066,934	Kaiser Aluminum and Chemical Corporation	18,085	18,671
453,800	Knight-Ridder Newspapers, Inc.	7,534	10,267
953,750	SAFECO Corporation	23,867	26,467
934,300	The Washington Post Company	10,628	43,445
	Total	$ 94,260	$163,889
	All other Holdings	39,506	57,040
	Total Equities	$133,766	$220,929

In some cases our indirect interest in earning power is becoming quite substantial. For example, note our holdings of 953,750 shares of SAFECO Corp. SAFECO probably is the best run large property and casualty insurance company in the United States. Their underwriting abilities are simply superb, their loss reserving is conservative, and their investment policies make great sense.

SAFECO is a much better insurance operation than our own (although we believe certain segments of ours are much better than average), is better than one we could develop and, similarly, is far better than any in which we might negotiate purchase of a controlling interest. Yet our purchase of SAFECO was made at substantially under book value. We paid less than 100 cents on the dollar for the best company in the business, when far more than 100 cents on the dollar is being paid for mediocre companies in corporate transactions. And there is no way to start a new operation—with necessarily uncertain prospects—at less than 100 cents on the dollar.

Of course, with a minor interest we do not have the right to direct or even influence management policies of SAFECO. But why should we wish to do this? The record would indicate that they do a better job of managing their operations than we could do ourselves. While there may be less excitement and prestige in sitting back and letting others do the work, we think that is all one loses by accepting a passive participation in excellent management. Because, quite clearly, if one controlled a company run as well as SAFECO, the proper policy also would be to sit back and let management do its job.

Earnings attributable to the shares of SAFECO owned by Berkshire at yearend amounted to $6.1 million during 1978, but only the dividends received (about 18% of earnings) are reflected in our operating earnings. We believe the balance, although not reportable, to be just as real in terms of eventual benefit to us as the amount distributed. In fact, SAFECO's retained earnings (or those of other well-run companies if they have opportunities to employ additional capital advantageously) may well eventually have a value to shareholders greater than 100 cents on the dollar.

We are not at all unhappy when our wholly-owned businesses retain all of their earnings if they can utilize internally those funds at attractive rates. Why should we feel differently about retention of earnings by companies in which we hold small equity interests, but where the record indicates even better prospects for profitable employment of capital? (This proposition cuts the other way, of course, in industries with low capital requirements, or if management has a record of plowing capital into projects of low profitability; then earnings should be paid out or used to repurchase shares—often by far the most attractive option for capital utilization.)

The aggregate level of such retained earnings attributable to our equity interests in fine companies is becoming quite substantial. It does not enter into our reported operating earnings, but we feel it well may have equal long-term significance to our shareholders. Our hope is that conditions continue to prevail in securities markets which allow our insurance companies to buy large amounts of underlying earning power for relatively modest outlays. At some point market conditions undoubtedly will again preclude such bargain buying but, in the meantime, we will try to make the most of opportunities.

Banking

Under Gene Abegg and Pete Jeffrey, the Illinois National Bank and Trust Company in Rockford continues to establish new records. Last year's earnings amounted to approximately 2.1% of average assets, about three times the level averaged by major banks. In our opinion, this extraordinary level of earnings is being achieved while maintaining significantly less asset risk than prevails at most of the larger banks.

We purchased the Illinois National Bank in March 1969. It was a first-class operation then, just as it had been ever since Gene Abegg opened the doors in 1931. Since 1968, consumer time deposits have quadrupled, net income has tripled and trust department income has more than doubled, while costs have been closely controlled.

Our experience has been that the manager of an already high-cost operation frequently is uncommonly resourceful in finding new ways to add to overhead, while the manager of a tightly-run operation usually continues to find additional methods to curtail costs, even when his costs are already well below those of his competitors. No one has demonstrated this latter ability better than Gene Abegg.

We are required to divest our bank by December 31, 1980. The most likely approach is to spin it off to Berkshire shareholders some time in the second half of 1980.

Retailing

Upon merging with Diversified, we acquired 100% ownership of Associated Retail Stores, Inc., a chain of about 75 popular priced women's apparel stores. Associated was launched in Chicago on March 7, 1931 with one store, $3200, and two extraordinary partners, Ben Rosner and Leo Simon. After Mr. Simon's death, the business was offered to Diversified for cash in 1967. Ben was to continue running the business—and run it, he has.

Associated's business has not grown, and it consistently has faced adverse demographic and retailing trends. But Ben's combination of merchandising, real estate and cost-containment skills has produced an outstanding record of profitability, with returns on capital necessarily employed in the business often in the 20% after-tax area.

Ben is now 75 and, like Gene Abegg, 81, at Illinois National and Louie Vincenti, 73, at Wesco, continues daily to bring an almost passionately proprietary attitude to the business. This group of top managers must appear to an outsider to be an overreaction on our part to an OEO bulletin on age discrimination. While unorthodox, these relationships have been exceptionally rewarding, both financially and personally. It is a real pleasure to work with managers who enjoy coming to work each morning and, once there, instinctively and unerringly think like owners. We are associated with some of the very best.

Warren E. Buffett, Chairman

March 26, 1979

Berkshire Hathaway Inc.

To the Shareholders of Berkshire Hathaway Inc.:

Again, we must lead off with a few words about accounting. Since our last annual report, the accounting profession has decided that equity securities owned by insurance companies must be carried on the balance sheet at market value. We previously have carried such equity securities at the lower of aggregate cost or aggregate market value. Because we have large unrealized gains in our insurance equity holdings, the result of this new policy is to increase substantially both the 1978 and 1979 yearend net worth, even after the appropriate liability is established for taxes on capital gains that would be payable should equities be sold at such market valuations.

As you know, Blue Chip Stamps, our 60% owned subsidiary, is fully consolidated in Berkshire Hathaway's financial statements. However, Blue Chip still is required to carry its equity investments at the lower of aggregate cost or aggregate market value, just as Berkshire Hathaway's insurance subsidiaries did prior to this year. Should the same equities be purchased at an identical price by an insurance subsidiary of Berkshire Hathaway and by Blue Chip Stamps, present accounting principles often would require that they end up carried on our consolidated balance sheet at two different values. (That should keep you on your toes.) Market values of Blue Chip Stamps' equity holdings are given in footnote 3 on page 18.

1979 Operating Results

We continue to feel that the ratio of operating earnings (before securities gains or losses) to shareholders' equity *with all securities valued at cost* is the most appropriate way to measure any single year's operating performance.

Measuring such results against shareholders' equity with securities valued at market could significantly distort the operating performance percentage because of wide year-to-year market value changes in the net worth figure that serves as the denominator. For example, a large decline in securities values could result in a very low "market value" net worth that, in turn, could cause mediocre operating earnings to look unrealistically good. Alternatively, the more successful that equity investments have been, the larger the net worth base becomes and the poorer the operating performance figure appears. Therefore, we will continue to report operating performance measured against beginning net worth, with securities valued at cost.

On this basis, we had a reasonably good operating performance in 1979—but not quite as good as that of 1978—with operating earnings amounting to 18.6% of beginning net worth. Earnings per share, of course, increased somewhat (about 20%) but we regard this as an improper figure upon which to focus. We had substantially more capital to work with in 1979 than in 1978, and our performance in utilizing that capital fell short of the earlier year, even though per-share earnings rose. "Earnings per share" will rise constantly on a dormant savings account or on a U.S. Savings Bond bearing a fixed rate of return simply because "earnings" (the stated interest rate) are continuously plowed back and added to the capital base. Thus, even a "stopped clock" can look like a growth stock if the dividend payout ratio is low.

The primary test of managerial economic performance is the achievement of a high earnings rate on equity capital employed (without undue leverage, accounting gimmickry, etc.) and not the achievement of consistent gains in earnings per share. In our view, many businesses would be better understood by their shareholder owners, as well as the general public, if managements and financial analysts modified the primary emphasis they place upon earnings per share, and upon yearly changes in that figure.

Long Term Results

In measuring long term economic performance—in contrast to yearly performance—we believe it is appropriate to recognize fully any realized capital gains or losses as well as extraordinary items, and also to utilize financial statements presenting equity securities at market value. Such capital gains or losses, either realized or unrealized, are fully as important to shareholders over a period of years as earnings realized in a more routine manner through operations; it is just that their impact is often extremely capricious in the short run, a characteristic that makes them inappropriate as an indicator of single year managerial performance.

The book value per share of Berkshire Hathaway on September 30, 1964 (the fiscal yearend prior to the time that your present management assumed responsibility) was $19.46 per share. At yearend 1979, book value with equity holdings carried at market value was $335.85 per share. The gain in book value comes to 20.5% compounded annually. This figure, of course, is far higher than any average of our yearly operating earnings calculations, and reflects the importance of capital appreciation of insurance equity investments in determining the overall results for our shareholders. It probably also is fair to say that the quoted book value in 1964 somewhat overstated the intrinsic value of the enterprise, since the assets owned at that time on either a going concern basis or a liquidating value basis were not worth 100 cents on the dollar. (The liabilities were solid, however.)

We have achieved this result while utilizing a low amount of leverage (both financial leverage measured by debt to equity, and operating leverage measured by premium volume to capital funds of our insurance business), and also without significant issuance or repurchase of shares. Basically, we have worked with the capital with which we started. From our textile base we, or our Blue Chip and Wesco subsidiaries, have acquired total ownership of thirteen businesses through negotiated purchases from private owners for cash, and have started six others. (It's worth a mention that those who have sold to us have, almost without exception, treated us with exceptional honor and fairness, both at the time of sale and subsequently.)

But before we drown in a sea of self-congratulation, a further—and crucial—observation must be made. A few years ago, a business whose per-share net worth compounded at 20% annually would have guaranteed its owners a highly successful real investment return. Now such an outcome seems less certain. For the inflation rate, coupled with individual tax rates, will be the ultimate determinant as to whether our internal operating performance produces successful investment results—i.e., a reasonable gain in purchasing power from funds committed—for you as shareholders.

Just as the original 3% savings bond, a 5% passbook savings account or an 8% U.S. Treasury Note have, in turn, been transformed by inflation into financial instruments that chew up, rather than enhance, purchasing power over their investment lives, a business earning 20% on capital can produce a negative real return for its owners under inflationary conditions not much more severe than presently prevail.

If we should continue to achieve a 20% compounded gain—not an easy or certain result by any means—and this gain is translated into a corresponding increase in the market value of Berkshire Hathaway stock as it has been over the last fifteen years, your after-tax purchasing power gain is likely to be very close to zero at a 14% inflation rate. Most of the remaining six percentage points will go for income tax any time you wish to convert your twenty percentage points of nominal annual gain into cash.

That combination—the inflation rate plus the percentage of capital that must be paid by the owner to transfer into his own pocket the annual earnings achieved by the business (i.e., ordinary income tax on dividends and capital gains tax on retained earnings)—can be thought of as an "investor's misery index". When this index exceeds the rate of return earned on equity by the business, the investor's purchasing power (real capital) shrinks even though he consumes nothing at all. *We have no corporate solution to this problem; high inflation rates will not help us earn higher rates of return on equity.*

One friendly but sharp-eyed commentator on Berkshire has pointed out that our book value at the end of 1964 would have bought about one-half ounce of gold and, fifteen years later, after we have plowed back all earnings along with much blood, sweat and tears, the book value produced will buy about the same half ounce. A similar comparison could be drawn with Middle Eastern oil. The rub has been that government has been exceptionally able in printing money and creating promises, but is unable to print gold or create oil.

We intend to continue to do as well as we can in managing the internal affairs of the business. But you should understand that external conditions affecting the stability of currency may very well be the most important factor in determining whether there are any real rewards from your investment in Berkshire Hathaway.

Sources of Earnings

We again present a table showing the sources of Berkshire's earnings. As explained last year, Berkshire owns about 60% of Blue Chip Stamps which, in turn, owns 80% of Wesco Financial Corporation. The table shows both aggregate earnings of the various business entities, as well as Berkshire's share. All of the significant capital gains or losses attributable to any of the business entities are aggregated in the realized securities gain figure at the bottom of the table, and are not included in operating earnings.

| (in thousands of dollars) | Earnings Before Income Taxes | | | | Net Earnings After Tax | |
| | Total | | Berkshire Share | | Berkshire Share | |
	1979	1978	1979	1978	1979	1978
Total – all entities	$68,632	$66,180	$56,427	$54,350	$42,817	$39,242
Earnings from operations:						
Insurance Group:						
Underwriting	$ 3,742	$ 3,001	$ 3,741	$ 3,000	$ 2,214	$ 1,560
Net investment income ..	24,224	19,705	24,216	19,691	20,106	16,400
Berkshire-Waumbec textiles.	1,723	2,916	1,723	2,916	848	1,342
Associated Retail Stores, Inc.	2,775	2,757	2,775	2,757	1,280	1,176
See's Candies	12,785	12,482	7,598	7,013	3,448	3,049
Buffalo Evening News	(4,617)	(2,913)	(2,744)	(1,637)	(1,333)	(738)
Blue Chip Stamps - Parent..	2,397	2,133	1,425	1,198	1,624	1,382
Illinois National Bank and Trust Company	5,747	4,822	5,614	4,710	5,027	4,262
Wesco Financial Corporation – Parent ..	2,413	1,771	1,098	777	937	665
Mutual Savings and Loan Association	10,447	10,556	4,751	4,638	3,261	3,042
Precision Steel	3,254	--	1,480	--	723	--
Interest on Debt	(8,248)	(5,566)	(5,860)	(4,546)	(2,900)	(2,349)
Other	1,342	720	996	438	753	261
Total Earnings from Operations	$57,984	$52,384	$46,813	$40,955	$35,988	$30,052
Realized Securities Gain.....	10,648	13,796	9,614	13,395	6,829	9,190
Total Earnings..........	$68,632	$66,180	$56,427	$54,350	$42,817	$39,242

Blue Chip and Wesco are public companies with reporting requirements of their own. On pages 37-43 of this report, we have reproduced the narrative reports of the principal executives of both companies, in which they describe 1979 operations. Some of the numbers they mention in their reports are not precisely identical to those in the above table because of accounting and tax complexities. (The Yanomamo Indians employ only three numbers: one, two, and more than two. Maybe their time will come.) However, the commentary in those reports should be helpful to you in understanding the underlying economic characteristics and future prospects of the important businesses that they manage.

A copy of the full annual report of either company will be mailed to any shareholder of Berkshire upon request to Mr. Robert H. Bird for Blue Chip Stamps, 5801 South Eastern Avenue, Los Angeles, California 90040, or to Mrs. Bette Deckard for Wesco Financial Corporation, 315 East Colorado Boulevard, Pasadena, California 91109.

Textiles and Retailing

The relative significance of these two areas has diminished somewhat over the years as our insurance business has grown dramatically in size and earnings. Ben Rosner, at Associated Retail Stores, continues to pull rabbits out of the hat—big rabbits from a small hat. Year after year, he produces very large earnings relative to capital employed—realized in cash and not in increased receivables and inventories as in many other retail businesses—in a segment of the market with little growth and unexciting demographics. Ben is now 76 and, like our other "up-and-comers", Gene

Abegg, 82, at Illinois National and Louis Vincenti, 74, at Wesco, regularly achieves more each year.

Our textile business also continues to produce some cash, but at a low rate compared to capital employed. This is not a reflection on the managers, but rather on the industry in which they operate. In some businesses—a network TV station, for example—it is virtually impossible to avoid earning extraordinary returns on tangible capital employed in the business. And assets in such businesses sell at equally extraordinary prices, one thousand cents or more on the dollar, a valuation reflecting the splendid, almost unavoidable, economic results obtainable. Despite a fancy price tag, the "easy" business may be the better route to go.

We can speak from experience, having tried the other route. Your Chairman made the decision a few years ago to purchase Waumbec Mills in Manchester, New Hampshire, thereby expanding our textile commitment. By any statistical test, the purchase price was an extraordinary bargain; we bought well below the working capital of the business and, in effect, got very substantial amounts of machinery and real estate for less than nothing. But the purchase was a mistake. While we labored mightily, new problems arose as fast as old problems were tamed.

Both our operating and investment experience cause us to conclude that "turnarounds" seldom turn, and that the same energies and talent are much better employed in a good business purchased at a fair price than in a poor business purchased at a bargain price. Although a mistake, the Waumbec acquisition has not been a disaster. Certain portions of the operation are proving to be valuable additions to our decorator line (our strongest franchise) at New Bedford, and it's possible that we may be able to run profitably on a considerably reduced scale at Manchester. However, our original rationale did not prove out.

Insurance Underwriting

We predicted last year that the combined underwriting ratio (see definition on page 36) for the insurance industry would "move up at least a few points, perhaps enough to throw the industry as a whole into an underwriting loss position". That is just about the way it worked out. The industry underwriting ratio rose in 1979 over three points, from roughly 97.4% to 100.7%. We also said that we thought our underwriting performance relative to the industry would improve somewhat in 1979 and, again, things worked out as expected. Our own underwriting ratio actually decreased from 98.2% to 97.1%. Our forecast for 1980 is similar in one respect; again we feel that the industry's performance will worsen by at least another few points. However, this year we have no reason to think that our performance relative to the industry will further improve. (Don't worry—we won't hold back to try to validate that forecast.)

Really extraordinary results were turned in by the portion of National Indemnity Company's insurance operation run by Phil Liesche. Aided by Roland Miller in Underwriting and Bill Lyons in Claims, this section of the business produced an underwriting profit of $8.4 million on about $82 million of earned premiums. Only a very few companies in the entire industry produced a result comparable to this.

You will notice that earned premiums in this segment were down somewhat from those of 1978. We hear a great many insurance managers talk about being willing to reduce volume in order to underwrite profitably, but we find that very few actually do so. Phil Liesche is an exception: if business makes sense, he writes it; if it doesn't, he rejects it. It is our policy not to lay off people because of the large fluctuations in work load produced by such voluntary volume changes. We would rather have some slack in the organization from time to time than keep everyone terribly busy writing business on which we are going to lose money. Jack Ringwalt, the founder of National Indemnity Company, instilled this underwriting discipline at the inception of the company, and Phil Liesche never has wavered in maintaining it. We believe such strong-mindedness is as rare as it is sound—and absolutely essential to the running of a first-class casualty insurance operation.

John Seward continues to make solid progress at Home and Automobile Insurance Company, in large part by significantly expanding the marketing scope of that company in general liability lines. These lines can be dynamite, but the record to date is excellent and, in John McGowan and Paul Springman, we have two cautious liability managers extending our capabilities.

Our reinsurance division, led by George Young, continues to give us reasonably satisfactory overall results after allowing for investment income, but underwriting performance remains unsatisfactory. We think the reinsurance business is a very tough business that is likely to get much tougher. In fact, the influx of capital into the business and the resulting softer price levels for continually increasing exposures may well produce disastrous results for many entrants (of which they may be blissfully unaware until they are in over their heads; much reinsurance business involves an exceptionally "long tail", a characteristic that allows catastrophic current loss experience to fester undetected for many years). It will be hard for us to be a whole lot smarter than the crowd and thus our reinsurance activity may decline substantially during the projected prolonged period of extraordinary competition.

The Homestate operation was disappointing in 1979. Excellent results again were turned in by George Billings at Texas United Insurance Company, winner of the annual award for the low loss ratio among Homestate companies, and Floyd Taylor at Kansas Fire and Casualty Company. But several of the other operations, particularly Cornhusker Casualty Company, our first and largest Homestate operation and historically a winner, had poor underwriting results which were accentuated by data processing, administrative and personnel problems. We have made some major mistakes in reorganizing our data processing activities, and those mistakes will not be cured immediately or without cost. However, John Ringwalt has thrown himself into the task of getting things straightened out and we have confidence that he, aided by several strong people who recently have been brought aboard, will succeed.

Our performance in Worker's Compensation was far, far better than we had any right to expect at the beginning of 1979. We had a very favorable climate in California for the achievement of good results but, beyond this, Milt Thornton at Cypress Insurance Company and Frank DeNardo at National Indemnity's California Worker's Compensation operation both performed in a simply outstanding manner. We have admitted—and with good reason—some mistakes on the acquisition front, but the Cypress purchase has turned out to be an absolute gem. Milt Thornton, like Phil Liesche, follows the policy of sticking with business that he understands and wants, without giving consideration to the impact on volume. As a result, he has an outstanding book of business and an exceptionally well functioning group of employees. Frank DeNardo has straightened out the mess he inherited in Los Angeles in a manner far beyond our expectations, producing savings measured in seven figures. He now can begin to build on a sound base.

At yearend we entered the specialized area of surety reinsurance under the management of Chet Noble. At least initially, this operation will be relatively small since our policy will be to seek client companies who appreciate the need for a long term "partnership" relationship with their reinsurers. We are pleased by the quality of the insurers we have attracted, and hope to add several more of the best primary writers as our financial strength and stability become better known in the surety field.

The conventional wisdom is that insurance underwriting overall will be poor in 1980, but that rates will start to firm in a year or so, leading to a turn in the cycle some time in 1981. We disagree with this view. Present interest rates encourage the obtaining of business at underwriting loss levels formerly regarded as totally unacceptable. Managers decry the folly of underwriting at a loss to obtain investment income, but we believe that many will. Thus we expect that competition will create a new threshold of tolerance for underwriting losses, and that combined ratios will average higher in the future than in the past.

To some extent, the day of reckoning has been postponed because of marked reduction in the frequency of auto accidents—probably brought on in major part by changes in driving habits induced by higher gas prices. In our opinion, if the habits hadn't changed, auto insurance rates would have been very little higher and underwriting results would have been much worse. This dosage of serendipity won't last indefinitely.

Our forecast is for an average combined ratio for the industry in the 105 area over the next five years. While we have a high degree of confidence that certain of our operations will do considerably better than average, it will be a challenge to us to operate below the industry figure. You can get a lot of surprises in insurance.

Nevertheless, we believe that insurance can be a very good business. It tends to magnify, to an unusual degree, human managerial talent—or the lack of it. We have a number of managers whose talent is both proven and growing. (And, in addition, we have a very large indirect interest in two truly outstanding management groups through our investments in SAFECO and GEICO.) Thus we expect to do well in insurance over a period of years. However, the business has the potential for really terrible results in a single specific year. If accident frequency should turn around quickly in the auto field, we, along with others, are likely to experience such a year.

Insurance Investments

In recent years we have written at length in this section about our insurance equity investments. In 1979 they continued to perform well, largely because the underlying companies in which we have invested, in practically all cases, turned in outstanding performances. Retained earnings applicable to our insurance equity investments, not reported in our financial statements, continue to mount annually and, in aggregate, now come to a very substantial number. We have faith that the managements of these companies will utilize those retained earnings effectively and will translate a dollar retained by them into a dollar or more of subsequent market value for us. In part, our unrealized gains reflect this process.

Below we show the equity investments which had a yearend market value of over $5 million:

No. of Shares	Company	Cost	Market
		(000's omitted)	
289,700	Affiliated Publications, Inc.	$ 2,821	$ 8,800
112,545	Amerada Hess.	2,861	5,487
246,450	American Broadcasting Companies, Inc.	6,082	9,673
5,730,114	GEICO Corp. (Common Stock)	28,288	68,045
328,700	General Foods, Inc.	11,437	11,053
1,007,500	Handy & Harman.	21,825	38,537
711,180	Interpublic Group of Companies, Inc.	4,531	23,736
1,211,834	Kaiser Aluminum & Chemical Corp.	20,629	23,328
282,500	Media General, Inc.	4,545	7,345
391,400	Ogilvy & Mather International	3,709	7,828
953,750	SAFECO Corporation	23,867	35,527
1,868,000	The Washington Post Company.	10,628	39,241
771,900	F. W. Woolworth Company	15,515	19,394
	Total	$156,738	$297,994
	All other Holdings	28,675	38,686
	Total Equities.	$185,413	$336,680

We currently believe that equity markets in 1980 are likely to evolve in a manner that will result in an underperformance by our portfolio for the first time in recent years. We very much like the companies in which we have major investments, and plan no changes to try to attune ourselves to the markets of a specific year.

Since we have covered our philosophy regarding equities extensively in recent annual reports, a more extended discussion of bond investments may be appropriate for this one, particularly in light of what has happened since yearend. An extraordinary amount of money has been lost by the insurance industry in the bond area—notwithstanding the accounting convention that allows insurance companies to carry their bond investments at amortized cost, regardless of impaired market value. Actually, that very accounting convention may have contributed in a major way to the losses; had management been forced to recognize market values, its attention might have been focused much earlier on the dangers of a very long-term bond contract.

Ironically, many insurance companies have decided that a one-year auto policy is inappropriate during a time of inflation, and six-month policies have been brought in as replacements. "How," say many of the insurance managers, "can we be expected to look forward twelve months and estimate such imponderables as hospital costs, auto parts prices, etc.?" But, having decided that one year is too long a period for which to set a fixed price for insurance in an inflationary world, they then have turned around, taken the proceeds from the sale of that six-month policy, and sold the money at a fixed price for thirty or forty years.

The very long-term bond contract has been the last major fixed price contract of extended duration still regularly initiated in an inflation-ridden world. The buyer of money to be used between 1980 and 2020 has been able to obtain a firm price now for each year of its use while the buyer of auto insurance, medical services, newsprint, office space—or just about any other product or service—would be greeted with laughter if he were to request a firm price now to apply through 1985. For in virtually all other areas of commerce, parties to long-term contracts now either index prices in some manner, or insist on the right to review the situation every year or so.

A cultural lag has prevailed in the bond area. The buyers (borrowers) and middlemen (underwriters) of money hardly could be expected to raise the question of whether it all made sense, and the sellers (lenders) slept through an economic and contractual revolution.

For the last few years our insurance companies have not been a net purchaser of any straight long-term bonds (those without conversion rights or other attributes offering profit possibilities). There have been some purchases in the straight bond area, of course, but they have been offset by sales or maturities. Even prior to this period, we never would buy thirty or forty-year bonds; instead we tried to concentrate in the straight bond area on shorter issues with sinking funds and on issues that seemed relatively undervalued because of bond market inefficiencies.

However, the mild degree of caution that we exercised was an improper response to the world unfolding about us. You do not adequately protect yourself by being half awake while others are sleeping. It was a mistake to buy fifteen-year bonds, and yet we did; we made an even more serious mistake in not selling them (at losses, if necessary) when our present views began to crystallize. (Naturally, those views are much clearer and definite in retrospect; it would be fair for you to ask why we weren't writing about this subject last year.)

Of course, we must hold significant amounts of bonds or other fixed dollar obligations in conjunction with our insurance operations. In the last several years our net fixed dollar commitments have been limited to the purchase of convertible bonds. We believe that the conversion options obtained, in effect, give that portion of the bond portfolio a far shorter average life than implied by the maturity terms of the issues (i.e., at an appropriate time of our choosing, we can terminate the bond contract by conversion into stock).

This bond policy has given us significantly lower unrealized losses than those experienced by the great majority of property and casualty insurance companies. We also have been helped by our strong preference for equities in recent years that has kept our overall bond segment relatively low. Nevertheless, we are taking our lumps in bonds and feel that, in a sense, our mistakes should be viewed less charitably than the mistakes of those who went about their business unmindful of the developing problems.

Harking back to our textile experience, we should have realized the futility of trying to be very clever (via sinking funds and other special type issues) in an area where the tide was running heavily against us.

We have severe doubts as to whether a very long-term fixed-interest bond, denominated in dollars, remains an appropriate business contract in a world where the value of dollars seems almost certain to shrink by the day. Those dollars, as well as paper creations of other governments, simply may have too many structural weaknesses to appropriately serve as a unit of long term commercial reference. If so, really long bonds may turn out to be obsolete instruments and insurers who have bought those maturities of 2010 or 2020 could have major and continuing problems on their hands. We, likewise, will be unhappy with our fifteen-year bonds and will annually pay a price in terms of earning power that reflects that mistake.

Some of our convertible bonds appear exceptionally attractive to us, and have the same sort of earnings retention factor (applicable to the stock into which they may be converted) that prevails in our conventional equity portfolio. We expect to make money in these bonds (we already have, in a few cases) and have hopes that our profits in this area may offset losses in straight bonds.

And, of course, there is the possibility that our present analysis is much too negative. The chances for very low rates of inflation are not nil. Inflation is man-made; perhaps it can be man-mastered. The threat which alarms us may also alarm legislators and other powerful groups, prompting some appropriate response.

Furthermore, present interest rates incorporate much higher inflation projections than those of a year or two ago. Such rates may prove adequate or more than adequate to protect bond buyers. We even may miss large profits from a major rebound in bond prices. However, our unwillingness to fix a price now for a pound of See's candy or a yard of Berkshire cloth to be delivered in 2010 or 2020 makes us equally unwilling to buy bonds which set a price on money now for use in those years. Overall, we opt for Polonius (slightly restated): "Neither a short-term borrower nor a long-term lender be."

Banking

This will be the last year that we can report on the Illinois National Bank and Trust Company as a subsidiary of Berkshire Hathaway. Therefore, it is particularly pleasant to report that, under Gene Abegg's and Pete Jeffrey's management, the bank broke all previous records and earned approximately 2.3% on average assets last year, a level again over three times that achieved by the average major bank, and more than double that of banks regarded as outstanding. The record is simply extraordinary, and the shareholders of Berkshire Hathaway owe a standing ovation to Gene Abegg for the performance this year and every year since our purchase in 1969.

As you know, the Bank Holding Company Act of 1969 requires that we divest the bank by December 31, 1980. For some years we have expected to comply by effecting a spin-off during 1980. However, the Federal Reserve Board has taken the firm position that if the bank is spun off, no officer or director of Berkshire Hathaway can be an officer or director of the spun-off bank or bank holding company, even in a case such as ours in which one individual would own over 40% of both companies.

Under these conditions, we are investigating the possible sale of between 80% and 100% of the stock of the bank. We will be most choosy about any purchaser, and our selection will not be based solely on price. The bank and its management have treated us exceptionally well and, if we have to sell, we want to be sure that they are treated equally as well. A spin-off still is a possibility if a fair price along with a proper purchaser cannot be obtained by early fall.

However, you should be aware that we do not expect to be able to fully, or even in very large part, replace the earning power represented by the bank from the proceeds of the sale of the bank. You simply can't buy high quality businesses at the sort of price/earnings multiple likely to prevail on our bank sale.

Financial Reporting

During 1979, NASDAQ trading was initiated in the stock of Berkshire Hathaway. This means that the stock now is quoted on the Over-the-Counter page of the *Wall Street Journal* under "Additional OTC Quotes". Prior to such listing, the *Wall Street Journal* and the Dow-Jones news ticker would not report our earnings, even though such earnings were one hundred or more times the level of some companies whose reports they regularly picked up.

Now, however, the Dow-Jones news ticker reports our quarterly earnings promptly after we release them and, in addition, both the ticker and the *Wall Street Journal* report our annual earnings. This solves a dissemination problem that had bothered us.

In some ways, our shareholder group is a rather unusual one, and this affects our manner of reporting to you. For example, at the end of each year about 98% of the shares outstanding are held by people who also were shareholders at the beginning of the year. Therefore, in our annual report we build upon what we have told you in previous years instead of restating a lot of material. You get more useful information this way, and we don't get bored.

Furthermore, perhaps 90% of our shares are owned by investors for whom Berkshire is their largest security holding, very often far and away the largest. Many of these owners are willing to spend a significant amount of time with the annual report, and we attempt to provide them with the same information we would find useful if the roles were reversed.

In contrast, we include no narrative with our quarterly reports. Our owners and managers both have very long time-horizons in regard to this business, and it is difficult to say anything new or meaningful each quarter about events of long-term significance.

But when you do receive a communication from us, it will come from the fellow you are paying to run the business. Your Chairman has a firm belief that owners are entitled to hear directly from the CEO as to what is going on and how he evaluates the business, currently and prospectively. You would demand that in a private company; you should expect no less in a public company. A once-a-year report of stewardship should not be turned over to a staff specialist or public relations consultant who is unlikely to be in a position to talk frankly on a manager-to-owner basis.

We feel that you, as owners, are entitled to the same sort of reporting by your manager as we feel is owed to us at Berkshire Hathaway by managers of our business units. Obviously, the degree of detail must be different, particularly where information would be useful to a business competitor or the like. But the general scope, balance, and level of candor should be similar. We don't expect a public relations document when our operating managers tell us what is going on, and we don't feel you should receive such a document.

In large part, companies obtain the shareholder constituency that they seek and deserve. If they focus their thinking and communications on short-term results or short-term stock market consequences they will, in large part, attract shareholders who focus on the same factors. And if they are cynical in their treatment of investors, eventually that cynicism is highly likely to be returned by the investment community.

Phil Fisher, a respected investor and author, once likened the policies of the corporation in attracting shareholders to those of a restaurant attracting potential customers. A restaurant could seek a given clientele—patrons of fast foods, elegant dining, Oriental food, etc.—and eventually obtain an appropriate group of devotees. If the job were expertly done, that clientele, pleased with the service, menu, and price level offered, would return consistently. But the restaurant could not change its character constantly and end up with a happy and stable clientele. If the business vacillated between French cuisine and take-out chicken, the result would be a revolving door of confused and dissatisfied customers.

So it is with corporations and the shareholder constituency they seek. You can't be all things to all men, simultaneously seeking different owners whose primary interests run from high current yield to long-term capital growth to stock market pyrotechnics, etc.

The reasoning of managements that seek large trading activity in their shares puzzles us. In effect, such managements are saying that they want a good many of the existing clientele continually to desert them in favor of new ones—because you can't add lots of new owners (with new expectations) without losing lots of former owners.

We much prefer owners who like our service and menu and who return year after year. It would be hard to find a better group to sit in the Berkshire Hathaway shareholder "seats" than those already occupying them. So we hope to continue to have a very low turnover among our owners, reflecting a constituency that understands our operation, approves of our policies, and shares our expectations. And we hope to deliver on those expectations.

Prospects

Last year we said that we expected operating earnings in dollars to improve but return on equity to decrease. This turned out to be correct. Our forecast for 1980 is the same. If we are wrong, it will be on the downside. In other words, we are virtually certain that our operating earnings expressed as a percentage of the new equity base of approximately $236 million, valuing securities at cost, will decline from the 18.6% attained in 1979. There is also a fair chance that operating earnings in aggregate dollars will fall short of 1979; the outcome depends partly upon the date of disposition of the bank, partly upon the degree of slippage in insurance underwriting profitability, and partly upon the severity of earnings problems in the savings and loan industry.

We continue to feel very good about our insurance equity investments. Over a period of years, we expect to develop very large and growing amounts of underlying earning power attributable to our fractional ownership of these companies. In most cases they are splendid businesses, splendidly managed, purchased at highly attractive prices.

Your company is run on the principle of centralization of financial decisions at the top (the very top, it might be added), and rather extreme delegation of operating authority to a number of key managers at the individual company or business unit level. We could just field a basketball team with our corporate headquarters group (which utilizes only about 1500 square feet of space).

This approach produces an occasional major mistake that might have been eliminated or minimized through closer operating controls. But it also eliminates large layers of costs and dramatically speeds decision-making. Because everyone has a great deal to do, a very great deal gets done. Most important of all, it enables us to attract and retain some extraordinarily talented individuals—people who simply can't be hired in the normal course of events—who find working for Berkshire to be almost identical to running their own show.

We have placed much trust in them—and their achievements have far exceeded that trust.

Warren E. Buffett, Chairman

March 3, 1980

BERKSHIRE HATHAWAY INC.

To the Shareholders of Berkshire Hathaway Inc.:

Operating earnings improved to $41.9 million in 1980 from $36.0 million in 1979, but return on beginning equity capital (with securities valued at cost) fell to 17.8% from 18.6%. We believe the latter yardstick to be the most appropriate measure of single-year managerial economic performance. In- formed use of that yardstick, however, requires an understanding of many factors, including accounting policies, historical carrying values of assets, financial leverage, and industry conditions.

In your evaluation of our economic performance, we suggest that two factors should receive your special attention—one of a positive nature peculiar, to a large extent, to our own operation, and one of a negative nature applicable to corporate performance generally. Let's look at the bright side first.

Non-Controlled Ownership Earnings

When one company owns part of another company, appropriate accounting procedures pertaining to that ownership interest must be selected from one of three major categories. The percentage of voting stock that is owned, in large part, determines which category of accounting principles should be utilized.

Generally accepted accounting principles require (subject to exceptions, naturally, as with our for- mer bank subsidiary) full consolidation of sales, expenses, taxes, and earnings of business holdings more than 50% owned. Blue Chip Stamps, 60% owned by Berkshire Hathaway Inc., falls into this category. Therefore, all Blue Chip income and expense items are included in full in Berkshire's Consolidated Statement of Earnings, with the 40% ownership interest of others in Blue Chip's net earnings reflected in the Statement as a deduction for "minority interest".

Full inclusion of underlying earnings from another class of holdings, companies owned 20% to 50% (usually called "investees"), also normally occurs. Earnings from such companies—for example, Wesco Financial, controlled by Berkshire but only 48% owned—are included via a one-line entry in the owner's Statement of Earnings. Unlike the over-50% category, all items of revenue and expense are omitted; just the proportional share of net income is included. Thus, if Corporation A owns one-third of Corporation B, one-third of B's earnings, whether or not distributed by B, will end up in A's earnings. There are some modifications, both in this and the over-50% category, for intercorporate taxes and pur- chase price adjustments, the explanation of which we will save for a later day. (We know you can hardly wait.)

Finally come holdings representing less than 20% ownership of another corporation's voting secu- rities. In these cases, accounting rules dictate that the owning companies include in their earnings only dividends received from such holdings. Undistributed earnings are ignored. Thus, should we own 10% of Corporation X with earnings of $10 million in 1980, we would report in our earnings (ignoring rela- tively minor taxes on intercorporate dividends) either (a) $1 million if X declared the full $10 million in dividends; (b) $500,000 if X paid out 50%, or $5 million, in dividends; or (c) zero if X reinvested all earn- ings.

We impose this short—and over-simplified—course in accounting upon you because Berkshire's concentration of resources in the insurance field produces a corresponding concentration of its assets in companies in that third (less than 20% owned) category. Many of these companies pay out relatively small proportions of their earnings in dividends. This means that only a small proportion of their current earning power is recorded in our own current operating earnings. But, while our reported operating earnings reflect only the dividends received from such companies, our economic well-being is determined by their earnings, not their dividends.

Our holdings in this third category of companies have increased dramatically in recent years as our insurance business has prospered and as securities markets have presented particularly attractive opportunities in the common stock area. The large increase in such holdings, plus the growth of earnings experienced by those partially-owned companies, has produced an unusual result; the part of "our" earnings that these companies retained last year (the part not paid to us in dividends) exceeded the total reported annual operating earnings of Berkshire Hathaway. Thus, conventional accounting only allows less than half of our earnings "iceberg" to appear above the surface, in plain view. Within the corporate world such a result is quite rare; in our case it is likely to be recurring.

Our own analysis of earnings reality differs somewhat from generally accepted accounting principles, particularly when those principles must be applied in a world of high and uncertain rates of inflation. (But it's much easier to criticize than to improve such accounting rules. The inherent problems are monumental.) We have owned 100% of businesses whose reported earnings were not worth close to 100 cents on the dollar to us even though, in an accounting sense, we totally controlled their disposition. (The "control" was theoretical. Unless we reinvested all earnings, massive deterioration in the value of assets already in place would occur. But those reinvested earnings had no prospect of earning anything close to a market return on capital.) We have also owned small fractions of businesses with extraordinary reinvestment possibilities whose retained earnings had an economic value to us far in excess of 100 cents on the dollar.

The value to Berkshire Hathaway of retained earnings is not determined by whether we own 100%, 50%, 20% or 1% of the businesses in which they reside. Rather, the value of those retained earnings is determined by the use to which they are put and the subsequent level of earnings produced by that usage. This is true whether we determine the usage, or whether managers we did not hire—but did elect to join—determine that usage. (It's the act that counts, not the actors.) And the value is in no way affected by the inclusion or non-inclusion of those retained earnings in our own reported operating earnings. If a tree grows in a forest partially owned by us, but we don't record the growth in our financial statements, we still own part of the tree.

Our view, we warn you, is non-conventional. But we would rather have earnings for which we did not get accounting credit put to good use in a 10%-owned company by a management we did not personally hire, than have earnings for which we did get credit put into projects of more dubious potential by another management—even if we are that management.

(We can't resist pausing here for a short commercial. One usage of retained earnings we often greet with special enthusiasm when practiced by companies in which we have an investment interest is repurchase of their own shares. The reasoning is simple: if a fine business is selling in the market place for far less than intrinsic value, what more certain or more profitable utilization of capital can there be than significant enlargement of the interests of all owners at that bargain price? The competitive nature of corporate acquisition activity almost guarantees the payment of a full—frequently more than full price when a company buys the entire ownership of another enterprise. But the auction nature of security markets often allows finely-run companies the opportunity to purchase portions of their own businesses at a price under 50% of that needed to acquire the same earning power through the negotiated acquisition of another enterprise.)

Long-Term Corporate Results

As we have noted, we evaluate single-year corporate performance by comparing operating earnings to shareholders' equity with securities valued at cost. Our long-term yardstick of performance, however, includes all capital gains or losses, realized or unrealized. We continue to achieve a long-term return on equity that considerably exceeds the average of our yearly returns. The major factor causing this pleasant result is a simple one: the retained earnings of those non-controlled holdings we discussed earlier have been translated into gains in market value.

Of course, this translation of retained earnings into market price appreciation is highly uneven (it goes in reverse some years), unpredictable as to timing, and unlikely to materialize on a precise dollar-for-dollar basis. And a silly purchase price for a block of stock in a corporation can negate the effects of a decade of earnings retention by that corporation. But when purchase prices are sensible, some long-term market recognition of the accumulation of retained earnings almost certainly will occur. Periodically you even will receive some frosting on the cake, with market appreciation far exceeding post-purchase retained earnings.

In the sixteen years since present management assumed responsibility for Berkshire, book value per share with insurance-held equities valued at market has increased from $19.46 to $400.80, or 20.5% compounded annually. (You've done better: the value of the mineral content in the human body compounded at 22% annually during the past decade.) It is encouraging, moreover, to realize that our record was achieved despite many mistakes. The list is too painful and lengthy to detail here. But it clearly shows that a reasonably competitive corporate batting average can be achieved in spite of a lot of managerial strikeouts.

Our insurance companies will continue to make large investments in well-run, favorably-situated, non-controlled companies that very often will pay out in dividends only small proportions of their earnings. Following this policy, we would expect our long-term returns to continue to exceed the returns derived annually from reported operating earnings. Our confidence in this belief can easily be quantified: if we were to sell the equities that we hold and replace them with long-term tax-free bonds, our reported operating earnings would rise immediately by over $30 million annually. Such a shift tempts us not at all.

So much for the good news.

Results for Owners

Unfortunately, earnings reported in corporate financial statements are no longer the dominant variable that determines whether there are any real earnings for you, the owner. For only gains in purchasing power represent real earnings on investment. If you (a) forego ten hamburgers to purchase an investment; (b) receive dividends which, after tax, buy two hamburgers; and (c) receive, upon sale of your holdings, after-tax proceeds that will buy eight hamburgers, then (d) you have had no real income from your investment, no matter how much it appreciated in dollars. You may feel richer, but you won't eat richer.

High rates of inflation create a tax on capital that makes much corporate investment unwise—at least if measured by the criterion of a positive real investment return to owners. This "hurdle rate" the return on equity that must be achieved by a corporation in order to produce any real return for its individual owners—has increased dramatically in recent years. The average tax-paying investor is now running up a down escalator whose pace has accelerated to the point where his upward progress is nil.

For example, in a world of 12% inflation a business earning 20% on equity (which very few manage consistently to do) and distributing it all to individuals in the 50% bracket is chewing up their real capital, not enhancing it. (Half of the 20% will go for income tax; the remaining 10% leaves the owners of the business with only 98% of the purchasing power they possessed at the start of the year—even though they have not spent a penny of their "earnings"). The investors in this bracket would actually be better off with a combination of stable prices and corporate earnings on equity capital of only a few per cent.

Explicit income taxes alone, unaccompanied by any implicit inflation tax, never can turn a positive corporate return into a negative owner return. (Even if there were 90% personal income tax rates on both dividends and capital gains, some real income would be left for the owner at a zero inflation rate.) But the inflation tax is not limited by reported income. Inflation rates not far from those recently experienced can turn the level of positive returns achieved by a majority of corporations into negative returns for all owners, including those not required to pay explicit taxes. (For example, if inflation reached 16%, owners of the 60% plus of corporate America earning less than this rate of return would be realizing a negative real return—even if income taxes on dividends and capital gains were eliminated.)

Of course, the two forms of taxation co-exist and interact since explicit taxes are levied on nominal, not real, income. Thus you pay income taxes on what would be deficits if returns to stockholders were measured in constant dollars.

At present inflation rates, we believe individual owners in medium or high tax brackets (as distinguished from tax-free entities such as pension funds, eleemosynary institutions, etc.) should expect no real long-term return from the average American corporation, even though these individuals reinvest the entire after-tax proceeds from all dividends they receive. The average return on equity of corporations is fully offset by the combination of the implicit tax on capital levied by inflation and the explicit taxes levied both on dividends and gains in value produced by retained earnings.

As we said last year, Berkshire has no corporate solution to the problem. (We'll say it again next year, too.) Inflation does not improve our return on equity.

Indexing is the insulation that all seek against inflation. But the great bulk (although there are important exceptions) of corporate capital is not even partially indexed. Of course, earnings and dividends per share usually will rise if significant earnings are "saved" by a corporation; i.e., reinvested instead of paid as dividends. But that would be true without inflation. A thrifty wage earner, likewise, could achieve regular annual increases in his total income without ever getting a pay increase—*if* he were willing to take only half of his paycheck in cash (his wage "dividend") and consistently add the other half (his "retained earnings") to a savings account. Neither this high-saving wage earner nor the stockholder in a high-saving corporation whose annual dividend rate increases while its rate of return on equity remains flat is truly indexed.

For capital to be truly indexed, return on equity must rise, i.e., business earnings consistently must increase in proportion to the increase in the price level *without any need for the business to add to capital—including working capital—employed.* (Increased earnings produced by increased investment don't count.) Only a few businesses come close to exhibiting this ability. And Berkshire Hathaway isn't one of them.

We, of course, have a corporate policy of reinvesting earnings for growth, diversity and strength, which has the incidental effect of minimizing the current imposition of explicit taxes on our owners. However, on a day-by-day basis, you will be subjected to the implicit inflation tax, and when you wish to transfer your investment in Berkshire into another form of investment, or into consumption, you also will face explicit taxes.

Sources of Earnings

The table below shows the sources of Berkshire's reported earnings. Berkshire owns about 60% of Blue Chip Stamps, which in turn owns 80% of Wesco Financial Corporation. The table shows aggregate earnings of the various business entities, as well as Berkshire's share of those earnings. All of the significant capital gains and losses attributable to any of the business entities are aggregated in the realized securities gains figure at the bottom of the table, and are not included in operating earnings. Our calculation of operating earnings also excludes the gain from sale of Mutual's branch offices. In this respect it differs from the presentation in our audited financial statements that includes this item in the calculation of "Earnings Before Realized Investment Gain".

| | Earnings Before Income Taxes | | | | Net Earnings After Tax | |
| | Total | | Berkshire Share | | Berkshire Share | |
(in thousands of dollars)	1980	1979	1980	1979	1980	1979
Total – all entities	$85,945	$68,632	$70,146	$56,427	$53,122	$42,817
Earnings from operations:						
Insurance Group:						
Underwriting	$ 6,738	$ 3,742	$ 6,737	$ 3,741	$ 3,637	$ 2,214
Net investment income ..	30,939	24,224	30,927	24,216	25,607	20,106
Berkshire-Waumbec textiles.	(508)	1,723	(508)	1,723	202	848
Associated Retail Stores. ...	2,440	2,775	2,440	2,775	1,169	1,280
See's Candies	15,031	12,785	8,958	7,598	4,212	3,448
Buffalo Evening News	(2,805)	(4,617)	(1,672)	(2,744)	(816)	(1,333)
Blue Chip Stamps – Parent .	7,699	2,397	4,588	1,425	3,060	1,624
Illinois National Bank.....	5,324	5,747	5,200	5,614	4,731	5,027
Wesco Financial – Parent ..	2,916	2,413	1,392	1,098	1,044	937
Mutual Savings and Loan ..	5,814	10,447	2,775	4,751	1,974	3,261
Precision Steel	2,833	3,254	1,352	1,480	656	723
Interest on Debt	(12,230)	(8,248)	(9,390)	(5,860)	(4,809)	(2,900)
Other	2,170	1,342	1,590	996	1,255	753
Total Earnings from Operations	$66,361	$57,984	$54,389	$46,813	$41,922	$35,988
Mutual Savings and Loan – sale of branches	5,873	--	2,803	--	1,293	--
Realized Securities Gain.....	13,711	10,648	12,954	9,614	9,907	6,829
Total Earnings..........	$85,945	$68,632	$70,146	$56,427	$53,122	$42,817

Blue Chip Stamps and Wesco are public companies with reporting requirements of their own. On pages 40 to 53 of this report we have reproduced the narrative reports of the principal executives of both companies, in which they describe 1980 operations. We recommend a careful reading, and suggest that you particularly note the superb job done by Louie Vincenti and Charlie Munger in repositioning Mutual Savings and Loan. A copy of the full annual report of either company will be mailed to any Berkshire shareholder upon request to Mr. Robert H. Bird for Blue Chip Stamps, 5801 South Eastern Avenue, Los Angeles, California 90040, or to Mrs. Bette Deckard for Wesco Financial Corporation, 315 East Colorado Boulevard, Pasadena, California 91109.

As indicated earlier, undistributed earnings in companies we do not control are now fully as important as the reported operating earnings detailed in the preceding table. The distributed portion, of course, finds its way into the table primarily through the net investment income section of Insurance Group earnings.

We show below Berkshire's proportional holdings in those non-controlled businesses for which only distributed earnings (dividends) are included in our own earnings.

No. of Shares	Company	Cost	Market
		(000's omitted)	
434,550	(a) Affiliated Publications, Inc.	$ 2,821	$ 12,222
464,317	(a) Aluminum Company of America	25,577	27,685
475,217	(b) Cleveland-Cliffs Iron Company	12,942	15,894
1,983,812	(b) General Foods, Inc.	62,507	59,889
7,200,000	(a) GEICO Corporation	47,138	105,300
2,015,000	(a) Handy & Harman	21,825	58,435
711,180	(a) Interpublic Group of Companies, Inc.	4,531	22,135
1,211,834	(a) Kaiser Aluminum & Chemical Corp.	20,629	27,569
282,500	(a) Media General	4,545	8,334
247,039	(b) National Detroit Corporation	5,930	6,299
881,500	(a) National Student Marketing	5,128	5,895
391,400	(a) Ogilvy & Mather Int'l. Inc.	3,709	9,981
370,088	(b) Pinkerton's, Inc.	12,144	16,489
245,700	(b) R. J. Reynolds Industries	8,702	11,228
1,250,525	(b) SAFECO Corporation	32,062	45,177
151,104	(b) The Times Mirror Company	4,447	6,271
1,868,600	(a) The Washington Post Company	10,628	42,277
667,124	(b) E W Woolworth Company	13,583	16,511
		$298,848	$497,591
	All Other Common Stockholdings	26,313	32,096
	Total Common Stocks	$325,161	$529,687

(a) All owned by Berkshire or its insurance subsidiaries.
(b) Blue Chip and/or Wesco own shares of these companies. All numbers represent Berkshire's net interest in the larger gross holdings of the group.

From this table, you can see that our sources of underlying earning power are distributed far differently among industries than would superficially seem the case. For example, our insurance subsidiaries own approximately 3% of Kaiser Aluminum, and 1¼% of Alcoa. Our share of the 1980 earnings of those companies amounts to about $13 million. (If translated dollar for dollar into a combination of eventual market value gain and dividends, this figure would have to be reduced by a significant, but not precisely determinable, amount of tax; perhaps 25% would be a fair assumption.) Thus, we have a much larger economic interest in the aluminum business than in practically any of the operating businesses we control and on which we report in more detail. If we maintain our holdings, our long-term performance will be more affected by the future economics of the aluminum industry than it will by direct operating decisions we make concerning most companies over which we exercise managerial control.

GEICO Corp.

Our largest non-controlled holding is 7.2 million shares of GEICO Corp., equal to about a 33% equity interest. Normally, an interest of this magnitude (over 20%) would qualify as an "investee" holding and would require us to reflect a proportionate share of GEICO's earnings in our own. However, we purchased our GEICO stock pursuant to special orders of the District of Columbia and New York Insurance Departments, which required that the right to vote the stock be placed with an independent party. Absent the vote, our 33% interest does not qualify for investee treatment. (Pinkerton's is a similar situation.)

Of course, whether or not the undistributed earnings of GEICO are picked up annually in our operating earnings figure has nothing to do with their economic value to us, or to you as owners of Berkshire. The value of these retained earnings will be determined by the skill with which they are put to use by GEICO management.

On this score, we simply couldn't feel better. GEICO represents the best of all investment worlds—the coupling of a very important and very hard to duplicate business advantage with an extraordinary management whose skills in operations are matched by skills in capital allocation.

As you can see, our holdings cost us $47 million, with about half of this amount invested in 1976 and most of the remainder invested in 1980. At the present dividend rate, our reported earnings from GEICO amount to a little over $3 million annually. But we estimate our share of its earning power is on the order of $20 million annually. Thus, undistributed earnings applicable to this holding alone may amount to 40% of total reported operating earnings of Berkshire.

We should emphasize that we feel as comfortable with GEICO management retaining an estimated $17 million of earnings applicable to our ownership as we would if that sum were in our own hands. In just the last two years GEICO, through repurchases of its own stock, has reduced the share equivalents it has outstanding from 34.2 million to 21.6 million, dramatically enhancing the interests of shareholders in a business that simply can't be replicated. The owners could not have been better served.

We have written in past reports about the disappointments that usually result from purchase and operation of "turnaround" businesses. Literally hundreds of turnaround possibilities in dozens of industries have been described to us over the years and, either as participants or as observers, we have tracked performance against expectations. Our conclusion is that, with few exceptions, when a management with a reputation for brilliance tackles a business with a reputation for poor fundamental economics, it is the reputation of the business that remains intact.

GEICO may appear to be an exception, having been turned around from the very edge of bankruptcy in 1976. It certainly is true that managerial brilliance was needed for its resuscitation, and that Jack Byrne, upon arrival in that year, supplied that ingredient in abundance.

But it also is true that the fundamental business advantage that GEICO had enjoyed—an advantage that previously had produced staggering success—was still intact within the company, although submerged in a sea of financial and operating troubles.

GEICO was designed to be the low-cost operation in an enormous marketplace (auto insurance) populated largely by companies whose marketing structures restricted adaptation. Run as designed, it could offer unusual value to its customers while earning unusual returns for itself. For decades it had been run in just this manner. Its troubles in the mid-70s were not produced by any diminution or disappearance of this essential economic advantage.

GEICO's problems at that time put it in a position analogous to that of American Express in 1964 following the salad oil scandal. Both were one-of-a-kind companies, temporarily reeling from the effects of a fiscal blow that did not destroy their exceptional underlying economics. The GEICO and American

Express situations, extraordinary business franchises with a localized excisable cancer (needing, to be sure, a skilled surgeon), should be distinguished from the true "turnaround" situation in which the managers expect—and need—to pull off a corporate Pygmalion.

Whatever the appellation, we are delighted with our GEICO holding which, as noted, cost us $47 million. To buy a similar $20 million of earning power in a business with first-class economic characteristics and bright prospects would cost a minimum of $200 million (much more in some industries) if it had to be accomplished through negotiated purchase of an entire company. A 100% interest of that kind gives the owner the options of leveraging the purchase, changing managements, directing cash flow, and selling the business. It may also provide some excitement around corporate headquarters (less frequently mentioned).

We find it perfectly satisfying that the nature of our insurance business dictates we buy many minority portions of already well-run businesses (at prices far below our share of the total value of the entire business) that do not need management change, re-direction of cash flow, or sale. There aren't many Jack Byrnes in the managerial world, or GEICOs in the business world. What could be better than buying into a partnership with both of them?

Insurance Industry Conditions

The insurance industry's underwriting picture continues to unfold about as we anticipated, with the combined ratio (see definition on page 37) rising from 100.6 in 1979 to an estimated 103.5 in 1980. It is virtually certain that this trend will continue and that industry underwriting losses will mount, significantly and progressively, in 1981 and 1982. To understand why, we recommend that you read the excellent analysis of property-casualty competitive dynamics done by Barbara Stewart of Chubb Corp. in an October 1980 paper. (Chubb's annual report consistently presents the most insightful, candid and well-written discussion of industry conditions; you should get on the company's mailing list.) Mrs. Stewart's analysis may not be cheerful, but we think it is very likely to be accurate.

And, unfortunately, a largely unreported but particularly pernicious problem may well prolong and intensify the coming industry agony. It is not only likely to keep many insurers scrambling for business when underwriting losses hit record levels—it is likely to cause them at such a time to redouble their efforts.

This problem arises from the decline in bond prices and the insurance accounting convention that allows companies to carry bonds at amortized cost, regardless of market value. Many insurers own long-term bonds that, at amortized cost, amount to two to three times net worth. If the level is three times, of course, a one-third shrink from cost in bond prices—if it were to be recognized on the books—would wipe out net worth. And shrink they have. Some of the largest and best known property-casualty companies currently find themselves with nominal, or even negative, net worth when bond holdings are valued at market. Of course their bonds could rise in price, thereby partially, or conceivably even fully, restoring the integrity of stated net worth. Or they could fall further. (We believe that short-term forecasts of stock or bond prices are useless. The forecasts may tell you a great deal about the forecaster; they tell you nothing about the future.)

It might strike some as strange that an insurance company's survival is threatened when its stock portfolio falls sufficiently in price to reduce net worth significantly, but that an even greater decline in bond prices produces no reaction at all. The industry would respond by pointing out that, no matter what the current price, the bonds will be paid in full at maturity, thereby eventually eliminating any interim price decline. It may take twenty, thirty, or even forty years, this argument says, but, as long as the bonds don't have to be sold, in the end they'll all be worth face value. Of course, if they are sold even if they are replaced with similar bonds offering better relative value—the loss must be booked immediately. And, just as promptly, published net worth must be adjusted downward by the amount of the loss.

Under such circumstances, a great many investment options disappear, perhaps for decades. For example, when large underwriting losses are in prospect, it may make excellent business logic for some insurers to shift from tax-exempt bonds into taxable bonds. Unwillingness to recognize major bond losses may be the sole factor that prevents such a sensible move.

But the full implications flowing from massive unrealized bond losses are far more serious than just the immobilization of investment intellect. For the source of funds to purchase *and hold* those bonds is a pool of money derived from policyholders and claimants (with changing faces)—money which, in effect, is temporarily on deposit with the insurer. As long as this pool retains its size, no bonds must be sold. If the pool of funds shrinks—which it will if the volume of business declines significantly—assets must be sold to pay off the liabilities. And if those assets consist of bonds with big unrealized losses, such losses will rapidly become realized, decimating net worth in the process.

Thus, an insurance company with a bond market value shrinkage approaching stated net worth (of which there are now many) and also faced with inadequate rate levels that are sure to deteriorate further has two options. One option for management is to tell the underwriters to keep pricing according to the exposure involved—"be sure to get a dollar of premium for every dollar of expense cost plus expectable loss cost".

The consequences of this directive are predictable: (a) with most business both price sensitive and renewable annually, many policies presently on the books will be lost to competitors in rather short order; (b) as premium volume shrinks significantly, there will be a lagged but corresponding decrease in liabilities (unearned premiums and claims payable); (c) assets (bonds) must be sold to match the decrease in liabilities; and (d) the formerly unrecognized disappearance of net worth will become partially recognized (depending upon the extent of such sales) in the insurer's published financial statements.

Variations of this depressing sequence involve a smaller penalty to stated net worth. The reaction of some companies at (c) would be to sell either stocks that are already carried at market values or recently purchased bonds involving less severe losses. This ostrich-like behavior—selling the better assets and keeping the biggest losers—while less painful in the short term, is unlikely to be a winner in the long term.

The second option is much simpler: just keep writing business regardless of rate levels and whopping prospective underwriting losses, thereby maintaining the present levels of premiums, assets and liabilities—and then pray for a better day, either for underwriting or for bond prices. There is much criticism in the trade press of "cash flow" underwriting; i.e., writing business regardless of prospective underwriting losses in order to obtain funds to invest at current high interest rates. This second option might properly be termed "asset maintenance" underwriting—the acceptance of terrible business just to keep the assets you now have.

Of course you know which option will be selected. And it also is clear that as long as many large insurers feel compelled to choose that second option, there will be no better day for underwriting. For if much of the industry feels it must maintain premium volume levels regardless of price adequacy, all insurers will have to come close to meeting those prices. Right behind having financial problems yourself, the next worst plight is to have a large group of competitors with financial problems that they can defer by a "sell-at-any-price" policy.

We mentioned earlier that companies that were unwilling—for any of a number of reasons, including public reaction, institutional pride, or protection of stated net worth—to sell bonds at price levels forcing recognition of major losses might find themselves frozen in investment posture for a decade or longer. But, as noted, that's only half of the problem. *Companies that have made extensive commitments to long-term bonds may have lost, for a considerable period of time, not only many of their investment options, but many of their underwriting options as well.*

Our own position in this respect is satisfactory. We believe our net worth, valuing bonds of all insurers at amortized cost, is the strongest relative to premium volume among all large property-casualty stockholder-owned groups. When bonds are valued at market, our relative strength becomes far more dramatic. (But lest we get too puffed up, we remind ourselves that our asset and liability maturities still are far more mismatched than we would wish and that we, too, lost important sums in bonds because your Chairman was talking when he should have been acting.)

Our abundant capital and investment flexibility will enable us to do whatever we think makes the most sense during the prospective extended period of inadequate pricing. But troubles for the industry mean troubles for us. Our financial strength doesn't remove us from the hostile pricing environment now enveloping the entire property-casualty insurance industry. It just gives us more staying power and more options.

Insurance Operations

The National Indemnity managers, led by Phil Liesche with the usual able assistance of Roland Miller and Bill Lyons, outdid themselves in 1980. While volume was flat, underwriting margins relative to the industry were at an all-time high. We expect decreased volume from this operation in 1981. But its managers will hear no complaints from corporate headquarters, nor will employment or salaries suffer. We enormously admire the National Indemnity underwriting discipline—embedded from origin by the founder, Jack Ringwalt—and know that this discipline, if suspended, probably could not be fully regained.

John Seward at Home and Auto continues to make good progress in replacing a diminishing number of auto policies with volume from less competitive lines, primarily small-premium general liability. Operations are being slowly expanded, both geographically and by product line, as warranted by underwriting results.

The reinsurance business continues to reflect the excesses and problems of the primary writers. Worse yet, it has the potential for magnifying such excesses. Reinsurance is characterized by extreme ease of entry, large premium payments in advance, and much-delayed loss reports and loss payments. Initially, the morning mail brings lots of cash and few claims. This state of affairs can produce a blissful, almost euphoric, feeling akin to that experienced by an innocent upon receipt of his first credit card.

The magnetic lure of such cash-generating characteristics, currently enhanced by the presence of high interest rates, is transforming the reinsurance market into "amateur night". Without a super catastrophe, industry underwriting will be poor in the next few years. If we experience such a catastrophe, there could be a bloodbath with some companies not able to live up to contractual commitments. George Young continues to do a first-class job for us in this business. Results, with investment income included, have been reasonably profitable. We will retain an active reinsurance presence but, for the foreseeable future, we expect no premium growth from this activity.

We continue to have serious problems in the Homestate operation. Floyd Taylor in Kansas has done an outstanding job but our underwriting record elsewhere is considerably below average. Our poorest performer has been Insurance Company of Iowa, at which large losses have been sustained annually since its founding in 1973. Late in the fall we abandoned underwriting in that state, and have merged the company into Cornhusker Casualty. There is potential in the homestate concept, but much work needs to be done in order to realize it.

Our Workers Compensation operation suffered a severe loss when Frank DeNardo died last year at 37. Frank instinctively thought like an underwriter. He was a superb technician and a fierce competitor; in short order he had straightened out major problems at the California Workers Compensation Division of National Indemnity. Dan Grossman, who originally brought Frank to us, stepped in immediately after Frank's death to continue that operation, which now utilizes Redwood Fire and Casualty, another Berkshire subsidiary, as the insuring vehicle.

Our major Workers Compensation operation, Cypress Insurance Company, run by Milt Thornton, continues its outstanding record. Year after year Milt, like Phil Liesche, runs an underwriting operation that far outpaces his competition. In the industry he is admired and copied, but not matched.

Overall, we look for a significant decline in insurance volume in 1981 along with a poorer underwriting result. We expect underwriting experience somewhat superior to that of the industry but, of course, so does most of the industry. There will be some disappointments.

Textile and Retail Operations

During the past year we have cut back the scope of our textile business. Operations at Waumbec Mills have been terminated, reluctantly but necessarily. Some equipment was transferred to New Bedford but most has been sold, or will be, along with real estate. Your Chairman made a costly mistake in not facing the realities of this situation sooner.

At New Bedford we have reduced the number of looms operated by about one-third, abandoning some high-volume lines in which product differentiation was insignificant. Even assuming everything went right—which it seldom did—these lines could not generate adequate returns related to investment. And, over a full industry cycle, losses were the most likely result.

Our remaining textile operation, still sizable, has been divided into a manufacturing and a sales division, each free to do business independent of the other. Thus, distribution strengths and mill capabilities will not be wedded to each other. We have more than doubled capacity in our most profitable textile segment through a recent purchase of used 130-inch Saurer looms. Current conditions indicate another tough year in textiles, but with substantially less capital employed in the operation.

Ben Rosner's record at Associated Retail Stores continues to amaze us. In a poor retailing year, Associated's earnings continued excellent—and those earnings all were translated into cash. On March 7, 1981 Associated will celebrate its 50th birthday. Ben has run the business (along with Leo Simon, his partner from 1931 to 1966) in each of those fifty years.

Disposition of Illinois National Bank and Trust of Rockford

On December 31, 1980 we completed the exchange of 41,086 shares of Rockford Bancorp Inc. (which owns 97.7% of Illinois National Bank) for a like number of shares of Berkshire Hathaway Inc.

Our method of exchange allowed all Berkshire shareholders to maintain their proportional interest in the Bank (except for me; I was permitted 80% of my proportional share). They were thus guaranteed an ownership position identical to that they would have attained had we followed a more conventional spinoff approach. Twenty-four shareholders (of our approximate 1300) chose this proportional exchange option.

We also allowed overexchanges, and thirty-nine additional shareholders accepted this option, thereby increasing their ownership in the Bank and decreasing their proportional ownership in Berkshire. All got the full amount of Bancorp stock they requested, since the total shares desired by these thirty-nine holders was just slightly less than the number left available by the remaining 1200-plus holders of Berkshire who elected not to part with any Berkshire shares at all. As the exchanger of last resort, I took the small balance (3% of Bancorp's stock). These shares, added to shares I received from my basic exchange allotment (80% of normal), gave me a slightly reduced proportional interest in the Bank and a slightly enlarged proportional interest in Berkshire.

Management of the Bank is pleased with the outcome. Bancorp will operate as an inexpensive and uncomplicated holding company owned by 65 shareholders. And all of those shareholders will have become Bancorp owners through a conscious affirmative decision.

Financing

In August we sold $60 million of 12¾% notes due August 1, 2005, with a sinking fund to begin in 1991.

The managing underwriters, Donaldson, Lufkin & Jenrette Securities Corporation, represented by Bill Fisher, and Chiles, Heider & Company, Inc., represented by Charlie Heider, did an absolutely first-class job from start to finish of the financing.

Unlike most businesses, Berkshire did not finance because of any specific immediate needs. Rather, we borrowed because we think that, over a period far shorter than the life of the loan, we will have many opportunities to put the money to good use. The most attractive opportunities may present themselves at a time when credit is extremely expensive—or even unavailable. At such a time we want to have plenty of financial firepower.

Our acquisition preferences run toward businesses that generate cash, not those that consume it. As inflation intensifies, more and more companies find that they must spend all funds they generate internally just to maintain their existing physical volume of business. There is a certain mirage-like quality to such operations. However attractive the earnings numbers, we remain leery of businesses that never seem able to convert such pretty numbers into no-strings-attached cash.

Businesses meeting our standards are not easy to find. (Each year we read of hundreds of corporate acquisitions; only a handful would have been of interest to us.) And logical expansion of our present operations is not easy to implement. But we'll continue to utilize both avenues in our attempts to further Berkshire's growth.

Under all circumstances we plan to operate with plenty of liquidity, with debt that is moderate in size and properly structured, and with an abundance of capital strength. Our return on equity is penalized somewhat by this conservative approach, but it is the only one with which we feel comfortable.

* * * * * * * * * * * *

Gene Abegg, founder of our long-owned bank in Rockford, died on July 2, 1980 at the age of 82. As a friend, banker and citizen, he was unsurpassed.

You learn a great deal about a person when you purchase a business from him and he then stays on to run it as an employee rather than as an owner. Before the purchase the seller knows the business intimately, whereas you start from scratch. The seller has dozens of opportunities to mislead the buyer—through omissions, ambiguities, and misdirection. After the check has changed hands, subtle (and not so subtle) changes of attitude can occur and implicit understandings can evaporate. As in the courtship-marriage sequence, disappointments are not infrequent.

From the time we first met, Gene shot straight 100% of the time—the only behavior pattern he had within him. At the outset of negotiations, he laid all negative factors face up on the table; on the other hand, for years after the transaction was completed he would tell me periodically of some previously undiscussed items of value that had come with our purchase.

Though he was already 71 years of age when he sold us the Bank, Gene subsequently worked harder for us than he had for himself. He never delayed reporting a problem for a minute, but problems were few with Gene. What else would you expect from a man who, at the time of the bank holiday in 1933, had enough cash on the premises to pay all depositors in full? Gene never forgot he was handling other people's money. Though this fiduciary attitude was always dominant, his superb managerial skills enabled the Bank to regularly achieve the top position nationally in profitability.

Gene was in charge of the Illinois National for close to fifty years—almost one-quarter of the lifetime of our country. George Mead, a wealthy industrialist, brought him in from Chicago to open a new bank after a number of other banks in Rockford had failed. Mr. Mead put up the money and Gene ran the show. His talent for leadership soon put its stamp on virtually every major civic activity in Rockford.

Dozens of Rockford citizens have told me over the years of help Gene extended to them. In some cases this help was financial; in all cases it involved much wisdom, empathy and friendship. He always offered the same to me. Because of our respective ages and positions I was sometimes the junior partner, sometimes the senior. Whichever the relationship, it always was a special one, and I miss it.

Warren E. Buffett
Chairman of the Board

February 27, 1981

BERKSHIRE HATHAWAY INC.

February 26, 1982

To the Shareholders of Berkshire Hathaway Inc.:

Operating earnings of $39.7 million in 1981 amounted to 15.2% of beginning equity capital (valuing securities at cost) compared to 17.8% in 1980. Our new plan that allows stockholders to designate corporate charitable contributions (detailed later) reduced earnings by about $900,000 in 1981. This program, which we expect to continue subject to annual evaluation of our corporate tax position, had not been initiated in 1980.

Non-Controlled Ownership Earnings

In the 1980 annual report we discussed extensively the concept of non-controlled ownership earnings, i.e., Berkshire's share of the undistributed earnings of companies we don't control or significantly influence but in which we, nevertheless, have important investments. (We will be glad to make available to new or prospective shareholders copies of that discussion or others from earlier reports to which we refer in this report.) No portion of those undistributed earnings is included in the operating earnings of Berkshire.

However, our belief is that, in aggregate, those undistributed and, therefore, unrecorded earnings will be translated into tangible value for Berkshire shareholders just as surely as if subsidiaries we control had earned, retained—and reported—similar earnings.

We know that this translation of non-controlled ownership earnings into corresponding realized and unrealized capital gains for Berkshire will be extremely irregular as to time of occurrence. While market values track business values quite well over long periods, in any given year the relationship can gyrate capriciously. Market recognition of retained earnings also will be unevenly realized among companies. It will be disappointingly low or negative in cases where earnings are employed non-productively, and far greater than dollar-for-dollar of retained earnings in cases of companies that achieve high returns with their augmented capital. Overall, if a group of non-controlled companies is selected with reasonable skill, the group result should be quite satisfactory.

In aggregate, our non-controlled business interests have more favorable underlying economic characteristics than our controlled businesses. That's understandable; the area of choice has been far wider. Small portions of exceptionally good businesses are usually available in the securities markets at reasonable prices. But such businesses are available for purchase in their entirety only rarely, and then almost always at high prices.

General Acquisition Behavior

As our history indicates, we are comfortable both with total ownership of businesses and with marketable securities representing small portions of businesses. We continually look for ways to employ large sums in each area. (But we try to avoid small commitments—"If something's not worth doing at all, it's not worth doing well".) Indeed, the liquidity requirements of our insurance and trading stamp businesses mandate major investments in marketable securities.

Our acquisition decisions will be aimed at maximizing real economic benefits, not at maximizing either managerial domain or reported numbers for accounting purposes. (In the long run, managements stressing accounting appearance over economic substance usually achieve little of either.)

Regardless of the impact upon immediately reportable earnings, we would rather buy 10% of Wonderful Business T at X per share than 100% of T at 2X per share. Most corporate managers prefer just the reverse, and have no shortage of stated rationales for their behavior.

However, we suspect three motivations—usually unspoken—to be, singly or in combination, the important ones in most high-premium takeovers:

(1) Leaders, business or otherwise, seldom are deficient in animal spirits and often relish increased activity and challenge. At Berkshire, the corporate pulse never beats faster than when an acquisition is in prospect.

(2) Most organizations, business or otherwise, measure themselves, are measured by others, and compensate their managers far more by the yardstick of size than by any other yardstick. (Ask a *Fortune 500* manager where his corporation stands on that famous list and, invariably, the number responded will be from the list ranked by size of sales; he may well not even know where his corporation places on the list *Fortune* just as faithfully compiles ranking the same 500 corporations by profitability.)

(3) Many managements apparently were overexposed in impressionable childhood years to the story in which the imprisoned handsome prince is released from a toad's body by a kiss from a beautiful princess. Consequently, they are certain their managerial kiss will do wonders for the profitability of Company T(arget).

Such optimism is essential. Absent that rosy view, why else should the shareholders of Company A(cquisitor) want to own an interest in T at the 2X takeover cost rather than at the X market price they would pay if they made direct purchases on their own?

In other words, investors can always buy toads at the going price for toads. If investors instead bankroll princesses who wish to pay double for the right to kiss the toad, those kisses had better pack some real dynamite. We've observed many kisses but very few miracles. Nevertheless, many managerial princesses remain serenely confident about the future potency of their kisses—even after their corporate backyards are knee-deep in unresponsive toads.

In fairness, we should acknowledge that some acquisition records have been dazzling. Two major categories stand out.

The first involves companies that, through design or accident, have purchased only businesses that are particularly well adapted to an inflationary environment. Such favored business must have two characteristics: (1) an ability to increase prices rather easily (even when product demand is flat and capacity is not fully utilized) without fear of significant loss of either market share or unit volume, and (2) an ability to accommodate large dollar volume increases in business (often produced more by inflation than by real growth) with only minor additional investment of capital. Managers of ordinary ability, focusing solely on acquisition possibilities meeting these tests, have achieved excellent results in recent decades. However, very few enterprises possess both characteristics, and competition to buy those that do has now become fierce to the point of being self-defeating.

The second category involves the managerial superstars—men who can recognize that rare prince who is disguised as a toad, and who have managerial abilities that enable them to peel away the disguise. We salute such managers as Ben Heineman at Northwest Industries, Henry Singleton at Teledyne, Erwin Zaban at National Service Industries, and especially Tom Murphy at Capital Cities Communications (a real managerial "twofer", whose acquisition efforts have been properly focused in Category 1 and whose operating talents also make him a leader of Category 2). From both direct and vicarious experience, we recognize the difficulty and rarity of these executives' achievements. (So do they; these champs have made very few deals in recent years, and often have found repurchase of their own shares to be the most sensible employment of corporate capital.)

Your Chairman, unfortunately, does not qualify for Category 2. And, despite a reasonably good understanding of the economic factors compelling concentration in Category 1, our actual acquisition activity in that category has been sporadic and inadequate. Our preaching was better than our performance. (We neglected the Noah principle: predicting rain doesn't count, building arks does.)

We have tried occasionally to buy toads at bargain prices with results that have been chronicled in past reports. Clearly our kisses fell flat. We have done well with a couple of princes—but they were princes when purchased. At least our kisses didn't turn them into toads. And, finally, we have occasionally been quite successful in purchasing fractional interests in easily-identifiable princes at toad-like prices.

Berkshire Acquisition Objectives

We will continue to seek the acquisition of businesses in their entirety at prices that will make sense, even should the future of the acquired enterprise develop much along the lines of its past. We may very well pay a fairly fancy price for a Category 1 business if we are reasonably confident of what we are getting. But we will not normally pay a lot in any purchase for what we are supposed to bring to the party—for we find that we ordinarily don't bring a lot.

During 1981 we came quite close to a major purchase involving both a business and a manager we liked very much. However, the price finally demanded, considering alternative uses for the funds involved, would have left our owners worse off than before the purchase. The empire would have been larger, but the citizenry would have been poorer.

Although we had no success in 1981, from time to time in the future we will be able to purchase 100% of businesses meeting our standards. Additionally, we expect an occasional offering of a major "non-voting partnership" as discussed under the Pinkerton's heading on page 47 of this report. We welcome suggestions regarding such companies where we, as a substantial junior partner, can achieve good economic results while furthering the long-term objectives of present owners and managers.

Currently, we find values most easily obtained through the open-market purchase of fractional positions in companies with excellent business franchises and competent, honest managements. We never expect to run these companies, but we do expect to profit from them.

We expect that undistributed earnings from such companies will produce full value (subject to tax when realized) for Berkshire and its shareholders. If they don't, we have made mistakes as to either: (1) the management we have elected to join; (2) the future economics of the business; or (3) the price we have paid.

We have made plenty of such mistakes—both in the purchase of non-controlling and controlling interests in businesses. Category (2) miscalculations are the most common. Of course, it is necessary to dig deep into our history to find illustrations of such mistakes—sometimes as deep as two or three months back. For example, last year your Chairman volunteered his expert opinion on the rosy future of the aluminum business. Several minor adjustments to that opinion—now aggregating approximately 180 degrees—have since been required.

For personal as well as more objective reasons, however, we generally have been able to correct such mistakes far more quickly in the case of non-controlled businesses (marketable securities) than in the case of controlled subsidiaries. Lack of control, in effect, often has turned out to be an economic plus.

As we mentioned last year, the magnitude of our non-recorded "ownership" earnings has grown to the point where their total is greater than our reported operating earnings. We expect this situation will continue. In just four ownership positions in this category—GEICO Corporation, General Foods Corporation, R. J. Reynolds Industries, Inc. and The Washington Post Company—our share of undistributed and therefore unrecorded earnings probably will total well over $35 million in 1982. The accounting rules that entirely ignore these undistributed earnings diminish the utility of our annual return on equity calculation, or any other single year measure of economic performance.

Long-Term Corporate Performance

In measuring long-term economic performance, equities held by our insurance subsidiaries are valued at market subject to a charge reflecting the amount of taxes that would have to be paid if unrealized gains were actually realized. If we are correct in the premise stressed in the preceding section of this report, our unreported ownership earnings will find their way, irregularly but inevitably, into our net worth. To date, this has been the case.

An even purer calculation of performance would involve a valuation of bonds and non-insurance held equities at market. However, GAAP accounting does not prescribe this procedure, and the added purity would change results only very slightly. Should any valuation difference widen to significant proportions, as it has at most major insurance companies, we will report its effect to you.

On a GAAP basis, during the present management's term of seventeen years, book value has increased from $19.46 per share to $526.02 per share, or 21.1% compounded annually. This rate of return number is highly likely to drift downward in future years. We hope, however, that it can be maintained significantly above the rate of return achieved by the average large American corporation.

Over half of the large gain in Berkshire's net worth during 1981—it totaled $124 million, or about 31%—resulted from the market performance of a single investment, GEICO Corporation. In aggregate, our market gain from securities during the year considerably outstripped the gain in underlying business values. Such market variations will not always be on the pleasant side.

In past reports we have explained how inflation has caused our apparently satisfactory long-term corporate performance to be illusory as a measure of true investment results for our owners. We applaud the efforts of Federal Reserve Chairman Volcker and note the currently more moderate increases in various price indices. Nevertheless, our views regarding long-term inflationary trends are as negative as ever. Like virginity, a stable price level seems capable of maintenance, but not of restoration.

Despite the overriding importance of inflation in the investment equation, we will not punish you further with another full recital of our views; inflation itself will be punishment enough. (Copies of previous discussions are available for masochists.) But, because of the unrelenting destruction of currency values, our corporate efforts will continue to do a much better job of filling your wallet than of filling your stomach.

Equity Value-Added

An additional factor should further subdue any residual enthusiasm you may retain regarding our long-term rate of return. The economic case justifying equity investment is that, in aggregate, additional earnings above passive investment returns—interest on fixed-income securities—will be derived through the employment of managerial and entrepreneurial skills in conjunction with that equity capital. Furthermore, the case says that since the equity capital position is associated with greater risk than passive forms of investment, it is "entitled" to higher returns. A "value-added" bonus from equity capital seems natural and certain.

But is it? Several decades back, a return on equity of as little as 10% enabled a corporation to be classified as a "good" business—i.e., one in which a dollar reinvested in the business logically could be expected to be valued by the market at more than one hundred cents. For, with long-term taxable bonds yielding 5% and long-term tax-exempt bonds 3%, a business operation that could utilize equity capital at 10% clearly was worth some premium to investors over the equity capital employed. That was true even though a combination of taxes on dividends and on capital gains would reduce the 10% earned by the corporation to perhaps 6%-8% in the hands of the individual investor.

Investment markets recognized this truth. During that earlier period, American business earned an average of 11% or so on equity capital employed and stocks, in aggregate, sold at valuations far above that equity capital (book value), averaging over 150 cents on the dollar. Most businesses were "good" businesses because they earned far more than their keep (the return on long-term passive money). The value-added produced by equity investment, in aggregate, was substantial.

That day is gone. But the lessons learned during its existence are difficult to discard. While investors and managers must place their feet in the future, their memories and nervous systems often remain plugged into the past. It is much easier for investors to utilize historic p/e ratios or for managers to utilize historic business valuation yardsticks than it is for either group to rethink their premises daily. When change is slow, constant rethinking is actually undesirable; it achieves little and slows response time. But when change is great, yesterday's assumptions can be retained only at great cost. And the pace of economic change has become breathtaking.

During the past year, long-term taxable bond yields exceeded 16% and long-term tax-exempts 14%. The total return achieved from such tax-exempts, of course, goes directly into the pocket of the individual owner. Meanwhile, American business is producing earnings of only about 14% on equity. And this 14% will be substantially reduced by taxation before it can be banked by the individual owner. The extent of such shrinkage depends upon the dividend policy of the corporation and the tax rates applicable to the investor.

Thus, *with interest rates on passive investments at late 1981 levels,* a typical American business is no longer worth one hundred cents on the dollar to owners who are individuals. (If the business is owned by pension funds or other tax-exempt investors, the arithmetic, although still unenticing, changes substantially for the better.) Assume an investor in a 50% tax bracket; if our typical company pays out all earnings, the income return to the investor will be equivalent to that from a 7% tax-exempt bond. And, if conditions persist—if all earnings are paid out and return on equity stays at 14%—the 7% tax-exempt equivalent to the higher-bracket individual investor is just as frozen as is the coupon on a tax-exempt bond. Such a perpetual 7% tax-exempt bond might be worth fifty cents on the dollar as this is written.

If, on the other hand, all earnings of our typical American business are retained and return on equity again remains constant, earnings will grow at 14% per year. If the p/e ratio remains constant, the price of our typical stock will also grow at 14% per year. But that 14% is not yet in the pocket of the shareholder. Putting it there will require the payment of a capital gains tax, presently assessed at a maximum rate of 20%. This net return, of course, works out to a poorer rate of return than the currently available passive after-tax rate.

Unless passive rates fall, companies achieving 14% per year gains in earnings per share while paying no cash dividend are an economic failure for their individual shareholders. The returns from passive capital outstrip the returns from active capital. This is an unpleasant fact for both investors and corporate managers and, therefore, one they may wish to ignore. But facts do not cease to exist, either because they are unpleasant or because they are ignored.

Most American businesses pay out a significant portion of their earnings and thus fall between the two examples. And most American businesses are currently "bad" businesses economically—producing less for their individual investors after-tax than the tax-exempt passive rate of return on money. Of course, some high-return businesses still remain attractive, even under present conditions. But American equity capital, in aggregate, produces no value-added for individual investors.

It should be stressed that this depressing situation does not occur because corporations are jumping, economically, less high than previously. In fact, they are jumping somewhat higher: return on equity has improved a few points in the past decade. But the crossbar of passive return has been elevated much faster. Unhappily, most companies can do little but hope that the bar will be lowered significantly; there are few industries in which the prospects seem bright for substantial gains in return on equity.

Inflationary experience and expectations will be major (but not the only) factors affecting the height of the crossbar in future years. If the causes of long-term inflation can be tempered, passive returns are likely to fall and the intrinsic position of American equity capital should significantly improve. Many businesses that now must be classified as economically "bad" would be restored to the "good" category under such circumstances.

A further, particularly ironic, punishment is inflicted by an inflationary environment upon the owners of the "bad" business. To continue operating in its present mode, such a low-return business usually must retain much of its earnings—no matter what penalty such a policy produces for shareholders.

Reason, of course, would prescribe just the opposite policy. An individual, stuck with a 5% bond with many years to run before maturity, does not take the coupons from that bond and pay one hundred cents on the dollar for more 5% bonds while similar bonds are available at, say, forty cents on the dollar. Instead, he takes those coupons from his low-return bond and—if inclined to reinvest—looks for the highest return with safety currently available. Good money is not thrown after bad.

What makes sense for the bondholder makes sense for the shareholder. Logically, a company with historic *and prospective* high returns on equity should retain much or all of its earnings so that shareholders can earn premium returns on enhanced capital. Conversely, low returns on corporate equity would suggest a very high dividend payout so that owners could direct capital toward more attractive areas. (The Scriptures concur. In the parable of the talents, the two high-earning servants are rewarded with 100% retention of earnings and encouraged to expand their operations. However, the non-earning third servant is not only chastised—"wicked and slothful"—but also is required to redirect all of his capital to the top performer. *Matthew 25: 14-30)*

But inflation takes us through the looking glass into the upside-down world of *Alice in Wonderland*. When prices continuously rise, the "bad" business must retain every nickel that it can. Not because it is attractive as a repository for equity capital, but precisely because it is so unattractive, the low-return business must follow a high retention policy. If it wishes to continue operating in the future as it has in the past—and most entities, including businesses, do—it simply has no choice.

For inflation acts as a gigantic corporate tapeworm. That tapeworm preemptively consumes its requisite daily diet of investment dollars regardless of the health of the host organism. Whatever the level of reported profits (even if nil), more dollars for receivables, inventory and fixed assets are continuously required by the business in order to merely match the unit volume of the previous year. The less prosperous the enterprise, the greater the proportion of available sustenance claimed by the tapeworm.

Under present conditions, a business earning 8% or 10% on equity often has no leftovers for expansion, debt reduction or "real" dividends. The tapeworm of inflation simply cleans the plate. (The low-return company's inability to pay dividends, understandably, is often disguised. Corporate America increasingly is turning to dividend reinvestment plans, sometimes even embodying a discount arrangement that all but forces shareholders to reinvest. Other companies sell newly issued shares to Peter in order to pay dividends to Paul. Beware of "dividends" that can be paid out only if someone promises to replace the capital distributed.)

Berkshire continues to retain its earnings for offensive, not defensive or obligatory, reasons. But in no way are we immune from the pressures that escalating passive returns exert on equity capital. We continue to clear the crossbar of after-tax passive return—but barely. Our historic 21% return—not at all assured for the future—still provides, after the current capital gain tax rate (which we expect to rise considerably in future years), a modest margin over current after-tax rates on passive money. It would be a bit humiliating to have our corporate value-added turn negative. But it can happen here as it has elsewhere, either from events outside anyone's control or from poor relative adaptation on our part.

Sources of Reported Earnings

The table below shows the sources of Berkshire's reported earnings. Berkshire owns about 60% of Blue Chip Stamps which, in turn, owns 80% of Wesco Financial Corporation. The table displays aggregate operating earnings of the various business entities, as well as Berkshire's share of those earnings. All of the significant gains and losses attributable to unusual sales of assets by any of the business entities are aggregated with securities transactions in the line near the bottom of the table and are not included in operating earnings.

| | Earnings Before Income Taxes | | | | Net Earnings After Tax | |
| | Total | | Berkshire Share | | Berkshire Share | |
	1981	1980	1981	1980	1981	1980
	(000s omitted)					
Operating Earnings:						
Insurance Group:						
Underwriting	$ 1,478	$ 6,738	$ 1,478	$ 6,737	$ 798	$ 3,637
Net Investment Income . . .	38,823	30,939	38,823	30,927	32,401	25,607
Berkshire-Waumbec Textiles . .	(2,669)	(508)	(2,669)	(508)	(1,493)	202
Associated Retail Stores	1,763	2,440	1,763	2,440	759	1,169
See's Candies.	21,891	15,475	13,046	9,223	6,289	4,459
Buffalo Evening News	(1,057)	(2,777)	(630)	(1,655)	(276)	(800)
Blue Chip Stamps – Parent . .	3,642	7,699	2,171	4,588	2,134	3,060
Wesco Financial – Parent	4,495	2,916	2,145	1,392	1,590	1,044
Mutual Savings and Loan	1,605	5,814	766	2,775	1,536	1,974
Precision Steel	3,453	2,833	1,648	1,352	841	656
Interest on Debt	(14,656)	(12,230)	(12,649)	(9,390)	(6,671)	(4,809)
Other*	1,895	1,698	1,344	1,308	1,513	992
Sub-total – Continuing Operations	$ 60,663	$ 61,037	$ 47,236	$ 49,189	$ 39,421	$ 37,191
Illinois National Bank**	--	5,324	--	5,200	--	4,731
Operating Earnings	60,663	66,361	47,236	54,389	39,421	41,922
Sales of securities and unusual sales of assets	37,801	19,584	33,150	15,757	23,183	11,200
Total Earnings – all entities	$ 98,464	$ 85,945	$ 80,386	$ 70,146	$ 62,604	$ 53,122

* *Amortization of intangibles arising in accounting for purchases of businesses (i.e. See's, Mutual and Buffalo Evening News) is reflected in the category designated as "Other".*
** *Berkshire divested itself of its ownership of the Illinois National Bank on December 31, 1980.*

Blue Chip Stamps and Wesco are public companies with reporting requirements of their own. On pages 38-50 of this report we have reproduced the narrative reports of the principal executives of both companies, in which they describe 1981 operations. A copy of the full annual report of either company will be mailed to any Berkshire shareholder upon request to Mr. Robert H. Bird for Blue Chip Stamps, 5801 South Eastern Avenue, Los Angeles, California 90040, or to Mrs. Jeanne Leach for Wesco Financial Corporation, 315 East Colorado Boulevard, Pasadena, California 91109.

As we indicated earlier, undistributed earnings in companies we do not control are now fully as important as the reported operating earnings detailed in the preceding table. The distributed portion of earnings, of course, finds its way into the table primarily through the net investment income segment of Insurance Group earnings.

We show below Berkshire's proportional holdings in those non-controlled businesses for which only distributed earnings (dividends) are included in our earnings.

No. of Shares	Company	Cost	Market
		(000's omitted)	
451,650	(a) Affiliated Publications, Inc.	$ 3,297	$ 14,114
703,634	(a) Aluminum Company of America	19,359	18,031
420,441	(a) Arcata Corporation (including common equivalents) . . .	14,076	15,136
475,217	(b) Cleveland-Cliffs Iron Company	12,942	14,362
441,522	(a) GATX Corporation	17,147	13,466
2,101,244	(b) General Foods, Inc.	66,277	66,714
7,200,000	(a) GEICO Corporation	47,138	199,800
2,015,000	(a) Handy & Harman	21,825	36,270
711,180	(a) Interpublic Group of Companies, Inc.	4,531	23,202
282,500	(a) Media General	4,545	11,088
391,400	(a) Ogilvy & Mather International Inc.	3,709	12,329
370,088	(b) Pinkerton's, Inc.	12,144	19,675
1,764,824	(b) R. J. Reynolds Industries, Inc.	76,668	83,127
785,225	(b) SAFECO Corporation	21,329	31,016
1,868,600	(a) The Washington Post Company	10,628	58,160
		$335,615	$616,490
	All Other Common Stockholdings	16,131	22,739
	Total Common Stocks	$351,746	$639,229

(a) All owned by Berkshire or its insurance subsidiaries.

(b) Blue Chip and/or Wesco own shares of these companies. All numbers represent Berkshire's net interest in the larger gross holdings of the group.

Our controlled and non-controlled businesses operate over such a wide spectrum of activities that detailed commentary here would prove too lengthy. Much additional financial information is included in Management's Discussion on pages 34-37 and in the narrative reports on pages 38-50. However, our largest area of both controlled and non-controlled activity has been, and almost certainly will continue to be, the property-casualty insurance area, and commentary on important developments in that industry is appropriate.

Insurance Industry Conditions

"Forecasts", said Sam Goldwyn, "are dangerous, particularly those about the future." (Berkshire shareholders may have reached a similar conclusion after rereading our past annual reports featuring your Chairman's prescient analysis of textile prospects.)

There is no danger, however, in forecasting that 1982 will be the worst year in recent history for insurance underwriting. That result already has been guaranteed by present pricing behavior, coupled with the term nature of the insurance contract.

While many auto policies are priced and sold at six-month intervals—and many property policies are sold for a three-year term—a weighted average of the duration of all property-casualty insurance policies probably runs a little under twelve months. And prices for the insurance coverage, of course, are frozen for the life of the contract. Thus, this year's sales contracts ("premium written" in the parlance of the industry) determine about one-half of next year's level of revenue ("premiums earned"). The remaining half will be determined by sales contracts written next year that will be about 50% earned in that year. The profitability consequences are automatic: if you make a mistake in pricing, you have to live with it for an uncomfortable period of time.

Note in the table below the year-over-year gain in industry-wide premiums written and the impact that it has on the current and following year's level of underwriting profitability. The result is exactly as you would expect in an inflationary world. When the volume gain is well up in double digits, it bodes well for profitability trends in the current and following year. When the industry volume gain is small, underwriting experience very shortly will get worse, no matter how unsatisfactory the current level.

The Best's data in the table reflect the experience of practically the entire industry, including stock, mutual and reciprocal companies. The combined ratio indicates total operating and loss costs as compared to premiums; a ratio below 100 indicates an underwriting profit, and one above 100 indicates a loss.

	Yearly Change in Premium Written (%)	Yearly Change in Premium Earned (%)	Combined Ratio after Policy-holder Dividends
1972	10.2	10.9	96.2
1973	8.0	8.8	99.2
1974	6.2	6.9	105.4
1975	11.0	9.6	107.9
1976	21.9	19.4	102.4
1977	19.8	20.5	97.2
1978	12.8	14.3	97.5
1979	10.3	10.4	100.6
1980	6.0	7.8	103.1
1981	3.6	4.1	105.7

Source: Best's Aggregates and Averages.

As Pogo would say, "The future isn't what it used to be." Current pricing practices promise devastating results, particularly if the respite from major natural disasters that the industry has enjoyed in recent years should end. *For underwriting experience has been getting worse in spite of good luck, not because of bad luck.* In recent years hurricanes have stayed at sea and motorists have reduced their driving. They won't always be so obliging.

And, of course the twin inflations, monetary and "social" (the tendency of courts and juries to stretch the coverage of policies beyond what insurers, relying upon contract terminology and precedent, had expected), are unstoppable. Costs of repairing both property and people—and the extent to which these repairs are deemed to be the responsibility of the insurer—will advance relentlessly.

Absent any bad luck (catastrophes, increased driving, etc.), an immediate industry volume gain of at least 10% per year probably is necessary to *stabilize* the record level of underwriting losses that will automatically prevail in mid-1982. (Most underwriters expect incurred losses in aggregate to rise at least 10% annually; each, of course, counts on getting less than his share.) Every percentage point of annual premium growth below the 10% equilibrium figure quickens the pace of deterioration. Quarterly data in 1981 underscore the conclusion that a terrible underwriting picture is worsening at an accelerating rate.

In the 1980 annual report we discussed the investment policies that have destroyed the integrity of many insurers' balance sheets, forcing them to abandon underwriting discipline and write business at any price in order to avoid negative cash flow. It was clear that insurers with large holdings of bonds valued, for accounting purposes, at nonsensically high prices would have little choice but to keep the money revolving by selling large numbers of policies at nonsensically low prices. Such insurers necessarily fear a major decrease in volume more than they fear a major underwriting loss.

But, unfortunately, all insurers are affected; it's difficult to price much differently than your most threatened competitor. This pressure continues unabated and adds a new motivation to the others that drive many insurance managers to push for business; worship of size over profitability, and the fear that market share surrendered never can be regained.

Whatever the reasons, we believe it is true that virtually no major property-casualty insurer—despite protests by the entire industry that rates are inadequate and great selectivity should be exercised—has been willing to turn down business to the point where cash flow has turned significantly negative. Absent such a willingness, prices will remain under severe pressure.

Commentators continue to talk of the underwriting cycle, usually implying a regularity of rhythm and a relatively constant midpoint of profitability. Our own view is different. We believe that very large, although obviously varying, underwriting losses will be the norm for the industry, and that the best underwriting years in the future decade may appear substandard against the average year of the past decade.

We have no magic formula to insulate our controlled insurance companies against this deteriorating future. Our managers, particularly Phil Liesche, Bill Lyons, Roland Miller, Floyd Taylor and Milt Thornton, have done a magnificent job of swimming against the tide. We have sacrificed much volume, but have maintained a substantial underwriting superiority in relation to industry-wide results. The outlook at Berkshire is for continued low volume. Our financial position offers us maximum flexibility, a very rare condition in the property-casualty insurance industry. And, at some point, should fear ever prevail throughout the industry, our financial strength could become an operational asset of immense value.

We believe that GEICO Corporation, our major non-controlled business operating in this field, is, by virtue of its extreme and improving operating efficiency, in a considerably more protected position than almost any other major insurer. GEICO is a brilliantly run implementation of a very important business idea.

Shareholder Designated Contributions

Our new program enabling shareholders to designate the recipients of corporate charitable contributions was greeted with extraordinary enthusiasm. A copy of the letter sent October 14, 1981 describing this program appears on pages 51-53. Of 932,206 shares eligible for participation (shares where the name of the actual owner appeared on our stockholder record), 95.6% responded. Even excluding Buffet-related shares, the response topped 90%.

In addition, more than 3% of our shareholders voluntarily wrote letters or notes, all but one approving of the program. Both the level of participation and of commentary surpass any shareholder response we have witnessed, even when such response has been intensively solicited by corporate staff and highly paid professional proxy organizations. In contrast, your extraordinary level of response occurred without even the nudge of a company-provided return envelope. This self-propelled behavior speaks well for the program, and speaks well for our shareholders.

Apparently the owners of our corporation like both possessing and exercising the ability to determine where gifts of their funds shall be made. The "father-knows-best" school of corporate governance will be surprised to find that none of our shareholders sent in a designation sheet with instructions that the officers of Berkshire—in their superior wisdom, of course—make the decision on charitable funds applicable to his shares. Nor did anyone suggest that his share of our charitable funds be used to match contributions made by our corporate directors to charities of the directors' choice (a popular, proliferating and non-publicized policy at many large corporations).

All told, $1,783,655 of shareholder-designed contributions were distributed to about 675 charities. In addition, Berkshire and subsidiaries continue to make certain contributions pursuant to local level decisions made by our operating managers.

There will be some years, perhaps two or three out of ten, when contributions by Berkshire will produce substandard tax deductions—or none at all. In those years we will not effect our shareholder designated charitable program. In all other years we expect to inform you about October 10th of the amount per share that you may designate. A reply form will accompany the notice, and you will be given about three weeks to respond with your designation. *To qualify, your shares must be registered in your own name or the name of an owning trust, corporation, partnership or estate, if applicable, on our stockholder list of September 30th, or the Friday preceding if such date falls on a Saturday or Sunday.*

Our only disappointment with this program in 1981 was that some of our shareholders, through no fault of their own, missed the opportunity to participate. The Treasury Department ruling allowing us to proceed without tax uncertainty was received early in October. The ruling did not cover participation by shareholders whose stock was registered in the name of nominees, such as brokers, and additionally required that the owners of all designating shares make certain assurances to Berkshire. These assurances could not be given us in effective form by nominee holders.

Under these circumstances, we attempted to communicate with all of our owners promptly (via the October 14th letter) so that, if they wished, they could prepare themselves to participate by the November 13th record date. It was particularly important that this information be communicated promptly to stockholders whose holdings were in nominee name, since they would not be eligible unless they took action to re-register their shares before the record date.

Unfortunately, communication to such non-record shareholders could take place only through the nominees. We therefore strongly urged those nominees, mostly brokerage houses, to promptly transmit our letter to the real owners. We explained that their failure to do so could deprive such owners of an important benefit.

The results from our urgings would not strengthen the case for private ownership of the U.S. Postal Service. Many of our shareholders never heard from their brokers (as some shareholders told us after reading news accounts of the program). Others were forwarded our letter too late for action.

One of the largest brokerage houses claiming to hold stock for sixty of its clients (about 4% of our shareholder population), apparently transmitted our letter about three weeks after receipt—too late for any of the sixty to participate. (Such lassitude did not pervade all departments of that firm; it billed Berkshire for mailing services within six days of that belated and ineffectual action.)

We recite such horror stories for two reasons: (1) if you wish to participate in future designated contribution programs, be sure to have your stock registered in your name well before September 30th; and (2) even if you don't care to participate and prefer to leave your stock in nominee form, it would be wise to have at least one share registered in your own name. By so doing, you can be sure that you will be notified of any important corporate news at the same time as all other shareholders.

The designated-contributions idea, along with many other ideas that have turned out well for us, was conceived by Charlie Munger, Vice Chairman of Berkshire and Chairman of Blue Chip. Irrespective of titles, Charlie and I work as partners in managing all controlled companies. To almost a sinful degree, we enjoy our work as managing partners. And we enjoy having you as our financial partners.

Warren E. Buffett
Chairman of the Board

BERKSHIRE HATHAWAY INC.

March 3, 1983

To the Shareholders of Berkshire Hathaway Inc.:

Operating earnings of $31.5 million in 1982 amounted to only 9.8% of beginning equity capital (valuing securities at cost), down from 15.2% in 1981 and far below our recent high of 19.4% in 1978. This decline largely resulted from:

(1) a significant deterioration in insurance underwriting results;

(2) a considerable expansion of equity capital without a corresponding growth in the businesses we operate directly; and

(3) a continually-enlarging commitment of our resources to investment in partially-owned, non-operated businesses; accounting rules dictate that a major part of our pro-rata share of earnings from such businesses must be excluded from Berkshire's reported earnings.

It was only a few years ago that we told you that the operating earnings/equity capital percentage, with proper allowance for a few other variables, was the most important yardstick of single-year managerial performance. While we still believe this to be the case with the vast majority of companies, we believe its utility in our own case has greatly diminished. You should be suspicious of such an assertion. Yardsticks seldom are discarded while yielding favorable readings. But when results deteriorate, most managers favor disposition of the yardstick rather than disposition of the manager.

To managers faced with such deterioration, a more flexible measurement system often suggests itself: just shoot the arrow of business performance into a blank canvas and then carefully draw the bullseye around the implanted arrow. We generally believe in pre-set, long-lived and small bullseyes. However, because of the importance of item (3) above, further explained in the following section, we believe our abandonment of the operating earnings/equity capital bullseye to be warranted.

Non-Reported Ownership Earnings

The appended financial statements reflect "accounting" earnings that generally include our proportionate share of earnings from any underlying business in which our ownership is at least 20%. Below the 20% ownership figure, however, only our share of dividends paid by the underlying business units is included in our accounting numbers; undistributed earnings of such less-than-20%-owned businesses are totally ignored.

There are a few exceptions to this rule; e.g., we own about 35% of GEICO Corporation but, because we have assigned our voting rights, the company is treated for accounting purposes as a less-than-20% holding. Thus, dividends received from GEICO in 1982 of $3.5 million after tax are the only item included in our "accounting" earnings. An additional $23 million that represents our share of GEICO's undistributed operating earnings for 1982 is totally excluded from our reported operating earnings. If GEICO had earned less money in 1982 but had paid an additional $1 million in dividends, our reported earnings would have been larger despite the poorer business results. Conversely, if GEICO had earned an additional $100 million—and retained it all—our reported earnings would have been unchanged. Clearly "accounting" earnings can seriously misrepresent economic reality.

We prefer a concept of "economic" earnings that includes all undistributed earnings, regardless of ownership percentage. In our view, the value to all owners of the retained earnings of a business enterprise is determined by the effectiveness with which those earnings are used—and not by the size of one's ownership percentage. If you have owned .01 of 1% of Berkshire during the past decade, you have benefited economically in full measure from your share of our retained earnings, no matter what your accounting system. Proportionately, you have done just as well as if you had owned the magic 20%. But if you have owned 100% of a great many capital-intensive businesses during the decade, retained earnings that were credited fully and with painstaking precision to you under standard accounting methods have resulted in minor or zero economic value. This is not a criticism of accounting procedures. We would not like to have the job of designing a better system. It's simply to say that managers and investors alike must understand that accounting numbers are the beginning, not the end, of business valuation.

In most corporations, less-than-20% ownership positions are unimportant (perhaps, in part, because they prevent maximization of cherished reported earnings) and the distinction between accounting and economic results we have just discussed matters little. But in our own case, such positions are of very large and growing importance. Their magnitude, we believe, is what makes our reported operating earnings figure of limited significance.

In our 1981 annual report we predicted that our share of undistributed earnings from four of our major non-controlled holdings would aggregate over $35 million in 1982. With no change in our holdings of three of these companies—GEICO, General Foods and The Washington Post—and a considerable increase in our ownership of the fourth, R. J. Reynolds Industries, our share of undistributed 1982 operating earnings of this group came to well over $40 million. This number—not reflected at all in our earnings—is greater than our total reported earnings, which include only the $14 million in dividends received from these companies. And, of course, we have a number of smaller ownership interests that, in aggregate, had substantial additional undistributed earnings.

We attach real significance to the general magnitude of these numbers, but we don't believe they should be carried to ten decimal places. Realization by Berkshire of such retained earnings through improved market valuations is subject to very substantial, but indeterminate, taxation. And while retained earnings over the years, and in the aggregate, have translated into at least equal market value for shareholders, the translation has been both extraordinarily uneven among companies and irregular and unpredictable in timing.

However, this very unevenness and irregularity offers advantages to the value-oriented purchaser of fractional portions of businesses. This investor may select from almost the entire array of major American corporations, including many far superior to virtually any of the businesses that could be bought in their entirety in a negotiated deal. And fractional-interest purchases can be made in an auction market where prices are set by participants with behavior patterns that sometimes resemble those of an army of manic-depressive lemmings.

Within this gigantic auction arena, it is our job to select businesses with economic characteristics allowing each dollar of retained earnings to be translated eventually into at least a dollar of market value. Despite a lot of mistakes, we have so far achieved this goal. In doing so, we have been greatly assisted by Arthur Okun's patron saint for economists—St. Offset. In some cases, that is, retained earnings attributable to our ownership position have had insignificant or even negative impact on market value, while in other major positions a dollar retained by an investee corporation has been translated into two or more dollars of market value. To date, our corporate over-achievers have more than offset the laggards. If we can continue this record, it will validate our efforts to maximize "economic" earnings, regardless of the impact upon "accounting" earnings.

Satisfactory as our partial-ownership approach has been, what really makes us dance is the purchase of 100% of good businesses at reasonable prices. We've accomplished this feat a few times (and expect to do so again), but it is an extraordinarily difficult job—far more difficult than the purchase at attractive prices of fractional interests.

As we look at the major acquisitions that others made during 1982, our reaction is not envy, but relief that we were non-participants. For in many of these acquisitions, managerial intellect wilted in competition with managerial adrenaline. The thrill of the chase blinded the pursuers to the consequences of the catch. Pascal's observation seems apt: "It has struck me that all men's misfortunes spring from the single cause that they are unable to stay quietly in one room."

(Your Chairman left the room once too often last year and almost starred in the Acquisition Follies of 1982. In retrospect, our major accomplishment of the year was that a very large purchase to which we had firmly committed was unable to be completed for reasons totally beyond our control. Had it come off, this transaction would have consumed extraordinary amounts of time and energy, all for a most uncertain payoff. If we were to introduce graphics to this report, illustrating favorable business developments of the past year, two blank pages depicting this blown deal would be the appropriate centerfold.)

Our partial-ownership approach can be continued soundly only as long as portions of attractive businesses can be acquired at attractive prices. We need a moderately-priced stock market to assist us in this endeavor. The market, like the Lord, helps those who help themselves. But, unlike the Lord, the market does not forgive those who know not what they do. For the investor, a too-high purchase price for the stock of an excellent company can undo the effects of a subsequent decade of favorable business developments.

Should the stock market advance to considerably higher levels, our ability to utilize capital effectively in partial-ownership positions will be reduced or eliminated. This will happen periodically: just ten years ago, at the height of the two-tier market mania (with high-return-on-equity businesses bid to the sky by institutional investors), Berkshire's insurance subsidiaries owned only $18 million in market value of equities, excluding their interest in Blue Chip Stamps. At that time, such equity holdings amounted to about 15% of our insurance company investments versus the present 80%. There were as many good businesses around in 1972 as in 1982, but the prices the stock market placed upon those businesses in 1972 looked absurd. While high stock prices in the future would make our performance look good temporarily, they would hurt our long-term business prospects rather than help them. We currently are seeing early traces of this problem.

Long-Term Corporate Performance

Our gain in net worth during 1982, valuing equities held by our insurance subsidiaries at market value (less capital gain taxes payable if unrealized gains were actually realized) amounted to $208 million. On a beginning net worth base of $519 million, the percentage gain was 40%.

During the 18-year tenure of present management, book value has grown from $19.46 per share to $737.43 per share, or 22.0% compounded annually. You can be certain that this percentage will diminish in the future. Geometric progressions eventually forge their own anchors.

Berkshire's economic goal remains to produce a long-term rate of return well above the return achieved by the average large American corporation. Our willingness to purchase either partial or total ownership positions in favorably-situated businesses, coupled with reasonable discipline about the prices we are willing to pay, should give us a good chance of achieving our goal.

Again this year the gain in market valuation of partially-owned businesses outpaced the gain in underlying economic value of those businesses. For example, $79 million of our $208 million gain is attributable to an increased market price for GEICO. This company continues to do exceptionally well, and we are more impressed than ever by the strength of GEICO's basic business idea and by the management skills of Jack Byrne. (Although not found in the catechism of the better business schools, "Let Jack Do It" works fine as a corporate creed for us.)

However, GEICO's increase in market value during the past two years has been considerably greater than the gain in its intrinsic business value, impressive as the latter has been. We expected such a favorable variation at some point, as the perception of investors converged with business reality. And we look forward to substantial future gains in underlying business value accompanied by irregular, but eventually full, market recognition of such gains.

Year-to-year variances, however, cannot consistently be in our favor. Even if our partially-owned businesses continue to perform well in an economic sense, there will be years when they perform poorly in the market. At such times our net worth could shrink significantly. We will not be distressed by such a shrinkage; if the businesses continue to look attractive and we have cash available, we simply will add to our holdings at even more favorable prices.

Sources of Reported Earnings

The table below shows the sources of Berkshire's reported earnings. In 1981 and 1982 Berkshire owned about 60% of Blue Chip Stamps which, in turn, owned 80% of Wesco Financial Corporation. The table displays aggregate operating earnings of the various business entities, as well as Berkshire's share of those earnings. All of the significant gains and losses attributable to unusual sales of assets by any of the business entities are aggregated with securities transactions in the line near the bottom of the table, and are not included in operating earnings.

| | Earnings Before Income Taxes | | | | Net Earnings After Tax | |
| | Total | | Berkshire Share | | Berkshire Share | |
	1982	1981	1982	1981	1982	1981
			(000s omitted)			
Operating Earnings:						
Insurance Group:						
Underwriting	$(21,558)	$ 1,478	$(21,558)	$ 1,478	$(11,345)	$ 798
Net Investment Income . . .	41,620	38,823	41,620	38,823	35,270	32,401
Berkshire-Waumbec Textiles . .	(1,545)	(2,669)	(1,545)	(2,669)	(862)	(1,493)
Associated Retail Stores	914	1,763	914	1,763	446	759
See's Candies.	23,884	20,961	14,235	12,493	6,914	5,910
Buffalo Evening News	(1,215)	(1,217)	(724)	(725)	(226)	(320)
Blue Chip Stamps – Parent . .	4,182	3,642	2,492	2,171	2,472	2,134
Wesco Financial – Parent	6,156	4,495	2,937	2,145	2,210	1,590
Mutual Savings and Loan	(6)	1,605	(2)	766	1,524	1,536
Precision Steel.	1,035	3,453	493	1,648	265	841
Interest on Debt	(14,996)	(14,656)	(12,977)	(12,649)	(6,951)	(6,671)
Other*	2,631	2,985	1,857	1,992	1,780	1,936
Operating Earnings	41,102	60,663	27,742	47,236	31,497	39,421
Sales of securities and						
unusual sales of assets	36,651	37,801	21,875	33,150	14,877	23,183
Total Earnings – all entities	$ 77,753	$ 98,464	$ 49,617	$ 80,386	$ 46,374	$ 62,604

* Amortization of intangibles arising in accounting for purchases of businesses (i.e. See's, Mutual and Buffalo Evening News) is reflected in the category designated as "Other".

On pages 45-61 of this report we have reproduced the narrative reports of the principal executives of Blue Chip and Wesco, in which they describe 1982 operations. A copy of the full annual report of either company will be mailed to any Berkshire shareholder upon request to Mr. Robert H. Bird for Blue Chip Stamps, 5801 South Eastern Avenue, Los Angeles, California 90040, or to Mrs. Jeanne Leach for Wesco Financial Corporation, 315 East Colorado Boulevard, Pasadena, California 91109.

I believe you will find the Blue Chip chronicle of developments in the Buffalo newspaper situation particularly interesting. There are now only 14 cities in the United States with a daily newspaper whose weekday circulation exceeds that of the Buffalo News. But the real story has been the growth in Sunday circulation. Six years ago, prior to introduction of a Sunday edition of the News, the long-established Courier-Express, as the only Sunday newspaper published in Buffalo, had circulation of 272,000. The News now has Sunday circulation of 367,000, a 35% gain—even though the number of households within the primary circulation area has shown little change during the six years. We know of no city in the United States with a long history of seven-day newspaper publication in which the percentage of households purchasing the Sunday newspaper has grown at anything like this rate. To the contrary, in most cities household penetration figures have grown negligibly, or not at all. Our key managers in Buffalo—Henry Urban, Stan Lipsey, Murray Light, Clyde Pinson, Dave Perona and Dick Feather—deserve great credit for this unmatched expansion in Sunday readership.

As we indicated earlier, undistributed earnings in companies we do not control are now fully as important as the reported operating earnings detailed in the preceding table. The distributed portion of non-controlled earnings, of course, finds its way into that table primarily through the net investment income segment of Insurance Group earnings.

We show below Berkshire's proportional holdings in those non-controlled businesses for which only distributed earnings (dividends) are included in our earnings.

No. of Shares or Share Equiv.		Cost	Market
		(000's omitted)	
460,650	(a) Affiliated Publications, Inc.	$ 3,516	$ 16,929
908,800	(c) Crum & Forster	47,144	48,962
2,101,244	(b) General Foods, Inc.	66,277	83,680
7,200,000	(a) GEICO Corporation	47,138	309,600
2,379,200	(a) Handy & Harman	27,318	46,692
711,180	(a) Interpublic Group of Companies, Inc.	4,531	34,314
282,500	(a) Media General.	4,545	12,289
391,400	(a) Ogilvy & Mather Int'l. Inc.	3,709	17,319
3,107,675	(b) R. J. Reynolds Industries.	142,343	158,715
1,531,391	(a) Time, Inc.	45,273	79,824
1,868,600	(a) The Washington Post Company	10,628	103,240
		$402,422	$911,564
	All Other Common Stockholdings.	21,611	34,058
	Total Common Stocks	$424,033	$945,622

(a) All owned by Berkshire or its insurance subsidiaries.
(b) Blue Chip and/or Wesco own shares of these companies. All numbers represent Berkshire's net interest in the larger gross holdings of the group.
(c) Temporary holding as cash substitute.

In case you haven't noticed, there is an important investment lesson to be derived from this table: nostalgia should be weighted heavily in stock selection. Our two largest unrealized gains are in Washington Post and GEICO, companies with which your Chairman formed his first commercial connections at the ages of 13 and 20, respectively After straying for roughly 25 years, we returned as investors in the mid-1970s. The table quantifies the rewards for even long-delayed corporate fidelity.

Our controlled and non-controlled businesses operate over such a wide spectrum that detailed commentary here would prove too lengthy. Much financial and operational information regarding the controlled businesses is included in Management's Discussion on pages 34-39, and in the narrative reports on pages 45-61. However, our largest area of business activity has been, and almost certainly will continue to be, the property-casualty insurance area. So commentary on developments in that industry is appropriate.

Insurance Industry Conditions

We show below an updated table of the industry statistics we utilized in last year's annual report. Its message is clear: underwriting results in 1983 will not be a sight for the squeamish.

	Yearly Change in Premium Written (%)	Yearly Change in Premium Earned (%)	Combined Ratio after Policy-holder Dividends
1972	10.2	10.9	96.2
1973	8.0	8.8	99.2
1974	6.2	6.9	105.4
1975	11.0	9.6	107.9
1976	21.9	19.4	102.4
1977	19.8	20.5	97.2
1978	12.8	14.3	97.5
1979	10.3	10.4	100.6
1980	6.0	7.8	103.1
1981 (Rev.)	3.9	4.1	106.0
1982 (Est.)	5.1	4.6	109.5

Source: Best's Aggregates and Averages.

The Best's data reflect the experience of practically the entire industry, including stock, mutual and reciprocal companies. The combined ratio represents total operating and loss costs as compared to revenue from premiums; a ratio below 100 indicates an underwriting profit, and one above 100 indicates a loss.

For reasons outlined in last year's report, as long as the annual gain in industry premiums written falls well below 10%, you can expect the underwriting picture in the next year to deteriorate. This will be true even at today's lower general rate of inflation. With the number of policies increasing annually, medical inflation far exceeding general inflation, and concepts of insured liability broadening, it is highly unlikely that yearly increases in insured losses will fall much below 10%.

You should be further aware that the 1982 combined ratio of 109.5 represents a "best case" estimate. In a given year, it is possible for an insurer to show almost any profit number it wishes, particularly if it (1) writes "long-tail" business (coverage where current costs can be only estimated, because claim payments are long delayed), (2) has been adequately reserved in the past, or (3) is growing very rapidly. There are indications that several large insurers opted in 1982 for obscure accounting and reserving maneuvers that masked significant deterioration in their underlying businesses. In insurance, as elsewhere, the reaction of weak managements to weak operations is often weak accounting. ("It's difficult for an empty sack to stand upright.")

The great majority of managements, however, try to play it straight. But even managements of integrity may subconsciously be less willing in poor profit years to fully recognize adverse loss trends. Industry statistics indicate some deterioration in loss reserving practices during 1982 and the true combined ratio is likely to be modestly worse than indicated by our table.

The conventional wisdom is that 1983 or 1984 will see the worst of underwriting experience and then, as in the past, the "cycle" will move, significantly and steadily, toward better results. We disagree because of a pronounced change in the competitive environment, hard to see for many years but now quite visible.

To understand the change, we need to look at some major factors that affect levels of corporate profitability generally. Businesses in industries with both substantial over-capacity and a "commodity" product (undifferentiated in any customer-important way by factors such as performance, appearance, service support, etc.) are prime candidates for profit troubles. These may be escaped, true, if prices or costs are administered in some manner and thereby insulated at least partially from normal market forces. This administration can be carried out (a) legally through government intervention (until recently, this category included pricing for truckers and deposit costs for financial institutions), (b) illegally through collusion, or (c) "extra-legally" through OPEC-style foreign cartelization (with tag-along benefits for domestic non-cartel operators).

If, however, costs and prices are determined by full-bore competition, there is more than ample capacity, and the buyer cares little about whose product or distribution services he uses, industry economics are almost certain to be unexciting. They may well be disastrous.

Hence the constant struggle of every vendor to establish and emphasize special qualities of product or service. This works with candy bars (customers buy by brand name, not by asking for a "two-ounce candy bar") but doesn't work with sugar (how often do you hear, "I'll have a cup of coffee with cream and C & H sugar, please").

In many industries, differentiation simply can't be made meaningful. A few producers in such industries may consistently do well if they have a cost advantage that is both wide and sustainable. By definition such exceptions are few, and, in many industries, are non-existent. For the great majority of companies selling "commodity" products, a depressing equation of business economics prevails: persistent over-capacity without administered prices (or costs) equals poor profitability.

Of course, over-capacity may eventually self-correct, either as capacity shrinks or demand expands. Unfortunately for the participants, such corrections often are long delayed. When they finally occur, the rebound to prosperity frequently produces a pervasive enthusiasm for expansion that, within a few years, again creates over-capacity and a new profitless environment. In other words, nothing fails like success.

What finally determines levels of long-term profitability in such industries is the ratio of supply-tight to supply-ample years. Frequently that ratio is dismal. (It seems as if the most recent supply-tight period in our textile business—it occurred some years back—lasted the better part of a morning.)

In some industries, however, capacity-tight conditions can last a long time. Sometimes actual growth in demand will outrun forecasted growth for an extended period. In other cases, adding capacity requires very long lead times because complicated manufacturing facilities must be planned and built.

But in the insurance business, to return to that subject, capacity can be instantly created by capital plus an underwriter's willingness to sign his name. (Even capital is less important in a world in which state-sponsored guaranty funds protect many policyholders against insurer insolvency.) Under almost all conditions except that of fear for survival—produced, perhaps, by a stock market debacle or a truly major natural disaster—the insurance industry operates under the competitive sword of substantial overcapacity. Generally, also, despite heroic attempts to do otherwise, the industry sells a relatively undifferentiated commodity-type product. (Many insureds, including the managers of large businesses, do not even know the names of their insurers.) Insurance, therefore, would seem to be a textbook case of an industry usually faced with the deadly combination of excess capacity and a "commodity" product.

Why, then, was underwriting, despite the existence of cycles, generally profitable over many decades? (From 1950 through 1970, the industry combined ratio averaged 99.0. allowing all investment income plus 1% of premiums to flow through to profits.) The answer lies primarily in the historic methods of regulation and distribution. For much of this century, a large portion of the industry worked, in effect, within a legal quasi-administered pricing system fostered by insurance regulators. While price competition existed, it was not pervasive among the larger companies. The main competition was for agents, who were courted via various non-price-related strategies.

For the giants of the industry, most rates were set through negotiations between industry "bureaus" (or through companies acting in accord with their recommendations) and state regulators. Dignified haggling occurred, but it was between company and regulator rather than between company and customer. When the dust settled, Giant A charged the same price as Giant B—and both companies and agents were prohibited by law from cutting such filed rates.

The company-state negotiated prices included specific profit allowances and, when loss data indicated that current prices were unprofitable, both company managements and state regulators expected that they would act together to correct the situation. Thus, most of the pricing actions of the giants of the industry were "gentlemanly", predictable, and profit-producing. Of prime importance—and in contrast to the way most of the business world operated—insurance companies could legally price their way to profitability even in the face of substantial over-capacity.

That day is gone. Although parts of the old structure remain, far more than enough new capacity exists outside of that structure to force all parties, old and new, to respond. The new capacity uses various methods of distribution and is not reluctant to use price as a prime competitive weapon. Indeed, it relishes that use. In the process, customers have learned that insurance is no longer a one-price business. They won't forget.

Future profitability of the industry will be determined by current competitive characteristics, not past ones. Many managers have been slow to recognize this. It's not only generals that prefer to fight the last war. Most business and investment analysis also comes from the rear-view mirror. It seems clear to us, however, that only one condition will allow the insurance industry to achieve significantly improved underwriting results. That is the same condition that will allow better results for the aluminum, copper, or corn producer—a major narrowing of the gap between demand and supply.

Unfortunately, there can be no surge in demand for insurance policies comparable to one that might produce a market tightness in copper or aluminum. Rather, the supply of available insurance coverage must be curtailed. "Supply", in this context, is mental rather than physical: plants or companies need not be shut; only the willingness of underwriters to sign their names need be curtailed.

This contraction will not happen because of generally poor profit levels. Bad profits produce much hand-wringing and finger-pointing. But they do not lead major sources of insurance capacity to turn their backs on very large chunks of business, thereby sacrificing market share and industry significance.

Instead, major capacity withdrawals require a shock factor such as a natural or financial "mega-disaster". One might occur tomorrow—or many years from now. The insurance business—even taking investment income into account—will not be particularly profitable in the meantime.

When supply ultimately contracts, large amounts of business will be available for the few with large capital capacity, a willingness to commit it, and an in-place distribution system. We would expect great opportunities for our insurance subsidiaries at such a time.

During 1982, our insurance underwriting deteriorated far more than did the industry's. From a profit position well above average, we, slipped to a performance modestly below average. The biggest swing was in National Indemnity's traditional coverages. Lines that have been highly profitable for us in the past are now priced at levels that guarantee underwriting losses. In 1983 we expect our insurance group to record an average performance in an industry in which average is very poor.

Two of our stars, Milt Thornton at Cypress and Floyd Taylor at Kansas Fire and Casualty, continued their outstanding records of producing an underwriting profit every year since joining us. Both Milt and Floyd simply are incapable of being average. They maintain a passionately proprietary attitude toward their operations and have developed a business culture centered upon unusual cost-consciousness and customer service. It shows on their scorecards.

During 1982, parent company responsibility for most of our insurance operations was given to Mike Goldberg. Planning, recruitment, and monitoring all have shown significant improvement since Mike replaced me in this role.

GEICO continues to be managed with a zeal for efficiency and value to the customer that virtually guarantees unusual success. Jack Byrne and Bill Snyder are achieving the most elusive of human goals—keeping things simple and remembering what you set out to do. In Lou Simpson, additionally, GEICO has the best investment manager in the property-casualty business. We are happy with every aspect of this operation. GEICO is a magnificent illustration of the high-profit exception we described earlier in discussing commodity industries with over-capacity—a company with a wide and sustainable cost advantage. Our 35% interest in GEICO represents about $250 million of premium volume, an amount considerably greater than all of the direct volume we produce.

Issuance of Equity

Berkshire and Blue Chip are considering merger in 1983. If it takes place, it will involve an exchange of stock based upon an identical valuation method applied to both companies. The one other significant issuance of shares by Berkshire or its affiliated companies that occurred during present management's tenure was in the 1978 merger of Berkshire with Diversified Retailing Company.

Our share issuances follow a simple basic rule: we will not issue shares unless we receive as much intrinsic business value as we give. Such a policy might seem axiomatic. Why, you might ask, would anyone issue dollar bills in exchange for fifty-cent pieces? Unfortunately, many corporate managers have been willing to do just that.

The first choice of these managers in making acquisitions may be to use cash or debt. But frequently the CEO's cravings outpace cash and credit resources (certainly mine always have). Frequently, also, these cravings occur when his own stock is selling far below intrinsic business value. This state of affairs produces a moment of truth. At that point, as Yogi Berra has said, "You can observe a lot just by watching." For shareholders then will find which objective the management truly prefers—expansion of domain or maintenance of owners' wealth.

The need to choose between these objectives occurs for some simple reasons. Companies often sell in the stock market below their intrinsic business value. But when a company wishes to sell out completely, in a negotiated transaction, it inevitably wants to—and usually can—receive full business value in whatever kind of currency the value is to be delivered. If cash is to be used in payment, the seller's calculation of value received couldn't be easier. If stock of the buyer is to be the currency, the seller's calculation is still relatively easy: just figure the market value in cash of what is to be received in stock.

Meanwhile, the buyer wishing to use his own stock as currency for the purchase has no problems if the stock is selling in the market at full intrinsic value.

But suppose it is selling at only half intrinsic value. In that case, the buyer is faced with the unhappy prospect of using a substantially undervalued currency to make its purchase.

Ironically, were the buyer to instead be a seller of its entire business, it too could negotiate for, and probably get, full intrinsic business value. But when the buyer makes a partial sale of itself—*and that is what the issuance of shares to make an acquisition amounts to*—it can customarily get no higher value set on its shares than the market chooses to grant it.

The acquirer who nevertheless barges ahead ends up using an undervalued (market value) currency to pay for a fully valued (negotiated value) property. In effect, the acquirer must give up $2 of value to receive $1 of value. Under such circumstances, a marvelous business purchased at a fair sales price becomes a terrible buy. For gold valued as gold cannot be purchased intelligently through the utilization of gold—or even silver—valued as lead.

If, however, the thirst for size and action is strong enough, the acquirer's manager will find ample rationalizations for such a value-destroying issuance of stock. Friendly investment bankers will reassure him as to the soundness of his actions. (Don't ask the barber whether you need a haircut.)

A few favorite rationalizations employed by stock-issuing managements follow:

(a) "The company we're buying is going to be worth a lot more in the future." (Presumably so is the interest in the old business that is being traded away; future prospects are implicit in the business valuation process. If 2X is issued for X, the imbalance still exists when both parts double in business value.)

(b) "We have to grow." (Who, it might be asked, is the "we"? For present shareholders, the reality is that all existing businesses shrink when shares are issued. Were Berkshire to issue shares tomorrow for an acquisition, Berkshire would own everything that it now owns plus the new business, but *your* interest in such hard-to-match businesses as See's Candy Shops, National Indemnity, etc. would automatically be reduced. If (1) your family owns a 120-acre farm and (2) you invite a neighbor with 60 acres of comparable land to merge his farm into an equal partnership—with you to be managing partner, then (3) your managerial domain will have grown to 180 acres but you will have permanently shrunk by 25% your family's ownership interest in both acreage and crops. Managers who want to expand their domain at the expense of owners might better consider a career in government.)

(c) "Our stock is undervalued and we've minimized its use in this deal—but we need to give the selling shareholders 51% in stock and 49% in cash so that certain of those shareholders can get the tax-free exchange they want." (This argument acknowledges that it is beneficial to the acquirer to hold down the issuance of shares, and we like that. But if it hurts the old owners to utilize shares on a 100% basis, it very likely hurts on a 51% basis. After all, a man is not charmed if a spaniel defaces his lawn, just because it's a spaniel and not a St. Bernard. And the wishes of sellers can't be the determinant of the best interests of the buyer—what would happen if, heaven forbid, the seller insisted that as a condition of merger the CEO of the acquirer be replaced?)

There are three ways to avoid destruction of value for old owners when shares are issued for acquisitions. One is to have a true business-value-for-business-value merger, such as the Berkshire-Blue Chip combination is intended to be. Such a merger attempts to be fair to shareholders of *both* parties, with each receiving just as much as it gives in terms of intrinsic business value. The Dart Industries-Kraft and Nabisco Standard Brands mergers appeared to be of this type, but they are the exceptions. It's not that acquirers wish to avoid such deals; it's just that they are very hard to do.

The second route presents itself when the acquirer's stock sells at or above its intrinsic business

11

value. In that situation, the use of stock as currency actually may enhance the wealth of the acquiring company's owners. Many mergers were accomplished on this basis in the 1965-69 period. The results were the converse of most of the activity since 1970: the shareholders of the *acquired* company received very inflated currency (frequently pumped up by dubious accounting and promotional techniques) and were the losers of wealth through such transactions.

During recent years the second solution has been available to very few large companies. The exceptions have primarily been those companies in glamorous or promotional businesses to which the market temporarily attaches valuations at or above intrinsic business valuation.

The third solution is for the acquirer to go ahead with the acquisition, but then subsequently repurchase a quantity of shares equal to the number issued in the merger. In this manner, what originally was a stock-for-stock merger can be converted, effectively, into a cash-for-stock acquisition. Repurchases of this kind are damage-repair moves. Regular readers will correctly guess that we much prefer repurchases that directly enhance the wealth of owners instead of repurchases that merely repair previous damage. Scoring touchdowns is more exhilarating than recovering one's fumbles. But, when a fumble has occurred, recovery is important and we heartily recommend damage-repair repurchases that turn a bad stock deal into a fair cash deal.

The language utilized in mergers tends to confuse the issues and encourage irrational actions by managers. For example, "dilution" is usually carefully calculated on a pro forma basis for both book value and current earnings per share. Particular emphasis is given to the latter item. When that calculation is negative (dilutive) from the acquiring company's standpoint, a justifying explanation will be made (internally, if not elsewhere) that the lines will cross favorably at some point in the future. (While deals often fail in practice, they never fail in projections—if the CEO is visibly panting over a prospective acquisition, subordinates and consultants will supply the requisite projections to rationalize any price.) Should the calculation produce numbers that are immediately positive—that is, anti-dilutive—for the acquirer, no comment is thought to be necessary.

The attention given this form of dilution is overdone: current earnings per share (or even earnings per share of the next few years) are an important variable in most business valuations, but far from all powerful.

There have been plenty of mergers, non-dilutive in this limited sense, that were instantly value destroying for the acquirer. And some mergers that have diluted current and near-term earnings per share have in fact been value-enhancing. What really counts is whether a merger is dilutive or anti-dilutive in terms of intrinsic business value (a judgment involving consideration of many variables). We believe calculation of dilution from this viewpoint to be all-important (and too seldom made).

A second language problem relates to the equation of exchange. If Company A announces that it will issue shares to merge with Company B, the process is customarily described as "Company A to Acquire Company B", or "B Sells to A". Clearer thinking about the matter would result if a more awkward but more accurate description were used: "Part of A sold to acquire B", or "Owners of B to receive part of A in exchange for their properties". In a trade, what you are giving is just as important as what you are getting. This remains true even when the final tally on what is being given is delayed. Subsequent sales of common stock or convertible issues, either to complete the financing for a deal or to restore balance sheet strength, must be fully counted in evaluating the fundamental mathematics of the original acquisition. (If corporate pregnancy is going to be the consequence of corporate mating, the time to face that fact is before the moment of ecstasy.)

Managers and directors might sharpen their thinking by asking themselves if they would sell 100%

of their business on the same basis they are being asked to sell part of it. And if it isn't smart to sell all on such a basis, they should ask themselves why it is smart to sell a portion. A cumulation of small managerial stupidities will produce a major stupidity—not a major triumph. (Las Vegas has been built upon the wealth transfers that occur when people engage in seemingly-small disadvantageous capital transactions.)

The "giving versus getting" factor can most easily be calculated in the case of registered investment companies. Assume Investment Company X, selling at 50% of asset value, wishes to merge with Investment Company Y. Assume, also, that Company X therefore decides to issue shares equal in market value to 100% of Y's asset value.

Such a share exchange would leave X trading $2 of its previous intrinsic value for $1 of Y's intrinsic value. Protests would promptly come forth from both X's shareholders and the SEC, which rules on the fairness of registered investment company mergers. Such a transaction simply would not be allowed.

In the case of manufacturing, service, financial companies, etc., values are not normally as precisely calculable as in the case of investment companies. But we have seen mergers in these industries that just as dramatically destroyed value for the owners of the acquiring company as was the case in the hypothetical illustration above. This destruction could not happen if management and directors would assess the fairness of any transaction by using the same yardstick in the measurement of both businesses.

Finally, a word should be said about the "double whammy" effect upon owners of the acquiring company when value-diluting stock issuances occur. Under such circumstances, the first blow is the loss of intrinsic business value that occurs through the merger itself. The second is the downward revision in market valuation that, quite rationally, is given to that now-diluted business value. For current and prospective owners understandably will not pay as much for assets lodged in the hands of a management that has a record of wealth-destruction through unintelligent share issuances as they will pay for assets entrusted to a management with precisely equal operating talents, but a known distaste for anti-owner actions. Once management shows itself insensitive to the interests of owners, shareholders will suffer a long time from the price/value ratio afforded their stock (relative to other stocks), no matter what assurances management gives that the value-diluting action taken was a one-of-a-kind event.

Those assurances are treated by the market much as one-bug-in-the-salad explanations are treated at restaurants. Such explanations, even when accompanied by a new waiter, do not eliminate a drop in the demand (and hence market value) for salads, both on the part of the offended customer and his neighbors pondering what to order. Other things being equal, the highest stock market prices relative to intrinsic business value are given to companies whose managers have demonstrated their unwillingness to issue shares at any time on terms unfavorable to the owners of the business.

At Berkshire, or any company whose policies we determine (including Blue Chip and Wesco), we will issue shares only if our owners receive in business value as much as we give. We will not equate activity with progress or corporate size with owner-wealth.

Miscellaneous

This annual report is read by a varied audience, and it is possible that some members of that audience may be helpful to us in our acquisition program.

We prefer:

(1) large purchases (at least $5 million of after-tax earnings),

(2) demonstrated consistent earning power (future projections are of little interest to us, nor are "turn-around" situations),

(3) businesses earning good returns on equity while employing little or no debt,

(4) management in place (we can't supply it),

(5) simple businesses (if there's lots of technology, we won't understand it),

(6) an offering price (we don't want to waste our time or that of the seller by talking, even preliminarily, about a transaction when price is unknown).

We will not engage in unfriendly transactions. We can promise complete confidentiality and a very fast answer as to possible interest—customarily within five minutes. Cash purchases are preferred, but we will consider the use of stock when it can be done on the basis described in the previous section.

* * * * *

Our shareholder-designated contributions program met with enthusiasm again this year; 95.8% of eligible shares participated. This response was particularly encouraging since only $1 per share was made available for designation, down from $2 in 1981. If the merger with Blue Chip takes place, a probable by-product will be the attainment of a consolidated tax position that will significantly enlarge our contribution base and give us a potential for designating bigger per-share amounts in the future.

If you wish to participate in future programs, we strongly urge that you immediately make sure that your shares are registered in the actual owner's name, not a "street" or nominee name. For new shareholders, a more complete description of the program is on pages 62-63.

* * * * *

In a characteristically rash move, we have expanded World Headquarters by 252 square feet (17%), coincidental with the signing of a new five-year lease at 1440 Kiewit Plaza. The five people who work here with me—Joan Atherton, Mike Goldberg, Gladys Kaiser, Verne McKenzie and Bill Scott—outproduce corporate groups many times their number. A compact organization lets all of us spend our time managing the business rather than managing each other.

Charlie Munger, my partner in management, will continue to operate from Los Angeles whether or not the Blue Chip merger occurs. Charlie and I are interchangeable in business decisions. Distance impedes us not at all: we've always found a telephone call to be more productive than a half-day committee meeting.

* * * * *

Two of our managerial stars retired this year: Phil Liesche at 65 from National Indemnity Company, and Ben Rosner at 79 from Associated Retail Stores. Both of these men made you, as shareholders of Berkshire, a good bit wealthier than you otherwise would have been. National Indemnity has been the most important operation in Berkshire's growth. Phil and Jack Ringwalt, his predecessor, were the two prime movers in National Indemnity's success. Ben Rosner sold Associated Retail Stores to Diversified Retailing Company for cash in 1967, promised to stay on only until the end of the year, and then hit business home runs for us for the next fifteen years.

Both Ben and Phil ran their businesses for Berkshire with every bit of the care and drive that they would have exhibited had they personally owned 100% of these businesses. No rules were necessary to enforce or even encourage this attitude; it was embedded in the character of these men long before we came on the scene. Their good character became our good fortune. If we can continue to attract managers with the qualities of Ben and Phil, you need not worry about Berkshire's future.

Warren E. Buffett
Chairman of the Board

BERKSHIRE HATHAWAY INC.

To the Shareholders of Berkshire Hathaway Inc.:

This past year our registered shareholders increased from about 1900 to about 2900. Most of this growth resulted from our merger with Blue Chip Stamps, but there also was an acceleration in the pace of "natural" increase that has raised us from the 1000 level a few years ago.

With so many new shareholders, it's appropriate to summarize the major business principles we follow that pertain to the manager-owner relationship:

o   Although our form is corporate, our attitude is partnership. Charlie Munger and I think of our shareholders as owner-partners, and of ourselves as managing partners. (Because of the size of our shareholdings we also are, for better or worse, controlling partners.) We do not view the company itself as the ultimate owner of our business assets but, instead, view the company as a conduit through which our shareholders own the assets.

o   In line with this owner-orientation, our directors are all major shareholders of Berkshire Hathaway. In the case of at least four of the five, over 50% of family net worth is represented by holdings of Berkshire. We eat our own cooking.

o   Our long-term economic goal (subject to some qualifications mentioned later) is to maximize the average annual rate of gain in intrinsic business value on a per-share basis. We do not measure the economic significance or performance of Berkshire by its size; we measure by per-share progress. We are certain that the rate of per-share progress will diminish in the future—a greatly enlarged capital base will see to that. But we will be disappointed if our rate does not exceed that of the average large American corporation.

o   Our preference would be to reach this goal by directly owning a diversified group of businesses that generate cash and consistently earn above-average returns on capital. Our second choice is to own parts of similar businesses, attained primarily through purchases of marketable common stocks by our insurance subsidiaries. The price and availability of businesses and the need for insurance capital determine any given year's capital allocation.

o   Because of this two-pronged approach to business ownership and because of the limitations of conventional accounting, consolidated reported earnings may reveal relatively little about our true economic performance. Charlie and I, both as owners and managers, virtually ignore such consolidated numbers. However, we will also report to you the earnings of each major business we control, numbers we consider of great importance. These figures, along with other information we will supply about the individual businesses, should generally aid you in making judgments about them.

o   Accounting consequences do not influence our operating or capital-allocation decisions. When acquisition costs are similar, we much prefer to purchase $2 of earnings that is not reportable by us under standard accounting principles than to purchase $1 of earnings that is reportable. This is precisely the choice that often faces us since entire businesses (whose earnings will be fully reportable) frequently sell for double the pro-rata price of small portions (whose earnings will be largely unreportable). In aggregate and over time, we expect the unreported earnings to

1

be fully reflected in our intrinsic business value through capital gains.

o We rarely use much debt and, when we do, we attempt to structure it on a long-term fixed rate basis. We will reject interesting opportunities rather than over-leverage our balance sheet. This conservatism has penalized our results but it is the only behavior that leaves us comfortable, considering our fiduciary obligations to policyholders, depositors, lenders and the many equity holders who have committed unusually large portions of their net worth to our care.

o A managerial "wish list" will not be filled at shareholder expense. We will not diversify by purchasing entire businesses at control prices that ignore long-term economic consequences to our shareholders. We will only do with your money what we would do with our own, weighing fully the values you can obtain by diversifying your own portfolios through direct purchases in the stock market.

o We feel noble intentions should be checked periodically against results. We test the wisdom of retaining earnings by assessing whether retention, over time, delivers shareholders at least $1 of market value for each $1 retained. To date, this test has been met. We will continue to apply it on a five-year rolling basis. As our net worth grows, it is more difficult to use retained earnings wisely.

o We will issue common stock only when we receive as much in business value as we give. This rule applies to all forms of issuance—not only mergers or public stock offerings, but stock for-debt swaps, stock options, and convertible securities as well. We will not sell small portions of your company—and that is what the issuance of shares amounts to—on a basis inconsistent with the value of the entire enterprise.

o You should be fully aware of one attitude Charlie and I share that hurts our financial performance: regardless of price, we have no interest at all in selling any good businesses that Berkshire owns, and are very reluctant to sell sub-par businesses as long as we expect them to generate at least some cash and as long as we feel good about their managers and labor relations. We hope not to repeat the capital-allocation mistakes that led us into such sub-par businesses. And we react with great caution to suggestions that our poor businesses can be restored to satisfactory profitability by major capital expenditures. (The projections will be dazzling—the advocates will be sincere—but, in the end, major additional investment in a terrible industry usually is about as rewarding as struggling in quicksand.) Nevertheless, gin rummy managerial behavior (discard your least promising business at each turn) is not our style. We would rather have our overall results penalized a bit than engage in it.

o We will be candid in our reporting to you, emphasizing the pluses and minuses important in appraising business value. Our guideline is to tell you the business facts that we would want to know if our positions were reversed. We owe you no less. Moreover, as a company with a major communications business, it would be inexcusable for us to apply lesser standards of accuracy, balance and incisiveness when reporting on ourselves than we would expect our news people to apply when reporting on others. We also believe candor benefits us as managers: the CEO who misleads others in public may eventually mislead himself in private.

o Despite our policy of candor, we will discuss our activities in marketable securities only to the extent legally required. Good investment ideas are rare, valuable and subject to competitive appropriation just as good product or business acquisition ideas are. Therefore, we normally will not talk about our investment ideas. This ban extends even to securities we have sold (because we may purchase them again) and to stocks we are incorrectly rumored to be buying. If we deny those reports but say "no comment" on other occasions, the no-comments become confirmation.

That completes the catechism, and we can now move on to the high point of 1983—the acquisition of a majority interest in Nebraska Furniture Mart and our association with Rose Blumkin and her family.

Nebraska Furniture Mart

Last year, in discussing how managers with bright, but adrenalin-soaked minds scramble after foolish acquisitions, I quoted Pascal: "It has struck me that all the misfortunes of men spring from the single cause that they are unable to stay quietly in one room."

Even Pascal would have left the room for Mrs. Blumkin.

About 67 years ago Mrs. Blumkin, then 23, talked her way past a border guard to leave Russia for America. She had no formal education, not even at the grammar school level, and knew no English. After some years in this country, she learned the language when her older daughter taught her, every evening, the words she had learned in school during the day.

In 1937, after many years of selling used clothing, Mrs. Blumkin had saved $500 with which to realize her dream of opening a furniture store. Upon seeing the American Furniture Mart in Chicago—then the center of the nation's wholesale furniture activity—she decided to christen her dream Nebraska Furniture Mart.

She met every obstacle you would expect (and a few you wouldn't) when a business endowed with only $500 and no locational or product advantage goes up against rich, long-entrenched competition. At one early point, when her tiny resources ran out, "Mrs. B" (a personal trademark now as well recognized in Greater Omaha as Coca-Cola or Sanka) coped in a way not taught at business schools: she simply sold the furniture and appliances from her home in order to pay creditors precisely as promised.

Omaha retailers began to recognize that Mrs. B would offer customers far better deals than they had been giving, and they pressured furniture and carpet manufacturers not to sell to her. But by various strategies she obtained merchandise and cut prices sharply. Mrs. B was then hauled into court for violation of Fair Trade laws. She not only won all the cases, but received invaluable publicity. At the end of one case, after demonstrating to the court that she could profitably sell carpet at a huge discount from the prevailing price, she sold the judge $1400 worth of carpet.

Today Nebraska Furniture Mart generates over $100 million of sales annually out of one 200,000 square-foot store. No other home furnishings store in the country comes close to that volume. That single store also sells more furniture, carpets, and appliances than do all Omaha competitors combined.

One question I always ask myself in appraising a business is how I would like, assuming I had ample capital and skilled personnel, to compete with it. I'd rather wrestle grizzlies than compete with Mrs. B and her progeny. They buy brilliantly, they operate at expense ratios competitors don't even dream about, and they then pass on to their customers much of the savings. It's the ideal business—one built upon exceptional value to the customer that in turn translates into exceptional economics for its owners.

Mrs. B is wise as well as smart and, for far-sighted family reasons, was willing to sell the business last year. I had admired both the family and the business for decades, and a deal was quickly made. But Mrs. B, now 90, is not one to go home and risk, as she puts it, "losing her marbles". She remains Chairman and is on the sales floor seven days a week. Carpet sales are her specialty. She personally sells quantities that would be a good departmental total for other carpet retailers.

We purchased 90% of the business—leaving 10% with members of the family who are involved in management—and have optioned 10% to certain key young family managers.

And what managers they are. Geneticists should do handsprings over the Blumkin family. Louie Blumkin, Mrs. B's son, has been President of Nebraska Furniture Mart for many years and is widely regarded as the shrewdest buyer of furniture and appliances in the country. Louie says he had the best teacher, and Mrs. B says she had the best student. They're both right. Louie and his three sons all have the Blumkin business ability, work ethic, and, most important, character. On top of that, they are really nice people. We are delighted to be in partnership with them.

Corporate Performance

During 1983 our book value increased from $737.43 per share to $975.83 per share, or by 32%. We never take the one-year figure very seriously. After all, why should the time required for a planet to circle the sun synchronize precisely with the time required for business actions to pay off? Instead, we recommend not less than a five-year test as a rough yardstick of economic performance. Red lights should start flashing if the five-year average annual gain falls much below the return on equity earned over the period by American industry in aggregate. (Watch out for our explanation if that occurs as Goethe observed, "When ideas fail, words come in very handy.")

During the 19-year tenure of present management, book value has grown from $19.46 per share to $975.83, or 22.6% compounded annually. Considering our present size, nothing close to this rate of return can be sustained. Those who believe otherwise should pursue a career in sales, but avoid one in mathematics.

We report our progress in terms of book value because in our case (though not, by any means, in all cases) it is a conservative but reasonably adequate proxy for growth in intrinsic business value—*the measurement that really counts*. Book value's virtue as a score-keeping measure is that it is easy to calculate and doesn't involve the subjective (but important) judgments employed in calculation of intrinsic business value. It is important to understand, however, that the two terms—book value and intrinsic business value—have very different meanings.

Book value is an accounting concept, recording the accumulated financial input from both contributed capital and retained earnings. Intrinsic business value is an economic concept, estimating future cash output discounted to present value. Book value tells you what has been put in; intrinsic business value estimates what can be taken out.

An analogy will suggest the difference. Assume you spend identical amounts putting each of two children through college. The book value (measured by financial input) of each child's education would be the same. But the present value of the future payoff (the intrinsic business value) might vary enormously—from zero to many times the cost of the education. So, also, do businesses having equal financial input end up with wide variations in value.

At Berkshire, at the beginning of fiscal 1965 when the present management took over, the $19.46 per share book value considerably overstated intrinsic business value. All of that book value consisted of textile assets that could not earn, on average, anything close to an appropriate rate of return. In the terms of our analogy, the investment in textile assets resembled investment in a largely-wasted education.

Now, however, our intrinsic business value considerably exceeds book value. There are two major reasons:

(1) Standard accounting principles require that common stocks held by our insurance subsidiaries be stated on our books at market value, but that other stocks we own be carried at the lower of aggregate cost or market. At the end of 1983, the market value of this latter group exceeded carrying value by $70 million pre-tax, or about $50 million after tax. This excess belongs in our intrinsic business value, but is not included in the calculation of book value;

(2) More important, we own several businesses that possess economic Goodwill (which is properly includable in intrinsic business value) far larger than the accounting Goodwill that is carried on our balance sheet and reflected in book value.

Goodwill, both economic and accounting, is an arcane subject and requires more explanation than is appropriate here. The appendix that follows this letter—"Goodwill and its Amortization: The Rules and The Realities"—explains why economic and accounting Goodwill can, and usually do, differ enormously.

You can live a full and rewarding life without ever thinking about Goodwill and its amortization. But students of investment and management should understand the nuances of the subject. My own thinking has changed drastically from 35 years ago when I was taught to favor tangible assets and to shun businesses whose value depended largely upon economic Goodwill. This bias caused me to make many important business mistakes of omission, although relatively few of commission.

Keynes identified my problem: "The difficulty lies not in the new ideas but in escaping from the old ones." My escape was long delayed, in part because most of what I had been taught by the same teacher had been (and continues to be) so extraordinarily valuable. Ultimately, business experience, direct and vicarious, produced my present strong preference for businesses that possess large amounts of enduring Goodwill and that utilize a minimum of tangible assets.

I recommend the Appendix to those who are comfortable with accounting terminology and who have an interest in understanding the business aspects of Goodwill. Whether or not you wish to tackle the Appendix, you should be aware that Charlie and I believe that Berkshire possesses very significant economic Goodwill value above that reflected in our book value.

Sources of Reported Earnings

The table below shows the sources of Berkshire's reported earnings. In 1982, Berkshire owned about 60% of Blue Chip Stamps whereas, in 1983, our ownership was 60% throughout the first six months and 100% thereafter. In turn, Berkshire's net interest in Wesco was 48% during 1982 and the first six months of 1983, and 80% for the balance of 1983. Because of these changed ownership percentages, the first two columns of the table provide the best measure of underlying business performance.

All of the significant gains and losses attributable to unusual sales of assets by any of the business entities are aggregated with securities transactions on the line near the bottom of the table, and are not included in operating earnings. (We regard any annual figure for realized capital gains or losses as meaningless, but we regard the aggregate realized and unrealized capital gains over a period of years as very important.) Furthermore, amortization of Goodwill is not charged against the specific businesses but, for reasons outlined in the Appendix, is set forth as a separate item.

| | Earnings Before Income Taxes | | | | Net Earnings After Tax | |
| | Total | | Berkshire Share | | Berkshire Share | |
	1983	1982	1983	1982	1983	1982
	(000s omitted)					
Operating Earnings:						
Insurance Group:						
Underwriting	$(33,872)	$(21,558)	$(33,872)	$(21,558)	$(18,400)	$(11,345)
Net Investment Income . . .	43,810	41,620	43,810	41,620	39,114	35,270
Berkshire-Waumbec Textiles. .	(100)	(1,545)	(100)	(1,545)	(63)	(862)
Associated Retail Stores	697	914	697	914	355	446
Nebraska Furniture Mart(1) . .	3,812	--	3,049	--	1,521	--
See's Candies.	27,411	23,884	24,526	14,235	12,212	6,914
Buffalo Evening News.	19,352	(1,215)	16,547	(724)	8,832	(226)
Blue Chip Stamps(2)	(1,422)	4,182	(1,876)	2,492	(353)	2,472
Wesco Financial – Parent	7,493	6,156	4,844	2,937	3,448	2,210
Mutual Savings and Loan	(798)	(6)	(467)	(2)	1,917	1,524
Precision Steel.	3,241	1,035	2,102	493	1,136	265
Interest on Debt	(15,104)	(14,996)	(13,844)	(12,977)	(7,346)	(6,951)
Special GEICO Distribution. .	21,000	--	21,000	--	19,551	--
Shareholder-Designated						
Contributions	(3,066)	(891)	(3,066)	(891)	(1,656)	(481)
Amortization of Goodwill. . . .	(532)	151	(563)	90	(563)	90
Other	10,121	3,371	9,623	2,658	8,490	2,171
Operating Earnings.	82,043	41,102	72,410	27,742	68,195	31,497
Sales of securities and						
unusual sales of assets	67,260	36,651	65,089	21,875	45,298	14,877
Total Earnings	$149,303	$ 77,753	$137,499	$ 49,617	$113,493	$ 46,374

(1) October through December
(2) 1982 and 1983 are not comparable; major assets were transferred in the merger.

For a discussion of the businesses owned by Wesco, please read Charlie Munger's report on pages 46-51. Charlie replaced Louie Vincenti as Chairman of Wesco late in 1983 when health forced Louie's retirement at age 77. In some instances, "health" is a euphemism, but in Louie's case nothing but health would cause us to consider his retirement. Louie is a marvelous man and has been a marvelous manager.

The special GEICO distribution reported in the table arose when that company made a tender offer for a portion of its stock, buying both from us and other shareholders. At GEICO's request, we tendered a quantity of shares that kept our ownership percentage the same after the transaction as before. The proportional nature of our sale permitted us to treat the proceeds as a dividend. Unlike individuals, corporations net considerably more when earnings are derived from dividends rather than from capital gains, since the effective Federal income tax rate on dividends is 6.9% versus 28% on capital gains.

Even with this special item added in, our total dividends from GEICO in 1983 were considerably less than our share of GEICO's earnings. Thus it is perfectly appropriate, from both an accounting and economic standpoint, to include the redemption proceeds in our reported earnings. It is because the item is large and unusual that we call your attention to it.

The table showing you our sources of earnings includes dividends from those non-controlled companies whose marketable equity securities we own. But the table does not include earnings those companies have retained that are applicable to our ownership. In aggregate and over time we expect those undistributed earnings to be reflected in market prices and to increase our intrinsic business value on a dollar-for-dollar basis, just as if those earnings had been under our control and reported as part of our profits. That does not mean we expect all of our holdings to behave uniformly; some will disappoint us, others will deliver pleasant surprises. To date our experience has been better than we originally anticipated, In aggregate, we have received far more than a dollar of market value gain for every dollar of earnings retained.

The following table shows our 1983 yearend net holdings in marketable equities. All numbers represent 100% of Berkshire's holdings, and 80% of Wesco's holdings. The portion attributable to minority shareholders of Wesco has been excluded.

No. of Shares		Cost	Market
		(000s omitted)	
690,975	Affiliated Publications, Inc.	$ 3,516	$ 26,603
4,451,544	General Foods Corporation(a)	163,786	228,698
6,850,000	GEICO Corporation	47,138	398,156
2,379,000	Handy & Harman	27,318	42,231
636,310	Interpublic Group of Companies, Inc.	4,056	33,088
197,200	Media General	3,191	11,191
250,400	Ogilvy & Mather International	2,580	12,833
5,618,661	R. J. Reynolds Industries(a)	268,918	314,334
901,788	Time, Inc.	27,732	56,860
1,868,600	The Washington Post Company	10,628	136,875
		$558,863	$1,287,869
	All Other Common Stockholdings	7,485	18,044
	Total Common Stocks	$566,348	$1,305,913

(a) WESCO owns shares in these companies.

Based upon present holdings and present dividend rates—excluding any special items such as the GEICO proportional redemption last year—we would expect reported dividends from this group to be approximately $39 million in 1984. We can also make a very rough guess about the earnings this group will retain that will be attributable to our ownership: these may total about $65 million for the year. These retained earnings could well have no immediate effect on market prices of the securities. Over time, however, we feel they will have real meaning.

In addition to the figures already supplied, information regarding the businesses we control appears in Management's Discussion on pages 40-44. The most significant of these are Buffalo Evening News, See's, and the Insurance Group, to which we will give some special attention here.

Buffalo Evening News

First, a clarification: our corporate name is Buffalo Evening News, Inc. but the name of the newspaper, since we began a morning edition a little over a year ago, is Buffalo News.

In 1983 the News somewhat exceeded its targeted profit margin of 10% after tax. Two factors were responsible: (1) a state income tax cost that was subnormal because of a large loss carry-forward, now fully utilized, and (2) a large drop in the per-ton cost of newsprint (an unanticipated fluke that will be reversed in 1984).

Although our profit margins in 1983 were about average for newspapers such as the News, the paper's performance, nevertheless, was a significant achievement considering the economic and retailing environment in Buffalo.

Buffalo has a concentration of heavy industry, a segment of the economy that was hit particularly hard by the recent recession and that has lagged the recovery. As Buffalo consumers have suffered, so also have the paper's retailing customers. Their numbers have shrunk over the past few years and many of those surviving have cut their linage.

Within this environment the News has one exceptional strength: its acceptance by the public, a matter measured by the paper's "penetration ratio"—the percentage of households within the community purchasing the paper each day. Our ratio is superb: for the six months ended September 30, 1983 the News stood number one in weekday penetration among the 100 largest papers in the United States (the ranking is based on "city zone" numbers compiled by the Audit Bureau of Circulations).

In interpreting the standings, it is important to note that many large cities have two papers, and that in such cases the penetration of either paper is necessarily lower than if there were a single paper, as in Buffalo. Nevertheless, the list of the 100 largest papers includes many that have a city to themselves. Among these, the News is at the top nationally, far ahead of many of the country's best-known dailies.

Among Sunday editions of these same large dailies, the News ranks number three in penetration—ten to twenty percentage points ahead of many well-known papers. It was not always this way in Buffalo. Below we show Sunday circulation in Buffalo in the years prior to 1977 compared with the present period. In that earlier period the Sunday paper was the Courier-Express (the News was not then publishing a Sunday paper). Now, of course, it is the News.

Average Sunday Circulation	
Year	*Circulation*
1970	314,000
1971	306,000
1972	302,000
1973	290,000
1974	278,000
1975	269,000
1976	270,000
1984 (Current)	376,000

We believe a paper's penetration ratio to be the best measure of the strength of its franchise. Papers with unusually high penetration in the geographical area that is of prime interest to major local retailers, and with relatively little circulation elsewhere, are exceptionally efficient buys for those retailers. Low-penetration papers have a far less compelling message to present to advertisers.

In our opinion, three factors largely account for the unusual acceptance of the News in the community. Among these, points 2 and 3 also may explain the popularity of the Sunday News compared to that of the Sunday Courier-Express when it was the sole Sunday paper:

(1) The first point has nothing to do with merits of the News. Both emigration and immigration are relatively low in Buffalo. A stable population is more interested and involved in the activities of its community than is a shifting population—and, as a result, is more interested in the content of the local daily paper. Increase the movement in and out of a city and penetration ratios will fall.

(2) The News has a reputation for editorial quality and integrity that was honed by our longtime editor, the legendary Alfred Kirchhofer, and that has been preserved and extended by Murray Light. This reputation was enormously important to our success in establishing a Sunday paper against entrenched competition. And without a Sunday edition, the News would not have survived in the long run.

(3) The News lives up to its name—it delivers a very unusual amount of news. During 1983, our "news hole" (editorial material—not ads) amounted to 50% of the newspaper's content (excluding preprinted inserts). Among papers that dominate their markets and that are of comparable or larger size, we know of only one whose news hole percentage exceeds that of the News. Comprehensive figures are not available, but a sampling indicates an average percentage in the high 30s. In other words, page for page, our mix gives readers over 25% more news than the typical paper. This news-rich mixture is by intent. Some publishers, pushing for higher profit margins, have cut their news holes during the past decade. We have maintained ours and will continue to do so. Properly written and edited, a full serving of news makes our paper more valuable to the reader and contributes to our unusual penetration ratio.

Despite the strength of the News' franchise, gains in ROP linage (advertising printed within the newspaper pages as contrasted to preprinted inserts) are going to be very difficult to achieve. We had an enormous gain in preprints during 1983: lines rose from 9.3 million to 16.4 million, revenues from $3.6 million to $8.1 million. These gains are consistent with national trends, but exaggerated in our case by business we picked up when the Courier-Express closed.

On balance, the shift from ROP to preprints has negative economic implications for us. Profitability on preprints is less and the business is more subject to competition from alternative means of delivery. Furthermore, a reduction in ROP linage means less absolute space devoted to news (since the news hole percentage remains constant), thereby reducing the utility of the paper to the reader.

Stan Lipsey became Publisher of the Buffalo News at midyear upon the retirement of Henry Urban. Henry never flinched during the dark days of litigation and losses following our introduction of the Sunday paper—an introduction whose wisdom was questioned by many in the newspaper business, including some within our own building. Henry is admired by the Buffalo business community, he's admired by all who worked for him, and he is admired by Charlie and me. Stan worked with Henry for several years, and has worked for Berkshire Hathaway since 1969. He has been personally involved in all nuts-and-bolts aspects of the newspaper business from editorial to circulation. We couldn't do better.

See's Candy Shops

The financial results at See's continue to be exceptional. The business possesses a valuable and solid consumer franchise and a manager equally valuable and solid.

In recent years See's has encountered two important problems, at least one of which is well on its way toward solution. That problem concerns costs, except those for raw materials. We have enjoyed a break on raw material costs in recent years though so, of course, have our competitors. One of these days we will get a nasty surprise in the opposite direction. In effect, raw material costs are largely beyond our

9

control since we will, as a matter of course, buy the finest ingredients that we can, regardless of changes in their price levels. We regard product quality as sacred.

But other kinds of costs are more controllable, and it is in this area that we have had problems. On a per-pound basis, our costs (not including those for raw materials) have increased in the last few years at a rate significantly greater than the increase in the general price level. It is vital to our competitive position and profit potential that we reverse this trend.

In recent months much better control over costs has been attained and we feel certain that our rate of growth in these costs in 1984 will be below the rate of inflation. This confidence arises out of our long experience with the managerial talents of Chuck Huggins. We put Chuck in charge the day we took over, and his record has been simply extraordinary, as shown by the following table:

52-53 Week Year Ended About December 31	Sales Revenues	Operating Profits After Taxes	Number of Pounds of Candy Sold	Number of Stores Open at Year End
1983 (53 weeks) . .	$133,531,000	$13,699,000	24,651,000	207
1982	123,662,000	11,875,000	24,216,000	202
1981	112,578,000	10,779,000	24,052,000	199
1980	97,715,000	7,547,000	24,065,000	191
1979	87,314,000	6,330,000	23,985,000	188
1978	73,653,000	6,178,000	22,407,000	182
1977	62,886,000	6,154,000	20,921,000	179
1976 (53 weeks) . .	56,333,000	5,569,000	20,553,000	173
1975	50,492,000	5,132,000	19,134,000	172
1974	41,248,000	3,021,000	17,883,000	170
1973	35,050,000	1,940,000	17,813,000	169
1972	31,337,000	2,083,000	16,954,000	167

The other problem we face, as the table suggests, is our recent inability to achieve meaningful gains in pounds sold. The industry has the same problem. But for many years we outperformed the industry in this respect and now we are not.

The poundage volume in our retail stores has been virtually unchanged each year for the past four, despite small increases every year in the number of shops (and in distribution expense as well). Of course, dollar volume has increased because we have raised prices significantly. But we regard the most important measure of retail trends to be units sold per store rather than dollar volume. On a same-store basis (counting only shops open throughout both years) with all figures adjusted to a 52-week year, poundage was down .8 of 1% during 1983. This small decline was our best same-store performance since 1979; the cumulative decline since then has been about 8%. Quantity-order volume, about 25% of our total, has plateaued in recent years following very large poundage gains throughout the 1970s.

We are not sure to what extent this flat volume—both in the retail shop area and the quantity order area—is due to our pricing policies and to what extent it is due to static industry volume, the recession, and the extraordinary share of market we already enjoy in our primary marketing area. Our price increase for 1984 is much more modest than has been the case in the past few years, and we hope that next year we can report better volume figures to you. But we have no basis to forecast these.

Despite the volume problem, See's strengths are many and important. In our primary marketing area, the West, our candy is preferred by an enormous margin to that of any competitor. In fact, we believe most lovers of chocolate prefer it to candy costing two or three times as much. (In candy, as in stocks, price and value can differ; price is what you give, value is what you get.) The quality of customer service in our shops—operated throughout the country by us and not by franchisees is every bit as good as the product. Cheerful, helpful personnel are as much a trademark of See's as is the logo on the box. That's no small achievement in a business that requires us to hire about 2000 seasonal workers. We know of no comparably-sized organization that betters the quality of customer service delivered by Chuck Huggins and his associates.

Because we have raised prices so modestly in 1984, we expect See's profits this year to be about the same as in 1983.

Insurance—Controlled Operations

We both operate insurance companies and have a large economic interest in an insurance business we don't operate, GEICO. The results for all can be summed up easily: in aggregate, the companies we operate and whose underwriting results reflect the consequences of decisions that were my responsibility a few years ago, had absolutely terrible results. Fortunately, GEICO, whose policies I do not influence, simply shot the lights out. The inference you draw from this summary is the correct one. I made some serious mistakes a few years ago that came home to roost.

The industry had its worst underwriting year in a long time, as indicated by the table below:

	Yearly Change in Premium Written (%)	Combined Ratio after Policy-holder Dividends
1972	10.2	96.2
1973	8.0	99.2
1974	6.2	105.4
1975	11.0	107.9
1976	21.9	102.4
1977	19.8	97.2
1978	12.8	97.5
1979	10.3	100.6
1980	6.0	103.1
1981	3.9	106.0
1982 (Revised)	4.4	109.7
1983 (Estimated)	4.6	111.0

Source: Best's Aggregates and Averages.

Best's data reflect the experience of practically the entire industry, including stock, mutual, and reciprocal companies. The combined ratio represents total insurance costs (losses incurred plus expenses) compared to revenue from premiums; a ratio below 100 indicates an underwriting profit and one above 100 indicates a loss.

For the reasons outlined in last year's report, we expect the poor industry experience of 1983 to be more or less typical for a good many years to come. (As Yogi Berra put it: "It will be deja vu all over again.") That doesn't mean we think the figures won't bounce around a bit; they are certain to. But we believe it highly unlikely that the combined ratio during the balance of the decade will average significantly below the 1981-1983 level. Based on our expectations regarding inflation—*and we are as pessimistic as ever on that front*—industry premium volume must grow about 10% annually merely to stabilize loss ratios at present levels.

Our own combined ratio in 1983 was 121. Since Mike Goldberg recently took over most of the responsibility for the insurance operation, it would be nice for me if our shortcomings could be placed at his doorstep rather than mine. But unfortunately, as we have often pointed out, the insurance business has a long lead-time. Though business policies may be changed and personnel improved, a significant period must pass before the effects are seen. (This characteristic of the business enabled us to make a great deal of money in GEICO; we could picture what was likely to happen well before it actually occurred.) So the roots of the 1983 results are operating and personnel decisions made two or more years back when I had direct managerial responsibility for the insurance group.

Despite our poor results overall, several of our managers did truly outstanding jobs. Roland Miller guided the auto and general liability business of National Indemnity Company and National Fire and Marine Insurance Company to improved results, while those of competitors deteriorated. In addition, Tom Rowley at Continental Divide Insurance—our fledgling Colorado homestate company—seems certain to be a winner. Mike found him a little over a year ago, and he was an important acquisition.

We have become active recently—and hope to become much more active—in reinsurance transactions where the buyer's overriding concern should be the seller's long-term creditworthiness. In such transactions our premier financial strength should make us the number one choice of both claimants and insurers who must rely on the reinsurer's promises for a great many years to come.

A major source of such business is structured settlements—a procedure for settling losses under which claimants receive periodic payments (almost always monthly, for life) rather than a single lump sum settlement. This form of settlement has important tax advantages for the claimant and also prevents his squandering a large lump-sum payment. Frequently, some inflation protection is built into the settlement. Usually the claimant has been seriously injured, and thus the periodic payments must be unquestionably secure for decades to come. We believe we offer unparalleled security. No other insurer we know of—even those with much larger gross assets—has our financial strength.

We also think our financial strength should recommend us to companies wishing to transfer loss reserves. In such transactions, other insurance companies pay us lump sums to assume all (or a specified portion of) future loss payments applicable to large blocks of expired business. Here also, the company transferring such claims needs to be certain of the transferee's financial strength for many years to come. Again, most of our competitors soliciting such business appear to us to have a financial condition that is materially inferior to ours.

Potentially, structured settlements and the assumption of loss reserves could become very significant to us. Because of their potential size and because these operations generate large amounts of investment income compared to premium volume, we will show underwriting results from those businesses on a separate line in our insurance segment data. We also will exclude their effect in reporting our combined ratio to you. We "front end" no profit on structured settlement or loss reserve transactions, and all attributable overhead is expensed currently. Both businesses are run by Don Wurster at National Indemnity Company.

Insurance—GEICO

Geico's performance during 1983 was as good as our own insurance performance was poor. Compared to the industry's combined ratio of 111, GEICO wrote at 96 *after* a large voluntary accrual for policyholder dividends. A few years ago I would not have thought GEICO could so greatly outperform the industry. Its superiority reflects the combination of a truly exceptional business idea and an exceptional management.

Jack Byrne and Bill Snyder have maintained extraordinary discipline in the underwriting area (including, crucially, provision for full and proper loss reserves), and their efforts are now being further rewarded by significant gains in new business. Equally important, Lou Simpson is the class of the field among insurance investment managers. The three of them are some team.

We have approximately a one-third interest in GEICO. That gives us a $270 million share in the company's premium volume, an amount some 80% larger than our own volume. Thus, the major portion of our total insurance business comes from the best insurance book in the country. This fact does not moderate by an iota the need for us to improve our own operation.

Stock Splits and Stock Activity

We often are asked why Berkshire does not split its stock. The assumption behind this question usually appears to be that a split would be a pro-shareholder action. We disagree. Let me tell you why.

One of our goals is to have Berkshire Hathaway stock sell at a price rationally related to its intrinsic business value. (But note "rationally related", not "identical": if well-regarded companies are generally selling in the market at large discounts from value, Berkshire might well be priced similarly.) The key to a rational stock price is rational shareholders, both current and prospective.

If the holders of a company's stock and/or the prospective buyers attracted to it are prone to make irrational or emotion-based decisions, some pretty silly stock prices are going to appear periodically. Manic-depressive personalities produce manic-depressive valuations. Such aberrations may help us in buying and selling the stocks of other companies. But we think it is in both your interest and ours to minimize their occurrence in the market for Berkshire.

To obtain only high quality shareholders is no cinch. Mrs. Astor could select her 400, but anyone can buy any stock. Entering members of a shareholder "club" cannot be screened for intellectual capacity, emotional stability, moral sensitivity or acceptable dress. Shareholder eugenics, therefore, might appear to be a hopeless undertaking.

In large part, however, we feel that high quality ownership can be attracted and maintained if we consistently communicate our business and ownership philosophy—*along with no other conflicting messages*—and then let self selection follow its course. For example, self selection will draw a far different crowd to a musical event advertised as an opera than one advertised as a rock concert even though anyone can buy a ticket to either.

Through our policies and communications—our "advertisements"—we try to attract investors who will understand our operations, attitudes and expectations. (And, fully as important, we try to dissuade those who won't.) We want those who think of themselves as business owners and invest in companies with the intention of staying a long time. And, we want those who keep their eyes focused on business results, not market prices.

Investors possessing those characteristics are in a small minority, but we have an exceptional collection of them. I believe well over 90%—probably over 95%—of our shares are held by those who were shareholders of Berkshire or Blue Chip five years ago. And I would guess that over 95% of our shares are held by investors for whom the holding is at least double the size of their next largest. Among companies with at least several thousand public shareholders and more than $1 billion of market value, we are almost certainly the leader in the degree to which our shareholders think and act like owners. Upgrading a shareholder group that possesses these characteristics is not easy.

Were we to split the stock or take other actions focusing on stock price rather than business value, we would attract an entering class of buyers inferior to the exiting class of sellers. At $1300, there are very few investors who can't afford a Berkshire share. Would a potential one-share purchaser be better off if we split 100 for 1 so he could buy 100 shares? Those who think so and who would buy the stock because of the split or in anticipation of one would definitely downgrade the quality of our present shareholder group. (Could we really improve our shareholder group by trading some of our present clear-thinking members for impressionable new ones who, preferring paper to value, feel wealthier with nine $10 bills than with one $100 bill?) People who buy for non-value reasons are likely to sell for non-value reasons. Their presence in the picture will accentuate erratic price swings unrelated to underlying business developments.

We will try to avoid policies that attract buyers with a short-term focus on our stock price and try to follow policies that attract informed long-term investors focusing on business values. just as you purchased your Berkshire shares in a market populated by rational informed investors, you deserve a chance to sell—should you ever want to—in the same kind of market. We will work to keep it in existence.

One of the ironies of the stock market is the emphasis on activity. Brokers, using terms such as "marketability" and "liquidity", sing the praises of companies with high share turnover (those who cannot fill your pocket will confidently fill your ear). But investors should understand that what is good for the croupier is not good for the customer. A hyperactive stock market is the pickpocket of enterprise.

For example, consider a typical company earning, say, 12% on equity. Assume a very high turnover rate in its shares of 100% per year. If a purchase and sale of the stock each extract commissions of 1% (the rate may be much higher on low-priced stocks) and if the stock trades at book value, the owners of our hypothetical company will pay, in aggregate, 2% of the company's net worth annually for the privilege of transferring ownership. This activity does nothing for the earnings of the business, and means that 1/6 of them are lost to the owners through the "frictional" cost of transfer. (And this calculation does not count option trading, which would increase frictional costs still further.)

All that makes for a rather expensive game of musical chairs. Can you imagine the agonized cry that would arise if a governmental unit were to impose a new 16 2/3% tax on earnings of corporations or investors? By market activity, investors can impose upon themselves the equivalent of such a tax.

Days when the market trades 100 million shares (and that kind of volume, when over-the-counter trading is included, is today abnormally low) are a curse for owners, not a blessing—for they mean that owners are paying twice as much to change chairs as they are on a 50-million-share day. If 100 million-share days persist for a year and the average cost on each purchase and sale is 15 cents a share, the chair-changing tax for investors in aggregate would total about $7.5 billion—an amount roughly equal to the combined 1982 profits of Exxon, General Motors, Mobil and Texaco, the four largest companies in the Fortune 500.

These companies had a combined net worth of $75 billion at yearend 1982 and accounted for over 12% of both net worth and net income of the entire Fortune 500 list. Under our assumption investors, in aggregate, every year forfeit all earnings from this staggering sum of capital merely to satisfy their penchant for "financial flip-flopping". In addition, investment management fees of over $2 billion annually—sums paid for chair-changing advice—require the forfeiture by investors of all earnings of the five largest banking organizations (Citicorp, Bank America, Chase Manhattan, Manufacturers Hanover and J. P. Morgan). These expensive activities may decide who eats the pie, but they don't enlarge it.

(We are aware of the pie-expanding argument that says that such activities improve the rationality of the capital allocation process. We think that this argument is specious and that, on balance, hyperactive equity markets subvert rational capital allocation and act as pie shrinkers. Adam Smith felt that all noncollusive acts in a free market were guided by an invisible hand that led an economy to maximum progress; our view is that casino-type markets and hair-trigger investment management act as an invisible foot that trips up and slows down a forward-moving economy.)

Contrast the hyperactive stock with Berkshire. The bid-and-ask spread in our stock currently is about 30 points, or a little over 2%. Depending on the size of the transaction, the difference between proceeds received by the seller of Berkshire and cost to the buyer may range downward from 4% (in trading involving only a few shares) to perhaps 1 1/2% (in large trades where negotiation can reduce both the market-maker's spread and the broker's commission). Because most Berkshire shares are traded in fairly large transactions, the spread on all trading probably does not average more than 2%.

Meanwhile, true turnover in Berkshire stock (excluding inter-dealer transactions, gifts and bequests) probably runs 3% per year. Thus our owners, in aggregate, are paying perhaps 6/100 of 1% of Berkshire's market value annually for transfer privileges. By this very rough estimate, that's $900,000—not a small cost, but far less than average. Splitting the stock would increase that cost, downgrade the quality of our shareholder population, and encourage a market price less consistently related to intrinsic business value. We see no offsetting advantages.

Miscellaneous

Last year in this section I ran a small ad to encourage acquisition candidates. In our communications businesses we tell our advertisers that repetition is a key to results (which it is), so we will again repeat our acquisition criteria.

We prefer: (1) large purchases (at least $5 million of after-tax earnings), (2) demonstrated consistent earning power (future projections are of little interest to us, nor are "turn-around" situations), (3) businesses earning good returns on equity while employing little or no debt, (4) management in place (we can't supply it), (5) simple businesses (if there's lots of technology, we won't understand it), (6) an offering price (we don't want to waste our time or that of the seller by talking, even preliminarily, about a transaction when price is unknown).

We will not engage in unfriendly takeovers. We can promise complete confidentiality and a very fast answer—customarily within five minutes—as to whether we're interested. We prefer to buy for cash, but will consider issuance of stock when we receive as much in intrinsic business value as we give. We invite potential sellers to check us out by contacting people with whom we have done business in the past. For the right business—and the right people—we can provide a good home.

* * * * *

About 96.4% of all eligible shares participated in our 1983 shareholder-designated contributions program. The total contributions made pursuant to this program—disbursed in the early days of 1984 but fully expensed in 1983—were $3,066,501, and 1353 charities were recipients. Although the response measured by the percentage of shares participating was extraordinarily good, the response measured by the percentage of holders participating was not as good. The reason may well be the large number of new shareholders acquired through the merger and their lack of familiarity with the program. We urge new shareholders to read the description of the program on pages 52-53.

If you wish to participate in future programs, we strongly urge that you immediately make sure that your shares are registered in the actual owner's name, not in "street" or nominee name. Shares not so registered on September 28, 1984 will not be eligible for any 1984 program.

* * * * *

The Blue Chip/Berkshire merger went off without a hitch. Less than one-tenth of 1% of the shares of each company voted against the merger, and no requests for appraisal were made. In 1983, we gained some tax efficiency from the merger and we expect to gain more in the future.

One interesting sidelight to the merger: Berkshire now has 1,146,909 shares outstanding compared to 1,137,778 shares at the beginning of fiscal 1965, the year present management assumed responsibility. For every 1% of the company you owned at that time, you now would own .99%. Thus, all of today's assets—the News, See's, Nebraska Furniture Mart, the Insurance Group, $1.3 billion in marketable stocks, etc.—have been added to the original textile assets with virtually no net dilution to the original owners.

We are delighted to have the former Blue Chip shareholders join us. To aid in your understanding of Berkshire Hathaway, we will be glad to send you the Compendium of Letters from the Annual Reports of 1977-1981, and/or the 1982 Annual report. Direct your request to the Company at 1440 Kiewit Plaza, Omaha, Nebraska 68131.

	Warren E. Buffett
March 14, 1984	Chairman of the Board

Appendix

BERKSHIRE HATHAWAY INC.

Goodwill and its Amortization: The Rules and The Realities

This appendix deals only with economic and accounting Goodwill—not the goodwill of everyday usage. For example, a business may be well liked, even loved, by most of its customers but possess no economic goodwill. (AT&T, before the breakup, was generally well thought of, but possessed not a dime of economic Goodwill.) And, regrettably, a business may be disliked by its customers but possess substantial, and growing, economic Goodwill. So, just for the moment, forget emotions and focus only on economics and accounting.

When a business is purchased, accounting principles require that the purchase price first be assigned to the fair value of the identifiable assets that are acquired. Frequently the sum of the fair values put on the assets (after the deduction of liabilities) is less than the total purchase price of the business. In that case, the difference is assigned to an asset account entitled "excess of cost over equity in net assets acquired". To avoid constant repetition of this mouthful, we will substitute "Goodwill".

Accounting Goodwill arising from businesses purchased before November 1970 has a special standing. Except under rare circumstances, it can remain an asset on the balance sheet as long as the business bought is retained. That means no amortization charges to gradually extinguish that asset need be made against earnings.

The case is different, however, with purchases made from November 1970 on. When these create Goodwill, it must be amortized over not more than 40 years through charges—of equal amount in every year—to the earnings account. Since 40 years is the maximum period allowed, 40 years is what managements (including us) usually elect. This annual charge to earnings is not allowed as a tax deduction and, thus, has an effect on after-tax income that is roughly double that of most other expenses.

That's how accounting Goodwill works. To see how it differs from economic reality, let's look at an example close at hand. We'll round some figures, and greatly oversimplify, to make the example easier to follow. We'll also mention some implications for investors and managers.

Blue Chip Stamps bought See's early in 1972 for $25 million, at which time See's had about $8 million of net tangible assets. (Throughout this discussion, accounts receivable will be classified as tangible assets, a definition proper for business analysis.) This level of tangible assets was adequate to conduct the business without use of debt, except for short periods seasonally. See's was earning about $2 million after tax at the time, and such earnings seemed conservatively representative of future earning power in constant 1972 dollars.

Thus our first lesson: businesses logically are worth far more than net tangible assets when they can be expected to produce earnings on such assets considerably in excess of market rates of return. The capitalized value of this excess return is economic Goodwill.

In 1972 (and now) relatively few businesses could be expected to consistently earn the 25% after tax on net tangible assets that was earned by See's—doing it, furthermore, with conservative accounting and no financial leverage. It was not the fair market value of the inventories, receivables or fixed assets that produced the premium rates of return. Rather it was a combination of intangible assets, particularly a pervasive favorable reputation with consumers based upon countless pleasant experiences they have had with both product and personnel.

Such a reputation creates a consumer franchise that allows the value of the product to the purchaser, rather than its production cost, to be the major determinant of selling price. Consumer franchises are a prime source of economic Goodwill. Other sources include governmental franchises not subject to profit regulation, such as television stations, and an enduring position as the low cost producer in an industry.

Let's return to the accounting in the See's example. Blue Chip's purchase of See's at $17 million over net tangible assets required that a Goodwill account of this amount be established as an asset on Blue Chip's books and that $425,000 be charged to income annually for 40 years to amortize that asset. By 1983, after 11 years of such charges, the $17 million had been reduced to about $12.5 million. Berkshire, meanwhile, owned 60% of Blue Chip and, therefore, also 60% of See's. This ownership meant that Berkshire's balance sheet reflected 60% of See's Goodwill, or about $7.5 million.

In 1983 Berkshire acquired the rest of Blue Chip in a merger that required purchase accounting as contrasted to the "pooling" treatment allowed for some mergers. Under purchase accounting, the "fair value" of the shares we gave to (or "paid") Blue Chip holders had to be spread over the net assets acquired from Blue Chip. This "fair value" was measured, as it almost always is when public companies use their shares to make acquisitions, by the market value of the shares given up.

The assets "purchased" consisted of 40% of everything owned by Blue Chip (as noted, Berkshire already owned the other 60%). What Berkshire "paid" was more than the net identifiable assets we received by $51.7 million, and was assigned to two pieces of Goodwill: $28.4 million to See's and $23.3 million to Buffalo Evening News.

After the merger, therefore, Berkshire was left with a Goodwill asset for See's that had two components: the $7.5 million remaining from the 1971 purchase, and $28.4 million newly created by the 40% "purchased" in 1983. Our amortization charge now will be about $1.0 million for the next 28 years, and $.7 million for the following 12 years, 2002 through 2013.

In other words, different purchase dates and prices have given us vastly different asset values and amortization charges for two pieces of the same asset. (We repeat our usual disclaimer: we have no better accounting system to suggest. The problems to be dealt with are mind boggling and require arbitrary rules.)

But what are the economic realities? One reality is that the amortization charges that have been deducted as costs in the earnings statement each year since acquisition of See's were not true economic costs. We know that because See's last year earned $13 million after taxes on about $20 million of net tangible assets—a performance indicating the existence of economic Goodwill far larger than the total original cost of our accounting Goodwill. In other words, while accounting Goodwill regularly decreased from the moment of purchase, economic Goodwill increased in irregular but very substantial fashion.

Another reality is that annual amortization charges in the future will not correspond to economic costs. It is possible, of course, that See's economic Goodwill will disappear. But it won't shrink in even decrements or anything remotely resembling them. What is more likely is that the Goodwill will *increase*—in current, if not in constant, dollars—because of inflation.

That probability exists because true economic Goodwill tends to rise in nominal value proportionally with inflation. To illustrate how this works, let's contrast a See's kind of business with a more mundane business. When we purchased See's in 1972, it will be recalled, it was earning about $2 million on $8 million of net tangible assets. Let us assume that our hypothetical mundane business then had $2 million of earnings also, but needed $18 million in net tangible assets for normal operations. Earning only 11% on required tangible assets, that mundane business would possess little or no economic Goodwill.

A business like that, therefore, might well have sold for the value of its net tangible assets, or for $18 million. In contrast, we paid $25 million for See's, even though it had no more in earnings and less than half as much in "honest-to-God" assets. Could less really have been more, as our purchase price implied? The answer is "yes"—*even if both businesses were expected to have flat unit volume*—as long as you anticipated, as we did in 1972, a world of continuous inflation.

To understand why, imagine the effect that a doubling of the price level would subsequently have on the two businesses. Both would need to double their nominal earnings to $4 million to keep themselves even with inflation. This would seem to be no great trick: just sell the same number of units at double earlier prices and, assuming profit margins remain unchanged, profits also must double.

But, crucially, to bring that about, both businesses probably would have to double their nominal investment in net tangible assets, since that is the kind of economic requirement that inflation usually imposes on businesses, both good and bad. A doubling of dollar sales means correspondingly more dollars must be employed immediately in receivables and inventories. Dollars employed in fixed assets will respond more slowly to inflation, but probably just as surely. And all of this inflation-required investment will produce no improvement in rate of return. The motivation for this investment is the survival of the business, not the prosperity of the owner.

Remember, however, that See's had net tangible assets of only $8 million. So it would only have had to commit an additional $8 million to finance the capital needs imposed by inflation. The mundane business, meanwhile, had a burden over twice as large—a need for $18 million of additional capital.

After the dust had settled, the mundane business, now earning $4 million annually, might still be worth the value of its tangible assets, or $36 million. That means its owners would have gained only a dollar of nominal value for every new dollar invested. (This is the same dollar-for-dollar result they would have achieved if they had added money to a savings account.)

See's, however, also earning $4 million, might be worth $50 million if valued (as it logically would be) on the same basis as it was at the time of our purchase. So it would have gained $25 million in nominal value while the owners were putting up only $8 million in additional capital—over $3 of nominal value gained for each $1 invested.

Remember, even so, that the owners of the See's kind of business were forced by inflation to ante up $8 million in additional capital just to stay even in real profits. Any unleveraged business that requires some net tangible assets to operate (and almost all do) is hurt by inflation. Businesses needing little in the way of tangible assets simply are hurt the least.

And that fact, of course, has been hard for many people to grasp. For years the traditional wisdom—long on tradition, short on wisdom—held that inflation protection was best provided by businesses laden with natural resources, plants and machinery, or other tangible assets ("In Goods We Trust"). It doesn't work that way. Asset-heavy businesses generally earn low rates of return—rates that often barely provide enough capital to fund the inflationary needs of the existing business, with nothing left over for real growth, for distribution to owners, or for acquisition of new businesses.

In contrast, a disproportionate number of the great business fortunes built up during the inflationary years arose from ownership of operations that combined intangibles of lasting value with relatively minor requirements for tangible assets. In such cases earnings have bounded upward in nominal dollars, and these dollars have been largely available for the acquisition of additional businesses. This phenomenon has been particularly evident in the communications business. That business has required little in the way of tangible investment—yet its franchises have endured. During inflation, Goodwill is the gift that keeps giving.

But that statement applies, naturally, only to true economic Goodwill. Spurious accounting Goodwill—and there is plenty of it around—is another matter. When an overexcited management purchases a business at a silly price, the same accounting niceties described earlier are observed. Because it can't go anywhere else, the silliness ends up in the Goodwill account. Considering the lack of managerial discipline that created the account, under such circumstances it might better be labeled "No-Will". Whatever the term, the 40-year ritual typically is observed and the adrenalin so capitalized remains on the books as an "asset" just as if the acquisition had been a sensible one.

* * * * *

If you cling to any belief that accounting treatment of Goodwill is the best measure of economic reality, I suggest one final item to ponder.

Assume a company with $20 per share of net worth, all tangible assets. Further assume the company has internally developed some magnificent consumer franchise, or that it was fortunate enough to obtain some important television stations by original FCC grant. Therefore, it earns a great deal on tangible assets, say $5 per share, or 25%.

With such economics, it might sell for $100 per share or more, and it might well also bring that price in a negotiated sale of the entire business.

Assume an investor buys the stock at $100 per share, paying in effect $80 per share for Goodwill (just as would a corporate purchaser buying the whole company). Should the investor impute a $2 per share amortization charge annually ($80 divided by 40 years) to calculate "true" earnings per share? And, if so, should the new "true" earnings of $3 per share cause him to rethink his purchase price?

* * * * *

We believe managers and investors alike should view intangible assets from two perspectives:

(1) In analysis of operating results—that is, in evaluating the underlying economics of a business unit—amortization charges should be ignored. What a business can be expected to earn on unleveraged net tangible assets, excluding any charges against earnings for amortization of Goodwill, is the best guide to the economic attractiveness of the operation. It is also the best guide to the current value of the operation's economic Goodwill.

(2) In evaluating the wisdom of business acquisitions, amortization charges should be ignored also. They should be deducted neither from earnings nor from the cost of the business. This means forever viewing purchased Goodwill at its full cost, before any amortization. Furthermore, cost should be defined as including the full intrinsic business value—not just the recorded accounting value—of all consideration given, irrespective of market prices of the securities involved at the time of merger and irrespective of whether pooling treatment was allowed. For example, what we truly paid in the Blue Chip merger for 40% of the Goodwill of See's and the News

was considerably more than the $51.7 million entered on our books. This disparity exists because the market value of the Berkshire shares given up in the merger was less than their intrinsic business value, which is the value that defines the true cost to us.

Operations that appear to be winners based upon perspective (1) may pale when viewed from perspective (2). A good business is not always a good purchase—although it's a good place to look for one.

We will try to acquire businesses that have excellent operating economics measured by (1) and that provide reasonable returns measured by (2). Accounting consequences will be totally ignored.

At yearend 1983, net Goodwill on our accounting books totaled $62 million, consisting of the $79 million you see stated on the asset side of our balance sheet, and $17 million of negative Goodwill that is offset against the carrying value of our interest in Mutual Savings and Loan.

We believe net economic Goodwill far exceeds the $62 million accounting number.

BERKSHIRE HATHAWAY INC.

To the Shareholders of Berkshire Hathaway Inc.:

Our gain in net worth during 1984 was $152.6 million, or $133 per share. This sounds pretty good but actually it's mediocre. Economic gains must be evaluated by comparison with the capital that produces them. Our twenty-year compounded annual gain in book value has been 22.1% (from $19.46 in 1964 to $1108.77 in 1984), but our gain in 1984 was only 13.6%.

As we discussed last year, the gain in per-share intrinsic business value is the economic measurement that really counts. But calculations of intrinsic business value are subjective. In our case, book value serves as a useful, although somewhat understated, proxy. In my judgment, intrinsic business value and book value increased during 1984 at about the same rate.

Using my academic voice, I have told you in the past of the drag that a mushrooming capital base exerts upon rates of return. Unfortunately, my academic voice is now giving way to a reportorial voice. Our historical 22% rate is just that—history. To earn even 15% annually over the next decade (assuming we continue to follow our present dividend policy, about which more will be said later in this letter) we would need profits aggregating about $3.9 billion. Accomplishing this will require a few big ideas—small ones just won't do. Charlie Munger, my partner in general management, and I do not have any such ideas at present, but our experience has been that they pop up occasionally. (How's that for a strategic plan?)

Sources of Reported Earnings

The table on the following page shows the sources of Berkshire's reported earnings. Berkshire's net ownership interest in many of the constituent businesses changed at midyear 1983 when the Blue Chip merger took place. Because of these changes, the first two columns of the table provide the best measure of underlying business performance.

All of the significant gains and losses attributable to unusual sales of assets by any of the business entities are aggregated with securities transactions on the line near the bottom of the table, and are not included in operating earnings. (We regard any annual figure for realized capital gains or losses as meaningless, but we regard the aggregate realized and unrealized capital gains over a period of years as very important.)

Furthermore, amortization of Goodwill is not charged against the specific businesses but, for reasons outlined in the Appendix to my letter in the 1983 annual report, is set forth as a separate item.

	(000s omitted)					
	Earnings Before Income Taxes				Net Earnings After Tax	
	Total		Berkshire Share		Berkshire Share	
	1984	1983	1984	1983	1984	1983
Operating Earnings:						
Insurance Group:						
Underwriting	$(48,060)	$(33,872)	$(48,060)	$(33,872)	$(25,955)	$(18,400)
Net Investment Income . . .	68,903	43,810	68,903	43,810	62,059	39,114
Buffalo News	27,328	19,352	27,328	16,547	13,317	8,832
Nebraska Furniture Mart(1) . .	14,511	3,812	11,609	3,049	5,917	1,521
See's Candies.	26,644	27,411	26,644	24,526	13,380	12,212
Associated Retail Stores	(1,072)	697	(1,072)	697	(579)	355
Blue Chip Stamps(2)	(1,843)	(1,422)	(1,843)	(1,876)	(899)	(353)
Mutual Savings and Loan	1,456	(798)	1,166	(467)	3,151	1,917
Precision Steel.	4,092	3,241	3,278	2,102	1,696	1,136
Textiles	418	(100)	418	(100)	226	(63)
Wesco Financial.	9,777	7,493	7,831	4,844	4,828	3,448
Amortization of Goodwill. . . .	(1,434)	(532)	(1,434)	(563)	(1,434)	(563)
Interest on Debt	(14,734)	(15,104)	(14,097)	(13,844)	(7,452)	(7,346)
Shareholder-Designated						
Contributions	(3,179)	(3,066)	(3,179)	(3,066)	(1,716)	(1,656)
Other	4,932	10,121	4,529	9,623	3,476	8,490
Operating Earnings.	87,739	61,043	82,021	51,410	70,015	48,644
Special GEICO Distribution . . .	--	19,575	--	19,575	--	18,224
Special Gen. Foods Distribution .	8,111	--	7,896	--	7,294	--
Sales of securities and						
unusual sales of assets	104,699	67,260	101,376	65,089	71,587	45,298
Total Earnings – all entities	$200,549	$147,878	$191,293	$136,074	$148,896	$112,166

(1) 1983 figures are those for October through December.
(2) 1984 and 1983 are not comparable; major assets were transferred in the mid-year 1983 merger of Blue Chip Stamps.

Sharp-eyed shareholders will notice that the amount of the special GEICO distribution and its location in the table have been changed from the presentation of last year. Though they reclassify and reduce "accounting" earnings, the changes are entirely of form, not of substance. The story behind the changes, however, is interesting.

As reported last year: (1) in mid-1983 GEICO made a tender offer to buy its own shares; (2) at the same time, we agreed by written contract to sell GEICO an amount of its shares that would be proportionately related to the aggregate number of shares GEICO repurchased via the tender from all other shareholders; (3) at completion of the tender, we delivered 350,000 shares to GEICO, received $21 million cash, and were left owning exactly the same percentage of GEICO that we owned before the tender; (4) GEICO's transaction with us amounted to a proportionate redemption, an opinion rendered us, without qualification, by a leading law firm; (5) the Tax Code logically regards such proportionate redemptions as substantially equivalent to dividends and, therefore, the $21 million we received was taxed at only the 6.9% inter-corporate dividend rate; (6) importantly, that $21 million was far less than the previously-undistributed earnings that had inured to our ownership in GEICO and, thus, from the standpoint of economic substance, was in our view equivalent to a dividend.

Because it was material and unusual, we highlighted the GEICO distribution last year to you, both in the applicable quarterly report and in this section of the annual report. Additionally, we emphasized the transaction to our auditors, Peat, Marwick, Mitchell & Co. Both the Omaha office of Peat Marwick and the reviewing Chicago partner, without objection, concurred with our dividend presentation.

In 1984, we had a virtually identical transaction with General Foods. The only difference was that General Foods repurchased its stock over a period of time in the open market, whereas GEICO had made a "one-shot" tender offer. In the General Foods case we sold to the company, on each day that it repurchased shares, a quantity of shares that left our ownership percentage precisely unchanged. Again our transaction was pursuant to a written contract executed before repurchases began. And again the money we received was far less than the retained earnings that had inured to our ownership interest since our purchase. Overall we received $21,843,601 in cash from General Foods, and our ownership remained at exactly 8.75%.

At this point the New York office of Peat Marwick came into the picture. Late in 1984 it indicated that it disagreed with the conclusions of the firm's Omaha office and Chicago reviewing partner. The New York view was that the GEICO and General Foods transactions should be treated as sales of stock by Berkshire rather than as the receipt of dividends. Under this accounting approach, a portion of the cost of our investment in the stock of each company would be charged against the redemption payment and any gain would be shown as a capital gain, not as dividend income. This is an accounting approach only, having no bearing on taxes: Peat Marwick agrees that the transactions were dividends for IRS purposes.

We disagree with the New York position from both the viewpoint of economic substance and proper accounting. But, to avoid a qualified auditor's opinion, we have adopted herein Peat Marwick's 1984 view and restated 1983 accordingly. None of this, however, has any effect on intrinsic business value: our ownership interests in GEICO and General Foods, our cash, our taxes, and the market value and tax basis of our holdings all remain the same.

This year we have again entered into a contract with General Foods whereby we will sell them shares concurrently with open market purchases that they make. The arrangement provides that our ownership interest will remain unchanged at all times. By keeping it so, we will insure ourselves dividend treatment for tax purposes. In our view also, the economic substance of this transaction again is the creation of dividend income. However, we will account for the redemptions as sales of stock rather than dividend income unless accounting rules are adopted that speak directly to this point. We will continue to prominently identify any such special transactions in our reports to you.

While we enjoy a low tax charge on these proportionate redemptions, and have participated in several of them, we view such repurchases as at least equally favorable for shareholders who do not sell. When companies with outstanding businesses and comfortable financial positions find their shares selling far below intrinsic value in the marketplace, no alternative action can benefit shareholders as surely as repurchases.

(Our endorsement of repurchases is limited to those dictated by price/value relationships and does not extend to the "greenmail" repurchase—a practice we find odious and repugnant. In these transactions, two parties achieve their personal ends by exploitation of an innocent and unconsulted third party. The players are: (1) the "shareholder" extortionist who, even before the ink on his stock certificate dries, delivers his "your-money-or-your-life" message to managers; (2) the corporate insiders who quickly seek peace at any price—as long as the price is paid by someone else; and (3) the shareholders whose money is used by (2) to make (1) go away. As the dust settles, the mugging, transient shareholder gives his speech on "free enterprise", the muggee management gives its speech on "the best interests of the company", and the innocent shareholder standing by mutely funds the payoff.)

The companies in which we have our largest investments have all engaged in significant stock repurchases at times when wide discrepancies existed between price and value. As shareholders, we find this encouraging and rewarding for two important reasons—one that is obvious, and one that is subtle and not always understood. The obvious point involves basic arithmetic: major repurchases at prices well below per-share intrinsic business value immediately increase, in a highly significant way, that value. When companies purchase their own stock, they often find it easy to get $2 of present value for $1. Corporate acquisition programs almost never do as well and, in a discouragingly large number of cases, fail to get anything close to $1 of value for each $1 expended.

The other benefit of repurchases is less subject to precise measurement but can be fully as important over time. By making repurchases when a company's market value is well below its business value, management clearly demonstrates that it is given to actions that enhance the wealth of shareholders, rather than to actions that expand management's domain but that do nothing for (or even harm) shareholders. Seeing this, shareholders and potential shareholders increase their estimates of future returns from the business. This upward revision, in turn, produces market prices more in line with intrinsic business value. These prices are entirely rational. Investors should pay more for a business that is lodged in the hands of a manager with demonstrated pro-shareholder leanings than for one in the hands of a self-interested manager marching to a different drummer. (To make the point extreme, how much would you pay to be a minority shareholder of a company controlled by Robert Wesco?)

The key word is "demonstrated". A manager who consistently turns his back on repurchases, when these clearly are in the interests of owners, reveals more than he knows of his motivations. No matter how often or how eloquently he mouths some public relations-inspired phrase such as "maximizing shareholder wealth" (this season's favorite), the market correctly discounts assets lodged with him. His heart is not listening to his mouth—and, after a while, neither will the market.

We have prospered in a very major way—as have other shareholders—by the large share repurchases of GEICO, Washington Post, and General Foods, our three largest holdings. (Exxon, in which we have our fourth largest holding, has also wisely and aggressively repurchased shares but, in this case, we have only recently established our position.) In each of these companies, shareholders have had their interests in outstanding businesses materially enhanced by repurchases made at bargain prices. We feel very comfortable owning interests in businesses such as these that offer excellent economics combined with shareholder-conscious managements.

The following table shows our 1984 yearend net holdings in marketable equities. All numbers exclude the interests attributable to minority shareholders of Wesco and Nebraska Furniture Mart.

No. of Shares		Cost	Market
		(000s omitted)	
690,975	Affiliated Publications, Inc.	$ 3,516	$ 32,908
740,400	American Broadcasting Companies, Inc.	44,416	46,738
3,895,710	Exxon Corporation.	173,401	175,307
4,047,191	General Foods Corporation	149,870	226,137
6,850,000	GEICO Corporation.	45,713	397,300
2,379,200	Handy & Harman	27,318	38,662
818,872	Interpublic Group of Companies, Inc.	2,570	28,149
555,949	Northwest Industries	26,581	27,242
2,553,488	Time, Inc.	89,327	109,162
1,868,600	The Washington Post Company	10,628	149,955
		$573,340	$1,231,560
	All Other Common Stockholdings	11,634	37,326
	Total Common Stocks	$584,974	$1,268,886

It's been over ten years since it has been as difficult as now to find equity investments that meet both our qualitative standards and our quantitative standards of value versus price. We try to avoid compromise of these standards, although we find doing nothing the most difficult task of all. (One English statesman attributed his country's greatness in the nineteenth century to a policy of "masterly inactivity". This is a strategy that is far easier for historians to commend than for participants to follow.)

In addition to the figures supplied at the beginning of this section, information regarding the businesses we own appears in Management's Discussion on pages 42-47. An amplified discussion of Wesco's businesses appears in Charlie Munger's report on pages 50-59. You will find particularly interesting his comments about conditions in the thrift industry. Our other major controlled businesses are Nebraska Furniture Mart, See's, Buffalo Evening News, and the Insurance Group, to which we will give some special attention here.

Nebraska Furniture Mart

Last year I introduced you to Mrs. B (Rose Blumkin) and her family. I told you they were terrific, and I understated the case. After another year of observing their remarkable talents and character, I can honestly say that I never have seen a managerial group that either functions or behaves better than the Blumkin family.

Mrs. B, Chairman of the Board, is now 91, and recently was quoted in the local newspaper as saying, "I come home to eat and sleep, and that's about it. I can't wait until it gets daylight so I can get back to the business". Mrs. B is at the store seven days a week, from opening to close, and probably makes more decisions in a day than most CEOs do in a year (better ones, too).

In May Mrs. B was granted an Honorary Doctorate in Commercial Science by New York University. (She's a "fast track" student: not one day in her life was spent in a school room prior to her receipt of the doctorate.) Previous recipients of honorary degrees in business from NYU include Clifton Garvin, Jr., CEO of Exxon Corp.; Walter Wriston, then CEO of Citicorp; Frank Cary, then CEO of IBM; Tom Murphy, then CEO of General Motors; and, most recently, Paul Volcker. (They are in good company.)

The Blumkin blood did not run thin. Louie, Mrs. B's son, and his three boys, Ron, Irv, and Steve, all contribute in full measure to NFM's amazing success. The younger generation has attended the best business school of them all—that conducted by Mrs. B and Louie—and their training is evident in their performance.

Last year NFM's net sales increased by $14.3 million, bringing the total to $115 million, all from the one store in Omaha. That is by far the largest volume produced by a single home furnishings store in the United States. In fact, the gain in sales last year was itself greater than the annual volume of many good-sized successful stores. The business achieves this success because it deserves this success. A few figures will tell you why.

In its fiscal 1984 10-K, the largest independent specialty retailer of home furnishings in the country, Levitz Furniture, described its prices as "generally lower than the prices charged by conventional furniture stores in its trading area". Levitz, in that year, operated at a gross margin of 44.4% (that is, on average, customers paid it $100 for merchandise that had cost it $55.60 to buy). The gross margin at NFM is not much more than half of that. NFM's low mark-ups are possible because of its exceptional efficiency: operating expenses (payroll, occupancy, advertising, etc.) are about 16.5% of sales versus 35.6% at Levitz.

None of this is in criticism of Levitz, which has a well-managed operation. But the NFM operation is simply extraordinary (and, remember, it all comes from a $500 investment by Mrs. B in 1937). By unparalleled efficiency and astute volume purchasing, NFM is able to earn excellent returns on capital while saving its customers at least $30 million annually from what, on average, it would cost them to buy the same merchandise at stores maintaining typical mark-ups. Such savings enable NFM to constantly widen its geographical reach and thus to enjoy growth well beyond the natural growth of the Omaha market.

I have been asked by a number of people just what secrets the Blumkins bring to their business. These are not very esoteric. All members of the family: (1) apply themselves with an enthusiasm and energy that would make Ben Franklin and Horatio Alger look like dropouts; (2) define with extraordinary realism their area of special competence and act decisively on all matters within it; (3) ignore even the most enticing propositions failing outside of that area of special competence; and, (4) unfailingly behave in a high-grade manner with everyone they deal with. (Mrs. B boils it down to "sell cheap and tell the truth".)

Our evaluation of the integrity of Mrs. B and her family was demonstrated when we purchased 90% of the business: NFM had never had an audit and we did not request one; we did not take an inventory nor verify the receivables; we did not check property titles. We gave Mrs. B a check for $55 million and she gave us her word. That made for an even exchange.

You and I are fortunate to be in partnership with the Blumkin family.

See's Candy Shops, Inc.

Below is our usual recap of See's performance since the time of purchase by Blue Chip Stamps:

52-53 Week Year Ended About December 31	Sales Revenues	Operating Profits After Taxes	Number of Pounds of Candy Sold	Number of Stores Open at Year End
1984.	$135,946,000	$13,380,000	24,759,000	214
1983 (53 weeks) . .	133,531,000	13,699,000	24,651,000	207
1982.	123,662,000	11,875,000	24,216,000	202
1981.	112,578,000	10,779,000	24,052,000	199
1980.	97,715,000	7,547,000	24,065,000	191
1979.	87,314,000	6,330,000	23,985,000	188
1978.	73,653,000	6,178,000	22,407,000	182
1977.	62,886,000	6,154,000	20,921,000	179
1976 (53 weeks) . .	56,333,000	5,569,000	20,553,000	173
1975.	50,492,000	5,132,000	19,134,000	172
1974.	41,248,000	3,021,000	17,883,000	170
1973.	35,050,000	1,940,000	17,813,000	169
1972.	31,337,000	2,083,000	16,954,000	167

This performance has not been produced by a generally rising tide. To the contrary, many well-known participants in the boxed-chocolate industry either have lost money in this same period or have been marginally profitable. To our knowledge, only one good-sized competitor has achieved high profitability. The success of See's reflects the combination of an exceptional product and an exceptional manager, Chuck Huggins.

During 1984 we increased prices considerably less than has been our practice in recent years: per-pound realization was $5.49, up only 1.4% from 1983. Fortunately, we made good progress on cost control, an area that has caused us problems in recent years. Per-pound costs—other than those for raw materials, a segment of expense largely outside of our control—increased by only 2.2% last year.

Our cost-control problem has been exacerbated by the problem of modestly declining volume (measured by pounds, not dollars) on a same-store basis. Total pounds sold through shops in recent years has been maintained at a roughly constant level only by the net addition of a few shops annually. This more-shops-to-get-the-same-volume situation naturally puts heavy pressure on per-pound selling costs.

In 1984, same-store volume declined 1.1%. Total shop volume, however, grew 0.6% because of an increase in stores. (Both percentages are adjusted to compensate for a 53-week fiscal year in 1983.)

See's business tends to get a bit more seasonal each year. In the four weeks prior to Christmas, we do 40% of the year's volume and earn about 75% of the year's profits. We also earn significant sums in the Easter and Valentine's Day periods, but pretty much tread water the rest of the year. In recent years, shop volume at Christmas has grown in relative importance, and so have quantity orders and mail orders. The increased concentration of business in the Christmas period produces a multitude of managerial problems, all of which have been handled by Chuck and his associates with exceptional skill and grace.

Their solutions have in no way involved compromises in either quality of service or quality of product. Most of our larger competitors could not say the same. Though faced with somewhat less extreme peaks and valleys in demand than we, they add preservatives or freeze the finished product in order to smooth the production cycle and thereby lower unit costs. We reject such techniques, opting, in effect, for production headaches rather than product modification.

Our mall stores face a host of new food and snack vendors that provide particularly strong competition at non-holiday periods. We need new products to fight back and during 1984 we introduced six candy bars that, overall, met with a good reception. Further product introductions are planned.

In 1985 we will intensify our efforts to keep per-pound cost increases below the rate of inflation. Continued success in these efforts, however, will require gains in same-store poundage. Prices in 1985 should average 6%—7% above those of 1984. Assuming no change in same-store volume, profits should show a moderate gain.

Buffalo Evening News

Profits at the News in 1984 were considerably greater than we expected. As at See's, excellent progress was made in controlling costs. Excluding hours worked in the newsroom, total hours worked decreased by about 2.8%. With this productivity improvement, overall costs increased only 4.9%. This performance by Stan Lipsey and his management team was one of the best in the industry.

However, we now face an acceleration in costs. In mid-1984 we entered into new multi-year union contracts that provided for a large "catch-up" wage increase. This catch-up is entirely appropriate: the cooperative spirit of our unions during the unprofitable 1977-1982 period was an important factor in our success in remaining cost competitive with The Courier-Express. Had we not kept costs down, the outcome of that struggle might well have been different.

Because our new union contracts took effect at varying dates, little of the catch-up increase was reflected in our 1984 costs. But the increase will be almost totally effective in 1985 and, therefore, our unit labor costs will rise this year at a rate considerably greater than that of the industry. We expect to mitigate this increase by continued small gains in productivity, but we cannot avoid significantly higher wage costs this year. Newsprint price trends also are less favorable now than they were in 1984. Primarily because of these two factors, we expect at least a minor contraction in margins at the News.

Working in our favor at the News are two factors of major economic importance:

(1) Our circulation is concentrated to an unusual degree in the area of maximum utility to our advertisers. "Regional" newspapers with wide-ranging circulation, on the other hand, have a significant portion of their circulation in areas that are of negligible utility to most advertisers. A subscriber several hundred miles away is not much of a prospect for the puppy you are offering to sell via a classified ad—nor for the grocer with stores only in the metropolitan area. "Wasted" circulation—as the advertisers call it -hurts profitability: expenses of a newspaper are determined largely by gross circulation while advertising revenues (usually 70%—80% of total revenues) are responsive only to useful circulation;

(2) Our penetration of the Buffalo retail market is exceptional; advertisers can reach almost all of their potential customers using only the News.

Last year I told you about this unusual reader acceptance: among the 100 largest newspapers in the country, we were then number one, daily, and number three, Sunday, in penetration. The most recent figures show us number one in penetration on weekdays and number two on Sunday. (Even so, the number of households in Buffalo has declined, so our current weekday circulation is down slightly; on Sundays it is unchanged.)

I told you also that one of the major reasons for this unusual acceptance by readers was the unusual quantity of news that we delivered to them: a greater percentage of our paper is devoted to news than is the case at any other dominant paper in our size range. In 1984 our "news hole" ratio was 50.9%, (versus 50.4% in 1983), a level far above the typical 35%-40%. We will continue to maintain this ratio in the 50% area. Also, though we last year reduced total hours worked in other departments, we maintained the level of employment in the newsroom and, again, will continue to do so. Newsroom costs advanced 9.1% in 1984, a rise far exceeding our overall cost increase of 4.9%.

Our news hole policy costs us significant extra money for newsprint. As a result, our news costs (newsprint for the news hole plus payroll and expenses of the newsroom) as a percentage of revenue run higher than those of most dominant papers of our size. There is adequate room, however, for our paper or any other dominant paper to sustain these costs: the difference between "high" and "low" news costs at papers of comparable size runs perhaps three percentage points while pre-tax profit margins are often ten times that amount.

The economics of a dominant newspaper are excellent, among the very best in the business world. Owners, naturally, would like to believe that their wonderful profitability is achieved only because they unfailingly turn out a wonderful product. That comfortable theory wilts before an uncomfortable fact. While first-class newspapers make excellent profits, the profits of third-rate papers are as good or better—as long as either class of paper is dominant within its community. Of course, product quality may have been crucial to the paper in achieving dominance. We believe this was the case at the News, in very large part because of people such as Alfred Kirchhofer who preceded us.

Once dominant, the newspaper itself, not the marketplace, determines just how good or how bad the paper will be. Good or bad, it will prosper. That is not true of most businesses: inferior quality generally produces inferior economics. But even a poor newspaper is a bargain to most citizens simply because of its "bulletin board" value. Other things being equal, a poor product will not achieve quite the level of readership achieved by a first-class product. A poor product, however, will still remain essential to most citizens, and what commands their attention will command the attention of advertisers.

Since high standards are not imposed by the marketplace, management must impose its own. Our commitment to an above-average expenditure for news represents an important quantitative standard. We have confidence that Stan Lipsey and Murray Light will continue to apply the far-more important qualitative standards. Charlie and I believe that newspapers are very special institutions in society. We are proud of the News, and intend an even greater pride to be justified in the years ahead.

Insurance Operations

Shown below is an updated version of our usual table listing two key figures for the insurance industry:

	Yearly Change in Premium Written (%)	Combined Ratio after Policy-holder Dividends
1972	10.2	96.2
1973	8.0	99.2
1974	6.2	105.4
1975	11.0	107.9
1976	21.9	102.4
1977	19.8	97.2
1978	12.8	97.5
1979	10.3	100.6
1980	6.0	103.1
1981	3.9	106.0
1982	4.4	109.7
1983 (Revised)	4.5	111.9
1984 (Estimated)	8.1	117.7

Source: Best's Aggregates and Averages.

Best's data reflect the experience of practically the entire industry, including stock, mutual, and reciprocal companies. The combined ratio represents total insurance costs (losses incurred plus expenses) compared to revenue from premiums; a ratio below 100 indicates an underwriting profit, and one above 100 indicates a loss.

For a number of years, we have told you that an annual increase by the industry of about 10% per year in premiums written is necessary for the combined ratio to remain roughly unchanged. We assumed in making that assertion that expenses as a percentage of premium volume would stay relatively stable and that losses would grow at about 10% annually because of the combined influence of unit volume increases, inflation, and judicial rulings that expand what is covered by the insurance policy.

Our opinion is proving dismayingly accurate: a premium increase of 10% per year since 1979 would have produced an aggregate increase through 1984 of 61% and a combined ratio in 1984 almost identical to the 100.6 of 1979. Instead, the industry had only a 30% increase in premiums and a 1984 combined ratio of 117.7. Today, we continue to believe that the key index to the trend of underwriting profitability is the year-to-year percentage change in industry premium volume.

It now appears that premium volume in 1985 will grow well over 10%. Therefore, assuming that catastrophes are at a "normal" level, we would expect the combined ratio to begin easing downward toward the end of the year. However, under our industrywide loss assumptions (i.e., increases of 10% annually), five years of 15%-per-year increases in premiums would be required to get the combined ratio back to 100. This would mean a doubling of industry volume by 1989, an outcome that seems highly unlikely to us. Instead, we expect several years of premium gains somewhat above the 10% level, followed by highly-competitive pricing that generally will produce combined ratios in the 108-113 range.

Our own combined ratio in 1984 was a humbling 134. (Here, as throughout this report, we exclude structured settlements and the assumption of loss reserves in reporting this ratio. Much additional detail, including the effect of discontinued operations on the ratio, appears on pages 42-43). This is the third year in a row that our underwriting performance has been far poorer than that of the industry. We expect an improvement in the combined ratio in 1985, and also expect our improvement to be substantially greater than that of the industry. Mike Goldberg has corrected many of the mistakes I made before he took over insurance operations. Moreover, our business is concentrated in lines that have experienced poorer-than-average results during the past several years, and that circumstance has begun to subdue many of our competitors and even eliminate some. With the competition shaken, we were able during the last half of 1984 to raise prices significantly in certain important lines with little loss of business.

For some years I have told you that there could be a day coming when our premier financial strength would make a real difference in the competitive position of our insurance operation. That day may have arrived. We are almost without question the strongest property/casualty insurance operation in the country, with a capital position far superior to that of well-known companies of much greater size.

Equally important, our corporate policy is to retain that superiority. The buyer of insurance receives only a promise in exchange for his cash. The value of that promise should be appraised against the possibility of adversity, not prosperity. At a minimum, the promise should appear able to withstand a prolonged combination of depressed financial markets and exceptionally unfavorable underwriting results. Our insurance subsidiaries are both willing and able to keep their promises in any such environment— and not too many other companies clearly are.

Our financial strength is a particular asset in the business of structured settlements and loss reserve assumptions that we reported on last year. The claimant in a structured settlement and the insurance company that has reinsured loss reserves need to be completely confident that payments will be forthcoming for decades to come. Very few companies in the property/casualty field can meet this test of unquestioned long-term strength. (In fact, only a handful of companies exists with which we will reinsure our own liabilities.)

We have grown in these new lines of business: funds that we hold to offset assumed liabilities grew from $16.2 million to $30.6 million during the year. We expect growth to continue and perhaps to greatly accelerate. To support this projected growth we have added substantially to the capital of Columbia Insurance Company, our reinsurance unit specializing in structured settlements and loss reserve assumptions. While these businesses are very competitive, returns should be satisfactory.

At GEICO the news, as usual, is mostly good. That company achieved excellent unit growth in its primary insurance business during 1984, and the performance of its investment portfolio continued to be extraordinary. Though underwriting results deteriorated late in the year, they still remain far better than those of the industry. Our ownership in GEICO at yearend amounted to 36% and thus our interest in their direct property/casualty volume of $885 million amounted to $320 million, or well over double our own premium volume.

I have reported to you in the past few years that the performance of GEICO's stock has considerably exceeded that company's business performance, brilliant as the latter has been. In those years, the carrying value of our GEICO investment on our balance sheet grew at a rate greater than the growth in GEICO's intrinsic business value. I warned you that over performance by the stock relative to the performance of the business obviously could not occur every year, and that in some years the stock must under perform the business. In 1984 that occurred and the carrying value of our interest in GEICO changed hardly at all, while the intrinsic business value of that interest increased substantially. Since 27% of Berkshire's net worth at the beginning of 1984 was represented by GEICO, its static market value had a significant impact upon our rate of gain for the year. We are not at all unhappy with such a result: we would far rather have the business value of GEICO increase by X during the year, while market value decreases, than have the intrinsic value increase by only 1/2 X with market value soaring. In GEICO's case, as in all of our investments, we look to business performance, not market performance. If we are correct in expectations regarding the business, the market eventually will follow along.

You, as shareholders of Berkshire, have benefited in enormous measure from the talents of GEICO's Jack Byrne, Bill Snyder, and Lou Simpson. In its core business—low-cost auto and homeowners insurance—GEICO has a major, sustainable competitive advantage. That is a rare asset in business generally, and it's almost non-existent in the field of financial services. (GEICO, itself, illustrates this point: despite the company's excellent management, superior profitability has eluded GEICO in all endeavors other than its core business.) In a large industry, a competitive advantage such as GEICO's provides the potential for unusual economic rewards, and Jack and Bill continue to exhibit great skill in realizing that potential.

Most of the funds generated by GEICO's core insurance operation are made available to Lou for investment. Lou has the rare combination of temperamental and intellectual characteristics that produce outstanding long-term investment performance. Operating with below-average risk, he has generated returns that have been by far the best in the insurance industry. I applaud and appreciate the efforts and talents of these three outstanding managers.

Errors in Loss Reserving

Any shareholder in a company with important interests in the property/casualty insurance business should have some understanding of the weaknesses inherent in the reporting of current earnings in that industry. Phil Graham, when publisher of the Washington Post, described the daily newspaper as "a first rough draft of history". Unfortunately, the financial statements of a property/casualty insurer provide, at best, only a first rough draft of earnings and financial condition.

The determination of costs is the main problem. Most of an insurer's costs result from losses on claims, and many of the losses that should be charged against the current year's revenue are exceptionally difficult to estimate. Sometimes the extent of these losses, or even their existence, is not known for decades.

The loss expense charged in a property/casualty company's current income statement represents: (1) losses that occurred and were paid during the year; (2) estimates for losses that occurred and were reported to the insurer during the year, but which have yet to be settled; (3) estimates of ultimate dollar costs for losses that occurred during the year but of which the insurer is unaware (termed "IBNR": incurred but not reported); and (4) the net effect of revisions this year of similar estimates for (2) and (3) made in past years.

Such revisions may be long delayed, but eventually any estimate of losses that causes the income for year X to be misstated must be corrected, whether it is in year X + 1, or X + 10. This, perforce, means that earnings in the year of correction also are misstated. For example, assume a claimant was injured by one of our insureds in 1979 and we thought a settlement was likely to be made for $10,000. That year we would have charged $10,000 to our earnings statement for the estimated cost of the loss and, correspondingly, set up a liability reserve on the balance sheet for that amount. If we settled the claim in 1984 for $100,000, we would charge earnings with a loss cost of $90,000 in 1984, although that cost was truly an expense of 1979. And if that piece of business was our only activity in 1979, we would have badly misled ourselves as to costs, and you as to earnings.

The necessarily-extensive use of estimates in assembling the figures that appear in such deceptively precise form in the income statement of property/casualty companies means that some error must seep in, no matter how proper the intentions of management. In an attempt to minimize error, most insurers use various statistical techniques to adjust the thousands of individual loss evaluations (called case reserves) that comprise the raw data for estimation of aggregate liabilities. The extra reserves created by these adjustments are variously labeled "bulk", "development", or "supplemental" reserves. The goal of the adjustments should be a loss-reserve total that has a 50-50 chance of being proved either slightly too high or slightly too low when all losses that occurred prior to the date of the financial statement are ultimately paid.

At Berkshire, we have added what we thought were appropriate supplemental reserves but in recent years they have not been adequate. It is important that you understand the magnitude of the errors that have been involved in our reserving. You can thus see for yourselves just how imprecise the process is, and also judge whether we may have some systemic bias that should make you wary of our current and future figures.

The following table shows the results from insurance underwriting as we have reported them to you in recent years, and also gives you calculations a year later on an "if-we-knew-then-what-we-think-we-know-now" basis. I say "what we think we know now" because the adjusted figures still include a great many estimates for losses that occurred in the earlier years. However, many claims from the earlier years have been settled so that our one-year-later estimate contains less guess work than our earlier estimate:

Year	Underwriting Results as Reported to You	Corrected Figures After One Year's Experience
1980	$ 6,738,000	$ 14,887,000
1981	1,478,000	(1,118,000)
1982	(21,462,000)	(25,066,000)
1983	(33,192,000)	(50,974,000)
1984	(45,413,000)	?

Our structured settlement and loss-reserve assumption businesses are not included in this table. Important additional information on loss reserve experience appears on pages 43-45.

To help you understand this table, here is an explanation of the most recent figures: 1984's reported pre-tax underwriting loss of $45.4 million consists of $27.6 million we estimate that we lost on 1984's business, plus the increased loss of $17.8 million reflected in the corrected figure for 1983.

As you can see from reviewing the table, my errors in reporting to you have been substantial and recently have always presented a better underwriting picture than was truly the case. This is a source of particular chagrin to me because: (1) I like for you to be able to count on what I say; (2) our insurance managers and I undoubtedly acted with less urgency than we would have had we understood the full extent of our losses; and (3) we paid income taxes calculated on overstated earnings and thereby gave the government money that we didn't need to. (These overpayments eventually correct themselves, but the delay is long and we don't receive interest on the amounts we overpaid.)

Because our business is weighted toward casualty and reinsurance lines, we have more problems in estimating loss costs than companies that specialize in property insurance. (When a building that you have insured burns down, you get a much faster fix on your costs than you do when an employer you have insured finds out that one of his retirees has contracted a disease attributable to work he did decades earlier.) But I still find our errors embarrassing. In our direct business, we have far underestimated the mushrooming tendency of juries and courts to make the "deep pocket" pay, regardless of the factual situation and the past precedents for establishment of liability. We also have underestimated the contagious effect that publicity regarding giant awards has on juries. In the reinsurance area, where we have had our worst experience in under reserving, our customer insurance companies have made the same mistakes. Since we set reserves based on information they supply us, their mistakes have become our mistakes.

I heard a story recently that is applicable to our insurance accounting problems: a man was traveling abroad when he received a call from his sister informing him that their father had died unexpectedly. It was physically impossible for the brother to get back home for the funeral, but he told his sister to take care of the funeral arrangements and to send the bill to him. After returning home he received a bill for several thousand dollars, which he promptly paid. The following month another bill came along for $15, and he paid that too. Another month followed, with a similar bill. When, in the next month, a third bill for $15 was presented, he called his sister to ask what was going on. "Oh", she said. "I forgot to tell you. We buried Dad in a rented suit."

If you've been in the insurance business in recent years—particularly the reinsurance business—this story hurts. We have tried to include all of our "rented suit" liabilities in our current financial statement, but our record of past error should make us humble, and you suspicious. I will continue to report to you the errors, plus or minus, that surface each year.

Not all reserving errors in the industry have been of the innocent-but-dumb variety. With underwriting results as bad as they have been in recent years—and with managements having as much discretion as they do in the presentation of financial statements—some unattractive aspects of human nature have manifested themselves. Companies that would be out of business if they realistically appraised their loss costs have, in some cases, simply preferred to take an extraordinarily optimistic view about these yet-to-be-paid sums. Others have engaged in various transactions to hide true current loss costs.

Both of these approaches can "work" for a considerable time: external auditors cannot effectively police the financial statements of property/casualty insurers. If liabilities of an insurer, correctly stated, would exceed assets, it falls to the insurer to volunteer this morbid information. In other words, the corpse is supposed to file the death certificate. Under this "honor system" of mortality, the corpse sometimes gives itself the benefit of the doubt.

In most businesses, of course, insolvent companies run out of cash. Insurance is different: you can be broke but flush. Since cash comes in at the inception of an insurance policy and losses are paid much later, insolvent insurers don't run out of cash until long after they have run out of net worth. In fact, these "walking dead" often redouble their efforts to write business, accepting almost any price or risk, simply to keep the cash flowing in. With an attitude like that of an embezzler who has gambled away his purloined funds, these companies hope that somehow they can get lucky on the next batch of business and thereby cover up earlier shortfalls. Even if they don't get lucky, the penalty to managers is usually no greater for a $100 million shortfall than one of $10 million; in the meantime, while the losses mount, the managers keep their jobs and perquisites.

The loss-reserving errors of other property/casualty companies are of more than academic interest to Berkshire. Not only does Berkshire suffer from sell-at-any-price competition by the "walking dead", but we also suffer when their insolvency is finally acknowledged. Through various state guarantee funds that levy assessments, Berkshire ends up paying a portion of the insolvent insurers' asset deficiencies, swollen as they usually are by the delayed detection that results from wrong reporting. There is even some potential for cascading trouble. The insolvency of a few large insurers and the assessments by state guarantee funds that would follow could imperil weak-but-previously-solvent insurers. Such dangers can be mitigated if state regulators become better at prompt identification and termination of insolvent insurers, but progress on that front has been slow.

Washington Public Power Supply System

From October, 1983 through June, 1984 Berkshire's insurance subsidiaries continuously purchased large quantities of bonds of Projects 1, 2, and 3 of Washington Public Power Supply System ("WPPSS"). This is the same entity that, on July 1, 1983, defaulted on $2.2 billion of bonds issued to finance partial construction of the now-abandoned Projects 4 and 5. While there are material differences in the obligors, promises, and properties underlying the two categories of bonds, the problems of Projects 4 and 5 have cast a major cloud over Projects 1, 2, and 3, and might possibly cause serious problems for the latter issues. In addition, there have been a multitude of problems related directly to Projects 1, 2, and 3 that could weaken or destroy an otherwise strong credit position arising from guarantees by Bonneville Power Administration.

Despite these important negatives, Charlie and I judged the risks *at the time we purchased the bonds and at the prices Berkshire paid* (much lower than present prices) to be considerably more than compensated for by prospects of profit.

As you know, we buy marketable stocks for our insurance companies based upon the criteria we would apply in the purchase of an entire business. This business-valuation approach is not widespread among professional money managers and is scorned by many academics. Nevertheless, it has served its followers well (to which the academics seem to say, "Well, it may be all right in practice, but it will never work in theory.") Simply put, we feel that if we can buy small pieces of businesses with satisfactory underlying economics at a fraction of the per-share value of the entire business, something good is likely to happen to us—particularly if we own a group of such securities.

We extend this business-valuation approach even to bond purchases such as WPPSS. We compare the $139 million cost of our yearend investment in WPPSS to a similar $139 million investment in an operating business. In the case of WPPSS, the "business" contractually earns $22.7 million after tax (via the interest paid on the bonds), and those earnings are available to us currently in cash. We are unable to buy operating businesses with economics close to these. Only a relatively few businesses earn the 16.3% after tax on unleveraged capital that our WPPSS investment does and those businesses, when available for purchase, sell at large premiums to that capital. In the average negotiated business transaction, unleveraged corporate earnings of $22.7 million after-tax (equivalent to about $45 million pre-tax) might command a price of $250—$300 million (or sometimes far more). For a business we understand well and strongly like, we will gladly pay that much. But it is double the price we paid to realize the same earnings from WPPSS bonds.

However, in the case of WPPSS, there is what we view to be a very slight risk that the "business" could be worth nothing within a year or two. There also is the risk that interest payments might be interrupted for a considerable period of time. Furthermore, the most that the "business" could be worth is about the $205 million face value of the bonds that we own, an amount only 48% higher than the price we paid.

This ceiling on upside potential is an important minus. It should be realized, however, that the great majority of operating businesses have a limited upside potential also unless more capital is continuously invested in them. That is so because most businesses are unable to significantly improve their average returns on equity—even under inflationary conditions, though these were once thought to automatically raise returns.

(Let's push our bond-as-a-business example one notch further: if you elect to "retain" the annual earnings of a 12% bond by using the proceeds from coupons to buy more bonds, earnings of that bond "business" will grow at a rate comparable to that of most operating businesses that similarly reinvest all earnings. In the first instance, a 30-year, zero-coupon, 12% bond purchased today for $10 million will be worth $300 million in 2015. In the second, a $10 million business that regularly earns 12% on equity and retains all earnings to grow, will also end up with $300 million of capital in 2015. Both the business and the bond will earn over $32 million in the final year.)

Our approach to bond investment—treating it as an unusual sort of "business" with special advantages and disadvantages—may strike you as a bit quirky. However, we believe that many staggering errors by investors could have been avoided if they had viewed bond investment with a businessman's perspective. For example, in 1946, 20-year AAA tax-exempt bonds traded at slightly below a 1% yield. In effect, the buyer of those bonds at that time bought a "business" that earned about 1% on "book value" (and that, moreover, could never earn a dime more than 1% on book), and paid 100 cents on the dollar for that abominable business.

If an investor had been business-minded enough to think in those terms—and that was the precise reality of the bargain struck—he would have laughed at the proposition and walked away. For, at the same time, businesses with excellent future prospects could have been bought at, or close to, book value while earning 10%, 12%, or 15% after tax on book. Probably no business in America changed hands in 1946 at book value that the buyer believed lacked the ability to earn more than 1% on book. But investors with bond-buying habits eagerly made economic commitments throughout the year on just that basis. Similar, although less extreme, conditions prevailed for the next two decades as bond investors happily signed up for twenty or thirty years on terms outrageously inadequate by business standards. (In what I think is by far the best book on investing ever written—"The Intelligent Investor", by Ben Graham—the last section of the last chapter begins with, "Investment is most intelligent when it is most businesslike." This section is called "A Final Word", and it is appropriately titled.)

We will emphasize again that there is unquestionably some risk in the WPPSS commitment. It is also the sort of risk that is difficult to evaluate. Were Charlie and I to deal with 50 similar evaluations over a lifetime, we would expect our judgment to prove reasonably satisfactory. But we do not get the chance to make 50 or even 5 such decisions in a single year. Even though our long-term results may turn out fine, in any given year we run a risk that we will look extraordinarily foolish. (That's why all of these sentences say "Charlie and I", or "we".)

Most managers have very little incentive to make the intelligent-but-with-some-chance-of-looking-like-an-idiot decision. Their personal gain/loss ratio is all too obvious: if an unconventional decision works out well, they get a pat on the back and, if it works out poorly, they get a pink slip. (Failing conventionally is the route to go; as a group, lemmings may have a rotten image, but no individual lemming has ever received bad press.)

Our equation is different. With 47% of Berkshire's stock, Charlie and I don't worry about being fired, and we receive our rewards as owners, not managers. Thus we behave with Berkshire's money as we would with our own. That frequently leads us to unconventional behavior both in investments and general business management.

We remain unconventional in the degree to which we concentrate the investments of our insurance companies, including those in WPPSS bonds. This concentration makes sense only because our insurance business is conducted from a position of exceptional financial strength. For almost all other insurers, a comparable degree of concentration (or anything close to it) would be totally inappropriate. Their capital positions are not strong enough to withstand a big error, no matter how attractive an investment opportunity might appear when analyzed on the basis of probabilities.

With our financial strength we can own large blocks of a few securities that we have thought hard about and bought at attractive prices. (Billy Rose described the problem of over-diversification: "If you have a harem of forty women, you never get to know any of them very well.") Over time our policy of concentration should produce superior results, though these will be tempered by our large size. When this policy produces a really bad year, as it must, at least you will know that our money was committed on the same basis as yours.

We made the major part of our WPPSS investment at different prices and under somewhat different factual circumstances than exist at present. If we decide to change our position, we will not inform shareholders until long after the change has been completed. (We may be buying or selling as you read this.) The buying and selling of securities is a competitive business, and even a modest amount of added competition on either side can cost us a great deal of money. Our WPPSS purchases illustrate this principle. From October, 1983 through June, 1984, we attempted to buy almost all the bonds that we could of Projects 1, 2, and 3. Yet we purchased less than 3% of the bonds outstanding. Had we faced even a few additional well-heeled investors, stimulated to buy because they knew we were, we could have ended up with a materially smaller amount of bonds, purchased at a materially higher price. (A couple of coat-tail riders easily could have cost us $5 million.) For this reason, we will not comment about our activities in securities—neither to the press, nor shareholders, nor to anyone else—unless legally required to do so.

One final observation regarding our WPPSS purchases: we dislike the purchase of most long-term bonds under most circumstances and have bought very few in recent years. That's because bonds are as sound as a dollar—and we view the long-term outlook for dollars as dismal. We believe substantial inflation lies ahead, although we have no idea what the average rate will turn out to be. Furthermore, we think there is a small, but not insignificant, chance of runaway inflation.

Such a possibility may seem absurd, considering the rate to which inflation has dropped. But we believe that present fiscal policy—featuring a huge deficit—is both extremely dangerous and difficult to reverse. (So far, most politicians in both parties have followed Charlie Brown's advice: "No problem is so big that it can't be run away from.") Without a reversal, high rates of inflation may be delayed (perhaps for a long time), but will not be avoided. If high rates materialize, they bring with them the potential for a runaway upward spiral.

While there is not much to choose between bonds and stocks (as a class) when annual inflation is in the 5%-10% range, runaway inflation is a different story. In that circumstance, a diversified stock portfolio would almost surely suffer an enormous loss in real value. But bonds already outstanding would suffer far more. Thus, we think an all-bond portfolio carries a small but unacceptable "wipe out" risk, and we require any purchase of long-term bonds to clear a special hurdle. Only when bond purchases appear decidedly superior to other business opportunities will we engage in them. Those occasions are likely to be few and far between.

Dividend Policy

Dividend policy is often reported to shareholders, but seldom explained. A company will say something like, "Our goal is to pay out 40% to 50% of earnings and to increase dividends at a rate at least equal to the rise in the CPI". And that's it—no analysis will be supplied as to why that particular policy is best for the owners of the business. Yet, allocation of capital is crucial to business and investment management. Because it is, we believe managers and owners should think hard about the circumstances under which earnings should be retained and under which they should be distributed.

The first point to understand is that all earnings are not created equal. In many businesses particularly those that have high asset/profit ratios—inflation causes some or all of the reported earnings to become ersatz. The ersatz portion—let's call these earnings "restricted"—cannot, if the business is to retain its economic position, be distributed as dividends. Were these earnings to be paid out, the business would lose ground in one or more of the following areas: its ability to maintain its unit volume of sales, its long-term competitive position, its financial strength. No matter how conservative its payout ratio, a company that consistently distributes restricted earnings is destined for oblivion unless equity capital is otherwise infused.

Restricted earnings are seldom valueless to owners, but they often must be discounted heavily. In effect, they are conscripted by the business, no matter how poor its economic potential. (This retention-no-matter-how-unattractive-the-return situation was communicated unwittingly in a marvelously ironic way by Consolidated Edison a decade ago. At the time, a punitive regulatory policy was a major factor causing the company's stock to sell as low as one-fourth of book value; i.e., every time a dollar of earnings was retained for reinvestment in the business, that dollar was transformed into only 25 cents of market value. But, despite this gold-into-lead process, most earnings were reinvested in the business rather than paid to owners. Meanwhile, at construction and maintenance sites throughout New York, signs proudly proclaimed the corporate slogan, "Dig We Must".)

Restricted earnings need not concern us further in this dividend discussion. Let's turn to the much-more-valued unrestricted variety. These earnings may, with equal feasibility, be retained or distributed. In our opinion, management should choose whichever course makes greater sense for the owners of the business.

This principle is not universally accepted. For a number of reasons managers like to withhold unrestricted, readily distributable earnings from shareholders—to expand the corporate empire over which the managers rule, to operate from a position of exceptional financial comfort, etc. But we believe there is only one valid reason for retention. Unrestricted earnings should be retained only when there is a reasonable prospect—backed preferably by historical evidence or, when appropriate, by a thoughtful analysis of the future—that *for every dollar retained by the corporation, at least one dollar of market value will be created for owners.* This will happen only if the capital retained produces incremental earnings equal to, or above, those generally available to investors.

To illustrate, let's assume that an investor owns a risk-free 10% perpetual bond with one very unusual feature. Each year the investor can elect either to take his 10% coupon in cash, or to reinvest the coupon in more 10% bonds with identical terms; i.e., a perpetual life and coupons offering the same cash-or-reinvest option. If, in any given year, the prevailing interest rate on long-term, risk-free bonds is 5%, it would be foolish for the investor to take his coupon in cash since the 10% bonds he could instead choose would be worth considerably more than 100 cents on the dollar. Under these circumstances, the investor wanting to get his hands on cash should take his coupon in additional bonds and then immediately sell them. By doing that, he would realize more cash than if he had taken his coupon directly in cash. Assuming all bonds were held by rational investors, no one would opt for cash in an era of 5% interest rates, not even those bondholders needing cash for living purposes.

If, however, interest rates were 15%, no rational investor would want his money invested for him at 10%. Instead, the investor would choose to take his coupon in cash, even if his personal cash needs were nil. The opposite course—reinvestment of the coupon—would give an investor additional bonds with market value far less than the cash he could have elected. If he should want 10% bonds, he can simply take the cash received and buy them in the market, where they will be available at a large discount.

An analysis similar to that made by our hypothetical bondholder is appropriate for owners in thinking about whether a company's unrestricted earnings should be retained or paid out. Of course, the analysis is much more difficult and subject to error because the rate earned on reinvested earnings is not a contractual figure, as in our bond case, but rather a fluctuating figure. Owners must guess as to what the rate will average over the intermediate future. However, once an informed guess is made, the rest of the analysis is simple: you should wish your earnings to be reinvested if they can be expected to earn high returns, and you should wish them paid to you if low returns are the likely outcome of reinvestment.

Many corporate managers reason very much along these lines in determining whether subsidiaries should distribute earnings to their parent company. At that level,. the managers have no trouble thinking like intelligent owners. But payout decisions at the parent company level often are a different story. Here managers frequently have trouble putting themselves in the shoes of their shareholder-owners.

With this schizoid approach, the CEO of a multi-divisional company will instruct Subsidiary A, whose earnings on incremental capital may be expected to average 5%, to distribute all available earnings in order that they may be invested in Subsidiary B, whose earnings on incremental capital are expected to be 15%. The CEO's business school oath will allow no lesser behavior. But if his own long-term record with incremental capital is 5%—and market rates are 10%—he is likely to impose a dividend policy on shareholders of the parent company that merely follows some historical or industry-wide payout pattern. Furthermore, he will expect managers of subsidiaries to give him a full account as to why it makes sense for earnings to be retained in their operations rather than distributed to the parent-owner. But seldom will he supply his owners with a similar analysis pertaining to the whole company.

In judging whether managers should retain earnings, shareholders should not simply compare total incremental earnings in recent years to total incremental capital because that relationship may be distorted by what is going on in a core business. During an inflationary period, companies with a core business characterized by extraordinary economics can use small amounts of incremental capital in that business at very high rates of return (as was discussed in last year's section on Goodwill). But, unless they are experiencing tremendous unit growth, outstanding businesses by definition generate large amounts of excess cash. If a company sinks most of this money in other businesses that earn low returns, the company's overall return on retained capital may nevertheless appear excellent because of the extraordinary returns being earned by the portion of earnings incrementally invested in the core business. The situation is analogous to a Pro-Am golf event: even if all of the amateurs are hopeless duffers, the team's best-ball score will be respectable because of the dominating skills of the professional.

Many corporations that consistently show good returns both on equity and on overall incremental capital have, indeed, employed a large portion of their retained earnings on an economically unattractive, even disastrous, basis. Their marvelous core businesses, however, whose earnings grow year after year, camouflage repeated failures in capital allocation elsewhere (usually involving high-priced acquisitions of businesses that have inherently mediocre economics). The managers at fault periodically report on the lessons they have learned from the latest disappointment. They then usually seek out future lessons. (Failure seems to go to their heads.)

In such cases, shareholders would be far better off if earnings were retained only to expand the high-return business, with the balance paid in dividends or used to repurchase stock (an action that increases the owners' interest in the exceptional business while sparing them participation in subpar businesses). Managers of high-return businesses who consistently employ much of the cash thrown off by those businesses in other ventures with low returns should be held to account for those allocation decisions, regardless of how profitable the overall enterprise is.

Nothing in this discussion is intended to argue for dividends that bounce around from quarter to quarter with each wiggle in earnings or in investment opportunities. Shareholders of public corporations understandably prefer that dividends be consistent and predictable. Payments, therefore, should reflect long-term expectations for both earnings and returns on incremental capital. Since the long-term corporate outlook changes only infrequently, dividend patterns should change no more often. But over time distributable earnings that have been withheld by managers should earn their keep. If earnings have been unwisely retained, it is likely that managers, too, have been unwisely retained.

Let's now turn to Berkshire Hathaway and examine how these dividend principles apply to it. Historically, Berkshire has earned well over market rates on retained earnings, thereby creating over one dollar of market value for every dollar retained. Under such circumstances, any distribution would have been contrary to the financial interest of shareholders, large or small.

In fact, significant distributions in the early years might have been disastrous, as a review of our starting position will show you. Charlie and I then controlled and managed three companies, Berkshire Hathaway Inc., Diversified Retailing Company, Inc., and Blue Chip Stamps (all now merged into our present operation). Blue Chip paid only a small dividend, Berkshire and DRC paid nothing. If, instead, the companies had paid out their entire earnings, we almost certainly would have no earnings at all now—and perhaps no capital as well. The three companies each originally made their money from a single business: (1) textiles at Berkshire; (2) department stores at Diversified; and (3) trading stamps at Blue Chip. These cornerstone businesses (carefully chosen, it should be noted, by your Chairman and Vice Chairman) have, respectively, (1) survived but earned almost nothing, (2) shriveled in size while incurring large losses, and (3) shrunk in sales volume to about 5% its size at the time of our entry. (Who says "you can't lose 'em all"?) Only by committing available funds to much better businesses were we able to overcome these origins. (It's been like overcoming a misspent youth.) Clearly, diversification has served us well.

We expect to continue to diversify while also supporting the growth of current operations though, as we've pointed out, our returns from these efforts will surely be below our historical returns. But as long as prospective returns are above the rate required to produce a dollar of market value per dollar retained, we will continue to retain all earnings. Should our estimate of future returns fall below that point, we will distribute all unrestricted earnings that we believe can not be effectively used. In making that judgment, we will look at both our historical record and our prospects. Because our year-to-year results are inherently volatile, we believe a five-year rolling average to be appropriate for judging the historical record.

Our present plan is to use our retained earnings to further build the capital of our insurance companies. Most of our competitors are in weakened financial condition and reluctant to expand substantially. Yet large premium-volume gains for the industry are imminent, amounting probably to well over $15 billion in 1985 versus less than $5 billion in 1983. These circumstances could produce major amounts of profitable business for us. Of course, this result is no sure thing, but prospects for it are far better than they have been for many years.

Miscellaneous

This is the spot where each year I run my small "business wanted" ad. In 1984 John Loomis, one of our particularly knowledgeable and alert shareholders, came up with a company that met all of our tests. We immediately pursued this idea, and only a chance complication prevented a deal. Since our ad is pulling, we will repeat it in precisely last year's form:

We prefer:

(1) large purchases (at least $5 million of after-tax earnings),

(2) demonstrated consistent earning power (future projections are of little interest to us, nor are "turn-around" situations),

(3) businesses earning good returns on equity while employing little or no debt,

(4) management in place (we can't supply it),

(5) simple businesses (if there's lots of technology, we won't understand it),

(6) an offering price (we don't want to waste our time or that of the seller by talking, even preliminarily, about a transaction when price is unknown).

We will not engage in unfriendly takeovers. We can promise complete confidentiality and a very fast answer—customarily within five minutes—as to whether we're interested. We prefer to buy for cash, but will consider issuance of stock when we receive as much in intrinsic business value as we give. We invite potential sellers to check us out by contacting people with whom we have done business in the past. For the right business—and the right people—we can provide a good home.

* * *

A record 97.2% of all eligible shares participated in Berkshire's 1984 shareholder-designated contributions program. Total contributions made through this program were $3,179,000, and 1,519 charities were recipients. Our proxy material for the annual meeting will allow you to cast an advisory vote expressing your views about this program—whether you think we should continue it and, if so, at what per-share level. (You may be interested to learn that we were unable to find a precedent for an advisory vote in which management seeks the opinions of shareholders about owner-related corporate policies. Managers who put their trust in capitalism seem in no hurry to put their trust in capitalists.)

We urge new shareholders to read the description of our shareholder-designated contributions program that appears on pages 60 and 61. If you wish to participate in future programs, we strongly urge that you immediately make sure that your shares are registered in the name of the actual owner, not in "street" name or nominee name. Shares not so registered on September 30, 1985 will be ineligible for the 1985 program.

* * *

Our annual meeting will be on May 21, 1985 in Omaha, and I hope that you attend. Many annual meetings are a waste of time, both for shareholders and for management. Sometimes that is true because management is reluctant to open up on matters of business substance. More often a nonproductive session is the fault of shareholder participants who are more concerned about their own moment on stage than they are about the affairs of the corporation. What should be a forum for business discussion becomes a forum for theatrics, spleen-venting and advocacy of issues. (The deal is irresistible: for the price of one share you get to tell a captive audience your ideas as to how the world should be run.) Under such circumstances, the quality of the meeting often deteriorates from year to year as the antics of those interested in themselves discourage attendance by those interested in the business.

Berkshire's meetings are a different story. The number of shareholders attending grows a bit each year and we have yet to experience a silly question or an ego-inspired commentary. Instead, we get a wide variety of thoughtful questions about the business. Because the annual meeting is the time and place for these, Charlie and I are happy to answer them all, no matter how long it takes. (We cannot, however, respond to written or phoned questions at other times of the year; one-person-at-a time reporting is a poor use of management time in a company with 3000 shareholders.) The only business matters that are off limits at the annual meeting are those about which candor might cost our company real money. Our activities in securities would be the main example.

We always have bragged a bit on these pages about the quality of our shareholder-partners. Come to the annual meeting and you will see why. Out-of-towners should schedule a stop at Nebraska Furniture Mart. If you make some purchases, you'll save far more than enough to pay for your trip, and you'll enjoy the experience.

February 25, 1985

Warren E. Buffett
Chairman of the Board

Subsequent Event: On March 18, a week after copy for this report went to the typographer but shortly before production, we agreed to purchase three million shares of Capital Cities Communications, Inc. at $172.50 per share. Our purchase is contingent upon the acquisition of American Broadcasting Companies, Inc. by Capital Cities, and will close when that transaction closes. At the earliest, that will be very late in 1985. Our admiration for the management of Capital Cities, led by Tom Murphy and Dan Burke, has been expressed several times in previous annual reports. Quite simply, they are tops in both ability and integrity. We will have more to say about this investment in next year's report.

BERKSHIRE HATHAWAY INC.

To the Shareholders of Berkshire Hathaway Inc.:

You may remember the wildly upbeat message of last year's report: nothing much was in the works but our experience had been that something big popped up occasionally. This carefully-crafted corporate strategy paid off in 1985. Later sections of this report discuss (a) our purchase of a major position in Capital Cities/ABC, (b) our acquisition of Scott & Fetzer, (c) our entry into a large, extended term participation in the insurance business of Fireman's Fund, and (d) our sale of our stock in General Foods.

Our gain in net worth during the year was $613.6 million, or 48.2%. It is fitting that the visit of Halley's Comet coincided with this percentage gain: neither will be seen again in my lifetime. Our gain in per-share book value over the last twenty-one years (that is, since present management took over) has been from $19.46 to $1643.71, or 23.2% compounded annually, another percentage that will not be repeated.

Two factors make anything approaching this rate of gain unachievable in the future. One factor probably transitory—is a stock market that offers very little opportunity compared to the markets that prevailed throughout much of the 1964-1984 period. Today we cannot find significantly-undervalued equities to purchase for our insurance company portfolios. The current situation is 180 degrees removed from that existing about a decade ago, when the only question was which bargain to choose.

This change in the market also has negative implications for our present portfolio. In our 1974 annual report I could say: "We consider several of our major holdings to have great potential for significantly increased values in future years." I can't say that now. It's true that our insurance companies currently hold major positions in companies with exceptional underlying economics and outstanding managements, just as they did in 1974. But current market prices generously appraise these attributes, whereas they were ignored in 1974. Today's valuations mean that our insurance companies have no chance for future portfolio gains on the scale of those achieved in the past.

The second negative factor, far more telling, is our size. Our equity capital is more than twenty times what it was only ten years ago. And an iron law of business is that growth eventually dampens exceptional economics. just look at the records of high-return companies once they have amassed even $1 billion of equity capital. None that I know of has managed subsequently, over a ten-year period, to keep on earning 20% or more on equity while reinvesting all or substantially all of its earnings. Instead, to sustain their high returns, such companies have needed to shed a lot of capital by way of either dividends or repurchases of stock. Their shareholders would have been far better off if all earnings could have been reinvested at the fat returns earned by these exceptional businesses. But the companies simply couldn't turn up enough high-return opportunities to make that possible.

Their problem is our problem. Last year I told you that we needed profits of $3.9 billion over the ten years then coming up to earn 15% annually. The comparable figure for the ten years now ahead is $5.7 billion, a 48% increase that corresponds—as it must mathematically—to the growth in our capital base during 1985. (Here's a little perspective: leaving aside oil companies, only about 15 U.S. businesses have managed to earn over $5.7 billion during the past ten years.)

Charlie Munger, my partner in managing Berkshire, and I are reasonably optimistic about Berkshire's ability to earn returns superior to those earned by corporate America generally, and you will benefit from the company's retention of all earnings as long as those returns are forthcoming. We have several things going for us: (1) we don't have to worry about quarterly or annual figures but, instead, can focus on whatever actions will maximize long-term value; (2) we can expand the business into any areas that make sense—our scope is not circumscribed by history, structure, or concept; and (3) we love our work. All of these help. Even so, we will also need a full measure of good fortune to average our hoped-for 15%—far more good fortune than was required for our past 23.2%.

We need to mention one further item in the investment equation that could affect recent purchasers of our stock. Historically, Berkshire shares have sold modestly below intrinsic business value. With the price there, purchasers could be certain (as long as they did not experience a widening of this discount) that their personal investment experience would at least equal the financial experience of the business. But recently the discount has disappeared, and occasionally a modest premium has prevailed.

The elimination of the discount means that Berkshire's market value increased even faster than business value (which, itself, grew at a pleasing pace). That was good news for any owner holding while that move took place, but it is bad news for the new or prospective owner. If the financial experience of new owners of Berkshire is merely to match the future financial experience of the company, any premium of market value over intrinsic business value that they pay must be maintained.

Management cannot determine market prices, although it can, by its disclosures and policies, encourage rational behavior by market participants. My own preference, as perhaps you'd guess, is for a market price that consistently approximates business value. Given that relationship, all owners prosper precisely as the business prospers during their period of ownership. Wild swings in market prices far above and below business value do not change the final gains for owners in aggregate; in the end, investor gains must equal business gains. But long periods of substantial undervaluation and/or overvaluation will cause the gains of the business to be inequitably distributed among various owners, with the investment result of any given owner largely depending upon how lucky, shrewd, or foolish he happens to be.

Over the long term there has been a more consistent relationship between Berkshire's market value and business value than has existed for any other publicly-traded equity with which I am familiar. This is a tribute to you. Because you have been rational, interested, and investment-oriented, the market price for Berkshire stock has almost always been sensible. This unusual result has been achieved by a shareholder group with unusual demographics: virtually all of our shareholders are individuals, not institutions. No other public company our size can claim the same.

You might think that institutions, with their large staffs of highly-paid and experienced investment professionals, would be a force for stability and reason in financial markets. They are not: stocks heavily owned and constantly monitored by institutions have often been among the most inappropriately valued.

Ben Graham told a story 40 years ago that illustrates why investment professionals behave as they do: An oil prospector, moving to his heavenly reward, was met by St. Peter with bad news. "You're qualified for residence", said St. Peter, "but, as you can see, the compound reserved for oil men is packed. There's no way to squeeze you in." After thinking a moment, the prospector asked if he might say just four words to the present occupants. That seemed harmless to St. Peter, so the prospector cupped his hands and yelled, "Oil discovered in hell." Immediately the gate to the compound opened and all of the oil men marched out to head for the nether regions. Impressed, St. Peter invited the prospector to move in and make himself comfortable. The prospector paused. "No," he said, "I think I'll go along with the rest of the boys. There might be some truth to that rumor after all."

Sources of Reported Earnings

The table on the next page shows the major sources of Berkshire's reported earnings. These numbers, along with far more detailed sub-segment numbers, are the ones that Charlie and I focus upon. We do not find consolidated figures an aid in either managing or evaluating Berkshire and, in fact, never prepare them for internal use.

Segment information is equally essential for investors wanting to know what is going on in a multi-line business. Corporate managers always have insisted upon such information before making acquisition decisions but, until a few years ago, seldom made it available to investors faced with acquisition and disposition decisions of their own. Instead, when owners wishing to understand the economic realities of their business asked for data, managers usually gave them a we-can't-tell-you-what-is-going-on-because-it-would-hurt-the-company answer. Ultimately the SEC ordered disclosure of segment data and management began supplying real answers. The change in their behavior recalls an insight of Al Capone: "You can get much further with a kind word and a gun than you can with a kind word alone."

In the table, amortization of Goodwill is not charged against the specific businesses but, for reasons outlined in the Appendix to my letter in the 1983 annual report, is aggregated as a separate item. (A compendium of the 1977-1984 letters is available upon request.) In the Business Segment Data and Management's Discussion sections on pages 39-41 and 49-55, much additional information regarding our businesses is provided, including Goodwill and Goodwill Amortization figures for each of the segments. I urge you to read those sections as well as Charlie Munger's letter to Wesco shareholders, which starts on page 56.

| | (000s omitted) | | | |
| | Pre-Tax Earnings | | Berkshire's Share of Net Earnings (after taxes and minority interests) | |
	1985	1984	1985	1984
Operating Earnings:				
Insurance Group:				
Underwriting	$(44,230)	$(48,060)	$(23,569)	$(25,955)
Net Investment Income	95,217	68,903	79,716	62,059
Associated Retail Stores	270	(1,072)	134	(579)
Blue Chip Stamps	5,763	(1,843)	2,813	(899)
Buffalo News	29,921	27,328	14,580	13,317
Mutual Savings and Loan	2,622	1,456	4,016	3,151
Nebraska Furniture Mart	12,686	14,511	5,181	5,917
Precision Steel	3,896	4,092	1,477	1,696
See's Candies	28,989	26,644	14,558	13,380
Textiles	(2,395)	418	(1,324)	226
Wesco Financial	9,500	9,777	4,191	4,828
Amortization of Goodwill	(1,475)	(1,434)	(1,475)	(1,434)
Interest on Debt	(14,415)	(14,734)	(7,288)	(7,452)
Shareholder-Designated Contributions	(4,006)	(3,179)	(2,164)	(1,716)
Other	3,106	4,932	2,102	3,475
Operating Earnings	125,449	87,739	92,948	70,014
Special General Foods Distribution	4,127	8,111	3,779	7,294
Special Washington Post Distribution	14,877	---	13,851	---
Sales of Securities	468,903	104,699	325,237	71,587
Total Earnings – all entities	$613,356	$200,549	$435,815	$148,895

Our 1985 results include unusually large earnings from the sale of securities. This fact, in itself, does not mean that we had a particularly good year (though, of course, we did). Security profits in a given year bear similarities to a college graduation ceremony in which the knowledge gained over four years is recognized on a day when nothing further is learned. We may hold a stock for a decade or more, and during that period it may grow quite consistently in both business and market value. In the year in which we finally sell it there may be no increase in value, or there may even be a decrease. But all growth in value since purchase will be reflected in the accounting earnings of the year of sale. (If the stock owned is in our insurance subsidiaries, however, any gain or loss in market value will be reflected in net worth annually.) Thus, reported capital gains or losses in any given year are meaningless as a measure of how well we have done in the current year.

A large portion of the realized gain in 1985 ($338 million pre-tax out of a total of $488 million) came about through the sale of our General Foods shares. We held most of these shares since 1980, when we had purchased them at a price far below what we felt was their per/share business value. Year by year, the managerial efforts of Jim Ferguson and Phil Smith substantially increased General Foods' business value and, last fall, Philip Morris made an offer for the company that reflected the increase. We thus benefited from four factors: a bargain purchase price, a business with fine underlying economics, an able management concentrating on the interests of shareholders, and a buyer willing to pay full business value. While that last factor is the only one that produces reported earnings, we consider identification of the first three to be the key to building value for Berkshire shareholders. In selecting common stocks, we devote our attention to attractive purchases, not to the possibility of attractive sales.

We have again reported substantial income from special distributions, this year from Washington Post and General Foods. (The General Foods transactions obviously took place well before the Philip Morris offer.) Distributions of this kind occur when we sell a portion of our shares in a company back to it simultaneously with its purchase of shares from other shareholders. The number of shares we sell is contractually set so as to leave our percentage ownership in the company precisely the same after the sale as before. Such a transaction is quite properly regarded by the IRS as substantially equivalent to a dividend since we, as a shareholder, receive cash while maintaining an unchanged ownership interest. This tax treatment benefits us because corporate taxpayers, unlike individual taxpayers, incur much lower taxes on dividend income than on income from long-term capital gains. (This difference will be widened further if the House-passed tax bill becomes law: under its provisions, capital gains realized by corporations will be taxed at the same rate as ordinary income.) However, accounting rules are unclear as to proper treatment for shareholder reporting. To conform with last year's treatment, we have shown these transactions as capital gains.

Though we have not sought out such transactions, we have agreed to them on several occasions when managements initiated the idea. In each case we have felt that non-selling shareholders (all of whom had an opportunity to sell at the same price we received) benefited because the companies made their repurchases at prices below intrinsic business value. The tax advantages we receive and our wish to cooperate with managements that are increasing values for all shareholders have sometimes led us to sell—but only to the extent that our proportional share of the business was undiminished.

At this point we usually turn to a discussion of some of our major business units. Before doing so, however, we should first look at a failure at one of our smaller businesses. Our Vice Chairman, Charlie Munger, has always emphasized the study of mistakes rather than successes, both in business and other aspects of life. He does so in the spirit of the man who said: "All I want to know is where I'm going to die so I'll never go there." You'll immediately see why we make a good team: Charlie likes to study errors and I have generated ample material for him, particularly in our textile and insurance businesses.

Shutdown of Textile Business

In July we decided to close our textile operation, and by yearend this unpleasant job was largely completed. The history of this business is instructive.

When Buffett Partnership, Ltd., an investment partnership of which I was general partner, bought control of Berkshire Hathaway 21 years ago, it had an accounting net worth of $22 million, all devoted to the textile business. The company's intrinsic business value, however, was considerably less because the textile assets were unable to earn returns commensurate with their accounting value. Indeed, during the previous nine years (the period in which Berkshire and Hathaway operated as a merged company) aggregate sales of $530 million had produced an aggregate loss of $10 million. Profits had been reported from time to time but the net effect was always one step forward, two steps back.

At the time we made our purchase, southern textile plants—largely non-union—were believed to have an important competitive advantage. Most northern textile operations had closed and many people thought we would liquidate our business as well.

We felt, however, that the business would be run much better by a long-time employee whom. we immediately selected to be president, Ken Chace. In this respect we were 100% correct: Ken and his recent successor, Garry Morrison, have been excellent managers, every bit the equal of managers at our more profitable businesses.

In early 1967 cash generated by the textile operation was used to fund our entry into insurance via the purchase of National Indemnity Company. Some of the money came from earnings and some from reduced investment in textile inventories, receivables, and fixed assets. This pullback proved wise: although much improved by Ken's management, the textile business never became a good earner, not even in cyclical upturns.

Further diversification for Berkshire followed, and gradually the textile operation's depressing effect on our overall return diminished as the business became a progressively smaller portion of the corporation. We remained in the business for reasons that I stated in the 1978 annual report (and summarized at other times also): "(1) our textile businesses are very important employers in their communities, (2) management has been straightforward in reporting on problems and energetic in attacking them, (3) labor has been cooperative and understanding in facing our common problems, and (4) the business should average modest cash returns relative to investment." I further said, "As long as these conditions prevail—and we expect that they will—we intend to continue to support our textile business despite more attractive alternative uses for capital."

It turned out that I was very wrong about (4). Though 1979 was moderately profitable, the business thereafter consumed major amounts of cash. By mid-1985 it became clear, even to me, that this condition was almost sure to continue. Could we have found a buyer who would continue operations, I would have certainly preferred to sell the business rather than liquidate it, even if that meant somewhat lower proceeds for us. But the economics that were finally obvious to me were also obvious to others, and interest was nil.

I won't close down businesses of sub-normal profitability merely to add a fraction of a point to our corporate rate of return. However, I also feel it inappropriate for even an exceptionally profitable company to fund an operation once it appears to have unending losses in prospect. Adam Smith would disagree with my first proposition, and Karl Marx would disagree with my second; the middle ground is the only position that leaves me comfortable.

I should reemphasize that Ken and Garry have been resourceful, energetic and imaginative in attempting to make our textile operation a success. Trying to achieve sustainable profitability, they reworked product lines, machinery configurations and distribution arrangements. We also made a major acquisition, Waumbec Mills, with the expectation of important synergy (a term widely used in business to explain an acquisition that otherwise makes no sense). But in the end nothing worked and I should be faulted for not quitting sooner. A recent *Business Week* article stated that 250 textile mills have closed since 1980. Their owners were not privy to any information that was unknown to me; they simply processed it more objectively. I ignored Comte's advice—"the intellect should be the servant of the heart, but not its slave"—and believed what I preferred to believe.

The domestic textile industry operates in a commodity business, competing in a world market in which substantial excess capacity exists. Much of the trouble we experienced was attributable, both directly and indirectly, to competition from foreign countries whose workers are paid a small fraction of the U.S. minimum wage. But that in no way means that our labor force deserves any blame for our closing. In fact, in comparison with employees of American industry generally, our workers were poorly paid, as has been the case throughout the textile business. In contract negotiations, union leaders and members were sensitive to our disadvantageous cost position and did not push for unrealistic wage increases or unproductive work practices. To the contrary, they tried just as hard as we did to keep us competitive. Even during our liquidation period they performed superbly. (Ironically, we would have been better off financially if our union had behaved unreasonably some years ago; we then would have recognized the impossible future that we faced, promptly closed down, and avoided significant future losses.)

Over the years, we had the option of making large capital expenditures in the textile operation that would have allowed us to somewhat reduce variable costs. Each proposal to do so looked like an immediate winner. Measured by standard return-on-investment tests, in fact, these proposals usually promised greater economic benefits than would have resulted from comparable expenditures in our highly-profitable candy and newspaper businesses.

But the promised benefits from these textile investments were illusory. Many of our competitors, both domestic and foreign, were stepping up to the same kind of expenditures and, once enough companies did so, their reduced costs became the baseline for reduced prices industrywide. Viewed individually, each company's capital investment decision appeared cost-effective and rational; viewed collectively, the decisions neutralized each other and were irrational (just as happens when each person watching a parade decides he can see a little better if he stands on tiptoes). After each round of investment, all the players had more money in the game and returns remained anemic.

Thus, we faced a miserable choice: huge capital investment would have helped to keep our textile business alive, but would have left us with terrible returns on ever-growing amounts of capital. After the investment, moreover, the foreign competition would still have retained a major, continuing advantage in labor costs. A refusal to invest, however, would make us increasingly non-competitive, even measured against domestic textile manufacturers. I always thought myself in the position described by Woody Allen in one of his movies: "More than any other time in history, mankind faces a crossroads. One path leads to despair and utter hopelessness, the other to total extinction. Let us pray we have the wisdom to choose correctly."

For an understanding of how the to-invest-or-not-to-invest dilemma plays out in a commodity business, it is instructive to look at Burlington Industries, by far the largest U.S. textile company both 21 years ago and now. In 1964 Burlington had sales of $1.2 billion against our $50 million. It had strengths in both distribution and production that we could never hope to match and also, of course, had an earnings record far superior to ours. Its stock sold at 60 at the end of 1964; ours was 13.

Burlington made a decision to stick to the textile business, and in 1985 had sales of about $2.8 billion. During the 1964-85 period, the company made capital expenditures of about $3 billion, far more than any other U.S. textile company and more than $200-per-share on that $60 stock. A very large part of the expenditures, I am sure, was devoted to cost improvement and expansion. Given Burlington's basic commitment to stay in textiles, I would also surmise that the company's capital decisions were quite rational.

Nevertheless, Burlington has lost sales volume in real dollars and has far lower returns on sales and equity now than 20 years ago. Split 2-for-1 in 1965, the stock now sells at 34—on an adjusted basis, just a little over its $60 price in 1964. Meanwhile, the CPI has more than tripled. Therefore, each share commands about one-third the purchasing power it did at the end of 1964. Regular dividends have been paid but they, too, have shrunk significantly in purchasing power.

This devastating outcome for the shareholders indicates what can happen when much brain power and energy are applied to a faulty premise. The situation is suggestive of Samuel Johnson's horse: "A horse that can count to ten is a remarkable horse—not a remarkable mathematician." Likewise, a textile company that allocates capital brilliantly within its industry is a remarkable textile company—but not a remarkable business.

My conclusion from my own experiences and from much observation of other businesses is that a good managerial record (measured by economic returns) is far more a function of what business boat you get into than it is of how effectively you row (though intelligence and effort help considerably, of course, in any business, good or bad). Some years ago I wrote: "When a management with a reputation for brilliance tackles a business with a reputation for poor fundamental economics, it is the reputation of the business that remains intact." Nothing has since changed my point of view on that matter. Should you find yourself in a chronically-leaking boat, energy devoted to changing vessels is likely to be more productive than energy devoted to patching leaks.

* * *

There is an investment postscript in our textile saga. Some investors weight book value heavily in their stock-buying decisions (as I, in my early years, did myself). And some economists and academicians believe replacement values are of considerable importance in calculating an appropriate price level for the stock market as a whole. Those of both persuasions would have received an education at the auction we held in early 1986 to dispose of our textile machinery.

The equipment sold (including some disposed of in the few months prior to the auction) took up about 750,000 square feet of factory space in New Bedford and was eminently usable. It originally cost us about $13 million, including $2 million spent in 1980-84, and had a current book value of $866,000 (after accelerated depreciation). Though no sane management would have made the investment, the equipment could have been replaced new for perhaps $30-$50 million.

Gross proceeds from our sale of this equipment came to $163,122. Allowing for necessary pre- and post-sale costs, our net was less than zero. Relatively modern looms that we bought for $5,000 apiece in 1981 found no takers at $50. We finally sold them for scrap at $26 each, a sum less than removal costs.

Ponder this: the economic goodwill attributable to two paper routes in Buffalo—or a single See's candy store—considerably exceeds the proceeds we received from this massive collection of tangible assets that not too many years ago, under different competitive conditions, was able to employ over 1,000 people.

Three Very Good Businesses (and a Few Thoughts About Incentive Compensation)

When I was 12, I lived with my grandfather for about four months. A grocer by trade, he was also working on a book and each night he dictated a few pages to me. The title—brace yourself—was "How to Run a Grocery Store and a Few Things I Have Learned About Fishing". My grandfather was sure that interest in these two subjects was universal and that the world awaited his views. You may conclude from this section's title and contents that I was overexposed to Grandpa's literary style (and personality).

I am merging the discussion of Nebraska Furniture Mart, See's Candy Shops, and Buffalo Evening News here because the economic strengths, weaknesses, and prospects of these businesses have changed little since I reported to you a year ago. The shortness of this discussion, however, is in no way meant to minimize the importance of these businesses to us: in 1985 they earned an aggregate of $72 million pre-tax. Fifteen years ago, before we had acquired any of them, their aggregate earnings were about $8 million pre-tax.

While an increase in earnings from $8 million to $72 million sounds terrific—and usually is—you should not automatically assume that to be the case. You must first make sure that earnings were not severely depressed in the base year. If they were instead substantial in relation to capital employed, an even more important point must be examined: how much additional capital was required to produce the additional earnings?

In both respects, our group of three scores well. First, earnings 15 years ago were excellent compared to capital then employed in the businesses. Second, although annual earnings are now $64 million greater, the businesses require only about $40 million more in invested capital to operate than was the case then.

The dramatic growth in earning power of these three businesses, accompanied by their need for only minor amounts of capital, illustrates very well the power of economic goodwill during an inflationary period (a phenomenon explained in detail in the 1983 annual report). The financial characteristics of these businesses have allowed us to use a very large portion of the earnings they generate elsewhere. Corporate America, however, has had a different experience: in order to increase earnings significantly, most companies have needed to increase capital significantly also. The average American business has required about $5 of additional capital to generate an additional $1 of annual pre-tax earnings. That business, therefore, would have required over $300 million in additional capital from its owners in order to achieve an earnings performance equal to our group of three.

When returns on capital are ordinary, an earn-more-by-putting-up-more record is no great managerial achievement. You can get the same result personally while operating from your rocking chair. just quadruple the capital you commit to a savings account and you will quadruple your earnings. You would hardly expect hosannas for that particular accomplishment. Yet, retirement announcements regularly sing the praises of CEOs who have, say, quadrupled earnings of their widget company during their reign—with no one examining whether this gain was attributable simply to many years of retained earnings and the workings of compound interest.

If the widget company consistently earned a superior return on capital throughout the period, or if capital employed only doubled during the CEO's reign, the praise for him may be well deserved. But if return on capital was lackluster and capital employed increased in pace with earnings, applause should be withheld. A savings account in which interest was reinvested would achieve the same year-by-year increase in earnings—and, at only 8% interest, would quadruple its annual earnings in 18 years.

The power of this simple math is often ignored by companies to the detriment of their shareholders. Many corporate compensation plans reward managers handsomely for earnings increases produced solely, or in large part, by retained earnings—i.e., earnings withheld from owners. For example, ten-year, fixed-price stock options are granted routinely, often by companies whose dividends are only a small percentage of earnings.

An example will illustrate the inequities possible under such circumstances. Let's suppose that you had a $100,000 savings account earning 8% interest and "managed" by a trustee who could decide each year what portion of the interest you were to be paid in cash. Interest not paid out would be "retained earnings" added to the savings account to compound. And let's suppose that your trustee, in his superior wisdom, set the "pay-out ratio" at one-quarter of the annual earnings.

Under these assumptions, your account would be worth $179,084 at the end of ten years. Additionally, your annual earnings would have increased about 70% from $8,000 to $13,515 under this inspired management. And, finally, your "dividends" would have increased commensurately, rising regularly from $2,000 in the first year to $3,378 in the tenth year. Each year, when your manager's public relations firm prepared his annual report to you, all of the charts would have had lines marching skyward.

Now, just for fun, let's push our scenario one notch further and give your trustee-manager a ten-year fixed-price option on part of your "business" (i.e., your savings account) based on its fair value in the first year. With such an option, your manager would reap a substantial profit at your expense—just from having held on to most of your earnings. If he were both Machiavellian and a bit of a mathematician, your manager might also have cut the pay-out ratio once he was firmly entrenched.

This scenario is not as farfetched as you might think. Many stock options in the corporate world have worked in exactly that fashion: they have gained in value simply because management retained earnings, not because it did well with the capital in its hands.

Managers actually apply a double standard to options. Leaving aside warrants (which deliver the issuing corporation immediate and substantial compensation), I believe it is fair to say that nowhere in the business world are ten-year fixed-price options on all or a portion of a business granted to outsiders. Ten months, in fact, would be regarded as extreme. It would be particularly unthinkable for managers to grant a long-term option on a business that was regularly adding to its capital. Any outsider wanting to secure such an option would be required to pay fully for capital added during the option period.

The unwillingness of managers to do-unto-outsiders, however, is not matched by an unwillingness to do-unto-themselves. (Negotiating with one's self seldom produces a barroom brawl.) Managers regularly engineer ten-year, fixed-price options for themselves and associates that, first, totally ignore the fact that retained earnings automatically build value and, second, ignore the carrying cost of capital. As a result, these managers end up profiting much as they would have had they had an option on that savings account that was automatically building up in value.

Of course, stock options often go to talented, value-adding managers and sometimes deliver them rewards that are perfectly appropriate. (Indeed, managers who are really exceptional almost always get far less than they should.) But when the result is equitable, it is accidental. Once granted, the option is blind to individual performance. Because it is irrevocable and unconditional (so long as a manager stays in the company), the sluggard receives rewards from his options precisely as does the star. A managerial Rip Van Winkle, ready to doze for ten years, could not wish for a better "incentive" system.

(I can't resist commenting on one long-term option given an "outsider": that granted the U.S. Government on Chrysler shares as partial consideration for the government's guarantee of some lifesaving loans. When these options worked out well for the government, Chrysler sought to modify the pay-off, arguing that the rewards to the government were both far greater than intended and outsize in relation to its contribution to Chrysler's recovery. The company's anguish over what it saw as an imbalance between payoff and performance made national news. That anguish may well be unique: to my knowledge, no managers—anywhere—have been similarly offended by unwarranted payoffs arising from options granted to themselves or their colleagues.)

Ironically, the rhetoric about options frequently describes them as desirable because they put managers and owners in the same financial boat. In reality, the boats are far different. No owner has ever escaped the burden of capital costs, whereas a holder of a fixed-price option bears no capital costs at all. An owner must weigh upside potential against downside risk; an option holder has no downside. In fact, the business project in which you would wish to have an option frequently is a project in which you would reject ownership. (I'll be happy to accept a lottery ticket as a gift—but I'll never buy one.)

In dividend policy also, the option holders' interests are best served by a policy that may ill serve the owner. Think back to the savings account example. The trustee, holding his option, would benefit from a no-dividend policy. Conversely, the owner of the account should lean to a total payout so that he can prevent the option-holding manager from sharing in the account's retained earnings.

Despite their shortcomings, options can be appropriate under some circumstances. My criticism relates to their indiscriminate use and, in that connection, I would like to emphasize three points:

First, stock options are inevitably tied to the overall performance of a corporation. Logically, therefore, they should be awarded only to those managers with overall responsibility. Managers with limited areas of responsibility should have incentives that pay off in relation to results under their control. The .350 hitter expects, and also deserves, a big payoff for his performance—even if he plays for a cellar-dwelling team. And the .150 hitter should get no reward—even if he plays for a pennant winner. Only those with overall responsibility for the team should have their rewards tied to its results.

Second, options should be structured carefully. Absent special factors, they should have built into them a retained-earnings or carrying-cost factor. Equally important, they should be priced realistically. When managers are faced with offers for their companies, they unfailingly point out how unrealistic market prices can be as an index of real value. But why, then, should these same depressed prices be the valuations at which managers sell portions of their businesses to themselves? (They may go further: officers and directors sometimes consult the Tax Code to determine the *lowest* prices at which they can, in effect, sell part of the business to insiders. While they're at it, they often elect plans that produce the worst tax result for the company.) Except in highly unusual cases, owners are not well served by the sale of part of their business at a bargain price—whether the sale is to outsiders or to insiders. The obvious conclusion: options should be priced at true business value.

Third, I want to emphasize that some managers whom I admire enormously—and whose operating records are far better than mine—disagree with me regarding fixed-price options. They have built corporate cultures that work, and fixed-price options have been a tool that helped them. By their leadership and example, and by the use of options as incentives, these managers have taught their colleagues to think like owners. Such a Culture is rare and when it exists should perhaps be left intact—despite inefficiencies and inequities that may infest the option program. "If it ain't broke, don't fix it" is preferable to "purity at any price".

At Berkshire, however, we use an incentive compensation system that rewards key managers for meeting targets in their own bailiwicks. If See's does well, that does not produce incentive compensation at the News—nor vice versa. Neither do we look at the price of Berkshire stock when we write bonus checks. We believe good unit performance should be rewarded whether Berkshire stock rises, falls, or stays even. Similarly, we think average performance should earn no special rewards even if our stock should soar. "Performance", furthermore, is defined in different ways depending upon the underlying economics of the business: in some our managers enjoy tailwinds not of their own making, in others they fight unavoidable headwinds.

The rewards that go with this system can be large. At our various business units, top managers sometimes receive incentive bonuses of five times their base salary, or more, and it would appear possible that one manager's bonus could top $2 million in 1986. (I hope so.) We do not put a cap on bonuses, and the potential for rewards is not hierarchical. The manager of a relatively small unit can earn far more than the manager of a larger unit if results indicate he should. We believe, further, that such factors as seniority and age should not affect incentive compensation (though they sometimes influence basic compensation). A 20-year-old who can hit .300 is as valuable to us as a 40-year-old performing as well.

Obviously, all Berkshire managers can use their bonus money (or other funds, including borrowed money) to buy our stock in the market. Many have done just that—and some now have large holdings. By accepting both the risks and the carrying costs that go with outright purchases, these managers truly walk in the shoes of owners.

Now let's get back—at long last—to our three businesses:

At Nebraska Furniture Mart our basic strength is an exceptionally low-cost operation that allows the business to regularly offer customers the best values available in home furnishings. NFM is the largest store of its kind in the country. Although the already-depressed farm economy worsened considerably in 1985, the store easily set a new sales record. I also am happy to report that NFM's Chairman, Rose Blumkin (the legendary "Mrs. B"), continues at age 92 to set a pace at the store that none of us can keep up with. She's there wheeling and dealing seven days a week, and I hope that any of you who visit Omaha will go out to the Mart and see her in action. It will inspire you, as it does me.

At See's we continue to get store volumes that are far beyond those achieved by any competitor we know of. Despite the unmatched consumer acceptance we enjoy, industry trends are not good, and we continue to experience slippage in poundage sales on a same-store basis. This puts pressure on per-pound costs. We now are willing to increase prices only modestly and, unless we can stabilize per-shop poundage, profit margins will narrow.

At the News volume gains are also difficult to achieve. Though linage increased during 1985, the gain was more than accounted for by preprints. ROP linage (advertising printed on our own pages) declined. Preprints are far less profitable than ROP ads, and also more vulnerable to competition. In 1985, the News again controlled costs well and our household penetration continues to be exceptional.

One problem these three operations do not have is management. At See's we have Chuck Huggins, the man we put in charge the day we bought the business. Selecting him remains one of our best business decisions. At the News we have Stan Lipsey, a manager of equal caliber. Stan has been with us 17 years, and his unusual business talents have become more evident with every additional level of responsibility he has tackled. And, at the Mart, we have the amazing Blumkins—Mrs. B, Louie, Ron, Irv, and Steve—a three-generation miracle of management.

I consider myself extraordinarily lucky to be able to work with managers such as these. I like them personally as much as I admire them professionally.

Insurance Operations

Shown below is an updated version of our usual table, listing two key figures for the insurance industry:

	Yearly Change in Premium Written (%)	Combined Ratio after Policyholder Dividends
1972	10.2	96.2
1973	8.0	99.2
1974	6.2	105.4
1975	11.0	107.9
1976	21.9	102.4
1977	19.8	97.2
1978	12.8	97.5
1979	10.3	100.6
1980	6.0	103.1
1981	3.9	106.0
1982	4.4	109.7
1983	4.5	111.9
1984 (Revised)	9.2	117.9
1985 (Estimated)	20.9	118.0

Source: Best's Aggregates and Averages

The combined ratio represents total insurance costs (losses incurred plus expenses) compared to revenue from premiums: a ratio below 100 indicates an underwriting profit, and one above 100 indicates a loss.

The industry's 1985 results were highly unusual. The revenue gain was exceptional, and had insured losses grown at their normal rate of most recent years—that is, a few points above the inflation rate—a significant drop in the combined ratio would have occurred. But losses in 1985 didn't cooperate, as they did not in 1984. Though inflation slowed considerably in these years, insured losses perversely accelerated, growing by 16% in 1984 and by an even more startling 17% in 1985. The year's growth in losses therefore exceeds the inflation rate by over 13 percentage points, a modern record.

Catastrophes were not the culprit in this explosion of loss cost. True, there were an unusual number of hurricanes in 1985, but the aggregate damage caused by all catastrophes in 1984 and 1985 was about 2% of premium volume, a not unusual proportion. Nor was there any burst in the number of insured autos, houses, employers, or other kinds of "exposure units".

A partial explanation for the surge in the loss figures is all the additions to reserves that the industry made in 1985. As results for the year were reported, the scene resembled a revival meeting: shouting "I've sinned, I've sinned", insurance managers rushed forward to confess they had under reserved in earlier years. Their corrections significantly affected 1985 loss numbers.

A more disturbing ingredient in the loss surge is the acceleration in "social" or "judicial" inflation. The insurer's ability to pay has assumed overwhelming importance with juries and judges in the assessment of both liability and damages. More and more, "the deep pocket" is being sought and found, no matter what the policy wording, the facts, or the precedents.

This judicial inflation represents a wild card in the industry's future, and makes forecasting difficult. Nevertheless, the short-term outlook is good. Premium growth improved as 1985 went along (quarterly gains were an estimated 15%, 19%, 24%, and 22%) and, barring a supercatastrophe, the industry's combined ratio should fall sharply in 1986.

The profit improvement, however, is likely to be of short duration. Two economic principles will see to that. First, commodity businesses achieve good levels of profitability only when prices are fixed in some manner or when capacity is short. Second, managers quickly add to capacity when prospects start to improve and capital is available.

In my 1982 report to you, I discussed the commodity nature of the insurance industry extensively. The typical policyholder does not differentiate between products but concentrates instead on price. For many decades a cartel-like procedure kept prices up, but this arrangement has disappeared for good. The insurance product now is priced as any other commodity for which a free market exists: when capacity is tight, prices will be set remuneratively; otherwise, they will not be.

Capacity currently is tight in many lines of insurance—though in this industry, unlike most, capacity is an attitudinal concept, not a physical fact. Insurance managers can write whatever amount of business they feel comfortable writing, subject only to pressures applied by regulators and Best's, the industry's authoritative rating service. The comfort level of both managers and regulators is tied to capital. More capital means more comfort, which in turn means more capacity. In the typical commodity business, furthermore, such as aluminum or steel, a long gestation precedes the birth of additional capacity. In the insurance industry, capital can be secured instantly. Thus, any capacity shortage can be eliminated in short order.

That's exactly what's going on right now. In 1985, about 15 insurers raised well over $3 billion, piling up capital so that they can write all the business possible at the better prices now available. The capital-raising trend has accelerated dramatically so far in 1986.

If capacity additions continue at this rate, it won't be long before serious price-cutting appears and next a fall in profitability. When the fall comes, it will be the fault of the capital-raisers of 1985 and 1986, not the price-cutters of 198X. (Critics should be understanding, however: as was the case in our textile example, the dynamics of capitalism cause each insurer to make decisions that for itself appear sensible, but that collectively slash profitability.)

In past reports, I have told you that Berkshire's strong capital position—the best in the industry—should one day allow us to claim a distinct competitive advantage in the insurance market. With the tightening of the market, that day arrived. Our premium volume more than tripled last year, following a long period of stagnation. Berkshire's financial strength (and our record of maintaining unusual strength through thick and thin) is now a major asset for us in securing good business.

We correctly foresaw a flight to quality by many large buyers of insurance and reinsurance who belatedly recognized that a policy is only an IOU—and who, in 1985, could not collect on many of their IOUs. These buyers today are attracted to Berkshire because of its strong capital position. But, in a development we did not foresee, we also are finding buyers drawn to us because our ability to insure substantial risks sets us apart from the crowd.

To understand this point, you need a few background facts about large risks. Traditionally, many insurers have wanted to write this kind of business. However, their willingness to do so has been almost always based upon reinsurance arrangements that allow the insurer to keep just a small portion of the risk itself while passing on ("laying off") most of the risk to its reinsurers. Imagine, for example, a directors and officers ("D & O") liability policy providing $25 million of coverage. By various "excess-of-loss" reinsurance contracts, the company issuing that policy might keep the liability for only the first $1 million of any loss that occurs. The liability for any loss above that amount up to $24 million would be borne by the reinsurers of the issuing insurer. In trade parlance, a company that issues large policies but retains relatively little of the risk for its own account writes a large gross line but a small net line.

In any reinsurance arrangement, a key question is how the premiums paid for the policy should be divided among the various "layers" of risk. In our D & O policy, for example. what part of the premium received should be kept by the issuing company to compensate it fairly for taking the first $1 million of risk and how much should be passed on to the reinsurers to compensate them fairly for taking the risk between $1 million and $25 million?

One way to solve this problem might be deemed the Patrick Henry approach: "I have but one lamp by which my feet are guided, and that is the lamp of experience." In other words, how much of the total premium would reinsurers have needed in the past to compensate them fairly for the losses they actually had to bear?

Unfortunately, the lamp of experience has always provided imperfect illumination for reinsurers because so much of their business is "long-tail", meaning it takes many years before they know what their losses are. Lately, however, the light has not only been dim but also grossly misleading in the images it has revealed. That is, the courts' tendency to grant awards that are both huge and lacking in precedent makes reinsurers' usual extrapolations or inferences from past data a formula for disaster. Out with Patrick Henry and in with Pogo: "The future ain't what it used to be."

The burgeoning uncertainties of the business, coupled with the entry into reinsurance of many unsophisticated participants, worked in recent years in favor of issuing companies writing a small net line: they were able to keep a far greater percentage of the premiums than the risk. By doing so, the issuing companies sometimes made money on business that was distinctly unprofitable for the issuing and reinsuring companies combined. (This result was not necessarily by intent: issuing companies generally knew no more than reinsurers did about the ultimate costs that would be experienced at higher layers of risk.) Inequities of this sort have been particularly pronounced in lines of insurance in which much change was occurring and losses were soaring; e.g., professional malpractice, D & O, products liability, etc. Given these circumstances, it is not surprising that issuing companies remained enthusiastic about writing business long after premiums became woefully inadequate on a gross basis.

An example of just how disparate results have been for issuing companies versus their reinsurers is provided by the 1984 financials of one of the leaders in large and unusual risks. In that year the company wrote about $6 billion of business and kept around $2 1/2 billion of the premiums, or about 40%. It gave the remaining $3 1/2 billion to reinsurers. On the part of the business kept, the company's underwriting loss was less than $200 million—an excellent result in that year. Meanwhile, the part laid off produced a loss of over $1.5 billion for the reinsurers. Thus, the issuing company wrote at a combined ratio of well under 110 while its reinsurers, participating in precisely the same policies, came in considerably over 140. This result was not attributable to natural catastrophes; it came from run-of-the-mill insurance losses (occurring, however, in surprising frequency and size). The issuing company's 1985 report is not yet available, but I would predict it will show that dramatically unbalanced results continued.

A few years such as this, and even slow-witted reinsurers can lose interest, particularly in explosive lines where the proper split in premium between issuer and reinsurer remains impossible to even roughly estimate. The behavior of reinsurers finally becomes like that of Mark Twain's cat: having once sat on a hot stove, it never did so again—but it never again sat on a cold stove, either. Reinsurers have had so many unpleasant surprises in long-tail casualty lines that many have decided (probably correctly) to give up the game entirely, regardless of price inducements. Consequently, there has been a dramatic pull-back of reinsurance capacity in certain important lines.

This development has left many issuing companies under pressure. They can no longer commit their reinsurers, time after time, for tens of millions per policy as they so easily could do only a year or two ago, and they do not have the capital and/or appetite to take on large risks for their own account. For many issuing companies, gross capacity has shrunk much closer to net capacity—and that is often small, indeed.

At Berkshire we have never played the lay-it-off-at-a-profit game and, until recently, that put us at a severe disadvantage in certain lines. Now the tables are turned: we have the underwriting capability whereas others do not. If we believe the price to be right, we are willing to write a net line larger than that of any but the largest insurers. For instance, we are perfectly willing to risk losing $10 million of our own money on a single event, as long as we believe that the price is right and that the risk of loss is not significantly correlated with other risks we are insuring. Very few insurers are willing to risk half that much on single events—although, just a short while ago, many were willing to lose five or ten times that amount as long as virtually all of the loss was for the account of their reinsurers.

In mid-1985 our largest insurance company, National Indemnity Company, broadcast its willingness to underwrite large risks by running an ad in three issues of an insurance weekly. The ad solicited policies of only large size: those with a minimum premium of $1 million. This ad drew a remarkable 600 replies and ultimately produced premiums totaling about $50 million. (Hold the applause: it's all long-tail business and it will be at least five years before we know whether this marketing success was also an underwriting success.) Today, our insurance subsidiaries continue to be sought out by brokers searching for large net capacity.

As I have said, this period of tightness will pass; insurers and reinsurers will return to underpricing. But for a year or two we should do well in several segments of our insurance business. Mike Goldberg has made many important improvements in the operation (prior mismanagement by your Chairman having provided him ample opportunity to do so). He has been particularly successful recently in hiring young managers with excellent potential. They will have a chance to show their stuff in 1986.

Our combined ratio has improved—from 134 in 1984 to 111 in 1985—but continues to reflect past misdeeds. Last year I told you of the major mistakes I had made in loss-reserving, and promised I would update you annually on loss-development figures. Naturally, I made this promise thinking my future record would be much improved. So far this has not been the case. Details on last year's loss development are on pages 50-52. They reveal significant underreserving at the end of 1984, as they did in the several years preceding.

The only bright spot in this picture is that virtually all of the underreserving revealed in 1984 occurred in the reinsurance area—and there, in very large part, in a few contracts that were discontinued several years ago. This explanation, however, recalls all too well a story told me many years ago by the then Chairman of General Reinsurance Company. He said that every year his managers told him that "except for the Florida hurricane" or "except for Midwestern tornadoes", they would have had a terrific year. Finally he called the group together and suggested that they form a new operation—the Except-For Insurance Company—in which they would henceforth place all of the business that they later wouldn't want to count.

In any business, insurance or otherwise, "except for" should be excised from the lexicon. If you are going to play the game, you must count the runs scored against you in all nine innings. Any manager who consistently says "except for" and then reports on the lessons he has learned from his mistakes may be missing the only important lesson—namely, that the real mistake is not the act, but the actor.

Inevitably, of course, business errors will occur and the wise manager will try to find the proper lessons in them. But the trick is to learn most lessons from the experiences of others. Managers who have learned much from personal experience in the past usually are destined to learn much from personal experience in the future.

GEICO, 38%-owned by Berkshire, reported an excellent year in 1985 in premium growth and investment results, but a poor year—by its lofty standards—in underwriting. Private passenger auto and homeowners insurance were the only important lines in the industry whose results deteriorated significantly during the year. GEICO did not escape the trend, although its record was far better than that of virtually all its major competitors.

Jack Byrne left GEICO at mid-year to head Fireman's Fund, leaving behind Bill Snyder as Chairman and Lou Simpson as Vice Chairman. Jack's performance in reviving GEICO from near-bankruptcy was truly extraordinary, and his work resulted in enormous gains for Berkshire. We owe him a great deal for that.

We are equally indebted to Jack for an achievement that eludes most outstanding leaders: he found managers to succeed him who have talents as valuable as his own. By his skill in identifying, attracting and developing Bill and Lou, Jack extended the benefits of his managerial stewardship well beyond his tenure.

Fireman's Fund Quota-Share Contract

Never one to let go of a meal ticket, we have followed Jack Byrne to Fireman's Fund ("FFIC") where he is Chairman and CEO of the holding company.

On September 1, 1985 we became a 7% participant in all of the business in force of the FFIC group, with the exception of reinsurance they write for unaffiliated companies. Our contract runs for four years, and provides that our losses and costs will be proportionate to theirs throughout the contract period. If there is no extension, we will thereafter have no participation in any ongoing business. However, for a great many years in the future, we will be reimbursing FFIC for our 7% of the losses that occurred in the September 1, 1985—August 31, 1989 period.

Under the contract FFIC remits premiums to us promptly and we reimburse FFIC promptly for expenses and losses it has paid. Thus, funds generated by our share of the business are held by us for investment. As part of the deal, I'm available to FFIC for consultation about general investment strategy. I'm not involved, however, in specific investment decisions of FFIC, nor is Berkshire involved in any aspect of the company's underwriting activities.

Currently FFIC is doing about $3 billion of business, and it will probably do more as rates rise. The company's September 1, 1985 unearned premium reserve was $1.324 billion, and it therefore transferred 7% of this, or $92.7 million, to us at initiation of the contract. We concurrently paid them $29.4 million representing the underwriting expenses that they had incurred on the transferred premium. All of the FFIC business is written by National Indemnity Company, but two-sevenths of it is passed along to Wesco-Financial Insurance Company ("Wes-FIC"), a new company organized by our 80%-owned subsidiary, Wesco Financial Corporation. Charlie Munger has some interesting comments about Wes-FIC and the reinsurance business on pages 60-62.

To the Insurance Segment tables on page 41, we have added a new line, labeled Major Quota Share Contracts. The 1985 results of the FFIC contract are reported there, though the newness of the arrangement makes these results only very rough approximations.

After the end of the year, we secured another quota-share contract, whose 1986 volume should be over $50 million. We hope to develop more of this business, and industry conditions suggest that we could: a significant number of companies are generating more business than they themselves can prudently handle. Our financial strength makes us an attractive partner for such companies.

Marketable Securities

We show below our 1985 yearend net holdings in marketable equities. All positions with a market value over $25 million are listed, and the interests attributable to minority shareholders of Wesco and Nebraska Furniture Mart are excluded.

No. of Shares		Cost	Market
		(000s omitted)	
1,036,461	Affiliated Publications, Inc.	$ 3,516	$ 55,710
900,800	American Broadcasting Companies, Inc.	54,435	108,997
2,350,922	Beatrice Companies, Inc.	106,811	108,142
6,850,000	GEICO Corporation	45,713	595,950
2,379,200	Handy & Harman	27,318	43,718
847,788	Time, Inc.	20,385	52,669
1,727,765	The Washington Post Company	9,731	205,172
		267,909	1,170,358
	All Other Common Stockholdings	7,201	27,963
	Total Common Stocks	$275,110	$1,198,321

We mentioned earlier that in the past decade the investment environment has changed from one in which great businesses were totally unappreciated to one in which they are appropriately recognized. The Washington Post Company ("WPC") provides an excellent example.

We bought all of our WPC holdings in mid-1973 at a price of not more than one-fourth of the then per-share business value of the enterprise. Calculating the price/value ratio required no unusual insights. Most security analysts, media brokers, and media executives would have estimated WPC's intrinsic business value at $400 to $500 million just as we did. And its $100 million stock market valuation was published daily for all to see. Our advantage, rather, was attitude: we had learned from Ben Graham that the key to successful investing was the purchase of shares in good businesses when market prices were at a large discount from underlying business values.

Most institutional investors in the early 1970s, on the other hand, regarded business value as of only minor relevance when they were deciding the prices at which they would buy or sell. This now seems hard to believe. However, these institutions were then under the spell of academics at prestigious business schools who were preaching a newly-fashioned theory: the stock market was totally efficient, and therefore calculations of business value—and even thought, itself—were of no importance in investment activities. (We are enormously indebted to those academics: what could be more advantageous in an intellectual contest—whether it be bridge, chess, or stock selection than to have opponents who have been taught that thinking is a waste of energy?)

Through 1973 and 1974, WPC continued to do fine as a business, and intrinsic value grew. Nevertheless, by yearend 1974 our WPC holding showed a loss of about 25%, with market value at $8 million against our cost of $10.6 million. What we had thought ridiculously cheap a year earlier had become a good bit cheaper as the market, in its infinite wisdom, marked WPC stock down to well below 20 cents on the dollar of intrinsic value.

You know the happy outcome. Kay Graham, CEO of WPC, had the brains and courage to repurchase large quantities of stock for the company at those bargain prices, as well as the managerial skills necessary to dramatically increase business values. Meanwhile, investors began to recognize the exceptional economics of the business and the stock price moved closer to underlying value. Thus, we experienced a triple dip: the company's business value soared upward, per-share business value increased considerably faster because of stock repurchases and, with a narrowing of the discount, the stock price outpaced the gain in per-share business value.

We hold all of the WPC shares we bought in 1973, except for those sold back to the company in 1985's proportionate redemption. Proceeds from the redemption plus yearend market value of our holdings total $221 million.

If we had invested our $10.6 million in any of a half-dozen media companies that were investment favorites in mid-1973, the value of our holdings at yearend would have been in the area of $40—$60 million. Our gain would have far exceeded the gain in the general market, an outcome reflecting the exceptional economics of the media business. The extra $160 million or so we gained through ownership of WPC came, in very large part, from the superior nature of the managerial decisions made by Kay as compared to those made by managers of most media companies. Her stunning business success has in large part gone unreported but among Berkshire shareholders it should not go unappreciated.

Our Capital Cities purchase, described in the next section, required me to leave the WPC Board early in 1986. But we intend to hold indefinitely whatever WPC stock FCC rules allow us to. We expect WPC's business values to grow at a reasonable rate, and we know that management is both able and shareholder-oriented. However, the market now values the company at over $1.8 billion, and there is no way that the value can progress from that level at a rate anywhere close to the rate possible when the company's valuation was only $100 million. Because market prices have also been bid up for our other holdings, we face the same vastly-reduced potential throughout our portfolio.

You will notice that we had a significant holding in Beatrice Companies at yearend. This is a short-term arbitrage holding—in effect, a parking place for money (though not a totally safe one, since deals sometimes fall through and create substantial losses). We sometimes enter the arbitrage field when we have more money than ideas, but only to participate in announced mergers and sales. We would be a lot happier if the funds currently employed on this short-term basis found a long-term home. At the moment, however, prospects are bleak.

At yearend our insurance subsidiaries had about $400 million in tax-exempt bonds, of which $194 million at amortized cost were issues of Washington Public Power Supply System ("WPPSS") Projects 1, 2, and 3. I discussed this position fully last year, and explained why we would not disclose further purchases or sales until well after the fact (adhering to the policy we follow on stocks). Our unrealized gain on the WPPSS bonds at yearend was $62 million, perhaps one-third arising from the upward movement of bonds generally, and the remainder from a more positive investor view toward WPPSS 1, 2, and 3s. Annual tax-exempt income from our WPPSS issues is about $30 million.

Capital Cities/ABC, Inc.

Right after yearend, Berkshire purchased 3 million shares of Capital Cities/ABC, Inc. ("Cap Cities") at $172.50 per share, the market price of such shares at the time the commitment was made early in March, 1985. I've been on record for many years about the management of Cap Cities: I think it is the best of any publicly-owned company in the country. And Tom Murphy and Dan Burke are not only great managers, they are precisely the sort of fellows that you would want your daughter to marry. It is a privilege to be associated with them—and also a lot of fun, as any of you who know them will understand.

Our purchase of stock helped Cap Cities finance the $3.5 billion acquisition of American Broadcasting Companies. For Cap Cities, ABC is a major undertaking whose economics are likely to be unexciting over the next few years. This bothers us not an iota; we can be very patient. (No matter how great the talent or effort, some things just take time: you can't produce a baby in one month by getting nine women pregnant.)

As evidence of our confidence, we have executed an unusual agreement: for an extended period Tom, as CEO (or Dan, should he be CEO) votes our stock. This arrangement was initiated by Charlie and me, not by Tom. We also have restricted ourselves in various ways regarding sale of our shares. The object of these restrictions is to make sure that our block does not get sold to anyone who is a large holder (or intends to become a large holder) without the approval of management, an arrangement similar to ones we initiated some years ago at GEICO and Washington Post.

Since large blocks frequently command premium prices, some might think we have injured Berkshire financially by creating such restrictions. Our view is just the opposite. We feel the long-term economic prospects for these businesses—and, thus, for ourselves as owners—are enhanced by the arrangements. With them in place, the first-class managers with whom we have aligned ourselves can focus their efforts entirely upon running the businesses and maximizing long-term values for owners. Certainly this is much better than having those managers distracted by "revolving-door capitalists" hoping to put the company "in play". (Of course, some managers place their own interests above those of the company and its owners and deserve to be shaken up—but, in making investments, we try to steer clear of this type.)

Today, corporate instability is an inevitable consequence of widely-diffused ownership of voting stock. At any time a major holder can surface, usually mouthing reassuring rhetoric but frequently harboring uncivil intentions. By circumscribing our blocks of stock as we often do, we intend to promote stability where it otherwise might be lacking. That kind of certainty, combined with a good manager and a good business, provides excellent soil for a rich financial harvest. That's the economic case for our arrangements.

The human side is just as important. We don't want managers we like and admire—and who have welcomed a major financial commitment by us—to ever lose any sleep wondering whether surprises might occur because of our large ownership. I have told them there will be no surprises, and these agreements put Berkshire's signature where my mouth is. That signature also means the managers have a corporate commitment and therefore need not worry if my personal participation in Berkshire's affairs ends prematurely (a term I define as any age short of three digits).

Our Cap Cities purchase was made at a full price, reflecting the very considerable enthusiasm for both media stocks and media properties that has developed in recent years (and that, in the case of some property purchases, has approached a mania). it's no field for bargains. However, our Cap Cities investment allies us with an exceptional combination of properties and people—and we like the opportunity to participate in size.

Of course, some of you probably wonder why we are now buying Cap Cities at $172.50 per share given that your Chairman, in a characteristic burst of brilliance, sold Berkshire's holdings in the same company at $43 per share in 1978-80. Anticipating your question, I spent much of 1985 working on a snappy answer that would reconcile these acts.

A little more time, please.

Acquisition of Scott & Fetzer

Right after yearend we acquired The Scott & Fetzer Company ("Scott Fetzer") of Cleveland for about $320 million. (In addition, about $90 million of pre-existing Scott Fetzer debt remains in place.) In the next section of this report I describe the sort of businesses that we wish to buy for Berkshire. Scott Fetzer is a prototype—understandable, large, well-managed, a good earner.

The company has sales of about $700 million derived from 17 businesses, many leaders in their fields. Return on invested capital is good to excellent for most of these businesses. Some well-known products are Kirby home-care systems, Campbell Hausfeld air compressors, and Wayne burners and water pumps.

World Book, Inc.—accounting for about 40% of Scott Fetzer's sales and a bit more of its income—is by far the company's largest operation. It also is by far the leader in its industry, selling more than twice as many encyclopedia sets annually as its nearest competitor. In fact, it sells more sets in the U.S. than its four biggest competitors combined.

Charlie and I have a particular interest in the World Book operation because we regard its encyclopedia as something special. I've been a fan (and user) for 25 years, and now have grandchildren consulting the sets just as my children did. World Book is regularly rated the most useful encyclopedia by teachers, librarians and consumer buying guides. Yet it sells for less than any of its major competitors. Childcraft, another World Book, Inc. product, offers similar value. This combination of exceptional products and modest prices at World Book, Inc. helped make us willing to pay the price demanded for Scott Fetzer, despite declining results for many companies in the direct-selling industry.

An equal attraction at Scott Fetzer is Ralph Schey, its CEO for nine years. When Ralph took charge, the company had 31 businesses, the result of an acquisition spree in the 1960s. He disposed of many that did not fit or had limited profit potential, but his focus on rationalizing the original potpourri was not so intense that he passed by World Book when it became available for purchase in 1978. Ralph's operating and capital-allocation record is superb, and we are delighted to be associated with him.

The history of the Scott Fetzer acquisition is interesting, marked by some zigs and zags before we became involved. The company had been an announced candidate for purchase since early 1984. A major investment banking firm spent many months canvassing scores of prospects, evoking interest from several. Finally, in mid-1985 a plan of sale, featuring heavy participation by an ESOP (Employee Stock Ownership Plan), was approved by shareholders. However, as difficulty in closing followed, the plan was scuttled.

I had followed this corporate odyssey through the newspapers. On October 10, well after the ESOP deal had fallen through, I wrote a short letter to Ralph, whom I did not know. I said we admired the company's record and asked if he might like to talk. Charlie and I met Ralph for dinner in Chicago on October 22 and signed an acquisition contract the following week.

The Scott Fetzer acquisition, plus major growth in our insurance business, should push revenues above $2 billion in 1986, more than double those of 1985.

Miscellaneous

The Scott Fetzer purchase illustrates our somewhat haphazard approach to acquisitions. We have no master strategy, no corporate planners delivering us insights about socioeconomic trends, and no staff to investigate a multitude of ideas presented by promoters and intermediaries. Instead, we simply hope that something sensible comes along—and, when it does, we act.

To give fate a helping hand, we again repeat our regular "business wanted" ad. The only change from last year's copy is in (1): because we continue to want any acquisition we make to have a measurable impact on Berkshire's financial results, we have raised our minimum profit requirement.

Here's what we're looking for:
(1) large purchases (at least $10 million of after-tax earnings),
(2) demonstrated consistent earning power (future projections are of little interest to us, nor are "turn-around" situations),
(3) businesses earning good returns on equity while employing little or no debt,
(4) management in place (we can't supply it),
(5) simple businesses (if there's lots of technology, we won't understand it),
(6) an offering price (we don't want to waste our time or that of the seller by talking, even preliminarily, about a transaction when price is unknown).

We will not engage in unfriendly takeovers. We can promise complete confidentiality and a very fast answer—customarily within five minutes—as to whether we're interested. We prefer to buy for cash, but will consider issuance of stock when we receive as much in intrinsic business value as we give. Indeed, following recent advances in the price of Berkshire stock, transactions involving stock issuance may be quite feasible. We invite potential sellers to check us out by contacting people with whom we have done business in the past. For the right business—and the right people—we can provide a good home.

On the other hand, we frequently get approached about acquisitions that don't come close to meeting our tests: new ventures, turnarounds, auction-like sales, and the ever-popular (among brokers) "I'm-sure-something-will-work-out-if-you-people-get-to-know-each-other". None of these attracts us in the least.

* * *

Besides being interested in the purchases of entire businesses as described above, we are also interested in the negotiated purchase of large, but not controlling, blocks of stock, as in our Cap Cities purchase. Such purchases appeal to us only when we are very comfortable with both the economics of the business and the ability and integrity of the people running the operation. We prefer large transactions: in the unusual case we might do something as small as $50 million (or even smaller), but our preference is for commitments many times that size.

* * *

About 96.8% of all eligible shares participated in Berkshire's 1985 shareholder-designated contributions program. Total contributions made through the program were $4 million, and 1,724 charities were recipients. We conducted a plebiscite last year in order to get your views about this program, as well as about our dividend policy. (Recognizing that it's possible to influence the answers to a question by the framing of it, we attempted to make the wording of ours as neutral as possible.) We present the ballot and the results in the Appendix on page 69. I think it's fair to summarize your response as highly supportive of present policies and your group preference—allowing for the tendency of people to vote for the status quo—to be for increasing the annual charitable commitment as our asset values build.

We urge new shareholders to read the description of our shareholder-designated contributions program that appears on pages 66 and 67. If you wish to participate in future programs, we strongly urge that you immediately make sure that your shares are registered in the name of the actual owner, not in "street" name or nominee name. Shares not so registered on September 30, 1986 will be ineligible for the 1986 program.

* * *

Five years ago we were required by the Bank Holding Company Act of 1969 to dispose of our holdings in The Illinois National Bank and Trust Company of Rockford, Illinois. Our method of doing so was unusual: we announced an exchange ratio between stock of Rockford Bancorp Inc. (the Illinois National's holding company) and stock of Berkshire, and then let each of our shareholders—except me—make the decision as to whether to exchange all, part, or none of his Berkshire shares for Rockford shares. I took the Rockford stock that was left over and thus my own holding in Rockford was determined by your decisions. At the time I said, "This technique embodies the world's oldest and most elementary system of fairly dividing an object. Just as when you were a child and one person cut the cake and the other got first choice, I have tried to cut the company fairly, but you get first choice as to which piece you want."

Last fall Illinois National was sold. When Rockford's liquidation is completed, its shareholders will have received per-share proceeds about equal to Berkshire's per-share intrinsic value at the time of the bank's sale. I'm pleased that this five-year result indicates that the division of the cake was reasonably equitable. Last year I put in a plug for our annual meeting, and you took me up on the invitation. Over 250 of our more than 3,000 registered shareholders showed up. Those attending behaved just as those present in previous years, asking the sort of questions you would expect from intelligent and interested owners. You can attend a great many annual meetings without running into a crowd like ours. (Lester Maddox, when Governor of Georgia, was criticized regarding the state's abysmal prison system. "The solution", he said, "is simple. All we need is a better class of prisoners." Upgrading annual meetings works the same way.)

I hope you come to this year's meeting, which will be held on May 20 in Omaha. There will be only one change: after 48 years of allegiance to another soft drink, your Chairman, in an unprecedented display of behavioral flexibility, has converted to the new Cherry Coke. Henceforth, it will be the Official Drink of the Berkshire Hathaway Annual Meeting.

And bring money: Mrs. B promises to have bargains galore if you will pay her a visit at The Nebraska Furniture Mart after the meeting.

Warren E. Buffett
Chairman of the Board

March 4, 1986

BERKSHIRE HATHAWAY INC.

To the Shareholders of Berkshire Hathaway Inc.:

Our gain in net worth during 1986 was $492.5 million, or 26.1%. Over the last 22 years (that is, since present management took over), our per-share book value has grown from $19.46 to $2,073.06, or 23.3% compounded annually. Both the numerator and denominator are important in the per-share book value calculation: during the 22-year period our corporate net worth has increased 10,600% while shares outstanding have increased less than 1%.

In past reports I have noted that book value at most companies differs widely from intrinsic business value—the number that really counts for owners. In our own case, however, book value has served for more than a decade as a reasonable if somewhat conservative proxy for business value. That is, our business value has moderately exceeded our book value, with the ratio between the two remaining fairly steady.

The good news is that in 1986 our percentage gain in business value probably exceeded the book value gain. I say "probably" because business value is a soft number: in our own case, two equally well-informed observers might make judgments more than 10% apart.

A large measure of our improvement in business value relative to book value reflects the outstanding performance of key managers at our major operating businesses. These managers—the Blumkins, Mike Goldberg, the Heldmans, Chuck Huggins, Stan Lipsey, and Ralph Schey—have over the years improved the earnings of their businesses dramatically while, except in the case of insurance, utilizing little additional capital. This accomplishment builds economic value, or "Goodwill," that does not show up in the net worth figure on our balance sheet, nor in our per-share book value. In 1986 this unrecorded gain was substantial.

So much for the good news. The bad news is that my performance did not match that of our managers. While they were doing a superb job in running our businesses, I was unable to skillfully deploy much of the capital they generated. Charlie Munger, our Vice Chairman, and I really have only two jobs. One is to attract and keep outstanding managers to run our various operations. This hasn't been all that difficult. Usually the managers came with the companies we bought, having demonstrated their talents throughout careers that spanned a wide variety of business circumstances. They were managerial stars long before they knew us, and our main contribution has been to not get in their way. This approach seems elementary: if my job were to manage a golf team—and if Jack Nicklaus or Arnold Palmer were willing to play for me—neither would get a lot of directives from me about how to swing.

Some of our key managers are independently wealthy (we hope they all become so), but that poses no threat to their continued interest: they work because they love what they do and relish the thrill of outstanding performance. They unfailingly think like owners (the highest compliment we can pay a manager) and find all aspects of their business absorbing.

(Our prototype for occupational fervor is the Catholic tailor who used his small savings of many years to finance a pilgrimage to the Vatican. When he returned, his parish held a special meeting to get his first-hand account of the Pope. "Tell us," said the eager faithful, "just what sort of fellow is he?" Our hero wasted no words: "He's a forty-four, medium.")

Charlie and I know that the right players will make almost any team manager look good. We subscribe to the philosophy of Ogilvy & Mather's founding genius, David Ogilvy: "If each of us hires people who are smaller than we are, we shall become a company of dwarfs. But, if each of us hires people who are bigger than we are, we shall become a company of giants."

A by-product of our managerial style is the ability it gives us to easily expand Berkshire's activities. We've read management treatises that specify exactly how many people should report to any one executive, but they make little sense to us. When you have able managers of high character running businesses about which they are passionate, you can have a dozen or more reporting to you and still have time for an afternoon nap. Conversely, if you have even one person reporting to you who is deceitful, inept or uninterested, you will find yourself with more than you can handle. Charlie and I could work with double the number of managers we now have, so long as they had the rare qualities of the present ones.

We intend to continue our practice of working only with people whom we like and admire. This policy not only maximizes our chances for good results, it also ensures us an extraordinarily good time. On the other hand, working with people who cause your stomach to churn seems much like marrying for money—probably a bad idea under any circumstances, but absolute madness if you are already rich.

The second job Charlie and I must handle is the allocation of capital, which at Berkshire is a considerably more important challenge than at most companies. Three factors make that so: we earn more money than average; we retain all that we earn; and, we are fortunate to have operations that, for the most part, require little incremental capital to remain competitive and to grow. Obviously, the future results of a business earning 23% annually and retaining it all are far more affected by today's capital allocations than are the results of a business earning 10% and distributing half of that to shareholders. If our retained earnings—and those of our major investees, GEICO and Capital Cities/ABC, Inc.—are employed in an unproductive manner, the economics of Berkshire will deteriorate very quickly. In a company adding only, say, 5% to net worth annually, capital-allocation decisions, though still important, will change the company's economics far more slowly.

Capital allocation at Berkshire was tough work in 1986. We did make one business acquisition—The Fechheimer Bros. Company, which we will discuss in a later section. Fechheimer is a company with excellent economics, run by exactly the kind of people with whom we enjoy being associated. But it is relatively small, utilizing only about 2% of Berkshire's net worth.

Meanwhile, we had no new ideas in the marketable equities field, an area in which once, only a few years ago, we could readily employ large sums in outstanding businesses at very reasonable prices. So our main capital allocation moves in 1986 were to pay off debt and stockpile funds. Neither is a fate worse than death, but they do not inspire us to do handsprings either. If Charlie and I were to draw blanks for a few years in our capital-allocation endeavors, Berkshire's rate of growth would slow significantly.

We will continue to look for operating businesses that meet our tests and, with luck, will acquire such a business every couple of years. But an acquisition will have to be large if it is to help our performance materially. Under current stock market conditions, we have little hope of finding equities to buy for our insurance companies. Markets will change significantly—you can be sure of that and some day we will again get our turn at bat. However, we haven't the faintest idea when that might happen.

It can't be said too often (although I'm sure you feel I've tried) that, even under favorable conditions, our returns are certain to drop substantially because of our enlarged size. We have told you that we hope to average a return of 15% on equity and we maintain that hope, despite some negative tax law changes described in a later section of this report. If we are to achieve this rate of return, our net worth must increase $7.2 billion in the next ten years. A gain of that magnitude will be possible only if, before too long, we come up with a few very big (and good) ideas. Charlie and I can't promise results, but we do promise you that we will keep our efforts focused on our goals.

Sources of Reported Earnings

The table on the next page shows the major sources of Berkshire's reported earnings. This table differs in several ways from the one presented last year. We have added four new lines of business because of the Scott Fetzer and Fechheimer acquisitions. In the case of Scott Fetzer, the two major units acquired were World Book and Kirby, and each is presented separately. Fourteen other businesses of Scott Fetzer are aggregated in Scott Fetzer—Diversified Manufacturing. SF Financial Group, a credit company holding both World Book and Kirby receivables, is included in "Other." This year, because Berkshire is so much larger, we also have eliminated separate reporting for several of our smaller businesses.

In the table, amortization of Goodwill is not charged against the specific businesses but, for reasons outlined in the Appendix to my letter in the 1983 Annual Report, is aggregated as a separate item. (A Compendium of earlier letters, including the Goodwill discussion, is available upon request.) Both the Scott Fetzer and Fechheimer acquisitions created accounting Goodwill, which is why the amortization charge for Goodwill increased in 1986.

Additionally, the Scott Fetzer acquisition required other major purchase-price accounting adjustments, as prescribed by generally accepted accounting principles (GAAP). The GAAP figures, of course, are the ones used in our consolidated financial statements. But, in our view, the GAAP figures are not necessarily the most useful ones for investors or managers. Therefore, the figures shown for specific operating units are earnings before purchase-price adjustments are taken into account. In effect, these are the earnings that would have been reported by the businesses if we had not purchased them.

A discussion of our reasons for preferring this form of presentation is in the Appendix to this letter. This Appendix will never substitute for a steamy novel and definitely is not required reading. However, I know that among our 6,000 shareholders there are those who are thrilled by my essays on accounting—and I hope that both of you enjoy the Appendix.

In the Business Segment Data on pages 41-43 and in the Management's Discussion section on pages 45-49, you will find much additional information about our businesses. I urge you to read those sections, as well as Charlie Munger's letter to Wesco shareholders, describing the various businesses of that subsidiary, which starts on page 50.

	(000s omitted)			
	Pre-Tax Earnings		Berkshire's Share of Net Earnings (after taxes and minority interests)	
	1986	1985	1986	1985
Operating Earnings:				
Insurance Group:				
Underwriting	$(55,844)	$(44,230)	$(29,864)	$(23,569)
Net Investment Income	107,143	95,217	96,440	79,716
Buffalo News	34,736	29,921	16,918	14,580
Fechheimer (Acquired 6/3/86)	8,400	---	3,792	---
Kirby	20,218	---	10,508	---
Nebraska Furniture Mart	17,685	12,686	7,192	5,181
Scott Fetzer – Diversified Mfg.	25,358	---	13,354	---
See's Candies	30,347	28,989	15,176	14,558
Wesco – other than insurance	5,542	16,018	5,550	9,684
World Book	21,978	---	11,670	---
Amortization of Goodwill	(2,555)	(1,475)	(2,555)	(1,475)
Other purchase-price accounting charges .	(10,033)	---	(11,031)	---
Interest on Debt and Pre-Payment penalty	(23,891)	(14,415)	(12,213)	(7,288)
Shareholder-Designated Contributions . .	(3,997)	(4,006)	(2,158)	(2,164)
Other	20,770	6,744	8,685	3,725
Operating Earnings	195,857	125,449	131,464	92,948
Special General Foods Distribution	---	4,127	---	3,779
Special Washington Post Distribution.	---	14,877	---	13,851
Sales of securities	216,242	468,903	150,897	325,237
Total Earnings – all entities	$412,099	$613,356	$282,361	$435,815

As you can see, operating earnings substantially improved during 1986. Some of the improvement came from the insurance operation, whose results I will discuss in a later section. Fechheimer also will be discussed separately. Our other major businesses performed as follows:

- Operating results at The Buffalo News continue to reflect a truly superb managerial job by Stan Lipsey. For the third year in a row, man-hours worked fell significantly and other costs were closely controlled. Consequently, our operating margins improved materially in 1986, even though our advertising rate increases were well below those of most major newspapers.

  Our cost-control efforts have in no way reduced our commitment to news. We continue to deliver a 50% "news hole" (the portion of the total space in the paper devoted to news), a higher percentage, we believe, than exists at any dominant newspaper in this country of our size or larger.

  The average news hole at papers comparable to the News is about 40%. The difference between 40% and 50% is more important than it might first seem: a paper with 30 pages of ads and a 40% news hole delivers 20 pages of news a day, whereas our paper matches 30 pages of ads with 30 pages of news. Therefore, given ad pages equal in number, we end up delivering our readers no less than 50% more news.

We believe this heavy commitment to news is one of the reasons The Buffalo News has the highest weekday penetration rate (the percentage of households in the paper's primary marketing area purchasing it each day) among any of the top 50 papers in the country. Our Sunday penetration, where we are also number one, is even more impressive. Ten years ago, the only Sunday paper serving Buffalo (the Courier-Express) had circulation of 271,000 and a penetration ratio of about 63%. The Courier-Express had served the area for many decades and its penetration ratio—which was similar to those existing in many metropolitan markets—was thought to be a "natural" one, accurately reflecting the local citizenry's appetite for a Sunday product.

Our Sunday paper was started in late 1977. It now has a penetration ratio of 83% and sells about 100,000 copies more each Sunday than did the Courier-Express ten years ago—even though population in our market area has declined during the decade. In recent history, no other city that has long had a local Sunday paper has experienced a penetration gain anywhere close to Buffalo's.

Despite our exceptional market acceptance, our operating margins almost certainly have peaked. A major newsprint price increase took effect at the end of 1986, and our advertising rate increases in 1987 will again be moderate compared to those of the industry. However, even if margins should materially shrink, we would not reduce our news-hole ratio.

As I write this, it has been exactly ten years since we purchased The News. The financial rewards it has brought us have far exceeded our expectations and so, too, have the non-financial rewards. Our respect for the News—high when we bought it—has grown consistently ever since the purchase, as has our respect and admiration for Murray Light, the editor who turns out the product that receives such extraordinary community acceptance. The efforts of Murray and Stan, which were crucial to the News during its dark days of financial reversals and litigation, have not in the least been lessened by prosperity. Charlie and I are grateful to them.

- The amazing Blumkins continue to perform business miracles at Nebraska Furniture Mart. Competitors come and go (mostly go), but Mrs. B. and her progeny roll on. In 1986 net sales increased 10.2% to $132 million. Ten years ago sales were $44 million and, even then, NFM appeared to be doing just about all of the business available in the Greater Omaha Area. Given NFM's remarkable dominance, Omaha's slow growth in population and the modest inflation rates that have applied to the goods NFM sells, how can this operation continue to rack up such large sales gains? The only logical explanation is that the marketing territory of NFM's one-and-only store continues to widen because of its ever-growing reputation for rock-bottom everyday prices and the broadest of selections. In preparation for further gains, NFM is expanding the capacity of its warehouse, located a few hundred yards from the store, by about one-third.

Mrs. B, Chairman of Nebraska Furniture Mart, continues at age 93 to outsell and out-hustle any manager I've ever seen. She's at the store seven days a week, from opening to close. Competing with her represents a triumph of courage over judgment.

It's easy to overlook what I consider to be the critical lesson of the Mrs. B saga: at 93, Omaha based Board Chairmen have yet to reach their peak. Please file this fact away to consult before you mark your ballot at the 2024 annual meeting of Berkshire.

- At See's, sales trends improved somewhat from those of recent years. Total pounds sold rose about 2%. (For you chocaholics who like to fantasize, one statistic: we sell over 12,000 tons annually.) Same-store sales, measured in pounds, were virtually unchanged. In the previous six years, same store poundage fell, and we gained or maintained poundage volume only by adding stores. But a particularly strong Christmas season in 1986 stemmed the decline. By stabilizing same-store volume and making a major effort to control costs, See's was able to maintain its excellent profit margin in 1986 though it put through only minimal price increases. We have Chuck Huggins, our long-time manager at See's, to thank for this significant achievement.

See's has a one-of-a-kind product "personality" produced by a combination of its candy's delicious taste and moderate price, the company's total control of the distribution process, and the exceptional service provided by store employees. Chuck rightfully measures his success by the satisfaction of our customers, and his attitude permeates the organization. Few major retailing companies have been able to sustain such a customer-oriented spirit, and we owe Chuck a great deal for keeping it alive and well at See's.

See's profits should stay at about their present level. We will continue to increase prices very modestly, merely matching prospective cost increases.

- World Book is the largest of 17 Scott Fetzer operations that joined Berkshire at the beginning of 1986. Last year I reported to you enthusiastically about the businesses of Scott Fetzer and about Ralph Schey, its manager. A year's experience has added to my enthusiasm for both. Ralph is a superb businessman and a straight shooter. He also brings exceptional versatility and energy to his job: despite the wide array of businesses that he manages, he is on top of the operations, opportunities and problems of each. And, like our other managers, Ralph is a real pleasure to work with. Our good fortune continues.

World Book's unit volume increased for the fourth consecutive year, with encyclopedia sales up 7% over 1985 and 45% over 1982. Childcraft's unit sales also grew significantly.

World Book continues to dominate the U.S. direct-sales encyclopedia market—and for good reasons. Extraordinarily well-edited and priced at under 5 cents per page, these books are a bargain for youngster and adult alike. You may find one editing technique interesting: World Book ranks over 44,000 words by difficulty. Longer entries in the encyclopedia include only the most easily comprehended words in the opening sections, with the difficulty of the material gradually escalating as the exposition proceeds. As a result, youngsters can easily and profitably read to the point at which subject matter gets too difficult, instead of immediately having to deal with a discussion that mixes up words requiring college-level comprehension with others of fourth-grade level.

Selling World Book is a calling. Over one-half of our active salespeople are teachers or former teachers, and another 5% have had experience as librarians. They correctly think of themselves as educators, and they do a terrific job. If you don't have a World Book set in your house, I recommend one.

- Kirby likewise recorded its fourth straight year of unit volume gains. Worldwide, unit sales grew 4% from 1985 and 33% from 1982. While the Kirby product is more expensive than most cleaners, it performs in a manner that leaves cheaper units far behind ("in the dust," so to speak). Many 30- and 40-year-old Kirby cleaners are still in active duty. If you want the best, you buy a Kirby.

Some companies that historically have had great success in direct sales have stumbled in recent years. Certainly the era of the working woman has created new challenges for direct sales organizations. So far, the record shows that both Kirby and World Book have responded most successfully.

The businesses described above, along with the insurance operation and Fechheimer, constitute our major business units. The brevity of our descriptions is in no way meant to diminish the importance of these businesses to us. All have been discussed in past annual reports and, because of the tendency of Berkshire owners to stay in the fold (about 98% of the stock at the end of each year is owned by people who were owners at the start of the year), we want to avoid undue repetition of basic facts. You can be sure that we will immediately report to you in detail if the underlying economics or competitive position of any of these businesses should materially change. In general, the businesses described in this section can be characterized as having very strong market positions, very high returns on capital employed, and the best of operating managements.

The Fechheimer Bros. Co.

Every year in Berkshire's annual report I include a description of the kind of business that we would like to buy. This "ad" paid off in 1986.

On January 15th of last year I received a letter from Bob Heldman of Cincinnati, a shareholder for many years and also Chairman of Fechheimer Bros. Until I read the letter, however, I did not know of either Bob or Fechheimer. Bob wrote that he ran a company that met our tests and suggested that we get together, which we did in Omaha after their results for 1985 were compiled.

He filled me in on a little history: Fechheimer, a uniform manufacturing and distribution business, began operations in 1842. Warren Heldman, Bob's father, became involved in the business in 1941 and his sons, Bob and George (now President), along with their sons, subsequently joined the company. Under the Heldmans' management, the business was highly successful.

In 1981 Fechheimer was sold to a group of venture capitalists in a leveraged buy out (an LBO), with management retaining an equity interest. The new company, as is the case with all LBOS, started with an exceptionally high debt/equity ratio. After the buy out, however, operations continued to be very successful. So by the start of last year debt had been paid down substantially and the value of the equity had increased dramatically. For a variety of reasons, the venture capitalists wished to sell and Bob, having dutifully read Berkshire's annual reports, thought of us.

Fechheimer is exactly the sort of business we like to buy. Its economic record is superb; its managers are talented, high-grade, and love what they do; and the Heldman family wanted to continue its financial interest in partnership with us. Therefore, we quickly purchased about 84% of the stock for a price that was based upon a $55 million valuation for the entire business.

The circumstances of this acquisition were similar to those prevailing in our purchase of Nebraska Furniture Mart: most of the shares were held by people who wished to employ funds elsewhere; family members who enjoyed running their business wanted to continue both as owners and managers; several generations of the family were active in the business, providing management for as far as the eye can see; and the managing family wanted a purchaser who would not re-sell, regardless of price, and who would let the business be run in the future as it had been in the past. Both Fechheimer and NFM were right for us, and we were right for them.

You may be amused to know that neither Charlie nor I have been to Cincinnati, headquarters for Fechheimer, to see their operation. (And, incidentally, it works both ways: Chuck Huggins, who has been running See's for 15 years, has never been to Omaha.) If our success were to depend upon insights we developed through plant inspections, Berkshire would be in big trouble. Rather, in considering an acquisition, we attempt to evaluate the economic characteristics of the business—its competitive strengths and weaknesses—and the quality of the people we will be joining. Fechheimer was a standout in both respects. In addition to Bob and George Heldman, who are in their mid-60s—spring chickens by our standards—there are three members of the next generation, Gary, Roger and Fred, to insure continuity.

As a prototype for acquisitions, Fechheimer has only one drawback: size. We hope our next acquisition is at least several times as large but a carbon copy in all other respects. Our threshold for minimum annual after-tax earnings of potential acquisitions has been moved up to $10 million from the $5 million level that prevailed when Bob wrote to me.

Flushed with success, we repeat our ad. If you have a business that fits, call me or, preferably, write.

Here's what we're looking for:
(1) large purchases (at least $10 million of after-tax earnings),
(2) demonstrated consistent earning power (future projections are of little interest to us, nor are "turn-around" situations),
(3) businesses earning good returns on equity while employing little or no debt.
(4) management in place (we can't supply it),
(5) simple businesses (if there's lots of technology, we won't understand it),
(6) an offering price (we don't want to waste our time or that of the seller by talking, even preliminarily, about a transaction when price is unknown).

We will not engage in unfriendly takeovers. We can promise complete confidentiality and a very fast answer—customarily within five minutes—as to whether we're interested. We prefer to buy for cash, but will consider issuing stock when we receive as much in intrinsic business value as we give. Indeed, following recent advances in the price of Berkshire stock, transactions involving stock issuance may be quite feasible. We invite potential sellers to check us out by contacting people with whom we have done business in the past. For the right business—and the right people—we can provide a good home.

On the other hand, we frequently get approached about acquisitions that don't come close to meeting our tests: new ventures, turnarounds, auction-like sales, and the ever-popular (among brokers) "I'm-sure-something-will-work-out-if-you-people-get-to-know-each-other." None of these attracts us in the least.

* * *

Besides being interested in the purchases of entire businesses as described above, we are also interested in the negotiated purchase of large, but not controlling, blocks of stock, as in our Cap Cities purchase. Such purchases appeal to us only when we are very comfortable with both the economics of the business and the ability and integrity of the people running the operation. We prefer large transactions: in the unusual case we might do something as small as $50 million (or even smaller), but our preference is for commitments many times that size.

Insurance Operations

We present our usual table of industry figures, expanded this year to include data about incurred losses and the GNP inflation index. The contrast in 1986 between the growth in premiums and growth in incurred losses will show you why underwriting results for the year improved materially:

	Yearly Change in Premiums Written (%)	Statutory Combined Ratio After Policyholder Dividends	Yearly Change in Incurred Losses (%)	Inflation Rate Measured by GNP Deflator (%)
1981	3.8	106.0	6.5	9.7
1982	4.4	109.8	8.4	6.4
1983	4.6	112.0	6.8	3.9
1984	9.2	117.9	16.9	3.8
1985	22.1	116.5	16.1	3.3
1986 (Est.)	22.6	108.5	15.5	2.6

Source: Best's Insurance Management Reports

The combined ratio represents total insurance costs (losses incurred plus expenses) compared to revenue from premiums: a ratio below 100 indicates an underwriting profit, and one above 100 indicates a loss. When the investment income that an insurer earns from holding on to policyholders' funds ("the float") is taken into account, a combined ratio in the 107-112 range typically produces an overall break-even result, exclusive of earnings on the funds provided by shareholders.

The math of the insurance business, encapsulated by the table, is not very complicated. In years when the industry's annual gain in revenues (premiums) pokes along at 4% or 5%, underwriting losses are sure to mount. This is not because auto accidents, fires, windstorms and the like are occurring more frequently, nor has it lately been the fault of general inflation. Today, social and judicial inflation are the major culprits; the cost of entering a courtroom has simply ballooned. Part of the jump in cost arises from skyrocketing verdicts, and part from the tendency of judges and juries to expand the coverage of insurance policies beyond that contemplated by the insurer when the policies were written. Seeing no let-up in either trend, we continue to believe that the industry's revenues must grow at close to 10% annually for it to just hold its own in terms of profitability, even though general inflation may be running only 2%—4%.

In 1986, as noted, the industry's premium volume soared even faster than loss costs. Consequently, the underwriting loss of the industry fell dramatically. In last year's report we predicted this sharp improvement but also predicted that prosperity would be fleeting. Alas, this second prediction is already proving accurate. The rate of gain in the industry's premium volume has slowed significantly (from an estimated 27.1% in 1986's first quarter, to 23.5% in the second, to 21.8% in the third, to 18.7% in the fourth), and we expect further slowing in 1987. Indeed, the rate of gain may well fall below my 10% "equilibrium" figure by the third quarter.

Nevertheless, underwriting results in 1987, assuming they are not dragged down by a major natural catastrophe, will again improve materially because price increases are recognized in revenues on a lagged basis. In effect, the good news in earnings follows the good news in prices by six to twelve months. But the improving trend in earnings will probably end by late 1988 or early 1989. Thereafter the industry is likely to head south in a hurry.

Pricing behavior in the insurance industry continues to be exactly what can be expected in a commodity-type business. Only under shortage conditions are high profits achieved, and such conditions don't last long. When the profit sun begins to shine, long-established insurers shower investors with new shares in order to build capital. In addition, newly-formed insurers rush to sell shares at the advantageous prices available in the new-issue market (prices advantageous, that is, to the insiders promoting the company but rarely to the new shareholders). These moves guarantee future trouble: capacity soars, competitive juices flow, and prices fade.

It's interesting to observe insurance leaders beseech their colleagues to behave in a more "statesmanlike" manner when pricing policies. "Why," they ask, "can't we learn from history, even out the peaks and valleys, and consistently price to make reasonable profits?" What they wish, of course, is pricing that resembles, say, that of The Wall Street journal, whose prices are ample to start with and rise consistently each year.

Such calls for improved behavior have all of the efficacy of those made by a Nebraska corn grower asking his fellow growers, worldwide, to market their corn with more statesmanship. What's needed is not more statesmen, but less corn. By raising large amounts of capital in the last two years, the insurance industry has, to continue our metaphor, vastly expanded its plantings of corn. The resulting increase in "crop"—i.e., the proliferation of insurance capacity—will have the same effect on prices and profits that surplus crops have had since time immemorial.

Our own insurance operation did well in 1986 and is also likely to do well in 1987. We have benefited significantly from industry conditions. But much of our prosperity arises from the efforts and ability of Mike Goldberg, manager of all insurance operations.

Our combined ratio (on a statutory basis and excluding structured settlements and financial reinsurance) fell from 111 in 1985 to 103 in 1986. In addition, our premium growth has been exceptional: although final figures aren't available, I believe that over the past two years we were the fastest growing company among the country's top 100 insurers. Some of our growth, it is true, came from our large quota-share contract with Fireman's Fund, described in last year's report and updated in Charlie's letter on page 54. But even if the premiums from that contract are excluded from the calculation, we probably still ranked first in growth.

Interestingly, we were the slowest-growing large insurer in the years immediately preceding 1985. In fact, we shrank—and we will do so again from time to time in the future. Our large swings in volume do not mean that we come and go from the insurance marketplace. Indeed, we are its most steadfast participant, always standing ready, at prices we believe adequate, to write a wide variety of high-limit coverages. The swings in our volume arise instead from the here-today, gone-tomorrow behavior of other insurers. When most insurers are "gone," because their capital is inadequate or they have been frightened by losses, insureds rush to us and find us ready to do business. But when hordes of insurers are "here," and are slashing prices far below expectable costs, many customers naturally leave us in order to take advantage of the bargains temporarily being offered by our competition.

Our firmness on prices works no hardship on the consumer: he is being bombarded by attractively priced insurance offers at those times when we are doing little business. And it works no hardship on our employees: we don't engage in layoffs when we experience a cyclical slowdown at one of our generally-profitable insurance operations. This no-layoff practice is in our self-interest. Employees who fear that large layoffs will accompany sizable reductions in premium volume will understandably produce scads of business through thick and thin (mostly thin).

The trends in National Indemnity's traditional business—the writing of commercial auto and general liability policies through general agents—suggest how gun-shy other insurers became for a while and how brave they are now getting. In the last quarter of 1984, NICO's monthly volume averaged $5 million, about what it had been running for several years. By the first quarter of 1986, monthly volume had climbed to about $35 million. In recent months, a sharp decline has set in. Monthly volume is currently about $20 million and will continue to fall as new competitors surface and prices are cut. Ironically, the managers of certain major new competitors are the very same managers that just a few years ago bankrupted insurers that were our old competitors. Through state-mandated guaranty funds, we must pay some of the losses these managers left unpaid, and now we find them writing the same sort of business under a new name. C'est la guerre.

The business we call "large risks" expanded significantly during 1986, and will be important to us in the future. In this operation, we regularly write policies with annual premiums of $1—$3 million, or even higher. This business will necessarily be highly volatile—both in volume and profitability—but our premier capital position and willingness to write large net lines make us a very strong force in the market when prices are right. On the other hand, our structured settlement business has become near-dormant because present prices make no sense to us.

The 1986 loss reserve development of our insurance group is chronicled on page 46. The figures show the amount of error in our yearend 1985 liabilities that a year of settlements and further evaluation has revealed. As you can see, what I told you last year about our loss liabilities was far from true—and that makes three years in a row of error. If the physiological rules that applied to Pinocchio were to apply to me, my nose would now draw crowds.

When insurance executives belatedly establish proper reserves, they often speak of "reserve strengthening," a term that has a rather noble ring to it. They almost make it sound as if they are adding extra layers of strength to an already-solid balance sheet. That's not the case: instead the term is a euphemism for what should more properly be called "correction of previous untruths" (albeit nonintentional ones).

We made a special effort at the end of 1986 to reserve accurately. However, we tried just as hard at the end of 1985. Only time will tell whether we have finally succeeded in correctly estimating our insurance liabilities.

Despite the difficulties we have had in reserving and the commodity economics of the industry, we expect our insurance business to both grow and make significant amounts of money—but progress will be distinctly irregular and there will be major unpleasant surprises from time to time. It's a treacherous business and a wary attitude is essential. We must heed Woody Allen: "While the lamb may lie down with the lion, the lamb shouldn't count on getting a whole lot of sleep."

In our insurance operations we have an advantage in attitude, we have an advantage in capital, and we are developing an advantage in personnel. Additionally, I like to think we have some long-term edge in investing the float developed from policyholder funds. The nature of the business suggests that we will need all of these advantages in order to prosper.

* * *

GEICO Corporation, 41% owned by Berkshire, had an outstanding year in 1986. Industrywide, underwriting experience in personal lines did not improve nearly as much as it did in commercial lines. But GEICO, writing personal lines almost exclusively, improved its combined ratio to 96.9 and recorded a 16% gain in premium volume. GEICO also continued to repurchase its own shares and ended the year with 5.5% fewer shares outstanding than it had at the start of the year. Our share of GEICO's premium volume is over $500 million, close to double that of only three years ago. GEICO's book of business is one of the best in the world of insurance, far better indeed than Berkshire's own book.

The most important ingredient in GEICO's success is rock-bottom operating costs, which set the company apart from literally hundreds of competitors that offer auto insurance. The total of GEICO's underwriting expense and loss adjustment expense in 1986 was only 23.5% of premiums. Many major companies show percentages 15 points higher than that. Even such huge direct writers as Allstate and State Farm incur appreciably higher costs than does GEICO.

The difference between GEICO's costs and those of its competitors is a kind of moat that protects a valuable and much-sought-after business castle. No one understands this moat-around-the-castle concept better than Bill Snyder, Chairman of GEICO. He continually widens the moat by driving down costs still more, thereby defending and strengthening the economic franchise. Between 1985 and 1986, GEICO's total expense ratio dropped from 24.1% to the 23.5% mentioned earlier and, under Bill's leadership, the ratio is almost certain to drop further. If it does—and if GEICO maintains its service and underwriting standards—the company's future will be brilliant indeed.

The second stage of the GEICO rocket is fueled by Lou Simpson, Vice Chairman, who has run the company's investments since late 1979. Indeed, it's a little embarrassing for me, the fellow responsible for investments at Berkshire, to chronicle Lou's performance at GEICO. Only my ownership of a controlling block of Berkshire stock makes me secure enough to give you the following figures, comparing the overall return of the equity portfolio at GEICO to that of the Standard & Poor's 500:

	GEICO's Equities	S&P 500
1980	23.7%	32.3%
1981	5.4	(5.0)
1982	45.8	21.4
1983	36.0	22.4
1984	21.8	6.2
1985	45.8	31.6
1986	38.7	18.6

These are not only terrific figures but, fully as important, they have been achieved in the right way. Lou has consistently invested in undervalued common stocks that, individually, were unlikely to present him with a permanent loss and that, collectively, were close to risk-free.

In sum, GEICO is an exceptional business run by exceptional managers. We are fortunate to be associated with them.

Marketable Securities

During 1986, our insurance companies purchased about $700 million of tax-exempt bonds, most having a maturity of 8 to 12 years. You might think that this commitment indicates a considerable enthusiasm for such bonds. Unfortunately, that's not so: at best, the bonds are mediocre investments. They simply seemed the least objectionable alternative at the time we bought them, and still seem so. (Currently liking neither stocks nor bonds, I find myself the polar opposite of Mae West as she declared: "I like only two kinds of men—foreign and domestic.")

We must, of necessity, hold marketable securities in our insurance companies and, as money comes in, we have only five directions to go: (1) long-term common stock investments; (2) long-term fixed-income securities; (3) medium-term fixed-income securities; (4) short-term cash equivalents; and (5) short-term arbitrage commitments.

Common stocks, of course, are the most fun. When conditions are right that is, when companies with good economics and good management sell well below intrinsic business value—stocks sometimes provide grand-slam home runs. But we currently find no equities that come close to meeting our tests.

This statement in no way translates into a stock market prediction: we have no idea—and never have had—whether the market is going to go up, down, or sideways in the near- or intermediate term future.

What we do know, however, is that occasional outbreaks of those two super-contagious diseases, fear and greed, will forever occur in the investment community. The timing of these epidemics will be unpredictable. And the market aberrations produced by them will be equally unpredictable, both as to duration and degree. Therefore, we never try to anticipate the arrival or departure of either disease. Our goal is more modest: we simply attempt to be fearful when others are greedy and to be greedy only when others are fearful.

As this is written, little fear is visible in Wall Street. Instead, euphoria prevails—and why not? What could be more exhilarating than to participate in a bull market in which the rewards to owners of businesses become gloriously uncoupled from the plodding performances of the businesses themselves. Unfortunately, however, stocks can't outperform businesses indefinitely.

Indeed, because of the heavy transaction and investment management costs they bear, stockholders as a whole and over the long term must inevitably underperform the companies they own. If American business, in aggregate, earns about 12% on equity annually, investors must end up earning significantly less. Bull markets can obscure mathematical laws, but they cannot repeal them.

The second category of investments open to our insurance companies is long-term bonds. These are unlikely to be of interest to us except in very special situations, such as the Washington Public Power Supply System #1, #2 and #3 issues, discussed in our 1984 report. (At yearend, we owned WPPSS issues having an amortized cost of $218 million and a market value of $310 million, paying us $31.7 million in annual tax-exempt income.) Our aversion to long-term bonds relates to our fear that we will see much higher rates of inflation within the next decade. Over time, the behavior of our currency will be determined by the behavior of our legislators. This relationship poses a continuing threat to currency stability—and a corresponding threat to the owners of long-term bonds.

We continue to periodically employ money in the arbitrage field. However, unlike most arbitrageurs, who purchase dozens of securities each year, we purchase only a few. We restrict ourselves to large deals that have been announced publicly and do not bet on the come. Therefore, our potential profits are apt to be small; but, with luck, our disappointments will also be few.

Our yearend portfolio shown below includes one arbitrage commitment, Lear-Siegler. Our balance sheet also includes a receivable for $145 million, representing the money owed us (and paid a few days later) by Unilever, then in the process of purchasing Chesebrough-Ponds, another of our arbitrage holdings. Arbitrage is an alternative to Treasury Bills as a short-term parking place for money—a choice that combines potentially higher returns with higher risks. To date, our returns from the funds committed to arbitrage have been many times higher than they would have been had we left those funds in Treasury Bills. Nonetheless, one bad experience could change the scorecard markedly.

We also, though it takes some straining, currently view medium-term tax-exempt bonds as an alternative to short-term Treasury holdings. Buying these bonds, we run a risk of significant loss if, as seems probable, we sell many of them well before maturity. However, we believe this risk is more than counter-balanced first, by the much higher after-tax returns currently realizable from these securities as compared to Treasury Bills and second, by the possibility that sales will produce an overall profit rather than a loss. Our expectation of a higher total return, after allowing for the possibility of loss and after taking into account all tax effects, is a relatively close call and could well be wrong. Even if we sell our bonds at a fairly large loss, however, we may end up reaping a higher after-tax return than we would have realized by repeatedly rolling over Treasury Bills.

In any event, you should know that our expectations for both the stocks and bonds we now hold are exceptionally modest, given current market levels. Probably the best thing that could happen to us is a market in which we would choose to sell many of our bond holdings at a significant loss in order to re-allocate funds to the far-better equity values then very likely to exist. The bond losses I am talking about would occur if high interest rates came along; the same rates would probably depress common stocks considerably more than medium-term bonds.

We show below our 1986 yearend net holdings in marketable equities. All positions with a market value of over $25 million are listed, and the interests attributable to minority shareholdings of Wesco Financial Corp. and Nebraska Furniture Mart are excluded.

No. of Shares		Cost	Market
		(000s omitted)	
2,990,000	Capital Cities/ABC, Inc.	$515,775	$ 801,694
6,850,000	GEICO Corporation	45,713	674,725
2,379,200	Handy & Harman	27,318	46,989
489,300	Lear Siegler, Inc.	44,064	44,587
1,727,765	The Washington Post Company	9,731	269,531
		642,601	1,837,526
	All Other Common Stockholdings	12,763	36,507
	Total Common Stocks	$655,364	$1,874,033

We should note that we expect to keep permanently our three primary holdings, Capital Cities/ABC, Inc., GEICO Corporation, and The Washington Post. Even if these securities were to appear significantly overpriced, we would not anticipate selling them, just as we would not sell See's or Buffalo Evening News if someone were to offer us a price far above what we believe those businesses are worth.

This attitude may seem old-fashioned in a corporate world in which activity has become the order of the day. The modern manager refers to his "portfolio" of businesses—meaning that all of them are candidates for "restructuring" whenever such a move is dictated by Wall Street preferences, operating conditions or a new corporate "concept." (Restructuring is defined narrowly, however: it extends only to dumping offending businesses, not to dumping the officers and directors who bought the businesses in the first place. "Hate the sin but love the sinner" is a theology as popular with the Fortune 500 as it is with the Salvation Army.)

Investment managers are even more hyperkinetic: their behavior during trading hours makes whirling dervishes appear sedated by comparison. Indeed, the term "institutional investor" is becoming one of those self-contradictions called an oxymoron, comparable to "jumbo shrimp," "lady mudwrestler" and "inexpensive lawyer."

Despite the enthusiasm for activity that has swept business and financial America, we will stick with our 'til-death-do-us-part policy. It's the only one with which Charlie and I are comfortable, it produces decent results, and it lets our managers and those of our investees run their businesses free of distractions.

NHP, Inc.

Last year we paid $23.7 million for about 50% of NHP, Inc., a developer, syndicator, owner and manager of multi-family rental housing. Should all executive stock options that have been authorized be granted and exercised, our equity interest will decline to slightly over 45%.

NHP, Inc. has a most unusual genealogy. In 1967, President Johnson appointed a commission of business and civic leaders, led by Edgar Kaiser, to study ways to increase the supply of multifamily housing for low- and moderate-income tenants. Certain members of the commission subsequently formed and promoted two business entities to foster this goal. Both are now owned by NHP, Inc. and one operates under unusual ground rules: three of its directors must be appointed by the President, with the advice and consent of the Senate, and it is also required by law to submit an annual report to the President.

Over 260 major corporations, motivated more by the idea of public service than profit, invested $42 million in the two original entities, which promptly began, through partnerships, to develop government-subsidized rental property. The typical partnership owned a single property and was largely financed by a non-recourse mortgage. Most of the equity money for each partnership was supplied by a group of limited partners who were primarily attracted by the large tax deductions that went with the investment. NHP acted as general partner and also purchased a small portion of each partnership's equity.

The Government's housing policy has, of course, shifted and NHP has necessarily broadened its activities to include non-subsidized apartments commanding market-rate rents. In addition, a subsidiary of NHP builds single-family homes in the Washington, D.C. area, realizing revenues of about $50 million annually.

NHP now oversees about 500 partnership properties that are located in 40 states, the District of Columbia and Puerto Rico, and that include about 80,000 housing units. The cost of these properties was more than $2.5 billion and they have been well maintained. NHP directly manages about 55,000 of the housing units and supervises the management of the rest. The company's revenues from management are about $16 million annually, and growing.

In addition to the equity interests it purchased upon the formation of each partnership, NHP owns varying residual interests that come into play when properties are disposed of and distributions are made to the limited partners. The residuals on many of NHP's "deep subsidy" properties are unlikely to be of much value. But residuals on certain other properties could prove quite valuable, particularly if inflation should heat up.

The tax-oriented syndication of properties to individuals has been halted by the Tax Reform Act of 1986. In the main, NHP is currently trying to develop equity positions or significant residual interests in non-subsidized rental properties of quality and size (typically 200 to 500 units). In projects of this kind, NHP usually works with one or more large institutional investors or lenders. NHP will continue to seek ways to develop low- and moderate-income apartment housing, but will not likely meet success unless government policy changes.

Besides ourselves, the large shareholders in NHP are Weyerhauser (whose interest is about 25%) and a management group led by Rod Heller, chief executive of NHP. About 60 major corporations also continue to hold small interests, none larger than 2%.

Taxation

The Tax Reform Act of 1986 affects our various businesses in important and divergent ways. Although we find much to praise in the Act, the net financial effect for Berkshire is negative: our rate of increase in business value is likely to be at least moderately slower under the new law than under the old. The net effect for our shareholders is even more negative: every dollar of increase in per-share business value, assuming the increase is accompanied by an equivalent dollar gain in the market value of Berkshire stock, will produce 72 cents of after-tax gain for our shareholders rather than the 80 cents produced under the old law. This result, of course, reflects the rise in the maximum tax rate on personal capital gains from 20% to 28%.

Here are the main tax changes that affect Berkshire:

- The tax rate on corporate ordinary income is scheduled to decrease from 46% in 1986 to 34% in 1988. This change obviously affects us positively—and it also has a significant positive effect on two of our three major investees, Capital Cities/ABC and The Washington Post Company.

I say this knowing that over the years there has been a lot of fuzzy and often partisan commentary about who really pays corporate taxes—businesses or their customers. The argument, of course, has usually turned around tax increases, not decreases. Those people resisting increases in corporate rates frequently argue that corporations in reality pay none of the taxes levied on them but, instead, act as a sort of economic pipeline, passing all taxes through to consumers. According to these advocates, any corporate-tax increase will simply lead to higher prices that, for the corporation, offset the increase. Having taken this position, proponents of the "pipeline" theory must also conclude that a tax decrease for corporations will not help profits but will instead flow through, leading to correspondingly lower prices for consumers.

Conversely, others argue that corporations not only pay the taxes levied upon them, but absorb them also. Consumers, this school says, will be unaffected by changes in corporate rates.

What really happens? When the corporate rate is cut, do Berkshire, The Washington Post, Cap Cities, etc., themselves soak up the benefits, or do these companies pass the benefits along to their customers in the form of lower prices? This is an important question for investors and managers, as well as for policymakers.

Our conclusion is that in some cases the benefits of lower corporate taxes fall exclusively, or almost exclusively, upon the corporation and its shareholders, and that in other cases the benefits are entirely, or almost entirely, passed through to the customer. What determines the outcome is the strength of the corporation's business franchise and whether the profitability of that franchise is regulated.

For example, when the franchise is strong and after-tax profits are regulated in a relatively precise manner, as is the case with electric utilities, changes in corporate tax rates are largely reflected in prices, not in profits. When taxes are cut, prices will usually be reduced in short order. When taxes are increased, prices will rise, though often not as promptly.

A similar result occurs in a second arena—in the price-competitive industry, whose companies typically operate with very weak business franchises. In such industries, the free market "regulates" after-tax profits in a delayed and irregular, but generally effective, manner. The marketplace, in effect, performs much the same function in dealing with the price-competitive industry as the Public Utilities Commission does in dealing with electric utilities. In these industries, therefore, tax changes eventually affect prices more than profits.

In the case of unregulated businesses blessed with strong franchises, however, it's a different story: the corporation and its shareholders are then the major beneficiaries of tax cuts. These companies benefit from a tax cut much as the electric company would if it lacked a regulator to force down prices.

Many of our businesses, both those we own in whole and in part, possess such franchises. Consequently, reductions in their taxes largely end up in our pockets rather than the pockets of our customers. While this may be impolitic to state, it is impossible to deny. If you are tempted to believe otherwise, think for a moment of the most able brain surgeon or lawyer in your area. Do you really expect the fees of this expert (the local "franchise-holder" in his or her specialty) to be reduced now that the top personal tax rate is being cut from 50% to 28%?

Your joy at our conclusion that lower rates benefit a number of our operating businesses and investees should be severely tempered, however, by another of our convictions: scheduled 1988 tax rates, both individual and corporate, seem totally unrealistic to us. These rates will very likely bestow a fiscal problem on Washington that will prove incompatible with price stability. We believe, therefore, that ultimately—within, say, five years—either higher tax rates or higher inflation rates are almost certain to materialize. And it would not surprise us to see both.

- Corporate capital gains tax rates have been increased from 28% to 34%, effective in 1987. This change will have an important adverse effect on Berkshire because we expect much of our gain in business value in the future, as in the past, to arise from capital gains. For example, our three major investment holdings—Cap Cities, GEICO, and Washington Post—at yearend had a market value of over $1.7 billion, close to 75% of the total net worth of Berkshire, and yet they deliver us only about $9 million in annual income. Instead, all three retain a very high percentage of their earnings, which we expect to eventually deliver us capital gains.

  The new law increases the rate for all gains realized in the future, including the unrealized gains that existed before the law was enacted. At yearend, we had $1.2 billion of such unrealized gains in our equity investments. The effect of the new law on our balance sheet will be delayed because a GAAP rule stipulates that the deferred tax liability applicable to unrealized gains should be stated at last year's 28% tax rate rather than the current 34% rate. This rule is expected to change soon. The moment it does, about $73 million will disappear from our GAAP net worth and be added to the deferred tax account.

- Dividend and interest income received by our insurance companies will be taxed far more heavily under the new law. First, all corporations will be taxed on 20% of the dividends they receive from other domestic corporations, up from 15% under the old law. Second, there is a change concerning the residual 80% that applies only to property/casualty companies: 15% of that residual will be taxed if the stocks paying the dividends were purchased after August 7, 1986. A third change, again applying only to property/casualty companies, concerns tax-exempt bonds: interest on bonds purchased by insurers after August 7, 1986 will only be 85% tax-exempt.

  The last two changes are very important. They mean that our income from the investments we make in future years will be significantly lower than would have been the case under the old law. My best guess is that these changes alone will eventually reduce the earning power of our insurance operation by at least 10% from what we could previously have expected.

- The new tax law also materially changes the timing of tax payments by property/casualty insurance companies. One new rule requires us to discount our loss reserves in our tax returns, a change that will decrease deductions and increase taxable income. Another rule, to be phased in over six years, requires us to include 20% of our unearned premium reserve in taxable income.

  Neither rule changes the amount of the annual tax accrual in our reports to you, but each materially accelerates the schedule of payments. That is, taxes formerly deferred will now be front-ended, a change that will significantly cut the profitability of our business. An analogy will suggest the toll: if, upon turning 21, you were required to immediately pay tax on all income you were due to receive throughout your life, both your lifetime wealth and your estate would be a small fraction of what they would be if all taxes on your income were payable only when you died.

Attentive readers may spot an inconsistency in what we say. Earlier, discussing companies in price-competitive industries, we suggested that tax increases or reductions affect these companies relatively little, but instead are largely passed along to their customers. But now we are saying that tax increases will affect profits of Berkshire's property/casualty companies even though they operate in an intensely price-competitive industry.

The reason this industry is likely to be an exception to our general rule is that not all major insurers will be working with identical tax equations. Important differences will exist for several reasons: a new alternative minimum tax will materially affect some companies but not others; certain major insurers have huge loss carry-forwards that will largely shield their income from significant taxes for at least a few years; and the results of some large insurers will be folded into the consolidated returns of companies with non-insurance businesses. These disparate conditions will produce widely varying marginal tax rates in the property/casualty industry. That will not be the case, however, in most other price-competitive industries, such as aluminum, autos and department stores, in which the major players will generally contend with similar tax equations.

The absence of a common tax calculus for property/casualty companies means that the increased taxes falling on the industry will probably not be passed along to customers to the degree that they would in a typical price-competitive industry. Insurers, in other words, will themselves bear much of the new tax burdens.

- A partial offset to these burdens is a "fresh start" adjustment that occurred on January 1, 1987 when our December 31, 1986 loss reserve figures were converted for tax purposes to the newly-required discounted basis. (In our reports to you, however, reserves will remain on exactly the same basis as in the past—undiscounted except in special cases such as structured settlements.) The net effect of the "fresh start" is to give us a double deduction: we will get a tax deduction in 1987 and future years for a portion of our-incurred-but-unpaid insurance losses that have already been fully deducted as costs in 1986 and earlier years.

The increase in net worth that is produced by this change is not yet reflected in our financial statements. Rather, under present GAAP rules (which may be changed), the benefit will flow into the earnings statement and, consequently, into net worth over the next few years by way of reduced tax charges. We expect the total benefit from the fresh-start adjustment to be in the $30—$40 million range. It should be noted, however, that this is a one-time benefit, whereas the negative impact of the other insurance-related tax changes is not only ongoing but, in important respects, will become more severe as time passes.

- The General Utilities Doctrine was repealed by the new tax law. This means that in 1987 and thereafter there will be a double tax on corporate liquidations, one at the corporate level and another at the shareholder level. In the past, the tax at the corporate level could be avoided, If Berkshire, for example, were to be liquidated—which it most certainly won't be—shareholders would, under the new law, receive far less from the sales of our properties than they would have if the properties had been sold in the past, assuming identical prices in each sale. Though this outcome is theoretical in our case, the change in the law will very materially affect many companies. Therefore, it also affects our evaluations of prospective investments. Take, for example, producing oil and gas businesses, selected media companies, real estate companies, etc. that might wish to sell out. The values that their shareholders can realize are likely to be significantly reduced simply because the General Utilities Doctrine has been repealed—though the companies' operating economics will not have changed adversely at all. My impression is that this important change in the law has not yet been fully comprehended by either investors or managers.

This section of our report has been longer and more complicated than I would have liked. But the changes in the law are many and important, particularly for property/casualty insurers. As I have noted, the new law will hurt Berkshire's results, but the negative impact is impossible to quantify with any precision.

Miscellaneous

We bought a corporate jet last year. What you have heard about such planes is true: they are very expensive and a luxury in situations like ours where little travel to out-of-the-way places is required. And planes not only cost a lot to operate, they cost a lot just to look at. Pre-tax, cost of capital plus depreciation on a new $15 million plane probably runs $3 million annually. On our own plane, bought for $850,000 used, such costs run close to $200,000 annually.

Cognizant of such figures, your Chairman, unfortunately, has in the past made a number of rather intemperate remarks about corporate jets. Accordingly, prior to our purchase, I was forced into my Galileo mode. I promptly experienced the necessary "counter-revelation" and travel is now considerably easier—and considerably costlier—than in the past. Whether Berkshire will get its money's worth from the plane is an open question, but I will work at achieving some business triumph that I can (no matter how dubiously) attribute to it. I'm afraid Ben Franklin had my number. Said he: "So convenient a thing it is to be a reasonable creature, since it enables one to find or make a reason for everything one has a mind to do."

About 97% of all eligible shares participated in Berkshire's 1986 shareholder-designated contributions program. Contributions made through the program were $4 million, and 1,934 charities were recipients.

We urge new shareholders to read the description of our shareholder-designated contributions program that appears on pages 58 and 59. If you wish to participate in future programs, we strongly urge that you immediately make sure your shares are registered in the name of the actual owner, not in "street" name or nominee name. Shares not so registered on September 30, 1987 will be ineligible for the 1987 program.

* * *

Last year almost 450 people attended our shareholders' meeting, up from about 250 the year before (and from about a dozen ten years ago). I hope you can join us on May 19th in Omaha. Charlie and I like to answer owner-related questions and I can promise you that our shareholders will pose many good ones. Finishing up the questions may take quite a while—we had about 65 last year so you should feel free to leave once your own have been answered.

Last year, after the meeting, one shareholder from New Jersey and another from New York went to the Furniture Mart, where each purchased a $5,000 Oriental rug from Mrs. B. (To be precise, they purchased rugs that might cost $10,000 elsewhere for which they were charged about $5,000.) Mrs. B was pleased—but not satisfied—and she will be looking for you at the store after this year's meeting. Unless our shareholders top last year's record, I'll be in trouble. So do me (and yourself) a favor, and go see her.

                                            Warren E. Buffett
February 27, 1987   Chairman of the Board

Appendix

Purchase-Price Accounting Adjustments and the "Cash Flow" Fallacy

First a short quiz: below are abbreviated 1986 statements of earnings for two companies. Which business is the more valuable?

	Company O	Company N
	(000s Omitted)	
Revenues	$ 677,240	$ 677,240
Costs of Goods Sold:		
Historical costs, excluding depreciation	$ 341,170	$341,170
Special non-cash inventory costs		4,979[1]
Depreciation of plant and equipment	8,301	13,355[2]
	349,471	359,504
Gross Profit	$ 327,769	$ 317,736
Selling & Admin. Expense.	$ 260,286	$260,286
Amortization of Goodwill		595[3]
	260,286	260,881
Operating Profit	$ 67,483	$ 56,855
Other Income, Net	4,135	4,135
Pre-Tax Income	$ 71,618	$ 60,990
Applicable Income Tax:		
Historical deferred and current tax . .	$ 31,387	$ 31,387
Non-Cash Inter-period Allocation Adjustment		998[4]
	31,387	32,385
Net Income	$ 40,231	$ 28,605

(Numbers (1) through (4) designate items discussed later in this section.)

As you've probably guessed, Companies O and N are the same business—Scott Fetzer. In the "O" (for "old") column we have shown what the company's 1986 GAAP earnings would have been if we had not purchased it; in the "N" (for "new") column we have shown Scott Fetzer's GAAP earnings as actually reported by Berkshire.

It should be emphasized that the two columns depict identical economics—i.e., the same sales, wages, taxes, etc. And both "companies" generate the same amount of cash for owners. Only the accounting is different.

So, fellow philosophers, which column presents truth? Upon which set of numbers should managers and investors focus?

Before we tackle those questions, let's look at what produces the disparity between O and N. We will simplify our discussion in some respects, but the simplification should not produce any inaccuracies in analysis or conclusions.

The contrast between O and N comes about because we paid an amount for Scott Fetzer that was different from its stated net worth. Under GAAP, such differences—such premiums or discounts—must be accounted for by "purchase-price adjustments." In Scott Fetzer's case, we paid $315 million for net assets that were carried on its books at $172.4 million. So we paid a premium of $142.6 million.

The first step in accounting for any premium paid is to adjust the carrying value of current assets to current values. In practice, this requirement usually does not affect receivables, which are routinely carried at current value, but often affects inventories. Because of a $22.9 million LIFO reserve and other accounting intricacies, Scott Fetzer's inventory account was carried at a $37.3 million discount from current value. So, making our first accounting move, we used $37.3 million of our $142.6 million premium to increase the carrying value of the inventory.

Assuming any premium is left after current assets are adjusted, the next step is to adjust fixed assets to current value. In our case, this adjustment also required a few accounting acrobatics relating to deferred taxes. Since this has been billed as a simplified discussion, I will skip the details and give you the bottom line: $68.0 million was added to fixed assets and $13.0 million was eliminated from deferred tax liabilities. After making this $81.0 million adjustment, we were left with $24.3 million of premium to allocate.

Had our situation called for them two steps would next have been required: the adjustment of intangible assets other than Goodwill to current fair values, and the restatement of liabilities to current fair values, a requirement that typically affects only long-term debt and unfunded pension liabilities. In Scott Fetzer's case, however, neither of these steps was necessary.

The final accounting adjustment we needed to make, after recording fair market values for all assets and liabilities, was the assignment of the residual premium to Goodwill (technically known as "excess of cost over the fair value of net assets acquired"). This residual amounted to $24.3 million. Thus, the balance sheet of Scott Fetzer immediately before the acquisition, which is summarized below in column O, was transformed by the purchase into the balance sheet shown in column N. In real terms, both balance sheets depict the same assets and liabilities—but, as you can see, certain figures differ significantly.

	Company O	Company N
	(000s Omitted)	
Assets		
Cash and Cash Equivalents	$ 3,593	$ 3,593
Receivables, net	90,919	90,919
Inventories	77,489	114,764
Other	5,954	5,954
Total Current Assets	177,955	215,230
Property, Plant, and Equipment, net	80,967	148,960
Investments in and Advances to Unconsolidated Subsidiaries and Joint Ventures	93,589	93,589
Other Assets, including Goodwill	9,836	34,210
	$362,347	$491,989
Liabilities		
Notes Payable and Current Portion of Long-term Debt	$ 4,650	$ 4,650
Accounts Payable	39,003	39,003
Accrued Liabilities	84,939	84,939
Total Current Liabilities	128,592	128,592
Long-term Debt and Capitalized Leases	34,669	34,669
Deferred Income Taxes	17,052	4,075
Other Deferred Credits	9,657	9,657
Total Liabilities	189,970	176,993
Shareholders' Equity	172,377	314,996
	$362,347	$491,989

The higher balance sheet figures shown in column N produce the lower income figures shown in column N of the earnings statement presented earlier. This is the result of the asset write-ups and of the fact that some of the written-up assets must be depreciated or amortized. The higher the asset figure, the higher the annual depreciation or amortization charge to earnings must be. The charges that flowed to the earnings statement because of the balance sheet write-ups were numbered in the statement of earnings shown earlier:

(1) $4,979,000 for non-cash inventory costs resulting, primarily, from reductions that Scott Fetzer made in its inventories during 1986; charges of this kind are apt to be small or non-existent in future years.

(2) $5,054,000 for extra depreciation attributable to the write-up of fixed assets; a charge approximating this amount will probably be made annually for 12 more years.

(3) $595,000 for amortization of Goodwill; this charge will be made annually for 39 more years in a slightly larger amount because our purchase was made on January 6 and, therefore, the 1986 figure applies to only 98% of the year.

(4) $998,000 for deferred-tax acrobatics that are beyond my ability to explain briefly (or perhaps even non-briefly); a charge approximating this amount will probably be made annually for 12 more years.

It is important to understand that none of these newly-created accounting costs, totaling $11.6 million, are deductible for income tax purposes. The "new" Scott Fetzer pays exactly the same tax as the "old" Scott Fetzer would have, even though the GAAP earnings of the two entities differ greatly. And, in respect to operating earnings, that would be true in the future also. However, in the unlikely event that Scott Fetzer sells one of its businesses, the tax consequences to the "old" and "new" company might differ widely.

By the end of 1986 the difference between the net worth of the "old" and "new" Scott Fetzer had been reduced from $142.6 million to $131.0 million by means of the extra $11.6 million that was charged to earnings of the new entity. As the years go by, similar charges to earnings will cause most of the premium to disappear, and the two balance sheets will converge. However, the higher land values and most of the higher inventory values that were established on the new balance sheet will remain unless land is disposed of or inventory levels are further reduced.

* * *

What does all this mean for owners? Did the shareholders of Berkshire buy a business that earned $40.2 million in 1986 or did they buy one earning $28.6 million? Were those $11.6 million of new charges a real economic cost to us? Should investors pay more for the stock of Company O than of Company N? And, if a business is worth some given multiple of earnings, was Scott Fetzer worth considerably more the day before we bought it than it was worth the following day?

If we think through these questions, we can gain some insights about what may be called "owner earnings." These represent (a) reported earnings plus (b) depreciation, depletion, amortization, and certain other non-cash charges such as Company N's items (1) and (4) less (c) the average annual amount of capitalized expenditures for plant and equipment, etc. that the business requires to fully maintain its long-term competitive position and its unit volume. (If the business requires additional working capital to maintain its competitive position and unit volume, the increment also should be included in (c) . However, businesses following the LIFO inventory method usually do not require additional working capital if unit volume does not change.)

Our owner-earnings equation does not yield the deceptively precise figures provided by GAAP, since(c) must be a guess—and one sometimes very difficult to make. Despite this problem, we consider the owner earnings figure, not the GAAP figure, to be the relevant item for valuation purposes—both for investors in buying stocks and for managers in buying entire businesses. We agree with Keynes's observation: "I would rather be vaguely right than precisely wrong."

The approach we have outlined produces "owner earnings" for Company O and Company N that are identical, which means valuations are also identical, just as common sense would tell you should be the case. This result is reached because the sum of (a) and (b) is the same in both columns O and N, and because(c) is necessarily the same in both cases.

And what do Charlie and I, as owners and managers, believe is the correct figure for the owner earnings of Scott Fetzer? Under current circumstances, we believe (c) is very close to the "old" company's (b) number of $8.3 million and much below the "new" company's (b) number of $19.9 million. Therefore, we believe that owner earnings are far better depicted by the reported earnings in the O column than by those in the N column. In other words, we feel owner earnings of Scott Fetzer are considerably larger than the GAAP figures that we report.

That is obviously a happy state of affairs. But calculations of this sort usually do not provide such pleasant news. Most managers probably will acknowledge that they need to spend something more than (b) on their businesses over the longer term just to hold their ground in terms of both unit volume and competitive position. When this imperative exists—that is, when (c) exceeds (b)—GAAP earnings over-state owner earnings. Frequently this overstatement is substantial. The oil industry has in recent years provided a conspicuous example of this phenomenon. Had most major oil companies spent only (b) each year, they would have guaranteed their shrinkage in real terms.

All of this points up the absurdity of the "cash flow" numbers that are often set forth in Wall Street reports. These numbers routinely include (a) plus (b)—but do not subtract (c) . Most sales brochures of investment bankers also feature deceptive presentations of this kind. These imply that the business being offered is the commercial counterpart of the Pyramids—forever state-of-the-art, never needing to be re-placed, improved or refurbished. Indeed, if all U.S. corporations were to be offered simultaneously for sale through our leading investment bankers—and if the sales brochures describing them were to be be-lieved—governmental projections of national plant and equipment spending would have to be slashed by 90%.

"Cash Flow", true, may serve as a shorthand of some utility in descriptions of certain real estate businesses or other enterprises that make huge initial outlays and only tiny outlays thereafter. A company whose only holding is a bridge or an extremely long-lived gas field would be an example. But "cash flow" is meaningless in such businesses as manufacturing, retailing, extractive companies, and utilities because, for them, (c) is always significant. To be sure, businesses of this kind may in a given year be able to defer capital spending. But over a five- or ten-year period, they must make the investment—or the business decays.

Why, then, are "cash flow" numbers so popular today? In answer, we confess our cynicism: we be-lieve these numbers are frequently used by marketers of businesses and securities in attempts to justify the unjustifiable (and thereby to sell what should be the unsalable). When (a)—that is, GAAP earnings—looks by itself inadequate to service debt of a junk bond or justify a foolish stock price, how convenient it becomes for salesmen to focus on (a) + (b). But you shouldn't add (b) without subtracting (c) : though dentists correctly claim that if you ignore your teeth they'll go away, the same is not true for (c) . The company or investor believing that the debt-servicing ability or the equity valuation of an enterprise can be measured by totaling (a) and (b) while ignoring (c) is headed for certain trouble.

* * *

To sum up: in the case of both Scott Fetzer and our other businesses, we feel that (b) on an histori-cal-cost basis—i.e., with both amortization of intangibles and other purchase-price adjustments exclud-ed—is quite close in amount to (c) . (The two items are not identical, of course. For example, at See's we annually make capitalized expenditures that exceed depreciation by $500,000 to $1 million, simply to hold our ground competitively.) Our conviction about this point is the reason we show our amortization and other purchase-price adjustment items separately in the table on page 8 and is also our reason for viewing the earnings of the individual businesses as reported there as much more closely approximating owner earnings than the GAAP figures.

Questioning GAAP figures may seem impious to some. After all, what are we paying the account-ants for if it is not to deliver us the "truth" about our business. But the accountants' job is to record, not to evaluate. The evaluation job falls to investors and managers.

Accounting numbers, of course, are the language of business and as such are of enormous help to anyone evaluating the worth of a business and tracking its progress. Charlie and I would be lost without these numbers: they invariably are the starting point for us in evaluating our own businesses and those of others. Managers and owners need to remember, however, that accounting is but an aid to business thinking, never a substitute for it.

BERKSHIRE HATHAWAY INC.

To the Shareholders of Berkshire Hathaway Inc.:

Our gain in net worth during 1987 was $464 million, or 19.5%. Over the last 23 years (that is, since present management took over), our per-share book value has grown from $19.46 to $2,477.47, or at a rate of 23.1% compounded annually.

What counts, of course, is the rate of gain in per-share business value, not book value. In many cases, a corporation's book value and business value are almost totally unrelated. For example, just before they went bankrupt, LTV and Baldwin-United published yearend audits showing their book values to be $652 million and $397 million, respectively. Conversely, Belridge Oil was sold to Shell in 1979 for $3.6 billion although its book value was only $177 million.

At Berkshire, however, the two valuations have tracked rather closely, with the growth rate in business value over the last decade moderately outpacing the growth rate in book value. This good news continued in 1987.

Our premium of business value to book value has widened for two simple reasons: We own some remarkable businesses and they are run by even more remarkable managers.

You have a right to question that second assertion. After all, CEOs seldom tell their shareholders that they have assembled a bunch of turkeys to run things. Their reluctance to do so makes for some strange annual reports. Oftentimes, in his shareholders' letter, a CEO will go on for pages detailing corporate performance that is woefully inadequate. He will nonetheless end with a warm paragraph describing his managerial comrades as "our most precious asset." Such comments sometimes make you wonder what the other assets can possibly be.

At Berkshire, however, my appraisal of our operating managers is, if anything, understated. To understand why, first take a look at page 7, where we show the earnings (on an historical-cost accounting basis) of our seven largest non-financial units: Buffalo News, Fechheimer, Kirby, Nebraska Furniture Mart, Scott Fetzer Manufacturing Group, See's Candies, and World Book. In 1987, these seven business units had combined operating earnings before interest and taxes of $180 million.

By itself, this figure says nothing about economic performance. To evaluate that, we must know how much total capital—debt and equity—was needed to produce these earnings. Debt plays an insignificant role at our seven units: Their net interest expense in 1987 was only $2 million. Thus, pre-tax earnings on the equity capital employed by these businesses amounted to $178 million. And this equity—again on an historical-cost basis—was only $175 million.

If these seven business units had operated as a single company, their 1987 *after*-tax earnings would have been approximately $100 million—a return of about 57% on equity capital. You'll seldom see such a percentage anywhere, let alone at large, diversified companies with nominal leverage. Here's a benchmark: In its 1988 Investor's Guide issue, Fortune reported that among the 500 largest industrial companies and 500 largest service companies, only six had averaged a return on equity of over 30% during the previous decade. The best performer among the 1000 was Commerce Clearing House at 40.2%.

1

Of course, the returns that Berkshire earns from these seven units are not as high as their underlying returns because, in aggregate, we bought the businesses at a substantial premium to underlying equity capital. Overall, these operations are carried on our books at about $222 million above the historical accounting values of the underlying assets. However, the managers of the units should be judged by the returns they achieve on the underlying assets; what we pay for a business does not affect the amount of capital its manager has to work with. (If, to become a shareholder and part owner of Commerce Clearing House, you pay, say, six times book value, that does not change CCH's return on equity.)

Three important inferences can be drawn from the figures I have cited. First, the current business value of these seven units is far above their historical book value and also far above the value at which they are carried on Berkshire's balance sheet. Second, because so little capital is required to run these businesses, they can grow while concurrently making almost all of their earnings available for deployment in new opportunities. Third, these businesses are run by truly extraordinary managers. The Blumkins, the Heldmans, Chuck Huggins, Stan Lipsey, and Ralph Schey all meld unusual talent, energy and character to achieve exceptional financial results.

For good reasons, we had very high expectations when we joined with these managers. In every case, however, our experience has greatly exceeded those expectations. We have received far more than we deserve, but we are willing to accept such inequities. (We subscribe to the view Jack Benny expressed upon receiving an acting award: "I don't deserve this, but then, I have arthritis and I don't deserve that either.")

Beyond the Sainted Seven, we have our other major unit, insurance, which I believe also has a business value well above the net assets employed in it. However, appraising the business value of a property-casualty insurance company is a decidedly imprecise process. The industry is volatile, reported earnings oftentimes are seriously inaccurate, and recent changes in the Tax Code will severely hurt future profitability. Despite these problems, we like the business and it will almost certainly remain our largest operation. Under Mike Goldberg's management, the insurance business should treat us well over time.

With managers like ours, my partner, Charlie Munger, and I have little to do with operations. in fact, it is probably fair to say that if we did more, less would be accomplished. We have no corporate meetings, no corporate budgets, and no performance reviews (though our managers, of course, oftentimes find such procedures useful at their operating units). After all, what can we tell the Blumkins about home furnishings, or the Heldmans about uniforms?

Our major contribution to the operations of our subsidiaries is applause. But it is not the indiscriminate applause of a Pollyanna. Rather it is informed applause based upon the two long careers we have spent intensively observing business performance and managerial behavior. Charlie and I have seen so much of the ordinary in business that we can truly appreciate a virtuoso performance. Only one response to the 1987 performance of our operating managers is appropriate: sustained, deafening applause.

Sources of Reported Earnings

The table on the following page shows the major sources of Berkshire's reported earnings. In the table, amortization of Goodwill and other major purchase-price accounting adjustments are not charged against the specific businesses to which they apply but, instead, are aggregated and shown separately. In effect, this procedure presents the earnings of our businesses as they would have been reported had we not purchased them. In appendixes to my letters in the 1983 and 1986 annual reports, I explained why this form of presentation seems to us to be more useful to investors and managers than the standard GAAP presentation, which makes purchase-price adjustments on a business-by business basis. The total net earnings we show in the table are, of course, identical to the GAAP figures in our audited financial statements.

In the Business Segment Data on pages 36-38 and in the Management's Discussion section on pages 40-44 you will find much additional information about our businesses. In these sections you will also find our segment earnings reported on a GAAP basis. I urge you to read that material, as well as Charlie Munger's letter to Wesco shareholders, describing the various businesses of that subsidiary, which starts on page 45.

| | (000s omitted) | | | |
| | Pre-Tax Earnings | | Berkshire's Share of Net Earnings (after taxes and minority interests) | |
	1987	1986	1987	1986
Operating Earnings:				
Insurance Group:				
Underwriting	$(55,429)	$(55,844)	$(20,696)	$(29,864)
Net Investment Income	152,483	107,143	136,658	96,440
Buffalo News	39,410	34,736	21,304	16,918
Fechheimer (Acquired 6/3/86)	13,332	8,400	6,580	3,792
Kirby	22,408	20,218	12,891	10,508
Nebraska Furniture Mart	16,837	17,685	7,554	7,192
Scott Fetzer Mfg. Group	30,591	25,358	17,555	13,354
See's Candies	31,693	30,347	17,363	15,176
Wesco – other than Insurance	6,209	5,542	4,978	5,550
World Book	25,745	21,978	15,136	11,670
Amortization of Goodwill	(2,862)	(2,555)	(2,862)	(2,555)
Other Purchase-Price Accounting Adjustments	(5,546)	(10,033)	(6,544)	(11,031)
Interest on Debt and Pre-Payment Penalty	(11,474)	(23,891)	(5,905)	(12,213)
Shareholder-Designated Contributions	(4,938)	(3,997)	(2,963)	(2,158)
Other	22,460	20,770	13,696	8,685
Operating Earnings	280,919	195,857	214,745	131,464
Sales of Securities	27,319	216,242	19,807	150,897
Total Earnings – All Entities	$308,238	$412,099	$234,552	$282,361

Gypsy Rose Lee announced on one of her later birthdays: "I have everything I had last year; it's just that it's all two inches lower." As the table shows, during 1987 almost all of our businesses aged in a more upbeat way.

There's not a lot new to report about these businesses—and that's good, not bad. Severe change and exceptional returns usually don't mix. Most investors, of course, behave as if just the opposite were true. That is, they usually confer the highest price-earnings ratios on exotic-sounding businesses that hold out the promise of feverish change. That prospect lets investors fantasize about future profitability rather than face today's business realities. For such investor-dreamers, any blind date is preferable to one with the girl next door, no matter how desirable she may be.

Experience, however, indicates that the best business returns are usually achieved by companies that are doing something quite similar today to what they were doing five or ten years ago. That is no argument for managerial complacency. Businesses always have opportunities to improve service, product lines, manufacturing techniques, and the like, and obviously these opportunities should be seized. But a business that constantly encounters major change also encounters many chances for major error. Furthermore, economic terrain that is forever shifting violently is ground on which it is difficult to build a fortress-like business franchise. Such a franchise is usually the key to sustained high returns.

The Fortune study I mentioned earlier supports our view. Only 25 of the 1,000 companies met two tests of economic excellence—an average return on equity of over 20% in the ten years, 1977 through 1986, and no year worse than 15%. These business superstars were also stock market superstars: During the decade, 24 of the 25 outperformed the S&P 500.

The Fortune champs may surprise you in two respects. First, most use very little leverage compared to their interest-paying capacity. Really good businesses usually don't need to borrow. Second, except for one company that is "high-tech" and several others that manufacture ethical drugs, the companies are in businesses that, on balance, seem rather mundane. Most sell non-sexy products or services in much the same manner as they did ten years ago (though in larger quantities now, or at higher prices, or both). The record of these 25 companies confirms that making the most of an already strong business franchise, or concentrating on a single winning business theme, is what usually produces exceptional economics.

Berkshire's experience has been similar. Our managers have produced extraordinary results by doing rather ordinary things—but doing them exceptionally well. Our managers protect their franchises, they control costs, they search for new products and markets that build on their existing strengths and they don't get diverted. They work exceptionally hard at the details of their businesses, and it shows.

Here's an update:

- Agatha Christie, whose husband was an archaeologist, said that was the perfect profession for one's spouse: "The older you become, the more interested they are in you." It is students of business management, not archaeologists, who should be interested in Mrs. B (Rose Blumkin), the 94-year-old chairman of Nebraska Furniture Mart.

  Fifty years ago Mrs. B started the business with $500, and today NFM is far and away the largest home furnishings store in the country. Mrs. B continues to work seven days a week at the job from the opening of each business day until the close. She buys, she sells, she manages—and she runs rings around the competition. It's clear to me that she's gathering speed and may well reach her full potential in another five or ten years. Therefore, I've persuaded the Board to scrap our mandatory retirement-at-100 policy. (And it's about time: With every passing year, this policy has seemed sillier to me.)

  Net sales of NFM were $142.6 million in 1987, up 8% from 1986. There's nothing like this store in the country, and there's nothing like the family Mrs. B has produced to carry on: Her son Louie, and his three boys, Ron, Irv and Steve, possess the business instincts, integrity and drive of Mrs. B. They work as a team and, strong as each is individually, the whole is far greater than the sum of the parts.

  The superb job done by the Blumkins benefits us as owners, but even more dramatically benefits NFM's customers. They saved about $30 million in 1987 by buying from NFM. In other words, the goods they bought would have cost that much more if purchased elsewhere.

You'll enjoy an anonymous letter I received last August: "Sorry to see Berkshire profits fall in the second quarter. One way you may gain back part of your lost. (sic) Check the pricing at The Furniture Mart. You will find that they are leaving 10% to 20% on the table. This additional profit on $140 million of sells (sic) is $28 million. Not small change in anyone's pocket! Check out other furniture, carpet, appliance and T.V. dealers. Your raising prices to a reasonable profit will help. Thank you. /signed/ A Competitor."

NFM will continue to grow and prosper by following Mrs. B's maxim: "Sell cheap and tell the truth."

- Among dominant papers of its size or larger, the Buffalo News continues to be the national leader in two important ways: (1) its weekday and Sunday penetration rate (the percentage of households in the paper's primary market area that purchase it); and (2) its "news-hole" percentage (the portion of the paper devoted to news).

It may not be coincidence that one newspaper leads in both categories: an exceptionally "news-rich" product makes for broad audience appeal, which in turn leads to high penetration. Of course, quantity must be matched by quality. This not only means good reporting and good writing; it means freshness and relevance. To be indispensable, a paper must promptly tell its readers many things they want to know but won't otherwise learn until much later, if ever.

At the News, we put out seven fresh editions every 24 hours, each one extensively changed in content. Here's a small example that may surprise you: We redo the obituary page in every edition of the News, or seven times a day. Any obituary added runs through the next six editions until the publishing cycle has been completed.

It's vital, of course, for a newspaper to cover national and international news well and in depth. But it is also vital for it to do what only a local newspaper can: promptly and extensively chronicle the personally-important, otherwise-unreported details of community life. Doing this job well requires a very broad range of news—and that means lots of space, intelligently used.

Our news hole was about 50% in 1987, just as it has been year after year. If we were to cut it to a more typical 40%, we would save approximately $4 million annually in newsprint costs. That interests us not at all—and it won't interest us even if, for one reason or another, our profit margins should significantly shrink.

Charlie and I do not believe in flexible operating budgets, as in "Non-direct expenses can be X if revenues are Y, but must be reduced if revenues are Y—5%." Should we really cut our news hole at the Buffalo News, or the quality of product and service at See's, simply because profits are down during a given year or quarter? Or, conversely, should we add a staff economist, a corporate strategist, an institutional advertising campaign or something else that does Berkshire no good simply because the money currently is rolling in?

That makes no sense to us. We neither understand the adding of unneeded people or activities because profits are booming, nor the cutting of essential people or activities because profitability is shrinking. That kind of yo-yo approach is neither business-like nor humane. Our goal is to do what makes sense for Berkshire's customers and employees at all times, and never to add the unneeded. ("But what about the corporate jet?" you rudely ask. Well, occasionally a man must rise above principle.)

Although the News' revenues have grown only moderately since 1984, superb management by Stan Lipsey, its publisher, has produced excellent profit growth. For several years, I have incorrectly predicted that profit margins at the News would fall. This year I will not let you down: Margins will, without question, shrink in 1988 and profit may fall as well. Skyrocketing newsprint costs will be the major cause.

- Fechheimer Bros. Company is another of our family businesses—and, like the Blumkins, what a family. Three generations of Heldmans have for decades consistently, built the sales and profits of this manufacturer and distributor of uniforms. In the year that Berkshire acquired its controlling interest in Fechheimer—1986—profits were a record. The Heldmans didn't slow down after that. Last year earnings increased substantially and the outlook is good for 1988.

There's nothing magic about the Uniform business; the only magic is in the Heldmans. Bob, George, Gary, Roger and Fred know the business inside and out, and they have fun running it. We are fortunate to be in partnership with them.

- Chuck Huggins continues to set new records at See's, just as he has ever since we put him in charge on the day of our purchase some 16 years ago. In 1987, volume hit a new high at slightly Under 25 million pounds. For the second year in a row, moreover, same-store sales, measured in pounds, were virtually unchanged. In case you are wondering, that represents improvement: In each of the previous six years, same-store sales had fallen.

Although we had a particularly strong 1986 Christmas season, we racked up better store-for-store comparisons in the 1987 Christmas season than at any other time of the year. Thus, the seasonal factor at See's becomes even more extreme. In 1987, about 85% of our profit was earned during December.

Candy stores are fun to visit, but most have not been fun for their owners. From what we can learn, practically no one besides See's has made significant profits in recent years from the operation of candy shops. Clearly, Chuck's record at See's is not due to a rising industry tide. Rather, it is a one-of-a-kind performance.

His achievement requires an excellent product—which we have—but it also requires genuine affection for the customer. Chuck is 100% customer-oriented, and his attitude sets the tone for the rest of the See's organization.

Here's an example of Chuck in action: At See's we regularly add new pieces of candy to our mix and also cull a few to keep our product line at about 100 varieties. Last spring we selected 14 items for elimination. Two, it turned out, were badly missed by our customers, who wasted no time in letting us know what they thought of our judgment: "A pox on all in See's who participated in the abominable decision…;" "May your new truffles melt in transit, may they sour in people's mouths, may your costs go up and your profits go down…;" "We are investigating the possibility of obtaining a mandatory injunction requiring you to supply…;" You get the picture. In all, we received many hundreds of letters.

Chuck not only reintroduced the pieces, he turned this miscue into an opportunity. Each person who had written got a complete and honest explanation in return. Said Chuck's letter: "Fortunately, when I make poor decisions, good things often happen as a result…;" And with the letter went a special gift certificate.

See's increased prices only slightly in the last two years. In 1988 we have raised prices somewhat more, though still moderately. To date, sales have been weak and it may be difficult for See's to improve its earnings this year.

- World Book, Kirby, and the Scott Fetzer Manufacturing Group are all under the management of Ralph Schey. And what a lucky thing for us that they are. I told you last year that Scott Fetzer performance in 1986 had far exceeded the expectations that Charlie and I had at the time of our purchase. Results in 1987 were even better. Pre-tax earnings rose 10% while average capital employed declined significantly.

Ralph's mastery of the 19 businesses for which he is responsible is truly amazing, and he has also attracted some outstanding managers to run them. We would love to find a few additional units that could be put under Ralph's wing.

The businesses of Scott Fetzer are too numerous to describe in detail. Let's just update you on one of our favorites: At the end of 1987, World Book introduced its most dramatically-revised edition since 1962. The number of color photos was increased from 14,000 to 24,000; over 6,000 articles were revised; 840 new contributors were added. Charlie and I recommend this product to you and your family, as we do World Book's products for younger children, Childcraft and Early World of Learning.

In 1987, World Book unit sales in the United States increased for the fifth consecutive year. International sales and profits also grew substantially. The outlook is good for Scott Fetzer operations in aggregate, and for World Book in particular.

Insurance Operations

Shown below is an updated version of our usual table presenting key figures for the insurance industry:

	Yearly Change in Premiums Written (%)	Statutory Combined Ratio After Policyholder Dividends	Yearly Change in Incurred Losses (%)	Inflation Rate Measured by GNP Deflator (%)
1981	3.8	106.0	6.5	9.7
1982	4.4	109.8	8.4	6.4
1983	4.6	112.0	6.8	3.9
1984	9.2	117.9	16.9	3.8
1985	22.1	116.3	16.1	3.3
1986 (Rev.)	22.2	108.0	13.5	2.6
1987 (Est.)	8.7	104.7	6.8	3.0

Source: Best's Insurance Management Reports

The combined ratio represents total insurance costs (losses incurred plus expenses) compared to revenue from premiums: A ratio below 100 indicates an underwriting profit, and one above 100 indicates a loss. When the investment income that an insurer earns from holding on to policyholders' funds ("the float") is taken into account, a combined ratio in the 107-111 range typically produces an overall break-even result, exclusive of earnings on the funds provided by shareholders.

The math of the insurance business, encapsulated by the table, is not very complicated. In years when the industry's annual gain in revenues (premiums) pokes along at 4% or 5%, underwriting losses are sure to mount. That is not because auto accidents, fires, windstorms and the like are occurring more frequently, nor has it lately been the fault of general inflation. Today, social and judicial inflation are the major culprits; the cost of entering a courtroom has simply ballooned. Part of the jump in cost arises from skyrocketing verdicts, and part from the tendency of judges and juries to expand the coverage of insurance policies beyond that contemplated by the insurer when the policies were written. Seeing no let-up in either trend, we continue to believe that the industry's revenues must grow at about 10% annually for it to just hold its own in terms of profitability, even though general inflation may be running at a considerably lower rate.

The strong revenue gains of 1985-87 almost guaranteed the industry an excellent underwriting performance in 1987 and, indeed, it was a banner year. But the news soured as the quarters rolled by: Best's estimates that year-over-year volume increases were 12.9%, 11.1%, 5.7%, and 5.6%. In 1988, the revenue gain is certain to be far below our 10% "equilibrium" figure. Clearly, the party is over.

However, earnings will not immediately sink. A lag factor exists in this industry: Because most policies are written for a one-year term, higher or lower insurance prices do not have their full impact on earnings until many months after they go into effect. Thus, to resume our metaphor, when the party ends and the bar is closed, you are allowed to finish your drink. If results are not hurt by a major natural catastrophe, we predict a small climb for the industry's combined ratio in 1988, followed by several years of larger increases.

The insurance industry is cursed with a set of dismal economic characteristics that make for a poor long-term outlook: hundreds of competitors, ease of entry, and a product that cannot be differentiated in any meaningful way. In such a commodity-like business, only a very low-cost operator or someone operating in a protected, and usually small, niche can sustain high profitability levels.

When shortages exist, however, even commodity businesses flourish. The insurance industry enjoyed that kind of climate for a while but it is now gone. One of the ironies of capitalism is that most managers in commodity industries abhor shortage conditions—even though those are the only circumstances permitting them good returns. Whenever shortages appear, the typical manager simply can't wait to expand capacity and thereby plug the hole through which money is showering upon him. This is precisely what insurance managers did in 1985-87, confirming again Disraeli's observation: "What we learn from history is that we do not learn from history."

At Berkshire, we work to escape the industry's commodity economics in two ways. First, we differentiate our product by our financial strength, which exceeds that of all others in the industry. This strength, however, is limited in its usefulness. It means nothing in the personal insurance field: The buyer of an auto or homeowners policy is going to get his claim paid even if his insurer fails (as many have). It often means nothing in the commercial insurance arena: When times are good, many major corporate purchasers of insurance and their brokers pay scant attention to the insurer's ability to perform under the more adverse conditions that may exist, say, five years later when a complicated claim is finally resolved. (Out of sight, out of mind—and, later on, maybe out-of-pocket.)

Periodically, however, buyers remember Ben Franklin's observation that it is hard for an empty sack to stand upright and recognize their need to buy promises only from insurers that have enduring financial strength. It is then that we have a major competitive advantage. When a buyer really focuses on whether a $10 million claim can be easily paid by his insurer five or ten years down the road, and when he takes into account the possibility that poor underwriting conditions may then coincide with depressed financial markets and defaults by reinsurer, he will find only a few companies he can trust. Among those, Berkshire will lead the pack.

Our second method of differentiating ourselves is the total indifference to volume that we maintain. In 1989, we will be perfectly willing to write five times as much business as we write in 1988—or only one-fifth as much. We hope, of course, that conditions will allow us large volume. But we cannot control market prices. If they are unsatisfactory, we will simply do very little business. No other major insurer acts with equal restraint.

Three conditions that prevail in insurance, but not in most businesses, allow us our flexibility. First, market share is not an important determinant of profitability: In this business, in contrast to the newspaper or grocery businesses, the economic rule is not survival of the fattest. Second, in many sectors of insurance, including most of those in which we operate, distribution channels are not proprietary and can be easily entered: Small volume this year does not preclude huge volume next year. Third, idle capacity—which in this industry largely means people—does not result in intolerable costs. In a way that industries such as printing or steel cannot, we can operate at quarter-speed much of the time and still enjoy long-term prosperity.

We follow a price-based-on-exposure, not-on-competition policy because it makes sense for our shareholders. But we're happy to report that it is also pro-social. This policy means that we are always available, given prices that we believe are adequate, to write huge volumes of almost any type of property-casualty insurance. Many other insurers follow an in-and-out approach. When they are "out"—because of mounting losses, capital inadequacy, or whatever—we are available. Of course, when others are panting to do business we are also available—but at such times we often find ourselves priced above the market. In effect, we supply insurance buyers and brokers with a large reservoir of standby capacity.

One story from mid-1987 illustrates some consequences of our pricing policy: One of the largest family-owned insurance brokers in the country is headed by a fellow who has long been a shareholder of Berkshire. This man handles a number of large risks that are candidates for placement with our New York office. Naturally, he does the best he can for his clients. And, just as naturally, when the insurance market softened dramatically in 1987 he found prices at other insurers lower than we were willing to offer. His reaction was, first, to place all of his business elsewhere and, second, to buy more stock in Berkshire. Had we been really competitive, he said, we would have gotten his insurance business but he would not have bought our stock.

Berkshire's underwriting experience was excellent in 1987, in part because of the lag factor discussed earlier. Our combined ratio (on a statutory basis and excluding structured settlements and financial reinsurance) was 105. Although the ratio was somewhat less favorable than in 1986, when it was 103, our profitability improved materially in 1987 because we had the use of far more float. This trend will continue to run in our favor: Our ratio of float to premium volume will increase very significantly during the next few years. Thus, Berkshire's insurance profits are quite likely to improve during 1988 and 1989, even though we expect our combined ratio to rise.

Our insurance business has also made some important non-financial gains during the last few years. Mike Goldberg, its manager, has assembled a group of talented professionals to write larger risks and unusual coverages. His operation is now well equipped to handle the lines of business that will occasionally offer us major opportunities.

Our loss reserve development, detailed on pages 41-42, looks better this year than it has previously. But we write lots of "long-tail" business—that is, policies generating claims that often take many years to resolve. Examples would be product liability, or directors and officers liability coverages. With a business mix like this, one year of reserve development tells you very little.

You should be very suspicious of any earnings figures reported by insurers (including our own, as we have unfortunately proved to you in the past). The record of the last decade shows that a great many of our best-known insurers have reported earnings to shareholders that later proved to be wildly erroneous. In most cases, these errors were totally innocent: The unpredictability of our legal system makes it impossible for even the most conscientious insurer to come close to judging the eventual cost of long-tail claims.

Nevertheless, auditors annually certify the numbers given them by management and in their opinions unqualifiedly state that these figures "present fairly" the financial position of their clients. The auditors use this reassuring language even though they know from long and painful experience that the numbers so certified are likely to differ dramatically from the true earnings of the period. Despite this history of error, investors understandably rely upon auditors' opinions. After all, a declaration saying that "the statements present fairly" hardly sounds equivocal to the non-accountant.

The wording in the auditor's standard opinion letter is scheduled to change next year. The new language represents improvement, but falls far short of describing the limitations of a casualty-insurer audit. If it is to depict the true state of affairs, we believe the standard opinion letter to shareholders of a property-casualty company should read something like: "We have relied upon representations of management in respect to the liabilities shown for losses and loss adjustment expenses, the estimate of which, in turn, very materially affects the earnings and financial condition herein reported. We can express no opinion about the accuracy of these figures. Subject to that important reservation, in our opinion, etc."

If lawsuits develop in respect to wildly inaccurate financial statements (which they do), auditors will definitely say something of that sort in court anyway. Why should they not be forthright about their role and its limitations from the outset?

We want to emphasize that we are not faulting auditors for their inability to accurately assess loss reserves (and therefore earnings). We fault them only for failing to publicly acknowledge that they can't do this job.

From all appearances, the innocent mistakes that are constantly made in reserving are accompanied by others that are deliberate. Various charlatans have enriched themselves at the expense of the investing public by exploiting, first, the inability of auditors to evaluate reserve figures and, second, the auditors' willingness to confidently certify those figures as if they had the expertise to do so. We will continue to see such chicanery in the future. Where "earnings" can be created by the stroke of a pen, the dishonest will gather. For them, long-tail insurance is heaven. The audit wording we suggest would at least serve to put investors on guard against these predators.

The taxes that insurance companies pay—which increased materially, though on a delayed basis, upon enactment of the Tax Reform Act of 1986—took a further turn for the worse at the end of 1987. We detailed the 1986 changes in last year's report. We also commented on the irony of a statute that substantially increased 1987 reported earnings for insurers even as it materially reduced both their long-term earnings potential and their business value. At Berkshire, the temporarily-helpful "fresh start" adjustment inflated 1987 earnings by $8.2 million.

In our opinion, the 1986 Act was the most important economic event affecting the insurance industry over the past decade. The 1987 Bill further reduced the intercorporate dividends-received credit from

80% to 70%, effective January 1, 1988, except for cases in which the taxpayer owns at least 20% of an investee.

Investors who have owned stocks or bonds through corporate intermediaries other than qualified investment companies have always been disadvantaged in comparison to those owning the same securities directly. The penalty applying to indirect ownership was greatly increased by the 1986 Tax Bill and, to a lesser extent, by the 1987 Bill, particularly in instances where the intermediary is an insurance company. We have no way of offsetting this increased level of taxation. It simply means that a given set of pre-tax investment returns will now translate into much poorer after-tax results for our shareholders.

All in all, we expect to do well in the insurance business, though our record is sure to be uneven. The immediate outlook is for substantially lower volume but reasonable earnings improvement. The decline in premium volume will accelerate after our quota-share agreement with Fireman's Fund expires in 1989. At some point, likely to be at least a few years away, we may see some major opportunities, for which we are now much better prepared than we were in 1985.

Marketable Securities—Permanent Holdings

Whenever Charlie and I buy common stocks for Berkshire's insurance companies (leaving aside arbitrage purchases, discussed later) we approach the transaction as if we were buying into a private business. We look at the economic prospects of the business, the people in charge of running it, and the price we must pay. We do not have in mind any time or price for sale. Indeed, we are willing to hold a stock indefinitely so long as we expect the business to increase in intrinsic value at a satisfactory rate. When investing, we view ourselves as business analysts—not as market analysts, not as macroeconomic analysts, and not even as security analysts.

Our approach makes an active trading market useful, since it periodically presents us with mouth-watering opportunities. But by no means is it essential: a prolonged suspension of trading in the securities we hold would not bother us any more than does the lack of daily quotations on World Book or Fechheimer. Eventually, our economic fate will be determined by the economic fate of the business we own, whether our ownership is partial or total.

Ben Graham, my friend and teacher, long ago described the mental attitude toward market fluctuations that I believe to be most conducive to investment success. He said that you should imagine market quotations as coming from a remarkably accommodating fellow named Mr. Market who is your partner in a private business. Without fail, Mr. Market appears daily and names a price at which he will either buy your interest or sell you his.

Even though the business that the two of you own may have economic characteristics that are stable, Mr. Market's quotations will be anything but. For, sad to say, the poor fellow has incurable emotional problems. At times he feels euphoric and can see only the favorable factors affecting the business. When in that mood, he names a very high buy-sell price because he fears that you will snap up his interest and rob him of imminent gains. At other times he is depressed and can see nothing but trouble ahead for both the business and the world. On these occasions he will name a very low price, since he is terrified that you will unload your interest on him.

Mr. Market has another endearing characteristic: He doesn't mind being ignored. If his quotation is uninteresting to you today, he will be back with a new one tomorrow. Transactions are strictly at your option. Under these conditions, the more manic-depressive his behavior, the better for you.

But, like Cinderella at the ball, you must heed one warning or everything will turn into pumpkins and mice: Mr. Market is there to serve you, not to guide you. It is his pocketbook, not his wisdom, that you will find useful. If he shows up some day in a particularly foolish mood, you are free to either ignore him or to take advantage of him, but it will be disastrous if you fall under his influence. Indeed, if you aren't certain that you understand and can value your business far better than Mr. Market, you don't belong in the game. As they say in poker, "If you've been in the game 30 minutes and you don't know who the patsy is, *you're* the patsy."

Ben's Mr. Market allegory may seem out-of-date in today's investment world, in which most professionals and academicians talk of efficient markets, dynamic hedging and betas. Their interest in such matters is understandable, since techniques shrouded in mystery clearly have value to the purveyor of investment advice. After all, what witch doctor has ever achieved fame and fortune by simply advising "Take two aspirins"?

The value of market esoterica to the consumer of investment advice is a different story. In my opinion, investment success will not be produced by arcane formulae, computer programs or signals flashed by the price behavior of stocks and markets. Rather an investor will succeed by coupling good business judgment with an ability to insulate his thoughts and behavior from the super-contagious emotions that swirl about the marketplace. In my own efforts to stay insulated, I have found it highly useful to keep Ben's Mr. Market concept firmly in mind.

Following Ben's teachings, Charlie and I let our marketable equities tell us by their operating results—not by their daily, or even yearly, price quotations—whether our investments are successful. The market may ignore business success for a while, but eventually will confirm it. As Ben said: "In the short run, the market is a voting machine but in the long run it is a weighing machine." The speed at which a business's success is recognized, furthermore, is not that important as long as the company's intrinsic value is increasing at a satisfactory rate. In fact, delayed recognition can be an advantage: It may give us the chance to buy more of a good thing at a bargain price.

Sometimes, of course, the market may judge a business to be more valuable than the underlying facts would indicate it is. In such a case, we will sell our holdings. Sometimes, also, we will sell a security that is fairly valued or even undervalued because we require funds for a still more undervalued investment or one we believe we understand better.

We need to emphasize, however, that we do not sell holdings just because they have appreciated or because we have held them for a long time. (Of Wall Street maxims the most foolish may be "You can't go broke taking a profit.") We are quite content to hold any security indefinitely, so long as the prospective return on equity capital of the underlying business is satisfactory, management is competent and honest, and the market does not overvalue the business.

However, our insurance companies own three marketable common stocks that we would not sell even though they became far overpriced in the market. In effect, we view these investments exactly like our successful controlled businesses—a permanent part of Berkshire rather than merchandise to be disposed of once Mr. Market offers us a sufficiently high price. To that, I will add one qualifier: These stocks are held by our insurance companies and we would, if absolutely necessary, sell portions of our holdings to pay extraordinary insurance losses. We intend, however, to manage our affairs so that sales are never required.

A determination to have and to hold, which Charlie and I share, obviously involves a mixture of personal and financial considerations. To some, our stand may seem highly eccentric. (Charlie and I have long followed David Oglivy's advice: "Develop your eccentricities while you are young. That way, when you get old, people won't think you're going ga-ga.") Certainly, in the transaction-fixated Wall Street of recent years, our posture must seem odd: To many in that arena, both companies and stocks are seen only as raw material for trades.

Our attitude, however, fits our personalities and the way we want to live our lives. Churchill once said, "You shape your houses and then they shape you." We know the manner in which we wish to be shaped. For that reason, we would rather achieve a return of X while associating with people whom we strongly like and admire than realize 110% of X by exchanging these relationships for uninteresting or unpleasant ones. And we will never find people we like and admire more than some of the main participants at the three companies—our permanent holdings—shown below:

No. of Shares		Cost	Market
		(000s omitted)	
3,000,000	Capital Cities/ABC, Inc.	$517,500	$1,035,000
6,850,000	GEICO Corporation	45,713	756,925
1,727,765	The Washington Post Company	9,731	323,092

We really don't see many fundamental differences between the purchase of a controlled business and the purchase of marketable holdings such as these. In each case we try to buy into businesses with favorable long-term economics. Our goal is to find an outstanding business at a sensible price, not a mediocre business at a bargain price. Charlie and I have found that making silk purses out of silk is the best that we can do; with sow's ears, we fail.

(It must be noted that your Chairman, always a quick study, required only 20 years to recognize how important it was to buy good businesses. In the interim, I searched for "bargains"—and had the misfortune to find some. My punishment was an education in the economics of short-line farm implement manufacturers, third-place department stores, and New England textile manufacturers.)

Of course, Charlie and I may misread the fundamental economics of a business. When that happens, we will encounter problems whether that business is a wholly-owned subsidiary or a marketable security, although it is usually far easier to exit from the latter. (Indeed, businesses can be misread: Witness the European reporter who, after being sent to this country to profile Andrew Carnegie, cabled his editor, "My God, you'll never believe the sort of money there is in running libraries.")

In making both control purchases and stock purchases, we try to buy not only good businesses, but ones run by high-grade, talented and likeable managers. If we make a mistake about the managers we link up with, the controlled company offers a certain advantage because we have the power to effect change. In practice, however, this advantage is somewhat illusory: Management changes, like marital changes, are painful, time-consuming and chancy. In any event, at our three marketable-but permanent holdings, this point is moot: With Tom Murphy and Dan Burke at Cap Cities, Bill Snyder and Lou Simpson at GEICO, and Kay Graham and Dick Simmons at The Washington Post, we simply couldn't be in better hands.

I would say that the controlled company offers two main advantages. First, when we control a company we get to allocate capital, whereas we are likely to have little or nothing to say about this process with marketable holdings. This point can be important because the heads of many companies are not skilled in capital allocation. Their inadequacy is not surprising. Most bosses rise to the top because they have excelled in an area such as marketing, production, engineering, administration or, sometimes, institutional politics.

Once they become CEOs, they face new responsibilities. They now must make capital allocation decisions, a critical job that they may have never tackled and that is not easily mastered. To stretch the point, it's as if the final step for a highly-talented musician was not to perform at Carnegie Hall but, instead, to be named Chairman of the Federal Reserve.

The lack of skill that many CEOs have at capital allocation is no small matter: After ten years on the job, a CEO whose company annually retains earnings equal to 10% of net worth will have been responsible for the deployment of more than 60% of all the capital at work in the business.

CEOs who recognize their lack of capital-allocation skills (which not all do) will often try to compensate by turning to their staffs, management consultants, or investment bankers. Charlie and I have frequently observed the consequences of such "help." On balance, we feel it is more likely to accentuate the capital-allocation problem than to solve it.

In the end, plenty of unintelligent capital allocation takes place in corporate America. (That's why you hear so much about "restructuring.") Berkshire, however, has been fortunate. At the companies that are our major non-controlled holdings, capital has generally been well-deployed and, in some cases, brilliantly so.

The second advantage of a controlled company over a marketable security has to do with taxes. Berkshire, as a corporate holder, absorbs some significant tax costs through the ownership of partial positions that we do not when our ownership is 80%, or greater. Such tax disadvantages have long been with us, but changes in the tax code caused them to increase significantly during the past year. As a consequence, a given business result can now deliver Berkshire financial results that are as much as 50% better if they come from an 80%-or-greater holding rather than from a lesser holding.

The disadvantages of owning marketable securities are sometimes offset by a huge advantage: Occasionally the stock market offers us the chance to buy non-controlling pieces of extraordinary businesses at truly ridiculous prices—dramatically below those commanded in negotiated transactions that transfer control. For example, we purchased our Washington Post stock in 1973 at $5.63 per share, and per-share operating earnings in 1987 after taxes were $10.30. Similarly, Our GEICO stock was purchased in 1976, 1979 and 1980 at an average of $6.67 per share, and after-tax operating earnings per share last year were $9.01. In cases such as these, Mr. Market has proven to be a mighty good friend.

An interesting accounting irony overlays a comparison of the reported financial results of our controlled companies with those of the permanent minority holdings listed above. As you can see, those three stocks have a market value of over $2 billion. Yet they produced only $11 million in reported after-tax earnings for Berkshire in 1987.

Accounting rules dictate that we take into income only the dividends these companies pay us—which are little more than nominal—rather than our share of their earnings, which in 1987 amounted to well over $100 million. On the other hand, accounting rules provide that the carrying value of these three holdings—owned, as they are, by insurance companies—must be recorded on our balance sheet at current market prices. The result: GAAP accounting lets us reflect in our net worth the up-to-date underlying values of the businesses we partially own, but does not let us reflect their underlying earnings in our income account.

In the case of our controlled companies, just the opposite is true. Here, we show full earnings in our income account but never change asset values on our balance sheet, no matter how much the value of a business might have increased since we purchased it.

Our mental approach to this accounting schizophrenia is to ignore GAAP figures and to focus solely on the future earning power of both our controlled and non-controlled businesses. Using this approach, we establish our own ideas of business value, keeping these independent from both the accounting values shown on our books for controlled companies and the values placed by a sometimes foolish market on our partially-owned companies. It is this business value that we hope to increase at a reasonable (or, preferably, unreasonable) rate in the years ahead.

Marketable Securities—Other

In addition to our three permanent common stock holdings, we hold large quantities of marketable securities in our insurance companies. In selecting these, we can choose among five major categories: (1) long-term common stock investments, (2) medium-term fixed-income securities, (3) long-term fixed income securities, (4) short-term cash equivalents, and (5) short-term arbitrage commitments.

We have no particular bias when it comes to choosing from these categories. We just continuously search among them for the highest after-tax returns as measured by "mathematical expectation," limiting ourselves always to investment alternatives we think we understand. Our criteria have nothing to do with maximizing immediately reportable earnings; our goal, rather, is to maximize eventual net worth.

- Let's look first at common stocks. During 1987 the stock market was an area of much excitement but little net movement: The Dow advanced 2.3% for the year. You are aware, of course, of the roller coaster ride that produced this minor change. Mr. Market was on a manic rampage until October and then experienced a sudden, massive seizure.

We have "professional" investors, those who manage many billions, to thank for most of this turmoil. Instead of focusing on what businesses will do in the years ahead, many prestigious money managers now focus on what they expect other money managers to do in the days ahead. For them, stocks are merely tokens in a game, like the thimble and flatiron in Monopoly.

An extreme example of what their attitude leads to is "portfolio insurance," a money-management strategy that many leading investment advisors embraced in 1986-1987. This strategy—which is simply an exotically-labeled version of the small speculator's stop-loss order dictates that ever increasing portions of a stock portfolio, or their index-future equivalents, be sold as prices decline. The strategy says nothing else matters: A downtick of a given magnitude automatically produces a huge sell order. According to the Brady Report, $60 billion to $90 billion of equities were poised on this hair trigger in mid-October of 1987.

If you've thought that investment advisors were hired to invest, you may be bewildered by this technique. After buying a farm, would a rational owner next order his real estate agent to start selling off pieces of it whenever a neighboring property was sold at a lower price? Or would you sell your house to whatever bidder was available at 9:31 on some morning merely because at 9:30 a similar house sold for less than it would have brought on the previous day?

Moves like that, however, are what portfolio insurance tells a pension fund or university to make when it owns a portion of enterprises such as Ford or General Electric. The less these companies are being valued at, says this approach, the more vigorously they should be sold. As a "logical" corollary, the approach commands the institutions to repurchase these companies— *I'm not making this up*—once their prices have rebounded significantly. Considering that huge sums are controlled by managers following such Alice-in-Wonderland practices, is it any surprise that markets sometimes behave in aberrational fashion?

Many commentators, however, have drawn an incorrect conclusion upon observing recent events: They are fond of saying that the small investor has no chance in a market now dominated by the erratic behavior of the big boys. This conclusion is dead wrong: Such markets are ideal for any investor—small or large—so long as he sticks to his investment knitting. Volatility caused by money managers who speculate irrationally with huge sums will offer the true investor more chances to make intelligent investment moves. He can be hurt by such volatility only if he is forced, by either financial or psychological pressures, to sell at untoward times.

At Berkshire, we have found little to do in stocks during the past few years. During the break in October, a few stocks fell to prices that interested us, but we were unable to make meaningful purchases before they rebounded. At yearend 1987 we had no major common stock investments (that is, over $50 million) other than those we consider permanent or arbitrage holdings. However, Mr. Market will offer us opportunities—you can be sure of that—and, when he does, we will be willing and able to participate.

- In the meantime, our major parking place for money is medium-term tax-exempt bonds, whose limited virtues I explained in last year's annual report. Though we both bought and sold some of these bonds in 1987, our position changed little overall, holding around $900 million. A large portion of our bonds are "grandfathered" under the Tax Reform Act of 1986, which means they are fully tax-exempt. Bonds currently purchased by insurance companies are not.

As an alternative to short-term cash equivalents, our medium-term tax-exempts have—so far served us well. They have produced substantial extra income for us and are currently worth a bit above our cost. Regardless of their market price, we are ready to dispose of our bonds whenever something better comes along.

- We continue to have an aversion to long-term bonds (and may be making a serious mistake by not disliking medium-term bonds as well). Bonds are no better than the currency in which they are denominated, and nothing we have seen in the past year—or past decade—makes us enthusiastic about the long-term future of U.S. currency.

Our enormous trade deficit is causing various forms of "claim checks"—U.S. government and corporate bonds, bank deposits, etc.—to pile up in the hands of foreigners at a distressing rate. By default, our government has adopted an approach to its finances patterned on that of Blanche DuBois, of *A Streetcar Named Desire*, who said, "I have always depended on the kindness of strangers." In this case, of course, the "strangers" are relying on the integrity of our claim checks although the plunging dollar has already made that proposition expensive for them.

The faith that foreigners are placing in us may be misfounded. When the claim checks outstanding grow sufficiently numerous and when the issuing party can unilaterally determine their purchasing power, the pressure on the issuer to dilute their value by inflating the currency becomes almost irresistible. For the debtor government, the weapon of inflation is the economic equivalent of the "H" bomb, and that is why very few countries have been allowed to swamp the world with debt denominated in their own currency. Our past, relatively good record for fiscal integrity has let us break this rule, but the generosity accorded us is likely to intensify, rather than relieve, the eventual pressure on us to inflate. If we do succumb to that pressure, it won't be just the foreign holders of our claim checks who will suffer. It will be all of us as well.

Of course, the U.S. may take steps to stem our trade deficit well before our position as a net debtor gets out of hand. (In that respect, the falling dollar will help, though unfortunately it will hurt in other ways.) Nevertheless, our government's behavior in this test of its mettle is apt to be consistent with its Scarlett O'Hara approach generally: "I'll think about it tomorrow." And, almost inevitably, procrastination in facing up to fiscal problems will have inflationary consequences. Both the timing and the sweep of those consequences are unpredictable. But our inability to quantify or time the risk does not mean we should ignore it. While recognizing the possibility that we may be wrong and that present interest rates may adequately compensate for the inflationary risk, we retain a general fear of long-term bonds.

We are, however, willing to invest a moderate portion of our funds in this category if we think we have a significant edge in a specific security. That willingness explains our holdings of the Washington Public Power Supply Systems #1, #2 and #3 issues, discussed in our 1984 report. We added to our WPPSS position during 1987. At yearend, we had holdings with an amortized cost of $240 million and a market value of $316 million, paying us tax-exempt income of $34 million annually.

- We continued to do well in arbitrage last year, though—or perhaps because—we operated on a very limited scale. We enter into only a few arbitrage commitments each year and restrict ourselves to large transactions that have been publicly announced. We do not participate in situations in which green-mailers are attempting to put a target company "in play."

We have practiced arbitrage on an opportunistic basis for decades and, to date, our results have been quite good. Though we've never made an exact calculation, I believe that overall we have averaged annual pre-tax returns of at least 25% from arbitrage. I'm quite sure we did better than that in 1987. But it should be emphasized that a really bad experience or two—such as many arbitrage operations suffered in late 1987—could change the figures dramatically.

Our only $50 million-plus arbitrage position at yearend 1987 was 1,096,200 shares of Allegis, with a cost of $76 million and a market value of $78 million.

- We had two other large holdings at yearend that do not fit precisely into any of our five categories. One was various Texaco, Inc. bonds with short maturities, all purchased after Texaco went into bankruptcy. Were it not for the extraordinarily strong capital position of our insurance companies, it would be inappropriate for us to buy defaulted bonds. At prices prevailing after Texaco's bankruptcy filing, however, we regarded these issues as by far the most attractive bond investment available to us.

On a worst-case basis with respect to the Pennzoil litigation, we felt the bonds were likely to be worth about what we paid for them. Given a sensible settlement, which seemed likely, we expected the bonds to be worth considerably more. At yearend our Texaco bonds were carried on our books at $104 million and had a market value of $119 million.

By far our largest—and most publicized—investment in 1987 was a $700 million purchase of Salomon Inc 9% preferred stock. This preferred is convertible after three years into Salomon common stock at $38 per share and, if not converted, will be redeemed ratably over five years beginning October 31, 1995. From most standpoints, this commitment fits into the medium-term fixed-income securities category. In addition, we have an interesting conversion possibility.

We, of course, have no special insights regarding the direction or future profitability of investment banking. By their nature, the economics of this industry are far less predictable than those of most other industries in which we have major Commitments. This unpredictability is one of the reasons why our participation is in the form of a convertible preferred.

What we do have a strong feeling about is the ability and integrity of John Gutfreund, CEO of Salomon Inc. Charlie and I like, admire and trust John. We first got to know him in 1976 when he played a key role in GEICO's escape from near-bankruptcy. Several times since, we have seen John steer clients away from transactions that would have been unwise, but that the client clearly wanted to make—even though his advice provided no fee to Salomon and acquiescence would have delivered a large fee. Such service-above-self behavior is far from automatic in Wall Street.

For the reasons Charlie outlines on page 50, at yearend we valued our Salomon investment at 98% of par, $14 million less than our cost. However, we believe there is a reasonable likelihood that a leading, high-quality capital-raising and market-making operation can average good returns on equity. If so, our conversion right will eventually prove to be valuable. Two further comments about our investments in marketable securities are appropriate. First, we give you our usual warning: Our holdings have changed since yearend and will continue to do so without notice.

The second comment is related: During 1987, as in some earlier years, there was speculation in the press from time to time about our purchase or sale of various securities. These stories were sometimes true, sometimes partially true, and other times completely untrue. Interestingly, there has been no correlation between the size and prestige of the publication and the accuracy of the report. One dead-wrong rumor was given considerable prominence by a major national magazine, and another leading publication misled its readers by writing about an arbitrage position as if it were a long-term investment commitment. (In not naming names, I am observing the old warning that it's not wise to pick fights with people who buy ink by the barrel.)

You should understand that we simply don't comment in any way on rumors, whether they are true or false. If we were to deny the incorrect reports and refuse comment on the correct ones, we would in effect be commenting on all.

In a world in which big investment ideas are both limited and valuable, we have no interest in telling potential competitors what we are doing except to the extent required by law. We certainly don't expect others to tell us of their investment ideas. Nor would we expect a media company to disclose news of acquisitions it was privately pursuing or a journalist to tell his competitors about stories on which he is working or sources he is using.

I find it uncomfortable when friends or acquaintances mention that they are buying X because it has been reported—incorrectly—that Berkshire is a buyer. However, I do not set them straight. If they want to participate in whatever Berkshire actually is buying, they can always purchase Berkshire stock. But perhaps that is too simple. Usually, I suspect, they find it more exciting to buy what is being talked about. Whether that strategy is more profitable is another question.

Financing

Shortly after yearend, Berkshire sold two issues of debentures, totaling $250 million. Both issues mature in 2018 and will be retired at an even pace through sinking fund operations that begin in 1999.

Our overall interest cost, after allowing for expenses of issuance, is slightly over 10%. Salomon was our investment banker, and its service was excellent.

Despite our pessimistic views about inflation, our taste for debt is quite limited. To be sure, it is likely that Berkshire could improve its return on equity by moving to a much higher, though still conventional, debt-to-business-value ratio. It's even more likely that we could handle such a ratio, without problems, under economic conditions far worse than any that have prevailed since the early 1930s.

But we do not wish it to be only likely that we can meet our obligations; we wish that to be certain. Thus we adhere to policies—both in regard to debt and all other matters—that will allow us to achieve acceptable long-term results under extraordinarily adverse conditions, rather than optimal results under a normal range of conditions.

Good business or investment decisions will eventually produce quite satisfactory economic results, with no aid from leverage. Therefore, it seems to us to be both foolish and improper to risk what is important (including, necessarily, the welfare of innocent bystanders such as policyholders and employees) for some extra returns that are relatively unimportant. This view is not the product of either our advancing age or prosperity: Our opinions about debt have remained constant.

However, we are not phobic about borrowing. (We're far from believing that there is no fate worse than debt.) We are willing to borrow an amount that we believe—on a worst-case basis—will pose no threat to Berkshire's well-being. Analyzing what that amount might be, we can look to some important strengths that would serve us well if major problems should engulf our economy: Berkshire's earnings come from many diverse and well-entrenched businesses; these businesses seldom require much capital investment; what debt we have is structured well; and we maintain major holdings of liquid assets. Clearly, we could be comfortable with a higher debt-to-business-value ratio than we now have.

One further aspect of our debt policy deserves comment: Unlike many in the business world, we prefer to finance in anticipation of need rather than in reaction to it. A business obtains the best financial results possible by managing both sides of its balance sheet well. This means obtaining the highest-possible return on assets and the lowest-possible cost on liabilities. It would be convenient if opportunities for intelligent action on both fronts coincided. However, reason tells us that just the opposite is likely to be the case: Tight money conditions, which translate into high costs for liabilities, will create the best opportunities for acquisitions, and cheap money will cause assets to be bid to the sky. Our conclusion: Action on the liability side should sometimes be taken independent of any action on the asset side.

Alas, what is "tight" and "cheap" money is far from clear at any particular time. We have no ability to forecast interest rates and—maintaining our usual open-minded spirit—believe that no one else can. Therefore, we simply borrow when conditions seem non-oppressive and hope that we will later find intelligent expansion or acquisition opportunities, which—as we have said—are most likely to pop up when conditions in the debt market are clearly oppressive. Our basic principle is that if you want to shoot rare, fast-moving elephants, you should always carry a loaded gun.

Our fund-first, buy-or-expand-later policy almost always penalizes near-term earnings. For example, we are now earning about 6½% on the $250 million we recently raised at 10%, a disparity that is currently costing us about $160,000 per week. This negative spread is unimportant to us and will not cause us to stretch for either acquisitions or higher-yielding short-term instruments. If we find the right sort of business elephant within the next five years or so, the wait will have been worthwhile.

Miscellaneous

We hope to buy more businesses that are similar to the ones we have, and we can use some help. If you have a business that fits the following criteria, call me or, preferably, write.

Here's what we're looking for:

(1) large purchases (at least $10 million of after-tax earnings),

(2) demonstrated consistent earning power (future projections are of little interest to us, nor are "turnaround" situations),

(3) businesses earning good returns on equity while employing little or no debt,

(4) management in place (we can't supply it),

(5) simple businesses (if there's lots of technology, we won't understand it),

(6) an offering price (we don't want to waste our time or that of the seller by talking, even preliminarily, about a transaction when price is unknown).

We will not engage in unfriendly takeovers. We can promise complete confidentiality and a very fast answer—customarily within five minutes—as to whether we're interested. We prefer to buy for cash, but will consider issuing stock when we receive as much in intrinsic business value as we give. We invite potential sellers to check us out by contacting people with whom we have done business in the past. For the right business—and the right people—we can provide a good home.

On the other hand, we frequently get approached about acquisitions that don't come close to meeting our tests: new ventures, turnarounds, auction-like sales, and the ever-popular (among brokers) "I'm-sure-something-will-work-out-if-you-people-get-to-know-each-other." None of these attracts us in the least.

Besides being interested in the purchases of entire businesses as described above, we are also interested in the negotiated purchase of large, but not controlling, blocks of stock comparable to those we hold in Cap Cities and Salomon. We have a special interest in purchasing convertible preferreds as a long-term investment, as we did at Salomon.

* * *

And now a bit of *deja vu*. Most of Berkshire's major stockholders received their shares at yearend 1969 in a liquidating distribution from Buffett Partnership, Ltd. Some of these former partners will remember that in 1962 I encountered severe managerial problems at Dempster Mill Manufacturing Co., a pump and farm implement manufacturing company that BPL controlled.

At that time, like now, I went to Charlie with problems that were too tough for me to solve. Charlie suggested the solution might lie in a California friend of his, Harry Bottle, whose special knack was never forgetting the fundamental. I met Harry in Los Angeles on April 17, 1962, and on April 23 he was in Beatrice, Nebraska, running Dempster. Our problems disappeared almost immediately. In my 1962 annual letter to partners, I named Harry "Man of the Year."

Fade to 24 years later: The scene is K & W Products, a small Berkshire subsidiary that produces automotive compounds. For years K & W did well, but in 1985-86 it stumbled badly, as it pursued the unattainable to the neglect of the achievable. Charlie, who oversees K & W, knew there was no need to consult me. Instead, he called Harry, now 68 years old, made him CEO, and sat back to await the inevitable. He didn't wait long. In 1987 K & W's profits set a record, up more than 300% from 1986. And, as profits went up, capital employed went down: K & W's investment in accounts receivable and inventories has decreased 20%.

If we run into another managerial problem ten or twenty years down the road, you know whose phone will ring.

* * *

About 97.2% of all eligible shares participated in Berkshire's 1987 shareholder-designated contributions program. Contributions made through the program were $4.9 million, and 2,050 charities were recipients.

A recent survey reported that about 50% of major American companies match charitable contributions made by directors (sometimes by a factor of three to one). In effect, these representatives of the owners direct funds to their favorite charities, and never consult the owners as to their charitable preferences. (I wonder how they would feel if the process were reversed and shareholders could invade the directors' pockets for charities favored by the shareholders.) When A takes money from B to give to C and A is a legislator, the process is called taxation. But when A is an officer or director of a corporation, it is called philanthropy. We continue to believe that contributions, aside from those with quite clear direct benefits to the company, should reflect the charitable preferences of owners rather than those of officers and directors.

We urge new shareholders to read the description of our shareholder-designated contributions program that appears on pages 54 and 55. If you wish to participate in future programs, we strongly urge that you immediately make sure your shares are registered in the name of the actual owner, not in "street" name or nominee name. Shares not so registered on September 30, 1988 will be ineligible for the 1988 program.

* * *

Last year we again had about 450 shareholders at our annual meeting. The 60 or so questions they asked were, as always, excellent. At many companies, the annual meeting is a waste of time because exhibitionists turn it into a sideshow. Ours, however, is different. It is informative for shareholders and fun for us. (At Berkshire's meetings, the exhibitionists are on the dais.)

This year our meeting will be on May 23, 1988 in Omaha, and we hope that you come. The meeting provides the forum for you to ask any owner-related questions you may have, and we will keep answering until all (except those dealing with portfolio activities or other proprietary information) have been dealt with.

Last year we rented two buses—for $100—to take shareholders interested in the trip to the Furniture Mart. Your actions demonstrated your good judgment: You snapped up about $40,000 of bargains. Mrs. B regards this expense/sales ratio as on the high side and attributes it to my chronic inattention to costs and generally sloppy managerial practices. But, gracious as always, she has offered me another chance and we will again have buses available following the meeting. Mrs. B says you must beat last year's sales figures, and I have told her she won't be disappointed.

| | Warren E. Buffett |
| February 29, 1988 | Chairman of the Board |

BERKSHIRE HATHAWAY INC.

To the Shareholders of Berkshire Hathaway Inc.:

Our gain in net worth during 1988 was $569 million, or 20.0%. Over the last 24 years (that is, since present management took over), our per-share book value has grown from $19.46 to $2,974.52, or at a rate of 23.0% compounded annually.

We've emphasized in past reports that what counts, however, is intrinsic business value—the figure, necessarily an estimate, indicating what all of our constituent businesses are worth. By our calculations, Berkshire's intrinsic business value significantly exceeds its book value. Over the 24 years, business value has grown somewhat faster than book value; in 1988, however, book value grew the faster, by a bit.

Berkshire's past rates of gain in both book value and business value were achieved under circumstances far different from those that now exist. Anyone ignoring these differences makes the same mistake that a baseball manager would were he to judge the future prospects of a 42-year-old center fielder on the basis of his lifetime batting average.

Important negatives affecting our prospects today are: (1) a less attractive stock market than generally existed over the past 24 years; (2) higher corporate tax rates on most forms of investment income; (3) a far more richly-priced market for the acquisition of businesses; and (4) industry conditions for Capital Cities/ABC, Inc., GEICO Corporation, and The Washington Post Company—Berkshire's three permanent investments, constituting about one-half of our net worth—that range from slightly to materially less favorable than those existing five to ten years ago. All of these companies have superb management and strong properties. But, at current prices, their upside potential looks considerably less exciting to us today than it did some years ago.

The major problem we face, however, is a growing capital base. You've heard that from us before, but this problem, like age, grows in significance each year. (And also, just as with age, it's better to have this problem continue to grow rather than to have it "solved.")

Four years ago I told you that we needed profits of $3.9 billion to achieve a 15% annual return over the decade then ahead. Today, for the next decade, a 15% return demands profits of $10.3 billion. That seems like a very big number to me and to Charlie Munger, Berkshire's Vice Chairman and my partner. (Should that number indeed prove too big, Charlie will find himself, in future reports, retrospectively identified as the senior partner.)

As a partial offset to the drag that our growing capital base exerts upon returns, we have a very important advantage now that we lacked 24 years ago. Then, all our capital was tied up in a textile business with inescapably poor economic characteristics. Today part of our capital is invested in some really exceptional businesses.

Last year we dubbed these operations the Sainted Seven: Buffalo News, Fechheimer, Kirby, Nebraska Furniture Mart, Scott Fetzer Manufacturing Group, See's, and World Book. In 1988 the Saints came marching in. You can see just how extraordinary their returns on capital were by examining the historical-cost financial statements on page 45, which combine the figures of the Sainted Seven with those of several smaller units. With no benefit from financial leverage, this group earned about 67% on average equity capital.

In most cases the remarkable performance of these units arises partially from an exceptional business franchise; in all cases an exceptional management is a vital factor. The contribution Charlie and I make is to leave these managers alone.

In my judgment, these businesses, in aggregate, will continue to produce superb returns. We'll need these: Without this help Berkshire would not have a chance of achieving our 15% goal. You can be sure that our operating managers will deliver; the question mark in our future is whether Charlie and I can effectively employ the funds that they generate.

In that respect, we took a step in the right direction early in 1989 when we purchased an 80% interest in Borsheim's, a jewelry business in Omaha. This purchase, described later in this letter, delivers exactly what we look for: an outstanding business run by people we like, admire, and trust. It's a great way to start the year.

Accounting Changes

We have made a significant accounting change that was mandated for 1988, and likely will have another to make in 1990. When we move figures around from year to year, without any change in economic reality, one of our always-thrilling discussions of accounting is necessary.

First, I'll offer my customary disclaimer: Despite the shortcomings of generally accepted accounting principles (GAAP), I would hate to have the job of devising a better set of rules. The limitations of the existing set, however, need not be inhibiting: CEOs are free to treat GAAP statements as a beginning rather than an end to their obligation to inform owners and creditors—and indeed they should. After all, any manager of a subsidiary company would find himself in hot water if he reported barebones GAAP numbers that omitted key information needed by his boss, the parent corporation's CEO. Why, then, should the CEO himself withhold information vitally useful to *his* bosses—the shareholder-owners of the corporation?

What needs to be reported is data—whether GAAP, non-GAAP, or extra-GAAP—that helps financially-literate readers answer three key questions: (1) Approximately how much is this company worth? (2) What is the likelihood that it can meet its future obligations? and (3) How good a job are its managers doing, given the hand they have been dealt?

In most cases, answers to one or more of these questions are somewhere between difficult and impossible to glean from the minimum GAAP presentation. The business world is simply too complex for a single set of rules to effectively describe economic reality for all enterprises, particularly those operating in a wide variety of businesses, such as Berkshire.

Further complicating the problem is the fact that many managements view GAAP not as a standard to be met, but as an obstacle to overcome. Too often their accountants willingly assist them. ("How much," says the client, "is two plus two?" Replies the cooperative accountant, "What number did you have in mind?") Even honest and well-intentioned managements sometimes stretch GAAP a bit in order to present figures they think will more appropriately describe their performance. Both the smoothing of earnings and the "big bath" quarter are "white lie" techniques employed by otherwise upright managements.

Then there are managers who actively use GAAP to deceive and defraud. They know that many investors and creditors accept GAAP results as gospel. So these charlatans interpret the rules "imaginatively" and record business transactions in ways that technically comply with GAAP but actually display an economic illusion to the world.

As long as investors—including supposedly sophisticated institutions—place fancy valuations on reported "earnings" that march steadily upward, you can be sure that some managers and promoters will exploit GAAP to produce such numbers, no matter what the truth may be. Over the years, Charlie and I have observed many accounting-based frauds of staggering size. Few of the perpetrators have been punished; many have not even been censured. It has been far safer to steal large sums with a pen than small sums with a gun.

Under one major change mandated by GAAP for 1988, we have been required to fully consolidate all our subsidiaries in our balance sheet and earnings statement. In the past, Mutual Savings and Loan, and Scott Fetzer Financial (a credit company that primarily finances installment sales of World Book and Kirby products) were consolidated on a "one-line" basis. That meant we (1) showed our equity in their combined net worths as a single-entry asset on Berkshire's consolidated balance sheet and (2) included our equity in their combined annual earnings as a single-line income entry in our consolidated statement of earnings. Now the rules require that we consolidate each asset and liability of these companies in our balance sheet and each item of their income and expense in our earnings statement.

This change underscores the need for companies also to report segmented data: The greater the number of economically diverse business operations lumped together in conventional financial statements, the less useful those presentations are and the less able investors are to answer the three questions posed earlier. Indeed, the only reason we ever prepare consolidated figures at Berkshire is to meet outside requirements. On the other hand, Charlie and I constantly study our segment data.

Now that we are required to bundle more numbers in our GAAP statements, we have decided to publish additional supplementary information that we think will help you measure both business value and managerial performance. (Berkshire's ability to discharge its obligations to creditors—the third question we listed—should be obvious, whatever statements you examine.) In these supplementary presentations, we will not necessarily follow GAAP procedures, or even corporate structure. Rather, we will attempt to lump major business activities in ways that aid analysis but do not swamp you with detail. Our goal is to give you important information in a form that we would wish to get it if our roles were reversed.

On pages 41-47 we show separate combined balance sheets and earnings statements for: (1) our subsidiaries engaged in finance-type operations, which are Mutual Savings and Scott Fetzer Financial; (2) our insurance operations, with their major investment positions itemized; (3) our manufacturing, publishing and retailing businesses, leaving aside certain non-operating assets and purchase-price accounting adjustments; and (4) an all-other category that includes the non-operating assets (primarily marketable securities) held by the companies in (3) as well as various assets and debts of the Wesco and Berkshire parent companies.

If you combine the earnings and the net worths of these four segments, you will derive totals matching those shown on our GAAP statements. However, we want to emphasize that our new presentation does not fall within the purview of our auditors, who in no way bless it. (In fact, they may be horrified; I don't want to ask.)

I referred earlier to a major change in GAAP that is expected in 1990. This change relates to the calculation of deferred taxes, and is both complicated and controversial—so much so that its imposition, originally scheduled for 1989, was postponed for a year.

When implemented, the new rule will affect us in various ways. Most important, we will be required to change the way we calculate our liability for deferred taxes on the unrealized appreciation of stocks held by our insurance companies.

Right now, our liability is layered. For the unrealized appreciation that dates back to 1986 and earlier years, $1.2 billion, we have booked a 28% tax liability. For the unrealized appreciation built up since, $600 million, the tax liability has been booked at 34%. The difference reflects the increase in tax rates that went into effect in 1987.

It now appears, however, that the new accounting rule will require us to establish the entire liability at 34% in 1990, taking the charge against our earnings. Assuming no change in tax rates by 1990, this step will reduce our earnings in that year (and thereby our reported net worth) by $71 million. The proposed rule will also affect other items on our balance sheet, but these changes will have only a minor impact on earnings and net worth.

We have no strong views about the desirability of this change in calculation of deferred taxes. We should point out, however, that neither a 28% nor a 34% tax liability precisely depicts economic reality at Berkshire since we have no plans to sell the stocks in which we have the great bulk of our gains.

To those of you who are uninterested in accounting, I apologize for this dissertation. I realize that many of you do not pore over our figures, but instead hold Berkshire primarily because you know that: (1) Charlie and I have the bulk of our money in Berkshire; (2) we intend to run things so that your gains or losses are in direct proportion to ours; and (3) the record has so far been satisfactory. There is nothing necessarily wrong with this kind of "faith" approach to investing. Other shareholders, however, prefer an "analysis" approach and we want to supply the information they need. In our own investing, we search for situations in which both approaches give us the same answer.

Sources of Reported Earnings

In addition to supplying you with our new four-sector accounting material, we will continue to list the major sources of Berkshire's reported earnings just as we have in the past.

In the following table, amortization of Goodwill and other major purchase-price accounting adjustments are not charged against the specific businesses to which they apply but are instead aggregated and shown separately. This procedure lets you view the earnings of our businesses as they would have been reported had we not purchased them. I've explained in past reports why this form of presentation seems to us to be more useful to investors and managers than the standard GAAP presentation, which makes purchase-price adjustments on a business-by-business basis. The total net earnings we show in the table are, of course, identical to the GAAP total in our audited financial statements.

Further information about these businesses is given in the Business Segment section on pages 32-34, and in the Management's Discussion section on pages 36-40. In these sections you also will find our segment earnings reported on a GAAP basis. For information on Wesco's businesses, I urge you to read Charlie Munger's letter, which starts on page 52. It contains the best description I have seen of the events that produced the present savings-and-loan crisis. Also, take special note of Dave Hillstrom's performance at Precision Steel Warehouse, a Wesco subsidiary. Precision operates in an extremely competitive industry, yet Dave consistently achieves good returns on invested capital. Though data is lacking to prove the point, I think it is likely that his performance, both in 1988 and years past, would rank him number one among his peers.

| | (000s omitted) | | | |
| | Pre-Tax Earnings | | Berkshire's Share of Net Earnings (after taxes and minority interests) | |
	1988	1987	1988	1987
Operating Earnings:				
Insurance Group:				
Underwriting	$(11,081)	$(55,429)	$ (1,045)	$(20,696)
Net Investment Income	231,250	152,483	197,779	136,658
Buffalo News	42,429	39,410	25,462	21,304
Fechheimer	14,152	13,332	7,720	6,580
Kirby	26,891	22,408	17,842	12,891
Nebraska Furniture Mart	18,439	16,837	9,099	7,554
Scott Fetzer Manufacturing Group	28,542	30,591	17,640	17,555
See's Candies	32,473	31,693	19,671	17,363
Wesco—other than Insurance	16,133	6,209	10,650	4,978
World Book	27,890	25,745	18,021	15,136
Amortization of Goodwill	(2,806)	(2,862)	(2,806)	(2,862)
Other Purchase-Price				
Accounting Charges	(6,342)	(5,546)	(7,340)	(6,544)
Interest on Debt*	(35,613)	(11,474)	(23,212)	(5,905)
Shareholder-Designated Contributions . .	(4,966)	(4,938)	(3,217)	(2,963)
Other	41,059	23,217	27,177	13,697
Operating Earnings	418,450	281,676	313,441	214,746
Sales of Securities	131,671	28,838	85,829	19,806
Total Earnings—All Entities	$550,121	$310,514	$399,270	$234,552

Excludes interest expense of Scott Fetzer Financial Group.

The earnings achieved by our operating businesses are superb, whether measured on an absolute basis or against those of their competitors. For that we thank our operating managers: You and I are fortunate to be associated with them.

At Berkshire, associations like these last a long time. We do not remove superstars from our lineup merely because they have attained a specified age—whether the traditional 65, or the 95 reached by Mrs. B on the eve of Hanukkah in 1988. Superb managers are too scarce a resource to be discarded simply because a cake gets crowded with candles. Moreover, our experience with newly-minted MBAs has not been that great. Their academic records always look terrific and the candidates always know just what to say; but too often they are short on personal commitment to the company and general business savvy. It's difficult to teach a new dog old tricks.

Here's an update on our major non-insurance operations:

- At Nebraska Furniture Mart, Mrs. B (Rose Blumkin) and her cart roll on and on. She's been the boss for 51 years, having started the business at 44 with $500. (Think what she would have done with $1,000!) With Mrs. B, old age will always be ten years away.

The Mart, long the largest home furnishings store in the country, continues to grow. In the fall, the store opened a detached 20,000 square foot Clearance Center, which expands our ability to offer bargains in all price ranges.

Recently Dillard's, one of the most successful department store operations in the country, entered the Omaha market. In many of its stores, Dillard's runs a full furniture department, undoubtedly doing well in this line. Shortly before opening in Omaha, however, William Dillard, chairman of the company, announced that his new store would not sell furniture. Said he, referring to NFM: "We don't want to compete with them. We think they are about the best there is."

At the Buffalo News we extol the value of advertising, and our policies at NFM prove that we practice what we preach. Over the past three years NFM has been the largest ROP advertiser in the Omaha World-Herald. (ROP advertising is the kind printed in the paper, as contrasted to the preprinted-insert kind.) In no other major market, to my knowledge, is a home furnishings operation the leading customer of the newspaper. At times, we also run large ads in papers as far away as Des Moines, Sioux City and Kansas City—always with good results. It truly does pay to advertise, as long as you have something worthwhile to offer.

Mrs. B's son, Louie, and his boys, Ron and Irv, complete the winning Blumkin team. It's a joy to work with this family. All its members have character that matches their extraordinary abilities.

- Last year I stated unequivocally that pre-tax margins at The Buffalo News would fall in 1988. That forecast would have proved correct at almost any other newspaper our size or larger. But Stan Lipsey—bless him—has managed to make me look foolish.

Though we increased our prices a bit less than the industry average last year, and though our newsprint costs and wage rates rose in line with industry norms, Stan actually improved margins a tad. No one in the newspaper business has a better managerial record. He has achieved it, furthermore, while running a paper that gives readers an extraordinary amount of news. We believe that our "newshole" percentage—the portion of the paper devoted to news—is bigger than that of any other dominant paper of our size or larger. The percentage was 49.5% in 1988 versus 49.8% in 1987. We are committed to keeping it around 50%, whatever the level or trend of profit margins.

Charlie and I have loved the newspaper business since we were youngsters, and we have had great fun with the News in the 12 years since we purchased it. We were fortunate to find Murray Light, a top-flight editor, on the scene when we arrived and he has made us proud of the paper ever since.

- See's Candies sold a record 25.1 million pounds in 1988. Prospects did not look good at the end of October, but excellent Christmas volume, considerably better than the record set in 1987, turned the tide.

As we've told you before, See's business continues to become more Christmas-concentrated. In 1988, the Company earned a record 90% of its full-year profits in December: $29 million out of $32.5 million before tax. (It's enough to make you believe in Santa Claus.) December's deluge of business produces a modest seasonal bulge in Berkshire's corporate earnings. Another small bulge occurs in the first quarter, when most World Book annuals are sold.

Charlie and I put Chuck Huggins in charge of See's about five minutes after we bought the company. Upon reviewing his record, you may wonder what took us so long.

- At Fechheimer, the Heldmans—Bob, George, Gary, Roger and Fred—are the Cincinnati counterparts of the Blumkins. Neither furniture retailing nor uniform manufacturing has inherently attractive economics. In these businesses, only exceptional managements can deliver high returns on invested capital. And that's exactly what the five Heldmans do. (As Mets announcer Ralph Kiner once said when comparing pitcher Steve Trout to his father, Dizzy Trout, the famous Detroit Tigers pitcher: "There's a lot of heredity in that family.")

  Fechheimer made a fairly good-sized acquisition in 1988. Charlie and I have such confidence in the business savvy of the Heldman family that we okayed the deal without even looking at it. There are very few managements anywhere—including those running the top tier companies of the Fortune 500—in which we would exhibit similar confidence.

  Because of both this acquisition and some internal growth, sales at Fechheimer should be up significantly in 1989.

- All of the operations managed by Ralph Schey—World Book, Kirby, and The Scott Fetzer Manufacturing Group—performed splendidly in 1988. Returns on the capital entrusted to Ralph continue to be exceptional.

  Within the Scott Fetzer Manufacturing Group, particularly fine progress was recorded at its largest unit, Campbell Hausfeld. This company, the country's leading producer of small and medium-sized air compressors, has more than doubled earnings since 1986.

  Unit sales at both Kirby and World Book were up significantly in 1988, with export business particularly strong. World Book became available in the Soviet Union in September, when that country's largest American book store opened in Moscow. Ours is the only general encyclopedia offered at the store.

  Ralph's personal productivity is amazing: In addition to running 19 businesses in superb fashion, he is active at The Cleveland Clinic, Ohio University, Case Western Reserve, and a venture capital operation that has spawned sixteen Ohio-based companies and resurrected many others. Both Ohio and Berkshire are fortunate to have Ralph on their side.

Borsheim's

It was in 1983 that Berkshire purchased an 80% interest in The Nebraska Furniture Mart. Your Chairman blundered then by neglecting to ask Mrs. B a question any schoolboy would have thought of: "Are there any more at home like you?" Last month I corrected the error: We are now 80% partners with another branch of the family.

After Mrs. B came over from Russia in 1917, her parents and five siblings followed. (Her two other siblings had preceded her.) Among the sisters was Rebecca Friedman who, with her husband, Louis, escaped in 1922 to the west through Latvia in a journey as perilous as Mrs. B's earlier odyssey to the east through Manchuria. When the family members reunited in Omaha they had no tangible assets. However, they came equipped with an extraordinary combination of brains, integrity, and enthusiasm for work—and that's all they needed. They have since proved themselves invincible.

In 1948 Mr. Friedman purchased Borsheim's, a small Omaha jewelry store. He was joined in the business by his son, Ike, in 1950 and, as the years went by, Ike's son, Alan, and his sons-in-law, Marvin Cohn and Donald Yale, came in also.

You won't be surprised to learn that this family brings to the jewelry business precisely the same approach that the Blumkins bring to the furniture business. The cornerstone for both enterprises is Mrs. B's creed: "Sell cheap and tell the truth." Other fundamentals at both businesses are: (1) single store operations featuring huge inventories that provide customers with an enormous selection across all price ranges, (2) daily attention to detail by top management, (3) rapid turnover, (4) shrewd buying, and (5) incredibly low expenses. The combination of the last three factors lets both stores offer everyday prices that no one in the country comes close to matching.

Most people, no matter how sophisticated they are in other matters, feel like babes in the woods when purchasing jewelry. They can judge neither quality nor price. For them only one rule makes sense: If you don't know jewelry, know the jeweler.

I can assure you that those who put their trust in Ike Friedman and his family will never be disappointed. The way in which we purchased our interest in their business is the ultimate testimonial. Borsheim's had no audited financial statements; nevertheless, we didn't take inventory, verify receivables or audit the operation in any way. Ike simply told us what was so—and on that basis we drew up a one-page contract and wrote a large check.

Business at Borsheim's has mushroomed in recent years as the reputation of the Friedman family has spread. Customers now come to the store from all over the country. Among them have been some friends of mine from both coasts who thanked me later for getting them there.

Borsheim's new links to Berkshire will change nothing in the way this business is run. All members of the Friedman family will continue to operate just as they have before; Charlie and I will stay on the sidelines where we belong. And when we say "all members," the words have real meaning. Mr. and Mrs. Friedman, at 88 and 87, respectively, are in the store daily. The wives of Ike, Alan, Marvin and Donald all pitch in at busy times, and a fourth generation is beginning to learn the ropes.

It is great fun to be in business with people you have long admired. The Friedmans, like the Blumkins, have achieved success because they have deserved success. Both families focus on what's right for the customer and that, inevitably, works out well for them, also. We couldn't have better partners.

Insurance Operations

Shown below is an updated version of our usual table presenting key figures for the insurance industry:

	Yearly Change in Premiums Written (%)	Statutory Combined Ratio After Policyholder Dividends	Yearly Change in Incurred Losses (%)	Inflation Rate Measured by GNP Deflator (%)
1981	3.8	106.0	6.5	9.6
1982	3.7	109.6	8.4	6.4
1983	5.0	112.0	6.8	3.8
1984	8.5	118.0	16.9	3.7
1985	22.1	116.3	16.1	3.2
1986	22.2	108.0	13.5	2.7
1987	9.4	104.6	7.8	3.3
1988 (Est.)	3.9	105.4	4.2	3.6

Source: A.M. Best Co.

The combined ratio represents total insurance costs (losses incurred plus expenses) compared to revenue from premiums: A ratio below 100 indicates an underwriting profit, and one above 100 indicates a loss. When the investment income that an insurer earns from holding on to policyholders' funds ("the float") is taken into account, a combined ratio in the 107-111 range typically produces an overall break-even result, exclusive of earnings on the funds provided by shareholders.

For the reasons laid out in previous reports, we expect the industry's incurred losses to grow by about 10% annually, even in years when general inflation runs considerably lower. If premium growth meanwhile materially lags that 10% rate, underwriting losses will mount, though the industry's tendency to underreserve when business turns bad may obscure their size for a time. As the table shows, the industry's underwriting loss grew in 1988. This trend is almost certain to continue—and probably will accelerate—for at least two more years.

The property-casualty insurance industry is not only subnormally profitable, it is subnormally popular. (As Sam Goldwyn philosophized: "In life, one must learn to take the bitter with the sour.") One of the ironies of business is that many relatively-unprofitable industries that are plagued by inadequate prices habitually find themselves beat upon by irate customers even while other, hugely profitable industries are spared complaints, no matter how high their prices.

Take the breakfast cereal industry, whose return on invested capital is more than double that of the auto insurance industry (which is why companies like Kellogg and General Mills sell at five times book value and most large insurers sell close to book). The cereal companies regularly impose price increases, few of them related to a significant jump in their costs. Yet not a peep is heard from consumers. But when auto insurers raise prices by amounts that do not even match cost increases, customers are outraged. If you want to be loved, it's clearly better to sell high-priced corn flakes than low-priced auto insurance.

The antagonism that the public feels toward the industry can have serious consequences: Proposition 103, a California initiative passed last fall, threatens to push auto insurance prices down sharply, even though costs have been soaring. The price cut has been suspended while the courts review the initiative, but the resentment that brought on the vote has not been suspended: Even if the initiative is overturned, insurers are likely to find it tough to operate profitably in California. (Thank heavens the citizenry isn't mad at bonbons: If Proposition 103 applied to candy as well as insurance, See's would be forced to sell its product for $5.76 per pound. rather than the $7.60 we charge—and would be losing money by the bucketful.)

The immediate direct effects on Berkshire from the initiative are minor, since we saw few opportunities for profit in the rate structure that existed in California prior to the vote. However, the forcing down of prices would seriously affect GEICO, our 44%-owned investee, which gets about 10% of its premium volume from California. Even more threatening to GEICO is the possibility that similar pricing actions will be taken in other states, through either initiatives or legislation.

If voters insist that auto insurance be priced below cost, it eventually must be sold by government. Stockholders can subsidize policyholders for a short period, but only taxpayers can subsidize them over the long term. At most property-casualty companies, socialized auto insurance would be no disaster for shareholders. Because of the commodity characteristics of the industry, most insurers earn mediocre returns and therefore have little or no economic goodwill to lose if they are forced by government to leave the auto insurance business. But GEICO, because it is a low-cost producer able to earn high returns on equity, has a huge amount of economic goodwill at risk. In turn, so do we.

At Berkshire, in 1988, our premium volume continued to fall, and in 1989 we will experience a large decrease for a special reason: The contract through which we receive 7% of the business of Fireman's Fund expires on August 31. At that time, we will return to Fireman's Fund the unearned premiums we hold that relate to the contract. This transfer of funds will show up in our "premiums written" account as a negative $85 million or so and will make our third-quarter figures look rather peculiar. However, the termination of this contract will not have a significant effect on profits.

Berkshire's underwriting results continued to be excellent in 1988. Our combined ratio (on a statutory basis and excluding structured settlements and financial reinsurance) was 104. Reserve development was favorable for the second year in a row, after a string of years in which it was very unsatisfactory. Details on both underwriting and reserve development appear on pages 36-38.

Our insurance volume over the next few years is likely to run very low, since business with a reasonable potential for profit will almost certainly be scarce. So be it. At Berkshire, we simply will not write policies at rates that carry the expectation of economic loss. We encounter enough troubles when we expect a gain.

Despite—or perhaps because of—low volume, our profit picture during the next few years is apt to be considerably brighter than the industry's. We are sure to have an exceptional amount of float compared to premium volume, and that augurs well for profits. In 1989 and 1990 we expect our float/premiums ratio to be at least three times that of the typical property/casualty company. Mike Goldberg, with special help from Ajit Jain, Dinos Iordanou, and the National Indemnity managerial team, has positioned us well in that respect.

At some point—we don't know when—we will be deluged with insurance business. The cause will probably be some major physical or financial catastrophe. But we could also experience an explosion in business, as we did in 1985, because large and increasing underwriting losses at other companies coincide with their recognition that they are far underreserved. in the meantime, we will retain our talented professionals, protect our capital, and try not to make major mistakes.

Marketable Securities

In selecting marketable securities for our insurance companies, we can choose among five major categories: (1) long-term common stock investments, (2) medium-term fixed-income securities, (3) long-term fixed-income securities, (4) short-term cash equivalents, and (5) short-term arbitrage commitments.

We have no particular bias when it comes to choosing from these categories. We just continuously search among them for the highest after-tax returns as measured by "mathematical expectation," limiting ourselves always to investment alternatives we think we understand. Our criteria have nothing to do with maximizing immediately reportable earnings; our goal, rather, is to maximize eventual net worth.

- Below we list our common stock holdings having a value over $100 million, not including arbitrage commitments, which will be discussed later. A small portion of these investments belongs to subsidiaries of which Berkshire owns less than 100%.

Shares	Company	Cost	Market
		(000s omitted)	
3,000,000	Capital Cities/ABC, Inc..	$517,500	$1,086,750
14,172,500	The Coca-Cola Company	592,540	632,448
2,400,000	Federal Home Loan Mortgage Corporation Preferred* .	71,729	121,200
6,850,000	GEICO Corporation	45,713	849,400
1,727,765	The Washington Post Company.	9,731	364,126

Although nominally a preferred stock, this security is financially equivalent to a common stock.

Our permanent holdings—Capital Cities/ABC, Inc., GEICO Corporation, and The Washington Post Company—remain unchanged. Also unchanged is our unqualified admiration of their managements: Tom Murphy and Dan Burke at Cap Cities, Bill Snyder and Lou Simpson at GEICO, and Kay Graham and Dick Simmons at The Washington Post. Charlie and I appreciate enormously the talent and integrity these managers bring to their businesses.

Their performance, which we have observed at close range, contrasts vividly with that of many CEOs, which we have fortunately observed from a safe distance. Sometimes these CEOs clearly do not belong in their jobs; their positions, nevertheless, are usually secure. The supreme irony of business management is that it is far easier for an inadequate CEO to keep his job than it is for an inadequate subordinate.

If a secretary, say, is hired for a job that requires typing ability of at least 80 words a minute and turns out to be capable of only 50 words a minute, she will lose her job in no time. There is a logical standard for this job; performance is easily measured; and if you can't make the grade, you're out. Similarly, if new sales people fail to generate sufficient business quickly enough, they will be let go. Excuses will not be accepted as a substitute for orders.

However, a CEO who doesn't perform is frequently carried indefinitely. One reason is that performance standards for his job seldom exist. When they do, they are often fuzzy or they may be waived or explained away, even when the performance shortfalls are major and repeated. At too many companies, the boss shoots the arrow of managerial performance and then hastily paints the bullseye around the spot where it lands.

Another important, but seldom recognized, distinction between the boss and the foot soldier is that the CEO has no immediate superior whose performance is itself getting measured. The sales manager who retains a bunch of lemons in his sales force will soon be in hot water himself. It is in his immediate self-interest to promptly weed out his hiring mistakes. Otherwise, he himself may be weeded out. An office manager who has hired inept secretaries faces the same imperative.

But the CEO's boss is a Board of Directors that seldom measures itself and is infrequently held to account for substandard corporate performance. If the Board makes a mistake in hiring, and perpetuates that mistake, so what? Even if the company is taken over because of the mistake, the deal will probably bestow substantial benefits on the outgoing Board members. (The bigger they are, the softer they fall.)

Finally, relations between the Board and the CEO are expected to be congenial. At board meetings, criticism of the CEO's performance is often viewed as the social equivalent of belching. No such inhibitions restrain the office manager from critically evaluating the substandard typist.

These points should not be interpreted as a blanket condemnation of CEOs or Boards of Directors: Most are able and hard-working, and a number are truly outstanding. But the management failings that Charlie and I have seen make us thankful that we are linked with the managers of our three permanent holdings. They love their businesses, they think like owners, and they exude integrity and ability.

- In 1988 we made major purchases of Federal Home Loan Mortgage Pfd. ("Freddie Mac") and Coca Cola. We expect to hold these securities for a long time. In fact, when we own portions of outstanding businesses with outstanding managements, our favorite holding period is forever. We are just the opposite of those who hurry to sell and book profits when companies perform well but who tenaciously hang on to businesses that disappoint. Peter Lynch aptly likens such behavior to cutting the flowers and watering the weeds. Our holdings of Freddie Mac are the maximum allowed by law, and are extensively described by Charlie in his letter. In our consolidated balance sheet these shares are carried at cost rather than market, since they are owned by Mutual Savings and Loan, a non-insurance subsidiary.

We continue to concentrate our investments in a very few companies that we try to understand well. There are only a handful of businesses about which we have strong long-term convictions. Therefore, when we find such a business, we want to participate in a meaningful way. We agree with Mae West: "Too much of a good thing can be wonderful."

- We reduced our holdings of medium-term tax-exempt bonds by about $100 million last year. All of the bonds sold were acquired after August 7, 1986. When such bonds are held by property-casualty insurance companies, 15% of the "tax-exempt" interest earned is subject to tax.

The $800 million position we still hold consists almost entirely of bonds "grandfathered" under the Tax Reform Act of 1986, which means they are entirely tax-exempt. Our sales produced a small profit and our remaining bonds, which have an average maturity of about six years, are worth modestly more than carrying value.

Last year we described our holdings of short-term and intermediate-term bonds of Texaco, which was then in bankruptcy. During 1988, we sold practically all of these bonds at a pre-tax profit of about $22 million. This sale explains close to $100 million of the reduction in fixed-income securities on our balance sheet.

We also told you last year about our holdings of another security whose predominant characteristics are those of an intermediate fixed-income issue: our $700 million position in Salomon Inc 9% convertible preferred. This preferred has a sinking fund that will retire it in equal annual installments from 1995 to 1999. Berkshire carries this holding at cost. For reasons discussed by Charlie on page 69, the estimated market value of our holding has improved from moderately under cost at the end of last year to moderately over cost at 1988 year end.

The close association we have had with John Gutfreund, CEO of Salomon, during the past year has reinforced our admiration for him. But we continue to have no great insights about the near, intermediate or long-term economics of the investment banking business: This is not an industry in which it is easy to forecast future levels of profitability. We continue to believe that our conversion privilege could well have important value over the life of our preferred. However, the overwhelming portion of the preferred's value resides in its fixed-income characteristics, not its equity characteristics.

- We have not lost our aversion to long-term bonds. We will become enthused about such securities only when we become enthused about prospects for long-term stability in the purchasing power of money. And that kind of stability isn't in the cards: Both society and elected officials simply have too many higher-ranking priorities that conflict with purchasing-power stability. The only long-term bonds we hold are those of Washington Public Power Supply Systems (WPPSS). A few of our WPPSS bonds have short maturities and many others, because of their high coupons, are likely to be refunded and paid off in a few years. Overall, our WPPSS holdings are carried on our balance sheet at $247 million and have a market value of about $352 million.

We explained the reasons for our WPPSS purchases in the 1983 annual report, and are pleased to tell you that this commitment has worked out about as expected. At the time of purchase, most of our bonds were yielding around 17% after taxes and carried no ratings, which had been suspended. Recently, the bonds were rated AA- by Standard & Poor's. They now sell at levels only slightly below those enjoyed by top-grade credits.

In the 1983 report, we compared the economics of our WPPSS purchase to those involved in buying a business. As it turned out, this purchase actually worked out better than did the general run of business acquisitions made in 1983, assuming both are measured on the basis of unleveraged, after tax returns achieved through 1988.

Our WPPSS experience, though pleasant, does nothing to alter our negative opinion about long-term bonds. It only makes us hope that we run into some other large stigmatized issue, whose troubles have caused it to be significantly misappraised by the market.

Arbitrage

In past reports we have told you that our insurance subsidiaries sometimes engage in arbitrage as an alternative to holding short-term cash equivalents. We prefer, of course, to make major long-term commitments, but we often have more cash than good ideas. At such times, arbitrage sometimes promises much greater returns than Treasury Bills and, equally important, cools any temptation we may have to relax our standards for long-term investments. (Charlie's sign off after we've talked about an arbitrage commitment is usually: "Okay, at least it will keep you out of bars.")

During 1988 we made unusually large profits from arbitrage, measured both by absolute dollars and rate of return. Our pre-tax gain was about $78 million on average invested funds of about $147 million.

This level of activity makes some detailed discussion of arbitrage and our approach to it appropriate. Once, the word applied only to the simultaneous purchase and sale of securities or foreign exchange in two different markets. The goal was to exploit tiny price differentials that might exist between, say, Royal Dutch stock trading in guilders in Amsterdam, pounds in London, and dollars in New York. Some people might call this scalping; it won't surprise you that practitioners opted for the French term, arbitrage.

Since World War I the definition of arbitrage—or "risk arbitrage," as it is now sometimes called—has expanded to include the pursuit of profits from an announced corporate event such as sale of the company, merger, recapitalization, reorganization, liquidation, self-tender, etc. In most cases the arbitrageur expects to profit regardless of the behavior of the stock market. The major risk he usually faces instead is that the announced event won't happen.

Some offbeat opportunities occasionally arise in the arbitrage field. I participated in one of these when I was 24 and working in New York for Graham-Newman Corp. Rockwood & Co., a Brooklyn based chocolate products company of limited profitability, had adopted LIFO inventory valuation in 1941 when cocoa was selling for 5¢ per pound. In 1954 a temporary shortage of cocoa caused the price to soar to over 60&cent. Consequently Rockwood wished to unload its valuable inventory—quickly, before the price dropped. But if the cocoa had simply been sold off, the company would have owed close to a 50% tax on the proceeds.

The 1954 Tax Code came to the rescue. It contained an arcane provision that eliminated the tax otherwise due on LIFO profits if inventory was distributed to shareholders as part of a plan reducing the scope of a corporation's business. Rockwood decided to terminate one of its businesses, the sale of cocoa butter, and said 13 million pounds of its cocoa bean inventory was attributable to that activity. Accordingly, the company offered to repurchase its stock in exchange for the cocoa beans it no longer needed, paying 80 pounds of beans for each share.

For several weeks I busily bought shares, sold beans, and made periodic stops at Schroeder Trust to exchange stock certificates for warehouse receipts. The profits were good and my only expense was subway tokens.

The architect of Rockwood's restructuring was an unknown, but brilliant Chicagoan, Jay Pritzker, then 32. If you're familiar with Jay's subsequent record, you won't be surprised to hear the action worked out rather well for Rockwood's continuing shareholders also. From shortly before the tender until shortly after it, Rockwood stock appreciated from 15 to 100, even though the company was experiencing large operating losses. Sometimes there is more to stock valuation than price-earnings ratios.

In recent years, most arbitrage operations have involved takeovers, friendly and unfriendly. With acquisition fever rampant, with anti-trust challenges almost non-existent, and with bids often ratcheting upward, arbitrageurs have prospered mightily. They have not needed special talents to do well; the trick, a la Peter Sellers in the movie, has simply been "Being There." In Wall Street the old proverb has been reworded: "Give a man a fish and you feed him for a day. Teach him how to arbitrage and you feed him forever." (If, however, he studied at the Ivan Boesky School of Arbitrage, it may be a state institution that supplies his meals.)

To evaluate arbitrage situations you must answer four questions: (1) How likely is it that the promised event will indeed occur? (2) How long will your money be tied up? (3) What chance is there that something still better will transpire—a competing takeover bid, for example? and (4) What will happen if the event does not take place because of anti-trust action, financing glitches, etc.?

Arcata Corp., one of our more serendipitous arbitrage experiences, illustrates the twists and turns of the business. On September 28, 1981 the directors of Arcata agreed in principle to sell the company to Kohlberg, Kravis, Roberts & Co. (KKR), then and now a major leveraged-buy out firm. Arcata was in the printing and forest products businesses and had one other thing going for it: In 1978 the U.S. Government had taken title to 10,700 acres of Arcata timber, primarily old-growth redwood, to expand Redwood National Park. The government had paid $97.9 million, in several installments, for this acreage, a sum Arcata was contesting as grossly inadequate. The parties also disputed the interest rate that should apply to the period between the taking of the property and final payment for it. The enabling legislation stipulated 6% simple interest; Arcata argued for a much higher and compounded rate.

Buying a company with a highly-speculative, large-sized claim in litigation creates a negotiating problem, whether the claim is on behalf of or against the company. To solve this problem, KKR offered $37.00 per Arcata share plus two-thirds of any additional amounts paid by the government for the redwood lands.

Appraising this arbitrage opportunity, we had to ask ourselves whether KKR would consummate the transaction since, among other things, its offer was contingent upon its obtaining "satisfactory financing." A clause of this kind is always dangerous for the seller: It offers an easy exit for a suitor whose ardor fades between proposal and marriage. However, we were not particularly worried about this possibility because KKR's past record for closing had been good.

We also had to ask ourselves what would happen if the KKR deal did fall through, and here we also felt reasonably comfortable: Arcata's management and directors had been shopping the company for some time and were clearly determined to sell. If KKR went away, Arcata would likely find another buyer, though of course, the price might be lower.

Finally, we had to ask ourselves what the redwood claim might be worth. Your Chairman, who can't tell an elm from an oak, had no trouble with that one: He coolly evaluated the claim at somewhere between zero and a whole lot.

We started buying Arcata stock, then around $33.50, on September 30 and in eight weeks purchased about 400,000 shares, or 5% of the company. The initial announcement said that the $37.00 would be paid in January, 1982. Therefore, if everything had gone perfectly, we would have achieved an annual rate of return of about 40%—not counting the redwood claim, which would have been frosting.

All did not go perfectly. In December it was announced that the closing would be delayed a bit. Nevertheless, a definitive agreement was signed on January 4. Encouraged, we raised our stake, buying at around $38.00 per share and increasing our holdings to 655,000 shares, or over 7% of the company. Our willingness to pay up—even though the closing had been postponed—reflected our leaning toward "a whole lot" rather than "zero" for the redwoods.

Then, on February 25 the lenders said they were taking a "second look" at financing terms " in view of the severely depressed housing industry and its impact on Arcata's outlook." The stockholders' meeting was postponed again, to April. An Arcata spokesman said he "did not think the fate of the acquisition itself was imperiled." When arbitrageurs hear such reassurances, their minds flash to the old saying: "He lied like a finance minister on the eve of devaluation."

On March 12 KKR said its earlier deal wouldn't work, first cutting its offer to $33.50, then two days later raising it to $35.00. On March 15, however, the directors turned this bid down and accepted another group's offer of $37.50 plus one-half of any redwood recovery. The shareholders okayed the deal, and the $37.50 was paid on June 4.

We received $24.6 million versus our cost of $22.9 million; our average holding period was close to six months. Considering the trouble this transaction encountered, our 15% annual rate of return—excluding any value for the redwood claim—was more than satisfactory.

But the best was yet to come. The trial judge appointed two commissions, one to look at the timber's value, the other to consider the interest rate questions. In January 1987, the first commission said the redwoods were worth $275.7 million and the second commission recommended a compounded, blended rate of return working out to about 14%.

In August 1987 the judge upheld these conclusions, which meant a net amount of about $600 million would be due Arcata. The government then appealed. In 1988, though, before this appeal was heard, the claim was settled for $519 million. Consequently, we received an additional $29.48 per share, or about $19.3 million. We will get another $800,000 or so in 1989.

Berkshire's arbitrage activities differ from those of many arbitrageurs. First, we participate in only a few, and usually very large, transactions each year. Most practitioners buy into a great many deals perhaps 50 or more per year. With that many irons in the fire, they must spend most of their time monitoring both the progress of deals and the market movements of the related stocks. This is not how Charlie nor I wish to spend our lives. (What's the sense in getting rich just to stare at a ticker tape all day?)

Because we diversify so little, one particularly profitable or unprofitable transaction will affect our yearly result from arbitrage far more than it will the typical arbitrage operation. So far, Berkshire has not had a really bad experience. But we will—and when it happens we'll report the gory details to you.

The other way we differ from some arbitrage operations is that we participate only in transactions that have been publicly announced. We do not trade on rumors or try to guess takeover candidates. We just read the newspapers, think about a few of the big propositions, and go by our own sense of probabilities.

At yearend, our only major arbitrage position was 3,342,000 shares of RJR Nabisco with a cost of $281.8 million and a market value of $304.5 million. In January we increased our holdings to roughly four million shares and in February we eliminated our position. About three million shares were accepted when we tendered our holdings to KKR, which acquired RJR, and the returned shares were promptly sold in the market. Our pre-tax profit was a better-than-expected $64 million.

Earlier, another familiar face turned up in the RJR bidding contest: Jay Pritzker, who was part of a First Boston group that made a tax-oriented offer. To quote Yogi Berra; "It was deja vu all over again."

During most of the time when we normally would have been purchasers of RJR, our activities in the stock were restricted because of Salomon's participation in a bidding group. Customarily, Charlie and I, though we are directors of Salomon, are walled off from information about its merger and acquisition work. We have asked that it be that way: The information would do us no good and could, in fact, occasionally inhibit Berkshire's arbitrage operations.

However, the unusually large commitment that Salomon proposed to make in the RJR deal required that all directors be fully informed and involved. Therefore, Berkshire's purchases of RJR were made at only two times: first, in the few days immediately following management's announcement of buyout plans, before Salomon became involved; and considerably later, after the RJR board made its decision in favor of KKR. Because we could not buy at other times, our directorships cost Berkshire significant money.

Considering Berkshire's good results in 1988, you might expect us to pile into arbitrage during 1989. Instead, we expect to be on the sidelines.

One pleasant reason is that our cash holdings are down—because our position in equities that we expect to hold for a very long time is substantially up. As regular readers of this report know, our new commitments are not based on a judgment about short-term prospects for the stock market. Rather, they reflect an opinion about long-term business prospects for specific companies. We do not have, never have had, and never will have an opinion about where the stock market, interest rates, or business activity will be a year from now.

Even if we had a lot of cash we probably would do little in arbitrage in 1989. Some extraordinary excesses have developed in the takeover field. As Dorothy says: "Toto, I have a feeling we're not in Kansas any more."

We have no idea how long the excesses will last, nor do we know what will change the attitudes of government, lender and buyer that fuel them. But we do know that the less the prudence with which others conduct their affairs, the greater the prudence with which we should conduct our own affairs. We have no desire to arbitrage transactions that reflect the unbridled—and, in our view, often unwarranted—optimism of both buyers and lenders. In our activities, we will heed the wisdom of Herb Stein: "If something can't go on forever, it will end."

Efficient Market Theory

The preceding discussion about arbitrage makes a small discussion of "efficient market theory" (EMT) also seem relevant. This doctrine became highly fashionable—indeed, almost holy scripture in academic circles during the 1970s. Essentially, it said that analyzing stocks was useless because all public information about them was appropriately reflected in their prices. In other words, the market always knew everything. As a corollary, the professors who taught EMT said that someone throwing darts at the stock tables could select a stock portfolio having prospects just as good as one selected by the brightest, most hard-working security analyst. Amazingly, EMT was embraced not only by academics, but by many investment professionals and corporate managers as well. Observing correctly that the market was *frequently* efficient, they went on to conclude incorrectly that it was *always* efficient. The difference between these propositions is night and day.

In my opinion, the continuous 63-year arbitrage experience of Graham-Newman Corp. Buffett Partnership, and Berkshire illustrates just how foolish EMT is. (There's plenty of other evidence, also.) While at Graham-Newman, I made a study of its earnings from arbitrage during the entire 1926-1956 lifespan of the company. Unleveraged returns averaged 20% per year. Starting in 1956, I applied Ben Graham's arbitrage principles, first at Buffett Partnership and then Berkshire. Though I've not made an exact calculation, I have done enough work to know that the 1956-1988 returns averaged well over 20%. (Of course, I operated in an environment far more favorable than Ben's; he had 1929-1932 to contend with.)

All of the conditions are present that are required for a fair test of portfolio performance: (1) the three organizations traded hundreds of different securities while building this 63-year record; (2) the results are not skewed by a few fortunate experiences; (3) we did not have to dig for obscure facts or develop keen insights about products or managements—we simply acted on highly-publicized events; and (4) our arbitrage positions were a clearly identified universe—they have not been selected by hindsight.

Over the 63 years, the general market delivered just under a 10% annual return, including dividends. That means $1,000 would have grown to $405,000 if all income had been reinvested. A 20% rate of return, however, would have produced $97 million. That strikes us as a statistically-significant differential that might, conceivably, arouse one's curiosity.

Yet proponents of the theory have never seemed interested in discordant evidence of this type. True, they don't talk quite as much about their theory today as they used to. But no one, to my knowledge, has ever said he was wrong, no matter how many thousands of students he has sent forth misinstructed. EMT, moreover, continues to be an integral part of the investment curriculum at major business schools. Apparently, a reluctance to recant, and thereby to demystify the priesthood, is not limited to theologians.

Naturally the disservice done students and gullible investment professionals who have swallowed EMT has been an extraordinary service to us and other followers of Graham. In any sort of a contest— financial, mental, or physical—it's an enormous advantage to have opponents who have been taught that it's useless to even try. From a selfish point of view, Grahamites should probably endow chairs to ensure the perpetual teaching of EMT.

All this said, a warning is appropriate. Arbitrage has looked easy recently. But this is not a form of investing that guarantees profits of 20% a year or, for that matter, profits of any kind. As noted, the market is reasonably efficient much of the time: For every arbitrage opportunity we seized in that 63-year period, many more were foregone because they seemed properly-priced.

An investor cannot obtain superior profits from stocks by simply committing to a specific investment category or style. He can earn them only by carefully evaluating facts and continuously exercising discipline. Investing in arbitrage situations, per se, is no better a strategy than selecting a portfolio by throwing darts.

New York Stock Exchange Listing

Berkshire's shares were listed on the New York Stock Exchange on November 29, 1988. On pages 50-51 we reproduce the letter we sent to shareholders concerning the listing.

Let me clarify one point not dealt with in the letter: Though our round lot for trading on the NYSE is ten shares, any number of shares from one on up can be bought or sold.

As the letter explains, our primary goal in listing was to reduce transaction costs, and we believe this goal is being achieved. Generally, the spread between the bid and asked price on the NYSE has been well below the spread that prevailed in the over-the-counter market.

Henderson Brothers, Inc., the specialist in our shares, is the oldest continuing specialist firm on the Exchange; its progenitor, William Thomas Henderson, bought his seat for $500 on September 8, 1861. (Recently, seats were selling for about $625,000.) Among the 54 firms acting as specialists, HBI ranks second in number of stocks assigned, with 83. We were pleased when Berkshire was allocated to HBI, and have been delighted with the firm's performance. Jim Maguire, Chairman of HBI, personally manages the trading in Berkshire, and we could not be in better hands.

In two respects our goals probably differ somewhat from those of most listed companies. First, we do not want to maximize the price at which Berkshire shares trade. We wish instead for them to trade in a narrow range centered at intrinsic business value (which we hope increases at a reasonable—or, better yet, unreasonable—rate). Charlie and I are bothered as much by significant overvaluation as significant undervaluation. Both extremes will inevitably produce results for many shareholders that will differ sharply from Berkshire's business results. If our stock price instead consistently mirrors business value, each of our shareholders will receive an investment result that roughly parallels the business results of Berkshire during his holding period.

Second, we wish for very little trading activity. If we ran a private business with a few passive partners, we would be disappointed if those partners, and their replacements, frequently wanted to leave the partnership. Running a public company, we feel the same way.

Our goal is to attract long-term owners who, at the time of purchase, have no timetable or price target for sale but plan instead to stay with us indefinitely. We don't understand the CEO who wants lots of stock activity, for that can be achieved only if many of his owners are constantly exiting. At what other organization—school, club, church, etc.—do leaders cheer when members leave? (However, if there were a broker whose livelihood depended upon the membership turnover in such organizations, you could be sure that there would be at least one proponent of activity, as in: "There hasn't been much going on in Christianity for a while; maybe we should switch to Buddhism next week.")

Of course, some Berkshire owners will need or want to sell from time to time, and we wish for good replacements who will pay them a fair price. Therefore we try, through our policies, performance, and communications, to attract new shareholders who understand our operations, share our time horizons, and measure us as we measure ourselves. If we can continue to attract this sort of shareholder—and, just as important, can continue to be uninteresting to those with short-term or unrealistic expectations—Berkshire shares should consistently sell at prices reasonably related to business value.

David L. Dodd

Dave Dodd, my friend and teacher for 38 years, died last year at age 93. Most of you don't know of him. Yet any long-time shareholder of Berkshire is appreciably wealthier because of the indirect influence he had upon our company.

Dave spent a lifetime teaching at Columbia University, and he co-authored *Security Analysis* with Ben Graham. From the moment I arrived at Columbia, Dave personally encouraged and educated me; one influence was as important as the other. Everything he taught me, directly or through his book, made sense. Later, through dozens of letters, he continued my education right up until his death.

I have known many professors of finance and investments but I have never seen any, except for Ben Graham, who was the match of Dave. The proof of his talent is the record of his students: No other teacher of investments has sent forth so many who have achieved unusual success.

When students left Dave's classroom, they were equipped to invest intelligently for a lifetime because the principles he taught were simple, sound, useful, and enduring. Though these may appear to be unremarkable virtues, the teaching of principles embodying them has been rare.

It's particularly impressive that Dave could practice as well as preach. just as Keynes became wealthy by applying his academic ideas to a very small purse, so, too, did Dave. Indeed, his financial performance far outshone that of Keynes, who began as a market-timer (leaning on business and credit-cycle theory) and converted, after much thought, to value investing. Dave was right from the start.

In Berkshire's investments, Charlie and I have employed the principles taught by Dave and Ben Graham. Our prosperity is the fruit of their intellectual tree.

Miscellaneous

We hope to buy more businesses that are similar to the ones we have, and we can use some help. If you have a business that fits the following criteria, call me or, preferably, write.

Here's what we're looking for:

(1) large purchases (at least $10 million of after-tax earnings),

(2) demonstrated consistent earning power (future projections are of little interest to us, nor are "turnaround" situations),

(3) businesses earning good returns on equity while employing little or no debt,

(4) management in place (we can't supply it),

(5) simple businesses (if there's lots of technology, we won't understand it),

(6) an offering price (we don't want to waste our time or that of the seller by talking, even preliminarily, about a transaction when price is unknown).

We will not engage in unfriendly takeovers. We can promise complete confidentiality and a very fast answer—customarily within five minutes—as to whether we're interested. We prefer to buy for cash, but will consider issuing stock when we receive as much in intrinsic business value as we give.

Our favorite form of purchase is one fitting the Blumkin-Friedman-Heldman mold. In cases like these, the company's owner-managers wish to generate significant amounts of cash, sometimes for themselves, but often for their families or inactive shareholders. However, these managers also wish to remain significant owners who continue to run their companies just as they have in the past. We think we offer a particularly good fit for owners with these objectives and invite potential sellers to check us out by contacting people with whom we have done business in the past.

Charlie and I frequently get approached about acquisitions that don't come close to meeting our tests: We've found that if you advertise an interest in buying collies, a lot of people will call hoping to sell you their cocker spaniels. Our interest in new ventures, turnarounds, or auction-like sales can best be expressed by another Goldwynism: "Please include me out."

Besides being interested in the purchase of businesses as described above, we are also interested in the negotiated purchase of large, but not controlling, blocks of stock comparable to those we hold in Cap Cities and Salomon. We have a special interest in purchasing convertible preferreds as a long-term investment, as we did at Salomon.

* * *

We received some good news a few weeks ago: Standard & Poor's raised our credit rating to AAA, which is the highest rating it bestows. Only 15 other U.S. industrial or property-casualty companies are rated AAA, down from 28 in 1980.

Corporate bondholders have taken their lumps in the past few years from "event risk." This term refers to the overnight degradation of credit that accompanies a heavily-leveraged purchase or recapitalization of a business whose financial policies, up to then, had been conservative. In a world of takeovers inhabited by few owner-managers, most corporations present such a risk. Berkshire does not. Charlie and I promise bondholders the same respect we afford shareholders.

* * *

About 97.4% of all eligible shares participated in Berkshire's 1988 shareholder-designated contributions program. Contributions made through the program were $5 million, and 2,319 charities were recipients. If we achieve reasonable business results, we plan to increase the per-share contributions in 1989.

We urge new shareholders to read the description of our shareholder-designated contributions program that appears on pages 48-49. If you wish to participate in future programs, we strongly urge that you immediately make sure your shares are registered in the name of the actual owner, not in the nominee name of a broker, bank or depository. Shares not so registered on September 30, 1989 will be ineligible for the 1989 program.

* * *

Berkshire's annual meeting will be held in Omaha on Monday, April 24, 1989, and I hope you will come. The meeting provides the forum for you to ask any owner-related questions you may have, and we will keep answering until all (except those dealing with portfolio activities or other proprietary information) have been dealt with.

After the meeting we will have several buses available to take you to visit Mrs. B at The Nebraska Furniture Mart and Ike Friedman at Borsheim's. Be prepared for bargains.

Out-of-towners may prefer to arrive early and visit Mrs. B during the Sunday store hours of noon to five. (These Sunday hours seem ridiculously short to Mrs. B, who feels they scarcely allow her time to warm up; she much prefers the days on which the store remains open from 10 a.m. to 9 p.m.) Borsheims, however, is not open on Sunday.

Ask Mrs. B the secret of her astonishingly low carpet prices. She will confide to you—as she does to everyone—how she does it: "I can sell so cheap 'cause I work for this dummy who doesn't know anything about carpet."

| | Warren E. Buffett |
| February 28, 1989 | Chairman of the Board |

BERKSHIRE HATHAWAY INC.

To the Shareholders of Berkshire Hathaway Inc.:

Our gain in net worth during 1989 was $1.515 billion, or 44.4%. Over the last 25 years (that is, since present management took over) our per-share book value has grown from $19.46 to $4,296.01, or at a rate of 23.8% compounded annually.

What counts, however, is intrinsic value—the figure indicating what all of our constituent businesses are rationally worth. With perfect foresight, this number can be calculated by taking all future cash flows of a business—in and out—and discounting them at prevailing interest rates. So valued, all businesses, from manufacturers of buggy whips to operators of cellular phones, become economic equals.

Back when Berkshire's book value was $19.46, intrinsic value was somewhat less because the book value was entirely tied up in a textile business not worth the figure at which it was carried. Now most of our businesses are worth far more than their carrying values. This agreeable evolution from a discount to a premium means that Berkshire's intrinsic business value has compounded at a rate that somewhat exceeds our 23.8% annual growth in book value.

The rear-view mirror is one thing; the windshield is another. A large portion of our book value is represented by equity securities that, with minor exceptions, are carried on our balance sheet at current market values. At yearend these securities were valued at higher prices, relative to their own intrinsic business values, than has been the case in the past. One reason is the buoyant 1989 stock market. More important, the virtues of these businesses have been widely recognized. Whereas once their stock prices were inappropriately low, they are not now.

We will keep most of our major holdings, regardless of how they are priced relative to intrinsic business value. This 'til-death-do-us-part attitude, combined with the full prices these holdings command, means that they cannot be expected to push up Berkshire's value in the future as sharply as in the past. In other words, our performance to date has benefited from a double-dip: (1) the exceptional gains in intrinsic value that our portfolio companies have achieved; (2) the additional bonus we realized as the market appropriately "corrected" the prices of these companies, raising their valuations in relation to those of the average business. We will continue to benefit from good gains in business value that we feel confident our portfolio companies will make. But our "catch-up" rewards have been realized, which means we'll have to settle for a single-dip in the future.

We face another obstacle: In a finite world, high growth rates must self-destruct. If the base from which the growth is taking place is tiny, this law may not operate for a time. But when the base balloons, the party ends: A high growth rate eventually forges its own anchor.

Carl Sagan has entertainingly described this phenomenon, musing about the destiny of bacteria that reproduce by dividing into two every 15 minutes. Says Sagan: "That means four doublings an hour, and 96 doublings a day. Although a bacterium weighs only about a trillionth of a gram, its descendants, after a day of wild asexual abandon, will collectively weigh as much as a mountain…in two days, more than the sun—and before very long, everything in the universe will be made of bacteria." Not to worry, says Sagan: Some obstacle always impedes this kind of exponential growth. "The bugs run out of food, or they poison each other, or they are shy about reproducing in public."

Even on bad days, Charlie Munger (Berkshire's Vice Chairman and my partner) and I do not think of Berkshire as a bacterium. Nor, to our unending sorrow, have we found a way to double its net worth every 15 minutes. Furthermore, we are not the least bit shy about reproducing—financially—in public. Nevertheless, Sagan's observations apply. From Berkshire's present base of $4.9 billion in net worth, we will find it much more difficult to average 15% annual growth in book value than we did to average 23.8% from the $22 million we began with.

Taxes

Our 1989 gain of $1.5 billion was achieved after we took a charge of about $712 million for income taxes. In addition, Berkshire's share of the income taxes paid by its five major investees totaled about $175 million.

Of this year's tax charge, about $172 million will be paid currently; the remainder, $540 million, is deferred. Almost all of the deferred portion relates to the 1989 increase in unrealized profits in our common stock holdings. Against this increase, we have reserved a 34% tax.

We also carry reserves at that rate against all unrealized profits generated in 1987 and 1988. But, as we explained last year, the unrealized gains we amassed before 1987—about $1.2 billion—carry reserves booked at the 28% tax rate that then prevailed.

A new accounting rule is likely to be adopted that will require companies to reserve against all gains at the current tax rate, whatever it may be. With the rate at 34%, such a rule would increase our deferred tax liability, and decrease our net worth, by about $71 million—the result of raising the reserve on our pre-1987 gain by six percentage points. Because the proposed rule has sparked widespread controversy and its final form is unclear, we have not yet made this change.

As you can see from our balance sheet on page 27, we would owe taxes of more than $1.1 billion were we to sell all of our securities at year-end market values. Is this $1.1 billion liability equal, or even similar, to a $1.1 billion liability payable to a trade creditor 15 days after the end of the year? Obviously not—despite the fact that both items have exactly the same effect on audited net worth, reducing it by $1.1 billion.

On the other hand, is this liability for deferred taxes a meaningless accounting fiction because its payment can be triggered only by the sale of stocks that, in very large part, we have no intention of selling? Again, the answer is no.

In economic terms, the liability resembles an interest-free loan from the U.S. Treasury that comes due only at our election (unless, of course, Congress moves to tax gains before they are realized). This "loan" is peculiar in other respects as well: It can be used only to finance the ownership of the particular, appreciated stocks and it fluctuates in size—daily as market prices change and periodically if tax rates change. In effect, this deferred tax liability is equivalent to a very large transfer tax that is payable only if we elect to move from one asset to another. Indeed, we sold some relatively small holdings in 1989, incurring about $76 million of "transfer" tax on $224 million of gains.

Because of the way the tax law works, the Rip Van Winkle style of investing that we favor—if successful—has an important mathematical edge over a more frenzied approach. Let's look at an extreme comparison.

Imagine that Berkshire had only $1, which we put in a security that doubled by yearend and was then sold. Imagine further that we used the after-tax proceeds to repeat this process in each of the next 19

2

years, scoring a double each time. At the end of the 20 years, the 34% capital gains tax that we would have paid on the profits from each sale would have delivered about $13,000 to the government and we would be left with about $25,250. Not bad. If, however, we made a single fantastic investment that *itself* doubled 20 times during the 20 years, our dollar would grow to $1,048,576. Were we then to cash out, we would pay a 34% tax of roughly $356,500 and be left with about $692,000.

The sole reason for this staggering difference in results would be the timing of tax payments. Interestingly, the government would gain from Scenario 2 in exactly the same 27:1 ratio as we—taking in taxes of $356,500 vs. $13,000—though, admittedly, it would have to wait for its money.

We have not, we should stress, adopted our strategy favoring long-term investment commitments because of these mathematics. Indeed, it is possible we could earn greater after-tax returns by moving rather frequently from one investment to another. Many years ago, that's exactly what Charlie and I did.

Now we would rather stay put, even if that means slightly lower returns. Our reason is simple: We have found splendid business relationships to be so rare and so enjoyable that we want to retain all we develop. This decision is particularly easy for us because we feel that these relationships will produce good—though perhaps not optimal—financial results. Considering that, we think it makes little sense for us to give up time with people we know to be interesting and admirable for time with others we do not know and who are likely to have human qualities far closer to average. That would be akin to marrying for money—a mistake under most circumstances, insanity if one is already rich.

Sources of Reported Earnings

The table below shows the major sources of Berkshire's reported earnings. In this presentation, amortization of Goodwill and other major purchase-price accounting adjustments are not charged against the specific businesses to which they apply, but are instead aggregated and shown separately. This procedure lets you view the earnings of our businesses as they would have been reported had we not purchased them. I've explained in past reports why this form of presentation seems to us to be more useful to investors and managers than one utilizing generally accepted accounting principles (GAAP), which require purchase-price adjustments to be made on a business-by-business basis. The total net earnings we show in the table are, of course, identical to the GAAP total in our audited financial statements.

Further information about these businesses is given in the Business Segment section on pages 37-39, and in the Management's Discussion section on pages 40-44. In these sections you also will find our segment earnings reported on a GAAP basis. For information on Wesco's businesses, I urge you to read Charlie Munger's letter, which starts on page 54. In addition, we have reprinted on page 71 Charlie's May 30, 1989 letter to the U. S. League of Savings Institutions, which conveyed our disgust with its policies and our consequent decision to resign.

	(000s omitted)			
	Pre-Tax Earnings		Berkshire's Share of Net Earnings (after taxes and minority interests)	
	1989	1988	1989	1988
Operating Earnings:				
Insurance Group:				
Underwriting	$(24,400)	$(11,081)	$ (12,259)	$ (1,045)
Net Investment Income	243,599	231,250	213,642	197,779
Buffalo News	46,047	42,429	27,771	25,462
Fechheimer	12,621	14,152	6,789	7,720
Kirby	26,114	26,891	16,803	17,842
Nebraska Furniture Mart	17,070	18,439	8,441	9,099
Scott Fetzer Manufacturing Group	33,165	28,542	19,996	17,640
See's Candies	34,235	32,473	20,626	19,671
Wesco—other than Insurance	13,008	16,133	9,810	10,650
World Book	25,583	27,890	16,372	18,021
Amortization of Goodwill	(3,387)	(2,806)	(3,372)	(2,806)
Other Purchase-Price				
Accounting Charges	(5,740)	(6,342)	(6,668)	(7,340)
Interest Expense*	(42,389)	(35,613)	(27,098)	(23,212)
Shareholder-Designated Contributions . .	(5,867)	(4,966)	(3,814)	(3,217)
Other	23,755	41,059	12,863	27,177
Operating Earnings	393,414	418,450	299,902	313,441
Sales of Securities	223,810	131,671	147,575	85,829
Total Earnings—All Entities	$617,224	$550,121	$447,477	$399,270

*Excludes interest expense of Scott Fetzer Financial Group and Mutual Savings & Loan.

We refer you also to pages 45-51, where we have rearranged Berkshire's financial data into four segments. These correspond to the way Charlie and I think about the business and should help you calculate Berkshire's intrinsic value. Shown on these pages are balance sheets and earnings statements for: (1) our insurance operations, with their major investment positions itemized; (2) our manufacturing, publishing and retailing businesses, leaving aside certain non-operating assets and purchase-price accounting adjustments; (3) our subsidiaries engaged in finance-type operations, which are Mutual Savings and Scott Fetzer Financial; and (4) an all-other category that includes the non-operating assets (primarily marketable securities) held by the companies in segment (2), all purchase price accounting adjustments, and various assets and debts of the Wesco and Berkshire parent companies.

If you combine the earnings and net worths of these four segments, you will derive totals matching those shown on our GAAP statements. However, I want to emphasize that this four-category presentation does not fall within the purview of our auditors, who in no way bless it.

In addition to our reported earnings, we also benefit from significant earnings of investees that standard accounting rules do not permit us to report. On page 15, we list five major investees from which we received dividends in 1989 of about $45 million, after taxes. However, our share of the *retained* earnings of these investees totaled about $212 million last year, not counting large capital gains realized by GEICO and Coca-Cola. If this $212 million had been distributed to us, our own operating earnings, after the payment of additional taxes, would have been close to $500 million rather than the $300 million shown in the table.

The question you must decide is whether these undistributed earnings are as valuable to us as those we report. We believe they are—and even think they may be more valuable. The reason for this a-bird-in-the-bush-may-be-worth-two-in-the-hand conclusion is that earnings retained by these investees will be deployed by talented, owner-oriented managers who sometimes have better uses for these funds in their own businesses than we would have in ours. I would not make such a generous assessment of most managements, but it is appropriate in these cases.

In our view, Berkshire's fundamental earning power is best measured by a "look-through" approach, in which we append our share of the operating earnings retained by our investees to our own reported operating earnings, excluding capital gains in both instances. For our intrinsic business value to grow at an average of 15% per year, our "look-through" earnings must grow at about the same pace. We'll need plenty of help from our present investees, and also need to add a new one from time to time, in order to reach this 15% goal.

Non-Insurance Operations

In the past, we have labeled our major manufacturing, publishing and retail operations "The Sainted Seven." With our acquisition of Borsheim's early in 1989, the challenge was to find a new title both alliterative and appropriate. We failed: Let's call the group "The Sainted Seven Plus One."

This divine assemblage—Borsheim's, The Buffalo News, Fechheimer Bros., Kirby, Nebraska Furniture Mart, Scott Fetzer Manufacturing Group, See's Candies, World Book—is a collection of businesses with economic characteristics that range from good to superb. Its managers range from superb to superb.

Most of these managers have no need to work for a living; they show up at the ballpark because they like to hit home runs. And that's exactly what they do. Their combined financial statements (including those of some smaller operations), shown on page 49, illustrate just how outstanding their performance is. On an historical accounting basis, after-tax earnings of these operations were 57% on average equity capital. Moreover, this return was achieved with no net leverage: Cash equivalents have matched funded debt. When I call off the names of our managers—the Blumkin, Friedman and Heldman families, Chuck Huggins, Stan Lipsey, and Ralph Schey—I feel the same glow that Miller Huggins must have experienced when he announced the lineup of his 1927 New York Yankees.

Let's take a look, business by business:

- In its first year with Berkshire, Borsheim's met all expectations. Sales rose significantly and are now considerably better than twice what they were four years ago when the company moved to its present location. In the six years prior to the move, sales had also doubled. Ike Friedman, Borsheim's managing genius—and I mean that—has only one speed: fast-forward.

  If you haven't been there, you've never seen a jewelry store like Borsheim's. Because of the huge volume it does at one location, the store can maintain an enormous selection across all price ranges. For the same reason, it can hold its expense ratio to about one-third that prevailing at jewelry stores offering comparable merchandise. The store's tight control of expenses, accompanied by its unusual buying power, enable it to offer prices far lower than those of other jewelers. These prices, in turn, generate even more volume, and so the circle goes 'round and 'round. The end result is store traffic as high as 4,000 people on seasonally-busy days.

Ike Friedman is not only a superb businessman and a great showman but also a man of integrity. We bought the business without an audit, and all of our surprises have been on the plus side. "If you don't know jewelry, know your jeweler" makes sense whether you are buying the whole business or a tiny diamond.

A story will illustrate why I enjoy Ike so much: Every two years I'm part of an informal group that gathers to have fun and explore a few subjects. Last September, meeting at Bishop's Lodge in Santa Fe, we asked Ike, his wife Roz, and his son Alan to come by and educate us on jewels and the jewelry business.

Ike decided to dazzle the group, so he brought from Omaha about $20 million of particularly fancy merchandise. I was somewhat apprehensive—Bishop's Lodge is no Fort Knox—and I mentioned my concern to Ike at our opening party the evening before his presentation. Ike took me aside. "See that safe?" he said. "This afternoon we changed the combination and now even the hotel management doesn't know what it is." I breathed easier. Ike went on: "See those two big fellows with guns on their hips? They'll be guarding the safe all night." I now was ready to rejoin the party. But Ike leaned closer: "And besides, Warren," he confided, "the jewels aren't in the safe."

How can we miss with a fellow like that—particularly when he comes equipped with a talented and energetic family, Alan, Marvin Cohn, and Don Yale.

- At See's Candies we had an 8% increase in pounds sold, even though 1988 was itself a record year. Included in the 1989 performance were excellent same-store poundage gains, our first in many years.

Advertising played an important role in this outstanding performance. We increased total advertising expenditures from $4 million to $5 million and also got copy from our agency, Hal Riney & Partners, Inc., that was 100% on the money in conveying the qualities that make See's special.

In our media businesses, such as the Buffalo News, we sell advertising. In other businesses, such as See's, we are buyers. When we buy, we practice exactly what we preach when we sell. At See's, we more than tripled our expenditures on newspaper advertising last year, to the highest percentage of sales that I can remember. The payoff was terrific, and we thank both Hal Riney and the power of well-directed newspaper advertising for this result.

See's splendid performances have become routine. But there is nothing routine about the management of Chuck Huggins: His daily involvement with all aspects of production and sales imparts a quality-and-service message to the thousands of employees we need to produce and distribute over 27 million pounds of candy annually. In a company with 225 shops and a massive mail order and phone business, it is no small trick to run things so that virtually every customer leaves happy. Chuck makes it look easy.

- The Nebraska Furniture Mart had record sales and excellent earnings in 1989, but there was one sad note. Mrs. B—Rose Blumkin, who started the company 52 years ago with $500—quit in May, after disagreeing with other members of the Blumkin family/management about the remodeling and operation of the carpet department.

Mrs. B probably has made more smart business decisions than any living American, but in this particular case I believe the other members of the family were entirely correct: Over the past three years, while the store's other departments increased sales by 24%, carpet sales declined by 17% (but not because of any lack of sales ability by Mrs. B, who has always personally sold far more merchandise than any other salesperson in the store).

You will be pleased to know that Mrs. B continues to make Horatio Alger's heroes look like victims of tired blood. At age 96 she has started a new business selling—what else?—carpet and furniture. And as always, she works seven days a week.

At the Mart Louie, Ron, and Irv Blumkin continue to propel what is by far the largest and most successful home furnishings store in the country. They are outstanding merchants, outstanding managers, and a joy to be associated with. One reading on their acumen: In the fourth quarter of 1989, the carpet department registered a 75.3% consumer share in the Omaha market, up from 67.7% a year earlier and over six times that of its nearest competitor.

NFM and Borsheim's follow precisely the same formula for success: (1) unparalleled depth and breadth of merchandise at one location; (2) the lowest operating costs in the business; (3) the shrewdest of buying, made possible in part by the huge volumes purchased; (4) gross margins, and therefore prices, far below competitors'; and (5) friendly personalized service with family members on hand at all times.

Another plug for newspapers: NFM increased its linage in the local paper by over 20% in 1989—off a record 1988—and remains the paper's largest ROP advertiser by far. (ROP advertising is the kind printed in the paper, as opposed to that in preprinted inserts.) To my knowledge, Omaha is the only city in which a home furnishings store is the advertising leader. Many retailers cut space purchases in 1989; our experience at See's and NFM would indicate they made a major mistake.

- The Buffalo News continued to star in 1989 in three important ways: First, among major metropolitan papers, both daily and Sunday, the News is number one in household penetration—the percentage of local households that purchase it each day. Second, in "news hole"—the portion of the paper devoted to news—the paper stood at 50.1% in 1989 vs. 49.5% in 1988, a level again making it more news-rich than any comparable American paper. Third, in a year that saw profits slip at many major papers, the News set its seventh consecutive profit record.

To some extent, these three factors are related, though obviously a high-percentage news hole, by itself, reduces profits significantly. A large and intelligently-utilized news hole, however, attracts a wide spectrum of readers and thereby boosts penetration. High penetration, in turn, makes a newspaper particularly valuable to retailers since it allows them to talk to the entire community through a single "megaphone." A low-penetration paper is a far less compelling purchase for many advertisers and will eventually suffer in both ad rates and profits.

It should be emphasized that our excellent penetration is neither an accident nor automatic. The population of Erie County, home territory of the News, has been falling—from 1,113,000 in 1970 to 1,015,000 in 1980 to an estimated 966,000 in 1988. Circulation figures tell a different story. In 1975, shortly before we started our Sunday edition, the Courier-Express, a long-established Buffalo paper, was selling 207,500 Sunday copies in Erie County. Last year—with population at least 5% lower—the News sold an average of 292,700 copies. I believe that in no other major Sunday market has there been anything close to that increase in penetration.

When this kind of gain is made—and when a paper attains an unequaled degree of acceptance in its home town—someone is doing something right. In this case major credit clearly belongs to Murray Light, our long-time editor who daily creates an informative, useful, and interesting product. Credit should go also to the Circulation and Production Departments: A paper that is frequently late, because of production problems or distribution weaknesses, will lose customers, no matter how strong its editorial content.

Stan Lipsey, publisher of the News, has produced profits fully up to the strength of our product. I believe Stan's managerial skills deliver at least five extra percentage points in profit margin compared to the earnings that would be achieved by an average manager given the same circumstances. That is an amazing performance, and one that could only be produced by a talented manager who knows—and cares—about every nut and bolt of the business.

Stan's knowledge and talents, it should be emphasized, extend to the editorial product. His early years in the business were spent on the news side and he played a key role in developing and editing a series of stories that in 1972 won a Pulitzer Prize for the Sun Newspaper of Omaha. Stan and I have worked together for over 20 years, through some bad times as well as good, and I could not ask for a better partner.

- At Fechheimer, the Heldman clan—Bob, George, Gary, Roger and Fred—continue their extraordinary performance. Profits in 1989 were down somewhat because of problems the business experienced in integrating a major 1988 acquisition. These problems will be ironed out in time. Meanwhile, return on invested capital at Fechheimer remains splendid.

Like all of our managers, the Heldmans have an exceptional command of the details of their business. At last year's annual meeting I mentioned that when a prisoner enters San Quentin, Bob and George probably know his shirt size. That's only a slight exaggeration: No matter what area of the country is being discussed, they know exactly what is going on with major customers and with the competition.

Though we purchased Fechheimer four years ago, Charlie and I have never visited any of its plants or the home office in Cincinnati. We're much like the lonesome Maytag repairman: The Heldman managerial product is so good that a service call is never needed.

- Ralph Schey continues to do a superb job in managing our largest group—World Book, Kirby, and the Scott Fetzer Manufacturing Companies. Aggregate earnings of these businesses have increased every year since our purchase and returns on invested capital continue to be exceptional. Ralph is running an enterprise large enough, were it standing alone, to be on the Fortune 500. And he's running it in a fashion that would put him high in the top decile, measured by return on equity.

For some years, World Book has operated out of a single location in Chicago's Merchandise Mart. Anticipating the imminent expiration of its lease, the business is now decentralizing into four locations. The expenses of this transition are significant; nevertheless profits in 1989 held up well. It will be another year before costs of the move are fully behind us.

Kirby's business was particularly strong last year, featuring large gains in export sales. International business has more than doubled in the last two years and quintupled in the past four; its share of unit sales has risen from 5% to 20%. Our largest capital expenditures in 1989 were at Kirby, in preparation for a major model change in 1990.

Ralph's operations contribute about 40% of the total earnings of the non-insurance group whose results are shown on page 49. When we bought Scott Fetzer at the start of 1986, our acquisition of Ralph as a manager was fully as important as our acquisition of the businesses. In addition to generating extraordinary earnings, Ralph also manages capital extremely well. These abilities have produced funds for Berkshire that, in turn, have allowed us to make many other profitable commitments.

And that completes our answer to the 1927 Yankees.

Insurance Operations

Shown below is an updated version of our usual table presenting key figures for the property-casualty insurance industry:

	Yearly Change in Premiums Written (%)	Statutory Combined Ratio After Policyholder Dividends	Yearly Change in Incurred Losses (%)	Inflation Rate Measured by GNP Deflator (%)
1981	3.8	106.0	6.5	9.6
1982	3.7	109.6	8.4	6.5
1983	5.0	112.0	6.8	3.8
1984	8.5	118.0	16.9	3.8
1985	22.1	116.3	16.1	3.0
1986	22.2	108.0	13.5	2.6
1987	9.4	104.6	7.8	3.1
1988	4.4	105.4	5.5	3.3
1989 (Est.)	2.1	110.4	8.7	4.2

Source: A.M. Best Co.

The combined ratio represents total insurance costs (losses incurred plus expenses) compared to revenue from premiums: A ratio below 100 indicates an underwriting profit, and one above 100 indicates a loss. When the investment income that an insurer earns from holding policyholders' funds ("the float") is taken into account, a combined ratio in the 107-111 range typically produces an overall breakeven result, exclusive of earnings on the funds provided by shareholders.

For the reasons laid out in previous reports, we expect the industry's incurred losses to grow by about 10% annually, even in years when general inflation runs considerably lower. (Actually, over the last 25 years, incurred losses have grown at a still faster rate, 11%.) If premium growth meanwhile materially lags that 10% rate, underwriting losses will mount, though the industry's tendency to underreserve when business turns bad may obscure their size for a time.

Last year we said the climb in the combined ratio was "almost certain to continue—and probably will accelerate—for at least two more years." This year we will not predict acceleration, but otherwise must repeat last year's forecast. Premium growth is running far below the 10% required annually. Remember also that a 10% rate would only stabilize the combined ratio, not bring it down.

The increase in the combined ratio in 1989 was a little more than we had expected because catastrophes (led by Hurricane Hugo) were unusually severe. These abnormalities probably accounted for about two points of the increase. If 1990 is more of a "normal" year, the combined ratio should rise only minimally from the catastrophe-swollen base of 1989. In 1991, though, the ratio is apt to climb by a greater degree.

Commentators frequently discuss the "underwriting cycle" and speculate about its next turn. If that term is used to connote rhythmic qualities, it is in our view a misnomer that leads to faulty thinking about the industry's fundamental economics.

The term was appropriate some decades ago when the industry and regulators cooperated to conduct the business in cartel fashion. At that time, the combined ratio fluctuated rhythmically for two reasons, both related to lags. First, data from the past were analyzed and then used to set new "corrected" rates, which were subsequently put into effect by virtually all insurers. Second, the fact that almost all policies were then issued for a one-to three-year term—which meant that it took a considerable time for mispriced policies to expire—delayed the impact of new rates on revenues. These two lagged responses made combined ratios behave much like alternating current. Meanwhile, the absence of significant price competition guaranteed that industry profits, averaged out over the cycle, would be satisfactory.

The cartel period is long gone. Now the industry has hundreds of participants selling a commodity-like product at independently-established prices. Such a configuration—whether the product being sold is steel or insurance policies—is certain to cause subnormal profitability in all circumstances but one: a shortage of usable capacity. Just how often these periods occur and how long they last determines the average profitability of the industry in question.

In most industries, capacity is described in physical terms. In the insurance world, however, capacity is customarily described in financial terms; that is, it's considered appropriate for a company to write no more than X dollars of business if it has Y dollars of net worth. In practice, however, constraints of this sort have proven ineffective. Regulators, insurance brokers, and customers are all slow to discipline companies that strain their resources. They also acquiesce when companies grossly overstate their true capital. Hence, a company can write a great deal of business with very little capital if it is so inclined. At bottom, therefore, the amount of industry capacity at any particular moment primarily depends on the mental state of insurance managers.

All this understood, it is not very difficult to prognosticate the industry's profits. Good profits will be realized only when there is a shortage of capacity. Shortages will occur only when insurers are frightened. That happens rarely—and most assuredly is not happening now.

Some analysts have argued that the more onerous taxes recently imposed on the insurance industry and 1989's catastrophes—Hurricane Hugo and the California earthquake—will cause prices to strengthen significantly. We disagree. These adversities have not destroyed the eagerness of insurers to write business at present prices. Therefore, premium volume won't grow by 10% in 1990, which means the negative underwriting trend will not reverse.

The industry will meantime say it needs higher prices to achieve profitability matching that of the average American business. Of course it does. So does the steel business. But needs and desires have nothing to do with the long-term profitability of industries. Instead, economic fundamentals determine the outcome. Insurance profitability will improve only when virtually all insurers are turning away business *despite* higher prices. And we're a long way from that point.

Berkshire's premium volume may drop to $150 million or so in 1990 (from a high of $1 billion in 1986), partly because our traditional business continues to shrink and partly because the contract under which we received 7% of the business of Fireman's Fund expired last August. Whatever the size of the drop, it will not disturb us. We have no interest in writing insurance that carries a mathematical expectation of loss; we experience enough disappointments doing transactions we believe to carry an expectation of profit.

However, our appetite for appropriately-priced business is ample, as one tale from 1989 will tell. It concerns "CAT covers," which are reinsurance contracts that primary insurance companies (and also re-insurers themselves) buy to protect themselves against a single catastrophe, such as a tornado or hurricane, that produces losses from a large number of policies. In these contracts, the primary insurer might retain the loss from a single event up to a maximum of, say, $10 million, buying various layers of reinsurance above that level. When losses exceed the retained amount, the reinsurer typically pays 95% of the excess up to its contractual limit, with the primary insurer paying the remainder. (By requiring the primary insurer to keep 5% of each layer, the reinsurer leaves him with a financial stake in each loss settlement and guards against his throwing away the reinsurer's money.)

CAT covers are usually one-year policies that also provide for one automatic reinstatement, which requires a primary insurer whose coverage has been exhausted by a catastrophe to buy a second cover for the balance of the year in question by paying another premium. This provision protects the primary company from being "bare" for even a brief period after a first catastrophic event. The duration of "an event" is usually limited by contract to any span of 72 hours designated by the primary company. Under this definition, a wide-spread storm, causing damage for three days, will be classified as a single event if it arises from a single climatic cause. If the storm lasts four days, however, the primary company will file a claim carving out the 72 consecutive hours during which it suffered the greatest damage. Losses that occurred outside that period will be treated as arising from a separate event.

In 1989, two unusual things happened. First, Hurricane Hugo generated $4 billion or more of insured loss, at a pace, however, that caused the vast damage in the Carolinas to occur slightly more than 72 hours after the equally severe damage in the Caribbean. Second, the California earthquake hit within weeks, causing insured damage that was difficult to estimate, even well after the event. Slammed by these two—or possibly three—major catastrophes, some primary insurers, and also many reinsurers that had themselves bought CAT protection, either used up their automatic second cover or became uncertain as to whether they had done so.

At that point sellers of CAT policies had lost a huge amount of money—perhaps twice because of the reinstatements—and not taken in much in premiums. Depending upon many variables, a CAT premium might generally have run 3% to 15% of the amount of protection purchased. For some years, we've thought premiums of that kind inadequate and have stayed away from the business.

But because the 1989 disasters left many insurers either actually or possibly bare, and also left most CAT writers licking their wounds, there was an immediate shortage after the earthquake of much-needed catastrophe coverage. Prices instantly became attractive, particularly for the reinsurance that CAT writers themselves buy. Just as instantly, Berkshire Hathaway offered to write up to $250 million of catastrophe coverage, advertising that proposition in trade publications. Though we did not write all the business we sought, we did in a busy ten days book a substantial amount.

Our willingness to put such a huge sum on the line for a loss that could occur tomorrow sets us apart from any reinsurer in the world. There are, of course, companies that sometimes write $250 million or even far more of catastrophe coverage. But they do so only when they can, in turn, reinsure a large percentage of the business with other companies. When they can't "lay off" in size, they disappear from the market.

Berkshire's policy, conversely, is to retain the business we write rather than lay it off. When rates carry an expectation of profit, we want to assume as much risk as is prudent. And in our case, that's a lot.

We will accept more reinsurance risk for our own account than any other company because of two factors: (1) by the standards of regulatory accounting, we have a net worth in our insurance companies of about $6 billion—the second highest amount in the United States; and (2) we simply don't care what earnings we report quarterly, or even annually, just as long as the decisions leading to those earnings (or losses) were reached intelligently.

Obviously, if we write $250 million of catastrophe coverage and retain it all ourselves, there is some probability that we will lose the full $250 million in a single quarter. That probability is low, but it is not zero. If we had a loss of that magnitude, our after-tax cost would be about $165 million. Though that is far more than Berkshire normally earns in a quarter, the damage would be a blow only to our pride, not to our well-being.

This posture is one few insurance managements will assume. Typically, they are willing to write scads of business on terms that almost guarantee them mediocre returns on equity. But they do not want to expose themselves to an embarrassing single-quarter loss, even if the managerial strategy that causes the loss promises, over time, to produce superior results. I can understand their thinking: What is best for their owners is not necessarily best for the managers. Fortunately Charlie and I have both total job security and financial interests that are identical with those of our shareholders. We are willing to *look* foolish as long as we don't feel we have *acted* foolishly.

Our method of operation, incidentally, makes us a stabilizing force in the industry. We add huge capacity when capacity is short and we become less competitive only when capacity is abundant. Of course, we don't follow this policy in the interest of stabilization—we follow it because we believe it to be the most sensible and profitable course of action. Nevertheless, our behavior steadies the market. In this case, Adam Smith's invisible hand works as advertised.

Currently, we hold an exceptional amount of float compared to premium volume. This circumstance should produce quite favorable insurance results for us during the next few years as it did in 1989. Our underwriting losses should be tolerable and our investment income from policyholder funds large. This pleasant situation, however, will gradually deteriorate as our float runs off.

At some point, however, there will be an opportunity for us to write large amounts of profitable business. Mike Goldberg and his management team of Rod Eldred, Dinos Iordanou, Ajit Jain, Phil Urban, and Don Wurster continue to position us well for this eventuality.

Marketable Securities

In selecting marketable securities for our insurance companies, we generally choose among five major categories: (1) long-term common stock investments, (2) medium-term fixed income securities, (3) long-term fixed income securities, (4) short-term cash equivalents, and (5) short-term arbitrage commitments.

We have no particular bias when it comes to choosing from these categories; we just continuously search among them for the highest after-tax returns as measured by "mathematical expectation," limiting ourselves always to investment alternatives we think we understand. Our criteria have nothing to do with maximizing immediately reportable earnings; our goal, rather, is to maximize eventual net worth.

- Below we list our common stock holdings having a value of over $100 million. A small portion of these investments belongs to subsidiaries of which Berkshire owns less than 100%.

Shares	Company	12/31/89 Cost	Market
		(000s omitted)	
3,000,000	Capital Cities/ABC, Inc..	$517,500	$1,692,375
23,350,000	The Coca-Cola Co.	1,023,920	1,803,787
2,400,000	Federal Home Loan Mortgage Corp..	71,729	161,100
6,850,000	GEICO Corp..	45,713	1,044,625
1,727,765	The Washington Post Company.	9,731	486,366

This list of companies is the same as last year's and in only one case has the number of shares changed: Our holdings of Coca-Cola increased from 14,172,500 shares at the end of 1988 to 23,350,000.

This Coca-Cola investment provides yet another example of the incredible speed with which your Chairman responds to investment opportunities, no matter how obscure or well-disguised they may be. I believe I had my first Coca-Cola in either 1935 or 1936. Of a certainty, it was in 1936 that I started buying Cokes at the rate of six for 25 cents from Buffett & Son, the family grocery store, to sell around the neighborhood for 5 cents each. In this excursion into high-margin retailing, I duly observed the extraordinary consumer attractiveness and commercial possibilities of the product.

I continued to note these qualities for the next 52 years as Coke blanketed the world. During this period, however, I carefully avoided buying even a single share, instead allocating major portions of my net worth to street railway companies, windmill manufacturers, anthracite producers, textile businesses, trading-stamp issuers, and the like. (If you think I'm making this up, I can supply the names.) Only in the summer of 1988 did my brain finally establish contact with my eyes.

What I then perceived was both clear and fascinating. After drifting somewhat in the 1970's, Coca-Cola had in 1981 become a new company with the move of Roberto Goizueta to CEO. Roberto, along with Don Keough, once my across-the-street neighbor in Omaha, first re-thought and focused the company's policies and then energetically carried them out. What was already the world's most ubiquitous product gained new momentum, with sales overseas virtually exploding.

Through a truly rare blend of marketing and financial skills, Roberto has maximized both the growth of his product and the rewards that this growth brings to shareholders. Normally, the CEO of a consumer products company, drawing on his natural inclinations or experience, will cause either marketing or finance to dominate the business at the expense of the other discipline. With Roberto, the mesh of marketing and finance is perfect and the result is a shareholder's dream.

Of course, we should have started buying Coke much earlier, soon after Roberto and Don began running things. In fact, if I had been thinking straight I would have persuaded my grandfather to sell the grocery store back in 1936 and put all of the proceeds into Coca-Cola stock. I've learned my lesson: My response time to the next glaringly attractive idea will be slashed to well under 50 years.

As I mentioned earlier, the yearend prices of our major investees were much higher relative to their intrinsic values than theretofore. While those prices may not yet cause nosebleeds, they are clearly vulnerable to a general market decline. A drop in their prices would not disturb us at all—it might in fact work to our eventual benefit—but it *would* cause at least a one-year reduction in Berkshire's net worth. We think such a reduction is almost certain in at least one of the next three years. Indeed, it would take only about a 10% year-to-year decline in the aggregate value of our portfolio investments to send Berkshire's net worth down.

We continue to be blessed with extraordinary managers at our portfolio companies. They are high-grade, talented, and shareholder-oriented. The exceptional results we have achieved while investing with them accurately reflect their exceptional personal qualities.

- We told you last year that we expected to do little in arbitrage during 1989, and that's the way it turned out. Arbitrage positions are a substitute for short-term cash equivalents, and during part of the year we held relatively low levels of cash. In the rest of the year we had a fairly good-sized cash position and even so chose not to engage in arbitrage. The main reason was corporate transactions that made no economic sense to us; arbitraging such deals comes too close to playing the greater-fool game. (As Wall Streeter Ray DeVoe says: "Fools rush in where angels fear to trade.") We will engage in arbitrage from time to time—sometimes on a large scale—but only when we like the odds.

- Leaving aside the three convertible preferreds discussed in the next section, we substantially reduced our holdings in both medium- and long-term fixed-income securities. In the long-terms, just about our only holdings have been Washington Public Power Supply Systems (WPPSS) bonds carrying coupons ranging from low to high. During the year we sold a number of the low-coupon issues, which we originally bought at very large discounts. Many of these issues had approximately doubled in price since we purchased them and in addition had paid us 15%-17% annually, tax-free. Our prices upon sale were only slightly cheaper than typical high-grade tax-exempts then commanded. We have kept all of our high-coupon WPPSS issues. Some have been called for redemption in 1991 and 1992, and we expect the rest to be called in the early to mid-1990s.

We also sold many of our medium-term tax-exempt bonds during the year. When we bought these bonds we said we would be happy to sell them—regardless of whether they were higher or lower than at our time of purchase—if something we liked better came along. Something did—and concurrently we unloaded most of these issues at modest gains. Overall, our 1989 profit from the sale of tax-exempt bonds was about $51 million pre-tax.

- The proceeds from our bond sales, along with our excess cash at the beginning of the year and that generated later through earnings, went into the purchase of three convertible preferred stocks. In the first transaction, which took place in July, we purchased $600 million of The Gillette Co. preferred with an 8 3/4% dividend, a mandatory redemption in ten years, and the right to convert into common at $50 per share. We next purchased $358 million of USAir Group, Inc. preferred stock with mandatory redemption in ten years, a dividend of 9 1/4%, and the right to convert into common at $60 per share. Finally, late in the year we purchased $300 million of Champion International Corp. preferred with mandatory redemption in ten years, a 9 1/4% dividend, and the right to convert into common at $38 per share.

Unlike standard convertible preferred stocks, the issues we own are either non-salable or non-convertible for considerable periods of time and there is consequently no way we can gain from short-term price blips in the common stock. I have gone on the board of Gillette, but I am not on the board of USAir or Champion. (I thoroughly enjoy the boards I am on, but can't handle any more.)

Gillette's business is very much the kind we like. Charlie and I think we understand the company's economics and therefore believe we can make a reasonably intelligent guess about its future. (If you haven't tried Gillette's new Sensor razor, go right out and get one.) However, we have no ability to forecast the economics of the investment banking business (in which we have a position through our 1987 purchase of Salomon convertible preferred), the airline industry, or the paper industry. This does not mean that we predict a negative future for these industries: we're agnostics, not atheists. Our lack of strong convictions about these businesses, however, means that we must structure our investments in them differently from what we do when we invest in a business appearing to have splendid economic characteristics.

In one major respect, however, these purchases are not different: We only want to link up with people whom we like, admire, and trust. John Gutfreund at Salomon, Colman Mockler, Jr. at Gillette, Ed Colodny at USAir, and Andy Sigler at Champion meet this test in spades.

They in turn have demonstrated some confidence in us, insisting in each case that our preferreds have unrestricted voting rights on a fully-converted basis, an arrangement that is far from standard in corporate finance. In effect they are trusting us to be intelligent owners, thinking about tomorrow *instead* of today, just as we are trusting them to be intelligent managers, thinking about tomorrow *as well* as today.

The preferred-stock structures we have negotiated will provide a mediocre return for us if industry economics hinder the performance of our investees, but will produce reasonably attractive results for us if they can earn a return comparable to that of American industry in general. We believe that Gillette, under Colman's management, will far exceed that return and believe that John, Ed, and Andy will reach it unless industry conditions are harsh.

Under almost any conditions, we expect these preferreds to return us our money plus dividends. If that is all we get, though, the result will be disappointing, because we will have given up flexibility and consequently will have missed some significant opportunities that are bound to present themselves during the decade. Under that scenario, we will have obtained only a preferred-stock yield during a period when the typical preferred stock will have held no appeal for us whatsoever. The only way Berkshire can achieve satisfactory results from its four preferred issues is to have the common stocks of the investee companies do well.

Good management and at least tolerable industry conditions will be needed if that is to happen. But we believe Berkshire's investment will also help and that the other shareholders of each investee will profit over the years ahead from our preferred-stock purchase. The help will come from the fact that each company now has a major, stable, and interested shareholder whose Chairman and Vice Chairman have, through Berkshire's investments, indirectly committed a very large amount of their own money to these undertakings. In dealing with our investees, Charlie and I will be supportive, analytical, and objective. We recognize that we are working with experienced CEOs who are very much in command of their own businesses but who nevertheless, at certain moments, appreciate the chance to test their thinking on someone without ties to their industry or to decisions of the past.

As a group, these convertible preferreds will not produce the returns we can achieve when we find a business with wonderful economic prospects that is unappreciated by the market. Nor will the returns be as attractive as those produced when we make our favorite form of capital deployment, the acquisition of 80% or more of a fine business with a fine management. But both opportunities are rare, particularly in a size befitting our present and anticipated resources.

In summation, Charlie and I feel that our preferred stock investments should produce returns moderately above those achieved by most fixed-income portfolios and that we can play a minor but enjoyable and constructive role in the investee companies.

Zero-Coupon Securities

In September, Berkshire issued $902.6 million principal amount of Zero-Coupon Convertible Subordinated Debentures, which are now listed on the New York Stock Exchange. Salomon Brothers handled the underwriting in superb fashion, providing us helpful advice and a flawless execution.

Most bonds, of course, require regular payments of interest, usually semi-annually. A zero-coupon bond, conversely, requires no current interest payments; instead, the investor receives his yield by purchasing the security at a significant discount from maturity value. The effective interest rate is determined by the original issue price, the maturity value, and the amount of time between issuance and maturity.

In our case, the bonds were issued at 44.314% of maturity value and are due in 15 years. For investors purchasing the bonds, that is the mathematical equivalent of a 5.5% current payment compounded semi-annually. Because we received only 44.31 cents on the dollar, our proceeds from this offering were $400 million (less about $9.5 million of offering expenses).

The bonds were issued in denominations of $10,000 and each bond is convertible into .4515 shares of Berkshire Hathaway. Because a $10,000 bond cost $4,431, this means that the conversion price was $9,815 per Berkshire share, a 15% premium to the market price then existing. Berkshire can call the bonds at any time after September 28, 1992 at their accreted value (the original issue price plus 5.5% compounded semi-annually) and on two specified days, September 28 of 1994 and 1999, the bondholders can require Berkshire to buy the securities at their accreted value.

For tax purposes, Berkshire is entitled to deduct the 5.5% interest accrual each year, even though we make no payments to the bondholders. Thus the net effect to us, resulting from the reduced taxes, is positive cash flow. That is a very significant benefit. Some unknowable variables prevent us from calculating our exact effective rate of interest, but under all circumstances it will be well below 5.5%. There is meanwhile a symmetry to the tax law: Any taxable holder of the bonds must pay tax each year on the 5.5% interest, even though he receives no cash.

Neither our bonds nor those of certain other companies that issued similar bonds last year (notably Loews and Motorola) resemble the great bulk of zero-coupon bonds that have been issued in recent years. Of these, Charlie and I have been, and will continue to be, outspoken critics. As I will later explain, such bonds have often been used in the most deceptive of ways and with deadly consequences to investors. But before we tackle that subject, let's travel back to Eden, to a time when the apple had not yet been bitten.

If you're my age you bought your first zero-coupon bonds during World War II, by purchasing the famous Series E U. S. Savings Bond, the most widely-sold bond issue in history. (After the war, these bonds were held by one out of two U. S. households.) Nobody, of course, called the Series E a zero-coupon bond, a term in fact that I doubt had been invented. But that's precisely what the Series E was.

These bonds came in denominations as small as $18.75. That amount purchased a $25 obligation of the United States government due in 10 years, terms that gave the buyer a compounded annual return of 2.9%. At the time, this was an attractive offer: the 2.9% rate was higher than that generally available on Government bonds and the holder faced no market-fluctuation risk, since he could at any time cash in his bonds with only a minor reduction in interest.

A second form of zero-coupon U. S. Treasury issue, also benign and useful, surfaced in the last decade. One problem with a normal bond is that even though it pays a given interest rate—say 10%—the holder cannot be assured that a compounded 10% return will be realized. For that rate to materialize, each semi-annual coupon must be reinvested at 10% as it is received. If current interest rates are, say, only 6% or 7% when these coupons come due, the holder will be unable to compound his money over the life of the bond at the advertised rate. For pension funds or other investors with long-term liabilities, "reinvestment risk" of this type can be a serious problem. Savings Bonds might have solved it, except that they are issued only to individuals and are unavailable in large denominations. What big buyers needed was huge quantities of "Savings Bond Equivalents."

Enter some ingenious and, in this case, highly useful investment bankers (led, I'm happy to say, by Salomon Brothers). They created the instrument desired by "stripping" the semi-annual coupons from standard Government issues. Each coupon, once detached, takes on the essential character of a Savings Bond since it represents a single sum due sometime in the future. For example, if you strip the 40 semi-annual coupons from a U. S. Government Bond due in the year 2010, you will have 40 zero-coupon bonds, with maturities from six months to 20 years, each of which can then be bundled with other coupons of like maturity and marketed. If current interest rates are, say, 10% for all maturities, the six-month issue will sell for 95.24% of maturity value and the 20-year issue will sell for 14.20%. The purchaser of any given maturity is thus guaranteed a compounded rate of 10% for his entire holding period. Stripping of government bonds has occurred on a large scale in recent years, as long-term investors, ranging from pension funds to individual IRA accounts, recognized these high-grade, zero-coupon issues to be well suited to their needs.

But as happens in Wall Street all too often, what the wise do in the beginning, fools do in the end. In the last few years zero-coupon bonds (and their functional equivalent, pay-in-kind bonds, which distribute additional PIK bonds semi-annually as interest instead of paying cash) have been issued in enormous quantities by ever-junkier credits. To these issuers, zero (or PIK) bonds offer one overwhelming advantage: It is impossible to default on a promise to pay nothing. Indeed, if LDC governments had issued no debt in the 1970's other than long-term zero-coupon obligations, they would now have a spotless record as debtors.

This principle at work—that you need not default for a long time if you solemnly promise to pay nothing for a long time—has not been lost on promoters and investment bankers seeking to finance ever-shakier deals. But its acceptance by lenders took a while: When the leveraged buy-out craze began some years back, purchasers could borrow only on a reasonably sound basis, in which conservatively-estimated *free* cash flow—that is, operating earnings plus depreciation and amortization less normalized capital expenditures—was adequate to cover both interest and modest reductions in debt.

Later, as the adrenalin of deal-makers surged, businesses began to be purchased at prices so high that all free cash flow necessarily had to be allocated to the payment of interest. That left nothing for the paydown of debt. In effect, a Scarlett O'Hara "I'll think about it tomorrow" position in respect to principal payments was taken by borrowers and accepted by a new breed of lender, the buyer of original-issue junk bonds. Debt now became something to be refinanced rather than repaid. The change brings to mind a *New Yorker* cartoon in which the grateful borrower rises to shake the hand of the bank's lending officer and gushes: "I don't know how I'll ever repay you."

Soon borrowers found even the new, lax standards intolerably binding. To induce lenders to finance even sillier transactions, they introduced an abomination, EBDIT—Earnings Before Depreciation,

Interest and Taxes—as the test of a company's ability to pay interest. Using this sawed-off yardstick, the borrower ignored depreciation as an expense on the theory that it did not require a current cash outlay.

Such an attitude is clearly delusional. At 95% of American businesses, capital expenditures that over time roughly approximate depreciation are a necessity and are every bit as real an expense as labor or utility costs. Even a high school dropout knows that to finance a car he must have income that covers not only interest and operating expenses, but also realistically-calculated depreciation. He would be laughed out of the bank if he started talking about EBDIT.

Capital outlays at a business can be skipped, of course, in any given month, just as a human can skip a day or even a week of eating. But if the skipping becomes routine and is not made up, the body weakens and eventually dies. Furthermore, a start-and-stop feeding policy will over time produce a less healthy organism, human or corporate, than that produced by a steady diet. As businessmen, Charlie and I relish having competitors who are unable to fund capital expenditures.

You might think that waving away a major expense such as depreciation in an attempt to make a terrible deal look like a good one hits the limits of Wall Street's ingenuity. If so, you haven't been paying attention during the past few years. Promoters needed to find a way to justify even pricier acquisitions. Otherwise, they risked—heaven forbid!—losing deals to other promoters with more "imagination."

So, stepping through the Looking Glass, promoters and their investment bankers proclaimed that EBDIT should now be measured against cash interest only, which meant that interest accruing on zero-coupon or PIK bonds could be ignored when the financial feasibility of a transaction was being assessed. This approach not only relegated depreciation expense to the let's-ignore-it corner, but gave similar treatment to what was usually a significant portion of interest expense. To their shame, many professional investment managers went along with this nonsense, though they usually were careful to do so only with clients' money, not their own. (Calling these managers "professionals" is actually too kind; they should be designated "promotees.")

Under this new standard, a business earning, say, $100 million pre-tax and having debt on which $90 million of interest must be paid currently, might use a zero-coupon or PIK issue to incur another $60 million of annual interest that would accrue and compound but not come due for some years. The rate on these issues would typically be very high, which means that the situation in year 2 might be $90 million cash interest plus $69 million accrued interest, and so on as the compounding proceeds. Such high-rate reborrowing schemes, which a few years ago were appropriately confined to the waterfront, soon became models of modern finance at virtually all major investment banking houses.

When they make these offerings, investment bankers display their humorous side: They dispense income and balance sheet projections extending five or more years into the future for companies they barely had heard of a few months earlier. If you are shown such schedules, I suggest that you join in the fun: Ask the investment banker for the *one-year* budgets that his own firm prepared as the last few years began and then compare these with what actually happened.

Some time ago Ken Galbraith, in his witty and insightful *The Great Crash*, coined a new economic term: "the bezzle," defined as the current amount of undiscovered embezzlement. This financial creature has a magical quality: The embezzlers are richer by the amount of the bezzle, while the embezzlees do not yet feel poorer.

Professor Galbraith astutely pointed out that this sum should be added to the National Wealth so that we might know the Psychic National Wealth. Logically, a society that wanted to *feel* enormously prosperous would both encourage its citizens to embezzle and try not to detect the crime. By this means, "wealth" would balloon though not an erg of productive work had been done.

The satirical nonsense of the bezzle is dwarfed by the real-world nonsense of the zero-coupon bond. With zeros, one party to a contract can experience "income" without his opposite experiencing the pain of expenditure. In our illustration, a company capable of earning only $100 million dollars annually—and therefore capable of paying only that much in interest—magically creates "earnings" for bondholders of $150 million. As long as major investors willingly don their Peter Pan wings and repeatedly say "I believe," there is no limit to how much "income" can be created by the zero-coupon bond.

Wall Street welcomed this invention with the enthusiasm less-enlightened folk might reserve for the wheel or the plow. Here, finally, was an instrument that would let the Street make deals at prices no longer limited by actual earning power. The result, obviously, would be more transactions: Silly prices will always attract sellers. And, as Jesse Unruh might have put it, transactions are the mother's milk of finance.

The zero-coupon or PIK bond possesses one additional attraction for the promoter and investment banker, which is that the time elapsing between folly and failure can be stretched out. This is no small benefit. If the period before all costs must be faced is long, promoters can create a string of foolish deals—and take in lots of fees—before any chickens come home to roost from their earlier ventures.

But in the end, alchemy, whether it is metallurgical or financial, fails. A base business can not be transformed into a golden business by tricks of accounting or capital structure. The man claiming to be a financial alchemist may become rich. But gullible investors rather than business achievements will usually be the source of his wealth.

Whatever their weaknesses, we should add, many zero-coupon and PIK bonds will not default. We have in fact owned some and may buy more if their market becomes sufficiently distressed. (We've not, however, even considered buying a new issue from a weak credit.) No financial instrument is evil per se; it's just that some variations have far more potential for mischief than others.

The blue ribbon for mischief-making should go to the zero-coupon issuer unable to make its interest payments on a current basis. Our advice: Whenever an investment banker starts talking about EBDIT—or whenever someone creates a capital structure that does not allow all interest, both payable and accrued, to be comfortably met out of current cash flow *net of ample capital expenditures*—zip up your wallet. Turn the tables by suggesting that the promoter and his high-priced entourage accept zero-coupon fees, deferring their take until the zero-coupon bonds have been paid in full. See then how much enthusiasm for the deal endures.

Our comments about investment bankers may seem harsh. But Charlie and I—in our hopelessly old-fashioned way—believe that they should perform a gatekeeping role, guarding investors against the promoter's propensity to indulge in excess. Promoters, after all, have throughout time exercised the same judgment and restraint in accepting money that alcoholics have exercised in accepting liquor. At a minimum, therefore, the banker's conduct should rise to that of a responsible bartender who, when necessary, refuses the profit from the next drink to avoid sending a drunk out on the highway. In recent years, unfortunately, many leading investment firms have found bartender morality to be an intolerably restrictive standard. Lately, those who have traveled the high road in Wall Street have not encountered heavy traffic.

One distressing footnote: The cost of the zero-coupon folly will not be borne solely by the direct participants. Certain savings and loan associations were heavy buyers of such bonds, using cash that came from FSLIC-insured deposits. Straining to show splendid earnings, these buyers recorded—but did not receive—ultra-high interest income on these issues. Many of these associations are now in major trouble. Had their loans to shaky credits worked, the owners of the associations would have pocketed the profits. In the many cases in which the loans will fail, the taxpayer will pick up the bill. To paraphrase Jackie Mason, at these associations it was the managers who should have been wearing the ski masks.

Mistakes of the First Twenty-five Years (A Condensed Version)

To quote Robert Benchley, "Having a dog teaches a boy fidelity, perseverance, and to turn around three times before lying down." Such are the shortcomings of experience. Nevertheless, it's a good idea to review past mistakes before committing new ones. So let's take a quick look at the last 25 years.

- My first mistake, of course, was in buying control of Berkshire. Though I knew its business— textile manufacturing—to be unpromising, I was enticed to buy because the price looked cheap. Stock purchases of that kind had proved reasonably rewarding in my early years, though by the time Berkshire came along in 1965 I was becoming aware that the strategy was not ideal.

  If you buy a stock at a sufficiently low price, there will usually be some hiccup in the fortunes of the business that gives you a chance to unload at a decent profit, even though the long-term performance of the business may be terrible. I call this the "cigar butt" approach to investing. A cigar butt found on the street that has only one puff left in it may not offer much of a smoke, but the "bargain purchase" will make that puff all profit.

  Unless you are a liquidator, that kind of approach to buying businesses is foolish. First, the original "bargain" price probably will not turn out to be such a steal after all. In a difficult business, no sooner is one problem solved than another surfaces— never is there just one cockroach in the kitchen. Second, any initial advantage you secure will be quickly eroded by the low return that the business earns. For example, if you buy a business for $8 million that can be sold or liquidated for $10 million and promptly take either course, you can realize a high return. But the investment will disappoint if the business is sold for $10 million in ten years and in the interim has annually earned and distributed only a few percent on cost. Time is the friend of the wonderful business, the enemy of the mediocre.

  You might think this principle is obvious, but I had to learn it the hard way—in fact, I had to learn it several times over. Shortly after purchasing Berkshire, I acquired a Baltimore department store, Hochschild Kohn, buying through a company called Diversified Retailing that later merged with Berkshire. I bought at a substantial discount from book value, the people were first-class, and the deal included some extras—unrecorded real estate values and a significant LIFO inventory cushion. How could I miss? So-o-o—three years later I was lucky to sell the business for about what I had paid. After ending our corporate marriage to Hochschild Kohn, I had memories like those of the husband in the country song, "My Wife Ran Away With My Best Friend and I Still Miss Him a Lot."

  I could give you other personal examples of "bargain-purchase" folly but I'm sure you get the picture: It's far better to buy a wonderful company at a fair price than a fair company at a wonderful price. Charlie understood this early; I was a slow learner. But now, when buying companies or common stocks, we look for first-class businesses accompanied by first-class managements.

- That leads right into a related lesson: Good jockeys will do well on good horses, but not on broken-down nags. Both Berkshire's textile business and Hochschild, Kohn had able and honest people running them. The same managers employed in a business with good economic characteristics would have achieved fine records. But they were never going to make any progress while running in quicksand.

I've said many times that when a management with a reputation for brilliance tackles a business with a reputation for bad economics, it is the reputation of the business that remains intact. I just wish I hadn't been so energetic in creating examples. My behavior has matched that admitted by Mae West: "I was Snow White, but I drifted."

• A further related lesson: Easy does it. After 25 years of buying and supervising a great variety of businesses, Charlie and I have *not* learned how to solve difficult business problems. What we have learned is to avoid them. To the extent we have been successful, it is because we concentrated on identifying one-foot hurdles that we could step over rather than because we acquired any ability to clear seven-footers.

The finding may seem unfair, but in both business and investments it is usually far more profitable to simply stick with the easy and obvious than it is to resolve the difficult. On occasion, tough problems *must* be tackled as was the case when we started our Sunday paper in Buffalo. In other instances, a great investment opportunity occurs when a marvelous business encounters a one-time huge, but solvable, problem as was the case many years back at both American Express and GEICO. Overall, however, we've done better by avoiding dragons than by slaying them.

• My most surprising discovery: the overwhelming importance in business of an unseen force that we might call "the institutional imperative." In business school, I was given no hint of the imperative's existence and I did not intuitively understand it when I entered the business world. I thought then that decent, intelligent, and experienced managers would automatically make rational business decisions. But I learned over time that isn't so. Instead, rationality frequently wilts when the institutional imperative comes into play.

For example: (1) As if governed by Newton's First Law of Motion, an institution will resist any change in its current direction; (2) Just as work expands to fill available time, corporate projects or acquisitions will materialize to soak up available funds; (3) Any business craving of the leader, however foolish, will be quickly supported by detailed rate-of-return and strategic studies prepared by his troops; and (4) The behavior of peer companies, whether they are expanding, acquiring, setting executive compensation or whatever, will be mindlessly imitated.

Institutional dynamics, not venality or stupidity, set businesses on these courses, which are too often misguided. After making some expensive mistakes because I ignored the power of the imperative, I have tried to organize and manage Berkshire in ways that minimize its influence. Furthermore, Charlie and I have attempted to concentrate our investments in companies that appear alert to the problem.

• After some other mistakes, I learned to go into business only with people whom I like, trust, and admire. As I noted before, this policy of itself will not ensure success: A second-class textile or department-store company won't prosper simply because its managers are men that you would be pleased to see your daughter marry. However, an owner—or investor—can accomplish wonders if he manages to associate himself with such people in businesses that possess decent economic characteristics. Conversely, we do not wish to join with managers who lack admirable qualities, no matter how attractive the prospects of their business. We've never succeeded in making a good deal with a bad person.

- Some of my worst mistakes were not publicly visible. These were stock and business purchases whose virtues I understood and yet didn't make. It's no sin to miss a great opportunity outside one's area of competence. But I have passed on a couple of really big purchases that were served up to me on a platter and that I was fully capable of understanding. For Berkshire's shareholders, myself included, the cost of this thumb-sucking has been huge.

- Our consistently-conservative financial policies may appear to have been a mistake, but in my view were not. In retrospect, it is clear that significantly higher, though still conventional, leverage ratios at Berkshire would have produced considerably better returns on equity than the 23.8% we have actually averaged. Even in 1965, perhaps we could have judged there to be a 99% probability that higher leverage would lead to nothing but good. Correspondingly, we might have seen only a 1% chance that some shock factor, external or internal, would cause a conventional debt ratio to produce a result falling somewhere between temporary anguish and default.

  We wouldn't have liked those 99:1 odds—and never will. A small chance of distress or disgrace cannot, in our view, be offset by a large chance of extra returns. If your actions are sensible, you are certain to get good results; in most such cases, leverage just moves things along faster. Charlie and I have never been in a big hurry: We enjoy the process far more than the proceeds—though we have learned to live with those also.

* * * * * * * * * * * *

We hope in another 25 years to report on the mistakes of the first 50. If we are around in 2015 to do that, you can count on this section occupying many more pages than it does here.

Miscellaneous

We hope to buy more businesses that are similar to the ones we have, and we can use some help. If you have a business that fits the following criteria, call me or, preferably, write.

Here's what we're looking for:

(1) Large purchases (at least $10 million of after-tax earnings),

(2) demonstrated consistent earning power (future projections are of little interest to us, nor are "turnaround" situations),

(3) businesses earning good returns on equity while employing little or no debt,

(4) management in place (we can't supply it),

(5) simple businesses (if there's lots of technology, we won't understand it),

(6) an offering price (we don't want to waste our time or that of the seller by talking, even preliminarily, about a transaction when price is unknown).

We will not engage in unfriendly takeovers. We can promise complete confidentiality and a very fast answer—customarily within five minutes—as to whether we're interested. We prefer to buy for cash, but will consider issuing stock when we receive as much in intrinsic business value as we give.

Our favorite form of purchase is one fitting the Blumkin-Friedman-Heldman mold. In cases like these, the company's owner-managers wish to generate significant amounts of cash, sometimes for themselves, but often for their families or inactive shareholders. At the same time, these managers wish to remain significant owners who continue to run their companies just as they have in the past. We think we offer a particularly good fit for owners with such objectives. We invite potential sellers to check us out by contacting people with whom we have done business in the past.

Charlie and I frequently get approached about acquisitions that don't come close to meeting our tests: We've found that if you advertise an interest in buying collies, a lot of people will call hoping to sell you their cocker spaniels. Our interest in new ventures, turnarounds, or auction-like sales can best be expressed by a Goldwynism: "Please include me out."

Besides being interested in the purchase of businesses as described above, we are also interested in the negotiated purchase of large, but not controlling, blocks of stock comparable to those we hold in Capital Cities, Salomon, Gillette, USAir and Champion. Last year we said we had a special interest in large purchases of convertible preferreds. We still have an appetite of that kind, but it is limited since we now are close to the maximum position we feel appropriate for this category of investment.

* * * * * * * * * * * *

Two years ago, I told you about Harry Bottle, who in 1962 quickly cured a major business mess at the first industrial company I controlled, Dempster Mill Manufacturing (one of my "bargain" purchases) and who 24 years later had reappeared to again rescue me, this time from problems at K&W Products, a small Berkshire subsidiary that produces automotive compounds. As I reported, in short order Harry reduced capital employed at K&W, rationalized production, cut costs, and quadrupled profits. You might think he would then have paused for breath. But last year Harry, now 70, attended a bankruptcy auction and, for a pittance, acquired a product line that is a natural for K&W. That company's profitability may well be increased 50% by this coup. Watch this space for future bulletins on Harry's triumphs.

* * * * * * * * * * * *

With more than a year behind him of trading Berkshire's stock on the New York Stock Exchange, our specialist, Jim Maguire of Henderson Brothers, Inc. ("HBI"), continues his outstanding performance. Before we listed, dealer spreads often were 3% or more of market price. Jim has maintained the spread at 50 points or less, which at current prices is well under 1%. Shareholders who buy or sell benefit significantly from this reduction in transaction costs.

Because we are delighted by our experience with Jim, HBI and the NYSE, I said as much in ads that have been run in a series placed by the NYSE. Normally I shun testimonials, but I was pleased in this instance to publicly compliment the Exchange.

* * * * * * * * * * * *

Last summer we sold the corporate jet that we purchased for $850,000 three years ago and bought another used jet for $6.7 million. Those of you who recall the mathematics of the multiplying bacteria on page 5 will understandably panic: If our net worth continues to increase at current rates, and the cost of replacing planes also continues to rise at the now-established rate of 100% compounded annually, it will not be long before Berkshire's entire net worth is consumed by its jet.

Charlie doesn't like it when I equate the jet with bacteria; he feels it's degrading to the bacteria. His idea of traveling in style is an air-conditioned bus, a luxury he steps up to only when bargain fares are in effect. My own attitude toward the jet can be summarized by the prayer attributed, apocryphally I'm sure, to St. Augustine as he contemplated leaving a life of secular pleasures to become a priest. Battling the conflict between intellect and glands, he pled: "Help me, Oh Lord, to become chaste—but not yet."

Naming the plane has not been easy. I initially suggested "The Charles T. Munger." Charlie countered with "The Aberration." We finally settled on "The Indefensible."

* * * * * * * * * * * *

About 96.9% of all eligible shares participated in Berkshire's 1989 shareholder-designated contributions program. Contributions made through the program were $5.9 million, and 2,550 charities were recipients.

We urge new shareholders to read the description of our shareholder-designated contributions program that appears on pages 52-53. If you wish to participate in future programs, we strongly urge that you immediately make sure your shares are registered in the name of the actual owner, not in the nominee name of a broker, bank or depository. Shares not so registered on August 31, 1990 will be ineligible for the 1990 program.

* * * * * * * * * * * *

The annual meeting this year will take place at 9:30 a.m. on Monday, April 30, 1990. Attendance grew last year to about 1,000, very close to the seating capacity of the Witherspoon Hall at Joslyn Museum. So this year's meeting will be moved to the Orpheum Theatre, which is in downtown Omaha, about one-quarter of a mile from the Red Lion Hotel. The Radisson-Redick Tower, a much smaller but nice hotel, is located across the street from the Orpheum. Or you may wish to stay at the Marriott, which is in west Omaha, about 100 yards from Borsheim's. We will have buses at the Marriott that will leave at 8:30 and 8:45 for the meeting and return after it ends.

Charlie and I always enjoy the meeting, and we hope you can make it. The quality of our shareholders is reflected in the quality of the questions we get: We have never attended an annual meeting anywhere that features such a consistently high level of intelligent, owner-related questions.

An attachment to our proxy material explains how you can obtain the card you will need for admission to the meeting. Because weekday parking can be tight around the Orpheum, we have lined up a number of nearby lots for our shareholders to use. The attachment also contains information about them.

As usual, we will have buses to take you to Nebraska Furniture Mart and Borsheim's after the meeting and to take you to downtown hotels or to the airport later. I hope that you will allow plenty of time to fully explore the attractions of both stores. Those of you arriving early can visit the Furniture Mart any day of the week; it is open from 10 a.m. to 5:30 p.m. on Saturdays, and from noon to 5:30 p.m. on Sundays.

Borsheim's normally is closed on Sunday, but we will open for shareholders and their guests from noon to 6 p.m. on Sunday, April 29th. Ike likes to put on a show, and you can rely on him to produce something very special for our shareholders.

In this letter we've had a lot to say about rates of compounding. If you can bear having your own rate turn negative for a day—not a pretty thought, I admit—visit Ike on the 29th.

March 2, 1990

Warren E. Buffett
Chairman of the Board

BERKSHIRE HATHAWAY INC.

To the Shareholders of Berkshire Hathaway Inc.:

Last year we made a prediction: "A reduction [in Berkshire's net worth] is almost certain in at least one of the next three years." During much of 1990's second half, we were on the road to quickly proving that forecast accurate. But some strengthening in stock prices late in the year enabled us to close 1990 with net worth up by $362 million, or 7.3%. Over the last 26 years (that is, since present management took over) our per-share book value has grown from $19.46 to $4,612.06, or at a rate of 23.2% compounded annually.

Our growth rate was lackluster in 1990 because our four major common stock holdings, in aggregate, showed little change in market value. Last year I told you that though these companies—Capital Cities/ABC, Coca-Cola, GEICO, and Washington Post—had fine businesses and superb managements, widespread recognition of these attributes had pushed the stock prices of the four to lofty levels. The market prices of the two media companies have since fallen significantly—for good reasons relating to evolutionary industry developments that I will discuss later—and the price of Coca-Cola stock has increased significantly for what I also believe are good reasons. Overall, yearend 1990 prices of our "permanent four," though far from enticing, were a bit more appealing than they were a year earlier.

Berkshire's 26-year record is meaningless in forecasting future results; so also, we hope, is the one-year record. We continue to aim for a 15% average annual gain in intrinsic value. But, as we never tire of telling you, this goal becomes ever more difficult to reach as our equity base, now $5.3 billion, increases.

If we do attain that 15% average, our shareholders should fare well. However, Berkshire's corporate gains will produce an identical gain for a specific shareholder only if he eventually sells his shares at the same relationship to intrinsic value that existed when he bought them. For example, if you buy at a 10% premium to intrinsic value; if intrinsic value subsequently grows at 15% a year; and if you then sell at a 10% premium, your own return will correspondingly be 15% compounded. (The calculation assumes that no dividends are paid.) If, however, you buy at a premium and sell at a smaller premium, your results will be somewhat inferior to those achieved by the company.

Ideally, the results of every Berkshire shareholder would closely mirror those of the company during his period of ownership. That is why Charlie Munger, Berkshire's Vice Chairman and my partner, and I hope for Berkshire to sell consistently at about intrinsic value. We prefer such steadiness to the value-ignoring volatility of the past two years: In 1989 intrinsic value grew less than did book value, which was up 44%, while the market price rose 85%; in 1990 book value and intrinsic value increased by a small amount, while the market price fell 23%.

Berkshire's intrinsic value continues to exceed book value by a substantial margin. We can't tell you the exact differential because intrinsic value is necessarily an estimate; Charlie and I might, in fact, differ by 10% in our appraisals. We do know, however, that we own some exceptional businesses that are worth considerably more than the values at which they are carried on our books.

Much of the extra value that exists in our businesses has been created by the managers now running them. Charlie and I feel free to brag about this group because we had nothing to do with developing the skills they possess: These superstars just came that way. Our job is merely to identify talented managers and provide an environment in which they can do their stuff. Having done it, they send their cash to headquarters and we face our only other task: the intelligent deployment of these funds.

My own role in operations may best be illustrated by a small tale concerning my granddaughter, Emily, and her fourth birthday party last fall. Attending were other children, adoring relatives, and Beemer the Clown, a local entertainer who includes magic tricks in his act.

Beginning these, Beemer asked Emily to help him by waving a "magic wand" over "the box of wonders." Green handkerchiefs went into the box, Emily waved the wand, and Beemer removed blue ones. Loose handkerchiefs went in and, upon a magisterial wave by Emily, emerged knotted. After four such transformations, each more amazing than its predecessor, Emily was unable to contain herself. Her face aglow, she exulted: "Gee, I'm really good at this."

And that sums up my contribution to the performance of Berkshire's business magicians—the Blumkins, the Friedman family, Mike Goldberg, the Heldmans, Chuck Huggins, Stan Lipsey and Ralph Schey. They deserve your applause.

Sources of Reported Earnings

The table below shows the major sources of Berkshire's reported earnings. In this presentation, amortization of Goodwill and other major purchase-price accounting adjustments are not charged against the specific businesses to which they apply, but are instead aggregated and shown separately. This procedure lets you view the earnings of our businesses as they would have been reported had we not purchased them. I've explained in past reports why this form of presentation seems to us to be more useful to investors and managers than one utilizing generally accepted accounting principles (GAAP), which require purchase-price adjustments to be made on a business-by-business basis. The total net earnings we show in the table are, of course, identical to the GAAP total in our audited financial statements.

Much additional information about these businesses is given on pages 39-46, where you also will find our segment earnings reported on a GAAP basis. For information on Wesco's businesses, I urge you to read Charlie Munger's letter, which starts on page 56. His letter also contains the clearest and most insightful discussion of the banking industry that I have seen.

		(000s omitted)		
			Berkshire's Share of Net Earnings (after taxes and minority interests)	
	Pre-Tax Earnings			
	1990	1989	1990	1989
Operating Earnings:				
Insurance Group:				
Underwriting	$(26,647)	$(24,400)	$(14,936)	$(12,259)
Net Investment Income	327,048	243,599	282,613	213,642
Buffalo News	43,954	46,047	25,981	27,771
Fechheimer	12,450	12,621	6,605	6,789
Kirby	27,445	26,114	17,613	16,803
Nebraska Furniture Mart	17,248	17,070	8,485	8,441
Scott Fetzer Manufacturing Group	30,378	33,165	18,458	19,996
See's Candies	39,580	34,235	23,892	20,626
Wesco – other than Insurance	12,441	13,008	9,676	9,810
World Book	31,896	25,583	20,420	16,372
Amortization of Goodwill	(3,476)	(3,387)	(3,461)	(3,372)
Other Purchase-Price Accounting Charges	(5,951)	(5,740)	(6,856)	(6,668)
Interest Expense*	(76,374)	(42,389)	(49,726)	(27,098)
Shareholder-Designated Contributions	(5,824)	(5,867)	(3,801)	(3,814)
Other	58,309	23,755	35,782	12,863
Operating Earnings	482,477	393,414	370,745	299,902
Sales of Securities	33,989	223,810	23,348	147,575
Total Earnings – All Entities	$516,466	$617,224	$394,093	$447,477

Excludes interest expense of Scott Fetzer Financial Group and Mutual Savings & Loan.

We refer you also to pages 47-53, where we have rearranged Berkshire's financial data into four segments. These correspond to the way Charlie and I think about the business and should help you more in estimating Berkshire's intrinsic value than consolidated figures would do. Shown on these pages are balance sheets and earnings statements for: (1) our insurance operations, with their major investment positions itemized; (2) our manufacturing, publishing and retailing businesses, leaving aside certain non- operating assets and purchase-price accounting adjustments; (3) our subsidiaries engaged in finance-type operations, which are Mutual Savings and Scott Fetzer Financial; and (4) an all-other category that includes the non-operating assets (primarily marketable securities) held by the companies in segment (2), all purchase- price accounting adjustments, and various assets and debts of the Wesco and Berkshire parent companies.

If you combine the earnings and net worths of these four segments, you will derive totals matching those shown on our GAAP statements. However, I want to emphasize that this four-category presentation does not fall within the purview of our auditors, who in no way bless it.

"Look-Through" Earnings

The term "earnings" has a precise ring to it. And when an earnings figure is accompanied by an unqualified auditor's certificate, a naive reader might think it comparable in certitude to pi, calculated to dozens of decimal places.

In reality, however, earnings can be as pliable as putty when a charlatan heads the company reporting them. Eventually truth will surface, but in the meantime a lot of money can change hands. Indeed, some important American fortunes have been created by the monetization of accounting mirages.

Funny business in accounting is not new. For connoisseurs of chicanery, I have attached as Appendix A on page 22 a previously unpublished satire on accounting practices written by Ben Graham in 1936. Alas, excesses similar to those he then lampooned have many times since found their way into the financial statements of major American corporations and been duly certified by big-name auditors. Clearly, investors must always keep their guard up and use accounting numbers as a beginning, not an end, in their attempts to calculate true "economic earnings" accruing to them.

Berkshire's own reported earnings are misleading in a different, but important, way: We have huge investments in companies ("investees") whose earnings far exceed their dividends and in which we record our share of earnings only to the extent of the dividends we receive. The extreme case is Capital Cities/ABC, Inc. Our 17% share of the company's earnings amounted to more than $83 million last year. Yet only about $530,000 ($600,000 of dividends it paid us less some $70,000 of tax) is counted in Berkshire's GAAP earnings. The residual $82 million-plus stayed with Cap Cities as retained earnings, which work for our benefit but go unrecorded on our books.

Our perspective on such "forgotten-but-not-gone" earnings is simple: The way they are accounted for is of no importance, but their ownership and subsequent utilization is all-important. We care not whether the auditors hear a tree fall in the forest; we do care who owns the tree and what's next done with it.

When Coca-Cola uses retained earnings to repurchase its shares, the company increases our percentage ownership in what I regard to be the most valuable franchise in the world. (Coke also, of course, uses retained earnings in many other value-enhancing ways.) Instead of repurchasing stock, Coca-Cola could pay those funds to us in dividends, which we could then use to purchase more Coke shares. That would be a less efficient scenario: Because of taxes we would pay on dividend income, we would not be able to increase our proportionate ownership to the degree that Coke can, acting for us. If this less efficient procedure were followed, however, Berkshire would report far greater "earnings."

I believe the best way to think about our earnings is in terms of "look-through" results, calculated as follows: Take $250 million, which is roughly our share of the 1990 operating earnings retained by our investees; subtract $30 million, for the incremental taxes we would have owed had that $250 million been paid to us in dividends; and add the remainder, $220 million, to our reported operating earnings of $371 million. Thus our 1990 "look-through earnings" were about $590 million.

As I mentioned last year, we hope to have look-through earnings grow about 15% annually. In 1990 we substantially exceeded that rate but in 1991 we will fall far short of it. Our Gillette preferred has been called and we will convert it into common stock on April 1. This will reduce reported earnings by about $35 million annually and look-through earnings by a much smaller, but still significant, amount. Additionally, our media earnings—both direct and look-through—appear sure to decline. Whatever the results, we will post you annually on how we are doing on a look-through basis.

Non-Insurance Operations

Take another look at the figures on page 51, which aggregate the earnings and balance sheets of our non-insurance operations. After-tax earnings on average equity in 1990 were 51%, a result that would have placed the group about 20th on the 1989 Fortune 500.

Two factors make this return even more remarkable. First, leverage did not produce it: Almost all our major facilities are owned, not leased, and such small debt as these operations have is basically offset by cash they hold. In fact, if the measurement was return on assets—a calculation that eliminates the effect of debt upon returns—our group would rank in Fortune's top ten.

Equally important, our return was not earned from industries, such as cigarettes or network television stations, possessing spectacular economics for all participating in them. Instead it came from a group of businesses operating in such prosaic fields as furniture retailing, candy, vacuum cleaners, and even steel warehousing. The explanation is clear: Our extraordinary returns flow from outstanding operating managers, not fortuitous industry economics.

Let's look at the larger operations:

- It was a poor year for retailing—particularly for big-ticket items—but someone forgot to tell Ike Friedman at Borsheim's. Sales were up 18%. That's both a same-stores and all-stores percentage, since Borsheim's operates but one establishment.

But, oh, what an establishment! We can't be sure about the fact (because most fine-jewelry retailers are privately owned) but we believe that this jewelry store does more volume than any other in the U.S., except for Tiffany's New York store.

Borsheim's could not do nearly that well if our customers came only from the Omaha metropolitan area, whose population is about 600,000. We have long had a huge percentage of greater Omaha's jewelry business, so growth in that market is necessarily limited. But every year business from non-Midwest customers grows dramatically. Many visit the store in person. A large number of others, however, buy through the mail in a manner you will find interesting.

These customers request a jewelry selection of a certain type and value—say, emeralds in the $10,000 - $20,000 range—and we then send them five to ten items meeting their specifications and from which they can pick. Last year we mailed about 1,500 assortments of all kinds, carrying values ranging from under $1,000 to hundreds of thousands of dollars.

The selections are sent all over the country, some to people no one at Borsheim's has ever met. (They must always have been well recommended, however.) While the number of mailings in 1990 was a record, Ike has been sending merchandise far and wide for decades. Misanthropes will be crushed to learn how well our "honor-system" works: We have yet to experience a loss from customer dishonesty.

We attract business nationwide because we have several advantages that competitors can't match. The most important item in the equation is our operating costs, which run about 18% of sales compared to 40% or so at the typical competitor. (Included in the 18% are occupancy and buying costs, which some public companies include in "cost of goods sold.") Just as Wal-Mart, with its 15% operating costs, sells at prices that high-cost competitors can't touch and thereby constantly increases its market share, so does Borsheim's. What works with diapers works with diamonds.

Our low prices create huge volume that in turn allows us to carry an extraordinarily broad inventory of goods, running ten or more times the size of that at the typical fine-jewelry store. Couple our breadth of selection and low prices with superb service and you can understand how Ike and his family have built a national jewelry phenomenon from an Omaha location.

And family it is. Ike's crew always includes son Alan and sons-in-law Marvin Cohn and Donald Yale. And when things are busy—that's often—they are joined by Ike's wife, Roz, and his daughters, Janis and Susie. In addition, Fran Blumkin, wife of Louie (Chairman of Nebraska Furniture Mart and Ike's cousin), regularly pitches in. Finally, you'll find Ike's 89-year-old mother, Rebecca, in the store most afternoons, Wall Street Journal in hand. Given a family commitment like this, is it any surprise that Borsheim's runs rings around competitors whose managers are thinking about how soon 5 o'clock will arrive?

- While Fran Blumkin was helping the Friedman family set records at Borsheim's, her sons, Irv and Ron, along with husband Louie, were setting records at The Nebraska Furniture Mart. Sales at our one-and-only location were $159 million, up 4% from 1989. Though again the fact can't be conclusively proved, we believe NFM does close to double the volume of any other home furnishings store in the country.

The NFM formula for success parallels that of Borsheim's. First, operating costs are rock-bottom—15% in 1990 against about 40% for Levitz, the country's largest furniture retailer, and 25% for Circuit City Stores, the leading discount retailer of electronics and appliances. Second, NFM's low costs allow the business to price well below all competitors. Indeed, major chains, knowing what they will face, steer clear of Omaha. Third, the huge volume generated by our bargain prices allows us to carry the broadest selection of merchandise available anywhere.

Some idea of NFM's merchandising power can be gleaned from a recent report of consumer behavior in Des Moines, which showed that NFM was Number 3 in popularity among 20 furniture retailers serving that city. That may sound like no big deal until you consider that 19 of those retailers are located in Des Moines, whereas our store is 130 miles away. This leaves customers driving a distance equal to that between Washington and Philadelphia in order to shop with us, even though they have a multitude of alternatives next door. In effect, NFM, like Borsheim's, has dramatically expanded the territory it serves—not by the traditional method of opening new stores but rather by creating an irresistible magnet that employs price and selection to pull in the crowds.

Last year at the Mart there occurred an historic event: I experienced a counterrevelation. Regular readers of this report know that I have long scorned the boasts of corporate executives about synergy, deriding such claims as the last refuge of scoundrels defending foolish acquisitions. But now I know better: In Berkshire's first synergistic explosion, NFM put a See's candy cart in the store late last year and sold more candy than that moved by some of the full-fledged stores See's operates in California. This success contradicts all tenets of retailing. With the Blumkins, though, the impossible is routine.

- At See's, physical volume set a record in 1990—but only barely and only because of good sales early in the year. After the invasion of Kuwait, mall traffic in the West fell. Our poundage volume at Christmas dropped slightly, though our dollar sales were up because of a 5% price increase.

That increase, and better control of expenses, improved profit margins. Against the backdrop of a weak retailing environment, Chuck Huggins delivered outstanding results, as he has in each of the nineteen years we have owned See's. Chuck's imprint on the business—a virtual fanaticism about quality and service—is visible at all of our 225 stores.

One happening in 1990 illustrates the close bond between See's and its customers. After 15 years of operation, our store in Albuquerque was endangered: The landlord would not renew our lease, wanting us instead to move to an inferior location in the mall and even so to pay a much higher rent. These changes would have wiped out the store's profit. After extended negotiations got us nowhere, we set a date for closing the store.

On her own, the store's manager, Ann Filkins, then took action, urging customers to protest the closing. Some 263 responded by sending letters and making phone calls to See's headquarters in San Francisco, in some cases threatening to boycott the mall. An alert reporter at the Albuquerque paper picked up the story. Supplied with this evidence of a consumer uprising, our landlord offered us a satisfactory deal. (He, too, proved susceptible to a counterrevelation.)

Chuck subsequently wrote personal letters of thanks to every loyalist and sent each a gift certificate. He repeated his thanks in a newspaper ad that listed the names of all 263. The sequel: Christmas sales in Albuquerque were up substantially.

- Charlie and I were surprised at developments this past year in the media industry, including newspapers such as our Buffalo News. The business showed far more vulnerability to the early stages of a recession than has been the case in the past. The question is whether this erosion is just part of an aberrational cycle—to be fully made up in the next upturn—or whether the business has slipped in a way that permanently reduces intrinsic business values.

Since I didn't predict what *has* happened, you may question the value of my prediction about what *will* happen. Nevertheless, I'll proffer a judgment: While many media businesses will remain economic marvels in comparison with American industry generally, they will prove considerably less marvelous than I, the industry, or lenders thought would be the case only a few years ago.

The reason media businesses have been so outstanding in the past was not physical growth, but rather the unusual pricing power that most participants wielded. Now, however, advertising dollars are growing slowly. In addition, retailers that do little or no media advertising (though they sometimes use the Postal Service) have gradually taken market share in certain merchandise categories. Most important of all, the number of both print and electronic advertising channels has substantially increased. As a consequence, advertising dollars are more widely dispersed and the pricing power of ad vendors has diminished. These circumstances materially reduce the intrinsic value of our major media investments and also the value of our operating unit, Buffalo News—though all remain fine businesses.

Notwithstanding the problems, Stan Lipsey's management of the News continues to be superb. During 1990, our earnings held up much better than those of most metropolitan papers, falling only 5%. In the last few months of the year, however, the rate of decrease was far greater.

I can safely make two promises about the News in 1991: (1) Stan will again rank at the top among newspaper publishers; and (2) earnings will fall substantially. Despite a slowdown in the demand for newsprint, the price per ton will average significantly more in 1991 and the paper's labor costs will also be considerably higher. Since revenues may meanwhile be down, we face a real squeeze.

Profits may be off but our pride in the product remains. We continue to have a larger "news hole"—the portion of the paper devoted to news—than any comparable paper. In 1990, the proportion rose to 52.3% against 50.1% in 1989. Alas, the increase resulted from a decline in advertising pages rather than from a gain in news pages. Regardless of earnings pressures, we will maintain at least a 50% news hole. Cutting product quality is not a proper response to adversity.

- The news at Fechheimer, our manufacturer and retailer of uniforms, is all good with one exception: George Heldman, at 69, has decided to retire. I tried to talk him out of it but he had one irrefutable argument: With four other Heldmans—Bob, Fred, Gary and Roger—to carry on, he was leaving us with an abundance of managerial talent.

Fechheimer's operating performance improved considerably in 1990, as many of the problems we encountered in integrating the large acquisition we made in 1988 were moderated or solved. However, several unusual items caused the earnings reported in the "Sources" table to be flat. In the retail operation, we continue to add stores and now have 42 in 22 states. Overall, prospects appear excellent for Fechheimer.

- At Scott Fetzer, Ralph Schey runs 19 businesses with a mastery few bring to running one. In addition to overseeing three entities listed on page 6—World Book, Kirby, and Scott Fetzer Manufacturing—Ralph directs a finance operation that earned a record $12.2 million pre-tax in 1990.

Were Scott Fetzer an independent company, it would rank close to the top of the Fortune 500 in terms of return on equity, although it is not in businesses that one would expect to be economic champs. The superior results are directly attributable to Ralph.

At World Book, earnings improved on a small decrease in unit volume. The costs of our decentralization move were considerably less in 1990 than 1989 and the benefits of decentralization are being realized. World Book remains far and away the leader in United States encyclopedia sales and we are growing internationally, though from a small base.

Kirby unit volume grew substantially in 1990 with the help of our new vacuum cleaner, The Generation 3, which was an unqualified success. Earnings did not grow as fast as sales because of both start-up expenditures and "learning-curve" problems we encountered in manufacturing the new product. International business, whose dramatic growth I described last year, had a further 20% sales gain in 1990. With the aid of a recent price increase, we expect excellent earnings at Kirby in 1991.

Within the Scott Fetzer Manufacturing Group, Campbell Hausfeld, its largest unit, had a particularly fine year. This company, the country's leading producer of small and medium-sized air compressors, achieved record sales of $109 million, more than 30% of which came from products introduced during the last five years.

* * * * * * * * * * * *

In looking at the figures for our non-insurance operations, you will see that net worth increased by only $47 million in 1990 although earnings were $133 million. This does not mean that our managers are in any way skimping on investments that strengthen their business franchises or that promote growth. Indeed, they diligently pursue both goals.

But they also never deploy capital without good reason. The result: In the past five years they have funneled well over 80% of their earnings to Charlie and me for use in new business and investment opportunities.

Insurance Operations

Shown below is an updated version of our usual table presenting key figures for the property-casualty insurance industry:

	Yearly Change in Premiums Written (%)	Statutory Combined Ratio After Policyholder Dividends	Yearly Change in Incurred Losses (%)	Inflation Rate Measured by GNP Deflator (%)
1981	3.8	106.0	6.5	9.6
1982	3.7	109.6	8.4	6.5
1983	5.0	112.0	6.8	3.8
1984	8.5	118.0	16.9	3.8
1985	22.1	116.3	16.1	3.0
1986	22.2	108.0	13.5	2.6
1987	9.4	104.6	7.8	3.1
1988	4.4	105.4	5.5	3.3
1989 (Revised)	3.2	109.2	7.7	4.1
1990 (Est.)	4.5	109.8	5.0	4.1

Source: A.M. Best Co.

The combined ratio represents total insurance costs (losses incurred plus expenses) compared to revenue from premiums: A ratio below 100 indicates an underwriting profit, and one above 100 indicates a loss. The higher the ratio, the worse the year. When the investment income that an insurer earns from holding policyholders' funds ("the float") is taken into account, a combined ratio in the 107—111 range typically produces an overall breakeven result, exclusive of earnings on the funds provided by shareholders.

For the reasons laid out in previous reports, we expect the industry's incurred losses to grow at an average of 10% annually, even in periods when general inflation runs considerably lower. (Over the last 25 years, incurred losses have in reality grown at a still faster rate, 11%.) If premium growth meanwhile materially lags that 10% rate, underwriting losses will mount, though the industry's tendency to under-reserve when business turns bad may obscure their size for a time.

Last year premium growth fell far short of the required 10% and underwriting results therefore worsened. (In our table, however, the severity of the deterioration in 1990 is masked because the industry's 1989 losses from Hurricane Hugo caused the ratio for that year to be somewhat above trendline.) The combined ratio will again increase in 1991, probably by about two points.

Results will improve only when most insurance managements become so fearful that they run from business, even though it can be done at much higher prices than now exist. At some point these managements will indeed get the message: The most important thing to do when you find yourself in a hole is to stop digging. But so far that point hasn't gotten across: Insurance managers continue to dig—sullenly but vigorously.

The picture would change quickly if a major physical or financial catastrophe were to occur. Absent such a shock, one to two years will likely pass before underwriting losses become large enough to raise management fear to a level that would spur major price increases. When that moment arrives, Berkshire will be ready—both financially and psychologically—to write huge amounts of business.

In the meantime, our insurance volume continues to be small but satisfactory. In the next section of this report we will give you a framework for evaluating insurance results. From that discussion, you will gain an understanding of why I am so enthusiastic about the performance of our insurance manager, Mike Goldberg, and his cadre of stars, Rod Eldred, Dinos Iordanou, Ajit Jain, and Don Wurster.

In assessing our insurance results over the next few years, you should be aware of one type of business we are pursuing that could cause them to be unusually volatile. If this line of business expands, as it may, our underwriting experience will deviate from the trendline you might expect: In most years we will somewhat exceed expectations and in an occasional year we will fall far below them.

The volatility I predict reflects the fact that we have become a large seller of insurance against truly major catastrophes ("super-cats"), which could for example be hurricanes, windstorms or earthquakes. The buyers of these policies are reinsurance companies that themselves are in the business of writing catastrophe coverage for primary insurers and that wish to "lay off," or rid themselves, of part of their exposure to catastrophes of special severity. Because the need for these buyers to collect on such a policy will only arise at times of extreme stress—perhaps even chaos—in the insurance business, they seek financially strong sellers. And here we have a major competitive advantage: In the industry, our strength is unmatched.

A typical super-cat contract is complicated. But in a plain-vanilla instance we might write a one-year, $10 million policy providing that the buyer, a reinsurer, would be paid that sum only if a catastrophe caused two results: (1) specific losses for the reinsurer above a threshold amount; and (2) aggregate losses for the insurance industry of, say, more than $5 billion. Under virtually all circumstances, loss levels that satisfy the second condition will also have caused the first to be met.

For this $10 million policy, we might receive a premium of, say, $3 million. Say, also, that we take in annual premiums of $100 million from super-cat policies of all kinds. In that case we are very likely in any given year to report either a profit of close to $100 million or a loss of well over $200 million. Note that we are not spreading risk as insurers typically do; we are concentrating it. Therefore, our yearly combined ratio on this business will almost never fall in the industry range of 100—120, but will instead be close to either zero or 300%.

Most insurers are financially unable to tolerate such swings. And if they have the ability to do so, they often lack the desire. They may back away, for example, because they write gobs of primary property insurance that would deliver them dismal results at the very time they would be experiencing major losses on super- cat reinsurance. In addition, most corporate managements believe that their shareholders dislike volatility in results.

We can take a different tack: Our business in primary property insurance is small and we believe that Berkshire shareholders, if properly informed, can handle unusual volatility in profits so long as the swings carry with them the prospect of superior long-term results. (Charlie and I always have preferred a lumpy 15% return to a smooth 12%.)

We want to emphasize three points: (1) While we expect our super-cat business to produce satisfactory results over, say, a decade, we're sure it will produce absolutely terrible results in at least an occasional year; (2) Our expectations can be based on little more than subjective judgments—for this kind of insurance, historical loss data are of very limited value to us as we decide what rates to charge today; and (3) Though we expect to write significant quantities of super-cat business, we will do so only at prices we believe to be commensurate with risk. If competitors become optimistic, our volume will fall. This insurance has, in fact, tended in recent years to be woefully underpriced; most sellers have left the field on stretchers.

At the moment, we believe Berkshire to be the largest U.S. writer of super-cat business. So when a major quake occurs in an urban area or a winter storm rages across Europe, light a candle for us.

Measuring Insurance Performance

In the previous section I mentioned "float," the funds of others that insurers, in the conduct of their business, temporarily hold. Because these funds are available to be invested, the typical property-casualty insurer can absorb losses and expenses that exceed premiums by 7% to 11% and still be able to break even on its business. Again, this calculation excludes the earnings the insurer realizes on net worth—that is, on the funds provided by shareholders.

However, many exceptions to this 7% to 11% range exist. For example, insurance covering losses to crops from hail damage produces virtually no float at all. Premiums on this kind of business are paid to the insurer just prior to the time hailstorms are a threat, and if a farmer sustains a loss he will be paid almost immediately. Thus, a combined ratio of 100 for crop hail insurance produces no profit for the insurer.

At the other extreme, malpractice insurance covering the potential liabilities of doctors, lawyers and accountants produces a very high amount of float compared to annual premium volume. The float materializes because claims are often brought long after the alleged wrongdoing takes place and because their payment may be still further delayed by lengthy litigation. The industry calls malpractice and certain other kinds of liability insurance "long-tail" business, in recognition of the extended period during which insurers get to hold large sums that in the end will go to claimants and their lawyers (and to the *insurer's* lawyers as well).

In long-tail situations a combined ratio of 115 (or even more) can prove profitable, since earnings produced by the float will exceed the 15% by which claims and expenses overrun premiums. The catch, though, is that "long-tail" means exactly that: Liability business written in a given year and presumed at first to have produced a combined ratio of 115 may eventually smack the insurer with 200, 300 or worse when the years have rolled by and all claims have finally been settled.

The pitfalls of this business mandate an operating principle that too often is ignored: Though certain long-tail lines may prove profitable at combined ratios of 110 or 115, insurers will invariably find it unprofitable to price using those ratios as targets. Instead, prices must provide a healthy margin of safety against the societal trends that are forever springing expensive surprises on the insurance industry. Setting a target of 100 can itself result in heavy losses; aiming for 110—115 is business suicide.

All of that said, what should the measure of an insurer's profitability be? Analysts and managers customarily look to the combined ratio—and it's true that this yardstick usually is a good indicator of where a company ranks in profitability. We believe a better measure, however, to be a comparison of underwriting loss to float developed.

This loss/float ratio, like any statistic used in evaluating insurance results, is meaningless over short time periods: Quarterly underwriting figures and even annual ones are too heavily based on estimates to be much good. But when the ratio takes in a period of years, it gives a rough indication of the cost of funds generated by insurance operations. A low cost of funds signifies a good business; a high cost translates into a poor business.

On the next page we show the underwriting loss, if any, of our insurance group in each year since we entered the business and relate that bottom line to the average float we have held during the year. From this data we have computed a "cost of funds developed from insurance."

	(1) Underwriting Loss *(In $ Millions)*	(2) Average Float	Approximate Cost of Funds *(Ratio of 1 to 2)*	Yearend Yield on Long-Term Govt. Bonds
1967	profit	$17.3	less than zero	5.50%
1968	profit	19.9	less than zero	5.90%
1969	profit	23.4	less than zero	6.79%
1970	$0.37	32.4	1.14%	6.25%
1971	profit	52.5	less than zero	5.81%
1972	profit	69.5	less than zero	5.82%
1973	profit	73.3	less than zero	7.27%
1974	7.36	79.1	9.30%	8.13%
1975	11.35	87.6	12.96%	8.03%
1976	profit	102.6	less than zero	7.30%
1977	profit	139.0	less than zero	7.97%
1978	profit	190.4	less than zero	8.93%
1979	profit	227.3	less than zero	10.08%
1980	profit	237.0	less than zero	11.94%
1981	profit	228.4	less than zero	13.61%
1982	21.56	220.6	9.77%	10.64%
1983	33.87	231.3	14.64%	11.84%
1984	48.06	253.2	18.98%	11.58%
1985	44.23	390.2	11.34%	9.34%
1986	55.84	797.5	7.00%	7.60%
1987	55.43	1,266.7	4.38%	8.95%
1988	11.08	1,497.7	0.74%	9.00%
1989	24.40	1,541.3	1.58%	7.97%
1990	26.65	1,637.3	1.63%	8.24%

The float figures are derived from the total of loss reserves, loss adjustment expense reserves and unearned premium reserves minus agents' balances, prepaid acquisition costs and deferred charges applicable to assumed reinsurance. At some insurers other items should enter into the calculation, but in our case these are unimportant and have been ignored.

During 1990 we held about $1.6 billion of float slated eventually to find its way into the hands of others. The underwriting loss we sustained during the year was $27 million and thus our insurance operation produced funds for us at a cost of about 1.6%. As the table shows, we managed in some years to underwrite at a profit and in those instances our cost of funds was less than zero. In other years, such as 1984, we paid a very high price for float. In 19 years out of the 24 we have been in insurance, though, we have developed funds at a cost below that paid by the government.

There are two important qualifications to this calculation. First, the fat lady has yet to gargle, let alone sing, and we won't know our true 1967—1990 cost of funds until all losses from this period have been settled many decades from now. Second, the value of the float to shareholders is somewhat undercut by the fact that they must put up their own funds to support the insurance operation and are subject to double taxation on the investment income these funds earn. Direct investments would be more tax-efficient.

The tax penalty that indirect investments impose on shareholders is in fact substantial. Though the calculation is necessarily imprecise, I would estimate that the owners of the average insurance company would find the tax penalty adds about one percentage point to their cost of float. I also think that approximates the correct figure for Berkshire.

Figuring a cost of funds for an insurance business allows anyone analyzing it to determine whether the operation has a positive or negative value for shareholders. If this cost (including the tax penalty) is higher than that applying to alternative sources of funds, the value is negative. If the cost is lower, the value is positive—and if the cost is *significantly* lower, the insurance business qualifies as a very valuable asset.

So far Berkshire has fallen into the significantly-lower camp. Even more dramatic are the numbers at GEICO, in which our ownership interest is now 48% and which customarily operates at an underwriting profit. GEICO's growth has generated an ever-larger amount of funds for investment that have an effective cost of considerably less than zero. Essentially, GEICO's policyholders, in aggregate, pay the company interest on the float rather than the other way around. (But handsome is as handsome does: GEICO's unusual profitability results from its extraordinary operating efficiency and its careful classification of risks, a package that in turn allows rock-bottom prices for policyholders.)

Many well-known insurance companies, on the other hand, incur an underwriting loss/float cost that, combined with the tax penalty, produces negative results for owners. In addition, these companies, like all others in the industry, are vulnerable to catastrophe losses that could exceed their reinsurance protection and take their cost of float right off the chart. Unless these companies can materially improve their underwriting performance—and history indicates that is an almost impossible task—their shareholders will experience results similar to those borne by the owners of a bank that pays a higher rate of interest on deposits than it receives on loans.

All in all, the insurance business has treated us very well. We have expanded our float at a cost that on the average is reasonable, and we have further prospered because we have earned good returns on these low-cost funds. Our shareholders, true, have incurred extra taxes, but they have been more than compensated for this cost (so far) by the benefits produced by the float.

A particularly encouraging point about our record is that it was achieved despite some colossal mistakes made by your Chairman prior to Mike Goldberg's arrival. Insurance offers a host of opportunities for error, and when opportunity knocked, too often I answered. Many years later, the bills keep arriving for these mistakes: In the insurance business, there is no statute of limitations on stupidity.

The intrinsic value of our insurance business will always be far more difficult to calculate than the value of, say, our candy or newspaper companies. By any measure, however, the business is worth far more than its carrying value. Furthermore, despite the problems this operation periodically hands us, it is the one—among all the fine businesses we own—that has the greatest potential.

Marketable Securities

Below we list our common stock holdings having a value of over $100 million. A small portion of these investments belongs to subsidiaries of which Berkshire owns less than 100%.

Shares	Company	Cost	Market
		(000s omitted)	
3,000,000	Capital Cities/ABC, Inc.	$517,500	$1,377,375
46,700,000	The Coca-Cola Co.	1,023,920	2,171,550
2,400,000	Federal Home Loan Mortgage Corp.	71,729	117,000
6,850,000	GEICO Corp.	45,713	1,110,556
1,727,765	The Washington Post Company	9,731	342,097
5,000,000	Wells Fargo & Company	289,431	289,375

11

Lethargy bordering on sloth remains the cornerstone of our investment style: This year we neither bought nor sold a share of five of our six major holdings. The exception was Wells Fargo, a superbly-managed, high-return banking operation in which we increased our ownership to just under 10%, the most we can own without the approval of the Federal Reserve Board. About one-sixth of our position was bought in 1989, the rest in 1990.

The banking business is no favorite of ours. When assets are twenty times equity—a common ratio in this industry—mistakes that involve only a small portion of assets can destroy a major portion of equity. And mistakes have been the rule rather than the exception at many major banks. Most have resulted from a managerial failing that we described last year when discussing the "institutional imperative:" the tendency of executives to mindlessly imitate the behavior of their peers, no matter how foolish it may be to do so. In their lending, many bankers played follow-the-leader with lemming-like zeal; now they are experiencing a lemming-like fate.

Because leverage of 20:1 magnifies the effects of managerial strengths and weaknesses, we have no interest in purchasing shares of a poorly-managed bank at a "cheap" price. Instead, our only interest is in buying into well-managed banks at fair prices.

With Wells Fargo, we think we have obtained the best managers in the business, Carl Reichardt and Paul Hazen. In many ways the combination of Carl and Paul reminds me of another—Tom Murphy and Dan Burke at Capital Cities/ABC. First, each pair is stronger than the sum of its parts because each partner understands, trusts and admires the other. Second, both managerial teams pay able people well, but abhor having a bigger head count than is needed. Third, both attack costs as vigorously when profits are at record levels as when they are under pressure. Finally, both stick with what they understand and let their abilities, not their egos, determine what they attempt. (Thomas J. Watson Sr. of IBM followed the same rule: "I'm no genius," he said. "I'm smart in spots—but I stay around those spots.")

Our purchases of Wells Fargo in 1990 were helped by a chaotic market in bank stocks. The disarray was appropriate: Month by month the foolish loan decisions of once well-regarded banks were put on public display. As one huge loss after another was unveiled—often on the heels of managerial assurances that all was well—investors understandably concluded that no bank's numbers were to be trusted. Aided by their flight from bank stocks, we purchased our 10% interest in Wells Fargo for $290 million, less than five times after-tax earnings, and less than three times pre-tax earnings.

Wells Fargo is big—it has $56 billion in assets—and has been earning more than 20% on equity and 1.25% on assets. Our purchase of one-tenth of the bank may be thought of as roughly equivalent to our buying 100% of a $5 billion bank with identical financial characteristics. But were we to make such a purchase, we would have to pay about twice the $290 million we paid for Wells Fargo. Moreover, that $5 billion bank, commanding a premium price, would present us with another problem: We would not be able to find a Carl Reichardt to run it. In recent years, Wells Fargo executives have been more avidly recruited than any others in the banking business; no one, however, has been able to hire the dean.

Of course, ownership of a bank—or about any other business—is far from riskless. California banks face the specific risk of a major earthquake, which might wreak enough havoc on borrowers to in turn destroy the banks lending to them. A second risk is systemic—the possibility of a business contraction or financial panic so severe that it would endanger almost every highly-leveraged institution, no matter how intelligently run. Finally, the market's major fear of the moment is that West Coast real estate values will tumble because of overbuilding and deliver huge losses to banks that have financed the expansion. Because it is a leading real estate lender, Wells Fargo is thought to be particularly vulnerable.

None of these eventualities can be ruled out. The probability of the first two occurring, however, is low and even a meaningful drop in real estate values is unlikely to cause major problems for well-managed institutions. Consider some mathematics: Wells Fargo currently earns well over $1 billion pre-tax annually after expensing more than $300 million for loan losses. If 10% of all $48 billion of the bank's loans—not just its real estate loans—were hit by problems in 1991, and these produced losses (including foregone interest) averaging 30% of principal, the company would roughly break even.

A year like that—which we consider only a low-level possibility, not a likelihood—would not distress us. In fact, at Berkshire we would love to acquire businesses or invest in capital projects that produced no return for a year, but that could then be expected to earn 20% on growing equity. Nevertheless, fears of a California real estate disaster similar to that experienced in New England caused the price of Wells Fargo stock to fall almost 50% within a few months during 1990. Even though we had bought some shares at the prices prevailing before the fall, we welcomed the decline because it allowed us to pick up many more shares at the new, panic prices.

Investors who expect to be ongoing buyers of investments throughout their lifetimes should adopt a similar attitude toward market fluctuations; instead many illogically become euphoric when stock prices rise and unhappy when they fall. They show no such confusion in their reaction to food prices: Knowing they are forever going to be buyers of food, they welcome falling prices and deplore price increases. (It's the seller of food who doesn't like declining prices.) Similarly, at the Buffalo News we would cheer lower prices for newsprint—even though it would mean marking down the value of the large inventory of newsprint we always keep on hand—because we know we are going to be perpetually buying the product.

Identical reasoning guides our thinking about Berkshire's investments. We will be buying businesses—or small parts of businesses, called stocks—year in, year out as long as I live (and longer, if Berkshire's directors attend the seances I have scheduled). Given these intentions, declining prices for businesses benefit us, and rising prices hurt us.

The most common cause of low prices is pessimism—some times pervasive, some times specific to a company or industry. We *want* to do business in such an environment, not because we like pessimism but because we like the prices it produces. It's optimism that is the enemy of the rational buyer.

None of this means, however, that a business or stock is an intelligent purchase simply because it is unpopular; a contrarian approach is just as foolish as a follow-the-crowd strategy. What's required is thinking rather than polling. Unfortunately, Bertrand Russell's observation about life in general applies with unusual force in the financial world: "Most men would rather die than think. Many do."

* * * * * * * * * * * *

Our other major portfolio change last year was large additions to our holdings of RJR Nabisco bonds, securities that we first bought in late 1989. At yearend 1990 we had $440 million invested in these securities, an amount that approximated market value. (As I write this, however, their market value has risen by more than $150 million.)

Just as buying into the banking business is unusual for us, so is the purchase of below-investment-grade bonds. But opportunities that interest us and that are also large enough to have a worthwhile impact on Berkshire's results are rare. Therefore, we will look at any category of investment, so long as we understand the business we're buying into and believe that price and value may differ significantly. (Woody Allen, in another context, pointed out the advantage of open-mindedness: "I can't understand why more people aren't bi-sexual because it doubles your chances for a date on Saturday night.")

In the past we have bought a few below-investment-grade bonds with success, though these were all old-fashioned "fallen angels"—bonds that were initially of investment grade but that were downgraded when the issuers fell on bad times. In the 1984 annual report we described our rationale for buying one fallen angel, the Washington Public Power Supply System.

A kind of bastardized fallen angel burst onto the investment scene in the 1980s—"junk bonds" that were far below investment- grade when issued. As the decade progressed, new offerings of manufactured junk became ever junkier and ultimately the predictable outcome occurred: Junk bonds lived up to their name. In 1990—even before the recession dealt its blows—the financial sky became dark with the bodies of failing corporations.

The disciples of debt assured us that this collapse wouldn't happen: Huge debt, we were told, would cause operating managers to focus their efforts as never before, much as a dagger mounted on the steering wheel of a car could be expected to make its driver proceed with intensified care. We'll acknowledge that such an attention-getter would produce a very alert driver. But another certain consequence would be a deadly—and unnecessary—accident if the car hit even the tiniest pothole or sliver of ice. The roads of business are riddled with potholes; a plan that requires dodging them all is a plan for disaster.

In the final chapter of <u>The Intelligent Investor</u> Ben Graham forcefully rejected the dagger thesis: "Confronted with a challenge to distill the secret of sound investment into three words, we venture the motto, Margin of Safety." Forty-two years after reading that, I still think those are the right three words. The failure of investors to heed this simple message caused them staggering losses as the 1990s began.

At the height of the debt mania, capital structures were concocted that guaranteed failure: In some cases, so much debt was issued that even highly favorable business results could not produce the funds to service it. One particularly egregious "kill- 'em-at-birth" case a few years back involved the purchase of a mature television station in Tampa, bought with so much debt that the interest on it exceeded the station's *gross revenues*. Even if you assume that all labor, programs and services were donated rather than purchased, this capital structure required revenues to explode—or else the station was doomed to go broke. (Many of the bonds that financed the purchase were sold to now-failed savings and loan associations; as a taxpayer, you are picking up the tab for this folly.)

All of this seems impossible now. When these misdeeds were done, however, dagger-selling investment bankers pointed to the "scholarly" research of academics, which reported that over the years the higher interest rates received from low-grade bonds had more than compensated for their higher rate of default. Thus, said the friendly salesmen, a diversified portfolio of junk bonds would produce greater net returns than would a portfolio of high-grade bonds. (Beware of past-performance "proofs" in finance: If history books were the key to riches, the Forbes 400 would consist of librarians.)

There was a flaw in the salesmen's logic—one that a first- year student in statistics is taught to recognize. An assumption was being made that the universe of newly-minted junk bonds was identical to the universe of low-grade fallen angels and that, therefore, the default experience of the latter group was meaningful in predicting the default experience of the new issues. (That was an error similar to checking the historical death rate from Kool-Aid before drinking the version served at Jonestown.)

The universes were of course dissimilar in several vital respects. For openers, the manager of a fallen angel almost invariably yearned to regain investment-grade status and worked toward that goal. The junk-bond operator was usually an entirely different breed. Behaving much as a heroin user might, he devoted his energies not to finding a cure for his debt-ridden condition, but rather to finding another fix. Additionally, the fiduciary sensitivities of the executives managing the typical fallen angel were often, though not always, more finely developed than were those of the junk-bond-issuing financiopath.

Wall Street cared little for such distinctions. As usual, the Street's enthusiasm for an idea was proportional not to its merit, but rather to the revenue it would produce. Mountains of junk bonds were sold by those who didn't care to those who didn't think—and there was no shortage of either.

Junk bonds remain a mine field, even at prices that today are often a small fraction of issue price. As we said last year, we have never bought a new issue of a junk bond. (The only time to buy these is on a day with no "y" in it.) We are, however, willing to look at the field, now that it is in disarray.

In the case of RJR Nabisco, we feel the Company's credit is considerably better than was generally perceived for a while and that the yield we receive, as well as the potential for capital gain, more than compensates for the risk we incur (though that is far from nil). RJR has made asset sales at favorable prices, has added major amounts of equity, and in general is being run well.

However, as we survey the field, most low-grade bonds still look unattractive. The handiwork of the Wall Street of the 1980s is even worse than we had thought: Many important businesses have been mortally wounded. We will, though, keep looking for opportunities as the junk market continues to unravel.

Convertible Preferred Stocks

We continue to hold the convertible preferred stocks described in earlier reports: $700 million of Salomon Inc, $600 million of The Gillette Company, $358 million of USAir Group, Inc. and $300 million of Champion International Corp. Our Gillette holdings will be converted into 12 million shares of common stock on April 1. Weighing interest rates, credit quality and prices of the related common stocks, we can assess our holdings in Salomon and Champion at yearend 1990 as worth about what we paid, Gillette as worth somewhat more, and USAir as worth substantially less.

In making the USAir purchase, your Chairman displayed exquisite timing: I plunged into the business at almost the exact moment that it ran into severe problems. (No one pushed me; in tennis parlance, I committed an "unforced error.") The company's troubles were brought on both by industry conditions and by the post-merger difficulties it encountered in integrating Piedmont, an affliction I should have expected since almost all airline mergers have been followed by operational turmoil.

In short order, Ed Colodny and Seth Schofield resolved the second problem: The airline now gets excellent marks for service. Industry-wide problems have proved to be far more serious. Since our purchase, the economics of the airline industry have deteriorated at an alarming pace, accelerated by the kamikaze pricing tactics of certain carriers. The trouble this pricing has produced for all carriers illustrates an important truth: In a business selling a commodity-type product, it's impossible to be a lot smarter than your dumbest competitor.

However, unless the industry is decimated during the next few years, our USAir investment should work out all right. Ed and Seth have decisively addressed the current turbulence by making major changes in operations. Even so, our investment is now less secure than at the time I made it.

Our convertible preferred stocks are relatively simple securities, yet I should warn you that, if the past is any guide, you may from time to time read inaccurate or misleading statements about them. Last year, for example, several members of the press calculated the value of all our preferreds as equal to that of the common stock into which they are convertible. By their logic, that is, our Salomon preferred, convertible into common at $38, would be worth 60% of face value if Salomon common were selling at $22.80. But there is a small problem with this line of reasoning: Using it, one must conclude that all of the value of a convertible preferred resides in the conversion privilege and that the value of a *non*-convertible preferred of Salomon would be zero, no matter what its coupon or terms for redemption.

The point you should keep in mind is that most of the value of our convertible preferreds is derived from their fixed-income characteristics. That means the securities cannot be worth less than the value they would possess as non-convertible preferreds and may be worth more because of their conversion options.

* * * * * * * * * * * *

I deeply regret having to end this section of the report with a note about my friend, Colman Mockler, Jr., CEO of Gillette, who died in January. No description better fitted Colman than "gentleman"—a word signifying integrity, courage and modesty. Couple these qualities with the humor and exceptional business ability that Colman possessed and you can understand why I thought it an undiluted pleasure to work with him and why I, and all others who knew him, will miss Colman so much.

A few days before Colman died, Gillette was richly praised in a Forbes cover story. Its theme was simple: The company's success in shaving products has come not from marketing savvy (though it exhibits that talent repeatedly) but has instead resulted from its devotion to quality. This mind-set has caused it to consistently focus its energies on coming up with something better, even though its existing products already ranked as the class of the field. In so depicting Gillette, Forbes in fact painted a portrait of Colman.

Help! Help!

Regular readers know that I shamelessly utilize the annual letter in an attempt to acquire businesses for Berkshire. And, as we constantly preach at the Buffalo News, advertising does work: Several businesses have knocked on our door because someone has read in these pages of our interest in making acquisitions. (Any good ad salesman will tell you that trying to sell something without advertising is like winking at a girl in the dark.)

In Appendix B (on pages 26-27) I've reproduced the essence of a letter I wrote a few years back to the owner/manager of a desirable business. If you have no personal connection with a business that might be of interest to us but have a friend who does, perhaps you can pass this report along to him.

Here's the sort of business we are looking for:

(1) Large purchases (at least $10 million of after-tax earnings),

(2) Demonstrated consistent earning power (future projections are of little interest to us, nor are "turnaround" situations),

(3) Businesses earning good returns on equity while employing little or no debt,

(4) Management in place (we can't supply it),

(5) Simple businesses (if there's lots of technology, we won't understand it),

(6) An offering price (we don't want to waste our time or that of the seller by talking, even preliminarily, about a transaction when price is unknown).

We will not engage in unfriendly takeovers. We can promise complete confidentiality and a very fast answer—customarily within five minutes—as to whether we're interested. We prefer to buy for cash, but will consider issuing stock when we receive as much in intrinsic business value as we give.

Our favorite form of purchase is one fitting the Blumkin- Friedman-Heldman mold. In cases like these, the company's owner- managers wish to generate significant amounts of cash, sometimes for themselves, but often for their families or inactive shareholders. At the same time, these managers wish to remain significant owners who continue to run their companies just as they have in the past. We think we offer a particularly good fit for owners with such objectives. We invite potential sellers to check us out by contacting people with whom we have done business in the past.

Charlie and I frequently get approached about acquisitions that don't come close to meeting our tests: We've found that if you advertise an interest in buying collies, a lot of people will call hoping to sell you their cocker spaniels. A line from a country song expresses our feeling about new ventures, turnarounds, or auction-like sales: "When the phone don't ring, you'll know it's me."

Besides being interested in the purchase of businesses as described above, we are also interested in the negotiated purchase of large, but not controlling, blocks of stock comparable to those we hold in Capital Cities, Salomon, Gillette, USAir, and Champion. We are not interested, however, in receiving suggestions about purchases we might make in the general stock market.

Miscellaneous

Ken Chace has decided not to stand for reelection as a director at our upcoming annual meeting. We have no mandatory retirement age for directors at Berkshire (and won't!), but Ken, at 75 and living in Maine, simply decided to cut back his activities.

Ken was my immediate choice to run the textile operation after Buffett Partnership, Ltd. assumed control of Berkshire early in 1965. Although I made an economic mistake in sticking with the textile business, I made no mistake in choosing Ken: He ran the operation well, he was always 100% straight with me about its problems, and he generated the funds that allowed us to diversify into insurance.

16

My wife, Susan, will be nominated to succeed Ken. She is now the second largest shareholder of Berkshire and if she outlives me will inherit all of my stock and effectively control the company. She knows, and agrees, with my thoughts on successor management and also shares my view that neither Berkshire nor its subsidiary businesses and important investments should be sold simply because some very high bid is received for one or all.

I feel strongly that the fate of our businesses and their managers should not depend on my health—which, it should be added, is excellent—and I have planned accordingly. Neither my estate plan nor that of my wife is designed to preserve the family fortune; instead, both are aimed at preserving the character of Berkshire and returning the fortune to society.

Were I to die tomorrow, you could be sure of three things: (1) None of my stock would have to be sold; (2) Both a controlling shareholder and a manager with philosophies similar to mine would follow me; and (3) Berkshire's earnings would increase by $1 million annually, since Charlie would immediately sell our corporate jet, The Indefensible (ignoring my wish that it be buried with me).

* * * * * * * * * * * *

About 97.3% of all eligible shares participated in Berkshire's 1990 shareholder-designated contributions program. Contributions made through the program were $5.8 million, and 2,600 charities were recipients.

We suggest that new shareholders read the description of our shareholder-designated contributions program that appears on pages 54-55. To participate in future programs, you must make sure your shares are registered in the name of the actual owner, not in the nominee name of a broker, bank or depository. Shares not so registered on August 31, 1991 will be ineligible for the 1991 program.

In addition to the shareholder-designated contributions that Berkshire distributes, managers of our operating businesses make contributions, including merchandise, averaging about $1.5 million annually. These contributions support local charities, such as The United Way, and produce roughly commensurate benefits for our businesses.

However, neither our operating managers nor officers of the parent company use Berkshire funds to make contributions to broad national programs or charitable activities of special personal interest to them, except to the extent they do so as shareholders. If your employees, including your CEO, wish to give to their alma maters or other institutions to which they feel a personal attachment, we believe they should use their own money, not yours.

* * * * * * * * * * * *

The annual meeting this year will be held at the Orpheum Theater in downtown Omaha at 9:30 a.m. on Monday, April 29, 1991. Attendance last year grew to a record 1,300, about a 100-fold increase from ten years ago.

We recommend getting your hotel reservations early at one of these hotels: (1) The Radisson-Redick Tower, a small (88 rooms) but nice hotel across the street from the Orpheum; (2) the much larger Red Lion Hotel, located about a five-minute walk from the Orpheum; or (3) the Marriott, located in West Omaha about 100 yards from Borsheim's and a twenty minute drive from downtown. We will have buses at the Marriott that will leave at 8:30 and 8:45 for the meeting, and return after it ends.

Charlie and I always enjoy the meeting, and we hope you can make it. The quality of our shareholders is reflected in the quality of the questions we get: We have never attended an annual meeting anywhere that features such a consistently high level of intelligent, owner-related questions.

An attachment to our proxy material explains how you can obtain the card you will need for admission to the meeting. Because weekday parking can be tight around the Orpheum, we have lined up a number of nearby lots for our shareholders to use. The attachment also contains information about them.

As usual, we will have buses to take you to Nebraska Furniture Mart and Borsheim's after the meeting and to take you to downtown hotels or to the airport later. I hope that you will allow plenty of time to fully explore the attractions of both stores. Those of you arriving early can visit the Furniture Mart any day of the week; it is open from 10 a.m. to 5:30 p.m. on Saturdays, and from noon to 5:30 p.m. on Sundays. While there, stop at the See's Candy cart and see for yourself the dawn of synergism at Berkshire.

Borsheim's normally is closed on Sunday, but we will open for shareholders and their guests from noon to 6 p.m. on Sunday, April 28. At our Sunday opening last year you made Ike very happy: After totaling the day's volume, he suggested to me that we start holding annual meetings quarterly. Join us at Borsheim's even if you just come to watch; it's a show you shouldn't miss.

Last year the first question at the annual meeting was asked by 11-year-old Nicholas Kenner, a third-generation shareholder from New York City. Nicholas plays rough: "How come the stock is down?" he fired at me. My answer was not memorable.

We hope that other business engagements won't keep Nicholas away from this year's meeting. If he attends, he will be offered the chance to again ask the first question; Charlie and I want to tackle him while we're *fresh*. This year, however, it's Charlie's turn to answer.

Warren E. Buffett
Chairman of the Board

March 1, 1991

APPENDIX A

U. S. STEEL ANNOUNCES SWEEPING MODERNIZATION SCHEME*

* An unpublished satire by Ben Graham, written in 1936 and given by the author to Warren Buffett in 1954.

Myron C. Taylor, Chairman of U. S. Steel Corporation, today announced the long awaited plan for completely modernizing the world's largest industrial enterprise. Contrary to expectations, no changes will be made in the company's manufacturing or selling policies. Instead, the bookkeeping system is to be entirely revamped. By adopting and further improving a number of modern accounting and financial devices the corporation's earning power will be amazingly transformed. Even under the subnormal conditions of 1935, it is estimated that the new bookkeeping methods would have yielded a reported profit of close to $50 per share on the common stock. The scheme of improvement is the result of a comprehensive survey made by Messrs. Price, Bacon, Guthrie & Colpitts; it includes the following six points:

1. Writing down of Plant Account to Minus $1,000,000,000.

2. Par value of common stock to be reduced to 1¢.

3. Payment of all wages and salaries in option warrants.

4. Inventories to be carried at $1.

5. Preferred Stock to be replaced by non-interest bearing bonds redeemable at 50% discount.

6. A $1,000,000,000 Contingency Reserve to be established.

The official statement of this extraordinary Modernization Plan follows in full:

The Board of Directors of U. S. Steel Corporation is pleased to announce that after intensive study of the problems arising from changed conditions in the industry, it has approved a comprehensive plan for remodeling the Corporation's accounting methods. A survey by a Special Committee, aided and abetted by Messrs. Price, Bacon, Guthrie & Colpitts, revealed that our company has lagged somewhat behind other American business enterprises in utilizing certain advanced bookkeeping methods, by means of which the earning power may be phenomenally enhanced without requiring any cash outlay or any changes in operating or sales conditions. It has been decided not only to adopt these newer methods, but to develop them to a still higher stage of perfection. The changes adopted by the Board may be summarized under six heads, as follows:

1. Fixed Assets to be written down to <u>Minus $1,000,000,000</u>.

Many representative companies have relieved their income accounts of all charges for depreciation by writing down their plant account to $1. The Special Committee points out that if their plants are worth only $1, the fixed assets of U. S. Steel Corporation are worth a good deal less than that sum. It is now a well-recognized fact that many plants are in reality a liability rather than an asset, entailing not only depreciation charges, but taxes, maintenance, and other expenditures. Accordingly, the Board has decided to extend the write-down policy initiated in the 1935 report, and to mark down the Fixed Assets from $1,338,522,858.96 to a round <u>Minus $1,000,000,000</u>.

The advantages of this move should be evident. As the plant wears out, the liability becomes correspondingly reduced. Hence, instead of the present depreciation charge of some $47,000,000 yearly there will be an annual <u>appreciation credit</u> of 5%, or $50,000,000. This will increase earnings by no less than $97,000,000 per annum.

2. Reduction of Par Value of Common Stock to 1¢, and

3. Payment of Salaries and Wages in Option Warrants.

Many corporations have been able to reduce their overhead expenses substantially by paying a large part of their executive salaries in the form of options to buy stock, which carry no charge against earnings. The full possibilities of this modern device have apparently not been adequately realized. The Board of Directors has adopted the following advanced form of this idea:

The entire personnel of the Corporation are to receive their compensation in the form of rights to buy common stock at $50 per share, at the rate of one purchase right for each $50 of salary and/or wages in their present amounts. The par value of the common stock is to be reduced to 1¢.

The almost incredible advantages of this new plan are evident from the following:

A. The payroll of the Corporation will be entirely eliminated, a saving of $250,000,000 per annum, based on 1935 operations.

B. At the same time, the effective compensation of all our employees will be increased severalfold. Because of the large earnings per share to be shown on our common stock under the new methods, it is certain that the shares will command a price in the market far above the option level of $50 per share, making the readily realizable value of these option warrants greatly in excess of the present cash wages that they will replace.

C. The Corporation will realize an additional large annual profit through the exercise of these warrants. Since the par value of the common stock will be fixed at 1¢, there will be a gain of $49.99 on each share subscribed for. In the interest of conservative accounting, however, this profit will not be included in the income account, but will be shown separately as a credit to Capital Surplus.

D. The Corporation's cash position will be enormously strengthened. In place of the present annual cash out-go of $250,000,000 for wages (1935 basis), there will be annual cash inflow of $250,000,000 through exercise of the subscription warrants for 5,000,000 shares of common stock. The Company's large earnings and strong cash position will permit the payment of a liberal dividend which, in turn, will result in the exercise of these option warrants immediately after issuance which, in turn, will further improve the cash position which, in turn, will permit a higher dividend rate—and so on, indefinitely.

4. Inventories to be carried at $1.

Serious losses have been taken during the depression due to the necessity of adjusting inventory value to market. Various enterprises—notably in the metal and cotton-textile fields—have successfully dealt with this problem by carrying all or part of their inventories at extremely low unit prices. The U. S. Steel Corporation has decided to adopt a still more progressive policy, and to carry its entire inventory at $1. This will be effected by an appropriate write-down at the end of each year, the amount of said write-down to be charged to the Contingency Reserve hereinafter referred to.

The benefits to be derived from this new method are very great. Not only will it obviate all possibility of inventory depreciation, but it will substantially enhance the annual earnings of the Corporation. The inventory on hand at the beginning of the year, valued at $1, will be sold during the year at an excellent profit. It is estimated that our income will be increased by means of this method to the extent of at least $150,000,000 per annum which, by a coincidence, will about equal the amount of the write-down to be made each year against Contingency Reserve.

A minority report of the Special Committee recommends that Accounts Receivable and Cash also be written down to $1, in the interest of consistency and to gain additional advantages similar to those just discussed. This proposal has been rejected for the time being because our auditors still require that any recoveries of receivables and cash so charged off be credited to surplus instead of to the year's income. It is expected, however, that this auditing rule—which is rather reminiscent of the horse-and-buggy days—will soon be changed in line with modern tendencies. Should this occur, the minority report will be given further and favorable consideration.

5. Replacement of Preferred Stock by Non-Interest-Bearing Bonds Redeemable at 50% Discount.

During the recent depression many companies have been able to offset their operating losses by including in income profits arising from repurchases of their own bonds at a substantial discount from par. Unfortunately the credit of U. S. Steel Corporation has always stood so high that this lucrative source of revenue has not hitherto been available to it. The Modernization Scheme will remedy this condition.

It is proposed that each share of preferred stock be exchanged for $300 face value of non-interest-bearing sinking-fund notes, redeemable by lot at 50% of face value in 10 equal annual installments. This will require the issuance of $1,080,000,000 of new notes, of which $108,000,000 will be retired each year at a cost to the Corporation of only $54,000,000, thus creating an annual profit of the same amount.

Like the wage-and/or-salary plan described under 3. above, this arrangement will benefit both the Corporation and its preferred stockholders. The latter are assured payment for their present shares at 150% of par value over an average period of five years. Since short-term securities yield practically no return at present, the non-interest-bearing feature is of no real importance. The Corporation will convert its present annual <u>charge</u> of $25,000,000 for preferred dividends into an annual bond-retirement <u>profit</u> of $54,000,000—an aggregate yearly gain of $79,000,000.

6. Establishment of a Contingency Reserve of $1,000,000,000.

The Directors are confident that the improvements hereinbefore described will assure the Corporation of a satisfactory earning power under all conditions in the future. Under modern accounting methods, however, it is unnecessary to incur the slightest risk of loss through adverse business developments of any sort, since all these may be provided for in advance by means of a Contingency Reserve.

The Special Committee has recommended that the Corporation create such a Contingency Reserve in the fairly substantial amount of $1,000,000,000. As previously set forth, the annual write-down of inventory to $1 will be absorbed by this reserve. To prevent eventual exhaustion of the Contingency Reserve, it has been further decided that it be replenished each year by transfer of an appropriate sum from Capital Surplus. Since the latter is expected to increase each year by not less than $250,000,000 through the exercise of the Stock Option Warrants (see 3. above), it will readily make good any drains on the Contingency Reserve.

In setting up this arrangement, the Board of Directors must confess regretfully that they have been unable to improve upon the devices already employed by important corporations in transferring large sums between Capital, Capital Surplus, Contingency Reserves and other Balance Sheet Accounts. In fact, it must be admitted that our entries will be somewhat too simple, and will lack that element of extreme mystification that characterizes the most advanced procedure in this field. The Board of Directors, however, have insisted upon clarity and simplicity in framing their Modernization Plan, even at the sacrifice of possible advantage to the Corporation's earning power.

In order to show the combined effect of the new proposals upon the Corporation's earning power, we submit herewith a condensed Income Account for 1935 on two bases, viz:

	A. As Reported	B. Pro-Forma Giving Effect to Changes Proposed Herewith
Gross Receipts from all Sources (Including Inter-Company)	$765,000,000	$765,000,000
Salaries and Wages.	251,000,000	—
Other Operating Expenses and Taxes.	461,000,000	311,000,000
Depreciation.	47,000,000	(50,000,000)
Interest	5,000,000	5,000,000
Discount on Bonds Retired	—	(54,000,000)
Preferred Dividends	25,000,000	—
Balance for Common	(24,000,000)	553,000,000
Average Shares Outstanding	8,703,252	11,203,252
Earned Per Share	($2.76)	$49.80

In accordance with a somewhat antiquated custom there is appended herewith a condensed pro-forma Balance Sheet of the U. S. Steel Corporation as of December 31, 1935, after giving effect to proposed changes in asset and liability accounts.

ASSETS

Fixed Assets, net	($1,000,000,000)
Cash Assets	142,000,000
Receivables	56,000,000
Inventory	1
Miscellaneous Assets	27,000,000
Total	($774,999,999)

LIABILITIES

Common Stock Par 1¢ (Par Value $87,032.52) Stated Value*	($3,500,000,000)
Subsidiaries' Bonds and Stocks	113,000,000
New Sinking Fund Notes	1,080,000,000
Current Liabilities	69,000,000
Contingency Reserve	1,000,000,000
Other Reserves	74,000,000
Initial Surplus	389,000,001
Total	($774,999,999)

*Given a Stated Value differing from Par Value, in accordance with the laws of the State of Virginia, where the company will be re-incorporated.

It is perhaps unnecessary to point out to our stockholders that modern accounting methods give rise to balance sheets differing somewhat in appearance from those of a less advanced period. In view of the very large earning power that will result from these changes in the Corporation's Balance Sheet, it is not expected that undue attention will be paid to the details of assets and liabilities.

In conclusion, the Board desires to point out that the combined procedure, whereby plant will be carried at a minus figure, our wage bill will be eliminated, and inventory will stand on our books at virtually nothing, will give U. S. Steel Corporation an enormous competitive advantage in the industry. We shall be able to sell our products at exceedingly low prices and still show a handsome margin of profit. It is the considered view of the Board of Directors that under the Modernization Scheme we shall be able to undersell all competitors to such a point that the antitrust laws will constitute the only barrier to 100% domination of the industry.

In making this statement, the Board is not unmindful of the possibility that some of our competitors may seek to offset our new advantages by adopting similar accounting improvements. We are confident, however, that U. S. Steel will be able to retain the loyalty of its customers, old and new, through the unique prestige that will accrue to it as the originator and pioneer in these new fields of service to the user of steel. Should necessity arise, moreover, we believe we shall be able to maintain our deserved superiority by introducing still more advanced bookkeeping methods, which are even now under development in our Experimental Accounting Laboratory.

APPENDIX B

Some Thoughts on Selling Your Business*

*This is an edited version of a letter I sent some years ago to a man who had indicated
that he might want to sell his family business. I present it here because it is a message I
would like to convey to other prospective sellers.—W.E.B.

Dear _____:

Here are a few thoughts pursuant to our conversation of the other day.

Most business owners spend the better part of their lifetimes building their businesses. By experience built
upon endless repetition, they sharpen their skills in merchandising, purchasing, personnel selection, etc. It's a learning process, and mistakes made in one year often contribute to competence and success in succeeding years.

In contrast, owner-managers sell their business only once—frequently in an emotionally-charged atmosphere
with a multitude of pressures coming from different directions. Often, much of the pressure comes from brokers
whose compensation is contingent upon consummation of a sale, regardless of its consequences for both buyer and
seller. The fact that the decision is so important, both financially and personally, to the owner can make the process
more, rather than less, prone to error. And, mistakes made in the once-in-a-lifetime sale of a business are not revers-
ible.

Price is very important, but often is not the most critical aspect of the sale. You and your family have an extraordinary business—one of a kind in your field—and any buyer is going to recognize that. It's also a business that
is going to get more valuable as the years go by. So if you decide not to sell now, you are very likely to realize more
money later on. With that knowledge you can deal from strength and take the time required to select the buyer you
want.

If you should decide to sell, I think Berkshire Hathaway offers some advantages that most other buyers do
not. Practically all of these buyers will fall into one of two categories:

(1) A company located elsewhere but operating in your business or in a business somewhat akin to yours.
Such a buyer—no matter what promises are made—will usually have managers who feel they know how to run your
business operations and, sooner or later, will want to apply some hands-on "help." If the acquiring company is much
larger, it often will have squads of managers, recruited over the years in part by promises that they will get to run
future acquisitions. They will have their own way of doing things and, even though your business record undoubtedly will be far better than theirs, human nature will at some point cause them to believe that their methods of operating are superior. You and your family probably have friends who have sold their businesses to larger companies, and
I suspect that their experiences will confirm the tendency of parent companies to take over the running of their subsidiaries, particularly when the parent knows the industry, or thinks it does.

(2) A financial maneuverer, invariably operating with large amounts of borrowed money, who plans to resell
either to the public or to another corporation as soon as the time is favorable. Frequently, this buyer's major contribution will be to change accounting methods so that earnings can be presented in the most favorable light just prior
to his bailing out. I'm enclosing a recent article that describes this sort of transaction, which is becoming much more
frequent because of a rising stock market and the great supply of funds available for such transactions.

If the sole motive of the present owners is to cash their chips and put the business behind them—and plenty
of sellers fall in this category—either type of buyer that I've just described is satisfactory. But if the sellers' business
represents the creative work of a lifetime and forms an integral part of their personality and sense of being, buyers of
either type have serious flaws.

Berkshire is another kind of buyer—a rather unusual one. We buy to keep, but we don't have, and don't expect to have, operating people in our parent organization. All of the businesses we own are run autonomously to an extraordinary degree. In most cases, the managers of important businesses we have owned for many years have not been to Omaha or even met each other. When we buy a business, the sellers go on running it just as they did before the sale; we adapt to their methods rather than vice versa.

We have no one—family, recently recruited MBAs, etc.—to whom we have promised a chance to run businesses we have bought from owner-managers. And we won't have.

You know of some of our past purchases. I'm enclosing a list of everyone from whom we have ever bought a business, and I invite you to check with them as to our performance versus our promises. You should be particularly interested in checking with the few whose businesses did not do well in order to ascertain how we behaved under difficult conditions.

Any buyer will tell you that he needs you personally—and if he has any brains, he most certainly does need you. But a great many buyers, for the reasons mentioned above, don't match their subsequent actions to their earlier words. We will behave exactly as promised, both because we have so promised, and because we need to in order to achieve the best business results.

This need explains why we would want the operating members of your family to retain a 20% interest in the business. We need 80% to consolidate earnings for tax purposes, which is a step important to us. It is equally important to us that the family members who run the business remain as owners. Very simply, we would not want to buy unless we felt key members of present management would stay on as our partners. Contracts cannot guarantee your continued interest; we would simply rely on your word.

The areas I get involved in are capital allocation and selection and compensation of the top man. Other personnel decisions, operating strategies, etc. are his bailiwick. Some Berkshire managers talk over some of their decisions with me; some don't. It depends upon their personalities and, to an extent, upon their own personal relationship with me.

If you should decide to do business with Berkshire, we would pay in cash. Your business would not be used as collateral for any loan by Berkshire. There would be no brokers involved.

Furthermore, there would be no chance that a deal would be announced and that the buyer would then back off or start suggesting adjustments (with apologies, of course, and with an explanation that banks, lawyers, boards of directors, etc. were to be blamed). And finally, you would know exactly with whom you are dealing. You would not have one executive negotiate the deal only to have someone else in charge a few years later, or have the president regretfully tell you that his board of directors required this change or that (or possibly required sale of your business to finance some new interest of the parent's).

It's only fair to tell you that you would be no richer after the sale than now. The ownership of your business already makes you wealthy and soundly invested. A sale would change the form of your wealth, but it wouldn't change its amount. If you sell, you will have exchanged a 100%-owned valuable asset that you understand for another valuable asset—cash—that will probably be invested in small pieces (stocks) of other businesses that you understand less well. There is often a sound reason to sell but, if the transaction is a fair one, the reason is not so that the seller can become wealthier.

I will not pester you; if you have any possible interest in selling, I would appreciate your call. I would be extraordinarily proud to have Berkshire, along with the key members of your family, own _____; I believe we would do very well financially; and I believe you would have just as much fun running the business over the next 20 years as you have had during the past 20.

Sincerely,

/s/ Warren E. Buffett

BERKSHIRE HATHAWAY INC.

To the Shareholders of Berkshire Hathaway Inc.:

Our gain in net worth during 1991 was $2.1 billion, or 39.6%. Over the last 27 years (that is, since present management took over) our per-share book value has grown from $19 to $6,437, or at a rate of 23.7% compounded annually.

The size of our equity capital—which now totals $7.4 billion—makes it certain that we cannot maintain our past rate of gain or, for that matter, come close to doing so. As Berkshire grows, the universe of opportunities that can significantly influence the company's performance constantly shrinks. When we were working with capital of $20 million, an idea or business producing $1 million of profit added five percentage points to our return for the year. Now we need a $370 million idea (i.e., one contributing over $550 million of pre-tax profit) to achieve the same result. And there are many more ways to make $1 million than to make $370 million.

Charlie Munger, Berkshire's Vice Chairman, and I have set a goal of attaining a 15% average annual increase in Berkshire's intrinsic value. If our growth in *book* value is to keep up with a 15% pace, we must earn $22 billion during the next decade. Wish us luck—we'll need it.

Our outsized gain in book value in 1991 resulted from a phenomenon not apt to be repeated: a dramatic rise in the price-earnings ratios of Coca-Cola and Gillette. These two stocks accounted for nearly $1.6 billion of our $2.1 billion growth in net worth last year. When we loaded up on Coke three years ago, Berkshire's net worth was $3.4 billion; now our Coke stock alone is worth more than that.

Coca-Cola and Gillette are two of the best companies in the world and we expect their earnings to grow at hefty rates in the years ahead. Over time, also, the value of our holdings in these stocks should grow in rough proportion. Last year, however, the valuations of these two companies rose far faster than their earnings. In effect, we got a double-dip benefit, delivered partly by the excellent earnings growth and even more so by the market's reappraisal of these stocks. We believe this reappraisal was warranted. But it can't recur annually: We'll have to settle for a single dip in the future.

A Second Job

In 1989 when I—a happy consumer of five cans of Cherry Coke daily—announced our purchase of $1 billion worth of Coca-Cola stock, I described the move as a rather extreme example of putting our money where my mouth was. On August 18 of last year, when I was elected Interim Chairman of Salomon Inc, it was a different story: I put my mouth where our money was.

You've all read of the events that led to my appointment. My decision to take the job carried with it an implicit but important message: Berkshire's operating managers are so outstanding that I knew I could materially reduce the time I was spending at the company and yet remain confident that its economic progress would not skip a beat. The Blumkins, the Friedman family, Mike Goldberg, the Heldmans, Chuck Huggins, Stan Lipsey, Ralph Schey and Frank Rooney (CEO of H.H. Brown, our latest acquisition, which I will describe later) are all masters of their operations and need no help from me. My job is merely to treat them right and to allocate the capital they generate. Neither function is impeded by my work at Salomon.

The role that Charlie and I play in the success of our operating units can be illustrated by a story about George Mira, the one-time quarterback of the University of Miami, and his coach, Andy Gustafson. Playing Florida and near its goal line, Mira dropped back to pass. He spotted an open receiver but found his right shoulder in the unshakable grasp of a Florida linebacker. The right-handed Mira thereupon switched the ball to his other hand and threw the only left-handed pass of his life—for a touchdown. As the crowd erupted, Gustafson calmly turned to a reporter and declared: "Now that's what I call coaching."

Given the managerial stars we have at our operating units, Berkshire's performance is not affected if Charlie or I slip away from time to time. You should note, however, the "interim" in my Salomon title. Berkshire is my first love and one that will never fade: At the Harvard Business School last year, a student asked me when I planned to retire and I replied, "About five to ten years after I die."

Sources of Reported Earnings

The table below shows the major sources of Berkshire's reported earnings. In this presentation, amortization of Goodwill and other major purchase-price accounting adjustments are not charged against the specific businesses to which they apply, but are instead aggregated and shown separately. This procedure lets you view the earnings of our businesses as they would have been reported had we not purchased them. I've explained in past reports why this form of presentation seems to us to be more useful to investors and managers than one utilizing generally accepted accounting principles (GAAP), which require purchase-price adjustments to be made on a business-by-business basis. The total net earnings we show in the table are, of course, identical to the GAAP total in our audited financial statements.

A large amount of additional information about these businesses is given on pages 33-47, where you also will find our segment earnings reported on a GAAP basis. However, we will not in this letter discuss each of our non-insurance operations, as we have in the past. Our businesses have grown in number—and will continue to grow—so it now makes sense to rotate coverage, discussing one or two in detail each year.

	(000s omitted)			
	Pre-Tax Earnings		Berkshire's Share of Net Earnings (after taxes and minority interests)	
	1991	1990	1991	1990
Operating Earnings:				
Insurance Group:				
Underwriting	$(119,593)	$ (26,647)	$ (77,229)	$ (14,936)
Net Investment Income	331,846	327,047	285,173	282,613
H. H. Brown (acquired 7/1/91)	13,616	---	8,611	---
Buffalo News	37,113	43,954	21,841	25,981
Fechheimer	12,947	12,450	6,843	6,605
Kirby	35,726	27,445	22,555	17,613
Nebraska Furniture Mart	14,384	17,248	6,993	8,485
Scott Fetzer Manufacturing Group	26,123	30,378	15,901	18,458
See's Candies	42,390	39,580	25,575	23,892
Wesco – other than Insurance	12,230	12,441	8,777	9,676
World Book	22,483	31,896	15,487	20,420
Amortization of Goodwill	(4,113)	(3,476)	(4,098)	(3,461)
Other Purchase-Price Accounting Charges	(6,021)	(5,951)	(7,019)	(6,856)
Interest Expense*	(89,250)	(76,374)	(57,165)	(49,726)
Shareholder-Designated Contributions	(6,772)	(5,824)	(4,388)	(3,801)
Other	77,399	58,310	47,896	35,782
Operating Earnings	400,508	482,477	315,753	370,745
Sales of Securities	192,478	33,989	124,155	23,348
Total Earnings – All Entities	$ 592,986	$ 516,466	$ 439,908	$ 394,093

*Excludes interest expense of Scott Fetzer Financial Group and Mutual Savings & Loan.

"Look-Through" Earnings

We've previously discussed look-through earnings, which consist of: (1) the operating earnings reported in the previous section, plus; (2) the retained operating earnings of major investees that, under GAAP accounting, are not reflected in our profits, less; (3) an allowance for the tax that would be paid by Berkshire if these retained earnings of investees had instead been distributed to us.

I've told you that over time look-through earnings must increase at about 15% annually if our intrinsic business value is to grow at that rate. Indeed, since present management took over in 1965, our look-through earnings have grown at almost the identical 23% rate of gain recorded for book value.

Last year, however, our look-through earnings did not grow at all but rather declined by 14%. To an extent, the decline was precipitated by two forces that I discussed in last year's report and that I warned you would have a negative effect on look-through earnings.

First, I told you that our media earnings—both direct and look-through—were "sure to decline" and they in fact did. The second force came into play on April 1, when the call of our Gillette preferred stock required us to convert it into common. The after-tax earnings in 1990 from our preferred had been about $45 million, an amount somewhat higher than the combination in 1991 of three months of dividends on our preferred plus nine months of look-through earnings on the common.

Two other outcomes that I did not foresee also hurt look-through earnings in 1991. First, we had a break-even result from our interest in Wells Fargo (dividends we received from the company were offset by negative retained earnings). Last year I said that such a result at Wells was "a low-level possibility—not a likelihood." Second, we recorded significantly lower—though still excellent—insurance profits.

The following table shows you how we calculate look-through earnings, although I warn you that the figures are necessarily very rough. (The dividends paid to us by these investees have been included in the operating earnings itemized on page 6, mostly under "Insurance Group: Net Investment Income.")

Berkshire's Major Investees	Berkshire's Approximate Ownership at Yearend		Berkshire's Share of Undistributed Operating Earnings (in millions)	
	1991	1990	1991	1990
Capital Cities/ABC Inc.	18.1%	17.9%	$ 61	$ 85
The Coca-Cola Company	7.0%	7.0%	69	58
Federal Home Loan Mortgage Corp.	3.4%[1]	3.2%[1]	15	10
The Gillette Company	11.0%	---	23[2]	---
GEICO Corp.	48.2%	46.1%	69	76
The Washington Post Company	14.6%	14.6%	10	18
Wells Fargo & Company	9.6%	9.7%	(17)	19[3]
Berkshire's share of undistributed earnings of major investees			$230	$266
Hypothetical tax on these undistributed investee earnings			(30)	(35)
Reported operating earnings of Berkshire			316	371
Total look-through earnings of Berkshire			$516	$602

(1) Net of minority interest at Wesco
(2) For the nine months after Berkshire converted its preferred on April
(3) Calculated on average ownership for the year

* * * * * * * * * * * *

We also believe that investors can benefit by focusing on their own look-through earnings. To calculate these, they should determine the underlying earnings attributable to the shares they hold in their portfolio and total these. The goal of each investor should be to create a portfolio (in effect, a "company") that will deliver him or her the highest possible look-through earnings a decade or so from now.

An approach of this kind will force the investor to think about long-term business prospects rather than short-term stock market prospects, a perspective likely to improve results. It's true, of course, that, in the long run, the scoreboard for investment decisions is market price. But prices will be determined by future earnings. In investing, just as in baseball, to put runs on the scoreboard one must watch the playing field, not the scoreboard.

A Change in Media Economics and Some Valuation Math

In last year's report, I stated my opinion that the decline in the profitability of media companies reflected secular as well as cyclical factors. The events of 1991 have fortified that case: The economic strength of once-mighty media enterprises continues to erode as retailing patterns change and advertising and entertainment choices proliferate. In the business world, unfortunately, the rear-view mirror is always clearer than the windshield: A few years back no one linked to the media business—neither lenders, owners nor financial analysts—saw the economic deterioration that was in store for the industry. (But give me a few years and I'll probably convince myself that I did.)

The fact is that newspaper, television, and magazine properties have begun to resemble *businesses* more than *franchises* in their economic behavior. Let's take a quick look at the characteristics separating these two classes of enterprise, keeping in mind, however, that many operations fall in some middle ground and can best be described as weak franchises or strong businesses.

An economic franchise arises from a product or service that: (1) is needed or desired; (2) is thought by its customers to have no close substitute and; (3) is not subject to price regulation. The existence of all three conditions will be demonstrated by a company's ability to regularly price its product or service aggressively and thereby to earn high rates of return on capital. Moreover, franchises can tolerate mis-management. Inept managers may diminish a franchise's profitability, but they cannot inflict mortal damage.

In contrast, "a business" earns exceptional profits only if it is the low-cost operator or if supply of its product or service is tight. Tightness in supply usually does not last long. With superior management, a company may maintain its status as a low-cost operator for a much longer time, but even then unceasingly faces the possibility of competitive attack. And a business, unlike a franchise, can be killed by poor management.

Until recently, media properties possessed the three characteristics of a franchise and consequently could both price aggressively and be managed loosely. Now, however, consumers looking for information and entertainment (their primary interest being the latter) enjoy greatly broadened choices as to where to find them. Unfortunately, demand can't expand in response to this new supply: 500 million American eyeballs and a 24-hour day are all that's available. The result is that competition has intensified, markets have fragmented, and the media industry has lost some—though far from all—of its franchise strength.

* * * * * * * * * * *

The industry's weakened franchise has an impact on its value that goes far beyond the immediate effect on earnings. For an understanding of this phenomenon, let's look at some much over-simplified, but relevant, math.

A few years ago the conventional wisdom held that a newspaper, television or magazine property would forever increase its earnings at 6% or so annually and would do so *without the employment of additional capital*, for the reason that depreciation charges would roughly match capital expenditures and working capital requirements would be minor. Therefore, reported earnings (before amortization of intangibles) were also freely-distributable earnings, which meant that ownership of a media property could be construed as akin to owning a perpetual annuity set to grow at 6% a year. Say, next, that a discount rate of 10% was used to determine the present value of that earnings stream. One could then calculate that it was appropriate to pay a whopping $25 million for a property with current after-tax earnings of $1 million. (This after-tax multiplier of 25 translates to a multiplier on pre-tax earnings of about 16.)

Now change the assumption and posit that the $1 million represents "normal earning power" and that earnings will bob around this figure cyclically. A "bob-around" pattern is indeed the lot of most businesses, whose income stream grows only if their owners are willing to commit more capital (usually in the form of retained earnings). Under our revised assumption, $1 million of earnings, discounted by the same 10%, translates to a $10 million valuation. Thus a seemingly modest shift in assumptions reduces the property's valuation to 10 times after-tax earnings (or about 6 1/2 times pre-tax earnings).

Dollars are dollars whether they are derived from the operation of media properties or of steel mills. What in the past caused buyers to value a dollar of earnings from media far higher than a dollar from steel was that the earnings of a media property were expected to constantly grow (without the business requiring much additional capital), whereas steel earnings clearly fell in the bob-around category. Now, however, expectations for media have moved toward the bob-around model. And, as our simplified example illustrates, valuations must change dramatically when expectations are revised.

We have a significant investment in media—both through our direct ownership of Buffalo News and our shareholdings in The Washington Post Company and Capital Cities/ABC—and the intrinsic value of this investment has declined materially because of the secular transformation that the industry is experiencing. (Cyclical factors have also hurt our current look-through earnings, but these factors do not reduce intrinsic value.) However, as our Business Principles on page 2-3 note, one of the rules by which we run Berkshire is that we do not sell businesses—or investee holdings that we have classified as permanent—simply because we see ways to use the money more advantageously elsewhere. (We did sell certain other media holdings sometime back, but these were relatively small.)

The intrinsic value losses that we have suffered have been moderated because the Buffalo News, under Stan Lipsey's leadership, has done far better than most newspapers and because both Cap Cities and Washington Post are exceptionally well-managed. In particular, these companies stayed on the sidelines during the late 1980's period in which purchasers of media properties regularly paid irrational prices. Also, the debt of both Cap Cities and Washington Post is small and roughly offset by cash that they hold. As a result, the shrinkage in the value of their assets has not been accentuated by the effects of leverage. Among publicly-owned media companies, our two investees are about the only ones essentially free of debt. Most of the other companies, through a combination of the aggressive acquisition policies they pursued and shrinking earnings, find themselves with debt equal to five or more times their current net income.

The strong balance sheets and strong managements of Cap Cities and Washington Post leave us more comfortable with these investments than we would be with holdings in any other media companies. Moreover, most media properties continue to have far better economic characteristics than those possessed by the average American business. But gone are the days of bullet-proof franchises and cornucopian economics.

Twenty Years in a Candy Store

We've just passed a milestone: Twenty years ago, on January 3, 1972, Blue Chip Stamps (then an affiliate of Berkshire and later merged into it) bought control of See's Candy Shops, a West Coast manufacturer and retailer of boxed-chocolates. The nominal price that the sellers were asking—calculated on the 100% ownership we ultimately attained—was $40 million. But the company had $10 million of excess cash, and therefore the true offering price was $30 million. Charlie and I, not yet fully appreciative of the value of an economic franchise, looked at the company's mere $7 million of tangible net worth and said $25 million was as high as we would go (and we meant it). Fortunately, the sellers accepted our offer.

The sales of trading stamps by Blue Chip thereafter declined from $102.5 million in 1972 to $1.2 million in 1991. But See's candy sales in the same period increased from $29 million to $196 million. Moreover, profits at See's grew even faster than sales, from $4.2 million pre-tax in 1972 to $42.4 million last year.

For an increase in profits to be evaluated properly, it must be compared with the incremental capital investment required to produce it. On this score, See's has been astounding: The company now operates comfortably with only $25 million of net worth, which means that our beginning base of $7 million has had to be supplemented by only $18 million of reinvested earnings. Meanwhile, See's remaining pre-tax profits of $410 million were distributed to Blue Chip/Berkshire during the 20 years for these companies to deploy (after payment of taxes) in whatever way made most sense.

In our See's purchase, Charlie and I had one important insight: We saw that the business had untapped pricing power. Otherwise, we were lucky twice over. First, the transaction was not derailed by our dumb insistence on a $25 million price. Second, we found Chuck Huggins, then See's executive vice-president, whom we instantly put in charge. Both our business and personal experiences with Chuck have been outstanding. One example: When the purchase was made, we shook hands with Chuck on a compensation arrangement—conceived in about five minutes and never reduced to a written contract—that remains unchanged to this day.

In 1991, See's sales volume, measured in dollars, matched that of 1990. In pounds, however, volume was down 4%. All of that slippage took place in the last two months of the year, a period that normally produces more than 80% of annual profits. Despite the weakness in sales, profits last year grew 7%, and our pre-tax profit margin was a record 21.6%.

Almost 80% of See's sales come from California and our business clearly was hurt by the recession, which hit the state with particular force late in the year. Another negative, however, was the mid-year initiation in California of a sales tax of 7%-8% (depending on the county involved) on "snack food" that was deemed applicable to our candy.

Shareholders who are students of epistemological shadings will enjoy California's classifications of "snack" and "non-snack" foods:

Taxable "Snack" Foods	Non-Taxable "Non-Snack" Foods
Ritz Crackers	Soda Crackers
Popped Popcorn	Unpopped Popcorn
Granola Bars	Granola Cereal
Slice of Pie (Wrapped)	Whole Pie
Milky Way Candy Bar	Milky Way Ice Cream Bar

What—you are sure to ask—is the tax status of a *melted* Milky Way ice cream bar? In that androgynous form, does it more resemble an ice cream bar or a candy bar that has been left in the sun? It's no wonder that Brad Sherman, Chairman of California's State Board of Equalization, who opposed the snack food bill but must now administer it, has said: "I came to this job as a specialist in tax law. Now I find my constituents should have elected Julia Child."

Charlie and I have many reasons to be thankful for our association with Chuck and See's. The obvious ones are that we've earned exceptional returns and had a good time in the process. Equally important, ownership of See's has taught us much about the evaluation of franchises. We've made significant money in certain common stocks because of the lessons we learned at See's.

H. H. Brown

We made a sizable acquisition in 1991—the H. H. Brown Company—and behind this business is an interesting history. In 1927 a 29-year-old businessman named Ray Heffernan purchased the company, then located in North Brookfield, Massachusetts, for $10,000 and began a 62-year career of running it. (He also found time for other pursuits: At age 90 he was still joining new golf clubs.) By Mr. Heffernan's retirement in early 1990 H. H. Brown had three plants in the United States and one in Canada; employed close to 2,000 people; and earned about $25 million annually before taxes.

Along the way, Frances Heffernan, one of Ray's daughters, married Frank Rooney, who was sternly advised by Mr. Heffernan before the wedding that he had better forget any ideas he might have about working for his father-in-law. That was one of Mr. Heffernan's few mistakes: Frank went on to become CEO of Melville Shoe (now Melville Corp.). During his 23 years as boss, from 1964 through 1986, Melville's earnings averaged more than 20% on equity and its stock (adjusted for splits) rose from $16 to $960. And a few years after Frank retired, Mr. Heffernan, who had fallen ill, asked him to run Brown.

After Mr. Heffernan died late in 1990, his family decided to sell the company—and here we got lucky. I had known Frank for a few years but not well enough for him to think of Berkshire as a possible buyer. He instead gave the assignment of selling Brown to a major investment banker, which failed also to think of us. But last spring Frank was playing golf in Florida with John Loomis, a long-time friend of mine as well as a Berkshire shareholder, who is always on the alert for something that might fit us. Hearing about the impending sale of Brown, John told Frank that the company should be right up Berkshire's alley, and Frank promptly gave me a call. I thought right away that we would make a deal and before long it was done.

Much of my enthusiasm for this purchase came from Frank's willingness to continue as CEO. Like most of our managers, he has no financial need to work but does so because he loves the game and likes to excel. Managers of this stripe cannot be "hired" in the normal sense of the word. What we must do is provide a concert hall in which business artists of this class will wish to perform.

Brown (which, by the way, has no connection to Brown Shoe of St. Louis) is the leading North American manufacturer of work shoes and boots, and it has a history of earning unusually fine margins on sales and assets. Shoes are a tough business—of the billion pairs purchased in the United States each year, about 85% are imported —and most manufacturers in the industry do poorly. The wide range of styles and sizes that producers offer causes inventories to be heavy; substantial capital is also tied up in receivables. In this kind of environment, only outstanding managers like Frank and the group developed by Mr. Heffernan can prosper.

A distinguishing characteristic of H. H. Brown is one of the most unusual compensation systems I've encountered—but one that warms my heart: A number of key managers are paid an annual salary of $7,800, to which is added a designated percentage of the profits of the company after these are reduced by a charge for capital employed. These managers therefore truly stand in the shoes of owners. In contrast, most managers talk the talk but don't walk the walk, choosing instead to employ compensation systems that are long on carrots but short on sticks (and that almost invariably treat equity capital as if it were cost-free). The arrangement at Brown, in any case, has served both the company and its managers exceptionally well, which should be no surprise: Managers eager to bet heavily on their abilities usually have plenty of ability to bet on.

* * * * * * * * * * *

It's discouraging to note that though we have on four occasions made major purchases of companies whose sellers were represented by prominent investment banks, we were in only one of these instances contacted by the investment bank. In the other three cases, I myself or a friend initiated the transaction at some point after the investment bank had solicited its own list of prospects. We would love to see an intermediary earn its fee by thinking of us—and therefore repeat here what we're looking for:

(1) Large purchases (at least $10 million of after-tax earnings),
(2) Demonstrated consistent earning power (future projections are of little interest to us, nor are "turnaround" situations),
(3) Businesses earning good returns on equity while employing little or no debt,
(4) Management in place (we can't supply it),
(5) Simple businesses (if there's lots of technology, we won't understand it),
(6) An offering price (we don't want to waste our time or that of the seller by talking, even preliminarily, about a transaction when price is unknown).

We will not engage in unfriendly takeovers. We can promise complete confidentiality and a very fast answer—customarily within five minutes—as to whether we're interested. (With Brown, we didn't even need to take five.) We prefer to buy for cash, but will consider issuing stock when we receive as much in intrinsic business value as we give.

Our favorite form of purchase is one fitting the pattern through which we acquired Nebraska Furniture Mart, Fechheimer's and Borsheim's. In cases like these, the company's owner-managers wish to generate significant amounts of cash, sometimes for themselves, but often for their families or inactive shareholders. At the same time, these managers wish to remain significant owners who continue to run their companies just as they have in the past. We think we offer a particularly good fit for owners with such objectives and we invite potential sellers to check us out by contacting people with whom we have done business in the past.

Charlie and I frequently get approached about acquisitions that don't come close to meeting our tests: We've found that if you advertise an interest in buying collies, a lot of people will call hoping to sell you their cocker spaniels. A line from a country song expresses our feeling about new ventures, turnarounds, or auction-like sales: "When the phone don't ring, you'll know it's me."

Besides being interested in the purchase of businesses as described above, we are also interested in the negotiated purchase of large, but not controlling, blocks of stock comparable to those we hold in Capital Cities, Salomon, Gillette, USAir, Champion, and American Express. We are not interested, however, in receiving suggestions about purchases we might make in the general stock market.

Insurance Operations

Shown below is an updated version of our usual table presenting key figures for the property-casualty insurance industry:

	Yearly Change in Premiums Written (%)	Statutory Combined Ratio After Policyholder Dividends	Yearly Change in Incurred Losses (%)	Inflation Rate Measured by GNP Deflator (%)
1981	3.8	106.0	6.5	10.0
1982	3.7	109.6	8.4	6.2
1983	5.0	112.0	6.8	4.0
1984	8.5	118.0	16.9	4.5
1985	22.1	116.3	16.1	3.7
1986	22.2	108.0	13.5	2.7
1987	9.4	104.6	7.8	3.1
1988	4.4	105.4	5.5	3.9
1989	3.2	109.2	7.7	4.4
1990 (Revised)	4.4	109.6	4.8	4.1
1991 (Est.)	3.1	109.1	2.9	3.7

The combined ratio represents total insurance costs (losses incurred plus expenses) compared to revenue from premiums: A ratio below 100 indicates an underwriting profit, and one above 100 indicates a loss. The higher the ratio, the worse the year. When the investment income that an insurer earns from holding policyholders' funds ("the float") is taken into account, a combined ratio in the 107—111 range typically produces an overall break-even result, exclusive of earnings on the funds provided by shareholders.

For the reasons laid out in previous reports, we expect the industry's incurred losses to grow at close to 10% annually, even in periods when general inflation runs considerably lower. (Over the last 25 years, incurred losses have in reality grown at a still faster rate, 11%.) If premium growth meanwhile materially lags that 10% rate, underwriting losses will mount.

However, the industry's tendency to under-reserve when business turns bad may obscure the picture for a time—and that could well describe the situation last year. Though premiums did not come close to growing 10%, the combined ratio failed to deteriorate as I had expected but instead slightly improved. Loss-reserve data for the industry indicate that there is reason to be skeptical of that outcome, and it may turn out that 1991's ratio should have been worse than was reported. In the long run, of course, trouble awaits managements that paper over operating problems with accounting maneuvers. Eventually, managements of this kind achieve the same result as the seriously-ill patient who tells his doctor: "I can't afford the operation, but would you accept a small payment to touch up the x-rays?"

Berkshire's insurance business has changed in ways that make combined ratios, our own or the industry's, largely irrelevant to our performance. What counts with us is the "cost of funds developed from insurance," or in the vernacular, "the cost of float."

Float—which we generate in exceptional amounts—is the total of loss reserves, loss adjustment expense reserves and unearned premium reserves minus agents balances, prepaid acquisition costs and deferred charges applicable to assumed reinsurance. And the cost of float is measured by our underwriting loss.

The table below shows our cost of float since we entered the business in 1967.

	(1) Underwriting Loss	(2) Average Float	Approximate Cost of Funds	Yearend Yield on Long-Term Govt. Bonds
	(In $ Millions)		(Ratio of 1 to 2)	
1967........	profit	$17.3	less than zero	5.50%
1968........	profit	19.9	less than zero	5.90%
1969........	profit	23.4	less than zero	6.79%
1970........	$0.37	32.4	1.14%	6.25%
1971........	profit	52.5	less than zero	5.81%
1972........	profit	69.5	less than zero	5.82%
1973........	profit	73.3	less than zero	7.27%
1974........	7.36	79.1	9.30%	8.13%
1975........	11.35	87.6	12.96%	8.03%
1976........	profit	102.6	less than zero	7.30%
1977........	profit	139.0	less than zero	7.97%
1978........	profit	190.4	less than zero	8.93%
1979........	profit	227.3	less than zero	10.08%
1980........	profit	237.0	less than zero	11.94%
1981........	profit	228.4	less than zero	13.61%
1982........	21.56	220.6	9.77%	10.64%
1983........	33.87	231.3	14.64%	11.84%
1984........	48.06	253.2	18.98%	11.58%
1985........	44.23	390.2	11.34%	9.34%
1986........	55.84	797.5	7.00%	7.60%
1987........	55.43	1,266.7	4.38%	8.95%
1988........	11.08	1,497.7	0.74%	9.00%
1989........	24.40	1,541.3	1.58%	7.97%
1990........	26.65	1,637.3	1.63%	8.24%
1991........	119.6	1,895.0	6.31%	7.40%

As you can see, our cost of funds in 1991 was well below the U. S. Government's cost on newly-issued long-term bonds. We have in fact beat the government's rate in 20 of the 25 years we have been in the insurance business, often by a wide margin. We have over that time also substantially increased the amount of funds we hold, which counts as a favorable development but only because the cost of funds has been satisfactory. Our float should continue to grow; the challenge will be to garner these funds at a reasonable cost.

Berkshire continues to be a very large writer—perhaps the largest in the world—of "super-cat" insurance, which is coverage that other insurance companies buy to protect themselves against major catastrophic losses. Profits in this business are enormously volatile. As I mentioned last year, $100 million in super-cat premiums, which is roughly our annual expectation, could deliver us anything from a $100 million profit (in a year with no big catastrophe) to a $200 million loss (in a year in which a couple of major hurricanes and/or earthquakes come along).

We price this business expecting to pay out, over the long term, about 90% of the premiums we receive. In any given year, however, we are likely to appear either enormously profitable or enormously unprofitable. That is true in part because GAAP accounting does not allow us to set up reserves in the catastrophe-free years for losses that are certain to be experienced in other years. In effect, a one-year accounting cycle is ill-suited to the nature of this business—and that is a reality you should be aware of when you assess our annual results.

Last year there appears to have been, by our definition, one super-cat, but it will trigger payments from only about 25% of our policies. Therefore, we currently estimate the 1991 underwriting profit from our catastrophe business to have been about $11 million. (You may be surprised to learn the identity of the biggest catastrophe in 1991: It was neither the Oakland fire nor Hurricane Bob, but rather a September typhoon in Japan that caused the industry an insured loss now estimated at about $4-$5 billion. At the higher figure, the loss from the typhoon would surpass that from Hurricane Hugo, the previous record-holder.)

Insurers will always need huge amounts of reinsurance protection for marine and aviation disasters as well as for natural catastrophes. In the 1980's much of this reinsurance was supplied by "innocents"—that is, by insurers that did not understand the risks of the business—but they have now been financially burned beyond recognition. (Berkshire itself was an innocent all too often when I was personally running the insurance operation.) Insurers, though, like investors, eventually repeat their mistakes. At some point—probably after a few catastrophe-scarce years—innocents will reappear and prices for super-cat policies will plunge to silly levels.

As long as apparently-adequate rates prevail, however, we will be a major participant in super-cat coverages. In marketing this product, we enjoy a significant competitive advantage because of our premier financial strength. Thinking insurers know that when "the big one" comes, many reinsurers who found it easy to write policies will find it difficult to write checks. (Some reinsurers can say what Jackie Mason does: "I'm fixed for life—as long as I don't buy anything.") Berkshire's ability to fulfill all its commitments under conditions of even extreme adversity is unquestioned.

Overall, insurance offers Berkshire its greatest opportunities. Mike Goldberg has accomplished wonders with this operation since he took charge and it has become a very valuable asset, albeit one that can't be appraised with any precision.

Marketable Common Stocks

On the next page we list our common stock holdings having a value of over $100 million. A small portion of these investments belongs to subsidiaries of which Berkshire owns less than 100%.

Shares	Company	12/31/91	
		Cost	Market
		(000s omitted)	
3,000,000	Capital Cities/ABC, Inc.	$ 517,500	$1,300,500
46,700,000	The Coca-Cola Co.	1,023,920	3,747,675
2,495,000	Federal Home Loan Mortgage Corp.	77,245	343,090
6,850,000	GEICO Corp.	45,713	1,363,150
24,000,000	The Gillette Company	600,000	1,347,000
31,247,000	Guinness PLC	264,782	296,755
1,727,765	The Washington Post Company	9,731	336,050
5,000,000	Wells Fargo & Company	289,431	290,000

As usual the list reflects our Rip Van Winkle approach to investing. Guinness is a new position. But we held the other seven stocks a year ago (making allowance for the conversion of our Gillette position from preferred to common) and in six of those we hold an unchanged number of shares. The exception is Federal Home Loan Mortgage ("Freddie Mac"), in which our shareholdings increased slightly. Our stay-put behavior reflects our view that the stock market serves as a relocation center at which money is moved from the active to the patient. (With tongue only partly in check, I suggest that recent events indicate that the much-maligned "idle rich" have received a bad rap: They have maintained or increased their wealth while many of the "energetic rich"—aggressive real estate operators, corporate acquirers, oil drillers, etc.—have seen their fortunes disappear.)

Our Guinness holding represents Berkshire's first significant investment in a company domiciled outside the United States. Guinness, however, earns its money in much the same fashion as Coca-Cola and Gillette, U.S.-based companies that garner most of their profits from international operations. Indeed, in the sense of where they earn their profits—continent-by-continent—Coca-Cola and Guinness display strong similarities. (But you'll never get their drinks confused—and your Chairman remains unmovably in the Cherry Coke camp.)

We continually search for large businesses with understandable, enduring and mouth-watering economics that are run by able and shareholder-oriented managements. This focus doesn't guarantee results: We both have to buy at a sensible price and get business performance from our companies that validates our assessment. But this investment approach—searching for the superstars—offers us our only chance for real success. Charlie and I are simply not smart enough, considering the large sums we work with, to get great results by adroitly buying and selling portions of far-from-great businesses. Nor do we think many others can achieve long-term investment success by flitting from flower to flower. Indeed, we believe that according the name "investors" to institutions that trade actively is like calling someone who repeatedly engages in one-night stands a romantic.

If my universe of business possibilities was limited, say, to private companies in Omaha, I would, first, try to assess the long-term economic characteristics of each business; second, assess the quality of the people in charge of running it; and, third, try to buy into a few of the best operations at a sensible price. I certainly would not wish to own an equal part of every business in town. Why, then, should Berkshire take a different tack when dealing with the larger universe of public companies? And since finding great businesses and outstanding managers is so difficult, why should we discard proven products? (I was tempted to say "the real thing.") Our motto is: "If at first you do succeed, quit trying."

John Maynard Keynes, whose brilliance as a practicing investor matched his brilliance in thought, wrote a letter to a business associate, F. C. Scott, on August 15, 1934 that says it all: "As time goes on, I get more and more convinced that the right method in investment is to put fairly large sums into enterprises which one thinks one knows something about and in the management of which one thoroughly believes. It is a mistake to think that one limits one's risk by spreading too much between enterprises about which one knows little and has no reason for special confidence. . . . One's knowledge and experience are definitely limited and there are seldom more than two or three enterprises at any given time in which I personally feel myself entitled to put *full* confidence."

Mistake Du Jour

In the 1989 annual report I wrote about "Mistakes of the First 25 Years" and promised you an update in 2015. My experiences in the first few years of this second "semester" indicate that my backlog of matters to be discussed will become unmanageable if I stick to my original plan. Therefore, I will occasionally unburden myself in these pages in the hope that public confession may deter further bumblings. (Post-mortems prove useful for hospitals and football teams; why not for businesses and investors?)

Typically, our most egregious mistakes fall in the omission, rather than the commission, category. That may spare Charlie and me some embarrassment, since you don't see these errors; but their invisibility does not reduce their cost. In this mea culpa, I am not talking about missing out on some company that depends upon an esoteric invention (such as Xerox), high-technology (Apple), or even brilliant merchandising (Wal-Mart). We will never develop the competence to spot such businesses early. Instead I refer to business situations that Charlie and I can understand and that seem clearly attractive—but in which we nevertheless end up sucking our thumbs rather than buying.

Every writer knows it helps to use striking examples, but I wish the one I now present wasn't quite so dramatic: In early 1988, we decided to buy 30 million shares (adjusted for a subsequent split) of Federal National Mortgage Association (Fannie Mae), which would have been a $350-$400 million investment. We had owned the stock some years earlier and understood the company's business. Furthermore, it was clear to us that David Maxwell, Fannie Mae's CEO, had dealt superbly with some problems that he had inherited and had established the company as a financial powerhouse—with the best yet to come. I visited David in Washington and confirmed that he would not be uncomfortable if we were to take a large position.

After we bought about 7 million shares, the price began to climb. In frustration, I stopped buying (a mistake that, thankfully, I did not repeat when Coca-Cola stock rose similarly during our purchase program). In an even sillier move, I surrendered to my distaste for holding small positions and sold the 7 million shares we owned.

I wish I could give you a halfway rational explanation for my amateurish behavior vis-a-vis Fannie Mae. But there isn't one. What I *can* give you is an estimate as of yearend 1991 of the approximate gain that Berkshire *didn't* make because of your Chairman's mistake: about $1.4 billion.

Fixed-Income Securities

We made several significant changes in our fixed-income portfolio during 1991. As I noted earlier, our Gillette preferred was called for redemption, which forced us to convert to common stock; we eliminated our holdings of an RJR Nabisco issue that was subject to an exchange offer and subsequent call; and we purchased fixed-income securities of American Express and First Empire State Corp., a Buffalo-based bank holding company. We also added to a small position in ACF Industries that we had established in late 1990. Our largest holdings at yearend were:

| | (000s omitted) | |
Issuer	Cost of Preferreds and Amortized Value of Bonds	Market
ACF Industries	$ 93,918[2]	$118,683
American Express	300,000	263,265[1][2]
Champion International	300,000[2]	300,000[1]
First Empire State	40,000	50,000[1][2]
RJR Nabisco	222,148[2]	285,683
Salomon	700,000[2]	714,000[1]
USAir	358,000[2]	232,700[1]
Washington Public Power Systems . .	158,553[2]	203,071

(1) Fair value as determined by Charlie and me
(2) Carrying value in our financial statements

Our $40 million of First Empire State preferred carries a 9% coupon, is non-callable until 1996 and is convertible at $78.91 per share. Normally I would think a purchase of this size too small for Berkshire, but I have enormous respect for Bob Wilmers, CEO of First Empire, and like being his partner on any scale.

Our American Express preferred is not a normal fixed-income security. Rather it is a "Perc," which carries a fixed dividend of 8.85% on our $300 million cost. Absent one exception mentioned later, our preferred must be converted three years after issuance, into a maximum of 12,244,898 shares. If necessary, a downward adjustment in the conversion ratio will be made in order to limit to $414 million the total value of the common we receive. Though there is thus a ceiling on the value of the common stock that we will receive upon conversion, there is no floor. The terms of the preferred, however, include a provision allowing us to extend the conversion date by one year if the common stock is below $24.50 on the third anniversary of our purchase.

Overall, our fixed-income investments have treated us well, both over the long term and recently. We have realized large capital gains from these holdings, including about $152 million in 1991. Additionally, our after-tax yields have considerably exceeded those earned by most fixed-income portfolios.

Nevertheless, we have had some surprises, none greater than the need for me to involve myself personally and intensely in the Salomon situation. As I write this letter, I am also writing a letter for inclusion in Salomon's annual report and I refer you to that report for an update on the company. (Write to: Corporate Secretary, Salomon Inc, Seven World Trade Center, New York, NY 10048) Despite the company's travails, Charlie and I believe our Salomon preferred stock increased slightly in value during 1991. Lower interest rates and a higher price for Salomon's common produced this result.

Last year I told you that our USAir investment "should work out all right unless the industry is decimated during the next few years." Unfortunately 1991 was a decimating period for the industry, as Midway, Pan Am and America West all entered bankruptcy. (Stretch the period to 14 months and you can add Continental and TWA.)

The low valuation that we have given USAir in our table reflects the risk that the industry will remain unprofitable for virtually all participants in it, a risk that is far from negligible. The risk is heightened by the fact that the courts have been encouraging bankrupt carriers to continue operating. These carriers can temporarily charge fares that are below the industry's costs because the bankrupts don't incur the capital costs faced by their solvent brethren and because they can fund their losses—and thereby stave off shutdown—by selling off assets. This burn-the-furniture-to-provide-firewood approach to fare-setting by bankrupt carriers contributes to the toppling of previously-marginal carriers, creating a domino effect that is perfectly designed to bring the industry to its knees.

Seth Schofield, who became CEO of USAir in 1991, is making major adjustments in the airline's operations in order to improve its chances of being one of the few industry survivors. There is no tougher job in corporate America than running an airline: Despite the huge amounts of equity capital that have been injected into it, the industry, in aggregate, has posted a net loss since its birth after Kitty Hawk. Airline managers need brains, guts, and experience—and Seth possesses all three of these attributes.

Miscellaneous

About 97.7% of all eligible shares participated in Berkshire's 1991 shareholder-designated contributions program. Contributions made through the program were $6.8 million, and 2,630 charities were recipients.

We suggest that new shareholders read the description of our shareholder-designated contributions program that appears on pages 48-49. To participate in future programs, you must make sure your shares are registered in the name of the actual owner, not in the nominee name of a broker, bank or depository. Shares not so registered on August 31, 1992 will be ineligible for the 1992 program.

In addition to the shareholder-designated contributions that Berkshire distributes, managers of our operating businesses make contributions, including merchandise, averaging about $1.5 million annually. These contributions support local charities, such as The United Way, and produce roughly commensurate benefits for our businesses.

However, neither our operating managers nor officers of the parent company use Berkshire funds to make contributions to broad national programs or charitable activities of special personal interest to them, except to the extent they do so as shareholders. If your employees, including your CEO, wish to give to their alma maters or other institutions to which they feel a personal attachment, we believe they should use their own money, not yours.

* * * * * * * * * * *

The faithful will notice that, for the first time in some years, Charlie's annual letter to Wesco shareholders is not reprinted in this report. Since his letter is relatively barebones this year, Charlie said he saw no point in including it in these pages; my own recommendation, however, is that you get a copy of the Wesco report. Simply write: Corporate Secretary, Wesco Financial Corporation, 315 East Colorado Boulevard, Pasadena, CA 91101.

* * * * * * * * * * *

Malcolm G. Chace, Jr., now 88, has decided not to stand for election as a director this year. But the association of the Chace family with Berkshire will not end: Malcolm III (Kim), Malcolm's son, will be nominated to replace him.

In 1931, Malcolm went to work for Berkshire Fine Spinning Associates, which merged with Hathaway Manufacturing Co. in 1955 to form our present company. Two years later, Malcolm became Berkshire Hathaway's Chairman, a position he held as well in early 1965 when he made it possible for Buffett Partnership, Ltd. to buy a key block of Berkshire stock owned by some of his relatives. This purchase gave our partnership effective control of the company. Malcolm's immediate family meanwhile kept its Berkshire stock and for the last 27 years has had the second-largest holding in the company, trailing only the Buffett family. Malcolm has been a joy to work with and we are delighted that the long-running relationship between the Chace family and Berkshire is continuing to a new generation.

* * * * * * * * * * *

The annual meeting this year will be held at the Orpheum Theater in downtown Omaha at 9:30 a.m. on Monday, April 27, 1992. Attendance last year grew to a record 1,550, but that still leaves plenty of room at the Orpheum.

We recommend that you get your hotel reservations early at one of these hotels: (1) The Radisson-Redick Tower, a small (88 rooms) but nice hotel across the street from the Orpheum; (2) the much larger Red Lion Hotel, located about a five-minute walk from the Orpheum; or (3) the Marriott, located in West Omaha about 100 yards from Borsheim's and a twenty minute drive from downtown. We will have buses at the Marriott that will leave at 8:30 and 8:45 for the meeting and return after it ends.

Charlie and I always enjoy the meeting, and we hope you can make it. The quality of our shareholders is reflected in the quality of the questions we get: We have never attended an annual meeting anywhere that features such a consistently high level of intelligent, owner-related questions.

An attachment to our proxy material explains how you can obtain the card you will need for admission to the meeting. With the admission card, we will enclose information about parking facilities located near the Orpheum. If you are driving, come a little early. Nearby lots fill up quickly and you may have to walk a few blocks.

As usual, we will have buses to take you to Nebraska Furniture Mart and Borsheim's after the meeting and to take you from there to downtown hotels or the airport later. I hope that you will allow plenty of time to fully explore the attractions of both stores. Those of you arriving early can visit the Furniture Mart any day of the week; it is open from 10 a.m. to 5:30 p.m. on Saturdays and from noon to 5:30 p.m. on Sundays. While there, stop at the See's Candy Cart and find out for yourself why Americans ate 26 million pounds of See's products last year.

Borsheim's normally is closed on Sunday, but we will be open for shareholders and their guests from noon to 6 p.m. on Sunday, April 26. Borsheim's will also have a special party the previous evening at which shareholders are welcome. (You must, however, write Mrs. Gladys Kaiser at our office for an invitation.) On display that evening will be a 150-year retrospective of the most exceptional timepieces made by Patek Philippe, including watches once owned by Queen Victoria, Pope Pius IX, Rudyard Kipling, Madame Curie and Albert Einstein. The centerpiece of the exhibition will be a $5 million watch whose design and manufacture required nine years of labor by Patek Philippe craftsmen. Along with the rest of the collection, this watch will be on display at the store on Sunday—unless Charlie has by then impulsively bought it.

Nicholas Kenner nailed me—again—at last year's meeting, pointing out that I had said in the 1990 annual report that he was 11 in May 1990, when actually he was 9. So, asked Nicholas rather caustically: "If you can't get that straight, how do I know the numbers in the back [the financials] are correct?" I'm still searching for a snappy response. Nicholas will be at this year's meeting—he spurned my offer of a trip to Disney World on that day—so join us to watch a continuation of this lop-sided battle of wits.

February 28, 1992

Warren E. Buffett
Chairman of the Board

BERKSHIRE HATHAWAY INC.

To the Shareholders of Berkshire Hathaway Inc.:

Our per-share book value increased 20.3% during 1992. Over the last 28 years (that is, since present management took over) book value has grown from $19 to $7,745, or at a rate of 23.6% compounded annually.

During the year, Berkshire's net worth increased by $1.52 billion. More than 98% of this gain came from earnings and appreciation of portfolio securities, with the remainder coming from the issuance of new stock. These shares were issued as a result of our calling our convertible debentures for redemption on January 4, 1993, and of some holders electing to receive common shares rather than the cash that was their alternative. Most holders of the debentures who converted into common waited until January to do it, but a few made the move in December and therefore received shares in 1992. To sum up what happened to the $476 million of bonds we had outstanding: $25 million were converted into shares before yearend; $46 million were converted in January; and $405 million were redeemed for cash. The conversions were made at $11,719 per share, so altogether we issued 6,106 shares.

Berkshire now has 1,152,547 shares outstanding. That compares, you will be interested to know, to 1,137,778 shares outstanding on October 1, 1964, the beginning of the fiscal year during which Buffett Partnership, Ltd. acquired control of the company.

We have a firm policy about issuing shares of Berkshire, doing so only when we receive as much value as we give. Equal value, however, has not been easy to obtain, since we have always valued our shares highly. So be it: We wish to increase Berkshire's size only when doing that also increases the wealth of its owners.

Those two objectives do not necessarily go hand-in-hand as an amusing but value-destroying experience in our past illustrates. On that occasion, we had a significant investment in a bank whose management was hell-bent on expansion. (Aren't they all?) When our bank wooed a smaller bank, its owner demanded a stock swap on a basis that valued the acquiree's net worth and earning power at over twice that of the acquirer's. Our management—visibly in heat—quickly capitulated. The owner of the acquiree then insisted on one other condition: "You must promise me," he said in effect, "that once our merger is done and I have become a major shareholder, you'll never again make a deal this dumb."

You will remember that our goal is to increase our per-share intrinsic value—for which our book value is a conservative, but useful, proxy—at a 15% annual rate. This objective, however, cannot be attained in a smooth manner. Smoothness is particularly elusive because of the accounting rules that apply to the common stocks owned by our insurance companies, whose portfolios represent a high proportion of Berkshire's net worth. Since 1979, generally accepted accounting principles (GAAP) have required that these securities be valued at their market prices (less an adjustment for tax on any net unrealized appreciation) rather than at the lower of cost or market. Run-of-the-mill fluctuations in equity prices therefore cause our annual results to gyrate, especially in comparison to those of the typical industrial company.

To illustrate just how volatile our progress has been—and to indicate the impact that market movements have on short-term results—we show on the facing page our annual change in per-share net worth and compare it with the annual results (including dividends) of the S&P 500.

You should keep at least three points in mind as you evaluate this data. The first point concerns the many businesses we operate whose annual earnings are unaffected by changes in stock market valuations. The impact of these businesses on both our absolute and relative performance has changed over the years. Early on, returns from our textile operation, which then represented a significant portion of our net worth, were a major drag on performance, averaging far less than would have been the case if the money invested in that business had instead been invested in the S&P 500. In more recent years, as we assembled our collection of exceptional businesses run by equally exceptional managers, the returns from our operating businesses have been high—usually well in excess of the returns achieved by the S&P.

1

A second important factor to consider—and one that significantly hurts our relative performance—is that both the income and capital gains from our securities are burdened by a substantial corporate tax liability whereas the S&P returns are pre-tax. To comprehend the damage, imagine that Berkshire had owned nothing other than the S&P index during the 28-year period covered. In that case, the tax bite would have caused our corporate performance to be appreciably below the record shown in the table for the S&P. Under present tax laws, a gain for the S&P of 18% delivers a corporate holder of that index a return well short of 13%. And this problem would be intensified if corporate tax rates were to rise. This is a structural disadvantage we simply have to live with; there is no antidote for it.

The third point incorporates two predictions: Charlie Munger, Berkshire's Vice Chairman and my partner, and I are virtually certain that the return over the next decade from an investment in the S&P index will be far less than that of the past decade, and we are dead certain that the drag exerted by Berkshire's expanding capital base will substantially reduce our historical advantage relative to the index.

Making the first prediction goes somewhat against our grain: We've long felt that the only value of stock forecasters is to make fortune tellers look good. Even now, Charlie and I continue to believe that short-term market forecasts are poison and should be kept locked up in a safe place, away from children and also from grown-ups who behave in the market like children. However, it is clear that stocks cannot forever overperform their underlying businesses, as they have so dramatically done for some time, and that fact makes us quite confident of our forecast that the rewards from investing in stocks over the next decade will be significantly smaller than they were in the last. Our second conclusion—that an increased capital base will act as an anchor on our relative performance—seems incontestable. The only open question is whether we can drag the anchor along at some tolerable, though slowed, pace.

We will continue to experience considerable volatility in our annual results. That's assured by the general volatility of the stock market, by the concentration of our equity holdings in just a few companies, and by certain business decisions we have made, most especially our move to commit large resources to super-catastrophe insurance. We not only accept this volatility but welcome it: A tolerance for short-term swings improves our long-term prospects. In baseball lingo, our performance yardstick is slugging percentage, not batting average.

The Salomon Interlude

Last June, I stepped down as Interim Chairman of Salomon Inc after ten months in the job. You can tell from Berkshire's 1991-92 results that the company didn't miss me while I was gone. But the reverse isn't true: I missed Berkshire and am delighted to be back full-time. There is no job in the world that is more fun than running Berkshire and I count myself lucky to be where I am.

The Salomon post, though far from fun, was interesting and worthwhile: In Fortune's annual survey of America's Most Admired Corporations, conducted last September, Salomon ranked second among 311 companies in the degree to which it improved its reputation. Additionally, Salomon Brothers, the securities subsidiary of Salomon Inc, reported record pre-tax earnings last year—34% above the previous high.

Many people helped in the resolution of Salomon's problems and the righting of the firm, but a few clearly deserve special mention. It is no exaggeration to say that without the combined efforts of Salomon executives Deryck Maughan, Bob Denham, Don Howard, and John Macfarlane, the firm very probably would not have survived. In their work, these men were tireless, effective, supportive and selfless, and I will forever be grateful to them.

Salomon's lead lawyer in its Government matters, Ron Olson of Munger, Tolles & Olson, was also key to our success in getting through this trouble. The firm's problems were not only severe, but complex. At least five authorities—the SEC, the Federal Reserve Bank of New York, the U.S. Treasury, the U.S. Attorney for the Southern District of New York, and the Antitrust Division of the Department of Justice—had important concerns about Salomon. If we were to resolve our problems in a coordinated and prompt manner, we needed a lawyer with exceptional legal, business and human skills. Ron had them all.

Acquisitions

Of all our activities at Berkshire, the most exhilarating for Charlie and me is the acquisition of a business with excellent economic characteristics and a management that we like, trust and admire. Such acquisitions are not easy to make but we look for them constantly. In the search, we adopt the same attitude one might find appropriate in looking for a spouse: It pays to be active, interested and open-minded, but it does not pay to be in a hurry.

In the past, I've observed that many acquisition-hungry managers were apparently mesmerized by their child-hood reading of the story about the frog-kissing princess. Remembering her success, they pay dearly for the right to kiss corporate toads, expecting wondrous transfigurations. Initially, disappointing results only deepen their desire to round up new toads. ("Fanaticism," said Santyana, "consists of redoubling your effort when you've forgotten your aim.") Ultimately, even the most optimistic manager must face reality. Standing knee-deep in unresponsive toads, he then announces an enormous "restructuring" charge. In this corporate equivalent of a Head Start program, the CEO receives the education but the stockholders pay the tuition.

In my early days as a manager I, too, dated a few toads. They were cheap dates—I've never been much of a sport—but my results matched those of acquirers who courted higher-priced toads. I kissed and they croaked.

After several failures of this type, I finally remembered some useful advice I once got from a golf pro (who, like all pros who have had anything to do with my game, wishes to remain anonymous). Said the pro: "Practice doesn't make perfect; practice makes permanent." And thereafter I revised my strategy and tried to buy good businesses at fair prices rather than fair businesses at good prices.

Last year, in December, we made an acquisition that is a prototype of what we now look for. The purchase was 82% of Central States Indemnity, an insurer that makes monthly payments for credit-card holders who are unable themselves to pay because they have become disabled or unemployed. Currently the company's annual premiums are about $90 million and profits about $10 million. Central States is based in Omaha and managed by Bill Kizer, a friend of mine for over 35 years. The Kizer family—which includes sons Bill, Dick and John—retains 18% ownership of the business and will continue to run things just as it has in the past. We could not be associated with better people.

Coincidentally, this latest acquisition has much in common with our first, made 26 years ago. At that time, we purchased another Omaha insurer, National Indemnity Company (along with a small sister company) from Jack Ringwalt, another long-time friend. Jack had built the business from scratch and, as was the case with Bill Kizer, thought of me when he wished to sell. (Jack's comment at the time: "If I don't sell the company, my executor will, and I'd rather pick the home for it.") National Indemnity was an outstanding business when we bought it and continued to be under Jack's management. Hollywood has had good luck with sequels; I believe we, too, will.

Berkshire's acquisition criteria are described on page 23. Beyond purchases made by the parent company, however, our subsidiaries sometimes make small "add-on" acquisitions that extend their product lines or distribution capabilities. In this manner, we enlarge the domain of managers we already know to be outstanding—and that's a low-risk and high-return proposition. We made five acquisitions of this type in 1992, and one was not so small: At yearend, H. H. Brown purchased Lowell Shoe Company, a business with $90 million in sales that makes Nurse-mates, a leading line of shoes for nurses, and other kinds of shoes as well. Our operating managers will continue to look for add-on opportunities, and we would expect these to contribute modestly to Berkshire's value in the future.

Then again, a trend has emerged that may make further acquisitions difficult. The parent company made one purchase in 1991, buying H. H. Brown, which is run by Frank Rooney, who has eight children. In 1992 our only deal was with Bill Kizer, father of nine. It won't be easy to keep this string going in 1993.

Sources of Reported Earnings

The table below shows the major sources of Berkshire's reported earnings. In this presentation, amortization of Goodwill and other major purchase-price accounting adjustments are not charged against the specific businesses to which they apply, but are instead aggregated and shown separately. This procedure lets you view the earnings of our businesses as they would have been reported had we not purchased them. I've explained in past reports why this form of presentation seems to us to be more useful to investors and managers than one utilizing GAAP, which requires purchase-price adjustments to be made on a business-by-business basis. The total net earnings we show in the table are, of course, identical to the GAAP total in our audited financial statements.

	(000s omitted)			
			Berkshire's Share of Net Earnings (after taxes and minority interests)	
	Pre-Tax Earnings			
	1992	1991	1992	1991
Operating Earnings:				
Insurance Group:				
Underwriting	$(108,961)	$(119,593)	$ (71,141)	$ (77,229)
Net Investment Income	355,067	331,846	305,763	285,173
H. H. Brown (acquired 7/1/91)	27,883	13,616	17,340	8,611
Buffalo News	47,863	37,113	28,163	21,841
Fechheimer	13,698	12,947	7,267	6,843
Kirby	35,653	35,726	22,795	22,555
Nebraska Furniture Mart	17,110	14,384	8,072	6,993
Scott Fetzer Manufacturing Group	31,954	26,123	19,883	15,901
See's Candies	42,357	42,390	25,501	25,575
Wesco – other than Insurance	15,153	12,230	9,195	8,777
World Book	29,044	22,483	19,503	15,487
Amortization of Goodwill	(4,702)	(4,113)	(4,687)	(4,098)
Other Purchase-Price Accounting Charges	(7,385)	(6,021)	(8,383)	(7,019)
Interest Expense*	(98,643)	(89,250)	(62,899)	(57,165)
Shareholder-Designated Contributions	(7,634)	(6,772)	(4,913)	(4,388)
Other	72,223	77,399	36,267	47,896
Operating Earnings	460,680	400,508	347,726	315,753
Sales of Securities	89,937	192,478	59,559	124,155
Total Earnings – All Entities	$ 550,617	$ 592,986	$ 407,285	$ 439,908

Excludes interest expense of Scott Fetzer Financial Group and Mutual Savings & Loan. Includes $22.5 million in 1992 and $5.7 million in 1991 of premiums paid on the early redemption of debt.

A large amount of additional information about these businesses is given on pages 37-47, where you will also find our segment earnings reported on a GAAP basis. Our goal is to give you all of the financial information that Charlie and I consider significant in making our own evaluation of Berkshire.

"Look-Through" Earnings

We've previously discussed look-through earnings, which consist of: (1) the operating earnings reported in the previous section, plus; (2) the retained operating earnings of major investees that, under GAAP accounting, are not reflected in our profits, less; (3) an allowance for the tax that would be paid by Berkshire if these retained earnings of investees had instead been distributed to us. Though no single figure can be perfect, we believe that the look-through number more accurately portrays the earnings of Berkshire than does the GAAP number.

I've told you that over time look-through earnings must increase at about 15% annually if our intrinsic business value is to grow at that rate. Our look-through earnings in 1992 were $604 million, and they will need to grow to more than $1.8 billion by the year 2000 if we are to meet that 15% goal. For us to get there, our operating subsidiaries and investees must deliver excellent performances, and we must exercise some skill in capital allocation as well.

We cannot promise to achieve the $1.8 billion target. Indeed, we may not even come close to it. But it does guide our decision-making: When we allocate capital today, we are thinking about what will maximize look-through earnings in 2000.

We do not, however, see this long-term focus as eliminating the need for us to achieve decent short-term results as well. After all, we were thinking long-range thoughts five or ten years ago, and the moves we made then should now be paying off. If plantings made confidently are repeatedly followed by disappointing harvests, something is wrong with the farmer. (Or perhaps with the farm: Investors should understand that for certain companies, and even for some industries, there simply is *no* good long-term strategy.) Just as you should be suspicious of managers who pump up short-term earnings by accounting maneuvers, asset sales and the like, so also should you be suspicious of those managers who fail to deliver for extended periods and blame it on their long-term focus. (Even Alice, after listening to the Queen lecture her about "jam tomorrow," finally insisted, "It must come sometimes to jam today.")

The following table shows you how we calculate look-through earnings, though I warn you that the figures are necessarily *very* rough. (The dividends paid to us by these investees have been included in the operating earnings itemized on page 8, mostly under "Insurance Group: Net Investment Income.")

Berkshire's Major Investees	Berkshire's Approximate Ownership at Yearend		Berkshire's Share of Undistributed Operating Earnings (in millions)	
	1992	1991	1992	1991
Capital Cities/ABC Inc.	18.2%	18.1%	$ 70	$ 61
The Coca-Cola Company	7.1%	7.0%	82	69
Federal Home Loan Mortgage Corp.	8.2%[1]	3.4%[1]	29	15
GEICO Corp.	48.1%	48.2%	34	69[3]
General Dynamics Corp.	14.1%	--	11[2]	--
The Gillette Company	10.9%	11.0%	38[3]	23[2]
Guinness PLC	2.0%	1.6%	7[2]	--
The Washington Post Company	14.6%	14.6%	11	10
Wells Fargo & Company	11.5%	9.6%	16[2]	(17)[2]
Berkshire's share of undistributed earnings of major investees.			$298	$230
Hypothetical tax on these undistributed investee earnings			(42)	(30)
Reported operating earnings of Berkshire			348	316
Total look-through earnings of Berkshire.			$604	$516

(1) Net of minority interest at Wesco
(2) Calculated on average ownership for the year
(3) Excludes realized capital gains, which have been both recurring and significant

Insurance Operations

Shown below is an updated version of our usual table presenting key figures for the property-casualty insurance industry:

	Yearly Change in Premiums Written (%)	*Combined Ratio After Policyholder Dividends*
1981.	3.8	106.0
1982.	3.7	109.6
1983.	5.0	112.0
1984.	8.5	118.0
1985.	22.1	116.3
1986	22.2	108.0
1987.	9.4	104.6
1988.	4.5	105.4
1989.	3.2	109.2
1990.	4.5	109.6
1991 (Revised)	2.4	108.8
1992 (Est.).	2.7	114.8

The combined ratio represents total insurance costs (losses incurred plus expenses) compared to revenue from premiums: A ratio below 100 indicates an underwriting profit, and one above 100 indicates a loss. The higher the ratio, the worse the year. When the investment income that an insurer earns from holding policyholders' funds ("the float") is taken into account, a combined ratio in the 106—110 range typically produces an overall break-even result, exclusive of earnings on the funds provided by shareholders.

About four points in the industry's 1992 combined ratio can be attributed to Hurricane Andrew, which caused the largest insured loss in history. Andrew destroyed a few small insurers. Beyond that, it awakened some larger companies to the fact that their reinsurance protection against catastrophes was far from adequate. (It's only when the tide goes out that you learn who's been swimming naked.) One major insurer escaped insolvency solely because it had a wealthy parent that could promptly supply a massive transfusion of capital.

Bad as it was, however, Andrew could easily have been far more damaging if it had hit Florida 20 or 30 miles north of where it actually did and had hit Louisiana further east than was the case. All in all, many companies will rethink their reinsurance programs in light of the Andrew experience.

As you know we are a large writer—perhaps the largest in the world—of "super-cat" coverages, which are the policies that other insurance companies buy to protect themselves against major catastrophic losses. Consequently, we too took our lumps from Andrew, suffering losses from it of about $125 million, an amount roughly equal to our 1992 super-cat premium income. Our other super-cat losses, though, were negligible. This line of business therefore produced an overall loss of only $2 million for the year. (In addition, our investee, GEICO, suffered a net loss from Andrew, after reinsurance recoveries and tax savings, of about $50 million, of which our share is roughly $25 million. This loss did not affect our operating earnings, but did reduce our look-through earnings.)

In last year's report I told you that I hoped that our super-cat business would over time achieve a 10% profit margin. But I also warned you that in any given year the line was likely to be "either enormously profitable or enormously unprofitable." Instead, both 1991 and 1992 have come in close to a break-even level. Nonetheless, I see these results as aberrations and stick with my prediction of huge annual swings in profitability from this business.

Let me remind you of some characteristics of our super-cat policies. Generally, they are activated only when two things happen. First, the direct insurer or reinsurer we protect must suffer losses of a given amount—that's the policyholder's "retention"—from a catastrophe; and second, industry-wide insured losses from the catastrophe must exceed some minimum level, which usually is $3 billion or more. In most cases, the policies we issue cover only a specific geographical area, such as a portion of the U.S., the entire U.S., or everywhere other than the U.S. Also, many policies are not activated by the first super-cat that meets the policy terms, but instead cover only a "second-event" or even a third- or fourth-event. Finally, some policies are triggered only by a catastrophe of a specific type, such as an earthquake. Our exposures are large: We have one policy that calls for us to pay $100 million to the policyholder if a specified catastrophe occurs. (Now you know why I suffer eyestrain: from watching The Weather Channel.)

Currently, Berkshire is second in the U.S. property-casualty industry in net worth (the leader being State Farm, which neither buys nor sells reinsurance). Therefore, we have the capacity to assume risk on a scale that interests virtually no other company. We have the appetite as well: As Berkshire's net worth and earnings grow, our willingness to write business increases also. But let me add that means good business. The saying, "a fool and his money are soon invited everywhere," applies in spades in reinsurance, and we actually reject more than 98% of the business we are offered. Our ability to choose between good and bad proposals reflects a management strength that matches our financial strength: Ajit Jain, who runs our reinsurance operation, is simply the best in this business. In combination, these strengths guarantee that we will stay a major factor in the super-cat business so long as prices are appropriate.

What constitutes an appropriate price, of course, is difficult to determine. Catastrophe insurers can't simply extrapolate past experience. If there is truly "global warming," for example, the odds would shift, since tiny changes in atmospheric conditions can produce momentous changes in weather patterns. Furthermore, in recent years there has been a mushrooming of population and insured values in U.S. coastal areas that are particularly vulnerable to hurricanes, the number one creator of super-cats. A hurricane that caused x dollars of damage 20 years ago could easily cost $10x$ now.

Occasionally, also, the unthinkable happens. Who would have guessed, for example, that a major earthquake could occur in Charleston, S.C.? (It struck in 1886, registered an estimated 6.6 on the Richter scale, and caused 60 deaths.) And who could have imagined that our country's most serious quake would occur at New Madrid, Missouri, which suffered an estimated 8.7 shocker in 1812. By comparison, the 1989 San Francisco quake was a 7.1—and remember that each one-point Richter increase represents a ten-fold increase in strength. Someday, a U.S. earthquake occurring far from California will cause enormous losses for insurers.

When viewing our quarterly figures, you should understand that our accounting for super-cat premiums differs from our accounting for other insurance premiums. Rather than recording our super-cat premiums on a pro-rata basis over the life of a given policy, we defer recognition of revenue until a loss occurs or until the policy expires. We take this conservative approach because the likelihood of super-cats causing us losses is particularly great toward the end of the year. It is then that weather tends to kick up: Of the ten largest insured losses in U.S. history, nine occurred in the last half of the year. In addition, policies that are not triggered by a first event are unlikely, by their very terms, to cause us losses until late in the year.

The bottom-line effect of our accounting procedure for super-cats is this: Large losses may be reported in any quarter of the year, but significant profits will only be reported in the fourth quarter.

* * * * * * * * * * * *

As I've told you in each of the last few years, what counts in our insurance business is "the cost of funds developed from insurance," or in the vernacular, "the cost of float." Float—which we generate in exceptional amounts—is the total of loss reserves, loss adjustment expense reserves and unearned premium reserves minus agents' balances, prepaid acquisition costs and deferred charges applicable to assumed reinsurance. The cost of float is measured by our underwriting loss.

The table below shows our cost of float since we entered the business in 1967.

	(1) Underwriting Loss *(In $ Millions)*	(2) Average Float	Approximate Cost of Funds *(Ratio of 1 to 2)*	Yearend Yield on Long-Term Govt. Bonds
1967	profit	$17.3	less than zero	5.50%
1968	profit	19.9	less than zero	5.90%
1969	profit	23.4	less than zero	6.79%
1970	$0.37	32.4	1.14%	6.25%
1971	profit	52.5	less than zero	5.81%
1972	profit	69.5	less than zero	5.82%
1973	profit	73.3	less than zero	7.27%
1974	7.36	79.1	9.30%	8.13%
1975	11.35	87.6	12.96%	8.03%
1976	profit	102.6	less than zero	7.30%
1977	profit	139.0	less than zero	7.97%
1978	profit	190.4	less than zero	8.93%
1979	profit	227.3	less than zero	10.08%
1980	profit	237.0	less than zero	11.94%
1981	profit	228.4	less than zero	13.61%
1982	21.56	220.6	9.77%	10.64%
1983	33.87	231.3	14.64%	11.84%
1984	48.06	253.2	18.98%	11.58%
1985	44.23	390.2	11.34%	9.34%
1986	55.84	797.5	7.00%	7.60%
1987	55.43	1,266.7	4.38%	8.95%
1988	11.08	1,497.7	0.74%	9.00%
1989	24.40	1,541.3	1.58%	7.97%
1990	26.65	1,637.3	1.63%	8.24%
1991	119.59	1,895.0	6.31%	7.40%
1992	108.96	2,290.4	4.76%	7.39%

Last year, our insurance operation again generated funds at a cost below that incurred by the U.S. Government on its newly-issued long-term bonds. This means that in 21 years out of the 26 years we have been in the insurance business we have beaten the Government's rate, and often we have done so by a wide margin. (If, on average, we didn't beat the Government's rate, there would be no economic reason for us to be in the business.)

In 1992, as in previous years, National Indemnity's commercial auto and general liability business, led by Don Wurster, and our homestate operation, led by Rod Eldred, made excellent contributions to our low cost of float. Indeed, both of these operations recorded an underwriting profit last year, thereby generating float at a less-than-zero cost. The bulk of our float, meanwhile, comes from large transactions developed by Ajit. His efforts are likely to produce a further growth in float during 1993.

Charlie and I continue to like the insurance business, which we expect to be our main source of earnings for decades to come. The industry is huge; in certain sectors we can compete world-wide; and Berkshire possesses an important competitive advantage. We will look for ways to expand our participation in the business, either indirectly as we have done through GEICO or directly as we did by acquiring Central States Indemnity.

Common Stock Investments

Below we list our common stock holdings having a value of over $100 million. A small portion of these investments belongs to subsidiaries of which Berkshire owns less than 100%.

Shares	Company	12/31/92	
		Cost	Market
		(000s omitted)	
3,000,000	Capital Cities/ABC, Inc.	$ 517,500	$1,523,500
93,400,000	The Coca-Cola Co.	1,023,920	3,911,125
16,196,700	Federal Home Loan Mortgage Corp. ("Freddie Mac")	414,257	783,515
34,250,000	GEICO Corp.	45,713	2,226,250
4,350,000	General Dynamics Corp.	312,438	450,769
24,000,000	The Gillette Company	600,000	1,365,000
38,335,000	Guinness PLC	333,019	299,581
1,727,765	The Washington Post Company	9,731	396,954
6,358,418	Wells Fargo & Company	380,983	485,624

Leaving aside splits, the number of shares we held in these companies changed during 1992 in only four cases: We added moderately to our holdings in Guinness and Wells Fargo, we more than doubled our position in Freddie Mac, and we established a new holding in General Dynamics. We like to buy.

Selling, however, is a different story. There, our pace of activity resembles that forced upon a traveler who found himself stuck in tiny Podunk's only hotel. With no T.V. in his room, he faced an evening of boredom. But his spirits soared when he spied a book on the night table entitled "Things to do in Podunk." Opening it, he found just a single sentence: "You're doing it."

We were lucky in our General Dynamics purchase. I had paid little attention to the company until last summer, when it announced it would repurchase about 30% of its shares by way of a Dutch tender. Seeing an arbitrage opportunity, I began buying the stock for Berkshire, expecting to tender our holdings for a small profit. We've made the same sort of commitment perhaps a half-dozen times in the last few years, reaping decent rates of return for the short periods our money has been tied up.

But then I began studying the company and the accomplishments of Bill Anders in the brief time he'd been CEO. And what I saw made my eyes pop: Bill had a clearly articulated and rational strategy; he had been focused and imbued with a sense of urgency in carrying it out; and the results were truly remarkable.

In short order, I dumped my arbitrage thoughts and decided that Berkshire should become a long-term investor with Bill. We were helped in gaining a large position by the fact that a tender greatly swells the volume of trading in a stock. In a one-month period, we were able to purchase 14% of the General Dynamics shares that remained outstanding after the tender was completed.

****

Our equity-investing strategy remains little changed from what it was fifteen years ago, when we said in the 1977 annual report: "We select our marketable equity securities in much the way we would evaluate a business for acquisition in its entirety. We want the business to be one (a) that we can understand; (b) with favorable long-term prospects; (c) operated by honest and competent people; and (d) available at a very attractive price." We have seen cause to make only one change in this creed: Because of both market conditions and our size, we now substitute "an attractive price" for "a very attractive price."

But how, you will ask, does one decide what's "attractive"? In answering this question, most analysts feel they must choose between two approaches customarily thought to be in opposition: "value" and "growth." Indeed, many investment professionals see any mixing of the two terms as a form of intellectual cross-dressing.

We view that as fuzzy thinking (in which, it must be confessed, I myself engaged some years ago). In our opinion, the two approaches are joined at the hip: Growth is *always* a component in the calculation of value, constituting a variable whose importance can range from negligible to enormous and whose impact can be negative as well as positive.

In addition, we think the very term "value investing" is redundant. What is "investing" if it is not the act of seeking value at least sufficient to justify the amount paid? Consciously paying more for a stock than its calculated value—in the hope that it can soon be sold for a still-higher price—should be labeled speculation (which is neither illegal, immoral nor—in our view—financially fattening).

Whether appropriate or not, the term "value investing" is widely used. Typically, it connotes the purchase of stocks having attributes such as a low ratio of price to book value, a low price-earnings ratio, or a high dividend yield. Unfortunately, such characteristics, even if they appear in combination, are far from determinative as to whether an investor is indeed buying something for what it is worth and is therefore truly operating on the principle of obtaining value in his investments. Correspondingly, opposite characteristics—a high ratio of price to book value, a high price-earnings ratio, and a low dividend yield—are in no way inconsistent with a "value" purchase.

Similarly, business growth, per se, tells us little about value. It's true that growth often has a positive impact on value, sometimes one of spectacular proportions. But such an effect is far from certain. For example, investors have regularly poured money into the domestic airline business to finance profitless (or worse) growth. For these investors, it would have been far better if Orville had failed to get off the ground at Kitty Hawk: The more the industry has grown, the worse the disaster for owners.

Growth benefits investors only when the business in point can invest at incremental returns that are enticing—in other words, only when each dollar used to finance the growth creates over a dollar of long-term market value. In the case of a low-return business requiring incremental funds, growth hurts the investor.

In The Theory of Investment Value, written over 50 years ago, John Burr Williams set forth the equation for value, which we condense here: *The value of any stock, bond or business today is determined by the cash inflows and outflows—discounted at an appropriate interest rate—that can be expected to occur during the remaining life of the asset.* Note that the formula is the same for stocks as for bonds. Even so, there is an important, and difficult to deal with, difference between the two: A bond has a coupon and maturity date that define future cash flows; but in the case of equities, the investment analyst must himself estimate the future "coupons." Furthermore, the quality of management affects the bond coupon only rarely—chiefly when management is so inept or dishonest that payment of interest is suspended. In contrast, the ability of management can dramatically affect the equity "coupons."

The investment shown by the discounted-flows-of-cash calculation to be the cheapest is the one that the investor should purchase—irrespective of whether the business grows or doesn't, displays volatility or smoothness in its earnings, or carries a high price or low in relation to its current earnings and book value. Moreover, though the value equation has usually shown equities to be cheaper than bonds, that result is not inevitable: When bonds are calculated to be the more attractive investment, they should be bought.

Leaving the question of price aside, the best business to own is one that over an extended period can employ large amounts of incremental capital at very high rates of return. The worst business to own is one that must, or *will*, do the opposite—that is, consistently employ ever-greater amounts of capital at very low rates of return. Unfortunately, the first type of business is very hard to find: Most high-return businesses need relatively little capital. Shareholders of such a business usually will benefit if it pays out most of its earnings in dividends or makes significant stock repurchases.

Though the mathematical calculations required to evaluate equities are not difficult, an analyst—even one who is experienced and intelligent—can easily go wrong in estimating future "coupons." At Berkshire, we attempt to deal with this problem in two ways. First, we try to stick to businesses we believe we understand. That means they must be relatively simple and stable in character. If a business is complex or subject to constant change, we're not smart enough to predict future cash flows. Incidentally, that shortcoming doesn't bother us. What counts for most people in investing is not how much they know, but rather how realistically they define what they don't know. An investor needs to do very few things right as long as he or she avoids big mistakes.

Second, and equally important, we insist on a margin of safety in our purchase price. If we calculate the value of a common stock to be only slightly higher than its price, we're not interested in buying. We believe this margin-of-safety principle, so strongly emphasized by Ben Graham, to be the cornerstone of investment success.

Fixed-Income Securities

Below we list our largest holdings of fixed-income securities:

	(000s omitted)	
Issuer	Cost of Preferreds and Amortized Value of Bonds	Market
ACF Industries Debentures............	$133,065[1]	$163,327
American Express "Percs"	300,000	309,000[1][2]
Champion International Conv. Pfd.......	300,000[1]	309,000[2]
First Empire State Conv. Pfd..........	40,000	68,000[1][2]
Salomon Conv. Pfd.................	700,000[1]	756,000[2]
USAir Conv. Pfd...................	358,000[1]	268,700[2]
Washington Public Power Systems Bonds .	58,768[1]	81,002

(1) Carrying value in our financial statements
(2) Fair value as determined by Charlie and me

During 1992 we added to our holdings of ACF debentures, had some of our WPPSS bonds called, and sold our RJR Nabisco position.

Over the years, we've done well with fixed-income investments, having realized from them both large capital gains (including $80 million in 1992) and exceptional current income. Chrysler Financial, Texaco, Time-Warner, WPPSS and RJR Nabisco were particularly good investments for us. Meanwhile, our fixed-income losses have been negligible: We've had thrills but so far no spills.

Despite the success we experienced with our Gillette preferred, which converted to common stock in 1991, and despite our reasonable results with other negotiated purchases of preferreds, our overall performance with such purchases has been inferior to that we have achieved with purchases made in the secondary market. This is actually the result we expected. It corresponds with our belief that an intelligent investor in common stocks will do better in the secondary market than he will do buying new issues.

The reason has to do with the way prices are set in each instance. The secondary market, which is periodically ruled by mass folly, is constantly setting a "clearing" price. No matter how foolish that price may be, it's what counts for the holder of a stock or bond who needs or wishes to sell, of whom there are always going to be a few at any moment. In many instances, shares worth x in business value have sold in the market for $1/2x$ or less.

The new-issue market, on the other hand, is ruled by controlling stockholders and corporations, who can usually select the timing of offerings or, if the market looks unfavorable, can avoid an offering altogether. Understandably, these sellers are not going to offer any bargains, either by way of a public offering or in a negotiated transaction: It's rare you'll find x for $1/2x$ here. Indeed, in the case of common-stock offerings, selling shareholders are often motivated to unload *only* when they feel the market is overpaying. (These sellers, of course, would state that proposition somewhat differently, averring instead that they simply resist selling when the market is underpaying for their goods.)

To date, our negotiated purchases, as a group, have fulfilled but not exceeded the expectation we set forth in our 1989 Annual Report: "Our preferred stock investments should produce returns modestly above those achieved by most fixed-income portfolios." In truth, we would have done better if we could have put the money that went into our negotiated transactions into open-market purchases of the type we like. But both our size and the general strength of the markets made that difficult to do.

There was one other memorable line in the 1989 Annual Report: "We have no ability to forecast the economics of the investment banking business, the airline industry, or the paper industry." At the time some of you may have doubted this confession of ignorance. Now, however, even my mother acknowledges its truth.

In the case of our commitment to USAir, industry economics had soured before the ink dried on our check. As I've previously mentioned, it was I who happily jumped into the pool; no one pushed me. Yes, I knew the industry would be ruggedly competitive, but I did not expect its leaders to engage in prolonged kamikaze behavior. In the last two years, airline companies have acted as if they are members of a competitive tontine, which they wish to bring to its conclusion as rapidly as possible.

Amidst this turmoil, Seth Schofield, CEO of USAir, has done a truly extraordinary job in repositioning the airline. He was particularly courageous in accepting a strike last fall that, had it been lengthy, might well have bankrupted the company. Capitulating to the striking union, however, would have been equally disastrous: The company was burdened with wage costs and work rules that were considerably more onerous than those encumbering its major competitors, and it was clear that over time any high-cost producer faced extinction. Happily for everyone, the strike was settled in a few days.

A competitively-beset business such as USAir requires far more managerial skill than does a business with fine economics. Unfortunately, though, the near-term reward for skill in the airline business is simply survival, not prosperity.

In early 1993, USAir took a major step toward assuring survival—and eventual prosperity—by accepting British Airways' offer to make a substantial, but minority, investment in the company. In connection with this transaction, Charlie and I were asked to join the USAir board. We agreed, though this makes five outside board memberships for me, which is more than I believe advisable for an active CEO. Even so, if an investee's management and directors believe it particularly important that Charlie and I join its board, we are glad to do so. We expect the managers of our investees to work hard to increase the value of the businesses they run, and there are times when large owners should do their bit as well.

Two New Accounting Rules and a Plea for One More

A new accounting rule having to do with deferred taxes becomes effective in 1993. It undoes a dichotomy in our books that I have described in previous annual reports and that relates to the accrued taxes carried against the unrealized appreciation in our investment portfolio. At yearend 1992, that appreciation amounted to $7.6 billion. Against $6.4 billion of that, we carried taxes at the current 34% rate. Against the remainder of $1.2 billion, we carried an accrual of 28%, the tax rate in effect when that portion of the appreciation occurred. The new accounting rule says we must henceforth accrue all deferred tax at the current rate, which to us seems sensible.

The new marching orders mean that in the first quarter of 1993 we will apply a 34% rate to all of our unrealized appreciation, thereby increasing the tax liability and reducing net worth by $70 million. The new rule also will cause us to make other minor changes in our calculation of deferred taxes.

Future changes in tax rates will be reflected immediately in the liability for deferred taxes and, correspondingly, in net worth. The impact could well be substantial. Nevertheless, what is important in the end is the tax rate at the time we sell securities, when unrealized appreciation becomes realized.

Another major accounting change, whose implementation is required by January 1, 1993, mandates that businesses recognize their present-value liability for post-retirement health benefits. Though GAAP has previously required recognition of pensions to be paid in the future, it has illogically ignored the costs that companies will then have to bear for health benefits. The new rule will force many companies to record a huge balance-sheet liability (and a consequent reduction in net worth) and also henceforth to recognize substantially higher costs when they are calculating annual profits.

In making acquisitions, Charlie and I have tended to avoid companies with significant post-retirement liabilities. As a result, Berkshire's present liability and future costs for post-retirement health benefits—though we now have 22,000 employees—are inconsequential. I need to admit, though, that we had a near miss: In 1982 I made a huge mistake in committing to buy a company burdened by extraordinary post-retirement health obligations. Luckily, though, the transaction fell through for reasons beyond our control. Reporting on this episode in the 1982 annual report, I said: "If we were to introduce graphics to this report, illustrating favorable business developments of the past year, two blank pages depicting this blown deal would be the appropriate centerfold." Even so, I wasn't expecting things to get as bad as they did. Another buyer appeared, the business soon went bankrupt and was shut down, and thousands of workers found those bountiful health-care promises to be largely worthless.

In recent decades, no CEO would have dreamed of going to his board with the proposition that his company become an insurer of uncapped post-retirement health benefits that other corporations chose to install. A CEO didn't need to be a medical expert to know that lengthening life expectancies and soaring health costs would guarantee an insurer a financial battering from such a business. Nevertheless, many a manager blithely committed his own company to a self-insurance plan embodying precisely the same promises—and thereby doomed his shareholders to suffer the inevitable consequences. In health-care, open-ended promises have created open-ended liabilities that in a few cases loom so large as to threaten the global competitiveness of major American industries.

I believe part of the reason for this reckless behavior was that accounting rules did not, for so long, require the booking of post-retirement health costs as they were incurred. Instead, the rules allowed cash-basis accounting, which vastly understated the liabilities that were building up. In effect, the attitude of both managements and their accountants toward these liabilities was "out-of-sight, out-of-mind." Ironically, some of these same managers would be quick to criticize Congress for employing "cash-basis" thinking in respect to Social Security promises or other programs creating future liabilities of size.

Managers thinking about accounting issues should never forget one of Abraham Lincoln's favorite riddles: "How many legs does a dog have if you call his tail a leg?" The answer: "Four, because calling a tail a leg does not make it a leg." It behooves managers to remember that Abe's right even if an auditor is willing to certify that the tail is a leg.

* * * * * * * * * * * *

The most egregious case of let's-not-face-up-to-reality behavior by executives and accountants has occurred in the world of stock options. In Berkshire's 1985 annual report, I laid out my opinions about the use and misuse of options. But even when options are structured properly, they are accounted for in ways that make no sense. The lack of logic is not accidental: For decades, much of the business world has waged war against accounting rulemakers, trying to keep the costs of stock options from being reflected in the profits of the corporations that issue them.

Typically, executives have argued that options are hard to value and that therefore their costs should be ignored. At other times managers have said that assigning a cost to options would injure small start-up businesses. Sometimes they have even solemnly declared that "out-of-the-money" options (those with an exercise price equal to or above the current market price) have no value when they are issued.

Oddly, the Council of Institutional Investors has chimed in with a variation on that theme, opining that options should not be viewed as a cost because they "aren't dollars out of a company's coffers." I see this line of reasoning as offering exciting possibilities to American corporations for instantly improving their reported profits. For example, they could eliminate the cost of insurance by paying for it with options. So if you're a CEO and subscribe to this "no cash-no cost" theory of accounting, I'll make you an offer you can't refuse: Give us a call at Berkshire and we will happily sell you insurance in exchange for a bundle of long-term options on your company's stock.

Shareholders should understand that companies incur costs when they deliver something of value to another party and not just when cash changes hands. Moreover, it is both silly and cynical to say that an important item of cost should not be recognized simply because it can't be quantified with pinpoint precision. Right now, accounting abounds with imprecision. After all, no manager or auditor knows how long a 747 is going to last, which means he also does not know what the yearly depreciation charge for the plane should be. No one knows with any certainty what a bank's annual loan loss charge ought to be. And the estimates of losses that property-casualty companies make are notoriously inaccurate.

Does this mean that these important items of cost should be ignored simply because they can't be quantified with absolute accuracy? Of course not. Rather, these costs should be estimated by honest and experienced people and then recorded. When you get right down to it, what other item of major but hard-to-precisely-calculate cost—other, that is, than stock options—does the accounting profession say should be ignored in the calculation of earnings?

Moreover, options are just not that difficult to value. Admittedly, the difficulty is increased by the fact that the options given to executives are restricted in various ways. These restrictions affect value. They do not, however, eliminate it. In fact, since I'm in the mood for offers, I'll make one to any executive who is granted a restricted option, even though it may be out of the money: On the day of issue, Berkshire will pay him or her a substantial sum for the right to any future gain he or she realizes on the option. So if you find a CEO who says his newly-issued options have little or no value, tell him to try us out. In truth, we have far more confidence in our ability to determine an appropriate price to pay for an option than we have in our ability to determine the proper depreciation rate for our corporate jet.

It seems to me that the realities of stock options can be summarized quite simply: If options aren't a form of compensation, what are they? If compensation isn't an expense, what is it? And, if expenses shouldn't go into the calculation of earnings, where in the world should they go?

The accounting profession and the SEC should be shamed by the fact that they have long let themselves be muscled by business executives on the option-accounting issue. Additionally, the lobbying that executives engage in may have an unfortunate by-product: In my opinion, the business elite risks losing its credibility on issues of significance to society—about which it may have much of value to say—when it advocates the incredible on issues of significance to itself.

Miscellaneous

We have two pieces of regrettable news this year. First, Gladys Kaiser, my friend and assistant for twenty-five years, will give up the latter post after the 1993 annual meeting, though she will certainly remain my friend forever. Gladys and I have been a team, and though I knew her retirement was coming, it is still a jolt.

Secondly, in September, Verne McKenzie relinquished his role as Chief Financial Officer after a 30-year association with me that began when he was the outside auditor of Buffett Partnership, Ltd. Verne is staying on as a consultant, and though that job description is often a euphemism, in this case it has real meaning. I expect Verne to continue to fill an important role at Berkshire but to do so at his own pace. Marc Hamburg, Verne's understudy for five years, has succeeded him as Chief Financial Officer.

I recall that one woman, upon being asked to describe the perfect spouse, specified an archeologist: "The older I get," she said, "the more he'll be interested in me." She would have liked my tastes: I treasure those extraordinary Berkshire managers who are working well past normal retirement age and who concomitantly are achieving results much superior to those of their younger competitors. While I understand and empathize with the decision of Verne and Gladys to retire when the calendar says it's time, theirs is not a step I wish to encourage. It's hard to teach a new dog old tricks.

* * * * * * * * * * * *

I am a moderate in my views about retirement compared to Rose Blumkin, better known as Mrs. B. At 99, she continues to work seven days a week. And about her, I have some particularly good news.

You will remember that after her family sold 80% of Nebraska Furniture Mart (NFM) to Berkshire in 1983, Mrs. B continued to be Chairman and run the carpet operation. In 1989, however, she left because of a managerial disagreement and opened up her own operation next door in a large building that she had owned for several years. In her new business, she ran the carpet section but leased out other home-furnishings departments.

At the end of last year, Mrs. B decided to sell her building and land to NFM. She'll continue, however, to run her carpet business at its current location (no sense slowing down just when you're hitting full stride). NFM will set up shop alongside her, in that same building, thereby making a major addition to its furniture business.

I am delighted that Mrs. B has again linked up with us. Her business story has no parallel and I have always been a fan of hers, whether she was a partner or a competitor. But believe me, partner is better.

This time around, Mrs. B graciously offered to sign a non-compete agreement—and I, having been incautious on this point when she was 89, snapped at the deal. Mrs. B belongs in the Guinness Book of World Records on many counts. Signing a non-compete at 99 merely adds one more.

* * * * * * * * * * * *

Ralph Schey, CEO of Scott Fetzer and a manager who I hope is with us at 99 also, hit a grand slam last year when that company earned a record $110 million pre-tax. What's even more impressive is that Scott Fetzer achieved such earnings while employing only $116 million of equity capital. This extraordinary result is not the product of leverage: The company uses only minor amounts of borrowed money (except for the debt it employs—appropriately—in its finance subsidiary).

Scott Fetzer now operates with a significantly smaller investment in both inventory and fixed assets than it had when we bought it in 1986. This means the company has been able to distribute more than 100% of its earnings to Berkshire during our seven years of ownership while concurrently increasing its earnings stream—which was excellent to begin with—by a lot. Ralph just keeps on outdoing himself, and Berkshire shareholders owe him a great deal.

* * * * * * * * * * * *

Those readers with particularly sharp eyes will note that our corporate expense fell from $5.6 million in 1991 to $4.2 million in 1992. Perhaps you will think that I have sold our corporate jet, The Indefensible. Forget it! I find the thought of retiring the plane even more revolting than the thought of retiring the Chairman. (In this matter I've demonstrated uncharacteristic flexibility: For years I argued passionately against corporate jets. But finally my dogma was run over by my karma.)

Our reduction in corporate overhead actually came about because those expenses were especially high in 1991, when we incurred a one-time environmental charge relating to alleged pre-1970 actions of our textile operation. Now that things are back to normal, our after-tax overhead costs are under 1% of our reported operating earnings and less than 1/2 of 1% of our look-through earnings. We have no legal, personnel, public relations, investor relations, or strategic planning departments. In turn this means we don't need support personnel such as guards, drivers, messengers, etc. Finally, except for Verne, we employ no consultants. Professor Parkinson would like our operation—though Charlie, I must say, still finds it outrageously fat.

At some companies, corporate expense runs 10% or more of operating earnings. The tithing that operations thus makes to headquarters not only hurts earnings, but more importantly slashes capital values. If the business that spends 10% on headquarters' costs achieves earnings at its operating levels identical to those achieved by the business that incurs costs of only 1%, shareholders of the first enterprise suffer a 9% loss in the value of their holdings simply because of corporate overhead. Charlie and I have observed no correlation between high corporate costs and good corporate performance. In fact, we see the simpler, low-cost operation as more likely to operate effectively than its bureaucratic brethren. We're admirers of the Wal-Mart, Nucor, Dover, GEICO, Golden West Financial and Price Co. models.

* * * * * * * * * * * *

Late last year Berkshire's stock price crossed $10,000. Several shareholders have mentioned to me that the high price causes them problems: They like to give shares away each year and find themselves impeded by the tax rule that draws a distinction between annual gifts of $10,000 or under to a single individual and those above $10,000. That is, those gifts no greater than $10,000 are completely tax-free; those above $10,000 require the donor to use up a portion of his or her lifetime exemption from gift and estate taxes, or, if that exemption has been exhausted, to pay gift taxes.

I can suggest three ways to address this problem. The first would be useful to a married shareholder, who can give up to $20,000 annually to a single recipient, as long as the donor files a gift tax return containing his or her spouse's written consent to gifts made during the year.

Secondly, a shareholder, married or not, can make a bargain sale. Imagine, for example, that Berkshire is selling for $12,000 and that one wishes to make only a $10,000 gift. In that case, sell the stock to the giftee for $2,000. (Caution: You will be taxed on the amount, if any, by which the sales price to your giftee exceeds your tax basis.)

Finally, you can establish a partnership with people to whom you are making gifts, fund it with Berkshire shares, and simply give percentage interests in the partnership away each year. These interests can be for any value that you select. If the value is $10,000 or less, the gift will be tax-free.

We issue the customary warning: Consult with your own tax advisor before taking action on any of the more esoteric methods of gift-making.

We hold to the view about stock splits that we set forth in the 1983 Annual Report. Overall, we believe our owner-related policies—including the no-split policy—have helped us assemble a body of shareholders that is the best associated with any widely-held American corporation. Our shareholders think and behave like rational long-term owners and view the business much as Charlie and I do. Consequently, our stock consistently trades in a price range that is sensibly related to intrinsic value.

Additionally, we believe that our shares turn over far less actively than do the shares of any other widely-held company. The frictional costs of trading—which act as a major "tax" on the owners of many companies—are virtually non-existent at Berkshire. (The market-making skills of Jim Maguire, our New York Stock Exchange specialist, definitely help to keep these costs low.) Obviously a split would not change this situation dramatically. Nonetheless, there is no way that our shareholder group would be upgraded by the new shareholders enticed by a split. Instead we believe that modest degradation would occur.

* * * * * * * * * * * *

As I mentioned earlier, on December 16th we called our zero-coupon, convertible debentures for payment on January 4, 1993. These obligations bore interest at 5 1/2%, a low cost for funds when they were issued in 1989, but an unattractive rate for us at the time of call.

The debentures could have been redeemed at the option of the holder in September 1994, and 5 1/2% money available for no longer than that is not now of interest to us. Furthermore, Berkshire shareholders are disadvantaged by having a conversion option outstanding. At the time we issued the debentures, this disadvantage was offset by the attractive interest rate they carried; by late 1992, it was not.

In general, we continue to have an aversion to debt, particularly the short-term kind. But we are willing to incur modest amounts of debt when it is both properly structured and of significant benefit to shareholders.

* * * * * * * * * * * *

About 97% of all eligible shares participated in Berkshire's 1992 shareholder-designated contributions program. Contributions made through the program were $7.6 million, and 2,810 charities were recipients. I'm considering increasing these contributions in the future at a rate greater than the increase in Berkshire's book value, and I would be glad to hear from you as to your thinking about this idea.

We suggest that new shareholders read the description of our shareholder-designated contributions program that appears on pages 48-49. To participate in future programs, you must make sure your shares are registered in the name of the actual owner, not in the nominee name of a broker, bank or depository. Shares not so registered on August 31, 1993 will be ineligible for the 1993 program.

In addition to the shareholder-designated contributions that Berkshire distributes, managers of our operating businesses make contributions, including merchandise, averaging about $2.0 million annually. These contributions support local charities, such as The United Way, and produce roughly commensurate benefits for our businesses.

However, neither our operating managers nor officers of the parent company use Berkshire funds to make contributions to broad national programs or charitable activities of special personal interest to them, except to the extent they do so as shareholders. If your employees, including your CEO, wish to give to their alma maters or other institutions to which they feel a personal attachment, we believe they should use their own money, not yours.

* * * * * * * * * * * *

This year the Annual Meeting will be held at the Orpheum Theater in downtown Omaha at 9:30 a.m. on Monday, April 26, 1993. A record 1,700 people turned up for the meeting last year, but that number still leaves plenty of room at the Orpheum.

We recommend that you get your hotel reservations early at one of these hotels: (1) The Radisson-Redick Tower, a small (88 rooms) but nice hotel across the street from the Orpheum; (2) the much larger Red Lion Hotel, located about a five-minute walk from the Orpheum; or (3) the Marriott, located in West Omaha about 100 yards from Borsheim's, which is a twenty minute drive from downtown. We will have buses at the Marriott that will leave at 8:30 and 8:45 for the meeting and return after it ends.

Charlie and I always enjoy the meeting, and we hope you can make it. The quality of our shareholders is reflected in the quality of the questions we get: We have never attended an annual meeting anywhere that features such a consistently high level of intelligent, owner-related questions.

An attachment to our proxy material explains how you can obtain the card you will need for admission to the meeting. With the admission card, we will enclose information about parking facilities located near the Orpheum. If you are driving, come a little early. Nearby lots fill up quickly and you may have to walk a few blocks.

As usual, we will have buses to take you to Nebraska Furniture Mart and Borsheim's after the meeting and to take you from there to downtown hotels or the airport later. I hope that you will allow plenty of time to fully explore the attractions of both stores. Those of you arriving early can visit the Furniture Mart any day of the week; it is open from 10 a.m. to 5:30 p.m. on Saturdays and from noon to 5:30 p.m. on Sundays. While there, stop at the See's Candy Cart and find out for yourself why Charlie and I are a good bit wider than we were back in 1972 when we bought See's.

Borsheim's normally is closed on Sunday but will be open for shareholders and their guests from noon to 6 p.m. on Sunday, April 25. Charlie and I will be in attendance, sporting our jeweler's loupes, and ready to give advice about gems to anyone foolish enough to listen. Also available will be plenty of Cherry Cokes, See's candies, and other lesser goodies. I hope you will join us.

March 1, 1993

Warren E. Buffett
Chairman of the Board

BERKSHIRE HATHAWAY INC.

To the Shareholders of Berkshire Hathaway Inc.:

Our per-share book value increased 14.3% during 1993. Over the last 29 years (that is, since present management took over) book value has grown from $19 to $8,854, or at a rate of 23.3% compounded annually.

During the year, Berkshire's net worth increased by $1.5 billion, a figure affected by two negative and two positive non-operating items. For the sake of completeness, I'll explain them here. If you aren't thrilled by accounting, however, feel free to fast-forward through this discussion:

1. The first negative was produced by a change in Generally Accepted Accounting Principles (GAAP) having to do with the taxes we accrue against unrealized appreciation in the securities we carry at market value. The old rule said that the tax rate used should be the one in effect when the appreciation took place. Therefore, at the end of 1992, we were using a rate of 34% on the $6.4 billion of gains generated after 1986 and 28% on the $1.2 billion of gains generated before that. The new rule stipulates that the current tax rate should be applied to all gains. The rate in the first quarter of 1993, when this rule went into effect, was 34%. Applying that rate to our pre-1987 gains reduced net worth by $70 million.

2. The second negative, related to the first, came about because the corporate tax rate was raised in the third quarter of 1993 to 35%. This change required us to make an additional charge of 1% against all of our unrealized gains, and that charge penalized net worth by $75 million. Oddly, GAAP required both this charge and the one described above to be deducted from the earnings we report, even though the unrealized appreciation that gave rise to the charges was never included in earnings, but rather was credited directly to net worth.

3. Another 1993 change in GAAP affects the value at which we carry the securities that we own. In recent years, both the common stocks and certain common-equivalent securities held by our insurance companies have been valued at market, whereas equities held by our non- insurance subsidiaries or by the parent company were carried at their aggregate cost or market, whichever was lower. Now GAAP says that *all* common stocks should be carried at market, a rule we began following in the fourth quarter of 1993. This change produced a gain in Berkshire's reported net worth of about $172 million.

4. Finally, we issued some stock last year. In a transaction described in last year's Annual Report, we issued 3,944 shares in early January, 1993 upon the conversion of $46 million convertible debentures that we had called for redemption. Additionally, we issued 25,203 shares when we acquired Dexter Shoe, a purchase discussed later in this report. The overall result was that our shares outstanding increased by 29,147 and our net worth by about $478 million. Per-share book value also grew, because the shares issued in these transactions carried a price above their book value.

Of course, it's per-share intrinsic value, not book value, that counts. Book value is an accounting term that measures the capital, including retained earnings, that has been put into a business. Intrinsic value is a present-value estimate of the cash that can be taken out of a business during its remaining life. At most companies, the two values are unrelated. Berkshire, however, is an exception: Our book value, though significantly below our intrinsic value, serves as a useful device for tracking that key figure. In 1993, each measure grew by roughly 14%, advances that I would call satisfactory but unexciting.

These gains, however, were outstripped by a much larger gain—39%—in Berkshire's market price. Over time, of course, market price and intrinsic value will arrive at about the same destination. But in the short run the two often diverge in a major way, a phenomenon I've discussed in the past. Two years ago, Coca-Cola and Gillette, both large holdings of ours, enjoyed market price increases that dramatically outpaced their earnings gains. In the 1991 Annual Report, I said that the stocks of these companies could not continuously overperform their businesses.

From 1991 to 1993, Coke and Gillette increased their annual operating earnings per share by 38% and 37% respectively, but their market prices moved up only 11% and 6%. In other words, the companies overperformed their stocks, a result that no doubt partly reflects Wall Street's new apprehension about brand names. Whatever the reason, what will count over time is the earnings performance of these companies. If they prosper, Berkshire will also prosper, though not in a lock-step manner.

Let me add a lesson from history: Coke went public in 1919 at $40 per share. By the end of 1920 the market, coldly reevaluating Coke's future prospects, had battered the stock down by more than 50%, to $19.50. At yearend 1993, that single share, with dividends reinvested, was worth more than $2.1 million. As Ben Graham said: "In the short-run, the market is a voting machine—reflecting a voter-registration test that requires only money, not intelligence or emotional stability—but in the long-run, the market is a weighing machine."

So how should Berkshire's over-performance in the market last year be viewed? Clearly, Berkshire was selling at a higher percentage of intrinsic value at the end of 1993 than was the case at the beginning of the year. On the other hand, in a world of 6% or 7% long-term interest rates, Berkshire's market price was not inappropriate if—and you should understand that this is a huge if—Charlie Munger, Berkshire's Vice Chairman, and I can attain our long-standing goal of increasing Berkshire's per-share intrinsic value at an average annual rate of 15%. We have not retreated from this goal. But we again emphasize, as we have for many years, that the growth in our capital base makes 15% an ever-more difficult target to hit.

What we have going for us is a growing collection of good-sized operating businesses that possess economic characteristics ranging from good to terrific, run by managers whose performance ranges from terrific to terrific. You need have no worries about this group.

The capital-allocation work that Charlie and I do at the parent company, using the funds that our managers deliver to us, has a less certain outcome: It is not easy to find new businesses and managers comparable to those we have. Despite that difficulty, Charlie and I relish the search, and we are happy to report an important success in 1993.

Dexter Shoe

What we did last year was build on our 1991 purchase of H. H. Brown, a superbly-run manufacturer of work shoes, boots and other footwear. Brown has been a real winner: Though we had high hopes to begin with, these expectations have been considerably exceeded thanks to Frank Rooney, Jim Issler and the talented managers who work with them. Because of our confidence in Frank's team, we next acquired Lowell Shoe, at the end of 1992. Lowell was a long-established manufacturer of women's and nurses' shoes, but its business needed some fixing. Again, results have surpassed our expectations. So we promptly jumped at the chance last year to acquire Dexter Shoe of Dexter, Maine, which manufactures popular-priced men's and women's shoes. Dexter, I can assure you, needs *no* fixing: It is one of the best-managed companies Charlie and I have seen in our business lifetimes.

Harold Alfond, who started working in a shoe factory at 25 cents an hour when he was 20, founded Dexter in 1956 with $10,000 of capital. He was joined in 1958 by Peter Lunder, his nephew. The two of them have since built a business that now produces over 7.5 million pairs of shoes annually, most of them made in Maine and the balance in Puerto Rico. As you probably know, the domestic shoe industry is generally thought to be unable to compete with imports from low-wage countries. But someone forgot to tell this to the ingenious managements of Dexter and H. H. Brown and to their skilled labor forces, which together make the U.S. plants of both companies highly competitive against all comers.

Dexter's business includes 77 retail outlets, located primarily in the Northeast. The company is also a major manufacturer of golf shoes, producing about 15% of U.S. output. Its bread and butter, though, is the manufacture of traditional shoes for traditional retailers, a job at which it excels: Last year both Nordstrom and J.C. Penney bestowed special awards upon Dexter for its performance as a supplier during 1992.

Our 1993 results include Dexter only from our date of merger, November 7th. In 1994, we expect Berkshire's shoe operations to have more than $550 million in sales, and we would not be surprised if the combined pre-tax earnings of these businesses topped $85 million. Five years ago we had no thought of getting into shoes. Now we have 7,200 employees in that industry, and I sing "There's No Business Like Shoe Business" as I drive to work. So much for strategic plans.

At Berkshire, we have no view of the future that dictates what businesses or industries we will enter. Indeed, we think it's usually poison for a corporate giant's shareholders if it embarks upon new ventures pursuant to some grand vision. We prefer instead to focus on the economic characteristics of businesses that we wish to own and the personal characteristics of managers with whom we wish to associate—and then to hope we get lucky in finding the two in combination. At Dexter, we did.

* * * * * * * * * * *

And now we pause for a short commercial: Though they owned a business jewel, we believe that Harold and Peter (who were not interested in cash) made a sound decision in exchanging their Dexter stock for shares of Berkshire. What they did, in effect, was trade a 100% interest in a single terrific business for a smaller interest in a large group of terrific businesses. They incurred no tax on this exchange and now own a security that can be easily used for charitable or personal gifts, or that can be converted to cash in amounts, and at times, of their own choosing. Should members of their families desire to, they can pursue varying financial paths without running into the complications that often arise when assets are concentrated in a private business.

For tax and other reasons, private companies also often find it difficult to diversify outside their industries. Berkshire, in contrast, can diversify with ease. So in shifting their ownership to Berkshire, Dexter's shareholders solved a reinvestment problem. Moreover, though Harold and Peter now have non-controlling shares in Berkshire, rather than controlling shares in Dexter, they know they will be treated as partners and that we will follow owner-oriented practices. If they elect to retain their Berkshire shares, their investment result from the merger date forward will exactly parallel my own result. Since I have a huge percentage of my net worth committed for life to Berkshire shares—and since the company will issue me neither restricted shares nor stock options—my gain-loss equation will always match that of all other owners.

Additionally, Harold and Peter know that at Berkshire we can keep our promises: There will be no changes of control or culture at Berkshire for many decades to come. Finally, and of paramount importance, Harold and Peter can be sure that they will get to run their business—an activity they dearly love—exactly as they did before the merger. At Berkshire, we do not tell .400 hitters how to swing.

What made sense for Harold and Peter probably makes sense for a few other owners of large private businesses. So, if you have a business that might fit, let me hear from you. Our acquisition criteria are set forth in the appendix on page 22.

Sources of Reported Earnings

The table below shows the major sources of Berkshire's reported earnings. In this presentation, amortization of Goodwill and other major purchase-price accounting adjustments are not charged against the specific businesses to which they apply, but are instead aggregated and shown separately. This procedure lets you view the earnings of our businesses as they would have been reported had we not purchased them. I've explained in past reports why this form of presentation seems to us to be more useful to investors and managers than one utilizing GAAP, which requires purchase-price adjustments to be made on a business-by-business basis. The total net earnings we show in the table are, of course, identical to the GAAP total in our audited financial statements.

	(000s omitted)			
	Pre-Tax Earnings		Berkshire's Share of Net Earnings (after taxes and minority interests)	
	1993	1992	1993	1992
Operating Earnings:				
Insurance Group:				
Underwriting	$ 30,876	$(108,961)	$ 20,156	$(71,141)
Net Investment Income	375,946	355,067	321,321	305,763
H. H. Brown, Lowell, and Dexter	44,025 *	27,883	28,829	17,340
Buffalo News	50,962	47,863	29,696	28,163
Commercial & Consumer Finance	22,695	19,836	14,161	12,664
Fechheimer	13,442	13,698	6,931	7,267
Kirby	39,147	35,653	25,056	22,795
Nebraska Furniture Mart	21,540	17,110	10,398	8,072
Scott Fetzer Manufacturing Group	38,196	31,954	23,809	19,883
See's Candies	41,150	42,357	24,367	25,501
World Book	19,915	29,044	13,537	19,503
Purchase-Price Accounting & Goodwill Charges	(17,033)	(12,087)	(13,996)	(13,070)
Interest Expense**	(56,545)	(98,643)	(35,614)	(62,899)
Shareholder-Designated Contributions	(9,448)	(7,634)	(5,994)	(4,913)
Other	28,428	67,540	15,094	32,798
Operating Earnings	643,296	460,680	477,751	347,726
Sales of Securities	546,422	89,937	356,702	59,559
Tax Accruals Caused by New Accounting Rules	---	---	(146,332)	---
Total Earnings – All Entities	$1,189,718	$ 550,617	$688,121	$407,285

*   *Includes Dexter's earnings only from the date it was acquired, November 7, 1993.*

**   *Excludes interest expense of Commercial and Consumer Finance businesses. In 1992 includes $22.5 million of premiums paid on the early redemption of debt.*

A large amount of information about these businesses is given on pages 38-49, where you will also find our segment earnings reported on a GAAP basis. In addition, on pages 52-59, we have rearranged Berkshire's financial data into four segments on a non-GAAP basis, a presentation that corresponds to the way Charlie and I think about the company. Our intent is to supply you with the financial information that we would wish you to give us if our positions were reversed.

"Look-Through" Earnings

We've previously discussed look-through earnings, which we believe more accurately portray the earnings of Berkshire than does our GAAP result. As we calculate them, look-through earnings consist of: (1) the operating earnings reported in the previous section, plus; (2) the retained operating earnings of major investees that, under GAAP accounting, are not reflected in our profits, less; (3) an allowance for the tax that would be paid by Berkshire if these retained earnings of investees had instead been distributed to us. The "operating earnings" of which we speak here exclude capital gains, special accounting items and major restructuring charges.

Over time, our look-through earnings need to increase at about 15% annually if our intrinsic value is to grow at that rate. Last year, I explained that we had to increase these earnings to about $1.8 billion in the year 2000, were we to meet the 15% goal. Because we issued additional shares in 1993, the amount needed has risen to about $1.85 billion.

That is a tough goal, but one that we expect you to hold us to. In the past, we've criticized the managerial practice of shooting the arrow of performance and *then* painting the target, centering it on whatever point the arrow happened to hit. We will instead risk embarrassment by painting first and shooting later.

If we are to hit the bull's-eye, we will need markets that allow the purchase of businesses and securities on sensible terms. Right now, markets are difficult, but they can—and will—change in unexpected ways and at unexpected times. In the meantime, we'll try to resist the temptation to do something marginal simply because we are long on cash. There's no use running if you're on the wrong road.

The following table shows how we calculate look-through earnings, though I warn you that the figures are necessarily *very* rough. (The dividends paid to us by these investees have been included in the operating earnings itemized on page 8, mostly under "Insurance Group: Net Investment Income.")

Berkshire's Major Investees	Berkshire's Approximate Ownership at Yearend		Berkshire's Share of Undistributed Operating Earnings (in millions)	
	1993	1992	1993	1992
Capital Cities/ABC Inc.	13.0%	18.2%	$ 83[2]	$ 70
The Coca-Cola Company	7.2%	7.1%	94	82
Federal Home Loan Mortgage Corp.	6.8%[1]	8.2%[1]	41[2]	29[2]
GEICO Corp.	48.4%	48.1%	76[3]	34[3]
General Dynamics Corp.	13.9%	14.1%	25	11[2]
The Gillette Company	10.9%	10.9%	44	38
Guinness PLC	1.9%	2.0%	8	7
The Washington Post Company	14.8%	14.6%	15	11
Wells Fargo & Company	12.2%	11.5%	53[2]	16[2]
Berkshire's share of undistributed earnings of major investees			$439	$298
Hypothetical tax on these undistributed investee earnings[4]			(61)	(42)
Reported operating earnings of Berkshire			478	348
Total look-through earnings of Berkshire			$856	$604

(1) Does not include shares allocable to the minority interest at Wesco
(2) Calculated on average ownership for the year
(3) Excludes realized capital gains, which have been both recurring and significant
(4) The tax rate used is 14%, which is the rate Berkshire pays on the dividends it receives

We have told you that we expect the undistributed, hypothetically-taxed earnings of our investees to produce at least equivalent gains in Berkshire's intrinsic value. To date, we have far exceeded that expectation. For example, in 1986 we bought three million shares of Capital Cities/ABC for $172.50 per share and late last year sold one-third of that holding for $630 per share. After paying 35% capital gains taxes, we realized a $297 million profit from the sale. In contrast, during the eight years we held these shares, the retained earnings of Cap Cities attributable to them—hypothetically taxed at a lower 14% in accordance with our look-through method—were only $152 million. In other words, we paid a much larger tax bill than our look-through presentations to you have assumed and nonetheless realized a gain that far exceeded the undistributed earnings allocable to these shares.

We expect such pleasant outcomes to recur often in the future and therefore believe our look-through earnings to be a conservative representation of Berkshire's true economic earnings.

Taxes

As our Cap Cities sale emphasizes, Berkshire is a substantial payer of federal income taxes. In aggregate, we will pay 1993 federal income taxes of $390 million, about $200 million of that attributable to operating earnings and $190 million to realized capital gains. Furthermore, our share of the 1993 federal and foreign income taxes paid by our investees is well over $400 million, a figure you don't see on our financial statements but that is nonetheless real. Directly and indirectly, Berkshire's 1993 federal income tax payments will be about 1/2 of 1% of the total paid last year by all American corporations.

Speaking for our own shares, Charlie and I have absolutely no complaint about these taxes. We know we work in a market-based economy that rewards our efforts far more bountifully than it does the efforts of others whose output is of equal or greater benefit to society. Taxation should, and does, partially redress this inequity. But we still remain extraordinarily well-treated.

Berkshire and its shareholders, in combination, would pay a much smaller tax if Berkshire operated as a partnership or "S" corporation, two structures often used for business activities. For a variety of reasons, that's not feasible for Berkshire to do. However, the penalty our corporate form imposes is mitigated—though far from eliminated—by our strategy of investing for the long term. Charlie and I would follow a buy-and-hold policy even if we ran a tax-exempt institution. We think it the soundest way to invest, and it also goes down the grain of our personalities. A third reason to favor this policy, however, is the fact that taxes are due only when gains are realized.

Through my favorite comic strip, Li'l Abner, I got a chance during my youth to see the benefits of delayed taxes, though I missed the lesson at the time. Making his readers feel superior, Li'l Abner bungled happily, but moronically, through life in Dogpatch. At one point he became infatuated with a New York temptress, Appassionatta Van Climax, but despaired of marrying her because he had only a single silver dollar and she was interested solely in millionaires. Dejected, Abner took his problem to Old Man Mose, the font of all knowledge in Dogpatch. Said the sage: Double your money 20 times and Appassionatta will be yours (1, 2, 4, 8 . . . . 1,048,576).

My last memory of the strip is Abner entering a roadhouse, dropping his dollar into a slot machine, and hitting a jackpot that spilled money all over the floor. Meticulously following Mose's advice, Abner picked up two dollars and went off to find his next double. Whereupon I dumped Abner and began reading Ben Graham.

Mose clearly was overrated as a guru: Besides failing to anticipate Abner's slavish obedience to instructions, he also forgot about taxes. Had Abner been subject, say, to the 35% federal tax rate that Berkshire pays, and had he managed one double annually, he would after 20 years only have accumulated $22,370. Indeed, had he kept on both getting his annual doubles and paying a 35% tax on each, he would have needed 7 1/2 years more to reach the $1 million required to win Appassionatta.

But what if Abner had instead put his dollar in a single investment and held it until it doubled the same 27 1/2 times? In that case, he would have realized about $200 million pre-tax or, after paying a $70 million tax in the final year, about $130 million after-tax. For that, Appassionatta would have crawled to Dogpatch. Of course, with 27 1/2 years having passed, how Appassionatta would have looked to a fellow sitting on $130 million is another question.

What this little tale tells us is that tax-paying investors will realize a far, far greater sum from a single investment that compounds internally at a given rate than from a succession of investments compounding at the same rate. But I suspect many Berkshire shareholders figured that out long ago.

Insurance Operations

At this point in the report we've customarily provided you with a table showing the annual "combined ratio" of the insurance industry for the preceding decade. This ratio compares total insurance costs (losses incurred plus expenses) to revenue from premiums. For many years, the ratio has been above 100, a level indicating an underwriting loss. That is, the industry has taken in less money each year from its policyholders than it has had to pay for operating expenses and for loss events that occurred during the year.

Offsetting this grim equation is a happier fact: Insurers get to hold on to their policyholders' money for a time before paying it out. This happens because most policies require that premiums be prepaid and, more importantly, because it often takes time to resolve loss claims. Indeed, in the case of certain lines of insurance, such as product liability or professional malpractice, many years may elapse between the loss event and payment.

To oversimplify the matter somewhat, the total of the funds prepaid by policyholders and the funds earmarked for incurred-but-not-yet-paid claims is called "the float." In the past, the industry was able to suffer a combined ratio of 107 to 111 and still break even from its insurance writings because of the earnings derived from investing this float.

As interest rates have fallen, however, the value of float has substantially declined. Therefore, the data that we have provided in the past are no longer useful for year-to-year comparisons of industry profitability. A company writing at the same combined ratio now as in the 1980's today has a far less attractive business than it did then.

Only by making an analysis that incorporates both underwriting results and the current risk-free earnings obtainable from float can one evaluate the true economics of the business that a property-casualty insurer writes. Of course, the *actual* investment results that an insurer achieves from the use of both float and stockholders' funds is also of major importance and should be carefully examined when an investor is assessing managerial performance. But that should be a separate analysis from the one we are discussing here. The value of float funds—in effect, their transfer price as they move from the insurance operation to the investment operation—should be determined simply by the risk-free, long-term rate of interest.

On the next page we show the numbers that count in an evaluation of Berkshire's insurance business. We calculate our float—which we generate in exceptional amounts relative to our premium volume—by adding loss reserves, loss adjustment reserves and unearned premium reserves and then subtracting agent's balances, prepaid acquisition costs and deferred charges applicable to assumed reinsurance. Our cost of float is determined by our underwriting loss or profit. In those years when we have had an underwriting profit, which includes 1993, our cost of float has been negative, and we have determined our insurance earnings by adding underwriting profit to float income.

	(1) Underwriting Loss	(2) Average Float	Approximate Cost of Funds	Yearend Yield on Long-Term Govt. Bonds
	(In $ Millions)		*(Ratio of 1 to 2)*	
1967	profit	$17.3	less than zero	5.50%
1968	profit	19.9	less than zero	5.90%
1969	profit	23.4	less than zero	6.79%
1970	$ 0.37	32.4	1.14%	6.25%
1971	profit	52.5	less than zero	5.81%
1972	profit	69.5	less than zero	5.82%
1973	profit	73.3	less than zero	7.27%
1974	7.36	79.1	9.30%	8.13%
1975	11.35	87.6	12.96%	8.03%
1976	profit	102.6	less than zero	7.30%
1977	profit	139.0	less than zero	7.97%
1978	profit	190.4	less than zero	8.93%
1979	profit	227.3	less than zero	10.08%
1980	profit	237.0	less than zero	11.94%
1981	profit	228.4	less than zero	13.61%
1982	21.56	220.6	9.77%	10.64%
1983	33.87	231.3	14.64%	11.84%
1984	48.06	253.2	18.98%	11.58%
1985	44.23	390.2	11.34%	9.34%
1986	55.84	797.5	7.00%	7.60%
1987	55.43	1,266.7	4.38%	8.95%
1988	11.08	1,497.7	0.74%	9.00%
1989	24.40	1,541.3	1.58%	7.97%
1990	26.65	1,637.3	1.63%	8.24%
1991	119.59	1,895.0	6.31%	7.40%
1992	108.96	2,290.4	4.76%	7.39%
1993	profit	2,624.7	less than zero	6.35%

As you can see, in our insurance operation last year we had the use of $2.6 billion at no cost; in fact we were paid $31 million, our underwriting profit, to hold these funds. This sounds good —is good—but is far from as good as it sounds.

We temper our enthusiasm because we write a large volume of "super-cat" policies (which other insurance and reinsurance companies buy to recover part of the losses they suffer from mega-catastrophes) and because last year we had no losses of consequence from this activity. As that suggests, the truly catastrophic Midwestern floods of 1993 did not trigger super-cat losses, the reason being that very few flood policies are purchased from private insurers.

It would be fallacious, however, to conclude from this single-year result that the super-cat business is a wonderful one, or even a satisfactory one. A simple example will illustrate the fallacy: Suppose there is an event that occurs 25 times in every century. If you annually give 5-for-1 odds against its occurrence *that* year, you will have many more winning years than losers. Indeed, you may go a straight six, seven or more years without loss. You also will eventually go broke.

At Berkshire, we naturally believe we are obtaining adequate premiums and giving more like 3 1/2-for-1 odds. But there is no way for us—or anyone else—to calculate the true odds on super-cat coverages. In fact, it will take decades for us to find out whether our underwriting judgment has been sound.

What we do know is that when a loss comes, it's likely to be a lulu. There may well be years when Berkshire will suffer losses from the super-cat business equal to three or four times what we earned from it in 1993. When Hurricane Andrew blew in 1992, we paid out about $125 million. Because we've since expanded our super-cat business, a similar storm today could cost us $600 million.

So far, we have been lucky in 1994. As I write this letter, we are estimating that our losses from the Los Angeles earthquake will be nominal. But if the quake had been a 7.5 instead of a 6.8, it would have been a different story.

Berkshire is ideally positioned to write super-cat policies. In Ajit Jain, we have by far the best manager in this business. Additionally, companies writing these policies need enormous capital, and our net worth is ten to twenty times larger than that of our main competitors. In most lines of insurance, huge resources aren't that important: An insurer can diversify the risks it writes and, if necessary, can lay off risks to reduce concentration in its portfolio. That isn't possible in the super-cat business. So these competitors are forced into offering far smaller limits than those we can provide. Were they bolder, they would run the risk that a mega-catastrophe—or a confluence of smaller catastrophes—would wipe them out.

One indication of our premier strength and reputation is that each of the four largest reinsurance companies in the world buys very significant reinsurance coverage from Berkshire. Better than anyone else, these giants understand that the test of a reinsurer is its ability and willingness to pay losses under trying circumstances, not its readiness to accept premiums when things look rosy.

One caution: There has recently been a substantial increase in reinsurance capacity. Close to $5 billion of equity capital has been raised by reinsurers, almost all of them newly-formed entities. Naturally these new entrants are hungry to write business so that they can justify the projections they utilized in attracting capital. This new competition won't affect our 1994 operations; we're filled up there, primarily with business written in 1993. But we are now seeing signs of price deterioration. If this trend continues, we will resign ourselves to much-reduced volume, keeping ourselves available, though, for the large, sophisticated buyer who requires a super-cat insurer with large capacity and a sure ability to pay losses.

In other areas of our insurance business, our homestate operation, led by Rod Eldred; our workers' compensation business, headed by Brad Kinstler; our credit-card operation, managed by the Kizer family; and National Indemnity's traditional auto and general liability business, led by Don Wurster, all achieved excellent results. In combination, these four units produced a significant underwriting profit and substantial float.

All in all, we have a first-class insurance business. Though its results will be highly volatile, this operation possesses an intrinsic value that exceeds its book value by a large amount—larger, in fact, than is the case at any other Berkshire business.

Common Stock Investments

Below we list our common stockholdings having a value of over $250 million. A small portion of these investments belongs to subsidiaries of which Berkshire owns less than 100%.

Shares	Company	12/31/93 Cost	Market
		(000s omitted)	
2,000,000	Capital Cities/ABC, Inc..	$ 345,000	$1,239,000
93,400,000	The Coca-Cola Company	1,023,920	4,167,975
13,654,600	Federal Home Loan Mortgage Corp. ("Freddie Mac")	307,505	681,023
34,250,000	GEICO Corp.	45,713	1,759,594
4,350,000	General Dynamics Corp.	94,938	401,287
24,000,000	The Gillette Company	600,000	1,431,000
38,335,000	Guinness PLC	333,019	270,822
1,727,765	The Washington Post Company	9,731	440,148
6,791,218	Wells Fargo & Company	423,680	878,614

Considering the similarity of this year's list and the last, you may decide your management is hopelessly comatose. But we continue to think that it is usually foolish to part with an interest in a business that is both understandable and durably wonderful. Business interests of that kind are simply too hard to replace.

Interestingly, corporate managers have no trouble understanding that point when they are focusing on a business they operate: A parent company that owns a subsidiary with superb long-term economics is not likely to sell that entity regardless of price. "Why," the CEO would ask, "should I part with my crown jewel?" Yet that same CEO, when it comes to running his personal investment portfolio, will offhandedly—and even impetuously—move from business to business when presented with no more than superficial arguments by his broker for doing so. The worst of these is perhaps, "You can't go broke taking a profit." Can you imagine a CEO using this line to urge his board to sell a star subsidiary? In our view, what makes sense in business also makes sense in stocks: An investor should ordinarily hold a small piece of an outstanding business with the same tenacity that an owner would exhibit if he owned all of that business.

Earlier I mentioned the financial results that could have been achieved by investing $40 in The Coca-Cola Co. in 1919. In 1938, more than 50 years after the introduction of Coke, and long after the drink was firmly established as an American icon, *Fortune* did an excellent story on the company. In the second paragraph the writer reported: "Several times every year a weighty and serious investor looks long and with profound respect at Coca-Cola's record, but comes regretfully to the conclusion that he is looking too late. The specters of saturation and competition rise before him."

Yes, competition there was in 1938 and in 1993 as well. But it's worth noting that in 1938 The Coca-Cola Co. sold 207 million cases of soft drinks (if its gallonage then is converted into the 192-ounce cases used for measurement today) and in 1993 it sold about 10.7 billion cases, a 50-fold increase in physical volume from a company that in 1938 was already dominant in its very major industry. Nor was the party over in 1938 for an investor: Though the $40 invested in 1919 in one share had (with dividends reinvested) turned into $3,277 by the end of 1938, a fresh $40 then invested in Coca-Cola stock would have grown to $25,000 by yearend 1993.

I can't resist one more quote from that 1938 *Fortune* story: "It would be hard to name any company comparable in size to Coca-Cola and selling, as Coca-Cola does, an unchanged product that can point to a ten-year record anything like Coca-Cola's." In the 55 years that have since passed, Coke's product line has broadened somewhat, but it's remarkable how well that description still fits.

Charlie and I decided long ago that in an investment lifetime it's just too hard to make hundreds of smart decisions. That judgment became ever more compelling as Berkshire's capital mushroomed and the universe of investments that could significantly affect our results shrank dramatically. Therefore, we adopted a strategy that required our being smart—and not too smart at that—only a very few times. Indeed, we'll now settle for one good idea a year. (Charlie says it's my turn.)

The strategy we've adopted precludes our following standard diversification dogma. Many pundits would therefore say the strategy must be riskier than that employed by more conventional investors. We disagree. We believe that a policy of portfolio concentration may well *decrease* risk if it raises, as it should, both the intensity with which an investor thinks about a business and the comfort-level he must feel with its economic characteristics before buying into it. In stating this opinion, we define risk, using dictionary terms, as "the possibility of loss or injury."

Academics, however, like to define investment "risk" differently, averring that it is the relative volatility of a stock or portfolio of stocks—that is, their volatility as compared to that of a large universe of stocks. Employing data bases and statistical skills, these academics compute with precision the "beta" of a stock—its relative volatility in the past—and then build arcane investment and capital-allocation theories around this calculation. In their hunger for a single statistic to measure risk, however, they forget a fundamental principle: It is better to be approximately right than precisely wrong.

For owners of a business—and that's the way we think of shareholders—the academics' definition of risk is far off the mark, so much so that it produces absurdities. For example, under beta-based theory, a stock that has dropped very sharply compared to the market—as had Washington Post when we bought it in 1973—becomes "riskier" at the lower price than it was at the higher price. Would that description have then made any sense to someone who was offered the entire company at a vastly-reduced price?

In fact, the true investor *welcomes* volatility. Ben Graham explained why in Chapter 8 of *The Intelligent Investor.* There he introduced "Mr. Market," an obliging fellow who shows up every day to either buy from you or sell to you, whichever you wish. The more manic-depressive this chap is, the greater the opportunities available to the investor. That's true because a wildly fluctuating market means that irrationally low prices will periodically be attached to solid businesses. It is impossible to see how the availability of such prices can be thought of as increasing the hazards for an investor who is totally free to either ignore the market or exploit its folly.

In assessing risk, a beta purist will disdain examining what a company produces, what its competitors are doing, or how much borrowed money the business employs. He may even prefer not to know the company's name. What he treasures is the price history of its stock. In contrast, we'll happily forgo knowing the price history and instead will seek whatever information will further our understanding of the company's business. After we buy a stock, consequently, we would not be disturbed if markets closed for a year or two. We don't need a daily quote on our 100% position in See's or H. H. Brown to validate our well-being. Why, then, should we need a quote on our 7% interest in Coke?

In our opinion, the real risk that an investor must assess is whether his aggregate after-tax receipts from an investment (including those he receives on sale) will, over his prospective holding period, give him at least as much purchasing power as he had to begin with, plus a modest rate of interest on that initial stake. Though this risk cannot be calculated with engineering precision, it can in some cases be judged with a degree of accuracy that is useful. The primary factors bearing upon this evaluation are:

1) The certainty with which the long-term economic characteristics of the business can be evaluated;

2) The certainty with which management can be evaluated, both as to its ability to realize the full potential of the business and to wisely employ its cash flows;

3) The certainty with which management can be counted on to channel the rewards from the business to the shareholders rather than to itself;

4) The purchase price of the business;

5) The levels of taxation and inflation that will be experienced and that will determine the degree by which an investor's purchasing-power return is reduced from his gross return.

These factors will probably strike many analysts as unbearably fuzzy, since they cannot be extracted from a data base of any kind. But the difficulty of precisely quantifying these matters does not negate their importance nor is it insuperable. Just as Justice Stewart found it impossible to formulate a test for obscenity but nevertheless asserted, "I know it when I see it," so also can investors—in an inexact but useful way—"see" the risks inherent in certain investments without reference to complex equations or price histories.

Is it really so difficult to conclude that Coca-Cola and Gillette possess far less business risk over the long term than, say, *any* computer company or retailer? Worldwide, Coke sells about 44% of all soft drinks, and Gillette has more than a 60% share (in value) of the blade market. Leaving aside chewing gum, in which Wrigley is dominant, I know of no other significant businesses in which the leading company has long enjoyed such global power.

Moreover, both Coke and Gillette have actually increased their worldwide shares of market in recent years. The might of their brand names, the attributes of their products, and the strength of their distribution systems give them an enormous competitive advantage, setting up a protective moat around their economic castles. The average company, in contrast, does battle daily without any such means of protection. As Peter Lynch says, stocks of companies selling commodity-like products should come with a warning label: "Competition may prove hazardous to human wealth."

The competitive strengths of a Coke or Gillette are obvious to even the casual observer of business. Yet the beta of their stocks is similar to that of a great many run-of-the-mill companies who possess little or no competitive advantage. Should we conclude from this similarity that the competitive strength of Coke and Gillette gains them nothing when business risk is being measured? Or should we conclude that the risk in owning a piece of a company—its stock—is somehow divorced from the long-term risk inherent in its business operations? We believe neither conclusion makes sense and that equating beta with investment risk also makes no sense.

The theoretician bred on beta has no mechanism for differentiating the risk inherent in, say, a single-product toy company selling pet rocks or hula hoops from that of another toy company whose sole product is Monopoly or Barbie. But it's quite possible for ordinary investors to make such distinctions if they have a reasonable understanding of consumer behavior and the factors that create long-term competitive strength or weakness. Obviously, every investor will make mistakes. But by confining himself to a relatively few, easy-to-understand cases, a reasonably intelligent, informed and diligent person can judge investment risks with a useful degree of accuracy.

In many industries, of course, Charlie and I can't determine whether we are dealing with a "pet rock" or a "Barbie." We couldn't solve this problem, moreover, even if we were to spend years intensely studying those industries. Sometimes our own intellectual shortcomings would stand in the way of understanding, and in other cases the nature of the industry would be the roadblock. For example, a business that must deal with fast-moving technology is not going to lend itself to reliable evaluations of its long-term economics. Did we foresee thirty years ago what would transpire in the television-manufacturing or computer industries? Of course not. (Nor did most of the investors and corporate managers who enthusiastically entered those industries.) Why, then, should Charlie and I now think we can predict the future of other rapidly-evolving businesses? We'll stick instead with the easy cases. Why search for a needle buried in a haystack when one is sitting in plain sight?

Of course, some investment strategies—for instance, our efforts in arbitrage over the years—require wide diversification. If significant risk exists in a single transaction, overall risk should be reduced by making that purchase one of many mutually-independent commitments. Thus, you may consciously purchase a risky investment—one that indeed has a significant possibility of causing loss or injury—if you believe that your gain, weighted for probabilities, considerably exceeds your loss, comparably weighted, and if you can commit to a number of similar, but unrelated opportunities. Most venture capitalists employ this strategy. Should you choose to pursue this course, you should adopt the outlook of the casino that owns a roulette wheel, which will want to see lots of action because it is favored by probabilities, but will refuse to accept a single, huge bet.

Another situation requiring wide diversification occurs when an investor who does not understand the economics of specific businesses nevertheless believes it in his interest to be a long-term owner of American industry. That investor should both own a large number of equities and space out his purchases. By periodically investing in an index fund, for example, the know-nothing investor can actually out-perform most investment professionals. Paradoxically, when "dumb" money acknowledges its limitations, it ceases to be dumb.

On the other hand, if you are a know-*something* investor, able to understand business economics and to find five to ten sensibly-priced companies that possess important long-term competitive advantages, conventional diversification makes no sense for you. It is apt simply to hurt your results and increase your risk. I cannot understand why an investor of that sort elects to put money into a business that is his 20th favorite rather than simply adding that money to his top choices—the businesses he understands best and that present the least risk, along with the greatest profit potential. In the words of the prophet Mae West: "Too much of a good thing can be wonderful."

Corporate Governance

At our annual meetings, someone usually asks "What happens to this place if you get hit by a truck?" I'm glad they are still asking the question in this form. It won't be too long before the query becomes: "What happens to this place if you *don't* get hit by a truck?"

Such questions, in any event, raise a reason for me to discuss corporate governance, a hot topic during the past year. In general, I believe that directors have stiffened their spines recently and that shareholders are now being treated somewhat more like true owners than was the case not long ago. Commentators on corporate governance, however, seldom make any distinction among three fundamentally different manager/owner situations that exist in publicly-held companies. Though the legal responsibility of directors is identical throughout, their ability to effect change differs in each of the cases. Attention usually falls on the first case, because it prevails on the corporate scene. Since Berkshire falls into the second category, however, and will someday fall into the third, we will discuss all three variations.

The first, and by far most common, board situation is one in which a corporation has no controlling shareholder. In that case, I believe directors should behave as if there is a single absentee owner, whose long-term interest they should try to further in all proper ways. Unfortunately, "long-term" gives directors a lot of wiggle room. If they lack either integrity or the ability to think independently, directors can do great violence to shareholders while still claiming to be acting in their long-term interest. But assume the board is functioning well and must deal with a management that is mediocre or worse. Directors then have the responsibility for changing that management, just as an intelligent owner would do if he were present. And if able but greedy managers over-reach and try to dip too deeply into the shareholders' pockets, directors must slap their hands.

In this plain-vanilla case, a director who sees something he doesn't like should attempt to persuade the other directors of his views. If he is successful, the board will have the muscle to make the appropriate change. Suppose, though, that the unhappy director can't get other directors to agree with him. He should then feel free to make his views known to the absentee owners. Directors seldom do that, of course. The temperament of many directors would in fact be incompatible with critical behavior of that sort. But I see nothing improper in such actions, assuming the issues are serious. Naturally, the complaining director can expect a vigorous rebuttal from the unpersuaded directors, a prospect that should discourage the dissenter from pursuing trivial or non-rational causes.

For the boards just discussed, I believe the directors ought to be relatively few in number—say, ten or less—and ought to come mostly from the outside. The outside board members should establish standards for the CEO's performance and should also periodically meet, without his being present, to evaluate his performance against those standards.

The requisites for board membership should be business savvy, interest in the job, and owner-orientation. Too often, directors are selected simply because they are prominent or add diversity to the board. That practice is a mistake. Furthermore, mistakes in selecting directors are particularly serious because appointments are so hard to undo: The pleasant but vacuous director need never worry about job security.

The second case is that existing at Berkshire, where the controlling owner is also the manager. At some companies, this arrangement is facilitated by the existence of two classes of stock endowed with disproportionate voting power. In these situations, it's obvious that the board does not act as an agent between owners and management and that the directors cannot effect change except through persuasion. Therefore, if the owner/manager is mediocre or worse—or is over-reaching—there is little a director can do about it except object. If the directors having no connections to the owner/manager make a unified argument, it may well have some effect. More likely it will not.

If change does not come, and the matter is sufficiently serious, the outside directors should resign. Their resignation will signal their doubts about management, and it will emphasize that no outsider is in a position to correct the owner/manager's shortcomings.

The third governance case occurs when there is a controlling owner who is not involved in management. This case, examples of which are Hershey Foods and Dow Jones, puts the outside directors in a potentially useful position. If they become unhappy with either the competence or integrity of the manager, they can go directly to the owner (who may also be on the board) and report their dissatisfaction. This situation is ideal for an outside director, since he need make his case only to a single, presumably interested owner, who can forthwith effect change if the argument is persuasive. Even so, the dissatisfied director has only that single course of action. If he remains unsatisfied about a critical matter, he has no choice but to resign.

Logically, the third case should be the most effective in insuring first-class management. In the second case the owner is not going to fire himself, and in the first case, directors often find it very difficult to deal with mediocrity or mild over-reaching. Unless the unhappy directors can win over a majority of the board—an awkward social and logistical task, particularly if management's behavior is merely odious, not egregious—their hands are effectively tied. In practice, directors trapped in situations of this kind usually convince themselves that by staying around they can do at least some good. Meanwhile, management proceeds unfettered.

In the third case, the owner is neither judging himself nor burdened with the problem of garnering a majority. He can also insure that outside directors are selected who will bring useful qualities to the board. These directors, in turn, will know that the good advice they give will reach the right ears, rather than being stifled by a recalcitrant management. If the controlling owner is intelligent and self-confident, he will make decisions in respect to management that are meritocratic and pro-shareholder. Moreover—and this is critically important—he can readily correct any mistake he makes.

At Berkshire we operate in the second mode now and will for as long as I remain functional. My health, let me add, is excellent. For better or worse, you are likely to have me as an owner/manager for some time.

After my death, all of my stock will go to my wife, Susie, should she survive me, or to a foundation if she dies before I do. In neither case will taxes and bequests require the sale of consequential amounts of stock.

When my stock is transferred to either my wife or the foundation, Berkshire will enter the third governance mode, going forward with a vitally interested, but non-management, owner and with a management that must perform for that owner. In preparation for that time, Susie was elected to the board a few years ago, and in 1993 our son, Howard, joined the board. These family members will not be managers of the company in the future, but they will represent the controlling interest should anything happen to me. Most of our other directors are also significant owners of Berkshire stock, and each has a strong owner-orientation. All in all, we're prepared for "the truck."

Shareholder-Designated Contributions

About 97% of all eligible shares participated in Berkshire's 1993 shareholder-designated contributions program. Contributions made through the program were $9.4 million and 3,110 charities were recipients.

Berkshire's practice in respect to discretionary philanthropy—as contrasted to its policies regarding contributions that are clearly related to the company's business activities—differs significantly from that of other publicly-held corporations. There, most corporate contributions are made pursuant to the wishes of the CEO (who often will be responding to social pressures), employees (through matching gifts), or directors (through matching gifts or requests they make of the CEO).

At Berkshire, we believe that the company's money is the owners' money, just as it would be in a closely-held corporation, partnership, or sole proprietorship. Therefore, if funds are to be given to causes unrelated to Berkshire's business activities, it is the charities favored by our owners that should receive them. We've yet to find a CEO who believes he should personally fund the charities favored by his shareholders. Why, then, should they foot the bill for his picks?

Let me add that our program is easy to administer. Last fall, for two months, we borrowed one person from National Indemnity to help us implement the instructions that came from our 7,500 registered shareholders. I'd guess that the average corporate program in which employee gifts are matched incurs far greater administrative costs. Indeed, our entire corporate overhead is less than half the size of our charitable contributions. *(Charlie, however, insists that I tell you that $1.4 million of our $4.9 million overhead is attributable to our corporate jet, The Indefensible.)*

Below is a list showing the largest categories to which our shareholders have steered their contributions.

(a) 347 churches and synagogues received 569 gifts
(b) 283 colleges and universities received 670 gifts
(c) 244 K-12 schools (about two-thirds secular, one- third religious) received 525 gifts

(d) 288 institutions dedicated to art, culture or the humanities received 447 gifts

(e) 180 religious social-service organizations (split about equally between Christian and Jewish) received 411 gifts

(f) 445 secular social-service organizations (about 40% youth-related) received 759 gifts

(g) 153 hospitals received 261 gifts

(h) 186 health-related organizations (American Heart Association, American Cancer Society, etc.) received 320 gifts

Three things about this list seem particularly interesting to me. First, to some degree it indicates what people choose to give money to when they are acting of their own accord, free of pressure from solicitors or emotional appeals from charities. Second, the contributions programs of publicly-held companies almost never allow gifts to churches and synagogues, yet clearly these institutions are what many shareholders would like to support. Third, the gifts made by our shareholders display conflicting philosophies: 130 gifts were directed to organizations that believe in making abortions readily available for women and 30 gifts were directed to organizations (other than churches) that discourage or are opposed to abortion.

Last year I told you that I was thinking of raising the amount that Berkshire shareholders can give under our designated-contributions program and asked for your comments. We received a few well-written letters opposing the entire idea, on the grounds that it was our job to run the business and not our job to force shareholders into making charitable gifts. Most of the shareholders responding, however, noted the tax efficiency of the plan and urged us to increase the designated amount. Several shareholders who have given stock to their children or grandchildren told me that they consider the program a particularly good way to get youngsters thinking at an early age about the subject of giving. These people, in other words, perceive the program to be an educational, as well as philanthropic, tool. The bottom line is that we did raise the amount in 1993, from $8 per share to $10.

In addition to the shareholder-designated contributions that Berkshire distributes, our operating businesses make contributions, including merchandise, averaging about $2.5 million annually. These contributions support local charities, such as The United Way, and produce roughly commensurate benefits for our businesses.

We suggest that new shareholders read the description of our shareholder-designated contributions program that appears on pages 50-51. *To participate in future programs, you must make sure your shares are registered in the name of the actual owner, not in the nominee name of a broker, bank or depository. Shares not so registered on August 31, 1994 will be ineligible for the 1994 program.*

A Few Personal Items

Mrs. B—Rose Blumkin—had her 100th birthday on December 3, 1993. (The candles cost more than the cake.) That was a day on which the store was scheduled to be open in the evening. Mrs. B, who works seven days a week, for however many hours the store operates, found the proper decision quite obvious: She simply postponed her party until an evening when the store was closed.

Mrs. B's story is well-known but worth telling again. She came to the United States 77 years ago, unable to speak English and devoid of formal schooling. In 1937, she founded the Nebraska Furniture Mart with $500. Last year the store had sales of $200 million, a larger amount by far than that recorded by any other home furnishings store in the United States. Our part in all of this began ten years ago when Mrs. B sold control of the business to Berkshire Hathaway, a deal we completed without obtaining audited financial statements, checking real estate records, or getting any warranties. In short, her word was good enough for us.

Naturally, I was delighted to attend Mrs. B's birthday party. After all, she's promised to attend *my* 100th.

* * * * * * * * * * *

Katharine Graham retired last year as the chairman of The Washington Post Company, having relinquished the CEO title three years ago. In 1973, we purchased our stock in her company for about $10 million. Our holding now garners $7 million a year in dividends and is worth over $400 million. At the time of our purchase, we knew that the economic prospects of the company were good. But equally important, Charlie and I concluded that Kay would prove to be an outstanding manager and would treat all shareholders honorably. That latter consideration was particularly important because The Washington Post Company has two classes of stock, a structure that we've seen some managers abuse.

All of our judgments about this investment have been validated by events. Kay's skills as a manager were underscored this past year when she was elected by *Fortune's* Board of Editors to the Business Hall of Fame. On behalf of our shareholders, Charlie and I had long ago put her in Berkshire's Hall of Fame.

* * * * * * * * * * * *

Another of last year's retirees was Don Keough of Coca-Cola, although, as he puts it, his retirement lasted "about 14 hours." Don is one of the most extraordinary human beings I've ever known—a man of enormous business talent, but, even more important, a man who brings out the absolute best in everyone lucky enough to associate with him. Coca-Cola wants its product to be present at the happy times of a person's life. Don Keough, as an individual, invariably increases the happiness of those around him. It's impossible to think about Don without feeling good.

I will edge up to how I met Don by slipping in a plug for my neighborhood in Omaha: Though Charlie has lived in California for 45 years, his home as a boy was about 200 feet away from the house where I now live; my wife, Susie, grew up 1 1/2 blocks away; and we have about 125 Berkshire shareholders in the zip code. As for Don, in 1958 he bought the house directly across the street from mine. He was then a coffee salesman with a big family and a small income.

The impressions I formed in those days about Don were a factor in my decision to have Berkshire make a record $1 billion investment in Coca-Cola in 1988-89. Roberto Goizueta had become CEO of Coke in 1981, with Don alongside as his partner. The two of them took hold of a company that had stagnated during the previous decade and moved it from $4.4 billion of market value to $58 billion in less than 13 years. What a difference a pair of managers like this makes, even when their product has been around for 100 years.

* * * * * * * * * * * *

Frank Rooney did double duty last year. In addition to leading H. H. Brown to record profits—35% above the 1992 high—he also was key to our merger with Dexter.

Frank has known Harold Alfond and Peter Lunder for decades, and shortly after our purchase of H. H. Brown, told me what a wonderful operation they managed. He encouraged us to get together and in due course we made a deal. Frank told Harold and Peter that Berkshire would provide an ideal corporate "home" for Dexter, and that assurance undoubtedly contributed to their decision to join with us.

I've told you in the past of Frank's extraordinary record in building Melville Corp. during his 23 year tenure as CEO. Now, at 72, he's setting an even faster pace at Berkshire. Frank has a low-key, relaxed style, but don't let that fool you. When he swings, the ball disappears far over the fence.

The Annual Meeting

This year the Annual Meeting will be held at the Orpheum Theater in downtown Omaha at 9:30 a.m. on Monday, April 25, 1994. A record 2,200 people turned up for the meeting last year, but the theater can handle many more. We will have a display in the lobby featuring many of our consumer products—candy, spray guns, shoes, cutlery, encyclopedias, and the like. Among my favorites slated to be there is a See's candy assortment that commemorates Mrs. B's 100th birthday and that features her picture, rather than Mrs. See's, on the package.

We recommend that you promptly get hotel reservations at one of these hotels: (1) The Radisson-Redick Tower, a small (88 rooms) but nice hotel across the street from the Orpheum; (2) the much larger Red Lion Hotel, located about a five-minute walk from the Orpheum; or (3) the Marriott, located in West Omaha about 100 yards from Borsheim's, which is a twenty-minute drive from downtown. We will have buses at the Marriott that will leave at 8:30 and 8:45 for the meeting and return after it ends.

An attachment to our proxy material explains how you can obtain the card you will need for admission to the meeting. With the admission card, we will enclose information about parking facilities located near the Orpheum. If

334

you are driving, come a little early. Nearby lots fill up quickly and you may have to walk a few blocks.

As usual, we will have buses to take you to Nebraska Furniture Mart and Borsheim's after the meeting and to take you from there to downtown hotels or the airport later. Those of you arriving early can visit the Furniture Mart any day of the week; it is open from 10 a.m. to 5:30 p.m. on Saturdays and from noon to 5:30 p.m. on Sundays. Borsheim's normally is closed on Sunday but will be open for shareholders and their guests from noon to 6 p.m. on Sunday, April 24.

In past trips to Borsheim's, many of you have met Susan Jacques. Early in 1994, Susan was made President and CEO of the company, having risen in 11 years from a $4-an-hour job that she took at the store when she was 23. Susan will be joined at Borsheim's on Sunday by many of the managers of our other businesses, and Charlie and I will be there as well.

On the previous evening, Saturday, April 23, there will be a baseball game at Rosenblatt Stadium between the Omaha Royals and the Nashville Sounds (which could turn out to be Michael Jordan's team). As you may know, a few years ago I bought 25% of the Royals (a capital-allocation decision for which I will not become famous) and this year the league has cooperatively scheduled a home stand at Annual Meeting time.

I will throw the first pitch on the 23rd, and it's a certainty that I will improve on last year's humiliating performance. On that occasion, the catcher inexplicably called for my "sinker" and I dutifully delivered a pitch that barely missed my foot. This year, I will go with my high hard one regardless of what the catcher signals, so bring your speed-timing devices. The proxy statement will include information about obtaining tickets to the game. I regret to report that you won't have to buy them from scalpers.

Warren E. Buffett
Chairman of the Board

March 1, 1994

BERKSHIRE HATHAWAY INC.

To the Shareholders of Berkshire Hathaway Inc.:

Our gain in net worth during 1994 was $1.45 billion or 13.9%. Over the last 30 years (that is, since present management took over) our per-share book value has grown from $19 to $10,083, or at a rate of 23% compounded annually.

Charlie Munger, Berkshire's Vice Chairman and my partner, and I make few predictions. One we will confidently offer, however, is that the future performance of Berkshire won't come close to matching the performance of the past.

The problem is not that what has worked in the past will cease to work in the future. To the contrary, we believe that our formula—the purchase at sensible prices of businesses that have good underlying economics and are run by honest and able people—is certain to produce reasonable success. We expect, therefore, to keep on doing well.

A fat wallet, however, is the enemy of superior investment results. And Berkshire now has a net worth of $11.9 billion compared to about $22 million when Charlie and I began to manage the company. Though there are as many good businesses as ever, it is useless for us to make purchases that are inconsequential in relation to Berkshire's capital. (As Charlie regularly reminds me, "If something is not worth doing at all, it's not worth doing well.") We now consider a security for purchase only if we believe we can deploy at least $100 million in it. Given that minimum, Berkshire's investment universe has shrunk dramatically.

Nevertheless, we will stick with the approach that got us here and try not to relax our standards. Ted Williams, in The Story of My Life, explains why: "My argument is, to be a good hitter, you've got to get a good ball to hit. It's the first rule in the book. If I have to bite at stuff that is out of my happy zone, I'm not a .344 hitter. I might only be a .250 hitter." Charlie and I agree and will try to wait for opportunities that are well within our own "happy zone."

We will continue to ignore political and economic forecasts, which are an expensive distraction for many investors and businessmen. Thirty years ago, no one could have foreseen the huge expansion of the Vietnam War, wage and price controls, two oil shocks, the resignation of a president, the dissolution of the Soviet Union, a one-day drop in the Dow of 508 points, or treasury bill yields fluctuating between 2.8% and 17.4%.

But, surprise—none of these blockbuster events made the slightest dent in Ben Graham's investment principles. Nor did they render unsound the negotiated purchases of fine businesses at sensible prices. Imagine the cost to us, then, if we had let a fear of unknowns cause us to defer or alter the deployment of capital. Indeed, we have usually made our best purchases when apprehensions about some macro event were at a peak. Fear is the foe of the faddist, but the friend of the fundamentalist.

A different set of major shocks is sure to occur in the next 30 years. We will neither try to predict these nor to profit from them. If we can identify businesses similar to those we have purchased in the past, external surprises will have little effect on our long-term results.

What we promise you—along with more modest gains—is that during your ownership of Berkshire, you will fare just as Charlie and I do. If you suffer, we will suffer; if we prosper, so will you. And we will not break this bond by introducing compensation arrangements that give us a greater participation in the upside than the downside.

We further promise you that our personal fortunes will remain overwhelmingly concentrated in Berkshire shares: We will not ask you to invest with us and then put our own money elsewhere. In addition, Berkshire dominates both the investment portfolios of most members of our families and of a great many friends who belonged to partnerships that Charlie and I ran in the 1960's. We could not be more motivated to do our best.

Luckily, we have a good base from which to work. Ten years ago, in 1984, Berkshire's insurance companies held securities having a value of $1.7 billion, or about $1,500 per Berkshire share. Leaving aside all income and capital gains from those securities, Berkshire's pre-tax earnings that year were only about $6 million. We had earnings, yes, from our various manufacturing, retailing and service businesses, but they were almost entirely offset by the combination of underwriting losses in our insurance business, corporate overhead and interest expense.

Now we hold securities worth $18 billion, or over $15,000 per Berkshire share. If you again exclude all income from these securities, our pre-tax earnings in 1994 were about $384 million. During the decade, employment has grown from 5,000 to 22,000 (including eleven people at World Headquarters).

We achieved our gains through the efforts of a superb corps of operating managers who get extraordinary results from some ordinary-appearing businesses. Casey Stengel described managing a baseball team as "getting paid for home runs other fellows hit." That's my formula at Berkshire, also.

The businesses in which we have partial interests are equally important to Berkshire's success. A few statistics will illustrate their significance: In 1994, Coca-Cola sold about 280 billion 8-ounce servings and earned a little less than a penny on each. But pennies add up. Through Berkshire's 7.8% ownership of Coke, we have an economic interest in 21 billion of its servings, which produce "soft-drink earnings" for us of nearly $200 million. Similarly, by way of its Gillette stock, Berkshire has a 7% share of the world's razor and blade market (measured by revenues, not by units), a proportion according us about $250 million of sales in 1994. And, at Wells Fargo, a $53 billion bank, our 13% ownership translates into a $7 billion "Berkshire Bank" that earned about $100 million during 1994.

It's far better to own a significant portion of the Hope diamond than 100% of a rhinestone, and the companies just mentioned easily qualify as rare gems. Best of all, we aren't limited to simply a few of this breed, but instead possess a growing collection.

Stock prices will continue to fluctuate—sometimes sharply—and the economy will have its ups and down. Over time, however, we believe it highly probable that the sort of businesses we own will continue to increase in value at a satisfactory rate.

Book Value and Intrinsic Value

We regularly report our per-share book value, an easily calculable number, though one of limited use. Just as regularly, we tell you that what counts is intrinsic value, a number that is impossible to pinpoint but essential to estimate.

For example, in 1964, we could state with certitude that Berkshire's per-share book value was $19.46. However, that figure considerably overstated the stock's intrinsic value since all of the company's resources were tied up in a sub-profitable textile business. Our textile assets had neither going-concern nor liquidation values equal to their carrying values. In 1964, then, anyone inquiring into the soundness of Berkshire's balance sheet might well have deserved the answer once offered up by a Hollywood mogul of dubious reputation: "Don't worry, the liabilities are solid."

Today, Berkshire's situation has reversed: Many of the businesses we control are worth far more than their carrying value. (Those we don't control, such as Coca-Cola or Gillette, are carried at current market values.) We continue to give you book value figures, however, because they serve as a rough, albeit significantly understated, tracking measure for Berkshire's intrinsic value. Last year, in fact, the two measures moved in concert: Book value gained 13.9%, and that was the approximate gain in intrinsic value also.

We define intrinsic value as the discounted value of the cash that can be taken out of a business during its remaining life. Anyone calculating intrinsic value necessarily comes up with a highly subjective figure that will change both as estimates of future cash flows are revised and as interest rates move. Despite its fuzziness, however, intrinsic value is all-important and is the only logical way to evaluate the relative attractiveness of investments and businesses.

To see how historical input (book value) and future output (intrinsic value) can diverge, let's look at another form of investment, a college education. Think of the education's cost as its "book value." If it is to be accurate, the cost should include the earnings that were foregone by the student because he chose college rather than a job.

For this exercise, we will ignore the important non-economic benefits of an education and focus strictly on its economic value. First, we must estimate the earnings that the graduate will receive over his lifetime and subtract from that figure an estimate of what he would have earned had he lacked his education. That gives us an excess earnings figure, which must then be discounted, at an appropriate interest rate, back to graduation day. The dollar result equals the intrinsic economic value of the education.

Some graduates will find that the book value of their education exceeds its intrinsic value, which means that whoever paid for the education didn't get his money's worth. In other cases, the intrinsic value of an education will far exceed its book value, a result that proves capital was wisely deployed. In all cases, what is clear is that book value is meaningless as an indicator of intrinsic value.

Now let's get less academic and look at Scott Fetzer, an example from Berkshire's own experience. This account will not only illustrate how the relationship of book value and intrinsic value can change but also will provide an accounting lesson that I know you have been breathlessly awaiting. Naturally, I've chosen here to talk about an acquisition that has turned out to be a huge winner.

Berkshire purchased Scott Fetzer at the beginning of 1986. At the time, the company was a collection of 22 businesses, and today we have exactly the same line-up—no additions and no disposals. Scott Fetzer's main operations are World Book, Kirby, and Campbell Hausfeld, but many other units are important contributors to earnings as well.

We paid $315.2 million for Scott Fetzer, which at the time had $172.6 million of book value. The $142.6 million premium we handed over indicated our belief that the company's intrinsic value was close to double its book value.

In the table below we trace the book value of Scott Fetzer, as well as its earnings and dividends, since our purchase.

Year	(1) Beginning Book Value	(2) Earnings	(3) Dividends	(4) Ending Book Value (1)+(2)-(3)
		(In $ Millions)		
1986	$172.6	$ 40.3	$125.0	$ 87.9
1987	87.9	48.6	41.0	95.5
1988	95.5	58.0	35.0	118.6
1989	118.6	58.5	71.5	105.5
1990	105.5	61.3	33.5	133.3
1991	133.3	61.4	74.0	120.7
1992	120.7	70.5	80.0	111.2
1993	111.2	77.5	98.0	90.7
1994	90.7	79.3	76.0	94.0

Because it had excess cash when our deal was made, Scott Fetzer was able to pay Berkshire dividends of $125 million in 1986, though it earned only $40.3 million. I should mention that we have not introduced leverage into Scott Fetzer's balance sheet. In fact, the company has gone from very modest debt when we purchased it to virtually no debt at all (except for debt used by its finance subsidiary). Similarly, we have not sold plants and leased them back, nor sold receivables, nor the like. Throughout our years of ownership, Scott Fetzer has operated as a conservatively-financed and liquid enterprise.

As you can see, Scott Fetzer's earnings have increased steadily since we bought it, but book value has not grown commensurately. Consequently, return on equity, which was exceptional at the time of our purchase, has now become truly extraordinary. Just how extraordinary is illustrated by comparing Scott Fetzer's performance to that of the Fortune 500, a group it would qualify for if it were a stand-alone company.

Had Scott Fetzer been on the 1993 500 list—the latest available for inspection—the company's return on equity would have ranked 4th. But that is far from the whole story. The top three companies in return on equity were

Insilco, LTV and Gaylord Container, each of which emerged from bankruptcy in 1993 and none of which achieved meaningful earnings that year except for those they realized when they were accorded debt forgiveness in bankruptcy proceedings. Leaving aside such non-operating windfalls, Scott Fetzer's return on equity would have ranked it first on the Fortune 500, well ahead of number two. Indeed, Scott Fetzer's return on equity was double that of the company ranking tenth.

You might expect that Scott Fetzer's success could only be explained by a cyclical peak in earnings, a monopolistic position, or leverage. But no such circumstances apply. Rather, the company's success comes from the managerial expertise of CEO Ralph Schey, of whom I'll tell you more later.

First, however, the promised accounting lesson: When we paid a $142.6 million premium over book value for Scott Fetzer, that figure had to be recorded on Berkshire's balance sheet. I'll spare you the details of how this worked (these were laid out in an appendix to our 1986 Annual Report) and get to the bottom line: After a premium is initially recorded, it must in almost all cases be written off over time through annual charges that are shown as costs in the acquiring company's earnings statement.

The following table shows, first, the annual charges Berkshire has made to gradually extinguish the Scott Fetzer acquisition premium and, second, the premium that remains on our books. These charges have no effect on cash or the taxes we pay, and are not, in our view, an economic cost (though many accountants would disagree with us). They are merely a way for us to reduce the carrying value of Scott Fetzer on our books so that the figure will eventually match the net worth that Scott Fetzer actually employs in its business.

Year	Beginning Purchase Premium	Purchase-Premium Charge to Berkshire Earnings	Ending Purchase Premium
		(In $ Millions)	
1986	$142.6	$ 11.6	$131.0
1987	131.0	7.1	123.9
1988	123.9	7.9	115.9
1989	115.9	7.0	108.9
1990	108.9	7.1	101.9
1991	101.9	6.9	95.0
1992	95.0	7.7	87.2
1993	87.2	28.1	59.1
1994	59.1	4.9	54.2

Note that by the end of 1994 the premium was reduced to $54.2 million. When this figure is added to Scott Fetzer's year-end book value of $94 million, the total is $148.2 million, which is the current carrying value of Scott Fetzer on Berkshire's books. That amount is less than half of our carrying value for the company when it was acquired. Yet Scott Fetzer is now earning about twice what it then did. Clearly, the intrinsic value of the business has consistently grown, even though we have just as consistently marked down its carrying value through purchase-premium charges that reduced Berkshire's earnings and net worth.

The difference between Scott Fetzer's intrinsic value and its carrying value on Berkshire's books is now huge. As I mentioned earlier—but am delighted to mention again—credit for this agreeable mismatch goes to Ralph Schey, a focused, smart and high-grade manager.

The reasons for Ralph's success are not complicated. Ben Graham taught me 45 years ago that in investing it is not necessary to do extraordinary things to get extraordinary results. In later life, I have been surprised to find that this statement holds true in business management as well. What a manager must do is handle the basics well and not get diverted. That's precisely Ralph's formula. He establishes the right goals and never forgets what he set out to do. On the personal side, Ralph is a joy to work with. He's forthright about problems and is self-confident without being self-important.

He is also experienced. Though I don't know Ralph's age, I do know that, like many of our managers, he is over 65. At Berkshire, we look to performance, not to the calendar. Charlie and I, at 71 and 64 respectively, now keep George Foreman's picture on our desks. You can make book that our scorn for a mandatory retirement age will grow stronger every year.

Intrinsic Value and Capital Allocation

Understanding intrinsic value is as important for managers as it is for investors. When managers are making capital allocation decisions—including decisions to repurchase shares—it's vital that they act in ways that increase per-share intrinsic value and avoid moves that decrease it. This principle may seem obvious but we constantly see it violated. And, when misallocations occur, shareholders are hurt.

For example, in contemplating business mergers and acquisitions, many managers tend to focus on whether the transaction is immediately dilutive or anti-dilutive to earnings per share (or, at financial institutions, to per-share book value). An emphasis of this sort carries great dangers. Going back to our college-education example, imagine that a 25-year-old first-year MBA student is considering merging his future economic interests with those of a 25-year-old day laborer. The MBA student, a non-earner, would find that a "share-for-share" merger of his equity interest in himself with that of the day laborer would enhance his near-term earnings (in a big way!). But what could be sillier for the student than a deal of this kind?

In corporate transactions, it's equally silly for the would-be purchaser to focus on current earnings when the prospective acquiree has either different prospects, different amounts of non-operating assets, or a different capital structure. At Berkshire, we have rejected many merger and purchase opportunities that would have boosted current and near-term earnings but that would have reduced per-share intrinsic value. Our approach, rather, has been to follow Wayne Gretzky's advice: "Go to where the puck is going to be, not to where it is." As a result, our shareholders are now many billions of dollars richer than they would have been if we had used the standard catechism.

The sad fact is that most major acquisitions display an egregious imbalance: They are a bonanza for the shareholders of the acquiree; they increase the income and status of the acquirer's management; and they are a honey pot for the investment bankers and other professionals on both sides. But, alas, they usually reduce the wealth of the acquirer's shareholders, often to a substantial extent. That happens because the acquirer typically gives up more intrinsic value than it receives. Do that enough, says John Medlin, the retired head of Wachovia Corp., and "you are running a chain letter in reverse."

Over time, the skill with which a company's managers allocate capital has an enormous impact on the enterprise's value. Almost by definition, a really good business generates far more money (at least after its early years) than it can use internally. The company could, of course, distribute the money to shareholders by way of dividends or share repurchases. But often the CEO asks a strategic planning staff, consultants or investment bankers whether an acquisition or two might make sense. That's like asking your interior decorator whether you need a $50,000 rug.

The acquisition problem is often compounded by a biological bias: Many CEO's attain their positions in part because they possess an abundance of animal spirits and ego. If an executive is heavily endowed with these qualities—which, it should be acknowledged, sometimes have their advantages—they won't disappear when he reaches the top. When such a CEO is encouraged by his advisors to make deals, he responds much as would a teenage boy who is encouraged by his father to have a normal sex life. It's not a push he needs.

Some years back, a CEO friend of mine—in jest, it must be said—unintentionally described the pathology of many big deals. This friend, who ran a property-casualty insurer, was explaining to his directors why he wanted to acquire a certain life insurance company. After droning rather unpersuasively through the economics and strategic rationale for the acquisition, he abruptly abandoned the script. With an impish look, he simply said: "Aw, fellas, all the other kids have one."

At Berkshire, our managers will continue to earn extraordinary returns from what appear to be ordinary businesses. As a first step, these managers will look for ways to deploy their earnings advantageously in their businesses. What's left, they will send to Charlie and me. We then will try to use those funds in ways that build per-share intrinsic value. Our goal will be to acquire either part or all of businesses that we believe we understand, that have good, sustainable underlying economics, and that are run by managers whom we like, admire and trust.

Compensation

At Berkshire, we try to be as logical about compensation as about capital allocation. For example, we compensate Ralph Schey based upon the results of Scott Fetzer rather than those of Berkshire. What could make more sense, since he's responsible for one operation but not the other? A cash bonus or a stock option tied to the fortunes of Berkshire would provide totally capricious rewards to Ralph. He could, for example, be hitting home runs at Scott Fetzer while Charlie and I rang up mistakes at Berkshire, thereby negating his efforts many times over. Conversely, why should option profits or bonuses be heaped upon Ralph if good things are occurring in other parts of Berkshire but Scott Fetzer is lagging?

In setting compensation, we like to hold out the promise of large carrots, but make sure their delivery is tied directly to results in the area that a manager controls. When capital invested in an operation is significant, we also both charge managers a high rate for incremental capital they employ and credit them at an equally high rate for capital they release.

The product of this money's-not-free approach is definitely visible at Scott Fetzer. If Ralph can employ incremental funds at good returns, it pays him to do so: His bonus increases when earnings on additional capital exceed a meaningful hurdle charge. But our bonus calculation is symmetrical: If incremental investment yields substandard returns, the shortfall is costly to Ralph as well as to Berkshire. The consequence of this two-way arrangement is that it pays Ralph—and pays him well—to send to Omaha any cash he can't advantageously use in his business.

It has become fashionable at public companies to describe almost every compensation plan as aligning the interests of management with those of shareholders. In our book, alignment means being a partner in both directions, not just on the upside. Many "alignment" plans flunk this basic test, being artful forms of "heads I win, tails you lose."

A common form of misalignment occurs in the typical stock option arrangement, which does not periodically increase the option price to compensate for the fact that retained earnings are building up the wealth of the company. Indeed, the combination of a ten-year option, a low dividend payout, and compound interest can provide lush gains to a manager who has done no more than tread water in his job. A cynic might even note that when payments to owners are held down, the profit to the option-holding manager increases. I have yet to see this vital point spelled out in a proxy statement asking shareholders to approve an option plan.

I can't resist mentioning that our compensation arrangement with Ralph Schey was worked out in about five minutes, immediately upon our purchase of Scott Fetzer and without the "help" of lawyers or compensation consultants. This arrangement embodies a few very simple ideas—not the kind of terms favored by consultants who cannot easily send a large bill unless they have established that you have a large problem (and one, of course, that requires an annual review). Our agreement with Ralph has never been changed. It made sense to him and to me in 1986, and it makes sense now. Our compensation arrangements with the managers of all our other units are similarly simple, though the terms of each agreement vary to fit the economic characteristics of the business at issue, the existence in some cases of partial ownership of the unit by managers, etc.

In all instances, we pursue rationality. Arrangements that pay off in capricious ways, unrelated to a manager's personal accomplishments, may well be welcomed by certain managers. Who, after all, refuses a free lottery ticket? But such arrangements are wasteful to the company and cause the manager to lose focus on what should be his real areas of concern. Additionally, irrational behavior at the parent may well encourage imitative behavior at subsidiaries.

At Berkshire, only Charlie and I have the managerial responsibility for the entire business. Therefore, we are the only parties who should logically be compensated on the basis of what the enterprise does as a whole. Even so, that is not a compensation arrangement we desire. We have carefully designed both the company and our jobs so that we do things we enjoy with people we like. Equally important, we are forced to do very few boring or unpleasant tasks. We are the beneficiaries as well of the abundant array of material and psychic perks that flow to the heads of corporations. Under such idyllic conditions, we don't expect shareholders to ante up loads of compensation for which we have no possible need.

Indeed, if we were not paid at all, Charlie and I would be delighted with the cushy jobs we hold. At bottom, we subscribe to Ronald Reagan's creed: "It's probably true that hard work never killed anyone, but I figure why take the chance."

Sources of Reported Earnings

The table on the next page shows the main sources of Berkshire's reported earnings. In this presentation, purchase-premium charges of the type we discussed in our earlier analysis of Scott Fetzer are not assigned to the specific businesses to which they apply, but are instead aggregated and shown separately. This procedure lets you view the earnings of our businesses as they would have been reported had we not purchased them. This form of presentation seems to us to be more useful to investors and managers than one utilizing GAAP, which requires purchase premiums to be charged off, business-by-business. The total earnings we show in the table are, of course, identical to the GAAP total in our audited financial statements.

	Pre-Tax Earnings		Berkshire's Share of Net Earnings (after taxes and minority interests)	
	1994	1993	1994	1993
	(000s omitted)			
Operating Earnings:				
Insurance Group:				
Underwriting	$129,926	$ 30,876	$ 80,860	$ 20,156
Net Investment Income	419,422	375,946	350,453	321,321
Buffalo News	54,238	50,962	31,685	29,696
Fechheimer	14,260	13,442	7,107	6,931
Finance Businesses	21,568	22,695	14,293	14,161
Kirby	42,349	39,147	27,719	25,056
Nebraska Furniture Mart	17,356	21,540	8,652	10,398
Scott Fetzer Manufacturing Group	39,435	38,196	24,909	23,809
See's Candies	47,539	41,150	28,247	24,367
Shoe Group	85,503	44,025 *	55,750	28,829
World Book	24,662	19,915	17,275	13,537
Purchase-Price Premium Charges	(22,595)	(17,033)	(19,355)	(13,996)
Interest Expense**	(60,111)	(56,545)	(37,264)	(35,614)
Shareholder-Designated Contributions	(10,419)	(9,448)	(6,668)	(5,994)
Other	36,232	28,428	22,576	15,094
Operating Earnings	839,365	643,296	606,239	477,751
Sales of Securities	91,332	546,422	61,138	356,702
Decline in Value of USAir Preferred Stock	(268,500)	---	(172,579)	---
Tax Accruals Caused by New Accounting Rules	---	---	---	(146,332)
Total Earnings – All Entities	$662,197	$1,189,718	$494,798	$688,121

*   *Includes Dexter's earnings only from the date it was acquired, November 7, 1993.*

** *Excludes interest expense of Finance Businesses.*

A large amount of information about these businesses is given on pages 37-48, where you will also find our segment earnings reported on a GAAP basis. In addition, on pages 53-59, we have rearranged Berkshire's financial data into four segments on a non-GAAP basis, a presentation that corresponds to the way Charlie and I think about the company. Our intent is to supply you with the financial information that we would wish you to give us if our positions were reversed.

"Look-Through" Earnings

In past reports, we've discussed look-through earnings, which we believe more accurately portray the earnings of Berkshire than does our GAAP result. As we calculate them, look-through earnings consist of: (1) the operating earnings reported in the previous section, plus; (2) the retained operating earnings of major investees that, under GAAP accounting, are not reflected in our profits, less; (3) an allowance for the tax that would be paid by Berkshire if these retained earnings of investees had instead been distributed to us. The "operating earnings" of which we speak here exclude capital gains, special accounting items and major restructuring charges.

If our intrinsic value is to grow at our target rate of 15%, our look-through earnings, over time, must also increase at about that pace. When I first explained this concept a few years back, I told you that meeting this 15% goal would require us to generate look-through earnings of about $1.8 billion by 2000. Because we've since issued about 3% more shares, that figure has grown to $1.85 billion.

We are now modestly ahead of schedule in meeting our goal, but to a significant degree that is because our super-cat insurance business has recently delivered earnings far above trend-line expectancy (an outcome I will discuss in the next section). Giving due weight to that abnormality, we still expect to hit our target but that, of course, is no sure thing.

The following table shows how we calculate look-through earnings, though I warn you that the figures are necessarily very rough. (The dividends paid to us by these investees have been included in the operating earnings itemized on page 12, mostly under "Insurance Group: Net Investment Income.")

Berkshire's Major Investees	Berkshire's Approximate Ownership at Yearend		Berkshire's Share of Undistributed Operating Earnings (in millions)	
	1994	1993	1994	1993
	5.5%	2.4%	$ 25[2]	$ 16
Capital Cities/ABC Inc.	13.0%	13.0%	85	83[2]
The Coca-Cola Company	7.8%	7.2%	116[2]	94
Federal Home Loan Mortgage Corp.	6.3%[1]	6.8%[1]	47[2]	41[2]
Gannett Co., Inc.	4.9%	---	4[2]	---
GEICO Corp.	50.2%	48.4%	63[2]	76[3]
The Gillette Company	10.8%	10.9%	51	44
PNC Bank Corp.	8.3%	---	10[2]	---
The Washington Post Company	15.2%	14.8%	18	15
Wells Fargo & Company	13.3%	12.2%	73	53[2]
Berkshire's share of undistributed earnings of major investees			492	$422
Hypothetical tax on these undistributed investee earnings[4]			(68)	(59)
Reported operating earnings of Berkshire			606	478
Total look-through earnings of Berkshire			$1,030	$ 841

(1) Does not include shares allocable to the minority interest at Wesco
(2) Calculated on average ownership for the year
(3) Excludes realized capital gains, which have been both recurring and significant
(4) The tax rate used is 14%, which is the rate Berkshire pays on the dividends it receives

Insurance Operations

As we've explained in past reports, what counts in our insurance business is, first, the amount of "float" we develop and, second, its cost to us. Float is money we hold but don't own. In an insurance operation, float arises because most policies require that premiums be prepaid and, more importantly, because it usually takes time for an insurer to hear about and resolve loss claims.

Typically, the premiums that an insurer takes in do not cover the losses and expenses it must pay. That leaves it running an "underwriting loss"—and that loss is the cost of float.

An insurance business is profitable over time if its cost of float is less than the cost the company would otherwise incur to obtain funds. But the business has a negative value if the cost of its float is higher than market rates for money.

As the numbers in the following table show, Berkshire's insurance business has been an enormous winner. For the table, we have compiled our float—which we generate in exceptional amounts relative to our premium volume—by adding loss reserves, loss adjustment reserves, funds held under reinsurance assumed and unearned premium reserves and then subtracting agents' balances, prepaid acquisition costs, prepaid taxes and deferred charges applicable to assumed reinsurance. Our cost of float is determined by our underwriting loss or profit. In those years when we have had an underwriting profit, such as the last two, our cost of float has been negative, and we have determined our insurance earnings by adding underwriting profit to float income.

	(1) Underwriting Loss	(2) Average Float	Approximate Cost of Funds	Yearend Yield on Long-Term Govt. Bonds
	(In $ Millions)		*(Ratio of 1 to 2)*	
1967	profit	$17.3	less than zero	5.50%
1968	profit	19.9	less than zero	5.90%
1969	profit	23.4	less than zero	6.79%
1970	$ 0.37	32.4	1.14%	6.25%
1971	profit	52.5	less than zero	5.81%
1972	profit	69.5	less than zero	5.82%
1973	profit	73.3	less than zero	7.27%
1974	7.36	79.1	9.30%	8.13%
1975	11.35	87.6	12.96%	8.03%
1976	profit	102.6	less than zero	7.30%
1977	profit	139.0	less than zero	7.97%
1978	profit	190.4	less than zero	8.93%
1979	profit	227.3	less than zero	10.08%
1980	profit	237.0	less than zero	11.94%
1981	profit	228.4	less than zero	13.61%
1982	21.56	220.6	9.77%	10.64%
1983	33.87	231.3	14.64%	11.84%
1984	48.06	253.2	18.98%	11.58%
1985	44.23	390.2	11.34%	9.34%
1986	55.84	797.5	7.00%	7.60%
1987	55.43	1,266.7	4.38%	8.95%
1988	11.08	1,497.7	0.74%	9.00%
1989	24.40	1,541.3	1.58%	7.97%
1990	26.65	1,637.3	1.63%	8.24%
1991	119.59	1,895.0	6.31%	7.40%
1992	108.96	2,290.4	4.76%	7.39%
1993	profit	2,624.7	less than zero	6.35%
1994	profit	3,056.6	less than zero	7.88%

Charlie and I are delighted that our float grew in 1994 and are even more pleased that it proved to be cost-free. But our message this year echoes the one we delivered in 1993: Though we have a fine insurance business, it is not as good as it currently looks.

The reason we must repeat this caution is that our "super-cat" business (which sells policies that insurance and reinsurance companies buy to protect themselves from the effects of mega-catastrophes) was again highly profitable. Since truly major catastrophes occur infrequently, our super-cat business can be expected to show large profits in most years but occasionally to record a huge loss. In other words, the attractiveness of our super-cat business will take many years to measure. Certainly 1994 should be regarded as close to a best-case. Our only significant losses arose from the California earthquake in January. I will add that we do not expect to suffer a major loss from the early-1995 Kobe earthquake.

Super-cat policies are small in number, large in size and non-standardized. Therefore, the underwriting of this business requires far more judgment than, say, the underwriting of auto policies, for which a mass of data is available. Here Berkshire has a major advantage: Ajit Jain, our super-cat manager, whose underwriting skills are the finest. His value to us is simply enormous.

In addition, Berkshire has a special advantage in the super-cat business because of our towering financial strength, which helps us in two ways. First, a prudent insurer will want its protection against true mega-catastrophes—such as a $50 billion windstorm loss on Long Island or an earthquake of similar cost in California—to be absolutely certain. But that same insurer knows that the disaster making it dependent on a large super-cat recovery is also the disaster that could cause many reinsurers to default. There's not much sense in paying premiums for coverage that will evaporate precisely when it is needed. So the certainty that Berkshire will be both solvent and liquid after a catastrophe of unthinkable proportions is a major competitive advantage for us.

The second benefit of our capital strength is that we can write policies for amounts that no one else can even consider. For example, during 1994, a primary insurer wished to buy a short-term policy for $400 million of California earthquake coverage and we wrote the policy immediately. We know of no one else in the world who would take a $400 million risk, or anything close to it, for their own account.

Generally, brokers attempt to place coverage for large amounts by spreading the burden over a number of small policies. But, at best, coverage of that sort takes considerable time to arrange. In the meantime, the company desiring reinsurance is left holding a risk it doesn't want and that may seriously threaten its well-being. At Berkshire, on the other hand, we will quote prices for coverage as great as $500 million on the same day that we are asked to bid. No one else in the industry will do the same.

By writing coverages in large lumps, we obviously expose Berkshire to lumpy financial results. That's totally acceptable to us: Too often, insurers (as well as other businesses) follow sub-optimum strategies in order to "smooth" their reported earnings. By accepting the prospect of volatility, we expect to earn higher long-term returns than we would by pursuing predictability.

Given the risks we accept, Ajit and I constantly focus on our "worst case," knowing, of course, that it is difficult to judge what this is, since you could conceivably have a Long Island hurricane, a California earthquake, and Super Cat X all in the same year. Additionally, insurance losses could be accompanied by non-insurance troubles. For example, were we to have super-cat losses from a large Southern California earthquake, they might well be accompanied by a major drop in the value of our holdings in See's, Wells Fargo and Freddie Mac.

All things considered, we believe our worst-case *insurance* loss from a super-cat is now about $600 million after-tax, an amount that would slightly exceed Berkshire's annual earnings from other sources. If you are not comfortable with this level of exposure, the time to sell your Berkshire stock is now, not after the inevitable mega-catastrophe.

Our super-cat volume will probably be down in 1995. Prices for garden-variety policies have fallen somewhat, and the torrent of capital that was committed to the reinsurance business a few years ago will be inclined to chase premiums, irrespective of their adequacy. Nevertheless, we have strong relations with an important group of clients who will provide us with a substantial amount of business in 1995.

Berkshire's other insurance operations had excellent results in 1994. Our homestate operation, led by Rod Eldred; our workers' compensation business, headed by Brad Kinstler; our credit card operation, managed by the Kizer family; National Indemnity's traditional auto and general liability business, led by Don Wurster—all of these generated significant underwriting profits accompanied by substantial float.

We can conclude this section as we did last year: All in all, we have a first-class insurance business. Though its results will be highly volatile, this operation possesses an intrinsic value that exceeds its book value by a large amount—larger, in fact, than is the case at any other Berkshire business.

Common Stock Investments

Below we list our common stockholdings having a value of over $300 million. A small portion of these investments belongs to subsidiaries of which Berkshire owns less than 100%.

Shares	Company	12/31/94	
		Cost	Market
		(000s omitted)	
27,759,941	American Express Company	$ 723,919	$ 818,918
20,000,000	Capital Cities/ABC, Inc.	345,000	1,705,000
100,000,000	The Coca-Cola Company	1,298,888	5,150,000
12,761,200	Federal Home Loan Mortgage Corp. ("Freddie Mac")	270,468	644,441
6,854,500	Gannett Co., Inc.	335,216	365,002
34,250,000	GEICO Corp.	45,713	1,678,250
24,000,000	The Gillette Company	600,000	1,797,000
19,453,300	PNC Bank Corporation	503,046	410,951
1,727,765	The Washington Post Company	9,731	418,983
6,791,218	Wells Fargo & Company	423,680	984,727

Our investments continue to be few in number and simple in concept: The truly big investment idea can usually be explained in a short paragraph. We like a business with enduring competitive advantages that is run by able and owner-oriented people. When these attributes exist, and when we can make purchases at sensible prices, it is hard to go wrong (a challenge we periodically manage to overcome).

Investors should remember that their scorecard is not computed using Olympic-diving methods: Degree-of-difficulty doesn't count. If you are right about a business whose value is largely dependent on a single key factor that is both easy to understand and enduring, the payoff is the same as if you had correctly analyzed an investment alternative characterized by many constantly shifting and complex variables.

We try to *price*, rather than *time*, purchases. In our view, it is folly to forego buying shares in an outstanding business whose long-term future is predictable, because of short-term worries about an economy or a stock market that we know to be unpredictable. Why scrap an informed decision because of an uninformed guess?

We purchased National Indemnity in 1967, See's in 1972, Buffalo News in 1977, Nebraska Furniture Mart in 1983, and Scott Fetzer in 1986 because those are the years they became available and because we thought the prices they carried were acceptable. In each case, we pondered what the business was likely to do, not what the Dow, the Fed, or the economy might do. If we see this approach as making sense in the purchase of businesses in their entirety, why should we change tack when we are purchasing small pieces of wonderful businesses in the stock market?

Before looking at new investments, we consider adding to old ones. If a business is attractive enough to buy once, it may well pay to repeat the process. We would love to increase our economic interest in See's or Scott Fetzer, but we haven't found a way to add to a 100% holding. In the stock market, however, an investor frequently gets the chance to increase his economic interest in businesses he knows and likes. Last year we went that direction by enlarging our holdings in Coca-Cola and American Express.

Our history with American Express goes way back and, in fact, fits the pattern of my pulling current investment decisions out of past associations. In 1951, for example, GEICO shares comprised 70% of my personal portfolio and GEICO was also the first stock I sold—I was then 20—as a security salesman (the sale was 100 shares to my Aunt Alice who, bless her, would have bought anything I suggested). Twenty-five years later, Berkshire purchased a major stake in GEICO at the time it was threatened with insolvency. In another instance, that of the Washington Post, about half of my initial investment funds came from delivering the paper in the 1940's. Three decades later Berkshire purchased a large position in the company two years after it went public. As for Coca-Cola, my first business venture—this was in the 1930's—was buying a six-pack of Coke for 25 cents and selling each bottle for 5 cents. It took only fifty years before I finally got it: The real money was in the syrup.

My American Express history includes a couple of episodes: In the mid-1960's, just after the stock was battered by the company's infamous salad-oil scandal, we put about 40% of Buffett Partnership Ltd.'s capital into the stock—the largest investment the partnership had ever made. I should add that this commitment gave us over 5% ownership in Amex at a cost of $13 million. As I write this, we own just under 10%, which has cost us $1.36 billion. (Amex earned $12.5 million in 1964 and $1.4 billion in 1994.)

My history with Amex's IDS unit, which today contributes about a third of the earnings of the company, goes back even further. I first purchased stock in IDS in 1953 when it was growing rapidly and selling at a price-earnings ratio of only 3. (There was a lot of low-hanging fruit in those days.) I even produced a long report—do I ever write a short one?—on the company that I sold for $1 through an ad in the Wall Street Journal.

Obviously American Express and IDS (recently renamed American Express Financial Advisors) are far different operations today from what they were then. Nevertheless, I find that a long-term familiarity with a company and its products is often helpful in evaluating it.

Mistake Du Jour

Mistakes occur at the time of decision. We can only make our mistake-du-jour award, however, when the foolishness of the decision become obvious. By this measure, 1994 was a vintage year with keen competition for the gold medal. Here, I would like to tell you that the mistakes I will describe originated with Charlie. But whenever I try to explain things that way, my nose begins to grow.

And the nominees are . . .

Late in 1993 I sold 10 million shares of Cap Cities at $63; at year-end 1994, the price was $85.25. (The difference is $222.5 million for those of you who wish to avoid the pain of calculating the damage yourself.) When we purchased the stock at $17.25 in 1986, I told you that I had previously sold our Cap Cities holdings at $4.30 per share during 1978-80, and added that I was at a loss to explain my earlier behavior. Now I've become a repeat offender. Maybe it's time to get a guardian appointed.

Egregious as it is, the Cap Cities decision earns only a silver medal. Top honors go to a mistake I made five years ago that fully ripened in 1994: Our $358 million purchase of USAir preferred stock, on which the dividend was suspended in September. In the 1990 Annual Report I correctly described this deal as an "unforced error," meaning that I was neither pushed into the investment nor misled by anyone when making it. Rather, this was a case of sloppy analysis, a lapse that may have been caused by the fact that we were buying a senior security or by hubris. Whatever the reason, the mistake was large.

Before this purchase, I simply failed to focus on the problems that would inevitably beset a carrier whose costs were both high and extremely difficult to lower. In earlier years, these life-threatening costs posed few problems. Airlines were then protected from competition by regulation, and carriers could absorb high costs because they could pass them along by way of fares that were also high.

When deregulation came along, it did not immediately change the picture: The capacity of low-cost carriers was so small that the high-cost lines could, in large part, maintain their existing fare structures. During this period, with the longer-term problems largely invisible but slowly metastasizing, the costs that were non-sustainable became further embedded.

As the seat capacity of the low-cost operators expanded, their fares began to force the old-line, high-cost airlines to cut their own. The day of reckoning for these airlines could be delayed by infusions of capital (such as ours into USAir), but eventually a fundamental rule of economics prevailed: In an unregulated commodity business, a company must lower its costs to competitive levels or face extinction. This principle should have been obvious to your Chairman, but I missed it.

Seth Schofield, CEO of USAir, has worked diligently to correct the company's historical cost problems but, to date, has not managed to do so. In part, this is because he has had to deal with a moving target, the result of certain major carriers having obtained labor concessions and other carriers having benefitted from "fresh-start" costs that came out of bankruptcy proceedings. (As Herb Kelleher, CEO of Southwest Airlines, has said: "Bankruptcy court for airlines has become a health spa.") Additionally, it should be no surprise to anyone that those airline employees who contractually receive above-market salaries will resist any reduction in these as long as their checks continue to clear.

Despite this difficult situation, USAir may yet achieve the cost reductions it needs to maintain its viability long-term. But it is far from sure that will happen.

Accordingly, we wrote our USAir investment down to $89.5 million, 25 cents on the dollar at yearend 1994. This valuation reflects both a possibility that our preferred will have its value fully or largely restored and an opposite possibility that the stock will eventually become worthless. Whatever the outcome, we will heed a prime rule of investing: You don't have to make it back the way that you lost it.

The accounting effects of our USAir writedown are complicated. Under GAAP accounting, insurance companies are required to carry all stocks on their balance sheets at estimated market value. Therefore, at the end of last year's third quarter, we were carrying our USAir preferred at $89.5 million, or 25% of cost. In other words, our net worth was at that time reflecting a value for USAir that was far below our $358 million cost.

But in the fourth quarter, we concluded that the decline in value was, in accounting terms, "other than temporary," and that judgment required us to send the writedown of $269 million through our income statement. The amount will have no other fourth-quarter effect. That is, it will not reduce our net worth, because the diminution of value had already been reflected.

Charlie and I will not stand for reelection to USAir's board at the upcoming annual meeting. Should Seth wish to consult with us, however, we will be pleased to be of any help that we can.

Miscellaneous

Two CEO's who have done great things for Berkshire shareholders retired last year: Dan Burke of Capital Cities/ABC and Carl Reichardt of Wells Fargo. Dan and Carl encountered very tough industry conditions in recent years. But their skill as managers allowed the businesses they ran to emerge from these periods with record earnings, added luster, and bright prospects. Additionally, Dan and Carl prepared well for their departure and left their companies in outstanding hands. We owe them our gratitude.

* * * * * * * * * * * *

About 95.7% of all eligible shares participated in Berkshire's 1994 shareholder-designated contributions program. Contributions made through the program were $10.4 million and 3,300 charities were recipients.

Every year a few shareholders miss participating in the program because they either do not have their shares registered in their own names on the prescribed record date or because they fail to get the designation form back to us within the 60-day period allowed for its return. Since we don't make exceptions when requirements aren't met, we urge that both new shareholders and old read the description of our shareholder-designated contributions program that appears on pages 50-51.

To participate in future programs, you must make sure your shares are registered in the name of the actual owner, not in the nominee name of a broker, bank or depository. Shares not so registered on August 31, 1995 will be ineligible for the 1995 program.

* * * * * * * * * * * *

We made only one minor acquisition during 1994—a small retail shoe chain—but our interest in finding good candidates remains as keen as ever. The criteria we employ for purchases or mergers is detailed in the appendix on page 21.

Last spring, we offered to merge with a large, family-controlled business on terms that included a Berkshire convertible preferred stock. Though we failed to reach an agreement, this episode made me realize that we needed to ask our shareholders to authorize preferred shares in case we wanted in the future to move quickly if a similar acquisition opportunity were to appear. Accordingly, our proxy presents a proposal that you authorize a large amount of preferred stock, which will be issuable on terms set by the Board of Directors. You can be sure that Charlie and I will not use these shares without being completely satisfied that we are receiving as much in intrinsic value as we are giving.

* * * * * * * * * * * *

Charlie and I hope you can come to the Annual Meeting—at a new site. Last year, we slightly overran the Orpheum Theater's seating capacity of 2,750, and therefore we will assemble at 9:30 a.m. on Monday, May 1, 1995, at the Holiday Convention Centre. The main ballroom at the Centre can handle 3,300, and if need be, we will have audio and video equipment in an adjacent room capable of handling another 1,000 people.

Last year we displayed some of Berkshire's products at the meeting, and as a result sold about 800 pounds of candy, 507 pairs of shoes, and over $12,000 of World Books and related publications. All these goods will be available again this year. Though we like to think of the meeting as a spiritual experience, we must remember that even the least secular of religions includes the ritual of the collection plate.

Of course, what you really should be purchasing is a video tape of the 1995 Orange Bowl. Your Chairman views this classic nightly, switching to slow motion for the fourth quarter. Our cover color this year is a salute to Nebraska's football coach, Tom Osborne, and his Cornhuskers, the country's top college team. I urge you to wear Husker red to the annual meeting and promise you that at least 50% of your managerial duo will be in appropriate attire.

We recommend that you promptly get hotel reservations for the meeting, as we expect a large crowd. Those of you who like to be downtown (about six miles from the Centre) may wish to stay at the Radisson Redick Tower, a small (88 rooms) but nice hotel or at the much larger Red Lion Hotel a few blocks away. In the vicinity of the Centre are the Holiday Inn (403 rooms), Homewood Suites (118 rooms) and Hampton Inn (136 rooms). Another recommended spot is the Marriott, whose west Omaha location is about 100 yards from Borsheim's and a ten-minute drive from the Centre. There will be buses at the Marriott that will leave at 8:45 and 9:00 for the meeting and return after it ends.

An attachment to our proxy material explains how you can obtain the card you will need for admission to the meeting. A good-sized parking area is available at the Centre, while those who stay at the Holiday Inn, Homewood Suites and Hampton Inn will be able to walk to the meeting.

As usual, we will have buses to take you to the Nebraska Furniture Mart and Borsheim's after the meeting and to take you from there to hotels or the airport later. I hope you make a special effort to visit the Nebraska Furniture Mart because it has opened the Mega Mart, a true retailing marvel that sells electronics, appliances, computers, CD's, cameras and audio equipment. Sales have been sensational since the opening, and you will be amazed by both the variety of products available and their display on the floor.

The Mega Mart, adjacent to NFM's main store, is on our 64-acre site about two miles north of the Centre. The stores are open from 10 a.m. to 9 p.m. on Fridays, 10 a.m. to 6 p.m. on Saturdays and noon to 6 p.m. on Sundays. When you're there be sure to say hello to Mrs. B, who, at 101, will be hard at work in our Mrs. B's Warehouse. She never misses a day at the store—or, for that matter, an hour.

Borsheim's normally is closed on Sunday but will be open for shareholders and their guests from noon to 6 p.m. on Sunday. This is always a special day, and we will try to have a few surprises. Usually this is the biggest sales day of the year, so for more reasons than one Charlie and I hope to see you there.

On Saturday evening, April 29, there will be a baseball game at Rosenblatt Stadium between the Omaha Royals and the Buffalo Bisons. The Buffalo team is owned by my friends, Mindy and Bob Rich, Jr., and I'm hoping they will attend. If so, I will try to entice Bob into a one-pitch duel on the mound. Bob is a capitalist's Randy Johnson—young, strong and athletic—and not the sort of fellow you want to face early in the season. So I will need plenty of vocal support.

The proxy statement will include information about obtaining tickets to the game. About 1,400 shareholders attended the event last year. Opening the game that night, I had my stuff and threw a strike that the scoreboard reported at eight miles per hour. What many fans missed was that I shook off the catcher's call for my fast ball and instead delivered my change-up. This year it will be all smoke.

Warren E. Buffett
Chairman of the Board

March 7, 1995

BERKSHIRE HATHAWAY INC.

To the Shareholders of Berkshire Hathaway Inc.:

Our gain in net worth during 1995 was $5.3 billion, or 45.0%. Per-share book value grew by a little less, 43.1%, because we paid stock for two acquisitions, increasing our shares outstanding by 1.3%. Over the last 31 years (that is, since present management took over) per-share book value has grown from $19 to $14,426, or at a rate of 23.6% compounded annually.

There's no reason to do handsprings over 1995's gains. This was a year in which any fool could make a bundle in the stock market. And we did. To paraphrase President Kennedy, a rising tide lifts all yachts.

Putting aside the financial results, there was plenty of good news at Berkshire last year: We negotiated three acquisitions of exactly the type we desire. Two of these, Helzberg's Diamond Shops and R.C. Willey Home Furnishings, are included in our 1995 financial statements, while our largest transaction, the purchase of GEICO, closed immediately after the end of the year. (I'll tell you more about all three acquisitions later in the report.)

These new subsidiaries roughly double our revenues. Even so, the acquisitions neither materially increased our shares outstanding nor our debt. And, though these three operations employ over 11,000 people, our headquarters staff grew only from 11 to 12. (No sense going crazy.)

Charlie Munger, Berkshire's Vice Chairman and my partner, and I want to build a collection of companies—both wholly- and partly-owned—that have excellent economic characteristics and that are run by outstanding managers. Our favorite acquisition is the negotiated transaction that allows us to purchase 100% of such a business at a fair price. But we are almost as happy when the stock market offers us the chance to buy a modest percentage of an outstanding business at a pro-rata price well below what it would take to buy 100%. This double-barrelled approach—purchases of entire businesses through negotiation or purchases of part-interests through the stock market—gives us an important advantage over capital-allocators who stick to a single course. Woody Allen once explained why eclecticism works: "The real advantage of being bisexual is that it doubles your chances for a date on Saturday night."

Over the years, we've been Woody-like in our thinking, attempting to increase our marketable investments in wonderful businesses, while simultaneously trying to buy similar businesses in their entirety. The following table illustrates our progress on both fronts. In the tabulation, we show the marketable securities owned per share of Berkshire at ten-year intervals. A second column lists our per-share operating earnings (before taxes and purchase-price adjustments but after interest and corporate overhead) from all other activities. In other words, the second column shows what we earned excluding the dividends, interest and capital gains that we realized from investments. Purchase-price accounting adjustments are ignored for reasons we have explained at length in previous reports and which, as an act of mercy, we won't repeat. (We'll be glad to send masochists the earlier explanations, however.)

Year	Marketable Securities Per Share	Pre-tax Earnings Per Share Excluding All Income from Investments
1965	$ 4	$ 4.08
1975	159	(6.48)
1985	2,443	18.86
1995	22,088	258.20
Yearly Growth Rate: 1965-95	33.4%	14.7%

These results have not sprung from some master plan that we concocted in 1965. In a general way, we knew then what we hoped to accomplish but had no idea what specific opportunities might make it possible. Today we remain similarly unstructured: Over time, we expect to improve the figures in both columns but have no road map to tell us how that will come about.

We proceed with two advantages: First, our operating managers are outstanding and, in most cases, have an unusually strong attachment to Berkshire. Second, Charlie and I have had considerable experience in allocating capital and try to go at that job rationally and objectively. The giant disadvantage we face is size: In the early years, we needed only good ideas, but now we need good *big* ideas. Unfortunately, the difficulty of finding these grows in direct proportion to our financial success, a problem that increasingly erodes our strengths.

I will have more to say about Berkshire's prospects later in this report, when I discuss our proposed recapitalization.

Acquisitions

It may seem strange that we exult over a year in which we made three acquisitions, given that we have regularly used these pages to question the acquisition activities of most managers. Rest assured, Charlie and I haven't lost our skepticism: We believe most deals do damage to the shareholders of the acquiring company. Too often, the words from *HMS Pinafore* apply: "Things are seldom what they seem, skim milk masquerades as cream." Specifically, sellers and their representatives invariably present financial projections having more entertainment value than educational value. In the production of rosy scenarios, Wall Street can hold its own against Washington.

In any case, why potential buyers even look at projections prepared by sellers baffles me. Charlie and I never give them a glance, but instead keep in mind the story of the man with an ailing horse. Visiting the vet, he said: "Can you help me? Sometimes my horse walks just fine and sometimes he limps." The vet's reply was pointed: "No problem—when he's walking fine, sell him." In the world of mergers and acquisitions, that horse would be peddled as Secretariat.

At Berkshire, we have all the difficulties in perceiving the future that other acquisition-minded companies do. Like they also, we face the inherent problem that the seller of a business practically always knows far more about it than the buyer and also picks the time of sale—a time when the business is likely to be walking "just fine."

Even so, we do have a few advantages, perhaps the greatest being that we *don't* have a strategic plan. Thus we feel no need to proceed in an ordained direction (a course leading almost invariably to silly purchase prices) but can instead simply decide what makes sense for our owners. In doing that, we always mentally compare any move we are contemplating with dozens of other opportunities open to us, including the purchase of small pieces of the best businesses in the world via the stock market. Our practice of making this comparison—acquisitions against passive investments—is a discipline that managers focused simply on expansion seldom use.

Talking to *Time Magazine* a few years back, Peter Drucker got to the heart of things: "I will tell you a secret: Dealmaking beats working. Dealmaking is exciting and fun, and working is grubby. Running anything is primarily an enormous amount of grubby detail work . . . dealmaking is romantic, sexy. That's why you have deals that make no sense."

In making acquisitions, we have a further advantage: As payment, we can offer sellers a stock backed by an extraordinary collection of outstanding businesses. An individual or a family wishing to dispose of a single fine business, but also wishing to defer personal taxes indefinitely, is apt to find Berkshire stock a particularly comfortable holding. I believe, in fact, that this calculus played an important part in the two acquisitions for which we paid shares in 1995.

Beyond that, sellers sometimes care about placing their companies in a corporate home that will both endure and provide pleasant, productive working conditions for their managers. Here again, Berkshire offers something special. Our managers operate with extraordinary autonomy. Additionally, our ownership structure enables sellers to know that when I say we are buying to keep, the promise means something. For our part, we like dealing with owners who care what happens to their companies and people. A buyer is likely to find fewer unpleasant surprises dealing with that type of seller than with one simply auctioning off his business.

2

In addition to the foregoing being an explanation of our acquisition style, it is, of course, a not-so-subtle sales pitch. If you own or represent a business earning $25 million or more before tax, and it fits the criteria listed on page 23, just give me a call. Our discussion will be confidential. And if you aren't interested now, file our proposition in the back of your mind: We are never going to lose our appetite for buying companies with good economics and excellent management.

Concluding this little dissertation on acquisitions, I can't resist repeating a tale told me last year by a corporate executive. The business he grew up in was a fine one, with a long-time record of leadership in its industry. Its main product, however, was distressingly glamorless. So several decades ago, the company hired a management consultant who—naturally—advised diversification, the then-current fad. ("Focus" was not yet in style.) Before long, the company acquired a number of businesses, each after the consulting firm had gone through a long—and expensive—acquisition study. And the outcome? Said the executive sadly, "When we started, we were getting 100% of our earnings from the original business. After ten years, we were getting 150%."

Helzberg's Diamond Shops

A few years back, management consultants popularized a technique called "management by walking around" (MBWA). At Berkshire, we've instituted ABWA (acquisitions by walking around).

In May 1994, a week or so after the Annual Meeting, I was crossing the street at 58th and Fifth Avenue in New York, when a woman called out my name. I listened as she told me she'd been to, and had enjoyed, the Annual Meeting. A few seconds later, a man who'd heard the woman stop me did so as well. He turned out to be Barnett Helzberg, Jr., who owned four shares of Berkshire and had also been at our meeting.

In our few minutes of conversation, Barnett said he had a business we might be interested in. When people say that, it usually turns out they have a lemonade stand—with potential, of course, to quickly grow into the next Microsoft. So I simply asked Barnett to send me particulars. That, I thought to myself. will be the end of that.

Not long after, Barnett sent me the financial statements of Helzberg's Diamond Shops. The company had been started by his grandfather in 1915 from a single store in Kansas City and had developed by the time we met into a group with 134 stores in 23 states. Sales had grown from $10 million in 1974 to $53 million in 1984 and $282 million in 1994. We weren't talking lemonade stands.

Barnett, then 60, loved the business but also wanted to feel free of it. In 1988, as a step in that direction, he had brought in Jeff Comment, formerly President of Wanamaker's, to help him run things. The hiring of Jeff turned out to be a homerun, but Barnett still found that he couldn't shake a feeling of ultimate responsibility. Additionally, he owned a valuable asset that was subject to the vagaries of a single, very competitive industry, and he thought it prudent to diversify his family's holdings.

Berkshire was made to order for him. It took us awhile to get together on price, but there was never any question in my mind that, first, Helzberg's was the kind of business that we wanted to own and, second, Jeff was our kind of manager. In fact, we would not have bought the business if Jeff had not been there to run it. Buying a retailer without good management is like buying the Eiffel Tower without an elevator.

We completed the Helzberg purchase in 1995 by means of a tax-free exchange of stock, the only kind of transaction that interested Barnett. Though he was certainly under no obligation to do so, Barnett shared a meaningful part of his proceeds from the sale with a large number of his associates. When someone behaves that generously, you know you are going to be treated right as a buyer.

The average Helzberg's store has annual sales of about $2 million, far more than competitors operating similarly-sized stores achieve. This superior per-store productivity is the key to Helzberg's excellent profits. If the company continues its first-rate performance—and we believe it will—it could grow rather quickly to several times its present size.

Helzberg's, it should be added, is an entirely different sort of operation from Borsheim's, our Omaha jewelry business, and the two companies will operate independently of each other. Borsheim's had an excellent year in 1995, with sales up 11.7%. Susan Jacques, its 36-year-old CEO, had an even better year, giving birth to her second son at the start of the Christmas season. Susan has proved to be a terrific leader in the two years since her promotion.

R.C. Willey Home Furnishings

It was Nebraska Furniture Mart's Irv Blumkin who did the walking around in the case of R.C. Willey, long the leading home furnishings business in Utah. Over the years, Irv had told me about the strengths of that company. And he had also told Bill Child, CEO of R.C. Willey, how pleased the Blumkin family had been with its Berkshire relationship. So in early 1995, Bill mentioned to Irv that for estate tax and diversification reasons, he and the other owners of R.C. Willey might be interested in selling.

From that point forward, things could not have been simpler. Bill sent me some figures, and I wrote him a letter indicating my idea of value. We quickly agreed on a number, and found our personal chemistry to be perfect. By mid-year, the merger was completed.

R.C. Willey is an amazing story. Bill took over the business from his father-in-law in 1954 when sales were about $250,000. From this tiny base, Bill employed Mae West's philosophy: "It's not what you've got—it's what you do with what you've got." Aided by his brother, Sheldon, Bill has built the company to its 1995 sales volume of $257 million, and it now accounts for over 50% of the furniture business in Utah. Like Nebraska Furniture Mart, R.C. Willey sells appliances, electronics, computers and carpets in addition to furniture. Both companies have about the same sales volume, but NFM gets all of its business from one complex in Omaha, whereas R.C. Willey will open its sixth major store in the next few months.

Retailing is a tough business. During my investment career, I have watched a large number of retailers enjoy terrific growth and superb returns on equity for a period, and then suddenly nosedive, often all the way into bankruptcy. This shooting-star phenomenon is far more common in retailing than it is in manufacturing or service businesses. In part, this is because a retailer must stay smart, day after day. Your competitor is always copying and then topping whatever you do. Shoppers are meanwhile beckoned in every conceivable way to try a stream of new merchants. In retailing, to coast is to fail.

In contrast to this have-to-be-smart-every-day business, there is what I call the have-to-be-smart-*once* business. For example, if you were smart enough to buy a network TV station very early in the game, you could put in a shiftless and backward nephew to run things, and the business would still do well for decades. You'd do far better, of course, if you put in Tom Murphy, but you could stay comfortably in the black without him. For a retailer, hiring that nephew would be an express ticket to bankruptcy.

The two retailing businesses we purchased this year are blessed with terrific managers who love to compete and have done so successfully for decades. Like the CEOs of our other operating units, they will operate autonomously: We want them to feel that the businesses they run are *theirs*. This means no second-guessing by Charlie and me. We avoid the attitude of the alumnus whose message to the football coach is "I'm 100% with you—win or tie." Our basic goal as an owner is to behave with our managers as we like our owners to behave with us.

As we add more operations, I'm sometimes asked how many people I can handle reporting to me. My answer to that is simple: If I have one person reporting to me and he is a lemon, that's one too many, and if I have managers like those we now have, the number can be almost unlimited. We are lucky to have Bill and Sheldon associated with us, and we hope that we can acquire other businesses that bring with them managers of similar caliber.

GEICO Corporation

Right after yearend, we completed the purchase of 100% of GEICO, the seventh largest auto insurer in the United States, with about 3.7 million cars insured. I've had a 45-year association with GEICO, and though the story has been told before, it's worth a short recap here.

I attended Columbia University's business school in 1950-51, not because I cared about the degree it offered, but because I wanted to study under Ben Graham, then teaching there. The time I spent in Ben's classes was a personal high, and quickly induced me to learn all I could about my hero. I turned first to *Who's Who in America*, finding there, among other things, that Ben was Chairman of Government Employees Insurance Company, to me an unknown company in an unfamiliar industry.

A librarian next referred me to Best's Fire and Casualty insurance manual, where I learned that GEICO was based in Washington, DC. So on a Saturday in January, 1951, I took the train to Washington and headed for GEICO's downtown headquarters. To my dismay, the building was closed, but I pounded on the door until a custodian appeared. I asked this puzzled fellow if there was anyone in the office I could talk to, and he said he'd seen one man working on the sixth floor.

And thus I met Lorimer Davidson, Assistant to the President, who was later to become CEO. Though my only credentials were that I was a student of Graham's, "Davy" graciously spent four hours or so showering me with both kindness and instruction. No one has ever received a better half-day course in how the insurance industry functions nor in the factors that enable one company to excel over others. As Davy made clear, GEICO's method of selling—direct marketing—gave it an enormous cost advantage over competitors that sold through agents, a form of distribution so ingrained in the business of these insurers that it was impossible for them to give it up. After my session with Davy, I was more excited about GEICO than I have ever been about a stock.

When I finished at Columbia some months later and returned to Omaha to sell securities, I naturally focused almost exclusively on GEICO. My first sales call—on my Aunt Alice, who always supported me 100%—was successful. But I was then a skinny, unpolished 20-year-old who looked about 17, and my pitch usually failed. Undaunted, I wrote a short report late in 1951 about GEICO for "The Security I Like Best" column in The *Commercial and Financial Chronicle,* a leading financial publication of the time. More important, I bought stock for my own account.

You may think this odd, but I have kept copies of every tax return I filed, starting with the return for 1944. Checking back, I find that I purchased GEICO shares on four occasions during 1951, the last purchase being made on September 26. This pattern of persistence suggests to me that my tendency toward self-intoxication was developed early. I probably came back on that September day from unsuccessfully trying to sell some prospect and decided—despite my already having more than 50% of my net worth in GEICO—to load up further. In any event, I accumulated 350 shares of GEICO during the year, at a cost of $10,282. At yearend, this holding was worth $13,125, more than 65% of my net worth.

You can see why GEICO was my first business love. Furthermore, just to complete this stroll down memory lane, I should add that I earned most of the funds I used to buy GEICO shares by delivering *The Washington Post,* the chief product of a company that much later made it possible for Berkshire to turn $10 million into $500 million.

Alas, I sold my entire GEICO position in 1952 for $15,259, primarily to switch into Western Insurance Securities. This act of infidelity can partially be excused by the fact that Western was selling for slightly more than one times its current earnings, a p/e ratio that for some reason caught my eye. But in the next 20 years, the GEICO stock I sold grew in value to about $1.3 million, which taught me a lesson about the inadvisability of selling a stake in an identifiably-wonderful company.

In the early 1970's, after Davy retired, the executives running GEICO made some serious errors in estimating their claims costs, a mistake that led the company to underprice its policies—and that almost caused it to go bankrupt. The company was saved only because Jack Byrne came in as CEO in 1976 and took drastic remedial measures.

Because I believed both in Jack and in GEICO's fundamental competitive strength, Berkshire purchased a large interest in the company during the second half of 1976, and also made smaller purchases later. By yearend 1980, we had put $45.7 million into GEICO and owned 33.3% of its shares. During the next 15 years, we did not make further purchases. Our interest in the company, nonetheless, grew to about 50% because it was a big repurchaser of its own shares.

Then, in 1995, we agreed to pay $2.3 billion for the half of the company we didn't own. That is a steep price. But it gives us full ownership of a growing enterprise whose business remains exceptional for precisely the same reasons that prevailed in 1951. In addition, GEICO has two extraordinary managers: Tony Nicely, who runs the insurance side of the operation, and Lou Simpson, who runs investments.

Tony, 52, has been with GEICO for 34 years. There's no one I would rather have managing GEICO's insurance operation. He has brains, energy, integrity and focus. If we're lucky, he'll stay another 34 years.

Lou runs investments just as ably. Between 1980 and 1995, the equities under Lou's management returned an average of 22.8% annually vs. 15.7% for the S&P. Lou takes the same conservative, concentrated approach to investments that we do at Berkshire, and it is an enormous plus for us to have him on board. One point that goes beyond Lou's GEICO work: His presence on the scene assures us that Berkshire would have an extraordinary professional immediately available to handle its investments if something were to happen to Charlie and me.

GEICO, of course, must continue both to attract good policyholders and keep them happy. It must also reserve and price properly. But the ultimate key to the company's success is its rock-bottom operating costs, which virtually no competitor can match. In 1995, moreover, Tony and his management team pushed underwriting and loss adjustment expenses down further to 23.6% of premiums, nearly one percentage point below 1994's ratio. In business, I look for economic castles protected by unbreachable "moats." Thanks to Tony and his management team, GEICO's moat widened in 1995.

Finally, let me bring you up to date on Davy. He's now 93 and remains my friend and teacher. He continues to pay close attention to GEICO and has always been there when the company's CEOs—Jack Byrne, Bill Snyder and Tony—have needed him. Our acquisition of 100% of GEICO caused Davy to incur a large tax. Characteristically, he still warmly supported the transaction.

Davy has been one of my heroes for the 45 years I've known him, and he's never let me down. You should understand that Berkshire would not be where it is today if Davy had not been so generous with his time on a cold Saturday in 1951. I've often thanked him privately, but it is fitting that I use this report to thank him on behalf of Berkshire's shareholders.

Insurance Operations

In addition to acquiring GEICO, we enjoyed other favorable developments in insurance during 1995.

As we've explained in past reports, what counts in our insurance business is, first, the amount of "float" we generate and, second, its cost to us. Float is money we hold but don't own. In an insurance operation, float arises because most policies require that premiums be prepaid and, more importantly, because it usually takes time for an insurer to hear about and resolve loss claims.

Typically, the premiums that an insurer takes in do not cover the losses and expenses it must pay. That leaves it running an "underwriting loss"—and that loss is the cost of float. An insurance business is profitable over time if its cost of float is less than the cost the company would otherwise incur to obtain funds. But the business has a negative value if the cost of its float is higher than market rates for money.

As the numbers in the following table show, Berkshire's insurance business has been a huge winner. For the table, we have calculated our float— which we generate in exceptional amounts relative to our premium volume— by adding loss reserves, loss adjustment reserves, funds held under reinsurance assumed and unearned premium reserves, and then subtracting agents' balances, prepaid acquisition costs, prepaid taxes and deferred charges applicable to assumed reinsurance. Our cost of float is determined by our underwriting loss or profit. In those years when we have had an underwriting profit, such as the last three, our cost of float has been negative, which means we have calculated our insurance earnings by adding underwriting profit to float income.

	(1) Underwriting Loss	(2) Average Float	Approximate Cost of Funds (Ratio of 1 to 2)	Yearend Yield on Long-Term Govt. Bonds
		(In $ Millions)		
1967	profit	$17.3	less than zero	5.50%
1968	profit	19.9	less than zero	5.90%
1969	profit	23.4	less than zero	6.79%
1970	$ 0.37	32.4	1.14%	6.25%
1971	profit	52.5	less than zero	5.81%
1972	profit	69.5	less than zero	5.82%
1973	profit	73.3	less than zero	7.27%
1974	7.36	79.1	9.30%	8.13%
1975	11.35	87.6	12.96%	8.03%
1976	profit	102.6	less than zero	7.30%
1977	profit	139.0	less than zero	7.97%
1978	profit	190.4	less than zero	8.93%
1979	profit	227.3	less than zero	10.08%
1980	profit	237.0	less than zero	11.94%
1981	profit	228.4	less than zero	13.61%
1982	21.56	220.6	9.77%	10.64%
1983	33.87	231.3	14.64%	11.84%
1984	48.06	253.2	18.98%	11.58%
1985	44.23	390.2	11.34%	9.34%
1986	55.84	797.5	7.00%	7.60%
1987	55.43	1,266.7	4.38%	8.95%
1988	11.08	1,497.7	0.74%	9.00%
1989	24.40	1,541.3	1.58%	7.97%
1990	26.65	1,637.3	1.63%	8.24%
1991	119.59	1,895.0	6.31%	7.40%
1992	108.96	2,290.4	4.76%	7.39%
1993	profit	2,624.7	less than zero	6.35%
1994	profit	3,056.6	less than zero	7.88%
1995	profit	3,607.2	less than zero	5.95%

Since 1967, when we entered the insurance business, our float has grown at an annual compounded rate of 20.7%. In more years than not, our cost of funds has been less than nothing. This access to "free" money has boosted Berkshire's performance in a major way.

Any company's level of profitability is determined by three items: (1) what its assets earn; (2) what its liabilities cost; and (3) its utilization of "leverage"—that is, the degree to which its assets are funded by liabilities rather than by equity. Over the years, we have done well on Point 1, having produced high returns on our assets. But we have also benefitted greatly—to a degree that is not generally well-understood—because our liabilities have cost us very little. An important reason for this low cost is that we have obtained float on very advantageous terms. The same cannot be said by many other property and casualty insurers, who may generate plenty of float, but at a cost that exceeds what the funds are worth to them. In those circumstances, leverage becomes a disadvantage.

Since our float has cost us virtually nothing over the years, it has in effect served as equity. Of course, it differs from true equity in that it doesn't belong to us. Nevertheless, let's assume that instead of our having $3.4 billion of float at the end of 1994, we had replaced it with $3.4 billion of equity. Under this scenario, we would have owned no more assets than we did during 1995. We would, however, have had somewhat lower earnings because the cost of float was negative last year. That is, our float threw off profits. And, of course, to obtain the replacement equity, we would have needed to sell many new shares of Berkshire. The net result—more shares, equal assets and lower earnings—would have materially reduced the value of our stock. So you can understand why float wonderfully benefits a business—if it is obtained at a low cost.

Our acquisition of GEICO will immediately increase our float by nearly $3 billion, with additional growth almost certain. We also expect GEICO to operate at a decent underwriting profit in most years, a fact that will increase the probability that our total float will cost us nothing. Of course, we paid a very substantial price for the GEICO float, whereas virtually all of the gains in float depicted in the table were developed internally.

Our enthusiasm over 1995's insurance results must be tempered once again because we had our third straight year of good fortune in the super-cat business. In this operation, we sell policies that insurance and reinsurance companies buy to protect themselves from the effects of mega-catastrophes. Since truly major catastrophes occur infrequently, our super-cat business can be expected to show large profits in most years but occasionally to record a huge loss. In other words, the attractiveness of our super-cat business will take many years to measure. We know that the results of years like the past three will be at least partially offset by some truly terrible year in the future. We just hope that "partially" turns out to be the proper adverb.

There were plenty of catastrophes last year, but no super-cats of the insured variety. The Southeast had a close call when Opal, sporting winds of 150 miles per hour, hovered off Florida. However, the storm abated before hitting land, and so a second Andrew was dodged. For insurers, the Kobe earthquake was another close call: The economic damage was huge—perhaps even a record—but only a tiny portion of it was insured. The insurance industry won't always be that lucky.

Ajit Jain is the guiding genius of our super-cat business and writes important non-cat business as well. In insurance, the term "catastrophe" is applied to an event, such as a hurricane or earthquake, that causes a great many insured losses. The other deals Ajit enters into usually cover only a single large loss. A simplified description of three transactions from last year will illustrate both what I mean and Ajit's versatility. We insured: (1) The life of Mike Tyson for a sum that is large initially and that, fight-by-fight, gradually declines to zero over the next few years; (2) Lloyd's against more than 225 of its "names" dying during the year; and (3) The launch, and a year of orbit, of two Chinese satellites. Happily, both satellites are orbiting, the Lloyd's folk avoided abnormal mortality, and if Mike Tyson looked any healthier, no one would get in the ring with him.

Berkshire is sought out for many kinds of insurance, both super-cat and large single-risk, because: (1) our financial strength is unmatched, and insureds know we can and will pay our losses under the most adverse of circumstances; (2) we can supply a quote faster than anyone in the business; and (3) we will issue policies with limits larger than anyone else is prepared to write. Most of our competitors have extensive reinsurance treaties and lay off much of their business. While this helps them avoid shock losses, it also hurts their flexibility and reaction time. As you know, Berkshire moves quickly to seize investment and acquisition opportunities; in insurance we respond with the same exceptional speed. In another important point, large coverages don't frighten us but, on the contrary, intensify our interest. We have offered a *policy* under which we could have lost $1 billion; the largest coverage that a client *accepted* was $400 million.

We will get hit from time to time with large losses. Charlie and I, however, are quite willing to accept relatively volatile results in exchange for better long-term earnings than we would otherwise have had. In other words, we prefer a lumpy 15% to a smooth 12%. Since most managers opt for smoothness, we are left with a competitive advantage that we try to maximize. We do, though, monitor our aggregate exposure in order to keep our "worst case" at a level that leaves us comfortable.

Indeed, our worst case from a "once-in-a-century" super-cat is far less severe—relative to net worth—than that faced by many well-known primary companies writing great numbers of property policies. These insurers don't issue single huge-limit policies as we do, but their small policies, in aggregate, can create a risk of staggering size. The "big one" would blow right through the reinsurance covers of some of these insurers, exposing them to uncapped losses that could threaten their survival. In our case, losses would be large, but capped at levels we could easily handle.

Prices are weakening in the super-cat field. That is understandable considering the influx of capital into the reinsurance business a few years ago and the natural desire of those holding the capital to employ it. No matter what others may do, we will not knowingly write business at inadequate rates. We unwittingly did this in the early 1970's and, after more than 20 years, regularly receive significant bills stemming from the mistakes of that era. My guess is that we will still be getting surprises from that business 20 years from now. A bad reinsurance contract is like hell: easy to enter and impossible to exit.

I actively participated in those early reinsurance decisions, and Berkshire paid a heavy tuition for my education in the business. Unfortunately, reinsurance students can't attend school on scholarship. GEICO, incidentally, suffered a similar, disastrous experience in the early 1980's, when it plunged enthusiastically into the writing of reinsurance and large risks. GEICO's folly was brief, but it will be cleaning things up for at least another decade. The well-publicized problems at Lloyd's further illustrate the perils of reinsurance and also underscore how vital it is that the interests of the people who write insurance business be aligned—on the downside as well as the upside—with those of the people putting up the capital. When that kind of symmetry is missing, insurers almost invariably run into trouble, though its existence may remain hidden for some time.

A small, apocryphal story about an insurance CEO who was visited by an analyst tells a lot about this industry. To the analyst's questions about his business, the CEO had nothing but gloomy answers: Rates were ridiculously low; the reserves on his balance sheet weren't adequate for ordinary claims, much less those likely to arise from asbestos and environmental problems; most of his reinsurers had long since gone broke, leaving him holding the sack. But then the CEO brightened: "Still, things could be a lot worse," he said. "It could be *my* money." At Berkshire, it's *our* money.

Berkshire's other insurance operations, though relatively small, performed magnificently in 1995. National Indemnity's traditional business had a combined ratio of 84.2 and developed, as usual, a large amount of float compared to premium volume. Over the last three years, this segment of our business, run by Don Wurster, has had an average combined ratio of 85.6. Our homestate operation, managed by Rod Eldred, grew at a good rate in 1995 and achieved a combined ratio of 81.4. Its three-year combined ratio is an amazing 82.4. Berkshire's California workers' compensation business, run by Brad Kinstler, faced fierce price-cutting in 1995 and lost a great many renewals when we refused to accept inadequate rates. Though this operation's volume dropped materially, it produced an excellent underwriting profit. Finally, John Kizer, at Central States Indemnity, continues to do an extraordinary job. His premium volume was up 23% in 1995, and underwriting profit grew by 59%. Ajit, Don, Rod, Brad and John are all under 45, an embarrassing fact demolishing my theory that managers only hit their stride after they reach 70.

To sum up, we entered 1995 with an exceptional insurance operation of moderate size. By adding GEICO, we entered 1996 with a business still better in quality, much improved in its growth prospects, and doubled in size. More than ever, insurance is our core strength.

Sources of Reported Earnings

The table below shows the main sources of Berkshire's reported earnings. In this presentation, purchase-premium charges are not assigned to the specific businesses to which they apply, but are instead aggregated and shown separately. This procedure lets you view the earnings of our businesses as they would have been reported had we not purchased them. This form of presentation seems to us to be more useful to investors and managers than one utilizing GAAP, which requires purchase-premiums to be charged off, business-by-business. The total earnings we show in the table are, of course, identical to the GAAP total in our audited financial statements.

| | (in millions) | | | |
| | Pre-Tax Earnings | | Berkshire's Share of Net Earnings (after taxes and minority interests) | |
	1995	1994	1995	1994
Operating Earnings:				
Insurance Group:				
Underwriting	$ 20.5	$129.9	$ 11.3	$ 80.9
Net Investment Income	501.6	419.4	417.7	350.5
Buffalo News	46.8	54.2	27.3	31.7
Fechheimer	16.9	14.3	8.8	7.1
Finance Businesses	20.8	22.1	12.6	14.6
Home Furnishings	29.7 [1]	17.4	16.7 [1]	8.7
Jewelry	33.9 [2]	--- [3]	19.1 [2]	--- [3]
Kirby	50.2	42.3	32.1	27.7
Scott Fetzer Manufacturing Group	34.1	39.5	21.2	24.9
See's Candies	50.2	47.5	29.8	28.2
Shoe Group	58.4	85.5	37.5	55.8
World Book	8.8	24.7	7.0	17.3
Purchase-Price Premium Charges	(27.0)	(22.6)	(23.4)	(19.4)
Interest Expense [4]	(56.0)	(60.1)	(34.9)	(37.3)
Shareholder-Designated Contributions	(11.6)	(10.4)	(7.0)	(6.7)
Other	37.4	35.7	24.4	22.3
Operating Earnings	814.7	839.4	600.2	606.2
Sales of Securities	194.1	91.3	125.0	61.1
Decline in Value of USAir Preferred Stock	---	(268.5)	---	(172.6)
Total Earnings – All Entities	$1,008.8	$662.2	$725.2	$494.8

(1) *Includes R.C. Willey from June 29, 1995.*
(2) *Includes Helzberg's from April 30, 1995.*
(3) *Jewelry earnings were included in "Other" in 1994.*
(4) *Excludes interest expense of Finance Businesses.*

A large amount of information about these businesses is given on pages 41-52, where you will also find our segment earnings reported on a GAAP basis. In addition, on pages 57-63, we have rearranged Berkshire's financial data into four segments on a non-GAAP basis, a presentation that corresponds to the way Charlie and I think about the company. Our intent is to supply you with the financial information that we would wish you to give us if our positions were reversed.

At Berkshire, we believe in Charlie's dictum—"Just tell me the bad news; the good news will take care of itself"—and that is the behavior we expect of our managers when they are reporting to us. Consequently, I also owe you—Berkshire's owners—a report on three operations that, though they continued to earn decent (or better) returns on invested capital, experienced a decline in earnings last year. Each encountered a different type of problem.

Our shoe business operated in an industry that suffered depressed earnings throughout last year, and many of our competitors made only marginal profits or worse. That means we at least maintained, and in some instances widened, our competitive superiority. So I have no doubt that our shoe operations will climb back to top-grade earnings in the future. In other words, though the turn has not yet occurred, we believe you should view last year's figures as reflecting a cyclical problem, not a secular one.

The Buffalo News, though still doing very well in comparison to other newspapers, is another story. In this case, industry trends are not good. In the 1991 Annual Report, I explained that newspapers had lost a notch in their economic attractiveness from the days when they appeared to have a bullet-proof franchise. Today, the industry retains its excellent economics, but has lost still another notch. Over time, we expect the competitive strength of newspapers to gradually erode, though the industry should nevertheless remain a fine business for many years to come.

Berkshire's most difficult problem is World Book, which operates in an industry beset by increasingly tough competition from CD-ROM and on-line offerings. True, we are still profitable, a claim that perhaps no other print encyclopedia can make. But our sales and earnings trends have gone in the wrong direction. At the end of 1995, World Book made major changes in the way it distributes its product, stepped up its efforts with electronic products and sharply reduced its overhead costs. It will take time for us to evaluate the effects of these initiatives, but we are confident they will significantly improve our viability.

All of our operations, including those whose earnings fell last year, benefit from exceptionally talented and dedicated managers. Were we to have the choice of any other executives now working in their industries, there is not one of our managers we would replace.

Many of our managers don't have to work for a living, but simply go out and perform every day for the same reason that wealthy golfers stay on the tour: They love both doing what they do and doing it well. To describe them as working may be a misnomer—they simply prefer spending much of their time on a productive activity at which they excel to spending it on leisure activities. Our job is to provide an environment that will keep them feeling this way, and so far we seem to have succeeded: Thinking back over the 1965-95 period, I can't recall that a single key manager has left Berkshire to join another employer.

Common Stock Investments

Below we present our common stock investments. Those with a market value of more than $600 million are itemized.

Shares	Company	12/31/95 Cost	Market
		(dollars in millions)	
49,456,900	American Express Company	$1,392.7	$2,046.3
20,000,000	Capital Cities/ABC, Inc.	345.0	2,467.5
100,000,000	The Coca-Cola Company	1,298.9	7,425.0
12,502,500	Federal Home Loan Mortgage Corp. ("Freddie Mac")	260.1	1,044.0
34,250,000	GEICO Corp.	45.7	2,393.2
48,000,000	The Gillette Company	600.0	2,502.0
6,791,218	Wells Fargo & Company	423.7	1,466.9
	Others	1,379.0	2,655.4
	Total Common Stocks	$5,745.1	$22,000.3

We continue in our Rip Van Winkle mode: Five of our six top positions at yearend 1994 were left untouched during 1995. The sixth was American Express, in which we increased our ownership to about 10%.

In early 1996, two major events affected our holdings: First, our purchase of the GEICO stock we did not already own caused that company to be converted into a wholly-owned subsidiary. Second, we exchanged our Cap Cities shares for a combination of cash and Disney stock.

In the Disney merger, Cap Cities shareholders had a choice of actions. If they chose, they could exchange each of their Cap Cities shares for one share of Disney stock plus $65. Or they could ask for—though not necessarily get—all cash or all stock, with their ultimate allotment of each depending on the choices made by other shareholders and certain decisions made by Disney. For our 20 million shares, we sought stock, but do not know, as this report goes to press, how much we were allocated. We are certain, however, to receive something over 20 million Disney shares. We have also recently bought Disney stock in the market.

One more bit of history: I first became interested in Disney in 1966, when its market valuation was less than $90 million, even though the company had earned around $21 million pre-tax in 1965 and was sitting with more cash than debt. At Disneyland, the $17 million Pirates of the Caribbean ride would soon open. Imagine my excitement—a company selling at only five times rides!

Duly impressed, Buffett Partnership Ltd. bought a significant amount of Disney stock at a split-adjusted price of 31¢ per share. That decision may appear brilliant, given that the stock now sells for $66. But your Chairman was up to the task of nullifying it: In 1967 I sold out at 48¢ per share.

Oh well—we're happy to be once again a large owner of a business with both unique assets and outstanding management.

Convertible Preferred Stocks

As many of you will remember, Berkshire made five private purchases of convertible preferred stocks during the 1987-91 period and the time seems right to discuss their status. Here are the particulars:

Company	Dividend Rate	Year of Purchase	Cost	Market Value
			(dollars in millions)	
Champion International Corp......	9 1/4%	1989	$300	$388[1]
First Empire State Corp..........	9%	1991	40	110
The Gillette Company	8 3/4%	1989	600	2,502[2]
Salomon Inc..................	9%	1987	700	728[3]
USAir Group, Inc.............	9 1/4%	1989	358	215

(1) Proceeds from sale of common we received through conversion in 1995.
(2) 12/31/95 value of common we received through conversion in 1991.
(3) Includes $140 we received in 1995 from partial redemption.

In each case we had the option of sticking with these preferreds as fixed-income securities or converting them into common stock. Initially, their value to us came primarily from their fixed-income characteristics. The option we had to convert was a kicker.

Our $300 million private purchase of American Express "Percs"—described in the 1991 Annual Report—is not included in the table because that security was a modified form of common stock whose fixed-income characteristics contributed only a minor portion of its initial value. Three years after we bought them, the Percs automatically were converted to common stock. In contrast, the five securities in the table were set to become common stocks only if we wished them to—a crucial difference.

When we purchased our convertible securities, I told you that we expected to earn after-tax returns from them that "moderately" exceeded what we could earn from the medium-term fixed-income securities they replaced. We beat this expectation—but only because of the performance of a single issue. I also told you that these securities, as a group, would "not produce the returns we can achieve when we find a business with wonderful economic prospects." Unfortunately, that prediction was fulfilled. Finally, I said that "under almost any conditions, we expect these preferreds to return us our money plus dividends." That's one I would like to have back. Winston Churchill once said that "eating my words has never given me indigestion." My assertion, however, that it was almost impossible for us to lose money on our preferreds has caused me some well-deserved heartburn.

Our best holding has been Gillette, which we told you from the start was a superior business. Ironically, though, this is also the purchase in which I made my biggest mistake—of a kind, however, never recognized on financial statements.

We paid $600 million in 1989 for Gillette preferred shares that were convertible into 48 million (split-adjusted) common shares. Taking an alternative route with the $600 million, I probably could have purchased 60 million shares of common from the company. The market on the common was then about $10.50, and given that this would have been a huge private placement carrying important restrictions, I probably could have bought the stock at a discount of at least 5%. I can't be sure about this, but it's likely that Gillette's management would have been just as happy to have Berkshire opt for common.

But I was far too clever to do that. Instead, for less than two years, we received some extra dividend income (the difference between the preferred's yield and that of the common), at which point the company—quite properly—called the issue, moving to do that as quickly as was possible. If I had negotiated for common rather than preferred, we would have been better off at yearend 1995 by $625 million, minus the "excess" dividends of about $70 million.

In the case of Champion, the ability of the company to call our preferred at 115% of cost forced a move out of us last August that we would rather have delayed. In this instance, we converted our shares just prior to the pending call and offered them to the company at a modest discount.

Charlie and I have never had a conviction about the paper industry—actually, I can't remember ever owning the common stock of a paper producer in my 54 years of investing—so our choice in August was whether to sell in the market or to the company. Champion's management had always been candid and honorable in dealing with us and wished to repurchase common shares, so we offered our stock to the company. Our Champion capital gain was moderate—about 19% after tax from a six-year investment—but the preferred delivered us a good after-tax dividend yield throughout our holding period. (That said, many press accounts have overstated the after-tax yields earned by property-casualty insurance companies on dividends paid to them. What the press has failed to take into account is a change in the tax law that took effect in 1987 and that significantly reduced the dividends received credit applicable to insurers. For details, see our 1986 Annual Report.)

Our First Empire preferred will be called on March 31, 1996, the earliest date allowable. We are comfortable owning stock in well-run banks, and we will convert and keep our First Empire common shares. Bob Wilmers, CEO of the company, is an outstanding banker, and we love being associated with him.

Our other two preferreds have been disappointing, though the Salomon preferred has modestly outperformed the fixed-income securities for which it was a substitute. However, the amount of management time Charlie and I have devoted to this holding has been vastly greater than its economic significance to Berkshire. Certainly I never dreamed I would take a new job at age 60—Salomon interim chairman, that is—because of an earlier purchase of a fixed-income security.

Soon after our purchase of the Salomon preferred in 1987, I wrote that I had "no special insights regarding the direction or future profitability of investment banking." Even the most charitable commentator would conclude that I have since proved my point.

To date, our option to convert into Salomon common has not proven of value. Furthermore, the Dow Industrials have doubled since I committed to buy the preferred, and the brokerage group has performed equally as well. That means my decision to go with Salomon because I saw value in the conversion option must be graded as very poor. Even so, the preferred has continued under some trying conditions to deliver as a fixed-income security, and the 9% dividend is currently quite attractive.

Unless the preferred is converted, its terms require redemption of 20% of the issue on October 31 of each year, 1995-99, and $140 million of our original $700 million was taken on schedule last year. (Some press reports labeled this a sale, but a senior security that matures is not "sold.") Though we did not elect to convert the preferred that matured last year, we have four more bites at the conversion apple, and I believe it quite likely that we will yet find value in our right to convert.

I discussed the USAir investment at length in last year's report. The company's results improved in 1995, but it still faces significant problems. On the plus side for us is the fact that our preferred is structurally well-designed: For example, though we have not been paid dividends since June 1994, the amounts owed us are compounding at 5% over the prime rate. On the minus side is the fact that we are dealing with a weak credit.

We feel much better about our USAir preferred than we did a year ago, but your guess is as good as mine as to its ultimate value. (Indeed, considering my record with this investment, it's fair to say that your guess may be *better* than mine.) At yearend we carried our preferred (in which there is no public market) at 60% of par, though USAir also has outstanding a junior preferred that is significantly inferior to ours in all respects except conversion price and that was then trading at 82% of par. As I write this, the junior issue has advanced to 97% of par. Let's hope the market is right.

Overall, our preferreds have performed well, but that is true only because of one huge winner, Gillette. Leaving aside Gillette, our preferreds as a group have delivered us after-tax returns no more than equal to those we could have earned from the medium-term fixed-income issues that they replaced.

A Proposed Recapitalization

At the Annual Meeting you will be asked to approve a recapitalization of Berkshire, creating two classes of stock. If the plan is adopted, our existing common stock will be designated as Class A Common Stock and a new Class B Common Stock will be authorized.

Each share of the "B" will have the rights of 1/30th of an "A" share with these exceptions: First, a B share will have 1/200th of the vote of an A share (rather than 1/30th of the vote). Second, the B will not be eligible to participate in Berkshire's shareholder-designated charitable contributions program.

When the recapitalization is complete, each share of A will become convertible, at the holder's option and at any time, into 30 shares of B. This conversion privilege will not extend in the opposite direction. That is, holders of B shares will not be able to convert them into A shares.

We expect to list the B shares on the New York Stock Exchange, where they will trade alongside the A stock. To create the shareholder base necessary for a listing—and to ensure a liquid market in the B stock—Berkshire expects to make a public offering for cash of at least $100 million of new B shares. The offering will be made only by means of a prospectus.

The market will ultimately determine the price of the B shares. Their price, though, should be in the neighborhood of 1/30th of the price of the A shares.

Class A shareholders who wish to give gifts may find it convenient to convert a share or two of their stock into Class B shares. Additionally, arbitrage-related conversions will occur if demand for the B is strong enough to push its price to slightly above 1/30th of the price of A.

However, because the Class A stock will entitle its holders to full voting rights and access to Berkshire's contributions program, these shares will be superior to the Class B shares and we would expect most shareholders to remain holders of the Class A—which is precisely what the Buffett and Munger families plan to do, except in those instances when we ourselves might convert a few shares to facilitate gifts. The prospect that most shareholders will stick to the A stock suggests that it will enjoy a somewhat more liquid market than the B.

There are tradeoffs for Berkshire in this recapitalization. But they do not arise from the proceeds of the offering—we will find constructive uses for the money—nor in any degree from the price at which we will sell the B shares. As I write this—with Berkshire stock at $36,000—Charlie and I do not believe it undervalued. Therefore, the offering we propose will not diminish the per-share intrinsic value of our existing stock. Let me also put our thoughts about valuation more baldly: Berkshire is selling at a price at which Charlie and I would not consider buying it.

What Berkshire will incur by way of the B stock are certain added costs, including those involving the mechanics of handling a larger number of shareholders. On the other hand, the stock should be a convenience for people wishing to make gifts. And those of you who have hoped for a split have gained a do-it-yourself method of bringing one about.

We are making this move, though, for other reasons—having to do with the appearance of expense-laden unit trusts purporting to be low-priced "clones" of Berkshire and sure to be aggressively marketed. The idea behind these vehicles is not new: In recent years, a number of people have told me about their wish to create an "all-Berkshire" investment fund to be sold at a low dollar price. But until recently, the promoters of these investments heard out my objections and backed off.

I did not discourage these people because I prefer large investors over small. Were it possible, Charlie and I would love to turn $1,000 into $3,000 for multitudes of people who would find that gain an important answer to their immediate problems.

In order to quickly triple small stakes, however, we would have to just as quickly turn our present market capitalization of $43 billion into $129 billion (roughly the market cap of General Electric, America's most highly valued company). *We can't come close to doing that.* The very best we hope for is—on average—to double Berkshire's per-share intrinsic value every five years, and we may well fall far short of that goal.

In the end, Charlie and I do not care whether our shareholders own Berkshire in large or small amounts. What we wish for are shareholders of any size who are knowledgeable about our operations, share our objectives and long-term perspective, and are aware of our limitations, most particularly those imposed by our large capital base.

The unit trusts that have recently surfaced fly in the face of these goals. They would be sold by brokers working for big commissions, would impose other burdensome costs on their shareholders, and would be marketed *en masse* to unsophisticated buyers, apt to be seduced by our past record and beguiled by the publicity Berkshire and I have received in recent years. The sure outcome: a multitude of investors destined to be disappointed.

Through our creation of the B stock—a low-denomination product far superior to Berkshire-only trusts—we hope to make the clones unmerchandisable.

But both present and prospective Berkshire shareholders should pay special attention to one point: Though the per-share intrinsic value of our stock has grown at an excellent rate during the past five years, its market price has grown still faster. The stock, in other words, has outperformed the business.

That kind of market overperformance cannot persist indefinitely, neither for Berkshire nor any other stock. *Inevitably, there will be periods of underperformance as well.* The price volatility that results, though endemic to public markets, is not to our liking. What we would prefer instead is to have the market price of Berkshire precisely track its intrinsic value. Were the stock to do that, every shareholder would benefit during his period of ownership in exact proportion to the progress Berkshire itself made in the period.

Obviously, the market behavior of Berkshire's stock will never conform to this ideal. But we will come closer to this goal than we would otherwise if our present and prospective shareholders are informed, business-oriented and not exposed to high-commission salesmanship when making their investment decisions. To that end, we are better off if we can blunt the merchandising efforts of the unit trusts—and that is the reason we are creating the B stock.

We look forward to answering your questions about the recapitalization at the Annual Meeting.

Miscellaneous

Berkshire isn't the only American corporation utilizing the new, exciting ABWA strategy. At about 1:15 p.m. on July 14, 1995, Michael Eisner, CEO of The Walt Disney Company, was walking up Wildflower Lane in Sun Valley. At the same time, I was leaving a lunch at Herbert Allen's home on that street to meet Tom Murphy, CEO of Cap Cities/ABC, for a golf game.

That morning, speaking to a large group of executives and money managers assembled by Allen's investment bank, Michael had made a brilliant presentation about Disney, and upon seeing him, I offered my congratulations. We chatted briefly—and the subject of a possible combination of Disney and Cap Cities came up. This wasn't the first time a merger had been discussed, but progress had never before been made, in part because Disney wanted to buy with cash and Cap Cities desired stock.

Michael and I waited a few minutes for Murph to arrive, and in the short conversation that ensued, both Michael and Murph indicated they might bend on the stock/cash question. Within a few weeks, they both did, at which point a contract was put together in three very busy days.

The Disney/Cap Cities deal makes so much sense that I'm sure it would have occurred without that chance encounter in Sun Valley. But when I ran into Michael that day on Wildflower Lane, he was heading for his plane, so without that accidental meeting the deal certainly wouldn't have happened in the time frame it did. I believe both Disney and Cap Cities will benefit from the fact that we all serendipitously met that day.

* * * * * * * * * * *

It's appropriate that I say a few words here about Murph. To put it simply, he is as fine an executive as I have ever seen in my long exposure to business. Equally important, he possesses human qualities every bit the equal of his managerial qualities. He's an extraordinary friend, parent, husband and citizen. In those rare instances in which Murph's personal interests diverged from those of shareholders, he unfailingly favored the owners. When I say that I like to be associated with managers whom I would love to have as a sibling, in-law, or trustee of my will, Murph is the exemplar of what I mean.

If Murph should elect to run another business, don't bother to study its value—just buy the stock. And don't later be as dumb as I was two years ago when I sold one-third of our holdings in Cap Cities for $635 million (versus the $1.27 billion those shares would bring in the Disney merger).

* * * * * * * * * * *

About 96.3% of all eligible shares participated in Berkshire's 1995 shareholder-designated contributions program. Contributions made were $11.6 million and 3,600 charities were recipients. A full description of the shareholder-designated contributions program appears on pages 54-55.

Every year a few shareholders miss out on the program because they don't have their shares registered in their own names on the prescribed record date or because they fail to get their designation form back to us within the 60-day period allowed. That second problem pained me especially this year because two good friends with substantial holdings missed the deadline. We had to deny their requests to be included because we can't make exceptions for some shareholders while refusing to make them for others.

To participate in future programs, you must own Class A shares that are registered in the name of the actual owner, not the nominee name of a broker, bank or depository. Shares not so registered on August 31, 1996, will be ineligible for the 1996 program. When you get the form, return it promptly so that it does not get put aside or forgotten.

* * * * * * * * * * *

When it comes to our Annual Meetings, Charlie and I are managerial oddballs: We thoroughly enjoy the event. So come join us on Monday, May 6. At Berkshire, we have no investor relations department and don't use financial analysts as a channel for disseminating information, earnings "guidance," or the like. Instead, we prefer direct manager-to-owner communication and believe that the Annual Meeting is the ideal place for this interchange of ideas. Talking to you there is efficient for us and also democratic in that all present simultaneously hear what we have to say.

Last year, for the first time, we had the Annual Meeting at the Holiday Convention Centre and the logistics seemed to work. The ballroom there was filled with about 3,200 people, and we had a video feed into a second room holding another 800 people. Seating in the main room was a little tight, so this year we will probably configure it to hold 3,000. This year we will also have two rooms for the overflow.

All in all, we will be able to handle 5,000 shareholders. The meeting will start at 9:30 a.m., but be warned that last year the main ballroom was filled shortly after 8:00 a.m.

Shareholders from 49 states attended our 1995 meeting—where were you, Vermont?—and a number of foreign countries, including Australia, Sweden and Germany, were represented. As always, the meeting attracted shareholders who were interested in Berkshire's business—as contrasted to shareholders who are primarily interested in themselves—and the questions were all good. Charlie and I ate lunch on stage and answered questions for about five hours.

We feel that if owners come from all over the world, we should try to make sure they have an opportunity to ask their questions. Most shareholders leave about noon, but a thousand or so hardcore types usually stay to see whether we will drop. Charlie and I are in training to last at least five hours again this year.

We will have our usual array of Berkshire products at the meeting and this year will add a sales representative from GEICO. At the 1995 meeting, we sold 747 pounds of candy, 759 pairs of shoes, and over $17,500 of World

Books and related publications. In a move that might have been dangerous had our stock been weak, we added knives last year from our Quikut subsidiary and sold 400 sets of these. (We draw the line at soft fruit, however.) All of these goods will again be available this year. We don't consider a cultural event complete unless a little business is mixed in.

Because we expect a large crowd for the meeting, we recommend that you promptly get both plane and hotel reservations. Those of you who like to be downtown (about six miles from the Centre) may wish to stay at the Radisson Redick Tower, a small (88 rooms) but nice hotel, or at the much larger Red Lion Hotel a few blocks away. In the vicinity of the Centre are the Holiday Inn (403 rooms), Homewood Suites (118 rooms) and Hampton Inn (136 rooms). Another recommended spot is the Marriott, whose west Omaha location is about 100 yards from Borsheim's and a ten-minute drive from the Centre. There will be buses at the Marriott that will leave at 7:30, 8:00 and 8:30 for the meeting and return after it ends.

An attachment to our proxy material explains how you can obtain the card you will need for admission to the meeting. A good-sized parking area is available at the Centre, while those who stay at the Holiday Inn, Homewood Suites and Hampton Inn will be able to walk to the meeting. As usual, we will have buses to take you to the Nebraska Furniture Mart and Borsheim's after the meeting and to take you from there to hotels or the airport later.

NFM's main store, on its 64-acre site about two miles north of the Centre, is open from 10 a.m. to 9 p.m. on weekdays, 10 a.m. to 6 p.m. on Saturdays, and noon to 6 p.m. on Sundays. Rose Blumkin—"Mrs. B"—is now 102, but will be hard at work in Mrs. B's Warehouse. She was honored in November at the opening of The Rose, a classic downtown theater of the 20's that has been magnificently restored, but that would have been demolished had she not saved it. Ask her to tell you the story.

Borsheim's normally is closed on Sunday but will be open for shareholders and their guests from 10 a.m. to 6 p.m. on May 5th. Additionally, we will have a special opening for shareholders on Saturday, the 4th, from 6 p.m. to 9 p.m. Last year, on Shareholders Day, we wrote 1,733 tickets in the six hours we were open—which is a sale every 13 seconds. Remember, though, that records are made to be broken.

At Borsheim's, we will also have the world's largest faceted diamond on display. Two years in the cutting, this inconspicuous bauble is 545 carats in size. Please inspect this stone and let it guide you in determining what size gem is appropriate for the one you love.

On Saturday evening, May 4, there will be a baseball game at Rosenblatt Stadium between the Omaha Royals and the Louisville Redbirds. I expect to make the opening pitch—owning a quarter of the team assures me of one start per year—but our manager, Mike Jirschele, will probably make his usual mistake and yank me immediately after. About 1,700 shareholders attended last year's game. Unfortunately, we had a rain-out, which greatly disappointed the many scouts in the stands. But the smart ones will be back this year, and I plan to show them my best stuff.

Our proxy statement will include information about obtaining tickets to the game. We will also offer an information packet this year listing restaurants that will be open on Sunday night and describing various things that you can do in Omaha on the weekend.

For years, I've unsuccessfully tried to get my grade school classmate, "Pal" Gorat, to open his steakhouse for business on the Sunday evening preceding the meeting. But this year he's relented. Gorat's is a family-owned enterprise that has thrived for 52 years, and if you like steaks, you'll love this place. I've told Pal he will get a good crowd, so call Gorat's at 402-551-3733 for a reservation. You'll spot me there—I'll be the one eating the rare T-bone with a double order of hash browns.

March 1, 1996

Warren E. Buffett
Chairman of the Board

BERKSHIRE HATHAWAY INC.

Chairman's Letter

To the Shareholders of Berkshire Hathaway Inc.:

Our gain in net worth during 1996 was $6.2 billion, or 36.1%. Per-share book value, however, grew by less, 31.8%, because the number of Berkshire shares increased: We issued stock in acquiring FlightSafety International and also sold new Class B shares.* Over the last 32 years (that is, since present management took over) per-share book value has grown from $19 to $19,011, or at a rate of 23.8% compounded annually.

For technical reasons, we have restated our 1995 financial statements, a matter that requires me to present one of my less-than-thrilling explanations of accounting arcana. I'll make it brief.

The restatement was required because GEICO became a wholly-owned subsidiary of Berkshire on January 2, 1996, whereas it was previously classified as an investment. From an economic viewpoint—taking into account major tax efficiencies and other benefits we gained—the value of the 51% of GEICO we owned at year-end 1995 *increased* significantly when we acquired the remaining 49% of the company two days later. Accounting rules applicable to this type of "step acquisition," however, required us to *write down* the value of our 51% at the time we moved to 100%. That writedown—which also, of course, reduced book value—amounted to $478.4 million. As a result, we now carry our original 51% of GEICO at a value that is both lower than its market value at the time we purchased the remaining 49% of the company and lower than the value at which we carry that 49% itself.

There is an offset, however, to the reduction in book value I have just described: Twice during 1996 we issued Berkshire shares at a premium to book value, first in May when we sold the B shares for cash and again in December when we used both A and B shares as part-payment for FlightSafety. In total, the three non-operational items affecting book value contributed less than one percentage point to our 31.8% per-share gain last year.

I dwell on this rise in per-share book value because it roughly indicates our economic progress during the year. But, as Charlie Munger, Berkshire's Vice Chairman, and I have repeatedly told you, what counts at Berkshire is intrinsic value, not book value. The last time you got that message from us was in the Owner's Manual, sent to you in June after we issued the Class B shares. In that manual, we not only defined certain key terms—such as intrinsic value— but also set forth our economic principles.

For many years, we have listed these principles in the front of our annual report, but in this report, on pages 58 to 67, we reproduce the entire Owner's Manual. In this letter, we will occasionally refer to the manual so that we can avoid repeating certain definitions and explanations. For example, if you wish to brush up on "intrinsic value," see pages 64 and 65.

Last year, for the first time, we supplied you with a table that Charlie and I believe will help anyone trying to estimate Berkshire's intrinsic value. In the updated version of that table, which follows, we trace two key indices of value. The first column lists our per-share ownership of investments (including cash and equivalents) and the second column shows our per-share earnings from Berkshire's operating businesses before taxes and purchase-accounting adjustments but after all interest and corporate overhead expenses. The operating-earnings column excludes all dividends, interest and capital gains that we realized from the investments presented in the first column. In effect, the two columns show what Berkshire would have reported had it been broken into two parts.

---

* Each Class B share has an economic interest equal to 1/30th of that possessed by a Class A share, which is the new designation for the only stock that Berkshire had outstanding before May 1996.Throughout this report, we state all per-share figures in terms of "Class A equivalents," which are the sum of the Class A shares outstanding and 1/30th of the Class B shares outstanding.

Year	Marketable Securities Per Share	Pre-tax Earnings Per Share Excluding All Income from Investments
1965	$ 4	$ 4.08
1975	159	(6.48)
1985	2,443	18.86
1995	22,088	258.20
1996	28,500	421.39
Annual Growth Rate: 1965-95	33.4%	14.7%
One-Year Growth Rate: 1965-95	29.0%	63.2%

As the table tells you, our investments per share increased in 1996 by 29.0% and our non-investment earnings grew by 63.2%. Our goal is to keep the numbers in both columns moving ahead at a reasonable (or, better yet, unreasonable) pace.

Our expectations, however, are tempered by two realities. First, our past rates of growth cannot be matched nor even approached: Berkshire's equity capital is now large—in fact, fewer than ten businesses in America have capital larger— and an abundance of funds tends to dampen returns. Second, whatever our rate of progress, it will not be smooth: Year-to-year moves in the first column of the table above will be influenced in a major way by fluctuations in securities markets; the figures in the second column will be affected by wide swings in the profitability of our catastrophe-reinsurance business.

In the table, the donations made pursuant to our shareholder-designated contributions program are charged against the second column, though we view them as a shareholder benefit rather than as an expense. All other corporate expenses are also charged against the second column. These costs may be lower than those of any other large American corporation: Our after-tax headquarters expense amounts to less than two basis points (1/50th of 1%) measured against net worth. Even so, Charlie used to think this expense percentage outrageously high, blaming it on my use of Berkshire's corporate jet, *The Indefensible*. But Charlie has recently experienced a "counter-revelation": With our purchase of FlightSafety, whose major activity is the training of corporate pilots, he now rhapsodizes at the mere mention of jets.

Seriously, costs matter. For example, equity mutual funds incur corporate expenses—largely payments to the funds' managers—that average about 100 basis points, a levy likely to cut the returns their investors earn by 10% or more over time. Charlie and I make no promises about Berkshire's results. We do promise you, however, that virtually all of the gains Berkshire makes will end up with shareholders. We are here to make money with you, not off you.

The Relationship of Intrinsic Value to Market Price

In last year's letter, with Berkshire shares selling at $36,000, I told you: (1) Berkshire's gain in market value in recent years had outstripped its gain in intrinsic value, even though the latter gain had been highly satisfactory; (2) that kind of overperformance could not continue indefinitely; (3) Charlie and I did not at that moment consider Berkshire to be undervalued.

Since I set down those cautions, Berkshire's intrinsic value has increased very significantly—aided in a major way by a stunning performance at GEICO that I will tell you more about later—while the market price of our shares has changed little. This, of course, means that in 1996 Berkshire's stock underperformed the business. Consequently, today's price/value relationship is both much different from what it was a year ago and, as Charlie and I see it, more appropriate.

Over time, the aggregate gains made by Berkshire shareholders must of necessity match the business gains of the company. When the stock temporarily overperforms or underperforms the business, a limited number of shareholders—either sellers or buyers—receive outsized benefits at the expense of those they trade with. Generally, the sophisticated have an edge over the innocents in this game.

Though our primary goal is to maximize the amount that our shareholders, in total, reap from their ownership of Berkshire, we wish also to minimize the benefits going to some shareholders at the expense of others. These are goals we would have were we managing a family partnership, and we believe they make equal sense for the manager of a public company. In a partnership, fairness requires that partnership interests be valued equitably when partners enter or exit; in a public company, fairness prevails when market price and intrinsic value are in sync. Obviously, they won't always meet that ideal, but a manager—by his policies and communications—can do much to foster equity.

Of course, the longer a shareholder holds his shares, the more bearing Berkshire's business results will have on his financial experience—and the less it will matter what premium or discount to intrinsic value prevails when he buys and sells his stock. That's one reason we hope to attract owners with long-term horizons. Overall, I think we have succeeded in that pursuit. Berkshire probably ranks number one among large American corporations in the percentage of its shares held by owners with a long-term view.

Acquisitions of 1996

We made two acquisitions in 1996, both possessing exactly the qualities we seek—excellent business economics and an outstanding manager.

The first acquisition was Kansas Bankers Surety (KBS), an insurance company whose name describes its specialty. The company, which does business in 22 states, has an extraordinary underwriting record, achieved through the efforts of Don Towle, an extraordinary manager. Don has developed first-hand relationships with hundreds of bankers and knows every detail of his operation. He thinks of himself as running a company that is "his," an attitude we treasure at Berkshire. Because of its relatively small size, we placed KBS with Wesco, our 80%-owned subsidiary, which has wanted to expand its insurance operations.

You might be interested in the carefully-crafted and sophisticated acquisition strategy that allowed Berkshire to nab this deal. Early in 1996 I was invited to the 40th birthday party of my nephew's wife, Jane Rogers. My taste for social events being low, I immediately, and in my standard, gracious way, began to invent reasons for skipping the event. The party planners then countered brilliantly by offering me a seat next to a man I always enjoy, Jane's dad, Roy Dinsdale—so I went.

The party took place on January 26. Though the music was loud—Why must bands play as if they will be paid by the decibel?—I just managed to hear Roy say he'd come from a directors meeting at Kansas Bankers Surety, a company I'd always admired. I shouted back that he should let me know if it ever became available for purchase.

On February 12, I got the following letter from Roy: "Dear Warren: Enclosed is the annual financial information on Kansas Bankers Surety. This is the company that we talked about at Janie's party. If I can be of any further help, please let me know." On February 13, I told Roy we would pay $75 million for the company—and before long we had a deal. I'm now scheming to get invited to Jane's next party.

Our other acquisition in 1996—FlightSafety International, the world's leader in the training of pilots—was far larger, at about $1.5 billion, but had an equally serendipitous origin. The heroes of this story are first, Richard Sercer, a Tucson aviation consultant, and second, his wife, Alma Murphy, an ophthalmology graduate of Harvard Medical School, who in 1990 wore down her husband's reluctance and got him to buy Berkshire stock. Since then, the two have attended all our Annual Meetings, but I didn't get to know them personally.

Fortunately, Richard had also been a long-time shareholder of FlightSafety, and it occurred to him last year that the two companies would make a good fit. He knew our acquisition criteria, and he thought that Al Ueltschi, FlightSafety's 79-year-old CEO, might want to make a deal that would both give him a home for his company and a security in payment that he would feel comfortable owning throughout his lifetime. So in July, Richard wrote Bob Denham, CEO of Salomon Inc, suggesting that he explore the possibility of a merger.

Bob took it from there, and on September 18, Al and I met in New York. I had long been familiar with FlightSafety's business, and in about 60 seconds I knew that Al was exactly our kind of manager. A month later, we had a contract. Because Charlie and I wished to minimize the issuance of Berkshire shares, the transaction we structured gave FlightSafety shareholders a choice of cash or stock but carried terms that encouraged those who were tax-indifferent to take cash. This nudge led to about 51% of FlightSafety's shares being exchanged for cash, 41% for Berkshire A and 8% for Berkshire B.

Al has had a lifelong love affair with aviation and actually piloted Charles Lindbergh. After a barnstorming career in the 1930s, he began working for Juan Trippe, Pan Am's legendary chief. In 1951, while still at Pan Am, Al founded FlightSafety, subsequently building it into a simulator manufacturer and a worldwide trainer of pilots (single-engine, helicopter, jet and marine). The company operates in 41 locations, outfitted with 175 simulators of planes ranging from the very small, such as Cessna 210s, to Boeing 747s. Simulators are not cheap—they can cost as much as $19 million —so this business, unlike many of our operations, is capital intensive. About half of the company's revenues are derived from the training of corporate pilots, with most of the balance coming from airlines and the military.

Al may be 79, but he looks and acts about 55. He will run operations just as he has in the past: We never fool with success. I have told him that though we don't believe in splitting Berkshire stock, we will split his age 2-for-1 when he hits 100.

An observer might conclude from our hiring practices that Charlie and I were traumatized early in life by an EEOC bulletin on age discrimination. The real explanation, however, is self-interest: It's difficult to teach a new dog old tricks. The many Berkshire managers who are past 70 hit home runs today at the same pace that long ago gave them reputations as young slugging sensations. Therefore, to get a job with us, just employ the tactic of the 76-year-old who persuaded a dazzling beauty of 25 to marry him. "How did you ever get her to accept?" asked his envious contemporaries. The comeback: "I told her I was 86."

* * * * * * * * * * * *

And now we pause for our usual commercial: If you own a large business with good economic characteristics and wish to become associated with an exceptional collection of businesses having similar characteristics, Berkshire may well be the home you seek. Our requirements are set forth on page 21. If your company meets them—and if I fail to make the next birthday party you attend—give me a call.

Insurance Operations—Overview

Our insurance business was terrific in 1996. In both primary insurance, where GEICO is our main unit, and in our "super-cat" reinsurance business, results were outstanding.

As we've explained in past reports, what counts in our insurance business is, first, the amount of "float" we generate and, second, its cost to us. These are matters that are important for you to understand because float is a major component of Berkshire's intrinsic value that is not reflected in book value.

To begin with, float is money we hold but don't own. In an insurance operation, float arises because premiums are received before losses are paid. Secondly, the premiums that an insurer takes in typically do not cover the losses and expenses it eventually must pay. That leaves it running an "underwriting loss," which is the cost of float. An insurance business has value if its cost of float over time is less than the cost the company would otherwise incur to obtain funds. But the business is an albatross if the cost of its float is higher than market rates for money.

As the numbers in the following table show, Berkshire's insurance business has been a huge winner. For the table, we have calculated our float— which we generate in large amounts relative to our premium volume—by adding loss reserves, loss adjustment reserves, funds held under reinsurance assumed and unearned premium reserves, and then subtracting agents' balances, prepaid acquisition costs, prepaid taxes and deferred charges applicable to assumed reinsurance. Our cost of float is determined by our underwriting loss or profit. In those years when we have had an underwriting profit, such as the last four, our cost of float has been negative. In effect, we have been paid for holding money.

	(1) Underwriting Loss (In $ Millions)	(2) Average Float	Approximate Cost of Funds (Ratio of 1 to 2)	Yearend Yield on Long-Term Govt. Bonds
1967	profit	$17.3	less than zero	5.50%
1968	profit	19.9	less than zero	5.90%
1969	profit	23.4	less than zero	6.79%
1970	$ 0.37	32.4	1.14%	6.25%
1971	profit	52.5	less than zero	5.81%
1972	profit	69.5	less than zero	5.82%
1973	profit	73.3	less than zero	7.27%
1974	7.36	79.1	9.30%	8.13%
1975	11.35	87.6	12.96%	8.03%
1976	profit	102.6	less than zero	7.30%
1977	profit	139.0	less than zero	7.97%
1978	profit	190.4	less than zero	8.93%
1979	profit	227.3	less than zero	10.08%
1980	profit	237.0	less than zero	11.94%
1981	profit	228.4	less than zero	13.61%
1982	21.56	220.6	9.77%	10.64%
1983	33.87	231.3	14.64%	11.84%
1984	48.06	253.2	18.98%	11.58%
1985	44.23	390.2	11.34%	9.34%
1986	55.84	797.5	7.00%	7.60%
1987	55.43	1,266.7	4.38%	8.95%
1988	11.08	1,497.7	0.74%	9.00%
1989	24.40	1,541.3	1.58%	7.97%
1990	26.65	1,637.3	1.63%	8.24%
1991	119.59	1,895.0	6.31%	7.40%
1992	108.96	2,290.4	4.76%	7.39%
1993	profit	2,624.7	less than zero	6.35%
1994	profit	3,056.6	less than zero	7.88%
1995	profit	3,607.2	less than zero	5.95%
1996	profit	6,702.0	less than zero	6.64%

Since 1967, when we entered the insurance business, our float has grown at an annual compounded rate of 22.3%. In more years than not, our cost of funds has been less than nothing. This access to "free" money has boosted Berkshire's performance in a major way. Moreover, our acquisition of GEICO materially increases the probability that we can continue to obtain "free" funds in increasing amounts.

Super-Cat Insurance

As in the past three years, we once again stress that the good results we are reporting for Berkshire stem in part from our super-cat business having a lucky year. In this operation, we sell policies that insurance and reinsurance companies buy to protect themselves from the effects of mega-catastrophes. Since truly major catastrophes are rare occurrences, our super-cat business can be expected to show large profits in most years—and to record a huge loss occasionally. In other words, the attractiveness of our super-cat business will take a great many years to measure. *What you must understand, however, is that a truly terrible year in the super-cat business is not a possibility— it's a certainty. The only question is when it will come.*

I emphasize this lugubrious point because I would not want you to panic and sell your Berkshire stock upon hearing that some large catastrophe had cost us a significant amount. If you would tend to react that way, you should not own Berkshire shares now, just as you should entirely avoid owning stocks if a crashing market would lead you to panic and sell. Selling fine businesses on "scary" news is usually a bad decision. (Robert Woodruff, the business genius who built Coca-Cola over many decades and who owned a huge position in the company, was once asked when it might be a good time to sell Coke stock. Woodruff had a simple answer: "I don't know. I've never sold any.")

In our super-cat operation, our customers are insurers that are exposed to major earnings volatility and that wish to reduce it. The product we sell— for what we hope is an appropriate price— is our willingness to shift that volatility to our own books. Gyrations in Berkshire's earnings don't bother us in the least: Charlie and I would much rather earn a lumpy 15% over time than a smooth 12%. (After all, our earnings swing wildly on a daily and weekly basis—why should we demand that smoothness accompany each orbit that the earth makes of the sun?) We are most comfortable with that thinking, however, when we have shareholder/partners who can also accept volatility, and that's why we regularly repeat our cautions.

We took on some major super-cat exposures during 1996. At mid-year we wrote a contract with Allstate that covers Florida hurricanes, and though there are no definitive records that would allow us to prove this point, we believe that to have *then* been the largest single catastrophe risk ever assumed by one company for its own account. Later in the year, however, we wrote a policy for the California Earthquake Authority that goes into effect on April 1, 1997, and that exposes us to a loss more than twice that possible under the Florida contract. Again we retained all the risk for our own account. Large as these coverages are, Berkshire's after-tax "worst-case" loss from a true mega-catastrophe is probably no more than $600 million, which is less than 3% of our book value and 1.5% of our market value. To gain some perspective on this exposure, look at the table on page 2 and note the much greater volatility that security markets have delivered us.

In the super-cat business, we have three major competitive advantages. First, the parties buying reinsurance from us know that we both can and will pay under the most adverse of circumstances. Were a truly cataclysmic disaster to occur, it is not impossible that a financial panic would quickly follow. If that happened, there could well be respected reinsurers that would have difficulty paying at just the moment that their clients faced extraordinary needs. Indeed, one reason we never "lay off" part of the risks we insure is that we have reservations about our ability to collect from others when disaster strikes. When it's Berkshire promising, insureds know with certainty that they can collect promptly.

Our second advantage—somewhat related—is subtle but important. After a mega-catastrophe, insurers might well find it difficult to obtain reinsurance even though their need for coverage would then be particularly great. At such a time, Berkshire would without question have very substantial capacity available—but it will naturally be our long-standing clients that have first call on it. That business reality has made major insurers and reinsurers throughout the world realize the desirability of doing business with us. Indeed, we are currently getting sizable "stand-by" fees from reinsurers that are simply nailing down their ability to get coverage from us should the market tighten.

Our final competitive advantage is that we can provide dollar coverages of a size neither matched nor approached elsewhere in the industry. Insurers looking for huge covers know that a single call to Berkshire will produce a firm and immediate offering.

A few facts about our exposure to California earthquakes—our largest risk—seem in order. The Northridge quake of 1994 laid homeowners' losses on insurers that greatly exceeded what computer models had told them to expect. Yet the intensity of that quake was mild compared to the "worst-case" possibility for California. Understandably, insurers became—ahem—shaken and started contemplating a retreat from writing earthquake coverage into their homeowners' policies.

In a thoughtful response, Chuck Quackenbush, California's insurance commissioner, designed a new residential earthquake policy to be written by a state-sponsored insurer, The California Earthquake Authority. This entity, which went into operation on December 1, 1996, needed large layers of reinsurance—and that's where we came in. Berkshire's layer of approximately $1 billion will be called upon if the Authority's aggregate losses in the period ending March 31, 2001 exceed about $5 billion. (The press originally reported larger figures, but these would have applied only if all California insurers had entered into the arrangement; instead only 72% signed up.)

So what are the true odds of our having to make a payout during the policy's term? We don't know—nor do we think computer models will help us, since we believe the precision they project is a chimera. In fact, such models can lull decision-makers into a false sense of security and thereby increase their chances of making a really huge mistake. We've already seen such debacles in both insurance and investments. Witness "portfolio insurance," whose destructive effects in the 1987 market crash led one wag to observe that it was the computers that should have been jumping out of windows.

Even if perfection in assessing risks is unattainable, insurers can underwrite sensibly. After all, you need not know a man's precise age to know that he is old enough to vote nor know his exact weight to recognize his need to diet. In insurance, it is essential to remember that virtually all surprises are unpleasant, and with that in mind we try to price our super-cat exposures so that about 90% of total premiums end up being eventually paid out in losses and expenses. Over time, we will find out how smart our pricing has been, but that will not be quickly. The super-cat business is just like the investment business in that it often takes a long time to find out whether you knew what you were doing.

What I can state with certainty, however, is that we have the best person in the world to run our super-cat business: Ajit Jain, whose value to Berkshire is simply enormous. In the reinsurance field, disastrous propositions abound. I know that because I personally embraced all too many of these in the 1970s and also because GEICO has a large runoff portfolio made up of foolish contracts written in the early-1980s, able though its then-management was. Ajit, I can assure you, won't make mistakes of this type.

I have mentioned that a mega-catastrophe might cause a catastrophe in the financial markets, a possibility that is unlikely but not far-fetched. Were the catastrophe a quake in California of sufficient magnitude to tap our coverage, we would almost certainly be damaged in other ways as well. For example, See's, Wells Fargo and Freddie Mac could be hit hard. All in all, though, we can handle this aggregation of exposures.

In this respect, as in others, we try to "reverse engineer" our future at Berkshire, bearing in mind Charlie's dictum: "All I want to know is where I'm going to die so I'll never go there." (Inverting really works: Try singing country western songs backwards and you will quickly regain your house, your car and your wife.) If we can't tolerate a possible consequence, remote though it may be, we steer clear of planting its seeds. That is why we don't borrow big amounts and why we make sure that our super-cat business losses, large though the maximums may sound, will not put a major dent in Berkshire's intrinsic value.

Insurance—GEICO and Other Primary Operations

When we moved to total ownership of GEICO early last year, our expectations were high—and they are all being exceeded. That is true from both a business and personal perspective: GEICO's operating chief, Tony Nicely, is a superb business manager and a delight to work with. Under almost any conditions, GEICO would be an exceptionally valuable asset. With Tony at the helm, it is reaching levels of performance that the organization would only a few years ago have thought impossible.

There's nothing esoteric about GEICO's success: The company's competitive strength flows directly from its position as a low-cost operator. Low costs permit low prices, and low prices attract and retain good policyholders. The final segment of a virtuous circle is drawn when policyholders recommend us to their friends. GEICO gets more than one million referrals annually and these produce more than half of our new business, an advantage that gives us enormous savings in acquisition expenses—and that makes our costs still lower.

This formula worked in spades for GEICO in 1996: Its voluntary auto policy count grew 10%. During the previous 20 years, the company's best-ever growth for a year had been 8%, a rate achieved only once. Better yet, the growth in voluntary policies accelerated during the year, led by major gains in the nonstandard market, which has been an underdeveloped area at GEICO. I focus here on voluntary policies because the involuntary business we get from assigned risk pools and the like is unprofitable. Growth in that sector is most unwelcome.

GEICO's growth would mean nothing if it did not produce reasonable underwriting profits. Here, too, the news is good: Last year we hit our underwriting targets and then some. Our goal, however, is not to widen our profit margin but rather to enlarge the price advantage we offer customers. Given that strategy, we believe that 1997's growth will easily top that of last year.

We expect new competitors to enter the direct-response market, and some of our existing competitors are likely to expand geographically. Nonetheless, the economies of scale we enjoy should allow us to maintain or even widen the protective moat surrounding our economic castle. We do best on costs in geographical areas in which we enjoy high market penetration. As our policy count grows, concurrently delivering gains in penetration, we expect to drive costs materially lower. GEICO's sustainable cost advantage is what attracted me to the company way back in 1951, when the entire business was valued at $7 million. It is also why I felt Berkshire should pay $2.3 billion last year for the 49% of the company that we didn't then own.

Maximizing the results of a wonderful business requires management and focus. Lucky for us, we have in Tony a superb manager whose business focus never wavers. Wanting also to get the entire GEICO organization concentrating as he does, we needed a compensation plan that was itself sharply focused—and immediately after our purchase, we put one in.

Today, the bonuses received by dozens of top executives, starting with Tony, are based upon only two key variables: (1) growth in voluntary auto policies and (2) underwriting profitability on "seasoned" auto business (meaning policies that have been on the books for more than one year). In addition, we use the same yardsticks to calculate the annual contribution to the company's profit-sharing plan. *Everyone* at GEICO knows what counts.

The GEICO plan exemplifies Berkshire's incentive compensation principles: Goals should be (1) tailored to the economics of the specific operating business; (2) simple in character so that the degree to which they are being realized can be easily measured; and (3) directly related to the daily activities of plan participants. As a corollary, we shun "lottery ticket" arrangements, such as options on Berkshire shares, whose ultimate value—which could range from zero to huge—is totally out of the control of the person whose behavior we would like to affect. In our view, a system that produces quixotic payoffs will not only be wasteful for owners but may actually discourage the focused behavior we value in managers.

Every quarter, all 9,000 GEICO associates can see the results that determine our profit-sharing plan contribution. In 1996, they enjoyed the experience because the plan literally went off the chart that had been constructed at the start of the year. Even I knew the answer to that problem: Enlarge the chart. Ultimately, the results called for a record contribution of 16.9% ($40 million), compared to a five-year average of less than 10% for the comparable plans previously in effect. Furthermore, at Berkshire, we never greet good work by raising the bar. If GEICO's performance continues to improve, we will happily keep on making larger charts.

Lou Simpson continues to manage GEICO's money in an outstanding manner: Last year, the equities in his portfolio outdid the S&P 500 by 6.2 percentage points. In Lou's part of GEICO's operation, we again tie compensation to performance—but to investment performance over a four-year period, not to underwriting results nor to the performance of GEICO as a whole. We think it foolish for an insurance company to pay bonuses that are tied to overall corporate results when great work on one side of the business—underwriting or investment—could conceivably be completely neutralized by bad work on the other. If you bat .350 at Berkshire, you can be sure you will get paid commensurately even if the rest of the team bats .200. In Lou and Tony, however, we are lucky to have Hall-of-Famers in both key positions.

* * * * * * * * * * *

Though they are, of course, smaller than GEICO, our other primary insurance operations turned in equally stunning results last year. National Indemnity's traditional business had a combined ratio of 74.2 and, as usual, developed a large amount of float compared to premium volume. Over the last three years, this segment of our business, run by Don Wurster, has had an average combined ratio of 83.0. Our homestate operation, managed by Rod Eldred, recorded a combined ratio of 87.1 even though it absorbed the expenses of expanding to new states. Rod's three-year combined ratio is an amazing 83.2. Berkshire's workers' compensation business, run out of California by Brad Kinstler, has now moved into six other states and, despite the costs of that expansion, again achieved an excellent underwriting profit. Finally, John Kizer, at Central States Indemnity, set new records for premium volume while generating good earnings from underwriting. In aggregate, our smaller insurance operations (now including Kansas Bankers Surety) have an underwriting record virtually unmatched in the industry. Don, Rod, Brad and John have all created significant value for Berkshire, and we believe there is more to come.

Taxes

In 1961, President Kennedy said that we should ask not what our country can do for us, but rather ask what we can do for our country. Last year we decided to give his suggestion a try—and who says it never hurts to ask? We were told to mail $860 million in income taxes to the U.S. Treasury.

Here's a little perspective on that figure: If an equal amount had been paid by only 2,000 other taxpayers, the government would have had a balanced budget in 1996 without needing a dime of taxes—income or Social Security or what have you—from *any* other American. Berkshire shareholders can truly say, "I gave at the office."

Charlie and I believe that large tax payments by Berkshire are entirely fitting. The contribution we thus make to society's well-being is at most only proportional to its contribution to ours. Berkshire prospers in America as it would nowhere else.

Sources of Reported Earnings

The table that follows shows the main sources of Berkshire's reported earnings. In this presentation, purchase-accounting adjustments are not assigned to the specific businesses to which they apply, but are instead aggregated and shown separately. This procedure lets you view the earnings of our businesses as they would have been reported had we not purchased them. For the reasons discussed on pages 65 and 66, this form of presentation seems to us to be more useful to investors and managers than one utilizing generally-accepted accounting principles (GAAP), which require purchase-premiums to be charged off business-by-business. The total earnings we show in the table are, of course, identical to the GAAP total in our audited financial statements.

			(in millions)	
			Berkshire's Share of Net Earnings (after taxes and minority interests)	
	Pre-Tax Earnings			
	1996	*1995(1)*	*1996*	*1995(1)*
Operating Earnings:				
Insurance Group:				
Underwriting	$ 222.1	$ 20.5	$ 142.8	$ 11.3
Net Investment Income	726.2	501.6	593.1	417.7
Buffalo News	50.4	46.8	29.5	27.3
Fechheimer	17.3	16.9	9.3	8.8
Finance Businesses	23.1	20.8	14.9	12.6
Home Furnishings	43.8	29.7 (2)	24.8	16.7 (2)
Jewelry	27.8	33.9 (3)	16.1	19.1 (3)
Kirby	58.5	50.2	39.9	32.1
Scott Fetzer Manufacturing Group	50.6	34.1	32.2	21.2
See's Candies	51.9	50.2	30.8	29.8
Shoe Group	61.6	58.4	41.0	37.5
World Book	12.6	8.8	9.5	7.0
Purchase-Accounting Adjustments	(75.7)	(27.0)	(70.5)	(23.4)
Interest Expense(4)	(94.3)	(56.0)	(56.6)	(34.9)
Shareholder-Designated Contributions	(13.3)	(11.6)	(8.5)	(7.0)
Other	58.8	37.4	34.8	24.4
Operating Earnings	1,221.4	814.7	883.1	600.2
Sales of Securities	2,484.5	194.1	1,605.5	125.0
Total Earnings – All Entities	$3,705.9	$1,008.8	$2,488.6	$ 725.2

(1) Before the GEICO-related restatement.
(2) Includes R.C. Willey from June 29, 1995.
(3) Includes Helzberg's from April 30, 1995.
(4) Excludes interest expense of Finance Businesses.

In this section last year, I discussed three businesses that reported a decline in earnings—Buffalo News, Shoe Group and World Book. All, I'm happy to say, recorded gains in 1996.

World Book, however, did not find it easy: Despite the operation's new status as the only direct-seller of encyclopedias in the country (Encyclopedia Britannica exited the field last year), its unit volume fell. Additionally, World Book spent heavily on a new CD-ROM product that began to take in revenues only in early 1997, when it was launched in association with IBM. In the face of these factors, earnings would have evaporated had World Book not revamped distribution methods and cut overhead at headquarters, thereby dramatically reducing its fixed costs. Overall, the company has gone a long way toward assuring its long-term viability in both the print and electronic marketplaces.

Our only disappointment last year was in jewelry: Borsheim's did fine, but Helzberg's suffered a material decline in earnings. Its expense levels had been geared to a sizable increase in same-store sales, consistent with the gains achieved in recent years. When sales were instead flat, profit margins fell. Jeff Comment, CEO of Helzberg's, is addressing the expense problem in a decisive manner, and the company's earnings should improve in 1997.

Overall, our operating businesses continue to perform exceptionally, far outdoing their industry norms. For this, Charlie and I thank our managers. If you should see any of them at the Annual Meeting, add your thanks as well.

More information about our various businesses is given on pages 36-46, where you will also find our segment earnings reported on a GAAP basis. In addition, on pages 51-57, we have rearranged Berkshire's financial data into four segments on a non-GAAP basis, a presentation that corresponds to the way Charlie and I think about the company. Our intent is to supply you with the financial information that we would wish you to give us if our positions were reversed.

"Look-Through" Earnings

Reported earnings are a poor measure of economic progress at Berkshire, in part because the numbers shown in the table presented earlier include only the dividends we receive from investees—though these dividends typically represent only a small fraction of the earnings attributable to our ownership. Not that we mind this division of money, since on balance we regard the undistributed earnings of investees as more valuable to us than the portion paid out. The reason is simple: Our investees often have the opportunity to reinvest earnings at high rates of return. So why should we want them paid out?

To depict something closer to economic reality at Berkshire than reported earnings, though, we employ the concept of "look-through" earnings. As we calculate these, they consist of: (1) the operating earnings reported in the previous section, plus; (2) our share of the retained operating earnings of major investees that, under GAAP accounting, are not reflected in our profits, less; (3) an allowance for the tax that would be paid by Berkshire if these retained earnings of investees had instead been distributed to us. When tabulating "operating earnings" here, we exclude purchase-accounting adjustments as well as capital gains and other major non-recurring items.

The following table sets forth our 1996 look-through earnings, though I warn you that the figures can be no more than approximate, since they are based on a number of judgment calls. (The dividends paid to us by these investees have been included in the operating earnings itemized on page 12, mostly under "Insurance Group: Net Investment Income.")

Berkshire's Major Investees	Berkshire's Approximate Ownership at Yearend[1]	Berkshire's Share of Undistributed Operating Earnings (in millions)[2]
American Express Company	10.5%	$ 132
The Coca-Cola Company	8.1%	180
The Walt Disney Company	3.6%	50
Federal Home Loan Mortgage Corp.	8.4%	77
The Gillette Company	8.6%	73
McDonald's Corporation	4.3%	38
The Washington Post Company	15.8%	27
Wells Fargo & Company	8.0%	84
Berkshire's share of undistributed earnings of major investees		661
Hypothetical tax on these undistributed investee earnings[3]		(93)
Reported operating earnings of Berkshire		954
Total look-through earnings of Berkshire		$1,522

(1) Does not include shares allocable to minority interests

(2) Calculated on average ownership for the year

(3) The tax rate used is 14%, which is the rate Berkshire pays on the dividends it receives

Common Stock Investments

Below we present our common stock investments. Those with a market value of more than $500 million are itemized.

Shares	Company	12/31/96 Cost*	Market
		(dollars in millions)	
49,456,900	American Express Company	$1,392.7	$ 2,794.3
100,000,000	The Coca-Cola Company	1,298.9	10,525.0
24,614,214	The Walt Disney Company	577.0	1,716.8
64,246,000	Federal Home Loan Mortgage Corp.	333.4	1,772.8
48,000,000	The Gillette Company	600.0	3,732.0
30,156,600	McDonald's Corporation	1,265.3	1,368.4
1,727,765	The Washington Post Company	10.6	579.0
7,291,418	Wells Fargo & Company	497.8	1,966.9
	Others	1,934.5	3,295.4
	Total Common Stocks	$7,910.2	$27,750.6

* Represents tax-basis cost which, in aggregate, is $1.2 billion less than GAAP cost.

Our portfolio shows little change: We continue to make more money when snoring than when active.

Inactivity strikes us as intelligent behavior. Neither we nor most business managers would dream of feverishly trading highly-profitable subsidiaries because a small move in the Federal Reserve's discount rate was predicted or because some Wall Street pundit had reversed his views on the market. Why, then, should we behave differently with our minority positions in wonderful businesses? The art of investing in public companies successfully is little different from the art of successfully acquiring subsidiaries. In each case you simply want to acquire, at a sensible price, a business with excellent economics and able, honest management. Thereafter, you need only monitor whether these qualities are being preserved.

When carried out capably, an investment strategy of that type will often result in its practitioner owning a few securities that will come to represent a very large portion of his portfolio. This investor would get a similar result if he followed a policy of purchasing an interest in, say, 20% of the future earnings of a number of outstanding college basketball stars. A handful of these would go on to achieve NBA stardom, and the investor's take from them would soon dominate his royalty stream. To suggest that this investor should sell off portions of his most successful investments simply because they have come to dominate his portfolio is akin to suggesting that the Bulls trade Michael Jordan because he has become so important to the team.

In studying the investments we have made in both subsidiary companies and common stocks, you will see that we favor businesses and industries unlikely to experience major change. The reason for that is simple: Making either type of purchase, we are searching for operations that we believe are virtually certain to possess enormous competitive strength ten or twenty years from now. A fast-changing industry environment may offer the chance for huge wins, but it precludes the certainty we seek.

I should emphasize that, as citizens, Charlie and I welcome change: Fresh ideas, new products, innovative processes and the like cause our country's standard of living to rise, and that's clearly good. As investors, however, our reaction to a fermenting industry is much like our attitude toward space exploration: We applaud the endeavor but prefer to skip the ride.

Obviously all businesses change to some extent. Today, See's is different in many ways from what it was in 1972 when we bought it: It offers a different assortment of candy, employs different machinery and sells through different distribution channels. But the reasons why people today buy boxed chocolates, and why they buy them from us rather than from someone else, are virtually unchanged from what they were in the 1920s when the See family was building the business. Moreover, these motivations are not likely to change over the next 20 years, or even 50.

We look for similar predictability in marketable securities. Take Coca-Cola: The zeal and imagination with which Coke products are sold has burgeoned under Roberto Goizueta, who has done an absolutely incredible job in creating value for his shareholders. Aided by Don Keough and Doug Ivester, Roberto has rethought and improved every aspect of the company. But the fundamentals of the business—the qualities that underlie Coke's competitive dominance and stunning economics—have remained constant through the years.

I was recently studying the 1896 report of Coke (and you think that *you* are behind in your reading!). At that time Coke, though it was already the leading soft drink, had been around for only a decade. But its blueprint for the next 100 years was already drawn. Reporting sales of $148,000 that year, Asa Candler, the company's president, said: "We have not lagged in our efforts to go into all the world teaching that Coca-Cola is the article, par excellence, for the health and good feeling of all people." Though "health" may have been a reach, I love the fact that Coke still relies on Candler's basic theme today—a century later. Candler went on to say, just as Roberto could now, "No article of like character has ever so firmly entrenched itself in public favor." Sales of syrup that year, incidentally, were 116,492 gallons versus about 3.2 billion in 1996.

I can't resist one more Candler quote: "Beginning this year about March 1st . . . we employed ten traveling salesmen by means of which, with systematic correspondence from the office, we covered almost the territory of the Union." That's my kind of sales force.

Companies such as Coca-Cola and Gillette might well be labeled "The Inevitables." Forecasters may differ a bit in their predictions of exactly how much soft drink or shaving-equipment business these companies will be doing in ten or twenty years. Nor is our talk of inevitability meant to play down the vital work that these companies must continue to carry out, in such areas as manufacturing, distribution, packaging and product innovation. In the end, however, no sensible observer—not even these companies' most vigorous competitors, assuming they are assessing the matter honestly—questions that Coke and Gillette will dominate their fields worldwide for an investment lifetime. Indeed, their dominance will probably strengthen. Both companies have significantly expanded their already huge shares of market during the past ten years, and all signs point to their repeating that performance in the next decade.

Obviously many companies in high-tech businesses or embryonic industries will grow much faster in percentage terms than will The Inevitables. But I would rather be certain of a good result than hopeful of a great one.

Of course, Charlie and I can identify only a few Inevitables, even after a lifetime of looking for them. Leadership alone provides no certainties: Witness the shocks some years back at General Motors, IBM and Sears, all of which had enjoyed long periods of seeming invincibility. Though some industries or lines of business exhibit characteristics that endow leaders with virtually insurmountable advantages, and that tend to establish Survival of the Fattest as almost a natural law, most do not. Thus, for every Inevitable, there are dozens of Impostors, companies now riding high but vulnerable to competitive attacks. Considering what it takes to be an Inevitable, Charlie and I recognize that we will never be able to come up with a Nifty Fifty or even a Twinkling Twenty. To the Inevitables in our portfolio, therefore, we add a few "Highly Probables."

You can, of course, pay too much for even the best of businesses. The overpayment risk surfaces periodically and, in our opinion, may now be quite high for the purchasers of virtually all stocks, The Inevitables included. Investors making purchases in an overheated market need to recognize that it may often take an extended period for the value of even an outstanding company to catch up with the price they paid.

A far more serious problem occurs when the management of a great company gets sidetracked and neglects its wonderful base business while purchasing other businesses that are so-so or worse. When that happens, the suffering of investors is often prolonged. Unfortunately, that is precisely what transpired years ago at both Coke and Gillette. (Would you believe that a few decades back they were growing shrimp at Coke and exploring for oil at Gillette?) Loss of focus is what most worries Charlie and me when we contemplate investing in businesses that in general look outstanding. All too often, we've seen value stagnate in the presence of hubris or of boredom that caused the attention of managers to wander. That's not going to happen again at Coke and Gillette, however—not given their current and prospective managements.

* * * * * * * * * * * *

Let me add a few thoughts about your own investments. Most investors, both institutional and individual, will find that the best way to own common stocks is through an index fund that charges minimal fees. Those following this path are sure to beat the net results (after fees and expenses) delivered by the great majority of investment professionals.

Should you choose, however, to construct your own portfolio, there are a few thoughts worth remembering. Intelligent investing is not complex, though that is far from saying that it is easy. What an investor needs is the ability to correctly evaluate selected businesses. Note that word "selected": You don't have to be an expert on every company, or even many. You only have to be able to evaluate companies within your circle of competence. The size of that circle is not very important; knowing its boundaries, however, is vital.

To invest successfully, you need not understand beta, efficient markets, modern portfolio theory, option pricing or emerging markets. You may, in fact, be better off knowing nothing of these. That, of course, is not the prevailing view at most business schools, whose finance curriculum tends to be dominated by such subjects. In our view, though, investment students need only two well-taught courses—How to Value a Business, and How to Think About Market Prices.

Your goal as an investor should simply be to purchase, at a rational price, a part interest in an easily-understandable business whose earnings are virtually certain to be materially higher five, ten and twenty years from now. Over time, you will find only a few companies that meet these standards—so when you see one that qualifies, you should buy a meaningful amount of stock. You must also resist the temptation to stray from your guidelines: If you aren't willing to own a stock for ten years, don't even think about owning it for ten minutes. Put together a portfolio of companies whose aggregate earnings march upward over the years, and so also will the portfolio's market value.

Though it's seldom recognized, this is the exact approach that has produced gains for Berkshire shareholders: Our look-through earnings have grown at a good clip over the years, and our stock price has risen correspondingly. Had those gains in earnings not materialized, there would have been little increase in Berkshire's value.

The greatly enlarged earnings base we now enjoy will inevitably cause our future gains to lag those of the past. We will continue, however, to push in the directions we always have. We will try to build earnings by running our present businesses well—a job made easy because of the extraordinary talents of our operating managers—and by purchasing other businesses, in whole or in part, that are not likely to be roiled by change and that possess important competitive advantages.

USAir

When Richard Branson, the wealthy owner of Virgin Atlantic Airways, was asked how to become a millionaire, he had a quick answer: "There's really nothing to it. Start as a billionaire and then buy an airline." Unwilling to accept Branson's proposition on faith, your Chairman decided in 1989 to test it by investing $358 million in a 9.25% preferred stock of USAir.

I liked and admired Ed Colodny, the company's then-CEO, and I still do. But my analysis of USAir's business was both superficial and wrong. I was so beguiled by the company's long history of profitable operations, and by the protection that ownership of a senior security seemingly offered me, that I overlooked the crucial point: USAir's revenues would increasingly feel the effects of an unregulated, fiercely-competitive market whereas its cost structure was a holdover from the days when regulation protected profits. These costs, if left unchecked, portended disaster, however reassuring the airline's past record might be. (If history supplied all of the answers, the Forbes 400 would consist of librarians.)

To rationalize its costs, however, USAir needed major improvements in its labor contracts—and that's something most airlines have found it extraordinarily difficult to get, short of credibly threatening, or actually entering, bankruptcy. USAir was to be no exception. Immediately after we purchased our preferred stock, the imbalance between the company's costs and revenues began to grow explosively. In the 1990-1994 period, USAir lost an aggregate of $2.4 billion, a performance that totally wiped out the book equity of its common stock.

For much of this period, the company paid us our preferred dividends, but in 1994 payment was suspended. A bit later, with the situation looking particularly gloomy, we wrote down our investment by 75%, to $89.5 million. Thereafter, during much of 1995, I offered to sell our shares at 50% of face value. Fortunately, I was unsuccessful.

Mixed in with my many mistakes at USAir was one thing I got right: Making our investment, we wrote into the preferred contract a somewhat unusual provision stipulating that "penalty dividends"—to run five percentage points over the prime rate—would be accrued on any arrearages. This meant that when our 9.25% dividend was omitted for two years, the unpaid amounts compounded at rates ranging between 13.25% and 14%.

Facing this penalty provision, USAir had every incentive to pay arrearages just as promptly as it could. And in the second half of 1996, when USAir turned profitable, it indeed began to pay, giving us $47.9 million. We owe Stephen Wolf, the company's CEO, a huge thank-you for extracting a performance from the airline that permitted this payment. Even so, USAir's performance has recently been helped significantly by an industry tailwind that may be cyclical in nature. The company still has basic cost problems that must be solved.

In any event, the prices of USAir's publicly-traded securities tell us that our preferred stock is now probably worth its par value of $358 million, give or take a little. In addition, we have over the years collected an aggregate of $240.5 million in dividends (including $30 million received in 1997).

Early in 1996, before any accrued dividends had been paid, I tried once more to unload our holdings—this time for about $335 million. You're lucky: I again failed in my attempt to snatch defeat from the jaws of victory.

In another context, a friend once asked me: "If you're so rich, why aren't you smart?" After reviewing my sorry performance with USAir, you may conclude he had a point.

Financings

We wrote four checks to Salomon Brothers last year and in each case were delighted with the work for which we were paying. I've already described one transaction: the FlightSafety purchase in which Salomon was the initiating investment banker. In a second deal, the firm placed a small debt offering for our finance subsidiary.

Additionally, we made two good-sized offerings through Salomon, both with interesting aspects. The first was our sale in May of 517,500 shares of Class B Common, which generated net proceeds of $565 million. As I have told you before, we made this sale in response to the threatened creation of unit trusts that would have marketed themselves as Berkshire look-alikes. In the process, they would have used our past, and definitely nonrepeatable, record to entice naive small investors and would have charged these innocents high fees and commissions.

I think it would have been quite easy for such trusts to have sold many billions of dollars worth of units, and I also believe that early marketing successes by these trusts would have led to the formation of others. (In the securities business, whatever can be sold will be sold.) The trusts would have meanwhile indiscriminately poured the proceeds of their offerings into a supply of Berkshire shares that is fixed and limited. The likely result: a speculative bubble in our stock. For at least a time, the price jump would have been self-validating, in that it would have pulled new waves of naive and impressionable investors into the trusts and set off still more buying of Berkshire shares.

Some Berkshire shareholders choosing to exit might have found that outcome ideal, since they could have profited at the expense of the buyers entering with false hopes. Continuing shareholders, however, would have suffered once reality set in, for at that point Berkshire would have been burdened with both hundreds of thousands of unhappy, indirect owners (trustholders, that is) and a stained reputation.

Our issuance of the B shares not only arrested the sale of the trusts, but provided a low-cost way for people to invest in Berkshire if they still wished to after hearing the warnings we issued. To blunt the enthusiasm that brokers normally have for pushing new issues—because that's where the money is—we arranged for our offering to carry a commission of only 1.5%, the lowest payoff that we have ever seen in a common stock underwriting. Additionally, we made the amount of the offering open-ended, thereby repelling the typical IPO buyer who looks for a short-term price spurt arising from a combination of hype and scarcity.

Overall, we tried to make sure that the B stock would be purchased only by investors with a long-term perspective. Those efforts were generally successful: Trading volume in the B shares immediately following the offering—a rough index of "flipping"—was far below the norm for a new issue. In the end we added about 40,000 shareholders, most of whom we believe both understand what they own and share our time horizons.

Salomon could not have performed better in the handling of this unusual transaction. Its investment bankers understood perfectly what we were trying to achieve and tailored every aspect of the offering to meet these objectives. The firm would have made far more money—perhaps ten times as much—if our offering had been standard in its make-up. But the investment bankers involved made no attempt to tweak the specifics in that direction. Instead they came up with ideas that were counter to Salomon's financial interest but that made it much more certain Berkshire's goals would be reached. Terry Fitzgerald captained this effort, and we thank him for the job that he did.

Given that background, it won't surprise you to learn that we again went to Terry when we decided late in the year to sell an issue of Berkshire notes that can be exchanged for a portion of the Salomon shares that we hold. In this instance, once again, Salomon did an absolutely first-class job, selling $500 million principal amount of five-year notes for $447.1 million. Each $1,000 note is exchangeable into 17.65 shares and is callable in three years at accreted value. Counting the original issue discount and a 1% coupon, the securities will provide a yield of 3% to maturity for holders who do not exchange them for Salomon stock. But it seems quite likely that the notes will be exchanged before their maturity. If that happens, our interest cost will be about 1.1% for the period prior to exchange.

In recent years, it has been written that Charlie and I are unhappy about all investment-banking fees. That's dead wrong. We have paid a great many fees over the last 30 years—beginning with the check we wrote to Charlie Heider upon our purchase of National Indemnity in 1967—and we are delighted to make payments that are commensurate with performance. In the case of the 1996 transactions at Salomon Brothers, we more than got our money's worth.

Miscellaneous

Though it was a close decision, Charlie and I have decided to enter the 20th Century. Accordingly, we are going to put future quarterly and annual reports of Berkshire on the Internet, where they can be accessed via http://www.berkshirehathaway.com. We will always "post" these reports on a Saturday so that anyone interested will have ample time to digest the information before trading begins. Our publishing schedule for the next 12 months is May 17, 1997, August 16, 1997, November 15, 1997, and March 14, 1998. We will also post any press releases that we issue.

At some point, we may stop mailing our quarterly reports and simply post these on the Internet. This move would eliminate significant costs. Also, we have a large number of "street name" holders and have found that the distribution of our quarterlies to them is highly erratic: Some holders receive their mailings weeks later than others.

The drawback to Internet-only distribution is that many of our shareholders lack computers. Most of these holders, however, could easily obtain printouts at work or through friends. Please let me know if you prefer that we continue mailing quarterlies. We want your input—starting with whether you even read these reports—and at a minimum will make no change in 1997. Also, we will definitely keep delivering the annual report in its present form in addition to publishing it on the Internet.

* * * * * * * * * * * *

About 97.2% of all eligible shares participated in Berkshire's 1996 shareholder-designated contributions program. Contributions made were $13.3 million, and 3,910 charities were recipients. A full description of the shareholder-designated contributions program appears on pages 48-49.

Every year a few shareholders miss out on the program because they don't have their shares registered in their own names on the prescribed record date or because they fail to get the designation form back to us within the 60-

day period allowed. This is distressing to Charlie and me. But if replies are received late, we have to reject them because we can't make exceptions for some shareholders while refusing to make them for others.

To participate in future programs, you must own Class A shares that are registered in the name of the actual owner, not the nominee name of a broker, bank or depository. Shares not so registered on August 31, 1997, will be ineligible for the 1997 program. When you get the form, return it promptly so that it does not get put aside or forgotten.

The Annual Meeting

Our capitalist's version of Woodstock -the Berkshire Annual Meeting-will be held on Monday, May 5. Charlie and I thoroughly enjoy this event, and we hope that you come. We will start at 9:30 a.m., break for about 15 minutes at noon (food will be available—but at a price, of course), and then continue talking to hard-core attendees until at least 3:30. Last year we had representatives from all 50 states, as well as Australia, Greece, Israel, Portugal, Singapore, Sweden, Switzerland, and the United Kingdom. The annual meeting is a time for owners to get their business-related questions answered, and therefore Charlie and I will stay on stage until we start getting punchy. (When that happens, I hope you notice a change.)

Last year we had attendance of 5,000 and strained the capacity of the Holiday Convention Centre, even though we spread out over three rooms. This year, our new Class B shares have caused a doubling of our stockholder count, and we are therefore moving the meeting to the Aksarben Coliseum, which holds about 10,000 and also has a huge parking lot. The doors will open for the meeting at 7:00 a.m., and at 8:30 we will—upon popular demand—show a new Berkshire movie produced by Marc Hamburg, our CFO. (In this company, no one gets by with doing only a single job.)

Overcoming our legendary repugnance for activities even faintly commercial, we will also have an abundant array of Berkshire products *for sale* in the halls outside the meeting room. Last year we broke all records, selling 1,270 pounds of See's candy, 1,143 pairs of Dexter shoes, $29,000 of World Books and related publications, and 700 sets of knives manufactured by our Quikut subsidiary. Additionally, many shareholders made inquiries about GEICO auto policies. If you would like to investigate possible insurance savings, bring your present policy to the meeting. We estimate that about 40% of our shareholders can save money by insuring with us. (We'd like to say 100%, but the insurance business doesn't work that way: Because insurers differ in their underwriting judgments, some of our shareholders are currently paying rates that are lower than GEICO's.)

An attachment to the proxy material enclosed with this report explains how you can obtain the card you will need for admission to the meeting. We expect a large crowd, so get both plane and hotel reservations promptly. American Express (800-799-6634) will be happy to help you with arrangements. As usual, we will have buses servicing the larger hotels to take you to and from the meeting, and also to take you to Nebraska Furniture Mart, Borsheim's and the airport after it is over.

NFM's main store, located on a 75-acre site about a mile from Aksarben, is open from 10 a.m. to 9 p.m. on weekdays, 10 a.m. to 6 p.m. on Saturdays, and noon to 6 p.m. on Sundays. Come by and say hello to "Mrs. B" (Rose Blumkin). She's 103 now and sometimes operates with an oxygen mask that is attached to a tank on her cart. But if you try to keep pace with her, it will be you who needs oxygen. NFM did about $265 million of business last year—a record for a single-location home furnishings operation—and you'll see why once you check out its merchandise and prices.

Borsheim's normally is closed on Sunday but will be open for shareholders from 10 a.m. to 6 p.m. on May 4th. Last year on "Shareholder Sunday" we broke every Borsheim's record in terms of tickets, dollar volume and, no doubt, attendees per square inch. Because we expect a capacity crowd this year as well, all shareholders attending on Sunday must bring their admission cards. Shareholders who prefer a somewhat less frenzied experience will get the same special treatment on Saturday, when the store is open from 10 a.m. to 5:30 p.m., or on Monday between 10 a.m. and 8 p.m. Come by at any time this year and let Susan Jacques, Borsheim's CEO, and her skilled associates perform a painless walletectomy on you.

My favorite steakhouse, Gorat's, was sold out last year on the weekend of the annual meeting, even though it added an additional seating at 4 p.m. on Sunday. You can make reservations beginning on April 1st *(but not earlier)* by calling 402-551-3733. I will be at Gorat's on Sunday after Borsheim's, having my usual rare T-bone and double order of hashbrowns. I can also recommend—this is the standard fare when Debbie Bosanek, my invaluable assistant, and I go to lunch—the hot roast beef sandwich with mashed potatoes and gravy. Mention Debbie's name and you will be given an extra boat of gravy.

The Omaha Royals and Indianapolis Indians will play baseball on Saturday evening, May 3rd, at Rosenblatt Stadium. Pitching in my normal rotation—one throw a year—I will start.

Though Rosenblatt is normal in appearance, it is anything but: The field sits on a unique geological structure that occasionally emits short gravitational waves causing even the most smoothly-delivered pitch to sink violently. I have been the victim of this weird phenomenon several times in the past but am hoping for benign conditions this year. There will be lots of opportunities for photos at the ball game, but you will need incredibly fast reflexes to snap my fast ball en route to the plate.

Our proxy statement includes information about obtaining tickets to the game. We will also provide an information packet listing restaurants that will be open on Sunday night and describing various things that you can do in Omaha on the weekend. The entire gang at Berkshire looks forward to seeing you.

Warren E. Buffett
Chairman of the Board

February 28, 1997

BERKSHIRE HATHAWAY INC.

1997 Chairman's Letter

To the Shareholders of Berkshire Hathaway Inc.:

Our gain in net worth during 1997 was $8.0 billion, which increased the per-share book value of both our Class A and Class B stock by 34.1%. Over the last 33 years (that is, since present management took over) per-share book value has grown from $19 to $25,488, a rate of 24.1% compounded annually.*

Given our gain of 34.1%, it is tempting to declare victory and move on. But last year's performance was no great triumph: *Any* investor can chalk up large returns when stocks soar, as they did in 1997. In a bull market, one must avoid the error of the preening duck that quacks boastfully after a torrential rainstorm, thinking that its paddling skills have caused it to rise in the world. A right-thinking duck would instead compare its position after the downpour to that of the other ducks on the pond.

So what's our duck rating for 1997? The table on the facing page shows that though we paddled furiously last year, passive ducks that simply invested in the S&P Index rose almost as fast as we did. Our appraisal of 1997's performance, then: Quack.

When the market booms, we tend to suffer in comparison with the S&P Index. The Index bears no tax costs, nor do mutual funds, since they pass through all tax liabilities to their owners. Last year, on the other hand, Berkshire paid or accrued $4.2 billion for federal income tax, or about 18% of our beginning net worth.

Berkshire will always have corporate taxes to pay, which means it needs to overcome their drag in order to justify its existence. Obviously, Charlie Munger, Berkshire's Vice Chairman and my partner, and I won't be able to lick that handicap every year. But we expect over time to maintain a modest advantage over the Index, and that is the yardstick against which you should measure us. We will not ask you to adopt the philosophy of the Chicago Cubs fan who reacted to a string of lackluster seasons by saying, "Why get upset? Everyone has a bad century now and then."

Gains in book value are, of course, not the bottom line at Berkshire. What truly counts are gains in per-share intrinsic business value. Ordinarily, though, the two measures tend to move roughly in tandem, and in 1997 that was the case: Led by a blow-out performance at GEICO, Berkshire's intrinsic value (which far exceeds book value) grew at nearly the same pace as book value.

For more explanation of the term, intrinsic value, you may wish to refer to our Owner's Manual, reprinted on pages 62 to 71. This manual sets forth our owner-related business principles, information that is important to all of Berkshire's shareholders.

In our last two annual reports, we furnished you a table that Charlie and I believe is central to estimating Berkshire's intrinsic value. In the updated version of that table, which follows, we trace our two key components of value. The first column lists our per-share ownership of investments (including cash and equivalents) and the second column shows our per-share earnings from Berkshire's operating businesses before taxes and purchase-accounting adjustments (discussed on pages 69 and 70), but after all interest and corporate expenses. The second column excludes all dividends, interest and capital gains that we realized from the investments presented in the first column. In effect, the columns show what Berkshire would look like were it split into two parts, with one entity holding our investments and the other operating all of our businesses and bearing all corporate costs.

---

* All figures used in this report apply to Berkshire's A shares, the successor to the only stock that the company had outstanding before 1996. The B shares have an economic interest equal to 1/30th that of the A.

Year	Investments Per Share	Pre-tax Earnings Per Share Excluding All Income from Investments
1967	$ 41	$ 1.09
1977	372	12.44
1987	3,910	108.14
1997	38,043	717.82

Pundits who ignore what our 38,000 employees contribute to the company, and instead simply view Berkshire as a de facto investment company, should study the figures in the second column. We made our first business acquisition in 1967, and since then our pre-tax operating earnings have grown from $1 million to $888 million. Furthermore, as noted, in this exercise we have assigned all of Berkshire's corporate expenses—overhead of $6.6 million, interest of $66.9 million and shareholder contributions of $15.4 million—to our business operations, even though a portion of these could just as well have been assigned to the investment side.

Here are the growth rates of the two segments by decade:

Decade Ending	Investments Per Share	Pre-tax Earnings Per Share Excluding All Income from Investments
1977	24.6%	27.6%
1987	26.5%	24.1%
1997	25.5%	20.8%
Annual Growth Rate, 1967-1997	25.6%	24.2%

During 1997, both parts of our business grew at a satisfactory rate, with investments increasing by $9,543 per share, or 33.5%, and operating earnings growing by $296.43 per share, or 70.3%. One important caveat: Because we were lucky in our super-cat insurance business (to be discussed later) and because GEICO's underwriting gain was well above what we can expect in most years, our 1997 operating earnings were much better than we anticipated and also more than we expect for 1998.

Our rate of progress in both investments and operations is *certain* to fall in the future. For anyone deploying capital, nothing recedes like success. My own history makes the point: Back in 1951, when I was attending Ben Graham's class at Columbia, an idea giving me a $10,000 gain improved my investment performance for the year by a full 100 percentage points. Today, an idea producing a $500 million pre-tax profit for Berkshire adds *one* percentage point to our performance. It's no wonder that my annual results in the 1950s were better by nearly thirty percentage points than my annual gains in any subsequent decade. Charlie's experience was similar. We weren't smarter then, just smaller. At our present size, any performance superiority we achieve will be minor.

We will be helped, however, by the fact that the businesses to which we have already allocated capital—both operating subsidiaries and companies in which we are passive investors—have splendid long-term prospects. We are also blessed with a managerial corps that is unsurpassed in ability and focus. Most of these executives are wealthy and do not need the pay they receive from Berkshire to maintain their way of life. They are motivated by the joy of accomplishment, not by fame or fortune.

Though we are delighted with what we own, we are not pleased with our prospects for committing incoming funds. Prices are high for both businesses and stocks. That does not mean that the prices of either will fall—we have absolutely no view on that matter—but it does mean that we get relatively little in prospective earnings when we commit fresh money.

Under these circumstances, we try to exert a Ted Williams kind of discipline. In his book *The Science of Hitting*, Ted explains that he carved the strike zone into 77 cells, each the size of a baseball. Swinging only at balls in his "best" cell, he knew, would allow him to bat .400; reaching for balls in his "worst" spot, the low outside corner of the strike zone, would reduce him to .230. In other words, waiting for the fat pitch would mean a trip to the Hall of Fame; swinging indiscriminately would mean a ticket to the minors.

If they are in the strike zone at all, the business "pitches" we now see are just catching the lower outside corner. If we swing, we will be locked into low returns. But if we let all of today's balls go by, there can be no assurance that the next ones we see will be more to our liking. Perhaps the attractive prices of the past were the aberrations, not the full prices of today. Unlike Ted, we can't be called out if we resist three pitches that are barely in the strike zone; nevertheless, just standing there, day after day, with my bat on my shoulder is not my idea of fun.

Unconventional Commitments

When we can't find our favorite commitment—a well-run and sensibly-priced business with fine economics—we usually opt to put new money into very short-term instruments of the highest quality. Sometimes, however, we venture elsewhere. Obviously we believe that the alternative commitments we make are more likely to result in profit than loss. But we also realize that they do not offer the certainty of profit that exists in a wonderful business secured at an attractive price. Finding that kind of opportunity, we *know* that we are going to make money—the only question being when. With alternative investments, we *think* that we are going to make money. But we also recognize that we will sometimes realize losses, occasionally of substantial size.

We had three non-traditional positions at yearend. The first was derivative contracts for 14.0 million barrels of oil, that being what was then left of a 45.7 million barrel position we established in 1994-95. Contracts for 31.7 million barrels were settled in 1995-97, and these supplied us with a pre-tax gain of about $61.9 million. Our remaining contracts expire during 1998 and 1999. In these, we had an unrealized gain of $11.6 million at yearend. Accounting rules require that commodity positions be carried at market value. Therefore, both our annual and quarterly financial statements reflect any unrealized gain or loss in these contracts. When we established our contracts, oil for future delivery seemed modestly underpriced. Today, though, we have no opinion as to its attractiveness.

Our second non-traditional commitment is in silver. Last year, we purchased 111.2 million ounces. Marked to market, that position produced a pre-tax gain of $97.4 million for us in 1997. In a way, this is a return to the past for me: Thirty years ago, I bought silver because I anticipated its demonetization by the U.S. Government. Ever since, I have followed the metal's fundamentals but not owned it. In recent years, bullion inventories have fallen materially, and last summer Charlie and I concluded that a higher price would be needed to establish equilibrium between supply and demand. Inflation expectations, it should be noted, play no part in our calculation of silver's value.

Finally, our largest non-traditional position at yearend was $4.6 billion, at amortized cost, of long-term zero-coupon obligations of the U.S. Treasury. These securities pay no interest. Instead, they provide their holders a return by way of the discount at which they are purchased, a characteristic that makes their market prices move rapidly when interest rates change. If rates rise, you lose heavily with zeros, and if rates fall, you make outsized gains. Since rates fell in 1997, we ended the year with an unrealized pre-tax gain of $598.8 million in our zeros. Because we carry the securities at market value, that gain is reflected in yearend book value.

In purchasing zeros, rather than staying with cash-equivalents, we risk looking very foolish: A macro-based commitment such as this never has anything close to a 100% probability of being successful. However, you pay Charlie and me to use our best judgment—not to avoid embarrassment—and we will occasionally make an unconventional move when we believe the odds favor it. Try to think kindly of us when we blow one. Along with President Clinton, we will be feeling your pain: The Munger family has more than 90% of its net worth in Berkshire and the Buffetts more than 99%.

How We Think About Market Fluctuations

A short quiz: If you plan to eat hamburgers throughout your life and are not a cattle producer, should you wish for higher or lower prices for beef? Likewise, if you are going to buy a car from time to time but are not an auto manufacturer, should you prefer higher or lower car prices? These questions, of course, answer themselves.

But now for the final exam: If you expect to be a net saver during the next five years, should you hope for a higher or lower stock market during that period? Many investors get this one wrong. Even though they are going to be net buyers of stocks for many years to come, they are elated when stock prices rise and depressed when they fall. In effect, they rejoice because prices have risen for the "hamburgers" they will soon be buying. This reaction makes no sense. Only those who will be sellers of equities in the near future should be happy at seeing stocks rise. Prospective purchasers should much prefer sinking prices.

For shareholders of Berkshire who do not expect to sell, the choice is even clearer. To begin with, our owners are automatically saving even if they spend every dime they personally earn: Berkshire "saves" for them by retaining all earnings, thereafter using these savings to purchase businesses and securities. Clearly, the more cheaply we make these buys, the more profitable our owners' indirect savings program will be.

Furthermore, through Berkshire you own major positions in companies that consistently repurchase their shares. The benefits that these programs supply us grow as prices fall: When stock prices are low, the funds that an investee spends on repurchases increase our ownership of that company by a greater amount than is the case when prices are higher. For example, the repurchases that Coca-Cola, The Washington Post and Wells Fargo made in past years at very low prices benefitted Berkshire far more than do today's repurchases, made at loftier prices.

At the end of every year, about 97% of Berkshire's shares are held by the same investors who owned them at the start of the year. That makes them savers. They should therefore rejoice when markets decline and allow both us and our investees to deploy funds more advantageously.

So smile when you read a headline that says "Investors lose as market falls." Edit it in your mind to "*Disin*vestors lose as market falls—but investors gain." Though writers often forget this truism, there is a buyer for every seller and what hurts one necessarily helps the other. (As they say in golf matches: "Every putt makes *someone* happy.")

We gained enormously from the low prices placed on many equities and businesses in the 1970s and 1980s. Markets that then were hostile to investment transients were friendly to those taking up permanent residence. In recent years, the actions we took in those decades have been validated, but we have found few new opportunities. In its role as a corporate "saver," Berkshire continually looks for ways to sensibly deploy capital, but it may be some time before we find opportunities that get us truly excited.

Insurance Operations—Overview

What does excite us, however, is our insurance business. GEICO is flying, and we expect that it will continue to do so. Before we expound on that, though, let's discuss "float" and how to measure its cost. Unless you understand this subject, it will be impossible for you to make an informed judgment about Berkshire's intrinsic value.

To begin with, float is money we hold but don't own. In an insurance operation, float arises because premiums are received before losses are paid, an interval that sometimes extends over many years. During that time, the insurer invests the money. Typically, this pleasant activity carries with it a downside: The premiums that an insurer takes in usually do not cover the losses and expenses it eventually must pay. That leaves it running an "underwriting loss," which is the cost of float. An insurance business has value if its cost of float over time is less than the cost the company would otherwise incur to obtain funds. But the business is a lemon if its cost of float is higher than market rates for money.

A caution is appropriate here: Because loss costs must be estimated, insurers have enormous latitude in figuring their underwriting results, and that makes it very difficult for investors to calculate a company's true cost of float. Estimating errors, usually innocent but sometimes not, can be huge. The consequences of these miscalculations flow directly into earnings. An experienced observer can usually detect large-scale errors in reserving, but the general public can typically do no more than accept what's presented, and at times I have been amazed by the numbers that big-name auditors have implicitly blessed. As for Berkshire, Charlie and I attempt to be conservative in presenting its underwriting results to you, because we have found that virtually all surprises in insurance are unpleasant ones.

As the numbers in the following table show, Berkshire's insurance business has been a huge winner. For the table, we have calculated our float—which we generate in large amounts relative to our premium volume—by adding net loss reserves, loss adjustment reserves, funds held under reinsurance assumed and unearned premium reserves, and then subtracting agents' balances, prepaid acquisition costs, prepaid taxes and deferred charges applicable to assumed reinsurance. Our cost of float is determined by our underwriting loss or profit. In those years when we have had an underwriting profit, such as the last five, our cost of float has been negative. In effect, we have been paid for holding money.

	(1) Underwriting Loss (In $ Millions)	(2) Average Float	Approximate Cost of Funds (Ratio of 1 to 2)	Yearend Yield on Long-Term Govt. Bonds
1967	profit	$17.3	less than zero	5.50%
1968	profit	19.9	less than zero	5.90%
1969	profit	23.4	less than zero	6.79%
1970	$ 0.37	32.4	1.14%	6.25%
1971	profit	52.5	less than zero	5.81%
1972	profit	69.5	less than zero	5.82%
1973	profit	73.3	less than zero	7.27%
1974	7.36	79.1	9.30%	8.13%
1975	11.35	87.6	12.96%	8.03%
1976	profit	102.6	less than zero	7.30%
1977	profit	139.0	less than zero	7.97%
1978	profit	190.4	less than zero	8.93%
1979	profit	227.3	less than zero	10.08%
1980	profit	237.0	less than zero	11.94%
1981	profit	228.4	less than zero	13.61%
1982	21.56	220.6	9.77%	10.64%
1983	33.87	231.3	14.64%	11.84%
1984	48.06	253.2	18.98%	11.58%
1985	44.23	390.2	11.34%	9.34%
1986	55.84	797.5	7.00%	7.60%
1987	55.43	1,266.7	4.38%	8.95%
1988	11.08	1,497.7	0.74%	9.00%
1989	24.40	1,541.3	1.58%	7.97%
1990	26.65	1,637.3	1.63%	8.24%
1991	119.59	1,895.0	6.31%	7.40%
1992	108.96	2,290.4	4.76%	7.39%
1993	profit	2,624.7	less than zero	6.35%
1994	profit	3,056.6	less than zero	7.88%
1995	profit	3,607.2	less than zero	5.95%
1996	profit	6,702.0	less than zero	6.64%
1997	profit	7,093.1	less than zero	5.92%

Since 1967, when we entered the insurance business, our float has grown at an annual compounded rate of 21.7%. Better yet, it has cost us nothing, and in fact has made us money. Therein lies an accounting irony: Though our float is shown on our balance sheet as a liability, it has had a value to Berkshire greater than an equal amount of net worth would have had.

The expiration of several large contracts will cause our float to decline during the first quarter of 1998, but we expect it to grow substantially over the long term. We also believe that our cost of float will continue to be highly favorable.

Super-Cat Insurance

Occasionally, however, the cost of our float will spike severely. That will occur because of our heavy involvement in the super-cat business, which by its nature is the most volatile of all insurance lines. In this operation, we sell policies that insurance and reinsurance companies purchase in order to limit their losses when mega-catastrophes strike. Berkshire is the preferred market for sophisticated buyers: When the "big one" hits, the financial strength of super-cat writers will be tested, and Berkshire has no peer in this respect.

Since truly major catastrophes are rare occurrences, our super-cat business can be expected to show large profits in most years—and to record a huge loss occasionally. In other words, the attractiveness of our super-cat business will take a great many years to measure. *What you must understand, however, is that a truly terrible year in the super-cat business is not a possibility—it's a certainty. The only question is when it will come.*

Last year, we were very lucky in our super-cat operation. The world suffered no catastrophes that caused huge amounts of insured damage, so virtually all premiums that we received dropped to the bottom line. This pleasant result has a dark side, however. Many investors who are "innocents"—meaning that they rely on representations of salespeople rather than on underwriting knowledge of their own—have come into the reinsurance business by means of purchasing pieces of paper that are called "catastrophe bonds." The second word in this term, though, is an Orwellian misnomer: A true bond obliges the issuer to pay; these bonds, in effect, are contracts that lay a provisional promise to pay on the *purchaser*.

This convoluted arrangement came into being because the promoters of the contracts wished to circumvent laws that prohibit the writing of insurance by entities that haven't been licensed by the state. A side benefit for the promoters is that calling the insurance contract a "bond" may also cause unsophisticated buyers to assume that these instruments involve far less risk than is actually the case.

Truly outsized risks will exist in these contracts if they are not properly priced. A pernicious aspect of catastrophe insurance, however, makes it likely that mispricing, even of a severe variety, will not be discovered for a very long time. Consider, for example, the odds of throwing a 12 with a pair of dice—1 out of 36. Now assume that the dice will be thrown once a year; that you, the "bond-buyer," agree to pay $50 million if a 12 appears; and that for "insuring" this risk you take in an annual "premium" of $1 million. That would mean you had significantly underpriced the risk. Nevertheless, you could go along for years thinking you were making money—indeed, easy money. There is actually a 75.4% probability that you would go for a decade without paying out a dime. Eventually, however, you would go broke.

In this dice example, the odds are easy to figure. Calculations involving monster hurricanes and earthquakes are necessarily much fuzzier, and the best we can do at Berkshire is to estimate a range of probabilities for such events. The lack of precise data, coupled with the rarity of such catastrophes, plays into the hands of promoters, who typically employ an "expert" to advise the potential bond-buyer about the probability of losses. The expert puts no money on the table. Instead, he receives an up-front payment that is forever his no matter how inaccurate his predictions. Surprise: When the stakes are high, an expert can invariably be found who will affirm—to return to our example—that the chance of rolling a 12 is not 1 in 36, but more like 1 in 100. (In fairness, we should add that the expert will probably believe that his odds are correct, a fact that makes him less reprehensible—but more dangerous.)

The influx of "investor" money into catastrophe bonds—which may well live up to their name—has caused super-cat prices to deteriorate materially. Therefore, we will write less business in 1998. We have some large multi-year contracts in force, however, that will mitigate the drop. The largest of these are two policies that we described in last year's report—one covering hurricanes in Florida and the other, signed with the California Earthquake Authority, covering earthquakes in that state. Our "worst-case" loss remains about $600 million after-tax, the maximum we could lose under the CEA policy. Though this loss potential may sound large, it is only about 1% of Berkshire's market value. Indeed, if we could get appropriate prices, we would be willing to significantly increase our "worst-case" exposure.

Our super-cat business was developed from scratch by Ajit Jain, who has contributed to Berkshire's success in a variety of other ways as well. Ajit possesses both the discipline to walk away from business that is inadequately priced and the imagination to then find other opportunities. Quite simply, he is one of Berkshire's major assets. Ajit would have been a star in whatever career he chose; fortunately for us, he enjoys insurance.

Insurance—GEICO (1-800-555-2756) and Other Primary Operations

Last year I wrote about GEICO's Tony Nicely and his terrific management skills. If I had known then what he had in store for us in 1997, I would have searched for still greater superlatives. Tony, now 54, has been with GEICO for 36 years and last year was his best. As CEO, he has transmitted vision, energy and enthusiasm to all members of the GEICO family—raising their sights from what *has* been achieved to what *can* be achieved.

We measure GEICO's performance by first, the net increase in its voluntary auto policies (that is, not including policies assigned us by the state) and, second, the profitability of "seasoned" auto business, meaning policies that have been with us for more than a year and are thus past the period in which acquisition costs cause them to be money-losers. In 1996, in-force business grew 10%, and I told you how pleased I was, since that rate was well above anything we had seen in two decades. Then, in 1997, growth jumped to 16%.

Below are the new business and in-force figures for the last five years:

Years	New Voluntary Auto Policies	Voluntary Auto Policies in Force
1993	354,882	2,011,055
1994	396,217	2,147,549
1995	461,608	2,310,037
1996	617,669	2,543,699
1997	913,176	2,949,439

Of course, any insurer can grow rapidly if it gets careless about underwriting. GEICO's underwriting profit for the year, though, was 8.1% of premiums, far above its average. Indeed, that percentage was higher than we wish it to be: Our goal is to pass on most of the benefits of our low-cost operation to our customers, holding ourselves to about 4% in underwriting profit. With that in mind, we reduced our average rates a bit during 1997 and may well cut them again this year. Our rate changes varied, of course, depending on the policyholder and where he lives; we strive to charge a rate that properly reflects the loss expectancy of each driver.

GEICO is not the only auto insurer obtaining favorable results these days. Last year, the industry recorded profits that were far better than it anticipated or can sustain. Intensified competition will soon squeeze margins very significantly. But this is a development we welcome: Long term, a tough market helps the low-cost operator, which is what we are and intend to remain.

Last year I told you about the record 16.9% profit-sharing contribution that GEICO's associates had earned and explained that two simple variables set the amount: policy growth and profitability of seasoned business. I further explained that 1996's performance was so extraordinary that we had to enlarge the chart delineating the possible payouts. The new configuration didn't make it through 1997: We enlarged the chart's boundaries again and awarded our 10,500 associates a profit-sharing contribution amounting to 26.9% of their base compensation, or $71 million. In addition, the same two variables—policy growth and profitability of seasoned business—determined the cash bonuses that we paid to dozens of top executives, starting with Tony.

At GEICO, we are paying in a way that makes sense for both our owners and our managers. We distribute merit badges, not lottery tickets: In none of Berkshire's subsidiaries do we relate compensation to our stock price, which our associates cannot affect in any meaningful way. Instead, we tie bonuses to each unit's business performance, which is the direct product of the unit's people. When that performance is terrific—as it has been at GEICO—there is nothing Charlie and I enjoy more than writing a big check.

GEICO's underwriting profitability will probably fall in 1998, but the company's growth could accelerate. We're planning to step on the gas: GEICO's marketing expenditures this year will top $100 million, up 50% from 1997. Our market share today is only 3%, a level of penetration that should increase dramatically in the next decade. The auto insurance industry is huge—it does about $115 billion of volume annually—and there are tens of millions of drivers who would save substantial money by switching to us.

* * * * * * * * * * * *

In the 1995 report, I described the enormous debt that you and I owe to Lorimer Davidson. On a Saturday early in 1951, he patiently explained the ins and outs of both GEICO and its industry to me—a 20-year-old stranger who'd arrived at GEICO's headquarters uninvited and unannounced. Davy later became the company's CEO and has remained my friend and teacher for 47 years. The huge rewards that GEICO has heaped on Berkshire would not have materialized had it not been for his generosity and wisdom. Indeed, had I not met Davy, I might never have grown to understand the whole field of insurance, which over the years has played such a key part in Berkshire's success.

Davy turned 95 last year, and it's difficult for him to travel. Nevertheless, Tony and I hope that we can persuade him to attend our annual meeting, so that our shareholders can properly thank him for his important contributions to Berkshire. Wish us luck.

* * * * * * * * * * * *

Though they are, of course, far smaller than GEICO, our other primary insurance operations turned in results last year that, in aggregate, were fully as stunning. National Indemnity's traditional business had an underwriting profit of 32.9% and, as usual, developed a large amount of float compared to premium volume. Over the last three years, this segment of our business, run by Don Wurster, has had a profit of 24.3%. Our homestate operation, managed by Rod Eldred, recorded an underwriting profit of 14.1% even though it continued to absorb the expenses of geographical expansion. Rod's three-year record is an amazing 15.1%. Berkshire's workers' compensation business, run out of California by Brad Kinstler, had a modest underwriting loss in a difficult environment; its three-year underwriting record is a positive 1.5%. John Kizer, at Central States Indemnity, set a new volume record while generating good underwriting earnings. At Kansas Bankers Surety, Don Towle more than lived up to the high expectations we had when we purchased the company in 1996.

In aggregate, these five operations recorded an underwriting profit of 15.0%. The two Dons, along with Rod, Brad and John, have created significant value for Berkshire, and we believe there is more to come.

Sources of Reported Earnings

The table that follows shows the main sources of Berkshire's reported earnings. In this presentation, purchase-accounting adjustments are not assigned to the specific businesses to which they apply, but are instead aggregated and shown separately. This procedure lets you view the earnings of our businesses as they would have been reported had we not purchased them. For the reasons discussed on pages 69 and 70, this form of presentation seems to us to be more useful to investors and managers than one utilizing generally-accepted accounting principles (GAAP), which require purchase-premiums to be charged off business-by-business. The total earnings we show in the table are, of course, identical to the GAAP total in our audited financial statements.

	(in millions)			
	Pre-Tax Earnings		Berkshire's Share of Net Earnings (after taxes and minority interests)	
	1997	1996	1997	1996
Operating Earnings:				
Insurance Group:				
Underwriting – Super-Cat	$ 283.0	$ 167.0	$ 182.7	$ 107.4
Underwriting – Other Reinsurance	(155.2)	(174.8)	(100.1)	(112.4)
Underwriting – GEICO	280.7	171.4	181.1	110.2
Underwriting – Other Primary	52.9	58.5	34.1	37.6
Net Investment Income	882.3	726.2	703.6	593.1
Buffalo News	55.9	50.4	32.7	29.5
Finance Businesses	28.1	23.1	18.0	14.9
FlightSafety	139.5	3.1 [1]	84.4	1.9 [1]
Home Furnishings	56.8 [2]	43.8	32.2 [2]	24.8
Jewelry	31.6	27.8	18.3	16.1
Scott Fetzer(excluding finance operation)	118.9	121.7	77.3	81.6
See's Candies	58.6	51.9	35.0	30.8
Shoe Group	48.8	61.6	32.2	41.0
Purchase-Accounting Adjustments	(104.9)	(75.7)	(97.0)	(70.5)
Interest Expense[3]	(106.6)	(94.3)	(67.1)	(56.6)
Shareholder-Designated Contributions	(15.4)	(13.3)	(9.9)	(8.5)
Other	60.7	73.0	37.0	42.2
Operating Earnings	1,715.7	1,221.4	1,194.5	883.1
Capital Gains from Investments	1,111.9	2,484.5	707.1	1,605.5
Total Earnings – All Entities	$2,827.6	$3,705.9	$1,901.6	$2,488.6

(1) From date of acquisition, December 23, 1996.
(2) Includes Star Furniture from July 1, 1997.
(3) Excludes interest expense of Finance Businesses.

Overall, our operating businesses continue to perform exceptionally well, far outdoing their industry norms. We are particularly pleased that profits improved at Helzberg's after a disappointing 1996. Jeff Comment, Helzberg's CEO, took decisive steps early in 1997 that enabled the company to gain real momentum by the crucial Christmas season. In the early part of this year, as well, sales remained strong.

Casual observers may not appreciate just how extraordinary the performance of many of our businesses has been: If the earnings history of, say, Buffalo News or Scott Fetzer is compared to the records of their publicly-owned peers, their performance might seem to have been unexceptional. But most public companies retain two-thirds or more of their earnings to fund their corporate growth. In contrast, those Berkshire subsidiaries have paid 100% of their earnings to us, their parent company, to fund *our* growth.

In effect, the records of the public companies reflect the cumulative benefits of the earnings they have retained, while the records of our operating subsidiaries get no such boost. Over time, however, the earnings these subsidiaries have distributed have created truly huge amounts of earning power elsewhere in Berkshire. The News, See's and Scott Fetzer have alone paid us $1.8 billion, which we have gainfully employed elsewhere. We owe their managements our gratitude for much more than the earnings that are detailed in the table.

Additional information about our various businesses is given on pages 36—50, where you will also find our segment earnings reported on a GAAP basis. In addition, on pages 55—61, we have rearranged Berkshire's financial data into four segments on a non-GAAP basis, a presentation that corresponds to the way Charlie and I think about the company. Our intent is to supply you with the financial information that we would wish you to give us if our positions were reversed.

Look-Through Earnings

Reported earnings are a poor measure of economic progress at Berkshire, in part because the numbers shown in the table presented earlier include only the dividends we receive from investees—though these dividends typically represent only a small fraction of the earnings attributable to our ownership. Not that we mind this division of money, since on balance we regard the undistributed earnings of investees as more valuable to us than the portion paid out. The reason is simple: Our investees often have the opportunity to reinvest earnings at high rates of return. So why should we want them paid out?

To depict something closer to economic reality at Berkshire than reported earnings, though, we employ the concept of "look-through" earnings. As we calculate these, they consist of: (1) the operating earnings reported in the previous section, plus; (2) our share of the retained operating earnings of major investees that, under GAAP accounting, are not reflected in our profits, less; (3) an allowance for the tax that would be paid by Berkshire if these retained earnings of investees had instead been distributed to us. When tabulating "operating earnings" here, we exclude purchase-accounting adjustments as well as capital gains and other major non-recurring items.

The following table sets forth our 1997 look-through earnings, though I warn you that the figures can be no more than approximate, since they are based on a number of judgment calls. (The dividends paid to us by these investees have been included in the operating earnings itemized on page 11, mostly under "Insurance Group: Net Investment Income.")

Berkshire's Major Investees	Berkshire's Approximate Ownership at Yearend[1]	Berkshire's Share of Undistributed Operating Earnings (in millions)[2]
American Express Company	10.7%	$161
The Coca-Cola Company	8.1%	216
The Walt Disney Company	3.2%	65
Freddie Mac	8.6%	86
The Gillette Company..................	8.6%	82
The Washington Post Company	16.5%	30
Wells Fargo & Company.................	7.8%	103
Berkshire's share of undistributed earnings of major investees		743
Hypothetical tax on these undistributed investee earnings[3]		(105)
Reported operating earnings of Berkshire		1,292
Total look-through earnings of Berkshire		$1,930

(1) Does not include shares allocable to minority interests
(2) Calculated on average ownership for the year
(3) The tax rate used is 14%, which is the rate Berkshire pays on the dividends it receives

Acquisitions of 1997

In 1997, we agreed to acquire Star Furniture and International Dairy Queen (a deal that closed early in 1998). Both businesses fully meet our criteria: They are understandable; possess excellent economics; and are run by outstanding people.

The Star transaction has an interesting history. Whenever we buy into an industry whose leading participants aren't known to me, I always ask our new partners, "Are there any more at home like you?" Upon our purchase of Nebraska Furniture Mart in 1983, therefore, the Blumkin family told me about three outstanding furniture retailers in other parts of the country. At the time, however, none was for sale.

Many years later, Irv Blumkin learned that Bill Child, CEO of R.C. Willey—one of the recommended three—might be interested in merging, and we promptly made the deal described in the 1995 report. We have been delighted with that association—Bill is the perfect partner. Furthermore, when we asked Bill about industry standouts, he came up with the remaining two names given me by the Blumkins, one of these being Star Furniture of Houston. But time went by without there being any indication that either of the two was available.

On the Thursday before last year's annual meeting, however, Bob Denham of Salomon told me that Melvyn Wolff, the long-time controlling shareholder and CEO of Star, wanted to talk. At our invitation, Melvyn came to the meeting and spent his time in Omaha confirming his positive feelings about Berkshire. I, meanwhile, looked at Star's financials, and liked what I saw.

A few days later, Melvyn and I met in New York and made a deal in a single, two-hour session. As was the case with the Blumkins and Bill Child, I had no need to check leases, work out employment contracts, etc. I knew I was dealing with a man of integrity and that's what counted.

Though the Wolff family's association with Star dates back to 1924, the business struggled until Melvyn and his sister Shirley Toomin took over in 1962. Today Star operates 12 stores—ten in Houston and one each in Austin and Bryan—and will soon move into San Antonio as well. We won't be surprised if Star is many times its present size a decade from now.

Here's a story illustrating what Melvyn and Shirley are like: When they told their associates of the sale, they also announced that Star would make large, special payments to those who had helped them succeed—and then defined that group as everyone in the business. Under the terms of our deal, it was Melvyn and Shirley's money, not ours, that funded this distribution. Charlie and I love it when we become partners with people who behave like that.

The Star transaction closed on July 1. In the months since, we've watched Star's already-excellent sales and earnings growth accelerate further. Melvyn and Shirley will be at the annual meeting, and I hope you get a chance to meet them.

Next acquisition: International Dairy Queen. There are 5,792 Dairy Queen stores operating in 23 countries—all but a handful run by franchisees—and in addition IDQ franchises 409 Orange Julius operations and 43 Karmel-korn operations. In 190 locations, "treat centers" provide some combination of the three products.

For many years IDQ had a bumpy history. Then, in 1970, a Minneapolis group led by John Mooty and Rudy Luther took control. The new managers inherited a jumble of different franchising agreements, along with some unwise financing arrangements that had left the company in a precarious condition. In the years that followed, management rationalized the operation, extended food service to many more locations, and, in general, built a strong organization.

Last summer Mr. Luther died, which meant his estate needed to sell stock. A year earlier, Dick Kiphart of William Blair & Co., had introduced me to John Mooty and Mike Sullivan, IDQ's CEO, and I had been impressed with both men. So, when we got the chance to merge with IDQ, we offered a proposition patterned on our FlightSafety acquisition, extending selling shareholders the option of choosing either cash or Berkshire shares having a slightly lower immediate value. By tilting the consideration as we did, we encouraged holders to opt for cash, the type of payment we by far prefer. Even then, only 45% of IDQ shares elected cash.

Charlie and I bring a modicum of product expertise to this transaction: He has been patronizing the Dairy Queens in Cass Lake and Bemidji, Minnesota, for decades, and I have been a regular in Omaha. We have put our money where our mouth is.

A Confession

I've mentioned that we strongly prefer to use cash rather than Berkshire stock in acquisitions. A study of the record will tell you why: If you aggregate all of our stock-only mergers (excluding those we did with two affiliated companies, Diversified Retailing and Blue Chip Stamps), you will find that our shareholders are slightly worse off than they would have been had I not done the transactions. Though it hurts me to say it, when I've issued stock, I've cost you money.

Be clear about one thing: This cost has *not* occurred because we were misled in any way by sellers or because they thereafter failed to manage with diligence and skill. On the contrary, the sellers were completely candid when we were negotiating our deals and have been energetic and effective ever since.

Instead, our problem has been that we own a truly marvelous collection of businesses, which means that trading away a portion of them for something new almost never makes sense. When we issue shares in a merger, we reduce your ownership in all of our businesses—partly-owned companies such as Coca-Cola, Gillette and American Express, and all of our terrific operating companies as well. An example from sports will illustrate the difficulty we face: For a baseball team, acquiring a player who can be expected to bat .350 is almost always a wonderful event—*except* when the team must trade a .380 hitter to make the deal.

Because our roster is filled with .380 hitters, we have tried to pay cash for acquisitions, and here our record has been far better. Starting with National Indemnity in 1967, and continuing with, among others, See's, Buffalo News, Scott Fetzer and GEICO, we have acquired—for cash—a number of large businesses that have performed incredibly well since we bought them. These acquisitions have delivered Berkshire tremendous value—indeed, far more than I anticipated when we made our purchases.

We believe that it is almost impossible for us to "trade up" from our present businesses and managements. Our situation is the opposite of Camelot's Mordred, of whom Guenevere commented, "The one thing I can say for him is that he is bound to marry well. Everybody is above him." Marrying well is extremely difficult for Berkshire.

So you can be sure that Charlie and I will be very reluctant to issue shares in the future. In those cases when we simply must do so—when certain shareholders of a desirable acquiree insist on getting stock—we will include an attractive cash option in order to tempt as many of the sellers to take cash as is possible.

Merging with public companies presents a special problem for us. If we are to offer *any* premium to the acquiree, one of two conditions must be present: Either our own stock must be overvalued relative to the acquiree's, or the two companies together must be expected to earn more than they would if operated separately. Historically, Berkshire has seldom been overvalued. In this market, moreover, undervalued acquirees are almost impossible to find. That other possibility—synergy gains—is usually unrealistic, since we expect acquirees to operate after we've bought them just as they did before. Joining with Berkshire does not normally raise their revenues nor cut their costs.

Indeed, their reported costs (but not their true ones) will *rise* after they are bought by Berkshire if the acquiree has been granting options as part of its compensation packages. In these cases, "earnings" of the acquiree have been overstated because they have followed the standard—but, in our view, dead wrong—accounting practice of ignoring the cost to a business of issuing options. When Berkshire acquires an option-issuing company, we promptly substitute a cash compensation plan having an economic value equivalent to that of the previous option plan. The acquiree's true compensation cost is thereby brought out of the closet and charged, as it should be, against earnings.

The reasoning that Berkshire applies to the merger of public companies *should* be the calculus for all buyers. Paying a takeover premium does not make sense for any acquirer unless a) its stock is overvalued relative to the acquiree's or b) the two enterprises will earn more combined than they would separately. Predictably, acquirers normally hew to the second argument because very few are willing to acknowledge that their stock is overvalued. However, voracious buyers—the ones that issue shares as fast as they can print them—are tacitly conceding that point. (Often, also, they are running Wall Street's version of a chain-letter scheme.)

In some mergers there truly are major synergies—though oftentimes the acquirer pays too much to obtain them—but at other times the cost and revenue benefits that are projected prove illusory. Of one thing, however, be certain: If a CEO is enthused about a particularly foolish acquisition, both his internal staff and his outside advisors will come up with whatever projections are needed to justify his stance. Only in fairy tales are emperors told that they are naked.

Common Stock Investments

Below we present our common stock investments. Those with a market value of more than $750 million are itemized.

		12/31/97	
Shares	Company	Cost*	Market
		(dollars in millions)	
49,456,900	American Express Company	$1,392.7	$ 4,414.0
200,000,000	The Coca-Cola Company	1,298.9	13,337.5
21,563,414	The Walt Disney Company	381.2	2,134.8
63,977,600	Freddie Mac	329.4	2,683.1
48,000,000	The Gillette Company	600.0	4,821.0
23,733,198	Travelers Group Inc.	604.4	1,278.6
1,727,765	The Washington Post Company	10.6	840.6
6,690,218	Wells Fargo & Company	412.6	2,270.9
	Others	2,177.1	4,467.2
	Total Common Stocks	$7,206.9	$36,247.7

* Represents tax-basis cost which, in aggregate, is $1.8 billion less than GAAP cost.

We made net sales during the year that amounted to about 5% of our beginning portfolio. In these, we significantly reduced a few of our holdings that are below the $750 million threshold for itemization, and we also modestly trimmed a few of the larger positions that we detail. Some of the sales we made during 1997 were aimed at changing our bond-stock ratio moderately in response to the relative values that we saw in each market, a realignment we have continued in 1998.

Our reported positions, we should add, sometimes reflect the investment decisions of GEICO's Lou Simpson. Lou independently runs an equity portfolio of nearly $2 billion that may at times overlap the portfolio that I manage, and occasionally he makes moves that differ from mine.

Though we don't attempt to predict the movements of the stock market, we do try, in a very rough way, to value it. At the annual meeting last year, with the Dow at 7,071 and long-term Treasury yields at 6.89%, Charlie and I stated that we did not consider the market overvalued *if* 1) interest rates remained where they were or fell, and 2) American business continued to earn the remarkable returns on equity that it had recently recorded. So far, interest rates have fallen—that's one requisite satisfied—and returns on equity still remain exceptionally high. If they stay there—and if interest rates hold near recent levels—there is no reason to think of stocks as generally overvalued. On the other hand, returns on equity are not a sure thing to remain at, or even near, their present levels.

In the summer of 1979, when equities looked cheap to me, I wrote a *Forbes* article entitled "You pay a very high price in the stock market for a cheery consensus." At that time skepticism and disappointment prevailed, and my point was that investors should be glad of the fact, since pessimism drives down prices to truly attractive levels. Now, however, we have a very cheery consensus. That does not necessarily mean this is the wrong time to buy stocks: Corporate America is now earning far more money than it was just a few years ago, and in the presence of lower interest rates, every dollar of earnings becomes more valuable. Today's price levels, though, have materially eroded the "margin of safety" that Ben Graham identified as the cornerstone of intelligent investing.

* * * * * * * * * * * *

In last year's annual report, I discussed Coca-Cola, our largest holding. Coke continues to increase its market dominance throughout the world, but, tragically, it has lost the leader responsible for its outstanding performance. Roberto Goizueta, Coke's CEO since 1981, died in October. After his death, I read every one of the more than 100 letters and notes he had written me during the past nine years. Those messages could well serve as a guidebook for success in both business and life.

In these communications, Roberto displayed a brilliant and clear strategic vision that was always aimed at advancing the well-being of Coke shareholders. Roberto knew where he was leading the company, how he was going to get there, and why this path made the most sense for his owners—and, equally important, he had a burning sense of urgency about reaching his goals. An excerpt from one handwritten note he sent to me illustrates his mind-set: "By the way, I have told Olguita that what she refers to as an obsession, you call focus. I like your term much better." Like all who knew Roberto, I will miss him enormously.

Consistent with his concern for the company, Roberto prepared for a seamless succession long before it seemed necessary. Roberto knew that Doug Ivester was the right man to take over and worked with Doug over the years to ensure that no momentum would be lost when the time for change arrived. The Coca-Cola Company will be the same steamroller under Doug as it was under Roberto.

Convertible Preferreds

Two years ago, I gave you an update on the five convertible preferreds that we purchased through private placements in the 1987-1991 period. At the time of that earlier report, we had realized a small profit on the sale of our Champion International holding. The four remaining preferred commitments included two, Gillette and First Empire State, that we had converted into common stock in which we had large unrealized gains, and two others, USAir and Salomon, that had been trouble-prone. At times, the last two had me mouthing a line from a country song: "How can I miss you if you won't go away?"

Since I delivered that report, all four holdings have grown significantly in value. The common stocks of both Gillette and First Empire have risen substantially, in line with the companies' excellent performance. At yearend, the $600 million we put into Gillette in 1989 had appreciated to $4.8 billion, and the $40 million we committed to First Empire in 1991 had risen to $236 million.

Our two laggards, meanwhile, have come to life in a very major way. In a transaction that finally rewarded its long-suffering shareholders, Salomon recently merged into Travelers Group. All of Berkshire's shareholders—including me, very personally—owe a huge debt to Deryck Maughan and Bob Denham for, first, playing key roles in saving Salomon from extinction following its 1991 scandal and, second, restoring the vitality of the company to a level that made it an attractive acquisition for Travelers. I have often said that I wish to work with executives that I like, trust and admire. No two fit that description better than Deryck and Bob.

Berkshire's final results from its Salomon investment won't be tallied for some time, but it is safe to say that they will be far better than I anticipated two years ago. Looking back, I think of my Salomon experience as having been both fascinating and instructional, though for a time in 1991-92 I felt like the drama critic who wrote: "I would have enjoyed the play except that I had an unfortunate seat. It faced the stage."

The resuscitation of US Airways borders on the miraculous. Those who have watched my moves in this investment know that I have compiled a record that is unblemished by success. I was wrong in originally purchasing the stock, and I was wrong later, in repeatedly trying to unload our holdings at 50 cents on the dollar.

Two changes at the company coincided with its remarkable rebound: 1) Charlie and I left the board of directors and 2) Stephen Wolf became CEO. Fortunately for our egos, the second event was the key: Stephen Wolf's accomplishments at the airline have been phenomenal.

There still is much to do at US Airways, but survival is no longer an issue. Consequently, the company made up the dividend arrearages on our preferred during 1997, adding extra payments to compensate us for the delay we suffered. The company's common stock, furthermore, has risen from a low of $4 to a recent high of $73.

Our preferred has been called for redemption on March 15. But the rise in the company's stock has given our conversion rights, which we thought worthless not long ago, great value. It is now almost certain that our US Airways shares will produce a decent profit—that is, if my cost for Maalox is excluded—and the gain could even prove indecent.

Next time I make a big, dumb decision, Berkshire shareholders will know what to do: *Phone Mr. Wolf.*

* * * * * * * * * * * *

In addition to the convertible preferreds, we purchased one other private placement in 1991, $300 million of American Express Percs. This security was essentially a common stock that featured a tradeoff in its first three years: We received extra dividend payments during that period, but we were also capped in the price appreciation we could realize. Despite the cap, this holding has proved extraordinarily profitable thanks to a move by your Chairman that combined luck and skill—110% luck, the balance skill.

Our Percs were due to convert into common stock in August 1994, and in the month before I was mulling whether to sell upon conversion. One reason to hold was Amex's outstanding CEO, Harvey Golub, who seemed likely to maximize whatever potential the company had (a supposition that has since been proved—in spades). But the size of that potential was in question: Amex faced relentless competition from a multitude of card-issuers, led by Visa. Weighing the arguments, I leaned toward sale.

Here's where I got lucky. During that month of decision, I played golf at Prouts Neck, Maine with Frank Olson, CEO of Hertz. Frank is a brilliant manager, with intimate knowledge of the card business. So from the first tee on I was quizzing him about the industry. By the time we reached the second green, Frank had convinced me that Amex's corporate card was a terrific franchise, and I had decided not to sell. On the back nine I turned buyer, and in a few months Berkshire owned 10% of the company.

We now have a $3 billion gain in our Amex shares, and I naturally feel very grateful to Frank. But George Gillespie, our mutual friend, says that I am confused about where my gratitude should go. After all, he points out, it was he who arranged the game and assigned me to Frank's foursome.

Quarterly Reports to Shareholders

In last year's letter, I described the growing costs we incur in mailing quarterly reports and the problems we have encountered in delivering them to "street-name" shareholders. I asked for your opinion about the desirability of our continuing to print reports, given that we now publish our quarterly and annual communications on the Internet, at our site, www.berkshirehathaway.com. Relatively few shareholders responded, but it is clear that at least a small number who want the quarterly information have no interest in getting it off the Internet. Being a life-long sufferer from technophobia, I can empathize with this group.

The cost of publishing quarterlies, however, continues to balloon, and we have therefore decided to send printed versions only to shareholders who request them. If you wish the quarterlies, please complete the reply card that is bound into this report. In the meantime, be assured that *all* shareholders will continue to receive the *annual* report in printed form.

Those of you who enjoy the computer should check out our home page. It contains a large amount of current information about Berkshire and also all of our annual letters since 1977. In addition, our website includes links to the home pages of many Berkshire subsidiaries. On these sites you can learn more about our subsidiaries' products and—yes—even place orders for them.

We are required to file our quarterly information with the SEC no later than 45 days after the end of each quarter. One of our goals in posting communications on the Internet is to make this material information—in full detail and in a form unfiltered by the media—simultaneously available to all interested parties at a time when markets are closed. Accordingly, we plan to send our 1998 quarterly information to the SEC on three Fridays, May 15, August 14, and November 13, and on those nights to post the same information on the Internet. This procedure will put all of our shareholders, whether they be direct or "street-name," on an equal footing. Similarly, we will post our 1998 annual report on the Internet on Saturday, March 13, 1999, and mail it at about the same time.

Shareholder-Designated Contributions

About 97.7% of all eligible shares participated in Berkshire's 1997 shareholder-designated contributions program. Contributions made were $15.4 million, and 3,830 charities were recipients. A full description of the program appears on pages 52—53.

Cumulatively, over the 17 years of the program, Berkshire has made contributions of $113.1 million pursuant to the instructions of our shareholders. The rest of Berkshire's giving is done by our subsidiaries, which stick to the philanthropic patterns that prevailed before they were acquired (except that their former owners themselves take on the responsibility for their personal charities). In aggregate, our subsidiaries made contributions of $8.1 million in 1997, including in-kind donations of $4.4 million.

Every year a few shareholders miss out on our contributions program because they don't have their shares registered in their own names on the prescribed record date or because they fail to get the designation form back to us within the 60-day period allowed. Charlie and I regret this. But if replies are received late, we have to reject them because we can't make exceptions for some shareholders while refusing to make them for others.

To participate in future programs, you must own Class A shares that are registered in the name of the actual owner, not the nominee name of a broker, bank or depository. Shares not so registered on August 31, 1998, will be ineligible for the 1998 program. When you get the contributions form from us, return it promptly so that it does not get put aside or forgotten.

The Annual Meeting

Woodstock Weekend at Berkshire will be May 2-4 this year. The finale will be the annual meeting, which will begin at 9:30 a.m. on Monday, May 4. Last year we met at Aksarben Coliseum, and both our staff and the crowd were delighted with the venue. There was only one crisis: The night before the meeting, I lost my voice, thereby fulfilling Charlie's wildest fantasy. He was crushed when I showed up the next morning with my speech restored.

Last year about 7,500 attended the meeting. They represented all 50 states, as well as 16 countries, including Australia, Brazil, Israel, Saudi Arabia, Singapore and Greece. Taking into account several overflow rooms, we believe that we can handle more than 11,000 people, and that should put us in good shape this year even though our shareholder count has risen significantly. Parking is ample at Aksarben; acoustics are excellent; and seats are comfortable.

The doors will open at 7 a.m. on Monday and at 8:30 we will again feature the world premiere of a movie epic produced by Marc Hamburg, our CFO. The meeting will last until 3:30, with a short break at noon. This interval will permit the exhausted to leave unnoticed and allow time for the hardcore to lunch at Aksarben's concession stands. Charlie and I enjoy questions from owners, so bring up whatever is on your mind.

Berkshire products will again be *for sale* in the halls outside the meeting room. Last year—not that I pay attention to this sort of thing—we again set sales records, moving 2,500 pounds of See's candy, 1,350 pairs of Dexter shoes, $75,000 of World Books and related publications, and 888 sets of Quikut knives. We also took orders for a new line of apparel, featuring our Berkshire logo, and sold about 1,000 polo, sweat, and T-shirts. At this year's meeting, we will unveil our 1998 collection.

GEICO will again be on hand with a booth staffed by star associates from its regional offices. Find out whether you can save money by shifting your auto insurance to GEICO. About 40% of those who check us out learn that savings are possible. The proportion is not 100% because insurers differ in their underwriting judgments, with some favoring drivers who live in certain geographical areas and work at certain occupations more than we do. We believe, however, that we more frequently offer the low price than does any other national carrier selling insurance to all comers. In the GEICO informational material that accompanies this report, you will see that in 38 states we now offer a special discount of as much as 8% to our shareholders. We also have applications pending that would extend this discount to drivers in other states.

An attachment to the proxy material that is enclosed with this report explains how you can obtain the card you will need for admission to the meeting. We expect a large crowd, so get plane, hotel and car reservations promptly. American Express (800-799-6634) will be happy to help you with arrangements. As usual, we will have buses at the larger hotels that will take you to and from the meeting and also deliver you to Nebraska Furniture Mart, Borsheim's and the airport after its conclusion. You are likely, however, to find a car handy.

NFM's main store, located on a 75-acre site about a mile from Aksarben, is open from 10 a.m. to 9 p.m. on weekdays, 10 a.m. to 6 p.m. on Saturdays, and noon to 6 p.m. on Sundays. During the period from May 1 to May 5, shareholders who present NFM with the coupon that will accompany their meeting ticket will be entitled to a discount that is otherwise restricted to its employees.

Borsheim's normally is closed on Sunday but will be open for shareholders from 10 a.m. to 6 p.m. on May 3rd. Last year was our second-best shareholder's day, exceeded only by 1996's. I regard this slippage as an anomaly and hope that you will prove me right this year. Charlie will be available for autographs. He smiles, however, only if the paper he signs is a Borsheim's sales ticket. Shareholders who wish to visit on Saturday (10 a.m. to 5:30 p.m.) or on Monday (10 a.m.-8 p.m.) should be sure to identify themselves as Berkshire owners so that Susan Jacques, Borsheim's CEO, can make you especially welcome. Susan, I should add, had a fabulous year in 1997. As a manager, she is everything that an owner hopes for.

On Sunday afternoon we will also have a special treat for bridge players in the mall outside of Borsheim's. There, Bob Hamman—a legend of the game for more than three decades—will take on all comers. Join in and dazzle Bob with your skill.

My favorite steakhouse, Gorat's, opens one Sunday a year—for Berkshire shareholders on the night before the annual meeting. Last year the restaurant started serving at 4 p.m. and finished about 1:30 a.m, an endurance trial that was the result of taking 1,100 reservations vs. a seating capacity of 235. If you make a reservation and then can't attend, be sure to let Gorat's know promptly, since it goes to great effort to help us and we want to reciprocate. You can make reservations beginning on April 1st (*but not before*) by calling 402-551-3733. Last year I had to leave Gorat's a little early because of my voice problem, but this year I plan to leisurely savor every bite of my rare T-bone and double order of hash browns.

After this warmup, Charlie and I will head for the Dairy Queen on 114th, just south of Dodge. There are 12 great Dairy Queens in metropolitan Omaha, but the 114th Street location is the best suited to handle the large crowd that we expect. South of the property, there are hundreds of parking spaces on both sides of the street. Also, this Dairy Queen will extend its Sunday hours to 11 p.m. in order to accommodate our shareholders.

The 114th Street operation is now run by two sisters, Coni Birge and Deb Novotny, whose grandfather put up the building in 1962 at what was then the outer edge of the city. Their mother, Jan Noble, took over in 1972, and Coni and Deb continue as third generation owner-managers. Jan, Coni and Deb will all be on hand Sunday evening, and I hope that you meet them. Enjoy one of their hamburgers if you can't get into Gorat's. And then, around eight o'clock, join me in having a Dusty Sundae for dessert. This item is a personal specialty—the Dairy Queen will furnish you a copy of my recipe—and will be offered only on Shareholder Sunday.

The Omaha Royals and Albuquerque Dukes will play baseball on Saturday evening, May 2nd, at Rosenblatt Stadium. As usual, your Chairman, shamelessly exploiting his 25% ownership of the team, will take the mound. But this year you will see something new.

In past games, much to the bafflement of the crowd, I have shaken off the catcher's first call. He has consistently asked for my sweeping curve, and I have just as regularly resisted. Instead, I have served up a pathetic fast ball, which on my best day was clocked at eight miles per hour (with a following wind).

There's a story behind my unwillingness to throw the curve ball. As some of you may know, Candy Cummings invented the curve in 1867 and used it to great effect in the National Association, where he never won less than 28 games in a season. The pitch, however, drew immediate criticism from the very highest of authorities, namely Charles Elliott, then president of Harvard University, who declared, "I have heard that this year we at Harvard won the baseball championship because we have a pitcher who has a fine curve ball. I am further instructed that the purpose of the curve ball is to deliberately deceive the batter. Harvard is not in the business of teaching deception." (I'm not making this up.)

Ever since I learned of President Elliott's moral teachings on this subject, I have scrupulously refrained from using my curve, however devastating its effect might have been on hapless batters. Now, however, it is time for my karma to run over Elliott's dogma and for me to quit holding back. Visit the park on Saturday night and marvel at the majestic arc of my breaking ball.

Our proxy statement includes information about obtaining tickets to the game. We will also provide an information packet describing the local hot spots, including, of course, those 12 Dairy Queens.

Come to Omaha—the cradle of capitalism—in May and enjoy yourself.

Warren E. Buffett
February 27, 1998   Chairman of the Board

BERKSHIRE HATHAWAY INC.

To the Shareholders of Berkshire Hathaway Inc.:

Our gain in net worth during 1998 was $25.9 billion, which increased the per-share book value of both our Class A and Class B stock by 48.3%. Over the last 34 years (that is, since present management took over) per-share book value has grown from $19 to $37,801, a rate of 24.7% compounded annually.*

Normally, a gain of 48.3% would call for handsprings — but not this year. Remember Wagner, whose music has been described as better than it sounds? Well, Berkshire's progress in 1998 — though more than satisfactory — was not as good as it looks. That's because most of that 48.3% gain came from our issuing shares in acquisitions.

To explain: Our stock sells at a large premium over book value, which means that any issuing of shares we do — whether for cash or as consideration in a merger — instantly increases our per-share book-value figure, even though we've earned not a dime. What happens is that we get more per-share book value in such transactions than we give up. These transactions, however, do not deliver us any immediate gain in per-share *intrinsic value*, because in this respect what we give and what we get are roughly equal. And, as Charlie Munger, Berkshire's Vice Chairman and my partner, and I can't tell you too often (though you may feel that we try), it's the per-share gain in intrinsic value that counts rather than the per-share gain in book value. Though Berkshire's intrinsic value grew very substantially in 1998, the gain fell well short of the 48.3% recorded for book value. Nevertheless, intrinsic value still *far* exceeds book value. (For a more extensive discussion of these terms, and other investment and accounting concepts, please refer to our Owner's Manual, on pages 56-64, in which we set forth our owner-related business principles. Intrinsic value is discussed on pages 61 and 62.)

We entered 1999 with the best collection of businesses and managers in our history. The two companies we acquired in 1998, General Re and Executive Jet, are first-class in every way — more about both later — and the performance of our operating businesses last year exceeded my hopes. GEICO, once again, simply shot the lights out. On the minus side, several of the public companies in which we have major investments experienced significant operating shortfalls that neither they nor I anticipated early in the year. Consequently, our equity portfolio did not perform nearly as well as did the S&P 500. The problems of these companies are almost certainly temporary, and Charlie and I believe that their long-term prospects are excellent.

In our last three annual reports, we furnished you a table that we regard as central to estimating Berkshire's intrinsic value. In the updated version of that table, which follows, we trace our two key components of value, including General Re on a pro-forma basis as if we had owned it throughout the year. The first column lists our per-share ownership of investments (including cash and equivalents but excluding securities held in our financial products operation) and the second column shows our per-share earnings from Berkshire's operating businesses before taxes and purchase-accounting adjustments (discussed on pages 62 and 63), but after all interest and corporate expenses. The second column excludes *all* dividends, interest and capital gains that we realized from the investments presented in the first column. In effect, the columns show how Berkshire would look if it were split into two parts, with one entity holding our investments and the other operating all of our businesses and bearing all corporate costs.

---

*All figures used in this report apply to Berkshire's A shares, the successor to the only stock that the company had outstanding before 1996. The B shares have an economic interest equal to 1/30th that of the A.

Year	Investments Per Share	Pre-tax Earnings Per Share With All Income from Investments Excluded
1968	$ 53	$ 2.87
1978	465	12.85
1988	4,876	145.77
1998	47,647	474.45

Here are the growth rates of the two segments by decade:

Decade Ending	Investments Per Share	Pre-tax Earnings Per Share With All Income from Investments Excluded
1978	24.2%	16.2%
1988	26.5%	27.5%
1998	25.6%	12.5%
Annual Growth Rate, 1968-1998	25.4%	18.6%

During 1998, our investments increased by $9,604 per share, or 25.2%, but per-share operating earnings fell by 33.9%. General Re (included, as noted, on a pro-forma basis) explains both facts. This company has very large investments, and these greatly increased our per-share investment figure. But General Re also had an underwriting loss in 1998, and that hurt operating earnings. Had we not acquired General Re, per-share operating earnings would have shown a modest gain.

Though certain of our acquisitions and operating strategies may from time to time affect one column more than the other, we continually work to increase the figures in both. But one thing is certain: Our future rates of gain will fall far short of those achieved in the past. Berkshire's capital base is now simply too large to allow us to earn truly outsized returns. If you believe otherwise, you should consider a career in sales but avoid one in mathematics (bearing in mind that there are really only three kinds of people in the world: those who can count and those who can't).

Currently we are working to compound a net worth of $57.4 billion, the largest of any American corporation (though our figure will be eclipsed if the merger of Exxon and Mobil takes place). Of course, our lead in net worth does not mean that Berkshire outranks all other businesses in value: Market value is what counts for owners and General Electric and Microsoft, for example, have valuations more than three times Berkshire's. Net worth, though, measures the capital that managers must deploy, and at Berkshire that figure has indeed become huge.

Nonetheless, Charlie and I will do our best to increase intrinsic value in the future at an average rate of 15%, a result we consider to be at the very peak of possible outcomes. We may have years when we exceed 15%, but we will most certainly have other years when we fall far short of that — including years showing negative returns — and those will bring our average down. In the meantime, you should understand just what an average gain of 15% over the next five years implies: It means we will need to increase net worth by $58 billion. Earning this daunting 15% will require us to come up with big ideas: Popcorn stands just won't do. Today's markets are not friendly to our search for "elephants," but you can be sure that we will stay focused on the hunt.

Whatever the future holds, I make you one promise: I'll keep at least 99% of my net worth in Berkshire for as long as I am around. How long will that be? My model is the loyal Democrat in Fort Wayne who asked to be buried in Chicago so that he could stay active in the party. To that end, I've already selected a "power spot" at the office for my urn.

* * * * * * * * * * *

Our financial growth has been matched by employment growth: We now have 47,566 on our payroll, with the acquisitions of 1998 bringing 7,074 employees to us and internal growth adding another 2,500. To balance this gain of 9,500 in hands-on employees, we have enlarged the staff at world headquarters from 12 to 12.8. (The .8 doesn't refer to me or Charlie: We have a new person in accounting, working four days a week.) Despite this alarming trend toward corporate bloat, our after-tax overhead last year was about $3.5 million, or well under one basis point (.01 of 1%) of the value of the assets we manage.

Taxes

One beneficiary of our increased size has been the U.S. Treasury. The federal income taxes that Berkshire and General Re have paid, or will soon pay, in respect to 1998 earnings total $2.7 billion. That means we shouldered *all* of the U.S. Government's expenses for more than a half-day.

Follow that thought a little further: If only 625 other U.S. taxpayers had paid the Treasury as much as we and General Re did last year, no one else — neither corporations nor 270 million citizens — would have had to pay federal income taxes or any other kind of federal tax (for example, social security or estate taxes). Our shareholders can truly say that they "gave at the office."

Writing checks to the IRS that include strings of zeros does not bother Charlie or me. Berkshire as a corporation, and we as individuals, have prospered in America as we would have in no other country. Indeed, if we lived in some other part of the world and completely escaped taxes, I'm sure we would be worse off financially (and in many other ways as well). Overall, we feel extraordinarily lucky to have been dealt a hand in life that enables us to write large checks to the government rather than one requiring the government to regularly write checks to us — say, because we are disabled or unemployed.

Berkshire's tax situation is sometimes misunderstood. First, capital gains have no special attraction for us: A corporation pays a 35% rate on taxable income, whether it comes from capital gains or from ordinary operations. This means that Berkshire's tax on a long-term capital gain is fully 75% higher than what an individual would pay on an identical gain.

Some people harbor another misconception, believing that we can exclude 70% of all dividends we receive from our taxable income. Indeed, the 70% rate applies to most corporations and also applies to Berkshire in cases where we hold stocks in non-insurance subsidiaries. However, almost all of our equity investments are owned by our insurance companies, and in that case the exclusion is 59.5%. That still means a dollar of dividends is considerably more valuable to us than a dollar of ordinary income, but not to the degree often assumed.

* * * * * * * * * * * *

Berkshire truly went all out for the Treasury last year. In connection with the General Re merger, we wrote a $30 million check to the government to pay an SEC fee tied to the new shares created by the deal. We understand that this payment set an SEC record. Charlie and I are enormous admirers of what the Commission has accomplished for American investors. We would rather, however, have found another way to show our admiration.

GEICO (1-800-847-7536)

Combine a great idea with a great manager and you're certain to obtain a great result. That mix is alive and well at GEICO. The idea is low-cost auto insurance, made possible by direct-to-customer marketing, and the manager is Tony Nicely. Quite simply, there is no one in the business world who could run GEICO better than Tony does. His instincts are unerring, his energy is boundless, and his execution is flawless. While maintaining underwriting discipline, Tony is building an organization that is gaining market share at an accelerating rate.

This pace has been encouraged by our compensation policies. The direct writing of insurance — that is, without there being an agent or broker between the insurer and its policyholder — involves a substantial front-end investment. First-year business is therefore unprofitable in a major way. At GEICO, we do not wish this cost to deter our associates from the aggressive pursuit of new business — which, as it renews, will deliver significant profits — so we leave it out of our compensation formulas. What's included then? We base 50% of our associates' bonuses and profit sharing on the earnings of our "seasoned" book, meaning policies that have been with us for more than a year. The other 50% is tied to growth in policyholders — and here we have stepped on the gas.

In 1995, the year prior to its acquisition by Berkshire, GEICO spent $33 million on marketing and had 652 telephone counselors. Last year the company spent $143 million, and the counselor count grew to 2,162. The effects that these efforts had at the company are shown by the new business and in-force figures below:

Years	New Auto Policies*	Auto Policies In-Force*
1993	354,882	2,011,055
1994	396,217	2,147,549
1995	461,608	2,310,037
1996	617,669	2,543,699
1997	913,176	2,949,439
1998	1,317,761	3,562,644

* "Voluntary" only; excludes assigned risks and the like.

In 1999, we will again increase our marketing budget, spending at least $190 million. In fact, there is no limit to what Berkshire is willing to invest in GEICO's new-business activity, as long as we can concurrently build the infrastructure the company needs to properly serve its policyholders.

Because of the first-year costs, companies that are concerned about quarterly or annual earnings would shy from similar investments, no matter how intelligent these might be in terms of building long-term value. Our calculus is different: We simply measure whether we are creating more than a dollar of value per dollar spent — and if that calculation is favorable, the more dollars we spend the happier I am.

There is far more to GEICO's success, of course, than low prices and a torrent of advertising. The handling of claims must also be fair, fast and friendly — and ours is. Here's an impartial scorecard on how we shape up: In New York, our largest-volume state, the Insurance Department recently reported that GEICO's complaint ratio in 1997 was not only the lowest of the five largest auto insurers but was also less than half the average of the other four.

GEICO's 1998 profit margin of 6.7% was better than we had anticipated — and, indeed, better than we wished. Our results reflect an industry-wide phenomenon: In recent years, both the frequency of auto accidents and their severity have unexpectedly declined. We responded by reducing rates 3.3% in 1998, and we will reduce them still more in 1999. These moves will soon bring profit margins down — at the least to 4%, which is our target, and perhaps considerably lower. Whatever the case, we believe that our margins will continue to be much better than those of the industry.

With GEICO's growth and profitability both outstanding in 1998, so also were its profit-sharing and bonus payments. Indeed, the profit-sharing payment of $103 million or 32.3% of salary — which went to all 9,313 associates who had been with us for more than a year — may well have been the highest percentage payment at any large company in the country. (In addition, associates benefit from a company-funded pension plan.)

The 32.3% may turn out to be a high-water mark, given that the profitability component in our profit-sharing calculation is almost certain to come down in the future. The growth component, though, may well increase. Overall, we expect the two benchmarks together to dictate very significant profit-sharing payments for decades to come. For our associates, growth pays off in other ways as well: Last year we promoted 4,612 people.

Impressive as the GEICO figures are, we have far more to do. Our market share improved significantly in 1998 — but only from 3% to 3½%. For every policyholder we now have, there are another ten who should be giving us their business.

Some of you who are reading this may be in that category. About 40% of those who check our rates find that they can save money by doing business with us. The proportion is not 100% because insurers differ in their underwriting judgements, with some giving more credit than we do to drivers who live in certain geographical areas or work at certain occupations. We believe, however, that we more frequently offer the low price than does any other national carrier selling insurance to all comers. Furthermore, in 40 states we can offer a special discount — usually 8% — to our shareholders. So give us a call and check us out.

* * * * * * * * * * * *

You may think that one commercial in this section is enough. But I have another to present, this one directed at managers of publicly-owned companies.

At Berkshire we feel that telling outstanding CEOs, such as Tony, how to run their companies would be the height of foolishness. Most of our managers wouldn't work for us if they got a lot of backseat driving. (Generally, they don't have to work for *anyone*, since 75% or so are independently wealthy.) Besides, they are the Mark McGwires of the business world and need no advice from us as to how to hold the bat or when to swing.

Nevertheless, Berkshire's ownership may make even the best of managers more effective. First, we eliminate all of the ritualistic and nonproductive activities that normally go with the job of CEO. Our managers are totally in charge of their personal schedules. Second, we give each a simple mission: Just run your business as if: 1) you own 100% of it; 2) it is the only asset in the world that you and your family have or will ever have; and 3) you can't sell or merge it for at least a century. As a corollary, we tell them they should not let any of their decisions be affected even slightly by accounting considerations. We want our managers to think about what counts, not how it will be counted.

Very few CEOs of public companies operate under a similar mandate, mainly because they have owners who focus on short-term prospects and reported earnings. Berkshire, however, has a shareholder base — which it will have for decades to come — that has the longest investment horizon to be found in the public-company universe. Indeed, a majority of our shares are held by investors who expect to die still holding them. We can therefore ask our CEOs to manage for maximum long-term value, rather than for next quarter's earnings. We certainly don't ignore the current results of our businesses — in most cases, they are of great importance — but we *never* want them to be achieved at the expense of our building ever-greater competitive strengths.

I believe the GEICO story demonstrates the benefits of Berkshire's approach. Charlie and I haven't taught Tony a thing — and never will — but we *have* created an environment that allows him to apply all of his talents to what's important. He does not have to devote his time or energy to board meetings, press interviews, presentations by investment bankers or talks with financial analysts. Furthermore, he need never spend a moment thinking about financing, credit ratings or "Street" expectations for earnings per share. Because of our ownership structure, he also knows that this operational framework will endure for decades to come. In this environment of freedom, both Tony and his company can convert their almost limitless potential into matching achievements.

If you are running a large, profitable business that will thrive in a GEICO-like environment, check our acquisition criteria on page 21 and give me a call. I promise a fast answer and will mention your inquiry to no one except Charlie.

Executive Jet Aviation (1-800-848-6436)

To understand the huge potential at Executive Jet Aviation (EJA), you need some understanding of its business, which is selling fractional shares of jets and operating the fleet for its many owners. Rich Santulli, CEO of EJA, created the fractional ownership industry in 1986, by visualizing an important new way of using planes. Then he combined guts and talent to turn his idea into a major business.

In a fractional ownership plan, you purchase a portion — say $^1/_8$th — of any of a wide variety of jets that EJA offers. That purchase entitles you to 100 hours of flying time annually. ("Dead-head" hours don't count against your allotment, and you are also allowed to average your hours over five years.) In addition, you pay both a monthly management fee and a fee for hours actually flown.

Then, on a few hours notice, EJA makes your plane, or another at least as good, available to you at your choice of the 5500 airports in the U.S. In effect, calling up your plane is like phoning for a taxi.

I first heard about the NetJets® program, as it is called, about four years ago from Frank Rooney, our manager at H.H. Brown. Frank had used and been delighted with the service and suggested that I meet Rich to investigate signing up for my family's use. It took Rich about 15 minutes to sell me a quarter (200 hours annually) of a Hawker 1000. Since then, my family has learned firsthand — through flying 900 hours on 300 trips — what a friendly, efficient, and safe operation EJA runs. Quite simply, they love this service. In fact, they quickly grew so enthusiastic that I did a testimonial ad for EJA long before I knew there was any possibility of our purchasing the business. I did, however, ask Rich to give me a call if he ever got interested in selling. Luckily, he phoned me last May, and we quickly made a $725 million deal, paying equal amounts of cash and stock.

EJA, which is by far the largest operator in its industry, has more than 1,000 customers and 163 aircraft (including 23 "core" aircraft that are owned or leased by EJA itself, so that it can make sure that service is first-class even during the times when demand is heaviest). Safety, of course, is the paramount issue in any flight operation, and Rich's pilots — now numbering about 650 — receive extensive training at least twice a year from FlightSafety International, another Berkshire subsidiary and the world leader in pilot training. The bottom line on our pilots: I've sold the Berkshire plane and will now do all of my business flying, as well as my personal flying, with NetJets' crews.

Being the leader in this industry is a major advantage for all concerned. Our customers gain because we have an armada of planes positioned throughout the country at all times, a blanketing that allows us to provide unmatched service. Meanwhile, we gain from the blanketing because it reduces dead-head costs. Another compelling attraction for our clients is that we offer products from Boeing, Gulfstream, Falcon, Cessna, and Raytheon, whereas our two competitors are owned by manufacturers that offer only their own planes. In effect, NetJets is like a physician who can recommend whatever medicine best fits the needs of each patient; our competitors, in contrast, are producers of a "house" brand that they must prescribe for one and all.

In many cases our clients, both corporate and individual, own fractions of several different planes and can therefore match specific planes to specific missions. For example, a client might own $1/16$th of three different jets (each giving it 50 hours of flying time), which in total give it a virtual fleet, obtained for a small fraction of the cost of a single plane.

Significantly, it is not only small businesses that can benefit from fractional ownership. Already, some of America's largest companies use NetJets as a supplement to their own fleet. This saves them big money in both meeting peak requirements and in flying missions that would require their wholly-owned planes to log a disproportionate amount of dead-head hours.

When a plane is slated for personal use, the clinching argument is that either the client signs up now or his children likely will later. That's an equation I explained to my wonderful Aunt Alice 40 years ago when she asked me whether she could afford a fur coat. My reply settled the issue: "Alice, *you* aren't buying it; your heirs are."

EJA's growth has been explosive: In 1997, it accounted for 31% of all corporate jets ordered in the world. Nonetheless, Rich and I believe that the potential of fractional ownership has barely been scratched. If many thousands of owners find it sensible to own 100% of a plane — which must be used 350-400 hours annually if it's to make economic sense — there must be a large multiple of that number for whom fractional ownership works.

In addition to being a terrific executive, Rich is fun. Like most of our managers, he has no economic need whatsoever to work. Rich spends his time at EJA because it's his baby — and he wants to see how far he can take it. We both already know the answer, both literally and figuratively: to the ends of the earth.

* * * * * * * * * * * *

And now a small hint to Berkshire directors: Last year I spent more than nine times my salary at Borsheim's and EJA. Just think how Berkshire's business would boom if you'd only spring for a raise.

General Re

On December 21, we completed our $22 billion acquisition of General Re Corp. In addition to owning 100% of General Reinsurance Corporation, the largest U.S. property-casualty reinsurer, the company also owns (including stock it has an arrangement to buy) 82% of the oldest reinsurance company in the world, Cologne Re. The two companies together reinsure all lines of insurance and operate in 124 countries.

For many decades, General Re's name has stood for quality, integrity and professionalism in reinsurance — and under Ron Ferguson's leadership, this reputation has been burnished still more. Berkshire can add absolutely nothing to the skills of General Re's and Cologne Re's managers. On the contrary, there is a lot that they can teach us.

Nevertheless, we believe that Berkshire's ownership will benefit General Re in important ways and that its earnings a decade from now will materially exceed those that would have been attainable absent the merger. We base this optimism on the fact that we can offer General Re's management a freedom to operate in whatever manner will best allow the company to exploit its strengths.

Let's look for a moment at the reinsurance business to understand why General Re could not on its own do what it can under Berkshire. Most of the demand for reinsurance comes from primary insurers who want to escape the wide swings in earnings that result from large and unusual losses. In effect, a reinsurer gets paid for absorbing the volatility that the client insurer wants to shed.

Ironically, though, a publicly-held reinsurer gets graded by both its owners and those who evaluate its credit on the smoothness of its own results. Wide swings in earnings hurt both credit ratings and p/e ratios, even when the business that produces such swings has an expectancy of satisfactory profits over time. This market reality sometimes causes a reinsurer to make costly moves, among them laying off a significant portion of the business it writes (in transactions that are called "retrocessions") or rejecting good business simply because it threatens to bring on too much volatility.

Berkshire, in contrast, happily accepts volatility, just as long as it carries with it the expectation of increased profits over time. Furthermore, we are a Fort Knox of capital, and that means volatile earnings can't impair our premier credit ratings. Thus we have the perfect structure for writing — and *retaining* — reinsurance in virtually any amount. In fact, we've used this strength over the past decade to build a powerful super-cat business.

What General Re gives us, however, is the distribution force, technical facilities and management that will allow us to employ our structural strength in every facet of the industry. In particular, General Re and Cologne Re can now accelerate their push into international markets, where the preponderance of industry growth will almost certainly occur. As the merger proxy statement spelled out, Berkshire also brings tax and investment benefits to General Re. But the most compelling reason for the merger is simply that General Re's outstanding management can now do what it does best, unfettered by the constraints that have limited its growth.

Berkshire is assuming responsibility for General Re's investment portfolio, though not for Cologne Re's. We will not, however, be involved in General Re's underwriting. We will simply ask the company to exercise the discipline of the past while increasing the proportion of its business that is retained, expanding its product line, and widening its geographical coverage — making these moves in recognition of Berkshire's financial strength and tolerance for wide swings in earnings. As we've long said, we prefer a lumpy 15% return to a smooth 12%.

Over time, Ron and his team will maximize General Re's new potential. He and I have known each other for many years, and each of our companies has initiated significant business that it has reinsured with the other. Indeed, General Re played a key role in the resuscitation of GEICO from its near-death status in 1976.

Both Ron and Rich Santulli plan to be at the annual meeting, and I hope you get a chance to say hello to them.

The Economics of Property-Casualty Insurance

With the acquisition of General Re — and with GEICO's business mushrooming — it becomes more important than ever that you understand how to evaluate an insurance company. The key determinants are: (1) the amount of float that the business generates; (2) its cost; and (3) most important of all, the long-term outlook for both of these factors.

To begin with, float is money we hold but don't own. In an insurance operation, float arises because premiums are received before losses are paid, an interval that sometimes extends over many years. During that time, the insurer invests the money. Typically, this pleasant activity carries with it a downside: The premiums that an insurer takes in usually do not cover the losses and expenses it eventually must pay. That leaves it running an "underwriting loss," which is the cost of float. An insurance business has value if its cost of float over time is less than the cost the company would otherwise incur to obtain funds. But the business is a lemon if its cost of float is higher than market rates for money.

A caution is appropriate here: Because loss costs must be estimated, insurers have enormous latitude in figuring their underwriting results, and that makes it very difficult for investors to calculate a company's true cost of float. Errors of estimation, usually innocent but sometimes not, can be huge. The consequences of these miscalculations flow directly into earnings. An experienced observer can usually detect large-scale errors in reserving, but the general public can typically do no more than accept what's presented, and at times I have been amazed by the numbers that big-name auditors have implicitly blessed. As for Berkshire, Charlie and I attempt to be conservative in presenting its underwriting results to you, because we have found that virtually all surprises in insurance are unpleasant ones.

The table that follows shows the float generated by Berkshire's insurance operations since we entered the business 32 years ago. The data are for every fifth year and also the last, which includes General Re's huge float. For the table we have calculated our float — which we generate in large amounts relative to our premium volume — by adding net loss reserves, loss adjustment reserves, funds held under reinsurance assumed and unearned premium reserves, and then subtracting agents balances, prepaid acquisition costs, prepaid taxes and deferred charges applicable to assumed reinsurance. (Got that?)

Year	Average Float (in $ millions)
1967	17
1972	70
1977	139
1982	221
1987	1,267
1992	2,290
1997	7,093
1998	22,762 (yearend)

Impressive as the growth in our float has been — 25.4% compounded annually — what really counts is the cost of this item. If that becomes too high, growth in float becomes a curse rather than a blessing.

At Berkshire, the news is all good: Our average cost over the 32 years has been well under zero. In aggregate, we have posted a substantial underwriting profit, which means that we have been paid for holding a large and growing amount of money. This is the best of all worlds. Indeed, though our net float is recorded on our balance sheet as a liability, it has had more economic value to us than an equal amount of net worth would have had. As long as we can continue to achieve an underwriting profit, float will continue to outrank net worth in value.

During the next few years, Berkshire's growth in float may well be modest. The reinsurance market is soft, and in this business, relationships change slowly. Therefore, General Re's float — ²/₃rds of our total — is unlikely to increase significantly in the near term. We do expect, however, that our cost of float will remain very attractive compared to that of other insurers.

Sources of Reported Earnings

The table that follows shows the main sources of Berkshire's reported earnings. In this presentation, purchase-accounting adjustments are not assigned to the specific businesses to which they apply, but are instead aggregated and shown separately. This procedure lets you view the earnings of our businesses as they would have been reported had we not purchased them. For the reasons discussed on pages 62 and 63, this form of presentation seems to us to be more useful to investors and managers than one utilizing generally-accepted accounting principles (GAAP), which require purchase-premiums to be charged off business-by-business. The total earnings we show in the table are, of course, identical to the GAAP total in our audited financial statements.

	Pre-Tax Earnings (in millions)		Berkshire's Share of Net Earnings (after taxes and minority interests)	
	1998	1997	1998	1997
Operating Earnings:				
Insurance Group:				
Underwriting — Super-Cat	$154	$283	$100	$183
Underwriting — Other Reinsurance	(175)	(155)	(114)	(100)
Underwriting — GEICO	269	281	175	181
Underwriting — Other Primary	17	53	10	34
Net Investment Income	974	882	731	704
Buffalo News	53	56	32	33
Finance and Financial Products Businesses	205	28	133	18
Flight Services	181 [1]	140 [2]	110 [1]	84 [2]
Home Furnishings	72	57	41	32
International Dairy Queen	58	—	35	—
Jewelry	39	32	23	18
Scott Fetzer (excluding finance operation)	137	119	85	77
See's Candies	62	59	40	35
Shoe Group	33	49	23	32
General Re	26 [3]	—	16 [3]	—
Purchase-Accounting Adjustments	(123)	(101)	(118)	(94)
Interest Expense [4]	(100)	(107)	(63)	(67)
Shareholder-Designated Contributions	(17)	(15)	(11)	(10)
Other	34	60	29	37
Operating Earnings	1,899	1,721	1,277	1,197
Capital Gains from Investments	2,415	1,106	1,553	704
Total Earnings - All Entities	$4,314	$2,827	$2,830	$1,901

[1] Includes Executive Jet from August 7, 1998 .   [3] From date of acquisition, December 21, 1998.
[2] Includes Star Furniture from July 1, 1997.   [4] Excludes interest expense of Finance Businesses.

You can be proud of our operating managers. They almost invariably deliver earnings that are at the very top of what conditions in their industries allow, meanwhile fortifying their businesses' long-term competitive strengths. In aggregate, they have created many billions of dollars of value for you.

An example: In my 1994 letter, I reported on Ralph Schey's extraordinary performance at Scott Fetzer. Little did I realize that he was just warming up. Last year Scott Fetzer, operating with no leverage (except for a conservative level of debt in its finance subsidiary), earned a record $96.5 million after-tax on its $112 million net worth.

Today, Berkshire has an unusually large number of individuals, such as Ralph, who are truly legends in their industries. Many of these joined us when we purchased their companies, but in recent years we have also identified a number of strong managers internally. We further expanded our corps of all-stars in an important way when we acquired General Re and EJA.

Charlie and I have the easy jobs at Berkshire: We do very little except allocate capital. And, even then, we are not all that energetic. We have one excuse, though: In allocating capital, activity does not correlate with achievement. Indeed, in the fields of investments and acquisitions, frenetic behavior is often counterproductive. Therefore, Charlie and I mainly just wait for the phone to ring.

Our managers, however, work very hard — and it shows. Naturally, they want to be paid fairly for their efforts, but pay alone can't explain their extraordinary accomplishments. Instead, each is primarily motivated by a vision of just how far his or her business can go — and by a desire to be the one who gets it there. Charlie and I thank them on your behalf and ours.

* * * * * * * * * * * *

Additional information about our various businesses is given on pages 39-53, where you will also find our segment earnings reported on a GAAP basis. In addition, on pages 65-71, we have rearranged Berkshire's financial data into four segments on a non-GAAP basis, a presentation that corresponds to the way Charlie and I think about the company.

Normally, we follow this section with one on "Look-Through" Earnings. Because the General Re acquisition occurred near yearend, though, neither a historical nor a pro-forma calculation of a 1998 number seems relevant. We will resume the look-through calculation in next year's report.

Investments

Below we present our common stock investments. Those with a market value of more than $750 million are itemized.

Shares	Company	12/31/98 Cost*	Market
		(dollars in millions)	
50,536,900	American Express Company	$1,470	$ 5,180
200,000,000	The Coca-Cola Company	1,299	13,400
51,202,242	The Walt Disney Company	281	1,536
60,298,000	Freddie Mac	308	3,885
96,000,000	The Gillette Company	600	4,590
1,727,765	The Washington Post Company	11	999
63,595,180	Wells Fargo & Company	392	2,540
	Others	2,683	5,135
	Total Common Stocks	$ 7,044	$ 37,265

* Represents tax-basis cost which, in aggregate, is $1.5 billion less than GAAP cost.

During the year, we slightly increased our holdings in American Express, one of our three largest commitments, and left the other two unchanged. However, we trimmed or substantially cut many of our smaller positions. Here, I need to make a confession (ugh): The portfolio actions I took in 1998 actually *decreased* our gain for the year. In particular, my decision to sell McDonald's was a very big mistake. Overall, you would have been better off last year if I had regularly snuck off to the movies during market hours.

At yearend, we held more than $15 billion in cash equivalents (including high-grade securities due in less than one year). Cash never makes us happy. But it's better to have the money burning a hole in Berkshire's pocket than resting comfortably in someone else's. Charlie and I will continue our search for large equity investments or, better yet, a really major business acquisition that would absorb our liquid assets. Currently, however, we see nothing on the horizon.

Once we knew that the General Re merger would definitely take place, we asked the company to dispose of the equities that it held. (As mentioned earlier, we do not manage the Cologne Re portfolio, which includes many equities.) General Re subsequently eliminated its positions in about 250 common stocks, incurring $935 million of taxes in the process. This "clean sweep" approach reflects a basic principle that Charlie and I employ in business and investing: We don't back into decisions.

Last year I deviated from my standard practice of not disclosing our investments (other than those we are legally required to report) and told you about three unconventional investments we had made. There were several reasons behind that disclosure. First, questions about our silver position that we had received from regulatory authorities led us to believe that they wished us to publicly acknowledge this investment. Second, our holdings of zero-coupon bonds were so large that we wanted our owners to know of this investment's potential impact on Berkshire's net worth. Third, we simply wanted to alert you to the fact that we sometimes *do* make unconventional commitments.

Normally, however, as discussed in the Owner's Manual on page 61, we see no advantage in talking about specific investment actions. Therefore — unless we again take a position that is particularly large — we will not post you as to what we are doing in respect to any specific holding of an unconventional sort. We can report, however, that we have eliminated certain of the positions discussed last year and added certain others.

Our never-comment-even-if-untrue policy in regard to investments may disappoint "piggybackers" but will benefit owners: Your Berkshire shares would be worth less if we discussed what we are doing. Incidentally, we should warn you that media speculation about our investment moves continues in most cases to be incorrect. People who rely on such commentary do so at their own peril.

Accounting — Part 1

Our General Re acquisition put a spotlight on an egregious flaw in accounting procedure. Sharp-eyed shareholders reading our proxy statement probably noticed an unusual item on page 60. In the pro-forma statement of income — which detailed how the combined 1997 earnings of the two entities would have been affected by the merger — there was an item stating that compensation expense would have been increased by $63 million.

This item, we hasten to add, does not signal that either Charlie or I have experienced a major personality change. (He still travels coach and quotes Ben Franklin.) Nor does it indicate any shortcoming in General Re's accounting practices, which have followed GAAP to the letter. Instead, the pro-forma adjustment came about because we are replacing General Re's longstanding stock option plan with a cash plan that ties the incentive compensation of General Re managers to their operating achievements. Formerly what counted for these managers was General Re's stock price; now their payoff will come from the business performance they deliver.

The new plan and the terminated option arrangement have matching economics, which means that the rewards they deliver to employees should, for a given level of performance, be the same. But what these people could have formerly anticipated earning from new option grants will now be paid in cash. (Options granted in past years remain outstanding.)

Though the two plans are an economic wash, the cash plan we are putting in will produce a vastly different accounting result. This Alice-in-Wonderland outcome occurs because existing accounting principles ignore the cost of stock options when earnings are being calculated, even though options are a huge and increasing expense at a great many corporations. In effect, accounting principles offer management a choice: Pay employees in one form and count the cost, or pay them in another form and ignore the cost. Small wonder then that the use of options has mushroomed. This lop-sided choice has a big downside for owners, however: Though options, if properly structured, can be an appropriate, *and even ideal*, way to compensate and motivate top managers, they are more often wildly capricious in their distribution of rewards, inefficient as motivators, and inordinately expensive for shareholders.

Whatever the merits of options may be, their accounting treatment is outrageous. Think for a moment of that $190 million we are going to spend for advertising at GEICO this year. Suppose that instead of paying cash for our ads, we paid the media in ten-year, at-the-market Berkshire options. Would anyone then care to argue that Berkshire had not borne a cost for advertising, or should not be charged this cost on its books?

Perhaps Bishop Berkeley — you may remember him as the philosopher who mused about trees falling in a forest when no one was around — would believe that an expense unseen by an accountant does not exist. Charlie and I, however, have trouble being philosophical about unrecorded costs. When we consider investing in an option-issuing company, we make an appropriate downward adjustment to reported earnings, simply subtracting an amount equal to what the company could have realized by publicly selling options of like quantity and structure. Similarly, if we contemplate an acquisition, we include in our evaluation the cost of replacing any option plan. Then, if we make a deal, we promptly take that cost out of hiding.

Readers who disagree with me about options will by this time be mentally quarreling with my equating the cost of options issued to employees with those that might theoretically be sold and traded publicly. It is true, to state one of these arguments, that employee options are sometimes forfeited — that lessens the damage done to shareholders — whereas publicly-offered options would not be. It is true, also, that companies receive a tax deduction when employee options are exercised; publicly-traded options deliver no such benefit. But there's an offset to these points: Options issued to employees are often repriced, a transformation that makes them much more costly than the public variety.

It's sometimes argued that a non-transferable option given to an employee is less valuable to him than would be a publicly-traded option that he could freely sell. That fact, however, does not reduce the *cost* of the non-transferable option: Giving an employee a company car that can only be used for certain purposes diminishes its value to the employee, but does not in the least diminish its cost to the employer.

The earning revisions that Charlie and I have made for options in recent years have frequently cut the reported per-share figures by 5%, with 10% not all that uncommon. On occasion, the downward adjustment has been so great that it has affected our portfolio decisions, causing us either to make a sale or to pass on a stock purchase we might otherwise have made.

A few years ago we asked three questions in these pages to which we have not yet received an answer: "If options aren't a form of compensation, what are they? If compensation isn't an expense, what is it? And, if expenses shouldn't go into the calculation of earnings, where in the world should they go?"

Accounting — Part 2

The role that managements have played in stock-option accounting has hardly been benign: A distressing number of both CEOs and auditors have in recent years bitterly fought FASB's attempts to replace option fiction with truth and virtually none have spoken out in support of FASB. Its opponents even enlisted Congress in the fight, pushing the case that inflated figures were in the national interest.

Still, I believe that the behavior of managements has been even worse when it comes to restructurings and merger accounting. Here, many managements purposefully work at manipulating numbers and deceiving investors. And, as Michael Kinsley has said about Washington: "The scandal isn't in what's done that's *illegal* but rather in what's *legal*."

It was once relatively easy to tell the good guys in accounting from the bad: The late 1960's, for example, brought on an orgy of what one charlatan dubbed "bold, imaginative accounting" (the practice of which, incidentally, made him loved for a time by Wall Street because he never missed expectations). But most investors of that period knew who was playing games. And, to their credit, virtually all of America's most-admired companies then shunned deception.

In recent years, probity has eroded. Many major corporations still play things straight, but a significant and growing number of otherwise high-grade managers — CEOs you would be happy to have as spouses for your children or as trustees under your will — have come to the view that it's okay to manipulate earnings to satisfy what they believe are Wall Street's desires. Indeed, many CEOs think this kind of manipulation is not only okay, but actually their *duty*.

These managers start with the assumption, all too common, that their job at all times is to encourage the highest stock price possible (a premise with which we adamantly disagree). To pump the price, they strive, admirably, for operational excellence. But when operations don't produce the result hoped for, these CEOs resort to unadmirable accounting stratagems. These either manufacture the desired "earnings" or set the stage for them in the future.

Rationalizing this behavior, these managers often say that their shareholders will be hurt if their currency for doing deals — that is, their stock — is not fully-priced, and they also argue that in using accounting shenanigans to get the figures they want, they are only doing what everybody else does. Once such an everybody's-doing-it attitude takes hold, ethical misgivings vanish. Call this behavior Son of Gresham: Bad accounting drives out good.

The distortion *du jour* is the "restructuring charge," an accounting entry that can, of course, be legitimate but that too often is a device for manipulating earnings. In this bit of legerdemain, a large chunk of costs that should properly be attributed to a number of years is dumped into a single quarter, typically one already fated to disappoint investors. In some cases, the purpose of the charge is to clean up earnings misrepresentations of the past, and in others it is to prepare the ground for future misrepresentations. In either case, the size and timing of these charges is dictated by the cynical proposition that Wall Street will not mind if earnings fall short by $5 per share in a given quarter, just as long as this deficiency ensures that quarterly earnings in the future will consistently exceed expectations by five cents per share.

This dump-everything-into-one-quarter behavior suggests a corresponding "bold, imaginative" approach to — golf scores. In his first round of the season, a golfer should ignore his actual performance and simply fill his card with atrocious numbers — double, triple, quadruple bogeys — and then turn in a score of, say, 140. Having established this "reserve," he should go to the golf shop and tell his pro that he wishes to "restructure" his imperfect swing. Next, as he takes his new swing onto the course, he should count his good holes, but not the bad ones. These remnants from his old swing should be charged instead to the reserve established earlier. At the end of five rounds, then, his record will be 140, 80, 80, 80, 80 rather than 91, 94, 89, 94, 92. On Wall Street, they will ignore the 140 — which, after all, came from a "discontinued" swing — and will classify our hero as an 80 shooter (and one who *never* disappoints).

For those who prefer to cheat up front, there would be a variant of this strategy. The golfer, playing alone with a cooperative caddy-auditor, should defer the recording of bad holes, take four 80s, accept the plaudits he gets for such athleticism and consistency, and then turn in a fifth card carrying a 140 score. After rectifying his earlier scorekeeping sins with this "big bath," he may mumble a few apologies but will refrain from returning the sums he has previously collected from comparing scorecards in the clubhouse. (The caddy, need we add, will have acquired a loyal patron.)

Unfortunately, CEOs who use variations of these scoring schemes in real life tend to become addicted to the games they're playing — after all, it's easier to fiddle with the scorecard than to spend hours on the practice tee — and never muster the will to give them up. Their behavior brings to mind Voltaire's comment on sexual experimentation: "Once a philosopher, twice a pervert."

In the acquisition arena, restructuring has been raised to an art form: Managements now frequently use mergers to dishonestly rearrange the value of assets and liabilities in ways that will allow them to both smooth and swell future earnings. Indeed, at deal time, major auditing firms sometimes point out the possibilities for a little accounting magic (or for a lot). Getting this push from the pulpit, first-class people will frequently stoop to third-class tactics. CEOs understandably do not find it easy to reject auditor-blessed strategies that lead to increased future "earnings."

An example from the property-casualty insurance industry will illuminate the possibilities. When a p-c company is acquired, the buyer sometimes simultaneously increases its loss reserves, often substantially. This boost may merely reflect the previous inadequacy of reserves — though it is uncanny how often an actuarial "revelation" of this kind coincides with the inking of a deal. In any case, the move sets up the possibility of 'earnings' flowing into income at some later date, as reserves are released.

Berkshire has kept entirely clear of these practices: If we are to disappoint you, we would rather it be with our earnings than with our accounting. In all of our acquisitions, we have left the loss reserve figures exactly as we found them. After all, we have consistently joined with insurance managers knowledgeable about their business and honest in their financial reporting. When deals occur in which liabilities are increased immediately and substantially, simple logic says that at least one of those virtues must have been lacking — or, alternatively, that the acquirer is laying the groundwork for future infusions of "earnings."

Here's a true story that illustrates an all-too-common view in corporate America. The CEOs of two large banks, one of them a man who'd made many acquisitions, were involved not long ago in a friendly merger discussion (which in the end didn't produce a deal). The veteran acquirer was expounding on the merits of the possible combination, only to be skeptically interrupted by the other CEO: "But won't that mean a huge charge," he asked, "perhaps as much as $1 billion?" The "sophisticate" wasted no words: "We'll make it bigger than that — that's why we're doing the deal."

A preliminary tally by R. G. Associates, of Baltimore, of special charges taken or announced during 1998 — that is, charges for restructuring, in-process R&D, merger-related items, and write-downs — identified no less than 1,369 of these, totaling $72.1 billion. That is a staggering amount as evidenced by this bit of perspective: The 1997 earnings of the 500 companies in Fortune's famous list totaled $324 billion.

Clearly the attitude of disrespect that many executives have today for accurate reporting is a business disgrace. And auditors, as we have already suggested, have done little on the positive side. Though auditors *should* regard the investing public as their client, they tend to kowtow instead to the managers who choose them and dole out their pay. ("Whose bread I eat, his song I sing.")

A big piece of news, however, is that the SEC, led by its chairman, Arthur Levitt, seems determined to get corporate America to clean up its act. In a landmark speech last September, Levitt called for an end to "earnings management." He correctly observed, "Too many corporate managers, auditors and analysts are participants in a game of nods and winks." And then he laid on a real indictment: "Managing may be giving way to manipulating; integrity may be losing out to illusion."

I urge you to read the Chairman's speech (you can find it on the Internet at www.sec.gov) and to support him in his efforts to get corporate America to deliver a straight story to its owners. Levitt's job will be Herculean, but it is hard to think of another more important for him to take on.

Reports to Shareholders

Berkshire's Internet site, www.berkshirehathaway.com, has become a prime source for information about the company. While we continue to send an annual report to all shareholders, we now send quarterlies only to those who request them, letting others read these at our site. In this report, we again enclose a card that can be returned by those wanting to get printed quarterlies in 1999.

Charlie and I have two simple goals in reporting: 1) We want to give you the information that we would wish you to give us if our positions were reversed; and 2) We want to make Berkshire's information accessible to all of you simultaneously. Our ability to reach that second goal is greatly helped by the Internet.

In another portion of his September speech, Arthur Levitt deplored what he called "selective disclosure." His remarks were timely: Today, many companies matter-of-factly favor Wall Street analysts and institutional investors in a variety of ways that often skirt or cross the line of unfairness. These practices leave the great bulk of shareholders at a distinct disadvantage to a favored class.

At Berkshire, we regard the holder of one share of B stock as the equal of our large institutional investors. We, of course, warmly welcome institutions as owners and have gained a number of them through the General Re merger. We hope also that these new holders find that our owner's manual and annual reports offer them more insights and information about Berkshire than they garner about other companies from the investor relations departments that these corporations typically maintain. But if it is "earnings guidance" or the like that shareholders or analysts seek, we will simply guide them to our public documents.

This year we plan to post our quarterly reports on the Internet after the close of the market on May 14, August 13, and November 12. We also expect to put the 1999 annual report on our website on Saturday, March 11, 2000, and to mail the print version at roughly the same time.

We promptly post press releases on our website. This means that you do not need to rely on the versions of these reported by the media but can instead read the full text on your computer.

Despite the pathetic technical skills of your Chairman, I'm delighted to report that GEICO, Borsheim's, See's, and The Buffalo News are now doing substantial business via the Internet. We've also recently begun to offer annuity products on our website. This business was developed by Ajit Jain, who over the last decade has personally accounted for a significant portion of Berkshire's operating earnings. While Charlie and I sleep, Ajit keeps thinking of new ways to add value to Berkshire.

Shareholder-Designated Contributions

About 97.5% of all eligible shares participated in Berkshire's 1998 shareholder-designated contributions program, with contributions totaling $16.9 million. A full description of the program appears on pages 54-55.

Cumulatively, over the 18 years of the program, Berkshire has made contributions of $130 million pursuant to the instructions of our shareholders. The rest of Berkshire's giving is done by our subsidiaries, which stick to the philanthropic patterns that prevailed before they were acquired (except that their former owners themselves take on the responsibility for their personal charities). In aggregate, our subsidiaries made contributions of $12.5 million in 1998, including in-kind donations of $2.0 million.

To participate in future programs, you must own Class A shares that are registered in the name of the actual owner, not the nominee name of a broker, bank or depository. Shares not so registered on August 31, 1999, will be ineligible for the 1999 program. When you get the contributions form from us, return it promptly so that it does not get put aside or forgotten. Designations received after the due date will not be honored.

The Annual Meeting

This year's Woodstock for Capitalists will be held May 1-3, and we may face a problem. Last year more than 10,000 people attended our annual meeting, and our shareholders list has since doubled. So we don't quite know what attendance to expect this year. To be safe, we have booked both Aksarben Coliseum, which holds about 14,000 and the Holiday Convention Centre, which can seat an additional 5,000. Because we know that our Omaha shareholders will want to be good hosts to the out-of-towners (many of them come from outside the U.S), we plan to give those visitors first crack at the Aksarben tickets and to subsequently allocate these to greater Omaha residents on a first-come, first-served basis. If we exhaust the Aksarben tickets, we will begin distributing Holiday tickets to Omaha shareholders.

If we end up using both locations, Charlie and I will split our pre-meeting time between the two. Additionally, we will have exhibits and also the Berkshire movie, large television screens and microphones at both sites. When we break for lunch, many attendees will leave Aksarben, which means that those at Holiday can, if they wish, make the five-minute trip to Aksarben and finish out the day there. Buses will be available to transport people who don't have cars.

The doors will open at both locations at 7 a.m. on Monday, and at 8:30 we will premier the 1999 Berkshire movie epic, produced by Marc Hamburg, our CFO. The meeting will last from 9:30 until 3:30, interrupted only by the short lunch break.

An attachment to the proxy material that is enclosed with this report explains how you can obtain the badge you will need for admission to the meeting and other events. As for plane, hotel and car reservations, we have again signed up American Express (800-799-6634) to give you special help. In our normal fashion, we will run buses from the larger hotels to the meeting. After the meeting, these will make trips back to the hotels and to Nebraska Furniture Mart, Borsheim's and the airport. Even so, you are likely to find a car useful.

The full line of Berkshire products will be available at Aksarben, and the more popular items will also be at Holiday. Last year we set sales records across-the-board, moving 3,700 pounds of See's candy, 1,635 pairs of Dexter shoes, 1,150 sets of Quikut knives and 3,104 Berkshire shirts and hats. Additionally, $26,944 of World Book products were purchased as well as more than 2,000 golf balls with the Berkshire Hathaway logo. Charlie and I are pleased but not satisfied with these numbers and confidently predict new records in all categories this year. Our 1999 apparel line will be unveiled at the meeting, so please defer your designer purchases until you view our collection.

Dairy Queen will also be on hand and will again donate all proceeds to the Children's Miracle Network. Last year we sold about 4,000 Dilly® bars, fudge bars and vanilla/orange bars. Additionally, GEICO will have a booth that will be manned by a number of our top counselors from around the country, all of them ready to supply you with auto insurance quotes. In almost all cases, GEICO will be able to offer you a special shareholder's discount. Check out whether we can save you some money.

The *piece de resistance* of our one-company trade show will be a 79-foot-long, nearly 12-foot-wide, fully-outfitted cabin of a 737 Boeing Business Jet ("BBJ"), which is NetJets' newest product. This plane has a 14-hour range; is designed to carry 19 passengers; and offers a bedroom, an office, and two showers. Deliveries to fractional owners will begin in the first quarter of 2000.

The BBJ will be available for your inspection on May 1-3 near the entrance to the Aksarben hall. You should be able to minimize your wait by making your visit on Saturday or Sunday. Bring along your checkbook in case you decide to make an impulse purchase.

NFM's multi-stored complex, located on a 75-acre site about a mile from Aksarben, is open from 10 a.m. to 9 p.m. on weekdays, and 10 a.m. to 6 p.m. on Saturdays and Sundays. This operation did $300 million in business during 1998 and offers an unrivaled breadth of merchandise — furniture, electronics, appliances, carpets and computers — all at can't-be-beat prices. During the April 30th to May 4th period, shareholders presenting their meeting badge will receive a discount that is customarily given only to its employees.

Borsheim's normally is closed on Sunday but will be open for shareholders from 10 a.m. to 6 p.m. on May 2nd. On annual meeting weekend last year, the store did an incredible amount of business. Sales were double those of the previous year, and the store's volume on Sunday greatly exceeded volume for any day in Borsheim's history. Charlie attributes this record to the fact that he autographed sales tickets that day and, while I have my doubts about this proposition, we are not about to mess with a winning formula. Please give him writer's cramp. On last year's Sunday, Borsheim's wrote 2,501 tickets during the eight hours it was open. For those of you who are mathematically challenged, that is one ticket every 11½ seconds.

Shareholders who wish to avoid Sunday's crowd can visit Borsheim's on Saturday (10 a.m.-5:30 p.m.) or on Monday (10 a.m.-8 p.m.). Be sure to identify yourself as a Berkshire owner so that Susan Jacques, Borsheim's CEO, can quote you a "shareholder-weekend" price. Susan joined us in 1983 as a $4-per-hour salesperson and was made CEO in 1994. This move ranks as one of my best managerial decisions.

Bridge players can look forward to a thrill on Sunday, when Bob Hamman — the best the game has ever seen — will turn up to play with our shareholders in the mall outside of Borsheim's. Bob plays without sorting his cards — hey, maybe that's what's wrong with my game. We will also have a couple of other tables at which another expert or two will be playing.

Gorat's — my favorite steakhouse — will again be open especially for Berkshire shareholders on the Sunday night before the meeting. Though Gorat's served from 4 p.m. until about 1 a.m. last year, its crew was swamped, and some of our shareholders had an uncomfortable wait. This year fewer reservations will be accepted, and we ask that you don't come on Sunday without a reservation. In other years, many of our shareholders have chosen to visit Gorat's on Friday, Saturday or Monday. You can make reservations beginning on April 1 *(but not before)* by calling 402-551-3733. The cognoscenti will continue to order rare T-bones with double orders of hash browns.

The Omaha Golden Spikes (neé the Omaha Royals) will meet the Iowa Cubs on Saturday evening, May 1st, at Rosenblatt Stadium. Your Chairman, whose breaking ball had the crowd buzzing last year, will again take the mound. This year I plan to introduce my "flutterball." It's a real source of irritation to me that many view our annual meeting as a financial event rather than the sports classic I consider it to be. Once the world sees my flutterball, that misperception will be erased.

Our proxy statement includes instructions about obtaining tickets to the game and also a large quantity of other information that should help you to enjoy your visit. I particularly urge the 60,000 shareholders that we gained through the Gen Re merger to join us. Come and meet your fellow capitalists.

* * * * * * * * * * * *

It wouldn't be right to close without a word about the 11.8 people who work with me in Berkshire's corporate office. In addition to handling the myriad of tax, regulatory and administrative matters that come with owning dozens of businesses, this group efficiently and cheerfully manages various special projects, some of which generate hundreds of inquiries. Here's a sample of what went on in 1998:

- 6,106 shareholders designated 3,880 charities to receive contributions.

- Kelly Muchemore processed about 17,500 admission tickets for the annual meeting, along with orders and checks for 3,200 baseball tickets.

- Kelly and Marc Hamburg produced and directed the Aksarben extravaganza, a job that required them to arrange the presentations made by our subsidiaries, prepare our movie, and sometimes lend people a hand with travel and lodging.

- Debbie Bosanek satisfied the varying needs of the 46 media organizations (13 of them non-U.S.) that covered the meeting, and meanwhile, as always, skillfully assisted me in every aspect of my job.

- Debbie and Marc assembled the data for our annual report and oversaw the production and distribution of 165,000 copies. (This year the number will be 325,000.)

- Marc handled 95% of the details — and much of the substance — connected with our completing two major mergers.

- Kelly, Debbie and Deb Ray dealt efficiently with tens of thousands of requests for annual reports and financial information that came through the office.

You and I are paying for only 11.8 people, but we are getting what would at most places be the output of 100. To all of the 11.8, my thanks.

March 1, 1999

Warren E. Buffett
Chairman of the Board

BERKSHIRE HATHAWAY INC.

To the Shareholders of Berkshire Hathaway Inc.:

Our gain in net worth during 1999 was $358 million, which increased the per-share book value of both our Class A and Class B stock by 0.5%. Over the last 35 years (that is, since present management took over) per-share book value has grown from $19 to $37,987, a rate of 24.0% compounded annually.*

The numbers on the facing page show just how poor our 1999 record was. We had the worst absolute performance of my tenure and, compared to the S&P, the worst relative performance as well. Relative results are what concern us: Over time, bad relative numbers will produce unsatisfactory absolute results.

Even Inspector Clouseau could find last year's guilty party: your Chairman. My performance reminds me of the quarterback whose report card showed four Fs and a D but who nonetheless had an understanding coach. "Son," he drawled, "I think you're spending too much time on that one subject."

My "one subject" is capital allocation, and my grade for 1999 most assuredly is a D. What most hurt us during the year was the inferior performance of Berkshire's equity portfolio — and responsibility for that portfolio, leaving aside the small piece of it run by Lou Simpson of GEICO, is entirely mine. Several of our largest investees badly lagged the market in 1999 because they've had disappointing operating results. We still like these businesses and are content to have major investments in them. But their stumbles damaged our performance last year, and it's no sure thing that they will quickly regain their stride.

The fallout from our weak results in 1999 was a more-than-commensurate drop in our stock price. In 1998, to go back a bit, the stock outperformed the business. Last year the business did much better than the stock, a divergence that has continued to the date of this letter. Over time, of course, the performance of the stock *must* roughly match the performance of the business.

Despite our poor showing last year, Charlie Munger, Berkshire's Vice Chairman and my partner, and I expect that the gain in Berkshire's intrinsic value over the next decade will modestly exceed the gain from owning the S&P. We can't guarantee that, of course. But we are willing to back our conviction with our own money. To repeat a fact you've heard before, well over 99% of my net worth resides in Berkshire. Neither my wife nor I have ever sold a share of Berkshire and — unless our checks stop clearing — we have no intention of doing so.

Please note that I spoke of hoping to beat the S&P "modestly." For Berkshire, truly large superiorities over that index are a thing of the past. They existed then because we could buy both businesses and stocks at far more attractive prices than we can now, and also because we then had a much smaller capital base, a situation that allowed us to consider a much wider range of investment opportunities than are available to us today.

Our optimism about Berkshire's performance is also tempered by the expectation — indeed, in our minds, the virtual certainty — that the S&P will do far less well in the next decade or two than it has done since 1982. A recent article in Fortune expressed my views as to why this is inevitable, and I'm enclosing a copy with this report.

Our goal is to run our present businesses well — a task made easy because of the outstanding managers we have in place — and to acquire additional businesses having economic characteristics and managers comparable to those we already own. We made important progress in this respect during 1999 by acquiring Jordan's Furniture and contracting to buy a major portion of MidAmerican Energy. We will talk more about these companies later in the report but let me emphasize one point here: We bought both for cash, issuing no Berkshire shares. Deals of that kind aren't always possible, but that is the method of acquisition that Charlie and I vastly prefer.

---

*All figures used in this report apply to Berkshire's A shares, the successor to the only stock that the company had outstanding before 1996. The B shares have an economic interest equal to 1/30th that of the A.

Guides to Intrinsic Value

I often talk in these pages about intrinsic value, a key, though far from precise, measurement we utilize in our acquisitions of businesses and common stocks. (For an extensive discussion of this, and other investment and accounting terms and concepts, please refer to our Owner's Manual on pages 55 - 62. Intrinsic value is discussed on page 60.)

In our last four reports, we have furnished you a table that we regard as useful in estimating Berkshire's intrinsic value. In the updated version of that table, which follows, we trace two key components of value. The first column lists our per-share ownership of investments (including cash and equivalents but excluding assets held in our financial products operation) and the second column shows our per-share earnings from Berkshire's operating businesses before taxes and purchase-accounting adjustments (discussed on page 61), but after all interest and corporate expenses. The second column excludes *all* dividends, interest and capital gains that we realized from the investments presented in the first column. In effect, the columns show how Berkshire would look if it were split into two parts, with one entity holding our investments and the other operating all of our businesses and bearing all corporate costs.

Year	Investments Per Share	Pre-tax Earnings (Loss) Per Share With All Income from Investments Excluded
1969	$ 45	$ 4.39
1979	577	13.07
1989	7,200	108.86
1999	47,339	(458.55)

Here are the growth rates of the two segments by decade:

Decade Ending	Investments Per Share	Pre-tax Earnings Per Share With All Income from Investments Excluded
1979	29.0%	11.5%
1989	28.7%	23.6%
1999	20.7%	N.A.
Annual Growth Rate, 1969-1999	25.4%	N.A.

In 1999, our per-share investments changed very little, but our operating earnings, affected by negatives that overwhelmed some strong positives, fell apart. Most of our operating managers deserve a grade of A for delivering fine results and for having widened the difference between the intrinsic value of their businesses and the value at which these are carried on our balance sheet. But, offsetting this, we had a huge — and, I believe, aberrational — underwriting loss at General Re. Additionally, GEICO's underwriting profit fell, as we had predicted it would. GEICO's overall performance, though, was terrific, outstripping my ambitious goals.

We do not expect our underwriting earnings to improve in any dramatic way this year. Though GEICO's intrinsic value should grow by a highly satisfying amount, its underwriting performance is almost certain to weaken. That's because auto insurers, as a group, will do worse in 2000, and because we will materially increase our marketing expenditures. At General Re, we are raising rates and, if there is no mega-catastrophe in 2000, the company's underwriting loss should fall considerably. It takes some time, however, for the full effect of rate increases to kick in, and General Re is therefore likely to have another unsatisfactory underwriting year.

You should be aware that one item regularly working to widen the amount by which intrinsic value exceeds book value is the annual charge against income we take for amortization of goodwill — an amount now running about $500 million. This charge reduces the amount of goodwill we show as an asset and likewise the amount that is included in our book value. This is an accounting matter having nothing to do with true economic goodwill, which increases in most years. But even if economic goodwill were to remain constant, the annual amortization charge would persistently widen the gap between intrinsic value and book value.

Though we can't give you a precise figure for Berkshire's intrinsic value, or even an approximation, Charlie and I can assure you that it far exceeds our $57.8 billion book value. Businesses such as See's and Buffalo News are now worth fifteen to twenty times the value at which they are carried on our books. Our goal is to continually widen this spread at all subsidiaries.

A Managerial Story You Will Never Read Elsewhere

Berkshire's collection of managers is unusual in several important ways. As one example, a very high percentage of these men and women are independently wealthy, having made fortunes in the businesses that they run. They work neither because they need the money nor because they are contractually obligated to — we have no contracts at Berkshire. Rather, they work long and hard because they love their businesses. And I use the word "their" advisedly, since these managers are truly in charge — there are no show-and-tell presentations in Omaha, no budgets to be approved by headquarters, no dictums issued about capital expenditures. We simply ask our managers to run their companies as if these are the sole asset of their families and will remain so for the next century.

Charlie and I try to behave with our managers just as we attempt to behave with Berkshire's shareholders, treating both groups as we would wish to be treated if our positions were reversed. Though "working" means nothing to me financially, I love doing it at Berkshire for some simple reasons: It gives me a sense of achievement, a freedom to act as I see fit and an opportunity to interact daily with people I like and trust. Why should our managers — accomplished artists at what they do — see things differently?

In their relations with Berkshire, our managers often appear to be hewing to President Kennedy's charge, "Ask not what your country can do for you; ask what you can do for your country." Here's a remarkable story from last year: It's about R. C. Willey, Utah's dominant home furnishing business, which Berkshire purchased from Bill Child and his family in 1995. Bill and most of his managers are Mormons, and for this reason R. C. Willey's stores have never operated on Sunday. This is a difficult way to do business: Sunday is the favorite shopping day for many customers. Bill, nonetheless, stuck to his principles -- and while doing so built his business from $250,000 of annual sales in 1954, when he took over, to $342 million in 1999.

Bill felt that R. C. Willey could operate successfully in markets outside of Utah and in 1997 suggested that we open a store in Boise. I was highly skeptical about taking a no-Sunday policy into a new territory where we would be up against entrenched rivals open seven days a week. Nevertheless, this was Bill's business to run. So, despite my reservations, I told him to follow both his business judgment and his religious convictions.

Bill then insisted on a truly extraordinary proposition: He would personally buy the land and build the store — for about $9 million as it turned out — and would sell it to us at his cost if it proved to be successful. On the other hand, if sales fell short of his expectations, we could exit the business without paying Bill a cent. This outcome, of course, would leave him with a huge investment in an empty building. I told him that I appreciated his offer but felt that if Berkshire was going to get the upside it should also take the downside. Bill said nothing doing: If there was to be failure because of his religious beliefs, he wanted to take the blow personally.

The store opened last August and immediately became a huge success. Bill thereupon turned the property over to us — including some extra land that had appreciated significantly — and we wrote him a check for his cost. And get this: *Bill refused to take a dime of interest on the capital he had tied up over the two years.*

If a manager has behaved similarly at some other public corporation, I haven't heard about it. You can understand why the opportunity to partner with people like Bill Child causes me to tap dance to work every morning.

* * * * * * * * * * * *

A footnote: After our "soft" opening in August, we had a grand opening of the Boise store about a month later. Naturally, I went there to cut the ribbon (your Chairman, I wish to emphasize, is good for *something*). In my talk I told the crowd how sales had far exceeded expectations, making us, by a considerable margin, the largest home furnishings store in Idaho. Then, as the speech progressed, my memory miraculously began to improve. By the end of my talk, it all had come back to me: Opening a store in Boise had been *my* idea.

The Economics of Property/Casualty Insurance

Our main business — though we have others of great importance — is insurance. To understand Berkshire, therefore, it is necessary that you understand how to evaluate an insurance company. The key determinants are: (1) the amount of float that the business generates; (2) its cost; and (3) most critical of all, the long-term outlook for both of these factors.

To begin with, float is money we hold but don't own. In an insurance operation, float arises because premiums are received before losses are paid, an interval that sometimes extends over many years. During that time, the insurer invests the money. This pleasant activity typically carries with it a downside: The premiums that an insurer takes in usually do not cover the losses and expenses it eventually must pay. That leaves it running an "underwriting loss," which is the cost of float. An insurance business has value if its cost of float over time is less than the cost the company would otherwise incur to obtain funds. But the business is a lemon if its cost of float is higher than market rates for money.

A caution is appropriate here: Because loss costs must be estimated, insurers have enormous latitude in figuring their underwriting results, and that makes it very difficult for investors to calculate a company's true cost of float. Errors of estimation, usually innocent but sometimes not, can be huge. The consequences of these miscalculations flow directly into earnings. An experienced observer can usually detect large-scale errors in reserving, but the general public can typically do no more than accept what's presented, and at times I have been amazed by the numbers that big-name auditors have implicitly blessed. In 1999 a number of insurers announced reserve adjustments that made a mockery of the "earnings" that investors had relied on earlier when making their buy and sell decisions. At Berkshire, we strive to be conservative and consistent in our reserving. Even so, we warn you that an unpleasant surprise is always possible.

The table that follows shows (at intervals) the float generated by the various segments of Berkshire's insurance operations since we entered the business 33 years ago upon acquiring National Indemnity Company (whose traditional lines are included in the segment "Other Primary"). For the table we have calculated our float — which we generate in large amounts relative to our premium volume — by adding net loss reserves, loss adjustment reserves, funds held under reinsurance assumed and unearned premium reserves, and then subtracting agents balances, prepaid acquisition costs, prepaid taxes and deferred charges applicable to assumed reinsurance. (Got that?)

Yearend Float (in $ millions)

Year	GEICO	General Re	Other Reinsurance	Other Primary	Total
1967				20	20
1977			40	131	171
1987			701	807	1,508
1997	2,917		4,014	455	7,386
1998	3,125	14,909	4,305	415	22,754
1999	3,444	15,166	6,285	403	25,298

Growth of float is important — but its cost is what's vital. Over the years we have usually recorded only a small underwriting loss — which means our cost of float was correspondingly low — or actually had an underwriting profit, which means we were being *paid* for holding other people's money. Indeed, our cumulative result through 1998 was an underwriting profit. In 1999, however, we incurred a $1.4 billion underwriting loss that left us with float cost of 5.8%. One mildly mitigating factor: We enthusiastically welcomed $400 million of the loss because it stems from business that will deliver us exceptional float over the next decade. The balance of the loss, however, was decidedly unwelcome, and our overall result must be judged extremely poor. Absent a mega-catastrophe, we expect float cost to fall in 2000, but any decline will be tempered by our aggressive plans for GEICO, which we will discuss later.

There are a number of people who deserve credit for manufacturing so much "no-cost" float over the years. Foremost is Ajit Jain. It's simply impossible to overstate Ajit's value to Berkshire: He has from scratch built an outstanding reinsurance business, which during his tenure has earned an underwriting profit and now holds $6.3 billion of float.

In Ajit, we have an underwriter equipped with the intelligence to properly rate most risks; the realism to forget about those he can't evaluate; the courage to write huge policies when the premium is appropriate; and the discipline to reject even the smallest risk when the premium is inadequate. It is rare to find a person possessing any one of these talents. For one person to have them all is remarkable.

Since Ajit specializes in super-cat reinsurance, a line in which losses are infrequent but extremely large when they occur, his business is sure to be far more volatile than most insurance operations. To date, we have benefitted from good luck on this volatile book. Even so, Ajit's achievements are truly extraordinary.

In a smaller but nevertheless important way, our "other primary" insurance operation has also added to Berkshire's intrinsic value. This collection of insurers has delivered a $192 million underwriting profit over the past five years while supplying us with the float shown in the table. In the insurance world, results like this are uncommon, and for their feat we thank Rod Eldred, Brad Kinstler, John Kizer, Don Towle and Don Wurster.

As I mentioned earlier, the General Re operation had an exceptionally poor underwriting year in 1999 (though investment income left the company well in the black). Our business was extremely underpriced, both domestically and internationally, a condition that is improving but not yet corrected. Over time, however, the company should develop a growing amount of low-cost float. At both General Re and its Cologne subsidiary, incentive compensation plans are now directly tied to the variables of float growth and cost of float, the same variables that determine value for owners.

Even though a reinsurer may have a tightly focused and rational compensation system, it cannot count on every year coming up roses. Reinsurance is a highly volatile business, and neither General Re nor Ajit's operation is immune to bad pricing behavior in the industry. But General Re has the distribution , the underwriting skills, the culture, and — with Berkshire's backing — the financial clout to become the world's most profitable reinsurance company. Getting there will take time, energy and discipline, but we have no doubt that Ron Ferguson and his crew can make it happen.

GEICO (1-800-847-7536 or GEICO.com)

GEICO made exceptional progress in 1999. The reasons are simple: We have a terrific business idea being implemented by an extraordinary manager, Tony Nicely. When Berkshire purchased GEICO at the beginning of 1996, we handed the keys to Tony and asked him to run the operation exactly as if he owned 100% of it. He has done the rest. Take a look at his scorecard:

Years	New Auto Policies[1][2]	Auto Policies In-Force[1]
1993	346,882	2,011,055
1994	384,217	2,147,549
1995	443,539	2,310,037
1996	592,300	2,543,699
1997	868,430	2,949,439
1998	1,249,875	3,562,644
1999	1,648,095	4,328,900

[1] "Voluntary" only; excludes assigned risks and the like.
[2] Revised to exclude policies moved from one GEICO company to another.

In 1995, GEICO spent $33 million on marketing and had 652 telephone counselors. Last year the company spent $242 million, and the counselor count grew to 2,631. And we are just starting: The pace will step up materially in 2000. Indeed, we would happily commit $1 billion annually to marketing if we knew we could handle the business smoothly and if we expected the last dollar spent to produce new business at an attractive cost.

Currently two trends are affecting acquisition costs. The bad news is that it has become more expensive to develop inquiries. Media rates have risen, and we are also seeing diminishing returns — that is, as both we and our competitors step up advertising, inquiries per ad fall for all of us. These negatives are partly offset, however, by the fact that our closure ratio — the percentage of inquiries converted to sales — has steadily improved. Overall, we believe that our cost of new business, though definitely rising, is well below that of the industry. Of even greater importance, our operating costs for renewal business are the lowest among broad-based national auto insurers. Both of these major competitive advantages are sustainable. Others may copy our model, but they will be unable to replicate our economics.

The table above makes it appear that GEICO's retention of policyholders is falling, but for two reasons appearances are in this case deceiving. First, in the last few years our business mix has moved away from "preferred" policyholders, for whom industrywide retention rates are high, toward "standard" and "non-standard" policyholders for whom retention rates are much lower. (Despite the nomenclature, the three classes have similar profit prospects.) Second, retention rates for relatively new policyholders are always lower than those for long-time customers — and because of our accelerated growth, our policyholder ranks now include an increased proportion of new customers. Adjusted for these two factors, our retention rate has changed hardly at all.

We told you last year that underwriting margins for both GEICO and the industry would fall in 1999, and they did. We make a similar prediction for 2000. A few years ago margins got too wide, having enjoyed the effects of an unusual and unexpected decrease in the frequency and severity of accidents. The industry responded by reducing rates — but now is having to contend with an increase in loss costs. We would not be surprised to see the margins of auto insurers deteriorate by around three percentage points in 2000.

Two negatives besides worsening frequency and severity will hurt the industry this year. First, rate increases go into effect only slowly, both because of regulatory delay and because insurance contracts must run their course before new rates can be put in. Second, reported earnings of many auto insurers have benefitted in the last few years from reserve releases, made possible because the companies overestimated their loss costs in still-earlier years. This reservoir of redundant reserves has now largely dried up, and future boosts to earnings from this source will be minor at best.

In compensating its associates — from Tony on down — GEICO continues to use two variables, and only two, in determining what bonuses and profit-sharing contributions will be: 1) its percentage growth in policyholders and 2) the earnings of its "seasoned" business, meaning policies that have been with us for more than a year. We did outstandingly well on both fronts during 1999 and therefore made a profit-sharing payment of 28.4% of salary (in total, $113.3 million) to the great majority of our associates. Tony and I love writing those checks.

At Berkshire, we want to have compensation policies that are both easy to understand and in sync with what we wish our associates to accomplish. Writing new business is expensive (and, as mentioned, getting more expensive). If we were to include those costs in our calculation of bonuses — as managements did before our arrival at GEICO — we would be penalizing our associates for garnering new policies, even though these are very much in Berkshire's interest. So, in effect, we say to our associates that we will foot the bill for new business. Indeed, because percentage growth in policyholders is part of our compensation scheme, we *reward* our associates for producing this initially-unprofitable business. And then we reward them additionally for holding down costs on our seasoned business.

Despite the extensive advertising we do, our best source of new business is word-of-mouth recommendations from existing policyholders, who on the whole are pleased with our prices and service. An article published last year by *Kiplinger's Personal Finance Magazine* gives a good picture of where we stand in customer satisfaction: The magazine's survey of 20 state insurance departments showed that GEICO's complaint ratio was well below the ratio for most of its major competitors.

Our strong referral business means that we probably could maintain our policy count by spending as little as $50 million annually on advertising. That's a guess, of course, and we will never know whether it is accurate because Tony's foot is going to stay on the advertising pedal (and my foot will be on his). Nevertheless, I want to emphasize that a major percentage of the $300-$350 million we will spend in 2000 on advertising, as well as large additional costs we will incur for sales counselors, communications and facilities, are optional outlays we choose to make so that we can both achieve significant growth and extend and solidify the promise of the GEICO brand in the minds of Americans.

Personally, I think these expenditures are the best investment Berkshire can make. Through its advertising, GEICO is acquiring a direct relationship with a huge number of households that, on average, will send us $1,100 year after year. That makes us — among all companies, selling whatever kind of product — one of the country's leading direct merchandisers. Also, as we build our long-term relationships with more and more families, cash is pouring in rather than going out (no Internet economics here). Last year, as GEICO increased its customer base by 766,256, it gained $590 million of cash from operating earnings and the increase in float.

In the past three years, we have increased our market share in personal auto insurance from 2.7% to 4.1%. But we rightfully belong in many more households — maybe even yours. Give us a call and find out. About 40% of those people checking our rates find that they can save money by doing business with us. The proportion is not 100% because insurers differ in their underwriting judgments, with some giving more credit than we do to drivers who live in certain geographic areas or work at certain occupations. Our closure rate indicates, however, that we more frequently offer the low price than does any other national carrier selling insurance to all comers. Furthermore, in 40 states we can offer a special discount — usually 8% — to our shareholders. Just be sure to identify yourself as a Berkshire owner so that our sales counselor can make the appropriate adjustment.

* * * * * * * * * * * *

It's with sadness that I report to you that Lorimer Davidson, GEICO's former Chairman, died last November, a few days after his 97th birthday. For GEICO, Davy was a business giant who moved the company up to the big leagues. For me, he was a friend, teacher and hero. I have told you of his lifelong kindnesses to me in past reports. Clearly, my life would have developed far differently had he not been a part of it. Tony, Lou Simpson and I visited Davy in August and marveled at his mental alertness — particularly in all matters regarding GEICO. He was the company's number one supporter right up to the end, and we will forever miss him.

Aviation Services

Our two aviation services companies — FlightSafety International ("FSI") and Executive Jet Aviation ("EJA") — are both runaway leaders in their field. EJA, which sells and manages the fractional ownership of jet aircraft, through its NetJets® program, is larger than its next two competitors combined. FSI trains pilots (as well as other transportation professionals) and is five times or so the size of its nearest competitor.

Another common characteristic of the companies is that they are still managed by their founding entrepreneurs. Al Ueltschi started FSI in 1951 with $10,000, and Rich Santulli invented the fractional-ownership industry in 1986. These men are both remarkable managers who have no financial need to work but thrive on helping their companies grow and excel.

Though these two businesses have leadership positions that are similar, they differ in their economic characteristics. FSI must lay out huge amounts of capital. A single flight simulator can cost as much as $15 million — and we have 222. Only one person at a time, furthermore, can be trained in a simulator, which means that the capital investment per dollar of revenue at FSI is exceptionally high. Operating margins must therefore also be high, if we are to earn a reasonable return on capital. Last year we made capital expenditures of $215 million at FSI and FlightSafety Boeing, its 50%-owned affiliate.

At EJA, in contrast, the customer owns the equipment, though we, of course, must invest in a core fleet of our own planes to ensure outstanding service. For example, the Sunday after Thanksgiving, EJA's busiest day of the year, strains our resources since fractions of 169 planes are owned by 1,412 customers, many of whom are bent on flying home between 3 and 6 p.m. On that day, and certain others, we need a supply of company-owned aircraft to make sure all parties get where they want, when they want.

Still, most of the planes we fly are owned by customers, which means that modest pre-tax margins in this business can produce good returns on equity. Currently, our customers own planes worth over $2 billion, and in addition we have $4.2 billion of planes on order. Indeed, the limiting factor in our business right now is the availability of planes. We now are taking delivery of about 8% of all business jets manufactured in the world, and we wish we could get a bigger share than that. Though EJA was supply-constrained in 1999, its recurring revenues — monthly management fees plus hourly flight fees — increased 46%.

The fractional-ownership industry is still in its infancy. EJA is now building critical mass in Europe, and over time we will expand around the world. Doing that will be expensive — very expensive — but we will spend what it takes. Scale is vital to both us and our customers: The company with the most planes in the air worldwide will be able to offer its customers the best service. "Buy a fraction, get a fleet" has real meaning at EJA.

EJA enjoys another important advantage in that its two largest competitors are both subsidiaries of aircraft manufacturers and sell only the aircraft their parents make. Though these are fine planes, these competitors are severely limited in the cabin styles and mission capabilities they can offer. EJA, in contrast, offers a wide array of planes from five suppliers. Consequently, we can give the customer whatever *he* needs to buy — rather than his getting what the competitor's parent needs to sell.

Last year in this report, I described my family's delight with the one-quarter (200 flight hours annually) of a Hawker 1000 that we had owned since 1995. I got so pumped up by my own prose that shortly thereafter I signed up for one-sixteenth of a Cessna V Ultra as well. Now my annual outlays at EJA and Borsheim's, combined, total ten times my salary. Think of this as a rough guideline for your own expenditures with us.

During the past year, two of Berkshire's outside directors have also signed on with EJA. (Maybe we're paying them too much.) You should be aware that they and I are charged exactly the same price for planes and service as is any other customer: EJA follows a "most favored nations" policy, with no one getting a special deal.

And now, brace yourself. Last year, EJA passed the ultimate test: *Charlie signed up.* No other endorsement could speak more eloquently to the value of the EJA service. Give us a call at 1-800-848-6436 and ask for our "white paper" on fractional ownership.

Acquisitions of 1999

At both GEICO and Executive Jet, our best source of new customers is the happy ones we already have. Indeed, about 65% of our new owners of aircraft come as referrals from current owners who have fallen in love with the service.

Our acquisitions usually develop in the same way. At other companies, executives may devote themselves to pursuing acquisition possibilities with investment bankers, utilizing an auction process that has become standardized. In this exercise the bankers prepare a "book" that makes me think of the Superman comics of my youth. In the Wall Street version, a formerly mild-mannered company emerges from the investment banker's phone booth able to leap over competitors in a single bound and with earnings moving faster than a speeding bullet. Titillated by the book's description of the acquiree's powers, acquisition-hungry CEOs — Lois Lanes all, beneath their cool exteriors — promptly swoon.

What's particularly entertaining in these books is the precision with which earnings are projected for many years ahead. If you ask the author-banker, however, what his own firm will earn *next month*, he will go into a protective crouch and tell you that business and markets are far too uncertain for him to venture a forecast.

Here's one story I can't resist relating: In 1985, a major investment banking house undertook to sell Scott Fetzer, offering it widely — but with no success. Upon reading of this strikeout, I wrote Ralph Schey, then and now Scott Fetzer's CEO, expressing an interest in buying the business. I had never met Ralph, but within a week we had a deal. Unfortunately, Scott Fetzer's letter of engagement with the banking firm provided it a $2.5 million fee upon sale, even if it had nothing to do with finding the buyer. I guess the lead banker felt he should do something for his payment, so he graciously offered us a copy of the book on Scott Fetzer that his firm had prepared. With his customary tact, Charlie responded: "I'll pay $2.5 million *not* to read it."

At Berkshire, our carefully-crafted acquisition strategy is simply to wait for the phone to ring. Happily, it sometimes does so, usually because a manager who sold to us earlier has recommended to a friend that he think about following suit.

Which brings us to the furniture business. Two years ago I recounted how the acquisition of Nebraska Furniture Mart in 1983 and my subsequent association with the Blumkin family led to follow-on transactions with R. C. Willey (1995) and Star Furniture (1997). For me, these relationships have all been terrific. Not only did Berkshire acquire three outstanding retailers; these deals also allowed me to become friends with some of the finest people you will ever meet.

Naturally, I have persistently asked the Blumkins, Bill Child and Melvyn Wolff whether there are any more out there like you. Their invariable answer was the Tatelman brothers of New England and their remarkable furniture business, Jordan's.

I met Barry and Eliot Tatelman last year and we soon signed an agreement for Berkshire to acquire the company. Like our three previous furniture acquisitions, this business had long been in the family — in this case since 1927, when Barry and Eliot's grandfather began operations in a Boston suburb. Under the brothers' management, Jordan's has grown ever more dominant in its region, becoming the largest furniture retailer in New Hampshire as well as Massachusetts.

The Tatelmans don't just sell furniture or manage stores. They also present customers with a dazzling entertainment experience called "shoppertainment." A family visiting a store can have a terrific time, while concurrently viewing an extraordinary selection of merchandise. The business results are also extraordinary: Jordan's has the highest sales per square foot of any major furniture operation in the country. I urge you to visit one of their stores if you are in the Boston area — particularly the one at Natick, which is Jordan's newest. Bring money.

Barry and Eliot are classy people — just like their counterparts at Berkshire's three other furniture operations. When they sold to us, they elected to give each of their employees at least 50¢ for every hour that he or she had worked for Jordan's. This payment added up to $9 million, which came from the Tatelmans' own pockets, not from Berkshire's. And Barry and Eliot were thrilled to write the checks.

Each of our furniture operations is number one in its territory. We now sell more furniture than anyone else in Massachusetts, New Hampshire, Texas, Nebraska, Utah and Idaho. Last year Star's Melvyn Wolff and his sister, Shirley Toomim, scored two major successes: a move into San Antonio and a significant enlargement of Star's store in Austin.

There's no operation in the furniture retailing business remotely like the one assembled by Berkshire. It's fun for me and profitable for you. W. C. Fields once said, "It was a woman who drove me to drink, but unfortunately I never had the chance to thank her." I don't want to make that mistake. My thanks go to Louie, Ron and Irv Blumkin for getting me started in the furniture business and for unerringly guiding me as we have assembled the group we now have.

* * * * * * * * * * * *

Now, for our second acquisition deal: It came to us through my good friend, Walter Scott, Jr., chairman of Level 3 Communications and a director of Berkshire. Walter has many other business connections as well, and one of them is with MidAmerican Energy, a utility company in which he has substantial holdings and on whose board he sits. At a conference in California that we both attended last September, Walter casually asked me whether Berkshire might be interested in making a large investment in MidAmerican, and from the start the idea of being in partnership with Walter struck me as a good one. Upon returning to Omaha, I read some of MidAmerican's public reports and had two short meetings with Walter and David Sokol, MidAmerican's talented and entrepreneurial CEO. I then said that, at an appropriate price, we would indeed like to make a deal.

Acquisitions in the electric utility industry are complicated by a variety of regulations including the Public Utility Holding Company Act of 1935. Therefore, we had to structure a transaction that would avoid Berkshire gaining voting control. Instead we are purchasing an 11% fixed-income security, along with a combination of common stock and exchangeable preferred that will give Berkshire just under 10% of the voting power of MidAmerican but about 76% of the equity interest. All told, our investment will be about $2 billion.

Walter characteristically backed up his convictions with real money: He and his family will buy more MidAmerican stock for cash when the transaction closes, bringing their total investment to about $280 million. Walter will also be the controlling shareholder of the company, and I can't think of a better person to hold that post.

Though there are many regulatory constraints in the utility industry, it's possible that we will make additional commitments in the field. If we do, the amounts involved could be large.

Acquisition Accounting

Once again, I would like to make some comments about accounting, in this case about its application to acquisitions. This is currently a very contentious topic and, before the dust settles, Congress may even intervene (a truly terrible idea).

When a company is acquired, generally accepted accounting principles ("GAAP") currently condone two very different ways of recording the transaction: "purchase" and "pooling." In a pooling, stock must be the currency; in a purchase, payment can be made in either cash or stock. Whatever the currency, managements usually detest purchase accounting because it almost always requires that a "goodwill" account be established and subsequently written off — a process that saddles earnings with a large annual charge that normally persists for decades. In contrast, pooling avoids a goodwill account, which is why managements love it.

Now, the Financial Accounting Standards Board ("FASB") has proposed an end to pooling, and many CEOs are girding for battle. It will be an important fight, so we'll venture some opinions. To begin with, we agree with the many managers who argue that goodwill amortization charges are usually spurious. You'll find my thinking about this in the appendix to our 1983 annual report, which is available on our website, and in the Owner's Manual on pages 55 - 62.

For accounting rules to mandate amortization that will, in the usual case, conflict with reality is deeply troublesome: Most accounting charges *relate* to what's going on, even if they don't precisely measure it. As an example, depreciation charges can't with precision calibrate the decline in value that physical assets suffer, but these charges do at least describe something that is truly occurring: Physical assets invariably deteriorate. Correspondingly, obsolescence charges for inventories, bad debt charges for receivables and accruals for warranties are among the charges that reflect true costs. The annual charges for these expenses can't be exactly measured, but the necessity for estimating them is obvious.

In contrast, economic goodwill does not, in many cases, diminish. Indeed, in a great many instances — perhaps most — it actually grows in value over time. In character, economic goodwill is much like land: The value of both assets is sure to fluctuate, but the direction in which value is going to go is in no way ordained. At See's, for example, economic goodwill has grown, in an irregular but very substantial manner, for 78 years. And, if we run the business right, growth of that kind will probably continue for at least another 78 years.

To escape from the fiction of goodwill charges, managers embrace the fiction of pooling. This accounting convention is grounded in the poetic notion that when two rivers merge their streams become indistinguishable. Under this concept, a company that has been merged into a larger enterprise has not been "purchased" (even though it will often have received a large "sell-out" premium). Consequently, no goodwill is created, and those pesky subsequent charges to earnings are eliminated. Instead, the accounting for the ongoing entity is handled as if the businesses had forever been one unit.

So much for poetry. The reality of merging is usually far different: There is indisputably an acquirer and an acquiree, and the latter has been "purchased," no matter how the deal has been structured. If you think otherwise, just ask employees severed from their jobs which company was the conqueror and which was the conquered. You will find no confusion. So on this point the FASB is correct: In most mergers, a purchase has been made. Yes, there are some true "mergers of equals," but they are few and far between.

Charlie and I believe there's a reality-based approach that should both satisfy the FASB, which correctly wishes to record a purchase, and meet the objections of managements to nonsensical charges for diminution of goodwill. We would first have the acquiring company record its purchase price — whether paid in stock or cash — at fair value. In most cases, this procedure would create a large asset representing economic goodwill. We would then leave this asset on the books, not requiring its amortization. Later, if the economic goodwill became impaired, as it sometimes would, it would be written down just as would any other asset judged to be impaired.

If our proposed rule were to be adopted, it should be applied retroactively so that acquisition accounting would be consistent throughout America — a far cry from what exists today. One prediction: If this plan were to take effect, managements would structure acquisitions more sensibly, deciding whether to use cash or stock based on the real consequences for their shareholders rather than on the unreal consequences for their reported earnings.

* * * * * * * * * * *

In our purchase of Jordan's, we followed a procedure that will maximize the cash produced for our shareholders but minimize the earnings we report to you. Berkshire purchased assets for cash, an approach that on our tax returns permits us to amortize the resulting goodwill over a 15-year period. Obviously, this tax deduction materially increases the amount of cash delivered by the business. In contrast, when stock, rather than assets, is purchased for cash, the resulting writeoffs of goodwill are not tax-deductible. The economic difference between these two approaches is substantial.

From the economic standpoint of the acquiring company, the worst deal of all is a stock-for-stock acquisition. Here, a huge price is often paid without there being any step-up in the tax basis of either the stock of the acquiree or its assets. If the acquired entity is subsequently sold, its owner may owe a large capital gains tax (at a 35% or greater rate), even though the sale may truly be producing a major economic loss.

We have made some deals at Berkshire that used far-from-optimal tax structures. These deals occurred because the sellers insisted on a given structure and because, overall, we still felt the acquisition made sense. We have never done an inefficiently-structured deal, however, in order to make our figures look better.

Sources of Reported Earnings

The table that follows shows the main sources of Berkshire's reported earnings. In this presentation, purchase-accounting adjustments are not assigned to the specific businesses to which they apply, but are instead aggregated and shown separately. This procedure lets you view the earnings of our businesses as they would have been reported had we not purchased them. For the reasons discussed on page 61, this form of presentation seems to us to be more useful to investors and managers than one utilizing generally accepted accounting principles (GAAP), which require purchase-premiums to be charged off business-by-business. The total earnings we show in the table are, of course, identical to the GAAP total in our audited financial statements.

| | (in millions) | | | |
| | Pre-Tax Earnings | | Berkshire's Share of Net Earnings (after taxes and minority interests) | |
	1999	1998	1999	1998
Operating Earnings:				
Insurance Group:				
Underwriting — Reinsurance	$(1,440)	$(21)	$(927)	$(14)
Underwriting — GEICO	24	269	16	175
Underwriting — Other Primary	22	17	14	10
Net Investment Income	2,482	974	1,764	731
Buffalo News	55	53	34	32
Finance and Financial Products Businesses	125	205	86	133
Flight Services	225 (2)	181 (1)	132 (2)	110 (1)
Home Furnishings	79	72	46	41
International Dairy Queen	56	58	35	35
Jewelry	51	39	31	23
Scott Fetzer (excluding finance operation)	147	137	92	85
See's Candies	74	62	46	40
Shoe Group	17	33	11	23
Purchase-Accounting Adjustments	(739)	(123)	(648)	(118)
Interest Expense (3)	(109)	(100)	(70)	(63)
Shareholder-Designated Contributions	(17)	(17)	(11)	(11)
Other	33	60 (4)	20	45 (4)
Operating Earnings	1,085	1,899	671	1,277
Capital Gains from Investments	1,365	2,415	886	1,553
Total Earnings - All Entities	$2,450	$4,314	$1,557	$2,830

(1) Includes Executive Jet from August 7, 1998 .   (3) Excludes interest expense of Finance Businesses.
(2) Includes Jordan's Furniture from November 13, 1999.   (4) Includes General Re operations for ten days in 1998.

Almost all of our manufacturing, retailing and service businesses had excellent results in 1999. The exception was Dexter Shoe, and there the shortfall did not occur because of managerial problems: In skills, energy and devotion to their work, the Dexter executives are every bit the equal of our other managers. But we manufacture shoes primarily in the U.S., and it has become extremely difficult for domestic producers to compete effectively. In 1999, approximately 93% of the 1.3 billion pairs of shoes purchased in this country came from abroad, where extremely low-cost labor is the rule.

Counting both Dexter and H. H. Brown, we are currently the leading domestic manufacturer of shoes, and we are likely to continue to be. We have loyal, highly-skilled workers in our U.S. plants, and we want to retain every job here that we can. Nevertheless, in order to remain viable, we are sourcing more of our output internationally. In doing that, we have incurred significant severance and relocation costs that are included in the earnings we show in the table.

A few years back, Helzberg's, our 200-store jewelry operation, needed to make operating adjustments to restore margins to appropriate levels. Under Jeff Comment's leadership, the job was done and profits have dramatically rebounded. In the shoe business, where we have Harold Alfond, Peter Lunder, Frank Rooney and Jim Issler in charge, I believe we will see a similar improvement over the next few years.

See's Candies deserves a special comment, given that it achieved a record operating margin of 24% last year. Since we bought See's for $25 million in 1972, it has earned $857 million pre-tax. And, despite its growth, the business has required very little additional capital. Give the credit for this performance to Chuck Huggins. Charlie and I put him in charge the day of our purchase, and his fanatical insistence on both product quality and friendly service has rewarded customers, employees and owners.

Chuck gets better every year. When he took charge of See's at age 46, the company's pre-tax profit, expressed in millions, was about 10% of his age. Today he's 74, and the ratio has increased to 100%. Having discovered this mathematical relationship — let's call it Huggins' Law — Charlie and I now become giddy at the mere thought of Chuck's birthday.

* * * * * * * * * * * *

Additional information about our various businesses is given on pages 39 - 54, where you will also find our segment earnings reported on a GAAP basis. In addition, on pages 63 - 69, we have rearranged Berkshire's financial data into four segments on a non-GAAP basis, a presentation that corresponds to the way Charlie and I think about the company.

Look-Through Earnings

Reported earnings are an inadequate measure of economic progress at Berkshire, in part because the numbers shown in the table presented earlier include only the dividends we receive from investees — though these dividends typically represent only a small fraction of the earnings attributable to our ownership. Not that we mind this division of money, since on balance we regard the undistributed earnings of investees as more valuable to us than the portion paid out. The reason for our thinking is simple: Our investees often have the opportunity to reinvest earnings at high rates of return. So why should we want them paid out?

To depict something closer to economic reality at Berkshire than reported earnings, though, we employ the concept of "look-through" earnings. As we calculate these, they consist of: (1) the operating earnings reported in the previous section, plus; (2) our share of the retained operating earnings of major investees that, under GAAP accounting, are not reflected in our profits, less; (3) an allowance for the tax that would be paid by Berkshire if these retained earnings of investees had instead been distributed to us. When tabulating "operating earnings" here, we exclude purchase-accounting adjustments as well as capital gains and other major non-recurring items.

The following table sets forth our 1999 look-through earnings, though I warn you that the figures can be no more than approximate, since they are based on a number of judgment calls. (The dividends paid to us by these investees have been included in the operating earnings itemized on page 13, mostly under "Insurance Group: Net Investment Income.")

Berkshire's Major Investees	Berkshire's Approximate Ownership at Yearend[1]	Berkshire's Share of Undistributed Operating Earnings (in millions)[2]
American Express Company	11.3%	$228
The Coca-Cola Company	8.1%	144
Freddie Mac	8.6%	127
The Gillette Company	9.0%	53
M&T Bank	6.5%	17
The Washington Post Company	18.3%	30
Wells Fargo & Company	3.6%	108

Berkshire's share of undistributed earnings of major investees	707
Hypothetical tax on these undistributed investee earnings[3]	(99)
Reported operating earnings of Berkshire	1,318
Total look-through earnings of Berkshire	$ 1,926

    (1) Does not include shares allocable to minority interests
    (2) Calculated on average ownership for the year
    (3) The tax rate used is 14%, which is the rate Berkshire pays on the dividends it receives

Investments

Below we present our common stock investments. Those that had a market value of more than $750 million at the end of 1999 are itemized.

		12/31/99	
Shares	Company	Cost*	Market
		(dollars in millions)	
50,536,900	American Express Company	$1,470	$ 8,402
200,000,000	The Coca-Cola Company	1,299	11,650
59,559,300	Freddie Mac	294	2,803
96,000,000	The Gillette Company	600	3,954
1,727,765	The Washington Post Company	11	960
59,136,680	Wells Fargo & Company	349	2,391
	Others	4,180	6,848
	Total Common Stocks	$8,203	$37,008

    * Represents tax-basis cost which, in aggregate, is $691 million less than GAAP cost.

We made few portfolio changes in 1999. As I mentioned earlier, several of the companies in which we have large investments had disappointing business results last year. Nevertheless, we believe these companies have important competitive advantages that will endure over time. This attribute, which makes for good long-term investment results, is one Charlie and I occasionally believe we can identify. More often, however, we can't — not at least with a high degree of conviction. This explains, by the way, why we don't own stocks of tech companies, even though we share the general view that our society will be transformed by their products and services. Our problem — which we can't solve by studying up — is that we have no insights into which participants in the tech field possess a truly *durable* competitive advantage.

Our lack of tech insights, we should add, does not distress us. After all, there are a great many business areas in which Charlie and I have no special capital-allocation expertise. For instance, we bring nothing to the table when it comes to evaluating patents, manufacturing processes or geological prospects. So we simply don't get into judgments in those fields.

If we have a strength, it is in recognizing when we are operating well within our circle of competence and when we are approaching the perimeter. Predicting the long-term economics of companies that operate in fast-changing industries is simply far beyond our perimeter. If others claim predictive skill in those industries — and seem to have their claims validated by the behavior of the stock market — we neither envy nor emulate them. Instead, we just stick with what we understand. If we stray, we will have done so inadvertently, not because we got restless and substituted hope for rationality. Fortunately, it's almost certain there will be opportunities from time to time for Berkshire to do well within the circle we've staked out.

Right now, the prices of the fine businesses we already own are just not that attractive. In other words, we feel much better about the businesses than their stocks. That's why we haven't added to our present holdings. Nevertheless, we haven't yet scaled back our portfolio in a major way: If the choice is between a questionable business at a comfortable price or a comfortable business at a questionable price, we much prefer the latter. What really gets our attention, however, is a comfortable business at a comfortable price.

Our reservations about the prices of securities we own apply also to the general level of equity prices. We have never attempted to forecast what the stock market is going to do in the next month or the next year, and we are not trying to do that now. But, as I point out in the enclosed article, equity investors currently seem wildly optimistic in their expectations about future returns.

We see the growth in corporate profits as being largely tied to the business done in the country (GDP), and we see GDP growing at a real rate of about 3%. In addition, we have hypothesized 2% inflation. Charlie and I have no particular conviction about the accuracy of 2%. However, it's the market's view: Treasury Inflation-Protected Securities (TIPS) yield about two percentage points less than the standard treasury bond, and if you believe inflation rates are going to be higher than that, you can profit by simply buying TIPS and shorting Governments.

If profits do indeed grow along with GDP, at about a 5% rate, the valuation placed on American business is unlikely to climb by much more than that. Add in something for dividends, and you emerge with returns from equities that are dramatically less than most investors have either experienced in the past or expect in the future. If investor expectations become more realistic — and they almost certainly will — the market adjustment is apt to be severe, particularly in sectors in which speculation has been concentrated.

Berkshire will someday have opportunities to deploy major amounts of cash in equity markets — we are confident of that. But, as the song goes, "Who knows where or when?" Meanwhile, if anyone starts explaining to you what is going on in the truly-manic portions of this "enchanted" market, you might remember still another line of song: "Fools give you reasons, wise men never try."

Share Repurchases

Recently, a number of shareholders have suggested to us that Berkshire repurchase its shares. Usually the requests were rationally based, but a few leaned on spurious logic.

There is only one combination of facts that makes it advisable for a company to repurchase its shares: First, the company has available funds — cash plus sensible borrowing capacity — beyond the near-term needs of the business and, second, finds its stock selling in the market below its intrinsic value, conservatively-calculated. To this we add a caveat: Shareholders should have been supplied all the information they need for estimating that value. Otherwise, insiders could take advantage of their uninformed partners and buy out their interests at a fraction of true worth. We have, on rare occasions, seen that happen. Usually, of course, chicanery is employed to drive stock prices up, not down.

The business "needs" that I speak of are of two kinds: First, expenditures that a company must make to maintain its competitive position (e.g., the remodeling of stores at Helzberg's) and, second, optional outlays, aimed at business growth, that management expects will produce more than a dollar of value for each dollar spent (R. C. Willey's expansion into Idaho).

When available funds exceed needs of those kinds, a company with a growth-oriented shareholder population can buy new businesses or repurchase shares. If a company's stock is selling well below intrinsic value, repurchases usually make the most sense. In the mid-1970s, the wisdom of making these was virtually screaming at managements, but few responded. In most cases, those that did made their owners much wealthier than if alternative courses of action had been pursued. Indeed, during the 1970s (and, spasmodically, for some years thereafter) we searched for companies that were large repurchasers of their shares. This often was a tipoff that the company was both undervalued and run by a shareholder-oriented management.

That day is past. Now, repurchases are all the rage, but are all too often made for an unstated and, in our view, ignoble reason: to pump or support the stock price. The shareholder who chooses to sell today, of course, is benefitted by any buyer, whatever his origin or motives. But the *continuing* shareholder is penalized by repurchases above intrinsic value. Buying dollar bills for $1.10 is not good business for those who stick around.

Charlie and I admit that we feel confident in estimating intrinsic value for only a portion of traded equities and then only when we employ a range of values, rather than some pseudo-precise figure. Nevertheless, it appears to us that many companies now making repurchases are overpaying departing shareholders at the expense of those who stay. In defense of those companies, I would say that it is natural for CEOs to be optimistic about their own businesses. They also know a whole lot more about them than I do. However, I can't help but feel that too often today's repurchases are dictated by management's desire to "show confidence" or be in fashion rather than by a desire to enhance per-share value.

Sometimes, too, companies say they are repurchasing shares to offset the shares issued when stock options granted at much lower prices are exercised. This "buy high, sell low" strategy is one many unfortunate investors have employed — but never intentionally! Managements, however, seem to follow this perverse activity very cheerfully.

Of course, both option grants and repurchases may make sense — but if that's the case, it's not because the two activities are logically related. Rationally, a company's decision to repurchase shares or to issue them should stand on its own feet. Just because stock has been issued to satisfy options — or for any other reason — does not mean that stock should be repurchased at a price above intrinsic value. Correspondingly, a stock that sells well below intrinsic value should be repurchased whether or not stock has previously been issued (or may be because of outstanding options).

You should be aware that, at certain times in the past, I have erred in *not* making repurchases. My appraisal of Berkshire's value was then too conservative or I was too enthused about some alternative use of funds. We have therefore missed some opportunities — though Berkshire's trading volume at these points was too light for us to have done much buying, which means that the gain in our per-share value would have been minimal. (A repurchase of, say, 2% of a company's shares at a 25% discount from per-share intrinsic value produces only a ½% gain in that value at most — and even less if the funds could alternatively have been deployed in value-building moves.)

Some of the letters we've received clearly imply that the writer is unconcerned about intrinsic value considerations but instead wants us to trumpet an intention to repurchase so that the stock will rise (or quit going down). If the writer wants to sell tomorrow, his thinking makes sense — for him! — but if he intends to hold, he should instead hope the stock falls and trades in enough volume for us to buy a lot of it. That's the only way a repurchase program can have any real benefit for a continuing shareholder.

We will not repurchase shares unless we believe Berkshire stock is selling well below intrinsic value, conservatively calculated. Nor will we attempt to talk the stock up or down. (Neither publicly or privately have I ever told anyone to buy or sell Berkshire shares.) Instead we will give all shareholders — and potential shareholders — the same valuation-related information we would wish to have if our positions were reversed.

Recently, when the A shares fell below $45,000, we considered making repurchases. We decided, however, to delay buying, if indeed we elect to do *any*, until shareholders have had the chance to review this report. If we do find that repurchases make sense, we will only rarely place bids on the New York Stock Exchange ("NYSE"). Instead, we will respond to offers made directly to us at or below the NYSE bid. If you wish to offer stock, have your broker call Mark Millard at 402-346-1400. When a trade occurs, the broker can either record it in the "third market" or on the NYSE. We will favor purchase of the B shares if they are selling at more than a 2% discount to the A. We will not engage in transactions involving fewer than 10 shares of A or 50 shares of B.

Please be clear about one point: We will *never* make purchases with the intention of stemming a decline in Berkshire's price. Rather we will make them if and when we believe that they represent an attractive use of the Company's money. At best, repurchases are likely to have only a very minor effect on the future rate of gain in our stock's intrinsic value.

Shareholder-Designated Contributions

About 97.3% of all eligible shares participated in Berkshire's 1999 shareholder-designated contributions program, with contributions totaling $17.2 million. A full description of the program appears on pages 70 - 71.

Cumulatively, over the 19 years of the program, Berkshire has made contributions of $147 million pursuant to the instructions of our shareholders. The rest of Berkshire's giving is done by our subsidiaries, which stick to the philanthropic patterns that prevailed before they were acquired (except that their former owners themselves take on the responsibility for their personal charities). In aggregate, our subsidiaries made contributions of $13.8 million in 1999, including in-kind donations of $2.5 million.

To participate in future programs, you must own Class A shares that are registered in the name of the actual owner, not the nominee name of a broker, bank or depository. Shares not so registered on August 31, 2000, will be ineligible for the 2000 program. When you get the contributions form from us, return it promptly so that it does not get put aside or forgotten. Designations received after the due date will not be honored.

The Annual Meeting

This year's Woodstock Weekend for Capitalists will follow a format slightly different from that of recent years. We need to make a change because the Aksarben Coliseum, which served us well the past three years, is gradually being closed down. Therefore, we are relocating to the Civic Auditorium (which is on Capitol Avenue between 18th and 19th, behind the Doubletree Hotel), the only other facility in Omaha offering the space we require.

The Civic, however, is located in downtown Omaha, and we would create a parking and traffic nightmare if we were to meet there on a weekday. We will, therefore, convene on Saturday, April 29, with the doors opening at 7 a.m., the movie beginning at 8:30 and the meeting itself commencing at 9:30. As in the past, we will run until 3:30 with a short break at noon for food, which will be available at the Civic's concession stands.

An attachment to the proxy material that is enclosed with this report explains how you can obtain the credential you will need for admission to the meeting and other events. As for plane, hotel and car reservations, we have again signed up American Express (800-799-6634) to give you special help. In our normal fashion, we will run buses from the larger hotels to the meeting. After the meeting, the buses will make trips back to the hotels and to Nebraska Furniture Mart, Borsheim's and the airport. Even so, you are likely to find a car useful.

We have scheduled the meeting in 2002 and 2003 on the customary first Saturday in May. In 2001, however, the Civic is already booked on that Saturday, so we will meet on April 28. The Civic should fit our needs well on any weekend, since there will then be more than ample parking in nearby lots and garages as well as on streets. We will also be able to greatly enlarge the space we give exhibitors. So, overcoming my normal commercial reticence, I will see that you have a wide display of Berkshire products at the Civic that you can *purchase*. As a benchmark, in 1999 shareholders bought 3,059 pounds of See's candy, $16,155 of World Book Products, 1,928 pairs of Dexter shoes, 895 sets of Quikut knives, 1,752 golf balls with the Berkshire Hathaway logo and 3,446 items of Berkshire apparel. I know you can do better.

Last year, we also initiated the sale of at least eight fractions of Executive Jet aircraft. We will again have an array of models at the Omaha airport for your inspection on Saturday and Sunday. Ask an EJA representative at the Civic about viewing any of these planes.

Dairy Queen will also be on hand at the Civic and again will donate all proceeds to the Children's Miracle Network. Last year we sold 4,586 Dilly® bars, fudge bars and vanilla/orange bars. Additionally, GEICO will have a booth that will be staffed by a number of our top counselors from around the country, all of them ready to supply you with auto insurance quotes. In most cases, GEICO will be able to offer you a special shareholder's discount. Bring the details of your existing insurance, and check out whether we can save you some money.

Finally, Ajit Jain and his associates will be on hand to offer both no-commission annuities and a liability policy with jumbo limits of a size rarely available elsewhere. Talk to Ajit and learn how to protect yourself and your family against a $10 million judgment.

NFM's newly remodeled complex, located on a 75-acre site on 72nd Street between Dodge and Pacific, is open from 10 a.m. to 9 p.m. on weekdays and 10 a.m. to 6 p.m. on Saturdays and Sundays. This operation offers an unrivaled breadth of merchandise — furniture, electronics, appliances, carpets and computers — all at can't-be-beat prices. In 1999 NFM did more than $300 million of business at its 72nd Street location, which in a metropolitan area of 675,000 is an absolute miracle. During the Thursday, April 27 to Monday, May 1 period, any shareholder presenting his or her meeting credential will receive a discount that is customarily given only to employees. We have offered this break to shareholders the last couple of years, and sales have been amazing. In last year's five-day "Berkshire Weekend," NFM's volume was $7.98 million, an increase of 26% from 1998 and 51% from 1997.

Borsheim's — the largest jewelry store in the country except for Tiffany's Manhattan store — will have two shareholder-only events. The first will be a champagne and dessert party from 6 p.m.-10 p.m. on Friday, April 28. The second, the main gala, will be from 9 a.m. to 6 p.m. on Sunday, April 30. On that day, Charlie and I will be on hand to sign *sales tickets*. Shareholder prices will be available Thursday through Monday, so if you wish to avoid the largest crowds, which will form on Friday evening and Sunday, come at other times and identify yourself as a shareholder. On Saturday, we will be open until 7 p.m. Borsheim's operates on a gross margin that is fully twenty percentage points below that of its major rivals, so be prepared to be blown away by both our prices and selection.

In the mall outside of Borsheim's, we will again have Bob Hamman — the best bridge player the game has ever seen — available to play with our shareholders on Sunday. We will also have a few other experts playing at additional tables. In 1999, we had more demand than tables, but we will cure that problem this year.

Patrick Wolff, twice US chess champion, will again be in the mall playing blindfolded against all comers. He tells me that he has never tried to play more than four games simultaneously while handicapped this way but might try to bump that limit to five or six this year. If you're a chess fan, take Patrick on — but be sure to check his blindfold before your first move.

Gorat's — my favorite steakhouse — will again be open exclusively for Berkshire shareholders on Sunday, April 30, and will be serving from 4 p.m. until about midnight. Please remember that you can't come to Gorat's on Sunday without a reservation. To make one, call 402-551-3733 on April 3 (*but not before*). If Sunday is sold out, try Gorat's on one of the other evenings you will be in town. I make a "quality check" of Gorat's about once a week and can report that their rare T-bone (with a double order of hash browns) is still unequaled throughout the country.

The usual baseball game will be held at Rosenblatt Stadium at 7 p.m. on Saturday night. This year the Omaha Golden Spikes will play the Iowa Cubs. Come early, because that's when the real action takes place. Those who attended last year saw your Chairman pitch to Ernie Banks.

This encounter proved to be the titanic duel that the sports world had long awaited. After the first few pitches — which were not my best, but when have I ever thrown my best? — I fired a brushback at Ernie just to let him know who was in command. Ernie charged the mound, and I charged the plate. But a clash was avoided because we became exhausted before reaching each other.

Ernie was dissatisfied with his performance last year and has been studying the game films all winter. As you may know, Ernie had 512 home runs in his career as a Cub. Now that he has spotted telltale weaknesses in my delivery, he expects to get #513 on April 29. I, however, have learned new ways to disguise my "flutterball." Come and watch this matchup.

I should add that I have extracted a promise from Ernie that he will not hit a "come-backer" at me since I would never be able to duck in time to avoid it. My reflexes are like Woody Allen's, who said his were so slow that he was once hit by a car being pushed by two guys.

Our proxy statement contains instructions about obtaining tickets to the game and also a large quantity of other information that should help you enjoy your visit in Omaha. Join us at the Capitalist Caper on Capitol Avenue.

March 1, 2000

Warren E. Buffett
Chairman of the Board

BERKSHIRE HATHAWAY INC.

To the Shareholders of Berkshire Hathaway Inc.:

Our gain in net worth during 2000 was \$3.96 billion, which increased the per-share book value of both our Class A and Class B stock by 6.5%. Over the last 36 years (that is, since present management took over) per-share book value has grown from \$19 to \$40,442, a gain of 23.6% compounded annually.[*]

Overall, we had a decent year, our book-value gain having outpaced the performance of the S&P 500. And, though this judgment is necessarily subjective, we believe Berkshire's gain in per-share intrinsic value moderately exceeded its gain in book value. (Intrinsic value, as well as other key investment and accounting terms and concepts, are explained in our Owner's Manual on pages 59-66. Intrinsic value is discussed on page 64.)

Furthermore, we completed two significant acquisitions that we negotiated in 1999 and initiated six more. All told, these purchases have cost us about \$8 billion, with 97% of that amount paid in cash and 3% in stock. The eight businesses we've acquired have aggregate sales of about \$13 billion and employ 58,000 people. Still, we incurred no debt in making these purchases, and our shares outstanding have increased only $^1/_3$ of 1%. Better yet, we remain awash in liquid assets and are both eager and ready for even larger acquisitions.

I will detail our purchases in the next section of the report. But I will tell you now that we have embraced the 21st century by entering such cutting-edge industries as brick, carpet, insulation and paint. Try to control your excitement.

On the minus side, policyholder growth at GEICO slowed to a halt as the year progressed. It has become much more expensive to obtain new business. I told you last year that we would get our money's worth from stepped-up advertising at GEICO in 2000, but I was wrong. We'll examine the reasons later in the report.

Another negative — which has persisted for several years — is that we see our equity portfolio as only mildly attractive. We own stocks of some excellent businesses, but most of our holdings are fully priced and are unlikely to deliver more than moderate returns in the future. We're not alone in facing this problem: The long-term prospect for equities in general is far from exciting.

Finally, there is the negative that recurs annually: Charlie Munger, Berkshire's Vice Chairman and my partner, and I are a year older than when we last reported to you. Mitigating this adverse development is the indisputable fact that the age of your top managers is increasing at a considerably lower rate — *percentage-wise* — than is the case at almost all other major corporations. Better yet, this differential will widen in the future.

Charlie and I continue to aim at increasing Berkshire's per-share value at a rate that, over time, will modestly exceed the gain from owning the S&P 500. As the table on the facing page shows, a small annual advantage in our favor can, if sustained, produce an anything-but-small long-term advantage. To reach our goal we will need to add a few good businesses to Berkshire's stable each year, have the businesses we own generally gain in value, and avoid any material increase in our outstanding shares. We are confident about meeting the last two objectives; the first will require some luck.

It's appropriate here to thank two groups that made my job both easy and fun last year — just as they do every year. First, our operating managers continue to run their businesses in splendid fashion, which allows me to spend my time allocating capital rather than supervising them. (I wouldn't be good at that anyway.)

---

[*]All figures used in this report apply to Berkshire's A shares, the successor to the only stock that the company had outstanding before 1996. The B shares have an economic interest equal to 1/30th that of the A.

Our managers are a very special breed. At most large companies, the truly talented divisional managers seldom have the job they really want. Instead they yearn to become CEOs, either at their present employer or elsewhere. Indeed, if they stay put, they and their colleagues are likely to feel they have failed.

At Berkshire, our all-stars have *exactly* the jobs they want, ones that they hope and expect to keep throughout their business lifetimes. They therefore concentrate solely on maximizing the long-term value of the businesses that they "own" and love. If the businesses succeed, they have succeeded. And they stick with us: In our last 36 years, Berkshire has never had a manager of a significant subsidiary voluntarily leave to join another business.

The other group to which I owe enormous thanks is the home-office staff. After the eight acquisitions more than doubled our worldwide workforce to about 112,000, Charlie and I went soft last year and added one more person at headquarters. (Charlie, bless him, never lets me forget Ben Franklin's advice: "A small leak can sink a great ship.") Now we have 13.8 people.

This tiny band works miracles. In 2000 it handled all of the details connected with our eight acquisitions, processed extensive regulatory and tax filings (our tax return covers 4,896 pages), smoothly produced an annual meeting to which 25,000 tickets were issued, and accurately dispensed checks to 3,660 charities designated by our shareholders. In addition, the group dealt with all the routine tasks served up by a company with a revenue run-rate of $40 billion and more than 300,000 owners. And, to add to all of this, the other 12.8 are a delight to be around.

I should pay to have my job.

Acquisitions of 2000

Our acquisition technique at Berkshire is simplicity itself: We answer the phone. I'm also glad to report that it rings a bit more often now, because owners and/or managers increasingly wish to join their companies with Berkshire. Our acquisition criteria are set forth on page 23, and the number to call is 402-346-1400.

Let me tell you a bit about the businesses we have purchased during the past 14 months, starting with the two transactions that were initiated in 1999, but closed in 2000. (This list excludes some smaller purchases that were made by the managers of our subsidiaries and that, in most cases, will be integrated into their operations.)

- I described the first purchase — 76% of **MidAmerican Energy** — in last year's report. Because of regulatory constraints on our voting privileges, we perform only a "one-line" consolidation of MidAmerican's earnings and equity in our financial statements. If we instead fully consolidated the company's figures, our revenues in 2000 would have been $5 billion greater than we reported, though net income would remain the same.

- On November 23, 1999, I received a one-page fax from Bruce Cort that appended a *Washington Post* article describing an aborted buyout of **CORT Business Services**. Despite his name, Bruce has no connection with CORT. Rather, he is an airplane broker who had sold Berkshire a jet in 1986 and who, before the fax, had not been in touch with me for about ten years.

  I knew nothing about CORT, but I immediately printed out its SEC filings and liked what I saw. That same day I told Bruce I had a possible interest and asked him to arrange a meeting with Paul Arnold, CORT's CEO. Paul and I got together on November 29, and I knew at once that we had the right ingredients for a purchase: a fine though unglamorous business, an outstanding manager, and a price (going by that on the failed deal) that made sense.

  Operating out of 117 showrooms, CORT is the national leader in "rent-to-rent" furniture, primarily used in offices but also by temporary occupants of apartments. This business, it should be noted, has no similarity to "rent-to-own" operations, which usually involve the sale of home furnishings and electronics to people having limited income and poor credit.

We quickly purchased CORT for Wesco, our 80%-owned subsidiary, paying about $386 million in cash. You will find more details about CORT's operations in Wesco's 1999 and 2000 annual reports. Both Charlie and I enjoy working with Paul, and CORT looks like a good bet to beat our original expectations.

- Early last year, Ron Ferguson of General Re put me in contact with Bob Berry, whose family had owned **U.S. Liability** for 49 years. This insurer, along with two sister companies, is a medium-sized, highly-respected writer of unusual risks — "excess and surplus lines" in insurance jargon. After Bob and I got in touch, we agreed by phone on a half-stock, half-cash deal.

In recent years, Tom Nerney has managed the operation for the Berry family and has achieved a rare combination of excellent growth and unusual profitability. Tom is a powerhouse in other ways as well. In addition to having four adopted children (two from Russia), he has an extended family: the Philadelphia Belles, a young-teen girls basketball team that Tom coaches. The team had a 62-4 record last year and finished second in the AAU national tournament.

Few property-casualty companies are outstanding businesses. We have far more than our share, and U.S. Liability adds luster to the collection.

- **Ben Bridge Jeweler** was another purchase we made by phone, prior to any face-to-face meeting between me and the management. Ed Bridge, who with his cousin, Jon, manages this 65-store West Coast retailer, is a friend of Barnett Helzberg, from whom we bought Helzberg Diamonds in 1995. Upon learning that the Bridge family proposed to sell its company, Barnett gave Berkshire a strong recommendation. Ed then called and explained his business to me, also sending some figures, and we made a deal, again half for cash and half for stock.

Ed and Jon are fourth generation owner-managers of a business started 89 years ago in Seattle. Both the business and the family— including Herb and Bob, the fathers of Jon and Ed — enjoy extraordinary reputations. Same-store sales have increased by 9%, 11%, 13%, 10%, 12%, 21% and 7% over the past seven years, a truly remarkable record.

It was vital to the family that the company operate in the future as in the past. No one wanted another jewelry chain to come in and decimate the organization with ideas about synergy and cost saving (which, though they would never work, were certain to be tried). I told Ed and Jon that they would be in charge, and they knew I could be believed: After all, it's obvious that your Chairman would be a disaster at actually running a store or selling jewelry (though there are members of his family who have earned black belts as purchasers).

In their typically classy way, the Bridges allocated a substantial portion of the proceeds from their sale to the hundreds of co-workers who had helped the company achieve its success. We're proud to be associated with both the family and the company.

- In July we acquired **Justin Industries**, the leading maker of Western boots — including the Justin, Tony Lama, Nocona, and Chippewa brands — and the premier producer of brick in Texas and five neighboring states.

Here again, our acquisition involved serendipity. On May 4th, I received a fax from Mark Jones, a stranger to me, proposing that Berkshire join a group to acquire an unnamed company. I faxed him back, explaining that with rare exceptions we don't invest with others, but would happily pay him a commission if he sent details and we later made a purchase. He replied that the "mystery company" was Justin. I then went to Fort Worth to meet John Roach, chairman of the company and John Justin, who had built the business and was its major shareholder. Soon after, we bought Justin for $570 million in cash.

John Justin loved Justin Industries but had been forced to retire because of severe health problems (which sadly led to his death in late February). John was a class act — as a citizen, businessman and human being. Fortunately, he had groomed two outstanding managers, Harrold Melton at Acme and Randy Watson at Justin Boot, each of whom runs his company autonomously.

Acme, the larger of the two operations, produces more than one billion bricks per year at its 22 plants, about 11.7% of the industry's national output. The brick business, however, is necessarily regional, and in its territory Acme enjoys unquestioned leadership. When Texans are asked to name a brand of brick, 75% respond Acme, compared to 16% for the runner-up. (Before our purchase, I couldn't have named a brand of brick. Could you have?) This brand recognition is not only due to Acme's product quality, but also reflects many decades of extraordinary community service by both the company and John Justin.

I can't resist pointing out that Berkshire — whose top management has long been mired in the 19th century — is now one of the very few authentic "clicks-and-bricks" businesses around. We went into 2000 with GEICO doing significant business on the Internet, and then we added Acme. You can bet this move by Berkshire is making them *sweat* in Silicon Valley.

- In June, Bob Shaw, CEO of **Shaw Industries**, the world's largest carpet manufacturer, came to see me with his partner, Julian Saul, and the CEO of a second company with which Shaw was mulling a merger. The potential partner, however, faced huge asbestos liabilities from past activities, and any deal depended on these being eliminated through insurance.

  The executives visiting me wanted Berkshire to provide a policy that would pay *all* future asbestos costs. I explained that though we could write an exceptionally large policy — far larger than any other insurer would ever think of offering — we would never issue a policy that lacked a cap.

  Bob and Julian decided that if we didn't want to bet the ranch on the extent of the acquiree's liability, neither did they. So their deal died. But my interest in Shaw was sparked, and a few months later Charlie and I met with Bob to work out a purchase by Berkshire. A key feature of the deal was that both Bob and Julian were to continue owning at least 5% of Shaw. This leaves us associated with the best in the business as shown by Bob and Julian's record: Each built a large, successful carpet business before joining forces in 1998.

  Shaw has annual sales of about $4 billion, and we own 87.3% of the company. Leaving aside our insurance operation, Shaw is by far our largest business. Now, if people walk all over us, we won't mind.

- In July, Bob Mundheim, a director of **Benjamin Moore Paint**, called to ask if Berkshire might be interested in acquiring it. I knew Bob from Salomon, where he was general counsel during some difficult times, and held him in very high regard. So my answer was "Tell me more."

  In late August, Charlie and I met with Richard Roob and Yvan Dupuy, past and present CEOs of Benjamin Moore. We liked them; we liked the business; and we made a $1 billion cash offer on the spot. In October, their board approved the transaction, and we completed it in December. Benjamin Moore has been making paint for 117 years and has thousands of independent dealers that are a vital asset to its business. Make sure you specify our product for your next paint job.

- Finally, in late December, we agreed to buy **Johns Manville Corp.** for about $1.8 billion. This company's incredible odyssey over the last few decades — too multifaceted to be chronicled here — was shaped by its long history as a manufacturer of asbestos products. The much-publicized health problems that affected many people exposed to asbestos led to JM's declaring bankruptcy in 1982.

  Subsequently, the bankruptcy court established a trust for victims, the major asset of which was a controlling interest in JM. The trust, which sensibly wanted to diversify its assets, agreed last June to sell the business to an LBO buyer. In the end, though, the LBO group was unable to obtain financing.

Consequently, the deal was called off on Friday, December 8th. The following Monday, Charlie and I called Bob Felise, chairman of the trust, and made an all-cash offer with no financing contingencies. The next day the trustees voted tentatively to accept our offer, and a week later we signed a contract.

JM is the nation's leading producer of commercial and industrial insulation and also has major positions in roofing systems and a variety of engineered products. The company's sales exceed $2 billion and the business has earned good, if cyclical, returns. Jerry Henry, JM's CEO, had announced his retirement plans a year ago, but I'm happy to report that Charlie and I have convinced him to stick around.

* * * * * * * * * * * *

Two economic factors probably contributed to the rush of acquisition activity we experienced last year. First, many managers and owners foresaw near-term slowdowns in their businesses — and, in fact, we purchased several companies whose earnings will almost certainly decline this year from peaks they reached in 1999 or 2000. The declines make no difference to us, given that we expect all of our businesses to now and then have ups and downs. (Only in the sales presentations of investment banks do earnings move forever upward.) We don't care about the bumps; what matters are the overall results. But the decisions of other people are sometimes affected by the near-term outlook, which can both spur sellers and temper the enthusiasm of purchasers who might otherwise compete with us.

A second factor that helped us in 2000 was that the market for junk bonds dried up as the year progressed. In the two preceding years, junk bond purchasers had relaxed their standards, buying the obligations of ever-weaker issuers at inappropriate prices. The effects of this laxity were felt last year in a ballooning of defaults. In this environment, "financial" buyers of businesses — those who wish to buy using only a sliver of equity — became unable to borrow all they thought they needed. What they could still borrow, moreover, came at a high price. Consequently, LBO operators became less aggressive in their bidding when businesses came up for sale last year. Because we analyze purchases on an all-equity basis, our evaluations did not change, which means we became considerably more competitive.

Aside from the economic factors that benefited us, we now enjoy a major and growing advantage in making acquisitions in that we are often the buyer of choice for the seller. That fact, of course, doesn't assure a deal — sellers have to like our price, and we have to like their business and management — but it does help.

We find it meaningful when an owner *cares* about whom he sells to. We like to do business with someone who loves his company, not just the money that a sale will bring him (though we certainly understand why he likes that as well). When this emotional attachment exists, it signals that important qualities will likely be found within the business: honest accounting, pride of product, respect for customers, and a loyal group of associates having a strong sense of direction. The reverse is apt to be true, also. When an owner auctions off his business, exhibiting a total lack of interest in what follows, you will frequently find that it has been dressed up for sale, particularly when the seller is a "financial owner." And if owners behave with little regard for their business and its people, their conduct will often contaminate attitudes and practices throughout the company.

When a business masterpiece has been created by a lifetime — or several lifetimes — of unstinting care and exceptional talent, it should be important to the owner what corporation is entrusted to carry on its history. Charlie and I believe Berkshire provides an almost unique home. We take our obligations to the people who created a business very seriously, and Berkshire's ownership structure ensures that we can fulfill our promises. When we tell John Justin that his business will remain headquartered in Fort Worth, or assure the Bridge family that its operation will not be merged with another jeweler, these sellers can take those promises to the bank.

How much better it is for the "painter" of a business Rembrandt to personally select its permanent home than to have a trust officer or uninterested heirs auction it off. Throughout the years we have had great experiences with those who recognize that truth and apply it to their business creations. We'll leave the auctions to others.

The Economics of Property/Casualty Insurance

Our main business — though we have others of great importance — is insurance. To understand Berkshire, therefore, it is necessary that you understand how to evaluate an insurance company. The key determinants are: (1) the amount of float that the business generates; (2) its cost; and (3) most critical of all, the long-term outlook for both of these factors.

To begin with, float is money we hold but don't own. In an insurance operation, float arises because premiums are received before losses are paid, an interval that sometimes extends over many years. During that time, the insurer invests the money. This pleasant activity typically carries with it a downside: The premiums that an insurer takes in usually do not cover the losses and expenses it eventually must pay. That leaves it running an "underwriting loss," which is the cost of float. An insurance business has value if its cost of float over time is less than the cost the company would otherwise incur to obtain funds. But the business is a lemon if its cost of float is higher than market rates for money.

A caution is appropriate here: Because loss costs must be estimated, insurers have enormous latitude in figuring their underwriting results, and that makes it very difficult for investors to calculate a company's true cost of float. Errors of estimation, usually innocent but sometimes not, can be huge. The consequences of these miscalculations flow directly into earnings. An experienced observer can usually detect large-scale errors in reserving, but the general public can typically do no more than accept what's presented, and at times I have been amazed by the numbers that big-name auditors have implicitly blessed. Both the income statements and balance sheets of insurers can be minefields.

At Berkshire, we strive to be both consistent and conservative in our reserving. But we will make mistakes. And we warn you that there is nothing symmetrical about surprises in the insurance business: They almost always are unpleasant.

The table that follows shows (at intervals) the float generated by the various segments of Berkshire's insurance operations since we entered the business 34 years ago upon acquiring National Indemnity Company (whose traditional lines are included in the segment "Other Primary"). For the table we have calculated our float — which we generate in large amounts relative to our premium volume — by adding net loss reserves, loss adjustment reserves, funds held under reinsurance assumed and unearned premium reserves, and then subtracting insurance-related receivables, prepaid acquisition costs, prepaid taxes and deferred charges applicable to assumed reinsurance. (Don't panic, there won't be a quiz.)

Yearend Float (in $ millions)

Year	GEICO	General Re	Other Reinsurance	Other Primary	Total
1967				20	20
1977			40	131	171
1987			701	807	1,508
1997	2,917		4,014	455	7,386
1998	3,125	14,909	4,305	415	22,754
1999	3,444	15,166	6,285	403	25,298
2000	3,943	15,525	7,805	598	27,871

We're pleased by the growth in our float during 2000 but not happy with its cost. Over the years, our cost of float has been very close to zero, with the underwriting profits realized in most years offsetting the occasional terrible year such as 1984, when our cost was a staggering 19%. In 2000, however, we had an underwriting loss of $1.6 billion, which gave us a float cost of 6%. Absent a mega-catastrophe, we expect our float cost to fall in 2001 — perhaps substantially — in large part because of corrections in pricing at General Re that should increasingly be felt as the year progresses. On a smaller scale, GEICO may experience the same improving trend.

There are two factors affecting our cost of float that are very rare at other insurers but that now loom large at Berkshire. First, a few insurers that are currently experiencing large losses have offloaded a significant portion of these on us in a manner that penalizes our current earnings but gives us float we can use for many years to come. After the loss that we incur in the first year of the policy, there are *no* further costs attached to this business.

When these policies are properly priced, we welcome the pain-today, gain-tomorrow effects they have. In 1999, $400 million of our underwriting loss (about 27.8% of the total) came from business of this kind and in 2000 the figure was $482 million (34.4% of our loss). We have no way of predicting how much similar business we will write in the future, but what we do get will typically be in large chunks. Because these transactions can materially distort our figures, we will tell you about them as they occur.

Other reinsurers have little taste for this insurance. They simply can't stomach what huge underwriting losses do to their reported results, even though these losses are produced by policies whose overall economics are certain to be favorable. You should be careful, therefore, in comparing our underwriting results with those of other insurers.

An even more significant item in our numbers — which, again, you won't find much of elsewhere — arises from transactions in which we assume *past* losses of a company that wants to put its troubles behind it. To illustrate, the XYZ insurance company might have last year bought a policy obligating us to pay the first $1 billion of losses and loss adjustment expenses from events that happened in, say, 1995 and earlier years. These contracts can be very large, though we always require a cap on our exposure. We entered into a number of such transactions in 2000 and expect to close several more in 2001.

Under GAAP accounting, this "retroactive" insurance neither benefits nor penalizes our current earnings. Instead, we set up an asset called "deferred charges applicable to assumed reinsurance," in an amount reflecting the difference between the premium we receive and the (higher) losses we expect to pay (for which reserves are immediately established). We then amortize this asset by making annual charges to earnings that create equivalent underwriting losses. You will find the amount of the loss that we incur from these transactions in both our quarterly and annual management discussion. By their nature, these losses will continue for many years, often stretching into decades. As an offset, though, we have the use of float — lots of it.

Clearly, float carrying an annual cost of this kind is not as desirable as float we generate from policies that are expected to produce an underwriting profit (of which we have plenty). Nevertheless, this retroactive insurance should be decent business for us.

The net of all this is that a) I expect our cost of float to be very attractive in the future but b) rarely to return to a "no-cost" mode because of the annual charge that retroactive reinsurance will lay on us. Also — obviously — the ultimate benefits that we derive from float will depend not only on its cost but, fully as important, how effectively we deploy it.

Our retroactive business is almost single-handedly the work of Ajit Jain, whose praises I sing annually. It is impossible to overstate how valuable Ajit is to Berkshire. Don't worry about my health; worry about his.

Last year, Ajit brought home a $2.4 billion reinsurance premium, perhaps the largest in history, from a policy that retroactively covers a major U.K. company. Subsequently, he wrote a large policy protecting the Texas Rangers from the possibility that Alex Rodriguez will become permanently disabled. As sports fans know, "A-Rod" was signed for $252 million, a record, and we think that our policy probably also set a record for disability insurance. We cover many other sports figures as well.

In another example of his versatility, Ajit last fall negotiated a very interesting deal with Grab.com, an Internet company whose goal was to attract millions of people to its site and there to extract information from them that would be useful to marketers. To lure these people, Grab.com held out the possibility of a $1 billion prize (having a $170 million present value) and we insured its payment. A message on the site explained that the chance of anyone winning the prize was low, and indeed no one won. But the possibility of a win was far from nil.

Writing such a policy, we receive a modest premium, face the possibility of a huge loss, and get good odds. Very few insurers like that equation. And they're unable to cure their unhappiness by reinsurance. Because each policy has unusual — and sometimes unique — characteristics, insurers can't lay off the occasional shock loss through their standard reinsurance arrangements. Therefore, any insurance CEO doing a piece of business like this must run the small, but real, risk of a horrible quarterly earnings number, one that he would not enjoy explaining to his board or shareholders. Charlie and I, however, like any proposition that makes compelling mathematical sense, regardless of its effect on reported earnings.

At General Re, the news has turned considerably better: Ron Ferguson, along with Joe Brandon, Tad Montross, and a talented supporting cast took many actions during 2000 to bring that company's profitability back to past standards. Though our pricing is not fully corrected, we have significantly repriced business that was severely unprofitable or dropped it altogether. If there's no mega-catastrophe in 2001, General Re's float cost should fall materially.

The last couple of years haven't been any fun for Ron and his crew. But they have stepped up to tough decisions, and Charlie and I applaud them for these. General Re has several important and enduring business advantages. Better yet, it has managers who will make the most of them.

In aggregate, our smaller insurance operations produced an excellent underwriting profit in 2000 while generating significant float — just as they have done for more than a decade. If these companies were a single and separate operation, people would consider it an outstanding insurer. Because the companies instead reside in an enterprise as large as Berkshire, the world may not appreciate their accomplishments — but I sure do. Last year I thanked Rod Eldred, John Kizer, Don Towle and Don Wurster, and I again do so. In addition, we now also owe thanks to Tom Nerney at U.S. Liability and Michael Stearns, the new head of Cypress.

You may notice that Brad Kinstler, who *was* CEO of Cypress and whose praises I've sung in the past, is no longer in the list above. That's because we needed a new manager at Fechheimer Bros., our Cincinnati-based uniform company, and called on Brad. We seldom move Berkshire managers from one enterprise to another, but maybe we should try it more often: Brad is hitting home runs in his new job, just as he always did at Cypress.

GEICO (1-800-847-7536 or GEICO.com)

We show below the usual table detailing GEICO's growth. Last year I enthusiastically told you that we would step up our expenditures on advertising in 2000 and that the added dollars were the best investment that GEICO could make. I was wrong: The extra money we spent did not produce a commensurate increase in inquiries. Additionally, the percentage of inquiries that we converted into sales fell for the first time in many years. These negative developments combined to produce a sharp increase in our per-policy acquisition cost.

Years	New Auto Policies[1]	Auto Policies In-Force[1]
1993	346,882	2,011,055
1994	384,217	2,147,549
1995	443,539	2,310,037
1996	592,300	2,543,699
1997	868,430	2,949,439
1998	1,249,875	3,562,644
1999	1,648,095	4,328,900
2000	1,472,853	4,696,842

[1] "Voluntary" only; excludes assigned risks and the like.

Agonizing over errors is a mistake. But acknowledging and analyzing them can be useful, though that practice is rare in corporate boardrooms. There, Charlie and I have almost never witnessed a candid post-mortem of a failed decision, *particularly one involving an acquisition*. A notable exception to this never-look-back approach is that of The Washington Post Company, which unfailingly and objectively reviews its acquisitions three years after they are made. Elsewhere, triumphs are trumpeted, but dumb decisions either get no follow-up or are rationalized.

The financial consequences of these boners are regularly dumped into massive restructuring charges or write-offs that are casually waved off as "nonrecurring." Managements just love these. Indeed, in recent years it has seemed that no earnings statement is complete without them. The origins of these charges, though, are never explored. When it comes to corporate blunders, CEOs invoke the concept of the Virgin Birth.

To get back to our examination of GEICO: There are at least four factors that could account for the increased costs we experienced in obtaining new business last year, and all probably contributed in some manner.

First, in our advertising we have pushed "frequency" very hard, and we probably overstepped in certain media. We've always known that increasing the number of messages through any medium would eventually produce diminishing returns. The third ad in an hour on a given cable channel is simply not going to be as effective as the first.

Second, we may have already picked much of the low-hanging fruit. Clearly, the willingness to do business with a direct marketer of insurance varies widely among individuals: Indeed, some percentage of Americans — particularly older ones — are reluctant to make direct purchases of any kind. Over the years, however, this reluctance will ebb. A new generation with new habits will find the savings from direct purchase of their auto insurance too compelling to ignore.

Another factor that surely decreased the conversion of inquiries into sales was stricter underwriting by GEICO. Both the frequency and severity of losses increased during the year, and rates in certain areas became inadequate, in some cases substantially so. In these instances, we necessarily tightened our underwriting standards. This tightening, as well as the many rate increases we put in during the year, made our offerings less attractive to some prospects.

A high percentage of callers, it should be emphasized, can still save money by insuring with us. Understandably, however, some prospects will switch to save $200 per year but will not switch to save $50. Therefore, rate increases that bring our prices closer to those of our competitors will hurt our acceptance rate, even when we continue to offer the best deal.

Finally, the competitive picture changed in at least one important respect: State Farm — by far the largest personal auto insurer, with about 19% of the market — has been very slow to raise prices. Its costs, however, are clearly increasing right along with those of the rest of the industry. Consequently, State Farm had an underwriting loss last year from auto insurance (including rebates to policyholders) of 18% of premiums, compared to 4% at GEICO. Our loss produced a float cost for us of 6.1%, an unsatisfactory result. (Indeed, at GEICO we expect float, over time, to be free.) But we estimate that State Farm's float cost in 2000 was about 23%. The willingness of the largest player in the industry to tolerate such a cost makes the economics difficult for other participants.

That does not take away from the fact that State Farm is one of America's greatest business stories. I've urged that the company be studied at business schools because it has achieved fabulous success while following a path that in many ways defies the dogma of those institutions. Studying counter-evidence is a highly useful activity, though not one always greeted with enthusiasm at citadels of learning.

State Farm was launched in 1922, by a 45-year-old, semi-retired Illinois farmer, to compete with long-established insurers — haughty institutions in New York, Philadelphia and Hartford — that possessed overwhelming advantages in capital, reputation, and distribution. Because State Farm is a mutual company, its board members and managers could not be owners, and it had no access to capital markets during its years of fast growth. Similarly, the business never had the stock options or lavish salaries that many people think vital if an American enterprise is to attract able managers and thrive.

In the end, however, State Farm eclipsed all its competitors. In fact, by 1999 the company had amassed a tangible net worth exceeding that of all but four American businesses. If you want to read how this happened, get a copy of *The Farmer from Merna*.

Despite State Farm's strengths, however, GEICO has much the better business model, one that embodies significantly lower operating costs. And, when a company is selling a product with commodity-like economic characteristics, being the low-cost producer is all-important. This enduring competitive advantage of GEICO — one it possessed in 1951 when, as a 20-year-old student, I first became enamored with its stock — is the reason that over time it will inevitably increase its market share significantly while simultaneously achieving excellent profits. Our growth will be slow, however, if State Farm elects to continue bearing the underwriting losses that it is now suffering.

Tony Nicely, GEICO's CEO, remains an owner's dream. Everything he does makes sense. He never engages in wishful thinking or otherwise distorts reality, as so many managers do when the unexpected happens. As 2000 unfolded, Tony cut back on advertising that was not cost-effective, and he will continue to do that in 2001 if cutbacks are called for (though we will always maintain a *massive* media presence). Tony has also aggressively filed for price increases where we need them. He looks at the loss reports every day and is never behind the curve. To steal a line from a competitor, we are in good hands with Tony.

I've told you about our profit-sharing arrangement at GEICO that targets only two variables — growth in policies and the underwriting results of seasoned business. Despite the headwinds of 2000, we still had a performance that produced an 8.8% profit-sharing payment, amounting to $40.7 million.

GEICO will be a huge part of Berkshire's future. Because of its rock-bottom operating costs, it offers a great many Americans the cheapest way to purchase a high-ticket product that they *must* buy. The company then couples this bargain with service that consistently ranks high in independent surveys. That's a combination inevitably producing growth and profitability.

In just the last few years, *far* more drivers have learned to associate the GEICO brand with saving money on their insurance. We will pound that theme relentlessly until all Americans are aware of the value that we offer.

Investments

Below we present our common stock investments. Those that had a market value of more than $1 billion at the end of 2000 are itemized.

		12/31/00	
Shares	*Company*	*Cost*	*Market*
		(dollars in millions)	
151,610,700	American Express Company	$1,470	$ 8,329
200,000,000	The Coca-Cola Company	1,299	12,188
96,000,000	The Gillette Company	600	3,468
1,727,765	The Washington Post Company	11	1,066
55,071,380	Wells Fargo & Company	319	3,067
	Others	6,703	9,501
	Total Common Stocks	$10,402	$ 37,619

In 2000, we sold nearly all of our Freddie Mac and Fannie Mae shares, established 15% positions in several mid-sized companies, bought the high-yield bonds of a few issuers (very few — the category is not labeled junk without reason) and added to our holdings of high-grade, mortgage-backed securities. There are no "bargains" among our current holdings: We're content with what we own but far from excited by it.

Many people assume that marketable securities are Berkshire's first choice when allocating capital, but that's not true: Ever since we first published our economic principles in 1983, we have consistently stated that we would rather purchase businesses than stocks. (See number 4 on page 60.) One reason for that preference is personal, in that I love working with our managers. They are high-grade, talented and loyal. And, frankly, I find their business behavior to be more rational and owner-oriented than that prevailing at many public companies.

12

But there's also a powerful financial reason behind the preference, and that has to do with taxes. The tax code makes Berkshire's owning 80% or more of a business far more profitable for us, proportionately, than our owning a smaller share. When a company we own all of earns $1 million after tax, the entire amount inures to our benefit. If the $1 million is upstreamed to Berkshire, we owe no tax on the dividend. And, if the earnings are retained and we were to sell the subsidiary — not likely at Berkshire! — for $1million more than we paid for it, we would owe no capital gains tax. That's because our "tax cost" upon sale would include both what we paid for the business and all earnings it subsequently retained.

Contrast that situation to what happens when we own an investment in a marketable security. There, if we own a 10% stake in a business earning $10 million after tax, our $1 million share of the earnings is subject to *additional* state and federal taxes of (1) about $140,000 if it is distributed to us (our tax rate on most dividends is 14%); or (2) no less than $350,000 if the $1 million is retained and subsequently captured by us in the form of a capital gain (on which our tax rate is usually about 35%, though it sometimes approaches 40%). We may defer paying the $350,000 by not immediately realizing our gain, but eventually we must pay the tax. In effect, the government is our "partner" twice when we own part of a business through a stock investment, but only once when we own at least 80%.

Leaving aside tax factors, the formula we use for evaluating stocks and businesses is identical. Indeed, the formula for valuing *all* assets that are purchased for financial gain has been unchanged since it was first laid out by a very smart man in about 600 B.C. (though he wasn't smart enough to know it was 600 B.C.).

The oracle was Aesop and his enduring, though somewhat incomplete, investment insight was "a bird in the hand is worth two in the bush." To flesh out this principle, you must answer only three questions. How certain are you that there are indeed birds in the bush? When will they emerge and how many will there be? What is the risk-free interest rate (which we consider to be the yield on long-term U.S. bonds)? If you can answer these three questions, you will know the maximum value of the bush — and the maximum number of the birds you now possess that should be offered for it. And, of course, don't literally think birds. Think dollars.

Aesop's investment axiom, thus expanded and converted into dollars, is immutable. It applies to outlays for farms, oil royalties, bonds, stocks, lottery tickets, and manufacturing plants. And neither the advent of the steam engine, the harnessing of electricity nor the creation of the automobile changed the formula one iota — nor will the Internet. Just insert the correct numbers, and you can rank the attractiveness of all possible uses of capital throughout the universe.

Common yardsticks such as dividend yield, the ratio of price to earnings or to book value, and even growth rates have *nothing* to do with valuation except to the extent they provide clues to the amount and timing of cash flows into and from the business. Indeed, growth can destroy value if it requires cash inputs in the early years of a project or enterprise that exceed the discounted value of the cash that those assets will generate in later years. Market commentators and investment managers who glibly refer to "growth" and "value" styles as contrasting approaches to investment are displaying their ignorance, not their sophistication. Growth is simply a component — usually a plus, sometimes a minus — in the value equation.

Alas, though Aesop's proposition and the third variable — that is, interest rates — are simple, plugging in numbers for the other two variables is a difficult task. Using precise numbers is, in fact, foolish; working with a range of possibilities is the better approach.

Usually, the range must be so wide that no useful conclusion can be reached. Occasionally, though, even very conservative estimates about the future emergence of birds reveal that the price quoted is startlingly low in relation to value. (Let's call this phenomenon the IBT — Inefficient Bush Theory.) To be sure, an investor needs some general understanding of business economics as well as the ability to think independently to reach a well-founded positive conclusion. But the investor does not need brilliance nor blinding insights.

At the other extreme, there are many times when the *most* brilliant of investors can't muster a conviction about the birds to emerge, not even when a very broad range of estimates is employed. This kind of uncertainty frequently occurs when new businesses and rapidly changing industries are under examination. In cases of this sort, *any* capital commitment must be labeled speculative.

Now, speculation — in which the focus is not on what an asset will produce but rather on what the next fellow will pay for it — is neither illegal, immoral nor un-American. But it is not a game in which Charlie and I wish to play. We bring nothing to the party, so why should we expect to take anything home?

The line separating investment and speculation, which is never bright and clear, becomes blurred still further when most market participants have recently enjoyed triumphs. Nothing sedates rationality like large doses of effortless money. After a heady experience of that kind, normally sensible people drift into behavior akin to that of Cinderella at the ball. They know that overstaying the festivities — that is, continuing to speculate in companies that have gigantic valuations relative to the cash they are likely to generate in the future — will eventually bring on pumpkins and mice. But they nevertheless hate to miss a single minute of what is one helluva party. Therefore, the giddy participants all plan to leave just seconds before midnight. There's a problem, though: They are dancing in a room in which the clocks have no hands.

Last year, we commented on the exuberance — and, yes, it was irrational — that prevailed, noting that investor expectations had grown to be several multiples of probable returns. One piece of evidence came from a Paine Webber-Gallup survey of investors conducted in December 1999, in which the participants were asked their opinion about the annual returns investors could expect to realize over the decade ahead. Their answers averaged 19%. That, for sure, was an irrational expectation: For American business as a whole, there couldn't possibly be enough birds in the 2009 bush to deliver such a return.

Far more irrational still were the huge valuations that market participants were then putting on businesses almost certain to end up being of modest or no value. Yet investors, mesmerized by soaring stock prices and ignoring all else, piled into these enterprises. It was as if some virus, racing wildly among investment professionals as well as amateurs, induced hallucinations in which the values of stocks in certain sectors became decoupled from the values of the businesses that underlay them.

This surreal scene was accompanied by much loose talk about "value creation." We readily acknowledge that there has been a huge amount of true value created in the past decade by new or young businesses, and that there is much more to come. But value is destroyed, not created, by any business that loses money over its lifetime, no matter how high its interim valuation may get.

What actually occurs in these cases is wealth *transfer*, often on a massive scale. By shamelessly merchandising birdless bushes, promoters have in recent years moved billions of dollars from the pockets of the public to their own purses (and to those of their friends and associates). The fact is that a bubble market has allowed the creation of bubble companies, entities designed more with an eye to making money *off* investors rather than *for* them. Too often, an IPO, not profits, was the primary goal of a company's promoters. At bottom, the "business model" for these companies has been the old-fashioned chain letter, for which many fee-hungry investment bankers acted as eager postmen.

But a pin lies in wait for every bubble. And when the two eventually meet, a new wave of investors learns some very old lessons: First, many in Wall Street — a community in which quality control is not prized — will sell investors anything they will buy. Second, speculation is most dangerous when it looks easiest.

At Berkshire, we make *no* attempt to pick the few winners that will emerge from an ocean of unproven enterprises. We're not smart enough to do that, and we know it. Instead, we try to apply Aesop's 2,600-year-old equation to opportunities in which we have reasonable confidence as to how many birds are in the bush and when they will emerge (a formulation that my grandsons would probably update to "A girl in a convertible is worth five in the phonebook."). Obviously, we can never precisely predict the timing of cash flows in and out of a business or their exact amount. We try, therefore, to keep our estimates conservative and to focus on industries where business surprises are unlikely to wreak havoc on owners. Even so, we make many mistakes: I'm the fellow, remember, who thought he understood the future economics of trading stamps, textiles, shoes and second-tier department stores.

Lately, the most promising "bushes" have been negotiated transactions for entire businesses, and that pleases us. You should clearly understand, however, that these acquisitions will at best provide us only reasonable returns. Really juicy results from negotiated deals can be anticipated only when capital markets are severely constrained and the whole business world is pessimistic. We are 180 degrees from that point.

Sources of Reported Earnings

The table that follows shows the main sources of Berkshire's reported earnings. In this presentation, purchase-accounting adjustments are not assigned to the specific businesses to which they apply, but are instead aggregated and shown separately. This procedure lets you view the earnings of our businesses as they would have been reported had we not purchased them. For the reasons discussed on page 65, this form of presentation seems to us to be more useful to investors and managers than one utilizing generally accepted accounting principles (GAAP), which require purchase-premiums to be charged off business-by-business. The total net earnings we show in the table are, of course, identical to the GAAP total in our audited financial statements.

	(in millions)			
			Berkshire's Share of Net Earnings (after taxes and minority interests)	
	Pre-Tax Earnings			
	2000	*1999*	*2000*	*1999*
Operating Earnings:				
Insurance Group:				
Underwriting – Reinsurance	$(1,399)	$(1,440)	$(899)	$(927)
Underwriting – GEICO	(224)	24	(146)	16
Underwriting – Other Primary	38	22	24	14
Net Investment Income	2,747	2,482	1,929	1,764
Finance and Financial Products Business	556	125	360	86
Flight Services	213	225	126	132
MidAmerican Energy (76% owned)	197	--	109	--
Retail Operations	175	130	104	77
Scott Fetzer (excluding finance operation)	122	147	80	92
Other Businesses	225	210	134	131
Purchase-Accounting Adjustments	(881)	(739)	(843)	(648)
Corporate Interest Expense	(92)	(109)	(61)	(70)
Shareholder-Designated Contributions	(17)	(17)	(11)	(11)
Other	39	25	30	15
Operating Earnings	1,699	1,085	936	671
Capital Gains from Investments	3,955	1,365	2,392	886
Total Earnings – All Entities	$5,654	$2,450	$3,328	$1,557

Most of our manufacturing, retailing and service businesses did at least reasonably well last year.

The exception was shoes, particularly at Dexter. In our shoe businesses generally, our attempt to keep the bulk of our production in domestic factories has cost us dearly. We face another very tough year in 2001 also, as we make significant changes in how we do business.

I clearly made a mistake in paying what I did for Dexter in 1993. Furthermore, I compounded that mistake in a huge way by using Berkshire shares in payment. Last year, to recognize my error, we charged off all the remaining accounting goodwill that was attributable to the Dexter transaction. We may regain some economic goodwill at Dexter in the future, but we clearly have none at present.

The managers of our shoe businesses are first-class from both a business and human perspective. They are working very hard at a tough — and often terribly painful — job, even though their personal financial circumstances don't require them to do so. They have my admiration and thanks.

On a more pleasant note, we continue to be the undisputed leader in two branches of Aircraft Services — pilot training at FlightSafety (FSI) and fractional ownership of business jets at Executive Jet (EJA). Both companies are run by their remarkable founders.

Al Ueltschi at FSI is now 83 and continues to operate at full throttle. Though I am not a fan of stock splits, I am planning to split Al's age 2-for-1 when he hits 100. (If it works, guess who's next.)

We spent $272 million on flight simulators in 2000, and we'll spend a similar amount this year. Anyone who thinks that the annual charges for depreciation don't reflect a real cost — every bit as real as payroll or raw materials — should get an internship at a simulator company. Every year we spend amounts equal to our depreciation charge simply to stay in the same economic place — and then spend additional sums to grow. And growth is in prospect for FSI as far as the eye can see.

Even faster growth awaits EJA (whose fractional-ownership program is called NetJets®). Rich Santulli is the dynamo behind this business.

Last year I told you that EJA's recurring revenue from monthly management fees and hourly usage grew by 46% in 1999. In 2000 the growth was 49%. I also told you that this was a low-margin business, in which survivors will be few. Margins were indeed slim at EJA last year, in part because of the major costs we are incurring in developing our business in Europe.

Regardless of the cost, you can be sure that EJA's spending on safety will be whatever is needed. Obviously, we would follow this policy under any circumstances, but there's some self-interest here as well: I, my wife, my children, my sisters, my 94-year-old aunt, all but one of our directors, and at least nine Berkshire managers regularly fly in the NetJets program. Given that cargo, I applaud Rich's insistence on unusually high amounts of pilot training (an average of 23 days a year). In addition, our pilots cement their skills by flying 800 or so hours a year. Finally, each flies only one model of aircraft, which means our crews do no switching around among planes with different cockpit and flight characteristics.

EJA's business continues to be constrained by the availability of new aircraft. Still, our customers will take delivery of more than 50 new jets in 2001, 7% of world output. We are confident we will remain the world leader in fractional ownership, in respect to number of planes flying, quality of service, and standards of safety.

* * * * * * * * * *

Additional information about our various businesses is given on pages 42-58, where you will also find our segment earnings reported on a GAAP basis. In addition, on pages 67-73, we have rearranged Berkshire's financial data into four segments on a non-GAAP basis, a presentation that corresponds to the way Charlie and I think about the company.

Look-Through Earnings

Reported earnings are an inadequate measure of economic progress at Berkshire, in part because the numbers shown in the table on page 15 include only the dividends we receive from investees — though these dividends typically represent only a small fraction of the earnings attributable to our ownership. To depict something closer to economic reality at Berkshire than reported earnings, though, we employ the concept of "look-through" earnings. As we calculate these, they consist of: (1) the operating earnings reported on page 15; plus; (2) our share of the retained operating earnings of major investees that, under GAAP accounting, are not reflected in our profits, less; (3) an allowance for the tax that would be paid by Berkshire if these retained earnings of investees had instead been distributed to us. When tabulating "operating earnings" here, we exclude purchase-accounting adjustments as well as capital gains and other major non-recurring items.

The following table sets forth our 2000 look-through earnings, though I warn you that the figures can be no more than approximate, since they are based on a number of judgment calls. (The dividends paid to us by these investees have been included in the operating earnings itemized on page 15, mostly under "Insurance Group: Net Investment Income.")

Berkshire's Major Investees	Berkshire's Approximate Ownership at Yearend[1]	Berkshire's Share of Undistributed Operating Earnings (in millions)[2]
American Express Company	11.4%	$265
The Coca-Cola Company	8.1%	160
Freddie Mac	0.3%	106
The Gillette Company	9.1%	51
M&T Bank	7.2%	23
The Washington Post Company	18.3%	18
Wells Fargo & Company	3.2%	117

Berkshire's share of undistributed earnings of major investees	740
Hypothetical tax on these undistributed investee earnings[3]	(104)
Reported operating earnings of Berkshire	1,779
Total look-through earnings of Berkshire	$ 2,415

(1) Does not include shares allocable to minority interests
(2) Calculated on average ownership for the year
(3) The tax rate used is 14%, which is the rate Berkshire pays on most dividends it receives

Full and Fair Reporting

At Berkshire, full reporting means giving you the information that we would wish you to give to us if our positions were reversed. What Charlie and I would want under that circumstance would be all the important facts about current operations as well as the CEO's frank view of the long-term economic characteristics of the business. We would expect both a lot of financial details and a discussion of any significant data we would need to interpret what was presented.

When Charlie and I read reports, we have no interest in pictures of personnel, plants or products. References to EBITDA make us shudder — does management think the tooth fairy pays for capital expenditures? We're very suspicious of accounting methodology that is vague or unclear, since too often that means management wishes to hide something. And we don't want to read messages that a public relations department or consultant has turned out. Instead, we expect a company's CEO to explain in his or her own words what's happening.

For us, fair reporting means getting information to our 300,000 "partners" simultaneously, or as close to that mark as possible. We therefore put our annual and quarterly financials on the Internet between the close of the market on a Friday and the following morning. By our doing that, shareholders and other interested investors have timely access to these important releases and also have a reasonable amount of time to digest the information they include before the markets open on Monday. This year our quarterly information will be available on the Saturdays of May 12, August 11, and November 10. The 2001 annual report will be posted on March 9.

We applaud the work that Arthur Levitt, Jr., until recently Chairman of the SEC, has done in cracking down on the corporate practice of "selective disclosure" that had spread like cancer in recent years. Indeed, it had become virtually standard practice for major corporations to "guide" analysts or large holders to earnings expectations that were intended either to be on the nose or a tiny bit below what the company truly expected to earn. Through the selectively dispersed hints, winks and nods that companies engaged in, speculatively-minded institutions and advisors were given an information edge over investment-oriented individuals. This was corrupt behavior, unfortunately embraced by both Wall Street and corporate America.

Thanks to Chairman Levitt, whose general efforts on behalf of investors were both tireless and effective, corporations are now required to treat all of their owners equally. The fact that this reform came about because of coercion rather than conscience should be a matter of shame for CEOs and their investor relations departments.

One further thought while I'm on my soapbox: Charlie and I think it is both deceptive and dangerous for CEOs to predict growth rates for their companies. They are, of course, frequently egged on to do so by both analysts and their own investor relations departments. They should resist, however, because too often these predictions lead to trouble.

It's fine for a CEO to have his own internal goals and, in our view, it's even appropriate for the CEO to publicly express some hopes about the future, if these expectations are accompanied by sensible caveats. But for a major corporation to predict that its per-share earnings will grow over the long term at, say, 15% annually is to court trouble.

That's true because a growth rate of that magnitude can only be maintained by a very small percentage of large businesses. Here's a test: Examine the record of, say, the 200 highest earning companies from 1970 or 1980 and tabulate how many have increased per-share earnings by 15% annually since those dates. You will find that only a handful have. I would wager you a very significant sum that fewer than 10 of the 200 most profitable companies in 2000 will attain 15% annual growth in earnings-per-share over the next 20 years.

The problem arising from lofty predictions is not just that they spread unwarranted optimism. Even more troublesome is the fact that they corrode CEO behavior. Over the years, Charlie and I have observed many instances in which CEOs engaged in uneconomic operating maneuvers so that they could meet earnings targets they had announced. Worse still, after exhausting all that operating acrobatics would do, they sometimes played a wide variety of accounting games to "make the numbers." These accounting shenanigans have a way of snowballing: Once a company moves earnings from one period to another, operating shortfalls that occur thereafter require it to engage in further accounting maneuvers that must be even more "heroic." These can turn fudging into fraud. (More money, it has been noted, has been stolen with the point of a pen than at the point of a gun.)

Charlie and I tend to be leery of companies run by CEOs who woo investors with fancy predictions. A few of these managers will prove prophetic — but others will turn out to be congenital optimists, or even charlatans. Unfortunately, it's not easy for investors to know in advance which species they are dealing with.

* * * * * * * * * * *

I've warned you in the past that you should not believe everything you read or hear about Berkshire — even when it is published or broadcast by a prestigious news organization. Indeed, erroneous reports are particularly dangerous when they are circulated by highly-respected members of the media, simply because most readers and listeners know these outlets to be generally credible and therefore believe what they say.

An example is a glaring error about Berkshire's activities that appeared in the December 29 issue of *The Wall Street Journal*, a generally excellent paper that I have for all of my life found useful. On the front page (and above the fold, as they say) *The Journal* published a news brief that said, in unequivocal terms, that we were buying bonds of Conseco and Finova. This item directed the reader to the lead story of the Money and Investing section. There, in the second paragraph of the story, *The Journal* reported, *again without any qualification*, that Berkshire was buying Conseco and Finova bonds, adding that Berkshire had invested "several hundred million dollars" in each. Only in the 18th paragraph of the story (which by that point had jumped to an inside page) did the paper hedge a bit, saying that our Conseco purchases had been disclosed by "people familiar with the matter."

Well, not *that* familiar. True, we had purchased bonds and bank debt of Finova — though the report was wildly inaccurate as to the amount. But to this day neither Berkshire nor I have *ever* bought a share of stock or a bond of Conseco.

Berkshire is normally covered by a *Journal* reporter in Chicago who is both accurate and conscientious. In this case, however, the "scoop" was the product of a New York reporter for the paper. Indeed, the 29th was a busy day for him: By early afternoon, he had repeated the story on CNBC. Immediately, in lemming-like manner, other respected news organizations, relying solely on the *Journal*, began relating the same "facts." The result: Conseco stock advanced sharply during the day on exceptional volume that placed it ninth on the NYSE most-active list.

During all of the story's iterations, I never heard or read the word "rumor." Apparently reporters and editors, who generally pride themselves on their careful use of language, just can't bring themselves to attach this word to their accounts. But what description would fit more precisely? Certainly not the usual "sources say" or "it has been reported."

A column entitled "Today's Rumors," however, would not equate with the self-image of the many news organizations that think themselves above such stuff. These members of the media would feel that publishing such acknowledged fluff would be akin to *L'Osservatore Romano* initiating a gossip column. But rumors are what these organizations often publish and broadcast, whatever euphemism they duck behind. At a minimum, readers deserve honest terminology — a warning label that will protect their financial health in the same way that smokers whose physical health is at risk are given a warning.

The Constitution's First Amendment allows the media to print or say almost anything. Journalism's First Principle should require that the media be scrupulous in deciding what that will be.

Miscellaneous

In last year's report we examined the battle then raging over the use of "pooling" in accounting for mergers. It seemed to us that both sides were voicing arguments that were strong in certain respects and seriously flawed in others. We are pleased that the Financial Accounting Standards Board has since gone to an alternative approach that strikes us as very sound.

If the proposed rule becomes final, we will no longer incur a large annual charge for amortization of intangibles. Consequently, our reported earnings will more closely reflect economic reality. (See page 65.) None of this will have an effect on Berkshire's intrinsic value. Your Chairman, however, will personally benefit in that there will be one less item to explain in these letters.

* * * * * * * * * * *

I'm enclosing a report — generously supplied by *Outstanding Investor Digest* — of Charlie's remarks at last May's Wesco annual meeting. Charlie thinks about business economics and investment matters better than anyone I know, and I've learned a lot over the years by listening to him. Reading his comments will improve your understanding of Berkshire.

* * * * * * * * * * *

In 1985, we purchased Scott Fetzer, acquiring not only a fine business but the services of Ralph Schey, a truly outstanding CEO, as well. Ralph was then 61. Most companies, focused on the calendar rather than ability, would have benefited from Ralph's talents for only a few years.

At Berkshire, in contrast, Ralph ran Scott Fetzer for 15 years until his retirement at the end of 2000. Under his leadership, the company distributed $1.03 billion to Berkshire against our net purchase price of $230 million. We used these funds, in turn, to purchase other businesses. All told, Ralph's contributions to Berkshire's present value extend well into the billions of dollars.

As a manager, Ralph belongs in Berkshire's Hall of Fame, and Charlie and I welcome him to it.

* * * * * * * * * * *

A bit of nostalgia: It was exactly 50 years ago that I entered Ben Graham's class at Columbia. During the decade before, I had enjoyed — make that *loved* — analyzing, buying and selling stocks. But my results were no better than average.

Beginning in 1951 my performance improved. No, I hadn't changed my diet or taken up exercise. The only new ingredient was Ben's ideas. Quite simply, a few hours spent at the feet of the master proved far more valuable to me than had ten years of supposedly original thinking.

In addition to being a great teacher, Ben was a wonderful friend. My debt to him is incalculable.

Shareholder-Designated Contributions

About 97% of all eligible shares participated in Berkshire's 2000 shareholder-designated contributions program, with contributions totaling $16.9 million. A full description of the program appears on pages 74-75.

Cumulatively, over the 20 years of the program, Berkshire has made contributions of $164 million pursuant to the instructions of our shareholders. The rest of Berkshire's giving is done by our subsidiaries, which stick to the philanthropic patterns that prevailed before they were acquired (except that their former owners themselves take on the responsibility for their personal charities). In aggregate, our subsidiaries made contributions of $18.3 million in 2000, including in-kind donations of $3 million.

To participate in future programs, you must own Class A shares that are registered in the name of the actual owner, not the nominee name of a broker, bank or depository. Shares not so registered on August 31, 2001 will be ineligible for the 2001 program. When you get the contributions form from us, return it promptly so that it does not get put aside or forgotten. Designations received after the due date will not be honored.

The Annual Meeting

Last year we moved the annual meeting to the Civic Auditorium, and it worked very well for us. We will meet there again on Saturday, April 28. The doors will open at 7 a.m., the movie will begin at 8:30, and the meeting itself will commence at 9:30. There will be a short break at noon for food, with sandwiches available at the Civic's concession stands. Except for that interlude, Charlie and I will answer questions until 3:30.

For the next couple of years, the Civic is our only choice. We must therefore hold the meeting on either Saturday or Sunday to avoid the traffic and parking nightmare that would occur on a weekday. Shortly, however, Omaha will have a new Convention Center with ample parking. Assuming that the Center is then available to us, I will poll shareholders to see whether you wish to return to a Monday meeting. We will decide that vote based on the wishes of a majority of shareholders, not shares.

An attachment to the proxy material that is enclosed with this report explains how you can obtain the credential you will need for admission to this year's meeting and other events. As for plane, hotel and car reservations, we have again signed up American Express (800-799-6634) to give you special help. In our normal fashion, we will run buses from the larger hotels to the meeting. After the meeting, the buses will make trips back to the hotels and to Nebraska Furniture Mart, Borsheim's and the airport. Even so, you are likely to find a car useful.

We have added so many new companies to Berkshire this year that I'm not going to detail all of the products that we will be *selling* at the meeting. But come prepared to carry home everything from bricks to candy. One new product, however, deserves special note: Bob Shaw has designed a 3 x 5 rug featuring an excellent likeness of Charlie. Obviously, it would be embarrassing for Charlie — make that humiliating — if slow sales forced us to slash the rug's price, so step up and do your part.

GEICO will have a booth staffed by a number of its top counselors from around the country, all of them ready to supply you with auto insurance quotes. In most cases, GEICO will be able to offer you a special shareholder's discount (usually 8%). Bring the details of your existing insurance and check out whether we can save you some money.

At the Omaha airport on Saturday, we will have the usual array of aircraft from Executive Jet available for your inspection. Just ask an EJA representative at the Civic about viewing any of these planes. If you buy what we consider an appropriate number of items during the weekend, you may well need your own plane to take them home.

At Nebraska Furniture Mart, located on a 75-acre site on 72nd Street between Dodge and Pacific, we will again be having "Berkshire Weekend" pricing, which means we will be offering our shareholders a discount that is customarily given only to employees. We initiated this special pricing at NFM four years ago and sales during the "Weekend" grew from $5.3 million in 1997 to $9.1 million in 2000.

To get the discount, you must make your purchases between Wednesday, April 25 and Monday, April 30 and also present your meeting credential. The period's special pricing will even apply to the products of several prestige manufacturers that normally have ironclad rules against discounting but that, in the spirit of our shareholder weekend, have made an exception for you. We appreciate their cooperation. NFM is open from 10 a.m. to 9 p.m. on weekdays and 10 a.m. to 6 p.m. on Saturdays and Sundays.

Borsheim's — the largest jewelry store in the country except for Tiffany's Manhattan store — will have two shareholder-only events. The first will be a cocktail reception from 6 p.m. to 10 p.m. on Friday, April 27. The second, the main gala, will be from 9 a.m. to 5 p.m. on Sunday, April 29. Shareholder prices will be available Thursday through Monday, so if you wish to avoid the large crowds that will assemble on Friday evening and Sunday, come at other times and identify yourself as a shareholder. On Saturday, we will be open until 6 p.m. Borsheim's operates on a gross margin that is fully twenty percentage points below that of its major rivals, so the more you buy, the more you save (or at least that's what my family always tells me).

In the mall outside of Borsheim's, we will have local bridge experts available to play with our shareholders on Sunday. Bob Hamman, who normally is with us, will be in Africa this year. He has promised, however, to be on hand in 2002. Patrick Wolff, twice U.S. chess champion, will also be in the mall, taking on all comers — blindfolded! Last year, Patrick played as many as six games simultaneously — with his blindfold securely in place — and demolished his opponents.

As if all this isn't enough to test your skills, our Borsheim's Olympiad this year will also include Bill Robertie, one of only two players to twice win the backgammon world championship. Backgammon can be a big money game, so bring along your stock certificates.

Gorat's — my favorite steakhouse — will again be open exclusively for Berkshire shareholders on Sunday, April 29, and will be serving from 4 p.m. until 10 p.m. Please remember that you can't come to Gorat's on Sunday without a reservation. To make one, call 402-551-3733 on April 2 (*but not before*). If Sunday is sold out, try Gorat's on one of the other evenings you will be in town. If you order a rare T-bone with a double order of hash browns, you will establish your credentials as an epicure.

The usual baseball game will be held at Rosenblatt Stadium at 7 p.m. on Saturday night. This year the Omaha Golden Spikes will play the New Orleans Zephyrs. Ernie Banks is again going to be on hand to — bravely — face my fastball (once clocked at 95 mpm — miles per month).

My performance last year was not my best: It took me five pitches to throw anything resembling a strike. And, believe me, it gets lonely on the mound when you can't find the plate. Finally, I got one over, and Ernie lashed a line drive to left field. After I was yanked from the game, the many sports writers present asked what I had served up to Ernie. I quoted what Warren Spahn said after Willie Mays hit one of his pitches for a home run (Willie's first in the majors): "It was a helluva pitch for the first sixty feet."

It will be a different story this year. I don't want to tip my hand, so let's just say Ernie will have to deal with a pitch he has never seen before.

Our proxy statement contains instructions about obtaining tickets to the game and also a large quantity of other information that should help you enjoy your visit in Omaha. There will be plenty of action in town. So come for Woodstock Weekend and join our Celebration of Capitalism at the Civic.

Warren E. Buffett
Chairman of the Board

February 28, 2001

BERKSHIRE HATHAWAY INC.

To the Shareholders of Berkshire Hathaway Inc.:

Berkshire's *loss* in net worth during 2001 was $3.77 billion, which decreased the per-share book value of both our Class A and Class B stock by 6.2%. Over the last 37 years (that is, since present management took over) per-share book value has grown from $19 to $37,920, a rate of 22.6% compounded annually.[*]

Per-share intrinsic grew somewhat faster than book value during these 37 years, and in 2001 it probably decreased a bit less. We explain intrinsic value in our Owner's Manual, which begins on page 62. I urge new shareholders to read this manual to become familiar with Berkshire's key economic principles.

Two years ago, reporting on 1999, I said that we had experienced both the worst absolute and relative performance in our history. I added that "relative results are what concern us," a viewpoint I've had since forming my first investment partnership on May 5, 1956. Meeting with my seven founding limited partners that evening, I gave them a short paper titled "The Ground Rules" that included this sentence: "Whether we do a good job or a poor job is to be measured against the general experience in securities." We initially used the Dow Jones Industrials as our benchmark, but shifted to the S&P 500 when that index became widely used. Our comparative record since 1965 is chronicled on the facing page; last year Berkshire's advantage was 5.7 percentage points.

Some people disagree with our focus on relative figures, arguing that "you can't eat relative performance." But if you expect – as Charlie Munger, Berkshire's Vice Chairman, and I do – that owning the S&P 500 will produce reasonably satisfactory results over time, it follows that, for long-term investors, gaining small advantages annually over that index *must* prove rewarding. Just as you can eat well throughout the year if you own a profitable, but highly seasonal, business such as See's (which loses considerable money during the summer months) so, too, can you regularly feast on investment returns that beat the averages, however variable the absolute numbers may be.

Though our corporate performance last year was satisfactory, *my* performance was anything but. I manage most of Berkshire's equity portfolio, and my results were poor, just as they have been for several years. Of even more importance, I allowed General Re to take on business without a safeguard I knew was important, and on September 11th, this error caught up with us. I'll tell you more about my mistake later and what we are doing to correct it.

Another of my 1956 Ground Rules remains applicable: "I cannot promise results to partners." But Charlie and I *can* promise that your economic result from Berkshire will parallel ours during the period of your ownership: We will not take cash compensation, restricted stock or option grants that would make our results superior to yours.

Additionally, I will keep well over 99% of my net worth in Berkshire. My wife and I have never sold a share nor do we intend to. Charlie and I are disgusted by the situation, so common in the last few years, in which shareholders have suffered billions in losses while the CEOs, promoters, and other higher-ups who fathered these disasters have walked away with extraordinary wealth. Indeed, many of these people were urging investors to buy shares while concurrently dumping their own, sometimes using methods that hid their actions. To their shame, these business leaders view shareholders as patsies, not partners.

Though Enron has become the symbol for shareholder abuse, there is no shortage of egregious conduct elsewhere in corporate America. One story I've heard illustrates the all-too-common attitude of managers toward

---

[*]All figures used in this report apply to Berkshire's A shares, the successor to the only stock that the company had outstanding before 1996. The B shares have an ec onomic interest equal to 1/30th that of the A.

owners: A gorgeous woman slinks up to a CEO at a party and through moist lips purrs, "I'll do anything – *anything* – you want. Just tell me what you would like." With no hesitation, he replies, "Reprice my options."

One final thought about Berkshire: In the future we won't come close to replicating our past record. To be sure, Charlie and I will strive for above-average performance and will not be satisfied with less. But two conditions at Berkshire are far different from what they once were: Then, we could often buy businesses and securities at much lower valuations than now prevail; and more important, we were then working with far less money than we now have. Some years back, a good $10 million idea could do wonders for us (witness our investment in Washington Post in 1973 or GEICO in 1976). Today, the combination of *ten* such ideas and a triple in the value of *each* would increase the net worth of Berkshire by only ¼ of 1%. We need "elephants" to make significant gains now – and they are hard to find.

On the positive side, we have as fine an array of operating managers as exists at any company. (You can read about many of them in a new book by Robert P. Miles: *The Warren Buffett CEO.*) In large part, moreover, they are running businesses with economic characteristics ranging from good to superb. The ability, energy and loyalty of these managers is simply extraordinary. We now have completed 37 Berkshire years without having a CEO of an operating business elect to leave us to work elsewhere.

Our star-studded group grew in 2001. First, we completed the purchases of two businesses that we had agreed to buy in 2000 – Shaw and Johns Manville. Then we acquired two others, MiTek and XTRA, and contracted to buy two more: Larson-Juhl, an acquisition that has just closed, and Fruit of the Loom, which will close shortly if creditors approve our offer. All of these businesses are led by smart, seasoned and trustworthy CEOs.

Additionally, all of our purchases last year were for cash, which means our shareholders became owners of these additional businesses without relinquishing any interest in the fine companies they already owned. We will continue to follow our familiar formula, striving to increase the value of the excellent businesses we have, adding new businesses of similar quality, and issuing shares only grudgingly.

Acquisitions of 2001

A few days before last year's annual meeting, I received a heavy package from St. Louis, containing an unprepossessing chunk of metal whose function I couldn't imagine. There was a letter in the package, though, from Gene Toombs, CEO of a company called MiTek. He explained that MiTek is the world's leading producer of this thing I'd received, a "connector plate," which is used in making roofing trusses. Gene also said that the U.K. parent of MiTek wished to sell the company and that Berkshire seemed to him the ideal buyer. Liking the sound of his letter, I gave Gene a call. It took me only a minute to realize that he was our kind of manager and MiTek our kind of business. We made a cash offer to the U.K. owner and before long had a deal.

Gene's managerial crew is exceptionally enthusiastic about the company and wanted to participate in the purchase. Therefore, we arranged for 55 members of the MiTek team to buy 10% of the company, with each putting up a minimum of $100,000 in cash. Many borrowed money so they could participate.

As they would *not* be if they had options, all of these managers are true *owners*. They face the downside of decisions as well as the upside. They incur a cost of capital. And they can't "reprice" their stakes: What they paid is what they live with.

Charlie and I love the high-grade, truly entrepreneurial attitude that exists at MiTek, and we predict it will be a winner for all involved.

* * * * * * * * * * *

In early 2000, my friend, Julian Robertson, announced that he would terminate his investment partnership, Tiger Fund, and that he would liquidate it entirely except for four large holdings. One of these was XTRA, a leading lessor of truck trailers. I then called Julian, asking whether he might consider selling his XTRA block or whether, for that matter, the company's management might entertain an offer for the entire company. Julian referred me to Lew Rubin, XTRA's CEO. He and I had a nice conversation, but it was apparent that no deal was to be done.

Then in June 2001, Julian called to say that he had decided to sell his XTRA shares, and I resumed conversations with Lew. The XTRA board accepted a proposal we made, which was to be effectuated through a tender offer expiring on September 11th. The tender conditions included the usual "out," allowing us to withdraw if the stock market were to close before the offer's expiration. Throughout much of the 11th, Lew went through a particularly wrenching experience: First, he had a son-in-law working in the World Trade Center who couldn't be located; and second, he knew we had the option of backing away from our purchase. The story ended happily: Lew's son-in-law escaped serious harm, and Berkshire completed the transaction.

Trailer leasing is a cyclical business but one in which we should earn decent returns over time. Lew brings a new talent to Berkshire, and we hope to expand in leasing.

* * * * * * * * * * *

On December 3rd, I received a call from Craig Ponzio, owner of Larson-Juhl, the U.S. leader in custom-made picture frames. Craig had bought the company in 1981 (after first working at its manufacturing plant while attending college) and thereafter increased its sales from $3 million to $300 million. Though I had never heard of Larson-Juhl before Craig's call, a few minutes talk with him made me think we would strike a deal. He was straightforward in describing the business, cared about who bought it, and was realistic as to price. Two days later, Craig and Steve McKenzie, his CEO, came to Omaha and in ninety minutes we reached an agreement. In ten days we had signed a contract.

Larson-Juhl serves about 18,000 framing shops in the U.S. and is also the industry leader in Canada and much of Europe. We expect to see opportunities for making complementary acquisitions in the future.

* * * * * * * * * * *

As I write this letter, creditors are considering an offer we have made for Fruit of the Loom. The company entered bankruptcy a few years back, a victim both of too much debt and poor management. And, a good many years before that, I had some Fruit of the Loom experience of my own.

In August 1955, I was one of five employees, including two secretaries, working for the three managers of Graham-Newman Corporation, a New York investment company. Graham-Newman controlled Philadelphia and Reading Coal and Iron ("P&R"), an anthracite producer that had excess cash, a tax loss carryforward, and a declining business. At the time, I had a significant portion of my limited net worth invested in P&R shares, reflecting my faith in the business talents of my bosses, Ben Graham, Jerry Newman and Howard (Micky) Newman.

This faith was rewarded when P&R purchased the Union Underwear Company from Jack Goldfarb for $15 million. Union (though it was then only a licensee of the name) produced Fruit of the Loom underwear. The company possessed $5 million in cash – $2.5 million of which P&R used for the purchase – and was earning about $3 million pre-tax, earnings that could be sheltered by the tax position of P&R. And, oh yes: Fully $9 million of the remaining $12.5 million due was satisfied by non-interest-bearing notes, payable from 50% of any earnings Union had in excess of $1 million. (*Those* were the days; I get goosebumps just thinking about such deals.)

Subsequently, Union bought the licensor of the Fruit of the Loom name and, along with P&R, was merged into Northwest Industries. Fruit went on to achieve annual pre-tax earnings exceeding $200 million.

John Holland was responsible for Fruit's operations in its most bountiful years. In 1996, however, John retired, and management loaded the company with debt, in part to make a series of acquisitions that proved disappointing. Bankruptcy followed. John was then rehired, and he undertook a major reworking of operations. Before John's return, deliveries were chaotic, costs soared and relations with key customers deteriorated. While correcting these problems, John also reduced employment from a bloated 40,000 to 23,000. In short, he's been restoring the old Fruit of the Loom, albeit in a much more competitive environment.

Stepping into Fruit's bankruptcy proceedings, we made a proposal to creditors to which we attached no financing conditions, even though our offer had to remain outstanding for many months. We did, however, insist on a very unusual proviso: John had to be available to continue serving as CEO after we took over. To us, John and the brand are Fruit's key assets.

I was helped in this transaction by my friend and former boss, Micky Newman, now 81. What goes around truly does come around.

* * * * * * * * * * *

Our operating companies made several "bolt-on" acquisitions during the year, and I can't resist telling you about one. In December, Frank Rooney called to tell me H.H. Brown was buying the inventory and trademarks of Acme Boot for $700,000.

That sounds like small potatoes. But – would you believe it? – Acme was the second purchase of P&R, an acquisition that took place just before I left Graham-Newman in the spring of 1956. The price was $3.2 million, part of it again paid with non-interest bearing notes, for a business with sales of $7 million.

After P&R merged with Northwest, Acme grew to be the world's largest bootmaker, delivering annual profits many multiples of what the company had cost P&R. But the business eventually hit the skids and never recovered, and that resulted in our purchasing Acme's remnants.

In the frontispiece to *Security Analysis*, Ben Graham and Dave Dodd quoted Horace: "Many shall be restored that now are fallen and many shall fall that are now in honor." Fifty-two years after I first read those lines, my appreciation for what they say about business and investments continues to grow.

* * * * * * * * * * * *

In addition to bolt-on acquisitions, our managers continually look for ways to grow internally. In that regard, here's a postscript to a story I told you two years ago about R.C. Willey's move to Boise. As you may remember, Bill Child, R.C. Willey's chairman, wanted to extend his home-furnishings operation beyond Utah, a state in which his company does more than $300 million of business (up, it should be noted, from $250,000 when Bill took over 48 years ago). The company achieved this dominant position, moreover, with a "closed on Sunday" policy that defied conventional retailing wisdom. I was skeptical that this policy could succeed in Boise or, for that matter, anyplace outside of Utah. After all, Sunday is the day many consumers most like to shop.

Bill then insisted on something extraordinary: He would invest $11 million of his own money to build the Boise store and would sell it to Berkshire at cost (without interest!) if the venture succeeded. If it failed, Bill would keep the store and eat the loss on its disposal. As I told you in the 1999 annual report, the store immediately became a huge success — and it has since grown.

Shortly after the Boise opening, Bill suggested we try Las Vegas, and this time I was even more skeptical. How could we do business in a metropolis of that size and be closed on Sundays, a day that all of our competitors would be exploiting? Buoyed by the Boise experience, however, we proceeded to locate in Henderson, a mushrooming city adjacent to Las Vegas.

The result: This store outsells all others in the R.C. Willey chain, doing a volume of business that far exceeds the volume of any competitor and that is twice what I had anticipated. I cut the ribbon at the grand opening in October – this was after a "soft" opening and a few weeks of exceptional sales – and, just as I did at Boise, I suggested to the crowd that the new store was my idea.

It didn't work. Today, when I pontificate about retailing, Berkshire people just say, "What does Bill think?" (I'm going to draw the line, however, if he suggests that we also close on Saturdays.)

The Economics of Property/Casualty Insurance

Our main business — though we have others of great importance — is insurance. To understand Berkshire, therefore, it is necessary that you understand how to evaluate an insurance company. The key determinants are: (1) the amount of float that the business generates; (2) its cost; and (3) most critical of all, the long-term outlook for both of these factors.

To begin with, float is money we hold but don't own. In an insurance operation, float arises because premiums are received before losses are paid, an interval that sometimes extends over many years. During that time, the insurer invests the money. This pleasant activity typically carries with it a downside: The premiums that an insurer takes in usually do not cover the losses and expenses it eventually must pay. That leaves it running an "underwriting loss," which is the cost of float. An insurance business has value if its cost of float over time is less than the cost the company would otherwise incur to obtain funds. But the business is a lemon if its cost of float is higher than market rates for money.

Historically, Berkshire has obtained its float at a very low cost. Indeed, our cost has been less than zero in about half of the years in which we've operated; that is, we've actually been paid for holding other people's money. Over the last few years, however, our cost has been too high, and in 2001 it was terrible.

The table that follows shows (at intervals) the float generated by the various segments of Berkshire's insurance operations since we entered the business 35 years ago upon acquiring National Indemnity Company (whose traditional lines are included in the segment "Other Primary"). For the table we have calculated our float — which we generate in large amounts relative to our premium volume — by adding net loss reserves, loss adjustment reserves, funds held under reinsurance assumed and unearned premium reserves, and then subtracting insurance-related receivables, prepaid acquisition costs, prepaid taxes and deferred charges applicable to assumed reinsurance. (Got that?)

Yearend Float (in $ millions)

Year	GEICO	General Re	Other Reinsurance	Other Primary	Total
1967				20	20
1977			40	131	171
1987			701	807	1,508
1997	2,917		4,014	455	7,386
1998	3,125	14,909	4,305	415	22,754
1999	3,444	15,166	6,285	403	25,298
2000	3,943	15,525	7,805	598	27,871
2001	4,251	19,310	11,262	685	35,508

Last year I told you that, barring a mega-catastrophe, our cost of float would probably drop from its 2000 level of 6%. I had in mind natural catastrophes when I said that, but instead we were hit by a man-made catastrophe on September 11th – an event that delivered the insurance industry its largest loss in history. Our float cost therefore came in at a staggering 12.8%. It was our worst year in float cost since 1984, and a result that to a significant degree, as I will explain in the next section, we brought upon ourselves.

If no mega-catastrophe occurs, I – once again – expect the cost of our float to be low in the coming year. We will indeed need a low cost, as will *all* insurers. Some years back, float costing, say, 4% was tolerable because government bonds yielded twice as much, and stocks prospectively offered still loftier returns. Today, fat returns are nowhere to be found (at least *we* can't find them) and short-term funds earn less than 2%. Under these conditions, each of our insurance operations, save one, must deliver an underwriting profit if it is to be judged a good business. The exception is our retroactive reinsurance operation (a business we explained in last year's annual report), which has desirable economics even though it currently hits us with an annual underwriting loss of about $425 million.

Principles of Insurance Underwriting

When property/casualty companies are judged by their cost of float, very few stack up as satisfactory businesses. And interestingly – unlike the situation prevailing in many other industries – neither size nor brand name determines an insurer's profitability. Indeed, many of the biggest and best-known companies regularly deliver mediocre results. What counts in this business is underwriting discipline. The winners are those that unfailingly stick to three key principles:

1. *They accept only those risks that they are able to properly evaluate (staying within their circle of competence) and that, after they have evaluated all relevant factors including remote loss scenarios, carry the expectancy of profit. These insurers ignore market-share considerations and are sanguine about losing business to competitors that are offering foolish prices or policy conditions.*

2. *They limit the business they accept in a manner that guarantees they will suffer no aggregation of losses from a single event or from related events that will threaten their solvency. They ceaselessly search for possible correlation among seemingly-unrelated risks.*

7

3.   *They avoid business involving moral risk: No matter what the rate, trying to write good contracts with bad people doesn't work. While most policyholders and clients are honorable and ethical, doing business with the few exceptions is usually expensive, sometimes extraordinarily so.*

The events of September 11th made it clear that our implementation of rules 1 and 2 at General Re had been dangerously weak. In setting prices and also in evaluating aggregation risk, we had either overlooked or dismissed the possibility of large-scale terrorism losses. That was a relevant underwriting factor, and we ignored it.

In pricing property coverages, for example, we had looked to the past and taken into account only costs we might expect to incur from windstorm, fire, explosion and earthquake. But what will be the largest insured property loss in history (after adding related business-interruption claims) originated from none of these forces. In short, all of us in the industry made a fundamental underwriting mistake by focusing on experience, rather than exposure, thereby assuming a huge terrorism risk for which we received no premium.

Experience, of course, is a highly useful starting point in underwriting most coverages. For example, it's important for insurers writing California earthquake policies to know how many quakes in the state during the past century have registered 6.0 or greater on the Richter scale. This information will not tell you the exact probability of a big quake next year, or where in the state it might happen. But the statistic has utility, particularly if you are writing a huge statewide policy, as National Indemnity has done in recent years.

At certain times, however, using experience as a guide to pricing is not only useless, but actually dangerous. Late in a bull market, for example, large losses from directors and officers liability insurance ("D&O") are likely to be relatively rare. When stocks are rising, there are a scarcity of targets to sue, and both questionable accounting and management chicanery often go undetected. At that juncture, experience on high-limit D&O may look great.

But that's just when *exposure* is likely to be exploding, by way of ridiculous public offerings, earnings manipulation, chain-letter-like stock promotions and a potpourri of other unsavory activities. When stocks fall, these sins surface, hammering investors with losses that can run into the hundreds of billions. Juries deciding whether those losses should be borne by small investors or big insurance companies can be expected to hit insurers with verdicts that bear little relation to those delivered in bull-market days. Even one jumbo judgment, moreover, can cause settlement costs in later cases to mushroom. Consequently, the correct rate for D&O "excess" (meaning the insurer or reinsurer will pay losses above a high threshold) might well, if based on *exposure*, be five or more times the premium dictated by *experience*.

Insurers have always found it costly to ignore new exposures. Doing that in the case of terrorism, however, could literally bankrupt the industry. No one knows the probability of a nuclear detonation in a major metropolis this year (or even multiple detonations, given that a terrorist organization able to construct one bomb might not stop there). Nor can anyone, with assurance, assess the probability in this year, or another, of deadly biological or chemical agents being introduced simultaneously (say, through ventilation systems) into multiple office buildings and manufacturing plants. An attack like that would produce astronomical workers' compensation claims.

Here's what we *do* know:

(a)   The probability of such mind-boggling disasters, though likely very low at present, is not zero.

(b)   The probabilities are increasing, in an irregular and immeasurable manner, as knowledge and materials become available to those who wish us ill. Fear may recede with time, but the danger won't – the war against terrorism can never be won. The best the nation can achieve is a long succession of stalemates. There can be no checkmate against hydra-headed foes.

(c)   Until now, insurers and reinsurers have blithely assumed the financial consequences from the incalculable risks I have described.

(d)   Under a "close-to-worst-case" scenario, which could conceivably involve $1 trillion of damage, the insurance industry would be destroyed unless it manages in some manner to dramatically limit its assumption of terrorism risks. Only the U.S. Government has the resources to absorb such a blow. If it is unwilling to do so on a prospective basis, the general citizenry must bear its own risks and count on the Government to come to its rescue after a disaster occurs.

Why, you might ask, didn't I recognize the above facts *before* September 11th? The answer, sadly, is that I did – but I didn't convert thought into action. I violated the Noah rule: Predicting rain doesn't count; building arks does. I consequently let Berkshire operate with a dangerous level of risk – at General Re in particular. I'm sorry to say that much risk for which we haven't been compensated remains on our books, but it is running off by the day.

At Berkshire, it should be noted, we have for some years been willing to assume more risk than any other insurer has *knowingly* taken on. That's still the case. We are perfectly willing to lose $2 billion to $2½ billion in a single event (as we did on September 11th) if we have been paid properly for assuming the risk that caused the loss (which on that occasion we weren't).

Indeed, we have a major competitive advantage because of our tolerance for huge losses. Berkshire has massive liquid resources, substantial non-insurance earnings, a favorable tax position and a knowledgeable shareholder constituency willing to accept volatility in earnings. This unique combination enables us to assume risks that far exceed the appetite of even our largest competitors. Over time, insuring these jumbo risks should be profitable, though periodically they will bring on a terrible year.

The bottom-line today is that we will write some coverage for terrorist-related losses, including a few non-correlated policies with very large limits. But we will not knowingly expose Berkshire to losses beyond what we can comfortably handle. We will control our total exposure, no matter what the competition does.

Insurance Operations in 2001

Over the years, our insurance business has provided ever-growing, low-cost funds that have fueled much of Berkshire's growth. Charlie and I believe this will continue to be the case. But we stumbled in a big way in 2001, largely because of underwriting losses at General Re.

In the past I have assured you that General Re was underwriting with discipline – and I have been proven wrong. Though its managers' intentions were good, the company broke each of the three underwriting rules I set forth in the last section and has paid a huge price for doing so. One obvious cause for its failure is that it did not reserve correctly – more about this in the next section – and therefore severely miscalculated the cost of the product it was selling. Not knowing your costs will cause problems in any business. In long-tail reinsurance, where years of unawareness will promote and prolong severe underpricing, ignorance of true costs is dynamite.

Additionally, General Re was overly-competitive in going after, and retaining, business. While all concerned may intend to underwrite with care, it is nonetheless difficult for able, hard-driving professionals to curb their urge to prevail over competitors. If "winning," however, is equated with market share rather than profits, trouble awaits. "No" must be an important part of any underwriter's vocabulary.

At the risk of sounding Pollyannaish, I now assure you that underwriting discipline is being restored at General Re (and its Cologne Re subsidiary) with appropriate urgency. Joe Brandon was appointed General Re's CEO in September and, along with Tad Montross, its new president, is committed to producing underwriting profits. Last fall, Charlie and I read Jack Welch's terrific book, *Jack, Straight from the Gut* (get a copy!). In discussing it, we agreed that Joe has many of Jack's characteristics: He is smart, energetic, hands-on, and expects much of both himself and his organization.

When it was an independent company, General Re often shone, and now it also has the considerable strengths Berkshire brings to the table. With that added advantage and with underwriting discipline restored, General Re should be a huge asset for Berkshire. I predict that Joe and Tad will make it so.

* * * * * * * * * * *

At the National Indemnity reinsurance operation, Ajit Jain continues to add enormous value to Berkshire. Working with only 18 associates, Ajit manages one of the world's largest reinsurance operations measured by assets, and *the* largest, based upon the size of individual risks assumed.

I have known the details of almost every policy that Ajit has written since he came with us in 1986, and never on even a single occasion have I seen him break any of our three underwriting rules. His extraordinary discipline, of course, does not eliminate losses; it does, however, prevent foolish losses. And that's the key: Just as is the case in investing, insurers produce outstanding long-term results primarily by avoiding dumb decisions, rather than by making brilliant ones.

Since September 11th, Ajit has been particularly busy. Among the policies we have written and retained entirely for our own account are (1) $578 million of property coverage for a South American refinery once a loss there exceeds $1 billion; (2) $1 billion of non-cancelable third-party liability coverage for losses arising from acts of terrorism at several large international airlines; (3) £500 million of property coverage on a large North Sea oil platform, covering losses from terrorism and sabotage, above £600 million that the insured retained or reinsured elsewhere; and (4) significant coverage on the Sears Tower, including losses caused by terrorism, above a $500 million threshold. We have written many other jumbo risks as well, such as protection for the World Cup Soccer Tournament and the 2002 Winter Olympics. In all cases, however, we have attempted to avoid writing groups of policies from which losses might seriously aggregate. We will not, for example, write coverages on a large number of office and apartment towers in a single metropolis without excluding losses from both a nuclear explosion and the fires that would follow it.

No one can match the speed with which Ajit can offer huge policies. After September 11th, his quickness to respond, always important, has become a major competitive advantage. So, too, has our unsurpassed financial strength. Some reinsurers – particularly those who, in turn, are accustomed to laying off much of their business on a second layer of reinsurers known as retrocessionaires – are in a weakened condition and would have difficulty surviving a second mega-cat. When a daisy chain of retrocessionaires exists, a single weak link can pose trouble for all. In assessing the soundness of their reinsurance protection, insurers must therefore apply a stress test to all participants in the chain, and must contemplate a catastrophe loss occurring during a very unfavorable economic environment. After all, you only find out who is swimming naked when the tide goes out. At Berkshire, we retain our risks and depend on no one. And whatever the world's problems, our checks will clear.

Ajit's business will ebb and flow – but his underwriting principles won't waver. It's impossible to overstate his value to Berkshire.

* * * * * * * * * * *

GEICO, by far our largest primary insurer, made major progress in 2001, thanks to Tony Nicely, its CEO, and his associates. Quite simply, Tony is an owner's dream.

GEICO's premium volume grew 6.6% last year, its float grew $308 million, and it achieved an underwriting profit of $221 million. This means we were actually paid that amount last year to hold the $4.25 billion in float, which of course doesn't belong to Berkshire but can be used by us for investment.

The only disappointment at GEICO in 2001 – and it's an important one – was our inability to add policyholders. Our preferred customers (81% of our total) grew by 1.6% but our standard and non-standard policies fell by 10.1%. Overall, policies in force fell .8%.

New business has improved in recent months. Our closure rate from telephone inquiries has climbed, and our Internet business continues its steady growth. We, therefore, expect at least a modest gain in policy count during 2002. Tony and I are eager to commit much more to marketing than the $219 million we spent last year, but at the moment we cannot see how to do so effectively. In the meantime, our operating costs are low and far below those of our major competitors; our prices are attractive; and our float is cost-free and growing.

* * * * * * * * * * *

Our other primary insurers delivered their usual fine results last year. These operations, run by Rod Eldred, John Kizer, Tom Nerney, Michael Stearns, Don Towle and Don Wurster had combined premium volume of $579 million, up 40% over 2000. Their float increased 14.5% to $685 million, and they recorded an underwriting profit of $30 million. In aggregate, these companies are one of the finest insurance operations in the country, and their 2002 prospects look excellent.

"Loss Development" and Insurance Accounting

Bad terminology is the enemy of good thinking. When companies or investment professionals use terms such as "EBITDA" and "pro forma," they want you to unthinkingly accept concepts that are dangerously flawed. (In golf, my score is frequently below par on a *pro forma* basis: I have firm plans to "restructure" my putting stroke and therefore only count the swings I take before reaching the green.)

In insurance reporting, "loss development" is a widely used term – and one that is seriously misleading. First, a definition: Loss reserves at an insurer are not funds tucked away for a rainy day, but rather a liability account. If properly calculated, the liability states the amount that an insurer will have to pay for *all* losses (including associated costs) that have occurred prior to the reporting date but have not yet been paid. When calculating the reserve, the insurer will have been notified of many of the losses it is destined to pay, but others will not yet have been reported to it. These losses are called IBNR, for incurred but not reported. Indeed, in some cases (involving, say, product liability or embezzlement) the insured itself will not yet be aware that a loss has occurred.

It's clearly difficult for an insurer to put a figure on the ultimate cost of all such reported and unreported events. But the ability to do so with reasonable accuracy is vital. Otherwise the insurer's managers won't know what its actual loss costs are and how these compare to the premiums being charged. GEICO got into huge trouble in the early 1970s because for several years it severely underreserved, and therefore believed its product (insurance protection) was costing considerably less than was truly the case. Consequently, the company sailed blissfully along, underpricing its product and selling more and more policies at ever-larger losses.

When it becomes evident that reserves at past reporting dates understated the liability that truly existed at the time, companies speak of "loss development." In the year discovered, these shortfalls penalize reported earnings because the "catch-up" costs from prior years must be added to current-year costs when results are calculated. This is what happened at General Re in 2001: a staggering $800 million of loss costs that actually occurred in earlier years, but that were not then recorded, were belatedly recognized last year and charged against current earnings. The mistake was an honest one, I can assure you of that. Nevertheless, for several years, this underreserving caused us to believe that our costs were much lower than they truly were, an error that contributed to woefully inadequate pricing. Additionally, the overstated profit figures led us to pay substantial incentive compensation that we should not have and to incur income taxes far earlier than was necessary.

We recommend scrapping the term "loss development" and its equally ugly twin, "reserve strengthening." (Can you imagine an insurer, upon finding its reserves excessive, describing the reduction that follows as "reserve weakening"?) "Loss development" suggests to investors that some natural, uncontrollable event has occurred in the current year, and "reserve strengthening" implies that adequate amounts have been further buttressed. The truth, however, is that management made an error in estimation that in turn produced an error in the earnings previously reported. The losses didn't "develop" – they were there all along. What developed was management's understanding of the losses (or, in the instances of chicanery, management's willingness to finally fess up).

A more forthright label for the phenomenon at issue would be "loss costs we failed to recognize when they occurred" (or maybe just "oops"). Underreserving, it should be noted, is a common – and serious – problem throughout the property/casualty insurance industry. At Berkshire we told you of our own problems with underestimation in 1984 and 1986. Generally, however, our reserving has been conservative.

Major underreserving is common in cases of companies struggling for survival. In effect, insurance accounting is a self-graded exam, in that the insurer gives some figures to its auditing firm and generally doesn't get an argument. (What the *auditor* gets, however, is a letter from management that is designed to take his firm off the hook if the numbers later look silly.) A company experiencing financial difficulties – of a kind that, if truly faced, could put it out of business – seldom proves to be a tough grader. Who, after all, wants to prepare his own execution papers?

Even when companies have the best of intentions, it's not easy to reserve properly. I've told the story in the past about the fellow traveling abroad whose sister called to tell him that their dad had died. The brother replied that it was impossible for him to get home for the funeral; he volunteered, however, to shoulder its cost. Upon returning, the brother received a bill from the mortuary for $4,500, which he promptly paid. A month later, and a month after that also, he paid $10 pursuant to an add-on invoice. When a third $10 invoice came, he called his sister for an explanation. "Oh," she replied, "I forgot to tell you. We buried dad in a rented suit."

There are a lot of "rented suits" buried in the past operations of insurance companies. Sometimes the problems they signify lie dormant for decades, as was the case with asbestos liability, before virulently manifesting themselves. Difficult as the job may be, it's management's responsibility to adequately account for *all* possibilities. Conservatism is essential. When a claims manager walks into the CEO's office and says "Guess what just happened," his boss, if a veteran, does not expect to hear it's good news. Surprises in the insurance world have been far from symmetrical in their effect on earnings.

Because of this one-sided experience, it is folly to suggest, as some are doing, that all property/casualty insurance reserves be *discounted*, an approach reflecting the fact that they will be paid in the future and that therefore their present value is less than the stated liability for them. Discounting might be acceptable *if* reserves could be precisely established. They can't, however, because a myriad of forces – judicial broadening of policy language and medical inflation, to name just two chronic problems – are constantly working to make reserves inadequate. Discounting would exacerbate this already-serious situation and, additionally, would provide a new tool for the companies that are inclined to fudge.

I'd say that the effects from telling a profit-challenged insurance CEO to lower reserves through discounting would be comparable to those that would ensue if a father told his 16-year-old son to have a normal sex life. Neither party needs that kind of push.

Sources of Reported Earnings

The table that follows shows the main sources of Berkshire's reported earnings. In this presentation, purchase-accounting adjustments (primarily relating to "goodwill") are not assigned to the specific businesses to which they apply, but are instead aggregated and shown separately. This procedure lets you view the earnings of our businesses as they would have been reported had we not purchased them. In recent years, our "expense" for goodwill amortization has been large. Going forward, generally accepted accounting principles ("GAAP") will no longer require amortization of goodwill. This change will increase our reported earnings (though not our true economic earnings) and simplify this section of the report.

	(in millions)			
			Berkshire's Share of Net Earnings (after taxes and	
	Pre-Tax Earnings		*Minority interests)*	
	2001	*2000*	*2001*	*2000*
Operating Earnings:				
Insurance Group:				
Underwriting – Reinsurance	$(4,318)	$(1,416)	$(2,824)	$(911)
Underwriting – GEICO	221	(224)	144	(146)
Underwriting – Other Primary	30	25	18	16
Net Investment Income	2,824	2,773	1,968	1,946
Building Products[1]	461	34	287	21
Finance and Financial Products Business	519	530	336	343
Flight Services	186	213	105	126
MidAmerican Energy (76% owned)	600	197	230	109
Retail Operations	175	175	101	104
Scott Fetzer (excluding finance operation)	129	122	83	80
Shaw Industries[2]	292	--	156	--
Other Businesses	179	221	103	133
Purchase-Accounting Adjustments	(726)	(881)	(699)	(843)
Corporate Interest Expense	(92)	(92)	(60)	(61)
Shareholder-Designated Contributions	(17)	(17)	(11)	(11)
Other	25	39	16	30
Operating Earnings	488	1,699	(47)	936
Capital Gains from Investments	1,320	3,955	842	2,392
Total Earnings – All Entities	$1,808	$5,654	$ 795	$3,328

[1] *Includes Acme Brick from August 1, 2000; Benjamin Moore from December 18, 2000; Johns Manville from February 27, 2001; and MiTek from July 31, 2001.*

[2] *From date of acquisition, January 8, 2001.*

Here are some highlights (and lowlights) from 2001 relating to our non-insurance activities:

- Our shoe operations (included in "other businesses") lost $46.2 million pre-tax, with profits at H.H. Brown and Justin swamped by losses at Dexter.

  I've made three decisions relating to Dexter that have hurt you in a major way: (1) buying it in the first place; (2) paying for it with stock and (3) procrastinating when the need for changes in its operations was obvious. I would like to lay these mistakes on Charlie (or anyone else, for that matter) but they were mine. Dexter, prior to our purchase – and indeed for a few years after – prospered despite low-cost foreign competition that was brutal. I concluded that Dexter could continue to cope with that problem, and I was wrong.

  We have now placed the Dexter operation – which is still substantial in size – under the management of Frank Rooney and Jim Issler at H.H. Brown. These men have performed outstandingly for Berkshire, skillfully contending with the extraordinary changes that have bedeviled the footwear industry. During part of 2002, Dexter will be hurt by unprofitable sales commitments it made last year. After that, we believe our shoe business will be reasonably profitable.

- MidAmerican Energy, of which we own 76% on a fully-diluted basis, had a good year in 2001. Its reported earnings should also increase considerably in 2002 given that the company has been shouldering a large charge for the amortization of goodwill and that this "cost" will disappear under the new GAAP rules.

  Last year MidAmerican swapped some properties in England, adding Yorkshire Electric, with its 2.1 million customers. We are now serving 3.6 million customers in the U.K. and are its 2nd largest electric utility. We have an equally important operation in Iowa as well as major generating facilities in California and the Philippines.

  At MidAmerican – this may surprise you – we also own the second-largest residential real estate brokerage business in the country. We are market-share leaders in a number of large cities, primarily in the Midwest, and have recently acquired important firms in Atlanta and Southern California. Last year, operating under various names that are locally familiar, we handled about 106,000 transactions involving properties worth nearly $20 billion. Ron Peltier has built this business for us, and it's likely he will make more acquisitions in 2002 and the years to come.

- Considering the recessionary environment plaguing them, our retailing operations did well in 2001. In jewelry, same-store sales fell 7.6% and pre-tax margins were 8.9% versus 10.7% in 2000. Return on invested capital remains high.

  Same-store sales at our home-furnishings retailers were unchanged and so was the margin – 9.1% pre-tax – these operations earned. Here, too, return on invested capital is excellent.

  We continue to expand in both jewelry and home-furnishings. Of particular note, Nebraska Furniture Mart is constructing a mammoth 450,000 square foot store that will serve the greater Kansas City area beginning in the fall of 2003. Despite Bill Child's counter-successes, we will keep this store open on Sundays.

- The large acquisitions we initiated in late 2000 – Shaw, Johns Manville and Benjamin Moore – all came through their first year with us in great fashion. Charlie and I knew at the time of our purchases that we were in good hands with Bob Shaw, Jerry Henry and Yvan Dupuy, respectively – and we admire their work even more now. Together these businesses earned about $659 million pre-tax.

  Shortly after yearend we exchanged 4,740 Berkshire A shares (or their equivalent in B shares) for the 12.7% minority interest in Shaw, which means we now own 100% of the company. Shaw is our largest non-insurance operation and will play a big part in Berkshire's future.

- All of the income shown for Flight Services in 2001 – and a bit more – came from FlightSafety, our pilot-training subsidiary. Its earnings increased 2.5%, though return on invested capital fell slightly because of the $258 million investment we made last year in simulators and other fixed assets. My 84-year-old friend, Al Ueltschi, continues to run FlightSafety with the same enthusiasm and competitive spirit that he has exhibited since 1951, when he invested $10,000 to start the company. If I line Al up with a bunch of 60-year-olds at the annual meeting, you will not be able to pick him out.

After September 11th, training for commercial airlines fell, and today it remains depressed. However, training for business and general aviation, our main activity, is at near-normal levels and should continue to grow. In 2002, we expect to spend $162 million for 27 simulators, a sum far in excess of our annual depreciation charge of $95 million. Those who believe that EBITDA is in any way equivalent to true earnings are welcome to pick up the tab.

Our NetJets® fractional ownership program sold a record number of planes last year and also showed a gain of 21.9% in service income from management fees and hourly charges. Nevertheless, it operated at a small loss, versus a small profit in 2000. We made a little money in the U.S., but these earnings were more than offset by European losses. Measured by the value of our customers' planes, NetJets accounts for about half of the industry. We believe the other participants, in aggregate, lost significant money.

Maintaining a premier level of safety, security and service was always expensive, and the cost of sticking to those standards was exacerbated by September 11th. No matter how much the cost, we will continue to be the industry leader in all three respects. An uncompromising insistence on delivering only the best to his customers is embedded in the DNA of Rich Santulli, CEO of the company and the inventor of fractional ownership. I'm delighted with his fanaticism on these matters for both the company's sake and my family's: I believe the Buffetts fly more fractional-ownership hours – we log in excess of 800 annually – than does any other family. In case you're wondering, we use exactly the same planes and crews that serve NetJet's other customers.

NetJets experienced a spurt in new orders shortly after September 11th, but its sales pace has since returned to normal. Per-customer usage declined somewhat during the year, probably because of the recession.

Both we and our customers derive significant operational benefits from our being the runaway leader in the fractional ownership business. We have more than 300 planes constantly on the go in the U.S. and can therefore be wherever a customer needs us on very short notice. The ubiquity of our fleet also reduces our "positioning" costs below those incurred by operators with smaller fleets.

These advantages of scale, and others we have, give NetJets a significant economic edge over competition. Under the competitive conditions likely to prevail for a few years, however, our advantage will at best produce modest profits.

- Our finance and financial products line of business now includes XTRA, General Re Securities (which is in a run-off mode that will continue for an extended period) and a few other relatively small operations. The bulk of the assets and liabilities in this segment, however, arise from a few fixed-income strategies, involving highly-liquid AAA securities, that I manage. This activity, which only makes sense when certain market relationships exist, has produced good returns in the past and has reasonable prospects for continuing to do so over the next year or two.

Investments

Below we present our common stock investments. Those that had a market value of more than $500 million at the end of 2001 are itemized.

Shares	Company	12/31/01	
		Cost	Market
		(dollars in millions)	
151,610,700	American Express Company	$ 1,470	$ 5,410
200,000,000	The Coca-Cola Company	1,299	9,430
96,000,000	The Gillette Company	600	3,206
15,999,200	H&R Block, Inc.	255	715
24,000,000	Moody's Corporation	499	957
1,727,765	The Washington Post Company	11	916
53,265,080	Wells Fargo & Company	306	2,315
	Others	4,103	5,726
	Total Common Stocks	$8,543	$28,675

We made few changes in our portfolio during 2001. As a group, our larger holdings have performed poorly in the last few years, some because of disappointing operating results. Charlie and I still like the basic businesses of all the companies we own. But we do not believe Berkshire's equity holdings as a group are undervalued.

Our restrained enthusiasm for these securities is matched by decidedly lukewarm feelings about the prospects for stocks in general over the next decade or so. I expressed my views about equity returns in a speech I gave at an Allen and Company meeting in July (which was a follow-up to a similar presentation I had made two years earlier) and an edited version of my comments appeared in a December 10th *Fortune* article. I'm enclosing a copy of that article. You can also view the *Fortune* version of my 1999 talk at our website www.berkshirehathaway.com.

Charlie and I believe that American business will do fine over time but think that today's equity prices presage only moderate returns for investors. The market outperformed business for a very long period, and that phenomenon had to end. A market that no more than parallels business progress, however, is likely to leave many investors disappointed, particularly those relatively new to the game.

Here's one for those who enjoy an odd coincidence: The Great Bubble ended on March 10, 2000 (though we didn't realize that fact until some months later). On that day, the NASDAQ (recently 1,731) hit its all-time high of 5,132. That same day, Berkshire shares traded at $40,800, their lowest price since mid-1997.

* * * * * * * * * * * *

During 2001, we were somewhat more active than usual in "junk" bonds. These are not, we should emphasize, suitable investments for the general public, because too often these securities live up to their name. We have *never* purchased a newly-issued junk bond, which is the only kind most investors are urged to buy. When losses occur in this field, furthermore, they are often disastrous: Many issues end up at a small fraction of their original offering price and some become entirely worthless.

Despite these dangers, we periodically find a few – a *very* few – junk securities that are interesting to us. And, so far, our 50-year experience in distressed debt has proven rewarding. In our 1984 annual report, we described our purchases of Washington Public Power System bonds when that issuer fell into disrepute. We've also, over the years, stepped into other apparent calamities such as Chrysler Financial, Texaco and RJR Nabisco – all of which returned to grace. Still, if we stay active in junk bonds, you can expect us to have losses from time to time.

Occasionally, a purchase of distressed bonds leads us into something bigger. Early in the Fruit of the Loom bankruptcy, we purchased the company's public and bank debt at about 50% of face value. This was an unusual bankruptcy in that interest payments on senior debt were continued without interruption, which meant we earned about a 15% current return. Our holdings grew to 10% of Fruit's senior debt, which will probably end up returning us about 70% of face value. Through this investment, we indirectly reduced our purchase price for the whole company by a small amount.

In late 2000, we began purchasing the obligations of FINOVA Group, a troubled finance company, and that, too, led to our making a major transaction. FINOVA then had about $11 billion of debt outstanding, of which we purchased 13% at about two-thirds of face value. We expected the company to go into bankruptcy, but believed that liquidation of its assets would produce a payoff for creditors that would be well above our cost. As default loomed in early 2001, we joined forces with Leucadia National Corporation to present the company with a prepackaged plan for bankruptcy.

The plan as subsequently modified (and I'm simplifying here) provided that creditors would be paid 70% of face value (along with full interest) and that they would receive a newly-issued 7½% note for the 30% of their claims not satisfied by cash. To fund FINOVA's 70% distribution, Leucadia and Berkshire formed a jointly-owned entity – mellifluently christened Berkadia – that borrowed $5.6 billion through FleetBoston and, in turn, re-lent this sum to FINOVA, concurrently obtaining a priority claim on its assets. Berkshire guaranteed 90% of the Berkadia borrowing and also has a secondary guarantee on the 10% for which Leucadia has primary responsibility. (Did I mention that I am simplifying?).

There is a spread of about two percentage points between what Berkadia pays on its borrowing and what it receives from FINOVA, with this spread flowing 90% to Berkshire and 10% to Leucadia. As I write this, each loan has been paid down to $3.9 billion.

As part of the bankruptcy plan, which was approved on August 10, 2001, Berkshire also agreed to offer 70% of face value for up to $500 million principal amount of the $3.25 billion of new 7½% bonds that were issued by FINOVA. (Of these, we had already received $426.8 million in principal amount because of our 13% ownership of the original debt.) Our offer, which was to run until September 26, 2001, could be withdrawn under a variety of conditions, one of which became operative if the New York Stock Exchange closed during the offering period. When that indeed occurred in the week of September 11th, we promptly terminated the offer.

Many of FINOVA's loans involve aircraft assets whose values were significantly diminished by the events of September 11th. Other receivables held by the company also were imperiled by the economic consequences of the attack that day. FINOVA's prospects, therefore, are not as good as when we made our proposal to the bankruptcy court. Nevertheless we feel that overall the transaction will prove satisfactory for Berkshire. Leucadia has day-to-day operating responsibility for FINOVA, and we have long been impressed with the business acumen and managerial talent of its key executives.

* * * * * * * * * * *

It's déjà vu time again: In early 1965, when the investment partnership I ran took control of Berkshire, that company had its main banking relationships with First National Bank of Boston and a large New York City bank. Previously, I had done no business with either.

Fast forward to 1969, when I wanted Berkshire to buy the Illinois National Bank and Trust of Rockford. We needed $10 million, and I contacted both banks. There was no response from New York. However, two representatives of the Boston bank immediately came to Omaha. They told me they would supply the money for our purchase and that we would work out the details later.

For the next three decades, we borrowed almost nothing from banks. (Debt is a four-letter word around Berkshire.) Then, in February, when we were structuring the FINOVA transaction, I again called Boston, where First National had morphed into FleetBoston. Chad Gifford, the company's president, responded just as Bill Brown and Ira Stepanian had back in 1969 – "you've got the money and we'll work out the details later."

And that's just what happened. FleetBoston syndicated a loan for $6 billion (as it turned out, we didn't need $400 million of it), and it was quickly oversubscribed by 17 banks throughout the world. Sooooo . . . if you ever need $6 billion, just give Chad a call – assuming, that is, your credit is AAA.

* * * * * * * * * * *

One more point about our investments: The media often report that "Buffett is buying" this or that security, having picked up the "fact" from reports that Berkshire files. These accounts are sometimes correct, but at other times the transactions Berkshire reports are actually being made by Lou Simpson, who runs a $2 billion portfolio for GEICO that is quite independent of me. Normally, Lou does not tell me what he is buying or selling, and I learn of his activities only when I look at a GEICO portfolio summary that I receive a few days after the end of each month. Lou's thinking, of course, is quite similar to mine, but we usually end up in different securities. That's largely because he's working with less money and can therefore invest in smaller companies than I. Oh, yes, there's also another minor difference between us: In recent years, Lou's performance has been far better than mine.

Charitable Contributions

Berkshire follows a highly unusual policy in respect to charitable contributions – but it's one that Charlie and I believe is both rational and fair to owners.

First, we let our operating subsidiaries make their own charitable decisions, requesting only that the owners/managers who once ran these as independent companies make all donations to their *personal* charities from their own funds, instead of using company money. When our managers are using company funds, we trust them to make gifts in a manner that delivers commensurate tangible or intangible benefits to the operations they manage. Last year contributions from Berkshire subsidiaries totaled $19.2 million.

At the parent company level, we make no contributions except those designated by shareholders. We do not match contributions made by directors or employees, nor do we give to the favorite charities of the Buffetts or the Mungers. However, prior to our purchasing them, a few of our subsidiaries had employee-match programs and we feel fine about their continuing them: It's not our style to tamper with successful business cultures.

To implement our *owners'* charitable desires, each year we notify registered holders of A shares (A's represent 86.6% of our equity capital) of a per-share amount that they can instruct us to contribute to as many as three charities. Shareholders name the charity; Berkshire writes the check. Any organization that qualifies under the Internal Revenue Code can be designated by shareholders. Last year Berkshire made contributions of $16.7 million at the direction of 5,700 shareholders, who named 3,550 charities as recipients. Since we started this program, our shareholders' gifts have totaled $181 million.

Most public corporations eschew gifts to religious institutions. These, however, are favorite charities of our shareholders, who last year named 437 churches and synagogues to receive gifts. Additionally, 790 schools were recipients. A few of our larger shareholders, including Charlie and me, designate their personal foundations to get gifts, so that those entities can, in turn, disburse their funds widely.

I get a few letters every week criticizing Berkshire for contributing to Planned Parenthood. These letters are usually prompted by an organization that wishes to see boycotts of Berkshire products. The letters are invariably polite and sincere, but their writers are unaware of a key point: It's not Berkshire, but rather its owners who are making charitable decisions – and these owners are about as diverse in their opinions as you can imagine. For example, they are probably on both sides of the abortion issue in roughly the same proportion as the American population. We'll follow their instructions, whether they designate Planned Parenthood or Metro Right to Life, just as long as the charity possesses 501(c)(3) status. It's as if we paid a dividend, which the shareholder then donated. Our form of disbursement, however, is more tax-efficient.

In neither the purchase of goods nor the hiring of personnel, do we ever consider the religious views, the gender, the race or the sexual orientation of the persons we are dealing with. It would not only be wrong to do so, it would be idiotic. We need all of the talent we can find, and we have learned that able and trustworthy managers, employees and suppliers come from a very wide spectrum of humanity.

* * * * * * * * * *

To participate in our future charitable contribution programs, you must own Class A shares that are registered in the name of the actual owner, not the nominee name of a broker, bank or depository. Shares not so registered on August 31, 2002 will be ineligible for the 2002 program. When you get the contributions form from us, return it promptly. Designations received after the due date will not be honored.

The Annual Meeting

This year's annual meeting will be on Saturday, May 4, and we will again be at the Civic Auditorium. The doors will open at 7 a.m., the movie will begin at 8:30, and the meeting itself will commence at 9:30. There will be a short break at noon for food. (Sandwiches can be bought at the Civic's concession stands.) Except for that interlude, Charlie and I will answer questions until 3:30. Give us your best shot.

For at least the next year, the Civic, located downtown, is the only site available to us. We must therefore hold the meeting on either Saturday or Sunday to avoid the traffic and parking nightmare sure to occur on a weekday. Shortly, however, Omaha will have a new Convention Center with plenty of parking facilities. Assuming that we then head for the Center, I will poll shareholders to see whether you wish to return to the Monday meeting that was standard until 2000. We will decide that vote based on a count of shareholders, not shares. (This is *not* a system, however, we will ever institute to decide who should be CEO.)

An attachment to the proxy material that is enclosed with this report explains how you can obtain the credential you will need for admission to the meeting and other events. As for plane, hotel and car reservations, we have again signed up American Express (800-799-6634) to give you special help. They do a terrific job for us each year, and I thank them for it.

In our usual fashion, we will run buses from the larger hotels to the meeting. Afterwards, the buses will make trips back to the hotels and to Nebraska Furniture Mart, Borsheim's and the airport. Even so, you are likely to find a car useful.

We have added so many new companies to Berkshire this year that I'm not going to detail all of the products that we will be *selling* at the meeting. But come prepared to carry home everything from bricks to candy. And underwear, of course. Assuming our Fruit of the Loom purchase has closed by May 4, we will be selling Fruit's latest styles, which will make you your neighborhood's fashion leader. Buy a lifetime supply.

GEICO will have a booth staffed by a number of its top counselors from around the country, all of them ready to supply you with auto insurance quotes. In most cases, GEICO will be able to give you a special shareholder discount (usually 8%). This special offer is permitted by 41 of the 49 jurisdictions in which we operate. Bring the details of your existing insurance and check out whether we can save you money.

At the Omaha airport on Saturday, we will have the usual array of aircraft from NetJets® available for your inspection. Just ask a representative at the Civic about viewing any of these planes. If you buy what we consider an appropriate number of items during the weekend, you may well need your own plane to take them home. And, if you buy a fraction of a plane, we might even throw in a three-pack of briefs or boxers.

At Nebraska Furniture Mart, located on a 75-acre site on 72nd Street between Dodge and Pacific, we will again be having "Berkshire Weekend" pricing, which means we will be offering our shareholders a discount that is customarily given only to employees. We initiated this special pricing at NFM five years ago, and sales during the "Weekend" grew from $5.3 million in 1997 to $11.5 million in 2001.

To get the discount, you must make your purchases on Thursday, May 2 through Monday, May 6 and also present your meeting credential. The period's special pricing will even apply to the products of several prestigious manufacturers that normally have ironclad rules against discounting but that, in the spirit of our shareholder weekend, have made an exception for you. We appreciate their cooperation. NFM is open from 10 a.m. to 9 p.m. on weekdays and 10 a.m. to 6 p.m. on Saturdays and Sundays.

Borsheim's — the largest jewelry store in the country except for Tiffany's Manhattan store — will have two shareholder-only events. The first will be a cocktail reception from 6 p.m. to 10 p.m. on Friday, May 3. The second, the main gala, will be from 9 a.m. to 5 p.m. on Sunday, May 5. Shareholder prices will be available Thursday through Monday, so if you wish to avoid the large crowds that will assemble on Friday evening and Sunday, come at other times and identify yourself as a shareholder. On Saturday, we will be open until 6 p.m. Borsheim's operates on a gross margin that is fully twenty percentage points below that of its major rivals, so the more you buy, the more you save (or at least that's what my wife and daughter tell me). Come by and let us perform a walletectomy on you.

In the mall outside of Borsheim's, we will have some of the world's top bridge experts available to play with our shareholders on Sunday afternoon. We expect Bob and Petra Hamman along with Sharon Osberg to host tables. Patrick Wolff, twice U.S. chess champion, will also be in the mall, taking on all comers — blindfolded!

Last year, Patrick played as many as six games simultaneously — with his blindfold securely in place — and this year will try for seven. Finally, Bill Robertie, one of only two players who have twice won the backgammon world championship, will be on hand to test your skill at that game. Come to the mall on Sunday for the Mensa Olympics.

Gorat's — my favorite steakhouse — will again be open exclusively for Berkshire shareholders on Sunday, May 5, and will be serving from 4 p.m. until 10 p.m. Please remember that to come to Gorat's on Sunday, you must have a reservation. To make one, call 402-551-3733 on April 1 (*but not before*). If Sunday is sold out, try Gorat's on one of the other evenings you will be in town. Show your sophistication by ordering a rare T-bone with a double order of hash browns.

The usual baseball game will be held at Rosenblatt Stadium at 7 p.m. on Saturday night. This year the Omaha Royals will play the Oklahoma RedHawks. Last year, in an attempt to emulate the career switch of Babe Ruth, I gave up pitching and tried batting. Bob Gibson, an Omaha native, was on the mound and I was terrified, fearing Bob's famous brush-back pitch. Instead, he delivered a fast ball in the strike zone, and with a Mark McGwire-like swing, I managed to connect for a hard grounder, which inexplicably died in the infield. I didn't run it out: At my age, I get winded playing a hand of bridge.

I'm not sure what will take place at the ballpark this year, but come out and be surprised. Our proxy statement contains instructions for obtaining tickets to the game. Those people ordering tickets to the annual meeting will receive a booklet containing all manner of information that should help you enjoy your visit in Omaha. There will be plenty of action in town. So come for Woodstock Weekend and join our Celebration of Capitalism at the Civic.

* * * * * * * * * * * *

Finally, I would like to thank the wonderful and incredibly productive crew at World Headquarters (all 5,246.5 square feet of it) who make my job so easy. Berkshire added about 40,000 employees last year, bringing our workforce to 110,000. At headquarters we added one employee and now have 14.8. (I've tried in vain to get JoEllen Rieck to change her workweek from four days to five; I think she likes the national recognition she gains by being .8.)

The smooth handling of the array of duties that come with our current size and scope – as well as some additional activities almost unique to Berkshire, such as our shareholder gala and designated-gifts program – takes a very special group of people. And that we most definitely have.

February 28, 2002

Warren E. Buffett
Chairman of the Board

BERKSHIRE HATHAWAY INC.

To the Shareholders of Berkshire Hathaway Inc.:

Our gain in net worth during 2002 was $6.1 billion, which increased the per-share book value of both our Class A and Class B stock by 10.0%. Over the last 38 years (that is, since present management took over) per-share book value has grown from $19 to $41,727, a rate of 22.2% compounded annually.[*]

In all respects 2002 was a banner year. I'll provide details later, but here's a summary:

- Our various non-insurance operations performed exceptionally well, despite a sluggish economy. A decade ago Berkshire's annual pre-tax earnings from our non-insurance businesses was $272 million. Now, from our ever-expanding collection of manufacturing, retailing, service and finance businesses, we earn that sum *monthly*.

- Our insurance group increased its float to $41.2 billion, a hefty gain of $5.7 billion. Better yet, the use of these funds in 2002 cost us only 1%. Getting back to low-cost float feels good, particularly after our poor results during the three previous years. Berkshire's reinsurance division and GEICO shot the lights out in 2002, and underwriting discipline was restored at General Re.

- Berkshire acquired some important new businesses – with economic characteristics ranging from good to great, run by managers ranging from great to great. Those attributes are two legs of our "entrance" strategy, the third being a sensible purchase price. Unlike LBO operators and private equity firms, we have no "exit" strategy – we buy to keep. That's one reason why Berkshire is usually the first – and sometimes the only – choice for sellers and their managers.

- Our marketable securities outperformed most indices. For Lou Simpson, who manages equities at GEICO, this was old stuff. But, for me, it was a welcome change from the last few years, during which my investment record was dismal.

The confluence of these favorable factors in 2002 caused our book-value gain to outstrip the performance of the S&P 500 by 32.1 percentage points. This result is aberrational: Charlie Munger, Berkshire's vice chairman and my partner, and I hope to achieve – *at most* – an average annual advantage of a few points. In the future, there will be years in which the S&P soundly trounces us. That will in fact almost certainly happen during a strong bull market, because the portion of our assets committed to common stocks has significantly declined. This change, of course, helps our relative performance in down markets such as we had in 2002.

I have another caveat to mention about last year's results. If you've been a reader of financial reports in recent years, you've seen a flood of "pro-forma" earnings statements – tabulations in which managers invariably show "earnings" far in excess of those allowed by their auditors. In these presentations, the CEO tells his owners "don't count this, don't count that – just count what makes earnings fat." Often, a forget-all-this-bad-stuff message is delivered year after year without management so much as blushing.

---

[*]All figures used in this report apply to Berkshire's A shares, the successor to the only stock that the company had outstanding before 1996. The B shares have an economic interest equal to 1/30th that of the A.

We've yet to see a pro-forma presentation disclosing that audited earnings were somewhat high. So let's make a little history: Last year, on a pro-forma basis, Berkshire had *lower* earnings than those we actually reported.

That is true because two favorable factors aided our reported figures. First, in 2002 there was no megacatastrophe, which means that Berkshire (and other insurers as well) earned more from insurance than if losses had been normal. In years when the reverse is true – because of a blockbuster hurricane, earthquake or man-made disaster – many insurers like to report that they would have earned X "except for" the unusual event. The implication is that since such megacats are infrequent, they shouldn't be counted when "true" earnings are calculated. That is deceptive nonsense. "Except for" losses will forever be part of the insurance business, and they will forever be paid with shareholders' money.

Nonetheless, for the purposes of this exercise, we'll take a page from the industry's book. For last year, when we didn't have any truly major disasters, a downward adjustment is appropriate if you wish to "normalize" our underwriting result.

Secondly, the bond market in 2002 favored certain strategies we employed in our finance and financial products business. Gains from those strategies will certainly diminish within a year or two – and may well disappear.

Soooo . . . "except for" a couple of favorable breaks, our pre-tax earnings last year would have been about $500 million less than we actually reported. We're happy, nevertheless, to bank the excess. As Jack Benny once said upon receiving an award: "I don't deserve this honor – but, then, I have arthritis, and I don't deserve that either."

* * * * * * * * * * * *

We continue to be blessed with an extraordinary group of managers, many of whom haven't the slightest financial need to work. They stick around, though: In 38 years, we've never had a single CEO of a subsidiary elect to leave Berkshire to work elsewhere. Counting Charlie, we now have six managers over 75, and I hope that in four years that number increases by at least two (Bob Shaw and I are both 72). Our rationale: "It's hard to teach a new dog old tricks."

Berkshire's operating CEOs are masters of their crafts and run their businesses as if they were their own. My job is to stay out of their way and allocate whatever excess capital their businesses generate. It's easy work.

My managerial model is Eddie Bennett, who was a batboy. In 1919, at age 19, Eddie began his work with the Chicago White Sox, who that year went to the World Series. The next year, Eddie switched to the Brooklyn Dodgers, and they, too, won their league title. Our hero, however, smelled trouble. Changing boroughs, he joined the Yankees in 1921, and they promptly won their first pennant in history. Now Eddie settled in, shrewdly seeing what was coming. In the next seven years, the Yankees won five American League titles.

What does this have to do with management? It's simple – to be a winner, work with winners. In 1927, for example, Eddie received $700 for the 1/8th World Series share voted him by the legendary Yankee team of Ruth and Gehrig. This sum, which Eddie earned by working only four days (because New York swept the Series) was roughly equal to the full-year pay then earned by batboys who worked with ordinary associates.

Eddie understood that how he lugged bats was unimportant; what counted instead was hooking up with the cream of those on the playing field. I've learned from Eddie. At Berkshire, I regularly hand bats to many of the heaviest hitters in American business.

Acquisitions

We added some sluggers to our lineup last year. Two acquisitions pending at yearend 2001 were completed: Albecca (which operates under the name Larson-Juhl), the U.S. leader in custom-made picture frames; and Fruit of the Loom, the producer of about 33.3% of the men's and boy's underwear sold in the U.S. and of other apparel as well.

Both companies came with outstanding CEOs: Steve McKenzie at Albecca and John Holland at Fruit. John, who had retired from Fruit in 1996, rejoined it three years ago and rescued the company from the disastrous path it had gone down after he'd left. He's now 70, and I am trying to convince him to make his next retirement coincident with mine (presently scheduled for five years after my death – a date subject, however, to extension).

We initiated and completed two other acquisitions last year that were somewhat below our normal size threshold. In aggregate, however, these businesses earn more than $60 million pre-tax annually. Both operate in industries characterized by tough economics, but both also have important competitive strengths that enable them to earn decent returns on capital.

The newcomers are:

(a)   CTB, a worldwide leader in equipment for the poultry, hog, egg production and grain industries; and

(b)   Garan, a manufacturer of children's apparel, whose largest and best-known line is Garanimals®.

These two companies came with the managers responsible for their impressive records: Vic Mancinelli at CTB and Seymour Lichtenstein at Garan.

The largest acquisition we initiated in 2002 was The Pampered Chef, a company with a fascinating history dating back to 1980. Doris Christopher was then a 34-year-old suburban Chicago home economics teacher with a husband, two little girls, and absolutely no business background. Wanting, however, to supplement her family's modest income, she turned to thinking about what she knew best – food preparation. Why not, she wondered, make a business out of marketing kitchenware, focusing on the items she herself had found most useful?

To get started, Doris borrowed $3,000 against her life insurance policy – all the money *ever* injected into the company – and went to the Merchandise Mart on a buying expedition. There, she picked up a dozen each of this and that, and then went home to set up operations in her basement.

Her plan was to conduct in-home presentations to small groups of women, gathered at the homes of their friends. While driving to her first presentation, though, Doris almost talked herself into returning home, convinced she was doomed to fail.

But the women she faced that evening loved her and her products, purchased $175 of goods, and TPC was underway. Working with her husband, Jay, Doris did $50,000 of business in the first year. Today – only 22 years later – TPC does more than $700 million of business annually, working through 67,000 kitchen consultants.

I've been to a TPC party, and it's easy to see why the business is a success. The company's products, in large part proprietary, are well-styled and highly useful, and the consultants are knowledgeable and enthusiastic. Everyone has a good time. Hurry to pamperedchef.com on the Internet to find where to attend a party near you.

Two years ago, Doris brought in Sheila O'Connell Cooper, now CEO, to share the management load, and in August they met with me in Omaha. It took me about ten seconds to decide that these were two managers with whom I wished to partner, and we promptly made a deal. Berkshire shareholders couldn't be luckier than to be associated with Doris and Sheila.

* * * * * * * * * * *

Berkshire also made some important acquisitions last year through MidAmerican Energy Holdings (MEHC), a company in which our equity interest is 80.2%. Because the Public Utility Holding Company Act (PUHCA) limits us to 9.9% voting control, however, we are unable to fully consolidate MEHC's financial statements.

Despite the voting-control limitation – and the somewhat strange capital structure at MEHC it has engendered – the company is a key part of Berkshire. Already it has $18 billion of assets and delivers our largest stream of non-insurance earnings. It could well grow to be huge.

Last year MEHC acquired two important gas pipelines. The first, Kern River, extends from Southwest Wyoming to Southern California. This line moves about 900 million cubic feet of gas a day and is undergoing a $1.2 billion expansion that will double throughput by this fall. At that point, the line will carry enough gas to generate electricity for ten million homes.

The second acquisition, Northern Natural Gas, is a 16,600 mile line extending from the Southwest to a wide range of Midwestern locations. This purchase completes a corporate odyssey of particular interest to Omahans.

From its beginnings in the 1930s, Northern Natural was one of Omaha's premier businesses, run by CEOs who regularly distinguished themselves as community leaders. Then, in July, 1985, the company – which in 1980 had been renamed InterNorth – merged with Houston Natural Gas, a business less than half its size. The companies announced that the enlarged operation would be headquartered in Omaha, with InterNorth's CEO continuing in that job.

Within a year, those promises were broken. By then, the former CEO of Houston Natural had taken over the top job at InterNorth, the company had been renamed, and the headquarters had been moved to Houston. These switches were orchestrated by the new CEO – Ken Lay – and the name he chose was Enron.

Fast forward 15 years to late 2001. Enron ran into the troubles we've heard so much about and borrowed money from Dynegy, putting up the Northern Natural pipeline operation as collateral. The two companies quickly had a falling out, and the pipeline's ownership moved to Dynegy. That company, in turn, soon encountered severe financial problems of its own.

MEHC received a call on Friday, July 26, from Dynegy, which was looking for a quick and certain cash sale of the pipeline. Dynegy phoned the right party: On July 29, we signed a contract, and shortly thereafter Northern Natural returned home.

When 2001 began, Charlie and I had no idea that Berkshire would be moving into the pipeline business. But upon completion of the Kern River expansion, MEHC will transport about 8% of all gas used in the U.S. We continue to look for large energy-related assets, though in the electric utility field PUHCA constrains what we can do.

* * * * * * * * * * * *

A few years ago, and somewhat by accident, MEHC found itself in the residential real estate brokerage business. It is no accident, however, that we have dramatically expanded the operation. Moreover, we are likely to keep on expanding in the future.

We call this business HomeServices of America. In the various communities it serves, though, it operates under the names of the businesses it has acquired, such as CBS in Omaha, Edina Realty in Minneapolis and Iowa Realty in Des Moines. In most metropolitan areas in which we operate, we are the clear market leader.

HomeServices is now the second largest residential brokerage business in the country. On one side or the other (or both), we participated in $37 billion of transactions last year, up 100% from 2001.

Most of our growth came from three acquisitions we made during 2002, the largest of which was Prudential California Realty. Last year, this company, the leading realtor in a territory consisting of Los Angeles, Orange and San Diego Counties, participated in $16 billion of closings.

In a very short period, Ron Peltier, the company's CEO, has increased HomeServices' revenues – and profits – dramatically. Though this business will always be cyclical, it's one we like and in which we continue to have an appetite for sensible acquisitions.

* * * * * * * * * * * *

Dave Sokol, MEHC's CEO, and Greg Abel, his key associate, are huge assets for Berkshire. They are dealmakers, and they are managers. Berkshire stands ready to inject massive amounts of money into MEHC – and it will be fun to watch how far Dave and Greg can take the business.

The Economics of Property/Casualty Insurance

Our core business — though we have others of great importance — is insurance. To understand Berkshire, therefore, it is necessary that you understand how to evaluate an insurance company. The key determinants are: (1) the amount of float that the business generates; (2) its cost; and (3) most critical of all, the long-term outlook for both of these factors.

To begin with, float is money we hold but don't own. In an insurance operation, float arises because premiums are received before losses are paid, an interval that sometimes extends over many years. During that time, the insurer invests the money. This pleasant activity typically carries with it a downside: The premiums that an insurer takes in usually do not cover the losses and expenses it eventually must pay. That leaves it running an "underwriting loss," which is the cost of float. An insurance business has value if its cost of float over time is less than the cost the company would otherwise incur to obtain funds. But the business is a lemon if its cost of float is higher than market rates for money. Moreover, the downward trend of interest rates in recent years has transformed underwriting losses that formerly were tolerable into burdens that move insurance businesses deeply into the lemon category.

Historically, Berkshire has obtained its float at a very low cost. Indeed, our cost has been less than zero in many years; that is, we've actually been paid for holding other people's money. In 2001, however, our cost was terrible, coming in at 12.8%, about half of which was attributable to World Trade Center losses. Back in 1983-84, we had years that were even worse. There's nothing automatic about cheap float.

The table that follows shows (at intervals) the float generated by the various segments of Berkshire's insurance operations since we entered the business 36 years ago upon acquiring National Indemnity Company (whose traditional lines are included in the segment "Other Primary"). For the table we have calculated our float — which we generate in large amounts relative to our premium volume — by adding net loss reserves, loss adjustment reserves, funds held under reinsurance assumed and unearned premium reserves, and then subtracting insurance-related receivables, prepaid acquisition costs, prepaid taxes and deferred charges applicable to assumed reinsurance. (Got that?)

Yearend Float (in $ millions)

Year	GEICO	General Re	Other Reinsurance	Other Primary	Total
1967				20	20
1977			40	131	171
1987			701	807	1,508
1997	2,917		4,014	455	7,386
1998	3,125	14,909	4,305	415	22,754
1999	3,444	15,166	6,285	403	25,298
2000	3,943	15,525	7,805	598	27,871
2001	4,251	19,310	11,262	685	35,508
2002	4,678	22,207	13,396	943	41,224

Last year our cost of float was 1%. As I mentioned earlier, you should temper your enthusiasm about this favorable result given that no megacatastrophe occurred in 2002. We're certain to get one of these disasters periodically, and when we do our float-cost will spike.

Our 2002 results were hurt by 1) a painful charge at General Re for losses that should have been recorded as costs in earlier years, and 2) a "desirable" charge we incur annually for retroactive insurance (see the next section for more about these items). These costs totaled $1.75 billion, or about 4.6% of float. Fortunately, our overall underwriting experience on 2002 business was excellent, which allowed us, even after the charges noted, to approach a no-cost result.

Absent a megacatastrophe, I expect our cost of float in 2003 to again be very low – perhaps even less than zero. In the rundown of our insurance operations that follows, you will see why I'm optimistic that, over time, our underwriting results will both surpass those achieved by the industry and deliver us investable funds at minimal cost.

Insurance Operations

If our insurance operations are to generate low-cost float over time, they must: (a) underwrite with unwavering discipline; (b) reserve conservatively; and (c) avoid an aggregation of exposures that would allow a supposedly "impossible" incident to threaten their solvency. All of our major insurance businesses, with one exception, have regularly met those tests.

The exception is General Re, and there was much to do at that company last year to get it up to snuff. I'm delighted to report that under Joe Brandon's leadership, and with yeoman assistance by Tad Montross, enormous progress has been made on each of the fronts described.

When I agreed in 1998 to merge Berkshire with Gen Re, I thought that company stuck to the three rules I've enumerated. I had studied the operation for decades and had observed underwriting discipline that was consistent and reserving that was conservative. At merger time, I detected no slippage in Gen Re's standards.

I was dead wrong. Gen Re's culture and practices had substantially changed and unbeknownst to management – and to me – the company was grossly mispricing its current business. In addition, Gen Re had accumulated an aggregation of risks that would have been fatal had, say, terrorists detonated several large-scale nuclear bombs in an attack on the U.S. A disaster of that scope was highly improbable, of course, but it is up to insurers to limit their risks in a manner that leaves their finances rock-solid if the "impossible" happens. Indeed, had Gen Re remained independent, the World Trade Center attack alone would have threatened the company's existence.

When the WTC disaster occurred, it exposed weaknesses in Gen Re's operations that I should have detected earlier. But I was lucky: Joe and Tad were on hand, freshly endowed with increased authority and eager to rapidly correct the errors of the past. They knew what to do – and they did it.

It takes time for insurance policies to run off, however, and 2002 was well along before we managed to reduce our aggregation of nuclear, chemical and biological risk (NCB) to a tolerable level. That problem is now behind us.

On another front, Gen Re's underwriting attitude has been dramatically altered: The entire organization now understands that we wish to write only properly-priced business, whatever the effect on volume. Joe and Tad judge themselves *only* by Gen Re's underwriting profitability. Size simply doesn't count.

Finally, we are making every effort to get our reserving right. If we fail at that, we can't know our true costs. And any insurer that has no idea what its costs are is heading for big trouble.

At yearend 2001, General Re attempted to reserve adequately for all losses that had occurred prior to that date and were not yet paid – but we failed badly. Therefore the company's 2002 underwriting results were penalized by an additional $1.31 billion that we recorded to correct the estimation mistakes of earlier years. When I review the reserving errors that have been uncovered at General Re, a line from a country song seems apt: "I wish I didn't know now what I didn't know then."

I can promise you that our top priority going forward is to avoid inadequate reserving. But I can't guarantee success. The natural tendency of most casualty-insurance managers is to underreserve, and they must have a particular mindset – which, it may surprise you, has nothing to do with actuarial expertise – if they are to overcome this devastating bias. Additionally, a reinsurer faces far more difficulties in reserving properly than does a primary insurer. Nevertheless, at Berkshire, we have generally been successful in our reserving, and we are determined to be at General Re as well.

In summary, I believe General Re is now well positioned to deliver huge amounts of no-cost float to Berkshire and that its sink-the-ship catastrophe risk has been eliminated. The company still possesses the important competitive strengths that I've outlined in the past. And it gained another highly significant advantage last year when each of its three largest worldwide competitors, previously rated AAA, was demoted by at least one rating agency. Among the giants, General Re, rated AAA across-the-board, is now in a class by itself in respect to financial strength.

No attribute is more important. Recently, in contrast, one of the world's largest reinsurers – a company regularly recommended to primary insurers by leading brokers – has all but ceased paying claims, including those both valid and due. This company owes many billions of dollars to hundreds of primary insurers who now face massive write-offs. "Cheap" reinsurance is a fool's bargain: When an insurer lays out money today in exchange for a reinsurer's promise to pay a decade or two later, it's dangerous – and possibly life-threatening – for the insurer to deal with any but the strongest reinsurer around.

Berkshire shareholders owe Joe and Tad a huge thank you for their accomplishments in 2002. They worked harder during the year than I would wish for anyone – and it is paying off.

* * * * * * * * * * * *

At GEICO, everything went so well in 2002 that we should pinch ourselves. Growth was substantial, profits were outstanding, policyholder retention was up and sales productivity jumped significantly. These trends continue in early 2003.

Thank Tony Nicely for all of this. As anyone who knows him will attest, Tony has been in love with GEICO for 41 years – ever since he went to work for the company at 18 – and his results reflect this passion. He is proud of the money we save policyholders – about $1 billion annually versus what other insurers, on average, would have charged them. He is proud of the service we provide these policyholders: In a key industry survey, GEICO was recently ranked above all major competitors. He is proud of his 19,162 associates, who last year were awarded profit-sharing payments equal to 19% of their base salary because of the splendid results they achieved. And he is proud of the growing profits he delivers to Berkshire shareholders.

GEICO took in $2.9 billion in premiums when Berkshire acquired full ownership in 1996. Last year, its volume was $6.9 billion, with plenty of growth to come. Particularly promising is the company's Internet operation, whose new business grew by 75% last year. Check us out at GEICO.com (or call 800-847-7536). In most states, shareholders get a special 8% discount.

Here's one footnote to GEICO's 2002 earnings that underscores the need for insurers to do business with only the strongest of reinsurers. In 1981-1983, the managers then running GEICO decided to try their hand at writing commercial umbrella and product liability insurance. The risks seemed modest: the company took in only $3,051,000 from this line and used almost all of it – $2,979,000 – to buy reinsurance in order to limit its losses. GEICO was left with a paltry $72,000 as compensation for the minor portion of the risk that it retained. But this small bite of the apple was more than enough to make the experience memorable. GEICO's losses from this venture now total a breathtaking $94.1 *million* or about 130,000% of the net premium it received. Of the total loss, uncollectable receivables from deadbeat reinsurers account for no less than $90.3 million (including $19 million charged in 2002). So much for "cheap" reinsurance.

* * * * * * * * * * * *

Ajit Jain's reinsurance division was the major reason our float cost us so little last year. If we ever put a photo in a Berkshire annual report, it will be of Ajit. In color!

Ajit's operation has amassed $13.4 billion of float, more than all but a handful of insurers have ever built up. He accomplished this from a standing start in 1986, and even now has a workforce numbering only 20. And, most important, he has produced underwriting profits.

His profits are particularly remarkable if you factor in some accounting arcana that I am about to lay on you. So prepare to eat your spinach (or, alternatively, if debits and credits aren't your thing, skip the next two paragraphs).

Ajit's 2002 underwriting profit of $534 million came *after* his operation recognized a charge of $428 million attributable to "retroactive" insurance he has written over the years. In this line of business, we assume from another insurer the obligation to pay up to a specified amount for losses they have already incurred – often for events that took place decades earlier – but that are yet to be paid (for example, because a worker hurt in 1980 will receive monthly payments for life). In these arrangements, an insurer pays us a large upfront premium, but one that is less than the losses we expect to pay. We willingly accept this differential because a) our payments are capped, and b) we get to use the money until loss payments are actually made, with these often stretching out over a decade or more. About 80% of the $6.6 billion in asbestos and environmental loss reserves that we carry arises from capped contracts, whose costs consequently can't skyrocket.

When we write a retroactive policy, we immediately record both the premium and a reserve for the expected losses. The difference between the two is entered as an asset entitled "deferred charges – reinsurance assumed." This is no small item: at yearend, for all retroactive policies, it was $3.4 billion. We then amortize this asset downward by charges to income over the expected life of each policy. These charges – $440 million in 2002, including charges at Gen Re – create an underwriting loss, but one that is intentional and desirable. And even after this drag on reported results, Ajit achieved a large underwriting gain last year.

We want to emphasize, however, that we assume risks in Ajit's operation that are huge – *far* larger than those retained by any other insurer in the world. Therefore, a single event could cause a major swing in Ajit's results in any given quarter or year. That bothers us not at all: As long as we are paid appropriately, we love taking on short-term volatility that others wish to shed. At Berkshire, we would rather earn a lumpy 15% over time than a smooth 12%.

If you see Ajit at our annual meeting, bow deeply.

* * * * * * * * * * * *

Berkshire's smaller insurers had an outstanding year. Their aggregate float grew by 38%, and they realized an underwriting profit of $32 million, or 4.5% of premiums. Collectively, these operations would make one of the finest insurance companies in the country.

Included in these figures, however, were terrible results in our California workers' compensation operation. There, we have work to do. There, too, our reserving severely missed the mark. Until we figure out how to get this business right, we will keep it small.

For the fabulous year they had in 2002, we thank Rod Eldred, John Kizer, Tom Nerney, Don Towle and Don Wurster. They added a lot of value to your Berkshire investment.

Sources of Reported Earnings

The table that follows shows the main sources of Berkshire's reported earnings. You will notice that "Purchase-Accounting Adjustments" dropped sharply in 2002, the reason being that GAAP rules changed then, no longer requiring the amortization of goodwill. This change increases our reported earnings, but has no effect on our economic earnings.

	(in millions)			
	Pre-Tax Earnings		*Berkshire's Share of Net Earnings (after taxes and Minority interests)*	
	2002	*2001*	*2002*	*2001*
Operating Earnings:				
Insurance Group:				
Underwriting – General Re	$(1,393)	$(3,671)	$(930)	$(2,391)
Underwriting – Berkshire Group	534	(647)	347	(433)
Underwriting – GEICO	416	221	271	144
Underwriting – Other Primary	32	30	20	18
Net Investment Income	3,050	2,824	2,096	1,968
Apparel[1]	229	(33)	156	(28)
Building Products[2]	516	461	313	287
Finance and Financial Products Business	1,016	519	659	336
Flight Services	225	186	133	105
MidAmerican Energy (80% owned)	613	565	359	230
Retail Operations	166	175	97	101
Scott Fetzer (excluding finance operation)	129	129	83	83
Shaw Industries[3]	424	292	258	156
Other Businesses	256	212	160	131
Purchase-Accounting Adjustments	(119)	(726)	(65)	(699)
Corporate Interest Expense	(86)	(92)	(55)	(60)
Shareholder-Designated Contributions	(17)	(17)	(11)	(11)
Other	19	25	12	16
Operating Earnings	6,010	453	3,903	(47)
Capital Gains from Investments	603	1,320	383	842
Total Earnings – All Entities	$6,613	$1,773	$4,286	$ 795

[1] *Includes Fruit of the Loom from April 30, 2002 and Garan from September 4, 2002.*

[2] *Includes Johns Manville from February 27, 2001 and MiTek from July 31, 2001.*

[3] *From date of acquisition, January 8, 2001.*

Here's a summary of major developments at our non-insurance businesses:

- MidAmerican Energy's earnings grew in 2002 and will likely do so again this year. Most of the increase, both present and expected, results from the acquisitions described earlier. To fund these, Berkshire purchased $1,273 million of MidAmerican junior debt (bringing our total holdings of these 11% obligations to $1,728 million) and also invested $402 million in a "common-equivalent" stock. We now own (on a fully-diluted basis) 80.2% of MidAmerican's equity. MidAmerican's financial statements are presented in detail on page 37.

- Last year I told you of the problems at Dexter that led to a huge loss in our shoe business. Thanks to Frank Rooney and Jim Issler of H.H. Brown, the Dexter operation has been turned around. Despite the cost of unwinding our problems there, we earned $24 million in shoes last year, an upward swing of $70 million from 2001.

  Randy Watson at Justin also contributed to this improvement, increasing margins significantly while trimming invested capital. Shoes are a tough business, but we have terrific managers and believe that in the future we will earn reasonable returns on the capital we employ in this operation.

- In a so-so year for home-furnishing and jewelry retailers, our operations did well. Among our eight retailing operations, the best performer was Homemaker's in Des Moines. There, the talented Merschman family achieved outstanding gains in both sales and profits.

  Nebraska Furniture Mart will open a new blockbuster store in metropolitan Kansas City in August. With 450,000 square feet of retail space, it could well produce the second largest volume of any furniture store in the country – the Omaha operation being the national champion. I hope Berkshire shareholders in the Kansas City area will come out for the opening (and keep coming).

- Our home and construction-related businesses – Acme Brick, Benjamin Moore Paint, Johns-Manville, MiTek and Shaw – delivered $941 million of pre-tax earnings last year. Of particular significance was Shaw's gain from $292 million in 2001 to $424 million. Bob Shaw and Julian Saul are terrific operators. Carpet prices increased only 1% last year, but Shaw's productivity gains and excellent expense control delivered significantly improved margins.

  We cherish cost-consciousness at Berkshire. Our model is the widow who went to the local newspaper to place an obituary notice. Told there was a 25-cents-a-word charge, she requested "Fred Brown died." She was then informed there was a seven-word minimum. "Okay" the bereaved woman replied, "make it 'Fred Brown died, golf clubs for sale'."

- Earnings from flight services increased last year – but only because we realized a special pre-tax gain of $60 million from the sale of our 50% interest in FlightSafety Boeing. Without this gain, earnings from our training business would have fallen slightly in concert with the slowdown in business-aviation activity. FlightSafety training continues to be the gold standard for the industry, and we expect growth in the years to come.

  At NetJets, our fractional-ownership operation, we are the runaway leader of the four-company field. FAA records indicate that our industry share in 2002 was 75%, meaning that clients purchased or leased planes from us that were valued at triple those recorded by our three competitors *combined*. Last year, our fleet flew 132.7 million nautical miles, taking clients to 130 countries.

  Our preeminence is directly attributable to Rich Santulli, NetJets' CEO. He invented the business in 1986 and ever since has exhibited an unbending devotion to the highest levels of service, safety and security. Rich, Charlie and I insist on planes (and personnel) worthy of carrying our own families – because they regularly do.

  Though NetJets revenues set a record in 2002, the company again lost money. A small profit in the U.S. was more than offset by losses in Europe. Overall, the fractional-ownership industry lost significant sums last year, and that is almost certain to be the outcome in 2003 as well. The bald fact is that airplanes are costly to operate.

  Over time, this economic reality should work to our advantage, given that for a great many companies, private aircraft are an essential business tool. And for most of these companies, NetJets makes compelling sense as either a primary or supplementary supplier of the aircraft they need.

  Many businesses could save millions of dollars annually by flying with us. Indeed, the yearly savings at some large companies could exceed $10 million. Equally important, these companies would actually increase their operational capabilities by using us. A fractional ownership of a single NetJets plane allows a client to have several planes in the air simultaneously. Additionally, through the interchange arrangement we make available, an owner of an interest in one plane can fly any of 12 other models, using whatever plane makes most sense for a mission. (One of my sisters owns a fraction of a Falcon 2000, which she uses for trips to Hawaii, but – exhibiting the Buffett gene – she interchanges to a more economical Citation Excel for short trips in the U.S.)

  The roster of NetJets users confirms the advantages we offer major businesses. Take General Electric, for example. It has a large fleet of its own but also has an unsurpassed knowledge of how to utilize aircraft effectively and economically. And it is our largest customer.

- Our finance and financial products line covers a variety of operations, among them certain activities in high-grade fixed-income securities that proved highly profitable in 2002. Earnings in this arena will probably continue for a while, but are certain to decrease – and perhaps disappear – in time.

This category also includes a highly satisfactory – but rapidly diminishing – income stream from our Berkadia investment in Finova (described in last year's report). Our partner, Leucadia National Corp., has managed this operation with great skill, willingly doing far more than its share of the heavy lifting. I like this division of labor and hope to join with Leucadia in future transactions.

On the minus side, the Finance line also includes the operations of General Re Securities, a derivatives and trading business. This entity lost $173 million pre-tax last year, a result that, in part, is a belated acknowledgment of faulty, albeit standard, accounting it used in earlier periods. Derivatives, in fact, deserve an extensive look, both in respect to the accounting their users employ and to the problems they may pose for both individual companies and our economy.

Derivatives

Charlie and I are of one mind in how we feel about derivatives and the trading activities that go with them: We view them as time bombs, both for the parties that deal in them and the economic system.

Having delivered that thought, which I'll get back to, let me retreat to explaining derivatives, though the explanation must be general because the word covers an extraordinarily wide range of financial contracts. Essentially, these instruments call for money to change hands at some future date, with the amount to be determined by one or more reference items, such as interest rates, stock prices or currency values. If, for example, you are either long or short an S&P 500 futures contract, you are a party to a very simple derivatives transaction – with your gain or loss *derived* from movements in the index. Derivatives contracts are of varying duration (running sometimes to 20 or more years) and their value is often tied to several variables.

Unless derivatives contracts are collateralized or guaranteed, their ultimate value also depends on the creditworthiness of the counterparties to them. In the meantime, though, before a contract is settled, the counterparties record profits and losses – often huge in amount – in their current earnings statements without so much as a penny changing hands.

The range of derivatives contracts is limited only by the imagination of man (or sometimes, so it seems, madmen). At Enron, for example, newsprint and broadband derivatives, due to be settled many years in the future, were put on the books. Or say you want to write a contract speculating on the number of twins to be born in Nebraska in 2020. No problem – at a price, you will easily find an obliging counterparty.

When we purchased Gen Re, it came with General Re Securities, a derivatives dealer that Charlie and I didn't want, judging it to be dangerous. We failed in our attempts to sell the operation, however, and are now terminating it.

But closing down a derivatives business is easier said than done. It will be a great many years before we are totally out of this operation (though we reduce our exposure daily). In fact, the reinsurance and derivatives businesses are similar: Like Hell, both are easy to enter and almost impossible to exit. In either industry, once you write a contract – which may require a large payment decades later – you are usually stuck with it. True, there are methods by which the risk can be laid off with others. But most strategies of that kind leave you with residual liability.

Another commonality of reinsurance and derivatives is that both generate reported earnings that are often wildly overstated. That's true because today's earnings are in a significant way based on estimates whose inaccuracy may not be exposed for many years.

Errors will usually be honest, reflecting only the human tendency to take an optimistic view of one's commitments. But the parties to derivatives also have enormous incentives to cheat in accounting for them. Those who trade derivatives are usually paid (in whole or part) on "earnings" calculated by mark-to-market accounting. But often there is no real market (think about our contract involving twins) and "mark-to-model" is utilized. This substitution can bring on large-scale mischief. As a general rule, contracts involving multiple reference items and distant settlement dates increase the opportunities for counterparties to use fanciful assumptions. In the twins scenario, for example, the two parties to the contract might well use differing models allowing *both* to show substantial profits for many years. In extreme cases, mark-to-model degenerates into what I would call mark-to-myth.

Of course, both internal and outside auditors review the numbers, but that's no easy job. For example, General Re Securities at yearend (after ten months of winding down its operation) had 14,384 contracts outstanding, involving 672 counterparties around the world. Each contract had a plus or minus value derived from one or more reference items, including some of mind-boggling complexity. Valuing a portfolio like that, expert auditors could easily and honestly have widely varying opinions.

The valuation problem is far from academic: In recent years, some huge-scale frauds and near-frauds have been facilitated by derivatives trades. In the energy and electric utility sectors, for example, companies used derivatives and trading activities to report great "earnings" – until the roof fell in when they actually tried to convert the derivatives-related receivables on their balance sheets into cash. "Mark-to-market" then turned out to be truly "mark-to-myth."

I can assure you that the marking errors in the derivatives business have not been symmetrical. Almost invariably, they have favored either the trader who was eyeing a multi-million dollar bonus or the CEO who wanted to report impressive "earnings" (or both). The bonuses were paid, and the CEO profited from his options. Only much later did shareholders learn that the reported earnings were a sham.

Another problem about derivatives is that they can exacerbate trouble that a corporation has run into for completely unrelated reasons. This pile-on effect occurs because many derivatives contracts require that a company suffering a credit downgrade immediately supply collateral to counterparties. Imagine, then, that a company is downgraded because of general adversity and that its derivatives instantly kick in with *their* requirement, imposing an unexpected and enormous demand for cash collateral on the company. The need to meet this demand can then throw the company into a liquidity crisis that may, in some cases, trigger still more downgrades. It all becomes a spiral that can lead to a corporate meltdown.

Derivatives also create a daisy-chain risk that is akin to the risk run by insurers or reinsurers that lay off much of their business with others. In both cases, huge receivables from many counterparties tend to build up over time. (At Gen Re Securities, we still have $6.5 billion of receivables, though we've been in a liquidation mode for nearly a year.) A participant may see himself as prudent, believing his large credit exposures to be diversified and therefore not dangerous. Under certain circumstances, though, an exogenous event that causes the receivable from Company A to go bad will also affect those from Companies B through Z. History teaches us that a crisis often causes problems to correlate in a manner undreamed of in more tranquil times.

In banking, the recognition of a "linkage" problem was one of the reasons for the formation of the Federal Reserve System. Before the Fed was established, the failure of weak banks would sometimes put sudden and unanticipated liquidity demands on previously-strong banks, causing them to fail in turn. The Fed now insulates the strong from the troubles of the weak. But there is no central bank assigned to the job of preventing the dominoes toppling in insurance or derivatives. In these industries, firms that are fundamentally solid can become troubled simply because of the travails of other firms further down the chain. When a "chain reaction" threat exists within an industry, it pays to minimize links of any kind. That's how we conduct our reinsurance business, and it's one reason we are exiting derivatives.

Many people argue that derivatives reduce systemic problems, in that participants who can't bear certain risks are able to transfer them to stronger hands. These people believe that derivatives act to stabilize the economy, facilitate trade, and eliminate bumps for individual participants. And, on a micro level, what they say is often true. Indeed, at Berkshire, I sometimes engage in large-scale derivatives transactions in order to facilitate certain investment strategies.

Charlie and I believe, however, that the macro picture is dangerous and getting more so. Large amounts of risk, particularly credit risk, have become concentrated in the hands of relatively few derivatives dealers, who in addition trade extensively with one other. The troubles of one could quickly infect the others. On top of that, these dealers are owed huge amounts by non-dealer counterparties. Some of these counterparties, as I've mentioned, are linked in ways that could cause them to contemporaneously run into a problem because of a single event (such as the implosion of the telecom industry or the precipitous decline in the value of merchant power projects). Linkage, when it suddenly surfaces, can trigger serious systemic problems.

Indeed, in 1998, the leveraged and derivatives-heavy activities of a single hedge fund, Long-Term Capital Management, caused the Federal Reserve anxieties so severe that it hastily orchestrated a rescue effort. In later Congressional testimony, Fed officials acknowledged that, had they not intervened, the outstanding trades of LTCM – a firm unknown to the general public and employing only a few hundred people – could well have posed a serious threat to the stability of American markets. In other words, the Fed acted because its leaders were fearful of what might have happened to other financial institutions had the LTCM domino toppled. And this affair, though it paralyzed many parts of the fixed-income market for weeks, was far from a worst-case scenario.

One of the derivatives instruments that LTCM used was total-return swaps, contracts that facilitate 100% leverage in various markets, including stocks. For example, Party A to a contract, usually a bank, puts up all of the money for the purchase of a stock while Party B, without putting up any capital, agrees that at a future date it will receive any gain or pay any loss that the bank realizes.

Total-return swaps of this type make a joke of margin requirements. Beyond that, other types of derivatives severely curtail the ability of regulators to curb leverage and generally get their arms around the risk profiles of banks, insurers and other financial institutions. Similarly, even experienced investors and analysts encounter major problems in analyzing the financial condition of firms that are heavily involved with derivatives contracts. When Charlie and I finish reading the long footnotes detailing the derivatives activities of major banks, the only thing we understand is that we *don't* understand how much risk the institution is running.

The derivatives genie is now well out of the bottle, and these instruments will almost certainly multiply in variety and number until some event makes their toxicity clear. Knowledge of how dangerous they are has already permeated the electricity and gas businesses, in which the eruption of major troubles caused the use of derivatives to diminish dramatically. Elsewhere, however, the derivatives business continues to expand unchecked. Central banks and governments have so far found no effective way to control, or even monitor, the risks posed by these contracts.

Charlie and I believe Berkshire should be a fortress of financial strength – for the sake of our owners, creditors, policyholders and employees. We try to be alert to any sort of megacatastrophe risk, and that posture may make us unduly apprehensive about the burgeoning quantities of long-term derivatives contracts and the massive amount of uncollateralized receivables that are growing alongside. In our view, however, derivatives are financial weapons of mass destruction, carrying dangers that, while now latent, are potentially lethal.

Investments

Below we show our common stock investments. Those that had a market value of more than $500 million at the end of 2002 are itemized.

Shares	Company	12/31/02 Cost	Market
		(dollars in millions)	
151,610,700	American Express Company	$ 1,470	$ 5,359
200,000,000	The Coca-Cola Company	1,299	8,768
96,000,000	The Gillette Company	600	2,915
15,999,200	H&R Block, Inc.	255	643
6,708,760	M&T Bank	103	532
24,000,000	Moody's Corporation	499	991
1,727,765	The Washington Post Company	11	1,275
53,265,080	Wells Fargo & Company	306	2,497
	Others	4,621	5,383
	Total Common Stocks	$9,164	$28,363

We continue to do little in equities. Charlie and I are increasingly comfortable with our holdings in Berkshire's major investees because most of them have increased their earnings while their valuations have decreased. But we are not inclined to add to them. Though these enterprises have good prospects, we don't yet believe their shares are undervalued.

In our view, the same conclusion fits stocks generally. Despite three years of falling prices, which have significantly improved the attractiveness of common stocks, we still find *very* few that even mildly interest us. That dismal fact is testimony to the insanity of valuations reached during The Great Bubble. Unfortunately, the hangover may prove to be proportional to the binge.

The aversion to equities that Charlie and I exhibit today is far from congenital. We love owning common stocks – if they can be purchased at attractive prices. In my 61 years of investing, 50 or so years have offered that kind of opportunity. There will be years like that again. Unless, however, we see a very high probability of at least 10% pre-tax returns (which translate to 6½-7% after corporate tax), we will sit on the sidelines. With short-term money returning less than 1% after-tax, sitting it out is no fun. But occasionally successful investing requires inactivity.

Last year we were, however, able to make sensible investments in a few "junk" bonds and loans. Overall, our commitments in this sector sextupled, reaching $8.3 billion by yearend.

Investing in junk bonds and investing in stocks are alike in certain ways: Both activities require us to make a price-value calculation and also to scan hundreds of securities to find the very few that have attractive reward/risk ratios. But there are important differences between the two disciplines as well. In stocks, we expect every commitment to work out well because we concentrate on conservatively financed businesses with strong competitive strengths, run by able and honest people. If we buy into these companies at sensible prices, losses should be rare. Indeed, during the 38 years we have run the company's affairs, gains from the equities we manage at Berkshire (that is, excluding those managed at General Re and GEICO) have exceeded losses by a ratio of about 100 to one.

Purchasing junk bonds, we are dealing with enterprises that are far more marginal. These businesses are usually overloaded with debt and often operate in industries characterized by low returns on capital. Additionally, the quality of management is sometimes questionable. Management may even have interests that are directly counter to those of debtholders. Therefore, we expect that we will have occasional large losses in junk issues. So far, however, we have done reasonably well in this field.

Corporate Governance

Both the ability and fidelity of managers have long needed monitoring. Indeed, nearly 2,000 years ago, Jesus Christ addressed this subject, speaking (Luke 16:2) approvingly of "a certain rich man" who told his manager, "Give an account of thy stewardship; for thou mayest no longer be steward."

Accountability and stewardship withered in the last decade, becoming qualities deemed of little importance by those caught up in the Great Bubble. As stock prices went up, the behavioral norms of managers went down. By the late '90s, as a result, CEOs who traveled the high road did not encounter heavy traffic.

Most CEOs, it should be noted, are men and women you would be happy to have as trustees for your children's assets or as next-door neighbors. Too many of these people, however, have in recent years behaved badly at the office, fudging numbers and drawing obscene pay for mediocre business achievements. These otherwise decent people simply followed the career path of Mae West: "I was Snow White but I drifted."

In theory, corporate boards should have prevented this deterioration of conduct. I last wrote about the responsibilities of directors in the 1993 annual report. (We will send you a copy of this discussion on request, or you may read it on the Internet in the Corporate Governance section of the 1993 letter.) There, I said that directors "should behave as if there was a single absentee owner, whose long-term interest they should try to further in all proper ways." This means that directors must get rid of a manager who is mediocre or worse, no matter how likable he may be. Directors must react as did the chorus-girl bride of an 85-year-old multimillionaire when he asked whether she would love him if he lost his money. "Of course," the young beauty replied, "I would miss you, but I would still love you."

In the 1993 annual report, I also said directors had another job: "If able but greedy managers over-reach and try to dip too deeply into the shareholders' pockets, directors must slap their hands." Since I wrote that, over-reaching has become common but few hands have been slapped.

Why have intelligent and decent directors failed so miserably? The answer lies not in inadequate laws – it's always been clear that directors are obligated to represent the interests of shareholders – but rather in what I'd call "boardroom atmosphere."

It's almost impossible, for example, in a boardroom populated by well-mannered people, to raise the question of whether the CEO should be replaced. It's equally awkward to question a proposed acquisition that has been endorsed by the CEO, particularly when his inside staff and outside advisors are present and unanimously support his decision. (They wouldn't be in the room if they didn't.) Finally, when the compensation committee – armed, as always, with support from a high-paid consultant – reports on a megagrant of options to the CEO, it would be like belching at the dinner table for a director to suggest that the committee reconsider.

These "social" difficulties argue for outside directors regularly meeting without the CEO – a reform that is being instituted and that I enthusiastically endorse. I doubt, however, that most of the other new governance rules and recommendations will provide benefits commensurate with the monetary and other costs they impose.

The current cry is for "independent" directors. It is certainly true that it is desirable to have directors who think and speak independently – but they must also be business-savvy, interested and shareholder-oriented. In my 1993 commentary, those are the three qualities I described as essential.

Over a span of 40 years, I have been on 19 public-company boards (excluding Berkshire's) and have interacted with perhaps 250 directors. Most of them were "independent" as defined by today's rules. But the great majority of these directors lacked at least one of the three qualities I value. As a result, their contribution to shareholder well-being was minimal at best and, too often, negative. These people, decent and intelligent though they were, simply did not know enough about business and/or care enough about shareholders to question foolish acquisitions or egregious compensation. My own behavior, I must ruefully add, frequently fell short as well: Too often I was silent when management made proposals that I judged to be counter to the interests of shareholders. In those cases, collegiality trumped independence.

So that we may further see the failings of "independence," let's look at a 62-year case study covering thousands of companies. Since 1940, federal law has mandated that a large proportion of the directors of investment companies (most of these mutual funds) be independent. The requirement was originally 40% and now it is 50%. In any case, the typical fund has long operated with a majority of directors who qualify as independent.

These directors and the entire board have many perfunctory duties, but in actuality have only two important responsibilities: obtaining the best possible investment manager and negotiating with that manager for the lowest possible fee. When you are seeking investment help yourself, those two goals are the only ones that count, and directors acting for other investors should have exactly the same priorities. Yet when it comes to independent directors pursuing either goal, their record has been absolutely pathetic.

Many thousands of investment-company boards meet annually to carry out the vital job of selecting who will manage the savings of the millions of owners they represent. Year after year the directors of Fund A select manager A, Fund B directors select manager B, etc. ... in a zombie-like process that makes a mockery of stewardship. Very occasionally, a board will revolt. But for the most part, a monkey will type out a Shakespeare play before an "independent" mutual-fund director will suggest that his fund look at other managers, even if the incumbent manager has persistently delivered substandard performance. When they are handling their own money, of course, directors will look to alternative advisors – but it never enters their minds to do so when they are acting as fiduciaries for others.

The hypocrisy permeating the system is vividly exposed when a fund management company – call it "A" – is sold for a huge sum to Manager "B". Now the "independent" directors experience a "counter-revelation" and decide that Manager B is the best that can be found – even though B was available (and ignored) in previous years. Not so incidentally, B also could formerly have been hired at a far lower rate than is possible now that it has bought Manager A. That's because B has laid out a fortune to acquire A, and B must now recoup that cost through fees paid by the A shareholders who were "delivered" as part of the deal. (For a terrific discussion of the mutual fund business, read John Bogle's *Common Sense on Mutual Funds*.)

A few years ago, my daughter was asked to become a director of a family of funds managed by a major institution. The fees she would have received as a director were very substantial, enough to have increased her annual income by about 50% (a boost, she will tell you, she could use!). Legally, she would have been an independent director. But did the fund manager who approached her think there was *any* chance that she would think independently as to what advisor the fund should employ? Of course not. I am proud to say that she showed *real* independence by turning down the offer. The fund, however, had no trouble filling the slot (and – surprise – the fund has not changed managers).

Investment company directors have failed as well in negotiating management fees (just as compensation committees of many American companies have failed to hold the compensation of their CEOs to sensible levels). If you or I were empowered, I can assure you that we could easily negotiate materially lower management fees with the incumbent managers of most mutual funds. And, believe me, if directors were promised a portion of any fee savings they realized, the skies would be filled with falling fees. Under the current system, though, reductions mean nothing to "independent" directors while meaning everything to managers. So guess who wins?

Having the right money manager, of course, is far more important to a fund than reducing the manager's fee. Both tasks are nonetheless the job of directors. And in stepping up to these all-important responsibilities, tens of thousands of "independent" directors, over more than six decades, have failed miserably. (They've succeeded, however, in taking care of themselves; their fees from serving on multiple boards of a single "family" of funds often run well into six figures.)

When the manager cares deeply and the directors don't, what's needed is a powerful countervailing force – and that's the missing element in today's corporate governance. Getting rid of mediocre CEOs and eliminating overreaching by the able ones requires action by owners – big owners. The logistics aren't that tough: The ownership of stock has grown increasingly concentrated in recent decades, and today it would be easy for institutional managers to exert their will on problem situations. Twenty, or even fewer, of the largest institutions, acting together, could effectively reform corporate governance at a given company, simply by withholding their votes for directors who were tolerating odious behavior. In my view, this kind of concerted action is the only way that corporate stewardship can be meaningfully improved.

Unfortunately, certain major investing institutions have "glass house" problems in arguing for better governance elsewhere; they would shudder, for example, at the thought of their own performance and fees being closely inspected by their own boards. But Jack Bogle of Vanguard fame, Chris Davis of Davis Advisors, and Bill Miller of Legg Mason are now offering leadership in getting CEOs to treat their owners properly. Pension funds, as well as other fiduciaries, will reap better investment returns in the future if they support these men.

The acid test for reform will be CEO compensation. Managers will cheerfully agree to board "diversity," attest to SEC filings and adopt meaningless proposals relating to process. What many will fight, however, is a hard look at their own pay and perks.

In recent years compensation committees too often have been tail-wagging puppy dogs meekly following recommendations by consultants, a breed not known for allegiance to the faceless shareholders who pay their fees. (If you can't tell whose side someone is on, they are *not* on yours.) True, each committee is required by the SEC to state its reasoning about pay in the proxy. But the words are usually boilerplate written by the company's lawyers or its human-relations department.

This costly charade should cease. Directors should not serve on compensation committees unless they are *themselves* capable of negotiating on behalf of owners. They should explain both how they think about pay and how they measure performance. Dealing with shareholders' money, moreover, they should behave as they would were it their own.

In the 1890s, Samuel Gompers described the goal of organized labor as "More!" In the 1990s, America's CEOs adopted his battle cry. The upshot is that CEOs have often amassed riches while their shareholders have experienced financial disasters.

Directors should stop such piracy. There's nothing wrong with paying well for truly exceptional business performance. But, for anything short of that, it's time for directors to shout "Less!" It would be a travesty if the bloated pay of recent years became a baseline for future compensation. Compensation committees should go back to the drawing boards.

* * * * * * * * * * * *

Rules that have been proposed and that are almost certain to go into effect will require changes in Berkshire's board, obliging us to add directors who meet the codified requirements for "independence."

Doing so, we will add a test that we believe is important, but far from determinative, in fostering independence: We will select directors who have huge and true ownership interests (that is, stock that they or their family have *purchased*, not been given by Berkshire or received via options), expecting those interests to influence their actions to a degree that dwarfs other considerations such as prestige and board fees.

That gets to an often-overlooked point about directors' compensation, which at public companies averages perhaps $50,000 annually. It baffles me how the many directors who look to these dollars for perhaps 20% or more of their annual income can be considered independent when Ron Olson, for example, who is on our board, may be deemed not independent because he receives a tiny percentage of his very large income from Berkshire legal fees. As the investment company saga suggests, a director whose moderate income is heavily dependent on directors' fees – and who hopes mightily to be invited to join other boards in order to earn more fees – is highly unlikely to offend a CEO or fellow directors, who in a major way will determine his reputation in corporate circles. If regulators believe that "significant" money taints independence (and it certainly can), they have overlooked a massive class of possible offenders.

At Berkshire, wanting our fees to be meaningless to our directors, we pay them only a pittance. Additionally, not wanting to insulate our directors from any corporate disaster we might have, we don't provide them with officers' and directors' liability insurance (an unorthodoxy that, not so incidentally, has saved our shareholders many millions of dollars over the years). Basically, we want the behavior of our directors to be driven by the effect their decisions will have on their family's net worth, not by their compensation. That's the equation for Charlie and me as managers, and we think it's the right one for Berkshire directors as well.

To find new directors, we will look through our shareholders list for people who directly, or in their family, have had large Berkshire holdings – in the millions of dollars – for a long time. Individuals making that cut should automatically meet two of our tests, namely that they be interested in Berkshire and shareholder-oriented. In our third test, we will look for business savvy, a competence that is far from commonplace.

Finally, we will continue to have members of the Buffett family on the board. They are not there to run the business after I die, nor will they then receive compensation of any kind. Their purpose is to ensure, for both our shareholders and managers, that Berkshire's special culture will be nurtured when I'm succeeded by other CEOs.

Any change we make in the composition of our board will not alter the way Charlie and I run Berkshire. We will continue to emphasize substance over form in our work and waste as little time as possible during board meetings in show-and-tell and perfunctory activities. The most important job of our board is likely to be the selection of successors to Charlie and me, and that is a matter upon which it will focus.

The board we have had up to now has overseen a shareholder-oriented business, consistently run in accord with the economic principles set forth on pages 68-74 (which I urge all new shareholders to read). Our goal is to obtain new directors who are equally devoted to those principles.

The Audit Committee

Audit committees can't audit. Only a company's outside auditor can determine whether the earnings that a management purports to have made are suspect. Reforms that ignore this reality and that instead focus on the structure and charter of the audit committee will accomplish little.

As we've discussed, far too many managers have fudged their company's numbers in recent years, using both accounting and operational techniques that are typically legal but that nevertheless materially mislead investors. Frequently, auditors knew about these deceptions. Too often, however, they remained silent. The key job of the audit committee is simply to get the auditors to divulge what they know.

To do this job, the committee must make sure that the auditors worry more about misleading its members than about offending management. In recent years auditors have not felt that way. They have instead generally viewed the CEO, rather than the shareholders or directors, as their client. That has been a natural result of day-to-day working relationships and also of the auditors' understanding that, no matter what the book says, the CEO and CFO pay their fees and determine whether they are retained for both auditing and other work. The rules that have been recently instituted won't materially change this reality. What *will* break this cozy relationship is audit committees unequivocally putting auditors on the spot, making them understand they will become liable for major monetary penalties if they don't come forth with what they know or suspect.

In my opinion, audit committees can accomplish this goal by asking four questions of auditors, the answers to which should be recorded and reported to shareholders. These questions are:

1. If the auditor were solely responsible for preparation of the company's financial statements, would they have in any way been prepared differently from the manner selected by management? This question should cover both material and nonmaterial differences. If the auditor would have done something differently, both management's argument and the auditor's response should be disclosed. The audit committee should then evaluate the facts.

2. If the auditor were an investor, would he have received – in plain English – the information essential to his understanding the company's financial performance during the reporting period?

3. Is the company following the same internal audit procedure that would be followed if the auditor himself were CEO? If not, what are the differences and why?

4. Is the auditor aware of any actions – either accounting or operational – that have had the purpose and effect of moving revenues or expenses from one reporting period to another?

If the audit committee asks these questions, its composition – the focus of most reforms – is of minor importance. In addition, the procedure will save time and expense. When auditors are put on the spot, they will do their duty. If they are not put on the spot . . . well, we have seen the results of that.

The questions we have enumerated should be asked at least a week before an earnings report is released to the public. That timing will allow differences between the auditors and management to be aired with the committee and resolved. If the timing is tighter – if an earnings release is imminent when the auditors and committee interact – the committee will feel pressure to rubberstamp the prepared figures. Haste is the enemy of accuracy. My thinking, in fact, is that the SEC's recent shortening of reporting deadlines will hurt the quality of information that shareholders receive. Charlie and I believe that rule is a mistake and should be rescinded.

The primary advantage of our four questions is that they will act as a prophylactic. Once the auditors know that the audit committee will require them to affirmatively endorse, rather than merely acquiesce to, management's actions, they will resist misdoings early in the process, well before specious figures become embedded in the company's books. Fear of the plaintiff's bar will see to that.

* * * * * * * * * * *

The Chicago Tribune ran a four-part series on Arthur Andersen last September that did a great job of illuminating how accounting standards and audit quality have eroded in recent years. A few decades ago, an Arthur Andersen audit opinion was the gold standard of the profession. Within the firm, an elite Professional Standards Group (PSG) insisted on honest reporting, no matter what pressures were applied by the client. Sticking to these principles, the PSG took a stand in 1992 that the cost of stock options should be recorded as the expense it clearly was. The PSG's position was reversed, however, by the "rainmaking" partners of Andersen who knew what their clients wanted – higher reported earnings no matter what the reality. Many CEOs also fought expensing because they knew that the obscene megagrants of options they craved would be slashed if the true costs of these had to be recorded.

Soon after the Andersen reversal, the independent accounting standards board (FASB) voted 7-0 for expensing options. Predictably, the major auditing firms and an army of CEOs stormed Washington to pressure the Senate – what better institution to decide accounting questions? – into castrating the FASB. The voices of the protesters were amplified by their large political contributions, usually made with corporate money belonging to the very owners about to be bamboozled. It was not a sight for a civics class.

To its shame, the Senate voted 88-9 against expensing. Several prominent Senators even called for the demise of the FASB if it didn't abandon its position. (So much for independence.) Arthur Levitt, Jr., then Chairman of the SEC – and generally a vigilant champion of shareholders – has since described his reluctant bowing to Congressional and corporate pressures as the act of his chairmanship that he most regrets. (The details of this sordid affair are related in Levitt's excellent book, *Take on the Street*.)

With the Senate in its pocket and the SEC outgunned, corporate America knew that it was now boss when it came to accounting. With that, a new era of anything-goes earnings reports – blessed and, in some cases, encouraged by big-name auditors – was launched. The licentious behavior that followed quickly became an air pump for The Great Bubble.

After being threatened by the Senate, FASB backed off its original position and adopted an "honor system" approach, declaring expensing to be preferable but also allowing companies to ignore the cost if they wished. The disheartening result: Of the 500 companies in the S&P, 498 adopted the method deemed less desirable, which of course let them report higher "earnings." Compensation-hungry CEOs loved this outcome: Let FASB have the honor; *they* had the system.

In our 1992 annual report, discussing the unseemly and self-serving behavior of so many CEOs, I said "the business elite risks losing its credibility on issues of significance to society – about which it may have much of value to say – when it advocates the incredible on issues of significance to itself."

That loss of credibility has occurred. The job of CEOs is now to regain America's trust – and for the country's sake it's important that they do so. They will not succeed in this endeavor, however, by way of fatuous ads, meaningless policy statements, or structural changes of boards and committees. Instead, CEOs must embrace stewardship as a way of life and treat their owners as partners, not patsies. It's time for CEOs to walk the walk.

* * * * * * * * * * *

Three suggestions for investors: First, beware of companies displaying weak accounting. If a company still does not expense options, or if its pension assumptions are fanciful, watch out. When managements take the low road in aspects that are visible, it is likely they are following a similar path behind the scenes. There is seldom just one cockroach in the kitchen.

Trumpeting EBITDA (earnings before interest, taxes, depreciation and amortization) is a particularly pernicious practice. Doing so implies that depreciation is not truly an expense, given that it is a "non-cash" charge. That's nonsense. In truth, depreciation is a particularly unattractive expense because the cash outlay it represents is paid up front, before the asset acquired has delivered any benefits to the business. Imagine, if you will, that at the beginning of this year a company paid all of its employees for the next ten years of their service (in the way they would lay out cash for a fixed asset to be useful for ten years). In the following nine years, compensation would be a "non-cash" expense – a reduction of a prepaid compensation asset established this year. Would anyone care to argue that the recording of the expense in years two through ten would be simply a bookkeeping formality?

Second, unintelligible footnotes usually indicate untrustworthy management. If you can't understand a footnote or other managerial explanation, it's usually because the CEO doesn't want you to. Enron's descriptions of certain transactions *still* baffle me.

Finally, be suspicious of companies that trumpet earnings projections and growth expectations. Businesses seldom operate in a tranquil, no-surprise environment, and earnings simply don't advance smoothly (except, of course, in the offering books of investment bankers).

Charlie and I not only don't know today what our businesses will earn *next year* – we don't even know what they will earn *next quarter*. We are suspicious of those CEOs who regularly claim they do know the future – and we become downright incredulous if they consistently reach their declared targets. Managers that always promise to "make the numbers" will at some point be tempted to *make up* the numbers.

Shareholder-Designated Contributions

About 97.3% of all eligible shares participated in Berkshire's 2002 shareholder-designated contributions program, with contributions totaling $16.5 million.

Cumulatively, over the 22 years of the program, Berkshire has made contributions of $197 million pursuant to the instructions of our shareholders. The rest of Berkshire's giving is done by our subsidiaries, which stick to the philanthropic patterns that prevailed before they were acquired (except that their former owners themselves take on the responsibility for their personal charities). In aggregate, our subsidiaries made contributions of $24 million in 2002, including in-kind donations of $4 million.

To participate in future programs, you must own Class A shares that are registered in the name of the actual owner, not the nominee name of a broker, bank or depository. Shares not so registered on August 31, 2003 will be ineligible for the 2003 program. When you get the contributions form from us, return it promptly so that it does not get put aside or forgotten. Designations received after the due date will not be honored.

The Annual Meeting

This year's annual meeting will be held on Saturday, May 3, and once again we will be at the Civic Auditorium. The doors will open at 7 a.m., the movie will begin at 8:30, and the meeting itself will commence at 9:30. There will be a short break at noon for food. (Sandwiches will be available at the Civic's concession stands.) That interlude aside, Charlie and I will answer questions until 3:30. Give us your best shot.

An attachment to the proxy material that is enclosed with this report explains how you can obtain the credential you will need for admission to the meeting and other events. As for plane, hotel and car reservations, we have again signed up American Express (800-799-6634) to give you special help. They do a terrific job for us each year, and I thank them for it.

In our usual fashion, we will run vans from the larger hotels to the meeting. Afterwards, the vans will make trips back to the hotels and to Nebraska Furniture Mart, Borsheim's and the airport. Even so, you are likely to find a car useful.

Our exhibit area for Berkshire goods and services will be bigger and better than ever this year. So be prepared to *spend*. I think you will particularly enjoy visiting The Pampered Chef display, where you may run into Doris and Sheila.

GEICO will have a booth staffed by a number of its top counselors from around the country, all of them ready to supply you with auto insurance quotes. In most cases, GEICO will be able to give you a special shareholder discount (usually 8%). This special offer is permitted by 41 of the 49 jurisdictions in which we operate. Bring the details of your existing insurance and check out whether we can save you money.

On Saturday, at the Omaha airport, we will have the usual array of aircraft from NetJets® available for your inspection. Just ask a representative at the Civic about viewing any of these planes. If you buy what we consider an appropriate number of items during the weekend, you may well need your own plane to take them home. Furthermore, if you buy a fraction of a plane, I'll personally see that you get a three-pack of briefs from Fruit of the Loom.

At Nebraska Furniture Mart, located on a 77-acre site on 72nd Street between Dodge and Pacific, we will again be having "Berkshire Weekend" pricing, which means we will be offering our shareholders a discount that is customarily given only to employees. We initiated this special pricing at NFM six years ago, and sales during the "Weekend" grew from $5.3 million in 1997 to $14.2 million in 2002.

To get the discount, you must make your purchases during the Thursday, May 1 through Monday, May 5 period and also present your meeting credential. The period's special pricing will even apply to the products of several prestigious manufacturers that normally have ironclad rules against discounting but that, in the spirit of our shareholder weekend, have made an exception for you. We appreciate their cooperation. NFM is open from 10 a.m. to 9 p.m. on weekdays and 10 a.m. to 6 p.m. on Sundays. On Saturday this year, from 6 p.m. to 10 p.m., we are having a special affair for shareholders only. I'll be there, eating hot dogs and drinking Coke.

Borsheim's — the largest jewelry store in the country except for Tiffany's Manhattan store — will have two shareholder-only events. The first will be a cocktail reception from 6 p.m. to 10 p.m. on Friday, May 2. The second, the main gala, will be from 9 a.m. to 5 p.m. on Sunday, May 4. Ask Charlie to autograph your *sales ticket*.

Shareholder prices will be available Thursday through Monday, so if you wish to avoid the large crowds that will assemble on Friday evening and Sunday, come at other times and identify yourself as a shareholder. On Saturday, we will be open until 6 p.m. Borsheim's operates on a gross margin that is fully twenty percentage points below that of its major rivals, so the more you buy, the more you save (or at least that's what my wife and daughter tell me).

In the mall outside of Borsheim's, we will have some of the world's top bridge experts available to play with our shareholders on Sunday afternoon. We expect Bob Hamman, Sharon Osberg, Fred Gitelman and Sheri Winestock to host tables. Patrick Wolff, twice U.S. chess champion, will also be in the mall, taking on all comers — blindfolded! Last year, Patrick played six games *simultaneously* — with his blindfold securely in place — and for the first time suffered a loss. (He won the other five games, however.) He's been training overtime ever since and is planning to start a new streak this year.

Additionally, Bill Robertie, one of only two players who have twice won the backgammon world championship, will be on hand to test your skill at that game. Finally, we will have a newcomer: Peter Morris, the winner of the World Scrabble Championship in 1991. Peter will play on five boards simultaneously (no blindfold for him, however) and will also allow his challengers to consult a Scrabble dictionary.

We are also going to test your vocal chords at the mall. My friend, Al Oehrle of Philadelphia, will be at the piano to play any song in any key. Susie and I will lead the singing. *She* is good.

Gorat's — my favorite steakhouse — will again be open exclusively for Berkshire shareholders on Sunday, May 4, and will be serving from 4 p.m. until 10 p.m. Please remember that to come to Gorat's on Sunday, you must have a reservation. To make one, call 402-551-3733 on April 1 (*but not before*). If Sunday is sold out, try Gorat's on one of the other evenings you will be in town. Show your sophistication by ordering a rare T-bone with a double order of hash browns.

There won't be a ball game this year. After my fastball was clocked at 5 mph last year, I decided to hang up my spikes. So I'll see you on Saturday night at NFM instead.

* * * * * * * * * * * *

Next year our meeting will be held at Omaha's new convention center. This switch in locations will allow us to hold the event on either Saturday or Monday, whichever the majority of you prefer. Using the enclosed special ballot, please vote for your preference – *but only if you are likely to attend in the future.*

We will make the Saturday/Monday decision based upon a count of shareholders, not shares. That is, a Class B shareholder owning one share will have a vote equal to that of a Class A shareholder owning many shares. If the vote is close, we will go with the preference of out-of-towners.

Again, please vote only if there is a reasonable chance that you will be attending some meetings in the future.

Warren E. Buffett
Chairman of the Board

February 21, 2003

BERKSHIRE HATHAWAY INC.

To the Shareholders of Berkshire Hathaway Inc.:

Our gain in net worth during 2003 was $13.6 billion, which increased the per-share book value of both our Class A and Class B stock by 21%. Over the last 39 years (that is, since present management took over) per-share book value has grown from $19 to $50,498, a rate of 22.2% compounded annually.*

It's per-share intrinsic value that counts, however, not book value. Here, the news is good: Between 1964 and 2003, Berkshire morphed from a struggling northern textile business whose intrinsic value was less than book into a widely diversified enterprise worth far more than book. Our 39-year gain in intrinsic value has therefore somewhat exceeded our 22.2% gain in book. (For a better understanding of intrinsic value and the economic principles that guide Charlie Munger, my partner and Berkshire's vice-chairman, and me in running Berkshire, please read our Owner's Manual, beginning on page 69.)

Despite their shortcomings, book value calculations are useful at Berkshire as a slightly understated gauge for measuring the *long-term* rate of increase in our intrinsic value. The calculation is less relevant, however, than it once was in rating any single year's performance versus the S&P 500 index (a comparison we display on the facing page). Our equity holdings, including convertible preferreds, have fallen considerably as a percentage of our net worth, from an average of 114% in the 1980s, for example, to an average of 50% in 2000-03. Therefore, yearly movements in the stock market now affect a much smaller portion of our net worth than was once the case.

Nonetheless, Berkshire's long-term performance versus the S&P remains all-important. Our shareholders can buy the S&P through an index fund at very low cost. Unless we achieve gains in per-share intrinsic value in the future that outdo the S&P's performance, Charlie and I will be adding nothing to what you can accomplish on your own.

If we fail, we will have no excuses. Charlie and I operate in an ideal environment. To begin with, we are supported by an incredible group of men and women who run our operating units. If there were a Corporate Cooperstown, its roster would surely include many of our CEOs. Any shortfall in Berkshire's results will not be caused by our managers.

Additionally, we enjoy a rare sort of managerial freedom. Most companies are saddled with institutional constraints. A company's history, for example, may commit it to an industry that now offers limited opportunity. A more common problem is a shareholder constituency that pressures its manager to dance to Wall Street's tune. Many CEOs resist, but others give in and adopt operating and capital-allocation policies far different from those they would choose if left to themselves.

At Berkshire, neither history nor the demands of owners impede intelligent decision-making. When Charlie and I make mistakes, they are – in tennis parlance – unforced errors.

---

*All figures used in this report apply to Berkshire's A shares, the successor to the only stock that the company had outstanding before 1996. The B shares have an economic interest equal to 1/30th that of the A.

Operating Earnings

When valuations are similar, we strongly prefer owning businesses to owning stocks. During most of our years of operation, however, stocks were much the cheaper choice. We therefore sharply tilted our asset allocation in those years toward equities, as illustrated by the percentages cited earlier.

In recent years, however, we've found it hard to find significantly undervalued stocks, a difficulty greatly accentuated by the mushrooming of the funds we must deploy. Today, the number of stocks that can be purchased in large enough quantities to move the performance needle at Berkshire is a small fraction of the number that existed a decade ago. (Investment managers often profit far more from piling up assets than from handling those assets well. So when one tells you that increased funds won't hurt his investment performance, step back: His nose is about to grow.)

The shortage of attractively-priced stocks in which we can put large sums doesn't bother us, *providing* we can find companies to purchase that (1) have favorable and enduring economic charac- teristics; (2) are run by talented and honest managers and (3) are available at a sensible price. We have purchased a number of such businesses in recent years, though not enough to fully employ the gusher of cash that has come our way. In buying businesses, I've made some terrible mistakes, both of commission and omission. Overall, however, our acquisitions have led to decent gains in per-share earnings.

Below is a table that quantifies that point. But first we need to warn you that growth-rate presentations can be significantly distorted by a calculated selection of either initial or terminal dates. For example, if earnings are tiny in a beginning year, a long-term performance that was only mediocre can be made to appear sensational. That kind of distortion can come about because the company at issue was minuscule in the base year – which means that only a handful of insiders actually benefited from the touted performance – or because a larger company was then operating at just above breakeven. Picking a terminal year that is particularly buoyant will also favorably bias a calculation of growth.

The Berkshire Hathaway that present management assumed control of in 1965 had long been sizable. But in 1964, it earned only $175,586 or 15 cents per share, so close to breakeven that any calculation of earnings growth from that base would be meaningless. At the time, however, even those meager earnings looked good: Over the decade following the 1955 merger of Berkshire Fine Spinning Associates and Hathaway Manufacturing, the combined operation had lost $10.1 million and many thousands of employees had been let go. It was not a marriage made in heaven.

Against this background, we give you a picture of Berkshire's earnings growth that begins in 1968, but also includes subsequent base years spaced five years apart. A series of calculations is presented so that you can decide for yourself which period is most meaningful. I've started with 1968 because it was the first full year we operated National Indemnity, the initial acquisition we made as we began to expand Berkshire's business.

I don't believe that using 2003 as the terminal year distorts our calculations. It was a terrific year for our insurance business, but the big boost that gave to earnings was largely offset by the pathetically low interest rates we earned on our large holdings of cash equivalents (a condition that will not last). All figures shown below, it should be noted, *exclude* capital gains.

Year	Operating Earnings in $ millions	Operating Earnings Per Share in $	Subsequent Compounded Growth Rate of Per-Share Earnings
1964	.2	.15	Not meaningful (1964-2003)
1968	2.7	2.69	22.8% (1968-2003)
1973	11.9	12.18	20.8% (1973-2003)
1978	30.0	29.15	21.1% (1978-2003)
1983	48.6	45.60	24.3% (1983-2003)
1988	313.4	273.37	18.6% (1988-2003)
1993	477.8	413.19	23.9% (1993-2003)
1998	1,277.0	1,020.49	28.2% (1998-2003)
2003	5,422.0	3,531.32	

We will continue the capital allocation practices we have used in the past. If stocks become significantly cheaper than entire businesses, we will buy them aggressively. If selected bonds become attractive, as they did in 2002, we will again load up on these securities. Under *any* market or economic conditions, we will be happy to buy businesses that meet our standards. And, for those that do, the bigger the better. Our capital is underutilized now, but that will happen periodically. It's a painful condition to be in – but not as painful as doing something stupid. (I speak from experience.)

Overall, we are certain Berkshire's performance in the future will fall *far* short of what it has been in the past. Nonetheless, Charlie and I remain hopeful that we can deliver results that are modestly above average. That's what we're being paid for.

Acquisitions

As regular readers know, our acquisitions have often come about in strange ways. None, however, had a more unusual genesis than our purchase last year of Clayton Homes.

The unlikely source was a group of finance students from the University of Tennessee, and their teacher, Dr. Al Auxier. For the past five years, Al has brought his class to Omaha, where the group tours Nebraska Furniture Mart and Borsheim's, eats at Gorat's and then comes to Kiewit Plaza for a session with me. Usually about 40 students participate.

After two hours of give-and-take, the group traditionally presents me with a thank-you gift. (The doors stay locked until they do.) In past years it's been items such as a football signed by Phil Fulmer and a basketball from Tennessee's famous women's team.

This past February, the group opted for a book – which, luckily for me, was the recently-published autobiography of Jim Clayton, founder of Clayton Homes. I already knew the company to be the class act of the manufactured housing industry, knowledge I acquired after earlier making the mistake of buying some distressed junk debt of Oakwood Homes, one of the industry's largest companies. At the time of that purchase, I did not understand how atrocious consumer-financing practices had become throughout most of the manufactured housing industry. But I learned: Oakwood rather promptly went bankrupt.

Manufactured housing, it should be emphasized, can deliver very good value to home purchasers. Indeed, for decades, the industry has accounted for more than 15% of the homes built in the U.S. During those years, moreover, both the quality and variety of manufactured houses consistently improved.

Progress in design and construction was not matched, however, by progress in distribution and financing. Instead, as the years went by, the industry's business model increasingly centered on the ability of both the retailer and manufacturer to unload terrible loans on naive lenders. When "securitization" then became popular in the 1990s, further distancing the supplier of funds from the lending transaction, the industry's conduct went from bad to worse. Much of its volume a few years back came from buyers who shouldn't have bought, financed by lenders who shouldn't have lent. The consequence has been huge numbers of repossessions and pitifully low recoveries on the units repossessed.

Oakwood participated fully in the insanity. But Clayton, though it could not isolate itself from industry practices, behaved considerably better than its major competitors.

Upon receiving Jim Clayton's book, I told the students how much I admired his record and they took that message back to Knoxville, home of both the University of Tennessee and Clayton Homes. Al then suggested that I call Kevin Clayton, Jim's son and the CEO, to express my views directly. As I talked with Kevin, it became clear that he was both able and a straight-shooter.

Soon thereafter, I made an offer for the business based solely on Jim's book, my evaluation of Kevin, the public financials of Clayton and what I had learned from the Oakwood experience. Clayton's board was receptive, since it understood that the large-scale financing Clayton would need in the future might be hard to get. Lenders had fled the industry and securitizations, when possible at all, carried far more expensive and restrictive terms than was previously the case. This tightening was particularly serious for Clayton, whose earnings significantly depended on securitizations.

Today, the manufactured housing industry remains awash in problems. Delinquencies continue high, repossessed units still abound and the number of retailers has been halved. A different business model is required, one that eliminates the ability of the retailer and salesman to pocket substantial money up front by making sales financed by loans that are destined to default. Such transactions cause hardship to both buyer and lender and lead to a flood of repossessions that then undercut the sale of new units. Under a proper model – one requiring significant down payments and shorter-term loans – the industry will likely remain much smaller than it was in the 90s. But it will deliver to home buyers an asset in which they will have equity, rather than disappointment, upon resale.

In the "full circle" department, Clayton has agreed to buy the assets of Oakwood. When the transaction closes, Clayton's manufacturing capacity, geographical reach and sales outlets will be substantially increased. As a byproduct, the debt of Oakwood that we own, which we bought at a deep discount, will probably return a small profit to us.

And the students? In October, we had a surprise "graduation" ceremony in Knoxville for the 40 who sparked my interest in Clayton. I donned a mortarboard and presented each student with both a PhD (for phenomenal, hard-working dealmaker) from Berkshire and a B share. Al got an A share. If you meet some of the new Tennessee shareholders at our annual meeting, give them your thanks. And ask them if they've read any good books lately.

* * * * * * * * * * * *

In early spring, Byron Trott, a Managing Director of Goldman Sachs, told me that Wal-Mart wished to sell its McLane subsidiary. McLane distributes groceries and nonfood items to convenience stores, drug stores, wholesale clubs, mass merchandisers, quick service restaurants, theaters and others. It's a good business, but one not in the mainstream of Wal-Mart's future. It's made to order, however, for us.

McLane has sales of about $23 billion, but operates on paper-thin margins – about 1% pre-tax – and will swell Berkshire's sales figures far more than our income. In the past, some retailers had shunned McLane because it was owned by their major competitor. Grady Rosier, McLane's superb CEO, has already landed some of these accounts – he was in full stride the day the deal closed – and more will come.

For several years, I have given my vote to Wal-Mart in the balloting for Fortune Magazine's "Most Admired" list. Our McLane transaction reinforced my opinion. To make the McLane deal, I had a single meeting of about two hours with Tom Schoewe, Wal-Mart's CFO, and we then shook hands. (He did, however, first call Bentonville). Twenty-nine days later Wal-Mart had its money. We did no "due diligence." We knew everything would be exactly as Wal-Mart said it would be – and it was.

I should add that Byron has now been instrumental in three Berkshire acquisitions. He understands Berkshire far better than any investment banker with whom we have talked and – it hurts me to say this – earns his fee. I'm looking forward to deal number four (as, I am sure, is he).

Taxes

On May 20, 2003, The Washington Post ran an op-ed piece by me that was critical of the Bush tax proposals. Thirteen days later, Pamela Olson, Assistant Secretary for Tax Policy at the U.S. Treasury, delivered a speech about the new tax legislation saying, "That means a certain midwestern oracle, who, it must be noted, has played the tax code like a fiddle, is still safe retaining all his earnings." I think she was talking about me.

Alas, my "fiddle playing" will not get me to Carnegie Hall – or even to a high school recital. Berkshire, on your behalf and mine, will send the Treasury $3.3 billion for tax on its 2003 income, a sum equaling 2½% of the total income tax paid by *all* U.S. corporations in fiscal 2003. (In contrast, Berkshire's market valuation is about 1% of the value of all American corporations.) Our payment will almost certainly place us among our country's top ten taxpayers. Indeed, if only 540 taxpayers paid the amount Berkshire will pay, no other individual or corporation would have to pay *anything* to Uncle Sam. That's right: 290 million Americans and all other businesses would not have to pay a dime in income, social security, excise or estate taxes to the federal government. (Here's the math: Federal tax receipts, including social security receipts, in fiscal 2003 totaled $1.782 trillion and 540 "Berkshires," each paying $3.3 billion, would deliver the same $1.782 trillion.)

Our federal tax return for 2002 (2003 is not finalized), when we paid $1.75 billion, covered a mere 8,905 pages. As is required, we dutifully filed two copies of this return, creating a pile of paper seven feet tall. At World Headquarters, our small band of 15.8, though exhausted, momentarily flushed with pride: Berkshire, we felt, was surely pulling its share of our country's fiscal load.

But Ms. Olson sees things otherwise. And if that means Charlie and I need to try harder, we are ready to do so.

I do wish, however, that Ms. Olson would give me *some* credit for the progress I've already made. In 1944, I filed my first 1040, reporting my income as a thirteen-year-old newspaper carrier. The return covered three pages. After I claimed the appropriate business deductions, such as $35 for a bicycle, my tax bill was $7. I sent my check to the Treasury and it – without comment – promptly cashed it. We lived in peace.

* * * * * * * * * * *

I can understand why the Treasury is now frustrated with Corporate America and prone to outbursts. But it should look to Congress and the Administration for redress, not to Berkshire.

Corporate income taxes in fiscal 2003 accounted for 7.4% of all federal tax receipts, down from a post-war peak of 32% in 1952. With one exception (1983), last year's percentage is the lowest recorded since data was first published in 1934.

Even so, tax breaks for corporations (and their investors, particularly large ones) were a major part of the Administration's 2002 and 2003 initiatives. If class warfare is being waged in America, my class is clearly winning. Today, many large corporations – run by CEOs whose fiddle-playing talents make your Chairman look like he is all thumbs – pay nothing close to the stated federal tax rate of 35%.

In 1985, Berkshire paid $132 million in federal income taxes, and all corporations paid $61 billion. The comparable amounts in 1995 were $286 million and $157 billion respectively. And, as mentioned, we will pay about $3.3 billion for 2003, a year when all corporations paid $132 billion. We hope our taxes continue to rise in the future – it will mean we are prospering – but we also hope that the rest of Corporate America antes up along with us. This might be a project for Ms. Olson to work on.

Corporate Governance

In judging whether Corporate America is serious about reforming itself, CEO pay remains the acid test. To date, the results aren't encouraging. A few CEOs, such as Jeff Immelt of General Electric, have led the way in initiating programs that are fair to managers and shareholders alike. Generally, however, his example has been more admired than followed.

It's understandable how pay got out of hand. When management hires employees, or when companies bargain with a vendor, the intensity of interest is equal on both sides of the table. One party's gain is the other party's loss, and the money involved has real meaning to both. The result is an honest-to-God negotiation.

But when CEOs (or their representatives) have met with compensation committees, too often one side – the CEO's – has cared far more than the other about what bargain is struck. A CEO, for example, will always regard the difference between receiving options for 100,000 shares or for 500,000 as monumental. To a comp committee, however, the difference may seem unimportant – particularly if, as has been the case at most companies, neither grant will have any effect on reported earnings. Under these conditions, the negotiation often has a "play-money" quality.

Overreaching by CEOs greatly accelerated in the 1990s as compensation packages gained by the most avaricious– a title for which there was vigorous competition – were promptly replicated elsewhere. The couriers for this epidemic of greed were usually consultants and human relations departments, which had no trouble perceiving who buttered their bread. As one compensation consultant commented: "There are two classes of clients you don't want to offend – actual and potential."

In proposals for reforming this malfunctioning system, the cry has been for "independent" directors. But the question of what truly motivates independence has largely been neglected.

In last year's report, I took a look at how "independent" directors – as defined by statute – had performed in the mutual fund field. The Investment Company Act of 1940 mandated such directors, and that means we've had an extended test of what statutory standards produce. In our examination last year, we looked at the record of fund directors in respect to the two key tasks board members should perform – whether at a mutual fund business or any other. These two all-important functions are, first, to obtain (or retain) an able and honest manager and then to compensate that manager fairly.

Our survey was not encouraging. Year after year, at literally thousands of funds, directors had routinely rehired the incumbent management company, however pathetic its performance had been. Just as routinely, the directors had mindlessly approved fees that in many cases far exceeded those that could have been negotiated. Then, when a management company was sold – invariably at a huge price relative to tangible assets – the directors experienced a "counter-revelation" and immediately signed on with the new manager and accepted its fee schedule. In effect, the directors decided that whoever would pay the most for the old management company was the party that should manage the shareholders' money in the future.

Despite the lapdog behavior of independent fund directors, we did not conclude that they are bad people. They're not. But sadly, "boardroom atmosphere" almost invariably sedates their fiduciary genes.

On May 22, 2003, not long after Berkshire's report appeared, the Chairman of the Investment Company Institute addressed its membership about "The State of our Industry." Responding to those who have "weighed in about our perceived failings," he mused, "It makes me wonder what life would be like if we'd actually done something wrong."

Be careful what you wish for.

Within a few months, the world began to learn that many fund-management companies had followed policies that hurt the owners of the funds they managed, while simultaneously boosting the fees of the managers. Prior to their transgressions, it should be noted, these management companies were earning profit margins and returns on tangible equity that were the envy of Corporate America. Yet to swell profits further, they trampled on the interests of fund shareholders in an appalling manner.

So what are the directors of these looted funds doing? As I write this, I have seen none that have terminated the contract of the offending management company (though naturally that entity has often fired some of its employees). Can you imagine directors who had been personally defrauded taking such a boys-will-be-boys attitude?

To top it all off, at least one miscreant management company has put itself up for sale, undoubtedly hoping to receive a huge sum for "delivering" the mutual funds it has managed to the highest bidder among other managers. This is a travesty. Why in the world don't the directors of those funds simply select whomever they think is best among the bidding organizations and sign up with that party directly? The winner would consequently be spared a huge "payoff" to the former manager who, having flouted the principles of stewardship, deserves not a dime. Not having to bear that acquisition cost, the winner could surely manage the funds in question for a far lower ongoing fee than would otherwise have been the case. Any truly independent director should insist on this approach to obtaining a new manager.

The reality is that neither the decades-old rules regulating investment company directors nor the new rules bearing down on Corporate America foster the election of truly independent directors. In both instances, an individual who is receiving 100% of his income from director fees – and who may wish to enhance his income through election to other boards – is deemed independent. That is nonsense. The same rules say that Berkshire director and lawyer Ron Olson, who receives from us perhaps 3% of his very large income, does not qualify as independent because that 3% comes from legal fees Berkshire pays his firm rather than from fees he earns as a Berkshire director. Rest assured, 3% from any source would not torpedo Ron's independence. But getting 20%, 30% or 50% of their income from director fees might well temper the independence of many individuals, particularly if their overall income is not large. Indeed, I think it's clear that at mutual funds, it has.

* * * * * * * * * * *

Let me make a small suggestion to "independent" mutual fund directors. Why not simply affirm in each annual report that "(1) We have looked at other management companies and believe the one we have retained for the upcoming year is among the better operations in the field; and (2) we have negotiated a fee with our managers comparable to what other clients with equivalent funds would negotiate."

It does not seem unreasonable for shareholders to expect fund directors – who are often receiving fees that exceed $100,000 annually – to declare themselves on these points. Certainly these directors would satisfy themselves on both matters were they handing over a large chunk of their own money to the manager. If directors are unwilling to make these two declarations, shareholders should heed the maxim "If you don't know whose side someone is on, he's probably not on yours."

Finally, a disclaimer. A great many funds have been run well and conscientiously despite the opportunities for malfeasance that exist. The shareholders of these funds have benefited, and their managers have earned their pay. Indeed, if I were a director of certain funds, including some that charge above-average fees, I would enthusiastically make the two declarations I have suggested. Additionally, those index funds that are very low-cost (such as Vanguard's) are investor-friendly by definition and are the best selection for most of those who wish to own equities.

I am on my soapbox now only because the blatant wrongdoing that has occurred has betrayed the trust of so many millions of shareholders. Hundreds of industry insiders had to know what was going on, yet none publicly said a word. It took Eliot Spitzer, and the whistleblowers who aided him, to initiate a housecleaning. We urge fund directors to continue the job. Like directors throughout Corporate America, these fiduciaries must now decide whether their job is to work for owners or for managers.

Berkshire Governance

True independence – meaning the willingness to challenge a forceful CEO when something is wrong or foolish – is an enormously valuable trait in a director. It is also rare. The place to look for it is among high-grade people whose interests are in line with those of rank-and-file shareholders – *and are in line in a very big way.*

We've made that search at Berkshire. We now have eleven directors and *each* of them, combined with members of their families, owns more than $4 million of Berkshire stock. Moreover, all have held major stakes in Berkshire for many years. In the case of six of the eleven, family ownership amounts to at least hundreds of millions and dates back at least three decades. All eleven directors purchased their holdings in the market just as you did; we've never passed out options or restricted shares. Charlie and I love such honest-to-God ownership. After all, who ever washes a rental car?

In addition, director fees at Berkshire are nominal (as my son, Howard, periodically reminds me). Thus, the upside from Berkshire for all eleven is proportionately the same as the upside for any Berkshire shareholder. And it always will be.

The downside for Berkshire directors is actually worse than yours because we carry *no* directors and officers liability insurance. Therefore, if something really catastrophic happens on our directors' watch, they are exposed to losses that will far exceed yours.

The bottom line for our directors: You win, they win big; you lose, they lose big. Our approach might be called owner-capitalism. We know of no better way to engender true independence. (This structure does not guarantee perfect behavior, however: I've sat on boards of companies in which Berkshire had huge stakes and remained silent as questionable proposals were rubber-stamped.)

In addition to being independent, directors should have business savvy, a shareholder orientation and a genuine interest in the company. The rarest of these qualities is business savvy – and if it is lacking, the other two are of little help. Many people who are smart, articulate and admired have no real understanding of business. That's no sin; they may shine elsewhere. But they don't belong on corporate boards. Similarly, I would be useless on a medical or scientific board (though I would likely be welcomed by a chairman who wanted to run things his way). My name would dress up the list of directors, but I wouldn't know enough to critically evaluate proposals. Moreover, to cloak my ignorance, I would keep my mouth shut (if you can imagine that). In effect, I could be replaced, without loss, by a potted plant.

Last year, as we moved to change our board, I asked for self-nominations from shareholders who believed they had the requisite qualities to be a Berkshire director. Despite the lack of either liability insurance or meaningful compensation, we received more than twenty applications. Most were good, coming from owner-oriented individuals having family holdings of Berkshire worth well over $1 million. After considering them, Charlie and I – with the concurrence of our incumbent directors – asked four shareholders who did not nominate themselves to join the board: David Gottesman, Charlotte Guyman, Don Keough and Tom Murphy. These four people are all friends of mine, and I know their strengths well. They bring an extraordinary amount of business talent to Berkshire's board.

The primary job of our directors is to select my successor, either upon my death or disability, or when I begin to lose my marbles. (David Ogilvy had it right when he said: "Develop your eccentricities when young. That way, when you get older, people won't think you are going gaga." Charlie's family and mine feel that we overreacted to David's advice.)

At our directors' meetings we cover the usual run of housekeeping matters. But the real discussion – both with me in the room and absent – centers on the strengths and weaknesses of the four internal candidates to replace me.

Our board knows that the ultimate scorecard on its performance will be determined by the record of my successor. He or she will need to maintain Berkshire's culture, allocate capital and keep a group of America's best managers happy in their jobs. This isn't the toughest task in the world – the train is already moving at a good clip down the track – and I'm totally comfortable about it being done well by any of the four candidates we have identified. I have more than 99% of my net worth in Berkshire and will be happy to have my wife or foundation (depending on the order in which she and I die) continue this concentration.

Sector Results

As managers, Charlie and I want to give our owners the financial information and commentary we would wish to receive if our roles were reversed. To do this with both clarity and reasonable brevity becomes more difficult as Berkshire's scope widens. Some of our businesses have vastly different economic characteristics from others, which means that our consolidated statements, with their jumble of figures, make useful analysis almost impossible.

On the following pages, therefore, we will present some balance sheet and earnings figures from our four major categories of businesses along with commentary about each. We particularly want you to understand the limited circumstances under which we will use debt, since typically we shun it. We will not, however, inundate you with data that has no real value in calculating Berkshire's intrinsic value. Doing so would likely obfuscate the most important facts. One warning: When analyzing Berkshire, be sure to remember that the company should be viewed as an unfolding movie, not as a still photograph. Those who focused in the past on only the snapshot of the day sometimes reached erroneous conclusions.

Insurance

Let's start with insurance – since that's where the money is.

The fountain of funds we enjoy in our insurance operations comes from "float," which is money that doesn't belong to us but that we temporarily hold. Most of our float arises because (1) premiums are paid upfront though the service we provide – insurance protection – is delivered over a period that usually covers a year and; (2) loss events that occur today do not always result in our immediately paying claims, since it sometimes takes years for losses to be reported (think asbestos), negotiated and settled.

Float is wonderful – *if* it doesn't come at a high price. The cost of float is determined by underwriting results, meaning how losses and expenses paid compare with premiums received. The property-casualty industry as a whole regularly operates at a substantial underwriting loss, and therefore often has a cost of float that is unattractive.

Overall, our results have been good. True, we've had five terrible years in which float cost us more than 10%. But in 18 of the 37 years Berkshire has been in the insurance business, we have operated at an underwriting profit, meaning we were actually *paid* for holding money. And the quantity of this cheap money has grown far beyond what I dreamed it could when we entered the business in 1967.

Yearend Float (in $ millions)

Year	GEICO	General Re	Other Reinsurance	Other Primary	Total
1967				20	20
1977			40	131	171
1987			701	807	1,508
1997	2,917		4,014	455	7,386
1998	3,125	14,909	4,305	415	22,754
1999	3,444	15,166	6,285	403	25,298
2000	3,943	15,525	7,805	598	27,871
2001	4,251	19,310	11,262	685	35,508
2002	4,678	22,207	13,396	943	41,224
2003	5,287	23,654	13,948	1,331	44,220

Last year was a standout. Float reached record levels and it came without cost as all major segments contributed to Berkshire's $1.7 billion pre-tax underwriting profit.

Our results have been exceptional for one reason: We have truly exceptional managers. Insurers sell a non-proprietary piece of paper containing a non-proprietary promise. Anyone can copy anyone else's product. No installed base, key patents, critical real estate or natural resource position protects an insurer's competitive position. Typically, brands do not mean much either.

The critical variables, therefore, are managerial brains, discipline and integrity. Our managers have all of these attributes – in spades. Let's take a look at these all-stars and their operations.

- General Re had been Berkshire's problem child in the years following our acquisition of it in 1998. Unfortunately, it was a 400-pound child, and its negative impact on our overall performance was large.

  That's behind us: Gen Re is fixed. Thank Joe Brandon, its CEO, and his partner, Tad Montross, for that. When I wrote you last year, I thought that discipline had been restored to both underwriting and reserving, and events during 2003 solidified my view.

That does not mean we will never have setbacks. Reinsurance is a business that is certain to deliver blows from time to time. But, under Joe and Tad, this operation will be a powerful engine driving Berkshire's future profitability.

Gen Re's financial strength, unmatched among reinsurers even as we started 2003, further improved during the year. Many of the company's competitors suffered credit downgrades last year, leaving Gen Re, and its sister operation at National Indemnity, as the only AAA-rated companies among the world's major reinsurers.

When insurers purchase reinsurance, they buy only a promise – one whose validity may not be tested for decades – and there are no promises in the reinsurance world equaling those offered by Gen Re and National Indemnity. Furthermore, unlike most reinsurers, we retain virtually all of the risks we assume. Therefore, our ability to pay is not dependent on the ability or willingness of others to reimburse us. This *independent* financial strength could be enormously important when the industry experiences the mega-catastrophe it surely will.

- Regular readers of our annual reports know of Ajit Jain's incredible contributions to Berkshire's prosperity over the past 18 years. He continued to pour it on in 2003. With a staff of only 23, Ajit runs one of the world's largest reinsurance operations, specializing in mammoth and unusual risks.

Often, these involve assuming catastrophe risks – say, the threat of a large California earthquake – of a size far greater than any other reinsurer will accept. This means Ajit's results (and Berkshire's) will be lumpy. You should, therefore, expect his operation to have an occasional horrible year. Over time, however, you can be confident of a terrific result from this one-of-a-kind manager.

Ajit writes some very unusual policies. Last year, for example, PepsiCo promoted a drawing that offered participants a chance to win a $1 billion prize. Understandably, Pepsi wished to lay off this risk, and we were the logical party to assume it. So we wrote a $1 billion policy, retaining the risk entirely for our own account. Because the prize, if won, was payable over time, our exposure in present-value terms was $250 million. (I helpfully suggested that any winner be paid $1 a year for a billion years, but that proposal didn't fly.) The drawing was held on September 14. Ajit and I held our breath, as did the finalist in the contest, and we left happier than he. PepsiCo has renewed for a repeat contest in 2004.

- GEICO was a fine insurance company when Tony Nicely took over as CEO in 1992. Now it is a great one. During his tenure, premium volume has increased from $2.2 billion to $8.1 billion, and our share of the personal-auto market has grown from 2.1% to 5.0%. More important, GEICO has paired these gains with outstanding underwriting performance.

(We now pause for a commercial)

It's been 67 years since Leo Goodwin created a great business idea at GEICO, one designed to save policyholders significant money. Go to Geico.com or call 1-800-847-7536 to see what we can do for you.

(End of commercial)

In 2003, both the number of inquiries coming into GEICO and its closure rate on these increased significantly. As a result our preferred policyholder count grew 8.2%, and our standard and non-standard policies grew 21.4%.

GEICO's business growth creates a never-ending need for more employees and facilities. Our most recent expansion, announced in December, is a customer service center in – I'm delighted to say – Buffalo. Stan Lipsey, the publisher of our Buffalo News, was instrumental in bringing the city and GEICO together.

The key figure in this matter, however, was Governor George Pataki. His leadership and tenacity are why Buffalo will have 2,500 new jobs when our expansion is fully rolled out. Stan, Tony, and I – along with Buffalo – thank him for his help.

- Berkshire's smaller insurers had another terrific year. This group, run by Rod Eldred, John Kizer, Tom Nerney, Don Towle and Don Wurster, increased its float by 41%, while delivering an excellent underwriting profit. These men, though operating in unexciting ways, produce truly exciting results.

* * * * * * * * * * * *

We should point out again that in any given year a company writing long-tail insurance (coverages giving rise to claims that are often settled many years after the loss-causing event takes place) can report almost any earnings that the CEO desires. Too often the industry has reported wildly inaccurate figures by misstating liabilities. Most of the mistakes have been innocent. Sometimes, however, they have been intentional, their object being to fool investors and regulators. Auditors and actuaries have usually failed to prevent both varieties of misstatement.

I have failed on occasion too, particularly in not spotting Gen Re's unwitting underreserving a few years back. Not only did that mean we reported inaccurate figures to you, but the error also resulted in our paying very substantial taxes earlier than was necessary. Aaarrrggghh. I told you last year, however, that I thought our current reserving was at appropriate levels. So far, that judgment is holding up.

Here are Berkshire's pre-tax underwriting results by segment:

	Gain (Loss) in $ millions	
	2003	*2002*
Gen Re	$ 145	$(1,393)
Ajit's business excluding retroactive contracts	1,434	980
Ajit's retroactive contracts*	(387)	(433)
GEICO	452	416
Other Primary	74	32
Total	$1,718	$ (398)

*These contracts were explained on page 10 of the 2002 annual report, available on the Internet at www.berkshirehathaway.com. In brief, this segment consists of a few jumbo policies that are likely to produce underwriting losses (which are capped) but also provide unusually large amounts of float.

Regulated Utility Businesses

Through MidAmerican Energy Holdings, we own an 80.5% (fully diluted) interest in a wide variety of utility operations. The largest are (1) Yorkshire Electricity and Northern Electric, whose 3.7 million electric customers make it the third largest distributor of electricity in the U.K.; (2) MidAmerican Energy, which serves 689,000 electric customers in Iowa and; (3) Kern River and Northern Natural pipelines, which carry 7.8% of the natural gas transported in the United States.

Berkshire has three partners, who own the remaining 19.5%: Dave Sokol and Greg Abel, the brilliant managers of the business, and Walter Scott, a long-time friend of mine who introduced me to the company. Because MidAmerican is subject to the Public Utility Holding Company Act ("PUHCA"), Berkshire's voting interest is limited to 9.9%. Walter has the controlling vote.

Our limited voting interest forces us to account for MidAmerican in our financial statements in an abbreviated manner. Instead of our fully including its assets, liabilities, revenues and expenses in our statements, we record only a one-line entry in both our balance sheet and income account. It's likely that some day, perhaps soon, either PUHCA will be repealed or accounting rules will change. Berkshire's consolidated figures would then take in all of MidAmerican, including the substantial debt it utilizes.

The size of this debt (which is not now, nor will it be, an obligation of Berkshire) is entirely appropriate. MidAmerican's diverse and stable utility operations assure that, even under harsh economic conditions, aggregate earnings will be ample to very comfortably service all debt.

At yearend, $1.578 billion of MidAmerican's most junior debt was payable to Berkshire. This debt has allowed acquisitions to be financed without our three partners needing to increase their already substantial investments in MidAmerican. By charging 11% interest, Berkshire is compensated fairly for putting up the funds needed for purchases, while our partners are spared dilution of their equity interests.

MidAmerican also owns a significant non-utility business, Home Services of America, the second largest real estate broker in the country. Unlike our utility operations, this business is highly cyclical, but nevertheless one we view enthusiastically. We have an exceptional manager, Ron Peltier, who, through both his acquisition and operational skills, is building a brokerage powerhouse.

Last year, Home Services participated in $48.6 billion of transactions, a gain of $11.7 billion from 2002. About 23% of the increase came from four acquisitions made during the year. Through our 16 brokerage firms – all of which retain their local identities – we employ 16,343 brokers in 16 states. Home Services is almost certain to grow substantially in the next decade as we continue to acquire leading localized operations.

****

Here's a tidbit for fans of free enterprise. On March 31, 1990, the day electric utilities in the U.K. were denationalized, Northern and Yorkshire had 6,800 employees in functions these companies continue today to perform. Now they employ 2,539. Yet the companies are serving about the same number of customers as when they were government owned and are distributing more electricity.

This is not, it should be noted, a triumph of deregulation. Prices and earnings continue to be regulated in a fair manner by the government, just as they should be. It is a victory, however, for those who believe that profit-motivated managers, even though they recognize that the benefits will largely flow to customers, will find efficiencies that government never will.

Here are some key figures on MidAmerican's operations:

	Earnings (in $ millions)	
	2003	2002
U.K. Utilities	$ 289	$ 267
Iowa	269	241
Pipelines	261	104
Home Services	113	70
Other (Net)	144	108
Earnings before corporate interest and tax	1,076	790
Corporate Interest, other than to Berkshire	(225)	(192)
Interest Payments to Berkshire	(184)	(118)
Tax	(251)	(100)
Net Earnings	$ 416	$ 380
Earnings Applicable to Berkshire*	$ 429	$ 359
Debt Owed to Others	10,296	10,286
Debt Owed to Berkshire	1,578	1,728

*Includes interest paid to Berkshire (net of related income taxes) of $118 in 2003 and $75 in 2002.

14

Finance and Financial Products

This sector includes a wide-ranging group of activities. Here's some commentary on the most important.

- I manage a few opportunistic strategies in AAA fixed-income securities that have been quite profitable in the last few years. These opportunities come and go – and at present, they are going. We sped their departure somewhat last year, thereby realizing 24% of the capital gains we show in the table that follows.

  Though far from foolproof, these transactions involve no credit risk and are conducted in exceptionally liquid securities. We therefore finance the positions almost entirely with borrowed money. As the assets are reduced, so also are the borrowings. The smaller portfolio we now have means that in the near future our earnings in this category will decline significantly. It was fun while it lasted, and at some point we'll get another turn at bat.

- A far less pleasant unwinding operation is taking place at Gen Re Securities, the trading and derivatives operation we inherited when we purchased General Reinsurance.

  When we began to liquidate Gen Re Securities in early 2002, it had 23,218 outstanding tickets with 884 counterparties (some having names I couldn't pronounce, much less creditworthiness I could evaluate). Since then, the unit's managers have been skillful and diligent in unwinding positions. Yet, at yearend – nearly two years later – we still had 7,580 tickets outstanding with 453 counterparties. (As the country song laments, "How can I miss you if you won't go away?")

  The shrinking of this business has been costly. We've had pre-tax losses of $173 million in 2002 and $99 million in 2003. These losses, it should be noted, came from a portfolio of contracts that – in full compliance with GAAP – had been regularly marked-to-market with standard allowances for future credit-loss and administrative costs. Moreover, our liquidation has taken place both in a benign market – we've had no credit losses of significance – and in an orderly manner. This is just the opposite of what might be expected if a financial crisis forced a number of derivatives dealers to cease operations simultaneously.

  If our derivatives experience – and the Freddie Mac shenanigans of mind-blowing size and audacity that were revealed last year – makes you suspicious of accounting in this arena, consider yourself wised up. No matter how financially sophisticated you are, you can't possibly learn from reading the disclosure documents of a derivatives-intensive company what risks lurk in its positions. Indeed, the more you know about derivatives, the less you will feel you can learn from the disclosures normally proffered you. In Darwin's words, "Ignorance more frequently begets confidence than does knowledge."

* * * * * * * * * * *

And now it's confession time: I'm sure I could have saved you $100 million or so, pre-tax, if I had acted more promptly to shut down Gen Re Securities. Both Charlie and I knew at the time of the General Reinsurance merger that its derivatives business was unattractive. Reported profits struck us as illusory, and we felt that the business carried sizable risks that could not effectively be measured or limited. Moreover, we knew that any major problems the operation might experience would likely correlate with troubles in the financial or insurance world that would affect Berkshire elsewhere. In other words, if the derivatives business were ever to need shoring up, it would commandeer the capital and credit of Berkshire at just the time we could otherwise deploy those resources to huge advantage. (A historical note: We had just such an experience in 1974 when we were the victim of a major insurance fraud. We could not determine for some time how much the fraud would ultimately cost us and therefore kept more funds in cash-equivalents than we normally would have.

Absent this precaution, we would have made larger purchases of stocks that were then extraordinarily cheap.)

Charlie would have moved swiftly to close down Gen Re Securities – no question about that. I, however, dithered. As a consequence, our shareholders are paying a far higher price than was necessary to exit this business.

- Though we include Gen Re's sizable life and health reinsurance business in the "insurance" sector, we show the results for Ajit Jain's life and annuity business in this section. That's because this business, in large part, involves arbitraging money. Our annuities range from a retail product sold directly on the Internet to structured settlements that require us to make payments for 70 years or more to people severely injured in accidents.

  We've realized some extra income in this business because of accelerated principal payments we received from certain fixed-income securities we had purchased at discounts. This phenomenon has ended, and earnings are therefore likely to be lower in this segment during the next few years.

- We have a $604 million investment in Value Capital, a partnership run by Mark Byrne, a member of a family that has helped Berkshire over the years in many ways. Berkshire is a limited partner in, and has no say in the management of, Mark's enterprise, which specializes in highly-hedged fixed-income opportunities. Mark is smart and honest and, along with his family, has a significant investment in Value.

  Because of accounting abuses at Enron and elsewhere, rules will soon be instituted that are likely to require that Value's assets and liabilities be consolidated on Berkshire's balance sheet. We regard this requirement as inappropriate, given that Value's liabilities – which usually are above $20 billion – are in no way ours. Over time, other investors will join us as partners in Value. When enough do, the need for us to consolidate Value will disappear.

- We have told you in the past about Berkadia, the partnership we formed three years ago with Leucadia to finance and manage the wind-down of Finova, a bankrupt lending operation. The plan was that we would supply most of the capital and Leucadia would supply most of the brains. And that's the way it has worked. Indeed, Joe Steinberg and Ian Cumming, who together run Leucadia, have done such a fine job in liquidating Finova's portfolio that the $5.6 billion guarantee we took on in connection with the transaction has been extinguished. The unfortunate byproduct of this fast payoff is that our future income will be much reduced. Overall, Berkadia has made excellent money for us, and Joe and Ian have been terrific partners.

- Our leasing businesses are XTRA (transportation equipment) and CORT (office furniture). Both operations have had poor earnings during the past two years as the recession caused demand to drop considerably more than was anticipated. They remain leaders in their fields, and I expect at least a modest improvement in their earnings this year.

- Through our Clayton purchase, we acquired a significant manufactured-housing finance operation. Clayton, like others in this business, had traditionally securitized the loans it originated. The practice relieved stress on Clayton's balance sheet, but a by-product was the "front-ending" of income (a result dictated by GAAP).

  We are in no hurry to record income, have enormous balance-sheet strength, and believe that over the long-term the economics of holding our consumer paper are superior to what we can now realize through securitization. So Clayton has begun to retain its loans.

  We believe it's appropriate to finance a soundly-selected book of interest-bearing receivables almost entirely with debt (just as a bank would). Therefore, Berkshire will borrow money to finance Clayton's portfolio and re-lend these funds to Clayton at our cost plus one percentage point. This markup fairly compensates Berkshire for putting its exceptional creditworthiness to work, but it still delivers money to Clayton at an attractive price.

In 2003, Berkshire did $2 billion of such borrowing and re-lending, with Clayton using much of this money to fund several large purchases of portfolios from lenders exiting the business. A portion of our loans to Clayton also provided "catch-up" funding for paper it had generated earlier in the year from its own operation and had found difficult to securitize.

You may wonder why we borrow money while sitting on a mountain of cash. It's because of our "every tub on its own bottom" philosophy. We believe that any subsidiary lending money should pay an appropriate rate for the funds needed to carry its receivables and should not be subsidized by its parent. Otherwise, having a rich daddy can lead to sloppy decisions. Meanwhile, the cash we accumulate at Berkshire is destined for business acquisitions or for the purchase of securities that offer opportunities for significant profit. Clayton's loan portfolio will likely grow to at least $5 billion in not too many years and, with sensible credit standards in place, should deliver significant earnings.

For simplicity's sake, we include all of Clayton's earnings in this sector, though a sizable portion is derived from areas other than consumer finance.

	(in $ millions)			
	Pre-Tax Earnings		Interest-bearing Liabilities	
	2003	2002	2003	2002
Trading – Ordinary Income	$ 379	$ 553	$7,826	$13,762
Gen Re Securities	(99)	(173)	8,041*	10,631*
Life and annuity operation	99	83	2,331	1,568
Value Capital	31	61	18,238*	20,359*
Berkadia	101	115	525	2,175
Leasing operations	34	34	482	503
Manufactured housing finance (Clayton)	37**	—	2,032	—
Other	84	102	618	630
Income before capital gains	666	775		
Trading – Capital Gains	1,215	578	N.A.	N.A.
Total	$1,881	$1,353		

* Includes all liabilities
** From date of acquisition, August 7, 2003

Manufacturing, Service and Retailing Operations

Our activities in this category cover the waterfront. But let's look at a simplified balance sheet and earnings statement consolidating the entire group.

Balance Sheet 12/31/03 (in $ millions)

Assets		Liabilities and Equity	
Cash and equivalents	$ 1,250	Notes payable	$ 1,593
Accounts and notes receivable	2,796	Other current liabilities	4,300
Inventory	3,656	Total current liabilities	5,893
Other current assets	262		
Total current assets	7,964		
Goodwill and other intangibles	8,351	Deferred taxes	105
Fixed assets	5,898	Term debt and other liabilities	1,890
Other assets	1,054	Equity	15,379
	$23,267		$23,267

Earnings Statement (in $ millions)

	2003	2002
Revenues	$32,106	$16,970
Operating expenses (including depreciation of $605 in 2003 and $477 in 2002)	29,885	14,921
Interest expense (net)	64	108
Pre-tax income	2,157	1,941
Income taxes	813	743
Net income	$ 1,344	$ 1,198

This eclectic group, which sells products ranging from Dilly Bars to B-737s, earned a hefty 20.7% on average tangible net worth last year. However, we purchased these businesses at substantial premiums to net worth – that fact is reflected in the goodwill item shown on the balance sheet – and that reduces the earnings on our average *carrying* value to 9.2%.

Here are the pre-tax earnings for the larger categories or units.

	Pre-Tax Earnings (in $ millions)	
	2003	2002
Building Products	$ 559	$ 516
Shaw Industries	436	424
Apparel	289	229
Retail Operations	224	219
Flight Services	72	225
McLane *	150	—
Other businesses	427	328
	$2,157	$1,941

* From date of acquisition, May 23, 2003.

- Three of our building-materials businesses – Acme Brick, Benjamin Moore and MiTek – had record operating earnings last year. And earnings at Johns Manville, the fourth, were trending upward at yearend. Collectively, these companies earned 21.0% on tangible net worth.

- Shaw Industries, the world's largest manufacturer of broadloom carpet, also had a record year. Led by Bob Shaw, who built this huge enterprise from a standing start, the company will likely set another earnings record in 2004. In November, Shaw acquired various carpet operations from Dixie Group, which should add about $240 million to sales this year, boosting Shaw's volume to nearly $5 billion.

- Within the apparel group, Fruit of the Loom is our largest operation. Fruit has three major assets: a 148-year-old universally-recognized brand, a low-cost manufacturing operation, and John Holland, its CEO. In 2003, Fruit accounted for 42.3% of the men's and boys' underwear that was sold by mass marketers (Wal-Mart, Target, K-Mart, etc.) and increased its share of the women's and girls' business in that channel to 13.9%, up from 11.3% in 2002.

- In retailing, our furniture group earned $106 million pre-tax, our jewelers $59 million and See's, which is both a manufacturer and retailer, $59 million.

Both R.C. Willey and Nebraska Furniture Mart ("NFM") opened hugely successful stores last year, Willey in Las Vegas and NFM in Kansas City, Kansas. Indeed, we believe the Kansas City store is the country's largest-volume home-furnishings store. (Our Omaha operation, while located on a single plot of land, consists of three units.)

NFM was founded by Rose Blumkin ("Mrs. B") in 1937 with $500. She worked until she was 103 (hmmm . . . not a bad idea). One piece of wisdom she imparted to the generations following her was, "If you have the lowest price, customers will find you at the bottom of a river." Our store serving greater Kansas City, which is located in one of the area's more sparsely populated parts, has proved Mrs. B's point. Though we have more than 25 acres of parking, the lot has at times overflowed.

"Victory," President Kennedy told us after the Bay of Pigs disaster, "has a thousand fathers, but defeat is an orphan." At NFM, we knew we had a winner a month after the boffo opening in Kansas City, when our new store attracted an unexpected paternity claim. A speaker there, referring to the Blumkin family, asserted, "They had enough confidence and the policies of the Administration were working such that they were able to provide work for 1,000 of our fellow citizens." The proud papa at the podium? President George W. Bush.

- In flight services, FlightSafety, our training operation, experienced a drop in "normal" operating earnings from $183 million to $150 million. (The abnormals: In 2002 we had a $60 million pre-tax gain from the sale of a partnership interest to Boeing, and in 2003 we recognized a $37 million loss stemming from the premature obsolescence of simulators.) The corporate aviation business has slowed significantly in the past few years, and this fact has hurt FlightSafety's results. The company continues, however, to be far and away the leader in its field. Its simulators have an original cost of $1.2 billion, which is more than triple the cost of those operated by our closest competitor.

NetJets, our fractional-ownership operation lost $41 million pre-tax in 2003. The company had a modest operating profit in the U.S., but this was more than offset by a $32 million loss on aircraft inventory and by continued losses in Europe.

NetJets continues to dominate the fractional-ownership field, and its lead is increasing: Prospects overwhelmingly turn to us rather than to our three major competitors. Last year, among the four of us, we accounted for 70% of net sales (measured by value).

An example of what sets NetJets apart from competitors is our Mayo Clinic Executive Travel Response program, a free benefit enjoyed by all of our owners. On land or in the air, anywhere in the world and at any hour of any day, our owners and their families have an immediate link to Mayo. Should an emergency occur while they are traveling here or abroad, Mayo will instantly direct them to an appropriate doctor or hospital. Any baseline data about the patient that Mayo possesses is simultaneously made available to the treating physician. Many owners have already found this service invaluable, including one who needed emergency brain surgery in Eastern Europe.

The $32 million inventory write-down we took in 2003 occurred because of falling prices for used aircraft early in the year. Specifically, we bought back fractions from withdrawing owners at prevailing prices, and these fell in value before we were able to remarket them. Prices are now stable.

The European loss is painful. But any company that forsakes Europe, as all of our competitors have done, is destined for second-tier status. Many of our U.S. owners fly extensively in Europe and want the safety and security assured by a NetJets plane and pilots. Despite a slow start, furthermore, we are now adding European customers at a good pace. During the years 2001 through 2003, we had gains of 88%, 61% and 77% in European management-and-flying revenues. We have not, however, yet succeeded in stemming the flow of red ink.

Rich Santulli, NetJets' extraordinary CEO, and I expect our European loss to diminish in 2004 and also anticipate that it will be more than offset by U.S. profits. Overwhelmingly, our owners love the NetJets experience. Once a customer has tried us, going back to commercial aviation is like going back to holding hands. NetJets will become a very big business over time and will be one in which we are preeminent in both customer satisfaction and profits. Rich will see to that.

Investments

The table that follows shows our common stock investments. Those that had a market value of more than $500 million at the end of 2003 are itemized.

Shares	Company	Percentage of Company Owned	Cost	12/31/03 Market
			(in $ millions)	
151,610,700	American Express Company	11.8	$ 1,470	$ 7,312
200,000,000	The Coca-Cola Company	8.2	1,299	10,150
96,000,000	The Gillette Company	9.5	600	3,526
14,610,900	H&R Block, Inc...................................	8.2	227	809
15,476,500	HCA Inc.	3.1	492	665
6,708,760	M&T Bank Corporation	5.6	103	659
24,000,000	Moody's Corporation	16.1	499	1,453
2,338,961,000	PetroChina Company Limited	1.3	488	1,340
1,727,765	The Washington Post Company	18.1	11	1,367
56,448,380	Wells Fargo & Company......................	3.3	463	3,324
	Others		2,863	4,682
	Total Common Stocks		$ 8,515	$35,287

We bought some Wells Fargo shares last year. Otherwise, among our six largest holdings, we last changed our position in Coca-Cola in 1994, American Express in 1998, Gillette in 1989, Washington Post in 1973, and Moody's in 2000. Brokers don't love us.

We are neither enthusiastic nor negative about the portfolio we hold. We own pieces of excellent businesses – all of which had good gains in intrinsic value last year – but their current prices reflect their excellence. The unpleasant corollary to this conclusion is that I made a big mistake in not selling several of our larger holdings during The Great Bubble. If these stocks are fully priced now, you may wonder what I was thinking four years ago when their intrinsic value was lower and their prices far higher. So do I.

In 2002, junk bonds became very cheap, and we purchased about $8 billion of these. The pendulum swung quickly though, and this sector now looks decidedly unattractive to us. Yesterday's weeds are today being priced as flowers.

We've repeatedly emphasized that realized gains at Berkshire are meaningless for analytical purposes. We have a huge amount of unrealized gains on our books, and our thinking about when, and if, to cash them depends not at all on a desire to report earnings at one specific time or another. Nevertheless, to see the diversity of our investment activities, you may be interested in the following table, categorizing the gains we reported during 2003:

Category	Pre-Tax Gain (in $ million)
Common Stocks	$ 448
U.S. Government Bonds..	1,485
Junk Bonds...	1,138
Foreign Exchange Contracts	825
Other...	233
	$4,129

The common stock profits occurred around the edges of our portfolio – not, as we already mentioned, from our selling down our major positions. The profits in governments arose from our liquidation of long-term strips (the most volatile of government securities) and from certain strategies I follow within our finance and financial products division. We retained most of our junk portfolio, selling only a few issues. Calls and maturing bonds accounted for the rest of the gains in the junk category.

During 2002 we entered the foreign currency market for the first time in my life, and in 2003 we enlarged our position, as I became increasingly bearish on the dollar. I should note that the cemetery for seers has a huge section set aside for macro forecasters. We have in fact made few macro forecasts at Berkshire, and we have seldom seen others make them with sustained success.

We have – and will continue to have – the bulk of Berkshire's net worth in U.S. assets. But in recent years our country's trade deficit has been force-feeding huge amounts of claims on, and ownership in, America to the rest of the world. For a time, foreign appetite for these assets readily absorbed the supply. Late in 2002, however, the world started choking on this diet, and the dollar's value began to slide against major currencies. Even so, prevailing exchange rates will not lead to a material letup in our trade deficit. So whether foreign investors like it or not, they will continue to be flooded with dollars. The consequences of this are anybody's guess. They could, however, be troublesome – and reach, in fact, well beyond currency markets.

As an American, I hope there is a benign ending to this problem. I myself suggested one possible solution – which, incidentally, leaves Charlie cold – in a November 10, 2003 article in Fortune Magazine. Then again, perhaps the alarms I have raised will prove needless: Our country's dynamism and resiliency have repeatedly made fools of naysayers. But Berkshire holds many billions of cash-equivalents denominated in dollars. So I feel more comfortable owning foreign-exchange contracts that are at least a partial offset to that position.

These contracts are subject to accounting rules that require changes in their value to be contemporaneously included in capital gains or losses, even though the contracts have not been closed. We show these changes each quarter in the Finance and Financial Products segment of our earnings statement. At yearend, our open foreign exchange contracts totaled about $12 billion at market values and were spread among five currencies. Also, when we were purchasing junk bonds in 2002, we tried when possible to buy issues denominated in Euros. Today, we own about $1 billion of these.

When we can't find anything exciting in which to invest, our "default" position is U.S. Treasuries, both bills and repos. No matter how low the yields on these instruments go, we never "reach" for a little more income by dropping our credit standards or by extending maturities. Charlie and I detest taking even small risks unless we feel we are being adequately compensated for doing so. About as far as we will go down that path is to occasionally eat cottage cheese a day after the expiration date on the carton.

* * * * * * * * * * * *

A 2003 book that investors can learn much from is *Bull!* by Maggie Mahar. Two other books I'd recommend are *The Smartest Guys in the Room* by Bethany McLean and Peter Elkind, and *In an Uncertain World* by Bob Rubin. All three are well-reported and well-written. Additionally, Jason Zweig last year did a first-class job in revising *The Intelligent Investor*, my favorite book on investing.

Designated Gifts Program

From 1981 through 2002, Berkshire administered a program whereby shareholders could direct Berkshire to make gifts to their favorite charitable organizations. Over the years we disbursed $197 million pursuant to this program. Churches were the most frequently named designees, and many thousands of other organizations benefited as well. We were the only major public company that offered such a program to shareholders, and Charlie and I were proud of it.

We reluctantly terminated the program in 2003 because of controversy over the abortion issue. Over the years numerous organizations on both sides of this issue had been designated by our shareholders to receive contributions. As a result, we regularly received some objections to the gifts designated for pro-choice operations. A few of these came from people and organizations that proceeded to boycott products of our subsidiaries. That did not concern us. We refused all requests to limit the right of our owners to make whatever gifts they chose (as long as the recipients had 501(c)(3) status).

In 2003, however, many *independent* associates of The Pampered Chef began to feel the boycotts. This development meant that people who trusted us – but who were neither employees of ours nor had a voice in Berkshire decision-making – suffered serious losses of income.

For our shareholders, there was some modest tax efficiency in Berkshire doing the giving rather than their making their gifts directly. Additionally, the program was consistent with our "partnership" approach, the first principle set forth in our Owner's Manual. But these advantages paled when they were measured against damage done loyal associates who had with great personal effort built businesses of their own. Indeed, Charlie and I see nothing charitable in harming decent, hard-working people just so we and other shareholders can gain some minor tax efficiencies.

Berkshire now makes no contributions at the parent company level. Our various subsidiaries follow philanthropic policies consistent with their practices prior to their acquisition by Berkshire, except that any personal contributions that former owners had earlier made from their corporate pocketbook are now funded by them personally.

The Annual Meeting

Last year, I asked you to vote as to whether you wished our annual meeting to be held on Saturday or Monday. I was hoping for Monday. Saturday won by 2 to 1. It will be a while before shareholder democracy resurfaces at Berkshire.

But you have spoken, and we will hold this year's annual meeting on Saturday, May 1 at the new Qwest Center in downtown Omaha. The Qwest offers us 194,000 square feet for exhibition by our subsidiaries (up from 65,000 square feet last year) and much more seating capacity as well. The Qwest's doors will open at 7 a.m., the movie will begin at 8:30, and the meeting itself will commence at 9:30. There will be a short break at noon for food. (Sandwiches will be available at the Qwest's concession stands.) That interlude aside, Charlie and I will answer questions until 3:30. We will tell you everything we know . . . and, at least in my case, more.

An attachment to the proxy material that is enclosed with this report explains how you can obtain the credential you will need for admission to the meeting and other events. As for plane, hotel and car reservations, we have again signed up American Express (800-799-6634) to give you special help. They do a terrific job for us each year, and I thank them for it.

In our usual fashion, we will run vans from the larger hotels to the meeting. Afterwards, the vans will make trips back to the hotels and to Nebraska Furniture Mart, Borsheim's and the airport. Even so, you are likely to find a car useful.

Our exhibition of Berkshire goods and services will blow you away this year. On the floor, for example, will be a 1,600 square foot Clayton home (featuring Acme brick, Shaw carpet, Johns-Manville insulation, MiTek fasteners, Carefree awnings, and outfitted with NFM furniture). You'll find it a far cry from the mobile-home stereotype of a few decades ago.

GEICO will have a booth staffed by a number of its top counselors from around the country, all of them ready to supply you with auto insurance quotes. In most cases, GEICO will be able to give you a special shareholder discount (usually 8%). This special offer is permitted by 41 of the 49 jurisdictions in which we operate. Bring the details of your existing insurance and check out whether we can save you money.

On Saturday, at the Omaha airport, we will have the usual array of aircraft from NetJets® available for your inspection. Stop by the NetJets booth at the Qwest to learn about viewing these planes. If you buy what we consider an appropriate number of items during the weekend, you may well need your own plane to take them home.

At Nebraska Furniture Mart, located on a 77-acre site on 72ⁿᵈ Street between Dodge and Pacific, we will again be having "Berkshire Weekend" pricing, which means we will be offering our shareholders a discount that is customarily given only to employees. We initiated this special pricing at NFM seven years ago, and sales during the "Weekend" grew from $5.3 million in 1997 to $17.3 million in 2003. Every year has set a new record.

To get the discount, you must make your purchases between Thursday, April 29 and Monday, May 3 inclusive, and also present your meeting credential. The period's special pricing will even apply to the products of several prestigious manufacturers that normally have ironclad rules against discounting but that, in the spirit of our shareholder weekend, have made an exception for you. We appreciate their cooperation. NFM is open from 10 a.m. to 9 p.m. Monday through Saturday, and 10 a.m. to 6 p.m. on Sunday. On Saturday this year, from 5:30 p.m. to 8 p.m., we are having a special affair for shareholders only. I'll be there, eating barbeque and drinking Coke.

Borsheim's — the largest jewelry store in the country except for Tiffany's Manhattan store — will have two shareholder-only events. The first will be a cocktail reception from 6 p.m. to 10 p.m. on Friday, April 30. The second, the main gala, will be from 9 a.m. to 4 p.m. on Sunday, May 2. Ask Charlie to autograph your *sales ticket*.

Shareholder prices will be available Thursday through Monday, so if you wish to avoid the large crowds that will assemble on Friday evening and Sunday, come at other times and identify yourself as a shareholder. On Saturday, we will be open until 6 p.m. Borsheim's operates on a gross margin that is fully twenty percentage points below that of its major rivals, so the more you buy, the more you save – at least that's what my wife and daughter tell me. (Both were impressed early in life by the story of the boy who, after missing a street car, walked home and proudly announced that he had saved 5¢ by doing so. His father was irate: "Why didn't you miss a cab and save 85¢?")

In the mall outside of Borsheim's, we will have Bob Hamman and Sharon Osberg, two of the world's top bridge experts, available to play with our shareholders on Sunday afternoon. Additionally, Patrick Wolff, twice U.S. chess champion, will be in the mall, taking on all comers — blindfolded! I've watched, and he doesn't peek.

Gorat's — my favorite steakhouse — will again be open exclusively for Berkshire shareholders on Sunday, May 2, and will be serving from 4 p.m. until 10 p.m. Please remember that to come to Gorat's on Sunday, you must have a reservation. To make one, call 402-551-3733 on April 1 (*but not before*). If Sunday is sold out, try Gorat's on one of the other evenings you will be in town. Flaunt your mastery of fine dining by ordering, as I do, a rare T-bone with a double order of hash browns.

We will have a special reception on Saturday afternoon from 4:00 to 5:00 for shareholders who come from outside of North America. Every year our meeting draws many people from around the globe, and Charlie and I want to be sure we personally meet those who have come so far. Any shareholder who comes from other than the U.S. or Canada will be given special credentials and instructions for attending this function.

Charlie and I have a great time at the annual meeting. And you will, too. So join us at the Qwest for our annual Woodstock for Capitalists.

February 27, 2004	Warren E. Buffett Chairman of the Board

BERKSHIRE HATHAWAY INC.

To the Shareholders of Berkshire Hathaway Inc.:

Our gain in net worth during 2004 was $8.3 billion, which increased the per-share book value of both our Class A and Class B stock by 10.5%. Over the last 40 years (that is, since present management took over) book value has grown from $19 to $55,824, a rate of 21.9% compounded annually.*

It's per-share intrinsic value that counts, however, not book value. Here, the news is good: Between 1964 and 2004, Berkshire morphed from a struggling northern textile business whose intrinsic value was less than book into a diversified enterprise worth far more than book. Our 40-year gain in intrinsic value has therefore somewhat exceeded our 21.9% gain in book. (For an explanation of intrinsic value and the economic principles that guide Charlie Munger, my partner and Berkshire's vice-chairman, and me in running Berkshire, please read our Owner's Manual, beginning on page 73.)

Despite their shortcomings, yearly calculations of book value are useful at Berkshire as a slightly understated gauge for measuring the *long-term* rate of increase in our intrinsic value. The calculations are less relevant, however, than they once were in rating any single year's performance versus the S&P 500 index (a comparison we display on the facing page). Our equity holdings (including convertible preferreds) have fallen considerably as a percentage of our net worth, from an average of 114% in the 1980s, for example, to less than 50% in recent years. Therefore, yearly movements in the stock market now affect a much smaller portion of our net worth than was once the case, a fact that will normally cause us to underperform in years when stocks rise substantially and overperform in years when they fall.

However the yearly comparisons work out, Berkshire's long-term performance versus the S&P remains all-important. Our shareholders can buy the S&P through an index fund at very low cost. Unless we achieve gains in per-share intrinsic value in the future that outdo the S&P, Charlie and I will be adding nothing to what you can accomplish on your own.

Last year, Berkshire's book-value gain of 10.5% fell short of the index's 10.9% return. Our lackluster performance was not due to any stumbles by the CEOs of our operating businesses: As always, they pulled more than their share of the load. My message to them is simple: Run your business as if it were the only asset your family will own over the next hundred years. Almost invariably they do just that and, after taking care of the needs of their business, send excess cash to Omaha for me to deploy.

I didn't do that job very well last year. My hope was to make several multi-billion dollar acquisitions that would add new and significant streams of earnings to the many we already have. But I struck out. Additionally, I found very few attractive securities to buy. Berkshire therefore ended the year with $43 billion of cash equivalents, not a happy position. Charlie and I will work to translate some of this hoard into more interesting assets during 2005, though we can't promise success.

In one respect, 2004 was a remarkable year for the stock market, a fact buried in the maze of numbers on page 2. If you examine the 35 years since the 1960s ended, you will find that an investor's return, including dividends, from owning the S&P has averaged 11.2% annually (well above what we expect future returns to be). But if you look for years with returns anywhere close to that 11.2% – say, between 8% and 14% – you will find only *one* before 2004. In other words, last year's "normal" return is anything but.

---

*All figures used in this report apply to Berkshire's A shares, the successor to the only stock that the company had outstanding before 1996. The B shares have an economic interest equal to 1/30th that of the A.

Over the 35 years, American business has delivered terrific results. It should therefore have been easy for investors to earn juicy returns: All they had to do was piggyback Corporate America in a diversified, low-expense way. An index fund that they never touched would have done the job. Instead many investors have had experiences ranging from mediocre to disastrous.

There have been three primary causes: first, high costs, usually because investors traded excessively or spent far too much on investment management; second, portfolio decisions based on tips and fads rather than on thoughtful, quantified evaluation of businesses; and third, a start-and-stop approach to the market marked by untimely entries (after an advance has been long underway) and exits (after periods of stagnation or decline). Investors should remember that excitement and expenses are their enemies. And if they insist on trying to time their participation in equities, they should try to be fearful when others are greedy and greedy only when others are fearful.

Sector Results

As managers, Charlie and I want to give our owners the financial information and commentary we would wish to receive if our roles were reversed. To do this with both clarity and reasonable brevity becomes more difficult as Berkshire's scope widens. Some of our businesses have vastly different economic characteristics from others, which means that our consolidated statements, with their jumble of figures, make useful analysis almost impossible.

On the following pages, therefore, we will present some balance sheet and earnings figures from our four major categories of businesses along with commentary about each. We particularly want you to understand the limited circumstances under which we will use debt, given that we typically shun it. We will not, however, inundate you with data that has no real value in estimating Berkshire's intrinsic value. Doing so would tend to obfuscate the facts that count.

Regulated Utility Businesses

We have an 80.5% (fully diluted) interest in MidAmerican Energy Holdings, which owns a wide variety of utility operations. The largest of these are (1) Yorkshire Electricity and Northern Electric, whose 3.7 million electric customers make it the third largest distributor of electricity in the U.K.; (2) MidAmerican Energy, which serves 698,000 electric customers, primarily in Iowa; and (3) Kern River and Northern Natural pipelines, which carry 7.9% of the natural gas consumed in the U.S.

The remaining 19.5% of MidAmerican is owned by three partners of ours: Dave Sokol and Greg Abel, the brilliant managers of these businesses, and Walter Scott, a long-time friend of mine who introduced me to the company. Because MidAmerican is subject to the Public Utility Holding Company Act ("PUHCA"), Berkshire's voting interest is limited to 9.9%. Voting control rests with Walter.

Our limited voting interest forces us to account for MidAmerican in an abbreviated manner. Instead of our fully incorporating the company's assets, liabilities, revenues and expenses into Berkshire's statements, we make one-line entries only in both our balance sheet and income account. It's likely, though, that PUHCA will someday – perhaps soon – be repealed or that accounting rules will change. Berkshire's consolidated figures would then incorporate all of MidAmerican, including the substantial debt it utilizes (though this debt is not now, nor will it ever be, an obligation of Berkshire).

At yearend, $1.478 billion of MidAmerican's junior debt was payable to Berkshire. This debt has allowed acquisitions to be financed without our partners needing to increase their already substantial investments in MidAmerican. By charging 11% interest, Berkshire is compensated fairly for putting up the funds needed for purchases, while our partners are spared dilution of their equity interests. Because MidAmerican made no large acquisitions last year, it paid down $100 million of what it owes us.

MidAmerican also owns a significant non-utility business, HomeServices of America, the second largest real estate broker in the country. Unlike our utility operations, this business is highly cyclical, but nevertheless one we view enthusiastically. We have an exceptional manager, Ron Peltier, who through both his acquisition and operational skills is building a brokerage powerhouse.

HomeServices participated in $59.8 billion of transactions in 2004, a gain of $11.2 billion from 2003. About 24% of the increase came from six acquisitions made during the year. Through our 17 brokerage firms – all of which retain their local identities – we employ more than 18,000 brokers in 18 states. HomeServices is almost certain to grow substantially in the next decade as we continue to acquire leading localized operations.

Last year MidAmerican wrote off a major investment in a zinc recovery project that was initiated in 1998 and became operational in 2002. Large quantities of zinc are present in the brine produced by our California geothermal operations, and we believed we could profitably extract the metal. For many months, it appeared that commercially-viable recoveries were imminent. But in mining, just as in oil exploration, prospects have a way of "teasing" their developers, and every time one problem was solved, another popped up. In September, we threw in the towel.

Our failure here illustrates the importance of a guideline – *stay with simple propositions* – that we usually apply in investments as well as operations. If only one variable is key to a decision, and the variable has a 90% chance of going your way, the chance for a successful outcome is obviously 90%. But if ten independent variables need to break favorably for a successful result, and each has a 90% probability of success, the likelihood of having a winner is only 35%. In our zinc venture, we solved most of the problems. But one proved intractable, and that was one too many. Since a chain is no stronger than its weakest link, it makes sense to look for – if you'll excuse an oxymoron – mono-linked chains.

A breakdown of MidAmerican's results follows. In 2004, the "other" category includes a $72.2 million profit from sale of an Enron receivable that was thrown in when we purchased Northern Natural two years earlier. Walter, Dave and I, as natives of Omaha, view this unanticipated gain as war reparations – partial compensation for the loss our city suffered in 1986 when Ken Lay moved Northern to Houston, after promising to leave the company here. (For details, see Berkshire's 2002 annual report.)

Here are some key figures on MidAmerican's operations:

	Earnings (in $ millions)	
	2004	2003
U.K. utilities	$ 326	$ 289
Iowa utility	268	269
Pipelines	288	261
HomeServices	130	113
Other (net)	172	190
Loss from zinc project	(579)	(46)
Earnings before corporate interest and taxes	605	1,076
Interest, other than to Berkshire	(212)	(225)
Interest on Berkshire junior debt	(170)	(184)
Income tax	(53)	(251)
Net earnings	$ 170	$ 416
Earnings applicable to Berkshire*	$ 237	$ 429
Debt owed to others	10,528	10,296
Debt owed to Berkshire	1,478	1,578

*Includes interest earned by Berkshire (net of related income taxes) of $110 in 2004 and $118 in 2003.

Insurance

Since Berkshire purchased National Indemnity ("NICO") in 1967, property-casualty insurance has been our core business and the propellant of our growth. Insurance has provided a fountain of funds with which we've acquired the securities and businesses that now give us an ever-widening variety of earnings streams. So in this section, I will be spending a little time telling you how we got where we are.

The source of our insurance funds is "float," which is money that doesn't belong to us but that we temporarily hold. Most of our float arises because (1) premiums are paid upfront though the service we provide – insurance protection – is delivered over a period that usually covers a year and; (2) loss events that occur today do not always result in our immediately paying claims, because it sometimes takes many years for losses to be reported (asbestos losses would be an example), negotiated and settled. The $20 million of float that came with our 1967 purchase has now increased – both by way of internal growth and acquisitions – to $46.1 billion.

Float is wonderful – *if* it doesn't come at a high price. Its cost is determined by underwriting results, meaning how the expenses and losses we will ultimately pay compare with the premiums we have received. When an underwriting profit is achieved – as has been the case at Berkshire in about half of the 38 years we have been in the insurance business – float is better than free. In such years, we are actually paid for holding other people's money. For most insurers, however, life has been far more difficult: In aggregate, the property-casualty industry almost invariably operates at an underwriting loss. When that loss is large, float becomes expensive, sometimes devastatingly so.

Insurers have generally earned poor returns for a simple reason: They sell a commodity-like product. Policy forms are standard, and the product is available from many suppliers, some of whom are mutual companies ("owned" by policyholders rather than stockholders) with profit goals that are limited. Moreover, most insureds don't care from whom they buy. Customers by the millions say "I need some Gillette blades" or "I'll have a Coke" but we wait in vain for "I'd like a National Indemnity policy, please." Consequently, price competition in insurance is usually fierce. Think airline seats.

So, you may ask, how do Berkshire's insurance operations overcome the dismal economics of the industry and achieve some measure of enduring competitive advantage? We've attacked that problem in several ways. Let's look first at NICO's strategy.

When we purchased the company – a specialist in commercial auto and general liability insurance – it did not appear to have any attributes that would overcome the industry's chronic troubles. It was not well-known, had no informational advantage (the company has never had an actuary), was not a low-cost operator, and sold through general agents, a method many people thought outdated. Nevertheless, for almost all of the past 38 years, NICO has been a star performer. Indeed, had we not made this acquisition, Berkshire would be lucky to be worth half of what it is today.

What we've had going for us is a managerial mindset that most insurers find impossible to replicate. Take a look at the facing page. Can you imagine *any* public company embracing a business model that would lead to the decline in revenue that we experienced from 1986 through 1999? That colossal slide, it should be emphasized, did not occur because business was unobtainable. Many billions of premium dollars were readily available to NICO had we only been willing to cut prices. But we instead consistently priced to make a profit, not to match our most optimistic competitor. We never left customers – but they left us.

Most American businesses harbor an "institutional imperative" that rejects extended decreases in volume. What CEO wants to report to his shareholders that not only did business contract last year but that it will continue to drop? In insurance, the urge to keep writing business is also intensified because the consequences of foolishly-priced policies may not become apparent for some time. If an insurer is optimistic in its reserving, reported earnings will be overstated, and years may pass before true loss costs are revealed (a form of self-deception that nearly destroyed GEICO in the early 1970s).

Portrait of a Disciplined Underwriter
National Indemnity Company

Year	Written Premium (In $ millions)	No. of Employees at Year-End	Ratio of Operating Expenses to Written Premium	Underwriting Profit (Loss) as a Percentage of Premiums (Calculated as of year end 2004)*
1980	$79.6	372	32.3%	8.2%
1981	59.9	353	36.1%	(.8%)
1982	52.5	323	36.7%	(15.3%)
1983	58.2	308	35.6%	(18.7%)
1984	62.2	342	35.5%	(17.0%)
1985	160.7	380	28.0%	1.9%
1986	366.2	403	25.9%	30.7%
1987	232.3	368	29.5%	27.3%
1988	139.9	347	31.7%	24.8%
1989	98.4	320	35.9%	14.8%
1990	87.8	289	37.4%	7.0%
1991	88.3	284	35.7%	13.0%
1992	82.7	277	37.9%	5.2%
1993	86.8	279	36.1%	11.3%
1994	85.9	263	34.6%	4.6%
1995	78.0	258	36.6%	9.2%
1996	74.0	243	36.5%	6.8%
1997	65.3	240	40.4%	6.2%
1998	56.8	231	40.4%	9.4%
1999	54.5	222	41.2%	4.5%
2000	68.1	230	38.4%	2.9%
2001	161.3	254	28.8%	(11.6%)
2002	343.5	313	24.0%	16.8%
2003	594.5	337	22.2%	18.1%
2004	605.6	340	22.5%	5.1%

*It takes a long time to learn the true profitability of any given year. First, many claims are received after the end of the year, and we must estimate how many of these there will be and what they will cost. (In insurance jargon, these claims are termed IBNR – incurred but not reported.) Second, claims often take years, or even decades, to settle, which means there can be many surprises along the way.

For these reasons, the results in this column simply represent our best estimate at the end of 2004 as to how we have done in prior years. Profit margins for the years through 1999 are probably close to correct because these years are "mature," in the sense that they have few claims still outstanding. The more recent the year, the more guesswork is involved. In particular, the results shown for 2003 and 2004 are apt to change significantly.

Finally, there is a fear factor at work, in that a shrinking business usually leads to layoffs. To avoid pink slips, employees will rationalize inadequate pricing, telling themselves that poorly-priced business must be tolerated in order to keep the organization intact and the distribution system happy. If this course isn't followed, these employees will argue, the company will not participate in the recovery that they invariably feel is just around the corner.

To combat employees' natural tendency to save their own skins, we have always promised NICO's workforce that *no one* will be fired because of declining volume, however severe the contraction. (This is not Donald Trump's sort of place.) NICO is not labor-intensive, and, as the table suggests, can live with excess overhead. It can't live, however, with underpriced business and the breakdown in underwriting discipline that accompanies it. An insurance organization that doesn't care deeply about underwriting at a profit *this* year is unlikely to care *next* year either.

Naturally, a business that follows a no-layoff policy must be especially careful to avoid overstaffing when times are good. Thirty years ago Tom Murphy, then CEO of Cap Cities, drove this point home to me with a hypothetical tale about an employee who asked his boss for permission to hire an assistant. The employee assumed that adding $20,000 to the annual payroll would be inconsequential. But his boss told him the proposal should be evaluated as a $3 million decision, given that an additional person would probably cost at least that amount over his lifetime, factoring in raises, benefits and other expenses (more people, more toilet paper). And unless the company fell on very hard times, the employee added would be unlikely to be dismissed, however marginal his contribution to the business.

It takes real fortitude – embedded deep within a company's culture – to operate as NICO does. Anyone examining the table can scan the years from 1986 to 1999 quickly. But living day after day with dwindling volume – while competitors are boasting of growth and reaping Wall Street's applause – is an experience few managers can tolerate. NICO, however, has had four CEOs since its formation in 1940 and *none* have bent. (It should be noted that only one of the four graduated from college. Our experience tells us that extraordinary business ability is largely innate.)

The current managerial star – make that superstar – at NICO is Don Wurster (yes, he's "the graduate"), who has been running things since 1989. His slugging percentage is right up there with Barry Bonds' because, like Barry, Don will accept a walk rather than swing at a bad pitch. Don has now amassed $950 million of float at NICO that over time is almost certain to be proved the negative-cost kind. Because insurance prices are falling, Don's volume will soon decline very significantly and, as it does, Charlie and I will applaud him ever more loudly.

* * * * * * * * * * * *

Another way to prosper in a commodity-type business is to be the low-cost operator. Among auto insurers operating on a broad scale, GEICO holds that cherished title. For NICO, as we have seen, an ebb-and-flow business model makes sense. But a company holding a low-cost advantage must pursue an unrelenting foot-to-the-floor strategy. And that's just what we do at GEICO.

A century ago, when autos first appeared, the property-casualty industry operated as a cartel. The major companies, most of which were based in the Northeast, established "bureau" rates and that was it. No one cut prices to attract business. Instead, insurers competed for strong, well-regarded agents, a focus that produced high commissions for agents and high prices for consumers.

In 1922, State Farm was formed by George Mecherle, a farmer from Merna, Illinois, who aimed to take advantage of the pricing umbrella maintained by the high-cost giants of the industry. State Farm employed a "captive" agency force, a system keeping its acquisition costs lower than those incurred by the bureau insurers (whose "independent" agents successfully played off one company against another). With its low-cost structure, State Farm eventually captured about 25% of the personal lines (auto and homeowners) business, far outdistancing its once-mighty competitors. Allstate, formed in 1931, put a similar distribution system into place and soon became the runner-up in personal lines to State Farm. Capitalism had worked its magic, and these low-cost operations looked unstoppable.

But a man named Leo Goodwin had an idea for an even more efficient auto insurer and, with a skimpy $200,000, started GEICO in 1936. Goodwin's plan was to eliminate the agent entirely and to deal instead directly with the auto owner. Why, he asked himself, should there be any unnecessary and expensive links in the distribution mechanism when the product, auto insurance, was both mandatory and costly. Purchasers of business insurance, he reasoned, might well require professional advice, but most consumers knew what they needed in an auto policy. That was a powerful insight.

Originally, GEICO mailed its low-cost message to a limited audience of government employees. Later, it widened its horizons and shifted its marketing emphasis to the phone, working inquiries that came from broadcast and print advertising. And today the Internet is coming on strong.

Between 1936 and 1975, GEICO grew from a standing start to a 4% market share, becoming the country's fourth largest auto insurer. During most of this period, the company was superbly managed, achieving both excellent volume gains and high profits. It looked unstoppable. But after my friend and hero Lorimer Davidson retired as CEO in 1970, his successors soon made a huge mistake by under-reserving for losses. This produced faulty cost information, which in turn produced inadequate pricing. By 1976, GEICO was on the brink of failure.

Jack Byrne then joined GEICO as CEO and, almost single-handedly, saved the company by heroic efforts that included major price increases. Though GEICO's survival required these, policyholders fled the company, and by 1980 its market share had fallen to 1.8%. Subsequently, the company embarked on some unwise diversification moves. This shift of emphasis away from its extraordinary core business stunted GEICO's growth, and by 1993 its market share had grown only fractionally, to 1.9%. Then Tony Nicely took charge.

And what a difference that's made: In 2005 GEICO will probably secure a 6% market share. Better yet, Tony has matched growth with profitability. Indeed, GEICO delivers all of its constituents major benefits: In 2004 its customers saved $1 billion or so compared to what they would otherwise have paid for coverage, its associates earned a $191 million profit-sharing bonus that averaged 24.3% of salary, and its owner – that's us – enjoyed excellent financial returns.

There's more good news. When Jack Byrne was rescuing the company in 1976, New Jersey refused to grant him the rates he needed to operate profitably. He therefore promptly – and properly – withdrew from the state. Subsequently, GEICO avoided both New Jersey and Massachusetts, recognizing them as two jurisdictions in which insurers were destined to struggle.

In 2003, however, New Jersey took a new look at its chronic auto-insurance problems and enacted legislation that would curb fraud and allow insurers a fair playing field. Even so, one might have expected the state's bureaucracy to make change slow and difficult.

But just the opposite occurred. Holly Bakke, the New Jersey insurance commissioner, who would be a success in *any* line of work, was determined to turn the law's intent into reality. With her staff's cooperation, GEICO ironed out the details for re-entering the state and was licensed last August. Since then, we've received a response from New Jersey drivers that is multiples of my expectations.

We are now serving 140,000 policyholders – about 4% of the New Jersey market – and saving them substantial sums (as we do drivers everywhere). Word-of-mouth recommendations within the state are causing inquiries to pour in. And once we hear from a New Jersey prospect, our closure rate – the percentage of policies issued to inquiries received – is far higher in the state than it is nationally.

We make no claim, of course, that we can save *everyone* money. Some companies, using rating systems that are different from ours, will offer certain classes of drivers a lower rate than we do. But we believe GEICO offers the lowest price more often than any other national company that serves all segments of the public. In addition, in most states, including New Jersey, Berkshire shareholders receive an 8% discount. So gamble fifteen minutes of your time and go to GEICO.com – or call 800-847-7536 – to see whether you can save big money (which you might want to use, of course, to buy other Berkshire products).

* * * * * * * * * * * *

Reinsurance – insurance sold to other insurers who wish to lay off part of the risks they have assumed – should *not* be a commodity product. At bottom, any insurance policy is simply a promise, and as everyone knows, promises vary enormously in their quality.

At the primary insurance level, nevertheless, just who makes the promise is often of minor importance. In personal-lines insurance, for example, states levy assessments on solvent companies to pay the policyholders of companies that go broke. In the business-insurance field, the same arrangement applies to workers' compensation policies. "Protected" policies of these types account for about 60% of the property-casualty industry's volume. Prudently-run insurers are irritated by the need to subsidize poor or reckless management elsewhere, but that's the way it is.

Other forms of business insurance at the primary level involve promises that carry greater risks for the insured. When Reliance Insurance and Home Insurance were run into the ground, for example, their promises proved to be worthless. Consequently, many holders of their business policies (other than those covering workers' compensation) suffered painful losses.

The solvency risk in primary policies, however, pales in comparison to that lurking in reinsurance policies. When a reinsurer goes broke, staggering losses almost always strike the primary companies it has dealt with. This risk is far from minor: GEICO has suffered tens of millions in losses from its careless selection of reinsurers in the early 1980s.

Were a true mega-catastrophe to occur in the next decade or two – and that's a real possibility – some reinsurers would not survive. The largest insured loss to date is the World Trade Center disaster, which cost the insurance industry an estimated $35 billion. Hurricane Andrew cost insurers about $15.5 billion in 1992 (though that loss would be far higher in today's dollars). Both events rocked the insurance and reinsurance world. But a $100 billion event, or even a larger catastrophe, remains a possibility if either a particularly severe earthquake or hurricane hits just the wrong place. Four significant hurricanes struck Florida during 2004, causing an aggregate of $25 billion or so in insured losses. Two of these – Charley and Ivan – could have done at least three times the damage they did had they entered the U.S. not far from their actual landing points.

Many insurers regard a $100 billion industry loss as "unthinkable" and won't even plan for it. But at Berkshire, we are fully prepared. Our share of the loss would probably be 3% to 5%, and earnings from our investments and other businesses would comfortably exceed that cost. When "the day after" arrives, Berkshire's checks will clear.

Though the hurricanes hit us with a $1.25 billion loss, our reinsurance operations did well last year. At General Re, Joe Brandon has restored a long-admired culture of underwriting discipline that, for a time, had lost its way. The excellent results he realized in 2004 on current business, however, were offset by adverse developments from the years before he took the helm. At NICO's reinsurance operation, Ajit Jain continues to successfully underwrite huge risks that no other reinsurer is willing or able to accept. Ajit's value to Berkshire is enormous.

* * * * * * * * * * * *

Our insurance managers, maximizing the competitive strengths I've mentioned in this section, again delivered first-class underwriting results last year. As a consequence, our float was better than costless. Here's the scorecard:

Insurance Operations	Underwriting Profit 2004	Yearend Float 2004	2003
General Re	$ 3	$23,120	$23,654
B-H Reinsurance	417	15,278	13,948
GEICO	970	5,960	5,287
Other Primary*	161	1,736	1,331
Total	$1,551	$46,094	$44,220

(in $ millions)

*Includes, in addition to National Indemnity, a variety of other exceptional insurance businesses, run by Rod Eldred, John Kizer, Tom Nerney and Don Towle.

Berkshire's float increased $1.9 billion in 2004, even though a few insureds opted to commute (that is, unwind) certain reinsurance contracts. We agree to such commutations only when we believe the economics are favorable to us (after giving due weight to what we might earn in the future on the money we are returning).

To summarize, last year we were paid more than $1.5 billion to hold an average of about $45.2 billion. In 2005 pricing will be less attractive than it has been. Nevertheless, absent a mega-catastrophe, we have a decent chance of achieving no-cost float again this year.

Finance and Finance Products

Last year in this section we discussed a potpourri of activities. In this report, we'll skip over several that are now of lesser importance: Berkadia is down to tag ends; Value Capital has added other investors, negating our expectation that we would need to consolidate its financials into ours; and the trading operation that I run continues to shrink.

- Both of Berkshire's leasing operations rebounded last year. At CORT (office furniture), earnings remain inadequate, but are trending upward. XTRA disposed of its container and intermodal businesses in order to concentrate on trailer leasing, long its strong suit. Overhead has been reduced, asset utilization is up and decent profits are now being achieved under Bill Franz, the company's new CEO.

- The wind-down of Gen Re Securities continues. We decided to exit this derivative operation three years ago, but getting out is easier said than done. Though derivative instruments are purported to be highly liquid – and though we have had the benefit of a benign market while liquidating ours – we still had 2,890 contracts outstanding at yearend, down from 23,218 at the peak. Like Hell, derivative trading is easy to enter but difficult to leave. (Other similarities come to mind as well.)

Gen Re's derivative contracts have always been required to be marked to market, and I believe the company's management conscientiously tried to make realistic "marks." The market prices of derivatives, however, can be very fuzzy in a world in which settlement of a transaction is sometimes decades away and often involves multiple variables as well. In the interim the marks influence the managerial and trading bonuses that are paid annually. It's small wonder that phantom profits are often recorded.

Investors should understand that in all types of financial institutions, rapid growth sometimes masks major underlying problems (and occasionally fraud). The real test of the earning power of a derivatives operation is what it achieves after operating for an extended period in a no-growth mode. You only learn who has been swimming naked when the tide goes out.

- After 40 years, we've finally generated a little synergy at Berkshire: Clayton Homes is doing well and that's in part due to its association with Berkshire. The manufactured home industry

11

continues to reside in the intensive care unit of Corporate America, having sold less than 135,000 new homes last year, about the same as in 2003. Volume in these years was the lowest since 1962, and it was also only about 40% of annual sales during the years 1995-99. That era, characterized by irresponsible financing and naïve funders, was a fool's paradise for the industry.

Because one major lender after another has fled the field, financing continues to bedevil manufacturers, retailers and purchasers of manufactured homes. Here Berkshire's support has proven valuable to Clayton. We stand ready to fund whatever makes sense, and last year Clayton's management found much that qualified.

As we explained in our 2003 report, we believe in using borrowed money to support profitable, interest-bearing receivables. At the beginning of last year, we had borrowed $2 billion to relend to Clayton (at a one percentage-point markup) and by January 2005 the total was $7.35 billion. Most of the dollars added were borrowed by us on January 4, 2005, to finance a seasoned portfolio that Clayton purchased on December 30, 2004 from a bank exiting the business.

We now have two additional portfolio purchases in the works, totaling about $1.6 billion, but it's quite unlikely that we will secure others of any significance. Therefore, Clayton's receivables (in which originations will roughly offset payoffs) will probably hover around $9 billion for some time and should deliver steady earnings. This pattern will be far different from that of the past, in which Clayton, like all major players in its industry, "securitized" its receivables, causing earnings to be front-ended. In the last two years, the securitization market has dried up. The limited funds available today come only at higher cost and with harsh terms. Had Clayton remained independent in this period, it would have had mediocre earnings as it struggled with financing.

In April, Clayton completed the acquisition of Oakwood Homes and is now the industry's largest producer and retailer of manufactured homes. We love putting more assets in the hands of Kevin Clayton, the company's CEO. He is a prototype Berkshire manager. Today, Clayton has 11,837 employees, up from 7,136 when we purchased it, and Charlie and I are pleased that Berkshire has been useful in facilitating this growth.

For simplicity's sake, we include all of Clayton's earnings in this sector, though a sizable portion of these are derived from areas other than consumer finance.

	(in $ millions)			
	Pre-Tax Earnings		*Interest-Bearing Liabilities*	
	2004	*2003*	*2004*	*2003*
Trading – ordinary income	$ 264	$ 355	$5,751	$7,826
Gen Re Securities	(44)	(99)	5,437*	8,041*
Life and annuity operation	(57)	85	2,467	2,331
Value Capital	30	31	N/A	N/A
Berkadia	1	101	—	525
Leasing operations	92	34	391	482
Manufactured housing finance (Clayton)	220	37**	3,636	2,032
Other	78	75	N/A	N/A
Income before capital gains	584	619		
Trading – capital gains	1,750	1,215		
Total	$2,334	$1,834		

*   Includes all liabilities
**   From date of acquisition, August 7, 2003

Manufacturing, Service and Retailing Operations

Our activities in this category cover the waterfront. But let's look at a summary balance sheet and earnings statement consolidating the entire group.

Balance Sheet 12/31/04 (in $ millions)

Assets		Liabilities and Equity	
Cash and equivalents	$ 899	Notes payable	$ 1,143
Accounts and notes receivable	3,074	Other current liabilities	4,685
Inventory	3,842	Total current liabilities	5,828
Other current assets	254		
Total current assets	8,069		
Goodwill and other intangibles	8,362	Deferred taxes	248
Fixed assets	6,161	Term debt and other liabilities	1,965
Other assets	1,044	Equity	15,595
	$23,636		$23,636

Earnings Statement (in $ millions)

	2004	2003
Revenues	$44,142	$32,106
Operating expenses (including depreciation of $676 in 2004 and $605 in 2003)	41,604	29,885
Interest expense (net)	57	64
Pre-tax earnings	2,481	2,157
Income taxes	941	813
Net income	$ 1,540	$ 1,344

This eclectic group, which sells products ranging from Dilly Bars to fractional interests in Boeing 737s, earned a very respectable 21.7% on average tangible net worth last year, compared to 20.7% in 2003. It's noteworthy that these operations used only minor financial leverage in achieving these returns. Clearly, we own some very good businesses. We purchased many of them, however, at substantial premiums to net worth – a matter that is reflected in the goodwill item shown on the balance sheet – and that fact reduces the earnings on our average *carrying* value to 9.9%.

Here are the pre-tax earnings for the larger categories or units.

	Pre-Tax Earnings (in $ millions)	
	2004	2003
Building Products	$ 643	$ 559
Shaw Industries	466	436
Apparel & Footwear	325	289
Retailing of Jewelry, Home Furnishings and Candy	215	224
Flight Services	191	72
McLane	228	150*
Other businesses	413	427
	$2,481	$2,157

* From date of acquisition, May 23, 2003.

- In the building-products sector and at Shaw, we've experienced staggering cost increases for both raw-materials and energy. By December, for example, steel costs at MiTek (whose primary business is connectors for roof trusses) were running 100% over a year earlier. And MiTek uses 665 million pounds of steel every year. Nevertheless, the company continues to be an outstanding performer.

Since we purchased MiTek in 2001, Gene Toombs, its CEO, has made some brilliant "bolt-on" acquisitions and is on his way to creating a mini-Berkshire.

Shaw fielded a barrage of price increases in its main fiber materials during the year, a hit that added more than $300 million to its costs. (When you walk on carpet you are, in effect, stepping on processed oil.) Though we followed these hikes in costs with price increases of our own, there was an inevitable lag. Therefore, margins narrowed as the year progressed and remain under pressure today. Despite these roadblocks, Shaw, led by Bob Shaw and Julian Saul, earned an outstanding 25.6% on tangible equity in 2004. The company is a powerhouse and has a bright future.

- In apparel, Fruit of the Loom increased unit sales by 10 million dozen, or 14%, with shipments of intimate apparel for women and girls growing by 31%. Charlie, who is far more knowledgeable than I am on this subject, assures me that women are *not* wearing more underwear. With this expert input, I can only conclude that our market share in the women's category must be growing rapidly. Thanks to John Holland, Fruit is on the move.

  A smaller operation, Garan, also had an excellent year. Led by Seymour Lichtenstein and Jerry Kamiel, this company manufactures the popular Garanimals line for children. Next time you are in a Wal-Mart, check out this imaginative product.

- Among our retailers, Ben Bridge (jewelry) and R. C. Willey (home furnishings) were particular standouts last year.

  At Ben Bridge same-store sales grew 11.4%, the best gain among the publicly-held jewelers whose reports I have seen. Additionally, the company's profit margin widened. Last year was not a fluke: During the past decade, the same-store sales gains of the company have averaged 8.8%.

  Ed and Jon Bridge are fourth-generation managers and run the business exactly as if it were their own – which it is in every respect except for Berkshire's name on the stock certificates. The Bridges have expanded successfully by securing the right locations and, more importantly, by staffing these stores with enthusiastic and knowledgeable associates. We will move into Minneapolis-St. Paul this year.

  At Utah-based R. C. Willey, the gains from expansion have been even more dramatic, with 41.9% of 2004 sales coming from out-of-state stores that didn't exist before 1999. The company also improved its profit margin in 2004, propelled by its two new stores in Las Vegas.

  I would like to tell you that these stores were my idea. In truth, I thought they were mistakes. I knew, of course, how brilliantly Bill Child had run the R. C. Willey operation in Utah, where its market share had long been huge. But I felt our closed-on-Sunday policy would prove disastrous away from home. Even our first out-of-state store in Boise, which was highly successful, left me unconvinced. I kept asking whether Las Vegas residents, conditioned to seven-day-a-week retailers, would adjust to us. Our first Las Vegas store, opened in 2001, answered this question in a resounding manner, immediately becoming our number one unit.

  Bill and Scott Hymas, his successor as CEO, then proposed a second Las Vegas store, only about 20 minutes away. I felt this expansion would cannibalize the first unit, adding significant costs but only modest sales. The result? Each store is now doing about 26% more volume than any other store in the chain and is consistently showing large year-over-year gains.

  R. C. Willey will soon open in Reno. Before making this commitment, Bill and Scott again asked for my advice. Initially, I was pretty puffed up about the fact that they were consulting me. But then it dawned on me that the opinion of someone who is *always* wrong has its own special utility to decision-makers.

- Earnings improved in flight services. At FlightSafety, the world's leader in pilot training, profits rose as corporate aviation rebounded and our business with regional airlines increased. We now operate 283 simulators with an original cost of $1.2 billion. Pilots are trained one at a time on this expensive equipment. This means that as much as $3.50 of capital investment is required to produce $1 of annual revenue. With this level of capital intensity, FlightSafety requires very high operating margins in order to obtain reasonable returns on capital, which means that utilization rates are all-important. Last year, FlightSafety's return on tangible equity improved to 15.1% from 8.4% in 2003.

In another 2004 event, Al Ueltschi, who founded FlightSafety in 1951 with $10,000, turned over the CEO position to Bruce Whitman, a 43-year veteran at the company. (But Al's not going anywhere; I won't let him.) Bruce shares Al's conviction that flying an aircraft is a privilege to be extended only to people who regularly receive the highest quality of training and are undeniably competent. A few years ago, Charlie was asked to intervene with Al on behalf of a tycoon friend whom FlightSafety had flunked. Al's reply to Charlie: "Tell your pal he belongs in the back of the plane, not the cockpit."

FlightSafety's number one customer is NetJets, our aircraft fractional-ownership subsidiary. Its 2,100 pilots spend an average of 18 days a year in training. Additionally, these pilots fly only one aircraft type whereas many flight operations juggle pilots among several types. NetJets' high standards on both fronts are two of the reasons I signed up with the company years before Berkshire bought it.

Fully as important in my decisions to both use and buy NetJets, however, was the fact that the company was managed by Rich Santulli, the creator of the fractional-ownership industry and a fanatic about safety and service. I viewed the selection of a flight provider as akin to picking a brain surgeon: you simply want the best. (Let someone else experiment with the low bidder.)

Last year NetJets again gained about 70% of the net new business (measured by dollar value) going to the four companies that dominate the industry. A portion of our growth came from the 25-hour card offered by Marquis Jet Partners. Marquis is not owned by NetJets, but is instead a customer that repackages the purchases it makes from us into smaller packages that it sells through its card. Marquis deals exclusively with NetJets, utilizing the power of our reputation in its marketing.

Our U.S. contracts, including Marquis customers, grew from 3,877 to 4,967 in 2004 (versus approximately 1,200 contracts when Berkshire bought NetJets in 1998). Some clients (including me) enter into multiple contracts because they wish to use more than one type of aircraft, selecting for any given trip whichever type best fits the mission at hand.

NetJets earned a modest amount in the U.S. last year. But what we earned domestically was largely offset by losses in Europe. We are now, however, generating real momentum abroad. Contracts (including 25-hour cards that we ourselves market in Europe) increased from 364 to 693 during the year. We will again have a very significant European loss in 2005, but domestic earnings will likely put us in the black overall.

Europe has been expensive for NetJets – far more expensive than I anticipated – but it is essential to building a flight operation that will forever be in a class by itself. Our U.S. owners already want a quality service wherever they travel and their wish for flight hours abroad is certain to grow dramatically in the decades ahead. Last year, U.S. owners made 2,003 flights in Europe, up 22% from the previous year and 137% from 2000. Just as important, our European owners made 1,067 flights in the U.S., up 65% from 2003 and 239% from 2000.

Investments

We show below our common stock investments. Those that had a market value of more than $600 million at the end of 2004 are itemized.

			12/31/04	
		Percentage of		
Shares	_Company_	_Company Owned_	_Cost*_	_Market_
				(in $ millions)
151,610,700	American Express Company	12.1	$1,470	$ 8,546
200,000,000	The Coca-Cola Company	8.3	1,299	8,328
96,000,000	The Gillette Company	9.7	600	4,299
14,350,600	H&R Block, Inc....................................	8.7	223	703
6,708,760	M&T Bank Corporation	5.8	103	723
24,000,000	Moody's Corporation	16.2	499	2,084
2,338,961,000	PetroChina "H" shares (or equivalents)...	1.3	488	1,249
1,727,765	The Washington Post Company	18.1	11	1,698
56,448,380	Wells Fargo & Company........................	3.3	463	3,508
1,724,200	White Mountains Insurance....................	16.0	369	1,114
	Others		3,531	5,465
	Total Common Stocks		$9,056	$37,717

*This is our actual purchase price and also our tax basis; GAAP "cost" differs in a few cases because of write-ups or write-downs that have been required.

Some people may look at this table and view it as a list of stocks to be bought and sold based upon chart patterns, brokers' opinions, or estimates of near-term earnings. Charlie and I ignore such distractions and instead view our holdings as fractional ownerships in businesses. This is an important distinction. Indeed, this thinking has been the cornerstone of my investment behavior since I was 19. At that time I read Ben Graham's _The Intelligent Investor_, and the scales fell from my eyes. (Previously, I had been entranced by the stock market, but didn't have a clue about how to invest.)

Let's look at how the _businesses_ of our "Big Four" – American Express, Coca-Cola, Gillette and Wells Fargo – have fared since we bought into these companies. As the table shows, we invested $3.83 billion in the four, by way of multiple transactions between May 1988 and October 2003. On a composite basis, our dollar-weighted purchase date is July 1992. By yearend 2004, therefore, we had held these "business interests," on a weighted basis, about 12½ years.

In 2004, Berkshire's share of the group's earnings amounted to $1.2 billion. These earnings might legitimately be considered "normal." True, they were swelled because Gillette and Wells Fargo omitted option costs in their presentation of earnings; but on the other hand they were reduced because Coke had a non-recurring write-off.

Our share of the earnings of these four companies has grown almost every year, and now amounts to about 31.3% of our cost. Their cash distributions to us have also grown consistently, totaling $434 million in 2004, or about 11.3% of cost. All in all, the Big Four have delivered us a satisfactory, though far from spectacular, business result.

That's true as well of our experience in the market with the group. Since our original purchases, valuation gains have somewhat exceeded earnings growth because price/earnings ratios have increased. On a year-to-year basis, however, the business and market performances have often diverged, sometimes to an extraordinary degree. During The Great Bubble, market-value gains far outstripped the performance of the businesses. In the aftermath of the Bubble, the reverse was true.

Clearly, Berkshire's results would have been far better if I had caught this swing of the pendulum. That may seem easy to do when one looks through an always-clean, rear-view mirror. Unfortunately, however, it's the windshield through which investors must peer, and that glass is invariably fogged. Our huge positions add to the difficulty of our nimbly dancing in and out of holdings as valuations swing.

Nevertheless, I can properly be criticized for merely clucking about nose-bleed valuations during the Bubble rather than acting on my views. Though I said at the time that certain of the stocks we held were priced ahead of themselves, I underestimated just how severe the overvaluation was. I talked when I should have walked.

What Charlie and I would like is a little action now. We don't enjoy sitting on $43 billion of cash equivalents that are earning paltry returns. Instead, we yearn to buy more fractional interests similar to those we now own or – better still – more large businesses outright. We will do either, however, only when purchases can be made at prices that offer us the prospect of a reasonable return on our investment.

* * * * * * * * * * *

We've repeatedly emphasized that the "realized" gains that we report quarterly or annually are meaningless for analytical purposes. We have a huge amount of unrealized gains on our books, and our thinking about when, and if, to cash them depends not at all on a desire to report earnings at one specific time or another. A further complication in our reported gains occurs because GAAP requires that foreign exchange contracts be marked to market, a stipulation that causes unrealized gains or losses in these holdings to flow through our published earnings as if we had sold our positions.

Despite the problems enumerated, you may be interested in a breakdown of the gains we reported in 2003 and 2004. The data reflect actual sales except in the case of currency gains, which are a combination of sales and marks to market.

Category	Pre-Tax Gain (in $ millions)	
	2004	2003
Common Stocks	$ 870	$ 448
U.S. Government Bonds	104	1,485
Junk Bonds	730	1,138
Foreign Exchange Contracts	1,839	825
Other	(47)	233
Total	$3,496	$4,129

The junk bond profits include a foreign exchange component. When we bought these bonds in 2001 and 2002, we focused first, of course, on the credit quality of the issuers, all of which were American corporations. Some of these companies, however, had issued bonds denominated in foreign currencies. Because of our views on the dollar, we favored these for purchase when they were available.

As an example, we bought €254 million of Level 3 bonds (10 ¾% of 2008) in 2001 at 51.7% of par, and sold these at 85% of par in December 2004. This issue was traded in Euros that cost us 88¢ at the time of purchase but that brought $1.29 when we sold. Thus, of our $163 million overall gain, about $85 million came from the market's revised opinion about Level 3's credit quality, with the remaining $78 million resulting from the appreciation of the Euro. (In addition, we received cash interest during our holding period that amounted to about 25% annually on our dollar cost.)

* * * * * * * * * * *

The media continue to report that "Buffett buys" this or that stock. Statements like these are almost always based on filings Berkshire makes with the SEC and are therefore wrong. As I've said before, the stories should say "*Berkshire* buys."

Portrait of a Disciplined Investor
Lou Simpson

Year		Return from GEICO Equities	S&P Return	Relative Results
1980	....	23.7%	32.3%	(8.6%)
1981	....	5.4%	(5.0%)	10.4%
1982	....	45.8%	21.4%	24.4%
1983	....	36.0%	22.4%	13.6%
1984	....	21.8%	6.1%	15.7%
1985	....	45.8%	31.6%	14.2%
1986	....	38.7%	18.6%	20.1%
1987	....	(10.0%)	5.1%	(15.1%)
1988	....	30.0%	16.6%	13.4%
1989	....	36.1%	31.7%	4.4%
1990	....	(9.9%)	(3.1%)	(6.8%)
1991	....	56.5%	30.5%	26.0%
1992	....	10.8%	7.6%	3.2%
1993	....	4.6%	10.1%	(5.5%)
1994	....	13.4%	1.3%	12.1%
1995	....	39.8%	37.6%	2.2%
1996	....	29.2%	23.0%	6.2%
1997	....	24.6%	33.4%	(8.8%)
1998	....	18.6%	28.6%	(10.0%)
1999	....	7.2%	21.0%	(13.8%)
2000	....	20.9%	(9.1%)	30.0%
2001	....	5.2%	(11.9%)	17.1%
2002	....	(8.1%)	(22.1%)	14.0%
2003	....	38.3%	28.7%	9.6%
2004	....	16.9%	10.9%	6.0%
Average Annual Gain 1980-2004		20.3%	13.5%	6.8%

Even then, it is typically not I who make the buying decisions. Lou Simpson manages about $2½ billion of equities that are held by GEICO, and it is his transactions that Berkshire is usually reporting. Customarily his purchases are in the $200-$300 million range and are in companies that are smaller than the ones I focus on. Take a look at the facing page to see why Lou is a cinch to be inducted into the investment Hall of Fame.

You may be surprised to learn that Lou does not necessarily inform me about what he is doing. When Charlie and I assign responsibility, we truly hand over the baton – and we give it to Lou just as we do to our operating managers. Therefore, I typically learn of Lou's transactions about ten days after the end of each month. Sometimes, it should be added, I silently disagree with his decisions. But he's usually right.

Foreign Currencies

Berkshire owned about $21.4 billion of foreign exchange contracts at yearend, spread among 12 currencies. As I mentioned last year, holdings of this kind are a decided change for us. Before March 2002, neither Berkshire nor I had *ever* traded in currencies. But the evidence grows that our trade policies will put unremitting pressure on the dollar for many years to come – so since 2002 we've heeded that warning in setting our investment course. (As W.C. Fields once said when asked for a handout: "Sorry, son, all my money's tied up in currency.")

Be clear on one point: In no way does our thinking about currencies rest on doubts about America. We live in an extraordinarily rich country, the product of a system that values market economics, the rule of law and equality of opportunity. Our economy is far and away the strongest in the world and will continue to be. We are lucky to live here.

But as I argued in a November 10, 2003 article in *Fortune*, (available at berkshirehathaway.com), our country's trade practices are weighing down the dollar. The decline in its value has already been substantial, but is nevertheless likely to continue. Without policy changes, currency markets could even become disorderly and generate spillover effects, both political and financial. No one knows whether these problems will materialize. But such a scenario is a far-from-remote possibility that policymakers should be considering *now*. Their bent, however, is to lean toward not-so-benign neglect: A 318-page Congressional study of the consequences of unremitting trade deficits was published in November 2000 and has been gathering dust ever since. The study was ordered after the deficit hit a then-alarming $263 billion in 1999; by last year it had risen to $618 billion.

Charlie and I, it should be emphasized, believe that true trade – that is, the exchange of goods and services with other countries – is enormously beneficial for both us and them. Last year we had $1.15 trillion of such honest-to-God trade and the more of this, the better. But, as noted, our country also purchased an additional $618 billion in goods and services from the rest of the world that was unreciprocated. That is a staggering figure and one that has important consequences.

The balancing item to this one-way pseudo-trade — in economics there is always an offset — is a transfer of wealth from the U.S. to the rest of the world. The transfer may materialize in the form of IOUs our private or governmental institutions give to foreigners, or by way of their assuming ownership of our assets, such as stocks and real estate. In either case, Americans end up owning a reduced portion of our country while non-Americans own a greater part. This force-feeding of American wealth to the rest of the world is now proceeding at the rate of $1.8 billion daily, an increase of 20% since I wrote you last year. Consequently, other countries and their citizens now own a net of about $3 trillion of the U.S. A decade ago their net ownership was negligible.

The mention of trillions numbs most brains. A further source of confusion is that the current account deficit (the sum of three items, the most important by far being the trade deficit) and our national budget deficit are often lumped as "twins." They are anything but. They have different causes and different consequences.

A budget deficit in no way reduces the portion of the national pie that goes to Americans. As long as other countries and their citizens have no net ownership of the U.S., 100% of our country's output belongs to our citizens under *any* budget scenario, even one involving a huge deficit.

As a rich "family" awash in goods, Americans will argue through their legislators as to how government should redistribute the national output – that is who pays taxes and who receives governmental benefits. If "entitlement" promises from an earlier day have to be reexamined, "family members" will angrily debate among themselves as to who feels the pain. Maybe taxes will go up; maybe promises will be modified; maybe more internal debt will be issued. But when the fight is finished, *all* of the family's huge pie remains available for its members, however it is divided. No slice must be sent abroad.

Large and persisting current account deficits produce an entirely different result. As time passes, and as claims against us grow, we own less and less of what we produce. In effect, the rest of the world enjoys an ever-growing royalty on American output. Here, we are like a family that consistently overspends its income. As time passes, the family finds that it is working more and more for the "finance company" and less for itself.

Should we continue to run current account deficits comparable to those now prevailing, the net ownership of the U.S. by other countries and their citizens a decade from now will amount to roughly $11 trillion. And, if foreign investors were to earn only 5% on that net holding, we would need to send a net of $.55 trillion of goods and services abroad *every year* merely to service the U.S. investments then held by foreigners. At that date, a decade out, our GDP would probably total about $18 trillion (assuming low inflation, which is far from a sure thing). Therefore, our U.S. "family" would then be delivering 3% of its annual output to the rest of the world simply as tribute for the overindulgences of the past. In this case, unlike that involving budget deficits, the sons would truly pay for the sins of their fathers.

This annual royalty paid the world – which would not disappear unless the U.S. massively underconsumed and began to run consistent and large trade surpluses – would undoubtedly produce significant political unrest in the U.S. Americans would still be living very well, indeed better than now because of the growth in our economy. But they would chafe at the idea of perpetually paying tribute to their creditors and owners abroad. A country that is now aspiring to an "Ownership Society" will not find happiness in – and I'll use hyperbole here for emphasis – a "Sharecropper's Society." But that's precisely where our trade policies, supported by Republicans and Democrats alike, are taking us.

Many prominent U.S. financial figures, both in and out of government, have stated that our current-account deficits cannot persist. For instance, the minutes of the Federal Reserve Open Market Committee of June 29-30, 2004 say: "The staff noted that outsized external deficits could not be sustained indefinitely." But, despite the constant handwringing by luminaries, they offer no substantive suggestions to tame the burgeoning imbalance.

In the article I wrote for *Fortune* 16 months ago, I warned that "a gently declining dollar would not provide the answer." And so far it hasn't. Yet policymakers continue to hope for a "soft landing," meanwhile counseling other countries to stimulate (read "inflate") their economies and Americans to save more. In my view these admonitions miss the mark: There are deep-rooted structural problems that will cause America to continue to run a huge current-account deficit unless trade policies either change materially or the dollar declines by a degree that could prove unsettling to financial markets.

Proponents of the trade status quo are fond of quoting Adam Smith: "What is prudence in the conduct of every family can scarce be folly in that of a great kingdom. If a foreign country can supply us with a commodity cheaper than we ourselves can make it, better buy it of them with some part of the produce of our own industry, employed in a way in which we have some advantage."

I agree. Note, however, that Mr. Smith's statement refers to trade of *product* for product, not of *wealth* for product as our country is doing to the tune of $.6 trillion annually. Moreover, I am sure that he would never have suggested that "prudence" consisted of his "family" selling off part of its farm every day in order to finance its overconsumption. Yet that is just what the "great kingdom" called the United States is doing.

If the U.S. was running a $.6 trillion current-account *surplus*, commentators worldwide would violently condemn our policy, viewing it as an extreme form of "mercantilism" – a long-discredited economic strategy under which countries fostered exports, discouraged imports, and piled up treasure. I would condemn such a policy as well. But, in effect if not in intent, the rest of the world is practicing mercantilism in respect to the U.S., an act made possible by our vast store of assets and our pristine credit history. Indeed, the world would never let any other country use a credit card denominated in its own currency to the insatiable extent we are employing ours. Presently, most foreign investors are sanguine: they may view us as spending junkies, but they know we are *rich* junkies as well.

Our spendthrift behavior won't, however, be tolerated indefinitely. And though it's impossible to forecast just when and how the trade problem will be resolved, it's improbable that the resolution will foster an *increase* in the value of our currency relative to that of our trading partners.

We hope the U.S. adopts policies that will quickly and substantially reduce the current-account deficit. True, a prompt solution would likely cause Berkshire to record losses on its foreign-exchange contracts. But Berkshire's resources remain heavily concentrated in dollar-based assets, and both a strong dollar and a low-inflation environment are very much in our interest.

If you wish to keep abreast of trade and currency matters, read *The Financial Times*. This London-based paper has long been the leading source for daily international financial news and now has an excellent American edition. Both its reporting and commentary on trade are first-class.

* * * * * * * * * * * *

And, again, our usual caveat: macro-economics is a tough game in which few people, Charlie and I included, have demonstrated skill. We may well turn out to be wrong in our currency judgments. (Indeed, the fact that so many pundits now predict weakness for the dollar makes us uneasy.) If so, our mistake will be very public. The irony is that if we chose the opposite course, leaving all of Berkshire's assets in dollars even as they declined significantly in value, no one would notice our mistake.

John Maynard Keynes said in his masterful *The General Theory*: "Worldly wisdom teaches that it is better for reputation to fail conventionally than to succeed unconventionally." (Or, to put it in less elegant terms, lemmings as a class may be derided but never does an *individual* lemming get criticized.) From a reputational standpoint, Charlie and I run a clear risk with our foreign-exchange commitment. But we believe in managing Berkshire as if we owned 100% of it ourselves. And, were that the case, we would not be following a dollar-only policy.

Miscellaneous

- Last year I told you about a group of University of Tennessee finance students who played a key role in our $1.7 billion acquisition of Clayton Homes. Earlier, they had been brought to Omaha by their professor, Al Auxier – he brings a class every year – to tour Nebraska Furniture Mart and Borsheim's, eat at Gorat's and have a Q&A session with me at Kiewit Plaza. These visitors, like those who come for our annual meeting, leave impressed by both the city and its friendly residents.

  Other colleges and universities have now come calling. This school year we will have visiting classes, ranging in size from 30 to 100 students, from Chicago, Dartmouth (Tuck), Delaware State, Florida State, Indiana, Iowa, Iowa State, Maryland, Nebraska, Northwest Nazarene, Pennsylvania (Wharton), Stanford, Tennessee, Texas, Texas A&M, Toronto (Rotman), Union and Utah. Most of the students are MBA candidates, and I've been impressed by their quality. They are keenly interested in business and investments, but their questions indicate that they also have more on their minds than simply making money. I always feel good after meeting them.

At our sessions, I tell the newcomers the story of the Tennessee group and its spotting of Clayton Homes. I do this in the spirit of the farmer who enters his hen house with an ostrich egg and admonishes the flock: "I don't like to complain, girls, but this is just a small sample of what the competition is doing." To date, our new scouts have not brought us deals. But their mission in life has been made clear to them.

- You should be aware of an accounting rule that mildly distorts our financial statements in a pain-today, gain-tomorrow manner. Berkshire purchases life insurance policies from individuals and corporations who would otherwise surrender them for cash. As the new holder of the policies, we pay any premiums that become due and ultimately – when the original holder dies – collect the face value of the policies.

The original policyholder is usually in good health when we purchase the policy. Still, the price we pay for it is always well above its cash surrender value ("CSV"). Sometimes the original policyholder has borrowed against the CSV to make premium payments. In that case, the remaining CSV will be tiny and our purchase price will be a large multiple of what the original policyholder would have received, had he cashed out by surrendering it.

Under accounting rules, we must immediately charge as a realized capital loss the excess over CSV that we pay upon purchasing the policy. We also must make additional charges each year for the amount by which the premium we pay to keep the policy in force exceeds the increase in CSV. But obviously, we don't think these bookkeeping charges represent economic losses. If we did, we wouldn't buy the policies.

During 2004, we recorded net "losses" from the purchase of policies (and from the premium payments required to maintain them) totaling $207 million, which was charged against realized investment gains in our earnings statement (included in "other" in the table on page 17). When the proceeds from these policies are received in the future, we will record as realized investment gain the excess over the then-CSV.

- Two post-bubble governance reforms have been particularly useful at Berkshire, and I fault myself for not putting them in place many years ago. The first involves regular meetings of directors without the CEO present. I've sat on 19 boards, and on many occasions this process would have led to dubious plans being examined more thoroughly. In a few cases, CEO changes that were needed would also have been made more promptly. There is no downside to this process, and there are many possible benefits.

The second reform concerns the "whistleblower line," an arrangement through which employees can send information to me and the board's audit committee without fear of reprisal. Berkshire's extreme decentralization makes this system particularly valuable both to me and the committee. (In a sprawling "city" of 180,000 – Berkshire's current employee count – not every sparrow that falls will be noticed at headquarters.) Most of the complaints we have received are of "the guy next to me has bad breath" variety, but on occasion I have learned of important problems at our subsidiaries that I otherwise would have missed. The issues raised are usually not of a type discoverable by audit, but relate instead to personnel and business practices. Berkshire would be more valuable today if I had put in a whistleblower line decades ago.

- Charlie and I love the idea of shareholders thinking and behaving like owners. Sometimes that requires them to be pro-active. And in this arena large institutional owners should lead the way.

So far, however, the moves made by institutions have been less than awe-inspiring. Usually, they've focused on minutiae and ignored the three questions that truly count. First, does the company have the right CEO? Second, is he/she overreaching in terms of compensation? Third, are proposed acquisitions more likely to create or destroy per-share value?

On such questions, the interests of the CEO may well differ from those of the shareholders. Directors, moreover, sometimes lack the knowledge or gumption to overrule the CEO. Therefore, it's vital that large owners focus on these three questions and speak up when necessary.

Instead many simply follow a "checklist" approach to the issue *du jour*. Last year I was on the receiving end of a judgment reached in that manner. Several institutional shareholders and their advisors decided I lacked "independence" in my role as a director of Coca-Cola. One group wanted me removed from the board and another simply wanted me booted from the audit committee.

My first impulse was to secretly fund the group behind the second idea. Why anyone would wish to be on an audit committee is beyond me. But since directors must be assigned to one committee or another, and since no CEO wants me on his compensation committee, it's often been my lot to get an audit committee assignment. As it turned out, the institutions that opposed me failed and I was re-elected to the audit job. (I fought off the urge to ask for a recount.)

Some institutions questioned my "independence" because, among other things, McLane and Dairy Queen buy lots of Coke products. (Do they want us to favor Pepsi?) But independence is defined in Webster's as "not subject to control by others." I'm puzzled how anyone could conclude that our Coke purchases would "control" my decision-making when the counterweight is the well-being of $8 billion of Coke stock held by Berkshire. Assuming I'm even marginally rational, elementary arithmetic should make it clear that my heart and mind belong to the owners of Coke, not to its management.

I can't resist mentioning that Jesus understood the calibration of independence far more clearly than do the protesting institutions. In Matthew 6:21 He observed: "For where your treasure is, there will your heart be also." Even to an institutional investor, $8 billion should qualify as "treasure" that dwarfs any profits Berkshire might earn on its routine transactions with Coke.

Measured by the biblical standard, the Berkshire board is a model: (a) *every* director is a member of a family owning at least $4 million of stock; (b) *none* of these shares were acquired from Berkshire via options or grants; (c) *no* directors receive committee, consulting or board fees from the company that are more than a tiny portion of their annual income; and (d) although we have a standard corporate indemnity arrangement, we carry no liability insurance for directors.

At Berkshire, board members travel the same road as shareholders.

* * * * * * * * * * *

Charlie and I have seen much behavior confirming the Bible's "treasure" point. In our view, based on our considerable boardroom experience, the *least* independent directors are likely to be those who receive an important fraction of their annual income from the fees they receive for board service (and who hope as well to be recommended for election to other boards and thereby to boost their income further). Yet these are the very board members most often classed as "independent."

Most directors of this type are decent people and do a first-class job. But they wouldn't be human if they weren't tempted to thwart actions that would threaten their livelihood. Some may go on to succumb to such temptations.

Let's look at an example based upon circumstantial evidence. I have first-hand knowledge of a recent acquisition proposal (not from Berkshire) that was favored by management, blessed by the company's investment banker and slated to go forward at a price above the level at which the stock had sold for some years (or now sells for). In addition, a number of directors favored the transaction and wanted it proposed to shareholders.

Several of their brethren, however, each of whom received board and committee fees totaling about $100,000 annually, scuttled the proposal, which meant that shareholders never learned of this multi-billion offer. Non-management directors owned little stock except for shares they had received from the company. Their open-market purchases in recent years had meanwhile been nominal, even though the stock had sold far below the acquisition price proposed. In other words, these directors didn't want the shareholders to be offered X even though they had consistently declined the opportunity to buy stock for their own account at a fraction of X.

I don't know which directors opposed letting shareholders see the offer. But I do know that $100,000 is an important portion of the annual income of some of those deemed "independent," clearly meeting the Matthew 6:21 definition of "treasure." If the deal had gone through, these fees would have ended.

Neither the shareholders nor I will ever know what motivated the dissenters. Indeed they themselves will not likely know, given that self-interest inevitably blurs introspection. We do know one thing, though: At the same meeting at which the deal was rejected, the board voted itself a significant increase in directors' fees.

- While we are on the subject of self-interest, let's turn again to the most important accounting mechanism still available to CEOs who wish to overstate earnings: the non-expensing of stock options. The accomplices in perpetuating this absurdity have been many members of Congress who have defied the arguments put forth by all Big Four auditors, all members of the Financial Accounting Standards Board and virtually all investment professionals.

I'm enclosing an op-ed piece I wrote for *The Washington Post* describing a truly breathtaking bill that was passed 312-111 by the House last summer. Thanks to Senator Richard Shelby, the Senate didn't ratify the House's foolishness. And, to his great credit, Bill Donaldson, the investor-minded Chairman of the SEC, has stood firm against massive political pressure, generated by the check-waving CEOs who first muscled Congress in 1993 about the issue of option accounting and then repeated the tactic last year.

Because the attempts to obfuscate the stock-option issue continue, it's worth pointing out that no one – neither the FASB, nor investors generally, nor I – are talking about restricting the use of options in any way. Indeed, my successor at Berkshire may well receive much of his pay via options, albeit logically-structured ones in respect to 1) an appropriate strike price, 2) an escalation in price that reflects the retention of earnings, and 3) a ban on his quickly disposing of any shares purchased through options. We cheer arrangements that motivate managers, whether these be cash bonuses or options. And if a company is truly receiving value for the options it issues, we see no reason why recording their cost should cut down on their use.

The simple fact is that certain CEOs know their own compensation would be far more rationally determined if options were expensed. They also suspect that their stock would sell at a lower price if realistic accounting were employed, meaning that they would reap less in the market when they unloaded their personal holdings. To these CEOs such unpleasant prospects are a fate to be fought with all the resources they have at hand – even though the funds they use in that fight normally don't belong to them, but are instead put up by their shareholders.

Option-expensing is scheduled to become mandatory on June 15th. You can therefore expect intensified efforts to stall or emasculate this rule between now and then. Let your Congressman and Senators know what you think on this issue.

The Annual Meeting

There are two changes this year concerning the annual meeting. First, we have scheduled the meeting for the last Saturday in April (the 30th), rather than the usual first Saturday in May. This year Mother's Day falls on May 8, and it would be unfair to ask the employees of Borsheim's and Gorat's to take care of us at that special time – so we've moved everything up a week. Next year we'll return to our regular timing, holding the meeting on May 6, 2006.

Additionally, we are changing the sequence of events on meeting day, April 30. Just as always, the doors will open at the Qwest Center at 7 a.m. and the movie will be shown at 8:30. At 9:30, however, we will go directly to the question and answer period, which (allowing for lunch at the Qwest's stands) will last until 3:00. Then, after a short recess, Charlie and I will convene the annual meeting at 3:15.

We have made this change because a number of shareholders complained last year about the time consumed by two speakers who advocated proposals of limited interest to the majority of the audience – and who were no doubt relishing their chance to talk to a captive group of about 19,500. With our new procedure, those shareholders who wish to hear it all can stick around for the formal meeting and those who don't can leave – or better yet shop.

There will be plenty of opportunity for that pastime in the vast exhibition hall that adjoins the meeting area. Kelly Muchemore, the Flo Ziegfeld of Berkshire, put on a magnificent shopping extravaganza last year, and she says that was just a warm-up for this year. (Kelly, I am delighted to report, is getting married in October. I'm giving her away and suggested that she make a little history by holding the wedding at the annual meeting. She balked, however, when Charlie insisted that he be the ringbearer.)

Again we will showcase a 2,100 square foot Clayton home (featuring Acme brick, Shaw carpet, Johns Manville insulation, MiTek fasteners, Carefree awnings and NFM furniture). Take a tour through the home. Better yet, buy it.

GEICO will have a booth staffed by a number of its top counselors from around the country, all of them ready to supply you with auto insurance quotes. In most cases, GEICO will be able to give you a special shareholder discount (usually 8%). This special offer is permitted by 45 of the 50 jurisdictions in which we operate. Bring the details of your existing insurance and check out whether we can save you money.

On Saturday, at the Omaha airport, we will have the usual array of aircraft from NetJets® available for your inspection. Stop by the NetJets booth at the Qwest to learn about viewing these planes. Come to Omaha by bus; leave in your new plane.

The Bookworm shop did a terrific business last year selling Berkshire-related books. Displaying 18 titles, they sold 2,920 copies for $61,000. Since we charge the shop no rent (I must be getting soft), it gives shareholders a 20% discount. This year I've asked The Bookworm to add Graham Allison's *Nuclear Terrorism: The Ultimate Preventable Catastrophe*, a must-read for those concerned with the safety of our country. In addition, the shop will premiere *Poor Charlie's Almanack*, a book compiled by Peter Kaufman. Scholars have for too long debated whether Charlie is the reincarnation of Ben Franklin. This book should settle the question.

An attachment to the proxy material that is enclosed with this report explains how you can obtain the credential you will need for admission to the meeting and other events. As for plane, hotel and car reservations, we have again signed up American Express (800-799-6634) to give you special help. They do a terrific job for us each year, and I thank them for it.

At Nebraska Furniture Mart, located on a 77-acre site on 72nd Street between Dodge and Pacific, we will again be having "Berkshire Weekend" pricing. We initiated this special event at NFM eight years ago, and sales during the "Weekend" grew from $5.3 million in 1997 to $25.1 million in 2004 (up 45%

from a year earlier). Every year has set a new record, and on Saturday of last year, we had the largest single-day sales in NFM's history – $6.1 million.

To get the discount, you must make your purchases between Thursday, April 28 and Monday, May 2 inclusive, and also present your meeting credential. The period's special pricing will even apply to the products of several prestigious manufacturers that normally have ironclad rules against discounting but that, in the spirit of our shareholder weekend, have made an exception for you. We appreciate their cooperation. NFM is open from 10 a.m. to 9 p.m. Monday through Saturday, and 10 a.m. to 6 p.m. on Sunday. On Saturday this year, from 5:30 p.m. to 8 p.m. we are having a special affair for shareholders only. I'll be there, eating barbeque and drinking Coke.

Borsheim's – the largest jewelry store in the country except for Tiffany's Manhattan store – will have two shareholder-only events. The first will be a cocktail reception from 6 p.m. to 10 p.m. on Friday, April 29. The second, the main gala, will be from 9 a.m. to 4 p.m. on Sunday, May 1. On Saturday, we will be open until 6 p.m.

We will have huge crowds at Borsheim's throughout the weekend. For your convenience, therefore, shareholder prices will be available from Monday, April 25 through Saturday, May 7. During that period, just identify yourself as a shareholder through your meeting credentials or a brokerage statement.

Borsheim's operates on a gross margin that is fully twenty percentage points below that of its major rivals, even before the shareholders' discount. Last year, business over the weekend increased 73% from 2003, setting a record that will be tough to beat. Show me it can be done.

In a tent outside of Borsheim's, Patrick Wolff, twice U.S. chess champion, will take on all comers in groups of six – blindfolded. Additionally, we will have Bob Hamman and Sharon Osberg, two of the world's top bridge experts, available to play with our shareholders on Sunday afternoon. They plan to keep their eyes *open* – but Bob never sorts his cards, even when playing for a national championship.

Gorat's – my favorite steakhouse – will again be open exclusively for Berkshire shareholders on Sunday, May 1, and will be serving from 4 p.m. until 10 p.m. Please remember that to come to Gorat's on that day, you must have a reservation. To make one, call 402-551-3733 on April 1 (*but not before*). If Sunday is sold out, try Gorat's on one of the other evenings you will be in town. Enhance your reputation as an epicure by ordering, as I do, a rare T-bone with a double helping of hash browns.

We will again have a special reception from 4:00 to 5:30 on Saturday afternoon for shareholders who have come from outside of North America. Every year our meeting draws many people from around the globe, and Charlie and I want to be sure we personally greet those who have come so far. Last year we enjoyed meeting more than 400 of you including at least 100 from Australia. Any shareholder who comes from other than the U.S. or Canada will be given a special credential and instructions for attending this function.

* * * * * * * * * * * *

Charlie and I are lucky. We have jobs that we love and are helped every day in a myriad of ways by talented and cheerful associates. No wonder we tap-dance to work. But nothing is more fun for us than getting together with our shareholder-partners at Berkshire's annual meeting. So join us on April 30th at the Qwest for our annual Woodstock for Capitalists.

February 28, 2005

Warren E. Buffett
Chairman of the Board

BERKSHIRE HATHAWAY INC.

To the Shareholders of Berkshire Hathaway Inc.:

Our gain in net worth during 2005 was $5.6 billion, which increased the per-share book value of both our Class A and Class B stock by 6.4%. Over the last 41 years (that is, since present management took over) book value has grown from $19 to $59,377, a rate of 21.5% compounded annually.*

Berkshire had a decent year in 2005. We initiated five acquisitions (two of which have yet to close) and most of our operating subsidiaries prospered. Even our insurance business in its entirety did well, though Hurricane Katrina inflicted record losses on both Berkshire and the industry. We estimate our loss from Katrina at $2.5 billion – and her ugly sisters, Rita and Wilma, cost us an additional $.9 billion.

Credit GEICO – and its brilliant CEO, Tony Nicely – for our stellar insurance results in a disaster-ridden year. One statistic stands out: In just two years, GEICO improved its productivity by *32%*. Remarkably, employment fell by 4% even as policy count grew by 26% – and more gains are in store. When we drive unit costs down in such a dramatic manner, we can offer ever-greater value to our customers. The payoff: Last year, GEICO gained market-share, earned commendable profits and strengthened its brand. If you have a new son or grandson in 2006, name him Tony.

* * * * * * * * * * * *

My goal in writing this report is to give you the information you need to estimate Berkshire's intrinsic value. I say "estimate" because calculations of intrinsic value, though all-important, are necessarily imprecise and often seriously wrong. The more uncertain the future of a business, the more possibility there is that the calculation will be wildly off-base. (For an explanation of intrinsic value, see pages 77 – 78.) Here Berkshire has some advantages: a wide variety of relatively-stable earnings streams, combined with great liquidity and minimum debt. These factors mean that Berkshire's intrinsic value can be more precisely calculated than can the intrinsic value of most companies.

Yet if precision is aided by Berkshire's financial characteristics, the job of calculating intrinsic value has been made more complex by the mere presence of so many earnings streams. Back in 1965, when we owned only a small textile operation, the task of calculating intrinsic value was a snap. Now we own 68 distinct businesses with widely disparate operating and financial characteristics. This array of unrelated enterprises, coupled with our massive investment holdings, makes it impossible for you to simply examine our consolidated financial statements and arrive at an informed estimate of intrinsic value.

We have attempted to ease this problem by clustering our businesses into four logical groups, each of which we discuss later in this report. In these discussions, we will provide the key figures for both the group and its important components. Of course, the value of Berkshire may be either greater or less than the sum of these four parts. The outcome depends on whether our many units function better or worse by being part of a larger enterprise and whether capital allocation improves or deteriorates when it is under the direction of a holding company. In other words, does Berkshire ownership bring anything to the party, or would our shareholders be better off if they directly owned shares in each of our 68 businesses? These are important questions but ones that you will have to answer for yourself.

Before we look at our individual businesses, however, let's review two sets of figures that show where we've come from and where we are now. The first set is the amount of investments (including cash and cash-equivalents) we own on a per-share basis. In making this calculation, we exclude investments held in our finance operation because these are largely offset by borrowings:

---

*All figures used in this report apply to Berkshire's A shares, the successor to the only stock that the company had outstanding before 1996. The B shares have an economic interest equal to 1/30th that of the A.

Year	Per-Share Investments*
1965	$ 4
1975	159
1985	2,407
1995	21,817
2005	$74,129
Compound Growth Rate 1965-2005	28.0%
Compound Growth Rate 1995-2005	13.0%

*Net of minority interests

In addition to these marketable securities, which with minor exceptions are held in our insurance companies, we own a wide variety of non-insurance businesses. Below, we show the pre-tax earnings (excluding goodwill amortization) of these businesses, again on a per-share basis:

Year	Per-Share Earnings*
1965	$ 4
1975	4
1985	52
1995	175
2005	$2,441
Compound Growth Rate 1965-2005	17.2%
Compound Growth Rate 1995-2005	30.2%

*Pre-tax and net of minority interests

When growth rates are under discussion, it will pay you to be suspicious as to why the beginning and terminal years have been selected. If either year was aberrational, any calculation of growth will be distorted. In particular, a base year in which earnings were poor can produce a breathtaking, but meaningless, growth rate. In the table above, however, the base year of 1965 was abnormally *good*; Berkshire earned more money in that year than it did in all but one of the previous ten.

As you can see from the two tables, the comparative growth rates of Berkshire's two elements of value have changed in the last decade, a result reflecting our ever-increasing emphasis on business acquisitions. Nevertheless, Charlie Munger, Berkshire's Vice Chairman and my partner, and I want to increase the figures in *both* tables. In this ambition, we hope – metaphorically – to avoid the fate of the elderly couple who had been romantically challenged for some time. As they finished dinner on their 50th anniversary, however, the wife – stimulated by soft music, wine and candlelight – felt a long-absent tickle and demurely suggested to her husband that they go upstairs and make love. He agonized for a moment and then replied, "I can do one or the other, but not both."

Acquisitions

Over the years, our current businesses, in aggregate, should deliver modest growth in operating earnings. But they will not in themselves produce truly satisfactory gains. We will need major acquisitions to get that job done.

In this quest, 2005 was encouraging. We agreed to five purchases: two that were completed last year, one that closed after yearend and two others that we expect to close soon. None of the deals involve the issuance of Berkshire shares. That's a crucial, but often ignored, point: When a management proudly acquires another company for stock, the shareholders of the acquirer are concurrently selling part of their interest in everything they own. I've made this kind of deal a few times myself – and, on balance, my actions have cost you money.

4

Here are last year's purchases:

- On June 30 we bought Medical Protective Company ("MedPro"), a 106-year-old medical malpractice insurer based in Fort Wayne. Malpractice insurance is tough to underwrite and has proved to be a graveyard for many insurers. MedPro nevertheless should do well. It will have the attitudinal advantage that all Berkshire insurers share, wherein underwriting discipline trumps all other goals. Additionally, as part of Berkshire, MedPro has financial strength far exceeding that of its competitors, a quality assuring doctors that long-to-settle claims will not end up back on their doorstep because their insurer failed. Finally, the company has a smart and energetic CEO, Tim Kenesey, who instinctively thinks like a Berkshire manager.

- Forest River, our second acquisition, closed on August 31. A couple of months earlier, on June 21, I received a two-page fax telling me – point by point – why Forest River met the acquisition criteria we set forth on page 25 of this report. I had not before heard of the company, a recreational vehicle manufacturer with $1.6 billion of sales, nor of Pete Liegl, its owner and manager. But the fax made sense, and I immediately asked for more figures. These came the next morning, and that afternoon I made Pete an offer. On June 28, we shook hands on a deal.

  Pete is a remarkable entrepreneur. Some years back, he sold his business, then far smaller than today, to an LBO operator who promptly began telling him how to run the place. Before long, Pete left, and the business soon sunk into bankruptcy. Pete then repurchased it. You can be sure that *I* won't be telling Pete how to manage his operation.

  Forest River has 60 plants, 5,400 employees and has consistently gained share in the RV business, while also expanding into other areas such as boats. Pete is 61 – and definitely in an acceleration mode. Read the piece from *RV Business* that accompanies this report, and you'll see why Pete and Berkshire are made for each other.

- On November 12, 2005, an article ran in The Wall Street Journal dealing with Berkshire's unusual acquisition and managerial practices. In it Pete declared, "It was easier to sell my business than to renew my driver's license."

  In New York, Cathy Baron Tamraz read the article, and it struck a chord. On November 21, she sent me a letter that began, "As president of Business Wire, I'd like to introduce you to my company, as I believe it fits the profile of Berkshire Hathaway subsidiary companies as detailed in a recent Wall Street Journal article."

  By the time I finished Cathy's two-page letter, I felt Business Wire and Berkshire were a fit. I particularly liked her penultimate paragraph: "We run a tight ship and keep unnecessary spending under wraps. No secretaries or management layers here. Yet we'll invest big dollars to gain a technological advantage and move the business forward."

  I promptly gave Cathy a call, and before long Berkshire had reached agreement with Business Wire's controlling shareholder, Lorry Lokey, who founded the company in 1961 (and who had just made Cathy CEO). I love success stories like Lorry's. Today 78, he has built a company that disseminates information in 150 countries for 25,000 clients. His story, like those of many entrepreneurs who have selected Berkshire as a home for their life's work, is an example of what can happen when a good idea, a talented individual and hard work converge.

- In December we agreed to buy 81% of Applied Underwriters, a company that offers a combination of payroll services and workers' compensation insurance to small businesses. A majority of Applied's customers are located in California.

5

In 1998, though, when the company had 12 employees, it acquired an Omaha-based operation with 24 employees that offered a somewhat-similar service. Sid Ferenc and Steve Menzies, who have built Applied's remarkable business, concluded that Omaha had many advantages as an operational base – a brilliant insight, I might add – and today 400 of the company's 479 employees are located here.

Less than a year ago, Applied entered into a large reinsurance contract with Ajit Jain, the extraordinary manager of National Indemnity's reinsurance division. Ajit was impressed by Sid and Steve, and they liked Berkshire's method of operation. So we decided to join forces. We are pleased that Sid and Steve retain 19% of Applied. They started on a shoestring only 12 years ago, and it will be fun to see what they can accomplish with Berkshire's backing.

- Last spring, MidAmerican Energy, our 80.5% owned subsidiary, agreed to buy PacifiCorp, a major electric utility serving six Western states. An acquisition of this sort requires many regulatory approvals, but we've now obtained these and expect to close this transaction soon. Berkshire will then buy $3.4 billion of MidAmerican's common stock, which MidAmerican will supplement with $1.7 billion of borrowing to complete the purchase. You can't expect to earn outsized profits in regulated utilities, but the industry offers owners the opportunity to deploy large sums at fair returns – and therefore, it makes good sense for Berkshire. A few years back, I said that we hoped to make some very large purchases in the utility field. Note the plural – we'll be looking for more.

In addition to buying these new operations, we continue to make "bolt-on" acquisitions. Some aren't so small: Shaw, our carpet operation, spent about $550 million last year on two purchases that furthered its vertical integration and should improve its profit margin in the future. XTRA and Clayton Homes also made value-enhancing acquisitions.

Unlike many business buyers, Berkshire has no "exit strategy." We buy to keep. We do, though, have an entrance strategy, looking for businesses in this country or abroad that meet our six criteria and are available at a price that will produce a reasonable return. If you have a business that fits, give me a call. Like a hopeful teenage girl, I'll be waiting by the phone.

Insurance

Let's now talk about our four sectors and start with insurance, our core business. What counts here is the amount of "float" and its cost over time.

For new readers, let me explain. "Float" is money that doesn't belong to us but that we temporarily hold. Most of our float arises because (1) premiums are paid upfront though the service we provide – insurance protection – is delivered over a period that usually covers a year and; (2) loss events that occur today do not always result in our immediately paying claims, because it sometimes takes many years for losses to be reported (asbestos losses would be an example), negotiated and settled. The $20 million of float that came with our 1967 entry into insurance has now increased – both by way of internal growth and acquisitions – to $49 billion.

Float is wonderful – *if* it doesn't come at a high price. Its cost is determined by underwriting results, meaning how the expenses and losses we will ultimately pay compare with the premiums we have received. When an insurer earns an underwriting profit – as has been the case at Berkshire in about half of the 39 years we have been in the insurance business – float is better than free. In such years, we are actually paid for holding other people's money. For most insurers, however, life has been far more difficult: In aggregate, the property-casualty industry almost invariably operates at an underwriting loss. When that loss is large, float becomes expensive, sometimes devastatingly so.

In 2004 our float cost us less than nothing, and I told you that we had a chance – absent a mega-catastrophe – of no-cost float in 2005. But we *had* the mega-cat, and as a specialist in that coverage, Berkshire suffered hurricane losses of $3.4 billion. Nevertheless, our float was costless in 2005 because of the superb results we had in our other insurance activities, particularly at GEICO.

* * * * * * * * * * *

Auto policies in force grew by 12.1% at GEICO, a gain increasing its market share of U.S. private passenger auto business from about 5.6% to about 6.1%. Auto insurance is a big business: Each share-point equates to $1.6 billion in sales.

While our brand strength is not quantifiable, I believe it also grew significantly. When Berkshire acquired control of GEICO in 1996, its annual advertising expenditures were $31 million. Last year we were up to $502 million. And I can't wait to spend more.

Our advertising works because we have a great story to tell: More people can save money by insuring with us than is the case with any other national carrier offering policies to all comers. (Some specialized auto insurers do particularly well for applicants fitting into their niches; also, because our national competitors use rating systems that differ from ours, they will sometimes beat our price.) Last year, we achieved by far the highest conversion rate – the percentage of internet and phone quotes turned into sales – in our history. This is powerful evidence that our prices are more attractive relative to the competition than ever before. Test us by going to GEICO.com or by calling 800-847-7536. Be sure to indicate you are a shareholder because that fact will often qualify you for a discount.

I told you last year about GEICO's entry into New Jersey in August, 2004. Drivers in that state love us. Our retention rate there for new policyholders is running higher than in any other state, and by sometime in 2007, GEICO is likely to become the third largest auto insurer in New Jersey. There, as elsewhere, our low costs allow low prices that lead to steady gains in profitable business.

That simple formula immediately impressed me 55 years ago when I first discovered GEICO. Indeed, at age 21, I wrote an article about the company – it's reproduced on page 24 – when its market value was $7 million. As you can see, I called GEICO "The Security I Like Best." And that's what I still call it.

* * * * * * * * * * *

We have major reinsurance operations at General Re and National Indemnity. The former is run by Joe Brandon and Tad Montross, the latter by Ajit Jain. Both units performed well in 2005 considering the extraordinary hurricane losses that battered the industry.

It's an open question whether atmospheric, oceanic or other causal factors have dramatically changed the frequency or intensity of hurricanes. Recent experience is worrisome. We know, for instance, that in the 100 years before 2004, about 59 hurricanes of Category 3 strength, or greater, hit the Southeastern and Gulf Coast states, and that only three of these were Category 5s. We further know that in 2004 there were three Category 3 storms that hammered those areas and that these were followed by four more in 2005, one of them, Katrina, the most destructive hurricane in industry history. Moreover, there were three Category 5s near the coast last year that fortunately weakened before landfall.

Was this onslaught of more frequent and more intense storms merely an anomaly? Or was it caused by changes in climate, water temperature or other variables we don't fully understand? And could these factors be developing in a manner that will soon produce disasters dwarfing Katrina?

Joe, Ajit and I don't know the answer to these all-important questions. What we do know is that our ignorance means we must follow the course prescribed by Pascal in his famous wager about the existence of God. As you may recall, he concluded that since he didn't know the answer, his personal gain/loss ratio dictated an affirmative conclusion.

So guided, we've concluded that we should now write mega-cat policies only at prices far higher than prevailed last year – and then only with an aggregate exposure that would not cause us distress if shifts in some important variable produce far more costly storms in the near future. To a lesser degree, we felt this way after 2004 – and cut back our writings when prices didn't move. Now our caution has intensified. If prices seem appropriate, however, we continue to have both the ability and the appetite to be the largest writer of mega-cat coverage in the world.

* * * * * * * * * * * *

Our smaller insurers, with MedPro added to the fold, delivered truly outstanding results last year. However, what you see in the table below does not do full justice to their performance. That's because we increased the loss reserves of MedPro by about $125 million immediately after our purchase.

No one knows with any precision what amount will be required to pay the claims we inherited. Medical malpractice insurance is a "long-tail" line, meaning that claims often take many years to settle. In addition, there are other losses that have occurred, but that we won't even hear about for some time. One thing, though, we have learned – the hard way – after many years in the business: Surprises in insurance are far from symmetrical. You are lucky if you get one that is pleasant for every ten that go the other way. Too often, however, insurers react to looming loss problems with optimism. They behave like the fellow in a switchblade fight who, after his opponent has taken a mighty swipe at his throat, exclaimed, "You never touched me." His adversary's reply: "Just wait until you try to shake your head."

Excluding the reserves we added for prior periods, MedPro wrote at an underwriting profit. And our other primary companies, in aggregate, had an underwriting profit of $324 million on $1,270 million of volume. This is an extraordinary result, and our thanks go to Rod Eldred of Berkshire Hathaway Homestate Companies, John Kizer of Central States Indemnity, Tom Nerney of U. S. Liability, Don Towle of Kansas Bankers Surety and Don Wurster of National Indemnity.

Here's the overall tally on our underwriting and float for each major sector of insurance:

	(in $ millions)			
	Underwriting Profit (Loss)		Yearend Float	
Insurance Operations	_2005_	_2004_	_2005_	_2004_
General Re	$(334)	$ 3	$22,920	$23,120
B-H Reinsurance..............	(1,069)	417	16,233	15,278
GEICO	1,221	970	6,692	5,960
Other Primary.................	235*	161	3,442	1,736
Total...............................	$ 53	$1,551	$49,287	$46,094

*Includes MedPro from June 30, 2005.

Regulated Utility Business

We have an 80.5% (fully diluted) interest in MidAmerican Energy Holdings, which owns a wide variety of utility operations. The largest of these are (1) Yorkshire Electricity and Northern Electric, whose 3.7 million electric customers make it the third largest distributor of electricity in the U.K.; (2) MidAmerican Energy, which serves 706,000 electric customers, primarily in Iowa; and (3) Kern River and Northern Natural pipelines, which carry 7.8% of the natural gas consumed in the U.S. When our PacifiCorp acquisition closes, we will add 1.6 million electric customers in six Western states, with Oregon and Utah providing us the most business. This transaction will increase MidAmerican's revenues by $3.3 billion and its assets by $14.1 billion.

The Public Utility Holding Company Act ("PUHCA") was repealed on August 8, 2005, a milestone that allowed Berkshire to convert its MidAmerican preferred stock into voting common shares on February 9, 2006. This conversion ended a convoluted corporate arrangement that PUHCA had forced upon us. Now we have 83.4% of both the common stock and the votes at MidAmerican, which allows us to consolidate the company's income for financial accounting and tax purposes. Our true economic interest, however, is the aforementioned 80.5%, since there are options outstanding that are sure to be exercised within a few years and that upon exercise will dilute our ownership.

Though our voting power has increased dramatically, the dynamics of our four-party ownership have not changed at all. We view MidAmerican as a partnership among Berkshire, Walter Scott, and two terrific managers, Dave Sokol and Greg Abel. It's unimportant how many votes each party has; we will make major moves only when we are unanimous in thinking them wise. Five years of working with Dave, Greg and Walter have underscored my original belief: Berkshire couldn't have better partners.

You will notice that this year we have provided you with two balance sheets, one representing our actual figures per GAAP on December 31, 2005 (which does *not* consolidate MidAmerican) and one that reflects the subsequent conversion of our preferred. All future financial reports of Berkshire will include MidAmerican's figures.

Somewhat incongruously, MidAmerican owns the second largest real estate brokerage firm in the U.S. And it's a gem. The parent company's name is HomeServices of America, but our 19,200 agents operate through 18 locally-branded firms. Aided by three small acquisitions, we participated in $64 billion of transactions last year, up 6.5% from 2004.

Currently, the white-hot market in residential real estate of recent years is cooling down, and that should lead to additional acquisition possibilities for us. Both we and Ron Peltier, the company's CEO, expect HomeServices to be far larger a decade from now.

Here are some key figures on MidAmerican's operations:

	Earnings (in $ millions)	
	2005	2004
U.K. utilities	$ 308	$ 326
Iowa utility	288	268
Pipelines	309	288
HomeServices	148	130
Other (net)	107	172
Income (loss) from discontinued zinc project	8	(579)
Earnings before corporate interest and taxes	1,168	605
Interest, other than to Berkshire	(200)	(212)
Interest on Berkshire junior debt	(157)	(170)
Income tax	(248)	(53)
Net earnings	$ 563	$ 170
Earnings applicable to Berkshire*	$ 523	$ 237
Debt owed to others	10,296	10,528
Debt owed to Berkshire	1,289	1,478

*Includes interest earned by Berkshire (net of related income taxes) of $102 in 2005 and $110 in 2004.

Finance and Financial Products

The star of our finance sector is Clayton Homes, masterfully run by Kevin Clayton. He does not owe his brilliant record to a rising tide: The manufactured-housing business has been disappointing since Berkshire purchased Clayton in 2003. Industry sales have stagnated at 40-year lows, and the recent uptick from Katrina-related demand will almost certainly be short-lived. In recent years, many industry participants have suffered losses, and only Clayton has earned significant money.

In this brutal environment Clayton has bought a large amount of manufactured-housing loans from major banks that found them unprofitable and difficult to service. Clayton's operating expertise and Berkshire's financial resources have made this an excellent business for us and one in which we are preeminent. We presently service $17 billion of loans, compared to $5.4 billon at the time of our purchase. Moreover, Clayton now owns $9.6 billion of its servicing portfolio, a position built up almost entirely since Berkshire entered the picture.

To finance this portfolio, Clayton borrows money from Berkshire, which in turn borrows the same amount publicly. For the use of its credit, Berkshire charges Clayton a one percentage-point markup on its borrowing cost. In 2005, the cost to Clayton for this arrangement was $83 million. That amount is included in "Other" income in the table on the facing page, and Clayton's earnings of $416 million are after deducting this payment.

On the manufacturing side, Clayton has also been active. To its original base of twenty plants, it first added twelve more in 2004 by way of the bankruptcy purchase of Oakwood, which just a few years earlier was one of the largest companies in the business. Then in 2005 Clayton purchased Karsten, a four-plant operation that greatly strengthens Clayton's position on the West Coast.

* * * * * * * * * * *

Long ago, Mark Twain said: "A man who tries to carry a cat home by its tail will learn a lesson that can be learned in no other way." If Twain were around now, he might try winding up a derivatives business. After a few days, he would opt for cats.

We lost $104 million pre-tax last year in our continuing attempt to exit Gen Re's derivative operation. Our aggregate losses since we began this endeavor total $404 million.

Originally we had 23,218 contracts outstanding. By the start of 2005 we were down to 2,890. You might expect that our losses would have been stemmed by this point, but the blood has kept flowing. Reducing our inventory to 741 contracts last year cost us the $104 million mentioned above.

Remember that the rationale for establishing this unit in 1990 was Gen Re's wish to meet the needs of insurance clients. Yet one of the contracts we liquidated in 2005 had a term of 100 years! It's difficult to imagine what "need" such a contract could fulfill except, perhaps, the need of a compensation-conscious trader to have a long-dated contract on his books. Long contracts, or alternatively those with multiple variables, are the most difficult to mark to market (the standard procedure used in accounting for derivatives) and provide the most opportunity for "imagination" when traders are estimating their value. Small wonder that traders promote them.

A business in which huge amounts of compensation flow from assumed numbers is obviously fraught with danger. When two traders execute a transaction that has several, sometimes esoteric, variables and a far-off settlement date, their respective firms must subsequently value these contracts whenever they calculate their earnings. A given contract may be valued at one price by Firm A and at another by Firm B. You can bet that the valuation differences – and I'm personally familiar with several that were *huge* – tend to be tilted in a direction favoring higher earnings at each firm. It's a strange world in which two parties can carry out a paper transaction that each can promptly report as profitable.

I dwell on our experience in derivatives each year for two reasons. One is personal and unpleasant. The hard fact is that I have cost you a lot of money by not moving immediately to close down

Gen Re's trading operation. Both Charlie and I knew at the time of the Gen Re purchase that it was a problem and told its management that we wanted to exit the business. It was my responsibility to make sure that happened. Rather than address the situation head on, however, I wasted several years while we attempted to sell the operation. That was a doomed endeavor because no realistic solution could have extricated us from the maze of liabilities that was going to exist for decades. Our obligations were particularly worrisome because their potential to explode could not be measured. Moreover, if severe trouble occurred, we knew it was likely to correlate with problems elsewhere in financial markets.

So I failed in my attempt to exit painlessly, and in the meantime more trades were put on the books. Fault me for dithering. (Charlie calls it thumb-sucking.) When a problem exists, whether in personnel or in business operations, the time to act is *now*.

The second reason I regularly describe our problems in this area lies in the hope that our experiences may prove instructive for managers, auditors and regulators. In a sense, we are a canary in this business coal mine and should sing a song of warning as we expire. The number and value of derivative contracts outstanding in the world continues to mushroom and is now a multiple of what existed in 1998, the last time that financial chaos erupted.

Our experience should be particularly sobering because we were a better-than-average candidate to exit gracefully. Gen Re was a relatively minor operator in the derivatives field. It has had the good fortune to unwind its supposedly liquid positions in a benign market, all the while free of financial or other pressures that might have forced it to conduct the liquidation in a less-than-efficient manner. Our accounting in the past was conventional and actually thought to be conservative. Additionally, we know of no bad behavior by anyone involved.

It could be a different story for others in the future. Imagine, if you will, one or more firms (troubles often spread) with positions that are many multiples of ours attempting to liquidate in chaotic markets and under extreme, and well-publicized, pressures. This is a scenario to which much attention should be given now rather than after the fact. The time to have considered – and improved – the reliability of New Orleans' levees was *before* Katrina.

When we finally wind up Gen Re Securities, my feelings about its departure will be akin to those expressed in a country song, "My wife ran away with my best friend, and I sure miss him a lot."

* * * * * * * * * * * *

Below are the results of our various finance and financial products activities:

| | Pre-Tax Earnings | | Interest-Bearing Liabilities | |
| | *(in $ millions)* | | | |
	2005	*2004*	*2005*	*2004*
Trading – ordinary income	$ 200	$ 264	$1,061	$5,751
Gen Re Securities (loss)	(104)	(44)	2,617*	5,437*
Life and annuity operation	11	(57)	2,461	2,467
Value Capital (loss)	(33)	30	N/A	N/A
Leasing operations	173	92	370	391
Manufactured-housing finance (Clayton)	416	192	9,299	3,636
Other	159	107	N/A	N/A
Income before capital gains	822	584		
Trading – capital gains (losses)	(234)	1,750		
Total	$ 588	$2,334		

*Includes all liabilities

Manufacturing, Service and Retailing Operations

Our activities in this part of Berkshire cover the waterfront. Let's look, though, at a summary balance sheet and earnings statement for the entire group.

Balance Sheet 12/31/05 (in $ millions)

Assets		Liabilities and Equity	
Cash and equivalents	$ 1,004	Notes payable	$ 1,469
Accounts and notes receivable	3,287	Other current liabilities	5,371
Inventory	4,143	Total current liabilities	6,840
Other current assets	342		
Total current assets	8,776		
Goodwill and other intangibles	9,260	Deferred taxes	338
Fixed assets	7,148	Term debt and other liabilities	2,188
Other assets	1,021	Equity	16,839
	$26,205		$26,205

Earnings Statement (in $ millions)

	2005	2004	2003
Revenues	$46,896	$44,142	$32,106
Operating expenses (including depreciation of $699 in 2005, $676 in 2004 and $605 in 2003)	44,190	41,604	29,885
Interest expense (net)	83	57	64
Pre-tax earnings	2,623	2,481	2,157
Income taxes	977	941	813
Net income	$ 1,646	$ 1,540	$ 1,344

This eclectic collection, which sells products ranging from Dilly Bars to fractional interests in Boeing 737s, earned a very respectable 22.2% on average tangible net worth last year. It's noteworthy also that these operations used only minor financial leverage in achieving that return. Clearly, we own some terrific businesses. We purchased many of them, however, at substantial premiums to net worth – a point reflected in the goodwill item shown on the balance sheet – and that fact reduces the earnings on our average *carrying* value to 10.1%.

Here are the pre-tax earnings for the larger categories or units.

	Pre-Tax Earnings (in $ millions)	
	2005	2004
Building Products	$ 751	$ 643
Shaw Industries	485	466
Apparel & Footwear	348	325
Retailing of Jewelry, Home Furnishings and Candy	257	215
Flight Services	120	191
McLane	217	228
Other businesses	445	413
	$2,623	$2,481

- In both our building-products companies and at Shaw, we continue to be hit by rising costs for raw materials and energy. Most of these operations are significant users of oil (or more specifically, petrochemicals) and natural gas. And prices for these commodities have soared.

  We, likewise, have raised prices on many products, but there are often lags before increases become effective. Nevertheless, both our building-products operations and Shaw delivered respectable results in 2005, a fact attributable to their strong business franchises and able managements.

- In apparel, our largest unit, Fruit of the Loom, again increased earnings and market-share. You know, of course, of our leadership position in men's and boys' underwear, in which we account for about 48.7% of the sales recorded by mass-marketers (Wal-Mart, Target, etc.). That's up from 44.2% in 2002, when we acquired the company. Operating from a smaller base, we have made still greater gains in intimate apparel for women and girls that is sold by the mass-marketers, climbing from 13.7% of their sales in 2002 to 24.7% in 2005. A gain like that in a major category doesn't come easy. Thank John Holland, Fruit's extraordinary CEO, for making this happen.

- I told you last year that Ben Bridge (jewelry) and R. C. Willey (home furnishings) had same-store sales gains far above the average of their industries. You might think that blow-out figures in one year would make comparisons difficult in the following year. But Ed and Jon Bridge at their operation and Scott Hymas at R. C. Willey were more than up to this challenge. Ben Bridge had a 6.6% same-store gain in 2005, and R. C. Willey came in at 9.9%.

  Our never-on-Sunday approach at R. C. Willey continues to overwhelm seven-day competitors as we roll out stores in new markets. The Boise store, about which I was such a skeptic a few years back, had a 21% gain in 2005, coming off a 10% gain in 2004. Our new Reno store, opened in November, broke out of the gate fast with sales that exceeded Boise's early pace, and we will begin business in Sacramento in June. If this store succeeds as I expect it to, Californians will see many more R. C. Willey stores in the years to come.

- In flight services, earnings improved at FlightSafety as corporate aviation continued its rebound. To support growth, we invest heavily in new simulators. Our most recent expansion, bringing us to 42 training centers, is a major facility at Farnborough, England that opened in September. When it is fully built out in 2007, we will have invested more than $100 million in the building and its 15 simulators. Bruce Whitman, FlightSafety's able CEO, makes sure that no competitor comes close to offering the breadth and depth of services that we do.

  Operating results at NetJets were a different story. I said last year that this business would earn money in 2005 – and I was dead wrong.

  Our European operation, it should be noted, showed both excellent growth and a reduced loss. Customer contracts there increased by 37%. We are the only fractional-ownership operation of any size in Europe, and our now-pervasive presence there is a key factor in making NetJets the worldwide leader in this industry.

  Despite a large increase in customers, however, our U.S. operation dipped far into the red. Its efficiency fell, and costs soared. We believe that our three largest competitors suffered similar problems, but each is owned by aircraft manufacturers that may think differently than we do about the necessity of making adequate profits. The *combined* value of the fleets managed by these three competitors, in any case, continues to be less valuable than the fleet that we operate.

  Rich Santulli, one of the most dynamic managers I've ever met, will solve our revenue/expense problem. He won't do it, however, in a manner that impairs the quality of the NetJets experience. Both he and I are committed to a level of service, security and safety that can't be matched by others.

- Our retailing category includes See's Candies, a company we bought early in 1972 (a date making it our oldest non-insurance business). At that time, Charlie and I immediately decided to put Chuck Huggins, then 46, in charge. Though we were new at the game of selecting managers, Charlie and I hit a home run with this appointment. Chuck's love for the customer and the brand permeated the organization, which in his 34-year tenure produced a more-than-tenfold increase in profits. This gain was achieved in an industry growing at best slowly and perhaps not at all. (Volume figures in this industry are hard to pin down.)

At yearend, Chuck turned the reins at See's over to Brad Kinstler, who previously had served Berkshire well while running Cypress Insurance and Fechheimer's. It's unusual for us to move managers around, but Brad's record made him an obvious choice for the See's job. I hope Chuck and his wife, Donna, are at the annual meeting. If they are, shareholders can join Charlie and me in giving America's number one candy maker a richly-deserved round of applause.

* * * * * * * * * * * *

Every day, in countless ways, the competitive position of each of our businesses grows either weaker or stronger. If we are delighting customers, eliminating unnecessary costs and improving our products and services, we gain strength. But if we treat customers with indifference or tolerate bloat, our businesses will wither. On a daily basis, the effects of our actions are imperceptible; cumulatively, though, their consequences are enormous.

When our long-term competitive position improves as a result of these almost unnoticeable actions, we describe the phenomenon as "widening the moat." And doing that is essential if we are to have the kind of business we want a decade or two from now. We always, of course, hope to earn more money in the short-term. But when short-term and long-term conflict, widening the moat *must* take precedence. If a management makes bad decisions in order to hit short-term earnings targets, and consequently gets behind the eight-ball in terms of costs, customer satisfaction or brand strength, no amount of subsequent brilliance will overcome the damage that has been inflicted. Take a look at the dilemmas of managers in the auto and airline industries today as they struggle with the huge problems handed them by their predecessors. Charlie is fond of quoting Ben Franklin's "An ounce of prevention is worth a pound of cure." But sometimes no amount of cure will overcome the mistakes of the past.

Our managers focus on moat-widening – and are brilliant at it. Quite simply, they are passionate about their businesses. Usually, they were running those long before we came along; our only function since has been to stay out of the way. If you see these heroes – and our four heroines as well – at the annual meeting, thank them for the job they do for you.

* * * * * * * * * * * *

The attitude of our managers vividly contrasts with that of the young man who married a tycoon's only child, a decidedly homely and dull lass. Relieved, the father called in his new son-in-law after the wedding and began to discuss the future:

"Son, you're the boy I always wanted and never had. Here's a stock certificate for 50% of the company. You're my equal partner from now on."

"Thanks, dad."

"Now, what would you like to run? How about sales?"

"I'm afraid I couldn't sell water to a man crawling in the Sahara."

"Well then, how about heading human relations?"

"I really don't care for people."

"No problem, we have lots of other spots in the business. What would you like to do?"

"Actually, nothing appeals to me. Why don't you just buy me out?"

Investments

We show below our common stock investments. Those that had a market value of more than $700 million at the end of 2005 are itemized.

			12/31/05	
		Percentage of		
Shares	Company	Company Owned	Cost*	Market
			(in $ millions)	
151,610,700	American Express Company	12.2	$1,287	$ 7,802
30,322,137	Ameriprise Financial, Inc.....................	12.1	183	1,243
43,854,200	Anheuser-Busch Cos., Inc....................	5.6	2,133	1,884
200,000,000	The Coca-Cola Company	8.4	1,299	8,062
6,708,760	M&T Bank Corporation	6.0	103	732
48,000,000	Moody's Corporation	16.2	499	2,948
2,338,961,000	PetroChina "H" shares (or equivalents)...	1.3	488	1,915
100,000,000	The Procter & Gamble Company	3.0	940	5,788
19,944,300	Wal-Mart Stores, Inc.	0.5	944	933
1,727,765	The Washington Post Company	18.0	11	1,322
95,092,200	Wells Fargo & Company........................	5.7	2,754	5,975
1,724,200	White Mountains Insurance....................	16.0	369	963
	Others		4,937	7,154
	Total Common Stocks		$15,947	$46,721

*This is our actual purchase price and also our tax basis; GAAP "cost" differs in a few cases because of write-ups or write-downs that have been required.

A couple of last year's changes in our portfolio occurred because of corporate events: Gillette was merged into Procter & Gamble, and American Express spun off Ameriprise. In addition, we substantially increased our holdings in Wells Fargo, a company that Dick Kovacevich runs brilliantly, and established positions in Anheuser-Busch and Wal-Mart.

Expect no miracles from our equity portfolio. Though we own major interests in a number of strong, highly-profitable businesses, they are not selling at anything like bargain prices. As a group, they may double in value in ten years. The likelihood is that their per-share earnings, in aggregate, will grow 6-8% per year over the decade and that their stock prices will more or less match that growth. (Their managers, of course, think my expectations are too modest – and I hope they're right.)

* * * * * * * * * * * *

The P&G-Gillette merger, closing in the fourth quarter of 2005, required Berkshire to record a $5.0 billion pre-tax capital gain. This bookkeeping entry, dictated by GAAP, is meaningless from an economic standpoint, and you should ignore it when you are evaluating Berkshire's 2005 earnings. We didn't intend to sell our Gillette shares before the merger; we don't intend to sell our P&G shares now; and we incurred no tax when the merger took place.

It's hard to overemphasize the importance of who is CEO of a company. Before Jim Kilts arrived at Gillette in 2001, the company was struggling, having particularly suffered from capital-allocation blunders. In the major example, Gillette's acquisition of Duracell cost Gillette shareholders billions of dollars, a loss never made visible by conventional accounting. Quite simply, what Gillette received in business value in this acquisition was not equivalent to what it gave up. (Amazingly, this most fundamental of yardsticks is almost always ignored by both managements and their investment bankers when acquisitions are under discussion.)

Upon taking office at Gillette, Jim quickly instilled fiscal discipline, tightened operations and energized marketing, moves that dramatically increased the intrinsic value of the company. Gillette's merger with P&G then expanded the potential of both companies. For his accomplishments, Jim was paid very well – but he earned every penny. (This is no academic evaluation: As a 9.7% owner of Gillette, Berkshire in effect paid that proportion of his compensation.) Indeed, it's difficult to overpay the *truly* extraordinary CEO of a giant enterprise. But this species is rare.

Too often, executive compensation in the U.S. is ridiculously out of line with performance. That won't change, moreover, because the deck is stacked against investors when it comes to the CEO's pay. The upshot is that a mediocre-or-worse CEO – aided by his handpicked VP of human relations and a consultant from the ever-accommodating firm of Ratchet, Ratchet and Bingo – all too often receives gobs of money from an ill-designed compensation arrangement.

Take, for instance, ten year, fixed-price options (and who wouldn't?). If Fred Futile, CEO of Stagnant, Inc., receives a bundle of these – let's say enough to give him an option on 1% of the company – his self-interest is clear: He should skip dividends entirely and instead use all of the company's earnings to repurchase stock.

Let's assume that under Fred's leadership Stagnant lives up to its name. In each of the ten years after the option grant, it earns $1 billion on $10 billion of net worth, which initially comes to $10 per share on the 100 million shares then outstanding. Fred eschews dividends and regularly uses all earnings to repurchase shares. If the stock constantly sells at ten times earnings per share, it will have appreciated 158% by the end of the option period. That's because repurchases would reduce the number of shares to 38.7 million by that time, and earnings per share would thereby increase to $25.80. Simply by withholding earnings from owners, Fred gets very rich, making a cool $158 million, despite the business itself improving not at all. Astonishingly, Fred could have made more than $100 million if Stagnant's earnings had *declined* by 20% during the ten-year period.

Fred can also get a splendid result for himself by paying no dividends and deploying the earnings he withholds from shareholders into a variety of disappointing projects and acquisitions. Even if these initiatives deliver a paltry 5% return, Fred will still make a bundle. Specifically – with Stagnant's p/e ratio remaining unchanged at ten – Fred's option will deliver him $63 million. Meanwhile, his shareholders will wonder what happened to the "alignment of interests" that was supposed to occur when Fred was issued options.

A "normal" dividend policy, of course – one-third of earnings paid out, for example – produces less extreme results but still can provide lush rewards for managers who achieve nothing.

CEOs understand this math and know that every dime paid out in dividends reduces the value of all outstanding options. I've never, however, seen this manager-owner conflict referenced in proxy materials that request approval of a fixed-priced option plan. Though CEOs invariably preach *internally* that capital comes at a cost, they somehow forget to tell shareholders that fixed-price options give them capital that is free.

It doesn't have to be this way: It's child's play for a board to design options that give effect to the automatic build-up in value that occurs when earnings are retained. But – surprise, surprise – options of that kind are almost never issued. Indeed, the very thought of options with strike prices that are adjusted for retained earnings seems foreign to compensation "experts," who are nevertheless encyclopedic about every management-friendly plan that exists. ("Whose bread I eat, his song I sing.")

Getting fired can produce a particularly bountiful payday for a CEO. Indeed, he can "earn" more in that single day, while cleaning out his desk, than an American worker earns in a lifetime of cleaning toilets. Forget the old maxim about nothing succeeding like success: Today, in the executive suite, the all-too-prevalent rule is that nothing succeeds like *failure*.

Huge severance payments, lavish perks and outsized payments for ho-hum performance often occur because comp committees have become slaves to comparative data. The drill is simple: Three or so directors – *not chosen by chance* – are bombarded for a few hours before a board meeting with pay statistics that perpetually ratchet upwards. Additionally, the committee is told about new perks that other managers are receiving. In this manner, outlandish "goodies" are showered upon CEOs simply because of a corporate version of the argument we all used when children: "But, Mom, all the other kids have one." When comp committees follow this "logic," yesterday's most egregious excess becomes today's baseline.

Comp committees should adopt the attitude of Hank Greenberg, the Detroit slugger and a boyhood hero of mine. Hank's son, Steve, at one time was a player's agent. Representing an outfielder in negotiations with a major league club, Steve sounded out his dad about the size of the signing bonus he should ask for. Hank, a true pay-for-performance guy, got straight to the point, "What did he hit last year?" When Steve answered ".246," Hank's comeback was immediate: "Ask for a uniform."

(Let me pause for a brief confession: In criticizing comp committee behavior, I don't speak as a true insider. Though I have served as a director of twenty public companies, only one CEO has put me on his comp committee. Hmmmm . . .)

* * * * * * * * * * * *

My views on America's long-term problem in respect to trade imbalances, which I have laid out in previous reports, remain unchanged. My conviction, however, cost Berkshire $955 million pre-tax in 2005. That amount is included in our earnings statement, a fact that illustrates the differing ways in which GAAP treats gains and losses. When we have a long-term position in stocks or bonds, year-to-year changes in value are reflected in our balance sheet but, as long as the asset is not sold, are rarely reflected in earnings. For example, our Coca-Cola holdings went from $1 billion in value early on to $13.4 billion at yearend 1998 and have since declined to $8.1 billion – with none of these moves affecting our earnings statement. Long-term currency positions, however, are daily marked to market and therefore have an effect on earnings in every reporting period. From the date we first entered into currency contracts, we are $2.0 billion in the black.

We reduced our direct position in currencies somewhat during 2005. We partially offset this change, however, by purchasing equities whose prices are denominated in a variety of foreign currencies and that earn a large part of their profits internationally. Charlie and I prefer this method of acquiring non-dollar exposure. That's largely because of changes in interest rates: As U.S. rates have risen relative to those of the rest of the world, holding most foreign currencies now involves a significant negative "carry." The carry aspect of our direct currency position indeed cost us money in 2005 and is likely to do so again in 2006. In contrast, the ownership of foreign equities is likely, over time, to create a positive carry – perhaps a substantial one.

The underlying factors affecting the U.S. current account deficit continue to worsen, and no letup is in sight. Not only did our trade deficit – the largest and most familiar item in the current account – hit an all-time high in 2005, but we also can expect a second item – the balance of investment income – to soon turn negative. As foreigners increase their ownership of U.S. assets (or of claims against us) relative to U.S. investments abroad, these investors will begin earning more on their holdings than we do on ours. Finally, the third component of the current account, unilateral transfers, is always negative.

The U.S., it should be emphasized, is extraordinarily rich and will get richer. As a result, the huge imbalances in its current account may continue for a long time without their having noticeable deleterious effects on the U.S. economy or on markets. I doubt, however, that the situation will forever remain benign. Either Americans address the problem soon in a way we select, or at some point the problem will likely address us in an unpleasant way of its own.

How to Minimize Investment Returns

It's been an easy matter for Berkshire and other owners of American equities to prosper over the years. Between December 31, 1899 and December 31, 1999, to give a really long-term example, the Dow rose from 66 to 11,497. (Guess what annual growth rate is required to produce this result; the surprising answer is at the end of this section.) This huge rise came about for a simple reason: Over the century American businesses did extraordinarily well and investors rode the wave of their prosperity. Businesses continue to do well. But now shareholders, through a series of self-inflicted wounds, are in a major way cutting the returns they will realize from their investments.

The explanation of how this is happening begins with a fundamental truth: With unimportant exceptions, such as bankruptcies in which some of a company's losses are borne by creditors, *the most that owners in aggregate can earn between now and Judgment Day is what their businesses in aggregate earn.* True, by buying and selling that is clever or lucky, investor A may take more than his share of the pie at the expense of investor B. And, yes, all investors *feel* richer when stocks soar. But an owner can exit only by having someone take his place. If one investor sells high, another must buy high. For owners as a whole, there is simply no magic – no shower of money from outer space – that will enable them to extract wealth from their companies beyond that created by the companies themselves.

Indeed, owners must earn less than their businesses earn because of "frictional" costs. And that's my point: These costs are now being incurred in amounts that will cause shareholders to earn *far* less than they historically have.

To understand how this toll has ballooned, imagine for a moment that all American corporations are, and always will be, owned by a single family. We'll call them the Gotrocks. After paying taxes on dividends, this family – generation after generation – becomes richer by the aggregate amount earned by its companies. Today that amount is about $700 billion annually. Naturally, the family spends some of these dollars. But the portion it saves steadily compounds for its benefit. In the Gotrocks household everyone grows wealthier at the same pace, and all is harmonious.

But let's now assume that a few fast-talking Helpers approach the family and persuade each of its members to try to outsmart his relatives by buying certain of their holdings and selling them certain others. The Helpers – for a fee, of course – obligingly agree to handle these transactions. The Gotrocks still own all of corporate America; the trades just rearrange who owns what. So the family's annual gain in wealth diminishes, equaling the earnings of American business *minus* commissions paid. The more that family members trade, the smaller their share of the pie and the larger the slice received by the Helpers. This fact is not lost upon these broker-Helpers: Activity is their friend and, in a wide variety of ways, they urge it on.

After a while, most of the family members realize that they are not doing so well at this new "beat-my-brother" game. Enter another set of Helpers. These newcomers explain to each member of the Gotrocks clan that by himself he'll never outsmart the rest of the family. The suggested cure: "Hire a manager – yes, us – and get the job done professionally." These manager-Helpers continue to use the broker-Helpers to execute trades; the managers may even increase their activity so as to permit the brokers to prosper still more. Overall, a bigger slice of the pie now goes to the two classes of Helpers.

The family's disappointment grows. Each of its members is now employing professionals. Yet overall, the group's finances have taken a turn for the worse. The solution? More help, of course.

It arrives in the form of financial planners and institutional consultants, who weigh in to advise the Gotrocks on selecting manager-Helpers. The befuddled family welcomes this assistance. By now its members know they can pick neither the right stocks nor the right stock-pickers. Why, one might ask, should they expect success in picking the right consultant? But this question does not occur to the Gotrocks, and the consultant-Helpers certainly don't suggest it to them.

The Gotrocks, now supporting three classes of expensive Helpers, find that their results get worse, and they sink into despair. But just as hope seems lost, a fourth group – we'll call them the hyper-Helpers – appears. These friendly folk explain to the Gotrocks that their unsatisfactory results are occurring because the existing Helpers – brokers, managers, consultants – are not sufficiently motivated and are simply going through the motions. "What," the new Helpers ask, "can you expect from such a bunch of zombies?"

The new arrivals offer a breathtakingly simple solution: *Pay more money.* Brimming with self-confidence, the hyper-Helpers assert that huge contingent payments – in addition to stiff fixed fees – are what each family member must fork over in order to *really* outmaneuver his relatives.

The more observant members of the family see that some of the hyper-Helpers are really just manager-Helpers wearing new uniforms, bearing sewn-on sexy names like HEDGE FUND or PRIVATE EQUITY. The new Helpers, however, assure the Gotrocks that this change of clothing is all-important, bestowing on its wearers magical powers similar to those acquired by mild-mannered Clark Kent when he changed into his Superman costume. Calmed by this explanation, the family decides to pay up.

And that's where we are today: A record portion of the earnings that would go in their entirety to owners – if they all just stayed in their rocking chairs – is now going to a swelling army of Helpers. Particularly expensive is the recent pandemic of profit arrangements under which Helpers receive large portions of the winnings when they are smart or lucky, and leave family members with all of the losses – and large fixed fees to boot – when the Helpers are dumb or unlucky (or occasionally crooked).

A sufficient number of arrangements like this – heads, the Helper takes much of the winnings; tails, the Gotrocks lose and pay dearly for the privilege of doing so – may make it more accurate to call the family the Hadrocks. Today, in fact, the family's frictional costs of all sorts may well amount to 20% of the earnings of American business. In other words, the burden of paying Helpers may cause American equity investors, overall, to earn only 80% or so of what they would earn if they just sat still and listened to no one.

Long ago, Sir Isaac Newton gave us three laws of motion, which were the work of genius. But Sir Isaac's talents didn't extend to investing: He lost a bundle in the South Sea Bubble, explaining later, "I can calculate the movement of the stars, but not the madness of men." If he had not been traumatized by this loss, Sir Isaac might well have gone on to discover the Fourth Law of Motion: *For investors as a whole, returns decrease as motion increases.*

* * * * * * * * * * * *

Here's the answer to the question posed at the beginning of this section: To get very specific, the Dow increased from 65.73 to 11,497.12 in the 20th century, and that amounts to a gain of 5.3% compounded annually. (Investors would also have received dividends, of course.) To achieve an equal rate of gain in the 21st century, the Dow will have to rise by December 31, 2099 to – brace yourself – precisely 2,011,011.23. But I'm willing to settle for 2,000,000; six years into this century, the Dow has gained not at all.

Debt and Risk

As we consolidate MidAmerican, our new balance sheet may suggest that Berkshire has expanded its tolerance for borrowing. But that's not so. Except for token amounts, we shun debt, turning to it for only three purposes:

1) We occasionally use repos as a part of certain short-term investing strategies that incorporate ownership of U.S. government (or agency) securities. Purchases of this kind are highly opportunistic and involve only the most liquid of securities. A few years ago, we entered into several interesting transactions that have since been unwound or are running off. The offsetting debt has likewise been cut substantially and before long may be gone.

2) We borrow money against portfolios of interest-bearing receivables whose risk characteristics we understand. We did this in 2001 when we guaranteed $5.6 billion of bank debt to take over, in partnership with Leucadia, a bankrupt Finova (which held a broad range of receivables). All of that debt has been repaid. More recently, we have borrowed to finance a widely-diversified, predictably-performing portfolio of manufactured-home receivables managed by Clayton. Alternatively, we could "securitize" – that is, sell – these receivables, but retain the servicing of them. If we followed this procedure, which is common in the industry, we would not show the debt that we do on our balance sheet, and we would also accelerate the earnings we report. In the end, however, we would earn less money. Were market variables to change so as to favor securitization (an unlikely event), we could sell part of our portfolio and eliminate the related debt. Until then, we prefer better profits to better cosmetics.

3) At MidAmerican, we have substantial debt, but it is that company's obligation only. Though it will appear on our consolidated balance sheet, Berkshire does *not* guarantee it.

Even so, this debt is unquestionably secure because it is serviced by MidAmerican's diversified stream of highly-stable utility earnings. If there were to be some bolt from the blue that hurt one of MidAmerican's utility properties, earnings from the others would still be more than ample to cover all debt requirements. Moreover, MidAmerican retains all of its earnings, an equity-building practice that is rare in the utility field.

From a risk standpoint, it is far safer to have earnings from ten diverse and uncorrelated utility operations that cover interest charges by, say, a 2:1 ratio than it is to have far greater coverage provided by a single utility. A catastrophic event can render a single utility insolvent – witness what Katrina did to the local electric utility in New Orleans – no matter how conservative its debt policy. A geographical disaster – say, an earthquake in a Western state – can't have the same effect on MidAmerican. And even a worrier like Charlie can't think of an event that would systemically decrease utility earnings in any major way. Because of MidAmerican's ever-widening diversity of regulated earnings, it will always utilize major amounts of debt.

And that's about it. We are not interested in incurring any significant debt at Berkshire for acquisitions or operating purposes. Conventional business wisdom, of course, would argue that we are being too conservative and that there are added profits that could be safely earned if we injected moderate leverage into our balance sheet.

Maybe so. But many of Berkshire's hundreds of thousands of investors have a large portion of their net worth in our stock (among them, it should be emphasized, a large number of our board and key managers) and a disaster for the company would be a disaster for them. Moreover, there are people who have been permanently injured to whom we owe insurance payments that stretch out for fifty years or more. To these and other constituencies we have promised total security, whatever comes: financial panics, stock-exchange closures (an extended one occurred in 1914) or even domestic nuclear, chemical or biological attacks.

We are quite willing to accept huge risks. Indeed, more than any other insurer, we write high-limit policies that are tied to single catastrophic events. We also own a large investment portfolio whose market value could fall dramatically and quickly under certain conditions (as happened on October 19, 1987). Whatever occurs, though, Berkshire will have the net worth, the earnings streams and the liquidity to handle the problem with ease.

Any other approach is dangerous. Over the years, a number of very smart people have learned the hard way that a long string of impressive numbers multiplied by a single zero always equals zero. That is not an equation whose effects I would like to experience personally, and I would like even less to be responsible for imposing its penalties upon others.

Management Succession

As owners, you are naturally concerned about whether I will insist on continuing as CEO after I begin to fade and, if so, how the board will handle that problem. You also want to know what happens if I should die tonight.

That second question is easy to answer. Most of our many businesses have strong market positions, significant momentum, and terrific managers. The special Berkshire culture is deeply ingrained throughout our subsidiaries, and these operations won't miss a beat when I die.

Moreover, we have three managers at Berkshire who are reasonably young and fully capable of being CEO. Any of the three would be much better at certain management aspects of my job than I. On the minus side, none has my crossover experience that allows me to be comfortable making decisions in either the business arena or in investments. That problem will be solved by having another person in the organization handle marketable securities. That's an interesting job at Berkshire, and the new CEO will have no problem in hiring a talented individual to do it. Indeed, that's what we have done at GEICO for 26 years, and our results have been terrific.

Berkshire's board has fully discussed each of the three CEO candidates and has unanimously agreed on the person who should succeed me if a replacement were needed today. The directors stay updated on this subject and could alter their view as circumstances change – new managerial stars may emerge and present ones will age. The important point is that the directors know now – and will always know in the future – exactly what they will do when the need arises.

The other question that must be addressed is whether the Board will be prepared to make a change if that need should arise not from my death but rather from my decay, particularly if this decay is accompanied by my delusionally thinking that I am reaching new peaks of managerial brilliance. That problem would not be unique to me. Charlie and I have faced this situation from time to time at Berkshire's subsidiaries. Humans age at greatly varying rates – but sooner or later their talents and vigor decline. Some managers remain effective well into their 80s – Charlie is a wonder at 82 – and others noticeably fade in their 60s. When their abilities ebb, so usually do their powers of self-assessment. Someone else often needs to blow the whistle.

When that time comes for me, our board will have to step up to the job. From a financial standpoint, its members are unusually motivated to do so. I know of no other board in the country in which the financial interests of directors are so completely aligned with those of shareholders. Few boards even come close. On a personal level, however, it is extraordinarily difficult for most people to tell someone, particularly a friend, that he or she is no longer capable.

If I become a candidate for that message, however, our board will be doing me a favor by delivering it. *Every* share of Berkshire that I own is destined to go to philanthropies, and I want society to reap the maximum good from these gifts and bequests. It would be a tragedy if the philanthropic potential of my holdings was diminished because my associates shirked their responsibility to (tenderly, I hope) show me the door. But don't worry about this. We have an outstanding group of directors, and they will always do what's right for shareholders.

And while we are on the subject, I feel terrific.

The Annual Meeting

Our meeting this year will be on Saturday, May 6. As always, the doors will open at the Qwest Center at 7 a.m., and the latest Berkshire movie will be shown at 8:30. At 9:30 we will go directly to the question-and-answer period, which (with a break for lunch at the Qwest's stands) will last until 3:00. Then, after a short recess, Charlie and I will convene the annual meeting at 3:15. This schedule worked well last year, because it let those who wanted to attend the formal session to do so, while freeing others to *shop*.

You certainly did your share in this respect last year. The 194,300 square foot hall adjoining the meeting area was filled with the products of Berkshire subsidiaries, and the 21,000 people who came to the meeting allowed every location to rack up sales records. Kelly Broz (neé Muchemore), the Flo Ziegfeld of Berkshire, orchestrates both this magnificent shopping extravaganza and the meeting itself. The exhibitors love her, and so do I. Kelly got married in October, and I gave her away. She asked me how I wanted to be listed in the wedding program. I replied "envious of the groom," and that's the way it went to press.

This year we will showcase two Clayton homes (featuring Acme brick, Shaw carpet, Johns Manville insulation, MiTek fasteners, Carefree awnings and NFM furniture). You will find that these homes, priced at $79,000 and $89,000, deliver excellent value. In fact, three shareholders came so firmly to that conclusion last year that they bought the $119,000 model we then showcased. Flanking the Clayton homes on the exhibition floor will be RVs from Forest River.

GEICO will have a booth staffed by a number of its top counselors from around the country, all of them ready to supply you with auto insurance quotes. In most cases, GEICO will be able to give you a special shareholder discount (usually 8%). This special offer is permitted by 45 of the 50 jurisdictions in which we operate. (One supplemental point: The discount is not additive if you qualify for another, such as that given certain groups.) Bring the details of your existing insurance and check out whether we can save you money. For at least 50% of you, I believe we can. And while you're at it, sign up for the new GEICO credit card. It's the one I now use.

On Saturday, at the Omaha airport, we will have the usual array of aircraft from NetJets® available for your inspection. Stop by the NetJets booth at the Qwest to learn about viewing these planes. Come to Omaha by bus; leave in your new plane.

The Bookworm boutique at the Qwest broke all records last year selling Berkshire-related books. An amazing 3,500 of these were *Poor Charlie's Almanack*, the collected wisdom of my partner. This means that a copy was sold every 9 seconds. And for good reason: You will never find a book with more useful ideas. Word-of-mouth recommendations have caused Charlie's first printing of 20,500 copies to sell out, and we will therefore have a revised and expanded edition on sale at our meeting. Among the other 22 titles and DVDs available last year at the Bookworm, 4,597 copies were sold for $84,746. Our shareholders are a bookseller's dream.

An attachment to the proxy material that is enclosed with this report explains how you can obtain the credential you will need for admission to the meeting and other events. As for plane, hotel and car reservations, we have again signed up American Express (800-799-6634) to give you special help. Carol Pedersen, who handles these matters, does a terrific job for us each year, and I thank her for it.

At Nebraska Furniture Mart, located on a 77-acre site on 72nd Street between Dodge and Pacific, we will again be having "Berkshire Weekend" pricing. We initiated this special event at NFM nine years ago, and sales during the "Weekend" grew from $5.3 million in 1997 to $27.4 million in 2005 (up 9% from a year earlier). I get goose bumps just thinking about this volume.

To obtain the discount, you must make your purchases between Thursday, May 4 and Monday, May 8 inclusive, and also present your meeting credential. The period's special pricing will even apply to the products of several prestigious manufacturers that normally have ironclad rules against discounting but that, in the spirit of our shareholder weekend, have made an exception for you. We appreciate their cooperation. NFM is open from 10 a.m. to 9 p.m. Monday through Saturday, and 10 a.m. to 6 p.m. on Sunday. On Saturday this year, from 5:30 p.m. to 8 p.m., we are having a special affair for shareholders only. I'll be there, eating barbeque, drinking Coke, and counting sales.

Borsheim's again will have two shareholder-only events. The first will be a cocktail reception from 6 p.m. to 10 p.m. on Friday, May 5. The second, the main gala, will be from 9 a.m. to 4 p.m. on Sunday, May 7. On Saturday, we will be open until 6 p.m.

We will have huge crowds at Borsheim's throughout the weekend. For your convenience, therefore, shareholder prices will be available from Monday, May 1 through Saturday, May 13. During that period, just identify yourself as a shareholder through your meeting credentials or a brokerage statement.

Borsheim's operates on a gross margin that, even before the shareholders' discount, is fully twenty percentage points below that of its major rivals. Last year, our shareholder-period business increased 9% from 2004, which came on top of a 73% gain the year before. The store sold 5,000 Berkshire Monopoly games – and then ran out. We've learned: Plenty will be in stock this year.

In a tent outside of Borsheim's, Patrick Wolff, twice U.S. chess champion, will take on all comers in groups of six – blindfolded. Additionally, we will have Bob Hamman and Sharon Osberg, two of the world's top bridge experts, available to play with our shareholders on Sunday afternoon. They plan to keep their eyes *open* – but Bob never sorts his cards, even when playing for a national championship.

Gorat's – my favorite steakhouse – will again be open exclusively for Berkshire shareholders on Sunday, May 7, and will be serving from 4 p.m. until 10 p.m. Please remember that to come to Gorat's on that day, you must have a reservation. To make one, call 402-551-3733 on April 1 (*but not before*).

In this school year, about 35 university classes will come to Omaha for sessions with me. I take almost all – in aggregate, perhaps 2,000 students – to lunch at Gorat's. And they love it. To learn why, come join us on Sunday.

We will again have a special reception from 4:00 to 5:30 on Saturday afternoon for shareholders who have come from outside of North America. Every year our meeting draws many people from around the globe, and Charlie and I want to be sure we personally greet those who have come so far. Last year we enjoyed meeting more than 400 of you from many dozens of countries. Any shareholder who comes from other than the U.S. or Canada will be given a special credential and instructions for attending this function.

* * * * * * * * * * * *

Charlie and I are extraordinarily lucky. We were born in America; had terrific parents who saw that we got good educations; have enjoyed wonderful families and great health; and came equipped with a "business" gene that allows us to prosper in a manner hugely disproportionate to other people who contribute as much or more to our society's well-being. Moreover, we have long had jobs that we love, in which we are helped every day in countless ways by talented and cheerful associates. No wonder we tap-dance to work. But nothing is more fun for us than getting together with our shareholder-partners at Berkshire's annual meeting. So join us on May 6th at the Qwest for our annual Woodstock for Capitalists. We'll see you there.

February 28, 2006

Warren E. Buffett
Chairman of the Board

BERKSHIRE HATHAWAY INC.

To the Shareholders of Berkshire Hathaway Inc.:

Our gain in net worth during 2006 was $16.9 billion, which increased the per-share book value of both our Class A and Class B stock by 18.4%. Over the last 42 years (that is, since present management took over) book value has grown from $19 to $70,281, a rate of 21.4% compounded annually.*

We believe that $16.9 billion is a record for a one-year gain in net worth – more than has ever been booked by *any* American business, leaving aside boosts that have occurred because of mergers (e.g., AOL's purchase of Time Warner). Of course, Exxon Mobil and other companies earn far more than Berkshire, but their earnings largely go to dividends and/or repurchases, rather than to building net worth.

All that said, a confession about our 2006 gain is in order. Our most important business, insurance, benefited from a large dose of luck: Mother Nature, bless her heart, went on vacation. After hammering us with hurricanes in 2004 and 2005 – storms that caused us to lose a bundle on super-cat insurance – she just vanished. Last year, the red ink from this activity turned black – *very* black.

In addition, the great majority of our 73 businesses did outstandingly well in 2006. Let me focus for a moment on one of our largest operations, GEICO. What management accomplished there was simply extraordinary.

As I've told you before, Tony Nicely, GEICO's CEO, went to work at the company 45 years ago, two months after turning 18. He became CEO in 1992, and from then on the company's growth exploded. In addition, Tony has delivered staggering productivity gains in recent years. Between yearend 2003 and yearend 2006, the number of GEICO policies increased from 5.7 million to 8.1 million, a jump of 42%. Yet during that same period, the company's employees (measured on a fulltime-equivalent basis) *fell* 3.5%. So productivity grew 47%. And GEICO didn't start fat.

That remarkable gain has allowed GEICO to maintain its all-important position as a low-cost producer, even though it has dramatically increased advertising expenditures. Last year GEICO spent $631 million on ads, up from $238 million in 2003 (and up from $31 million in 1995, when Berkshire took control). Today, GEICO spends far more on ads than any of its competitors, even those much larger. We will continue to raise the bar.

Last year I told you that if you had a new son or grandson to be sure to name him Tony. But Don Keough, a Berkshire director, recently had a better idea. After reviewing GEICO's performance in 2006, he wrote me, "Forget births. Tell the shareholders to immediately change the names of their *present* children to Tony or Antoinette." Don signed his letter "Tony."

* * * * * * * * * * * *

Charlie Munger – my partner and Berkshire's vice chairman – and I run what has turned out to be a big business, one with 217,000 employees and annual revenues approaching $100 billion. We certainly didn't plan it that way. Charlie began as a lawyer, and I thought of myself as a security analyst. Sitting in those seats, we both grew skeptical about the ability of big entities of any type to function well. Size seems to make many organizations slow-thinking, resistant to change and smug. In Churchill's words: "We shape our buildings, and afterwards our buildings shape us." Here's a telling fact: Of the ten non-oil companies having the largest market capitalization in 1965 – titans such as General Motors, Sears, DuPont and Eastman Kodak – only one made the 2006 list.

---

*All per-share figures used in this report apply to Berkshire's A shares. Figures for the B shares are 1/30th of those shown for the A.

In fairness, we've seen plenty of successes as well, some truly outstanding. There are many giant-company managers whom I greatly admire; Ken Chenault of American Express, Jeff Immelt of G.E. and Dick Kovacevich of Wells Fargo come quickly to mind. But I don't think I could do the management job they do. And I know I wouldn't enjoy many of the duties that come with their positions – meetings, speeches, foreign travel, the charity circuit and governmental relations. For me, Ronald Reagan had it right: "It's probably true that hard work never killed anyone – but why take the chance?"

So I've taken the easy route, just sitting back and working through great managers who run their own shows. My only tasks are to cheer them on, sculpt and harden our corporate culture, and make major capital-allocation decisions. Our managers have returned this trust by working hard and effectively.

For their performance over the last 42 years – and particularly for 2006 – Charlie and I thank them.

Yardsticks

Charlie and I measure Berkshire's progress and evaluate its intrinsic value in a number of ways. No single criterion is effective in doing these jobs, and even an avalanche of statistics will not capture some factors that are important. For example, it's essential that we have managers much younger than I available to succeed me. Berkshire has never been in better shape in this regard – but I can't prove it to you with numbers.

There are two statistics, however, that are of real importance. The first is the amount of investments (including cash and cash-equivalents) that we own on a per-share basis. Arriving at this figure, we exclude investments held in our finance operation because these are largely offset by borrowings. Here's the record since present management acquired control of Berkshire:

Year	Per-Share Investments*
1965	$ 4
1975	159
1985	2,407
1995	21,817
2006	$80,636
Compound Growth Rate 1965-2006	27.5%
Compound Growth Rate 1995-2006	12.6%

*Net of minority interests

In our early years we put most of our retained earnings and insurance float into investments in marketable securities. Because of this emphasis, and because the securities we purchased generally did well, our growth rate in investments was for a long time quite high.

Over the years, however, we have focused more and more on the acquisition of operating businesses. Using our funds for these purchases has both slowed our growth in investments and accelerated our gains in pre-tax earnings from non-insurance businesses, the second yardstick we use. Here's how those earnings have looked:

Year	Pre-Tax Earnings Per Share*
1965	$ 4
1975	4
1985	52
1995	175
2006	$3,625
Compound Growth Rate 1965-2006	17.9%
Compound Growth Rate 1995-2006	31.7%

*Excluding purchase-accounting adjustments and net of minority interests

Last year we had a good increase in non-insurance earnings – 38%. Large gains from here on in, though, will come only if we are able to make major, *and sensible*, acquisitions. That will not be easy. We do, however, have one advantage: More and more, Berkshire has become "the buyer of choice" for business owners and managers. Initially, we were viewed that way only in the U.S. (and more often than not by private companies). We've long wanted, nonetheless, to extend Berkshire's appeal beyond U.S. borders. And last year, our globe-trotting finally got underway.

Acquisitions

We began 2006 by completing the three acquisitions pending at yearend 2005, spending about $6 billion for PacifiCorp, Business Wire and Applied Underwriters. All are performing very well.

The highlight of the year, however, was our July 5th acquisition of most of ISCAR, an Israeli company, and our new association with its chairman, Eitan Wertheimer, and CEO, Jacob Harpaz. The story here began on October 25, 2005, when I received a 1¼-page letter from Eitan, of whom I then knew nothing. The letter began, "I am writing to introduce you to ISCAR," and proceeded to describe a cutting-tool business carried on in 61 countries. Then Eitan wrote, "We have for some time considered the issues of generational transfer and ownership that are typical for large family enterprises, and have given much thought to ISCAR's future. Our conclusion is that Berkshire Hathaway would be the ideal home for ISCAR. We believe that ISCAR would continue to thrive as a part of your portfolio of businesses."

Overall, Eitan's letter made the quality of the company and the character of its management leap off the page. It also made me want to learn more, and in November, Eitan, Jacob and ISCAR's CFO, Danny Goldman, came to Omaha. A few hours with them convinced me that if we were to make a deal, we would be teaming up with extraordinarily talented managers who could be trusted to run the business after a sale with all of the energy and dedication that they had exhibited previously. However, having never bought a business based outside of the U.S. (though I had bought a number of foreign stocks), I needed to get educated on some tax and jurisdictional matters. With that task completed, Berkshire purchased 80% of ISCAR for $4 billion. The remaining 20% stays in the hands of the Wertheimer family, making it our valued partner.

ISCAR's products are small, consumable cutting tools that are used in conjunction with large and expensive machine tools. It's a business without magic except for that imparted by the people who run it. But Eitan, Jacob and their associates are true managerial magicians who constantly develop tools that make their customers' machines more productive. The result: ISCAR makes money because it enables its customers to make *more* money. There is no better recipe for continued success.

In September, Charlie and I, along with five Berkshire associates, visited ISCAR in Israel. We – and I mean every one of us – have never been more impressed with any operation. At ISCAR, as throughout Israel, brains and energy are ubiquitous. Berkshire shareholders are lucky to have joined with Eitan, Jacob, Danny and their talented associates.

* * * * * * * * * * *

A few months later, Berkshire again became "the buyer of choice" in a deal brought to us by my friend, John Roach, of Fort Worth. John, many of you will remember, was Chairman of Justin Industries, which we bought in 2000. At that time John was helping John Justin, who was terminally ill, find a permanent home for his company. John Justin died soon after we bought Justin Industries, but it has since been run exactly as we promised him it would be.

Visiting me in November, John Roach brought along Paul Andrews, Jr., owner of about 80% of TTI, a Fort Worth distributor of electronic components. Over a 35-year period, Paul built TTI from $112,000 of sales to $1.3 billion. He is a remarkable entrepreneur and operator.

Paul, 64, loves running his business. But not long ago he happened to witness how disruptive the death of a founder can be both to a private company's employees and the owner's family. What starts out as disruptive, furthermore, often evolves into destructive. About a year ago, therefore, Paul began to think about selling TTI. His goal was to put his business in the hands of an owner he had carefully chosen, rather than allowing a trust officer or lawyer to conduct an auction after his death.

Paul rejected the idea of a "strategic" buyer, knowing that in the pursuit of "synergies," an owner of that type would be apt to dismantle what he had so carefully built, a move that would uproot hundreds of his associates (and perhaps wound TTI's business in the process). He also ruled out a private equity firm, which would very likely load the company with debt and then flip it as soon as possible.

That left Berkshire. Paul and I met on the morning of November 15th and made a deal before lunch. Later he wrote me: "After our meeting, I am confident that Berkshire is the right owner for TTI . . . I am proud of our past and excited about our future." And so are Charlie and I.

* * * * * * * * * * *

We also made some "tuck-in" acquisitions during 2006 at Fruit of the Loom ("Fruit"), MiTek, CTB, Shaw and Clayton. Fruit made the largest purchases. First, it bought Russell Corp., a leading producer of athletic apparel and uniforms for about $1.2 billion (including assumed debt) and in December it agreed to buy the intimate apparel business of VF Corp. Together, these acquisitions add about $2.2 billion to Fruit's sales and bring with them about 23,000 employees.

Charlie and I love it when we can acquire businesses that can be placed under managers, such as John Holland at Fruit, who have already shown their stuff at Berkshire. MiTek, for example, has made 14 acquisitions since we purchased it in 2001, and Gene Toombs has delivered results from these deals far in excess of what he had predicted. In effect, we leverage the managerial talent already with us by these tuck-in deals. We will make many more.

* * * * * * * * * * *

We continue, however, to need "elephants" in order for us to use Berkshire's flood of incoming cash. Charlie and I must therefore ignore the pursuit of mice and focus our acquisition efforts on much bigger game.

Our exemplar is the older man who crashed his grocery cart into that of a much younger fellow while both were shopping. The elderly man explained apologetically that he had lost track of his wife and was preoccupied searching for her. His new acquaintance said that by coincidence his wife had also wandered off and suggested that it might be more efficient if they jointly looked for the two women. Agreeing, the older man asked his new companion what his wife looked like. "She's a gorgeous blonde," the fellow answered, "with a body that would cause a bishop to go through a stained glass window, and she's wearing tight white shorts. How about yours?" The senior citizen wasted no words: "Forget her, we'll look for yours."

What *we* are looking for is described on page 25. If you have an acquisition candidate that fits, call me – day or night. And then watch me shatter a stained glass window.

* * * * * * * * * * * *

Now, let's examine the four major operating sectors of Berkshire. Lumping their financial figures together impedes analysis. So we'll look at them as four separate businesses, starting with the all–important insurance group.

Insurance

Next month marks the 40th anniversary of our entrance into the insurance business. It was on March 9, 1967, that Berkshire purchased National Indemnity and its companion company, National Fire & Marine, from Jack Ringwalt for $8.6 million.

Jack was a long-time friend of mine and an excellent, but somewhat eccentric, businessman. For about ten minutes every year he would get the urge to sell his company. But those moods – perhaps brought on by a tiff with regulators or an unfavorable jury verdict – quickly vanished.

In the mid-1960s, I asked investment banker Charlie Heider, a mutual friend of mine and Jack's, to alert me the next time Jack was "in heat." When Charlie's call came, I sped to meet Jack. We made a deal in a few minutes, with me waiving an audit, "due diligence" or anything else that would give Jack an opportunity to reconsider. We just shook hands, and that was that.

When we were due to close the purchase at Charlie's office, Jack was late. Finally arriving, he explained that he had been driving around looking for a parking meter with some unexpired time. That was a magic moment for me. I knew then that Jack was going to be my kind of manager.

When Berkshire purchased Jack's two insurers, they had "float" of $17 million. We've regularly offered a long explanation of float in earlier reports, which you can read on our website. Simply put, float is money we hold that is not ours but which we get to invest.

At the end of 2006, our float had grown to $50.9 billion, and we have since written a huge retroactive reinsurance contract with Equitas – which I will describe in the next section – that boosts float by another $7 billion. Much of the gain we've made has come through our acquisition of other insurers, but we've also had outstanding internal growth, particularly at Ajit Jain's amazing reinsurance operation. Naturally, I had no notion in 1967 that our float would develop as it has. There's much to be said for just putting one foot in front of the other every day.

The float from retroactive reinsurance contracts, of which we have many, automatically drifts down over time. Therefore, it will be difficult for us to increase float in the future unless we make new acquisitions in the insurance field. Whatever its size, however, the all-important *cost* of Berkshire's float over time is likely to be significantly below that of the industry, perhaps even falling to less than zero. Note the words "over time." There will be bad years periodically. You can be sure of that.

In 2006, though, everything went right in insurance – *really* right. Our managers – Tony Nicely (GEICO), Ajit Jain (B-H Reinsurance), Joe Brandon and Tad Montross (General Re), Don Wurster (National Indemnity Primary), Tom Nerney (U.S. Liability), Tim Kenesey (Medical Protective), Rod Eldred (Homestate Companies and Cypress), Sid Ferenc and Steve Menzies (Applied Underwriters), John Kizer (Central States) and Don Towle (Kansas Bankers Surety) – simply shot the lights out. When I recite their names, I feel as if I'm at Cooperstown, reading from the Hall of Fame roster. Of course, the overall insurance industry also had a terrific year in 2006. But our managers delivered results generally superior to those of their competitors.

Below is the tally on our underwriting and float for each major sector of insurance. Enjoy the view, because you won't soon see another like it.

(in $ millions)

Insurance Operations	Underwriting Profit (Loss)		Yearend Float	
	2006	2005	2006	2005
General Re	$ 526	$(334)	$22,827	$22,920
B-H Reinsurance.............	1,658	(1,069)	16,860	16,233
GEICO	1,314	1,221	7,171	6,692
Other Primary..................	340**	235*	4,029	3,442
Total................................	$3,838	$ 53	$50,887	$49,287

* Includes MedPro from June 30, 2005.
** Includes Applied Underwriters from May 19, 2006.

* * * * * * * * * * *

In 2007, our results from the bread-and-butter lines of insurance will deteriorate, though I think they will remain satisfactory. The big unknown is super-cat insurance. Were the terrible hurricane seasons of 2004-05 aberrations? Or were they our planet's first warning that the climate of the 21st Century will differ materially from what we've seen in the past? If the answer to the second question is yes, 2006 will soon be perceived as a misleading period of calm preceding a series of devastating storms. These could rock the insurance industry. It's naïve to think of Katrina as anything close to a worst-case event.

Neither Ajit Jain, who manages our super-cat operation, nor I know what lies ahead. We do know that it would be a huge mistake to bet that evolving atmospheric changes are benign in their implications for insurers.

Don't think, however, that we have lost our taste for risk. We remain prepared to lose $6 billion in a single event, *if* we have been paid appropriately for assuming that risk. We are not willing, though, to take on even very small exposures at prices that don't reflect our evaluation of loss probabilities. Appropriate prices don't guarantee profits in any given year, but inappropriate prices most certainly guarantee eventual losses. Rates have recently fallen because a flood of capital has entered the super-cat field. We have therefore sharply reduced our wind exposures. Our behavior here parallels that which we employ in financial markets: Be fearful when others are greedy, and be greedy when others are fearful.

Lloyd's, Equitas and Retroactive Reinsurance

Last year – we are getting now to Equitas – Berkshire agreed to enter into a huge retroactive reinsurance contract, a policy that protects an insurer against losses that have already happened, but whose cost is not yet known. I'll give you details of the agreement shortly. But let's first take a journey through insurance history, following the route that led to our deal.

Our tale begins around 1688, when Edward Lloyd opened a small coffee house in London. Though no Starbucks, his shop was destined to achieve worldwide fame because of the commercial activities of its clientele – shipowners, merchants and venturesome British capitalists. As these parties sipped Edward's brew, they began to write contracts transferring the risk of a disaster at sea from the owners of ships and their cargo to the capitalists, who wagered that a given voyage would be completed without incident. These capitalists eventually became known as "underwriters at Lloyd's."

Though many people believe Lloyd's to be an insurance company, that is not the case. It is instead a *place* where many member-insurers transact business, just as they did centuries ago.

Over time, the underwriters solicited passive investors to join in syndicates. Additionally, the business broadened beyond marine risks into every imaginable form of insurance, including exotic coverages that spread the fame of Lloyd's far and wide. The underwriters left the coffee house, found grander quarters and formalized some rules of association. And those persons who passively backed the underwriters became known as "names."

Eventually, the names came to include many thousands of people from around the world, who joined expecting to pick up some extra change without effort or serious risk. True, prospective names were always solemnly told that they would have unlimited and everlasting liability for the consequences of their syndicate's underwriting – "down to the last cufflink," as the quaint description went. But that warning came to be viewed as perfunctory. Three hundred years of retained cufflinks acted as a powerful sedative to the names poised to sign up.

Then came asbestos. When its prospective costs were added to the tidal wave of environmental and product claims that surfaced in the 1980s, Lloyd's began to implode. Policies written decades earlier – and largely forgotten about – were developing huge losses. No one could intelligently estimate their total, but it was certain to be many tens of billions of dollars. The specter of unending and unlimited losses terrified existing names and scared away prospects. Many names opted for bankruptcy; some even chose suicide.

From these shambles, there came a desperate effort to resuscitate Lloyd's. In 1996, the powers that be at the institution allotted £11.1 billion to a new company, Equitas, and made it responsible for paying all claims on policies written before 1993. In effect, this plan pooled the misery of the many syndicates in trouble. Of course, the money allotted could prove to be insufficient – and if that happened, the names remained liable for the shortfall.

But the new plan, by concentrating all of the liabilities in one place, had the advantage of eliminating much of the costly intramural squabbling that went on among syndicates. Moreover, the pooling allowed claims evaluation, negotiation and litigation to be handled more intelligently than had been the case previously. Equitas embraced Ben Franklin's thinking: "We must all hang together, or assuredly we shall hang separately."

From the start, many people predicted Equitas would eventually fail. But as Ajit and I reviewed the facts in the spring of 2006 – 13 years after the last exposed policy had been written and after the payment of £11.3 billion in claims – we concluded that the patient was likely to survive. And so we decided to offer a huge reinsurance policy to Equitas.

Because plenty of imponderables continue to exist, Berkshire could not provide Equitas, and its 27,972 names, unlimited protection. But we said – and I'm simplifying – that if Equitas would give us $7.12 billion in cash and securities (this is the float I spoke about), we would pay all of its future claims and expenses up to $13.9 billion. That amount was $5.7 billion above what Equitas had recently guessed its ultimate liabilities to be. Thus the names received a huge – and almost certainly sufficient – amount of future protection against unpleasant surprises. Indeed the protection is so large that Equitas plans a cash payment to its thousands of names, an event few of them had ever dreamed possible.

And how will Berkshire fare? That depends on how much "known" claims will end up costing us, how many yet-to-be-presented claims will surface and what they will cost, how soon claim payments will be made and how much we earn on the cash we receive before it must be paid out. Ajit and I think the odds are in our favor. And should we be wrong, Berkshire can handle it.

Scott Moser, the CEO of Equitas, summarized the transaction neatly: "Names wanted to sleep easy at night, and we think we've just bought them the world's best mattress."

* * * * * * * * * * *

Warning: It's time to eat your broccoli – I am now going to talk about accounting matters. I owe this to those Berkshire shareholders who love reading about debits and credits. I hope both of you find this discussion helpful. All others can skip this section; there will be no quiz.

Berkshire has done many retroactive transactions – in both number and amount a multiple of such policies entered into by any other insurer. We are the reinsurer of choice for these coverages because the obligations that are transferred to us – for example, lifetime indemnity and medical payments to be made to injured workers – may not be fully satisfied for 50 years or more. No other company can offer the certainty that Berkshire can, in terms of guaranteeing the full and fair settlement of these obligations. This fact is important to the original insurer, policyholders and regulators.

The accounting procedure for retroactive transactions is neither well known nor intuitive. The best way for shareholders to understand it, therefore, is for us to simply lay out the debits and credits. Charlie and I would like to see this done more often. We sometimes encounter accounting footnotes about important transactions that leave us baffled, and we go away suspicious that the reporting company wished it that way. (For example, try comprehending transactions "described" in the old 10-Ks of Enron, even after you *know* how the movie ended.)

So let us summarize our accounting for the Equitas transaction. The major debits will be to Cash and Investments, Reinsurance Recoverable, and Deferred Charges for Reinsurance Assumed ("DCRA"). The major credit will be to Reserve for Losses and Loss Adjustment Expense. No profit or loss will be recorded at the inception of the transaction, but underwriting losses will thereafter be incurred annually as the DCRA asset is amortized downward. The amount of the annual amortization charge will be primarily determined by how our end-of-the-year estimates as to the timing and amount of future loss payments compare to the estimates made at the beginning of the year. Eventually, when the last claim has been paid, the DCRA account will be reduced to zero. That day is 50 years or more away.

What's important to remember is that retroactive insurance contracts always produce underwriting losses for us. Whether these losses are worth experiencing depends on whether the cash we have received produces investment income that exceeds the losses. Recently our DCRA charges have annually delivered $300 million or so of underwriting losses, which have been more than offset by the income we have realized through use of the cash we received as a premium. Absent new retroactive contracts, the amount of the annual charge would normally decline over time. After the Equitas transaction, however, the annual DCRA cost will initially increase to about $450 million a year. This means that our other insurance operations must generate at least that much underwriting gain for our overall float to be cost-free. That amount is quite a hurdle but one that I believe we will clear in many, if not most, years.

Aren't you glad that I promised you there would be no quiz?

Manufacturing, Service and Retailing Operations

Our activities in this part of Berkshire cover the waterfront. Let's look, though, at a summary balance sheet and earnings statement for the entire group.

Balance Sheet 12/31/06 (in millions)

Assets		Liabilities and Equity	
Cash and equivalents	$ 1,543	Notes payable	$ 1,468
Accounts and notes receivable	3,793	Other current liabilities	6,635
Inventory	5,257	Total current liabilities	8,103
Other current assets	363		
Total current assets	10,956		
Goodwill and other intangibles	13,314	Deferred taxes	540
Fixed assets	8,934	Term debt and other liabilities	3,014
Other assets	1,168	Equity	22,715
	$34,372		$34,372

Earnings Statement (in millions)

	2006	2005	2004
Revenues	$52,660	$46,896	$44,142
Operating expenses (including depreciation of $823 in 2006, $699 in 2005 and $676 in 2004)	49,002	44,190	41,604
Interest expense	132	83	57
Pre-tax earnings	3,526*	2,623*	2,481*
Income taxes and minority interests	1,395	977	941
Net income	$ 2,131	$ 1,646	$ 1,540

*Does not include purchase-accounting adjustments.

This motley group, which sells products ranging from lollipops to motor homes, earned a pleasing 25% on average tangible net worth last year. It's noteworthy also that these operations used only minor financial leverage in achieving that return. Clearly we own some terrific businesses. We purchased many of them, however, at large premiums to net worth – a point reflected in the goodwill item shown on the balance sheet – and that fact reduces the earnings on our average *carrying* value to 10.8%.

Here are a few newsworthy items about companies in this sector:

- Bob Shaw, a remarkable entrepreneur who from a standing start built Shaw Industries into the country's largest carpet producer, elected last year, at age 75, to retire. To succeed him, Bob recommended Vance Bell, a 31-year veteran at Shaw, and Bob, as usual, made the right call. Weakness in housing has caused the carpet business to slow. Shaw, however, remains a powerhouse and a major contributor to Berkshire's earnings.

- MiTek, a manufacturer of connectors for roof trusses at the time we purchased it in 2001, is developing into a mini-conglomerate. At the rate it is growing, in fact, "mini" may soon be inappropriate. In purchasing MiTek for $420 million, we lent the company $200 million at 9% and bought $198 million of stock, priced at $10,000 per share. Additionally, 55 employees bought 2,200 shares for $22 million. Each employee paid *exactly* the same price that we did, in most cases borrowing money to do so.

  And are they ever glad they did! Five years later, MiTek's sales have tripled and the stock is valued at $71,699 per share. Despite its making 14 acquisitions, at a cost of $291 million, MiTek has paid off its debt to Berkshire and holds $35 million of cash. We celebrated the fifth anniversary of our purchase with a party in July. I told the group that it would be embarrassing if MiTek's stock price soared beyond that of Berkshire "A" shares. Don't be surprised, however, if that happens (though Charlie and I will try to make our shares a moving target).

- Not all of our businesses are destined to increase profits. When an industry's underlying economics are crumbling, talented management may slow the rate of decline. Eventually, though, eroding fundamentals will overwhelm managerial brilliance. (As a wise friend told me long ago, "If you want to get a reputation as a good businessman, be sure to get into a good business.") And fundamentals are definitely eroding in the newspaper industry, a trend that has caused the profits of our Buffalo News to decline. The skid will almost certainly continue.

  When Charlie and I were young, the newspaper business was as easy a way to make huge returns as existed in America. As one not-too-bright publisher famously said, "I owe my fortune to two great American institutions: monopoly and nepotism." No paper in a one-paper city, however bad the product or however inept the management, could avoid gushing profits.

  The industry's staggering returns could be simply explained. For most of the 20th Century, newspapers were the primary source of information for the American public. Whether the subject was sports, finance, or politics, newspapers reigned supreme. Just as important, their ads were the easiest way to find job opportunities or to learn the price of groceries at your town's supermarkets.

The great majority of families therefore felt the need for a paper every day, but understandably most didn't wish to pay for two. Advertisers preferred the paper with the most circulation, and readers tended to want the paper with the most ads and news pages. This circularity led to a law of the newspaper jungle: Survival of the Fattest.

Thus, when two or more papers existed in a major city (which was almost universally the case a century ago), the one that pulled ahead usually emerged as the stand-alone winner. After competition disappeared, the paper's pricing power in both advertising and circulation was unleashed. Typically, rates for both advertisers and readers would be raised annually – and the profits rolled in. For owners this was economic heaven. (Interestingly, though papers regularly – and often in a disapproving way – reported on the profitability of, say, the auto or steel industries, they never enlightened readers about their own Midas-like situation. Hmmm . . .)

As long ago as my 1991 letter to shareholders, I nonetheless asserted that this insulated world was changing, writing that "the media businesses . . . will prove considerably less marvelous than I, the industry, or lenders thought would be the case only a few years ago." Some publishers took umbrage at both this remark and other warnings from me that followed. Newspaper properties, moreover, continued to sell as if they were indestructible slot machines. In fact, many intelligent newspaper executives who regularly chronicled and analyzed important worldwide events were either blind or indifferent to what was going on under their noses.

Now, however, almost all newspaper owners realize that they are constantly losing ground in the battle for eyeballs. Simply put, if cable and satellite broadcasting, as well as the internet, had come along first, newspapers as we know them probably would never have existed.

In Berkshire's world, Stan Lipsey does a terrific job running the Buffalo News, and I am enormously proud of its editor, Margaret Sullivan. The News' penetration of its market is the highest among that of this country's large newspapers. We also do better financially than most metropolitan newspapers, even though Buffalo's population and business trends are not good. Nevertheless, this operation faces unrelenting pressures that will cause profit margins to slide.

True, we have the leading online news operation in Buffalo, and it will continue to attract more viewers and ads. However, the economic potential of a newspaper internet site – given the many alternative sources of information and entertainment that are free and only a click away – is at best a small fraction of that existing in the past for a print newspaper facing no competition.

For a local resident, ownership of a city's paper, like ownership of a sports team, still produces instant prominence. With it typically comes power and influence. These are ruboffs that appeal to many people with money. Beyond that, civic-minded, wealthy individuals may feel that local ownership will serve their community well. That's why Peter Kiewit bought the Omaha paper more than 40 years ago.

We are likely therefore to see non-economic individual buyers of newspapers emerge, just as we have seen such buyers acquire major sports franchises. Aspiring press lords should be careful, however: There's no rule that says a newspaper's revenues can't fall below its expenses and that losses can't mushroom. Fixed costs are high in the newspaper business, and that's bad news when unit volume heads south. As the importance of newspapers diminishes, moreover, the "psychic" value of possessing one will wane, whereas owning a sports franchise will likely retain its cachet.

Unless we face an irreversible cash drain, we will stick with the News, just as we've said that we would. (Read economic principle 11, on page 76.) Charlie and I love newspapers – we each read five a day – and believe that a free and energetic press is a key ingredient for maintaining a great democracy. We hope that some combination of print and online will ward off economic doomsday for newspapers, and we will work hard in Buffalo to develop a sustainable business model. I think we will be successful. But the days of lush profits from our newspaper are over.

- A *much* improved situation is emerging at NetJets, which sells and manages fractionally-owned aircraft. This company has never had a problem growing: Revenues from flight operations have increased 596% since our purchase in 1998. But profits had been erratic.

Our move to Europe, which began in 1996, was particularly expensive. After five years of operation there, we had acquired only 80 customers. And by mid-year 2006 our cumulative pre-tax loss had risen to $212 million. But European demand has now exploded, with a net of 589 customers having been added in 2005-2006. Under Mark Booth's brilliant leadership, NetJets is now operating profitably in Europe, and we expect the positive trend to continue.

Our U.S. operation also had a good year in 2006, which led to worldwide pre-tax earnings of $143 million at NetJets last year. We made this profit even though we suffered a loss of $19 million in the first quarter.

Credit Rich Santulli, along with Mark, for this turnaround. Rich, like many of our managers, has no financial need to work. But you'd never know it. He's absolutely tireless – monitoring operations, making sales, and traveling the globe to constantly widen the already-enormous lead that NetJets enjoys over its competitors. Today, the value of the fleet we manage is far greater than that managed by our three largest competitors *combined*.

There's a reason NetJets is the runaway leader: It offers the ultimate in safety and service. At Berkshire, and at a number of our subsidiaries, NetJets aircraft are an indispensable business tool. I also have a contract for personal use with NetJets and so do members of my family and most Berkshire directors. (None of us, I should add, gets a discount.) Once you've flown NetJets, returning to commercial flights is like going back to holding hands.

Regulated Utility Business

Berkshire has an 86.6% (fully diluted) interest in MidAmerican Energy Holdings, which owns a wide variety of utility operations. The largest of these are (1) Yorkshire Electricity and Northern Electric, whose 3.7 million electric customers make it the third largest distributor of electricity in the U.K.; (2) MidAmerican Energy, which serves 706,000 electric customers, primarily in Iowa; (3) Pacific Power and Rocky Mountain Power, serving about 1.7 million electric customers in six western states; and (4) Kern River and Northern Natural pipelines, which carry about 8% of the natural gas consumed in the U.S.

Our partners in ownership of MidAmerican are Walter Scott, and its two terrific managers, Dave Sokol and Greg Abel. It's unimportant how many votes each party has; we will make major moves only when we are unanimous in thinking them wise. Six years of working with Dave, Greg and Walter have underscored my original belief: Berkshire couldn't have better partners.

Somewhat incongruously, MidAmerican owns the second largest real estate brokerage firm in the U.S., HomeServices of America. This company operates through 20 locally-branded firms with 20,300 agents. Despite HomeServices' purchase of two operations last year, the company's overall volume fell 9% to $58 billion, and profits fell 50%.

The slowdown in residential real estate activity stems in part from the weakened lending practices of recent years. The "optional" contracts and "teaser" rates that have been popular have allowed borrowers to make payments in the early years of their mortgages that fall far short of covering normal interest costs. Naturally, there are few defaults when virtually nothing is required of a borrower. As a cynic has said, "A rolling loan gathers no loss." But payments *not* made add to principal, and borrowers who can't afford normal monthly payments early on are hit later with *above-normal* monthly obligations. This is the Scarlett O'Hara scenario: "I'll think about that tomorrow." For many home owners, "tomorrow" has now arrived. Consequently there is a huge overhang of offerings in several of HomeServices' markets.

Nevertheless, we will be seeking to purchase additional brokerage operations. A decade from now, HomeServices will almost certainly be much larger.

Here are some key figures on MidAmerican's operations:

	Earnings (in $ millions)	
	2006	2005
U.K. utilities	$ 338	$ 308
Iowa utility	348	288
Western utilities (acquired March 21, 2006)	356	N/A
Pipelines	376	309
HomeServices	74	148
Other (net)	226	115
Earnings before corporate interest and taxes	1,718	1,168
Interest, other than to Berkshire	(261)	(200)
Interest on Berkshire junior debt	(134)	(157)
Income tax	(407)	(248)
Net earnings	$ 916	$ 563
Earnings applicable to Berkshire*	$ 885	$ 523
Debt owed to others	16,946	10,296
Debt owed to Berkshire	1,055	1,289

*Includes interest earned by Berkshire (net of related income taxes) of $87 in 2006 and $102 in 2005.

Finance and Financial Products

You will be happy to hear – and I'm even happier – that this will be my last discussion of the losses at Gen Re's derivative operation. When we started to wind this business down early in 2002, we had 23,218 contracts outstanding. Now we have 197. Our cumulative pre-tax loss from this operation totals $409 million, but only $5 million occurred in 2006. Charlie says that if we had properly classified the $409 million on our 2001 balance sheet, it would have been labeled "Good Until Reached For." In any event, a Shakespearean thought – slightly modified – seems appropriate for the tombstone of this derivative business: "All's well that ends."

We've also wound up our investment in Value Capital. So earnings or losses from these two lines of business are making their final appearance in the table that annually appears in this section.

Clayton Homes remains an anomaly in the manufactured-housing industry, which last year recorded its lowest unit sales since 1962. Indeed, the industry's volume last year was only about one-third that of 1999. Outside of Clayton, I doubt if the industry, overall, made *any* money in 2006.

Yet Clayton earned $513 million pre-tax and paid Berkshire an additional $86 million as a fee for our obtaining the funds to finance Clayton's $10 billion portfolio of installment receivables. Berkshire's financial strength has clearly been of huge help to Clayton. But the driving force behind the company's success is Kevin Clayton. Kevin knows the business forward and backward, is a rational decision-maker and a joy to work with. Because of acquisitions, Clayton now employs 14,787 people, compared to 6,661 at the time of our purchase.

We have two leasing operations: CORT (furniture), run by Paul Arnold, and XTRA (truck trailers), run by Bill Franz. CORT's earnings improved significantly last year, and XTRA's remained at the high level attained in 2005. We continue to look for tuck-in acquisitions to be run by Paul or Bill, and also are open to ideas for new leasing opportunities.

Here's a breakdown of earnings in this sector:

	Pre-Tax Earnings		Interest-Bearing Liabilities	
(in millions)	*2006*	*2005*	*2006*	*2005*
Trading – ordinary income	$ 274	$ 200	$ 600	$1,061
Gen Re Securities (loss)	(5)	(104)	1,204*	2,617*
Life and annuity operation	29	11	2,459	2,461
Value Capital (loss)	6	(33)	N/A	N/A
Leasing operations	182	173	261	370
Manufactured-housing finance (Clayton)	513	416	10,498	9,299
Other	158	159	N/A	N/A
Income before capital gains	1,157	822		
Trading – capital gains (losses)	938	(234)		
Total	$ 2,095	$ 588		

*Includes all liabilities

Investments

We show below our common stock investments. With two exceptions, those that had a market value of more than $700 million at the end of 2006 are itemized. We don't itemize the two securities referred to, which have a market value of $1.9 billion, because we continue to buy them. I could, of course, tell you their names. But then I would have to kill you.

			12/31/06	
Shares	Company	Percentage of Company Owned	Cost*	Market
			(in millions)	
151,610,700	American Express Company	12.6	$ 1,287	$ 9,198
36,417,400	Anheuser-Busch Cos., Inc.	4.7	1,761	1,792
200,000,000	The Coca-Cola Company	8.6	1,299	9,650
17,938,100	Conoco Phillips	1.1	1,066	1,291
21,334,900	Johnson & Johnson	0.7	1,250	1,409
6,708,760	M&T Bank Corporation	6.1	103	820
48,000,000	Moody's Corporation	17.2	499	3,315
2,338,961,000	PetroChina "H" shares (or equivalents)	1.3	488	3,313
3,486,006	POSCO	4.0	572	1,158
100,000,000	The Procter & Gamble Company	3.2	940	6,427
229,707,000	Tesco	2.9	1,340	1,820
31,033,800	US Bancorp	1.8	969	1,123
17,072,192	USG Corp	19.0	536	936
19,944,300	Wal-Mart Stores, Inc.	0.5	942	921
1,727,765	The Washington Post Company	18.0	11	1,288
218,169,300	Wells Fargo & Company	6.5	3,697	7,758
1,724,200	White Mountains Insurance	16.0	369	999
	Others		5,866	8,315
	Total Common Stocks		$22,995	$61,533

*This is our actual purchase price and also our tax basis; GAAP "cost" differs in a few cases because of write-ups or write-downs that have been required.

We are delighted by the 2006 business performance of virtually all of our investees. Last year, we told you that our expectation was that these companies, in aggregate, would increase their earnings by 6% to 8% annually, a rate that would double their earnings every ten years or so. In 2006 American Express,

15

Coca-Cola, Procter & Gamble and Wells Fargo, our largest holdings, increased per-share earnings by 18%, 9%, 8% and 11%. These are stellar results, and we thank their CEOs.

* * * * * * * * * * * *

We've come close to eliminating our direct foreign-exchange position, from which we realized about $186 million in pre-tax profits in 2006 (earnings that were included in the Finance and Financial Products table shown earlier). That brought our total gain since inception of this position in 2002 to $2.2 billion. Here's a breakdown by currency:

Total Gain (Loss) in Millions

Australian dollar	$247.1	Mexican peso	$106.1
British pound	287.2	New Zealand dollar	102.6
Canadian dollar	398.3	Singapore dollar	(2.6)
Chinese yuan	(12.7)	South Korean won	261.3
Euro	839.2	Swiss franc	9.6
Hong Kong dollar	(2.5)	Taiwan dollar	(45.3)
Japanese yen	1.9	Miscellaneous options	22.9

We've made large indirect currency profits as well, though I've never tallied the precise amount. For example, in 2002-2003 we spent about $82 million buying – of all things – Enron bonds, some of which were denominated in Euros. Already we've received distributions of $179 million from these bonds, and our remaining stake is worth $173 million. That means our overall gain is $270 million, part of which came from the appreciation of the Euro that took place after our bond purchase.

When we first began making foreign exchange purchases, interest-rate differentials between the U.S. and most foreign countries favored a direct currency position. But that spread turned negative in 2005. We therefore looked for other ways to gain foreign-currency exposure, such as the ownership of foreign equities or of U.S. stocks with major earnings abroad. The currency factor, we should emphasize, is not dominant in our selection of equities, but is merely one of many considerations.

As our U.S. trade problems worsen, the probability that the dollar will weaken over time continues to be high. I fervently believe in *real* trade – the more the better for both us and the world. We had about $1.44 trillion of this honest-to-God trade in 2006. But the U.S. also had $.76 trillion of *pseudo*-trade last year – imports for which we exchanged no goods or services. (Ponder, for a moment, how commentators would describe the situation if our imports were $.76 trillion – a full 6% of GDP – and we had *no* exports.) Making these purchases that weren't reciprocated by sales, the U.S. necessarily transferred ownership of its assets or IOUs to the rest of the world. Like a very wealthy but self-indulgent family, we peeled off a bit of what we owned in order to consume more than we produced.

The U.S. can do a lot of this because we are an extraordinarily rich country that has behaved responsibly in the past. The world is therefore willing to accept our bonds, real estate, stocks and businesses. And we have a vast store of these to hand over.

These transfers will have consequences, however. Already the prediction I made last year about one fall-out from our spending binge has come true: The "investment income" account of our country – positive in every previous year since *1915* – turned negative in 2006. Foreigners now earn more on their U.S. investments than we do on our investments abroad. In effect, we've used up our bank account and turned to our credit card. And, like everyone who gets in hock, the U.S. will now experience "reverse compounding" as we pay ever-increasing amounts of interest on interest.

I want to emphasize that even though our course is unwise, Americans will live better ten or twenty years from now than they do today. Per-capita wealth will increase. But our citizens will also be forced every year to ship a significant portion of their current production abroad merely to service the cost of our huge debtor position. It won't be pleasant to work part of each day to pay for the over-consumption of your ancestors. I believe that at some point in the future U.S. workers and voters will find this annual "tribute" so onerous that there will be a severe political backlash. How that will play out in markets is impossible to predict – but to expect a "soft landing" seems like wishful thinking.

* * * * * * * * * * *

I should mention that all of the direct currency profits we have realized have come from forward contracts, which are derivatives, and that we have entered into other types of derivatives contracts as well. That may seem odd, since you know of our expensive experience in unwinding the derivatives book at Gen Re and also have heard me talk of the systemic problems that could result from the enormous growth in the use of derivatives. Why, you may wonder, are we fooling around with such potentially toxic material?

The answer is that derivatives, just like stocks and bonds, are sometimes wildly mispriced. For many years, accordingly, we have selectively written derivative contracts – few in number but sometimes for large dollar amounts. We currently have 62 contracts outstanding. I manage them personally, and they are free of counterparty credit risk. So far, these derivative contracts have worked out well for us, producing pre-tax profits in the hundreds of millions of dollars (above and beyond the gains I've itemized from forward foreign-exchange contracts). Though we will experience losses from time to time, we are likely to continue to earn – overall – significant profits from mispriced derivatives.

* * * * * * * * * * *

I have told you that Berkshire has three outstanding candidates to replace me as CEO and that the Board knows exactly who should take over if I should die tonight. Each of the three is much younger than I. The directors believe it's important that my successor have the prospect of a long tenure.

Frankly, we are not as well-prepared on the investment side of our business. There's a history here: At one time, Charlie was my potential replacement for investing, and more recently Lou Simpson has filled that slot. Lou is a top-notch investor with an outstanding long-term record of managing GEICO's equity portfolio. But he is only six years younger than I. If I were to die soon, he would fill in magnificently for a short period. For the long-term, though, we need a different answer.

At our October board meeting, we discussed that subject fully. And we emerged with a plan, which I will carry out with the help of Charlie and Lou.

Under this plan, I intend to hire a younger man or woman with the potential to manage a very large portfolio, who we hope will succeed me as Berkshire's chief investment officer when the need for someone to do that arises. As part of the selection process, we may in fact take on several candidates.

Picking the right person(s) will not be an easy task. It's not hard, of course, to find smart people, among them individuals who have impressive investment records. But there is far more to successful long-term investing than brains and performance that has recently been good.

Over time, markets will do extraordinary, even bizarre, things. A single, big mistake could wipe out a long string of successes. We therefore need someone genetically programmed to recognize and avoid serious risks, *including those never before encountered*. Certain perils that lurk in investment strategies cannot be spotted by use of the models commonly employed today by financial institutions.

Temperament is also important. Independent thinking, emotional stability, and a keen understanding of both human and institutional behavior is vital to long-term investment success. I've seen a lot of very smart people who have lacked these virtues.

Finally, we have a special problem to consider: our ability to keep the person we hire. Being able to list Berkshire on a resume would materially enhance the marketability of an investment manager. We will need, therefore, to be sure we can retain our choice, even though he or she could leave and make much more money elsewhere.

There are surely people who fit what we need, but they may be hard to identify. In 1979, Jack Byrne and I felt we had found such a person in Lou Simpson. We then made an arrangement with him whereby he would be paid well for sustained overperformance. Under this deal, he has earned large amounts. Lou, however, could have left us long ago to manage far greater sums on more advantageous terms. If money alone had been the object, that's exactly what he would have done. But Lou never considered such a move. We need to find a younger person or two made of the same stuff.

* * * * * * * * * * * *

The good news: At 76, I feel terrific and, according to all measurable indicators, am in excellent health. It's amazing what Cherry Coke and hamburgers will do for a fellow.

Some Changes on Berkshire's Board

The composition of our board will change in two ways this spring. One change will involve the Chace family, which has been connected to Berkshire and its predecessor companies for more than a century. In 1929, the first Malcolm G. Chace played an important role in merging four New England textile operations into Berkshire Fine Spinning Associates. That company merged with Hathaway Manufacturing in 1955 to form Berkshire Hathaway, and Malcolm G. Chace, Jr. became its chairman.

Early in 1965, Malcolm arranged for Buffett Partnership Ltd. to buy a key block of Berkshire shares and welcomed us as the new controlling shareholder of the company. Malcolm continued as non-executive chairman until 1969. He was both a wonderful gentleman and helpful partner.

That description also fits his son, Malcolm "Kim" Chace, who succeeded his father on Berkshire's board in 1992. But last year Kim, now actively and successfully running a community bank that he founded in 1996, suggested that we find a younger person to replace him on our board. We have done so, and Kim will step down as a director at the annual meeting. I owe much to the Chaces and wish to thank Kim for his many years of service to Berkshire.

In selecting a new director, we were guided by our long-standing criteria, which are that board members be owner-oriented, business-savvy, interested and truly independent. I say "truly" because many directors who are now deemed independent by various authorities and observers are far from that, relying heavily as they do on directors' fees to maintain their standard of living. These payments, which come in many forms, often range between $150,000 and $250,000 annually, compensation that may approach or even exceed all other income of the "independent" director. And – surprise, surprise – director compensation has soared in recent years, pushed up by recommendations from corporate America's favorite consultant, Ratchet, Ratchet and Bingo. (The name may be phony, but the action it conveys is not.)

Charlie and I believe our four criteria are essential if directors are to do their job – which, by law, is to faithfully represent *owners*. Yet these criteria are usually ignored. Instead, consultants and CEOs seeking board candidates will often say, "We're looking for a woman," or "a Hispanic," or "someone from abroad," or what have you. It sometimes sounds as if the mission is to stock Noah's ark. Over the years I've been queried many times about potential directors and have yet to hear *anyone* ask, "Does he think like an intelligent owner?"

The questions I instead get would sound ridiculous to someone seeking candidates for, say, a football team, or an arbitration panel or a military command. In those cases, the selectors would look for people who had the specific talents and attitudes that were required for a specialized job. At Berkshire, we are in the specialized activity of running a business well, and therefore we seek *business* judgment.

That's exactly what we've found in Susan Decker, CFO of Yahoo!, who will join our board at the annual meeting. We are lucky to have her: She scores very high on our four criteria and additionally, at 44, is young – an attribute, as you may have noticed, that your Chairman has long lacked. We will seek more young directors in the future, but never by slighting the four qualities that we insist upon.

This and That

Berkshire will pay about $4.4 billion in federal income tax on its 2006 earnings. In its last fiscal year the U.S. Government spent $2.6 trillion, or about $7 billion per day. Thus, for more than half of one day, Berkshire picked up the tab for *all* federal expenditures, ranging from Social Security and Medicare payments to the cost of our armed services. Had there been only 600 taxpayers like Berkshire, no one else in America would have needed to pay *any* federal income or payroll taxes.

* * * * * * * * * * * *

Our federal return last year, we should add, ran to 9,386 pages. To handle this filing, state and foreign tax returns, a myriad of SEC requirements, and all of the other matters involved in running Berkshire, we have gone all the way up to 19 employees at World Headquarters.

This crew occupies 9,708 square feet of space, and Charlie – at World Headquarters West in Los Angeles – uses another 655 square feet. Our home-office payroll, including benefits and counting both locations, totaled $3,531,978 last year. We're careful when spending your money.

Corporate bigwigs often complain about government spending, criticizing bureaucrats who they say spend taxpayers' money differently from how they would if it were their own. But sometimes the financial behavior of executives will also vary based on whose wallet is getting depleted. Here's an illustrative tale from my days at Salomon. In the 1980s the company had a barber, Jimmy by name, who came in weekly to give free haircuts to the top brass. A manicurist was also on tap. Then, because of a cost-cutting drive, patrons were told to pay their own way. One top executive (not the CEO) who had previously visited Jimmy weekly went immediately to a once-every-three-weeks schedule.

* * * * * * * * * * * *

Every now and then Charlie and I catch on early to a tide-like trend, one brimming over with commercial promise. For example, though American Airlines (with its "miles") and American Express (with credit card points) are credited as being trailblazers in granting customers "rewards," Charlie and I were far ahead of them in spotting the appeal of this powerful idea. Excited by our insight, the two of us jumped into the reward business way back in 1970 by buying control of a trading stamp operation, Blue Chip Stamps. In that year, Blue Chip had sales of $126 million, and its stamps papered California.

In 1970, indeed, about 60 *billion* of our stamps were licked by savers, pasted into books, and taken to Blue Chip redemption stores. Our catalog of rewards was 116 pages thick and chock full of tantalizing items. When I was told that even certain brothels and mortuaries gave stamps to their patrons, I felt I had finally found a sure thing.

Well, not quite. From the day Charlie and I stepped into the Blue Chip picture, the business went straight downhill. By 1980, sales had fallen to $19.4 million. And, by 1990, sales were bumping along at $1.5 million. No quitter, I redoubled my managerial efforts.

Sales then fell another 98%. Last year, in Berkshire's $98 billion of revenues, all of $25,920 (*no* zeros omitted) came from Blue Chip. Ever hopeful, Charlie and I soldier on.

* * * * * * * * * * * *

I mentioned last year that in my service on 19 corporate boards (not counting Berkshire or other controlled companies), I have been the Typhoid Mary of compensation committees. At only one company was I assigned to comp committee duty, and then I was promptly outvoted on the most crucial decision that we faced. My ostracism has been peculiar, considering that I certainly haven't lacked experience in setting CEO pay. At Berkshire, after all, I am a one-man compensation committee who determines the salaries and incentives for the CEOs of around 40 significant operating businesses.

How much time does this aspect of my job take? Virtually none. How many CEOs have voluntarily left us for other jobs in our 42-year history? Precisely none.

Berkshire employs many different incentive arrangements, with their terms depending on such elements as the economic potential or capital intensity of a CEO's business. Whatever the compensation arrangement, though, I try to keep it both simple and fair.

When we use incentives – and these can be large – they are always tied to the operating results for which a given CEO has authority. We issue no lottery tickets that carry payoffs unrelated to business performance. If a CEO bats .300, he gets paid for being a .300 hitter, even if circumstances outside of his control cause Berkshire to perform poorly. And if he bats .150, he doesn't get a payoff just because the successes of others have enabled Berkshire to prosper mightily. An example: We now own $61 billion of equities at Berkshire, whose value can easily rise or fall by 10% in a given year. Why in the world should the pay of our operating executives be affected by such $6 billion swings, however important the gain or loss may be for shareholders?

You've read loads about CEOs who have received astronomical compensation for mediocre results. Much less well-advertised is the fact that America's CEOs also generally live the good life. Many, it should be emphasized, are exceptionally able, and almost all work far more than 40 hours a week. But they are usually treated like royalty in the process. (And we're certainly going to keep it that way at Berkshire. Though Charlie still favors sackcloth and ashes, I prefer to be spoiled rotten. Berkshire owns The Pampered Chef; our wonderful office group has made me The Pampered Chief.)

CEO perks at one company are quickly copied elsewhere. "All the other kids have one" may seem a thought too juvenile to use as a rationale in the boardroom. But consultants employ precisely this argument, phrased more elegantly of course, when they make recommendations to comp committees.

Irrational and excessive comp practices will not be materially changed by disclosure or by "independent" comp committee members. Indeed, I think it's likely that the reason I was rejected for service on so many comp committees was that I was regarded as *too* independent. Compensation reform will only occur if the largest institutional shareholders – it would only take a few – demand a *fresh* look at the whole system. The consultants' present drill of deftly selecting "peer" companies to compare with their clients will only perpetuate present excesses.

* * * * * * * * * * * *

Last year I arranged for the bulk of my Berkshire holdings to go to five charitable foundations, thus carrying out part of my lifelong plan to eventually use all of my shares for philanthropic purposes. Details of the commitments I made, as well as the rationale for them, are posted on our website, www.berkshirehathaway.com. Taxes, I should note, had nothing to do with my decision or its timing. My federal and state income taxes in 2006 were exactly what they would have been had I not made my first contributions last summer, and the same point will apply to my 2007 contributions.

In my will I've stipulated that the proceeds from all Berkshire shares I still own at death are to be used for philanthropic purposes within ten years after my estate is closed. Because my affairs are not complicated, it should take three years at most for this closing to occur. Adding this 13-year period to my expected lifespan of about 12 years (though, naturally, I'm aiming for more) means that proceeds from *all* of my Berkshire shares will likely be distributed for societal purposes over the next 25 years or so.

I've set this schedule because I want the money to be spent relatively promptly by people I *know* to be capable, vigorous and motivated. These managerial attributes sometimes wane as institutions – particularly those that are exempt from market forces – age. Today, there are terrific people in charge at the five foundations. So at my death, why should they not move with dispatch to judiciously spend the money that remains?

Those people favoring perpetual foundations argue that in the future there will most certainly be large and important societal problems that philanthropy will need to address. I agree. But there will then also be many super-rich individuals and families whose wealth will exceed that of today's Americans and to whom philanthropic organizations can make their case for funding. These funders can *then* judge firsthand which operations have both the vitality and the focus to best address the major societal problems that *then* exist. In this way, a market test of ideas and effectiveness can be applied. Some organizations will deserve major support while others will have outlived their usefulness. Even if the people above ground make their decisions imperfectly, they should be able to allocate funds more rationally than a decedent six feet under will have ordained decades earlier. Wills, of course, can always be rewritten, but it's very unlikely that my thinking will change in a material way.

A few shareholders have expressed concern that sales of Berkshire by the foundations receiving shares will depress the stock. These fears are unwarranted. The annual trading volume of many stocks exceeds 100% of the outstanding shares, but nevertheless these stocks usually sell at prices approximating their intrinsic value. Berkshire also tends to sell at an appropriate price, but with annual volume that is only 15% of shares outstanding. At most, sales by the foundations receiving my shares will add three percentage points to annual trading volume, which will still leave Berkshire with a turnover ratio that is the lowest around.

Overall, Berkshire's business performance will determine the price of our stock, and most of the time it will sell in a zone of reasonableness. It's important that the foundations receive appropriate prices as they periodically sell Berkshire shares, but it's also important that incoming shareholders don't overpay. (See economic principle 14 on page 77.) By both our policies and shareholder communications, Charlie and I will do our best to ensure that Berkshire sells at neither a large discount nor large premium to intrinsic value.

The existence of foundation ownership will in no way influence our board's decisions about dividends, repurchases, or the issuance of shares. We will follow exactly the same rule that has guided us in the past: What action will be likely to deliver the best result for shareholders over time?

* * * * * * * * * * * * * *

In last year's report I allegorically described the Gotrocks family – a clan that owned all of America's businesses and that counterproductively attempted to increase its investment returns by paying ever-greater commissions and fees to "helpers." Sad to say, the "family" continued its self-destructive ways in 2006.

In part the family persists in this folly because it harbors unrealistic expectations about obtainable returns. Sometimes these delusions are self-serving. For example, private pension plans can temporarily overstate their earnings, and public pension plans can defer the need for increased taxes, by using investment assumptions that are likely to be out of reach. Actuaries and auditors go along with these tactics, and it can be decades before the chickens come home to roost (at which point the CEO or public official who misled the world is apt to be gone).

Meanwhile, Wall Street's Pied Pipers of Performance will have encouraged the futile hopes of the family. The hapless Gotrocks will be assured that they *all* can achieve above-average investment performance – but only by paying ever-higher fees. Call this promise the adult version of Lake Woebegon.

In 2006, promises and fees hit new highs. A flood of money went from institutional investors to the 2-and-20 crowd. For those innocent of this arrangement, let me explain: It's a lopsided system whereby 2% of your *principal* is paid each year to the manager even if he accomplishes nothing – or, for that matter, loses you a bundle – and, additionally, 20% of your profit is paid to him if he succeeds, even if his success is due simply to a rising tide. For example, a manager who achieves a gross return of 10% in a year will keep 3.6 percentage points – two points off the top plus 20% of the residual 8 points – leaving only 6.4 percentage points for his investors. On a $3 billion fund, this 6.4% net "performance" will deliver the manager a cool $108 million. He will receive this bonanza even though an index fund might have returned 15% to investors in the same period and charged them only a token fee.

The inexorable math of this grotesque arrangement is certain to make the Gotrocks family poorer over time than it would have been had it never heard of these "hyper-helpers." Even so, the 2-and-20 action spreads. Its effects bring to mind the old adage: When someone with experience proposes a deal to someone with money, too often the fellow with money ends up with the experience, and the fellow with experience ends up with the money.

* * * * * * * * * * * *

Let me end this section by telling you about one of the good guys of Wall Street, my long-time friend Walter Schloss, who last year turned 90. From 1956 to 2002, Walter managed a remarkably successful investment partnership, from which he took not a dime unless his investors made money. My admiration for Walter, it should be noted, is not based on hindsight. A full fifty years ago, Walter was my sole recommendation to a St. Louis family who wanted an honest and able investment manager.

Walter did not go to business school, or for that matter, college. His office contained one file cabinet in 1956; the number mushroomed to four by 2002. Walter worked without a secretary, clerk or bookkeeper, his only associate being his son, Edwin, a graduate of the North Carolina School of the Arts. Walter and Edwin never came within a mile of inside information. Indeed, they used "outside" information only sparingly, generally selecting securities by certain simple statistical methods Walter learned while working for Ben Graham. When Walter and Edwin were asked in 1989 by *Outstanding Investors Digest*, "How would you summarize your approach?" Edwin replied, "We try to buy stocks cheap." So much for Modern Portfolio Theory, technical analysis, macroeconomic thoughts and complex algorithms.

Following a strategy that involved no real risk – defined as permanent loss of capital – Walter produced results over his 47 partnership years that dramatically surpassed those of the S&P 500. It's particularly noteworthy that he built this record by investing in about 1,000 securities, mostly of a lackluster type. A few big winners did not account for his success. It's safe to say that had millions of investment managers made trades by a) drawing stock names from a hat; b) purchasing these stocks in comparable amounts when Walter made a purchase; and then c) selling when Walter sold his pick, the *luckiest* of them would not have come close to equaling his record. There is simply *no* possibility that what Walter achieved over 47 years was due to chance.

I first publicly discussed Walter's remarkable record in 1984. At that time "efficient market theory" (EMT) was the centerpiece of investment instruction at most major business schools. This theory, as then most commonly taught, held that the price of any stock at any moment is not demonstrably mispriced, which means that no investor can be *expected* to overperform the stock market averages using only publicly-available information (though some will do so by luck). When I talked about Walter 23 years ago, his record forcefully contradicted this dogma.

And what did members of the academic community do when they were exposed to this new and important evidence? Unfortunately, they reacted in all-too-human fashion: Rather than opening their minds, they closed their eyes. To my knowledge *no* business school teaching EMT made any attempt to study Walter's performance and what it meant for the school's cherished theory.

Instead, the faculties of the schools went merrily on their way presenting EMT as having the certainty of scripture. Typically, a finance instructor who had the nerve to question EMT had about as much chance of major promotion as Galileo had of being named Pope.

Tens of thousands of students were therefore sent out into life believing that on every day the price of every stock was "right" (or, more accurately, not demonstrably wrong) and that attempts to evaluate businesses – that is, stocks – were useless. Walter meanwhile went on overperforming, his job made easier by the misguided instructions that had been given to those young minds. After all, if you are in the shipping business, it's helpful to have all of your potential competitors be taught that the earth is flat.

Maybe it was a good thing for his investors that Walter didn't go to college.

The Annual Meeting

Our meeting this year will be held on Saturday, May 5th. As always, the doors will open at the Qwest Center at 7 a.m., and a new Berkshire movie will be shown at 8:30. At 9:30 we will go directly to the question-and-answer period, which (with a break for lunch at the Qwest's stands) will last until 3:00. Then, after a short recess, Charlie and I will convene the annual meeting at 3:15. If you decide to leave during the day's question periods, please do so while *Charlie* is talking.

The best reason to exit, of course is to *shop*. We will help you do that by filling the 194,300 square foot hall that adjoins the meeting area with the products of Berkshire subsidiaries. Last year, the 24,000 people who came to the meeting did their part, and almost every location racked up record sales. But records are made to be broken, and I know you can do better.

This year we will again showcase a Clayton home (featuring Acme brick, Shaw carpet, Johns Manville insulation, MiTek fasteners, Carefree awnings and NFM furniture). You will find that the home, priced at $139,900, delivers excellent value. Last year, a helper at the Qwest bought one of two homes on display well before we opened the doors to shareholders. Flanking the Clayton home on the exhibition floor this year will be an RV and pontoon boat from Forest River.

GEICO will have a booth staffed by a number of its top counselors from around the country, all of them ready to supply you with auto insurance quotes. In most cases, GEICO will be able to give you a special shareholder discount (usually 8%). This special offer is permitted by 45 of the 50 jurisdictions in which we operate. (One supplemental point: The discount is not additive if you qualify for another, such as that given certain groups.) Bring the details of your existing insurance and check out whether we can save you money. For at least 50% of you, I believe we can. And while you're at it, sign up for the new GEICO credit card. It's the one I now use (sparingly, of course).

On Saturday, at the Omaha airport, we will have the usual array of aircraft from NetJets available for your inspection. Stop by the NetJets booth at the Qwest to learn about viewing these planes. Come to Omaha by bus; leave in your new plane. And take all the hair gel that you wish on board with you.

In the Bookworm's corner of our bazaar, there will be about 25 books and DVDs – all discounted – led again by *Poor Charlie's Almanack*. (One hapless soul last year asked Charlie what he should do if he didn't enjoy the book. Back came a Mungerism: "No problem – just give it to someone more intelligent.") We've added a few titles this year. Among them are *Seeking Wisdom: From Darwin to Munger* by Peter Bevelin, a long-time Swedish shareholder of Berkshire, and Fred Schwed's classic, *Where are the Customers' Yachts?* This book was first published in 1940 and is now in its 4th edition. The funniest book ever written about investing, it lightly delivers many truly important messages on the subject.

An attachment to the proxy material that is enclosed with this report explains how you can obtain the credential you will need for admission to the meeting and other events. As for plane, hotel and car reservations, we have again signed up American Express (800-799-6634) to give you special help. Carol Pedersen, who handles these matters, does a terrific job for us each year, and I thank her for it. Hotel rooms can be hard to find, but work with Carol and you will get one.

At Nebraska Furniture Mart, located on a 77-acre site on 72nd Street between Dodge and Pacific, we will again be having "Berkshire Weekend" discount pricing. We initiated this special event at NFM ten years ago, and sales during the "Weekend" grew from $5.3 million in 1997 to $30 million in 2006. I get goose bumps just thinking about this volume.

To obtain the Berkshire discount, you must make your purchases between Thursday, May 3rd and Monday, May 7th inclusive, and also present your meeting credential. The period's special pricing will even apply to the products of several prestigious manufacturers that normally have ironclad rules against discounting but which, in the spirit of our shareholder weekend, have made an exception for you. We appreciate their cooperation. NFM is open from 10 a.m. to 9 p.m. Monday through Saturday, and 10 a.m.

to 6 p.m. on Sunday. On Saturday this year, from 5:30 p.m. to 8 p.m., NFM is having a special shareholder picnic featuring chicken and beef tacos (and hamburgers for traditionalists like me).

At a remodeled and expanded Borsheim's, we will again have two shareholder-only events. The first will be a cocktail reception from 6 p.m. to 10 p.m. on Friday, May 4th. The second, the main gala, will be held on Sunday, May 6th, from 9 a.m. to 4 p.m. On Saturday, we will be open until 6 p.m.

We will have huge crowds at Borsheim's throughout the weekend. For your convenience, therefore, shareholder prices will be available from Monday, April 30th through Saturday, May 12th. During that period, please identify yourself as a shareholder by presenting your meeting credentials or a brokerage statement that shows you are a Berkshire holder.

On Sunday, in a tent outside of Borsheim's, a blindfolded Patrick Wolff, twice U.S. chess champion, will take on all comers – who will have their eyes wide open – in groups of six. Last year I carried on a conversation with Patrick while he played in this manner. Nearby, Norman Beck, a remarkable magician from Dallas, will bewilder onlookers. Additionally, we will have Bob Hamman and Sharon Osberg, two of the world's top bridge experts, available to play bridge with our shareholders on Sunday afternoon.

To add to the Sunday fun at Borsheim's, Ariel Hsing will play table tennis (ping-pong to the uninitiated) from 1 p.m. to 4 p.m. against anyone brave enough to take her on. Ariel, though only 11, is ranked number one among girls under 16 in the U.S. (and number 1 among both boys and girls under 12). The week I turned 75 I played Ariel, then 9 and barely tall enough to see across the table, thinking I would take it easy on her so as not to crush her young spirit. Instead she crushed me. I've since devised a plan that will give me a chance against her. At 1 p.m. on Sunday, I will initiate play with a *2-point* game against Ariel. If I somehow win the first point, I will then feign injury and claim victory. After this strenuous encounter wears Ariel down, our shareholders can then try their luck against her.

Gorat's will again be open exclusively for Berkshire shareholders on Sunday, May 6th, and will be serving from 4 p.m. until 10 p.m. Please remember that to come to Gorat's on that day, you must have a reservation. To make one, call 402-551-3733 on April 1st (*but not before*).

In the 2006-2007 school year, 35 university classes, including one from IBMEC in Brazil, will come to Omaha for sessions with me. I take almost all – in aggregate, more than 2,000 students – to lunch at Gorat's. And they love it. To learn why, come join us on Sunday.

We will again have a reception at 4 p.m. on Saturday afternoon for shareholders who have come from outside of North America. Every year our meeting draws many people from around the globe, and Charlie and I want to be sure we personally greet those who have come so far. Last year we enjoyed meeting more than 400 of you from many dozens of countries. Any shareholder who comes from other than the U.S. or Canada will be given a special credential and instructions for attending this function.

* * * * * * * * * * * *

Charlie and I are extraordinarily lucky. We were born in America; had terrific parents who saw that we got good educations; have enjoyed wonderful families and great health; and came equipped with a "business" gene that allows us to prosper in a manner hugely disproportionate to other people who contribute as much or more to our society's well-being. Moreover, we have long had jobs that we love, in which we are helped every day in countless ways by talented and cheerful associates. No wonder we tap-dance to work. But nothing is more fun for us than getting together with our shareholder-partners at Berkshire's annual meeting. So join us on May 5th at the Qwest for our annual Woodstock for Capitalists. We'll see you there.

February 28, 2007

Warren E. Buffett
Chairman of the Board

BERKSHIRE HATHAWAY INC.

To the Shareholders of Berkshire Hathaway Inc.:

Our gain in net worth during 2007 was $12.3 billion, which increased the per-share book value of both our Class A and Class B stock by 11%. Over the last 43 years (that is, since present management took over) book value has grown from $19 to $78,008, a rate of 21.1% compounded annually.*

Overall, our 76 operating businesses did well last year. The few that had problems were primarily those linked to housing, among them our brick, carpet and real estate brokerage operations. Their setbacks are minor and temporary. Our competitive position in these businesses remains strong, and we have first-class CEOs who run them right, in good times or bad.

Some major financial institutions have, however, experienced staggering problems because they engaged in the "weakened lending practices" I described in last year's letter. John Stumpf, CEO of Wells Fargo, aptly dissected the recent behavior of many lenders: "It is interesting that the industry has invented new ways to lose money when the old ways seemed to work just fine."

You may recall a 2003 Silicon Valley bumper sticker that implored, "Please, God, Just One More Bubble." Unfortunately, this wish was promptly granted, as just about all Americans came to believe that house prices would forever rise. That conviction made a borrower's income and cash equity seem unimportant to lenders, who shoveled out money, confident that HPA – house price appreciation – would cure all problems. Today, our country is experiencing widespread pain because of that erroneous belief. As house prices fall, a huge amount of financial folly is being exposed. You only learn who has been swimming naked when the tide goes out – and what we are witnessing at some of our largest financial institutions is an ugly sight.

Turning to happier thoughts, we can report that Berkshire's newest acquisitions of size, TTI and Iscar, led by their CEOs, Paul Andrews and Jacob Harpaz respectively, performed magnificently in 2007. Iscar is as impressive a manufacturing operation as I've seen, a view I reported last year and that was confirmed by a visit I made in the fall to its extraordinary plant in Korea.

Finally, our insurance business – the cornerstone of Berkshire – had an excellent year. Part of the reason is that we have the best collection of insurance managers in the business – more about them later. But we also were very lucky in 2007, the second year in a row free of major insured catastrophes.

That party is over. It's a *certainty* that insurance-industry profit margins, including ours, will fall significantly in 2008. Prices are down, and exposures inexorably rise. Even if the U.S. has its third consecutive catastrophe-light year, industry profit margins will probably shrink by four percentage points or so. If the winds roar or the earth trembles, results could be *far* worse. So be prepared for lower insurance earnings during the next few years.

Yardsticks

Berkshire has two major areas of value. The first is our investments: stocks, bonds and cash equivalents. At yearend these totaled $141 billion (not counting those in our finance or utility operations, which we assign to our second bucket of value).

---

*All per-share figures used in this report apply to Berkshire's A shares. Figures for the B shares are 1/30th of those shown for the A.

Insurance float – money we temporarily hold in our insurance operations that does not belong to us – funds $59 billion of our investments. This float is "free" as long as insurance underwriting breaks even, meaning that the premiums we receive equal the losses and expenses we incur. Of course, insurance underwriting is volatile, swinging erratically between profits and losses. Over our entire history, however, we've been profitable, and I expect we will average breakeven results or better in the future. If we do that, our investments can be viewed as an unencumbered source of value for Berkshire shareholders.

Berkshire's second component of value is earnings that come from sources other than investments and insurance. These earnings are delivered by our 66 non-insurance companies, itemized on page 76. In our early years, we focused on the investment side. During the past two decades, however, we have put ever more emphasis on the development of earnings from non-insurance businesses.

The following tables illustrate this shift. In the first we tabulate per-share investments at 14-year intervals. We exclude those applicable to minority interests.

Year	Per-Share Investments	Years	Compounded Annual Gain in Per-Share Investments
1965	$ 4		
1979	577	1965-1979	42.8%
1993	13,961	1979-1993	25.6%
2007	90,343	1993-2007	14.3%

For the entire 42 years, our compounded annual gain in per-share investments was 27.1%. But the trend has been downward as we increasingly used our available funds to buy operating businesses.

Here's the record on how earnings of our non-insurance businesses have grown, again on a per-share basis and after applicable minority interests.

Year	Per Share Pre-Tax Earnings	Years	Compounded Annual Gain in Per-Share Pre-Tax Earnings
1965	$ 4		
1979	18	1965-1979	11.1%
1993	212	1979-1993	19.1%
2007	4,093	1993-2007	23.5%

For the entire period, the compounded annual gain was 17.8%, with gains accelerating as our focus shifted.

Though these tables may help you gain historical perspective and be useful in valuation, they are completely misleading in predicting future possibilities. *Berkshire's past record can't be duplicated or even approached. Our base of assets and earnings is now far too large for us to make outsized gains in the future.*

Charlie Munger, my partner at Berkshire, and I will continue to measure our progress by the two yardsticks I have just described and will regularly update you on the results. Though we can't come close to duplicating the past, we will do our best to make sure the future is not disappointing.

* * * * * * * * * * * *

In our efforts, we will be aided enormously by the managers who have joined Berkshire. This is an unusual group in several ways. First, most of them have no financial need to work. Many sold us their businesses for large sums and run them because they love doing so, not because they need the money. Naturally they wish to be paid fairly, but money alone is not the reason they work hard and productively.

A second, somewhat related, point about these managers is that they have exactly the job they want for the rest of their working years. At almost any other company, key managers below the top aspire to keep climbing the pyramid. For them, the subsidiary or division they manage today is a way station – or so they hope. Indeed, if they are in their present positions five years from now, they may well feel like failures.

Conversely, our CEOs' scorecards for success are not whether they obtain my job but instead are the long-term performances of their businesses. Their decisions flow from a here-today, here-forever mindset. I think our rare and hard-to-replicate managerial structure gives Berkshire a real advantage.

Acquisitions

Though our managers may be the best, we will need large and sensible acquisitions to get the growth in operating earnings we wish. Here, we made little progress in 2007 until very late in the year. Then, on Christmas day, Charlie and I finally earned our paychecks by contracting for the largest cash purchase in Berkshire's history.

The seeds of this transaction were planted in 1954. That fall, only three months into a new job, I was sent by my employers, Ben Graham and Jerry Newman, to a shareholders' meeting of Rockwood Chocolate in Brooklyn. A young fellow had recently taken control of this company, a manufacturer of assorted cocoa-based items. He had then initiated a one-of-a-kind tender, offering 80 pounds of cocoa beans for each share of Rockwood stock. I described this transaction in a section of the 1988 annual report that explained arbitrage. I also told you that Jay Pritzker – the young fellow mentioned above – was the business genius behind this tax-efficient idea, the possibilities for which had escaped all the other experts who had thought about buying Rockwood, including my bosses, Ben and Jerry.

At the meeting, Jay was friendly and gave me an education on the 1954 tax code. I came away very impressed. Thereafter, I avidly followed Jay's business dealings, which were many and brilliant. His valued partner was his brother, Bob, who for nearly 50 years ran Marmon Group, the home for most of the Pritzker businesses.

Jay died in 1999, and Bob retired early in 2002. Around then, the Pritzker family decided to gradually sell or reorganize certain of its holdings, including Marmon, a company operating 125 businesses, managed through nine sectors. Marmon's largest operation is Union Tank Car, which together with a Canadian counterpart owns 94,000 rail cars that are leased to various shippers. The original cost of this fleet is $5.1 billion. All told, Marmon has $7 billion in sales and about 20,000 employees.

We will soon purchase 60% of Marmon and will acquire virtually all of the balance within six years. Our initial outlay will be $4.5 billion, and the price of our later purchases will be based on a formula tied to earnings. Prior to our entry into the picture, the Pritzker family received substantial consideration from Marmon's distribution of cash, investments and certain businesses.

This deal was done in the way Jay would have liked. We arrived at a price using only Marmon's financial statements, employing no advisors and engaging in no nit-picking. I knew that the business would be exactly as the Pritzkers represented, and they knew that we would close on the dot, however chaotic financial markets might be. During the past year, many large deals have been renegotiated or killed entirely. With the Pritzkers, as with Berkshire, a deal is a deal.

Marmon's CEO, Frank Ptak, works closely with a long-time associate, John Nichols. John was formerly the highly successful CEO of Illinois Tool Works (ITW), where he teamed with Frank to run a mix of industrial businesses. Take a look at their ITW record; you'll be impressed.

Byron Trott of Goldman Sachs – whose praises I sang in the 2003 report – facilitated the Marmon transaction. Byron is the rare investment banker who puts himself in his client's shoes. Charlie and I trust him completely.

You'll like the code name that Goldman Sachs assigned the deal. Marmon entered the auto business in 1902 and exited it in 1933. Along the way it manufactured the Wasp, a car that won the first Indianapolis 500 race, held in 1911. So this deal was labeled "Indy 500."

* * * * * * * * * * * *

In May 2006, I spoke at a lunch at Ben Bridge, our Seattle-based jewelry chain. The audience was a number of its vendors, among them Dennis Ulrich, owner of a company that manufactured gold jewelry.

In January 2007, Dennis called me, suggesting that with Berkshire's support he could build a large jewelry supplier. We soon made a deal for his business, simultaneously purchasing a supplier of about equal size. The new company, Richline Group, has since made two smaller acquisitions. Even with those, Richline is far below the earnings threshold we normally require for purchases. I'm willing to bet, however, that Dennis – with the help of his partner, Dave Meleski – will build a large operation, earning good returns on capital employed.

Businesses – The Great, the Good and the Gruesome

Let's take a look at what kind of businesses turn us on. And while we're at it, let's also discuss what we wish to avoid.

Charlie and I look for companies that have a) a business we understand; b) favorable long-term economics; c) able and trustworthy management; and d) a sensible price tag. We like to buy the whole business or, if management is our partner, at least 80%. When control-type purchases of quality aren't available, though, we are also happy to simply buy small portions of great businesses by way of stock-market purchases. It's better to have a part interest in the Hope Diamond than to own all of a rhinestone.

A truly great business must have an enduring "moat" that protects excellent returns on invested capital. The dynamics of capitalism guarantee that competitors will repeatedly assault any business "castle" that is earning high returns. Therefore a formidable barrier such as a company's being the low-cost producer (GEICO, Costco) or possessing a powerful world-wide brand (Coca-Cola, Gillette, American Express) is essential for sustained success. Business history is filled with "Roman Candles," companies whose moats proved illusory and were soon crossed.

Our criterion of "enduring" causes us to rule out companies in industries prone to rapid and continuous change. Though capitalism's "creative destruction" is highly beneficial for society, it precludes investment certainty. A moat that must be continuously rebuilt will eventually be no moat at all.

Additionally, this criterion eliminates the business whose success *depends* on having a great manager. Of course, a terrific CEO is a huge asset for any enterprise, and at Berkshire we have an abundance of these managers. Their abilities have created billions of dollars of value that would never have materialized if typical CEOs had been running their businesses.

But if a business *requires* a superstar to produce great results, the business itself cannot be deemed great. A medical partnership led by your area's premier brain surgeon may enjoy outsized and growing earnings, but that tells little about its future. The partnership's moat will go when the surgeon goes. You can count, though, on the moat of the Mayo Clinic to endure, even though you can't name its CEO.

Long-term competitive advantage in a stable industry is what we seek in a business. If that comes with rapid organic growth, great. But even without organic growth, such a business is rewarding. We will simply take the lush earnings of the business and use them to buy similar businesses elsewhere. There's no rule that you have to invest money where you've earned it. Indeed, it's often a mistake to do so: Truly great businesses, earning huge returns on tangible assets, *can't* for any extended period reinvest a large portion of their earnings internally at high rates of return.

Let's look at the prototype of a dream business, our own See's Candy. The boxed-chocolates industry in which it operates is unexciting: Per-capita consumption in the U.S. is extremely low and doesn't grow. Many once-important brands have disappeared, and only three companies have earned more than token profits over the last forty years. Indeed, I believe that See's, though it obtains the bulk of its revenues from only a few states, accounts for nearly half of the entire industry's earnings.

At See's, annual sales were 16 million pounds of candy when Blue Chip Stamps purchased the company in 1972. (Charlie and I controlled Blue Chip at the time and later merged it into Berkshire.) Last year See's sold 31 million pounds, a growth rate of only 2% annually. Yet its durable competitive advantage, built by the See's family over a 50-year period, and strengthened subsequently by Chuck Huggins and Brad Kinstler, has produced extraordinary results for Berkshire.

We bought See's for $25 million when its sales were $30 million and pre-tax earnings were less than $5 million. The capital then required to conduct the business was $8 million. (Modest seasonal debt was also needed for a few months each year.) Consequently, the company was earning 60% pre-tax on invested capital. Two factors helped to minimize the funds required for operations. First, the product was sold for cash, and that eliminated accounts receivable. Second, the production and distribution cycle was short, which minimized inventories.

Last year See's sales were $383 million, and pre-tax profits were $82 million. The capital now required to run the business is $40 million. This means we have had to reinvest only $32 million since 1972 to handle the modest physical growth – and somewhat immodest financial growth – of the business. In the meantime pre-tax earnings have totaled $1.35 billion. *All of that*, except for the $32 million, has been sent to Berkshire (or, in the early years, to Blue Chip). After paying corporate taxes on the profits, we have used the rest to buy other attractive businesses. Just as Adam and Eve kick-started an activity that led to six billion humans, See's has given birth to multiple new streams of cash for us. (The biblical command to "be fruitful and multiply" is one we take seriously at Berkshire.)

There aren't many See's in Corporate America. Typically, companies that increase their earnings from $5 million to $82 million require, say, $400 million or so of capital investment to finance their growth. That's because growing businesses have both working capital needs that increase in proportion to sales growth and significant requirements for fixed asset investments.

A company that needs large increases in capital to engender its growth may well prove to be a satisfactory investment. There is, to follow through on our example, nothing shabby about earning $82 million pre-tax on $400 million of net tangible assets. But that equation for the owner is vastly different from the See's situation. It's far better to have an ever-increasing stream of earnings with virtually no major capital requirements. Ask Microsoft or Google.

One example of good, but far from sensational, business economics is our own FlightSafety. This company delivers benefits to its customers that are the equal of those delivered by any business that I know of. It also possesses a durable competitive advantage: Going to any other flight-training provider than the best is like taking the low bid on a surgical procedure.

Nevertheless, this business requires a significant reinvestment of earnings if it is to grow. When we purchased FlightSafety in 1996, its pre-tax operating earnings were $111 million, and its net investment in fixed assets was $570 million. Since our purchase, depreciation charges have totaled $923 million. But capital expenditures have totaled $1.635 billion, most of that for simulators to match the new airplane models that are constantly being introduced. (A simulator can cost us more than $12 million, and we have 273 of them.) Our fixed assets, after depreciation, now amount to $1.079 billion. Pre-tax operating earnings in 2007 were $270 million, a gain of $159 million since 1996. That gain gave us a good, but far from See's-like, return on our incremental investment of $509 million.

Consequently, if measured only by economic returns, FlightSafety is an excellent but not extraordinary business. Its put-up-more-to-earn-more experience is that faced by most corporations. For example, our large investment in regulated utilities falls squarely in this category. We will earn considerably more money in this business ten years from now, but we will invest many billions to make it.

Now let's move to the gruesome. The worst sort of business is one that grows rapidly, requires significant capital to engender the growth, and then earns little or no money. Think airlines. Here a *durable* competitive advantage has proven elusive ever since the days of the Wright Brothers. Indeed, if a farsighted capitalist had been present at Kitty Hawk, he would have done his successors a huge favor by shooting Orville down.

The airline industry's demand for capital ever since that first flight has been insatiable. Investors have poured money into a bottomless pit, attracted by growth when they should have been repelled by it. And I, to my shame, participated in this foolishness when I had Berkshire buy U.S. Air preferred stock in 1989. As the ink was drying on our check, the company went into a tailspin, and before long our preferred dividend was no longer being paid. But we then got very lucky. In one of the recurrent, but always misguided, bursts of optimism for airlines, we were actually able to sell our shares in 1998 for a hefty gain. In the decade following our sale, the company went bankrupt. Twice.

To sum up, think of three types of "savings accounts." The great one pays an extraordinarily high interest rate that will rise as the years pass. The good one pays an attractive rate of interest that will be earned also on deposits that are added. Finally, the gruesome account both pays an inadequate interest rate and requires you to keep adding money at those disappointing returns.

* * * * * * * * * * *

And now it's confession time. It should be noted that no consultant, board of directors or investment banker pushed me into the mistakes I will describe. In tennis parlance, they were all unforced errors.

To begin with, I almost blew the See's purchase. The seller was asking $30 million, and I was adamant about not going above $25 million. Fortunately, he caved. Otherwise I would have balked, and that $1.35 billion would have gone to somebody else.

About the time of the See's purchase, Tom Murphy, then running Capital Cities Broadcasting, called and offered me the Dallas-Fort Worth NBC station for $35 million. The station came with the Fort Worth paper that Capital Cities was buying, and under the "cross-ownership" rules Murph had to divest it. I knew that TV stations were See's-like businesses that required virtually no capital investment and had excellent prospects for growth. They were simple to run and showered cash on their owners.

Moreover, Murph, then as now, was a close friend, a man I admired as an extraordinary manager and outstanding human being. He knew the television business forward and backward and would not have called me unless he felt a purchase was certain to work. In effect Murph whispered "buy" into my ear. But I didn't listen.

In 2006, the station earned $73 million pre-tax, bringing its total earnings since I turned down the deal to at least $1 billion – almost all available to its owner for other purposes. Moreover, the property now has a capital value of about $800 million. Why did I say "no"? The only explanation is that my brain had gone on vacation and forgot to notify me. (My behavior resembled that of a politician Molly Ivins once described: "If his I.Q. was any lower, you would have to water him twice a day.")

Finally, I made an even worse mistake when I said "yes" to Dexter, a shoe business I bought in 1993 for $433 million in Berkshire stock (25,203 shares of A). What I had assessed as durable competitive advantage vanished within a few years. But that's just the beginning: By using Berkshire stock, I compounded this error hugely. That move made the cost to Berkshire shareholders not $400 million, but rather $3.5 billion. In essence, I gave away 1.6% of a wonderful business – one now valued at $220 billion – to buy a worthless business.

To date, Dexter is the worst deal that I've made. But I'll make more mistakes in the future – you can bet on that. A line from Bobby Bare's country song explains what too often happens with acquisitions: "I've never gone to bed with an ugly woman, but I've sure woke up with a few."

* * * * * * * * * * * *

Now, let's examine the four major operating sectors of Berkshire. Each sector has vastly different balance sheet and income account characteristics. Therefore, lumping them together impedes analysis. So we'll present them as four separate businesses, which is how Charlie and I view them.

Insurance

The best anecdote I've heard during the current presidential campaign came from Mitt Romney, who asked his wife, Ann, "When we were young, did you ever in your wildest dreams think I might be president?" To which she replied, "Honey, you weren't *in* my wildest dreams."

When we first entered the property/casualty insurance business in 1967, my wildest dreams did not envision our current operation. Here's how we did in the first five years after purchasing National Indemnity:

Year	Underwriting Profit (Loss)	Float
	(in millions)	
1967	$ 0.4	$18.5
1968	0.6	21.3
1969	0.1	25.4
1970	(0.4)	39.4
1971	1.4	65.6

To put it charitably, we were a slow starter. But things changed. Here's the record of the last five years:

Year	Underwriting Profit (Loss)	Float
	(in millions)	
2003	$1,718	$44,220
2004	1,551	46,094
2005	53	49,287
2006	3,838	50,887
2007	3,374	58,698

This metamorphosis has been accomplished by some extraordinary managers. Let's look at what each has achieved.

- GEICO possesses the widest moat of any of our insurers, one carefully protected and expanded by Tony Nicely, its CEO. Last year – again – GEICO had the best growth record among major auto insurers, increasing its market share to 7.2%. When Berkshire acquired control in 1995, that share was 2.5%. Not coincidentally, annual ad expenditures by GEICO have increased from $31 million to $751 million during the same period.

  Tony, now 64, joined GEICO at 18. Every day since, he has been passionate about the company – proud of how it could both save money for its customers and provide growth opportunities for its associates. Even now, with sales at $12 billion, Tony feels GEICO is just getting started. So do I.

  Here's some evidence. In the last three years, GEICO has increased its share of the motorcycle market from 2.1% to 6%. We've also recently begun writing policies on ATVs and RVs. And in November we wrote our first *commercial* auto policy. GEICO and National Indemnity are working together in the commercial field, and early results are very encouraging.

  Even in aggregate, these lines will remain a small fraction of our personal auto volume. Nevertheless, they should deliver a growing stream of underwriting profits and float.

- General Re, our international reinsurer, is by far our largest source of "home-grown" float – $23 billion at yearend. This operation is now a huge asset for Berkshire. Our ownership, however, had a shaky start.

  For decades, General Re was the Tiffany of reinsurers, admired by all for its underwriting skills and discipline. This reputation, unfortunately, outlived its factual underpinnings, a flaw that I completely missed when I made the decision in 1998 to merge with General Re. The General Re of 1998 was not operated as the General Re of 1968 or 1978.

  Now, thanks to Joe Brandon, General Re's CEO, and his partner, Tad Montross, the luster of the company has been restored. Joe and Tad have been running the business for six years and have been doing first-class business in a first-class way, to use the words of J. P. Morgan. They have restored discipline to underwriting, reserving and the selection of clients.

  Their job was made more difficult by costly and time-consuming legacy problems, both in the U.S. and abroad. Despite that diversion, Joe and Tad have delivered excellent underwriting results while skillfully repositioning the company for the future.

- Since joining Berkshire in 1986, Ajit Jain has built a truly great specialty reinsurance operation from scratch. For one-of-a-kind mammoth transactions, the world now turns to him.

  Last year I told you in detail about the Equitas transfer of huge, but capped, liabilities to Berkshire for a single premium of $7.1 billion. At this very early date, our experience has been good. But this doesn't tell us much because it's just one straw in a fifty-year-or-more wind. What we know for sure, however, is that the London team who joined us, headed by Scott Moser, is first-rate and has become a valuable asset for our insurance business.

- Finally, we have our smaller operations, which serve specialized segments of the insurance market. In aggregate, these companies have performed extraordinarily well, earning above-average underwriting profits and delivering valuable float for investment.

  Last year BoatU.S., headed by Bill Oakerson, was added to the group. This company manages an association of about 650,000 boat owners, providing them services similar to those offered by AAA auto clubs to drivers. Among the association's offerings is boat insurance. Learn more about this operation by visiting its display at the annual meeting.

Below we show the record of our four categories of property/casualty insurance.

Insurance Operations	Underwriting Profit (in millions) 2007	2006	Yearend Float 2007	2006
General Re	$ 555	$ 526	$23,009	$22,827
BH Reinsurance	1,427	1,658	23,692	16,860
GEICO	1,113	1,314	7,768	7,171
Other Primary	279	340*	4,229	4,029*
	$3,374	$3,838	$58,698	$50,887

* Includes Applied Underwriters from May 19, 2006.

Regulated Utility Business

Berkshire has an 87.4% (diluted) interest in MidAmerican Energy Holdings, which owns a wide variety of utility operations. The largest of these are (1) Yorkshire Electricity and Northern Electric, whose 3.8 million electric customers make it the third largest distributor of electricity in the U.K.; (2) MidAmerican Energy, which serves 720,000 electric customers, primarily in Iowa; (3) Pacific Power and Rocky Mountain Power, serving about 1.7 million electric customers in six western states; and (4) Kern River and Northern Natural pipelines, which carry about 8% of the natural gas consumed in the U.S.

Our partners in ownership of MidAmerican are Walter Scott, and its two terrific managers, Dave Sokol and Greg Abel. It's unimportant how many votes each party has; we make major moves only when we are unanimous in thinking them wise. Eight years of working with Dave, Greg and Walter have underscored my original belief: Berkshire couldn't have better partners.

Somewhat incongruously, MidAmerican also owns the second largest real estate brokerage firm in the U.S., HomeServices of America. This company operates through 20 locally-branded firms with 18,800 agents. Last year was a slow year for residential sales, and 2008 will probably be slower. We will continue, however, to acquire quality brokerage operations when they are available at sensible prices.

Here are some key figures on MidAmerican's operation:

	Earnings (in millions) 2007	2006
U.K. utilities	$ 337	$ 338
Iowa utility	412	348
Western utilities (acquired March 21, 2006)	692	356
Pipelines	473	376
HomeServices	42	74
Other (net)	130	245
Earnings before corporate interest and taxes	2,086	1,737
Interest, other than to Berkshire	(312)	(261)
Interest on Berkshire junior debt	(108)	(134)
Income tax	(477)	(426)
Net earnings	$ 1,189	$ 916
Earnings applicable to Berkshire*	$ 1,114	$ 885
Debt owed to others	19,002	16,946
Debt owed to Berkshire	821	1,055

*Includes interest earned by Berkshire (net of related income taxes) of $70 in 2007 and $87 in 2006.

We agreed to purchase 35,464,337 shares of MidAmerican at $35.05 per share in 1999, a year in which its per-share earnings were $2.59. Why the odd figure of $35.05? I originally decided the business was worth $35.00 per share to Berkshire. Now, I'm a "one-price" guy (remember See's?) and for several days the investment bankers representing MidAmerican had no luck in getting me to increase Berkshire's offer. But, finally, they caught me in a moment of weakness, and I caved, telling them I would go to $35.05. With that, I explained, they could tell their client they had wrung the last nickel out of me. At the time, it hurt.

Later on, in 2002, Berkshire purchased 6,700,000 shares at $60 to help finance the acquisition of one of our pipelines. Lastly, in 2006, when MidAmerican bought PacifiCorp, we purchased 23,268,793 shares at $145 per share.

In 2007, MidAmerican earned $15.78 per share. However, 77¢ of that was non-recurring – a reduction in deferred tax at our British utility, resulting from a lowering of the U.K. corporate tax rate. So call normalized earnings $15.01 per share. And yes, I'm glad I wilted and offered the extra nickel.

Manufacturing, Service and Retailing Operations

Our activities in this part of Berkshire cover the waterfront. Let's look, though, at a summary balance sheet and earnings statement for the entire group.

Balance Sheet 12/31/07 (in millions)

Assets		Liabilities and Equity	
Cash and equivalents	$ 2,080	Notes payable	$ 1,278
Accounts and notes receivable	4,488	Other current liabilities	7,652
Inventory	5,793	Total current liabilities	8,930
Other current assets	470		
Total current assets	12,831		
Goodwill and other intangibles	14,201	Deferred taxes	828
Fixed assets	9,605	Term debt and other liabilities	3,079
Other assets	1,685	Equity	25,485
	$38,322		$38,322

Earnings Statement (in millions)

	2007	2006	2005
Revenues	$59,100	$52,660	$46,896
Operating expenses (including depreciation of $955 in 2007, $823 in 2006 and $699 in 2005)	55,026	49,002	44,190
Interest expense	127	132	83
Pre-tax earnings	3,947*	3,526*	2,623*
Income taxes and minority interests	1,594	1,395	977
Net income	$ 2,353	$ 2,131	$ 1,646

*Does not include purchase-accounting adjustments.

This motley group, which sells products ranging from lollipops to motor homes, earned a pleasing 23% on average tangible net worth last year. It's noteworthy also that these operations used only minor financial leverage in achieving that return. Clearly we own some terrific businesses. We purchased many of them, however, at large premiums to net worth – a point reflected in the goodwill item shown on the balance sheet – and that fact reduces the earnings on our average *carrying* value to 9.8%.

Here are a few newsworthy items about companies in this sector:

- Shaw, Acme Brick, Johns Manville and MiTek were all hurt in 2007 by the sharp housing downturn, with their pre-tax earnings declining 27%, 41%, 38%, and 9% respectively. Overall, these companies earned $941 million pre-tax compared to $1.296 billion in 2006.

  Last year, Shaw, MiTek and Acme contracted for tuck-in acquisitions that will help future earnings. You can be sure they will be looking for more of these.

- In a tough year for retailing, our standouts were See's, Borsheims and Nebraska Furniture Mart.

  Two years ago Brad Kinstler was made CEO of See's. We very seldom move managers from one industry to another at Berkshire. But we made an exception with Brad, who had previously run our uniform company, Fechheimer, and Cypress Insurance. The move could not have worked out better. In his two years, profits at See's have increased more than 50%.

  At Borsheims, sales increased 15.1%, helped by a 27% gain during Shareholder Weekend. Two years ago, Susan Jacques suggested that we remodel and expand the store. I was skeptical, but Susan was right.

  Susan came to Borsheims 25 years ago as a $4-an-hour saleswoman. Though she lacked a managerial background, I did not hesitate to make her CEO in 1994. She's smart, she loves the business, and she loves her associates. That beats having an MBA degree any time.

  (An aside: Charlie and I are not big fans of resumes. Instead, we focus on brains, passion and integrity. Another of our great managers is Cathy Baron Tamraz, who has significantly increased Business Wire's earnings since we purchased it early in 2006. She is an owner's dream. It is positively *dangerous* to stand between Cathy and a business prospect. Cathy, it should be noted, began her career as a cab driver.)

  Finally, at Nebraska Furniture Mart, earnings hit a record as our Omaha and Kansas City stores each had sales of about $400 million. These, by some margin, are the two top home furnishings stores in the country. In a disastrous year for many furniture retailers, sales at Kansas City increased 8%, while in Omaha the gain was 6%.

  Credit the remarkable Blumkin brothers, Ron and Irv, for this performance. Both are close personal friends of mine and great businessmen.

- Iscar continues its wondrous ways. Its products are small carbide cutting tools that make large and very expensive machine tools more productive. The raw material for carbide is tungsten, mined in China. For many decades, Iscar moved tungsten to Israel, where brains turned it into something far more valuable. Late in 2007, Iscar opened a large plant in Dalian, China. In effect, we've now moved the brains to the tungsten. Major opportunities for growth await Iscar. Its management team, led by Eitan Wertheimer, Jacob Harpaz, and Danny Goldman, is certain to make the most of them.

- Flight services set a record in 2007 with pre-tax earnings increasing 49% to $547 million. Corporate aviation had an extraordinary year worldwide, and both of our companies – as runaway leaders in their fields – fully participated.

  FlightSafety, our pilot training business, gained 14% in revenues and 20% in pre-tax earnings. We estimate that we train about 58% of U.S. corporate pilots. Bruce Whitman, the company's CEO, inherited this leadership position in 2003 from Al Ueltschi, the father of advanced flight training, and has proved to be a worthy successor.

At NetJets, the inventor of fractional-ownership of jets, we also remain the unchallenged leader. We now operate 487 planes in the U.S. and 135 in Europe, a fleet more than twice the size of that operated by our three major competitors *combined*. Because our share of the large-cabin market is near 90%, our lead in value terms is far greater.

The NetJets brand – with its promise of safety, service and security – grows stronger every year. Behind this is the passion of one man, Richard Santulli. If you were to pick someone to join you in a foxhole, you couldn't do better than Rich. No matter what the obstacles, he just doesn't stop.

Europe is the best example of how Rich's tenacity leads to success. For the first ten years we made little financial progress there, actually running up cumulative losses of $212 million. After Rich brought Mark Booth on board to run Europe, however, we began to gain traction. Now we have real momentum, and last year earnings tripled.

In November, our directors met at NetJets headquarters in Columbus and got a look at the sophisticated operation there. It is responsible for 1,000 or so flights a day in all kinds of weather, with customers expecting top-notch service. Our directors came away impressed by the facility and its capabilities – but even more impressed by Rich and his associates.

Finance and Finance Products

Our major operation in this category is Clayton Homes, the largest U.S. manufacturer and marketer of manufactured homes. Clayton's market share hit a record 31% last year. But industry volume continues to shrink: Last year, manufactured home sales were 96,000, down from 131,000 in 2003, the year we bought Clayton. (At the time, it should be remembered, some commentators criticized its directors for selling at a cyclical bottom.)

Though Clayton earns money from both manufacturing and retailing its homes, most of its earnings come from an $11 billion loan portfolio, covering 300,000 borrowers. That's why we include Clayton's operation in this finance section. Despite the many problems that surfaced during 2007 in real estate finance, the Clayton portfolio is performing well. Delinquencies, foreclosures and losses during the year were at rates similar to those we experienced in our previous years of ownership.

Clayton's loan portfolio is financed by Berkshire. For this funding, we charge Clayton one percentage point over Berkshire's borrowing cost – a fee that amounted to $85 million last year. Clayton's 2007 pre-tax earnings of $526 million are *after* its paying this fee. The flip side of this transaction is that Berkshire recorded $85 million as income, which is included in "other" in the following table.

	Pre-Tax Earnings (in millions)	
	2007	*2006*
Trading – ordinary income	$ 272	$ 274
Life and annuity operation	(60)	29
Leasing operations	111	182
Manufactured-housing finance (Clayton)	526	513
Other	157	159
Income before capital gains	1,006	1,157
Trading – capital gains	105	938
	$1,111	$2,095

The leasing operations tabulated are XTRA, which rents trailers, and CORT, which rents furniture. Utilization of trailers was down considerably in 2007 and that led to a drop in earnings at XTRA. That company also borrowed $400 million last year and distributed the proceeds to Berkshire. The resulting higher interest it is now paying further reduced XTRA's earnings.

Clayton, XTRA and CORT are all good businesses, very ably run by Kevin Clayton, Bill Franz and Paul Arnold. Each has made tuck-in acquisitions during Berkshire's ownership. More will come.

Investments

We show below our common stock investments at yearend, itemizing those with a market value of at least $600 million.

| | | | 12/31/07 | |
Shares	Company	Percentage of Company Owned	Cost*	Market
			(in millions)	
151,610,700	American Express Company	13.1	$ 1,287	$ 7,887
35,563,200	Anheuser-Busch Companies, Inc.	4.8	1,718	1,861
60,828,818	Burlington Northern Santa Fe	17.5	4,731	5,063
200,000,000	The Coca-Cola Company	8.6	1,299	12,274
17,508,700	Conoco Phillips	1.1	1,039	1,546
64,271,948	Johnson & Johnson	2.2	3,943	4,287
124,393,800	Kraft Foods Inc.	8.1	4,152	4,059
48,000,000	Moody's Corporation	19.1	499	1,714
3,486,006	POSCO	4.5	572	2,136
101,472,000	The Procter & Gamble Company	3.3	1,030	7,450
17,170,953	Sanofi-Aventis	1.3	1,466	1,575
227,307,000	Tesco plc	2.9	1,326	2,156
75,176,026	U.S. Bancorp	4.4	2,417	2,386
17,072,192	USG Corp	17.2	536	611
19,944,300	Wal-Mart Stores, Inc.	0.5	942	948
1,727,765	The Washington Post Company	18.2	11	1,367
303,407,068	Wells Fargo & Company	9.2	6,677	9,160
1,724,200	White Mountains Insurance Group Ltd.	16.3	369	886
	Others		5,238	7,633
	Total Common Stocks		$39,252	$74,999

*This is our actual purchase price and also our tax basis; GAAP "cost" differs in a few cases because of write-ups or write-downs that have been required.

Overall, we are delighted by the business performance of our investees. In 2007, American Express, Coca-Cola and Procter & Gamble, three of our four largest holdings, increased per-share earnings by 12%, 14% and 14%. The fourth, Wells Fargo, had a small decline in earnings because of the popping of the real estate bubble. Nevertheless, I believe its intrinsic value increased, even if only by a minor amount.

In the strange world department, note that American Express and Wells Fargo were both organized by Henry Wells and William Fargo, Amex in 1850 and Wells in 1852. P&G and Coke began business in 1837 and 1886 respectively. Start-ups are not our game.

I should emphasize that we do not measure the progress of our investments by what their market prices do during any given year. Rather, we evaluate their performance by the two methods we apply to the businesses we own. The first test is improvement in earnings, with our making due allowance for industry conditions. The second test, more subjective, is whether their "moats" – a metaphor for the superiorities they possess that make life difficult for their competitors – have widened during the year. All of the "big four" scored positively on that test.

We made one large sale last year. In 2002 and 2003 Berkshire bought 1.3% of PetroChina for $488 million, a price that valued the entire business at about $37 billion. Charlie and I then felt that the company was worth about $100 billion. By 2007, two factors had materially increased its value: the price of oil had climbed significantly, and PetroChina's management had done a great job in building oil and gas reserves. In the second half of last year, the market value of the company rose to $275 billion, about what we thought it was worth compared to other giant oil companies. So we sold our holdings for $4 billion.

A footnote: We paid the IRS tax of $1.2 billion on our PetroChina gain. This sum paid *all* costs of the U.S. government – defense, social security, you name it – for about four hours.

* * * * * * * * * * * *

Last year I told you that Berkshire had 62 derivative contracts that I manage. (We also have a few left in the General Re runoff book.) Today, we have 94 of these, and they fall into two categories.

First, we have written 54 contracts that require us to make payments if certain bonds that are included in various high-yield indices default. These contracts expire at various times from 2009 to 2013. At yearend we had received $3.2 billion in premiums on these contracts; had paid $472 million in losses; and in the worst case (though it is extremely unlikely to occur) could be required to pay an additional $4.7 billion.

We are certain to make many more payments. But I believe that on premium revenues alone, these contracts will prove profitable, leaving aside what we can earn on the large sums we hold. Our yearend liability for this exposure was recorded at $1.8 billion and is included in "Derivative Contract Liabilities" on our balance sheet.

The second category of contracts involves various put options we have sold on four stock indices (the S&P 500 plus three foreign indices). These puts had original terms of either 15 or 20 years and were struck at the market. We have received premiums of $4.5 billion, and we recorded a liability at yearend of $4.6 billion. The puts in these contracts are exercisable *only* at their expiration dates, which occur between 2019 and 2027, and Berkshire will then need to make a payment only if the index in question is quoted at a level below that existing on the day that the put was written. Again, I believe these contracts, in aggregate, will be profitable and that we will, in addition, receive substantial income from our investment of the premiums we hold during the 15- or 20-year period.

Two aspects of our derivative contracts are particularly important. First, in all cases we hold the money, which means that we have *no* counterparty risk.

Second, accounting rules for our derivative contracts differ from those applying to our investment portfolio. In that portfolio, changes in value are applied to the net worth shown on Berkshire's balance sheet, but do not affect earnings unless we sell (or write down) a holding. Changes in the value of a derivative contract, however, must be applied each quarter to earnings.

Thus, our derivative positions will sometimes cause large swings in reported earnings, even though Charlie and I might believe the intrinsic value of these positions has changed little. He and I will not be bothered by these swings – even though they could easily amount to $1 billion or more in a quarter – and we hope you won't be either. You will recall that in our catastrophe insurance business, we are always ready to trade increased volatility in reported earnings in the short run for greater gains in net worth in the long run. That is our philosophy in derivatives as well.

* * * * * * * * * * * *

The U.S. dollar weakened further in 2007 against major currencies, and it's no mystery why: Americans like buying products made elsewhere more than the rest of the world likes buying products made in the U.S. Inevitably, that causes America to ship about $2 billion of IOUs and assets *daily* to the rest of the world. And over time, that puts pressure on the dollar.

When the dollar falls, it both makes our products cheaper for foreigners to buy and their products more expensive for U.S. citizens. That's why a falling currency is supposed to cure a trade deficit. Indeed, the U.S. deficit has undoubtedly been tempered by the large drop in the dollar. But ponder this: In 2002 when the Euro averaged 94.6¢, our trade deficit with Germany (the fifth largest of our trading partners) was $36 billion, whereas in 2007, with the Euro averaging $1.37, our deficit with Germany was up to $45 billion. Similarly, the Canadian dollar averaged 64¢ in 2002 and 93¢ in 2007. Yet our trade deficit with Canada rose as well, from $50 billion in 2002 to $64 billion in 2007. So far, at least, a plunging dollar has not done much to bring our trade activity into balance.

There's been much talk recently of sovereign wealth funds and how they are buying large pieces of American businesses. This is *our* doing, not some nefarious plot by foreign governments. Our trade equation guarantees massive foreign investment in the U.S. When we force-feed $2 billion daily to the rest of the world, they must invest in *something* here. Why should we complain when they choose stocks over bonds?

Our country's weakening currency is not the fault of OPEC, China, etc. Other developed countries rely on imported oil and compete against Chinese imports just as we do. In developing a sensible trade policy, the U.S. should not single out countries to punish or industries to protect. Nor should we take actions likely to evoke retaliatory behavior that will reduce America's exports, true trade that benefits both our country and the rest of the world.

Our legislators should recognize, however, that the current imbalances are unsustainable and should therefore adopt policies that will materially reduce them sooner rather than later. Otherwise our $2 billion daily of force-fed dollars to the rest of the world may produce global indigestion of an unpleasant sort. (For other comments about the unsustainability of our trade deficits, see Alan Greenspan's comments on November 19, 2004, the Federal Open Market Committee's minutes of June 29, 2004, and Ben Bernanke's statement on September 11, 2007.)

* * * * * * * * * * *

At Berkshire we held only one direct currency position during 2007. That was in – hold your breath – the Brazilian real. Not long ago, swapping dollars for reals would have been unthinkable. After all, during the past century *five* versions of Brazilian currency have, in effect, turned into confetti. As has been true in many countries whose currencies have periodically withered and died, wealthy Brazilians sometimes stashed large sums in the U.S. to preserve their wealth.

But any Brazilian who followed this apparently prudent course would have lost *half* his net worth over the past five years. Here's the year-by-year record (indexed) of the real versus the dollar from the end of 2002 to yearend 2007: 100; 122; 133; 152; 166; 199. Every year the real went up and the dollar fell. Moreover, during much of this period the Brazilian government was actually holding down the value of the real and supporting *our* currency by buying dollars in the market.

Our direct currency positions have yielded $2.3 billion of pre-tax profits over the past five years, and in addition we have profited by holding bonds of U.S. companies that are denominated in other currencies. For example, in 2001 and 2002 we purchased €310 million Amazon.com, Inc. 6 7/8 of 2010 at 57% of par. At the time, Amazon bonds were priced as "junk" credits, though they were anything but. (Yes, Virginia, you can occasionally find markets that are ridiculously inefficient – or at least you can find them anywhere except at the finance departments of some leading business schools.)

The Euro denomination of the Amazon bonds was a further, and important, attraction for us. The Euro was at 95¢ when we bought in 2002. Therefore, our cost in dollars came to only $169 million. Now the bonds sell at 102% of par and the Euro is worth $1.47. In 2005 and 2006 some of our bonds were called and we received $253 million for them. Our remaining bonds were valued at $162 million at yearend. Of our $246 million of realized and unrealized gain, about $118 million is attributable to the fall in the dollar. Currencies do matter.

At Berkshire, we will attempt to further increase our stream of direct and indirect foreign earnings. Even if we are successful, however, our assets and earnings will always be concentrated in the U.S. Despite our country's many imperfections and unrelenting problems of one sort or another, America's rule of law, market-responsive economic system, and belief in meritocracy are almost certain to produce ever-growing prosperity for its citizens.

* * * * * * * * * * * *

As I have told you before, we have for some time been well-prepared for CEO succession because we have three outstanding internal candidates. The board knows exactly whom it would pick if I were to become unavailable, either because of death or diminishing abilities. And that would still leave the board with two backups.

Last year I told you that we would also promptly complete a succession plan for the investment job at Berkshire, and we have indeed now identified four candidates who could succeed me in managing investments. All manage substantial sums currently, and all have indicated a strong interest in coming to Berkshire if called. The board knows the strengths of the four and would expect to hire one or more if the need arises. The candidates are young to middle-aged, well-to-do to rich, and all wish to work for Berkshire for reasons that go beyond compensation.

(I've reluctantly discarded the notion of my continuing to manage the portfolio after my death – abandoning my hope to give new meaning to the term "thinking outside the box.")

Fanciful Figures – How Public Companies Juice Earnings

Former Senator Alan Simpson famously said: "Those who travel the high road in Washington need not fear heavy traffic." If he had sought truly deserted streets, however, the Senator should have looked to Corporate America's accounting.

An important referendum on which road businesses prefer occurred in 1994. America's CEOs had just strong-armed the U.S. Senate into ordering the Financial Accounting Standards Board to shut up, by a vote that was 88-9. Before that rebuke the FASB had shown the audacity – by unanimous agreement, no less – to tell corporate chieftains that the stock options they were being awarded represented a form of compensation and that their value should be recorded as an expense.

After the senators voted, the FASB – now educated on accounting principles by the Senate's 88 closet CPAs – decreed that companies could choose between two methods of reporting on options. The *preferred* treatment would be to expense their value, but it would also be allowable for companies to ignore the expense as long as their options were issued at market value.

A moment of truth had now arrived for America's CEOs, and their reaction was not a pretty sight. During the next six years, exactly *two* of the 500 companies in the S&P chose the preferred route. CEOs of the rest opted for the low road, thereby ignoring a large and obvious expense in order to report higher "earnings." I'm sure some of them also felt that if they opted for expensing, their directors might in future years think twice before approving the mega-grants the managers longed for.

It turned out that for many CEOs even the low road wasn't good enough. Under the weakened rule, there remained earnings consequences if options were issued with a strike price below market value. No problem. To avoid that bothersome rule, a number of companies surreptitiously backdated options to falsely indicate that they were granted at current market prices, when in fact they were dished out at prices well below market.

Decades of option-accounting nonsense have now been put to rest, but other accounting choices remain – important among these the investment-return assumption a company uses in calculating pension expense. It will come as no surprise that many companies continue to choose an assumption that allows them to report less-than-solid "earnings." For the 363 companies in the S&P that have pension plans, this assumption in 2006 averaged 8%. Let's look at the chances of that being achieved.

The average holdings of bonds and cash for all pension funds is about 28%, and on these assets returns can be expected to be no more than 5%. Higher yields, of course, are obtainable but they carry with them a risk of commensurate (or greater) loss.

This means that the remaining 72% of assets – which are mostly in equities, either held directly or through vehicles such as hedge funds or private-equity investments – must earn 9.2% in order for the fund overall to achieve the postulated 8%. And that return must be delivered *after* all fees, which are now far higher than they have ever been.

How realistic is this expectation? Let's revisit some data I mentioned two years ago: During the 20th Century, the Dow advanced from 66 to 11,497. This gain, though it appears huge, shrinks to 5.3% when compounded annually. An investor who owned the Dow throughout the century would also have received generous dividends for much of the period, but only about 2% or so in the final years. It was a wonderful century.

Think now about *this* century. For investors to merely match that 5.3% market-value gain, the Dow – recently below 13,000 – would need to close at about *2,000,000* on December 31, 2099. We are now eight years into this century, and we have racked up less than 2,000 of the 1,988,000 Dow points the market needed to travel in this hundred years to equal the 5.3% of the last.

It's amusing that commentators regularly hyperventilate at the prospect of the Dow crossing an even number of thousands, such as 14,000 or 15,000. If they keep reacting that way, a 5.3% annual gain for the century will mean they experience at least 1,986 seizures during the next 92 years. While anything is possible, does anyone really believe this is the most likely outcome?

Dividends continue to run about 2%. Even if stocks were to average the 5.3% annual appreciation of the 1900s, the equity portion of plan assets – allowing for expenses of .5% – would produce no more than 7% or so. And .5% may well understate costs, given the presence of layers of consultants and high-priced managers ("helpers").

Naturally, everyone expects to be above average. And those helpers – bless their hearts – will certainly encourage their clients in this belief. But, as a class, the helper-aided group must be *below* average. The reason is simple: 1) Investors, overall, will necessarily earn an average return, minus costs they incur; 2) Passive and index investors, through their very inactivity, will earn that average minus costs that are very low; 3) With that group earning average returns, so must the remaining group – the active investors. But this group will incur high transaction, management, and advisory costs. Therefore, the active investors will have their returns diminished by a far greater percentage than will their inactive brethren. That means that the passive group – the "know-nothings" – must win.

I should mention that people who expect to earn 10% annually from equities during this century – envisioning that 2% of that will come from dividends and 8% from price appreciation – are implicitly forecasting a level of about *24,000,000* on the Dow by 2100. If your adviser talks to you about double-digit returns from equities, explain this math to him – not that it will faze him. Many helpers are apparently direct descendants of the queen in Alice in Wonderland, who said: "Why, sometimes I've believed as many as six impossible things before breakfast." Beware the glib helper who fills your head with fantasies while he fills his pockets with fees.

Some companies have pension plans in Europe as well as in the U.S. and, in their accounting, almost all assume that the U.S. plans will earn more than the non-U.S. plans. This discrepancy is puzzling: Why should these companies not put their U.S. managers in charge of the non-U.S. pension assets and let them work their magic on these assets as well? I've never seen this puzzle explained. But the auditors and actuaries who are charged with vetting the return assumptions seem to have no problem with it.

What is no puzzle, however, is why CEOs opt for a high investment assumption: It lets them report higher earnings. And if they are wrong, as I believe they are, the chickens won't come home to roost until long after they retire.

After decades of pushing the envelope – or worse – in its attempt to report the highest number possible for current earnings, Corporate America should ease up. It should listen to my partner, Charlie: "If you've hit three balls out of bounds to the left, aim a little to the right on the next swing."

* * * * * * * * * * *

Whatever pension-cost surprises are in store for shareholders down the road, these jolts will be surpassed many times over by those experienced by taxpayers. Public pension promises are huge and, in many cases, funding is woefully inadequate. Because the fuse on this time bomb is long, politicians flinch from inflicting tax pain, given that problems will only become apparent long after these officials have departed. Promises involving very early retirement – sometimes to those in their low 40s – and generous cost-of-living adjustments are easy for these officials to make. In a world where people are living longer and inflation is certain, those promises will be anything but easy to keep.

* * * * * * * * * * *

Having laid out the failures of an "honor system" in American accounting, I need to point out that this is exactly the system existing at Berkshire for a truly huge balance-sheet item. In every report we make to you, we must guesstimate the loss reserves for our insurance units. If our estimate is wrong, it means that both our balance sheet and our earnings statement will be wrong. So naturally we do our best to make these guesses accurate. *Nevertheless, in every report our estimate is sure to be wrong.*

At yearend 2007, we show an insurance liability of $56 billion that represents our guess as to what we will eventually pay for all loss events that occurred before yearend (except for about $3 billion of the reserve that has been discounted to present value). We know of many thousands of events and have put a dollar value on each that reflects what we believe we will pay, including the associated costs (such as attorney's fees) that we will incur in the payment process. In some cases, among them claims for certain serious injuries covered by worker's compensation, payments will be made for 50 years or more.

We also include a large reserve for losses that occurred before yearend but that we have yet to hear about. Sometimes, the insured itself does not know that a loss has occurred. (Think of an embezzlement that remains undiscovered for years.) We sometimes hear about losses from policies that covered our insured many decades ago.

A story I told you some years back illustrates our problem in accurately estimating our loss liability: A fellow was on an important business trip in Europe when his sister called to tell him that their dad had died. Her brother explained that he couldn't get back but said to spare nothing on the funeral, whose cost he would cover. When he returned, his sister told him that the service had been beautiful and presented him with bills totaling $8,000. He paid up but a month later received a bill from the mortuary for $10. He paid that, too – and still another $10 charge he received a month later. When a third $10 invoice was sent to him the following month, the perplexed man called his sister to ask what was going on. "Oh," she replied, "I forgot to tell you. We buried Dad in a rented suit."

At our insurance companies we have an unknown, but most certainly large, number of "rented suits" buried around the world. We try to estimate the bill for them accurately. In ten or twenty years, we will even be able to make a good guess as to how inaccurate our present guess is. But even *that* guess will be subject to surprises. I personally believe our stated reserves are adequate, but I've been wrong several times in the past.

The Annual Meeting

Our meeting this year will be held on Saturday, May 3rd. As always, the doors will open at the Qwest Center at 7 a.m., and a new Berkshire movie will be shown at 8:30. At 9:30 we will go directly to the question-and-answer period, which (with a break for lunch at the Qwest's stands) will last until 3:00. Then, after a short recess, Charlie and I will convene the annual meeting at 3:15. If you decide to leave during the day's question periods, please do so while *Charlie* is talking.

The best reason to exit, of course is to *shop*. We will help you do that by filling the 194,300-square-foot hall that adjoins the meeting area with the products of Berkshire subsidiaries. Last year, the 27,000 people who came to the meeting did their part, and almost every location racked up record sales. But you can do better. (If necessary, I'll lock the doors.)

This year we will again showcase a Clayton home (featuring Acme brick, Shaw carpet, Johns Manville insulation, MiTek fasteners, Carefree awnings and NFM furniture). You will find that this 1,550-square-foot home, priced at $69,500, delivers exceptional value. And after you purchase the house, consider also acquiring the Forest River RV and pontoon boat on display nearby.

GEICO will have a booth staffed by a number of its top counselors from around the country, all of them ready to supply you with auto insurance quotes. In most cases, GEICO will be able to give you a special shareholder discount (usually 8%). This special offer is permitted by 45 of the 50 jurisdictions in which we operate. (One supplemental point: The discount is not additive if you qualify for another, such as that given certain groups.) Bring the details of your existing insurance and check out whether we can save you money. For at least 50% of you, I believe we can.

On Saturday, at the Omaha airport, we will have the usual array of aircraft from NetJets available for your inspection. Stop by the NetJets booth at the Qwest to learn about viewing these planes. Come to Omaha by bus; leave in your new plane. And take all the hair gel and scissors that you wish on board with you.

Next, if you have any money left, visit the Bookworm, where you will find about 25 books and DVDs – all discounted – led again by *Poor Charlie's Almanack*. Without any advertising or bookstore placement, Charlie's book has now remarkably sold nearly 50,000 copies. For those of you who can't make the meeting, go to poorcharliesalmanack.com to order a copy.

An attachment to the proxy material that is enclosed with this report explains how you can obtain the credential you will need for admission to the meeting and other events. As for plane, hotel and car reservations, we have again signed up American Express (800-799-6634) to give you special help. Carol Pedersen, who handles these matters, does a terrific job for us each year, and I thank her for it. Hotel rooms can be hard to find, but work with Carol and you will get one.

At Nebraska Furniture Mart, located on a 77-acre site on 72nd Street between Dodge and Pacific, we will again be having "Berkshire Weekend" discount pricing. We initiated this special event at NFM eleven years ago, and sales during the "Weekend" grew from $5.3 million in 1997 to $30.9 million in 2007. This is more volume than most furniture stores register in a year.

To obtain the Berkshire discount, you must make your purchases between Thursday, May 1st and Monday, May 5th inclusive, and also present your meeting credential. The period's special pricing will even apply to the products of several prestigious manufacturers that normally have ironclad rules against discounting but which, in the spirit of our shareholder weekend, have made an exception for you. We appreciate their cooperation. NFM is open from 10 a.m. to 9 p.m. Monday through Saturday, and 10 a.m. to 6 p.m. on Sunday. On Saturday this year, from 5:30 p.m. to 8 p.m., NFM is having a Baja Beach Bash featuring beef and chicken tacos.

At Borsheims, we will again have two shareholder-only events. The first will be a cocktail reception from 6 p.m. to 10 p.m. on Friday, May 2nd. The second, the main gala, will be held on Sunday, May 4th, from 9 a.m. to 4 p.m. On Saturday, we will be open until 6 p.m.

We will have huge crowds at Borsheims throughout the weekend. For your convenience, therefore, shareholder prices will be available from Monday, April 28th through Saturday, May 10th. During that period, please identify yourself as a shareholder by presenting your meeting credentials or a brokerage statement that shows you are a Berkshire holder.

On Sunday, in a tent outside of Borsheims, a blindfolded Patrick Wolff, twice U.S. chess champion, will take on all comers – who will have their eyes wide open – in groups of six. Nearby, Norman Beck, a remarkable magician from Dallas, will bewilder onlookers. Additionally, we will have Bob Hamman and Sharon Osberg, two of the world's top bridge experts, available to play bridge with our shareholders on Sunday afternoon.

Gorat's will again be open exclusively for Berkshire shareholders on Sunday, May 4th, and will be serving from 4 p.m. until 10 p.m. Last year Gorat's, which seats 240, served 915 dinners on Shareholder Sunday. The three-day total was 2,487 including 656 T-bone steaks, the entrée preferred by the *cognoscenti*. Please remember that to come to Gorat's on that day, you must have a reservation. To make one, call 402-551-3733 on April 1st (*but not before*).

We will again have a reception at 4 p.m. on Saturday afternoon for shareholders who have come from outside of North America. Every year our meeting draws many people from around the globe, and Charlie and I want to be sure we personally greet those who have come so far. Last year we enjoyed meeting more than 400 of you from many dozens of countries. Any shareholder who comes from other than the U.S. or Canada will be given a special credential and instructions for attending this function.

* * * * * * * * * * * *

At 84 and 77, Charlie and I remain lucky beyond our dreams. We were born in America; had terrific parents who saw that we got good educations; have enjoyed wonderful families and great health; and came equipped with a "business" gene that allows us to prosper in a manner hugely disproportionate to that experienced by many people who contribute as much or more to our society's well-being. Moreover, we have long had jobs that we love, in which we are helped in countless ways by talented and cheerful associates. Every day is exciting to us; no wonder we tap-dance to work. But nothing is more fun for us than getting together with our shareholder-partners at Berkshire's annual meeting. So join us on May 3rd at the Qwest for our annual Woodstock for Capitalists. We'll see you there.

February 2008   Warren E. Buffett
                                                     Chairman of the Board

BERKSHIRE HATHAWAY INC.

To the Shareholders of Berkshire Hathaway Inc.:

Our *decrease* in net worth during 2008 was $11.5 billion, which reduced the per-share book value of both our Class A and Class B stock by 9.6%. Over the last 44 years (that is, since present management took over) book value has grown from $19 to $70,530, a rate of 20.3% compounded annually.*

The table on the preceding page, recording both the 44-year performance of Berkshire's book value and the S&P 500 index, shows that 2008 was the worst year for each. The period was devastating as well for corporate and municipal bonds, real estate and commodities. By yearend, investors of all stripes were bloodied and confused, much as if they were small birds that had strayed into a badminton game.

As the year progressed, a series of life-threatening problems within many of the world's great financial institutions was unveiled. This led to a dysfunctional credit market that in important respects soon turned non-functional. The watchword throughout the country became the creed I saw on restaurant walls when I was young: "In God we trust; all others pay cash."

By the fourth quarter, the credit crisis, coupled with tumbling home and stock prices, had produced a paralyzing fear that engulfed the country. A freefall in business activity ensued, accelerating at a pace that I have never before witnessed. The U.S. – and much of the world – became trapped in a vicious negative-feedback cycle. Fear led to business contraction, and that in turn led to even greater fear.

This debilitating spiral has spurred our government to take massive action. In poker terms, the Treasury and the Fed have gone "all in." Economic medicine that was previously meted out by the cupful has recently been dispensed by the barrel. These once-unthinkable dosages will almost certainly bring on unwelcome aftereffects. Their precise nature is anyone's guess, though one likely consequence is an onslaught of inflation. Moreover, major industries have become dependent on Federal assistance, and they will be followed by cities and states bearing mind-boggling requests. Weaning these entities from the public teat will be a political challenge. They won't leave willingly.

Whatever the downsides may be, strong and immediate action by government was essential last year if the financial system was to avoid a total breakdown. Had one occurred, the consequences for every area of our economy would have been cataclysmic. Like it or not, the inhabitants of Wall Street, Main Street and the various Side Streets of America were all in the same boat.

Amid this bad news, however, never forget that our country has faced far worse travails in the past. In the 20th Century alone, we dealt with two great wars (one of which we initially appeared to be losing); a dozen or so panics and recessions; virulent inflation that led to a 21½% prime rate in 1980; and the Great Depression of the 1930s, when unemployment ranged between 15% and 25% for many years. America has had no shortage of challenges.

Without fail, however, we've overcome them. In the face of those obstacles – and many others – the real standard of living for Americans improved nearly *seven*-fold during the 1900s, while the Dow Jones Industrials rose from 66 to 11,497. Compare the record of this period with the dozens of centuries during which humans secured only tiny gains, if any, in how they lived. Though the path has not been smooth, our economic system has worked extraordinarily well over time. It has unleashed human potential as no other system has, and it will continue to do so. America's best days lie ahead.

---

*All per-share figures used in this report apply to Berkshire's A shares. Figures for the B shares are 1/30th of those shown for A.

Take a look again at the 44-year table on page 2. In 75% of those years, the S&P stocks recorded a gain. I would guess that a roughly similar percentage of years will be positive in the next 44. But neither Charlie Munger, my partner in running Berkshire, nor I can predict the winning and losing years in advance. (In our usual opinionated view, we don't think anyone else can either.) We're certain, for example, that the economy will be in shambles throughout 2009 – and, for that matter, probably well beyond – but that conclusion does not tell us whether the stock market will rise or fall.

In good years and bad, Charlie and I simply focus on four goals:

(1)   maintaining Berkshire's Gibraltar-like financial position, which features huge amounts of excess liquidity, near-term obligations that are modest, and dozens of sources of earnings and cash;

(2)   widening the "moats" around our operating businesses that give them durable competitive advantages;

(3)   acquiring and developing new and varied streams of earnings;

(4)   expanding and nurturing the cadre of outstanding operating managers who, over the years, have delivered Berkshire exceptional results.

Berkshire in 2008

Most of the Berkshire businesses whose results are significantly affected by the economy earned below their potential last year, and that will be true in 2009 as well. Our retailers were hit particularly hard, as were our operations tied to residential construction. In aggregate, however, our manufacturing, service and retail businesses earned substantial sums and most of them – particularly the larger ones – continue to strengthen their competitive positions. Moreover, we are fortunate that Berkshire's two most important businesses – our insurance and utility groups – produce earnings that are not correlated to those of the general economy. Both businesses delivered outstanding results in 2008 and have excellent prospects.

As predicted in last year's report, the exceptional underwriting profits that our insurance businesses realized in 2007 were not repeated in 2008. Nevertheless, the insurance group delivered an underwriting gain for the sixth consecutive year. This means that our $58.5 billion of insurance "float" – money that doesn't belong to us but that we hold and invest for our own benefit – cost us less than zero. In fact, we were *paid* $2.8 billion to hold our float during 2008. Charlie and I find this enjoyable.

Over time, most insurers experience a substantial underwriting loss, which makes their economics far different from ours. Of course, we too will experience underwriting losses in some years. But we have the best group of managers in the insurance business, and in most cases they oversee entrenched and valuable franchises. Considering these strengths, I believe that we will earn an underwriting profit over the years and that our float will therefore cost us nothing. Our insurance operation, the core business of Berkshire, is an economic powerhouse.

Charlie and I are equally enthusiastic about our utility business, which had record earnings last year and is poised for future gains. Dave Sokol and Greg Abel, the managers of this operation, have achieved results unmatched elsewhere in the utility industry. I love it when they come up with new projects because in this capital-intensive business these ventures are often large. Such projects offer Berkshire the opportunity to put out substantial sums at decent returns.

Things also went well on the capital-allocation front last year. Berkshire is always a buyer of both businesses and securities, and the disarray in markets gave us a tailwind in our purchases. When investing, pessimism is your friend, euphoria the enemy.

In our insurance portfolios, we made three large investments on terms that would be unavailable in normal markets. These should add about $1½ billion pre-tax to Berkshire's annual earnings and offer possibilities for capital gains as well. We also closed on our Marmon acquisition (we own 64% of the company now and will purchase its remaining stock over the next six years). Additionally, certain of our subsidiaries made "tuck-in" acquisitions that will strengthen their competitive positions and earnings.

That's the good news. But there's another less pleasant reality: During 2008 I did some dumb things in investments. I made at least one major mistake of commission and several lesser ones that also hurt. I will tell you more about these later. Furthermore, I made some errors of omission, sucking my thumb when new facts came in that should have caused me to re-examine my thinking and promptly take action.

Additionally, the market value of the bonds and stocks that we continue to hold suffered a significant decline along with the general market. This does not bother Charlie and me. Indeed, we enjoy such price declines if we have funds available to increase our positions. Long ago, Ben Graham taught me that "Price is what you pay; value is what you get." Whether we're talking about socks or stocks, I like buying quality merchandise when it is marked down.

Yardsticks

Berkshire has two major areas of value. The first is our investments: stocks, bonds and cash equivalents. At yearend those totaled $122 billion (not counting the investments held by our finance and utility operations, which we assign to our second bucket of value). About $58.5 billion of that total is funded by our insurance float.

Berkshire's second component of value is earnings that come from sources other than investments and insurance. These earnings are delivered by our 67 non-insurance companies, itemized on page 96. We exclude our insurance earnings from this calculation because the value of our insurance operation comes from the investable funds it generates, and we have already included this factor in our first bucket.

In 2008, our investments fell from $90,343 per share of Berkshire (after minority interest) to $77,793, a decrease that was caused by a decline in market prices, not by net sales of stocks or bonds. Our second segment of value fell from pre-tax earnings of $4,093 per Berkshire share to $3,921 (again after minority interest).

Both of these performances are unsatisfactory. Over time, we need to make decent gains in each area if we are to increase Berkshire's intrinsic value at an acceptable rate. Going forward, however, our focus will be on the earnings segment, just as it has been for several decades. We like buying underpriced securities, but we like buying fairly-priced operating businesses even more.

Now, let's take a look at the four major operating sectors of Berkshire. Each of these has vastly different balance sheet and income account characteristics. Therefore, lumping them together, as is done in standard financial statements, impedes analysis. So we'll present them as four separate businesses, which is how Charlie and I view them.

Regulated Utility Business

Berkshire has an 87.4% (diluted) interest in MidAmerican Energy Holdings, which owns a wide variety of utility operations. The largest of these are (1) Yorkshire Electricity and Northern Electric, whose 3.8 million end users make it the U.K.'s third largest distributor of electricity; (2) MidAmerican Energy, which serves 723,000 electric customers, primarily in Iowa; (3) Pacific Power and Rocky Mountain Power, serving about 1.7 million electric customers in six western states; and (4) Kern River and Northern Natural pipelines, which carry about 9% of the natural gas consumed in the U.S.

Our partners in ownership of MidAmerican are its two terrific managers, Dave Sokol and Greg Abel, and my long-time friend, Walter Scott. It's unimportant how many votes each party has; we make major moves only when we are unanimous in thinking them wise. Nine years of working with Dave, Greg and Walter have reinforced my original belief: Berkshire couldn't have better partners.

Somewhat incongruously, MidAmerican also owns the second largest real estate brokerage firm in the U.S., HomeServices of America. This company operates through 21 locally-branded firms that have 16,000 agents. Last year was a terrible year for home sales, and 2009 looks no better. We will continue, however, to acquire quality brokerage operations when they are available at sensible prices.

Here are some key figures on MidAmerican's operations:

	Earnings (in millions)	
	2008	2007
U.K. utilities	$ 339	$ 337
Iowa utility	425	412
Western utilities	703	692
Pipelines	595	473
HomeServices	(45)	42
Other (net)	186	130
Operating earnings before corporate interest and taxes	2,203	2,086
Constellation Energy*	1,092	–
Interest, other than to Berkshire	(332)	(312)
Interest on Berkshire junior debt	(111)	(108)
Income tax	(1,002)	(477)
Net earnings	$ 1,850	$ 1,189
Earnings applicable to Berkshire**	$ 1,704	$ 1,114
Debt owed to others	19,145	19,002
Debt owed to Berkshire	1,087	821

 *Consists of a breakup fee of $175 million and a profit on our investment of $917 million.
**Includes interest earned by Berkshire (net of related income taxes) of $72 in 2008 and $70 in 2007.

MidAmerican's record in operating its regulated electric utilities and natural gas pipelines is truly outstanding. Here's some backup for that claim.

Our two pipelines, Kern River and Northern Natural, were both acquired in 2002. A firm called Mastio regularly ranks pipelines for customer satisfaction. Among the 44 rated, Kern River came in 9th when we purchased it and Northern Natural ranked 39th. There was work to do.

In Mastio's 2009 report, Kern River ranked 1st and Northern Natural 3rd. Charlie and I couldn't be more proud of this performance. It came about because hundreds of people at each operation committed themselves to a new culture and then delivered on their commitment.

Achievements at our electric utilities have been equally impressive. In 1995, MidAmerican became the major provider of electricity in Iowa. By judicious planning and a zeal for efficiency, the company has kept electric prices unchanged since our purchase and has promised to hold them steady through 2013.

MidAmerican has maintained this extraordinary price stability while making Iowa number one among all states in the percentage of its generation capacity that comes from wind. Since our purchase, MidAmerican's wind-based facilities have grown from zero to almost 20% of total capacity.

Similarly, when we purchased PacifiCorp in 2006, we moved aggressively to expand wind generation. Wind capacity was then 33 megawatts. It's now 794, with more coming. (Arriving at PacifiCorp, we found "wind" of a different sort: The company had 98 committees that met frequently. Now there are 28. Meanwhile, we generate and deliver considerably more electricity, doing so with 2% fewer employees.)

In 2008 alone, MidAmerican spent $1.8 billion on wind generation at our two operations, and today the company is number one in the nation among regulated utilities in ownership of wind capacity. By the way, compare that $1.8 billion to the $1.1 billion of pre-tax earnings of PacifiCorp (shown in the table as "Western") and Iowa. In our utility business, we spend all we earn, and then some, in order to fulfill the needs of our service areas. Indeed, MidAmerican has not paid a dividend since Berkshire bought into the company in early 2000. Its earnings have instead been reinvested to develop the utility systems our customers require and deserve. In exchange, we have been allowed to earn a fair return on the huge sums we have invested. It's a great partnership for all concerned.

* * * * * * * * * * * *

Our long-avowed goal is to be the "buyer of choice" for businesses – particularly those built and owned by families. The way to achieve this goal is to deserve it. That means we must keep our promises; avoid leveraging up acquired businesses; grant unusual autonomy to our managers; and hold the purchased companies through thick and thin (though we prefer thick and thicker).

Our record matches our rhetoric. Most buyers competing against us, however, follow a different path. For them, acquisitions are "merchandise." Before the ink dries on their purchase contracts, these operators are contemplating "exit strategies." We have a decided advantage, therefore, when we encounter sellers who truly care about the future of their businesses.

Some years back our competitors were known as "leveraged-buyout operators." But LBO became a bad name. So in Orwellian fashion, the buyout firms decided to change their moniker. What they did not change, though, were the essential ingredients of their previous operations, including their cherished fee structures and love of leverage.

Their new label became "private equity," a name that turns the facts upside-down: A purchase of a business by these firms almost invariably results in dramatic *reductions* in the equity portion of the acquiree's capital structure compared to that previously existing. A number of these acquirees, purchased only two to three years ago, are now in mortal danger because of the debt piled on them by their private-equity buyers. Much of the bank debt is selling below 70¢ on the dollar, and the public debt has taken a far greater beating. The private-equity firms, it should be noted, are not rushing in to inject the equity their wards now desperately need. Instead, they're keeping their remaining funds *very* private.

In the regulated utility field there are no large family-owned businesses. Here, Berkshire hopes to be the "buyer of choice" of *regulators*. It is they, rather than selling shareholders, who judge the fitness of purchasers when transactions are proposed.

There is no hiding your history when you stand before these regulators. They can – and do – call their counterparts in other states where you operate and ask how you have behaved in respect to all aspects of the business, including a willingness to commit adequate equity capital.

When MidAmerican proposed its purchase of PacifiCorp in 2005, regulators in the six new states we would be serving immediately checked our record in Iowa. They also carefully evaluated our financing plans and capabilities. We passed this examination, just as we expect to pass future ones.

There are two reasons for our confidence. First, Dave Sokol and Greg Abel are going to run any businesses with which they are associated in a first-class manner. They don't know of any other way to operate. Beyond that is the fact that we hope to buy more regulated utilities in the future – and we know that our business behavior in jurisdictions where we are operating today will determine how we are welcomed by new jurisdictions tomorrow.

Insurance

Our insurance group has propelled Berkshire's growth since we first entered the business in 1967. This happy result has not been due to general prosperity in the industry. During the 25 years ending in 2007, return on net worth for insurers averaged 8.5% versus 14.0% for the Fortune 500. Clearly our insurance CEOs have not had the wind at their back. Yet these managers have excelled to a degree Charlie and I never dreamed possible in the early days. Why do I love them? Let me count the ways.

At GEICO, Tony Nicely – now in his 48th year at the company after joining it when he was 18 – continues to gobble up market share while maintaining disciplined underwriting. When Tony became CEO in 1993, GEICO had 2.0% of the auto insurance market, a level at which the company had long been stuck. Now we have a 7.7% share, up from 7.2% in 2007.

The combination of new business gains and an improvement in the renewal rate on existing business has moved GEICO into the number three position among auto insurers. In 1995, when Berkshire purchased control, GEICO was number seven. Now we trail only State Farm and Allstate.

GEICO grows because it saves money for motorists. No one *likes* to buy auto insurance. But virtually everyone likes to drive. So, sensibly, drivers look for the lowest-cost insurance consistent with first-class service. Efficiency is the key to low cost, and efficiency is Tony's specialty. Five years ago the number of policies per employee was 299. In 2008, the number was 439, a huge increase in productivity.

As we view GEICO's current opportunities, Tony and I feel like two hungry mosquitoes in a nudist camp. Juicy targets are everywhere. First, and most important, our new business in auto insurance is now exploding. Americans are focused on saving money as never before, and they are flocking to GEICO. In January 2009, we set a monthly record – by a wide margin – for growth in policyholders. That record will last exactly 28 days: As we go to press, it's clear February's gain will be even better.

Beyond this, we are gaining ground in allied lines. Last year, our motorcycle policies increased by 23.4%, which raised our market share from about 6% to more than 7%. Our RV and ATV businesses are also growing rapidly, albeit from a small base. And, finally, we recently began insuring commercial autos, a big market that offers real promise.

GEICO is now saving money for millions of Americans. Go to GEICO.com or call 1-800-847-7536 and see if we can save you money as well.

General Re, our large international reinsurer, also had an outstanding year in 2008. Some time back, the company had serious problems (which I totally failed to detect when we purchased it in late 1998). By 2001, when Joe Brandon took over as CEO, assisted by his partner, Tad Montross, General Re's culture had further deteriorated, exhibiting a loss of discipline in underwriting, reserving and expenses. After Joe and Tad took charge, these problems were decisively and successfully addressed. Today General Re has regained its luster. Last spring Joe stepped down, and Tad became CEO. Charlie and I are grateful to Joe for righting the ship and are certain that, with Tad, General Re's future is in the best of hands.

Reinsurance is a business of long-term promises, sometimes extending for fifty years or more. This past year has retaught clients a crucial principle: A promise is no better than the person or institution making it. That's where General Re excels: It is the *only* reinsurer that is backed by an AAA corporation. Ben Franklin once said, "It's difficult for an empty sack to stand upright." That's no worry for General Re clients.

Our third major insurance operation is Ajit Jain's reinsurance division, headquartered in Stamford and staffed by only 31 employees. This may be one of the most remarkable businesses in the world, hard to characterize but easy to admire.

From year to year, Ajit's business is never the same. It features very large transactions, incredible speed of execution and a willingness to quote on policies that leave others scratching their heads. When there is a huge and unusual risk to be insured, Ajit is almost certain to be called.

Ajit came to Berkshire in 1986. Very quickly, I realized that we had acquired an extraordinary talent. So I did the logical thing: I wrote his parents in New Delhi and asked if they had another one like him at home. Of course, I knew the answer before writing. There *isn't* anyone like Ajit.

Our smaller insurers are just as outstanding in their own way as the "big three," regularly delivering valuable float to us at a negative cost. We aggregate their results below under "Other Primary." For space reasons, we don't discuss these insurers individually. But be assured that Charlie and I appreciate the contribution of each.

Here is the record for the four legs to our insurance stool. The underwriting profits signify that all four provided funds to Berkshire last year without cost, just as they did in 2007. And in both years our underwriting profitability was considerably better than that achieved by the industry. Of course, we ourselves will periodically have a terrible year in insurance. But, overall, I expect us to *average* an underwriting profit. If so, we will be using free funds of large size for the indefinite future.

| | Underwriting Profit | | Yearend Float | |
| | *(in millions)* | | | |
Insurance Operations	2008	2007	2008	2007
General Re	$ 342	$ 555	$21,074	$23,009
BH Reinsurance	1,324	1,427	24,221	23,692
GEICO	916	1,113	8,454	7,768
Other Primary	210	279	4,739	4,229
	$2,792	$3,374	$58,488	$58,698

Manufacturing, Service and Retailing Operations

Our activities in this part of Berkshire cover the waterfront. Let's look, though, at a summary balance sheet and earnings statement for the entire group.

Balance Sheet 12/31/08 (in millions)

Assets		Liabilities and Equity	
Cash and equivalents	$ 2,497	Notes payable	$ 2,212
Accounts and notes receivable	5,047	Other current liabilities	8,087
Inventory	7,500	Total current liabilities	10,299
Other current assets	752		
Total current assets	15,796		
Goodwill and other intangibles	16,515	Deferred taxes	2,786
Fixed assets	16,338	Term debt and other liabilities	6,033
Other assets	1,248	Equity	30,779
	$49,897		$49,897

9

Earnings Statement *(in millions)*

	2008	2007	2006
Revenues	$66,099	$59,100	$52,660
Operating expenses (including depreciation of $1,280 in 2008, $955 in 2007 and $823 in 2006)	61,937	55,026	49,002
Interest expense	139	127	132
Pre-tax earnings	4,023*	3,947*	3,526*
Income taxes and minority interests	1,740	1,594	1,395
Net income	$ 2,283	$ 2,353	$ 2,131

*Does not include purchase-accounting adjustments.

This motley group, which sells products ranging from lollipops to motor homes, earned an impressive 17.9% on average tangible net worth last year. It's also noteworthy that these operations used only minor financial leverage in achieving that return. Clearly we own some terrific businesses. We purchased many of them, however, at large premiums to net worth – a point reflected in the goodwill item shown on our balance sheet – and that fact reduces the earnings on our average *carrying* value to 8.1%.

Though the full-year result was satisfactory, earnings of many of the businesses in this group hit the skids in last year's fourth quarter. Prospects for 2009 look worse. Nevertheless, the group retains strong earning power even under today's conditions and will continue to deliver significant cash to the parent company. Overall, these companies improved their competitive positions last year, partly because our financial strength let us make advantageous tuck-in acquisitions. In contrast, many competitors were treading water (or sinking).

The most noteworthy of these acquisitions was Iscar's late-November purchase of Tungaloy, a leading Japanese producer of small tools. Charlie and I continue to look with astonishment – and appreciation! – at the accomplishments of Iscar's management. To secure one manager like Eitan Wertheimer, Jacob Harpaz or Danny Goldman when we acquire a company is a blessing. Getting three is like winning the Triple Crown. Iscar's growth since our purchase has exceeded our expectations – which were high – and the addition of Tungaloy will move performance to the next level.

MiTek, Benjamin Moore, Acme Brick, Forest River, Marmon and CTB also made one or more acquisitions during the year. CTB, which operates worldwide in the agriculture equipment field, has now picked up six small firms since we purchased it in 2002. At that time, we paid $140 million for the company. Last year its pre-tax earnings were $89 million. Vic Mancinelli, its CEO, followed Berkshire-like operating principles long before our arrival. He focuses on blocking and tackling, day by day doing the little things right and never getting off course. Ten years from now, Vic will be running a much larger operation and, more important, will be earning excellent returns on invested capital.

Finance and Financial Products

I will write here at some length about the mortgage operation of Clayton Homes and skip any financial commentary, which is summarized in the table at the end of this section. I do this because Clayton's recent experience may be useful in the public-policy debate about housing and mortgages. But first a little background.

Clayton is the largest company in the manufactured home industry, delivering 27,499 units last year. This came to about 34% of the industry's 81,889 total. Our share will likely grow in 2009, partly because much of the rest of the industry is in acute distress. Industrywide, units sold have steadily declined since they hit a peak of 372,843 in 1998.

At that time, much of the industry employed sales practices that were atrocious. Writing about the period somewhat later, I described it as involving "borrowers who shouldn't have borrowed being financed by lenders who shouldn't have lent."

To begin with, the need for meaningful down payments was frequently ignored. Sometimes fakery was involved. ("That certainly looks like a $2,000 cat to me" says the salesman who will receive a $3,000 commission if the loan goes through.) Moreover, impossible-to-meet monthly payments were being agreed to by borrowers who signed up because they had nothing to lose. The resulting mortgages were usually packaged ("securitized") and sold by Wall Street firms to unsuspecting investors. This chain of folly had to end badly, and it did.

Clayton, it should be emphasized, followed far more sensible practices in its own lending throughout that time. Indeed, no purchaser of the mortgages it originated and then securitized has ever lost a dime of principal or interest. But Clayton was the exception; industry losses were staggering. And the hangover continues to this day.

This 1997-2000 fiasco should have served as a canary-in-the-coal-mine warning for the far-larger conventional housing market. But investors, government and rating agencies learned exactly nothing from the manufactured-home debacle. Instead, in an eerie rerun of that disaster, the same mistakes were repeated with conventional homes in the 2004-07 period: Lenders happily made loans that borrowers couldn't repay out of their incomes, and borrowers just as happily signed up to meet those payments. Both parties counted on "house-price appreciation" to make this otherwise impossible arrangement work. It was Scarlett O'Hara all over again: "I'll think about it tomorrow." The consequences of this behavior are now reverberating through every corner of our economy.

Clayton's 198,888 borrowers, however, have continued to pay normally throughout the housing crash, handing us no unexpected losses. This is *not* because these borrowers are unusually creditworthy, a point proved by FICO scores (a standard measure of credit risk). Their median FICO score is 644, compared to a national median of 723, and about 35% are below 620, the segment usually designated "sub-prime." Many disastrous pools of mortgages on conventional homes are populated by borrowers with far better credit, as measured by FICO scores.

Yet at yearend, our delinquency rate on loans we have originated was 3.6%, up only modestly from 2.9% in 2006 and 2.9% in 2004. (In addition to our originated loans, we've also bought bulk portfolios of various types from other financial institutions.) Clayton's foreclosures during 2008 were 3.0% of originated loans compared to 3.8% in 2006 and 5.3% in 2004.

Why are our borrowers – characteristically people with modest incomes and far-from-great credit scores – performing so well? The answer is elementary, going right back to Lending 101. Our borrowers simply looked at how full-bore mortgage payments would compare with their actual – not hoped-for – income and then decided whether they could live with that commitment. Simply put, they took out a mortgage with the intention of paying it off, whatever the course of home prices.

Just as important is what our borrowers did *not* do. They did not count on making their loan payments by means of refinancing. They did not sign up for "teaser" rates that upon reset were outsized relative to their income. And they did not assume that they could always sell their home at a profit if their mortgage payments became onerous. Jimmy Stewart would have loved these folks.

Of course, a number of our borrowers will run into trouble. They generally have no more than minor savings to tide them over if adversity hits. The major cause of delinquency or foreclosure is the loss of a job, but death, divorce and medical expenses all cause problems. If unemployment rates rise – as they surely will in 2009 – more of Clayton's borrowers will have troubles, and we will have larger, though still manageable, losses. But our problems will not be driven to any extent by the trend of home prices.

Commentary about the current housing crisis often ignores the crucial fact that most foreclosures do *not* occur because a house is worth less than its mortgage (so-called "upside-down" loans). Rather, foreclosures take place because borrowers can't pay the monthly payment that they agreed to pay. Homeowners who have made a meaningful down-payment – derived from savings and not from other borrowing – seldom walk away from a primary residence simply because its value today is less than the mortgage. Instead, they walk when they can't make the monthly payments.

Home ownership is a wonderful thing. My family and I have enjoyed my present home for 50 years, with more to come. But enjoyment and utility should be the primary motives for purchase, not profit or refi possibilities. And the home purchased ought to fit the income of the purchaser.

The present housing debacle should teach home buyers, lenders, brokers and government some simple lessons that will ensure stability in the future. Home purchases should involve an honest-to-God down payment of at least 10% and monthly payments that can be comfortably handled by the borrower's income. That income should be carefully verified.

Putting people into homes, though a desirable goal, shouldn't be our country's primary objective. Keeping them in their homes should be the ambition.

* * * * * * * * * * * *

Clayton's lending operation, though not damaged by the performance of its borrowers, is nevertheless threatened by an element of the credit crisis. Funders that have access to any sort of government guarantee – banks with FDIC-insured deposits, large entities with commercial paper now backed by the Federal Reserve, and others who are using imaginative methods (or lobbying skills) to come under the government's umbrella – have money costs that are minimal. Conversely, highly-rated companies, such as Berkshire, are experiencing borrowing costs that, in relation to Treasury rates, are at record levels. Moreover, funds are abundant for the government-guaranteed borrower but often scarce for others, no matter how creditworthy they may be.

This unprecedented "spread" in the cost of money makes it unprofitable for any lender who doesn't enjoy government-guaranteed funds to go up against those with a favored status. Government is determining the "haves" and "have-nots." That is why companies are rushing to convert to bank holding companies, not a course feasible for Berkshire.

Though Berkshire's credit is pristine – we are one of only seven AAA corporations in the country – our cost of borrowing is now *far* higher than competitors with shaky balance sheets but government backing. At the moment, it is much better to be a financial cripple with a government guarantee than a Gibraltar without one.

Today's extreme conditions may soon end. At worst, we believe we will find at least a partial solution that will allow us to continue much of Clayton's lending. Clayton's earnings, however, will surely suffer if we are forced to compete for long against government-favored lenders.

| | Pre-Tax Earnings (in millions) | |
	2008	2007
Net investment income	$330	$ 272
Life and annuity operation	23	(60)
Leasing operations	87	111
Manufactured-housing finance (Clayton)	206	526
Other*	141	157
Income before investment and derivatives gains or losses	$787	$1,006

*Includes $92 million in 2008 and $85 million in 2007 of fees that Berkshire charges Clayton for the use of Berkshire's credit.

Tax-Exempt Bond Insurance

Early in 2008, we activated Berkshire Hathaway Assurance Company ("BHAC") as an insurer of the tax-exempt bonds issued by states, cities and other local entities. BHAC insures these securities for issuers both at the time their bonds are sold to the public (primary transactions) and later, when the bonds are already owned by investors (secondary transactions).

By yearend 2007, the half dozen or so companies that had been the major players in this business had all fallen into big trouble. The cause of their problems was captured long ago by Mae West: "I was Snow White, but I drifted."

The monolines (as the bond insurers are called) initially insured only tax-exempt bonds that were low-risk. But over the years competition for this business intensified, and rates fell. Faced with the prospect of stagnating or declining earnings, the monoline managers turned to ever-riskier propositions. Some of these involved the insuring of residential mortgage obligations. When housing prices plummeted, the monoline industry quickly became a basket case.

Early in the year, Berkshire offered to assume all of the insurance issued on tax-exempts that was on the books of the three largest monolines. These companies were all in life-threatening trouble (though they said otherwise.) We would have charged a 1½% rate to take over the guarantees on about $822 billion of bonds. If our offer had been accepted, we would have been required to pay any losses suffered by investors who owned these bonds – a guarantee stretching for 40 years in some cases. Ours was not a frivolous proposal: For reasons we will come to later, it involved substantial risk for Berkshire.

The monolines summarily rejected our offer, in some cases appending an insult or two. In the end, though, the turndowns proved to be *very* good news for us, because it became apparent that I had severely underpriced our offer.

Thereafter, we wrote about $15.6 billion of insurance in the secondary market. And here's the punch line: About 77% of this business was on bonds that were already insured, largely by the three aforementioned monolines. In these agreements, we have to pay for defaults *only* if the original insurer is financially unable to do so.

We wrote this "second-to-pay" insurance for rates averaging 3.3%. That's right; we have been paid far more for becoming the second to pay than the 1.5% we would have earlier charged to be the first to pay. In one extreme case, we actually agreed to be *fourth* to pay, nonetheless receiving about three times the 1% premium charged by the monoline that remains *first* to pay. In other words, three other monolines have to first go broke before we need to write a check.

Two of the three monolines to which we made our initial bulk offer later raised substantial capital. This, of course, directly helps *us*, since it makes it less likely that we will have to pay, at least in the near term, any claims on our second-to-pay insurance because these two monolines fail. In addition to our book of secondary business, we have also written $3.7 billion of primary business for a premium of $96 million. In primary business, of course, we are first to pay if the issuer gets in trouble.

We have a great many more multiples of capital behind the insurance we write than does any other monoline. Consequently, our guarantee is far more valuable than theirs. This explains why many sophisticated investors have bought second-to-pay insurance from us even though they were already insured by another monoline. BHAC has become not only the insurer of preference, but in many cases the *sole* insurer acceptable to bondholders.

Nevertheless, we remain very cautious about the business we write and regard it as far from a sure thing that this insurance will ultimately be profitable for us. The reason is simple, though I have never seen even a passing reference to it by any financial analyst, rating agency or monoline CEO.

The rationale behind very low premium rates for insuring tax-exempts has been that defaults have historically been few. But that record largely reflects the experience of entities that issued *uninsured* bonds. Insurance of tax-exempt bonds didn't exist before 1971, and even after that most bonds remained uninsured.

A universe of tax-exempts fully covered by insurance would be certain to have a somewhat different loss experience from a group of uninsured, but otherwise similar bonds, the only question being *how* different. To understand why, let's go back to 1975 when New York City was on the edge of bankruptcy. At the time its bonds – virtually all uninsured – were heavily held by the city's wealthier residents as well as by New York banks and other institutions. These local bondholders deeply desired to solve the city's fiscal problems. So before long, concessions and cooperation from a host of involved constituencies produced a solution. Without one, it was apparent to all that New York's citizens and businesses would have experienced widespread and severe financial losses from their bond holdings.

Now, imagine that all of the city's bonds had instead been insured by Berkshire. Would similar belt-tightening, tax increases, labor concessions, etc. have been forthcoming? Of course not. At a minimum, Berkshire would have been asked to "share" in the required sacrifices. And, considering our deep pockets, the required contribution would most certainly have been substantial.

Local governments are going to face *far* tougher fiscal problems in the future than they have to date. The pension liabilities I talked about in last year's report will be a huge contributor to these woes. Many cities and states were surely horrified when they inspected the status of their funding at yearend 2008. The gap between assets and a realistic actuarial valuation of present liabilities is simply staggering.

When faced with large revenue shortfalls, communities that have all of their bonds insured will be more prone to develop "solutions" less favorable to bondholders than those communities that have uninsured bonds held by local banks and residents. Losses in the tax-exempt arena, when they come, are also likely to be highly correlated among issuers. If a few communities stiff their creditors and get away with it, the chance that others will follow in their footsteps will grow. What mayor or city council is going to choose pain to local citizens in the form of major tax increases over pain to a far-away bond insurer?

Insuring tax-exempts, therefore, has the look today of a dangerous business – one with similarities, in fact, to the insuring of natural catastrophes. In both cases, a string of loss-free years can be followed by a devastating experience that more than wipes out all earlier profits. We will try, therefore, to proceed carefully in this business, eschewing many classes of bonds that other monolines regularly embrace.

* * * * * * * * * * * *

The type of fallacy involved in projecting loss experience from a universe of non-insured bonds onto a deceptively-similar universe in which many bonds are insured pops up in other areas of finance. "Back-tested" models of many kinds are susceptible to this sort of error. Nevertheless, they are frequently touted in financial markets as guides to future action. (If merely looking up past financial data would tell you what the future holds, the Forbes 400 would consist of librarians.)

Indeed, the stupefying losses in mortgage-related securities came in large part because of flawed, history-based models used by salesmen, rating agencies and investors. These parties looked at loss experience over periods when home prices rose only moderately and speculation in houses was negligible. They then made this experience a yardstick for evaluating future losses. They blissfully ignored the fact that house prices had recently skyrocketed, loan practices had deteriorated and many buyers had opted for houses they couldn't afford. In short, universe "past" and universe "current" had very different characteristics. But lenders, government and media largely failed to recognize this all-important fact.

Investors should be skeptical of history-based models. Constructed by a nerdy-sounding priesthood using esoteric terms such as beta, gamma, sigma and the like, these models tend to look impressive. Too often, though, investors forget to examine the assumptions behind the symbols. Our advice: Beware of geeks bearing formulas.

* * * * * * * * * * * *

A final post-script on BHAC: Who, you may wonder, runs this operation? While I help set policy, all of the heavy lifting is done by Ajit and his crew. Sure, they were already generating $24 billion of float along with hundreds of millions of underwriting profit annually. But how busy can that keep a 31-person group? Charlie and I decided it was high time for them to start doing a full day's work.

Investments

Because of accounting rules, we divide our large holdings of common stocks this year into two categories. The table below, presenting the first category, itemizes investments that are carried on our balance sheet at market value and that had a yearend value of more than $500 million.

| | | | 12/31/08 | |
Shares	Company	Percentage of Company Owned	Cost*	Market
			(in millions)	
151,610,700	American Express Company	13.1	$ 1,287	$ 2,812
200,000,000	The Coca-Cola Company	8.6	1,299	9,054
84,896,273	ConocoPhillips	5.7	7,008	4,398
30,009,591	Johnson & Johnson	1.1	1,847	1,795
130,272,500	Kraft Foods Inc.	8.9	4,330	3,498
3,947,554	POSCO	5.2	768	1,191
91,941,010	The Procter & Gamble Company	3.1	643	5,684
22,111,966	Sanofi-Aventis	1.7	1,827	1,404
11,262,000	Swiss Re	3.2	773	530
227,307,000	Tesco plc	2.9	1,326	1,193
75,145,426	U.S. Bancorp	4.3	2,337	1,879
19,944,300	Wal-Mart Stores, Inc.	0.5	942	1,118
1,727,765	The Washington Post Company	18.4	11	674
304,392,068	Wells Fargo & Company	7.2	6,702	8,973
	Others		6,035	4,870
	Total Common Stocks Carried at Market		$37,135	$49,073

*This is our actual purchase price and also our tax basis; GAAP "cost" differs in a few cases because of write-ups or write-downs that have been required.

In addition, we have holdings in Moody's and Burlington Northern Santa Fe that we now carry at "equity value" – our cost plus retained earnings since our purchase, minus the tax that would be paid if those earnings were paid to us as dividends. This accounting treatment is usually required when ownership of an investee company reaches 20%.

We purchased 15% of Moody's some years ago and have not since bought a share. Moody's, though, has repurchased its own shares and, by late 2008, those repurchases reduced its outstanding shares to the point that our holdings rose above 20%. Burlington Northern has also repurchased shares, but our increase to 20% primarily occurred because we continued to buy this stock.

Unless facts or rules change, you will see these holdings reflected in our balance sheet at "equity accounting" values, whatever their market prices. You will also see our share of their earnings (less applicable taxes) regularly included in our quarterly and annual earnings.

I told you in an earlier part of this report that last year I made a major mistake of commission (and maybe more; this one sticks out). Without urging from Charlie or anyone else, I bought a large amount of ConocoPhillips stock when oil and gas prices were near their peak. I in no way anticipated the dramatic fall in energy prices that occurred in the last half of the year. I still believe the odds are good that oil sells far higher in the future than the current $40-$50 price. But so far I have been dead wrong. Even if prices should rise, moreover, the terrible timing of my purchase has cost Berkshire several billion dollars.

I made some other already-recognizable errors as well. They were smaller, but unfortunately not *that* small. During 2008, I spent $244 million for shares of two Irish banks that appeared cheap to me. At yearend we wrote these holdings down to market: $27 million, for an 89% loss. Since then, the two stocks have declined even further. The tennis crowd would call my mistakes "unforced errors."

On the plus side last year, we made purchases totaling $14.5 billion in fixed-income securities issued by Wrigley, Goldman Sachs and General Electric. We very much like these commitments, which carry high current yields that, in themselves, make the investments more than satisfactory. But in each of these three purchases, we also acquired a substantial equity participation as a bonus. To fund these large purchases, I had to sell portions of some holdings that I would have preferred to keep (primarily Johnson & Johnson, Procter & Gamble and ConocoPhillips). However, I have pledged – to you, the rating agencies and myself – to always run Berkshire with more than ample cash. We never want to count on the kindness of strangers in order to meet tomorrow's obligations. When forced to choose, I will not trade even a night's sleep for the chance of extra profits.

The investment world has gone from underpricing risk to overpricing it. This change has not been minor; the pendulum has covered an extraordinary arc. A few years ago, it would have seemed unthinkable that yields like today's could have been obtained on good-grade municipal or corporate bonds even while risk-free governments offered near-zero returns on short-term bonds and no better than a pittance on long-terms. When the financial history of this decade is written, it will surely speak of the Internet bubble of the late 1990s and the housing bubble of the early 2000s. But the U.S. Treasury bond bubble of late 2008 may be regarded as almost equally extraordinary.

Clinging to cash equivalents or long-term government bonds at present yields is almost certainly a terrible policy if continued for long. Holders of these instruments, of course, have felt increasingly comfortable – in fact, almost smug – in following this policy as financial turmoil has mounted. They regard their judgment confirmed when they hear commentators proclaim "cash is king," even though that wonderful cash is earning close to nothing and will surely find its purchasing power eroded over time.

Approval, though, is not the goal of investing. In fact, approval is often counter-productive because it sedates the brain and makes it less receptive to new facts or a re-examination of conclusions formed earlier. Beware the investment activity that produces applause; the great moves are usually greeted by yawns.

Derivatives

Derivatives are dangerous. They have dramatically increased the leverage and risks in our financial system. They have made it almost impossible for investors to understand and analyze our largest commercial banks and investment banks. They allowed Fannie Mae and Freddie Mac to engage in massive misstatements of earnings for years. So indecipherable were Freddie and Fannie that their federal regulator, OFHEO, whose more than 100 employees had no job except the oversight of these two institutions, totally missed their cooking of the books.

Indeed, recent events demonstrate that certain big-name CEOs (or former CEOs) at major financial institutions were simply incapable of managing a business with a huge, complex book of derivatives. Include Charlie and me in this hapless group: When Berkshire purchased General Re in 1998, we knew we could not get our minds around its book of 23,218 derivatives contracts, made with 884 counterparties (many of which we had never heard of). So we decided to close up shop. Though we were under no pressure and were operating in benign markets as we exited, it took us five years and more than $400 million in losses to largely complete the task. Upon leaving, our feelings about the business mirrored a line in a country song: "I liked you better before I got to know you so well."

Improved "transparency" – a favorite remedy of politicians, commentators and financial regulators for averting future train wrecks – won't cure the problems that derivatives pose. I know of no reporting mechanism that would come close to describing and measuring the risks in a huge and complex portfolio of derivatives. Auditors can't audit these contracts, and regulators can't regulate them. When I read the pages of "disclosure" in 10-Ks of companies that are entangled with these instruments, all I end up knowing is that I *don't* know what is going on in their portfolios (and then I reach for some aspirin).

For a case study on regulatory effectiveness, let's look harder at the Freddie and Fannie example. These giant institutions were created by Congress, which retained control over them, dictating what they could and could not do. To aid its oversight, Congress created OFHEO in 1992, admonishing it to make sure the two behemoths were behaving themselves. With that move, Fannie and Freddie became the most intensely-regulated companies of which I am aware, as measured by manpower assigned to the task.

On June 15, 2003, OFHEO (whose annual reports are available on the Internet) sent its 2002 report to Congress – specifically to its four bosses in the Senate and House, among them none other than Messrs. Sarbanes and Oxley. The report's 127 pages included a self-congratulatory cover-line: "Celebrating 10 Years of Excellence." The transmittal letter and report were delivered nine days *after* the CEO and CFO of Freddie had resigned in disgrace and the COO had been fired. No mention of their departures was made in the letter, even while the report concluded, as it always did, that "Both Enterprises were financially sound and well managed."

In truth, both enterprises had engaged in massive accounting shenanigans for some time. Finally, in 2006, OFHEO issued a 340-page scathing chronicle of the sins of Fannie that, more or less, blamed the fiasco on every party but – you guessed it – Congress and OFHEO.

The Bear Stearns collapse highlights the counterparty problem embedded in derivatives transactions, a time bomb I first discussed in Berkshire's 2002 report. On April 3, 2008, Tim Geithner, then the able president of the New York Fed, explained the need for a rescue: "The sudden discovery by Bear's derivative counterparties that important financial positions they had put in place to protect themselves from financial risk were no longer operative would have triggered substantial further dislocation in markets. This would have precipitated a rush by Bear's counterparties to liquidate the collateral they held against those positions and to attempt to replicate those positions in already very fragile markets." This is Fedspeak for "We stepped in to avoid a financial chain reaction of unpredictable magnitude." In my opinion, the Fed was right to do so.

A normal stock or bond trade is completed in a few days with one party getting its cash, the other its securities. Counterparty risk therefore quickly disappears, which means credit problems can't accumulate. This rapid settlement process is key to maintaining the integrity of markets. That, in fact, is a reason for NYSE and NASDAQ *shortening* the settlement period from five days to three days in 1995.

Derivatives contracts, in contrast, often go unsettled for years, or even decades, with counterparties building up huge claims against each other. "Paper" assets and liabilities – often hard to quantify – become important parts of financial statements though these items will not be validated for many years. Additionally, a frightening web of mutual dependence develops among huge financial institutions. Receivables and payables by the billions become concentrated in the hands of a few large dealers who are apt to be highly-leveraged in other ways as well. Participants seeking to dodge troubles face the same problem as someone seeking to avoid venereal disease: It's not just whom *you* sleep with, but also whom *they* are sleeping with.

Sleeping around, to continue our metaphor, can actually be useful for large derivatives dealers because it assures them government aid if trouble hits. In other words, only companies having problems that can infect the entire neighborhood – I won't mention names – are certain to become a concern of the state (an outcome, I'm sad to say, that is proper). From this irritating reality comes *The First Law of Corporate Survival* for ambitious CEOs who pile on leverage and run large and unfathomable derivatives books: Modest incompetence simply won't do; it's mindboggling screw-ups that are required.

Considering the ruin I've pictured, you may wonder why Berkshire is a party to 251 derivatives contracts (other than those used for operational purposes at MidAmerican and the few left over at Gen Re). The answer is simple: I believe each contract we own was mispriced at inception, sometimes dramatically so. I both initiated these positions and monitor them, a set of responsibilities consistent with my belief that the CEO of any large financial organization *must* be the Chief Risk Officer as well. If we lose money on our derivatives, it will be my fault.

Our derivatives dealings require our counterparties to make payments to us when contracts are initiated. Berkshire therefore always holds the money, which leaves us assuming no meaningful counterparty risk. As of yearend, the payments made to us less losses we have paid – our derivatives "float," so to speak – totaled $8.1 billion. This float is similar to insurance float: If we break even on an underlying transaction, we will have enjoyed the use of free money for a long time. Our expectation, though it is far from a sure thing, is that we will do better than break even and that the substantial investment income we earn on the funds will be frosting on the cake.

Only a small percentage of our contracts call for any posting of collateral when the market moves against us. Even under the chaotic conditions existing in last year's fourth quarter, we had to post less than 1% of our securities portfolio. (When we post collateral, we deposit it with third parties, meanwhile retaining the investment earnings on the deposited securities.) In our 2002 annual report, we warned of the lethal threat that posting requirements create, real-life illustrations of which we witnessed last year at a variety of financial institutions (and, for that matter, at Constellation Energy, which was within hours of bankruptcy when MidAmerican arrived to effect a rescue).

Our contracts fall into four major categories. With apologies to those who are not fascinated by financial instruments, I will explain them in excruciating detail.

- We have added modestly to the "equity put" portfolio I described in last year's report. Some of our contracts come due in 15 years, others in 20. We must make a payment to our counterparty at maturity if the reference index to which the put is tied is then below what it was at the inception of the contract. Neither party can elect to settle early; it's only the price on the final day that counts.

  To illustrate, we might sell a $1 billion 15-year put contract on the S&P 500 when that index is at, say, 1300. If the index is at 1170 – down 10% – on the day of maturity, we would pay $100 million. If it is above 1300, we owe nothing. For us to lose $1 billion, the index would have to go to zero. In the meantime, the sale of the put would have delivered us a premium – perhaps $100 million to $150 million – that we would be free to invest as we wish.

  Our put contracts total $37.1 billion (at current exchange rates) and are spread among four major indices: the S&P 500 in the U.S., the FTSE 100 in the U.K., the Euro Stoxx 50 in Europe, and the Nikkei 225 in Japan. Our first contract comes due on September 9, 2019 and our last on January 24, 2028. We have received premiums of $4.9 billion, money we have invested. We, meanwhile, have paid nothing, since all expiration dates are far in the future. Nonetheless, we have used Black-Scholes valuation methods to record a yearend liability of $10 billion, an amount that will change on every reporting date. The two financial items – this estimated loss of $10 billion minus the $4.9 billion in premiums we have received – means that we have so far reported a mark-to-market loss of $5.1 billion from these contracts.

18

616

We endorse mark-to-market accounting. I will explain later, however, why I believe the Black-Scholes formula, even though it is the standard for establishing the dollar liability for options, produces strange results when the long-term variety are being valued.

One point about our contracts that is sometimes not understood: For us to lose the full $37.1 billion we have at risk, all stocks in all four indices would have to go to *zero* on their various termination dates. If, however – as an example – all indices fell 25% from their value at the inception of each contract, and foreign-exchange rates remained as they are today, we would owe about $9 billion, payable between 2019 and 2028. Between the inception of the contract and those dates, we would have held the $4.9 billion premium and earned investment income on it.

- The second category we described in last year's report concerns derivatives requiring us to pay when credit losses occur at companies that are included in various high-yield indices. Our standard contract covers a five-year period and involves 100 companies. We modestly expanded our position last year in this category. But, of course, the contracts on the books at the end of 2007 moved one year closer to their maturity. Overall, our contracts now have an average life of 2⅓ years, with the first expiration due to occur on September 20, 2009 and the last on December 20, 2013.

  By yearend we had received premiums of $3.4 billion on these contracts and paid losses of $542 million. Using mark-to-market principles, we also set up a liability for future losses that at yearend totaled $3.0 billion. Thus we had to that point recorded a loss of about $100 million, derived from our $3.5 billion total in paid and estimated future losses minus the $3.4 billion of premiums we received. In our quarterly reports, however, the amount of gain or loss has swung wildly from a profit of $327 million in the second quarter of 2008 to a loss of $693 million in the fourth quarter of 2008.

  Surprisingly, we made payments on these contracts of only $97 million last year, far below the estimate I used when I decided to enter into them. This year, however, losses have accelerated sharply with the mushrooming of large bankruptcies. In last year's letter, I told you I expected these contracts to show a profit at expiration. Now, with the recession deepening at a rapid rate, the possibility of an eventual loss has increased. Whatever the result, I will keep you posted.

- In 2008 we began to write "credit default swaps" on individual companies. This is simply credit insurance, similar to what we write in BHAC, except that here we bear the credit risk of corporations rather than of tax-exempt issuers.

  If, say, the XYZ company goes bankrupt, and we have written a $100 million contract, we are obligated to pay an amount that reflects the shrinkage in value of a comparable amount of XYZ's debt. (If, for example, the company's bonds are selling for 30 after default, we would owe $70 million.) For the typical contract, we receive quarterly payments for five years, after which our insurance expires.

  At yearend we had written $4 billion of contracts covering 42 corporations, for which we receive annual premiums of $93 million. This is the only derivatives business we write that has any counterparty risk; the party that buys the contract from us must be good for the quarterly premiums it will owe us over the five years. We are unlikely to expand this business to any extent because most buyers of this protection now insist that the seller post collateral, and we will not enter into such an arrangement.

- At the request of our customers, we write a few tax-exempt bond insurance contracts that are similar to those written at BHAC, but that are structured as derivatives. The only meaningful difference between the two contracts is that mark-to-market accounting is required for derivatives whereas standard accrual accounting is required at BHAC.

But this difference can produce some strange results. The bonds covered – in effect, insured – by these derivatives are largely general obligations of states, and we feel good about them. At yearend, however, mark-to-market accounting required us to record a loss of $631 million on these derivatives contracts. Had we instead insured the same bonds at the same price in BHAC, and used the accrual accounting required at insurance companies, we would have recorded a small *profit* for the year. The two methods by which we insure the bonds will eventually produce the same accounting result. In the short term, however, the variance in reported profits can be substantial.

We have told you before that our derivative contracts, subject as they are to mark-to-market accounting, will produce wild swings in the earnings we report. The ups and downs neither cheer nor bother Charlie and me. Indeed, the "downs" can be helpful in that they give us an opportunity to expand a position on favorable terms. I hope this explanation of our dealings will lead you to think similarly.

* * * * * * * * * * * *

The Black-Scholes formula has approached the status of holy writ in finance, and we use it when valuing our equity put options for financial statement purposes. Key inputs to the calculation include a contract's maturity and strike price, as well as the analyst's expectations for volatility, interest rates and dividends.

If the formula is applied to extended time periods, however, it can produce absurd results. In fairness, Black and Scholes almost certainly understood this point well. But their devoted followers may be ignoring whatever caveats the two men attached when they first unveiled the formula.

It's often useful in testing a theory to push it to extremes. So let's postulate that we sell a 100- year $1 billion put option on the S&P 500 at a strike price of 903 (the index's level on 12/31/08). Using the implied volatility assumption for long-dated contracts that we do, and combining that with appropriate interest and dividend assumptions, we would find the "proper" Black-Scholes premium for this contract to be $2.5 million.

To judge the rationality of that premium, we need to assess whether the S&P will be valued a century from now at less than today. Certainly the dollar will then be worth a small fraction of its present value (at only 2% inflation it will be worth roughly 14¢). So that will be a factor pushing the stated value of the index higher. Far more important, however, is that one hundred years of retained earnings will hugely increase the value of most of the companies in the index. In the 20th Century, the Dow-Jones Industrial Average increased by about 175-fold, mainly because of this retained-earnings factor.

Considering everything, I believe the probability of a decline in the index over a one-hundred-year period to be *far* less than 1%. But let's use that figure and also assume that the most likely decline – should one occur – is 50%. Under these assumptions, the mathematical expectation of loss on our contract would be $5 million ($1 billion X 1% X 50%).

But if we had received our theoretical premium of $2.5 million up front, we would have only had to invest it at 0.7% compounded annually to cover this loss expectancy. Everything earned above that would have been profit. Would you like to borrow money for 100 years at a 0.7% rate?

Let's look at my example from a worst-case standpoint. Remember that 99% of the time we would pay nothing if my assumptions are correct. But even in the worst case among the remaining 1% of possibilities – that is, one assuming a *total* loss of $1 billion – our borrowing cost would come to only 6.2%. Clearly, either my assumptions are crazy or the formula is inappropriate.

The ridiculous premium that Black-Scholes dictates in my extreme example is caused by the inclusion of volatility in the formula and by the fact that volatility is determined by how much stocks have moved around in some past period of days, months or years. This metric is simply irrelevant in estimating the probability-weighted range of values of American business 100 years from now. (Imagine, if you will, getting a quote every day on a farm from a manic-depressive neighbor and then using the volatility calculated from these changing quotes as an important ingredient in an equation that predicts a probability-weighted range of values for the farm a century from now.)

Though historical volatility is a useful – but far from foolproof – concept in valuing short-term options, its utility diminishes rapidly as the duration of the option lengthens. In my opinion, the valuations that the Black-Scholes formula now place on our long-term put options overstate our liability, though the overstatement will diminish as the contracts approach maturity.

Even so, we will continue to use Black-Scholes when we are estimating our financial-statement liability for long-term equity puts. The formula represents conventional wisdom and any substitute that I might offer would engender extreme skepticism. That would be perfectly understandable: CEOs who have concocted their own valuations for esoteric financial instruments have seldom erred on the side of conservatism. That club of optimists is one that Charlie and I have no desire to join.

The Annual Meeting

Our meeting this year will be held on Saturday, May 2nd. As always, the doors will open at the Qwest Center at 7 a.m., and a new Berkshire movie will be shown at 8:30. At 9:30 we will go directly to the question-and-answer period, which (with a break for lunch at the Qwest's stands) will last until 3:00. Then, after a short recess, Charlie and I will convene the annual meeting at 3:15. If you decide to leave during the day's question periods, please do so while *Charlie* is talking.

The best reason to exit, of course, is to *shop*. We will help you do that by filling the 194,300-square-foot hall that adjoins the meeting area with the products of Berkshire subsidiaries. Last year, the 31,000 people who came to the meeting did their part, and almost every location racked up record sales. But you can do better. (A friendly warning: If I find sales are lagging, I lock the exits.)

This year Clayton will showcase its new *i-house* that includes Shaw flooring, Johns Manville insulation and MiTek fasteners. This innovative "green" home, featuring solar panels and numerous other energy-saving products, is truly a home of the future. Estimated costs for electricity and heating total only about $1 per day when the home is sited in an area like Omaha. After purchasing the *i-house*, you should next consider the Forest River RV and pontoon boat on display nearby. Make your neighbors jealous.

GEICO will have a booth staffed by a number of its top counselors from around the country, all of them ready to supply you with auto insurance quotes. In most cases, GEICO will be able to give you a shareholder discount (usually 8%). This special offer is permitted by 44 of the 50 jurisdictions in which we operate. (One supplemental point: The discount is not additive if you qualify for another, such as that given certain groups.) Bring the details of your existing insurance and check out whether we can save you money. For at least 50% of you, I believe we can.

On Saturday, at the Omaha airport, we will have the usual array of NetJets aircraft available for your inspection. Stop by the NetJets booth at the Qwest to learn about viewing these planes. Come to Omaha by bus; leave in your new plane. And take along – with no fear of a strip search – the Ginsu knives that you've purchased at the exhibit of our Quikut subsidiary.

Next, if you have any money left, visit the Bookworm, which will be selling about 30 books and DVDs. A shipping service will be available for those whose thirst for knowledge exceeds their carrying capacity.

Finally, we will have three fascinating cars on the exhibition floor, including one from the past and one of the future. Paul Andrews, CEO of our subsidiary, TTI, will bring his 1935 Duesenberg, a car that once belonged to Mrs. Forrest Mars, Sr., parent and grandparent of our new partners in the Wrigley purchase. The future will be represented by a new plug-in electric car developed by BYD, an amazing Chinese company in which we have a 10% interest.

An attachment to the proxy material that is enclosed with this report explains how you can obtain the credential you will need for admission to the meeting and other events. As for plane, hotel and car reservations, we have again signed up American Express (800-799-6634) to give you special help. Carol Pedersen, who handles these matters, does a terrific job for us each year, and I thank her for it. Hotel rooms can be hard to find, but work with Carol and you will get one.

At Nebraska Furniture Mart, located on a 77-acre site on 72nd Street between Dodge and Pacific, we will again be having "Berkshire Weekend" discount pricing. We initiated this special event at NFM twelve years ago, and sales during the "Weekend" grew from $5.3 million in 1997 to a record $33.3 million in 2008. On Saturday of that weekend, we also set a single day record of $7.2 million. Ask any retailer what he thinks of such volume.

To obtain the Berkshire discount, you must make your purchases between Thursday, April 30th and Monday, May 4th inclusive, and also present your meeting credential. The period's special pricing will even apply to the products of several prestigious manufacturers that normally have ironclad rules against discounting but which, in the spirit of our shareholder weekend, have made an exception for you. We appreciate their cooperation. NFM is open from 10 a.m. to 9 p.m. Monday through Saturday, and 10 a.m. to 6 p.m. on Sunday. On Saturday this year, from 5:30 p.m. to 8 p.m., NFM is having a western cookout to which you are all invited.

At Borsheims, we will again have two shareholder-only events. The first will be a cocktail reception from 6 p.m. to 10 p.m. on Friday, May 1st. The second, the main gala, will be held on Sunday, May 3rd, from 9 a.m. to 4 p.m. On Saturday, we will be open until 6 p.m.

We will have huge crowds at Borsheims throughout the weekend. For your convenience, therefore, shareholder prices will be available from Monday, April 27th through Saturday, May 9th. During that period, please identify yourself as a shareholder by presenting your meeting credentials or a brokerage statement that shows you are a Berkshire holder.

On Sunday, in the mall outside of Borsheims, a blindfolded Patrick Wolff, twice U.S. chess champion, will take on all comers – who will have their eyes wide open – in groups of six. Nearby, Norman Beck, a remarkable magician from Dallas, will bewilder onlookers. Additionally, we will have Bob Hamman and Sharon Osberg, two of the world's top bridge experts, available to play bridge with our shareholders on Sunday afternoon.

Gorat's will again be open exclusively for Berkshire shareholders on Sunday, May 3rd, and will be serving from 1 p.m. until 10 p.m. Last year Gorat's, which seats 240, served 975 dinners on Shareholder Sunday. The three-day total was 2,448 including 702 T-bone steaks, the entrée preferred by the *cognoscenti*. Please don't embarrass me by ordering foie gras. Remember: To come to Gorat's on that day, you must have a reservation. To make one, call 402-551-3733 on April 1st (*but not before*).

We will again have a reception at 4 p.m. on Saturday afternoon for shareholders who have come from outside North America. Every year our meeting draws many people from around the globe, and Charlie and I want to be sure we personally greet those who have come so far. Last year we enjoyed meeting more than 700 of you from many dozens of countries. Any shareholder who comes from outside the U.S. or Canada will be given a special credential and instructions for attending this function.

* * * * * * * * * * *

This year we will be making important changes in how we handle the meeting's question periods. In recent years, we have received only a handful of questions directly related to Berkshire and its operations. Last year there were practically none. So we need to steer the discussion back to Berkshire's businesses.

In a related problem, there has been a mad rush when the doors open at 7 a.m., led by people who wish to be first in line at the 12 microphones available for questioners. This is not desirable from a safety standpoint, nor do we believe that sprinting ability should be the determinant of who gets to pose questions. (At age 78, I've concluded that speed afoot is a ridiculously overrated talent.) Again, a new procedure is desirable.

In our first change, several financial journalists from organizations representing newspapers, magazines and television will participate in the question-and-answer period, asking Charlie and me questions that shareholders have submitted by e-mail. The journalists and their e-mail addresses are: Carol Loomis, of Fortune, who may be emailed at cloomis@fortunemail.com; Becky Quick, of CNBC, at BerkshireQuestions@cnbc.com, and Andrew Ross Sorkin, of The New York Times, at arsorkin@nytimes.com. From the questions submitted, each journalist will choose the dozen or so he or she decides are the most interesting and important. (In your e-mail, let the journalist know if you would like your name mentioned if your question is selected.)

Neither Charlie nor I will get so much as a clue about the questions to be asked. We know the journalists will pick some tough ones and that's the way we like it.

In our second change, we will have a drawing at 8:15 at each microphone for those shareholders hoping to ask questions themselves. At the meeting, I will alternate the questions asked by the journalists with those from the winning shareholders. At least half the questions – those selected by the panel from your submissions – are therefore certain to be Berkshire-related. We will meanwhile continue to get some good – and perhaps entertaining – questions from the audience as well.

So join us at our Woodstock for Capitalists and let us know how you like the new format. Charlie and I look forward to seeing you.

February 27, 2009   Warren E. Buffett
Chairman of the Board

BERKSHIRE HATHAWAY INC.

To the Shareholders of Berkshire Hathaway Inc.:

Our gain in net worth during 2009 was $21.8 billion, which increased the per-share book value of both our Class A and Class B stock by 19.8%. Over the last 45 years (that is, since present management took over) book value has grown from $19 to $84,487, a rate of 20.3% compounded annually.*

Berkshire's recent acquisition of Burlington Northern Santa Fe (BNSF) has added at least 65,000 shareholders to the 500,000 or so already on our books. It's important to Charlie Munger, my long-time partner, and me that *all* of our owners understand Berkshire's operations, goals, limitations and culture. In each annual report, consequently, we restate the economic principles that guide us. This year these principles appear on pages 89-94 and I urge all of you – but particularly our new shareholders – to read them. Berkshire has adhered to these principles for decades and will continue to do so long after I'm gone.

In this letter we will also review some of the basics of our business, hoping to provide both a freshman orientation session for our BNSF newcomers and a refresher course for Berkshire veterans.

How We Measure Ourselves

Our metrics for evaluating our managerial performance are displayed on the facing page. From the start, Charlie and I have believed in having a rational and unbending standard for measuring what we have – or have not – accomplished. That keeps us from the temptation of seeing where the arrow of performance lands and *then* painting the bull's eye around it.

Selecting the S&P 500 as our bogey was an easy choice because our shareholders, at virtually no cost, can match its performance by holding an index fund. Why should they pay us for merely duplicating that result?

A more difficult decision for us was how to measure the progress of Berkshire versus the S&P. There are good arguments for simply using the change in our stock price. Over an extended period of time, in fact, that is the best test. But year-to-year market prices can be extraordinarily erratic. Even evaluations covering as long as a decade can be greatly distorted by foolishly high or low prices at the beginning or end of the measurement period. Steve Ballmer, of Microsoft, and Jeff Immelt, of GE, can tell you about that problem, suffering as they do from the nosebleed prices at which their stocks traded when they were handed the managerial baton.

The ideal standard for measuring our yearly progress would be the change in Berkshire's per-share intrinsic value. Alas, that value cannot be calculated with anything close to precision, so we instead use a crude proxy for it: per-share book value. Relying on this yardstick has its shortcomings, which we discuss on pages 92 and 93. Additionally, book value at most companies understates intrinsic value, and that is certainly the case at Berkshire. In aggregate, our businesses are worth considerably more than the values at which they are carried on our books. In our all-important insurance business, moreover, the difference is huge. Even so, Charlie and I believe that our book value – understated though it is – supplies the most useful tracking device for changes in intrinsic value. By this measurement, as the opening paragraph of this letter states, our book value since the start of fiscal 1965 has grown at a rate of 20.3% compounded annually.

---

*All per-share figures used in this report apply to Berkshire's A shares. Figures for the B shares are 1/1500th of those shown for A.

3

We should note that had we instead chosen *market prices* as our yardstick, Berkshire's results would look better, showing a gain since the start of fiscal 1965 of 22% compounded annually. Surprisingly, this modest difference in annual compounding rate leads to an 801,516% market-value gain for the entire 45-year period compared to the book-value gain of 434,057% (shown on page 2). Our market gain is better because in 1965 Berkshire shares sold at an appropriate discount to the book value of its underearning textile assets, whereas today Berkshire shares regularly sell at a premium to the accounting values of its first-class businesses.

Summed up, the table on page 2 conveys three messages, two positive and one hugely negative. First, we have never had *any* five-year period beginning with 1965-69 and ending with 2005-09 – and there have been 41 of these – during which our gain in book value did not exceed the S&P's gain. Second, though we have lagged the S&P in some years that were positive for the market, we have consistently done better than the S&P in the eleven years during which it delivered negative results. In other words, our defense has been better than our offense, and that's likely to continue.

The big minus is that our performance advantage has shrunk dramatically as our size has grown, an unpleasant trend that is *certain* to continue. To be sure, Berkshire has many outstanding businesses and a cadre of truly great managers, operating within an unusual corporate culture that lets them maximize their talents. Charlie and I believe these factors will continue to produce better-than-average results over time. But huge sums forge their own anchor and our future advantage, if any, will be a small fraction of our historical edge.

What We Don't Do

Long ago, Charlie laid out his strongest ambition: "All I want to know is where I'm going to die, so I'll never go there." That bit of wisdom was inspired by Jacobi, the great Prussian mathematician, who counseled "Invert, always invert" as an aid to solving difficult problems. (I can report as well that this inversion approach works on a less lofty level: Sing a country song in reverse, and you will quickly recover your car, house and wife.)

Here are a few examples of how we apply Charlie's thinking at Berkshire:

- Charlie and I avoid businesses whose futures we can't evaluate, no matter how exciting their products may be. In the past, it required no brilliance for people to foresee the fabulous growth that awaited such industries as autos (in 1910), aircraft (in 1930) and television sets (in 1950). But the future then also included competitive dynamics that would decimate almost all of the companies entering those industries. Even the survivors tended to come away bleeding.

 Just because Charlie and I can clearly see dramatic growth ahead for an industry does not mean we can judge what its profit margins and returns on capital will be as a host of competitors battle for supremacy. At Berkshire we will stick with businesses whose profit picture for decades to come seems reasonably predictable. Even then, we will make plenty of mistakes.

- We will never become dependent on the kindness of strangers. Too-big-to-fail is not a fallback position at Berkshire. Instead, we will always arrange our affairs so that any requirements for cash we may conceivably have will be dwarfed by our own liquidity. Moreover, that liquidity will be constantly refreshed by a gusher of earnings from our many and diverse businesses.

 When the financial system went into cardiac arrest in September 2008, Berkshire was a *supplier* of liquidity and capital to the system, not a supplicant. At the very peak of the crisis, we poured $15.5 billion into a business world that could otherwise look only to the federal government for help. Of that, $9 billion went to bolster capital at three highly-regarded and previously-secure American businesses that needed – *without delay* – our tangible vote of confidence. The remaining $6.5 billion satisfied our commitment to help fund the purchase of Wrigley, a deal that was completed without pause while, elsewhere, panic reigned.

We pay a steep price to maintain our premier financial strength. The $20 billion-plus of cash-equivalent assets that we customarily hold is earning a pittance at present. But we sleep well.

- We tend to let our many subsidiaries operate on their own, without our supervising and monitoring them to any degree. That means we are sometimes late in spotting management problems and that both operating and capital decisions are occasionally made with which Charlie and I would have disagreed had we been consulted. Most of our managers, however, use the independence we grant them magnificently, rewarding our confidence by maintaining an owner-oriented attitude that is invaluable and too seldom found in huge organizations. We would rather suffer the visible costs of a few bad decisions than incur the many invisible costs that come from decisions made too slowly – or not at all – because of a stifling bureaucracy.

  With our acquisition of BNSF, we now have about 257,000 employees and literally hundreds of different operating units. We hope to have many more of each. But we will never allow Berkshire to become some monolith that is overrun with committees, budget presentations and multiple layers of management. Instead, we plan to operate as a collection of separately-managed medium-sized and large businesses, most of whose decision-making occurs at the operating level. Charlie and I will limit ourselves to allocating capital, controlling enterprise risk, choosing managers and setting their compensation.

- We make no attempt to woo Wall Street. Investors who buy and sell based upon media or analyst commentary are not for us. Instead we want *partners* who join us at Berkshire because they wish to make a long-term investment in a *business* they themselves understand and because it's one that follows policies with which they concur. If Charlie and I were to go into a small venture with a few partners, we would seek individuals in sync with us, knowing that common goals and a shared destiny make for a happy business "marriage" between owners and managers. Scaling up to giant size doesn't change that truth.

  To build a compatible shareholder population, we try to communicate with our owners directly and informatively. Our goal is to tell you what we would like to know if our positions were reversed. Additionally, we try to post our quarterly and annual financial information on the Internet early on weekends, thereby giving you and other investors plenty of time during a non-trading period to digest just what has happened at our multi-faceted enterprise. (Occasionally, SEC deadlines force a non-Friday disclosure.) These matters simply can't be adequately summarized in a few paragraphs, nor do they lend themselves to the kind of catchy headline that journalists sometimes seek.

  Last year we saw, in one instance, how sound-bite reporting can go wrong. Among the 12,830 words in the annual letter was this sentence: "We are certain, for example, that the economy will be in shambles throughout 2009 – and probably well beyond – but that conclusion does not tell us whether the market will rise or fall." Many news organizations reported – indeed, blared – the first part of the sentence while making no mention whatsoever of its ending. I regard this as terrible journalism: Misinformed readers or viewers may well have thought that Charlie and I were forecasting bad things for the stock market, though we had not only in that sentence, but also elsewhere, made it clear we weren't predicting the market at all. Any investors who were misled by the sensationalists paid a big price: The Dow closed the day of the letter at 7,063 and finished the year at 10,428.

  Given a few experiences we've had like that, you can understand why I prefer that our communications with you remain as direct and unabridged as possible.

* * * * * * * * * * * *

Let's move to the specifics of Berkshire's operations. We have four major operating sectors, each differing from the others in balance sheet and income account characteristics. Therefore, lumping them together, as is standard in financial statements, impedes analysis. So we'll present them as four separate businesses, which is how Charlie and I view them.

Insurance

Our property-casualty (P/C) insurance business has been the engine behind Berkshire's growth and will continue to be. It has worked wonders for us. We carry our P/C companies on our books at $15.5 billion more than their net tangible assets, an amount lodged in our "Goodwill" account. These companies, however, are worth *far* more than their carrying value – and the following look at the economic model of the P/C industry will tell you why.

Insurers receive premiums upfront and pay claims later. In extreme cases, such as those arising from certain workers' compensation accidents, payments can stretch over decades. This collect-now, pay-later model leaves us holding large sums – money we call "float" – that will eventually go to others. Meanwhile, we get to invest this float for Berkshire's benefit. Though individual policies and claims come and go, the amount of float we hold remains remarkably stable in relation to premium volume. Consequently, as our business grows, so does our float.

If premiums exceed the total of expenses and eventual losses, we register an underwriting profit that adds to the investment income produced from the float. This combination allows us to enjoy the use of free money – and, better yet, get *paid* for holding it. Alas, the hope of this happy result attracts intense competition, so vigorous in most years as to cause the P/C industry as a whole to operate at a significant underwriting *loss*. This loss, in effect, is what the industry pays to hold its float. Usually this cost is fairly low, but in some catastrophe-ridden years the cost from underwriting losses more than eats up the income derived from use of float.

In my perhaps biased view, Berkshire has the best large insurance operation in the world. And I will absolutely state that we have the best managers. Our float has grown from $16 million in 1967, when we entered the business, to $62 billion at the end of 2009. Moreover, we have now operated at an underwriting profit for seven consecutive years. I believe it likely that we will continue to underwrite profitably in most – though certainly not all – future years. If we do so, our float will be cost-free, much as if someone deposited $62 billion with us that we could invest for our own benefit without the payment of interest.

Let me emphasize again that cost-free float is *not* a result to be expected for the P/C industry as a whole: In most years, premiums have been inadequate to cover claims plus expenses. Consequently, the industry's overall return on tangible equity has for many decades fallen far short of that achieved by the S&P 500. Outstanding economics exist at Berkshire only because we have some outstanding managers running some unusual businesses. Our insurance CEOs deserve your thanks, having added many billions of dollars to Berkshire's value. It's a pleasure for me to tell you about these all-stars.

* * * * * * * * * * * *

Let's start at GEICO, which is known to all of you because of its $800 million annual advertising budget (close to twice that of the runner-up advertiser in the auto insurance field). GEICO is managed by Tony Nicely, who joined the company at 18. Now 66, Tony still tap-dances to the office every day, just as I do at 79. We both feel lucky to work at a business we love.

GEICO's customers have warm feelings toward the company as well. Here's proof: Since Berkshire acquired control of GEICO in 1996, its market share has increased from 2.5% to 8.1%, a gain reflecting the net addition of seven million policyholders. Perhaps they contacted us because they thought our gecko was cute, but they bought from us to save important money. (Maybe you can as well; call 1-800-847-7536 or go to www.GEICO.com.) And they've stayed with us because they like our service as well as our price.

Berkshire acquired GEICO in two stages. In 1976-80 we bought about one-third of the company's stock for $47 million. Over the years, large repurchases by the company of its own shares caused our position to grow to about 50% without our having bought any more shares. Then, on January 2, 1996, we acquired the remaining 50% of GEICO for $2.3 *billion* in cash, about 50 times the cost of our original purchase.

An old Wall Street joke gets close to our experience:

Customer: Thanks for putting me in XYZ stock at 5. I hear it's up to 18.

Broker: Yes, and that's just the beginning. In fact, the company is doing so well now, that it's an even better buy at 18 than it was when you made your purchase.

Customer: Damn, I knew I should have waited.

GEICO's growth may slow in 2010. U.S. vehicle registrations are actually down because of slumping auto sales. Moreover, high unemployment is causing a growing number of drivers to go uninsured. (That's illegal almost everywhere, but if you've lost your job and still want to drive . . .) Our "low-cost producer" status, however, is sure to give us significant gains in the future. In 1995, GEICO was the country's sixth largest auto insurer; now we are number three. The company's float has grown from $2.7 billion to $9.6 billion. Equally important, GEICO has operated at an underwriting profit in 13 of the 14 years Berkshire has owned it.

I became excited about GEICO in January 1951, when I first visited the company as a 20-year-old student. Thanks to Tony, I'm even more excited today.

* * * * * * * * * * * *

A hugely important event in Berkshire's history occurred on a Saturday in 1985. Ajit Jain came into our office in Omaha – and I immediately knew we had found a superstar. (He had been discovered by Mike Goldberg, now elevated to St. Mike.)

We immediately put Ajit in charge of National Indemnity's small and struggling reinsurance operation. Over the years, he has built this business into a one-of-a-kind giant in the insurance world.

Staffed today by only 30 people, Ajit's operation has set records for transaction size in several areas of insurance. Ajit writes billion-dollar limits – and then keeps every dime of the risk instead of laying it off with other insurers. Three years ago, he took over huge liabilities from Lloyds, allowing it to clean up its relationship with 27,972 participants ("names") who had written problem-ridden policies that at one point threatened the survival of this 322-year-old institution. The premium for that single contract was $7.1 billion. During 2009, he negotiated a life reinsurance contract that could produce $50 billion of premium for us over the next 50 or so years.

Ajit's business is just the opposite of GEICO's. At that company, we have millions of small policies that largely renew year after year. Ajit writes relatively few policies, and the mix changes significantly from year to year. Throughout the world, he is known as the man to call when something both very large and unusual needs to be insured.

If Charlie, I and Ajit are ever in a sinking boat – and you can only save one of us – swim to Ajit.

* * * * * * * * * * * *

Our third insurance powerhouse is General Re. Some years back this operation was troubled; now it is a gleaming jewel in our insurance crown.

Under the leadership of Tad Montross, General Re had an outstanding underwriting year in 2009, while also delivering us unusually large amounts of float per dollar of premium volume. Alongside General Re's P/C business, Tad and his associates have developed a major life reinsurance operation that has grown increasingly valuable.

Last year General Re finally attained 100% ownership of Cologne Re, which since 1995 has been a key – though only partially-owned – part of our presence around the world. Tad and I will be visiting Cologne in September to thank its managers for their important contribution to Berkshire.

Finally, we own a group of smaller companies, most of them specializing in odd corners of the insurance world. In aggregate, their results have consistently been profitable and, as the table below shows, the float they provide us is substantial. Charlie and I treasure these companies and their managers.

Here is the record of all four segments of our property-casualty and life insurance businesses:

| Insurance Operations | Underwriting Profit | | Yearend Float | |
| | (in millions) | | | |
	2009	2008	2009	2008
General Re	$ 477	$ 342	$21,014	$21,074
BH Reinsurance	349	1,324	26,223	24,221
GEICO	649	916	9,613	8,454
Other Primary	84	210	5,061	4,739
	$1,559	$2,792	$61,911	$58,488

* * * * * * * * * * * *

And now a painful confession: Last year your chairman closed the book on a very expensive business fiasco entirely of his own making.

For many years I had struggled to think of side products that we could offer our millions of loyal GEICO customers. Unfortunately, I finally succeeded, coming up with a brilliant insight that we should market our own credit card. I reasoned that GEICO policyholders were likely to be good credit risks and, assuming we offered an attractive card, would likely favor us with their business. We got business all right – but of the wrong type.

Our pre-tax losses from credit-card operations came to about $6.3 million before I finally woke up. We then sold our $98 million portfolio of troubled receivables for 55¢ on the dollar, losing an additional $44 million.

GEICO's managers, it should be emphasized, were never enthusiastic about my idea. They warned me that instead of getting the cream of GEICO's customers we would get the – – – – – well, let's call it the non-cream. I subtly indicated that I was older and wiser.

I was just older.

Regulated Utility Business

Berkshire has an 89.5% interest in MidAmerican Energy Holdings, which owns a wide variety of utility operations. The largest of these are (1) Yorkshire Electricity and Northern Electric, whose 3.8 million end users make it the U.K.'s third largest distributor of electricity; (2) MidAmerican Energy, which serves 725,000 electric customers, primarily in Iowa; (3) Pacific Power and Rocky Mountain Power, serving about 1.7 million electric customers in six western states; and (4) Kern River and Northern Natural pipelines, which carry about 8% of the natural gas consumed in the U.S.

MidAmerican has two terrific managers, Dave Sokol and Greg Abel. In addition, my long-time friend, Walter Scott, along with his family, has a major ownership position in the company. Walter brings extraordinary business savvy to *any* operation. Ten years of working with Dave, Greg and Walter have reinforced my original belief: Berkshire couldn't have better partners. They are truly a dream team.

Somewhat incongruously, MidAmerican also owns the second largest real estate brokerage firm in the U.S., HomeServices of America. This company operates through 21 locally-branded firms that have 16,000 agents. Though last year was again a terrible year for home sales, HomeServices earned a modest sum. It also acquired a firm in Chicago and will add other quality brokerage operations when they are available at sensible prices. A decade from now, HomeServices is likely to be much larger.

Here are some key figures on MidAmerican's operations:

	Earnings (in millions)	
	2009	2008
U.K. utilities	$ 248	$ 339
Iowa utility	285	425
Western utilities	788	703
Pipelines	457	595
HomeServices	43	(45)
Other (net)	25	186
Operating earnings before corporate interest and taxes	1,846	2,203
Constellation Energy *	—	1,092
Interest, other than to Berkshire	(318)	(332)
Interest on Berkshire junior debt	(58)	(111)
Income tax	(313)	(1,002)
Net earnings	$ 1,157	$ 1,850
Earnings applicable to Berkshire **	$ 1,071	$ 1,704
Debt owed to others	19,579	19,145
Debt owed to Berkshire	353	1,087

*Consists of a breakup fee of $175 million and a profit on our investment of $917 million.
**Includes interest earned by Berkshire (net of related income taxes) of $38 in 2009 and $72 in 2008.

Our regulated electric utilities, offering monopoly service in most cases, operate in a symbiotic manner with the customers in their service areas, with those users depending on us to provide first-class service and invest for their future needs. Permitting and construction periods for generation and major transmission facilities stretch way out, so it is incumbent on us to be far-sighted. We, in turn, look to our utilities' regulators (acting on behalf of our customers) to allow us an appropriate return on the huge amounts of capital we must deploy to meet future needs. We shouldn't expect our regulators to live up to their end of the bargain unless we live up to ours.

Dave and Greg make sure we do just that. National research companies consistently rank our Iowa and Western utilities at or near the top of their industry. Similarly, among the 43 U.S. pipelines ranked by a firm named Mastio, our Kern River and Northern Natural properties tied for second place.

Moreover, we continue to pour huge sums of money into our operations so as to not only prepare for the future but also make these operations more environmentally friendly. Since we purchased MidAmerican ten years ago, it has *never* paid a dividend. We have instead used earnings to improve and expand our properties in each of the territories we serve. As one dramatic example, in the last three years our Iowa and Western utilities have earned $2.5 billion, while in this same period spending $3 billion on wind generation facilities.

MidAmerican has consistently kept its end of the bargain with society and, to society's credit, it has reciprocated: With few exceptions, our regulators have promptly allowed us to earn a fair return on the ever-increasing sums of capital we must invest. Going forward, we will do whatever it takes to serve our territories in the manner they expect. We believe that, in turn, we will be allowed the return we deserve on the funds we invest.

In earlier days, Charlie and I shunned capital-intensive businesses such as public utilities. Indeed, the best businesses by far for owners continue to be those that have high returns on capital and that require little incremental investment to grow. We are fortunate to own a number of such businesses, and we would love to buy more. Anticipating, however, that Berkshire will generate ever-increasing amounts of cash, we are today quite willing to enter businesses that regularly require large capital expenditures. We expect only that these businesses have reasonable expectations of earning decent returns on the incremental sums they invest. If our expectations are met – and we believe that they will be – Berkshire's ever-growing collection of good to great businesses should produce above-average, though certainly not spectacular, returns in the decades ahead.

Our BNSF operation, it should be noted, has certain important economic characteristics that resemble those of our electric utilities. In both cases we provide fundamental services that are, and will remain, essential to the economic well-being of our customers, the communities we serve, and indeed the nation. Both will require heavy investment that greatly exceeds depreciation allowances for decades to come. Both must also plan far ahead to satisfy demand that is expected to outstrip the needs of the past. Finally, both require wise regulators who will provide certainty about allowable returns so that we can confidently make the huge investments required to maintain, replace and expand the plant.

We see a "social compact" existing between the public and our railroad business, just as is the case with our utilities. If either side shirks its obligations, both sides will inevitably suffer. Therefore, both parties to the compact should – and we believe will – understand the benefit of behaving in a way that encourages good behavior by the other. It is inconceivable that our country will realize anything close to its full economic potential without its possessing first-class electricity and railroad systems. We will do our part to see that they exist.

In the future, BNSF results will be included in this "regulated utility" section. Aside from the two businesses having similar underlying economic characteristics, both are logical users of substantial amounts of debt that is *not* guaranteed by Berkshire. Both will retain most of their earnings. Both will earn and invest large sums in good times or bad, though the railroad will display the greater cyclicality. Overall, we expect this regulated sector to deliver significantly increased earnings over time, albeit at the cost of our investing many tens – yes, tens – of billions of dollars of incremental equity capital.

Manufacturing, Service and Retailing Operations

Our activities in this part of Berkshire cover the waterfront. Let's look, though, at a summary balance sheet and earnings statement for the entire group.

Balance Sheet 12/31/09 (in millions)

Assets		Liabilities and Equity	
Cash and equivalents	$ 3,018	Notes payable	$ 1,842
Accounts and notes receivable	5,066	Other current liabilities	7,414
Inventory	6,147	Total current liabilities	9,256
Other current assets	625		
Total current assets	14,856		
Goodwill and other intangibles	16,499	Deferred taxes	2,834
Fixed assets	15,374	Term debt and other liabilities	6,240
Other assets	2,070	Equity	30,469
	$48,799		$48,799

Earnings Statement (in millions)

	2009	2008	2007
Revenues	$61,665	$66,099	$59,100
Operating expenses (including depreciation of $1,422 in 2009, $1,280 in 2008 and $955 in 2007)	59,509	61,937	55,026
Interest expense	98	139	127
Pre-tax earnings	2,058*	4,023*	3,947*
Income taxes and minority interests	945	1,740	1,594
Net income	$ 1,113	$ 2,283	$ 2,353

*Does not include purchase-accounting adjustments.

Almost all of the many and widely-diverse operations in this sector suffered to one degree or another from 2009's severe recession. The major exception was McLane, our distributor of groceries, confections and non-food items to thousands of retail outlets, the largest by far Wal-Mart.

Grady Rosier led McLane to record pre-tax earnings of $344 million, which even so amounted to only slightly more than one cent per dollar on its huge sales of $31.2 billion. McLane employs a vast array of physical assets – practically all of which it owns – including 3,242 trailers, 2,309 tractors and 55 distribution centers with 15.2 million square feet of space. McLane's prime asset, however, is Grady.

We had a number of companies at which profits improved even as sales contracted, always an exceptional managerial achievement. Here are the CEOs who made it happen:

COMPANY	*CEO*
Benjamin Moore (paint)	Denis Abrams
Borsheims (jewelry retailing)	Susan Jacques
H. H. Brown (manufacturing and retailing of shoes)	Jim Issler
CTB (agricultural equipment)	Vic Mancinelli
Dairy Queen	John Gainor
Nebraska Furniture Mart (furniture retailing)	Ron and Irv Blumkin
Pampered Chef (direct sales of kitchen tools)	Marla Gottschalk
See's (manufacturing and retailing of candy)	Brad Kinstler
Star Furniture (furniture retailing)	Bill Kimbrell

Among the businesses we own that have major exposure to the depressed industrial sector, both Marmon and Iscar turned in relatively strong performances. Frank Ptak's Marmon delivered a 13.5% pre-tax profit margin, a record high. Though the company's sales were down 27%, Frank's cost-conscious management mitigated the decline in earnings.

Nothing stops Israel-based Iscar – not wars, recessions or competitors. The world's two other leading suppliers of small cutting tools both had very difficult years, each operating at a loss throughout much of the year. Though Iscar's results were down significantly from 2008, the company regularly reported profits, even while it was integrating and rationalizing Tungaloy, the large Japanese acquisition that we told you about last year. When manufacturing rebounds, Iscar will set new records. Its incredible managerial team of Eitan Wertheimer, Jacob Harpaz and Danny Goldman will see to that.

Every business we own that is connected to residential and commercial construction suffered severely in 2009. Combined pre-tax earnings of Shaw, Johns Manville, Acme Brick, and MiTek were $227 million, an 82.5% decline from $1.295 billion in 2006, when construction activity was booming. These businesses continue to bump along the bottom, though their competitive positions remain undented.

The major problem for Berkshire last year was NetJets, an aviation operation that offers fractional ownership of jets. Over the years, it has been enormously successful in establishing itself as the premier company in its industry, with the value of its fleet far exceeding that of its three major competitors *combined*. Overall, our dominance in the field remains unchallenged.

NetJets' business operation, however, has been another story. In the eleven years that we have owned the company, it has recorded an aggregate pre-tax loss of $157 million. Moreover, the company's debt has soared from $102 million at the time of purchase to $1.9 billion in April of last year. Without Berkshire's guarantee of this debt, NetJets would have been out of business. It's clear that I failed you in letting NetJets descend into this condition. But, luckily, I have been bailed out.

Dave Sokol, the enormously talented builder and operator of MidAmerican Energy, became CEO of NetJets in August. His leadership has been transforming: Debt has already been reduced to $1.4 billion, and, after suffering a staggering loss of $711 million in 2009, the company is now solidly profitable.

Most important, none of the changes wrought by Dave have in any way undercut the top-of-the-line standards for safety and service that Rich Santulli, NetJets' previous CEO and the father of the fractional-ownership industry, insisted upon. Dave and I have the strongest possible personal interest in maintaining these standards because we and our families use NetJets for almost all of our flying, as do many of our directors and managers. None of us are assigned special planes nor crews. We receive exactly the same treatment as any other owner, meaning we pay the same prices as everyone else does when we are using our personal contracts. In short, we eat our own cooking. In the aviation business, no other testimonial means more.

Finance and Financial Products

Our largest operation in this sector is Clayton Homes, the country's leading producer of modular and manufactured homes. Clayton was not always number one: A decade ago the three leading manufacturers were Fleetwood, Champion and Oakwood, which together accounted for 44% of the output of the industry. All have since gone bankrupt. Total industry output, meanwhile, has fallen from 382,000 units in 1999 to 60,000 units in 2009.

The industry is in shambles for two reasons, the first of which must be lived with if the U.S. economy is to recover. This reason concerns U.S. housing starts (including apartment units). In 2009, starts were 554,000, by far the lowest number in the 50 years for which we have data. Paradoxically, this is *good* news.

People *thought* it was good news a few years back when housing starts – the supply side of the picture – were running about two million annually. But household formations – the demand side – only amounted to about 1.2 million. After a few years of such imbalances, the country unsurprisingly ended up with far too many houses.

There were three ways to cure this overhang: (1) blow up a lot of houses, a tactic similar to the destruction of autos that occurred with the "cash-for-clunkers" program; (2) speed up household formations by, say, encouraging teenagers to cohabitate, a program not likely to suffer from a lack of volunteers or; (3) reduce new housing starts to a number far below the rate of household formations.

Our country has wisely selected the third option, which means that within a year or so residential housing problems should largely be behind us, the exceptions being only high-value houses and those in certain localities where overbuilding was particularly egregious. Prices will remain far below "bubble" levels, of course, but for every seller (or lender) hurt by this there will be a buyer who benefits. Indeed, many families that couldn't afford to buy an appropriate home a few years ago now find it well within their means because the bubble burst.

The second reason that manufactured housing is troubled is specific to the industry: the punitive differential in mortgage rates between factory-built homes and site-built homes. Before you read further, let me underscore the obvious: Berkshire has a dog in this fight, and you should therefore assess the commentary that follows with special care. That warning made, however, let me explain why the rate differential causes problems for both large numbers of lower-income Americans and Clayton.

The residential mortgage market is shaped by government rules that are expressed by FHA, Freddie Mac and Fannie Mae. Their lending standards are all-powerful because the mortgages they insure can typically be securitized and turned into what, in effect, is an obligation of the U.S. government. Currently buyers of conventional site-built homes who qualify for these guarantees can obtain a 30-year loan at about $5\frac{1}{4}\%$. In addition, these are mortgages that have recently been purchased in massive amounts by the Federal Reserve, an action that also helped to keep rates at bargain-basement levels.

In contrast, very few factory-built homes qualify for agency-insured mortgages. Therefore, a meritorious buyer of a factory-built home must pay about 9% on his loan. For the all-cash buyer, Clayton's homes offer terrific value. If the buyer needs mortgage financing, however – and, of course, most buyers do – the difference in financing costs too often negates the attractive price of a factory-built home.

Last year I told you why our buyers – generally people with low incomes – performed so well as credit risks. Their attitude was all-important: They signed up to live in the home, not resell or refinance it. Consequently, our buyers usually took out loans with payments geared to their verified incomes (we weren't making "liar's loans") and looked forward to the day they could burn their mortgage. If they lost their jobs, had health problems or got divorced, we could of course expect defaults. But they seldom walked away simply because house values had fallen. Even today, though job-loss troubles have grown, Clayton's delinquencies and defaults remain reasonable and will not cause us significant problems.

We have tried to qualify more of our customers' loans for treatment similar to those available on the site-built product. So far we have had only token success. Many families with modest incomes but responsible habits have therefore had to forego home ownership simply because the financing differential attached to the factory-built product makes monthly payments too expensive. If qualifications aren't broadened, so as to open low-cost financing to *all* who meet down-payment and income standards, the manufactured-home industry seems destined to struggle and dwindle.

Even under these conditions, I believe Clayton will operate profitably in coming years, though well below its potential. We couldn't have a better manager than CEO Kevin Clayton, who treats Berkshire's interests as if they were his own. Our product is first-class, inexpensive and constantly being improved. Moreover, we will continue to use Berkshire's credit to support Clayton's mortgage program, convinced as we are of its soundness. Even so, Berkshire can't borrow at a rate approaching that available to government agencies. This handicap will limit sales, hurting both Clayton and a multitude of worthy families who long for a low-cost home.

In the following table, Clayton's earnings are net of the company's payment to Berkshire for the use of its credit. Offsetting this cost to Clayton is an identical amount of income credited to Berkshire's finance operation and included in "Other Income." The cost and income amount was $116 million in 2009 and $92 million in 2008.

The table also illustrates how severely our furniture (CORT) and trailer (XTRA) leasing operations have been hit by the recession. Though their competitive positions remain as strong as ever, we have yet to see any bounce in these businesses.

	Pre-Tax Earnings	
	(in millions)	
	2009	2008
Net investment income	$278	$330
Life and annuity operation	116	23
Leasing operations	14	87
Manufactured-housing finance (Clayton)	187	206
Other income *	186	141
Income before investment and derivatives gains or losses	$781	$787

*Includes $116 million in 2009 and $92 million in 2008 of fees that Berkshire charges Clayton for the use of Berkshire's credit.

* * * * * * * * * * * *

At the end of 2009, we became a 50% owner of Berkadia Commercial Mortgage (formerly known as Capmark), the country's third-largest servicer of commercial mortgages. In addition to servicing a $235 billion portfolio, the company is an important originator of mortgages, having 25 offices spread around the country. Though commercial real estate will face major problems in the next few years, long-term opportunities for Berkadia are significant.

Our partner in this operation is Leucadia, run by Joe Steinberg and Ian Cumming, with whom we had a terrific experience some years back when Berkshire joined with them to purchase Finova, a troubled finance business. In resolving that situation, Joe and Ian did far more than their share of the work, an arrangement I always encourage. Naturally, I was delighted when they called me to partner again in the Capmark purchase.

Our first venture was also christened Berkadia. So let's call this one Son of Berkadia. Someday I'll be writing you about Grandson of Berkadia.

Investments

Below we show our common stock investments that at yearend had a market value of more than $1 billion.

Shares	Company	Percentage of Company Owned	Cost *	Market
			(in millions)	
151,610,700	American Express Company	12.7	$ 1,287	$ 6,143
225,000,000	BYD Company, Ltd.	9.9	232	1,986
200,000,000	The Coca-Cola Company	8.6	1,299	11,400
37,711,330	ConocoPhillips	2.5	2,741	1,926
28,530,467	Johnson & Johnson	1.0	1,724	1,838
130,272,500	Kraft Foods Inc.	8.8	4,330	3,541
3,947,554	POSCO	5.2	768	2,092
83,128,411	The Procter & Gamble Company	2.9	533	5,040
25,108,967	Sanofi-Aventis	1.9	2,027	1,979
234,247,373	Tesco plc	3.0	1,367	1,620
76,633,426	U.S. Bancorp	4.0	2,371	1,725
39,037,142	Wal-Mart Stores, Inc.	1.0	1,893	2,087
334,235,585	Wells Fargo & Company	6.5	7,394	9,021
	Others		6,680	8,636
	Total Common Stocks Carried at Market		$34,646	$59,034

*This is our actual purchase price and also our tax basis; GAAP "cost" differs in a few cases because of write-ups or write-downs that have been required.

In addition, we own positions in non-traded securities of Dow Chemical, General Electric, Goldman Sachs, Swiss Re and Wrigley with an aggregate cost of $21.1 billion and a carrying value of $26.0 billion. We purchased these five positions in the last 18 months. Setting aside the significant equity potential they provide us, these holdings deliver us an aggregate of $2.1 billion annually in dividends and interest. Finally, we owned 76,777,029 shares (22.5%) of BNSF at yearend, which we then carried at $85.78 per share, but which have subsequently been melded into our purchase of the entire company.

In 2009, our largest sales were in ConocoPhillips, Moody's, Procter & Gamble and Johnson & Johnson (sales of the latter occurring after we had built our position earlier in the year). Charlie and I believe that all of these stocks will likely trade higher in the future. We made some sales early in 2009 to raise cash for our Dow and Swiss Re purchases and late in the year made other sales in anticipation of our BNSF purchase.

We told you last year that very unusual conditions then existed in the corporate and municipal bond markets and that these securities were ridiculously cheap relative to U.S. Treasuries. We backed this view with some purchases, but I should have done far more. Big opportunities come infrequently. When it's raining gold, reach for a bucket, not a thimble.

We entered 2008 with $44.3 billion of cash-equivalents, and we have since retained operating earnings of $17 billion. Nevertheless, at yearend 2009, our cash was down to $30.6 billion (with $8 billion earmarked for the BNSF acquisition). We've put a lot of money to work during the chaos of the last two years. It's been an ideal period for investors: A climate of fear is their best friend. Those who invest only when commentators are upbeat end up paying a heavy price for meaningless reassurance. In the end, what counts in investing is what you pay for a business – through the purchase of a small piece of it in the stock market – and what that business earns in the succeeding decade or two.

* * * * * * * * * * * *

Last year I wrote extensively about our derivatives contracts, which were then the subject of both controversy and misunderstanding. For that discussion, please go to www.berkshirehathaway.com.

We have since changed only a few of our positions. Some credit contracts have run off. The terms of about 10% of our equity put contracts have also changed: Maturities have been shortened and strike prices materially reduced. In these modifications, no money changed hands.

A few points from last year's discussion are worth repeating:

(1) Though it's no sure thing, I expect our contracts in aggregate to deliver us a profit over their lifetime, even when investment income on the huge amount of float they provide us is excluded in the calculation. Our derivatives float – which is not included in the $62 billion of insurance float I described earlier – was about $6.3 billion at yearend.

(2) Only a handful of our contracts require us to post collateral under any circumstances. At last year's low point in the stock and credit markets, our posting requirement was $1.7 billion, a small fraction of the derivatives-related float we held. When we do post collateral, let me add, the securities we put up continue to earn money for our account.

(3) Finally, you should expect large swings in the carrying value of these contracts, items that can affect our reported quarterly earnings in a huge way but that do not affect our cash or investment holdings. That thought certainly fit 2009's circumstances. Here are the pre-tax quarterly gains and losses from derivatives valuations that were part of our reported earnings last year:

Quarter	$ Gain (Loss) in Billions
1	(1.517)
2	2.357
3	1.732
4	1.052

As we've explained, these wild swings neither cheer nor bother Charlie and me. When we report to you, we will continue to separate out these figures (as we do realized investment gains and losses) so that you can more clearly view the earnings of our operating businesses. We are delighted that we hold the derivatives contracts that we do. To date we have significantly profited from the float they provide. We expect also to earn further investment income over the life of our contracts.

634

We have long invested in derivatives contracts that Charlie and I think are mispriced, just as we try to invest in mispriced stocks and bonds. Indeed, we first reported to you that we held such contracts in early 1998. The dangers that derivatives pose for both participants and society – dangers of which we've long warned, and that can be dynamite – arise when these contracts lead to leverage and/or counterparty risk that is extreme. At Berkshire nothing like that has occurred – nor will it.

It's my job to keep Berkshire far away from such problems. Charlie and I believe that a CEO must not delegate risk control. It's simply too important. At Berkshire, I both initiate and monitor *every* derivatives contract on our books, with the exception of operations-related contracts at a few of our subsidiaries, such as MidAmerican, and the minor runoff contracts at General Re. If Berkshire ever gets in trouble, it will be *my* fault. It will not be because of misjudgments made by a Risk Committee or Chief Risk Officer.

* * * * * * * * * * *

In my view a board of directors of a huge financial institution is *derelict* if it does not insist that its CEO bear full responsibility for risk control. If he's incapable of handling that job, he should look for other employment. And if he fails at it – with the government thereupon required to step in with funds or guarantees – the financial consequences for him and his board should be severe.

It has not been shareholders who have botched the operations of some of our country's largest financial institutions. Yet they have borne the burden, with 90% or more of the value of their holdings wiped out in most cases of failure. Collectively, they have lost more than $500 billion in just the four largest financial fiascos of the last two years. To say these *owners* have been "bailed-out" is to make a mockery of the term.

The CEOs and directors of the failed companies, however, have largely gone unscathed. Their fortunes may have been diminished by the disasters they oversaw, but they still live in grand style. It is the behavior of these CEOs and directors that needs to be changed: If their institutions and the country are harmed by their recklessness, they should pay a heavy price – one not reimbursable by the companies they've damaged nor by insurance. CEOs and, in many cases, directors have long benefitted from oversized financial carrots; some *meaningful* sticks now need to be part of their employment picture as well.

An Inconvenient Truth (Boardroom Overheating)

Our subsidiaries made a few small "bolt-on" acquisitions last year for cash, but our blockbuster deal with BNSF required us to issue about 95,000 Berkshire shares that amounted to 6.1% of those previously outstanding. Charlie and I enjoy issuing Berkshire stock about as much as we relish prepping for a colonoscopy.

The reason for our distaste is simple. If we wouldn't dream of selling Berkshire in its entirety at the current market price, why in the world should we "sell" a significant part of the company at that same inadequate price by issuing our stock in a merger?

In evaluating a stock-for-stock offer, shareholders of the target company quite understandably focus on the market price of the acquirer's shares that are to be given them. But they also expect the transaction to deliver them the *intrinsic* value of their own shares – the ones they are giving up. If shares of a prospective acquirer are selling below their intrinsic value, it's impossible for that buyer to make a sensible deal in an all-stock deal. You simply can't exchange an undervalued stock for a fully-valued one without hurting your shareholders.

Imagine, if you will, Company A and Company B, of equal size and both with businesses intrinsically worth $100 per share. Both of their stocks, however, sell for $80 per share. The CEO of A, long on confidence and short on smarts, offers 1 ¼ shares of A for each share of B, correctly telling his directors that B is worth $100 per share. He will neglect to explain, though, that what he is giving will cost his shareholders $125 in intrinsic value. If the directors are mathematically challenged as well, and a deal is therefore completed, the shareholders of B will end up owning 55.6% of A & B's combined assets and A's shareholders will own 44.4%. Not everyone at A, it should be noted, is a loser from this nonsensical transaction. Its CEO now runs a company twice as large as his original domain, in a world where size tends to correlate with both prestige and compensation.

If an acquirer's stock is overvalued, it's a different story: Using it as a currency works to the acquirer's advantage. That's why bubbles in various areas of the stock market have invariably led to serial issuances of stock by sly promoters. Going by the market value of their stock, they can afford to overpay because they are, in effect, using counterfeit money. Periodically, many air-for-assets acquisitions have taken place, the late 1960s having been a particularly obscene period for such chicanery. Indeed, certain large companies were built in this way. (No one involved, of course, ever publicly acknowledges the reality of what is going on, though there is plenty of private snickering.)

In our BNSF acquisition, the selling shareholders quite properly evaluated our offer at $100 per share. The cost to us, however, was somewhat higher since 40% of the $100 was delivered in our shares, which Charlie and I believed to be worth more than their market value. Fortunately, we had long owned a substantial amount of BNSF stock that we purchased in the market for cash. All told, therefore, only about 30% of our cost overall was paid with Berkshire shares.

In the end, Charlie and I decided that the disadvantage of paying 30% of the price through stock was offset by the opportunity the acquisition gave us to deploy $22 billion of cash in a business we understood and liked for the long term. It has the additional virtue of being run by Matt Rose, whom we trust and admire. We also like the prospect of investing additional billions over the years at reasonable rates of return. But the final decision was a close one. If we had needed to use more stock to make the acquisition, it would in fact have made no sense. We would have then been giving up more than we were getting.

* * * * * * * * * * * *

I have been in dozens of board meetings in which acquisitions have been deliberated, often with the directors being instructed by high-priced investment bankers (are there any other kind?). Invariably, the bankers give the board a detailed assessment of the value of the company being purchased, with emphasis on why it is worth far more than its market price. In more than fifty years of board memberships, however, never have I heard the investment bankers (or management!) discuss the true value of what is being *given*. When a deal involved the issuance of the acquirer's stock, they simply used market value to measure the cost. *They did this even though they would have argued that the acquirer's stock price was woefully inadequate – absolutely no indicator of its real value – had a takeover bid for the acquirer instead been the subject up for discussion.*

When stock is the currency being contemplated in an acquisition and when directors are hearing from an advisor, it appears to me that there is only one way to get a rational and balanced discussion. Directors should hire a second advisor to make the case *against* the proposed acquisition, with its fee contingent on the deal *not* going through. Absent this drastic remedy, our recommendation in respect to the use of advisors remains: "Don't ask the barber whether you need a haircut."

* * * * * * * * * * * *

I can't resist telling you a true story from long ago. We owned stock in a large well-run bank that for decades had been statutorily prevented from acquisitions. Eventually, the law was changed and our bank immediately began looking for possible purchases. Its managers – fine people and able bankers – not unexpectedly began to behave like teenage boys who had just discovered girls.

They soon focused on a much smaller bank, also well-run and having similar financial characteristics in such areas as return on equity, interest margin, loan quality, etc. Our bank sold at a modest price (that's why we had bought into it), hovering near book value and possessing a very low price/earnings ratio. Alongside, though, the small-bank owner was being wooed by other large banks in the state and was holding out for a price close to three times book value. Moreover, he wanted stock, not cash.

Naturally, our fellows caved in and agreed to this value-destroying deal. "We need to show that we are in the hunt. Besides, it's only a small deal," they said, as if only *major* harm to shareholders would have been a legitimate reason for holding back. Charlie's reaction at the time: "Are we supposed to applaud because the dog that fouls our lawn is a Chihuahua rather than a Saint Bernard?"

The seller of the smaller bank – no fool – then delivered one final demand in his negotiations. "After the merger," he in effect said, perhaps using words that were phrased more diplomatically than these, "I'm going to be a large shareholder of your bank, and it will represent a huge portion of my net worth. You have to promise me, therefore, that you'll never again do a deal this dumb."

Yes, the merger went through. The owner of the small bank became richer, we became poorer, and the managers of the big bank – newly bigger – lived happily ever after.

The Annual Meeting

Our best guess is that 35,000 people attended the annual meeting last year (up from 12 – *no* zeros omitted – in 1981). With our shareholder population much expanded, we expect even more this year. Therefore, we will have to make a few changes in the usual routine. There will be no change, however, in our enthusiasm for having you attend. Charlie and I like to meet you, answer your questions and – best of all – have you *buy* lots of goods from our businesses.

The meeting this year will be held on Saturday, May 1st. As always, the doors will open at the Qwest Center at 7 a.m., and a new Berkshire movie will be shown at 8:30. At 9:30 we will go directly to the question-and-answer period, which (with a break for lunch at the Qwest's stands) will last until 3:30. After a short recess, Charlie and I will convene the annual meeting at 3:45. If you decide to leave during the day's question periods, please do so while *Charlie* is talking. (Act fast; he can be terse.)

The best reason to exit, of course, is to *shop*. We will help you do that by filling the 194,300-square-foot hall that adjoins the meeting area with products from dozens of Berkshire subsidiaries. Last year, you did your part, and most locations racked up record sales. But you can do better. (A friendly warning: If I find sales are lagging, I get testy and lock the exits.)

GEICO will have a booth staffed by a number of its top counselors from around the country, all of them ready to supply you with auto insurance quotes. In most cases, GEICO will be able to give you a shareholder discount (usually 8%). This special offer is permitted by 44 of the 51 jurisdictions in which we operate. (One supplemental point: The discount is not additive if you qualify for another, such as that given certain groups.) Bring the details of your existing insurance and check out whether we can save you money. For at least 50% of you, I believe we can.

Be sure to visit the Bookworm. Among the more than 30 books and DVDs it will offer are two new books by my sons: Howard's *Fragile*, a volume filled with photos and commentary about lives of struggle around the globe and Peter's *Life Is What You Make It*. Completing the family trilogy will be the debut of my sister Doris's biography, a story focusing on her remarkable philanthropic activities. Also available will be *Poor Charlie's Almanac*, the story of my partner. This book is something of a publishing miracle – never advertised, yet year after year selling many thousands of copies from its Internet site. (Should you need to ship your book purchases, a nearby shipping service will be available.)

If you are a big spender – or, for that matter, merely a gawker – visit Elliott Aviation on the east side of the Omaha airport between noon and 5:00 p.m. on Saturday. There we will have a fleet of NetJets aircraft that will get your pulse racing.

An attachment to the proxy material that is enclosed with this report explains how you can obtain the credential you will need for admission to the meeting and other events. As for plane, hotel and car reservations, we have again signed up American Express (800-799-6634) to give you special help. Carol Pedersen, who handles these matters, does a terrific job for us each year, and I thank her for it. Hotel rooms can be hard to find, but work with Carol and you will get one.

At Nebraska Furniture Mart, located on a 77-acre site on 72nd Street between Dodge and Pacific, we will again be having "Berkshire Weekend" discount pricing. To obtain the Berkshire discount, you must make your purchases between Thursday, April 29th and Monday, May 3rd inclusive, and also present your meeting credential. The period's special pricing will even apply to the products of several prestigious manufacturers that normally have ironclad rules against discounting but which, in the spirit of our shareholder weekend, have made an exception for you. We appreciate their cooperation. NFM is open from 10 a.m. to 9 p.m. Monday through Saturday, and 10 a.m. to 6 p.m. on Sunday. On Saturday this year, from 5:30 p.m. to 8 p.m., NFM is having a Berkyville BBQ to which you are all invited.

At Borsheims, we will again have two shareholder-only events. The first will be a cocktail reception from 6 p.m. to 10 p.m. on Friday, April 30th. The second, the main gala, will be held on Sunday, May 2nd, from 9 a.m. to 4 p.m. On Saturday, we will be open until 6 p.m.

We will have huge crowds at Borsheims throughout the weekend. For your convenience, therefore, shareholder prices will be available from Monday, April 26th through Saturday, May 8th. During that period, please identify yourself as a shareholder by presenting your meeting credentials or a brokerage statement that shows you are a Berkshire holder. Enter with rhinestones; leave with diamonds. My daughter tells me that the more you buy, the more you save (kids say the darnedest things).

On Sunday, in the mall outside of Borsheims, a blindfolded Patrick Wolff, twice U.S. chess champion, will take on all comers – who will have their eyes wide open – in groups of six. Nearby, Norman Beck, a remarkable magician from Dallas, will bewilder onlookers.

Our special treat for shareholders this year will be the return of my friend, Ariel Hsing, the country's top-ranked junior table tennis player (and a good bet to win at the Olympics some day). Now 14, Ariel came to the annual meeting four years ago and demolished all comers, including me. (You can witness my humiliating defeat on YouTube; just type in Ariel Hsing Berkshire.)

Naturally, I've been plotting a comeback and will take her on outside of Borsheims at 1:00 p.m. on Sunday. It will be a three-point match, and after I soften her up, all shareholders are invited to try their luck at similar three-point contests. Winners will be given a box of See's candy. We will have equipment available, but bring your own paddle if you think it will help. (It won't.)

Gorat's will again be open exclusively for Berkshire shareholders on Sunday, May 2nd, and will be serving from 1 p.m. until 10 p.m. Last year, though, it was overwhelmed by demand. With many more diners expected this year, I've asked my friend, Donna Sheehan, at Piccolo's – another favorite restaurant of mine – to serve shareholders on Sunday as well. (Piccolo's giant root beer float is mandatory for any fan of fine dining.) I plan to eat at both restaurants: All of the weekend action makes me *really* hungry, and I have favorite dishes at each spot. Remember: To make a reservation at Gorat's, call 402-551-3733 on April 1st (*but not before*) and at Piccolo's call 402-342-9038.

Regrettably, we will not be able to have a reception for international visitors this year. Our count grew to about 800 last year, and my simply signing one item per person took about 2½ hours. Since we expect even more international visitors this year, Charlie and I decided we must drop this function. But be assured, we welcome every international visitor who comes.

Last year we changed our method of determining what questions would be asked at the meeting and received many dozens of letters applauding the new arrangement. We will therefore again have the same three financial journalists lead the question-and-answer period, asking Charlie and me questions that shareholders have submitted to them by e-mail.

The journalists and their e-mail addresses are: Carol Loomis, of Fortune, who may be e-mailed at cloomis@fortunemail.com; Becky Quick, of CNBC, at BerkshireQuestions@cnbc.com, and Andrew Ross Sorkin, of The New York Times, at arsorkin@nytimes.com. From the questions submitted, each journalist will choose the dozen or so he or she decides are the most interesting and important. The journalists have told me your question has the best chance of being selected if you keep it concise and include no more than two questions in any e-mail you send them. (In your e-mail, let the journalist know if you would like your name mentioned if your question is selected.)

Neither Charlie nor I will get so much as a clue about the questions to be asked. We know the journalists will pick some tough ones and that's the way we like it.

We will again have a drawing at 8:15 on Saturday at each of 13 microphones for those shareholders wishing to ask questions themselves. At the meeting, I will alternate the questions asked by the journalists with those from the winning shareholders. We've added 30 minutes to the question time and will probably have time for about 30 questions from each group.

* * * * * * * * * *

At 86 and 79, Charlie and I remain lucky beyond our dreams. We were born in America; had terrific parents who saw that we got good educations; have enjoyed wonderful families and great health; and came equipped with a "business" gene that allows us to prosper in a manner hugely disproportionate to that experienced by many people who contribute as much or more to our society's well-being. Moreover, we have long had jobs that we love, in which we are helped in countless ways by talented and cheerful associates. Indeed, over the years, our work has become ever more fascinating; no wonder we tap-dance to work. If pushed, we would gladly pay substantial sums to have our jobs (but don't tell the Comp Committee).

Nothing, however, is more fun for us than getting together with our shareholder-partners at Berkshire's annual meeting. So join us on May 1st at the Qwest for our annual Woodstock for Capitalists. We'll see you there.

February 26, 2010

Warren E. Buffett
Chairman of the Board

P.S. Come by rail.

BERKSHIRE HATHAWAY INC.

To the Shareholders of Berkshire Hathaway Inc.:

The per-share book value of both our Class A and Class B stock increased by 13% in 2010. Over the last 46 years (that is, since present management took over), book value has grown from $19 to $95,453, a rate of 20.2% compounded annually.*

The highlight of 2010 was our acquisition of Burlington Northern Santa Fe, a purchase that's working out even better than I expected. It now appears that owning this railroad will increase Berkshire's "normal" earning power by nearly 40% pre-tax and by well over 30% after-tax. Making this purchase increased our share count by 6% and used $22 billion of cash. Since we've quickly replenished the cash, the economics of this transaction have turned out very well.

A "normal year," of course, is not something that either Charlie Munger, Vice Chairman of Berkshire and my partner, or I can define with anything like precision. But for the purpose of estimating our current earning power, we are envisioning a year free of a mega-catastrophe in insurance and possessing a general business climate somewhat better than that of 2010 but weaker than that of 2005 or 2006. Using these assumptions, and several others that I will explain in the "Investment" section, I can estimate that the normal earning power of the assets we currently own is about $17 billion pre-tax and $12 billion after-tax, excluding any capital gains or losses. Every day Charlie and I think about how we can build on this base.

Both of us are enthusiastic about BNSF's future because railroads have major cost and environmental advantages over trucking, their main competitor. Last year BNSF moved each ton of freight it carried a record 500 miles on a single gallon of diesel fuel. That's *three* times more fuel-efficient than trucking is, which means our railroad owns an important advantage in operating costs. Concurrently, our country gains because of reduced greenhouse emissions and a much smaller need for imported oil. When traffic travels by rail, society benefits.

Over time, the movement of goods in the United States will increase, and BNSF should get its full share of the gain. The railroad will need to invest massively to bring about this growth, but no one is better situated than Berkshire to supply the funds required. However slow the economy, or chaotic the markets, our checks will clear.

Last year – in the face of widespread pessimism about our economy – we demonstrated our enthusiasm for capital investment at Berkshire by spending $6 billion on property and equipment. Of this amount, $5.4 billion – or 90% of the total – was spent in the United States. Certainly our businesses will expand abroad in the future, but an overwhelming part of their future investments will be at home. In 2011, we will set a new record for capital spending – $8 billion – and spend *all* of the $2 billion increase in the United States.

Money will always flow toward opportunity, and there is an abundance of that in America. Commentators today often talk of "great uncertainty." But think back, for example, to December 6, 1941, October 18, 1987 and September 10, 2001. No matter how serene today may be, tomorrow is *always* uncertain.

---

* All per-share figures used in this report apply to Berkshire's A shares. Figures for the B shares are 1/1500th of those shown for A.

Don't let that reality spook you. Throughout my lifetime, politicians and pundits have constantly moaned about terrifying problems facing America. Yet our citizens now live an astonishing six times better than when I was born. The prophets of doom have overlooked the all-important factor that *is* certain: Human potential is far from exhausted, and the American system for unleashing that potential – a system that has worked wonders for over two centuries despite frequent interruptions for recessions and even a Civil War – remains alive and effective.

We are not natively smarter than we were when our country was founded nor do we work harder. But look around you and see a world beyond the dreams of any colonial citizen. Now, as in 1776, 1861, 1932 and 1941, America's best days lie ahead.

Performance

Charlie and I believe that those entrusted with handling the funds of others should establish performance goals at the onset of their stewardship. Lacking such standards, managements are tempted to shoot the arrow of performance and then paint the bull's-eye around wherever it lands.

In Berkshire's case, we long ago told you that our job is to increase per-share intrinsic value at a rate greater than the increase (including dividends) of the S&P 500. In some years we succeed; in others we fail. But, if we are unable over time to reach that goal, we have done nothing for our investors, who by themselves could have realized an equal or better result by owning an index fund.

The challenge, of course, is the calculation of intrinsic value. Present that task to Charlie and me separately, and you will get two different answers. Precision just isn't possible.

To eliminate subjectivity, we therefore use an *understated* proxy for intrinsic-value – book value – when measuring our performance. To be sure, some of our businesses are worth far more than their carrying value on our books. (Later in this report, we'll present a case study.) But since that premium seldom swings wildly from year to year, book value can serve as a reasonable device for tracking how we are doing.

The table on page 2 shows our 46-year record against the S&P, a performance quite good in the earlier years and now only satisfactory. The bountiful years, we want to emphasize, will never return. The huge sums of capital we currently manage eliminate *any* chance of exceptional performance. We will strive, however, for better-than-average results and feel it fair for you to hold us to that standard.

Yearly figures, it should be noted, are neither to be ignored nor viewed as all-important. The pace of the earth's movement around the sun is not synchronized with the time required for either investment ideas or operating decisions to bear fruit. At GEICO, for example, we enthusiastically spent $900 million last year on advertising to obtain policyholders who deliver us no immediate profits. If we could spend twice that amount productively, we would happily do so though short-term results would be further penalized. Many large investments at our railroad and utility operations are also made with an eye to payoffs well down the road.

To provide you a longer-term perspective on performance, we present on the facing page the yearly figures from page 2 recast into a series of five-year periods. Overall, there are 42 of these periods, and they tell an interesting story. On a comparative basis, our best years ended in the early 1980s. The *market's* golden period, however, came in the 17 following years, with Berkshire achieving stellar absolute returns even as our relative advantage narrowed.

After 1999, the market stalled (or have you already noticed that?). Consequently, the satisfactory performance relative to the S&P that Berkshire has achieved since then has delivered only moderate absolute results.

Looking forward, we hope to average several points better than the S&P – though that result is, of course, far from a sure thing. If we succeed in that aim, we will almost certainly produce better relative results in bad years for the stock market and suffer poorer results in strong markets.

Berkshire's Corporate Performance vs. the S&P 500 by Five-Year Periods

Five-Year Period	Annual Percentage Change		
	in Per-Share Book Value of Berkshire (1)	in S&P 500 with Dividends Included (2)	Relative Results (1)-(2)
1965-1969	17.2	5.0	12.2
1966-1970	14.7	3.9	10.8
1967-1971	13.9	9.2	4.7
1968-1972	16.8	7.5	9.3
1969-1973	17.7	2.0	15.7
1970-1974	15.0	(2.4)	17.4
1971-1975	13.9	3.2	10.7
1972-1976	20.8	4.9	15.9
1973-1977	23.4	(0.2)	23.6
1974-1978	24.4	4.3	20.1
1975-1979	30.1	14.7	15.4
1976-1980	33.4	13.9	19.5
1977-1981	29.0	8.1	20.9
1978-1982	29.9	14.1	15.8
1979-1983	31.6	17.3	14.3
1980-1984	27.0	14.8	12.2
1981-1985	32.6	14.6	18.0
1982-1986	31.5	19.8	11.7
1983-1987	27.4	16.4	11.0
1984-1988	25.0	15.2	9.8
1985-1989	31.1	20.3	10.8
1986-1990	22.9	13.1	9.8
1987-1991	25.4	15.3	10.1
1988-1992	25.6	15.8	9.8
1989-1993	24.4	14.5	9.9
1990-1994	18.6	8.7	9.9
1991-1995	25.6	16.5	9.1
1992-1996	24.2	15.2	9.0
1993-1997	26.9	20.2	6.7
1994-1998	33.7	24.0	9.7
1995-1999	30.4	28.5	1.9
1996-2000	22.9	18.3	4.6
1997-2001	14.8	10.7	4.1
1998-2002	10.4	(0.6)	11.0
1999-2003	6.0	(0.6)	6.6
2000-2004	8.0	(2.3)	10.3
2001-2005	8.0	0.6	7.4
2002-2006	13.1	6.2	6.9
2003-2007	13.3	12.8	0.5
2004-2008	6.9	(2.2)	9.1
2005-2009	8.6	0.4	8.2
2006-2010	10.0	2.3	7.7

Notes: The first two periods cover the five years beginning September 30 of the previous year. The third period covers 63 months beginning September 30, 1966 to December 31, 1971. All other periods involve calendar years.

The other notes on page 2 also apply to this table.

Intrinsic Value – Today and Tomorrow

Though Berkshire's intrinsic value cannot be precisely calculated, two of its three key pillars can be measured. Charlie and I rely heavily on these measurements when we make our own estimates of Berkshire's value.

The first component of value is our investments: stocks, bonds and cash equivalents. At yearend these totaled $158 billion at market value.

Insurance float – money we temporarily hold in our insurance operations that does not belong to us – funds $66 billion of our investments. This float is "free" as long as insurance underwriting breaks even, meaning that the premiums we receive equal the losses and expenses we incur. Of course, underwriting results are volatile, swinging erratically between profits and losses. Over our entire history, though, we've been significantly profitable, and I also expect us to average breakeven results or better in the future. If we do that, all of our investments – those funded both by float and by retained earnings – can be viewed as an element of value for Berkshire shareholders.

Berkshire's second component of value is earnings that come from sources other than investments and insurance underwriting. These earnings are delivered by our 68 non-insurance companies, itemized on page 106. In Berkshire's early years, we focused on the investment side. During the past two decades, however, we've increasingly emphasized the development of earnings from non-insurance businesses, a practice that will continue.

The following tables illustrate this shift. In the first table, we present per-share investments at decade intervals beginning in 1970, three years after we entered the insurance business. We exclude those investments applicable to minority interests.

Yearend	Per-Share Investments	Period	Compounded Annual Increase in Per-Share Investments
1970	$ 66		
1980	754	1970-1980	27.5%
1990	7,798	1980-1990	26.3%
2000	50,229	1990-2000	20.5%
2010	94,730	2000-2010	6.6%

Though our compounded annual increase in per-share investments was a healthy 19.9% over the 40-year period, our rate of increase has slowed sharply as we have focused on using funds to buy operating businesses.

The payoff from this shift is shown in the following table, which illustrates how earnings of our non-insurance businesses have increased, again on a per-share basis and after applicable minority interests.

Year	Per-Share Pre-Tax Earnings	Period	Compounded Annual Increase in Per-Share Pre-Tax Earnings
1970	$ 2.87		
1980	19.01	1970-1980	20.8%
1990	102.58	1980-1990	18.4%
2000	918.66	1990-2000	24.5%
2010	5,926.04	2000-2010	20.5%

For the forty years, our compounded annual gain in pre-tax, non-insurance earnings per share is 21.0%. During the same period, Berkshire's stock price increased at a rate of 22.1% annually. Over time, you can expect our stock price to move in rough tandem with Berkshire's investments and earnings. Market price and intrinsic value often follow very different paths – sometimes for extended periods – but eventually they meet.

There is a third, more subjective, element to an intrinsic value calculation that can be either positive or negative: the efficacy with which retained earnings will be deployed in the future. We, as well as many other businesses, are likely to retain earnings over the next decade that will equal, or even exceed, the capital we presently employ. Some companies will turn these retained dollars into fifty-cent pieces, others into two-dollar bills.

This "what-will-they-do-with-the-money" factor must always be evaluated along with the "what-do-we-have-now" calculation in order for us, or anybody, to arrive at a sensible estimate of a company's intrinsic value. That's because an outside investor stands by helplessly as management reinvests his share of the company's earnings. If a CEO can be expected to do this job well, the reinvestment prospects add to the company's current value; if the CEO's talents or motives are suspect, today's value must be discounted. The difference in outcome can be huge. A dollar of then-value in the hands of Sears Roebuck's or Montgomery Ward's CEOs in the late 1960s had a far different destiny than did a dollar entrusted to Sam Walton.

* * * * * * * * * * * *

Charlie and I hope that the per-share earnings of our non-insurance businesses continue to increase at a decent rate. But the job gets tougher as the numbers get larger. We will need both good performance from our current businesses and more *major* acquisitions. We're prepared. Our elephant gun has been reloaded, and my trigger finger is itchy.

Partially offsetting our anchor of size are several important advantages we have. First, we possess a cadre of truly skilled managers who have an unusual commitment to their own operations and to Berkshire. Many of our CEOs are independently wealthy and work only because they love what they do. They are volunteers, not mercenaries. Because no one can offer them a job they would enjoy more, they can't be lured away.

At Berkshire, managers can focus on running their businesses: They are not subjected to meetings at headquarters nor financing worries nor Wall Street harassment. They simply get a letter from me every two years (it's reproduced on pages 104-105) and call me when they wish. And their wishes do differ: There are managers to whom I have not talked in the last year, while there is one with whom I talk almost daily. Our trust is in people rather than process. A "hire well, manage little" code suits both them and me.

Berkshire's CEOs come in many forms. Some have MBAs; others never finished college. Some use budgets and are by-the-book types; others operate by the seat of their pants. Our team resembles a baseball squad composed of all-stars having vastly different batting styles. Changes in our line-up are seldom required.

Our second advantage relates to the allocation of the money our businesses earn. After meeting the needs of those businesses, we have very substantial sums left over. Most companies limit themselves to reinvesting funds within the industry in which they have been operating. That often restricts them, however, to a "universe" for capital allocation that is both tiny and quite inferior to what is available in the wider world. Competition for the few opportunities that *are* available tends to become fierce. The seller has the upper hand, as a girl might if she were the only female at a party attended by many boys. That lopsided situation would be great for the girl, but terrible for the boys.

At Berkshire we face no institutional restraints when we deploy capital. Charlie and I are limited only by our ability to understand the likely future of a possible acquisition. If we clear that hurdle – and frequently we can't – we are then able to compare any one opportunity against a host of others.

When I took control of Berkshire in 1965, I didn't exploit this advantage. Berkshire was then only in textiles, where it had in the previous decade lost significant money. The dumbest thing I could have done was to pursue "opportunities" to improve and expand the existing textile operation – so for years that's exactly what I did. And then, in a final burst of brilliance, I went out and bought *another* textile company. Aaaaaaargh! Eventually I came to my senses, heading first into insurance and then into other industries.

There is even a supplement to this world-is-our-oyster advantage: In addition to evaluating the attractions of one business against a host of others, we also measure businesses against opportunities available in marketable securities, a comparison most managements don't make. Often, businesses are priced ridiculously high against what can likely be earned from investments in stocks or bonds. At such moments, we buy securities and bide our time.

Our flexibility in respect to capital allocation has accounted for much of our progress to date. We have been able to take money we earn from, say, See's Candies or Business Wire (two of our best-run businesses, but also two offering limited reinvestment opportunities) and use it as part of the stake we needed to buy BNSF.

Our final advantage is the hard-to-duplicate culture that permeates Berkshire. And in businesses, culture counts.

To start with, the directors who represent you think and act like owners. They receive token compensation: no options, no restricted stock and, for that matter, virtually no cash. We do not provide them directors and officers liability insurance, a given at almost every other large public company. If they mess up with your money, they will lose their money as well. Leaving my holdings aside, directors and their families own Berkshire shares worth more than $3 billion. Our directors, therefore, monitor Berkshire's actions and results with keen interest and an owner's eye. You and I are lucky to have them as stewards.

This same owner-orientation prevails among our managers. In many cases, these are people who have sought out Berkshire as an acquirer for a business that they and their families have long owned. They came to us with an owner's mindset, and we provide an environment that encourages them to retain it. Having managers who love their businesses is no small advantage.

Cultures self-propagate. Winston Churchill once said, "You shape your houses and then they shape you." That wisdom applies to businesses as well. Bureaucratic procedures beget more bureaucracy, and imperial corporate palaces induce imperious behavior. (As one wag put it, "You know you're no longer CEO when you get in the back seat of your car and it doesn't move.") At Berkshire's "World Headquarters" our annual rent is $270,212. Moreover, the home-office investment in furniture, art, Coke dispenser, lunch room, high-tech equipment – you name it – totals $301,363. As long as Charlie and I treat your money as if it were our own, Berkshire's managers are likely to be careful with it as well.

Our compensation programs, our annual meeting and even our annual reports are all designed with an eye to reinforcing the Berkshire culture, and making it one that will repel and expel managers of a different bent. This culture grows stronger every year, and it will remain intact long after Charlie and I have left the scene.

We will need all of the strengths I've just described to do reasonably well. Our managers will deliver; you can count on that. But whether Charlie and I can hold up our end in capital allocation depends in part on the competitive environment for acquisitions. You will get our best efforts.

GEICO

Now let me tell you a story that will help you understand how the intrinsic value of a business can far exceed its book value. Relating this tale also gives me a chance to relive some great memories.

Sixty years ago last month, GEICO entered my life, destined to shape it in a huge way. I was then a 20-year-old graduate student at Columbia, having elected to go there because my hero, Ben Graham, taught a once-a-week class at the school.

One day at the library, I checked out Ben's entry in Who's Who in America and found he was chairman of Government Employees Insurance Co. (now called GEICO). I knew nothing of insurance and had never heard of the company. The librarian, however, steered me to a large compendium of insurers and, after reading the page on GEICO, I decided to visit the company. The following Saturday, I boarded an early train for Washington.

Alas, when I arrived at the company's headquarters, the building was closed. I then rather frantically started pounding on a door, until finally a janitor appeared. I asked him if there was anyone in the office I could talk to, and he steered me to the only person around, Lorimer Davidson.

That was my lucky moment. During the next four hours, "Davy" gave me an education about both insurance and GEICO. It was the beginning of a wonderful friendship. Soon thereafter, I graduated from Columbia and became a stock salesman in Omaha. GEICO, of course, was my prime recommendation, which got me off to a great start with dozens of customers. GEICO also jump-started my net worth because, soon after meeting Davy, I made the stock 75% of my $9,800 investment portfolio. (Even so, I felt *over*-diversified.)

Subsequently, Davy became CEO of GEICO, taking the company to undreamed-of heights before it got into trouble in the mid-1970s, a few years after his retirement. When that happened – with the stock falling by more than 95% – Berkshire bought about one-third of the company in the market, a position that over the years increased to 50% because of GEICO's repurchases of its own shares. Berkshire's cost for this half of the business was $46 million. (Despite the size of our position, we exercised no control over operations.)

We then purchased the remaining 50% of GEICO at the beginning of 1996, which spurred Davy, at 95, to make a video tape saying how happy he was that his beloved GEICO would permanently reside with Berkshire. (He also playfully concluded with, "Next time, Warren, please make an appointment.")

A lot has happened at GEICO during the last 60 years, but its core goal – saving Americans substantial money on their purchase of auto insurance – remains unchanged. (Try us at 1-800-847-7536 or www.GEICO.com.) In other words, get the policyholder's business by *deserving* his business. Focusing on this objective, the company has grown to be America's third-largest auto insurer, with a market share of 8.8%.

When Tony Nicely, GEICO's CEO, took over in 1993, that share was 2.0%, a level at which it had been stuck for more than a decade. GEICO became a different company under Tony, finding a path to consistent growth while simultaneously maintaining underwriting discipline and keeping its costs low.

Let me quantify Tony's achievement. When, in 1996, we bought the 50% of GEICO we didn't already own, it cost us about $2.3 billion. That price implied a value of $4.6 billion for 100%. GEICO then had tangible net worth of $1.9 billion.

The excess over tangible net worth of the implied value – $2.7 billion – was what we estimated GEICO's "goodwill" to be worth at that time. That goodwill represented the economic value of the policyholders who were then doing business with GEICO. In 1995, those customers had paid the company $2.8 billion in premiums. Consequently, we were valuing GEICO's customers at about 97% (2.7/2.8) of what they were annually paying the company. By industry standards, that was a very high price. But GEICO was no ordinary insurer: Because of the company's low costs, its policyholders were consistently profitable and unusually loyal.

Today, premium volume is $14.3 billion and growing. Yet we carry the goodwill of GEICO on our books at only $1.4 billion, an amount that will remain unchanged no matter how much the value of GEICO increases. (Under accounting rules, you write down the carrying value of goodwill if its economic value decreases, but leave it unchanged if economic value increases.) Using the 97%-of-premium-volume yardstick we applied to our 1996 purchase, the real value today of GEICO's economic goodwill is about $14 billion. And this value is likely to be much higher ten and twenty years from now. GEICO – off to a strong start in 2011 – is the gift that keeps giving.

One not-so-small footnote: Under Tony, GEICO has developed one of the country's largest personal-lines insurance *agencies*, which primarily sells homeowners policies to our GEICO auto insurance customers. In this business, we represent a number of insurers that are not affiliated with us. They take the risk; we simply sign up the customers. Last year we sold 769,898 new policies at this agency operation, up 34% from the year before. The obvious way this activity aids us is that it produces commission revenue; equally important is the fact that it further strengthens our relationship with our policyholders, helping us retain them.

I owe an enormous debt to Tony and Davy (and, come to think of it, to that janitor as well).

* * * * * * * * * * * *

Now, let's examine the four major sectors of Berkshire. Each has vastly different balance sheet and income characteristics from the others. Lumping them together therefore impedes analysis. So we'll present them as four separate businesses, which is how Charlie and I view them.

We will look first at insurance, Berkshire's core operation and the engine that has propelled our expansion over the years.

Insurance

Property-casualty ("P/C") insurers receive premiums upfront and pay claims later. In extreme cases, such as those arising from certain workers' compensation accidents, payments can stretch over decades. This collect-now, pay-later model leaves us holding large sums – money we call "float" – that will eventually go to others. Meanwhile, we get to invest this float for Berkshire's benefit. Though individual policies and claims come and go, the amount of float we hold remains remarkably stable in relation to premium volume. Consequently, as our business grows, so does our float. And how we have grown: Just take a look at the following table:

Yearend	Float (in $ millions)
1970	$ 39
1980	237
1990	1,632
2000	27,871
2010	65,832

If our premiums exceed the total of our expenses and eventual losses, we register an underwriting profit that adds to the investment income that our float produces. When such a profit occurs, we enjoy the use of free money – and, better yet, get *paid* for holding it. Alas, the wish of all insurers to achieve this happy result creates intense competition, so vigorous in most years that it causes the P/C industry as a whole to operate at a significant underwriting *loss*. This loss, in effect, is what the industry pays to hold its float. For example, State Farm, by far the country's largest insurer and a well-managed company, has incurred an underwriting loss in seven of the last ten years. During that period, its aggregate underwriting loss was more than $20 billion.

At Berkshire, we have now operated at an underwriting profit for eight consecutive years, our total underwriting gain for the period having been $17 billion. I believe it likely that we will continue to underwrite profitably in most – though certainly not all – future years. If we accomplish that, our float will be better than cost-free. We will benefit just as we would if some party deposited $66 billion with us, paid us a fee for holding its money and then let us invest its funds for our own benefit.

Let me emphasize again that cost-free float is *not* an outcome to be expected for the P/C industry as a whole: In most years, industry premiums have been inadequate to cover claims plus expenses. Consequently, the industry's overall return on tangible equity has for many decades fallen far short of the average return realized by American industry, a sorry performance almost certain to continue. Berkshire's outstanding economics exist only because we have some terrific managers running some unusual businesses. We've already told you about GEICO, but we have two other very large operations, and a bevy of smaller ones as well, each a star in its own way.

* * * * * * * * * * * *

First off is the Berkshire Hathaway Reinsurance Group, run by Ajit Jain. Ajit insures risks that no one else has the desire or the capital to take on. His operation combines capacity, speed, decisiveness and, most importantly, brains in a manner that is unique in the insurance business. Yet he never exposes Berkshire to risks that are inappropriate in relation to our resources. Indeed, we are *far* more conservative than most large insurers in that respect. In the past year, Ajit has significantly increased his life reinsurance operation, developing annual premium volume of about $2 billion that will repeat for decades.

From a standing start in 1985, Ajit has created an insurance business with float of $30 billion and significant underwriting profits, a feat that no CEO of any other insurer has come close to matching. By his accomplishments, he has added a great many billions of dollars to the value of Berkshire. Even kryptonite bounces off Ajit.

* * * * * * * * * * * *

We have another insurance powerhouse in General Re, managed by Tad Montross.

At bottom, a sound insurance operation requires four disciplines: (1) An understanding of *all* exposures that might cause a policy to incur losses; (2) A conservative evaluation of the likelihood of any exposure actually causing a loss and the probable cost if it does; (3) The setting of a premium that will deliver a profit, on average, after both prospective loss costs and operating expenses are covered; and (4) The willingness to walk away if the appropriate premium can't be obtained.

Many insurers pass the first three tests and flunk the fourth. The urgings of Wall Street, pressures from the agency force and brokers, or simply a refusal by a testosterone-driven CEO to accept shrinking volumes has led too many insurers to write business at inadequate prices. "The other guy is doing it so we must as well" spells trouble in any business, but none more so than insurance.

Tad has observed all four of the insurance commandments, and it shows in his results. General Re's huge float has been better than cost-free under his leadership, and we expect that, on average, it will continue to be.

* * * * * * * * * * * *

Finally, we own a group of smaller companies, most of them specializing in odd corners of the insurance world. In aggregate, their results have consistently been profitable and, as the table below shows, the float they provide us is substantial. Charlie and I treasure these companies and their managers.

Here is the record of all four segments of our property-casualty and life insurance businesses:

| | Underwriting Profit | | Yearend Float | |
| | (in millions) | | | |
Insurance Operations	2010	2009	2010	2009
General Re	$ 452	$ 477	$20,049	$21,014
BH Reinsurance	176	250	30,370	27,753
GEICO	1,117	649	10,272	9,613
Other Primary	268	84	5,141	5,061
	$2,013	$1,460	$65,832	$63,441

Among large insurance operations, Berkshire's impresses me as the best in the world.

Manufacturing, Service and Retailing Operations

Our activities in this part of Berkshire cover the waterfront. Let's look, though, at a summary balance sheet and earnings statement for the entire group.

Balance Sheet 12/31/10 (in millions)

Assets		Liabilities and Equity	
Cash and equivalents	$ 2,673	Notes payable	$ 1,805
Accounts and notes receivable	5,396	Other current liabilities	8,169
Inventory	7,101	Total current liabilities	9,974
Other current assets	550		
Total current assets	15,720		
Goodwill and other intangibles	16,976	Deferred taxes	3,001
Fixed assets	15,421	Term debt and other liabilities	6,621
Other assets	3,029	Equity	31,550
	$51,146		$51,146

Earnings Statement (in millions)

	2010	2009	2008
Revenues	$66,610	$61,665	$66,099
Operating expenses (including depreciation of $1,362 in 2010, $1,422 in 2009 and $1,280 in 2008)	62,225	59,509	61,937
Interest expense	111	98	139
Pre-tax earnings	4,274*	2,058*	4,023*
Income taxes and non-controlling interests	1,812	945	1,740
Net earnings	$ 2,462	$ 1,113	$ 2,283

*Does not include purchase-accounting adjustments.

This group of companies sells products ranging from lollipops to jet airplanes. Some of the businesses enjoy terrific economics, measured by earnings on unleveraged net *tangible* assets that run from 25% after-tax to more than 100%. Others produce good returns in the area of 12-20%. Unfortunately, a few have very poor returns, a result of some serious mistakes I have made in my job of capital allocation. These errors came about because I misjudged either the competitive strength of the business I was purchasing or the future economics of the industry in which it operated. I try to look out ten or twenty years when making an acquisition, but sometimes my eyesight has been poor.

Most of the companies in this section improved their earnings last year and four set records. Let's look first at the record-breakers.

- TTI, our electronic components distributor, had sales 21% above its previous high (recorded in 2008) and pre-tax earnings that topped its earlier record by 58%. Its sales gains spanned three continents, with North America at 16%, Europe at 26%, and Asia at 50%. The thousands of items TTI distributes are pedestrian, many selling for less than a dollar. The magic of TTI's exceptional performance is created by Paul Andrews, its CEO, and his associates.

- Forest River, our RV and boat manufacturer, had record sales of nearly $2 billion and record earnings as well. Forest River has 82 plants, and I have yet to visit one (or the home office, for that matter). There's no need; Pete Liegl, the company's CEO, runs a terrific operation. Come view his products at the annual meeting. Better yet, buy one.

- CTB, our farm-equipment company, again set an earnings record. I told you in the 2008 Annual Report about Vic Mancinelli, the company's CEO. He just keeps getting better. Berkshire paid $140 million for CTB in 2002. It has since paid us dividends of $160 million and eliminated $40 million of debt. Last year it earned $106 million pre-tax. Productivity gains have produced much of this increase. When we bought CTB, sales per employee were $189,365; now they are $405,878.

- Would you believe shoes? H. H. Brown, run by Jim Issler and best known for its Born brand, set a new record for sales and earnings (helped by its selling 1,110 pairs of shoes at our annual meeting). Jim has brilliantly adapted to major industry changes. His work, I should mention, is overseen by Frank Rooney, 89, a superb businessman and still a dangerous fellow with whom to have a bet on the golf course.

A huge story in this sector's year-to-year improvement occurred at NetJets. I can't overstate the breadth and importance of Dave Sokol's achievements at this company, the leading provider of fractional ownership of jet airplanes. NetJets has long been an operational success, owning a 2010 market share five times that of its nearest competitor. Our overwhelming leadership stems from a wonderful team of pilots, mechanics and service personnel. This crew again did its job in 2010, with customer satisfaction, as delineated in our regular surveys, hitting new highs.

Even though NetJets was consistently a runaway winner with customers, our financial results, since its acquisition in 1998, were a failure. In the 11 years through 2009, the company reported an aggregate pre-tax loss of $157 million, a figure that was far understated since borrowing costs at NetJets were heavily subsidized by its free use of Berkshire's credit. Had NetJets been operating on a stand-alone basis, its loss over the years would have been several hundreds of millions greater.

We are now charging NetJets an appropriate fee for Berkshire's guarantee. Despite this fee (which came to $38 million in 2010), NetJets earned $207 million pre-tax in 2010, a swing of $918 million from 2009. Dave's quick restructuring of management and the company's rationalization of its purchasing and spending policies has ended the hemorrhaging of cash and turned what was Berkshire's only major business problem into a solidly profitable operation.

Dave has meanwhile maintained NetJets' industry-leading reputation for safety and service. In many important ways, our training and operational standards are considerably stronger than those required by the FAA. Maintaining top-of-the-line standards is the right thing to do, but I also have a selfish reason for championing this policy. My family and I have flown more than 5,000 hours on NetJets (that's equal to being airborne 24 hours a day for seven months) and will fly thousands of hours more in the future. We receive no special treatment and have used a random mix of at least 100 planes and 300 crews. Whichever the plane or crew, we always know we are flying with the best-trained pilots in private aviation.

The largest earner in our manufacturing, service and retailing sector is Marmon, a collection of 130 businesses. We will soon increase our ownership in this company to 80% by carrying out our scheduled purchase of 17% of its stock from the Pritzker family. The cost will be about $1.5 billion. We will then purchase the remaining Pritzker holdings in 2013 or 2014, whichever date is selected by the family. Frank Ptak runs Marmon wonderfully, and we look forward to 100% ownership.

Next to Marmon, the two largest earners in this sector are Iscar and McLane. Both had excellent years. In 2010, Grady Rosier's McLane entered the wine and spirits distribution business to supplement its $32 billion operation as a distributor of food products, cigarettes, candy and sundries. In purchasing Empire Distributors, an operator in Georgia and North Carolina, we teamed up with David Kahn, the company's dynamic CEO. David is leading our efforts to expand geographically. By yearend he had already made his first acquisition, Horizon Wine and Spirits in Tennessee.

At Iscar, profits were up 159% in 2010, and we may well surpass pre-recession levels in 2011. Sales are improving throughout the world, particularly in Asia. Credit Eitan Wertheimer, Jacob Harpaz and Danny Goldman for an exceptional performance, one far superior to that of Iscar's main competitors.

All that is good news. Our businesses related to home construction, however, continue to struggle. Johns Manville, MiTek, Shaw and Acme Brick have maintained their competitive positions, but their profits are far below the levels of a few years ago. Combined, these operations earned $362 million pre-tax in 2010 compared to $1.3 billion in 2006, and their employment has fallen by about 9,400.

A housing recovery will probably begin within a year or so. In any event, it is certain to occur at some point. Consequently: (1) At MiTek, we have made, or committed to, five bolt-on acquisitions during the past eleven months; (2) At Acme, we just recently acquired the leading manufacturer of brick in Alabama for $50 million; (3) Johns Manville is building a $55 million roofing membrane plant in Ohio, to be completed next year; and (4) Shaw will spend $200 million in 2011 on plant and equipment, all of it situated in America. These businesses entered the recession strong and will exit it stronger. At Berkshire, our time horizon is forever.

Regulated, Capital-Intensive Businesses

We have two very large businesses, BNSF and MidAmerican Energy, with important common characteristics that distinguish them from our many others. Consequently, we give them their own sector in this letter and split out their financial statistics in our GAAP balance sheet and income statement.

A key characteristic of both companies is the huge investment they have in very long-lived, regulated assets, with these funded by large amounts of long-term debt that is *not* guaranteed by Berkshire. Our credit is not needed: Both businesses have earning power that, even under very adverse business conditions, amply covers their interest requirements. For example, in recessionary 2010 with BNSF's car loadings far off peak levels, the company's interest coverage was 6:1.

Both companies are heavily regulated, and both will have a never-ending need to make major investments in plant and equipment. Both also need to provide efficient, customer-satisfying service to earn the respect of their communities and regulators. In return, both need to be assured that they will be allowed to earn reasonable earnings on future capital investments.

Earlier I explained just how important railroads are to our country's future. Rail moves 42% of America's inter-city freight, measured by ton-miles, and BNSF moves more than any other railroad – about 28% of the industry total. A little math will tell you that more than 11% of *all* inter-city ton-miles of freight in the U.S. is transported by BNSF. Given the shift of population to the West, our share may well inch higher.

All of this adds up to a huge responsibility. We are a major and essential part of the American economy's circulatory system, obliged to constantly maintain and improve our 23,000 miles of track along with its ancillary bridges, tunnels, engines and cars. In carrying out this job, we must anticipate society's needs, not merely react to them. Fulfilling our societal obligation, we will regularly spend far more than our depreciation, with this excess amounting to $2 billion in 2011. I'm confident we will earn appropriate returns on our huge incremental investments. Wise regulation and wise investment are two sides of the same coin.

At MidAmerican, we participate in a similar "social compact." We are expected to put up ever-increasing sums to satisfy the future needs of our customers. If we meanwhile operate reliably and efficiently, we know that we will obtain a fair return on these investments.

MidAmerican supplies 2.4 million customers in the U.S. with electricity, operating as the largest supplier in Iowa, Wyoming and Utah and as an important provider in other states as well. Our pipelines transport 8% of the country's natural gas. Obviously, many millions of Americans depend on us every day.

MidAmerican has delivered outstanding results for both its owners (Berkshire's interest is 89.8%) and its customers. Shortly after MidAmerican purchased Northern Natural Gas pipeline in 2002, that company's performance as a pipeline was rated dead last, 43 out of 43, by the leading authority in the field. In the most recent report published, Northern Natural was ranked second. The top spot was held by our other pipeline, Kern River.

In its electric business, MidAmerican has a comparable record. Iowa rates have not increased since we purchased our operation there in 1999. During the same period, the other major electric utility in the state has raised prices more than 70% and now has rates far above ours. In certain metropolitan areas in which the two utilities operate side by side, electric bills of our customers run far below those of their neighbors. I am told that comparable houses sell at higher prices in these cities if they are located in our service area.

MidAmerican will have 2,909 megawatts of wind generation in operation by the end of 2011, more than any other regulated electric utility in the country. The total amount that MidAmerican has invested or committed to wind is a staggering $5.4 billion. We can make this sort of investment because MidAmerican retains *all* of its earnings, unlike other utilities that generally pay out most of what they earn.

As you can tell by now, I am proud of what has been accomplished for our society by Matt Rose at BNSF and by David Sokol and Greg Abel at MidAmerican. I am also both proud and grateful for what they have accomplished for Berkshire shareholders. Below are the relevant figures:

MidAmerican	*Earnings (in millions)*	
	2010	*2009*
U.K. utilities	$ 333	$ 248
Iowa utility	279	285
Western utilities	783	788
Pipelines	378	457
HomeServices	42	43
Other (net)	47	25
Operating earnings before corporate interest and taxes	1,862	1,846
Interest, other than to Berkshire	(323)	(318)
Interest on Berkshire junior debt	(30)	(58)
Income tax	(271)	(313)
Net earnings	$1,238	$1,157
Earnings applicable to Berkshire*	$1,131	$1,071

*Includes interest earned by Berkshire (net of related income taxes) of $19 in 2010 and $38 in 2009.

BNSF		
(Historical accounting through 2/12/10; purchase accounting subsequently)	*(in millions)*	
	2010	*2009*
Revenues	$16,850	$14,016
Operating earnings	4,495	3,254
Interest (Net)	507	613
Pre-Tax earnings	3,988	2,641
Net earnings	2,459	1,721

Finance and Financial Products

This, our smallest sector, includes two rental companies, XTRA (trailers) and CORT (furniture), and Clayton Homes, the country's leading producer and financer of manufactured homes.

Both of our leasing businesses improved their performances last year, albeit from a very low base. XTRA increased the utilization of its equipment from 63% in 2009 to 75% in 2010, thereby raising pre-tax earnings to $35 million from $17 million in 2009. CORT experienced a pickup in business as the year progressed and also significantly tightened its operations. The combination increased its pre-tax results from a loss of $3 million in 2009 to $18 million of profit in 2010.

At Clayton, we produced 23,343 homes, 47% of the industry's total of 50,046. Contrast this to the peak year of 1998, when 372,843 homes were manufactured. (We then had an industry share of 8%.) Sales would have been terrible last year under any circumstances, but the financing problems I commented upon in the 2009 report continue to exacerbate the distress. To explain: Home-financing policies of our government, expressed through the loans found acceptable by FHA, Freddie Mac and Fannie Mae, favor site-built homes and work to negate the price advantage that manufactured homes offer.

We finance more manufactured-home buyers than any other company. Our experience, therefore, should be instructive to those parties preparing to overhaul our country's home-loan practices. Let's take a look.

Clayton owns 200,804 mortgages that it originated. (It also has some mortgage portfolios that it purchased.) At the origination of these contracts, the average FICO score of our borrowers was 648, and 47% were 640 or below. Your banker will tell you that people with such scores are generally regarded as questionable credits.

Nevertheless, our portfolio has performed well during conditions of stress. Here's our loss experience during the last five years for originated loans:

Year	Net Losses as a Percentage of Average Loans
2006	1.53%
2007	1.27%
2008	1.17%
2009	1.86%
2010	1.72%

Our borrowers get in trouble when they lose their jobs, have health problems, get divorced, etc. The recession has hit them hard. But they want to stay in their homes, and generally they borrowed sensible amounts in relation to their income. In addition, we were keeping the originated mortgages for our own account, which means we were not securitizing or otherwise reselling them. If we were stupid in our lending, *we* were going to pay the price. That concentrates the mind.

If home buyers throughout the country had behaved like our buyers, America would not have had the crisis that it did. Our approach was simply to get a meaningful down-payment and gear *fixed* monthly payments to a sensible percentage of income. This policy kept Clayton solvent and also kept buyers in their homes.

Home ownership makes sense for most Americans, particularly at today's lower prices and bargain interest rates. All things considered, the third best investment I ever made was the purchase of my home, though I would have made far more money had I instead rented and used the purchase money to buy stocks. (The two best investments were wedding rings.) For the $31,500 I paid for our house, my family and I gained 52 years of terrific memories with more to come.

But a house can be a nightmare if the buyer's eyes are bigger than his wallet and if a lender – often protected by a government guarantee – facilitates his fantasy. Our country's social goal should not be to put families into the house of their dreams, but rather to put them into a house they can afford.

Investments

Below we show our common stock investments that at yearend had a market value of more than $1 billion.

| | | | 12/31/10 | | |
| | | | Percentage of Company | | |
Shares	Company		Owned	Cost *	Market
				(in millions)	
151,610,700	American Express Company		12.6	$ 1,287	$ 6,507
225,000,000	BYD Company, Ltd.		9.9	232	1,182
200,000,000	The Coca-Cola Company		8.6	1,299	13,154
29,109,637	ConocoPhillips		2.0	2,028	1,982
45,022,563	Johnson & Johnson		1.6	2,749	2,785
97,214,584	Kraft Foods Inc.		5.6	3,207	3,063
19,259,600	Munich Re		10.5	2,896	2,924
3,947,555	POSCO		4.6	768	1,706
72,391,036	The Procter & Gamble Company		2.6	464	4,657
25,848,838	Sanofi-Aventis		2.0	2,060	1,656
242,163,773	Tesco plc		3.0	1,414	1,608
78,060,769	U.S. Bancorp		4.1	2,401	2,105
39,037,142	Wal-Mart Stores, Inc.		1.1	1,893	2,105
358,936,125	Wells Fargo & Company		6.8	8,015	11,123
	Others			3,020	4,956
	Total Common Stocks Carried at Market			$33,733	$61,513

*This is our actual purchase price and also our tax basis; GAAP "cost" differs in a few cases because of write-ups or write-downs that have been required.

In our reported earnings we reflect only the dividends our portfolio companies pay us. Our share of the undistributed earnings of these investees, however, was more than $2 billion last year. These retained earnings are important. In our experience – and, for that matter, in the experience of investors over the past century – undistributed earnings have been either matched or exceeded by market gains, albeit in a highly irregular manner. (Indeed, sometimes the correlation goes in reverse. As one investor said in 2009: "This is worse than divorce. I've lost half my net worth – and I still have my wife.") In the future, we expect our market gains to eventually at least equal the earnings our investees retain.

* * * * * * * * * * * *

In our earlier estimate of Berkshire's normal earning power, we made three adjustments that relate to future investment income (but did *not* include anything for the undistributed earnings factor I have just described).

The first adjustment was decidedly negative. Last year, we discussed five large fixed-income investments that have been contributing substantial sums to our reported earnings. One of these – our Swiss Re note – was redeemed in the early days of 2011, and two others – our Goldman Sachs and General Electric preferred stocks – are likely to be gone by yearend. General Electric is entitled to call our preferred in October and has stated its intention to do so. Goldman Sachs has the right to call our preferred on 30 days notice, but has been held back by the Federal Reserve (bless it!), which unfortunately will likely give Goldman the green light before long.

All three of the companies redeeming must pay us a premium to do so – in aggregate about $1.4 billion – but all of the redemptions are nevertheless unwelcome. After they occur, our earning power will be significantly reduced. That's the bad news.

There are two probable offsets. At yearend we held $38 billion of cash equivalents that have been earning a pittance throughout 2010. At some point, however, better rates will return. They will add at least $500 million – and perhaps much more – to our investment income. That sort of increase in money-market yields is unlikely to come soon. It is appropriate, nevertheless, for us to include improved rates in an estimate of "normal" earning power. Even before higher rates come about, furthermore, we could get lucky and find an opportunity to use some of our cash hoard at decent returns. That day can't come too soon for me: To update Aesop, a girl in a convertible is worth five in the phone book.

In addition, dividends on our current common stock holdings will almost certainly increase. The largest gain is likely to come at Wells Fargo. The Federal Reserve, our friend in respect to Goldman Sachs, has frozen dividend levels at major banks, whether strong or weak, during the last two years. Wells Fargo, though consistently prospering throughout the worst of the recession and currently enjoying enormous financial strength and earning power, has therefore been forced to maintain an artificially low payout. (We don't fault the Fed: For various reasons, an across-the-board freeze made sense during the crisis and its immediate aftermath.)

At some point, probably soon, the Fed's restrictions will cease. Wells Fargo can then reinstate the rational dividend policy that its owners deserve. At that time, we would expect our annual dividends from just this one security to increase by several hundreds of millions of dollars annually.

Other companies we hold are likely to increase their dividends as well. Coca-Cola paid us $88 million in 1995, the year after we finished purchasing the stock. Every year since, Coke has increased its dividend. In 2011, we will almost certainly receive $376 million from Coke, up $24 million from last year. Within ten years, I would expect that $376 million to double. By the end of that period, I wouldn't be surprised to see our share of Coke's *annual* earnings exceed 100% of what we paid for the investment. Time is the friend of the wonderful business.

Overall, I believe our "normal" investment income will at least equal what we realized in 2010, though the redemptions I described will cut our take in 2011 and perhaps 2012 as well.

* * * * * * * * * * *

Last summer, Lou Simpson told me he wished to retire. Since Lou was a mere 74 – an age Charlie and I regard as appropriate only for trainees at Berkshire – his call was a surprise.

Lou joined GEICO as its investment manager in 1979, and his service to that company has been invaluable. In the 2004 Annual Report, I detailed his record with equities, and I have omitted updates only because his performance made mine look bad. Who needs that?

Lou has never been one to advertise his talents. But I will: Simply put, Lou is one of the investment greats. We will miss him.

* * * * * * * * * * *

Four years ago, I told you that we needed to add one or more younger investment managers to carry on when Charlie, Lou and I weren't around. At that time we had multiple outstanding candidates immediately available for my CEO job (as we do now), but we did not have backup in the investment area.

It's easy to identify many investment managers with great recent records. But past results, though important, do not suffice when prospective performance is being judged. How the record has been achieved is crucial, as is the manager's understanding of – and sensitivity to – risk (which in no way should be measured by beta, the choice of too many academics). In respect to the risk criterion, we were looking for someone with a hard-to-evaluate skill: the ability to anticipate the effects of economic scenarios not previously observed. Finally, we wanted someone who would regard working for Berkshire as far more than a job.

When Charlie and I met Todd Combs, we knew he fit our requirements. Todd, as was the case with Lou, will be paid a salary plus a contingent payment based on his performance relative to the S&P. We have arrangements in place for deferrals and carryforwards that will prevent see-saw performance being met by undeserved payments. The hedge-fund world has witnessed some terrible behavior by general partners who have received huge payouts on the upside and who then, when bad results occurred, have walked away rich, with their limited partners losing back their earlier gains. Sometimes these same general partners thereafter quickly started another fund so that they could immediately participate in future profits without having to overcome their past losses. Investors who put money with such managers should be labeled patsies, not partners.

As long as I am CEO, I will continue to manage the great majority of Berkshire's holdings, both bonds and equities. Todd initially will manage funds in the range of one to three billion dollars, an amount he can reset annually. His focus will be equities but he is not restricted to that form of investment. (Fund consultants like to require style boxes such as "long-short," "macro," "international equities." At Berkshire our only style box is "smart.")

Over time, we may add one or two investment managers if we find the right individuals. Should we do that, we will probably have 80% of each manager's performance compensation be dependent on his or her own portfolio and 20% on that of the other manager(s). We want a compensation system that pays off big for individual success but that also fosters cooperation, not competition.

When Charlie and I are no longer around, our investment manager(s) will have responsibility for the entire portfolio in a manner then set by the CEO and Board of Directors. Because good investors bring a useful perspective to the purchase of businesses, we would expect them to be consulted – but not to have a vote – on the wisdom of possible acquisitions. In the end, of course, the Board will make the call on any major acquisition.

One footnote: When we issued a press release about Todd's joining us, a number of commentators pointed out that he was "little-known" and expressed puzzlement that we didn't seek a "big-name." I wonder how many of them would have known of Lou in 1979, Ajit in 1985, or, for that matter, Charlie in 1959. Our goal was to find a 2-year-old Secretariat, not a 10-year-old Seabiscuit. (Whoops – that may not be the smartest metaphor for an 80-year-old CEO to use.)

Derivatives

Two years ago, in the 2008 Annual Report, I told you that Berkshire was a party to 251 derivatives contracts (other than those used for operations at our subsidiaries, such as MidAmerican, and the few left over at Gen Re). Today, the comparable number is 203, a figure reflecting both a few additions to our portfolio and the unwinding or expiration of some contracts.

Our continuing positions, all of which I am personally responsible for, fall largely into two categories. We view both categories as engaging us in insurance-like activities in which we receive premiums for assuming risks that others wish to shed. Indeed, the thought processes we employ in these derivatives transactions are identical to those we use in our insurance business. You should also understand that we get paid up-front when we enter into the contracts and therefore run no counterparty risk. That's important.

Our first category of derivatives consists of a number of contracts, written in 2004-2008, that required payments by us if there were bond defaults by companies included in certain high-yield indices. With minor exceptions, we were exposed to these risks for five years, with each contract covering 100 companies.

In aggregate, we received premiums of $3.4 billion for these contracts. When I originally told you in our 2007 Annual Report about them, I said that I expected the contracts would deliver us an "underwriting profit," meaning that our losses would be less than the premiums we received. In addition, I said we would benefit from the use of float.

Subsequently, as you know too well, we encountered both a financial panic and a severe recession. A number of the companies in the high-yield indices failed, which required us to pay losses of $2.5 billion. Today, however, our exposure is largely behind us because most of our higher-risk contracts have expired. Consequently, it appears almost certain that we will earn an underwriting profit as we originally anticipated. In addition, we have had the use of interest-free float that averaged about $2 billion over the life of the contracts. In short, we charged the right premium, and that protected us when business conditions turned terrible three years ago.

Our other large derivatives position – whose contracts go by the name of "equity puts" – involves insurance we wrote for parties wishing to protect themselves against a possible decline in equity prices in the U.S., U.K., Europe and Japan. These contracts are tied to various equity indices, such as the S&P 500 in the U.S. and the FTSE 100 in the U.K. In the 2004-2008 period, we received $4.8 billion of premiums for 47 of these contracts, most of which ran for 15 years. On these contracts, only the price of the indices on the termination date counts: No payments can be required before then.

As a first step in updating you about these contracts, I can report that late in 2010, at the instigation of our counterparty, we unwound eight contracts, all of them due between 2021 and 2028. We had originally received $647 million in premiums for these contracts, and the unwinding required us to pay $425 million. Consequently, we realized a gain of $222 million and also had the interest-free and unrestricted use of that $647 million for about three years.

Those 2010 transactions left us with 39 equity put contracts remaining on our books at yearend. On these, at their initiation, we received premiums of $4.2 billion.

The future of these contracts is, of course, uncertain. But here is one perspective on them. If the prices of the relevant indices are the same at the contract expiration dates as these prices were on December 31, 2010 – and foreign exchange rates are unchanged – we would owe $3.8 billion on expirations occurring from 2018 to 2026. You can call this amount "settlement value."

On our yearend balance sheet, however, we carry the liability for those remaining equity puts at $6.7 billion. In other words, if the prices of the relevant indices remain unchanged from that date, we will record a $2.9 billion gain in the years to come, that being the difference between the liability figure of $6.7 billion and the settlement value of $3.8 billion. I believe that equity prices will very likely increase and that our liability will fall significantly between now and settlement date. If so, our gain from this point will be even greater. But that, of course, is far from a sure thing.

What is sure is that we will have the use of our remaining "float" of $4.2 billion for an average of about 10 more years. (Neither this float nor that arising from the high-yield contracts is included in the insurance float figure of $66 billion.) Since money is fungible, think of a portion of these funds as contributing to the purchase of BNSF.

As I have told you before, almost all of our derivatives contracts are free of any obligation to post collateral – a fact that cut the premiums we could otherwise have charged. But that fact also left us feeling comfortable during the financial crisis, allowing us in those days to commit to some advantageous purchases. Foregoing some additional derivatives premiums proved to be well worth it.

On Reporting and Misreporting: The Numbers That Count and Those That Don't

Earlier in this letter, I pointed out some numbers that Charlie and I find useful in valuing Berkshire and measuring its progress.

Let's focus here on a number we omitted, but which many in the media feature above all others: net income. Important though that number may be at most companies, it is almost always *meaningless* at Berkshire. Regardless of how our businesses might be doing, Charlie and I could – quite legally – cause net income in any given period to be almost any number we would like.

We have that flexibility because *realized* gains or losses on investments go into the net income figure, whereas *unrealized* gains (and, in most cases, losses) are excluded. For example, imagine that Berkshire had a $10 billion increase in unrealized gains in a given year and concurrently had $1 billion of realized losses. Our net income – which would count only the loss – would be reported as *less* than our operating income. If we had meanwhile realized gains in the *previous* year, headlines might proclaim that our earnings were down X% when in reality our business might be much improved.

If we really thought net income important, we could regularly feed realized gains into it simply because we have a huge amount of unrealized gains upon which to draw. Rest assured, though, that Charlie and I have *never* sold a security because of the effect a sale would have on the net income we were soon to report. We both have a deep disgust for "game playing" with numbers, a practice that was rampant throughout corporate America in the 1990s and still persists, though it occurs less frequently and less blatantly than it used to.

Operating earnings, despite having some shortcomings, are in general a reasonable guide as to how our businesses are doing. Ignore our net income figure, however. Regulations require that we report it to you. But if you find reporters focusing on it, that will speak more to their performance than ours.

Both realized and unrealized gains and losses are fully reflected in the calculation of our book value. Pay attention to the changes in that metric and to the course of our operating earnings, and you will be on the right track.

* * * * * * * * * * * *

As a p.s., I can't resist pointing out just how capricious reported net income can be. Had our equity puts had a termination date of June 30, 2010, we would have been required to pay $6.4 billion to our counterparties at that date. Security prices then generally rose in the next quarter, a move that brought the corresponding figure down to $5.8 billion on September 30th. Yet the Black-Scholes formula that we use in valuing these contracts required us to *increase* our balance-sheet liability during this period from $8.9 billion to $9.6 billion, a change that, after the effect of tax accruals, reduced our net income for the quarter by $455 million.

Both Charlie and I believe that Black-Scholes produces wildly inappropriate values when applied to long-dated options. We set out one absurd example in these pages two years ago. More tangibly, we put our money where our mouth was by entering into our equity put contracts. By doing so, we implicitly asserted that the Black-Scholes calculations used by our counterparties or their customers were faulty.

We continue, nevertheless, to use that formula in presenting our financial statements. Black-Scholes is the accepted standard for option valuation – almost all leading business schools teach it – and we would be accused of shoddy accounting if we deviated from it. Moreover, we would present our auditors with an insurmountable problem were we to do that: They have clients who are our counterparties and who use Black-Scholes values for the same contracts we hold. It would be impossible for our auditors to attest to the accuracy of both their values and ours were the two far apart.

Part of the appeal of Black-Scholes to auditors and regulators is that it produces a precise number. Charlie and I can't supply one of those. We believe the true liability of our contracts to be far lower than that calculated by Black-Scholes, but we can't come up with an exact figure – anymore than we can come up with a *precise* value for GEICO, BNSF, or for Berkshire Hathaway itself. Our inability to pinpoint a number doesn't bother us: We would rather be approximately right than precisely wrong.

John Kenneth Galbraith once slyly observed that economists were most economical with ideas: They made the ones learned in graduate school last a lifetime. University finance departments often behave similarly. Witness the tenacity with which almost all clung to the theory of efficient markets throughout the 1970s and 1980s, dismissively calling powerful facts that refuted it "anomalies." (I always love explanations of that kind: The Flat Earth Society probably views a ship's circling of the globe as an annoying, but inconsequential, anomaly.)

Academics' current practice of teaching Black-Scholes as revealed truth needs re-examination. For that matter, so does the academic's inclination to dwell on the valuation of options. You can be highly successful as an investor without having the slightest ability to value an option. What students *should* be learning is how to value a business. That's what investing is all about.

Life and Debt

The fundamental principle of auto racing is that to finish first, you must first finish. That dictum is equally applicable to business and guides our every action at Berkshire.

Unquestionably, some people have become very rich through the use of borrowed money. However, that's also been a way to get very poor. When leverage works, it magnifies your gains. Your spouse thinks you're clever, and your neighbors get envious. But leverage is addictive. Once having profited from its wonders, very few people retreat to more conservative practices. And as we all learned in third grade – and some relearned in 2008 – any series of positive numbers, however impressive the numbers may be, evaporates when multiplied by a single zero. History tells us that leverage all too often produces zeroes, even when it is employed by very smart people.

Leverage, of course, can be lethal to businesses as well. Companies with large debts often assume that these obligations can be refinanced as they mature. That assumption is usually valid. Occasionally, though, either because of company-specific problems or a worldwide shortage of credit, maturities must actually be met by payment. For that, only cash will do the job.

Borrowers then learn that credit is like oxygen. When either is abundant, its presence goes unnoticed. When either is missing, that's *all* that is noticed. Even a short absence of credit can bring a company to its knees. In September 2008, in fact, its overnight disappearance in many sectors of the economy came dangerously close to bringing our entire country to its knees.

Charlie and I have *no* interest in any activity that could pose the slightest threat to Berkshire's well-being. (With our having a combined age of 167, starting over is not on our bucket list.) We are forever conscious of the fact that you, our partners, have entrusted us with what in many cases is a major portion of your savings. In addition, important philanthropy is dependent on our prudence. Finally, many disabled victims of accidents caused by our insureds are counting on us to deliver sums payable decades from now. It would be irresponsible for us to risk what all these constituencies need just to pursue a few points of extra return.

A little personal history may partially explain our extreme aversion to financial adventurism. I didn't meet Charlie until he was 35, though he grew up within 100 yards of where I have lived for 52 years and also attended the same inner-city public high school in Omaha from which my father, wife, children and two grandchildren graduated. Charlie and I did, however, both work as young boys at my grandfather's grocery store, though our periods of employment were separated by about five years. My grandfather's name was Ernest, and perhaps no man was more aptly named. No one worked for Ernest, even as a stock boy, without being shaped by the experience.

On the facing page you can read a letter sent in 1939 by Ernest to his youngest son, my Uncle Fred. Similar letters went to his other four children. I still have the letter sent to my Aunt Alice, which I found – along with $1,000 of cash – when, as executor of her estate, I opened her safe deposit box in 1970.

Ernest never went to business school – he never in fact finished high school – but he understood the importance of liquidity as a condition for *assured* survival. At Berkshire, we have taken his $1,000 solution a bit further and have pledged that we will hold at least $10 billion of cash, excluding that held at our regulated utility and railroad businesses. Because of that commitment, we customarily keep at least $20 billion on hand so that we can both withstand unprecedented insurance losses (our largest to date having been about $3 billion from Katrina, the insurance industry's most expensive catastrophe) and quickly seize acquisition or investment opportunities, even during times of financial turmoil.

Dear Fred & Catherine:

Over a period of a good many years I have known a great many people who at some time or another have suffered in various ways simply because they did not have ready cash. I have known people who have had to sacrifice some of their holdings in order to have money that was necessary at that time.

For a good many years your grandfather kept a certain amount of money where he could put his hands on it in very short notice.

For a number of years I have made it a point to keep a reserve, should some occasion come up where I would need money quickly, without disturbing the money that I have in my business. There have been a couple occasions when I found it very convenient to go to this fund.

Thus, I feel that everyone should have a reserve. I hope it never happens to you, but the chances are that some day you will need money, and need it badly, and with this thought in view, I started a fund by placing $200.00 in an envelope, with your name on it, when you were married. Each year I added something to it, until there is now $1000.00 in the fund.

Ten years have elapsed since you were married, and this fund is now completed.

It is my wish that you place this envelope in your safety deposit box, and keep it for the purpose that it was created for. Should the time come when you need part, I would suggest that you use as little as possible, and replace it as soon as possible.

You might feel that this should be invested and bring you an income. Forget it -- the mental satisfaction of having $1000.00 laid away where you can put your hands on it, is worth more than what interest it might bring, especially if you have the investment in something that you could not realize on quickly.

If in after years you feel this has been a good idea, you might repeat it with your own children.

For your information, I might mention that there has never been a Buffett who ever left a very large estate, but there has never been one that did not leave something. They never spent all they made, but always saved part of what they made, and it has all worked out pretty well.

This letter is being written at the expiration of ten years after you were married.

Ernest Buffett

"Dad"

We keep our cash largely in U.S. Treasury bills and avoid other short-term securities yielding a few more basis points, a policy we adhered to long before the frailties of commercial paper and money market funds became apparent in September 2008. We agree with investment writer Ray DeVoe's observation, "More money has been lost reaching for yield than at the point of a gun." At Berkshire, we don't rely on bank lines, and we don't enter into contracts that could require postings of collateral except for amounts that are tiny in relation to our liquid assets.

Furthermore, not a dime of cash has left Berkshire for dividends or share repurchases during the past 40 years. Instead, we have retained *all* of our earnings to strengthen our business, a reinforcement now running about $1 billion per month. Our net worth has thus increased from $48 million to $157 billion during those four decades and our intrinsic value has grown far more. No other American corporation has come close to building up its financial strength in this unrelenting way.

By being so cautious in respect to leverage, we penalize our returns by a minor amount. Having loads of liquidity, though, lets us sleep well. Moreover, during the episodes of financial chaos that occasionally erupt in our economy, we will be equipped both financially and emotionally to play offense while others scramble for survival. That's what allowed us to invest $15.6 billion in 25 days of panic following the Lehman bankruptcy in 2008.

The Annual Meeting

The annual meeting will be held on Saturday, April 30th. Carrie Kizer from our home office will be the ringmaster, and her theme this year is Planes, Trains and Automobiles. This gives NetJets, BNSF and BYD a chance to show off.

As always, the doors will open at the Qwest Center at 7 a.m., and a new Berkshire movie will be shown at 8:30. At 9:30 we will go directly to the question-and-answer period, which (with a break for lunch at the Qwest's stands) will last until 3:30. After a short recess, Charlie and I will convene the annual meeting at 3:45. If you decide to leave during the day's question periods, please do so while *Charlie* is talking. (Act fast; he can be terse.)

The best reason to exit, of course, is to *shop*. We will help you do that by filling the 194,300-square-foot hall that adjoins the meeting area with products from dozens of Berkshire subsidiaries. Last year, you did your part, and most locations racked up record sales. In a nine-hour period, we sold 1,053 pairs of Justin boots, 12,416 pounds of See's candy, 8,000 Dairy Queen Blizzards® and 8,800 Quikut knives (that's 16 knives per minute). But you can do better. Remember: Anyone who says money can't buy happiness simply hasn't learned where to shop.

GEICO will have a booth staffed by a number of its top counselors from around the country, all of them ready to supply you with auto insurance quotes. In most cases, GEICO will be able to give you a shareholder discount (usually 8%). This special offer is permitted by 44 of the 51 jurisdictions in which we operate. (One supplemental point: The discount is not additive if you qualify for another, such as that given certain groups.) Bring the details of your existing insurance and check out whether we can save you money. For at least half of you, I believe we can.

Be sure to visit the Bookworm. It will carry more than 60 books and DVDs, including the Chinese language edition of Poor Charlie's Almanack, the ever-popular book about my partner. So what if you can't read Chinese? Just buy a copy and carry it around; it will make you look urbane and erudite. Should you need to ship your book purchases, a shipping service will be available nearby.

If you are a big spender – or merely a gawker – visit Elliott Aviation on the east side of the Omaha airport between noon and 5:00 p.m. on Saturday. There we will have a fleet of NetJets aircraft that will get your pulse racing. Come by bus; leave by private jet.

An attachment to the proxy material that is enclosed with this report explains how you can obtain the credential you will need for admission to the meeting and other events. As for plane, hotel and car reservations, we have again signed up American Express (800-799-6634) to give you special help. Carol Pedersen, who handles these matters, does a terrific job for us each year, and I thank her for it. Hotel rooms can be hard to find, but work with Carol and you will get one.

Airlines have often jacked up prices – sometimes dramatically so – for the Berkshire weekend. If you are coming from far away, compare the cost of flying to Kansas City versus Omaha. The drive is about 2 ½ hours and it may be that you can save significant money, particularly if you had planned to rent a car in Omaha.

At Nebraska Furniture Mart, located on a 77-acre site on 72nd Street between Dodge and Pacific, we will again be having "Berkshire Weekend" discount pricing. Last year the store did $33.3 million of business during its annual meeting sale, a volume that – as far as I know – exceeds the one-week total of *any* retail store anyplace. To obtain the Berkshire discount, you must make your purchases between Tuesday, April 26th and Monday, May 2nd inclusive, and also present your meeting credential. The period's special pricing will even apply to the products of several prestigious manufacturers that normally have ironclad rules against discounting but which, in the spirit of our shareholder weekend, have made an exception for you. We appreciate their cooperation. NFM is open from 10 a.m. to 9 p.m. Monday through Saturday, and 10 a.m. to 6 p.m. on Sunday. On Saturday this year, from 5:30 p.m. to 8 p.m., NFM is having a picnic to which you are all invited.

At Borsheims, we will again have two shareholder-only events. The first will be a cocktail reception from 6 p.m. to 9 p.m. on Friday, April 29th. The second, the main gala, will be held on Sunday, May 1st, from 9 a.m. to 4 p.m. On Saturday, we will be open until 6 p.m. On Sunday, around 1 p.m., I will be at Borsheims with a smile and a shoeshine, selling jewelry just as I sold men's shirts at J.C. Penney's 63 years ago. I've told Susan Jacques, Borsheims' CEO, that I'm still a hotshot salesman. But I see doubt in her eyes. So cut loose and buy something from me for your wife or sweetheart (presumably the same person). Make me look good.

We will have huge crowds at Borsheims throughout the weekend. For your convenience, therefore, shareholder prices will be available from Monday, April 25th through Saturday, May 7th. During that period, please identify yourself as a shareholder by presenting your meeting credentials or a brokerage statement that shows you are a Berkshire shareholder.

On Sunday, in the mall outside of Borsheims, a blindfolded Patrick Wolff, twice U.S. chess champion, will take on all comers – who will have their eyes wide open – in groups of six. Nearby, Norman Beck, a remarkable magician from Dallas, will bewilder onlookers. Additionally, we will have Bob Hamman and Sharon Osberg, two of the world's top bridge experts, available to play bridge with our shareholders on Sunday afternoon.

Gorat's and Piccolo's will again be open exclusively for Berkshire shareholders on Sunday, May 1st. Both will be serving until 10 p.m., with Gorat's opening at 1 p.m. and Piccolo's opening at 4 p.m. These restaurants are my favorites and – still being a growing boy – I will eat at both of them on Sunday evening. Remember: To make a reservation at Gorat's, call 402-551-3733 on April 1st (*but not before*) and at Piccolo's call 402-342-9038.

We will again have the same three financial journalists lead the question-and-answer period, asking Charlie and me questions that shareholders have submitted to them by e-mail. The journalists and their e-mail addresses are: Carol Loomis, of Fortune, who may be emailed at cloomis@fortunemail.com; Becky Quick, of CNBC, at BerkshireQuestions@cnbc.com, and Andrew Ross Sorkin, of The New York Times, at arsorkin@nytimes.com.

From the questions submitted, each journalist will choose the dozen or so he or she decides are the most interesting and important. The journalists have told me your question has the best chance of being selected if you keep it concise, avoid sending it in at the last moment, make it Berkshire-related and include no more than two questions in any email you send them. (In your email, let the journalist know if you would like your name mentioned if your question is selected.)

Neither Charlie nor I will get so much as a clue about the questions to be asked. We know the journalists will pick some tough ones, and that's the way we like it.

We will again have a drawing at 8:15 a.m. on Saturday at each of 13 microphones for those shareholders wishing to ask questions themselves. At the meeting, I will alternate the questions asked by the journalists with those from the winning shareholders. We hope to answer at least 60 questions. From our standpoint, the more the better. Our goal, which we pursue both through these annual letters and by our meeting discussions, is to give you a better understanding of the business that *you* own.

* * * * * * * * * * * *

For good reason, I regularly extol the accomplishments of our operating managers. Equally important, however, are the 20 men and women who work with me at our corporate office (all on one floor, which is the way we intend to keep it!).

This group efficiently deals with a multitude of SEC and other regulatory requirements, files a 14,097-page Federal income tax return along with state and foreign returns, responds to countless shareholder and media inquiries, gets out the annual report, prepares for the country's largest annual meeting, coordinates the Board's activities – and the list goes on and on.

They handle all of these business tasks cheerfully and with unbelievable efficiency, making my life easy and joyful. Their efforts go beyond activities strictly related to Berkshire: They deal with 48 universities (selected from 200 applicants) who will send students to Omaha this school year for a day with me and also handle all kinds of requests that I receive, arrange my travel, and even get me hamburgers for lunch. No CEO has it better.

This home office crew has my deepest thanks and deserves yours as well. Come to our Woodstock for Capitalism on April 30th and tell them so.

February 26, 2011   Warren E. Buffett
                                              Chairman of the Board

Memo

To: Berkshire Hathaway Managers ("The All-Stars")

cc: Berkshire Directors

From: Warren E. Buffett

Date: July 26, 2010

This is my biennial letter to reemphasize Berkshire's top priority and to get your help on succession planning (yours, not mine!).

The priority is that all of us continue to zealously guard Berkshire's reputation. We can't be perfect but we can try to be. As I've said in these memos for more than 25 years: "We can afford to lose money – even a lot of money. But we can't afford to lose reputation – even a shred of reputation." We *must* continue to measure every act against not only what is legal but also what we would be happy to have written about on the front page of a national newspaper in an article written by an unfriendly but intelligent reporter.

Sometimes your associates will say "Everybody else is doing it." This rationale is almost always a bad one if it is the main justification for a business action. It is totally unacceptable when evaluating a moral decision. Whenever somebody offers that phrase as a rationale, in effect they are saying that they can't come up with a *good* reason. If anyone gives this explanation, tell them to try using it with a reporter or a judge and see how far it gets them.

If you see anything whose propriety or legality causes you to hesitate, be sure to give me a call. However, it's very likely that if a given course of action evokes such hesitation, it's too close to the line and should be abandoned. There's plenty of money to be made in the center of the court. If it's questionable whether some action is close to the line, just assume it is outside and forget it.

As a corollary, let me know promptly if there's any significant bad news. I can handle bad news but I don't like to deal with it after it has festered for awhile. A reluctance to face up immediately to bad news is what turned a problem at Salomon from one that could have easily been disposed of into one that almost caused the demise of a firm with 8,000 employees.

Somebody is doing something today at Berkshire that you and I would be unhappy about if we knew of it. That's inevitable: We now employ more than 250,000 people and the chances of that number getting through the day without any bad behavior occurring is nil. But we can have a huge effect in minimizing such activities by jumping on anything immediately when there is the slightest odor of impropriety. Your attitude on such matters, expressed by behavior as well as words, will be the most important factor in how the culture of your business develops. Culture, more than rule books, determines how an organization behaves.

In other respects, talk to me about what is going on as little or as much as you wish. Each of you does a first-class job of running your operation with your own individual style and you don't need me to help. The only items you need to clear with me are any changes in post-retirement benefits and any unusually large capital expenditures or acquisitions.

* * * * * * * * * * * *

I need your help in respect to the question of succession. I'm not looking for any of you to retire and I hope you all live to 100. (In Charlie's case, 110.) But just in case you don't, please send me a letter (at home if you wish) giving your recommendation as who should take over tomorrow if you should become incapacitated overnight. These letters will be seen by no one but me unless I'm no longer CEO, in which case my successor will need the information. Please summarize the strengths and weaknesses of your primary candidate as well as any possible alternates you may wish to include. Most of you have participated in this exercise in the past and others have offered your ideas verbally. However, it's important to me to get a periodic update, and now that we have added so many businesses, I need to have your thoughts in writing rather than trying to carry them around in my memory. Of course, there are a few operations that are run by two or more of you – such as the Blumkins, the Merschmans, the pair at Applied Underwriters, etc. – and in these cases, just forget about this item. Your note can be short, informal, handwritten, etc. Just mark it "Personal for Warren."

Thanks for your help on all of this. And thanks for the way you run your businesses. You make my job easy.

WEB/db

P.S. Another minor request: Please turn down all proposals for me to speak, make contributions, intercede with the Gates Foundation, etc. Sometimes these requests for you to act as intermediary will be accompanied by "It can't hurt to ask." It will be easier for both of us if you just say "no." As an added favor, don't suggest that they instead write or call me. Multiply 76 businesses by the periodic "I think he'll be interested in this one" and you can understand why it is better to say no firmly and immediately.

BERKSHIRE HATHAWAY INC.

To the Shareholders of Berkshire Hathaway Inc.:

The per-share book value of both our Class A and Class B stock increased by 4.6% in 2011. Over the last 47 years (that is, since present management took over), book value has grown from $19 to $99,860, a rate of 19.8% compounded annually.*

Charlie Munger, Berkshire's Vice Chairman and my partner, and I feel good about the company's progress during 2011. Here are the highlights:

- The primary job of a Board of Directors is to see that the right people are running the business and to be sure that the next generation of leaders is identified and ready to take over *tomorrow*. I have been on 19 corporate boards, and Berkshire's directors are at the top of the list in the time and diligence they have devoted to succession planning. What's more, their efforts have paid off.

  As 2011 started, Todd Combs joined us as an investment manager, and shortly after yearend Ted Weschler came aboard. Both of these men have outstanding investment skills and a deep commitment to Berkshire. Each will be handling a few billion dollars in 2012, but they have the brains, judgment and character to manage our entire portfolio when Charlie and I are no longer running Berkshire.

  Your Board is equally enthusiastic about my successor as CEO, an individual to whom they have had a great deal of exposure and whose managerial and human qualities they admire. (We have two superb back-up candidates as well.) When a transfer of responsibility is required, it will be seamless, and Berkshire's prospects will remain bright. More than 98% of my net worth is in Berkshire stock, all of which will go to various philanthropies. Being so heavily concentrated in one stock defies conventional wisdom. But I'm fine with this arrangement, knowing both the quality and diversity of the businesses we own and the caliber of the people who manage them. With these assets, my successor will enjoy a running start. Do not, however, infer from this discussion that Charlie and I are going anywhere; we continue to be in excellent health, and we love what we do.

- On September 16th we acquired Lubrizol, a worldwide producer of additives and other specialty chemicals. The company has had an outstanding record since James Hambrick became CEO in 2004, with pre-tax profits increasing from $147 million to $1,085 million. Lubrizol will have many opportunities for "bolt-on" acquisitions in the specialty chemical field. Indeed, we've already agreed to three, costing $493 million. James is a disciplined buyer and a superb operator. Charlie and I are eager to expand his managerial domain.

- Our major businesses did well last year. In fact, *each* of our five largest non-insurance companies – BNSF, Iscar, Lubrizol, Marmon Group and MidAmerican Energy – delivered record operating earnings. In aggregate these businesses earned more than $9 billion pre-tax in 2011. Contrast that to seven years ago, when we owned only one of the five, MidAmerican, whose pre-tax earnings were $393 million. Unless the economy weakens in 2012, *each* of our fabulous five should again set a record, with aggregate earnings comfortably topping $10 billion.

---

* All per-share figures used in this report apply to Berkshire's A shares. Figures for the B shares are 1/1500th of those shown for A.

- In total, our entire string of operating companies spent $8.2 billion for property, plant and equipment in 2011, smashing our previous record by more than $2 billion. About 95% of these outlays were made in the U.S., a fact that may surprise those who believe our country lacks investment opportunities. We welcome projects abroad, but expect the overwhelming majority of Berkshire's future capital commitments to be in America. In 2012, these expenditures will again set a record.

- Our insurance operations continued their delivery of costless capital that funds a myriad of other opportunities. This business produces "float" – money that doesn't belong to us, but that we get to invest for Berkshire's benefit. And if we pay out less in losses and expenses than we receive in premiums, we additionally earn an underwriting profit, meaning the float costs us less than nothing. Though we are sure to have underwriting losses from time to time, we've now had nine consecutive years of underwriting profits, totaling about $17 billion. Over the same nine years our float increased from $41 billion to its current record of $70 billion. Insurance has been good to us.

- Finally, we made two major investments in marketable securities: (1) a $5 billion 6% preferred stock of Bank of America that came with warrants allowing us to buy 700 million common shares at $7.14 per share any time before September 2, 2021; and (2) 63.9 million shares of IBM that cost us $10.9 billion. Counting IBM, we now have large ownership interests in four exceptional companies: 13.0% of American Express, 8.8% of Coca-Cola, 5.5% of IBM and 7.6% of Wells Fargo. (We also, of course, have many smaller, but important, positions.)

We view these holdings as partnership interests in wonderful businesses, not as marketable securities to be bought or sold based on their near-term prospects. Our share of *their* earnings, however, are far from fully reflected in *our* earnings; only the dividends we receive from these businesses show up in our financial reports. Over time, though, the undistributed earnings of these companies that are attributable to our ownership are of huge importance to us. That's because they will be used in a variety of ways to increase future earnings and dividends of the investee. They may also be devoted to stock repurchases, which will increase our share of the company's future earnings.

Had we owned our present positions throughout last year, our dividends from the "Big Four" would have been $862 million. That's all that would have been reported in Berkshire's income statement. Our share of this quartet's earnings, however, would have been far greater: $3.3 billion. Charlie and I believe that the $2.4 billion that goes unreported on our books creates at least that amount of value for Berkshire as it fuels earnings gains in future years. We expect the combined earnings of the four – and their dividends as well – to increase in 2012 and, for that matter, almost every year for a long time to come. A decade from now, our current holdings of the four companies might well account for earnings of $7 billion, of which $2 billion in dividends would come to us.

I've run out of good news. Here are some developments that hurt us during 2011:

- A few years back, I spent about $2 billion buying several bond issues of Energy Future Holdings, an electric utility operation serving portions of Texas. That was a mistake – a *big* mistake. In large measure, the company's prospects were tied to the price of natural gas, which tanked shortly after our purchase and remains depressed. Though we have annually received interest payments of about $102 million since our purchase, the company's ability to pay will soon be exhausted unless gas prices rise substantially. We wrote down our investment by $1 billion in 2010 and by an additional $390 million last year.

At yearend, we carried the bonds at their market value of $878 million. If gas prices remain at present levels, we will likely face a further loss, perhaps in an amount that will virtually wipe out our current carrying value. Conversely, a substantial increase in gas prices might allow us to recoup some, or even all, of our write-down. However things turn out, I totally miscalculated the gain/loss probabilities when I purchased the bonds. In tennis parlance, this was a major unforced error by your chairman.

- Three large and very attractive fixed-income investments were called away from us by their issuers in 2011. Swiss Re, Goldman Sachs and General Electric paid us an aggregate of $12.8 billion to redeem securities that were producing about $1.2 billion of pre-tax earnings for Berkshire. That's a lot of income to replace, though our Lubrizol purchase did offset most of it.

- Last year, I told you that "a housing recovery will probably begin within a year or so." I was dead wrong. We have five businesses whose results are significantly influenced by housing activity. The connection is direct at Clayton Homes, which is the largest producer of homes in the country, accounting for about 7% of those constructed during 2011.

  Additionally, Acme Brick, Shaw (carpet), Johns Manville (insulation) and MiTek (building products, primarily connector plates used in roofing) are all materially affected by construction activity. In aggregate, our five housing-related companies had pre-tax profits of $513 million in 2011. That's similar to 2010 but down from $1.8 billion in 2006.

  Housing will come back – you can be sure of that. Over time, the number of housing units necessarily matches the number of households (after allowing for a normal level of vacancies). For a period of years prior to 2008, however, America added more housing units than households. Inevitably, we ended up with far too many units and the bubble popped with a violence that shook the entire economy. That created still another problem for housing: Early in a recession, household formations slow, and in 2009 the decrease was dramatic.

  That devastating supply/demand equation is now reversed: Every day we are creating more households than housing units. People may postpone hitching up during uncertain times, but eventually hormones take over. And while "doubling-up" may be the initial reaction of some during a recession, living with in-laws can quickly lose its allure.

  At our current annual pace of 600,000 housing starts – considerably less than the number of new households being formed – buyers and renters are sopping up what's left of the old oversupply. (This process will run its course at different rates around the country; the supply-demand situation varies widely by locale.) While this healing takes place, however, our housing-related companies sputter, employing only 43,315 people compared to 58,769 in 2006. This hugely important sector of the economy, which includes not only construction but everything that feeds off of it, remains in a *depression* of its own. I believe this is the major reason a recovery in employment has so severely lagged the steady and substantial comeback we have seen in almost all other sectors of our economy.

  Wise monetary and fiscal policies play an important role in tempering recessions, but these tools don't create households nor eliminate excess housing units. Fortunately, demographics and our market system will restore the needed balance – probably before long. When that day comes, we will again build one million or more residential units annually. I believe pundits will be surprised at how far unemployment drops once that happens. They will then reawake to what has been true since 1776: America's best days lie ahead.

Intrinsic Business Value

Charlie and I measure our performance by the rate of gain in Berkshire's per-share intrinsic business value. If our gain over time outstrips the performance of the S&P 500, we have earned our paychecks. If it doesn't, we are overpaid at any price.

We have no way to pinpoint intrinsic value. But we do have a useful, *though considerably understated*, proxy for it: per-share book value. This yardstick is meaningless at most companies. At Berkshire, however, book value very roughly tracks business values. That's because the amount by which Berkshire's intrinsic value exceeds book value does not swing wildly from year to year, though it increases in most years. Over time, the divergence will likely become ever more substantial in absolute terms, remaining reasonably steady, however, on a percentage basis as both the numerator and denominator of the business-value/book-value equation increase.

We've regularly emphasized that our book-value performance is almost certain to outpace the S&P 500 in a bad year for the stock market and just as certainly will fall short in a strong up-year. The test is how we do over time. Last year's annual report included a table laying out results for the 42 five-year periods since we took over at Berkshire in 1965 (i.e., 1965-69, 1966-70, etc.). All showed our book value beating the S&P, and our string held for 2007-11. It will almost certainly snap, though, if the S&P 500 should put together a five-year winning streak (which it may well be on its way to doing as I write this).

* * * * * * * * * * * *

I also included two tables last year that set forth the key quantitative ingredients that will help you estimate our per-share intrinsic value. I won't repeat the full discussion here; you can find it reproduced on pages 99-100. To update the tables shown there, our per-share investments in 2011 increased 4% to $98,366, and our pre-tax earnings from businesses other than insurance and investments increased 18% to $6,990 per share.

Charlie and I like to see gains in both areas, but our primary focus is on building operating earnings. Over time, the businesses we currently own should increase their aggregate earnings, and we hope also to purchase some large operations that will give us a further boost. We now have eight subsidiaries that would each be included in the Fortune 500 were they stand-alone companies. That leaves only 492 to go. My task is clear, and I'm on the prowl.

Share Repurchases

Last September, we announced that Berkshire would repurchase its shares at a price of up to 110% of book value. We were in the market for only a few days – buying $67 million of stock – before the price advanced beyond our limit. Nonetheless, the general importance of share repurchases suggests I should focus for a bit on the subject.

Charlie and I favor repurchases when two conditions are met: first, a company has ample funds to take care of the operational and liquidity needs of its business; second, its stock is selling at a material discount to the company's intrinsic business value, conservatively calculated.

We have witnessed many bouts of repurchasing that failed our second test. Sometimes, of course, infractions – even serious ones – are innocent; many CEOs never stop believing their stock is cheap. In other instances, a less benign conclusion seems warranted. It doesn't suffice to say that repurchases are being made to offset the dilution from stock issuances or simply because a company has excess cash. Continuing shareholders are *hurt* unless shares are purchased below intrinsic value. The first law of capital allocation – whether the money is slated for acquisitions or share repurchases – is that what is smart at one price is dumb at another. (One CEO who always stresses the price/value factor in repurchase decisions is Jamie Dimon at J.P. Morgan; I recommend that you read his annual letter.)

Charlie and I have mixed emotions when Berkshire shares sell well below intrinsic value. We like making money for continuing shareholders, and there is no surer way to do that than by buying an asset – our own stock – that we know to be worth *at least* x for less than that – for .9x, .8x or even lower. (As one of our directors says, it's like shooting fish in a barrel, *after* the barrel has been drained and the fish have quit flopping.) Nevertheless, we don't enjoy cashing out partners at a discount, even though our doing so may give the selling shareholders a slightly higher price than they would receive if our bid was absent. When we are buying, therefore, we want those exiting partners to be fully informed about the value of the assets they are selling.

At our limit price of 110% of book value, repurchases clearly increase Berkshire's per-share intrinsic value. And the more and the cheaper we buy, the greater the gain for continuing shareholders. Therefore, if given the opportunity, we will likely repurchase stock aggressively at our price limit or lower. You should know, however, that we have no interest in supporting the stock and that our bids will fade in particularly weak markets. Nor will we buy shares if our cash-equivalent holdings are below $20 billion. At Berkshire, financial strength that is unquestionable takes precedence over all else.

* * * * * * * * * * * *

This discussion of repurchases offers me the chance to address the irrational reaction of many investors to changes in stock prices. When Berkshire buys stock in a company that is repurchasing shares, we hope for two events: First, we have the normal hope that earnings of the business will increase at a good clip for a long time to come; and second, we also hope that the stock *underperforms* in the market for a long time as well. A corollary to this second point: "Talking our book" about a stock we own – were that to be effective – would actually be harmful to Berkshire, not helpful as commentators customarily assume.

Let's use IBM as an example. As all business observers know, CEOs Lou Gerstner and Sam Palmisano did a superb job in moving IBM from near-bankruptcy twenty years ago to its prominence today. Their operational accomplishments were truly extraordinary.

But their financial management was equally brilliant, particularly in recent years as the company's financial flexibility improved. Indeed, I can think of no major company that has had better financial management, a skill that has materially increased the gains enjoyed by IBM shareholders. The company has used debt wisely, made value-adding acquisitions almost exclusively for cash and aggressively repurchased its own stock.

Today, IBM has 1.16 billion shares outstanding, of which we own about 63.9 million or 5.5%. Naturally, what happens to the company's earnings over the next five years is of enormous importance to us. Beyond that, the company will likely spend $50 billion or so in those years to repurchase shares. Our quiz for the day: What should a long-term shareholder, such as Berkshire, cheer for during that period?

I won't keep you in suspense. We should wish for IBM's stock price to *languish* throughout the five years.

Let's do the math. If IBM's stock price averages, say, $200 during the period, the company will acquire 250 million shares for its $50 billion. There would consequently be 910 million shares outstanding, and we would own about 7% of the company. If the stock conversely sells for an average of $300 during the five-year period, IBM will acquire only 167 million shares. That would leave about 990 million shares outstanding after five years, of which we would own 6.5%.

If IBM were to earn, say, $20 billion in the fifth year, our share of those earnings would be a full $100 million greater under the "disappointing" scenario of a lower stock price than they would have been at the higher price. At some later point our shares would be worth perhaps $1½ billion more than if the "high-price" repurchase scenario had taken place.

The logic is simple: If you are going to be a net buyer of stocks in the future, either directly with your own money or indirectly (through your ownership of a company that is repurchasing shares), you are *hurt* when stocks rise. You benefit when stocks swoon. *Emotions*, however, too often complicate the matter: Most people, including those who will be net buyers in the future, take comfort in seeing stock prices advance. These shareholders resemble a commuter who rejoices after the price of gas increases, simply because his tank contains a day's supply.

Charlie and I don't expect to win many of you over to our way of thinking – we've observed enough human behavior to know the futility of that – but we do want you to be aware of our personal calculus. And here a confession is in order: In my early days I, too, rejoiced when the market rose. Then I read Chapter Eight of Ben Graham's *The Intelligent Investor*, the chapter dealing with how investors should view fluctuations in stock prices. Immediately the scales fell from my eyes, and low prices became my friend. Picking up that book was one of the luckiest moments in my life.

In the end, the success of our IBM investment will be determined primarily by its future earnings. But an important secondary factor will be how many shares the company purchases with the substantial sums it is likely to devote to this activity. And if repurchases ever reduce the IBM shares outstanding to 63.9 million, I will abandon my famed frugality and give Berkshire employees a paid holiday.

* * * * * * * * * * * *

Now, let's examine the four major sectors of our operations. Each has vastly different balance sheet and income characteristics from the others. Lumping them together therefore impedes analysis. So we'll present them as four separate businesses, which is how Charlie and I view them. Because we may be repurchasing Berkshire shares from some of you, we will offer our thoughts in each section as to how intrinsic value compares to carrying value.

Insurance

Let's look first at insurance, Berkshire's core operation and the engine that has propelled our expansion over the years.

Property-casualty ("P/C") insurers receive premiums upfront and pay claims later. In extreme cases, such as those arising from certain workers' compensation accidents, payments can stretch over decades. This collect-now, pay-later model leaves us holding large sums – money we call "float" – that will eventually go to others. Meanwhile, we get to invest this float for Berkshire's benefit. Though individual policies and claims come and go, the amount of float we hold remains remarkably stable in relation to premium volume. Consequently, as our business grows, so does our float. And how we have grown, as the following table shows:

Year	Float (in $ millions)
1970	$ 39
1980	237
1990	1,632
2000	27,871
2010	65,832
2011	70,571

It's unlikely that our float will grow much – if at all – from its current level. That's mainly because we already have an outsized amount relative to our premium volume. Were there to be a *decline* in float, I will add, it would almost certainly be *very* gradual and therefore impose no unusual demand for funds on us.

If our premiums exceed the total of our expenses and eventual losses, we register an underwriting profit that adds to the investment income our float produces. When such a profit occurs, we enjoy the use of free money – and, better yet, get *paid* for holding it. Unfortunately, the wish of all insurers to achieve this happy result creates intense competition, so vigorous in most years that it causes the P/C industry as a whole to operate at a significant underwriting *loss*. For example, State Farm, by far the country's largest insurer and a well-managed company besides, has incurred an underwriting loss in eight of the last eleven years. There are a lot of ways to lose money in insurance, and the industry is resourceful in creating new ones.

As noted in the first section of this report, we have now operated at an underwriting profit for nine consecutive years, our gain for the period having totaled $17 billion. I believe it likely that we will continue to underwrite profitably in most – though certainly not all – future years. If we accomplish that, our float will be better than cost-free. We will profit just as we would if some party deposited $70.6 billion with us, paid us a fee for holding its money and then let us invest its funds for our own benefit.

So how does this attractive float affect intrinsic value calculations? Our float is deducted *in full* as a liability in calculating Berkshire's book value, just as if we had to pay it out tomorrow and were unable to replenish it. But that's an incorrect way to view float, which should instead be viewed as a revolving fund. If float is both costless and long-enduring, the true value of this liability is *far* lower than the accounting liability.

Partially offsetting this overstated liability is $15.5 billion of "goodwill" attributable to our insurance companies that is included in book value as an asset. In effect, this goodwill represents the price we paid for the float-generating capabilities of our insurance operations. The cost of the goodwill, however, has *no* bearing on its true value. If an insurance business produces large and sustained underwriting losses, any goodwill asset attributable to it should be deemed valueless, whatever its original cost.

Fortunately, that's not the case at Berkshire. Charlie and I believe the true economic value of our insurance goodwill – what *we* would pay to purchase float *of similar quality* – to be far in excess of its historic carrying value. The value of our float is one reason – a huge reason – why we believe Berkshire's intrinsic business value substantially exceeds book value.

Let me emphasize once again that cost-free float is *not* an outcome to be expected for the P/C industry as a whole: We don't think there is much "Berkshire-quality" float existing in the insurance world. In most years, including 2011, the industry's premiums have been inadequate to cover claims plus expenses. Consequently, the industry's overall return on tangible equity has for many decades fallen far short of the average return realized by American industry, a sorry performance almost certain to continue. Berkshire's outstanding economics exist only because we have some terrific managers running some extraordinary insurance operations. Let me tell you about the major units.

* * * * * * * * * * *

First by float size is the Berkshire Hathaway Reinsurance Group, run by Ajit Jain. Ajit insures risks that no one else has the desire or the capital to take on. His operation combines capacity, speed, decisiveness and, most importantly, brains in a manner that is unique in the insurance business. Yet he never exposes Berkshire to risks that are inappropriate in relation to our resources. Indeed, we are *far* more conservative in that respect than most large insurers. For example, if the insurance industry should experience a $250 billion loss from some mega-catastrophe – a loss about triple anything it has ever faced – Berkshire as a whole would likely record a moderate profit for the year because of its many streams of earnings. Concurrently, all other major insurers and reinsurers would be far in the red, and some would face insolvency.

From a standing start in 1985, Ajit has created an insurance business with float of $34 billion and significant underwriting profits, a feat that no CEO of any other insurer has come close to matching. By these accomplishments, he has added a great many billions of dollars to the value of Berkshire. Charlie would gladly trade me for a second Ajit. Alas, there is none.

* * * * * * * * * * *

We have another insurance powerhouse in General Re, managed by Tad Montross.

At bottom, a sound insurance operation needs to adhere to four disciplines. It must (1) understand *all* exposures that might cause a policy to incur losses; (2) conservatively evaluate the likelihood of any exposure actually causing a loss and the probable cost if it does; (3) set a premium that will deliver a profit, on average, after both prospective loss costs and operating expenses are covered; and (4) be willing to walk away if the appropriate premium can't be obtained.

Many insurers pass the first three tests and flunk the fourth. They simply can't turn their back on business that their competitors are eagerly writing. That old line, "The other guy is doing it so we must as well," spells trouble in any business, but in none more so than insurance. Indeed, a good underwriter needs an independent mindset akin to that of the senior citizen who received a call from his wife while driving home. "Albert, be careful," she warned, "I just heard on the radio that there's a car going the wrong way down the Interstate." "Mabel, they don't know the half of it," replied Albert, "It's not just one car, there are hundreds of them."

Tad has observed all four of the insurance commandments, and it shows in his results. General Re's huge float has been better than cost-free under his leadership, and we expect that, on average, it will continue to be. In the first few years after we acquired it, General Re was a major headache. Now it's a treasure.

* * * * * * * * * * *

Finally, there is GEICO, the insurer on which I cut my teeth 61 years ago. GEICO is run by Tony Nicely, who joined the company at 18 and completed 50 years of service in 2011.

GEICO's much-envied record comes from Tony's brilliant execution of a superb and almost-impossible-to-replicate business model. During Tony's 18-year tenure as CEO, our market share has grown from 2.0% to 9.3%. If it had instead remained static – as it had for more than a decade before he took over – our premium volume would now be $3.3 billion rather than the $15.4 billion we attained in 2011. The extra value created by Tony and his associates is a major element in Berkshire's excess of intrinsic value over book value.

There is still more than 90% of the auto-insurance market left for GEICO to rake in. Don't bet against Tony acquiring chunks of it year after year in the future. Our low costs permit low prices, and every day more Americans discover that the Gecko is doing them a favor when he urges them to visit GEICO.com for a quote. (Our lizard has another endearing quality: Unlike human spokesmen or spokeswomen who expensively represent other insurance companies, our little fellow has no agent.)

* * * * * * * * * * *

In addition to our three major insurance operations, we own a group of smaller companies, most of them plying their trade in odd corners of the insurance world. In aggregate, their results have consistently been profitable and the float they provide us is substantial. Charlie and I treasure these companies and their managers.

At yearend, we acquired Princeton Insurance, a New Jersey writer of medical malpractice policies. This bolt-on transaction expands the managerial domain of Tim Kenesey, the star CEO of Medical Protective, our Indiana-based med-mal insurer. Princeton brings with it more than $600 million of float, an amount that is included in the following table.

Here is the record of all four segments of our property-casualty and life insurance businesses:

	Underwriting Profit		Yearend Float	
	(in millions)			
Insurance Operations	2011	2010	2011	2010
BH Reinsurance	$(714)	$ 176	$33,728	$30,370
General Re	144	452	19,714	20,049
GEICO	576	1,117	11,169	10,272
Other Primary	242	268	5,960	5,141
	$ 248	$2,013	$70,571	$65,832

Among large insurance operations, Berkshire's impresses me as the best in the world.

Regulated, Capital-Intensive Businesses

We have two very large businesses, BNSF and MidAmerican Energy, that have important common characteristics distinguishing them from our many other businesses. Consequently, we assign them their own sector in this letter and also split out their combined financial statistics in our GAAP balance sheet and income statement.

A key characteristic of both companies is the huge investment they have in very long-lived, regulated assets, with these partially funded by large amounts of long-term debt that is *not* guaranteed by Berkshire. Our credit is not needed: Both businesses have earning power that even under terrible business conditions amply covers their interest requirements. In a less than robust economy during 2011, for example, BNSF's interest coverage was 9.5x. At MidAmerican, meanwhile, two key factors ensure its ability to service debt under all circumstances: The stability of earnings that is inherent in our exclusively offering an essential service and a diversity of earnings streams, which shield it from the actions of any single regulatory body.

Measured by ton-miles, rail moves 42% of America's inter-city freight, and BNSF moves more than any other railroad – about 37% of the industry total. A little math will tell you that about 15% of *all* inter-city ton-miles of freight in the U.S. is transported by BNSF. It is no exaggeration to characterize railroads as the circulatory system of our economy. Your railroad is the largest artery.

All of this places a huge responsibility on us. We must, without fail, maintain and improve our 23,000 miles of track along with 13,000 bridges, 80 tunnels, 6,900 locomotives and 78,600 freight cars. This job requires us to have ample financial resources under *all* economic scenarios and to have the human talent that can instantly and effectively deal with the vicissitudes of nature, such as the widespread flooding BNSF labored under last summer.

To fulfill its societal obligation, BNSF regularly invests far more than its depreciation charge, with the excess amounting to $1.8 billion in 2011. The three other major U.S. railroads are making similar outlays. Though many people decry our country's inadequate infrastructure spending, that criticism cannot be levied against the railroad industry. It is pouring money – *funds from the private sector* – into the investment projects needed to provide better and more extensive service in the future. If railroads were not making these huge expenditures, our country's publicly-financed highway system would face even greater congestion and maintenance problems than exist today.

Massive investments of the sort that BNSF is making would be foolish if it could not earn appropriate returns on the incremental sums it commits. But I am confident it will do so because of the value it delivers. Many years ago Ben Franklin counseled, "Keep thy shop, and thy shop will keep thee." Translating this to our regulated businesses, he might today say, "Take care of your customer, and the regulator – your customer's representative – will take care of you." Good behavior by each party begets good behavior in return.

At MidAmerican, we participate in a similar "social compact." We are expected to put up ever-increasing sums to satisfy the future needs of our customers. If we meanwhile operate reliably and efficiently, we know that we will obtain a fair return on these investments.

MidAmerican, 89.8% owned by Berkshire, supplies 2.5 million customers in the U.S. with electricity, operating as the largest supplier in Iowa, Utah and Wyoming and as an important provider in six other states as well. Our pipelines transport 8% of the country's natural gas. Obviously, many millions of Americans depend on us every day. They haven't been disappointed.

When MidAmerican purchased Northern Natural Gas pipeline in 2002, that company's performance as a pipeline was rated dead last, 43 out of 43, by the leading authority in the field. In the most recent report, Northern Natural was ranked second. The top spot was held by our other pipeline, Kern River.

In its electric business, MidAmerican has a comparable record. In the most recent survey of customer satisfaction, MidAmerican's U.S. utilities ranked second among 60 utility groups surveyed. The story was far different not many years back when MidAmerican acquired these properties.

MidAmerican will have 3,316 megawatts of wind generation in operation by the end of 2012, far more than any other regulated electric utility in the country. The total amount that we have invested or committed to wind is a staggering $6 billion. We can make this sort of investment because MidAmerican retains *all* of its earnings, unlike other utilities that generally pay out most of what they earn. In addition, late last year we took on two solar projects – one 100%-owned in California and the other 49%-owned in Arizona – that will cost about $3 billion to construct. Many more wind and solar projects will almost certainly follow.

As you can tell by now, I am proud of what has been accomplished for our society by Matt Rose at BNSF and by Greg Abel at MidAmerican. I am also both proud and grateful for what they have accomplished for Berkshire shareholders. Below are the relevant figures:

MidAmerican	Earnings (in millions)	
	_2011_	_2010_
U.K. utilities	$ 469	$ 333
Iowa utility	279	279
Western utilities	771	783
Pipelines	388	378
HomeServices	39	42
Other (net)	36	47
Operating earnings before corporate interest and taxes	1,982	1,862
Interest, other than to Berkshire	(323)	(323)
Interest on Berkshire junior debt	(13)	(30)
Income tax	(315)	(271)
Net earnings	$1,331	$1,238
Earnings applicable to Berkshire*	$1,204	$1,131

*Includes interest earned by Berkshire (net of related income taxes) of $8 in 2011 and $19 in 2010.

BNSF (Historical accounting through 2/12/10; purchase accounting subsequently)	(in millions)	
	_2011_	_2010_
Revenues	$19,548	$16,850
Operating earnings	5,310	4,495
Interest (Net)	560	507
Pre-Tax earnings	4,741	3,988
Net earnings	2,972	2,459

In the book value recorded on our balance sheet, BNSF and MidAmerican carry substantial goodwill components totaling $20 billion. In each instance, however, Charlie and I believe current intrinsic value is far greater than book value.

Manufacturing, Service and Retailing Operations

Our activities in this part of Berkshire cover the waterfront. Let's look, though, at a summary balance sheet and earnings statement for the entire group.

Balance Sheet 12/31/11 (in millions)

Assets		Liabilities and Equity	
Cash and equivalents	$ 4,241	Notes payable	$ 1,611
Accounts and notes receivable	6,584	Other current liabilities	15,124
Inventory	8,975	Total current liabilities	16,735
Other current assets	631		
Total current assets	20,431		
		Deferred taxes	4,661
Goodwill and other intangibles	24,755	Term debt and other liabilities	6,214
Fixed assets	17,866	Non-controlling interests	2,410
Other assets	3,661	Berkshire equity	36,693
	$66,713		$66,713

Earnings Statement (in millions)

	2011**	2010	2009
Revenues	$72,406	$66,610	$61,665
Operating expenses (including depreciation of $1,431 in 2011, $1,362 in 2010 and $1,422 in 2009)	67,239	62,225	59,509
Interest expense	130	111	98
Pre-tax earnings	5,037*	4,274*	2,058*
Income taxes and non-controlling interests	1,998	1,812	945
Net earnings	$ 3,039	$ 2,462	$ 1,113

*Does not include purchase-accounting adjustments.
**Includes earnings of Lubrizol from September 16.

This group of companies sells products ranging from lollipops to jet airplanes. Some of the businesses enjoy terrific economics, measured by earnings on unleveraged net *tangible* assets that run from 25% after-tax to more than 100%. Others produce good returns in the area of 12-20%. A few, however, have very poor returns, a result of some serious mistakes I made in my job of capital allocation. These errors came about because I misjudged either the competitive strength of the business being purchased or the future economics of the industry in which it operated. I try to look out ten or twenty years when making an acquisition, but sometimes my eyesight has been poor. Charlie's has been better; he voted no more than "present" on several of my errant purchases.

Berkshire's newer shareholders may be puzzled over our decision to hold on to my mistakes. After all, their earnings can never be consequential to Berkshire's valuation, and problem companies require more managerial time than winners. Any management consultant or Wall Street advisor would look at our laggards and say "dump them."

That won't happen. For 29 years, we have regularly laid out Berkshire's economic principles in these reports (pages 93-98) and Number 11 describes our general reluctance to sell poor performers (which, in most cases, lag because of industry factors rather than managerial shortcomings). Our approach is far from Darwinian, and many of you may disapprove of it. I can understand your position. However, we have made – and continue to make – a commitment to the sellers of businesses we buy that we will retain those businesses through thick and thin. So far, the dollar cost of that commitment has not been substantial and may well be offset by the goodwill it builds among prospective sellers looking for the right permanent home for their treasured business and loyal associates. These owners know that what they get with us can't be delivered by others and that our commitments will be good for many decades to come.

Please understand, however, that Charlie and I are neither masochists nor Pollyannas. If either of the failings we set forth in Rule 11 is present – if the business will likely be a cash drain over the longer term, or if labor strife is endemic – we will take prompt and decisive action. Such a situation has happened only a couple of times in our 47-year history, and none of the businesses we now own is in straits requiring us to consider disposing of it.

* * * * * * * * * * * *

The steady and substantial comeback in the U.S. economy since mid-2009 is clear from the earnings shown at the front of this section. This compilation includes 54 of our companies. But one of these, Marmon, is itself the owner of 140 operations in eleven distinct business sectors. In short, when you look at Berkshire, you are looking across corporate America. So let's dig a little deeper to gain a greater insight into what has happened in the last few years.

The four housing-related companies in this section (a group that excludes Clayton, which is carried under Finance and Financial Products) had aggregate pre-tax earnings of $227 million in 2009, $362 million in 2010 and $359 million in 2011. If you subtract these earnings from those in the combined statement, you will see that our multiple and diverse *non-housing* operations earned $1,831 million in 2009, $3,912 million in 2010 and $4,678 million in 2011. About $291 million of the 2011 earnings came from the Lubrizol acquisition. The profile of the remaining 2011 earnings – $4,387 million – illustrates the comeback of much of America from the devastation wrought by the 2008 financial panic. Though housing-related businesses remain in the emergency room, most other businesses have left the hospital with their health fully restored.

* * * * * * * * * * * *

Almost all of our managers delivered outstanding performances last year, among them those managers who run housing-related businesses and were therefore fighting hurricane-force headwinds. Here are a few examples:

- Vic Mancinelli again set a record at CTB, our agricultural equipment operation. We purchased CTB in 2002 for $139 million. It has subsequently distributed $180 million to Berkshire, last year earned $124 million pre-tax and has $109 million in cash. Vic has made a number of bolt-on acquisitions over the years, including a meaningful one he signed up after yearend.

- TTI, our electric components distributor, increased its sales to a record $2.1 billion, up 12.4% from 2010. Earnings also hit a record, up 127% from 2007, the year in which we purchased the business. In 2011, TTI performed far better than the large publicly-traded companies in its field. That's no surprise: Paul Andrews and his associates have been besting them for years. Charlie and I are delighted that Paul negotiated a large bolt-on acquisition early in 2012. We hope more follow.

- Iscar, our 80%-owned cutting-tools operation, continues to amaze us. Its sales growth and overall performance are unique in its industry. Iscar's managers – Eitan Wertheimer, Jacob Harpaz and Danny Goldman – are brilliant strategists and operators. When the economic world was cratering in November 2008, they stepped up to buy Tungaloy, a leading Japanese cutting-tool manufacturer. Tungaloy suffered significant damage when the tsunami hit north of Tokyo last spring. But you wouldn't know that now: Tungaloy went on to set a sales record in 2011. I visited the Iwaki plant in November and was inspired by the dedication and enthusiasm of Tungaloy's management, as well as its staff. They are a wonderful group and deserve your admiration and thanks.

- McLane, our huge distribution company that is run by Grady Rosier, added important new customers in 2011 and set a pre-tax earnings record of $370 million. Since its purchase in 2003 for $1.5 billion, the company has had pre-tax earnings of $2.4 billion and also increased its LIFO reserve by $230 million because the prices of the retail products it distributes (candy, gum, cigarettes, etc.) have risen. Grady runs a logistical machine second to none. You can look for bolt-ons at McLane, particularly in our new wine-and-spirits distribution business.

- Jordan Hansell took over at NetJets in April and delivered 2011 pre-tax earnings of $227 million. That is a particularly impressive performance because the sale of new planes was slow during most of the year. In December, however, there was an uptick that was more than seasonally normal. How permanent it will be is uncertain.

  A few years ago NetJets was my number one worry: Its costs were far out of line with revenues, and cash was hemorrhaging. Without Berkshire's support, NetJets would have gone broke. These problems are behind us, and Jordan is now delivering steady profits from a well-controlled and smoothly-running operation. NetJets is proceeding on a plan to enter China with some first-class partners, a move that will widen our business "moat." No other fractional-ownership operator has remotely the size and breadth of the NetJets operation, and none ever will. NetJets' unrelenting focus on safety and service has paid off in the marketplace.

- It's a joy to watch Marmon's progress under Frank Ptak's leadership. In addition to achieving internal growth, Frank regularly makes bolt-on acquisitions that, in aggregate, will materially increase Marmon's earning power. (He did three, costing about $270 million, in the last few months.) Joint ventures around the world are another opportunity for Marmon. At midyear Marmon partnered with the Kundalia family in an Indian crane operation that is already delivering substantial profits. This is Marmon's second venture with the family, following a successful wire and cable partnership instituted a few years ago.

  Of the eleven major sectors in which Marmon operates, ten delivered gains in earnings last year. You can be confident of higher earnings from Marmon in the years ahead.

- "Buy commodities, sell brands" has long been a formula for business success. It has produced enormous and sustained profits for Coca-Cola since 1886 and Wrigley since 1891. On a smaller scale, we have enjoyed good fortune with this approach at See's Candy since we purchased it 40 years ago.

  Last year See's had record pre-tax earnings of $83 million, bringing its total since we bought it to $1.65 billion. Contrast that figure with our purchase price of $25 million and our yearend carrying-value (net of cash) of less than zero. (Yes, you read that right; capital employed at See's fluctuates seasonally, hitting a low after Christmas.) Credit Brad Kinstler for taking the company to new heights since he became CEO in 2006.

- Nebraska Furniture Mart (80% owned) set an earnings record in 2011, netting more than ten times what it did in 1983, when we acquired our stake.

  But that's not the big news. More important was NFM's acquisition of a 433-acre tract north of Dallas on which we will build what is almost certain to be the highest-volume home-furnishings store in the country. Currently, that title is shared by our two stores in Omaha and Kansas City, each of which had record-setting sales of more than $400 million in 2011. It will be several years before the Texas store is completed, but I look forward to cutting the ribbon at the opening. (At Berkshire, the managers do the work; I take the bows.)

  Our new store, which will offer an unequalled variety of merchandise sold at prices that can't be matched, will bring huge crowds from near and far. This drawing power and our extensive holdings of land at the site should enable us to attract a number of other major stores. (If any high-volume retailers are reading this, contact me.)

  Our experience with NFM and the Blumkin family that runs it has been a real joy. The business was built by Rose Blumkin (known to all as "Mrs. B"), who started the company in 1937 with $500 and a dream. She sold me our interest when she was 89 and worked until she was 103. (After retiring, she died the next year, a sequence I point out to any other Berkshire manager who even thinks of retiring.)

  Mrs. B's son, Louie, now 92, helped his mother build the business after he returned from World War II and, along with his wife, Fran, has been my friend for 55 years. In turn, Louie's sons, Ron and Irv, have taken the company to new heights, first opening the Kansas City store and now gearing up for Texas.

The "boys" and I have had many great times together, and I count them among my best friends. The Blumkins are a remarkable family. Never inclined to let an extraordinary gene pool go to waste, I am rejoicing these days because several members of the fourth Blumkin generation have joined NFM.

Overall, the intrinsic value of the businesses in this Berkshire sector significantly exceeds their book value. For many of the smaller companies, however, this is not true. I have made more than my share of mistakes buying small companies. Charlie long ago told me, "If something's not worth doing at all, it's not worth doing well," and I should have listened harder. In any event, our large purchases have generally worked well – extraordinarily well in a few cases – and overall this sector is a winner for us.

* * * * * * * * * * * *

Certain shareholders have told me they hunger for more discussions of accounting arcana. So here's a bit of GAAP-mandated nonsense I hope both of them enjoy.

Common sense would tell you that our varied subsidiaries should be carried on our books at their cost plus the earnings they have retained since our purchase (unless their economic value has materially decreased, in which case an appropriate write-down must be taken). And that's essentially the reality at Berkshire – except for the weird situation at Marmon.

We purchased 64% of the company in 2008 and put this interest on our books at our cost, $4.8 billion. So far, so good. Then, in early 2011, pursuant to our original contract with the Pritzker family, we purchased an additional 16%, paying $1.5 billion as called for by a formula that reflected Marmon's increased value. In this instance, however, we were required to immediately write off $614 million of the purchase price retroactive to the end of 2010. (Don't ask!) Obviously, this write-off had no connection to economic reality. The excess of Marmon's intrinsic value over its carrying value is widened by this meaningless write-down.

Finance and Financial Products

This sector, our smallest, includes two rental companies, XTRA (trailers) and CORT (furniture), and Clayton Homes, the country's leading producer and financer of manufactured homes. Aside from these 100%-owned subsidiaries, we also include in this category a collection of financial assets and our 50% interest in Berkadia Commercial Mortgage.

It's instructive to look at what transpired at our three operating businesses after the economy fell off a cliff in late 2008, because their experiences illuminate the fractured recovery that later came along.

Results at our two leasing companies mirrored the "non-housing" economy. Their combined pre-tax earnings were $13 million in 2009, $53 million in 2010 and $155 million in 2011, an improvement reflecting the steady recovery we have seen in almost all of our non-housing businesses. In contrast, Clayton's world of manufactured housing (just like site-built housing) has endured a veritable depression, experiencing no recovery to date. Manufactured housing sales in the nation were 49,789 homes in 2009, 50,046 in 2010 and 51,606 in 2011. (When housing was booming in 2005, they were 146,744.)

Despite these difficult times, Clayton has continued to operate profitably, largely because its mortgage portfolio has performed well under trying circumstances. Because we are the largest lender in the manufactured homes sector and are also normally lending to lower-and-middle-income families, you might expect us to suffer heavy losses during a housing meltdown. But by sticking to old-fashioned loan policies – meaningful down payments and monthly payments with a sensible relationship to regular income – Clayton has kept losses to acceptable levels. It has done so even though many of our borrowers have had negative equity for some time.

As is well-known, the U.S. went off the rails in its home-ownership and mortgage-lending policies, and for these mistakes our economy is now paying a huge price. All of us participated in the destructive behavior – government, lenders, borrowers, the media, rating agencies, you name it. At the core of the folly was the almost universal belief that the value of houses was certain to increase over time and that any dips would be inconsequential. The acceptance of this premise justified almost any price and practice in housing transactions. Homeowners everywhere felt richer and rushed to "monetize" the increased value of their homes by refinancings. These massive cash infusions fueled a consumption binge throughout our economy. It all seemed great fun while it lasted. (A largely unnoted fact: Large numbers of people who have "lost" their house through foreclosure have actually realized a profit because they carried out refinancings earlier that gave them cash in excess of their cost. In these cases, the evicted homeowner was the winner, and the victim was the lender.)

In 2007, the bubble burst, just as all bubbles must. We are now in the fourth year of a cure that, though long and painful, is sure to succeed. Today, household formations are consistently exceeding housing starts.

Clayton's earnings should improve materially when the nation's excess housing inventory is worked off. As I see things today, however, I believe the intrinsic value of the three businesses in this sector does not differ materially from their book value.

Investments

Below we show our common stock investments that at yearend had a market value of more than $1 billion.

| | | | 12/31/11 | |
Shares	Company	Percentage of Company Owned	Cost*	Market
			(in millions)	
151,610,700	American Express Company	13.0	$ 1,287	$ 7,151
200,000,000	The Coca-Cola Company	8.8	1,299	13,994
29,100,937	ConocoPhillips	2.3	2,027	2,121
63,905,931	International Business Machines Corp.	5.5	10,856	11,751
31,416,127	Johnson & Johnson	1.2	1,880	2,060
79,034,713	Kraft Foods Inc.	4.5	2,589	2,953
20,060,390	Munich Re	11.3	2,990	2,464
3,947,555	POSCO	5.1	768	1,301
72,391,036	The Procter & Gamble Company	2.6	464	4,829
25,848,838	Sanofi	1.9	2,055	1,900
291,577,428	Tesco plc	3.6	1,719	1,827
78,060,769	U.S. Bancorp	4.1	2,401	2,112
39,037,142	Wal-Mart Stores, Inc.	1.1	1,893	2,333
400,015,828	Wells Fargo & Company	7.6	9,086	11,024
	Others		6,895	9,171
	Total Common Stocks Carried at Market		$48,209	$76,991

*This is our actual purchase price and also our tax basis; GAAP "cost" differs in a few cases because of write-ups or write-downs that have been required.

We made few changes in our investment holdings during 2011. But three moves were important: our purchases of IBM and Bank of America and the $1 billion addition we made to our Wells Fargo position.

The banking industry is back on its feet, and Wells Fargo is prospering. Its earnings are strong, its assets solid and its capital at record levels. At Bank of America, some huge mistakes were made by prior management. Brian Moynihan has made excellent progress in cleaning these up, though the completion of that process will take a number of years. Concurrently, he is nurturing a huge and attractive underlying business that will endure long after today's problems are forgotten. Our warrants to buy 700 million Bank of America shares will likely be of great value before they expire.

As was the case with Coca-Cola in 1988 and the railroads in 2006, I was late to the IBM party. I have been reading the company's annual report for more than 50 years, but it wasn't until a Saturday in March last year that my thinking crystallized. As Thoreau said, "It's not what you look at that matters, it's what you see."

Todd Combs built a $1.75 billion portfolio (at cost) last year, and Ted Weschler will soon create one of similar size. Each of them receives 80% of his performance compensation from his own results and 20% from his partner's. When our quarterly filings report relatively small holdings, these are not likely to be buys I made (though the media often overlook that point) but rather holdings denoting purchases by Todd or Ted.

One additional point about these two new arrivals. Both Ted and Todd will be helpful to the next CEO of Berkshire in making acquisitions. They have excellent "business minds" that grasp the economic forces likely to determine the future of a wide variety of businesses. They are aided in their thinking by an understanding of what is predictable and what is unknowable.

* * * * * * * * * * * *

There is little new to report on our derivatives positions, which we have described in detail in past reports. (Annual reports since 1977 are available at www.berkshirehathaway.com.) One important industry change, however, must be noted: Though our existing contracts have very minor collateral requirements, the rules have changed for new positions. Consequently, we will not be initiating any major derivatives positions. We shun contracts of any type that could require the instant posting of collateral. The possibility of some sudden and huge posting requirement – arising from an out-of-the-blue event such as a worldwide financial panic or massive terrorist attack – is inconsistent with our primary objectives of redundant liquidity and unquestioned financial strength.

Our insurance-like derivatives contracts, whereby we pay if various issues included in high-yield bond indices default, are coming to a close. The contracts that most exposed us to losses have already expired, and the remainder will terminate soon. In 2011, we paid out $86 million on two losses, bringing our total payments to $2.6 billion. We are almost certain to realize a final "underwriting profit" on this portfolio because the premiums we received were $3.4 billion, and our future losses are apt to be minor. In addition, we will have averaged about $2 billion of float over the five-year life of these contracts. This successful result during a time of great credit stress underscores the importance of obtaining a premium that is commensurate with the risk.

Charlie and I continue to believe that our equity-put positions will produce a significant profit, considering both the $4.2 billion of float we will have held for more than fifteen years and the $222 million profit we've already realized on contracts that we repurchased. At yearend, Berkshire's book value reflected a liability of $8.5 billion for the remaining contracts; if they had all come due at that time our payment would have been $6.2 billion.

The Basic Choices for Investors and the One We Strongly Prefer

Investing is often described as the process of laying out money now in the expectation of receiving more money in the future. At Berkshire we take a more demanding approach, defining investing as the transfer to others of purchasing power now with the reasoned expectation of receiving more purchasing power – *after taxes have been paid on nominal gains* – in the future. More succinctly, investing is forgoing consumption now in order to have the ability to consume more at a later date.

From our definition there flows an important corollary: The riskiness of an investment is *not* measured by beta (a Wall Street term encompassing volatility and often used in measuring risk) but rather by the probability – the *reasoned* probability – of that investment causing its owner a loss of purchasing-power over his contemplated holding period. Assets can fluctuate greatly in price and not be risky as long as they are reasonably certain to deliver increased purchasing power over their holding period. And as we will see, a non-fluctuating asset can be laden with risk.

Investment possibilities are both many and varied. There are three major categories, however, and it's important to understand the characteristics of each. So let's survey the field.

- Investments that are denominated in a given currency include money-market funds, bonds, mortgages, bank deposits, and other instruments. Most of these currency-based investments are thought of as "safe." In truth they are among the most dangerous of assets. Their beta may be zero, but their risk is huge.

Over the past century these instruments have destroyed the purchasing power of investors in many countries, even as the holders continued to receive timely payments of interest and principal. This ugly result, moreover, will forever recur. Governments determine the ultimate value of money, and systemic forces will sometimes cause them to gravitate to policies that produce inflation. From time to time such policies spin out of control.

Even in the U.S., where the wish for a stable currency is strong, the dollar has fallen a staggering 86% in value since 1965, when I took over management of Berkshire. It takes no less than $7 today to buy what $1 did at that time. Consequently, a tax-free institution would have needed 4.3% interest annually from bond investments over that period to simply maintain its purchasing power. Its managers would have been kidding themselves if they thought of *any* portion of that interest as "income."

For tax-paying investors like you and me, the picture has been far worse. During the same 47-year period, continuous rolling of U.S. Treasury bills produced 5.7% annually. That sounds satisfactory. But if an individual investor paid personal income taxes at a rate averaging 25%, this 5.7% return would have yielded *nothing* in the way of real income. This investor's visible income tax would have stripped him of 1.4 points of the stated yield, and the invisible inflation tax would have devoured the remaining 4.3 points. It's noteworthy that the implicit inflation "tax" was more than triple the explicit income tax that our investor probably thought of as his main burden. "In God We Trust" may be imprinted on our currency, but the hand that activates our government's printing press has been all too human.

High interest rates, of course, can compensate purchasers for the inflation risk they face with currency-based investments – and indeed, rates in the early 1980s did that job nicely. Current rates, however, do not come close to offsetting the purchasing-power risk that investors assume. Right now bonds should come with a warning label.

Under today's conditions, therefore, I do not like currency-based investments. Even so, Berkshire holds significant amounts of them, primarily of the short-term variety. At Berkshire the need for ample liquidity occupies center stage and will *never* be slighted, however inadequate rates may be. Accommodating this need, we primarily hold U.S. Treasury bills, the only investment that can be counted on for liquidity under the most chaotic of economic conditions. Our working level for liquidity is $20 billion; $10 billion is our absolute minimum.

Beyond the requirements that liquidity and regulators impose on us, we will purchase currency-related securities only if they offer the possibility of unusual gain – either because a particular credit is mispriced, as can occur in periodic junk-bond debacles, or because rates rise to a level that offers the possibility of realizing substantial capital gains on high-grade bonds when rates fall. Though we've exploited both opportunities in the past – and may do so again – we are now 180 degrees removed from such prospects. Today, a wry comment that Wall Streeter Shelby Cullom Davis made long ago seems apt: "Bonds promoted as offering risk-free returns are now priced to deliver return-free risk."

• The second major category of investments involves assets that will never produce anything, but that are purchased in the buyer's hope that someone else – who also knows that the assets will be forever unproductive – will pay more for them in the future. Tulips, of all things, briefly became a favorite of such buyers in the 17th century.

This type of investment requires an expanding pool of buyers, who, in turn, are enticed because they believe the buying pool will expand still further. Owners are *not* inspired by what the asset itself can produce – it will remain lifeless forever – but rather by the belief that others will desire it even more avidly in the future.

The major asset in this category is gold, currently a huge favorite of investors who fear almost all other assets, especially paper money (of whose value, as noted, they are right to be fearful). Gold, however, has two significant shortcomings, being neither of much use nor procreative. True, gold has some industrial and decorative utility, but the demand for these purposes is both limited and incapable of soaking up new production. Meanwhile, if you own one ounce of gold for an eternity, you will still own one ounce at its end.

What motivates most gold purchasers is their belief that the ranks of the fearful will grow. During the past decade that belief has proved correct. Beyond that, the rising price has on its own generated additional buying enthusiasm, attracting purchasers who see the rise as validating an investment thesis. As "bandwagon" investors join any party, they create their own truth – *for a while*.

Over the past 15 years, both Internet stocks and houses have demonstrated the extraordinary excesses that can be created by combining an initially sensible thesis with well-publicized rising prices. In these bubbles, an army of originally skeptical investors succumbed to the "proof" delivered by the market, and the pool of buyers – for a time – expanded sufficiently to keep the bandwagon rolling. But bubbles blown large enough inevitably pop. And then the old proverb is confirmed once again: "What the wise man does in the beginning, the fool does in the end."

Today the world's gold stock is about 170,000 metric tons. If all of this gold were melded together, it would form a cube of about 68 feet per side. (Picture it fitting comfortably within a baseball infield.) At $1,750 per ounce – gold's price as I write this – its value would be $9.6 trillion. Call this cube pile A.

Let's now create a pile B costing an equal amount. For that, we could buy *all* U.S. cropland (400 million acres with output of about $200 billion annually), plus 16 Exxon Mobils (the world's most profitable company, one earning more than $40 billion annually). After these purchases, we would have about $1 trillion left over for walking-around money (no sense feeling strapped after this buying binge). Can you imagine an investor with $9.6 trillion selecting pile A over pile B?

Beyond the staggering valuation given the existing stock of gold, current prices make today's annual production of gold command about $160 billion. Buyers – whether jewelry and industrial users, frightened individuals, or speculators – must continually absorb this additional supply to merely maintain an equilibrium at present prices.

A century from now the 400 million acres of farmland will have produced staggering amounts of corn, wheat, cotton, and other crops – and will continue to produce that valuable bounty, whatever the currency may be. Exxon Mobil will probably have delivered trillions of dollars in dividends to its owners and will also hold assets worth many more trillions (and, remember, you get *16* Exxons). The 170,000 tons of gold will be unchanged in size and still incapable of producing anything. You can fondle the cube, but it will not respond.

Admittedly, when people a century from now are fearful, it's likely many will still rush to gold. I'm confident, however, that the $9.6 trillion current valuation of pile A will compound over the century at a rate far inferior to that achieved by pile B.

• Our first two categories enjoy maximum popularity at peaks of fear: Terror over economic collapse drives individuals to currency-based assets, most particularly U.S. obligations, and fear of currency collapse fosters movement to sterile assets such as gold. We heard "cash is king" in late 2008, just when cash should have been deployed rather than held. Similarly, we heard "cash is trash" in the early 1980s just when fixed-dollar investments were at their most attractive level in memory. On those occasions, investors who required a supportive crowd paid dearly for that comfort.

My own preference – and you knew this was coming – is our third category: investment in productive assets, whether businesses, farms, or real estate. Ideally, these assets should have the ability in inflationary times to deliver output that will retain its purchasing-power value while requiring a minimum of new capital investment. Farms, real estate, and many businesses such as Coca-Cola, IBM and our own See's Candy meet that double-barreled test. Certain other companies – think of our regulated utilities, for example – fail it because inflation places heavy capital requirements on them. To earn more, their owners must invest more. Even so, these investments will remain superior to nonproductive or currency-based assets.

Whether the currency a century from now is based on gold, seashells, shark teeth, or a piece of paper (as today), people will be willing to exchange a couple of minutes of their daily labor for a Coca-Cola or some See's peanut brittle. In the future the U.S. population will move more goods, consume more food, and require more living space than it does now. People will forever exchange what they produce for what others produce.

Our country's businesses will continue to efficiently deliver goods and services wanted by our citizens. Metaphorically, these commercial "cows" will live for centuries and give ever greater quantities of "milk" to boot. Their value will be determined not by the medium of exchange but rather by their capacity to deliver milk. Proceeds from the sale of the milk will compound for the owners of the cows, just as they did during the 20th century when the Dow increased from 66 to 11,497 (and paid loads of dividends as well). Berkshire's goal will be to increase its ownership of first-class businesses. Our first choice will be to own them in their entirety – but we will also be owners by way of holding sizable amounts of marketable stocks. I believe that over any extended period of time this category of investing will prove to be the runaway winner among the three we've examined. More important, it will be *by far* the safest.

The Annual Meeting

The annual meeting will be held on Saturday, May 5th at the CenturyLink Center (renamed from "Qwest"). Last year, Carrie Kizer debuted as the ringmaster and earned a lifetime assignment. Everyone loved the job she did – especially me.

Soon after the 7 a.m. opening of the doors, we will have a new activity: The Newspaper Tossing Challenge. Late last year, Berkshire purchased the Omaha World-Herald and, in my meeting with its shareholder-employees, I told of the folding and throwing skills I developed while delivering 500,000 papers as a teenager.

I immediately saw skepticism in the eyes of the audience. That was no surprise to me. After all, the reporters' mantra is: "If your mother says she loves you, check it out." So now I have to back up my claim. At the meeting, I will take on all comers in making 35-foot tosses of the World-Herald to a Clayton porch. Any challenger whose paper lands closer to the doorstep than mine will receive a dilly bar. I've asked Dairy Queen to supply several for the contest, though I doubt that any will be needed. We will have a large stack of papers. Grab one. Fold it (no rubber bands). Take your best shot. Make my day.

At 8:30, a new Berkshire movie will be shown. An hour later, we will start the question-and-answer period, which (with a break for lunch at the CenturyLink's stands) will last until 3:30. After a short recess, Charlie and I will convene the annual meeting at 3:45. If you decide to leave during the day's question periods, please do so while *Charlie* is talking.

The best reason to exit, of course, is to *shop*. We will help you do so by filling the 194,300-square-foot hall that adjoins the meeting area with products from dozens of Berkshire subsidiaries. Last year, you did your part, and most locations racked up record sales. In a nine-hour period, we sold 1,249 pairs of Justin boots, 11,254 pounds of See's candy, 8,000 Quikut knives (that's 15 knives per minute) and 6,126 pairs of Wells Lamont gloves, a Marmon product whose very existence was news to me. (The product I focus on is money.) But you can do better. Remember: Anyone who says money can't buy happiness simply hasn't shopped at our meeting.

Among the new exhibitors this year will be Brooks, our running-shoe company. Brooks has been gobbling up market share and in 2011 had a sales gain of 34%, its tenth consecutive year of record volume. Drop by and congratulate Jim Weber, the company's CEO. And be sure to buy a couple of pairs of limited edition "Berkshire Hathaway Running Shoes."

GEICO will have a booth staffed by a number of its top counselors from around the country, all of them ready to supply you with auto insurance quotes. In most cases, GEICO will be able to give you a shareholder discount (usually 8%). This special offer is permitted by 44 of the 51 jurisdictions in which we operate. (One supplemental point: The discount is not additive if you qualify for another, such as that given certain groups.) Bring the details of your existing insurance and check out whether we can save you money. For at least half of you, I believe we can.

Be sure to visit the Bookworm. It will carry more than 35 books and DVDs, including a couple of new ones. I recommend *MiTek*, an informative history of one of our very successful subsidiaries. You'll learn how my interest in the company was originally piqued by my receiving in the mail a hunk of ugly metal whose purpose I couldn't fathom. Since we bought MiTek in 2001, it has made 33 "tuck-in" acquisitions, almost all successful. I think you'll also like a short book that Peter Bevelin has put together explaining Berkshire's investment and operating principles. It sums up what Charlie and I have been saying over the years in annual reports and at annual meetings. Should you need to ship your book purchases, a shipping service will be available nearby.

If you are a big spender – or aspire to become one – visit Elliott Aviation on the east side of the Omaha airport between noon and 5:00 p.m. on Saturday. There we will have a fleet of NetJets aircraft that will get your pulse racing. Come by bus; leave by private jet. I'll OK your credit.

An attachment to the proxy material that is enclosed with this report explains how you can obtain the credential you will need for admission to the meeting and other events. Airlines have sometimes jacked up prices for the Berkshire weekend. If you are coming from far away, compare the cost of flying to Kansas City versus Omaha. The drive between the two cities is about 2½ hours, and it may be that you can save significant money, particularly if you had planned to rent a car in Omaha. Spend the savings with us.

At Nebraska Furniture Mart, located on a 77-acre site on 72nd Street between Dodge and Pacific, we will again be having "Berkshire Weekend" discount pricing. Last year the store did $32.7 million of business during its annual meeting sale, a volume that exceeds the yearly sales of most furniture stores. To obtain the Berkshire discount, you must make your purchases between Tuesday, May 1st and Monday, May 7th inclusive, and also present your meeting credential. The period's special pricing will even apply to the products of several prestigious manufacturers that normally have ironclad rules against discounting but which, in the spirit of our shareholder weekend, have made an exception for you. We appreciate their cooperation. NFM is open from 10 a.m. to 9 p.m. Monday through Saturday, and 10 a.m. to 6 p.m. on Sunday. On Saturday this year, from 5:30 p.m. to 8 p.m., NFM is having a picnic to which you are all invited.

At Borsheims, we will again have two shareholder-only events. The first will be a cocktail reception from 6 p.m. to 9 p.m. on Friday, May 4th. The second, the main gala, will be held on Sunday, May 6th, from 9 a.m. to 4 p.m. On Saturday, we will be open until 6 p.m. On Sunday, around 2 p.m., I will be clerking at Borsheims, desperate to beat my sales figure from last year. So come take advantage of me. Ask me for my "Crazy Warren" price.

We will have huge crowds at Borsheims throughout the weekend. For your convenience, therefore, shareholder prices will be available from Monday, April 30th through Saturday, May 12th. During that period, please identify yourself as a shareholder by presenting your meeting credentials or a brokerage statement that shows you are a Berkshire holder.

On Sunday, in the mall outside of Borsheims, a blindfolded Patrick Wolff, twice U.S. chess champion, will take on all comers – who will have their eyes wide open – in groups of six. Nearby, Norman Beck, a remarkable magician from Dallas, will bewilder onlookers. Additionally, we will have Bob Hamman and Sharon Osberg, two of the world's top bridge experts, available to play bridge with our shareholders on Sunday afternoon. Two non-experts – Charlie and I – will also be at the tables.

Gorat's and Piccolo's will again be open exclusively for Berkshire shareholders on Sunday, May 6th. Both will be serving until 10 p.m., with Gorat's opening at 1 p.m. and Piccolo's opening at 4 p.m. These restaurants are my favorites, and I will eat at both of them on Sunday evening. (Actuarial tables tell me that I can consume another 12 million calories before my death. I'm terrified at the thought of leaving any of these behind, so will be frontloading on Sunday.) Remember: To make a reservation at Gorat's, call 402-551-3733 on April 1st (*but not before*) and at Piccolo's, call 402-342-9038. At Piccolo's, show some class and order a giant root beer float for dessert. Only sissies get the small one.

We will again have the same three financial journalists lead the question-and-answer period at the meeting, asking Charlie and me questions that shareholders have submitted to them by e-mail. The journalists and their e-mail addresses are: Carol Loomis, of Fortune, who may be e-mailed at cloomis@fortunemail.com; Becky Quick, of CNBC, at BerkshireQuestions@cnbc.com, and Andrew Ross Sorkin, of The New York Times, at arsorkin@nytimes.com.

From the questions submitted, each journalist will choose the dozen or so he or she decides are the most interesting and important. The journalists have told me your question has the best chance of being selected if you keep it concise, avoid sending it in at the last moment, make it Berkshire-related and include no more than two questions in any e-mail you send them. (In your e-mail, let the journalist know if you would like your name mentioned if your question is selected.)

This year we are adding a second panel of three financial analysts who follow Berkshire. They are Cliff Gallant of KBW, Jay Gelb of Barclays Capital and Gary Ransom of Dowling and Partners. These analysts will bring their own Berkshire-specific questions and alternate with the journalists and the audience.

Charlie and I believe that all shareholders should have access to new Berkshire information simultaneously and should also have adequate time to analyze it, which is why we try to issue financial information after the market close on a Friday. We do not talk one-on-one to large institutional investors or analysts. Our new panel will let analysts ask questions – perhaps even a few technical ones – in a manner that may be helpful to many shareholders.

Neither Charlie nor I will get so much as a clue about the questions to be asked. We know the journalists and analysts will come up with some tough ones, and that's the way we like it. All told, we expect at least 54 questions, which will allow for six from each analyst and journalist and 18 from the audience. If there is some extra time, we will take more from the audience. Audience questioners will be determined by drawings that will take place at 8:15 a.m. at each of the 13 microphones located in the arena and main overflow room.

* * * * * * * * * * * *

For good reason, I regularly extol the accomplishments of our operating managers. They are truly All-Stars, who run their businesses as if they were the only asset owned by their families. I believe their mindset to be as shareholder-oriented as can be found in the universe of large publicly-owned companies. Most have no financial need to work; the joy of hitting business "home runs" means as much to them as their paycheck.

Equally important, however, are the 23 men and women who work with me at our corporate office (all on one floor, which is the way we intend to keep it!).

This group efficiently deals with a multitude of SEC and other regulatory requirements and files a 17,839-page Federal income tax return – hello, Guinness! – as well as state and foreign returns. Additionally, they respond to countless shareholder and media inquiries, get out the annual report, prepare for the country's largest annual meeting, coordinate the Board's activities – and the list goes on and on.

They handle all of these business tasks cheerfully and with unbelievable efficiency, making my life easy and pleasant. Their efforts go beyond activities strictly related to Berkshire: They deal with 48 universities (selected from 200 applicants) who will send students to Omaha this school year for a day with me and also handle all kinds of requests that I receive, arrange my travel, and even get me hamburgers for lunch. No CEO has it better.

This home office crew, along with our operating managers, has my deepest thanks and deserves yours as well. Come to Omaha – the cradle of capitalism – on May 5th and tell them so.

February 25, 2012   Warren E. Buffett
                                                     Chairman of the Board

BERKSHIRE HATHAWAY INC.

To the Shareholders of Berkshire Hathaway Inc.:

In 2012, Berkshire achieved a total gain for its shareholders of $24.1 billion. We used $1.3 billion of that to repurchase our stock, which left us with an increase in net worth of $22.8 billion for the year. The per-share book value of both our Class A and Class B stock increased by 14.4%. Over the last 48 years (that is, since present management took over), book value has grown from $19 to $114,214, a rate of 19.7% compounded annually.*

A number of good things happened at Berkshire last year, but let's first get the bad news out of the way.

- When the partnership I ran took control of Berkshire in 1965, I could never have dreamed that a year in which we had a gain of $24.1 billion would be subpar, in terms of the comparison we present on the facing page.

  But subpar it was. For the ninth time in 48 years, Berkshire's percentage increase in book value was less than the S&P's percentage gain (a calculation that includes dividends as well as price appreciation). In eight of those nine years, it should be noted, the S&P had a gain of 15% or more. We do better when the wind is in our face.

  To date, we've never had a five-year period of underperformance, having managed 43 times to surpass the S&P over such a stretch. (The record is on page 103.) But the S&P has now had gains in each of the last four years, outpacing us over that period. If the market continues to advance in 2013, our streak of five-year wins will end.

  One thing of which you can be certain: Whatever Berkshire's results, my partner Charlie Munger, the company's Vice Chairman, and I will not change yardsticks. It's our *job* to increase intrinsic business value – for which we use book value as a *significantly understated* proxy – at a faster rate than the market gains of the S&P. If we do so, Berkshire's share price, though unpredictable from year to year, will itself outpace the S&P over time. If we fail, however, our management will bring no value to our investors, who themselves can earn S&P returns by buying a low-cost index fund.

  Charlie and I believe the gain in Berkshire's intrinsic value will over time likely surpass the S&P returns by a small margin. We're confident of that because we have some outstanding businesses, a cadre of terrific operating managers and a shareholder-oriented culture. Our relative performance, however, is almost certain to be better when the market is down or flat. In years when the market is particularly strong, expect us to fall short.

- The second disappointment in 2012 was my inability to make a major acquisition. I pursued a couple of elephants, but came up empty-handed.

---

* All per-share figures used in this report apply to Berkshire's A shares. Figures for the B shares are 1/1500th of those shown for A.

Our luck, however, changed early this year. In February, we agreed to buy 50% of a holding company that will own all of H. J. Heinz. The other half will be owned by a small group of investors led by Jorge Paulo Lemann, a renowned Brazilian businessman and philanthropist.

We couldn't be in better company. Jorge Paulo is a long-time friend of mine and an extraordinary manager. His group and Berkshire will each contribute about $4 billion for common equity in the holding company. Berkshire will also invest $8 billion in preferred shares that pay a 9% dividend. The preferred has two other features that materially increase its value: at some point it will be redeemed at a significant premium price and the preferred also comes with warrants permitting us to buy 5% of the holding company's common stock for a nominal sum.

Our total investment of about $12 billion soaks up much of what Berkshire earned last year. But we still have plenty of cash and are generating more at a good clip. So it's back to work; Charlie and I have again donned our safari outfits and resumed our search for elephants.

Now to some good news from 2012:

- Last year I told you that BNSF, Iscar, Lubrizol, Marmon Group and MidAmerican Energy – our five most profitable non-insurance companies – were likely to earn more than $10 billion pre-tax in 2012. They delivered. Despite tepid U.S. growth and weakening economies throughout much of the world, our "powerhouse five" had aggregate earnings of $10.1 billion, about $600 million more than in 2011.

  Of this group, only MidAmerican, then earning $393 million pre-tax, was owned by Berkshire eight years ago. Subsequently, we purchased another three of the five on an all-cash basis. In acquiring the fifth, BNSF, we paid about 70% of the cost in cash, and for the remainder, issued shares that increased the amount outstanding by 6.1%. Consequently, the $9.7 billion gain in annual earnings delivered Berkshire by the five companies has been accompanied by only minor dilution. That satisfies our goal of not simply growing, but rather increasing *per-share* results.

  Unless the U.S. economy tanks – which we don't expect – our powerhouse five should again deliver higher earnings in 2013. The five outstanding CEOs who run them will see to that.

- Though I failed to land a major acquisition in 2012, the managers of our subsidiaries did far better. We had a record year for "bolt-on" purchases, spending about $2.3 billion for 26 companies that were melded into our existing businesses. These transactions were completed without Berkshire issuing *any* shares.

  Charlie and I love these acquisitions: Usually they are low-risk, burden headquarters not at all, and expand the scope of our proven managers.

- Our insurance operations shot the lights out last year. While giving Berkshire $73 billion of *free* money to invest, they also delivered a $1.6 billion underwriting gain, the tenth consecutive year of profitable underwriting. This is truly having your cake and eating it too.

  GEICO led the way, continuing to gobble up market share without sacrificing underwriting discipline. Since 1995, when we obtained control, GEICO's share of the personal-auto market has grown from 2.5% to 9.7%. Premium volume meanwhile increased from $2.8 billion to $16.7 billion. Much more growth lies ahead.

  The credit for GEICO's extraordinary performance goes to Tony Nicely and his 27,000 associates. And to that cast, we should add our Gecko. Neither rain nor storm nor gloom of night can stop him; the little lizard just soldiers on, telling Americans how they can save big money by going to GEICO.com.

  When I count my blessings, I count GEICO twice.

- Todd Combs and Ted Weschler, our new investment managers, have proved to be smart, models of integrity, helpful to Berkshire in many ways beyond portfolio management, and a perfect cultural fit. We hit the jackpot with these two. In 2012 each outperformed the S&P 500 by double-digit margins. They left me in the dust as well.

  Consequently, we have increased the funds managed by each to almost $5 billion (some of this emanating from the pension funds of our subsidiaries). Todd and Ted are young and will be around to manage Berkshire's massive portfolio long after Charlie and I have left the scene. You can rest easy when they take over.

- Berkshire's yearend employment totaled a record 288,462 (see page 106 for details), up 17,604 from last year. Our headquarters crew, however, remained unchanged at 24. No sense going crazy.

- Berkshire's "Big Four" investments – American Express, Coca-Cola, IBM and Wells Fargo – all had good years. Our ownership interest in each of these companies increased during the year. We purchased additional shares of Wells Fargo (our ownership now is 8.7% versus 7.6% at yearend 2011) and IBM (6.0% versus 5.5%). Meanwhile, stock repurchases at Coca-Cola and American Express raised our percentage ownership. Our equity in Coca-Cola grew from 8.8% to 8.9% and our interest at American Express from 13.0% to 13.7%.

  Berkshire's ownership interest in all four companies is likely to increase in the future. Mae West had it right: "Too much of a good thing can be wonderful."

  The four companies possess marvelous businesses and are run by managers who are both talented and shareholder-oriented. At Berkshire we much prefer owning a non-controlling but substantial portion of a wonderful business to owning 100% of a so-so business. Our flexibility in capital allocation gives us a significant advantage over companies that limit themselves only to acquisitions they can operate.

  Going by our yearend share count, our portion of the "Big Four's" 2012 earnings amounted to $3.9 billion. In the earnings we report to you, however, we include only the dividends we receive – about $1.1 billion. But make no mistake: The $2.8 billion of earnings we do not report is every bit as valuable to us as what we record.

  The earnings that the four companies retain are often used for repurchases – which enhance our share of future earnings – and also for funding business opportunities that are usually advantageous. Over time we expect substantially greater earnings from these four investees. If we are correct, dividends to Berkshire will increase and, even more important, so will our unrealized capital gains (which, for the four, totaled $26.7 billion at yearend).

- There was a lot of hand-wringing last year among CEOs who cried "uncertainty" when faced with capital-allocation decisions (despite many of their businesses having enjoyed record levels of both earnings and cash). At Berkshire, we didn't share their fears, instead spending a record $9.8 billion on plant and equipment in 2012, about 88% of it in the United States. That's 19% more than we spent in 2011, our previous high. Charlie and I love investing large sums in worthwhile projects, whatever the pundits are saying. We instead heed the words from Gary Allan's new country song, "Every Storm Runs Out of Rain."

  We will keep our foot to the floor and will almost certainly set still another record for capital expenditures in 2013. Opportunities abound in America.

* * * * * * * * * * *

A thought for my fellow CEOs: Of course, the immediate future is uncertain; America has faced the unknown since 1776. It's just that sometimes people focus on the myriad of uncertainties that always exist while at other times they ignore them (usually because the recent past has been uneventful).

American business will do fine over time. And stocks will do well just as certainly, since their fate is tied to business performance. Periodic setbacks will occur, yes, but investors and managers are in a game that is heavily stacked in their favor. (The Dow Jones Industrials advanced from 66 to 11,497 in the 20th Century, a staggering 17,320% increase that materialized despite four costly wars, a Great Depression and many recessions. And don't forget that shareholders received substantial dividends throughout the century as well.)

Since the basic game is so favorable, Charlie and I believe it's a terrible mistake to try to dance in and out of it based upon the turn of tarot cards, the predictions of "experts," or the ebb and flow of business activity. The risks of being out of the game are huge compared to the risks of being in it.

My own history provides a dramatic example: I made my first stock purchase in the spring of 1942 when the U.S. was suffering major losses throughout the Pacific war zone. Each day's headlines told of more setbacks. Even so, there was no talk about uncertainty; *every* American I knew believed we would prevail.

The country's success since that perilous time boggles the mind: On an inflation-adjusted basis, GDP per capita more than *quadrupled* between 1941 and 2012. Throughout that period, *every* tomorrow has been uncertain. America's destiny, however, has always been clear: ever-increasing abundance.

If you are a CEO who has some large, profitable project you are shelving because of short-term worries, call Berkshire. Let us unburden you.

* * * * * * * * * * *

In summary, Charlie and I hope to build per-share intrinsic value by (1) improving the earning power of our many subsidiaries; (2) further increasing their earnings through bolt-on acquisitions; (3) participating in the growth of our investees; (4) repurchasing Berkshire shares when they are available at a meaningful discount from intrinsic value; and (5) making an occasional large acquisition. We will also try to maximize results for *you* by rarely, if ever, issuing Berkshire shares.

Those building blocks rest on a rock-solid foundation. A century hence, BNSF and MidAmerican Energy will continue to play major roles in the American economy. Insurance, moreover, will always be essential for both businesses and individuals – and no company brings greater resources to that arena than Berkshire. As we view these and other strengths, Charlie and I like your company's prospects.

Intrinsic Business Value

As much as Charlie and I talk about intrinsic business value, we cannot tell you precisely what that number is for Berkshire shares (or, for that matter, any other stock). In our 2010 annual report, however, we laid out the three elements – one of which was qualitative – that we believe are the keys to a sensible estimate of Berkshire's intrinsic value. That discussion is reproduced in full on pages 104-105.

Here is an update of the two quantitative factors: In 2012 our per-share investments increased 15.7% to $113,786, and our per-share pre-tax earnings from businesses other than insurance and investments also increased 15.7% to $8,085.

Since 1970, our per-share investments have increased at a rate of 19.4% compounded annually, and our per-share earnings figure has grown at a 20.8% clip. It is no coincidence that the price of Berkshire stock over the 42-year period has increased at a rate very similar to that of our two measures of value. Charlie and I like to see gains in both areas, but our strong emphasis will always be on building operating earnings.

* * * * * * * * * * *

Now, let's examine the four major sectors of our operations. Each has vastly different balance sheet and income characteristics from the others. Lumping them together therefore impedes analysis. So we'll present them as four separate businesses, which is how Charlie and I view them.

Insurance

Let's look first at insurance, Berkshire's core operation and the engine that has propelled our expansion over the years.

Property-casualty ("P/C") insurers receive premiums upfront and pay claims later. In extreme cases, such as those arising from certain workers' compensation accidents, payments can stretch over decades. This collect-now, pay-later model leaves us holding large sums – money we call "float" – that will eventually go to others. Meanwhile, we get to invest this float for Berkshire's benefit. Though individual policies and claims come and go, the amount of float we hold remains quite stable in relation to premium volume. Consequently, as our business grows, so does our float. And *how* we have grown, as the following table shows:

Year	Float (in $ millions)
1970	$ 39
1980	237
1990	1,632
2000	27,871
2010	65,832
2012	73,125

Last year I told you that our float was likely to level off or even decline a bit in the future. Our insurance CEOs set out to prove me wrong and *did*, increasing float last year by $2.5 billion. I now expect a further increase in 2013. But further gains will be tough to achieve. On the plus side, GEICO's float will almost certainly grow. In National Indemnity's reinsurance division, however, we have a number of run-off contracts whose float drifts downward. If we do experience a decline in float at some future time, it will be *very* gradual – at the outside no more than 2% in any year.

If our premiums exceed the total of our expenses and eventual losses, we register an underwriting profit that adds to the investment income our float produces. When such a profit is earned, we enjoy the use of free money – and, better yet, get *paid* for holding it. That's like your taking out a loan and having the bank pay *you* interest.

Unfortunately, the wish of all insurers to achieve this happy result creates intense competition, so vigorous in most years that it causes the P/C industry as a whole to operate at a significant underwriting *loss*. This loss, in effect, is what the industry pays to hold its float. For example, State Farm, by far the country's largest insurer and a well-managed company besides, incurred an underwriting loss in eight of the eleven years ending in 2011. (Their financials for 2012 are not yet available.) There are a lot of ways to lose money in insurance, and the industry never ceases searching for new ones.

As noted in the first section of this report, we have now operated at an underwriting profit for ten consecutive years, our pre-tax gain for the period having totaled $18.6 billion. Looking ahead, I believe we will continue to underwrite profitably in most years. If we do, our float will be better than free money.

So how does our attractive float affect the calculations of intrinsic value? When Berkshire's book value is calculated, the *full* amount of our float is deducted as a liability, just as if we had to pay it out tomorrow and were unable to replenish it. But that's an incorrect way to look at float, which should instead be viewed as a revolving fund. If float is both costless and long-enduring, which I believe Berkshire's will be, the true value of this liability is *dramatically* less than the accounting liability.

A partial offset to this overstated liability is $15.5 billion of "goodwill" that is attributable to our insurance companies and included in book value as an asset. In effect, this goodwill represents the price we paid for the float-generating capabilities of our insurance operations. The cost of the goodwill, however, has *no* bearing on its true value. For example, if an insurance business sustains large and prolonged underwriting losses, any goodwill asset carried on the books should be deemed valueless, whatever its original cost.

Fortunately, that's not the case at Berkshire. Charlie and I believe the true economic value of our insurance goodwill – what we would happily pay to purchase an insurance operation producing float *of similar quality* – to be far in excess of its historic carrying value. The value of our float is one reason – a huge reason – why we believe Berkshire's intrinsic business value substantially exceeds its book value.

Let me emphasize once again that cost-free float is *not* an outcome to be expected for the P/C industry as a whole: There is very little "Berkshire-quality" float existing in the insurance world. In 37 of the 45 years ending in 2011, the industry's premiums have been inadequate to cover claims plus expenses. Consequently, the industry's overall return on tangible equity has for many decades fallen far short of the average return realized by American industry, a sorry performance almost certain to continue.

A further unpleasant reality adds to the industry's dim prospects: Insurance earnings are now benefitting from "legacy" bond portfolios that deliver much higher yields than will be available when funds are reinvested during the next few years – and perhaps for many years beyond that. Today's bond portfolios are, in effect, wasting assets. Earnings of insurers will be hurt in a significant way as bonds mature and are rolled over.

* * * * * * * * * * *

Berkshire's outstanding economics exist only because we have some terrific managers running some extraordinary insurance operations. Let me tell you about the major units.

First by float size is the Berkshire Hathaway Reinsurance Group, run by Ajit Jain. Ajit insures risks that no one else has the desire or the capital to take on. His operation combines capacity, speed, decisiveness and, most important, brains in a manner unique in the insurance business. Yet he never exposes Berkshire to risks that are inappropriate in relation to our resources. Indeed, we are *far* more conservative in avoiding risk than most large insurers. For example, if the insurance industry should experience a $250 billion loss from some mega-catastrophe – a loss about triple anything it has ever experienced – Berkshire as a whole would likely record a significant profit for the year because it has so many streams of earnings. All other major insurers and reinsurers would meanwhile be far in the red, with some facing insolvency.

From a standing start in 1985, Ajit has created an insurance business with float of $35 billion and a significant cumulative underwriting profit, a feat that no other insurance CEO has come close to matching. He has thus added a great many billions of dollars to the value of Berkshire. If you meet Ajit at the annual meeting, bow deeply.

* * * * * * * * * * *

We have another reinsurance powerhouse in General Re, managed by Tad Montross.

At bottom, a sound insurance operation needs to adhere to four disciplines. It must (1) understand *all* exposures that might cause a policy to incur losses; (2) conservatively assess the likelihood of any exposure actually causing a loss and the probable cost if it does; (3) set a premium that, on average, will deliver a profit after both prospective loss costs and operating expenses are covered; and (4) be willing to walk away if the appropriate premium can't be obtained.

Many insurers pass the first three tests and flunk the fourth. They simply can't turn their back on business that is being eagerly written by their competitors. That old line, "The other guy is doing it, so we must as well," spells trouble in any business, but none more so than insurance.

Tad has observed all four of the insurance commandments, and it shows in his results. General Re's huge float has been better than cost-free under his leadership, and we expect that, on average, it will continue to be. We are particularly enthusiastic about General Re's international life reinsurance business, which has achieved consistent and profitable growth since we acquired the company in 1998.

* * * * * * * * * * * *

Finally, there is GEICO, the insurer on which I cut my teeth 62 years ago. GEICO is run by Tony Nicely, who joined the company at 18 and completed 51 years of service in 2012.

I rub my eyes when I look at what Tony has accomplished. Last year, it should be noted, his record was considerably better than is indicated by GEICO's GAAP underwriting profit of $680 million. Because of a change in accounting rules at the beginning of the year, we recorded a charge to GEICO's underwriting earnings of $410 million. This item had *nothing* to do with 2012's operating results, changing neither cash, revenues, expenses nor taxes. In effect, the writedown simply widened the already huge difference between GEICO's intrinsic value and the value at which we carry it on our books.

GEICO earned its underwriting profit, moreover, despite the company suffering its largest single loss in history. The cause was Hurricane Sandy, which cost GEICO more than three times the loss it sustained from Katrina, the previous record-holder. We insured 46,906 vehicles that were destroyed or damaged in the storm, a staggering number reflecting GEICO's leading market share in the New York metropolitan area.

Last year GEICO enjoyed a meaningful increase in both the renewal rate for existing policyholders ("persistency") and in the percentage of rate quotations that resulted in sales ("closures"). Big dollars ride on those two factors: A sustained gain in persistency of a bare one percentage point increases intrinsic value by more than $1 billion. GEICO's gains in 2012 offer dramatic proof that when people check the company's prices, they usually find they can save important sums. (Give us a try at 1-800-847-7536 or GEICO.com. Be sure to mention that you are a shareholder; that fact will usually result in a discount.)

* * * * * * * * * * * *

In addition to our three major insurance operations, we own a group of smaller companies, most of them plying their trade in odd corners of the insurance world. In aggregate, these companies have consistently delivered an underwriting profit. Moreover, as the table below shows, they also provide us with substantial float. Charlie and I treasure these companies and their managers.

Late in 2012, we enlarged this group by acquiring Guard Insurance, a Wilkes-Barre company that writes workers compensation insurance, primarily for smaller businesses. Guard's annual premiums total about $300 million. The company has excellent prospects for growth in both its traditional business and new lines it has begun to offer.

Insurance Operations	Underwriting Profit (in millions)		Yearend Float	
	2012	2011	2012	2011
BH Reinsurance	$ 304	$(714)	$34,821	$33,728
General Re	355	144	20,128	19,714
GEICO	680*	576	11,578	11,169
Other Primary	286	242	6,598	5,960
	$1,625	$ 248	$73,125	$70,571

*After a $410 million charge against earnings arising from an industry-wide accounting change.

Among large insurance operations, Berkshire's impresses me as the best in the world. It was our lucky day when, in March 1967, Jack Ringwalt sold us his two property-casualty insurers for $8.6 million.

Regulated, Capital-Intensive Businesses

We have two major operations, BNSF and MidAmerican Energy, that have important common characteristics distinguishing them from our other businesses. Consequently, we assign them their own section in this letter and split out their combined financial statistics in our GAAP balance sheet and income statement.

A key characteristic of both companies is their huge investment in very long-lived, regulated assets, with these partially funded by large amounts of long-term debt that is *not* guaranteed by Berkshire. Our credit is in fact not needed because each business has earning power that even under terrible conditions amply covers its interest requirements. In last year's tepid economy, for example, BNSF's interest coverage was 9.6x. (Our definition of coverage is pre-tax earnings/interest, *not* EBITDA/interest, a commonly-used measure we view as deeply flawed.) At MidAmerican, meanwhile, two key factors ensure its ability to service debt under all circumstances: the company's recession-resistant earnings, which result from our exclusively offering an essential service, and its great diversity of earnings streams, which shield it from being seriously harmed by any single regulatory body.

Every day, our two subsidiaries power the American economy in major ways:

- BNSF carries about 15% (measured by ton-miles) of *all* inter-city freight, whether it is transported by truck, rail, water, air, or pipeline. Indeed, we move more ton-miles of goods than *anyone* else, a fact making BNSF the most important artery in our economy's circulatory system.

  BNSF also moves its cargo in an extraordinarily fuel-efficient and environmentally friendly way, carrying a ton of freight about 500 miles on a single gallon of diesel fuel. Trucks taking on the same job guzzle about four times as much fuel.

- MidAmerican's electric utilities serve regulated retail customers in ten states. Only one utility holding company serves more states. In addition, we are the leader in renewables: first, from a standing start nine years ago, we now account for 6% of the country's wind generation capacity. Second, when we complete three projects now under construction, we will own about 14% of U.S. solar-generation capacity.

Projects like these require huge capital investments. Upon completion, indeed, our renewables portfolio will have cost $13 billion. We relish making such commitments if they promise reasonable returns – and on that front, we put a large amount of trust in future regulation.

Our confidence is justified both by our past experience and by the knowledge that society will forever need massive investment in both transportation and energy. It is in the self-interest of governments to treat capital providers in a manner that will ensure the continued flow of funds to essential projects. And it is in our self-interest to conduct our operations in a manner that earns the approval of our regulators and the people they represent.

Our managers must think today of what the country will need far down the road. Energy and transportation projects can take many years to come to fruition; a growing country simply can't afford to get behind the curve.

We have been doing our part to make sure that doesn't happen. Whatever you may have heard about our country's crumbling infrastructure in no way applies to BNSF or railroads generally. America's rail system has never been in better shape, a consequence of huge investments by the industry. We are not, however, resting on our laurels: BNSF will spend about $4 billion on the railroad in 2013, roughly double its depreciation charge and more than any railroad has spent in a single year.

In Matt Rose, at BNSF, and Greg Abel, at MidAmerican, we have two outstanding CEOs. They are extraordinary managers who have developed businesses that serve both their customers and owners well. Each has my gratitude and each deserves yours. Here are the key figures for their businesses:

MidAmerican (89.8% owned)	*Earnings (in millions)*	
	2012	*2011*
U.K. utilities	$ 429	$ 469
Iowa utility	236	279
Western utilities	737	771
Pipelines	383	388
HomeServices	82	39
Other (net)	91	36
Operating earnings before corporate interest and taxes	1,958	1,982
Interest	314	336
Income taxes	172	315
Net earnings	$ 1,472	$ 1,331
Earnings applicable to Berkshire	$ 1,323	$ 1,204

BNSF	*Earnings (in millions)*	
	2012	*2011*
Revenues	$20,835	$19,548
Operating expenses	14,835	14,247
Operating earnings before interest and taxes	6,000	5,301
Interest (net)	623	560
Income taxes	2,005	1,769
Net earnings	$ 3,372	$ 2,972

Sharp-eyed readers will notice an incongruity in the MidAmerican earnings tabulation. What in the world is HomeServices, a real estate brokerage operation, doing in a section entitled "Regulated, Capital-Intensive Businesses?"

Well, its ownership came with MidAmerican when we bought control of that company in 2000. At that time, I focused on MidAmerican's utility operations and barely noticed HomeServices, which then owned only a few real estate brokerage companies.

Since then, however, the company has regularly added residential brokers – three in 2012 – and now has about 16,000 agents in a string of major U.S. cities. (Our real estate brokerage companies are listed on page 107.) In 2012, our agents participated in $42 billion of home sales, up 33% from 2011.

Additionally, HomeServices last year purchased 67% of the Prudential and Real Living franchise operations, which together license 544 brokerage companies throughout the country and receive a small royalty on their sales. We have an arrangement to purchase the balance of those operations within five years. In the coming years, we will gradually rebrand both our franchisees and the franchise firms we own as Berkshire Hathaway HomeServices.

Ron Peltier has done an outstanding job in managing HomeServices during a depressed period. Now, as the housing market continues to strengthen, we expect earnings to rise significantly.

Manufacturing, Service and Retailing Operations

Our activities in this part of Berkshire cover the waterfront. Let's look, though, at a summary balance sheet and earnings statement for the entire group.

Balance Sheet 12/31/12 (in millions)

Assets		Liabilities and Equity	
Cash and equivalents	$ 5,338	Notes payable	$ 1,454
Accounts and notes receivable	7,382	Other current liabilities	8,527
Inventory	9,675	Total current liabilities	9,981
Other current assets	734		
Total current assets	23,129		
		Deferred taxes	4,907
Goodwill and other intangibles	26,017	Term debt and other liabilities	5,826
Fixed assets	18,871	Non-controlling interests	2,062
Other assets	3,416	Berkshire equity	48,657
	$71,433		$71,433

Earnings Statement (in millions)

	2012	2011*	2010
Revenues	$83,255	$72,406	$66,610
Operating expenses	76,978	67,239	62,225
Interest expense	146	130	111
Pre-tax earnings	6,131	5,037	4,274
Income taxes and non-controlling interests	2,432	1,998	1,812
Net earnings	$ 3,699	$ 3,039	$ 2,462

*Includes earnings of Lubrizol from September 16.

Our income and expense data conforming to Generally Accepted Accounting Principles ("GAAP") is on page 29. In contrast, the operating expense figures above are non-GAAP. In particular, they exclude some purchase-accounting items, primarily the amortization of certain intangible assets. We present the data in this manner because Charlie and I believe the adjusted numbers more accurately reflect the real expenses and profits of the businesses aggregated in the table.

I won't explain all of the adjustments – some are small and arcane – but serious investors should understand the disparate nature of intangible assets: Some truly deplete over time while others never lose value. With software, for example, amortization charges are very real expenses. Charges against other intangibles such as the amortization of customer relationships, however, arise through purchase-accounting rules and are clearly not real expenses. GAAP accounting draws no distinction between the two types of charges. Both, that is, are recorded as expenses when calculating earnings – even though from an investor's viewpoint they could not be more different.

In the GAAP-compliant figures we show on page 29, amortization charges of $600 million for the companies included in this section are deducted as expenses. We would call about 20% of these "real" – and indeed that is the portion we have included in the table above – and the rest not. This difference has become significant because of the many acquisitions we have made.

"Non-real" amortization expense also looms large at some of our major investees. IBM has made many small acquisitions in recent years and now regularly reports "adjusted operating earnings," a non-GAAP figure that excludes certain purchase-accounting adjustments. Analysts focus on this number, as they should.

A "non-real" amortization charge at Wells Fargo, however, is not highlighted by the company and never, to my knowledge, has been noted in analyst reports. The earnings that Wells Fargo reports are heavily burdened by an "amortization of core deposits" charge, the implication being that these deposits are disappearing at a fairly rapid clip. Yet core deposits regularly *increase*. The charge last year was about $1.5 billion. In *no* sense, except GAAP accounting, is this whopping charge an expense.

And that ends today's accounting lecture. Why is no one shouting "More, more?"

* * * * * * * * * * * *

The crowd of companies in this section sell products ranging from lollipops to jet airplanes. Some of the businesses enjoy terrific economics, measured by earnings on unleveraged net *tangible* assets that run from 25% after-tax to more than 100%. Others produce good returns in the area of 12-20%. A few, however, have very poor returns, a result of some serious mistakes I made in my job of capital allocation.

More than 50 years ago, Charlie told me that it was far better to buy a wonderful business at a fair price than to buy a fair business at a wonderful price. Despite the compelling logic of his position, I have sometimes reverted to my old habit of bargain-hunting, with results ranging from tolerable to terrible. Fortunately, my mistakes have usually occurred when I made smaller purchases. Our large acquisitions have generally worked out well and, in a few cases, more than well.

Viewed as a single entity, therefore, the companies in this group are an excellent business. They employ $22.6 billion of net tangible assets and, on that base, earned 16.3% after-tax.

Of course, a business with terrific economics can be a bad investment if the price paid is excessive. We have paid substantial premiums to net tangible assets for most of our businesses, a cost that is reflected in the large figure we show for intangible assets. Overall, however, we are getting a decent return on the capital we have deployed in this sector. Furthermore, the intrinsic value of the businesses, in aggregate, exceeds their carrying value by a good margin. Even so, the difference between intrinsic value and carrying value in the insurance and regulated-industry segments is *far* greater. It is there that the huge winners reside.

* * * * * * * * * * * *

Marmon provides an example of a clear and substantial gap existing between book value and intrinsic value. Let me explain the odd origin of this differential.

Last year I told you that we had purchased additional shares in Marmon, raising our ownership to 80% (up from the 64% we acquired in 2008). I also told you that GAAP accounting required us to immediately record the 2011 purchase on our books at far less than what we paid. I've now had a year to think about this weird accounting rule, but I've yet to find an explanation that makes *any* sense – nor can Charlie or Marc Hamburg, our CFO, come up with one. My confusion increases when I am told that if we hadn't already owned 64%, the 16% we purchased in 2011 would have been entered on our books at our cost.

In 2012 (and in early 2013, retroactive to yearend 2012) we acquired an additional 10% of Marmon and the same bizarre accounting treatment was required. The $700 million write-off we immediately incurred had no effect on earnings but did reduce book value and, therefore, 2012's gain in net worth.

The cost of our recent 10% purchase implies a $12.6 billion value for the 90% of Marmon we now own. Our balance-sheet carrying value for the 90%, however, is $8 billion. Charlie and I believe our current purchase represents excellent value. If we are correct, our Marmon holding is worth at least $4.6 billion more than its carrying value.

Marmon is a diverse enterprise, comprised of about 150 companies operating in a wide variety of industries. Its largest business involves the ownership of tank cars that are leased to a variety of shippers, such as oil and chemical companies. Marmon conducts this business through two subsidiaries, Union Tank Car in the U.S. and Procor in Canada.

Union Tank Car has been around a long time, having been owned by the Standard Oil Trust until that empire was broken up in 1911. Look for its UTLX logo on tank cars when you watch trains roll by. As a Berkshire shareholder, you own the cars with that insignia. When you spot a UTLX car, puff out your chest a bit and enjoy the same satisfaction that John D. Rockefeller undoubtedly experienced as he viewed *his* fleet a century ago.

Tank cars are owned by either shippers or lessors, not by railroads. At yearend Union Tank Car and Procor together owned 97,000 cars having a net book value of $4 billion. A new car, it should be noted, costs upwards of $100,000. Union Tank Car is also a major manufacturer of tank cars – some of them to be sold but most to be owned by it and leased out. Today, its order book extends well into 2014.

At both BNSF and Marmon, we are benefitting from the resurgence of U.S. oil production. In fact, our railroad is now transporting about 500,000 barrels of oil daily, roughly 10% of the total produced in the "lower 48" (i.e. not counting Alaska and offshore). All indications are that BNSF's oil shipments will grow substantially in coming years.

* * * * * * * * * * * *

Space precludes us from going into detail about the many other businesses in this segment. Company-specific information about the 2012 operations of some of the larger units appears on pages 76 to 79.

Finance and Financial Products

This sector, our smallest, includes two rental companies, XTRA (trailers) and CORT (furniture), as well as Clayton Homes, the country's leading producer and financer of manufactured homes. Aside from these 100%-owned subsidiaries, we also include in this category a collection of financial assets and our 50% interest in Berkadia Commercial Mortgage.

We include Clayton in this sector because it owns and services 332,000 mortgages, totaling $13.7 billion. In large part, these loans have been made to lower and middle-income families. Nevertheless, the loans have performed well throughout the housing collapse, thereby validating our conviction that a reasonable down payment and a sensible payments-to-income ratio will ward off outsized foreclosure losses, even during stressful times.

Clayton also produced 25,872 manufactured homes last year, up 13.5% from 2011. That output accounted for about 4.8% of all single-family residences built in the country, a share that makes Clayton America's number one homebuilder.

CORT and XTRA are leaders in their industries as well. Our expenditures for new rental equipment at XTRA totaled $256 million in 2012, more than double its depreciation expense. While competitors fret about today's uncertainties, XTRA is preparing for tomorrow.

Berkadia continues to do well. Our partners at Leucadia do most of the work in this venture, an arrangement that Charlie and I happily embrace.

Here's the pre-tax earnings recap for this sector:

	2012	2011
	(in millions)	
Berkadia	$ 35	$ 25
Clayton	255	154
CORT	42	29
XTRA	106	126
Net financial income*	410	440
	$848	$774

*Excludes capital gains or losses

Investments

Below we show our common stock investments that at yearend had a market value of more than $1 billion.

Shares	Company	Percentage of Company Owned	Cost*	Market
			12/31/12	
			(in millions)	
151,610,700	American Express Company	13.7	$ 1,287	$ 8,715
400,000,000	The Coca-Cola Company	8.9	1,299	14,500
24,123,911	ConocoPhillips	2.0	1,219	1,399
22,999,600	DIRECTV	3.8	1,057	1,154
68,115,484	International Business Machines Corp.	6.0	11,680	13,048
28,415,250	Moody's Corporation	12.7	287	1,430
20,060,390	Munich Re	11.3	2,990	3,599
20,668,118	Phillips 66	3.3	660	1,097
3,947,555	POSCO	5.1	768	1,295
52,477,678	The Procter & Gamble Company	1.9	336	3,563
25,848,838	Sanofi	2.0	2,073	2,438
415,510,889	Tesco plc	5.2	2,350	2,268
78,060,769	U.S. Bancorp	4.2	2,401	2,493
54,823,433	Wal-Mart Stores, Inc.	1.6	2,837	3,741
456,170,061	Wells Fargo & Company	8.7	10,906	15,592
	Others		7,646	11,330
	Total Common Stocks Carried at Market		$49,796	$87,662

*This is our actual purchase price and also our tax basis; GAAP "cost" differs in a few cases because of write-ups or write-downs that have been required.

One point about the composition of this list deserves mention. In Berkshire's past annual reports, every stock itemized in this space has been bought by me, in the sense that I made the decision to buy it for Berkshire. But starting with this list, any investment made by Todd Combs or Ted Weschler – or a combined purchase by them – that meets the dollar threshold for the list ($1 billion this year) will be included. Above is the first such stock, DIRECTV, which both Todd and Ted hold in their portfolios and whose combined holdings at the end of 2012 were valued at the $1.15 billion shown.

Todd and Ted also manage the pension funds of certain Berkshire subsidiaries, while others, for regulatory reasons, are managed by outside advisers. We do not include holdings of the pension funds in our annual report tabulations, though their portfolios often overlap Berkshire's.

****

We continue to wind down the part of our derivatives portfolio that involved the assumption by Berkshire of insurance-like risks. (Our electric and gas utility businesses, however, will continue to use derivatives for operational purposes.) New commitments would require us to post collateral and, with minor exceptions, we are unwilling to do that. Markets can behave in extraordinary ways, and we have no interest in exposing Berkshire to some out-of-the-blue event in the financial world that might require our posting mountains of cash on a moment's notice.

Charlie and I believe in operating with many redundant layers of liquidity, and we avoid any sort of obligation that could drain our cash in a material way. That reduces our returns in 99 years out of 100. But we will survive in the 100th while many others fail. And we will sleep well in all 100.

The derivatives we have sold that provide credit protection for corporate bonds will all expire in the next year. It's now almost certain that our profit from these contracts will approximate $1 billion pre-tax. We also received very substantial sums upfront on these derivatives, and the "float" attributable to them has averaged about $2 billion over their five-year lives. All told, these derivatives have provided a more-than-satisfactory result, especially considering the fact that we were guaranteeing corporate credits – mostly of the high-yield variety – throughout the financial panic and subsequent recession.

In our other major derivatives commitment, we sold long-term puts on four leading stock indices in the U.S., U.K., Europe and Japan. These contracts were initiated between 2004 and 2008 and even under the worst of circumstances have only minor collateral requirements. In 2010 we unwound about 10% of our exposure at a profit of $222 million. The remaining contracts expire between 2018 and 2026. Only the index value at expiration date counts; our counterparties have no right to early termination.

Berkshire received premiums of $4.2 billion when we wrote the contracts that remain outstanding. If all of these contracts had come due at yearend 2011, we would have had to pay $6.2 billion; the corresponding figure at yearend 2012 was $3.9 billion. With this large drop in immediate settlement liability, we reduced our GAAP liability at yearend 2012 to $7.5 billion from $8.5 billion at the end of 2011. Though it's no sure thing, Charlie and I believe it likely that the final liability will be considerably less than the amount we currently carry on our books. In the meantime, we can invest the $4.2 billion of float derived from these contracts as we see fit.

We Buy Some Newspapers . . . Newspapers?

During the past fifteen months, we acquired 28 daily newspapers at a cost of $344 million. This may puzzle you for two reasons. First, I have long told you in these letters and at our annual meetings that the circulation, advertising and profits of the newspaper industry overall are *certain* to decline. That prediction still holds. Second, the properties we purchased fell far short of meeting our off-stated size requirements for acquisitions.

We can address the second point easily. Charlie and I love newspapers and, *if their economics make sense*, will buy them even when they fall far short of the size threshold we would require for the purchase of, say, a widget company. Addressing the first point requires me to provide a more elaborate explanation, including some history.

News, to put it simply, is what people don't know that they want to know. And people will seek their news – what's important to *them* – from whatever sources provide the best combination of immediacy, ease of access, reliability, comprehensiveness and low cost. The relative importance of these factors varies with the nature of the news and the person wanting it.

Before television and the Internet, newspapers were the *primary* source for an incredible variety of news, a fact that made them indispensable to a very high percentage of the population. Whether your interests were international, national, local, sports or financial quotations, your newspaper usually was first to tell you the latest information. Indeed, your paper contained so much you wanted to learn that you received your money's worth, even if only a small number of its pages spoke to your specific interests. Better yet, advertisers typically paid almost all of the product's cost, and readers rode their coattails.

Additionally, the ads themselves delivered information of vital interest to hordes of readers, in effect providing even more "news." Editors would cringe at the thought, but for many readers learning what jobs or apartments were available, what supermarkets were carrying which weekend specials, or what movies were showing where and when was far more important than the views expressed on the editorial page.

In turn, the local paper was indispensable to advertisers. If Sears or Safeway built stores in Omaha, they required a "megaphone" to tell the city's residents why their stores should be visited *today*. Indeed, big department stores and grocers vied to outshout their competition with multi-page spreads, knowing that the goods they advertised would fly off the shelves. With no other megaphone remotely comparable to that of the newspaper, ads sold themselves.

As long as a newspaper was the only one in its community, its profits were certain to be extraordinary; whether it was managed well or poorly made little difference. (As one Southern publisher famously confessed, "I owe my exalted position in life to two great American institutions – nepotism and monopoly.")

Over the years, almost all cities became one-newspaper towns (or harbored two competing papers that joined forces to operate as a single economic unit). This contraction was inevitable because most people wished to read and pay for only one paper. When competition existed, the paper that gained a significant lead in circulation almost automatically received the most ads. That left ads drawing readers and readers drawing ads. This symbiotic process spelled doom for the weaker paper and became known as "survival of the fattest."

Now the world has changed. Stock market quotes and the details of national sports events are old news long before the presses begin to roll. The Internet offers extensive information about both available jobs and homes. Television bombards viewers with political, national and international news. In one area of interest after another, newspapers have therefore lost their "primacy." And, as their audiences have fallen, so has advertising. (Revenues from "help wanted" classified ads – long a huge source of income for newspapers – have plunged more than 90% in the past 12 years.)

Newspapers continue to reign supreme, however, in the delivery of local news. If you want to know what's going on in *your* town – whether the news is about the mayor or taxes or high school football – there is no substitute for a local newspaper that is doing its job. A reader's eyes may glaze over after they take in a couple of paragraphs about Canadian tariffs or political developments in Pakistan; a story about the reader himself or his neighbors will be read to the end. Wherever there is a pervasive sense of community, a paper that serves the special informational needs of that community will remain indispensable to a significant portion of its residents.

Even a valuable product, however, can self-destruct from a faulty business strategy. And that process has been underway during the past decade at almost all papers of size. Publishers – including Berkshire in Buffalo – have offered their paper free on the Internet while charging meaningful sums for the physical specimen. How could this lead to anything other than a sharp and steady drop in sales of the printed product? Falling circulation, moreover, makes a paper less essential to advertisers. Under these conditions, the "virtuous circle" of the past reverses.

The Wall Street Journal went to a pay model early. But the main exemplar for local newspapers is the *Arkansas Democrat-Gazette*, published by Walter Hussman, Jr. Walter also adopted a pay format early, and over the past decade his paper has retained its circulation far better than any other large paper in the country. Despite Walter's powerful example, it's only been in the last year or so that other papers, including Berkshire's, have explored pay arrangements. Whatever works best – and the answer is not yet clear – will be copied widely.

* * * * * * * * * * * *

Charlie and I believe that papers delivering comprehensive and reliable information to tightly-bound communities *and* having a sensible Internet strategy will remain viable for a long time. We do not believe that success will come from cutting either the news content or frequency of publication. Indeed, skimpy news coverage will almost certainly lead to skimpy readership. And the less-than-daily publication that is now being tried in some large towns or cities – while it may improve profits in the short term – seems certain to diminish the papers' relevance over time. Our goal is to keep our papers loaded with content of interest to our readers and to be paid appropriately by those who find us useful, whether the product they view is in their hands or on the Internet.

Our confidence is buttressed by the availability of Terry Kroeger's outstanding management group at the *Omaha World-Herald*, a team that has the ability to oversee a large group of papers. The individual papers, however, will be independent in their news coverage and editorial opinions. (I voted for Obama; of our 12 dailies that endorsed a presidential candidate, 10 opted for Romney.)

Our newspapers are certainly not insulated from the forces that have been driving revenues downward. Still, the six small dailies we owned throughout 2012 had unchanged revenues for the year, a result far superior to that experienced by big-city dailies. Moreover, the two large papers we operated throughout the year – *The Buffalo News* and the *Omaha World-Herald* – held their revenue loss to 3%, which was also an above-average outcome. Among newspapers in America's 50 largest metropolitan areas, our Buffalo and Omaha papers rank near the top in circulation penetration of their home territories.

This popularity is no accident: Credit the editors of those papers – Margaret Sullivan at the *News* and Mike Reilly at the *World-Herald* — for delivering information that has made their publications indispensable to community-interested readers. (Margaret, I regret to say, recently left us to join *The New York Times*, whose job offers are tough to turn down. That paper made a great hire, and we wish her the best.)

Berkshire's cash earnings from its papers will almost certainly trend downward over time. Even a sensible Internet strategy will not be able to prevent modest erosion. At our cost, however, I believe these papers will meet or exceed our economic test for acquisitions. Results to date support that belief.

Charlie and I, however, still operate under economic principle 11 (detailed on page 99) and will not continue the operation of *any* business doomed to unending losses. One daily paper that we acquired in a bulk purchase from Media General was significantly unprofitable under that company's ownership. After analyzing the paper's results, we saw no remedy for the losses and reluctantly shut it down. All of our remaining dailies, however, should be profitable for a long time to come. (They are listed on page 108.) At appropriate prices – and that means at a *very* low multiple of current earnings – we will purchase more papers of the type we like.

* * * * * * * * * * * *

A milestone in Berkshire's newspaper operations occurred at yearend when Stan Lipsey retired as publisher of *The Buffalo News*. It's no exaggeration for me to say that the *News* might now be extinct were it not for Stan.

Charlie and I acquired the *News* in April 1977. It was an evening paper, dominant on weekdays but lacking a Sunday edition. Throughout the country, the circulation trend was toward morning papers. Moreover, Sunday was becoming ever more critical to the profitability of metropolitan dailies. Without a Sunday paper, the *News* was destined to lose out to its morning competitor, which had a fat and entrenched Sunday product.

We therefore began to print a Sunday edition late in 1977. And then all hell broke loose. Our competitor sued us, and District Judge Charles Brieant, Jr. authored a harsh ruling that crippled the introduction of our paper. His ruling was later reversed – after 17 long months – in a 3-0 sharp rebuke by the Second Circuit Court of Appeals. While the appeal was pending, we lost circulation, hemorrhaged money and stood in constant danger of going out of business.

Enter Stan Lipsey, a friend of mine from the 1960s, who, with his wife, had sold Berkshire a small Omaha weekly. I found Stan to be an extraordinary newspaperman, knowledgeable about every aspect of circulation, production, sales and editorial. (He was a key person in gaining that small weekly a Pulitzer Prize in 1973.) So when I was in big trouble at the *News*, I asked Stan to leave his comfortable way of life in Omaha to take over in Buffalo.

He never hesitated. Along with Murray Light, our editor, Stan persevered through four years of very dark days until the *News* won the competitive struggle in 1982. Ever since, despite a difficult Buffalo economy, the performance of the *News* has been exceptional. As both a friend and as a manager, Stan is simply the best.

Dividends

A number of Berkshire shareholders – including some of my good friends – would like Berkshire to pay a cash dividend. It puzzles them that we relish the dividends we receive from most of the stocks that Berkshire owns, but pay out nothing ourselves. So let's examine when dividends do and don't make sense for shareholders.

A profitable company can allocate its earnings in various ways (which are not mutually exclusive). A company's management should first examine reinvestment possibilities offered by its current business – projects to become more efficient, expand territorially, extend and improve product lines or to otherwise widen the economic moat separating the company from its competitors.

I ask the managers of our subsidiaries to unendingly focus on moat-widening opportunities, and they find many that make economic sense. But sometimes our managers misfire. The usual cause of failure is that they start with the answer they want and then work backwards to find a supporting rationale. Of course, the process is subconscious; that's what makes it so dangerous.

Your chairman has not been free of this sin. In Berkshire's 1986 annual report, I described how twenty years of management effort and capital improvements in our original textile business were an exercise in futility. I *wanted* the business to succeed and *wished* my way into a series of bad decisions. (I even bought *another* New England textile company.) But wishing makes dreams come true only in Disney movies; it's poison in business.

Despite such past miscues, our first priority with available funds will always be to examine whether they can be *intelligently* deployed in our various businesses. Our record $12.1 billion of fixed-asset investments and bolt-on acquisitions in 2012 demonstrate that this is a fertile field for capital allocation at Berkshire. And here we have an advantage: Because we operate in so many areas of the economy, we enjoy a range of choices far wider than that open to most corporations. In deciding what to do, we can water the flowers and skip over the weeds.

Even after we deploy hefty amounts of capital in our current operations, Berkshire will regularly generate a lot of additional cash. Our next step, therefore, is to search for acquisitions unrelated to our current businesses. Here our test is simple: Do Charlie and I think we can effect a transaction that is likely to leave our shareholders wealthier on a per-share basis than they were prior to the acquisition?

I have made plenty of mistakes in acquisitions and will make more. Overall, however, our record is satisfactory, which means that our shareholders are *far* wealthier today than they would be if the funds we used for acquisitions had instead been devoted to share repurchases or dividends.

But, to use the standard disclaimer, past performance is no guarantee of future results. That's particularly true at Berkshire: Because of our present size, making acquisitions that are both meaningful and sensible is now more difficult than it has been during most of our years.

Nevertheless, a large deal still offers us possibilities to add materially to per-share intrinsic value. BNSF is a case in point: It is now worth considerably more than our carrying value. Had we instead allocated the funds required for this purchase to dividends or repurchases, you and I would have been worse off. Though large transactions of the BNSF kind will be rare, there are still some whales in the ocean.

The third use of funds – repurchases – is sensible for a company when its shares sell at a meaningful discount to conservatively calculated intrinsic value. Indeed, disciplined repurchases are the *surest* way to use funds intelligently: It's hard to go wrong when you're buying dollar bills for 80¢ or less. We explained our criteria for repurchases in last year's report and, if the opportunity presents itself, we will buy large quantities of our stock. We originally said we would not pay more than 110% of book value, but that proved unrealistic. Therefore, we increased the limit to 120% in December when a large block became available at about 116% of book value.

But never forget: In repurchase decisions, price is all-important. Value is *destroyed* when purchases are made above intrinsic value. The directors and I believe that continuing shareholders are benefitted in a meaningful way by purchases up to our 120% limit.

And that brings us to dividends. Here we have to make a few assumptions and use some math. The numbers will require careful reading, but they are essential to understanding the case for and against dividends. So bear with me.

We'll start by assuming that you and I are the equal owners of a business with $2 million of net worth. The business earns 12% on tangible net worth – $240,000 – and can reasonably expect to earn the same 12% on reinvested earnings. Furthermore, there are outsiders who always wish to buy into our business at 125% of net worth. Therefore, the value of what we each own is now $1.25 million.

You would like to have the two of us shareholders receive one-third of our company's annual earnings and have two-thirds be reinvested. That plan, you feel, will nicely balance your needs for both current income and capital growth. So you suggest that we pay out $80,000 of current earnings and retain $160,000 to increase the future earnings of the business. In the first year, your dividend would be $40,000, and as earnings grew and the one-third payout was maintained, so too would your dividend. In total, dividends and stock value would increase 8% each year (12% earned on net worth less 4% of net worth paid out).

After ten years our company would have a net worth of $4,317,850 (the original $2 million compounded at 8%) and your dividend in the upcoming year would be $86,357. Each of us would have shares worth $2,698,656 (125% of our half of the company's net worth). And we would live happily ever after – with dividends and the value of our stock continuing to grow at 8% annually.

There is an alternative approach, however, that would leave us even happier. Under this scenario, we would leave *all* earnings in the company and each sell 3.2% of our shares annually. Since the shares would be sold at 125% of book value, this approach would produce the same $40,000 of cash initially, a sum that would grow annually. Call this option the "sell-off" approach.

Under this "sell-off" scenario, the net worth of our company increases to $6,211,696 after ten years ($2 million compounded at 12%). Because we would be selling shares each year, our *percentage* ownership would have declined, and, after ten years, we would each own 36.12% of the business. Even so, your share of the net worth of the company at that time would be $2,243,540. And, remember, every dollar of net worth attributable to each of us can be sold for $1.25. Therefore, the market value of your remaining shares would be $2,804,425, about 4% greater than the value of your shares if we had followed the dividend approach.

Moreover, your annual cash receipts from the sell-off policy would now be running 4% more than you would have received under the dividend scenario. Voila! – you would have both more cash to spend annually *and* more capital value.

This calculation, of course, assumes that our hypothetical company can earn an average of 12% annually on net worth and that its shareholders can sell their shares for an average of 125% of book value. To that point, the S&P 500 earns considerably more than 12% on net worth and sells at a price far above 125% of that net worth. Both assumptions also seem reasonable for Berkshire, though certainly not assured.

Moreover, on the plus side, there also is a possibility that the assumptions will be exceeded. If they are, the argument for the sell-off policy becomes even stronger. Over Berkshire's history – admittedly one that won't come close to being repeated – the sell-off policy would have produced results for shareholders *dramatically* superior to the dividend policy.

Aside from the favorable math, there are two further – *and important* – arguments for a sell-off policy. First, dividends impose a specific cash-out policy upon all shareholders. If, say, 40% of earnings is the policy, those who wish 30% or 50% will be thwarted. Our 600,000 shareholders cover the waterfront in their desires for cash. It is safe to say, however, that a great many of them – perhaps even most of them – are in a net-savings mode and logically should prefer no payment at all.

The sell-off alternative, on the other hand, lets each shareholder make his own choice between cash receipts and capital build-up. One shareholder can elect to cash out, say, 60% of annual earnings while other shareholders elect 20% or nothing at all. Of course, a shareholder in our dividend-paying scenario could turn around and use his dividends to purchase more shares. But he would take a beating in doing so: He would both incur taxes and also pay a 25% premium to get his dividend reinvested. (Keep remembering, open-market purchases of the stock take place at 125% of book value.)

The second disadvantage of the dividend approach is of equal importance: The tax consequences for *all* taxpaying shareholders are inferior – usually *far* inferior – to those under the sell-off program. Under the dividend program, all of the cash received by shareholders each year is taxed whereas the sell-off program results in tax on only the gain portion of the cash receipts.

Let me end this math exercise – and I can hear you cheering as I put away the dentist drill – by using my own case to illustrate how a shareholder's regular disposals of shares can be accompanied by an *increased* investment in his or her business. For the last seven years, I have annually given away about 4¼% of my Berkshire shares. Through this process, my original position of 712,497,000 B-equivalent shares (split-adjusted) has decreased to 528,525,623 shares. Clearly my ownership *percentage* of the company has significantly decreased.

Yet my investment in the business has actually increased: The book value of my current interest in Berkshire considerably exceeds the book value attributable to my holdings of seven years ago. (The actual figures are $28.2 billion for 2005 and $40.2 billion for 2012.) In other words, I now have *far* more money working for me at Berkshire even though my ownership of the company has materially decreased. It's also true that my share of both Berkshire's intrinsic business value and the company's normal earning power is far greater than it was in 2005. Over time, I expect this accretion of value to continue – albeit in a decidedly irregular fashion – even as I now annually give away more than 4½% of my shares (the increase having occurred because I've recently doubled my lifetime pledges to certain foundations).

* * * * * * * * * * * *

Above all, dividend policy should always be clear, consistent and rational. A capricious policy will confuse owners and drive away would-be investors. Phil Fisher put it wonderfully 54 years ago in Chapter 7 of his *Common Stocks and Uncommon Profits*, a book that ranks behind only *The Intelligent Investor* and the 1940 edition of *Security Analysis* in the all-time-best list for the serious investor. Phil explained that you can successfully run a restaurant that serves hamburgers or, alternatively, one that features Chinese food. But you can't switch capriciously between the two and retain the fans of either.

Most companies pay consistent dividends, generally trying to increase them annually and cutting them very reluctantly. Our "Big Four" portfolio companies follow this sensible and understandable approach and, in certain cases, also repurchase shares quite aggressively.

We applaud their actions and hope they continue on their present paths. We like increased dividends, and we love repurchases at appropriate prices.

At Berkshire, however, we have consistently followed a different approach that we know has been sensible and that we hope has been made understandable by the paragraphs you have just read. We will stick with this policy as long as we believe our assumptions about the book-value buildup and the market-price premium seem reasonable. If the prospects for either factor change materially for the worse, we will reexamine our actions.

The Annual Meeting

The annual meeting will be held on Saturday, May 4th at the CenturyLink Center. Carrie Sova will be in charge. (Though that's a new name, it's the same wonderful Carrie as last year; she got married in June to a very lucky guy.) All of our headquarters group pitches in to help her; the whole affair is a homemade production, and I couldn't be more proud of those who put it together.

The doors will open at 7 a.m., and at 7:30 we will have our second International Newspaper Tossing Challenge. The target will be the porch of a Clayton Home, precisely 35 feet from the throwing line. Last year I successfully fought off all challengers. But now Berkshire has acquired a large number of newspapers and with them came much tossing talent (or so the throwers claim). Come see whether their talent matches their talk. Better yet, join in. The papers will be 36 to 42 pages and you must fold them yourself (no rubber bands).

At 8:30, a new Berkshire movie will be shown. An hour later, we will start the question-and-answer period, which (with a break for lunch at the CenturyLink's stands) will last until 3:30. After a short recess, Charlie and I will convene the annual meeting at 3:45. If you decide to leave during the day's question periods, please do so while *Charlie* is talking.

The best reason to exit, of course, is to *shop*. We will help you do so by filling the 194,300-square-foot hall that adjoins the meeting area with products from dozens of Berkshire subsidiaries. Last year, you did your part, and most locations racked up record sales. In a nine-hour period, we sold 1,090 pairs of Justin boots, (that's a pair every 30 seconds), 10,010 pounds of See's candy, 12,879 Quikut knives (24 knives per minute) and 5,784 pairs of Wells Lamont gloves, always a hot item. But you can do better. Remember: Anyone who says money can't buy happiness simply hasn't shopped at our meeting.

Last year, Brooks, our running shoe company, exhibited for the first time and ran up sales of $150,000. Brooks is on fire: Its volume in 2012 grew 34%, and that was on top of a similar 34% gain in 2011. The company's management expects another jump of 23% in 2013. We will again have a special commemorative shoe to offer at the meeting.

On Sunday at 8 a.m., we will initiate the "Berkshire 5K," a race starting at the CenturyLink. Full details for participating will be included in the Visitor's Guide that you will receive with your credentials for the meeting. We will have plenty of categories for competition, including one for the media. (It will be fun to report on *their* performance.) Regretfully, I will forego running; *someone* has to man the starting gun.

I should warn you that we have a lot of home-grown talent. Ted Weschler has run the marathon in 3:01. Jim Weber, Brooks' dynamic CEO, is another speedster with a 3:31 best. Todd Combs specializes in the triathlon, but has been clocked at 22 minutes in the 5K.

That, however, is just the beginning: Our directors are also fleet of foot (that is, *some* of our directors are). Steve Burke has run an amazing 2:39 Boston marathon. (It's a family thing; his wife, Gretchen, finished the New York marathon in 3:25.) Charlotte Guyman's best is 3:37, and Sue Decker crossed the tape in New York in 3:36. Charlie did not return his questionnaire.

GEICO will have a booth in the shopping area, staffed by a number of its top counselors from around the country. Stop by for a quote. In most cases, GEICO will be able to give you a shareholder discount (usually 8%). This special offer is permitted by 44 of the 51 jurisdictions in which we operate. (One supplemental point: The discount is not additive if you qualify for another, such as that given certain groups.) Bring the details of your existing insurance and check out whether we can save you money. For at least half of you, I believe we can.

Be sure to visit the Bookworm. It will carry about 35 books and DVDs, including a couple of new ones. Carol Loomis, who has been invaluable to me in editing this letter since 1977, has recently authored *Tap Dancing to Work: Warren Buffett on Practically Everything*. She and I have cosigned 500 copies, available exclusively at the meeting.

The Outsiders, by William Thorndike, Jr., is an outstanding book about CEOs who excelled at capital allocation. It has an insightful chapter on our director, Tom Murphy, overall the best business manager I've ever met. I also recommend *The Clash of the Cultures* by Jack Bogle and Laura Rittenhouse's *Investing Between the Lines*. Should you need to ship your book purchases, a shipping service will be available nearby.

The *Omaha World-Herald* will again have a booth, offering a few books it has recently published. Red-blooded Husker fans – is there any Nebraskan who isn't one? – will surely want to purchase *Unbeatable*. It tells the story of Nebraska football during 1993-97, a golden era in which Tom Osborne's teams went 60-3.

If you are a big spender – or aspire to become one – visit Signature Aviation on the east side of the Omaha airport between noon and 5:00 p.m. on Saturday. There we will have a fleet of NetJets aircraft that will get your pulse racing. Come by bus; leave by private jet. Live a little.

An attachment to the proxy material that is enclosed with this report explains how you can obtain the credential you will need for admission to the meeting and other events. Airlines have sometimes jacked up prices for the Berkshire weekend. If you are coming from far away, compare the cost of flying to Kansas City versus Omaha. The drive between the two cities is about 2½ hours, and it may be that you can save significant money, particularly if you had planned to rent a car in Omaha. Spend the savings with us.

At Nebraska Furniture Mart, located on a 77-acre site on 72nd Street between Dodge and Pacific, we will again be having "Berkshire Weekend" discount pricing. Last year the store did $35.9 million of business during its annual meeting sale, an all-time record that makes other retailers turn green. To obtain the Berkshire discount, you must make your purchases between Tuesday, April 30th and Monday, May 6th inclusive, and also present your meeting credential. The period's special pricing will even apply to the products of several prestigious manufacturers that normally have ironclad rules against discounting but which, in the spirit of our shareholder weekend, have made an exception for you. We appreciate their cooperation. NFM is open from 10 a.m. to 9 p.m. Monday through Saturday, and 10 a.m. to 6 p.m. on Sunday. On Saturday this year, from 5:30 p.m. to 8 p.m., NFM is having a picnic to which you are all invited.

At Borsheims, we will again have two shareholder-only events. The first will be a cocktail reception from 6 p.m. to 9 p.m. on Friday, May 3rd. The second, the main gala, will be held on Sunday, May 5th, from 9 a.m. to 4 p.m. On Saturday, we will be open until 6 p.m. In recent years, our three-day volume has far exceeded sales in all of December, normally a jeweler's best month.

Around 1 p.m. on Sunday, I will begin clerking at Borsheims. Last year my sales totaled $1.5 million. This year I won't quit until I hit $2 million. Because I need to leave well before sundown, I will be desperate to do business. Come take advantage of me. Ask for my "Crazy Warren" price.

We will have huge crowds at Borsheims throughout the weekend. For your convenience, therefore, shareholder prices will be available from Monday, April 29th through Saturday, May 11th. During that period, please identify yourself as a shareholder by presenting your meeting credentials or a brokerage statement that shows you are a Berkshire holder.

On Sunday, in the mall outside of Borsheims, a blindfolded Patrick Wolff, twice U.S. chess champion, will take on all comers – who will have their eyes wide open – in groups of six. Nearby, Norman Beck, a remarkable magician from Dallas, will bewilder onlookers. Additionally, we will have Bob Hamman and Sharon Osberg, two of the world's top bridge experts, available to play bridge with our shareholders on Sunday afternoon. Don't play them for money.

Gorat's and Piccolo's will again be open exclusively for Berkshire shareholders on Sunday, May 5th. Both will be serving until 10 p.m., with Gorat's opening at 1 p.m. and Piccolo's opening at 4 p.m. These restaurants are my favorites, and I will eat at both of them on Sunday evening. Remember: To make a reservation at Gorat's, call 402-551-3733 on April 1st (*but not before*) and at Piccolo's call 402-342-9038. At Piccolo's, order a giant root beer float for dessert. Only sissies get the small one. (I once saw Bill Gates polish off two of the giant variety *after* a full-course dinner; that's when I knew he would make a great director.)

We will again have the same three financial journalists lead the question-and-answer period at the meeting, asking Charlie and me questions that shareholders have submitted to them by e-mail. The journalists and their e-mail addresses are: Carol Loomis, of Fortune, who may be emailed at cloomis@fortunemail.com; Becky Quick, of CNBC, at BerkshireQuestions@cnbc.com, and Andrew Ross Sorkin, of The New York Times, at arsorkin@nytimes.com.

From the questions submitted, each journalist will choose the six he or she decides are the most interesting and important. The journalists have told me your question has the best chance of being selected if you keep it concise, avoid sending it in at the last moment, make it Berkshire-related and include no more than two questions in any email you send them. (In your email, let the journalist know if you would like your name mentioned if your question is selected.)

Last year we had a second panel of three analysts who follow Berkshire. All were insurance specialists, and shareholders subsequently indicated they wanted a little more variety. Therefore, this year we will have one insurance analyst, Cliff Gallant of Nomura Securities. Jonathan Brandt of Ruane, Cunniff & Goldfarb will join the analyst panel to ask questions that deal with our non-insurance operations.

Finally – to spice things up – we would like to add to the panel a credentialed bear on Berkshire, preferably one who is short the stock. Not yet having a bear identified, we would like to hear from applicants. The only requirement is that you be an investment professional and negative on Berkshire. The three analysts will bring their own Berkshire-specific questions and alternate with the journalists and the audience in asking them.

Charlie and I believe that all shareholders should have access to new Berkshire information simultaneously and should also have adequate time to analyze it, which is why we try to issue financial information after the market close on a Friday and why our annual meeting is held on Saturdays. We do not talk one-on-one to large institutional investors or analysts. Our hope is that the journalists and analysts will ask questions that will further educate shareholders about their investment.

Neither Charlie nor I will get so much as a clue about the questions to be asked. We know the journalists and analysts will come up with some tough ones, and that's the way we like it. All told, we expect at least 54 questions, which will allow for six from each analyst and journalist and 18 from the audience. If there is some extra time, we will take more from the audience. Audience questioners will be determined by drawings that will take place at 8:15 a.m. at each of the 11 microphones located in the arena and main overflow room.

* * * * * * * * * * * *

For good reason, I regularly extol the accomplishments of our operating managers. They are truly All-Stars, who run their businesses as if they were the only asset owned by their families. I believe their mindset to be as shareholder-oriented as can be found in the universe of large publicly-owned companies. Most have no financial need to work; the joy of hitting business "home runs" means as much to them as their paycheck.

Equally important, however, are the 23 men and women who work with me at our corporate office (all on one floor, which is the way we intend to keep it!).

This group efficiently deals with a multitude of SEC and other regulatory requirements, files a 21,500-page Federal income tax return as well as state and foreign returns, responds to countless shareholder and media inquiries, gets out the annual report, prepares for the country's largest annual meeting, coordinates the Board's activities – and the list goes on and on.

They handle all of these business tasks cheerfully and with unbelievable efficiency, making my life easy and pleasant. Their efforts go beyond activities strictly related to Berkshire: Last year they dealt with 48 universities (selected from 200 applicants) who sent students to Omaha for a Q&A day with me. They also handle all kinds of requests that I receive, arrange my travel, and even get me hamburgers for lunch. No CEO has it better; I truly do feel like tap dancing to work every day.

This home office crew, along with our operating managers, has my deepest thanks and deserves yours as well. Come to Omaha – the cradle of capitalism – on May 4th and chime in.

March 1, 2013

Warren E. Buffett
Chairman of the Board

Company Index

Person Index